Get to Know Microsoft Office Common Features

Backstage View and Info tab

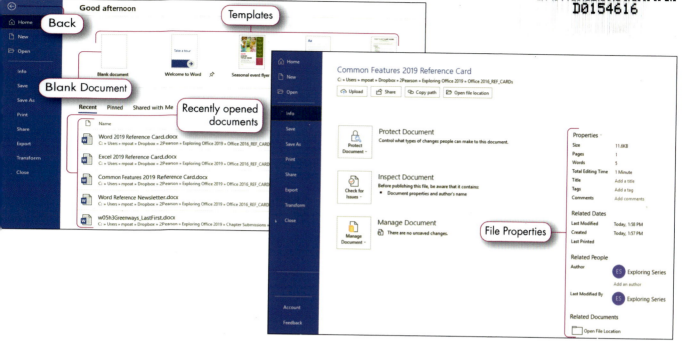

Creating, Opening, and Saving

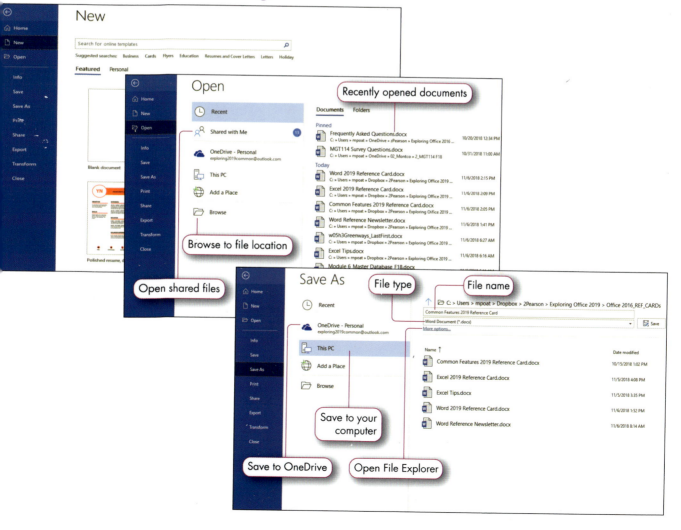

Common Ribbon Components

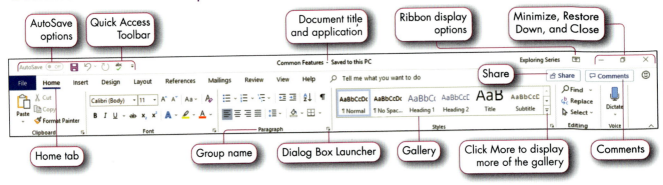

Using Office on Windows PC and Mac

Show group names on ribbon in Mac for Office:

1. Open the application.
2. Click Word menu and select Preferences.
3. Click View in Authoring and Proofing Tools.
4. Click to select Show group titles in the Ribbon section.

Selecting on a PC vs. a Mac	
On a PC	**On a Mac**
Double-click	Press Control+Click
Right-click	Press mousepad with two fingers

Using the Mini Toolbar

Using Cut, Copy, and Paste Options	
Command	**Actions**
Cut	• Click Cut in Clipboard group. • Right-click selection and select Cut. • Press Ctrl+X.
Copy	• Click Copy in Clipboard group. • Right-click selection and select Copy. • Press Ctrl+C.
Paste	• Click in destination location and select Paste in Clipboard group. • Click in destination location and press Ctrl+V. • Right-click in destination location and select one of the choices under Paste Options in the shortcut menu. • Click Clipboard Dialog Box Launcher to open Clipboard pane. Click in destination location. With Clipboard pane open, click the arrow beside the intended selection and select Paste.

(ex·ploring) SERIES

1. Investigating in a systematic way: examining. 2. Searching into or ranging over for the purpose of discovery.

Microsoft®

Office 365® 2019 Edition

INTRODUCTORY

Series Editor **Mary Anne Poatsy**

Mulbery | Hogan | Davidson | Lau | Lawson | Williams | Rutledge | Kosharek

Pearson

Vice President of Courseware Portfolio Management: Andrew Gilfillan
Executive Portfolio Manager: Samantha Lewis
Team Lead, Content Production: Laura Burgess
Content Producer: Alexandrina Wolf
Development Editor: Barbara Stover
Portfolio Management Assistant: Bridget Daly
Director of Product Marketing: Brad Parkins
Director of Field Marketing: Jonathan Cottrell
Product Marketing Manager: Heather Taylor
Field Marketing Manager: Bob Nisbet
Product Marketing Assistant: Liz Bennett
Field Marketing Assistant: Derrica Moser
Senior Operations Specialist: Maura Garcia
Senior Art Director: Mary Seiner
Interior and Cover Design: Pearson CSC
Cover Photo: Courtesy of Shutterstock® Images
Senior Product Model Manager: Eric Hakanson
Manager, Digital Studio: Heather Darby
Digital Content Producer, MyLab IT: Becca Golden
Course Producer, MyLab IT: Amanda Losonsky
Digital Studio Producer: Tanika Henderson
Full-Service Project Management: Pearson CSC (Amy Kopperude)
Composition: Pearson CSC

Credits and acknowledgments borrowed from other sources and reproduced, with permission, in this textbook appear on the appropriate page within text.

Microsoft and/or its respective suppliers make no representations about the suitability of the information contained in the documents and related graphics published as part of the services for any purpose. All such documents and related graphics are provided "as is" without warranty of any kind. Microsoft and/or its respective suppliers hereby disclaim all warranties and conditions with regard to this information, including all warranties and conditions of merchantability, whether express, implied or statutory, fitness for a particular purpose, title and non-infringement. In no event shall Microsoft and/or its respective suppliers be liable for any special, indirect or consequential damages or any damages whatsoever resulting from loss of use, data or profits, whether in an action of contract, negligence or other tortious action, arising out of or in connection with the use or performance of information available from the services.

The documents and related graphics contained herein could include technical inaccuracies or typographical errors. Changes are periodically added to the information herein. Microsoft and/or its respective suppliers may make improvements and/or changes in the product(s) and/or the program(s) described herein at any time. Partial screen shots may be viewed in full within the software version specified.

Microsoft® and Windows® are registered trademarks of the Microsoft Corporation in the U.S.A. and other countries. This book is not sponsored or endorsed by or affiliated with the Microsoft Corporation.

Many of the designations by manufacturers and sellers to distinguish their products are claimed as trademarks. Where those designations appear in this book, and the publisher was aware of a trademark claim, the designations have been printed in initial caps or all caps.

Cataloging-in-Publication Data is available on file at the Library of Congress.

ISBN 10:   0-13-540254-9
ISBN 13: 978-0-13-540254-2

3 2019

Dedications

For my husband, Ted, who <u>unselfishly</u> continues to take on more than his share to support me throughout the process; and for my children, Laura, Carolyn, and Teddy, whose encouragement and love have been inspiring.

Mary Anne Poatsy

I dedicate this book to my nephew Peyton and nieces MaKynlee and Tenley. I further dedicate this book to the loving memory of Aunt Barbara.

Keith Mulbery

For my father, Lawrence Conwill, a lifelong educator and administrator who has inspired so many both in and out of a classroom. His legacy in education and his love of family can never be truly matched, but is something I will always aspire to and admire in him. He is my hero.

Lynn Hogan

I dedicate this book to my beautiful wife Sarah. Thank you for your love, support, and amazing home-cooked meals. Your love is still my greatest achievement.

Jason Davidson

I dedicate this book to my only child, Catherine Shen, who taught me that there is another wonderful life outside of my work. My life has been more fulfilling and exciting with her in it. I also dedicate this book to the loving memory of my dog, Harry, who was by my side, through thick and thin, for 16 years. I miss him dearly every day.

Linda K. Lau

This book is dedicated to my children and to my students to inspire them to never give up and to always keep reaching for their dreams.

Rebecca Lawson

I offer thanks to my family and colleagues who have supported me on this journey. I would like to dedicate the work I have performed toward this undertaking to my little grandson, Yonason Meir (known for now as Mei-Mei), who as his name suggests, is the illumination in my life.

Jerri Williams

To Zac: thank you so much for your hard work and dedication on this project. The long (late) hours you spent did not go unnoticed. I have very much enjoyed working with you and hope there's more to come. To my husband Dan, whose encouragement, patience, and love helped make this endeavor possible. Thank you for taking on the many additional tasks at home so that I could focus on writing. To Emma and Jane, I love you. You inspire me to reach for my goals and never settle for less.

Amy Rutledge

I dedicate this book to my husband John, for his understanding, patience and encouragement; my son Justin and daughter-in-law Jennifer, for their love and unending support; my son Alex, whose strength through so many challenges continues to inspire me; and my grandsons, who make each day a new adventure.

Diane Kosharek

Mary Anne Poatsy, Series Editor, Common Features Author

Mary Anne is a senior faculty member at Montgomery County Community College, teaching various computer application and concepts courses in face-to-face and online environments. She holds a B.A. in Psychology and Education from Mount Holyoke College and an M.B.A. in Finance from Northwestern University's Kellogg Graduate School of Management.

Mary Anne has more than 20 years of educational experience. She has taught at Gwynedd Mercy College, Bucks County Community College, and Muhlenberg College. She also engages in corporate training. Before teaching, she was Vice President at Shearson Lehman in the Municipal Bond Investment Banking Department.

Dr. Keith Mulbery, Excel Author

Dr. Keith Mulbery is the Department Chair and a Professor in the Information Systems and Technology Department at Utah Valley University (UVU), where he currently teaches systems analysis and design, and global and ethical issues in information systems and technology. He has also taught computer applications, C# programming, and management information systems. Keith served as Interim Associate Dean, School of Computing, in the College of Technology and Computing at UVU.

Keith received the Utah Valley State College Board of Trustees Award of Excellence in 2001, School of Technology and Computing Scholar Award in 2007, and School of Technology and Computing Teaching Award in 2008. He has authored more than 17 textbooks, served as Series Editor for the Exploring Office 2007 series, and served as developmental editor on two textbooks for the Essentials Office 2000 series.

Keith received his B.S. and M.Ed. in Business Education from Southwestern Oklahoma State University and earned his Ph.D. in Education with an emphasis in Business Information Systems at Utah State University. His dissertation topic was computer-assisted instruction using Prentice Hall's Train and Assess IT program (the predecessor to MyITLab) to supplement traditional instruction in basic computer proficiency courses.

Dr. Lynn Hogan, Word Author

Dr. Lynn Hogan currently teaches at the University of North Alabama, providing instruction in the area of computer applications. Prior to her current assignment, she taught for more than 25 years at the community college level, serving in academic administration and teaching applications, programming, and concepts courses in both online and classroom environments. She has served as an author for several Pearson publications over the past 14 years, including Exploring 2010, 2013, and 2016. She also contributed Word chapters for the first edition of Your Office, and developed and wrote Practical Computing. She received an M.B.A. from the University of North Alabama, and a Ph.D. from the University of Alabama.

Lynn has two daughters and resides with her husband, Paul, in Alabama. Her interests include creative writing, photography, traveling, and helping manage a family horse farm.

Jason Davidson, Excel Author

Jason Davidson is a faculty member in the Lacey School of Business at Butler University, where he teaches Advanced Web Design, Data Networks, Data Analysis and Business Modeling, and introductory information systems courses. He has served as a co-author on the Exploring series since 2013. Prior to joining the faculty at Butler, he worked in the technical publishing industry using his background in media development. Along with teaching, he currently serves as an IT consultant for regional businesses in the Indianapolis area. He holds a B.A. in Media Arts from Butler University and an M.B.A. from Morehead State University. He lives in Indianapolis, Indiana, with his wife Sarah, and in his free time enjoys road biking, photography, and spending time with his family.

Dr. Linda K. Lau, Word Author

Since 1994, Dr. Linda K. Lau is a Management Information Systems (MIS) faculty at the College of Business and Economics, Longwood University, located in Farmville, Virginia. She received the Outstanding Academic Advisor Award in 2006. Besides teaching and advising, Linda has authored and co-authored numerous journal and conference articles and textbooks, edited two books, and sat on several editorial boards. Her current research interest focuses on cyber security and forensics, and she is a member of the *Journal of Digital Forensics, Security and Law (JDFSL)* editorial board. Linda earned her Ph.D. from Rensselaer Polytechnic Institute in 1993, and her M.B.A. and B.S. from Illinois State University in 1987 and 1986, respectively. In her younger days, Linda worked as a flight attendant for Singapore International Airlines for six years before coming to America to pursue her academic dream. She also worked as a financial consultant with Salomon Smith Barney from 1999 to 2000 before returning to the academic world. Linda resides in Richmond with her family.

Rebecca Lawson, PowerPoint Author

Rebecca Lawson is a professor in the Computer Information Technologies program at Lansing Community College. She coordinates the curriculum, develops the instructional materials, and teaches for the E-Business curriculum. She also serves as the Online Faculty Coordinator at the Center for Teaching Excellence at LCC. In that role, she develops and facilitates online workshops for faculty learning to teach online. Her major areas of interest include online curriculum quality assurance, the review and development of printed and online instructional materials, the assessment of computer and Internet literacy skill levels to facilitate student retention, and the use of social networking tools to support learning in blended and online learning environments.

Jerri Williams, Access Author

Jerri Williams is a Senior Instructor at Montgomery County Community College in Pennsylvania, and currently works as a technical editor and content developer in addition to her teaching responsibilities. Jerri worked as a live and virtual corporate trainer and developer in major pharmaceutical and other companies for many years prior to joining the Exploring Access 2013, 2016, and 2019 teams. She is interested in travel, history, cooking, theater, movies, and tending to her colonial farmhouse (a work in progress). Jerri is married to Gareth and is the mother of two daughters, Holly (an accountant/office manager, and mother of an adorable son, Meir) and Gwyneth (a corporate defense/employment attorney). Jerri and Gareth live outside of Philadelphia, and enjoy their home and garden, spending time with family and friends, watching the Philadelphia Eagles, and visiting the Jersey Shore any time of the year.

Amy Rutledge, Access Author

Amy Rutledge is a Special Instructor of Management Information Systems at Oakland University in Rochester, Michigan. She coordinates academic programs in Microsoft Office applications and introductory management information systems courses for the School of Business Administration. Before joining Oakland University as an instructor, Amy spent several years working for a music distribution company and automotive manufacturer in various corporate roles including IT project management. She holds a B.S. in Business Administration specializing in Management Information Systems, and a B.A. in French Modern Language and Literature. She holds an M.B.A from Oakland University. She resides in Michigan with her husband, Dan and daughters Emma and Jane.

Diane Kosharek, PowerPoint Author

Diane Kosharek holds a Bachelor's Degree in Education from the University of Wisconsin-Madison and a Master's Degree in Educational Computing from Cardinal Stritch University. She has spent the past 18 years teaching business technology courses at Madison College. In addition to her teaching role, she works closely with business and industry specialists developing and delivering tailored training solutions for area employers in areas such as customer service, software applications, and business writing skills. Prior to joining Madison College, she worked as a Technology Training Consultant, providing consultation and production assistance to teaching faculty and staff to incorporate appropriate technology in their courses to enhance learning.

Dr. Robert T. Grauer, Creator of the Exploring Series

Bob Grauer is an Associate Professor in the Department of Computer Information Systems at the University of Miami, where he is a multiple winner of the Outstanding Teaching Award in the School of Business, most recently in 2009. He has written numerous COBOL texts and is the vision behind the Exploring Office series, with more than three million books in print. His work has been translated into three foreign languages and is used in all aspects of higher education at both national and international levels. Bob Grauer has consulted for several major corporations including IBM and American Express. He received his Ph.D. in Operations Research in 1972 from the Polytechnic Institute of Brooklyn.

Brief Contents

Contents

Microsoft Office Excel 2019

Microsoft Office Access 2019

Microsoft Office PowerPoint 2019

Application Capstone Exercises

Acknowledgments

The Exploring team would like to acknowledge and thank all the reviewers who helped us throughout the years by providing us with their invaluable comments, suggestions, and constructive criticism.

A. D. Knight
Northwestern State University
Natchitoches–Louisiana

Aaron Montanino
Davenport University

Adriana Lumpkin
Midland College

Alan S. Abrahams
Virginia Tech

Alexandre C. Probst
Colorado Christian University

Ali Berrached
University of Houston–Downtown

Allen Alexander
Delaware Technical & Community College

Amy Rutledge
Oakland University

Andrea Marchese
Maritime College
State University of New York

Andrew Blitz
Broward College; Edison State College

Angel Norman
University of Tennessee–Knoxville

Angela Clark
University of South Alabama

Ann Rovetto
Horry–Georgetown Technical College

Astrid Todd
Guilford Technical Community College

Audrey Gillant
Maritime College, State University of
New York

Barbara Stover
Marion Technical College

Barbara Tollinger
Sinclair Community College

Ben Brahim Taha
Auburn University

Beverly Amer
Northern Arizona University

Beverly Fite
Amarillo College

Biswadip Ghosh
Metropolitan State University of Denver

Bonita Volker
Tidewater Community College

Bonnie Homan
San Francisco State University

Brad West
Sinclair Community College

Brian Kovar
Kansas State University

Brian Powell
West Virginia University

Carmen Morrison
North Central State College

Carol Buser
Owens Community College

Carol Roberts
University of Maine

Carol Wiggins
Blinn College

Carole Pfeiffer
Southeast Missouri State University

Carolyn Barren
Macomb Community College

Carolyn Borne
Louisiana State University

Cathy Poyner
Truman State University

Charles Hodgson
Delgado Community College

Chen Zhang
Bryant University

Cheri Higgins
Illinois State University

Cheryl Brown
Delgado Community College

Cheryl Hinds
Norfolk State University

Cheryl Sypniewski
Macomb Community College

Chris Robinson
Northwest State Community College

Cindy Herbert
Metropolitan Community College–Longview

Craig J. Peterson
American InterContinental University

Craig Watson
Bristol Community College

Dana Hooper
University of Alabama

Dana Johnson
North Dakota State University

Daniela Marghitu
Auburn University

David Noel
University of Central Oklahoma

David Pulis
Maritime College, State University of
New York

David Thornton
Jacksonville State University

Dawn Medlin
Appalachian State University

Debby Keen
University of Kentucky

Debra Chapman
University of South Alabama

Debra Hoffman
Southeast Missouri State University

Derrick Huang
Florida Atlantic University

Diana Baran
Henry Ford Community College

Diane Cassidy
The University of North Carolina at
Charlotte

Diane L. Smith
Henry Ford Community College

Dick Hewer
Ferris State College

Don Danner
San Francisco State University

Don Hoggan
Solano College

Don Riggs
SUNY Schenectady County Community
College

Doncho Petkov
Eastern Connecticut State University

Donna Ehrhart
Genesee Community College

Elaine Crable
Xavier University

Elizabeth Duett
Delgado Community College

Erhan Uskup
Houston Community College–Northwest

Eric Martin
University of Tennessee

Erika Nadas
Wilbur Wright College

Evelyn Schenk
Saginaw Valley State University

Floyd Winters
Manatee Community College

Frank Lucente
Westmoreland County Community College

G. Jan Wilms
Union University

Gail Cope
Sinclair Community College

Gary DeLorenzo
California University of Pennsylvania

Gary Garrison
Belmont University

Gary McFall
Purdue University

George Cassidy
Sussex County Community College

Gerald Braun
Xavier University

Gerald Burgess
Western New Mexico University

Gladys Swindler
Fort Hays State University

Gurinder Mehta
Sam Houston State University

Hector Frausto
California State University Los Angeles

Heith Hennel
Valencia Community College

Henry Rudzinski
Central Connecticut State University

Irene Joos
La Roche College

Iwona Rusin
Baker College; Davenport University

J. Roberto Guzman
San Diego Mesa College

Jacqueline D. Lawson
Henry Ford Community College

Jakie Brown, Jr.
Stevenson University

James Brown
Central Washington University

James Powers
University of Southern Indiana

Jane Stam
Onondaga Community College

Janet Bringhurst
Utah State University

Janice Potochney
Gateway Community College

Jean Luoma
Davenport University

Jean Welsh
Lansing Community College

Jeanette Dix
Ivy Tech Community College

Jennifer Day
Sinclair Community College

Jill Canine
Ivy Tech Community College

Jill Young
Southeast Missouri State University

Jim Chaffee
The University of Iowa Tippie College of
Business

Joanne Lazirko
University of Wisconsin–Milwaukee

Jodi Milliner
Kansas State University

John Hollenbeck
Blue Ridge Community College

John Meir
Midlands Technical College

John Nelson
Texas Christian University

John Seydel
Arkansas State University

Judith A. Scheeren
Westmoreland County Community College

Judith Brown
The University of Memphis

Juliana Cypert
Tarrant County College

Kamaljeet Sanghera
George Mason University

Karen Priestly
Northern Virginia Community College

Karen Ravan
Spartanburg Community College

Karen Tracey
Central Connecticut State University

Kathleen Brenan
Ashland University

Ken Busbee
Houston Community College

Kent Foster
Winthrop University

Kevin Anderson
Solano Community College

Kim Wright
The University of Alabama

Kirk Atkinson
Western Kentucky University

Kristen Hockman
University of Missouri–Columbia

Kristi Smith
Allegany College of Maryland

Laura Marcoulides
Fullerton College

Laura McManamon
University of Dayton

Laurence Boxer
Niagara University

Leanne Chun
Leeward Community College

Lee McClain
Western Washington University

Lewis Cappelli
Hudson Valley Community College

Linda D. Collins
Mesa Community College

Linda Johnsonius
Murray State University

Linda Lau
Longwood University

Linda Theus
Jackson State Community College

Linda Williams
Marion Technical College

Lisa Miller
University of Central Oklahoma

Lister Horn
Pensacola Junior College

Lixin Tao
Pace University

Loraine Miller
Cayuga Community College

Lori Kielty
Central Florida Community College

Lorna Wells
Salt Lake Community College

Lorraine Sauchin
Duquesne University

Lucy Parakhovnik
California State University–Northridge

Lynn Baldwin
Madison College

Lynn Keane
University of South Carolina

Lynn Mancini
Delaware Technical Community
College

Lynne Seal
Amarillo College

Mackinzee Escamilla
South Plains College

Marcia Welch
Highline Community College

Margaret McManus
Northwest Florida State College

Margaret Warrick
Allan Hancock College

Marilyn Hibbert
Salt Lake Community College

Mark Choman
Luzerne County Community College

Mary Beth Tarver
Northwestern State University

Mary Duncan
University of Missouri–St. Louis

Maryann Clark
University of New Hampshire

Melissa Nemeth
Indiana University–Purdue University
Indianapolis

Melody Alexander
Ball State University

Michael Douglas
University of Arkansas at Little Rock

Michael Dunklebarger
Alamance Community College

Michael G. Skaff
College of the Sequoias

Michele Budnovitch
Pennsylvania College of Technology

Mike Jochen
East Stroudsburg University

Mike Michaelson
Palomar College

Mike Scroggins
Missouri State University

Mimi Spain
Southern Maine Community College

Muhammed Badamas
Morgan State University

NaLisa Brown
University of the Ozarks

Nancy Grant
Community College of Allegheny
County–South Campus

Nanette Lareau
University of Arkansas Community
College–Morrilton

Nikia Robinson
Indian River State University

Pam Brune
Chattanooga State Community College

Pam Uhlenkamp
Iowa Central Community College

Patrick Smith
Marshall Community and Technical College

Paul Addison
Ivy Tech Community College

Paul Hamilton
New Mexico State University

Paula Ruby
Arkansas State University

Peggy Burrus
Red Rocks Community College

Peter Ross
SUNY Albany

Philip H. Nielson
Salt Lake Community College

Philip Valvalides
Guilford Technical Community College

Ralph Hooper
University of Alabama

Ranette Halverson
Midwestern State University

Richard Blamer
John Carroll University

Richard Cacace
Pensacola Junior College

Richard Hewer
Ferris State University

Richard Sellers
Hill College

Rob Murray
Ivy Tech Community College

Robert Banta
Macomb Community College

Robert Dus˘ek
Northern Virginia Community College

Robert G. Phipps, Jr.
West Virginia University

Robert Sindt
Johnson County Community College

Robert Warren
Delgado Community College

Robyn Barrett
St. Louis Community College–Meramec

Rocky Belcher
Sinclair Community College

Roger Pick
University of Missouri at Kansas City

Ronnie Creel
Troy University

Rosalie Westerberg
Clover Park Technical College

Ruth Neal
Navarro College

Sandra Thomas
Troy University

Sheila Gionfriddo
Luzerne County Community College

Sherrie Geitgey
Northwest State Community College

Sherry Lenhart
Terra Community College

Shohreh Hashemi
University of Houston–Downtown

Sophia Wilberscheid
Indian River State College

Sophie Lee
California State University–Long Beach

Stacy Johnson
Iowa Central Community College

Stephanie Kramer
Northwest State Community College

Stephen Z. Jourdan
Auburn University at Montgomery

Steven Schwarz
Raritan Valley Community College

Sue A. McCrory
Missouri State University

Sumathy Chandrashekar
Salisbury University

Susan Fuschetto
Cerritos College

Susan Medlin
UNC Charlotte

Susan N. Dozier
Tidewater Community College

Suzan Spitzberg
Oakton Community College

Suzanne M. Jeska
County College of Morris

Sven Aelterman
Troy University

Sy Hirsch
Sacred Heart University

Sylvia Brown
Midland College

Tommy Lu
Delaware Technical Community College

Wes Anthony
Houston Community College

Tanya Patrick
Clackamas Community College

Troy S. Cash
Northwest Arkansas Community College

William Ayen
University of Colorado at Colorado Springs

Terri Holly
Indian River State College

Vicki Robertson
Southwest Tennessee Community

Wilma Andrews
Virginia Commonwealth University

Terry Ray Rigsby
Hill College

Vickie Pickett
Midland College

Yvonne Galusha
University of Iowa

Thomas Rienzo
Western Michigan University

Vivianne Moore
Davenport University

Tina Johnson
Midwestern State University

Weifeng Chen
California University of Pennsylvania

Special thanks to our content development and technical team:

Barbara Stover

LeeAnn Bates
MyLab IT content author

Lisa Bucki

Becca Golden
Media Producer

Lori Damanti

Sallie Dodson

Jennifer Hurley
MyLab IT content author

Morgan Hetzler

Ken Mayer

Kevin Marino
MyLab IT content author

Joyce Nielsen

Chris Parent

Ralph Moore
MyLab IT content author

Sean Portnoy

Jerri Williams
MyLab IT content author

Steven Rubin

The Exploring Series and You

Exploring is Pearson's Office Application series that requires students like you to think "beyond the point and click." In this edition, the *Exploring* experience has evolved to be even more in tune with the student of today. With an emphasis on Mac compatibility, critical thinking, and continual updates to stay in sync with the changing Microsoft Office 365, and by providing additional valuable assignments and resources, the *Exploring* series is able to offer you the most usable, current, and beneficial learning experience ever.

The goal of *Exploring* is, as it has always been, to go farther than teaching just the steps to accomplish a task—the series provides the theoretical foundation for you to understand when and why to apply a skill. As a result, you achieve a deeper understanding of each application and can apply this critical thinking beyond Office and the classroom.

New to This Edition

Continual eText Updates: This edition of *Exploring* is written to Microsoft® Office 365®, which is constantly updating. In order to stay current with the software, we are committed to twice annual updates of the eText and Content Updates document available as an instructor resource for text users.

Focus on Mac: Mac usage is growing, and even outstripping PC usage at some four-year institutions. In response, new features such as Mac Tips, On a Mac step boxes, Mac Troubleshooting, and Mac tips on Student Reference Cards help ensure Mac users have a flawless experience using *Exploring*.

Expanded Running Case: In this edition, the Running Case has been expanded to all applications, with one exercise per chapter focusing on the New Castle County Technical Services case, providing a continuous and real-world project for students to work on throughout the semester.

Pre-Built Learning Modules: Pre-built inside MyLab IT, these make course setup a snap. The modules are based on research and instructor best practices, and can be easily customized to meet your course requirements.

Critical Thinking Modules: Pre-built inside MyLab IT, these pair a Grader Project with a critical thinking quiz that requires students to first complete a hands-on project, then reflect on what they did and the data or information they interacted with, to answer a series of objective critical thinking questions. These are offered both at the chapter level for regular practice, as well as at the Application level where students can earn a Critical Thinking badge.

What's New for MyLab IT Graders

Graders with WHY: All Grader project instructions now incorporate the scenario and the WHY to help students critically think and understand why they're performing the steps in the project.

Hands-On Exercise Assessment Graders: A new Grader in each chapter that mirrors the Hands-On Exercise. Using an alternate scenario and data files, this new Grader is built to be more instructional and features Learning Aids such as Read (eText), Watch (video), and Practice (guided simulation) in the Grader report to help students learn, remediate, and resubmit.

Auto-Graded Critical Thinking Quizzes:

- Application Capstones that allow students to earn a Critical Thinking badge
- Chapter-level quizzes for each Mid-Level Exercise Grader project

Improved Mac Compatibility in Graders: All Graders are tested for Mac compatibility and any that can be made 100% Mac compatible are identified in the course. This excludes Access projects as well as any that use functionality not available in Mac Office.

Autograded Integrated Grader Projects: Based on the discipline-specific integrated projects, covering Word, Excel, PowerPoint, and Access in various combinations.

Final Solution Image: Included with Grader student downloads, final output images allows students to visualize what their solution should look like.

What's New for MyLab IT Simulations

Updated Office 365, 2019 Edition Simulations: Written by the *Exploring* author team, ensures one-to-one content to directly match the Hands-On Exercises (Simulation Training) and mirror them with an alternate scenario (Simulation Assessment).

Student Action Visualization: Provides a playback of student actions within the simulation for remediation by students and review by instructors when there is a question about why an action is marked as incorrect.

Series Hallmarks

The **How/Why Approach** helps students move beyond the point and click to a true understanding of how to apply Microsoft Office skills.

- **White Pages/Yellow Pages** clearly distinguish the theory (white pages) from the skills covered in the Hands-On Exercises (yellow pages) so students always know what they are supposed to be doing and why.

- **Case Study** presents a scenario for the chapter, creating a story that ties the Hands-On Exercises together and gives context to the skills being introduced.

- **Hands-On Exercise Videos** are tied to each Hands-On Exercise and walk students through the steps of the exercise while weaving in conceptual information related to the Case Study and the objectives as a whole.

An **Outcomes focus** allows students and instructors to know the higher-level learning goals and how those are achieved through discreet objectives and skills.

- **Outcomes** presented at the beginning of each chapter identify the learning goals for students and instructors.

- **Enhanced Objective Mapping** enables students to follow a directed path through each chapter, from the objectives list at the chapter opener through the exercises at the end of the chapter.
  - **Objectives List:** This provides a simple list of key objectives covered in the chapter. This includes page numbers so students can skip between objectives where they feel they need the most help.
  - **Step Icons:** These icons appear in the white pages and reference the step numbers in the Hands-On Exercises, providing a correlation between the two so students can easily find conceptual help when they are working hands-on and need a refresher.
  - **Quick Concepts Check:** A series of questions that appear briefly at the end of each white page section. These questions cover the most essential concepts in the white pages required for students to be successful in working the Hands-On Exercises. Page numbers are included for easy reference to help students locate the answers.
  - **Chapter Objectives Review:** Located near the end of the chapter and reviews all important concepts covered in the chapter. Designed in an easy-to-read bulleted format.

- **MOS Certification Guide** for instructors and students to direct anyone interested in prepping for the MOS exam to the specific locations to find all content required for the test.

End-of-Chapter Exercises offer instructors several options for assessment. Each chapter has approximately 11–12 exercises ranging from multiple choice questions to open-ended projects.

- **Multiple Choice, Key Terms Matching, Practice Exercises, Mid-Level Exercises, Running Case, Disaster Recovery, and Capstone Exercises** are at the end of all chapters.
  - **Enhanced Mid-Level Exercises** include a **Creative Case** (for PowerPoint and Word), which allows students some flexibility and creativity, not being bound by a definitive solution, and an **Analysis Case** (for Excel and Access), which requires students to interpret the data they are using to answer an analytic question.

- **Application Capstone** exercises are included in the book to allow instructors to test students on the contents of a single application.

The Exploring Series and MyLab IT

The *Exploring Series* has been a market leader for more than 20 years, with a hallmark focus on both the *how* and *why* behind what students do within the Microsoft Office software. In this edition, the pairing of the text with MyLab IT Simulations, Graders, Objective Quizzes, and Resources as a fully complementary program allows students and instructors to get the very most out of their use of the *Exploring Series*.

To maximize student results, we recommend pairing the text content with MyLab IT, which is the teaching and learning platform that empowers you to reach every student. By combining trusted author content with digital tools and a flexible platform, MyLab personalizes the learning experience and helps your students learn and retain key course concepts while developing skills that future employers are seeking in their candidates.

Solving Teaching and Learning Challenges

Pearson addresses these teaching and learning challenges with *Exploring* and MyLab IT 2019.

Reach Every Student

MyLab IT 2019 delivers trusted content and resources through easy-to-use, Prebuilt Learning Modules that promote student success. Through an authentic learning experience, students become sharp critical thinkers and proficient in Microsoft Office, developing essential skills employers seek.

Practice and Feedback: What do I do when I get stuck or need more practice?

MyLab IT features **Integrated Learning Aids** within the Simulations and now also within the Grader Reports, allowing students to choose to Read (via the eText), Watch (via an author-created hands-on video), or Practice (via a guided simulation) whenever they get stuck. These are conveniently accessible directly within the simulation training so that students do not have to leave the graded assignment to access these helpful resources. The **Student Action Visualization** captures all the work students do in the Simulation for both Training and Assessment and allows students and instructors to watch a detailed playback for the purpose of remediation or guidance when students get stuck. MyLab IT offers **Grader project reports** for coaching, remediation, and defensible grading. Score Card Detail allows you to easily see where students were scored correctly or incorrectly, pointing out how many points were deducted on each step. Live Comments Report allows you and the students to see the actual files the student submitted with mark-ups/comments on what they missed and now includes Learning Aids to provide immediate remediation for incorrect steps.

Application, Motivation, and Employability Skills: Why am I taking this course, and will this help me get a job?

Students want to know that what they are doing in this class is setting them up for their ultimate goal—to get a job. With an emphasis on **employability skills** like critical thinking and other soft skills, **digital badges** to prove student proficiency in Microsoft skills and critical thinking, and **MOS Certification practice materials** in MyLab IT, the *Exploring Series* is putting students on the path to differentiate themselves in the job market, so that they can find and land a job that values their schools once they leave school.

Application: How do I get students to apply what they've learned in a meaningful way?

The *Exploring Series* and MyLab IT offer instructors the ability to provide students with authentic formative and summative assessments. The realistic and hi-fidelity **simulations** help students feel like they are working in the real Microsoft applications and allow them to explore, use 96% of Microsoft methods, and do so without penalty. The **Grader projects** allow students to gain real-world context as they work live in the application, applying both an understanding of how and why to perform certain skills to complete a project. New **Critical Thinking quizzes** require students to demonstrate their understanding of why, by answering questions that force them to analyze and interpret the project they worked on to answer a series of objective questions. The new **Running Case** woven through all applications requires students to apply their knowledge in a realistic way to a long-running, semester-long project focused on the same company.

Ease of Use: I need a course solution that is easy to use for both me and my students

MyLab IT 2019 is the easiest and most accessible in its history. With new **Prebuilt Learning** and **Critical Thinking Modules** course set-up is simple! **LMS integration capabilities** allow users seamless access to MyLab IT with single sign-on, grade sync, and asset-level deep linking. Continuing a focus on accessibility, MyLab IT includes an **integrated Accessibility Toolbar** with translation feature for students with disabilities, as well as a **Virtual Keyboard** that allows students to complete keyboard actions entirely on screen. There is also an enhanced focus on Mac compatibility with even more Mac-compatible Grader projects.

Developing Employability Skills

High-Demand Office Skills are taught to help students gain these skills and prepare for the Microsoft Office Certification exams (MOS). The MOS objectives are covered throughout the content, and a MOS Objective Appendix provides clear mapping of where to find each objective. Practice exams in the form of Graders and Simulations are available in MyLab IT.

Badging Digital badges are available for students in Introductory and Advanced Microsoft Word, Excel, Access, and PowerPoint. This digital credential is issued to students upon successful completion (90%+ score) of an Application Capstone Badging Grader project. MyLab IT badges provide verified evidence that learners have demonstrated specific skills and competencies using Microsoft Office tools in a real project and help distinguish students within the job pool. Badges are issued through the Acclaim system and can be placed in a LinkedIn ePortfolio, posted on social media (Facebook, Twitter), and/or included in a résumé. Badges include tags with relevant information that allow students to be discoverable by potential employers, as well as search for jobs for which they are qualified.

> "The badge is a way for employers to actually verify that a potential employee is actually somewhat fluent with Excel."—Bunker Hill Community College Student

The new **Critical Thinking Badge** in MyLab IT for 2019 provides verified evidence that learners have demonstrated the ability to not only complete a real project, but also analyze and problem-solve using Microsoft Office applications. Students prove this by completing an objective quiz that requires them to critically think about the project, interpret data, and explain why they performed the actions they did in the project. Critical Thinking is a hot button issue at many institutions and is highly sought after in job candidates, allowing students with the Critical Thinking Badge to stand out and prove their skills.

Soft Skills Videos are included in MyLab IT for educators who want to emphasize key employability skills such as Accepting Criticism and Being Coachable, Customer Service, and Resume and Cover Letter Best Practices.

Resources

Instructor Teaching Resources	
Supplements Available to Instructors at www.pearsonhighered.com/exploring	**Features of the Supplement**
Instructor's Manual	Available for each chapter and includes: • List of all Chapter Resources, File Names, and Where to Find • Chapter Overview • Class Run-Down • Key Terms • Discussion Questions • Practice Projects & Applications • Teaching Notes • Additional Web Resources • Projects and Exercises with File Names • Solutions to Multiple Choice, Key Terms Matching, and Quick Concepts Checks
Solutions Files, Annotated Solution Files, Scorecards	• Available for all exercises with definitive solutions • Annotated Solution Files in PDF feature callouts to enable easy grading • Scorecards to allow for easy scoring for hand-grading all exercises with definitive solutions, and scoring by step adding to 100 points.
Rubrics	For Mid-Level Exercises without a definitive solution. Available in Microsoft Word format, enabling instructors to customize the assignments for their classes
Test Bank	Approximately 75–100 total questions per chapter, made up of multiple-choice, true/false, and matching. Questions include these annotations: • Correct Answer • Difficulty Level • Learning Objective Alternative versions of the Test Bank are available for the following LMS: Blackboard CE/Vista, Blackboard, Desire2Learn, Moodle, Sakai, and Canvas
Computerized TestGen	TestGen allows instructors to: • Customize, save, and generate classroom tests • Edit, add, or delete questions from the Test Item Files • Analyze test results • Organize a database of tests and student results
PowerPoint Presentations	PowerPoints for each chapter cover key topics, feature key images from the text, and include detailed speaker notes in addition to the slide content. PowerPoints meet accessibility standards for students with disabilities. Features include, but are not limited to: • Keyboard and Screen Reader access • Alternative text for images • High color contrast between background and foreground colors

Scripted Lectures	• A lecture guide that provides the actions and language to help demonstrate skills from the chapter • Follows the activity similar to the Hands-On Exercises but with an alternative scenario and data files
Prepared Exams	• An optional Hands-On Exercise that can be used to assess students' ability to perform the skills from each chapter, or across all chapters in an application. • Each Prepared Exam folder includes the needed data files, instruction file, solution, annotated solution, and scorecard.
Outcome and Objective Maps	• Available for each chapter to help you determine what to assign • Includes every exercise and identifies which outcomes, objectives, and skills are included from the chapter
MOS Mapping, MOS Online Appendix	• Based on the Office 2019 MOS Objectives • Includes a full mapping of where each objective is covered in the materials • For any content not covered in the textbook, additional material is available in the Online Appendix document
Transition Guide	A detailed spreadsheet that provides a clear mapping of content from Exploring Microsoft Office 2016 to Exploring Microsoft Office 365, 2019 Edition
Content Updates Guide	A living document that features any changes in content based on Microsoft Office 365 changes as well as any errata
Assignment Sheets	Document with a grid of suggested student deliverables per chapter that can be passed out to students with columns for Due Date, Possible Points, and Actual Points
Sample Syllabus	Syllabus templates set up for 8-week, 12-week, and 16-week courses
Answer Keys for Multiple Choice, Key Terms Matching, and Quick Concepts Check	Answer keys for each objective, matching, or short-answer question type from each chapter

Student Resources

Supplements Available to Students at www.pearsonhighered.com/ exploring	**Features of the Supplement**
Student Data Files	All data files needed for the following exercises, organized by chapter: • Hands-On Exercises • Practice Exercises • Mid-Level Exercises • Running Case • Disaster Recovery Case • Capstone Exercise
MOS Certification Material	• Based on the Office 2019 MOS Objectives • Includes a full mapping of where each objective is covered in the materials • For any content not covered in the textbook, additional material is available in the Online Appendix document

(ex·ploring)

SERIES

1. Investigating in a systematic way: examining. 2. Searching into or ranging over for the purpose of discovery.

Microsoft®

Office 365®

2019 Edition

INTRODUCTORY

Office 365 Common Features

LEARNING OUTCOME

You will apply skills common across the Microsoft Office suite to create and format documents and edit content in Office 365 applications.

OBJECTIVES & SKILLS: After you read this chapter, you will be able to:

CASE STUDY | Spotted Begonia Art Gallery

You are an administrative assistant for Spotted Begonia, a local art gallery. The gallery does a lot of community outreach to help local artists develop a network of clients and supporters. Local schools are invited to bring students to the gallery for enrichment programs.

As the administrative assistant for Spotted Begonia, you are responsible for overseeing the production of documents, spreadsheets, newspaper articles, and presentations that will be used to increase public awareness of the gallery. Other clerical assistants who are familiar with Microsoft Office will prepare the promotional materials, and you will proofread, make necessary corrections, adjust page layouts, save and print documents, and identify appropriate templates to simplify tasks. Your experience with Microsoft Office is limited, but you know that certain fundamental tasks that are common to Word, Excel, and PowerPoint will help you accomplish your oversight task. You are excited to get started with your work!

Taking the First Step

Dean Drobot/Shutterstock

CHAPTER 1

FIGURE 1.1 Spotted Begonia Art Gallery Documents

CASE STUDY | Spotted Begonia Art Gallery

Starting Files	Files to be Submitted
cf01h1Letter.docx	cf01h1Letter_LastFirst.docx
Seasonal Event Flyer Template	cf01h3Flyer_LastFirst.docx

MyLab IT Grader An alternate version of this project is available as a MyLab IT Grader Assessment

Get Started with Office Applications

Organizations around the world rely heavily on Microsoft Office software to produce documents, spreadsheets, presentations, and databases. **Microsoft Office** is a productivity software suite that includes a set of software applications, each one specializing in a specific type of output. There are different versions of Office. Office 365 is purchased as a monthly or annual subscription and is fully installed on your PC, tablet, and phone. With Office 365, you receive periodic updates of new features and security measures. Office 365 also includes access to OneDrive storage. Office 2019 is a one-time purchase and fully installed on your PC. Periodic upgrades are not available. Both Office 365 and Office 2019 have versions that run on a Mac.

All versions of Microsoft Office include Word, Excel, and PowerPoint, as well as some other applications. Some versions of Office also include Access. Office 365 for Mac and Office for Mac include Word, Excel, and PowerPoint, but not Access. **Microsoft Word** (Word) is a word processing application, used to produce all sorts of documents, including memos, newsletters, reports, and brochures. **Microsoft Excel** (Excel) is a financial spreadsheet program, used to organize records, financial transactions, and business information in the form of worksheets. **Microsoft PowerPoint** (PowerPoint) is presentation software, used to create dynamic presentations to inform and persuade audiences. Finally, **Microsoft Access** (Access) is a database program, used to record and link data, query databases, and create forms and reports. The choice of which software application to use really depends on what type of output you are producing. Table 1.1 describes the major tasks of the four primary applications in Microsoft Office.

TABLE 1.1 Microsoft Office Applications	
Office Application	**Application Characteristics**
Word	Word processing software used with text and graphics to create, edit, and format documents.
Excel	Spreadsheet software used to store quantitative data and to perform accurate and rapid calculations, what-if analyses, and charting, with results ranging from simple budgets to sophisticated financial and statistical analyses.
PowerPoint	Presentation graphics software used to create slide shows for presentation by a speaker or delivered online, to be published as part of a website, or to run as a stand-alone application on a computer kiosk.
Access	Relational database software used to store data and convert it into information. Database software is used primarily for decision making by businesses that compile data from multiple records stored in tables to produce informative reports.

These programs are designed to work together, so you can integrate components created in one application into a file created by another application. For example, you could integrate a chart created in Excel into a Word document or a PowerPoint presentation, or you could export a table created in Access into Excel for further analysis. You can use two or more Office applications to produce your intended output.

In addition, Microsoft Office applications share common features. Such commonality gives a similar feel to each software application so that learning and working with each Office software application is easier. This chapter focuses on many common features that the Office applications share. Although Word is primarily used to illustrate many examples, you are encouraged to open and explore Excel and PowerPoint (and to some degree, Access) to examine the same features in those applications. As a note, most of the content in this chapter and book are for the Windows-based Office applications. Some basic information about Office for Mac is included in TIP boxes and in the Step boxes when there are significant differences to point out.

In this section, you will learn how to log in with your Microsoft account, open an application, and open and save a file. You will also learn to identify interface components common to Office software applications, such as the ribbon, Backstage view, and the Quick Access Toolbar. You will experience Live Preview. You will learn how to get help with an application. You will also learn about customizing the ribbon and using Office add-ins.

Starting an Office Application

Microsoft Office applications are launched from the Start menu. Select the Start icon to display the Start menu and select the app tile for the application in which you want to work (see Figure 1.2). Note: The Start menu in Figure 1.2 may show different tiles and arrangement of tiles than what is on your Start menu. If the application tile you want is not on the Start menu, you can open the program from the list of all apps on the left side of the Start menu, or alternatively, you can use search on the taskbar. Just type the name of the program in the search box and press Enter. The program will open automatically.

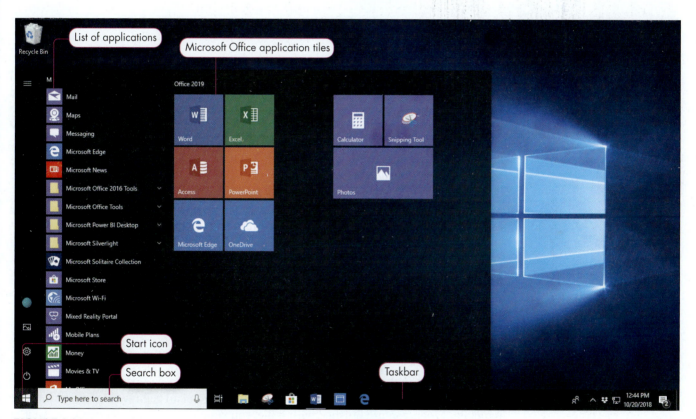

FIGURE 1.2 Windows Start Menu

Use Your Microsoft Account

When you have a Microsoft account, you can sign in to any Windows computer and you will be able to access the saved settings associated with your Microsoft account. That means any computer can have the same familiar look that you are used to seeing on your home or school computers and devices. Your Microsoft account will automatically sign in to all the apps and services that use a Microsoft account, such as OneDrive and Outlook. If you share your computer with another user, each user can have access to his or her own Microsoft account, and can easily switch between accounts by logging out of one Microsoft account and logging in to another Microsoft account. You can switch accounts within an application as well.

To switch between accounts in an application such as Word, complete the following steps:

1. Click the profile name at the top-right of the application.
2. Select Switch account.
3. Select an account from the list, if the account has already been added to the computer, or add a new account.

On a Mac, to switch between accounts in an application, complete the following steps:

1. Click the application menu (Word, Excel, etc.), click Sign Out, and then click Sign Out again.
2. Click File, click New From Template, and then click Sign in at top of the left pane.
3. Click Sign in again, type your user email, click Next, type password, and then click Sign in.

Use OneDrive

Having a Microsoft account also provides additional benefits, such as being connected to all of Microsoft's resources on the Internet. These resources include an Outlook email account and access to OneDrive cloud storage. *Cloud storage* is a technology used to store files and work with programs that are stored in a central location on the Internet. *OneDrive* is a Microsoft app used to store, access, and share files and folders on the Internet. OneDrive is the default storage location when saving Office files. Because OneDrive stores files on the Internet, when a document has been saved in OneDrive the most recent version of the document will be accessible when you log in from any computer connected to the Internet. Files and folders saved to OneDrive can be available offline and accessed through File Explorer—Windows' file management system. Moreover, changes made to any document saved to OneDrive will be automatically updated across all devices, so each device you access with your Windows account will all have the same version of the file.

OneDrive enables you to collaborate with others. You can share your documents with others or edit a document on which you are collaborating. You can even work with others simultaneously on the same document.

STEP 1   Working with Files

When working with an Office application, you can begin by opening an existing file that has already been saved to a storage medium or you can begin work on a new file or template. When you are finished with a file, you should save it, so you can retrieve it at another time.

Create a New File

After opening an Office application, you will be presented with template choices. Use the Blank document (workbook, presentation, database, etc.) template to start a new blank file. You can also create a new Office file from within an application by selecting New from the File tab.

The File tab is located at the far left of the ribbon. When you select the File tab, you see *Backstage view*. Backstage view is where you manage your files and the data about them—creating, saving, printing, sharing, inspecting for accessibility, compatibility, and other document issues, and accessing other setting options. The File tab and Backstage view is where you do things "to" a file, whereas the other tabs on the ribbon enable you to do things "in" a file.

Save a File

Saving a file enables you to open it for additional updates or reference later. Files are saved to a storage medium such as a hard drive, flash drive, or to OneDrive.

The first time you save a file, you indicate where the file will be saved and assign a file name. It is best to save the file in an appropriately named folder so you can find it easily later. Thereafter, you can continue to save the file with the same name and location using the Save command. If the file is saved in OneDrive, any changes to the file will be automatically saved. You do not have to actively save the document. If you want more control over when changes to your document are saved, you have the option to turn this feature off (or back on) with the AutoSave feature in the Quick Access Toolbar.

There are instances where you will want to rename the file or save it to a different location. For example, you might reuse a budget saved as an Excel worksheet, modifying it for another year, and want to keep a copy of both the old and revised budgets. In this instance, you would save the new workbook with a new name, and perhaps save it in a different folder. To do so, use the Save As command, and continue with the same procedure to save a new file: navigating to the new storage location and changing the file name. Figure 1.3 shows a typical Save As pane that enables you to select a location before saving the file. Notice that OneDrive is listed as well as This PC. To navigate to a specific location, use Browse.

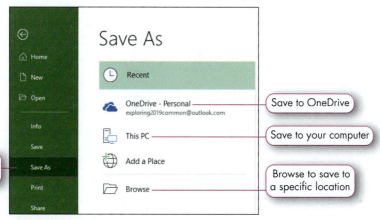

FIGURE 1.3 Save As in Backstage View

To save a file with a different name and/or file location, complete the following steps:

1. Click the File tab.
2. Click Save As.
3. Select a location or click Browse to navigate to the file storage location.
4. Type the file name.
5. Click Save.

STEP 2 **Open a Saved File**

Often you will need to work on an existing file that has been saved to a storage location. This may be an email attachment that you have downloaded to a storage device, a file that has been shared with you in OneDrive, or a file you have previously created. To open an existing file, navigate in File Explorer to the folder or drive where the document is stored, and then double-click the file name to open the file. The application and the file will open. Alternatively, if the application is already open, from Backstage view, click Open, and then click Browse, This PC, or OneDrive to locate and open the file (see Figure 1.4).

> **MAC TIP:** To open an existing file, navigate in Finder to the folder or drive where the document is stored and double-click the file name to open the file.

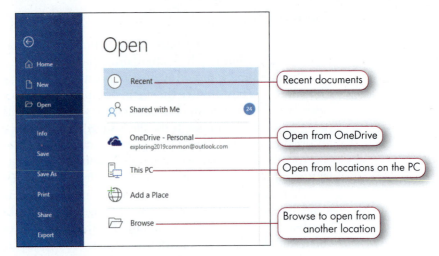

FIGURE 1.4 Open in Backstage View

Office simplifies the task of reopening files by providing a Recent documents list with links to your most recently used files, as shown in Figure 1.5. When opening the application, the Recent list displays in the center pane. The Recent list changes to reflect only the most recently opened files, so if it has been quite some time since you worked with a particular file, or if you have worked on several other files in between and you do not see your file listed, you can click More documents (or Workbooks, Presentations, etc).

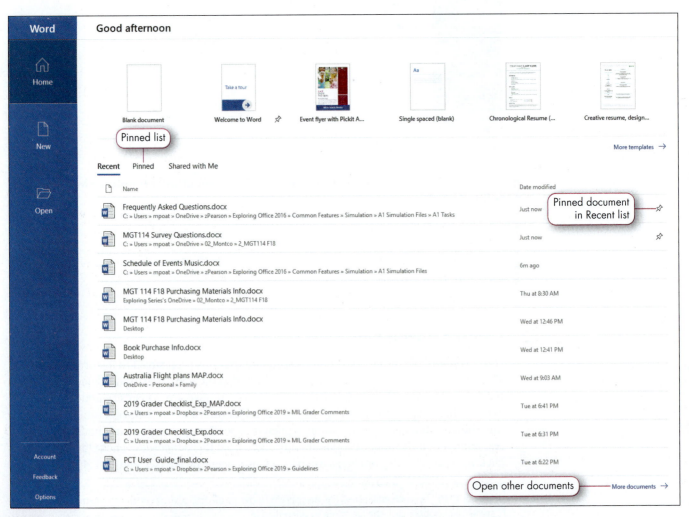

FIGURE 1.5 Recent Documents List

Using Common Interface Components

When you open any Office application, you will first notice the title bar and ribbon (see Figure 1.6) at the top of the document. These features enable you to identify the document, provide easy access to frequently used commands, and controls the window in which the document displays. The *title bar* identifies the current file name and the application in which you are working. It also includes control buttons that enable you to minimize, restore down, or close the application window. The Quick Access Toolbar, on the left side of the title bar, enables you to turn AutoSave on or off, save the file, undo or redo editing, and customize the Quick Access Toolbar. Located just below the title bar is the ribbon. The *ribbon* is the command center of Office applications containing tabs, groups, and commands. If you are working with a large project, you can maximize your workspace by temporarily hiding the ribbon. There are several methods that can be used to hide and then redisplay the ribbon:

- Double-click any tab name to collapse; click any tab name to expand
- Click the Collapse Ribbon arrow at the far-right side of the ribbon
- Use the Ribbon Display Option on the right side of the Title bar. These controls enable you to not only collapse or expand the ribbon, but also to choose whether you want to see the tabs or no tabs at all.

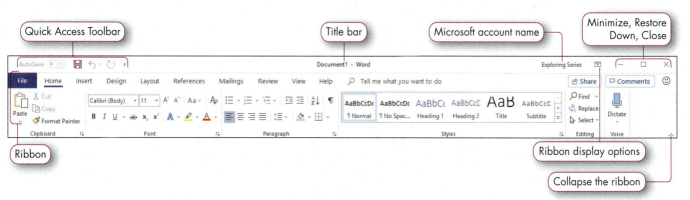

FIGURE 1.6 The Title Bar, Quick Access Toolbar, and Document Controls

Use the Ribbon

The main organizational grouping on the ribbon is tabs. The *tab* name indicates the type of commands located on the tab. On each tab, the ribbon displays several task-oriented groups. A *group* is a subset of a tab that organizes similar commands together. A *command* is a button or task within a group that you select to perform a task (see Figure 1.7). The ribbon with the tabs and groups of commands is designed to provide efficient functionality. For that reason, the Home tab displays when you first open a file in an Office software application and contains groups with the most commonly used commands for that application. For example, because you often want to change the way text is displayed, the Home tab in an Office application includes a Font group, with commands related to modifying text. Similarly, other tabs contain groups of related actions, or commands, many of which are unique to each Office application. The active tab in Figure 1.7 is the Home tab.

> **MAC TIP:** Office for Mac does not display group names in the ribbon by default. On a Mac, to display group names on the ribbon, click the application name menu (Word, Excel, PowerPoint) and select Preferences. Click View and click to select Show group titles in the Ribbon section of the View dialog box.

FIGURE 1.7 The Ribbon

As shown in Figure 1.7, some ribbon commands, such as Paste in the Clipboard group, contain two parts: the main command and an arrow. The arrow may be below or to the right of the main command, depending on the command, window size, or screen resolution. When selected, the arrow brings up additional commands or options associated with the main command. For example, selecting the Paste arrow enables you to access the Paste Options commands, and the Font color arrow displays a set of colors from which to choose. Instructions in the *Exploring* series use the command name to instruct you to click the main command to perform the default action, such as click Paste. Instructions include the word *arrow* when you need to select the arrow to access an additional option, such as click the Paste arrow.

Office applications enable you to work with objects such as images, shapes, charts, and tables. When you include such objects in a project, they are considered separate components that you can manage independently. To work with an object, you must first select it. When an object is selected, the ribbon is modified to include one or more **contextual tabs** that contain groups of commands related to the selected object. These tabs are designated as Tool tabs; for example, Picture Tools is the contextual tab that displays when a picture is selected. When the object is no longer selected, the contextual tab disappears.

Word, PowerPoint, Excel, and Access all share a similar ribbon structure. Although the specific tabs, groups, and commands vary among the Office programs, the way in which you use the ribbon and the descriptive nature of tab titles is the same, regardless of which program you are using. For example, if you want to insert a chart in Excel, a header in Word, or a shape in PowerPoint, those commands are found on the Insert tab in those programs. The first thing you should do as you begin to work with an Office application is to study the ribbon. Look at all tabs and their contents. That way, you will have a good idea of where to find specific commands, and how the ribbon with which you are currently working differs from one that you might have used in another application.

STEP 3 ▶ Use a Dialog Box and Gallery

Some commands and features do not display on the ribbon because they are not as commonly used. For example, you might want to apply a special effect such as Small caps or apply character spacing to some text. Because these effects are not found on the ribbon, they will most likely be found in a **dialog box** (in this case, the Font dialog box). When you open a dialog box, you gain access to more precise or less frequently used commands. Dialog boxes are accessed by clicking a **Dialog Box Launcher** ⌐, found in the lower right corner of some ribbon groups. Figure 1.8 shows the Font group Dialog Box Launcher and the Font dialog box.

> **MAC TIP:** Dialog box launchers are not available in Office for Mac. Instead, click a menu option such as Format, Edit, or Insert for additional options.

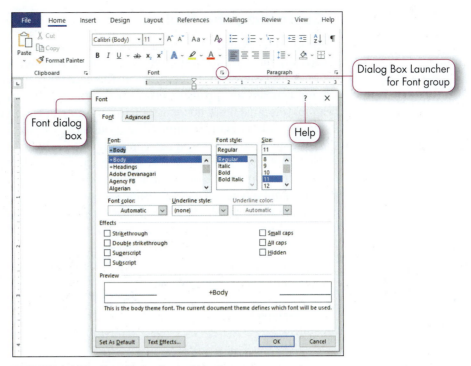

FIGURE 1.8 The Font Dialog Box in Word

Similarly, some formatting and design options are too numerous to include in the ribbon's limited space. For example, the Styles group displays on the Home tab of the Word ribbon. Because there are more styles than can easily display at once, the Styles group can be expanded to display a gallery of additional styles. A *gallery* is an Office feature that displays additional formatting and design options. Galleries in Excel and PowerPoint provide additional choices of chart styles and slide themes, respectively. Figure 1.9 shows an example of a PowerPoint Themes gallery. From the ribbon, you can display a gallery of additional choices by clicking More ⬇, which is located at the bottom right of the group's scroll bar found in some ribbon selections (see Figure 1.9).

FIGURE 1.9 The Variants Gallery in PowerPoint

When editing a document, worksheet, or presentation, it is helpful to see the results of formatting changes before you make final selections. The feature that displays a preview of the results of a selection is called *Live Preview*. For example, you might be considering modifying the color of an image in a document or worksheet. As you place the pointer over a color selection in a ribbon gallery or group, the selected image will temporarily display the color to which you are pointing. Similarly, you can get a preview of how theme designs would display on PowerPoint slides by pointing to specific themes in the PowerPoint Themes group and noting the effect on a displayed slide. When you click the item, the selection is applied. Live Preview is available in various ribbon selections among the Office applications.

Customize the Ribbon

Although the ribbon is designed to put the tasks you need most in an easily accessible location, there may be tasks that are specific to your job or hobby that are on various tabs, or not displayed on the ribbon at all. In this case, you can personalize the ribbon by creating your own tabs and group together the commands you want to use. To add a command to a tab, you must first add a custom group. You can create as many new tabs and custom groups with as many commands as you need. You can also create a custom group on any of the default tabs and add commands to the new group or hide any commands you use less often (see Figure 1.10). Keep in mind that when you customize the ribbon, the customization applies only to the Office program in which you are working at the time. If you want a new tab with the same set of commands in both Word and PowerPoint, for example, the new tab would need to be created in each application.

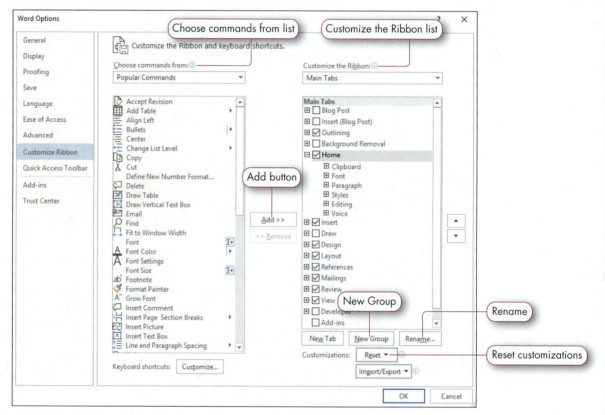

FIGURE 1.10 Customize the Ribbon in Word

There are several ways to access the Customize the Ribbon options:

- Right-click in an empty space in the ribbon and select Customize the Ribbon on the shortcut menu.
- Click the File tab, select Options, and then select Customize Ribbon.
- Click the Customize Quick Access Toolbar button, select More Commands, and then select Customize Ribbon.

The left side of the Customize the Ribbon window displays popular commands associated with the active application, but all available commands can be displayed by selecting All Commands in the *Choose commands from* list. On the right side of the Customize the Ribbon window is a list of the Main Tabs and Groups in the active application. You can also access the contextual Tool tabs by selecting the arrow in the Customize the Ribbon list and selecting Tool Tabs.

To customize the ribbon by adding a command to an existing tab, complete the following steps:

1. Click the File tab, click Options, and then select Customize Ribbon. (Alternatively, follow the other steps above to access the Customize the Ribbon window.)
2. Click the tab name that you want to add a group to under the Customize the Ribbon list. Ensure a blue background displays behind the tab name. Note that checking or unchecking the tab is not selecting the tab for this feature.
3. Click New Group. New Group (Custom) displays as a group on the selected tab.
4. Click Rename and give the new group a meaningful name.
5. Click the command to be added under the Choose commands from list.
6. Click Add.
7. Repeat as necessary, click OK when you have made all your selections.

On a Mac, to customize the ribbon, complete the following steps:

1. Click the Word menu (or whichever application you are working in) and select Preferences.
2. Click Ribbon & Toolbar in the Authoring and Proofing Tools (or in Excel, Authoring).
3. Click the plus sign at the bottom of the Main Tabs box and select New Group.
4. Click the Settings icon and click Rename. Give the new group a meaningful name. Click Save.
5. Continue using steps 5 and 6 in the PC step box above.

To revert all tabs or to reset select tabs to original settings, click Reset, and then click Reset all customizations or Reset only selected Ribbon tab (refer to Figure 1.10).

STEP 4 ## Use and Customize the Quick Access Toolbar

The **Quick Access Toolbar (QAT)**, located at the top-left corner of every Office application window (refer to Figure 1.6), provides one-click access to commonly executed tasks. By default, the QAT includes commands for saving a file and for undoing or redoing recent actions. You can recover from a mistake by clicking Undo on the QAT. If you click the Undo command arrow on the QAT, you can select from a list of previous actions in order of occurrence. The Undo list is not maintained when you close a file or exit the application, so you can only erase an action that took place during the current Office session. You can also Redo (or Replace) an action that you have just undone.

You can also customize the QAT to include commands you frequently use (see Figure 1.11). One command you may want to add is Quick Print. Rather than clicking

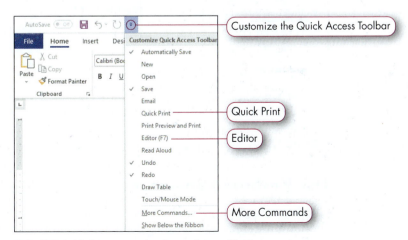

FIGURE 1.11 Customize the Quick Access Toolbar

the File tab, selecting Print, and then selecting various print options, you can add Quick Print to the QAT so that with one click you can print your document with the default Print settings. Other convenient commands can be added, such as Editor to run a spell check of the document.

You customize the QAT by selecting Customize Quick Access Toolbar arrow on the right side of the displayed QAT commands or by right-clicking an empty area on the QAT, and then selecting or deselecting the options from the displayed list of commands. Alternatively, you can right-click any command on the ribbon and select Add to Quick Access Toolbar from the shortcut menu.

To remove a command from the QAT, right-click the command and select Remove from Quick Access Toolbar. If you want to move the QAT to display under the ribbon, select Customize Quick Access Toolbar and click Show below the Ribbon.

STEP 5 ## Use a Shortcut Menu

In Office, you can usually accomplish the same task in several ways. Although the ribbon and QAT provide efficient access to commands, in some situations you might find it more convenient to access the same commands on a shortcut menu. A ***shortcut menu*** is a context-sensitive menu that displays commands and options relevant to the active object. Shortcut menus are accessed by selecting text or an object or by placing the insertion point in a document and pressing the right mouse button or pressing the right side of a trackpad. (On a Mac, press the Control key when you tap the mouse or use a two-finger tap on a trackpad). The shortcut menu will always include options to cut, copy, and paste. In addition, a shortcut menu features tasks that are specifically related to the document content where the insertion point is placed. For example, if your insertion point is on a selected word or group of words, the shortcut menu would include tasks such as to find a synonym or add a comment. If the active object is a picture, the shortcut menu includes options to group objects, provide a caption, or wrap text. As shown in Figure 1.12, when right-clicking a slide thumbnail in PowerPoint, the shortcut menu displays options to add a new slide, duplicate or delete slides, or to change slide layout.

FIGURE 1.12 A Shortcut Menu in PowerPoint

Use Keyboard Shortcuts

Another way to simplify initiating commands is to use ***keyboard shortcuts***. Keyboard shortcuts are created by pressing combinations of two or more keys to initiate a software command. Keyboard shortcuts are viewed as being more efficient because you do not have to take your fingers off the keyboard. Some of the most common keyboard shortcuts in Office include Ctrl+C (Copy), Ctrl+X (Cut), Ctrl+V (Paste), and Ctrl+Z (Undo). Pressing Ctrl+Home moves the insertion point to the beginning of a Word document, to cell A1 in Excel, or to the first PowerPoint slide. To move to the end of those files, press Ctrl+End. There are many other keyboard shortcuts. To discover a keyboard shortcut for a command, point to a command icon on the ribbon to display the ScreenTip. If a keyboard shortcut exists, it will display in the ScreenTip. Many similar keyboard shortcuts exist for Office for Mac applications; however, press the Command key rather than the Ctrl key, such as Command+C for Copy.

> **TIP: USING KEYTIPS**
> Another way to use shortcuts, especially those that do not have a keyboard shortcut, is to press Alt to display KeyTips. You can use KeyTips to do tasks quickly without using the mouse by pressing a few keys—no matter where you are in an Office program. You can get to every command on the ribbon by using an access key—usually by pressing two to four keys sequentially. To stop displaying KeyTips, press Alt again.

Getting Help

No matter whether you are a skilled or a novice user of an Office application, there are times when you need help in either finding a certain ribbon command or need additional assistance or training for a task. Fortunately, there are features included in every Office application to offer you support.

STEP 6 ### Use the Tell Me Box

To the right of the last ribbon tab is a magnifying glass icon and the phrase "Tell me what you want to do." This is the ***Tell me box*** (see Figure 1.13). Use Tell me to enter words and phrases to search for help and information about a command or task you want to perform. Alternatively, use Tell me for a shortcut to a command or, in some instances (like Bold), to complete the action for you. Tell me can also help you research or define a term you entered. Perhaps you want to find an instance of a word in your document and replace it with another word but cannot locate the Find command on the ribbon. As shown in Figure 1.13, you can type *find* in the Tell me box and a list of commands related to the skill will display, including Find & Select and Replace. Find & Select gives options for the Find command. If you click Replace, the Find and Replace dialog box opens without you having to locate the command on the ribbon.

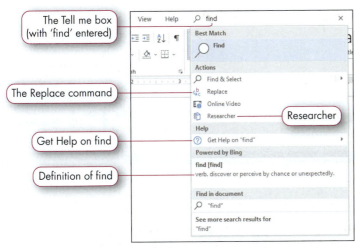

FIGURE 1.13 The Tell Me Box

Should you want to read about the feature instead of applying it, you can click *Get Help on "find,"* which will open Office Help for the feature. Another feature is Smart Lookup on the References tab. This feature opens the Smart Lookup pane that shows results from various online sources based on the search term. **Smart Lookup** provides information about tasks or commands in Office and can also be used to search for general information on a topic, such as *President George Washington.* Smart Lookup is also available on the shortcut menu when you right-click text as well as on the References tab in Word. Depending on your search, Researcher may display instead of, or in addition to, Smart Lookup. Researcher can be used to find quotes, citable sources, and images. Researcher is shown in Figure 1.13.

Use the Help Tab

If you are looking for additional help or training on certain features in any Microsoft Office application, you can access this support on the Help tab (see Figure 1.14). The Help command opens the Help pane with a list of tutorials on a variety of application-specific topics. Show Training displays application-specific training videos in the Help pane. Besides Help and Show Training, the Help tab also includes means to contact Microsoft support and to share your feedback. If you are using Office 365, you receive periodic updates with new features as they are released. To learn more about these features, or simply to discover what a new or previous update includes, use the What's New command. What's New brings you to a webpage that discusses all the newly added features organized by release date. You can also access What's New by clicking Account in Backstage view.

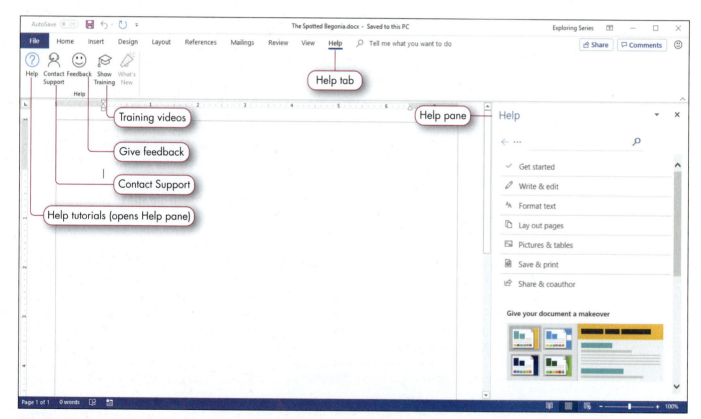

FIGURE 1.14 Help Tab

Use Enhanced ScreenTips

As you use the commands on the ribbon, there may be some that you would like to know more about its purpose, or would like assurance that you are selecting the correct command. For quick summary information on the name and purpose of a command button, point to the command until an *Enhanced ScreenTip* displays, with the name and a brief description of the command. If applicable, a keyboard shortcut is also included. Some ScreenTips include a *Tell me more* option for additional help. The Enhanced ScreenTip, shown for *Format Painter* in Figure 1.15, provides a short description of the command in addition to the steps that discuss how to use Format Painter. Use Format Painter to copy all applied formatting from one set of text to another.

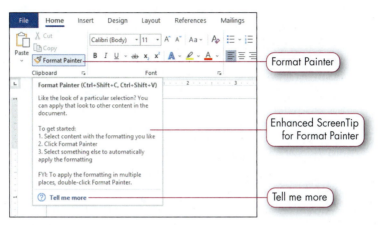

FIGURE 1.15 Enhanced ScreenTip

> **TIP: COPY FORMAT WITH FORMAT PAINTER**
> Use Format Painter to quickly apply the same formatting, such as color, font style, and size to other text. Format Painter can also be used to copy border styles to shapes. Format Painter is available in Word, Excel, and PowerPoint, and can be extremely useful when applying multiple formats to other text. Using Format Painter also ensures consistency in appearance between sets of text. To copy formatting to one location, single-click Format Painter, and then click where you want the format applied. To copy formatting to multiple locations, double-click Format Painter. Press Esc or click Format Painter again to turn off the command.

Installing Add-ins

As complete as the Office applications are, you still might want an additional feature that is not a part of the program. Fortunately, there are Microsoft and third-party programs called add-ins that you can add to the program. An *add-in* is a custom program that extends the functionality of a Microsoft Office application (see Figure 1.16). For example, in PowerPoint, you could add capability for creating diagrams, access free images, or obtain assistance with graphic design. In Excel, add-ins could provide additional functionality that can help with statistics and data mining. In Word, add-ins could provide survey or resume-creating capabilities. Some add-ins will be available for several applications. For example, the Pickit image app shown in Figure 1.16 is available for Word and PowerPoint. You can access add-ins through the My Add-ins or Get Add-ins commands on the Insert tab. Some templates may come with an add-in associated with it. Some add-ins are available for free, whereas others may have a cost.

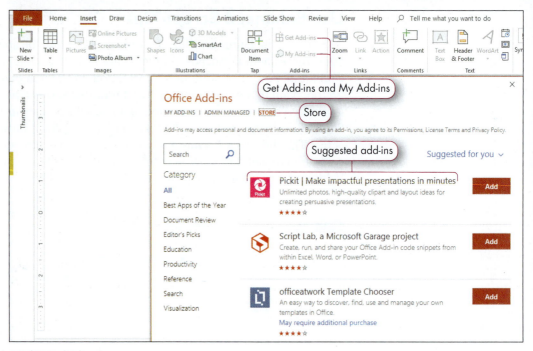

FIGURE 1.16 Add-ins for PowerPoint

Quick Concepts

1. Explain the benefits of logging in with your Microsoft account. **_p. 5_**

2. Describe when you would use Save and when you would use Save As when saving a document. **_p. 7_**

3. Explain how the ribbon is organized. **_p. 9_**

4. Describe the Office application features that are available to assist you in getting help with a task. **_p. 15_**

Hands-On Exercises

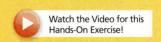
Watch the Video for this Hands-On Exercise!

1 Get Started with Office Applications

The Spotted Begonia Art Gallery just hired several new clerical assistants to help you develop materials for the various activities coming up throughout the year. A coworker sent you a letter and asked for your assistance in making a few minor formatting changes. The letter is an invitation to the *Discover the Artist in You!* program Children's Art Festival. To begin, you will open Word and open an existing document. You will use the Shortcut menu to make simple changes to the document. Finally, you will use the Tell me box to apply a style to the first line of text.

STEP 1 OPEN AND SAVE A FILE

You start Microsoft Word and open an event invitation letter that you will later modify. You rename the file to preserve the original and to save the changes you will make later. Refer to Figure 1.17 as you complete Step 1.

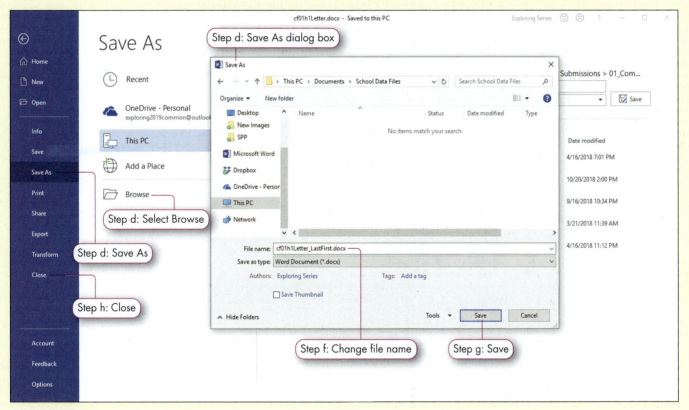

FIGURE 1.17 The Save As Dialog Box

a. Open the Word document *cf01h1Letter*.

The event invitation letter opens.

> **TROUBLESHOOTING:** When you open a file from the student files associated with this book, you may see an Enable Content warning in the Message Bar. This is a security measure to alert a user when there is potentially unsafe content in the file you want to open. You may be confident of the trustworthiness of the files for this book, and should click Enable Content to begin working on the file.

b. Click the **File tab**, click **Save As**, and then click **Browse** to display the Save As dialog box.

Because you will change the name of an existing file, you use the Save As command to give the file a new name. On a Mac, click the File menu and click Save As.

c. Navigate to the location where you are saving your files.

If you are saving the file in a different location than that of your data files, then you will also change the location of where the file is saved.

d. Click in the **File name box** (or the Save As box in Office for Mac) and type **cf01h1Letter_LastFirst**.

You save the document with a different name to preserve the original file.

When you save files, use your last and first names. For example, as the Common Features author, I would name my document "cf01h1Letter_PoatsyMaryAnne."

e. Click **Save**.

> **TROUBLESHOOTING:** If you make any major mistakes in this exercise, you can close the file, open *cf01h1Letter* again, and then start this exercise over.

The file is now saved as cf01h1Letter_LastFirst. Check the title bar of the document to confirm that the file has been saved with the correct name.

f. Click **File** and click **Close** to close the file. Keep Word open.

STEP 2 OPEN A SAVED FILE AND USE THE RIBBON

You now have time to modify the letter, so you open the saved file. You use ribbon commands to modify parts of the letter. Refer to Figure 1.18 as you complete Step 2.

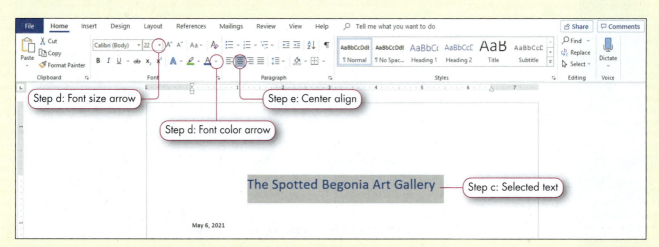

FIGURE 1.18 Use Ribbon Commands to Modify Text

a. Click the **File tab** and click **Open** from the left menu.

The Open window displays.

b. Click **cf01h1Letter_LastFirst** from the list of Recent documents on the right side of the Open window.

The letter you saved earlier opens and is ready to be modified.

c. Place the insertion point in the left margin just before the first line of text *The Spotted Begonia Art Gallery* so an angled right-pointing arrow displays and click.

This is an efficient way of selecting an entire line of text. Alternatively, you can drag the pointer across the text while holding down the left mouse button to select the text.

d. Click the **Font color arrow** in the Font group on the Home tab and select **Blue** in the Standard Colors section. With the text still selected, click the **Font Size arrow** in the Font group and select **22**.

You have changed the color and size of the Art Gallery's name.

e. Click **Center** in the Paragraph group.

f. Click **File** and click **Save**.

Because the file has already been saved, and the name and location are not changing, you use the Save command to save the changes.

USE A DIALOG BOX AND GALLERY

Some of the modifications you want to make to the letter require using tasks that are in dialog boxes and galleries. You will use a Dialog Box Launcher and More to expand the galleries to access the needed commands and features. Refer to Figure 1.19 as you complete Step 3.

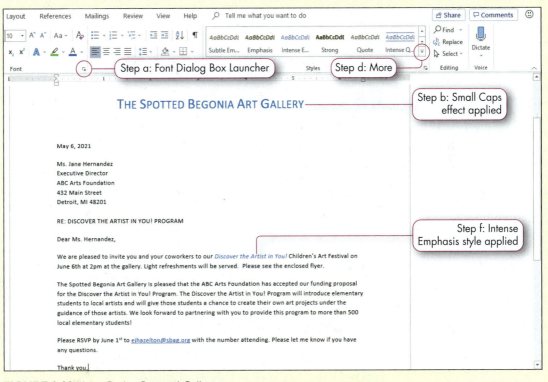

FIGURE 1.19 Use a Dialog Box and Gallery

a. Select the text **The Spotted Begonia Art Gallery**, if it is not already selected. Click the **Font Dialog Box Launcher** ⬜ in the Font group.

The Font dialog box displays.

> **MAC TROUBLESHOOTING:** Office for Mac does not have Dialog Box Launchers. Instead, open a menu and select an option. For example, to access Font options that display in the Font Dialog Box, click the Format menu, and then click Font.

b. Click the **Small caps check box** in the Effects section to select it and click **OK**.

The Small caps text effect is applied to the selected text.

c. Place the insertion point immediately to the left of the text *Discover the Artist in You!* in the first sentence of the paragraph beginning *We are pleased*. Hold the left mouse button down and drag the pointer to select the text up to and including the exclamation point.

> **TROUBLESHOOTING:** Be sure the file you are working on is displayed as a full window. Otherwise, use the vertical scroll bar to bring the paragraph into view.

d. Click **More** in the Styles group to display the Styles gallery. (On a Mac, click the right gallery arrow or click the down arrow to view more options.)

e. Point to Heading 1 style.

Notice how Live Preview shows how that effect will look on the selected text.

f. Click **Intense Emphasis**.

The Intense Emphasis style is applied to the program name.

g. Click **File** and click **Save**.

STEP 4 ## USE AND CUSTOMIZE THE QUICK ACCESS TOOLBAR

You make a change to the document and immediately change your mind. You use the Undo button on the QAT to revert to the original word. You also anticipate checking the spelling on the letter before sending it out. Because you use Spell Check often, you decide to add the command to the QAT. Finally, you realize that you could be saving the document more efficiently by using Save on the QAT. Refer to Figure 1.20 as you complete Step 4.

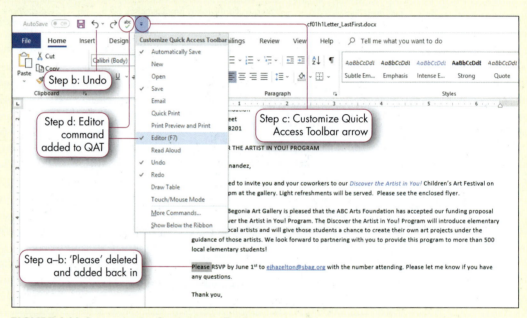

FIGURE 1.20 Customize the Quick Access Toolbar

a. Scroll down so the third paragraph beginning with *Please RSVP* is visible. Double-click **Please** and press **Delete** on the keyboard.

Please is deleted from the letter, but you decide to add it back in.

b. Click **Undo** on the QAT.

Please displays again.

c. Click the **Customize Quick Access Toolbar arrow** on the right side of the QAT.

A list of commands that can be added to the QAT displays.

d. Click **Editor**.

The Editor icon displays on the QAT so you can check for spelling, grammar, and writing issues.

e. Click **Save** on the QAT.

USE A SHORTCUT MENU

The letter inviting Ms. Hernandez also extends the invitation to her coworkers. Ms. Hazelton has asked that you use a different word for coworkers, so you use a shortcut menu to find a synonym. Refer to Figure 1.21 as you complete Step 5.

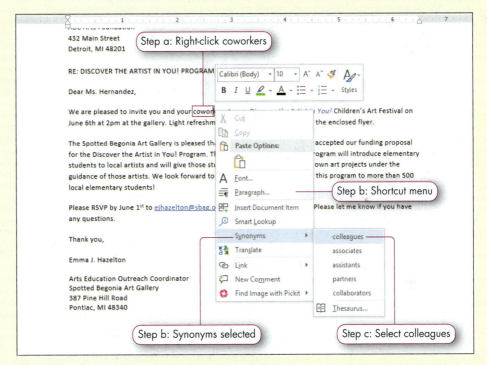

FIGURE 1.21 Use the Shortcut Menu to Find a Synonym

a. Point to and right-click the word **coworkers** in the first sentence of the letter that starts with *We are pleased*.

A shortcut menu displays.

> **MAC TROUBLESHOOTING:** To open a shortcut menu, use Control+click.

b. Select **Synonyms** on the shortcut menu.

A list of alternate words for coworkers displays.

c. Select **colleagues** from the list.

The synonym *colleagues* replaces the word *coworkers*.

d. Click **Save** on the QAT.

You would like to apply the Intense Effect style you used to format *Discover the Artist in You!* to other instances of the program name in the second paragraph. You think there is a more efficient way of applying the same format to other text, but you do not know how to complete the task. Therefore, you use the Tell me box to search for the command and then you apply the change. Refer to Figure 1.22 as you complete Step 6.

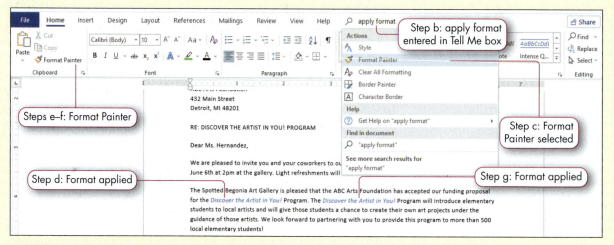

FIGURE 1.22 Use the Tell Me Box

a. Click anywhere in the text **Discover the Artist in You!** in the first sentence of the letter that starts with *We are pleased.*

b. Click the **Tell me box** and type **apply format**.

The Tell me box displays a list of options related to apply format.

c. Select **Format Painter** from the list of options in the Tell Me results.

Notice that the Format Painter command in the Clipboard group is selected and a paint-brush is added to the insertion point .

d. Drag the pointer over the first instance of **Discover the Artist in You!** in the second line of the second paragraph beginning with *The Spotted Begonia.*

The Intense Emphasis style was applied to the selected text.

> **TROUBLESHOOTING:** If the format is not applied to the text, move to the next step, but double-click Format Painter and apply the format to both instances of Discover the Artist in You!

e. Point to **Format Painter** in the Clipboard group and read the Enhanced ScreenTip.

You notice that to apply formatting to more than one selection, you must double-click Format Painter, but because you need to apply the format to only one more set of text, you will single-click the command.

f. Click **Format Painter** in the Clipboard group.

g. Drag the pointer over the second instance of **Discover the Artist in You!** in the second paragraph beginning with *The Spotted Begonia.*

You used the Format Painter to copy the formatting applied to text to other text.

> **TROUBLESHOOTING:** Press Esc on the keyboard to turn off Format Painter if you had to double-click Format Painter in Step d above.

h. Save and close the document. You will submit this file to your instructor at the end of the last Hands-On Exercise.

Format Document Content

In the process of creating a document, worksheet, or presentation, you will most likely make some formatting changes. You might center a title, or format budget worksheet totals as currency. You can change the font so that typed characters are larger or in a different style. You might even want to bold text to add emphasis. Sometimes, it may be more efficient to start with a document that has formatting already applied or apply a group of coordinated fonts, font styles, and colors. You might also want to add, delete, or reposition text. Inserting and formatting images can add interest to a document or illustrate content. Finally, no document is finished until all spelling and grammar has been checked and all errors removed.

In this section, you will explore themes and templates. You will learn to use the Mini Toolbar to quickly make formatting changes. You will learn how to select and edit text, as well as check your grammar and spelling. You will learn how to move, copy, and paste text, and how to insert pictures. And, finally, you will learn how to resize and format pictures and graphics.

Using Templates and Applying Themes

You can enhance your documents by using a template or applying a theme. A ***template*** is a predesigned file that incorporates formatting elements and layouts and may include content that can be modified. A ***theme*** is a collection of design choices that includes colors, fonts, and special effects used to give a consistent look to a document, workbook, or presentation. Microsoft provides high-quality templates and themes, designed to make it faster and easier to create professional-looking documents.

STEP 1 Open a Template

When you launch any Office program and click New, the screen displays thumbnail images of a sampling of templates for that application (see Figure 1.23). Alternatively, if you are already working in an application, click the File tab and select New on the Backstage

FIGURE 1.23 Templates in Excel

Navigation Pane. One benefit of starting with a template is if you know only a little bit about the software, with only a few simple changes you would have a well-formatted document that represents your specific needs. Even if you know a lot about the program, starting with a template can be much more efficient than if you designed it yourself from a blank file. Templates in Excel often use complex formulas and formatting to achieve a dynamic workbook that would automatically adjust with only a few inputs. Using a resume template in Word greatly simplifies potentially complex formatting, enabling you to concentrate on just inputting your personal experiences. PowerPoint templates can include single element slides (such as organization charts) but also include comprehensive presentations on topics such as Business Plans or a Quiz show game presentation similar to *Jeopardy!*

The Templates list is composed of template groups available within each Office application. The search box enables you to locate other templates that are available online. When you select a template, you can view more information about the template, including author information, a general overview about the template, and additional views (if applicable).

To search for and use a template, complete the following steps:

1. Open the Microsoft Office application with which you will be working. Or, if the application is already open, click File and click New.
2. Type a search term in the *Search for online templates box* or click one of the Suggested searches.
3. Scroll through the template options or after selecting a search term, use the list at the right to narrow your search further.
4. Select a template and review its information in the window that opens.
5. Click Create to open the template in the application.

On a Mac, to search for and use a template, complete the following steps:

1. Open the Microsoft Office application with which you will be working. Or, if the application is already open, click the File menu and click New from Template.
2. Continue with steps 2 through 5 in the PC steps above.

STEP 2 Apply a Theme

Applying a theme enables you to visually coordinate various page elements. Themes are different for each of the Office applications. In Word, a theme is a set of coordinating fonts, colors, and special effects, such as shadowing or glows, that are combined into a package to provide a stylish appearance (see Figure 1.24). In PowerPoint, a theme is a file that includes the formatting elements such as a background, a color scheme, and slide layouts that position content placeholders. Themes in Excel are like those in Word in that they are a set of coordinating fonts, colors, and special effects. Themes also affect any SmartArt or charts in a document, workbook, or presentation. Access also has a set of themes that coordinate the appearance of fonts and colors for objects such as Forms and Reports. In Word and PowerPoint, themes are accessed from the Design tab. In Excel, they are accessed from the Page Layout tab. In Access, themes can be applied to forms and reports and are accessed from the respective object's Tools Design tab. In any application, themes can be modified with different fonts, colors, or effects, or you can design your own theme and set it as a default.

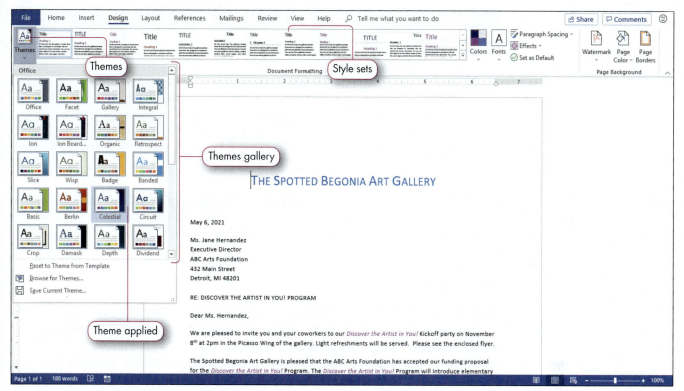

FIGURE 1.24 Themes in Word

Modifying Text

Formatting and modifying text in documents, worksheets, or presentations is an essential function when using Office applications. Centering a title, formatting cells, or changing the font color or size are tasks that occur frequently. In all Office applications, the Home tab provides tools for editing text.

STEP 3 ## Select Text

Before making any changes to existing text or numbers, you must first select the characters. A common way to select text or numbers is to place the pointer before the first character of the text you want to select, hold down the left mouse button, and then drag to highlight the intended selection. Note that in Word and PowerPoint when the pointer is used to select text in this manner, it takes on the shape of the letter *I*, called the *I-beam* $\boxed{\text{I}}$.

Sometimes it can be difficult to precisely select a small amount of text, such as a few letters or a punctuation mark. Other times, the task can be overwhelmingly large, such as when selecting an entire multi-page document. Or, you might need to select a single word, sentence, or paragraph. In these situations, you should use one of the shortcuts to selecting large or small blocks of text. The shortcuts shown in Table 1.2 are primarily applicable to text in Word and PowerPoint. When working with Excel, you will more often need to select multiple cells. To select multiple cells, drag the selection when the pointer displays as a large white plus sign $\boxed{\oplus}$.

Once you have selected the text, besides applying formatting, you can delete or simply type over to replace the text.

TABLE 1.2	Shortcut Selection in Word and PowerPoint
Item Selected	**Action**
One word	Double-click the word.
One line of text	Place the pointer at the left of the line, in the margin area. When the pointer changes to an angled right-pointing arrow, click to select the line.
One sentence	Press and hold Ctrl and click in the sentence to select it.
One paragraph	Triple-click in the paragraph.
One character to the left of the insertion point	Press and hold Shift and press the left arrow on the keyboard.
One character to the right of the insertion point	Press and hold Shift and press the right arrow on the keyboard.
Entire document	Press and hold Ctrl and press A on the keyboard.

Format Text

At times, you will want to make the font size larger or smaller, change the font color, or apply other font attributes, for example, to emphasize key information such as titles, headers, dates, and times. Because formatting text is commonplace, Office places formatting commands in many convenient places within each Office application.

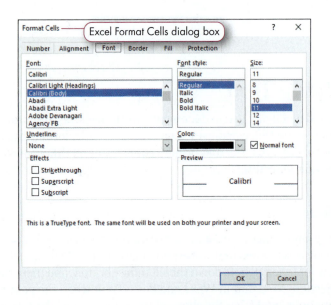

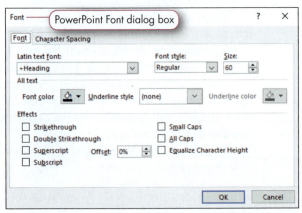

FIGURE 1.25 The Font Dialog Boxes

You can find the most common formatting commands in the Font group on the Home tab. As noted earlier, Word, Excel, and PowerPoint all share very similar Font groups that provide access to tasks related to changing the font, size, and color. Remember that you can place the pointer over any command icon to view a summary of the command's purpose, so although the icons might appear cryptic at first, you can use the pointer to quickly determine the purpose and applicability to your potential text change.

If the font change that you plan to make is not included as a choice on the Home tab, you may find what you are looking for in the Font dialog box. If you are making many formatting choices at once, using the Font dialog box may be more efficient. Depending on the application, the contents of the Font dialog box vary slightly, but the purpose is consistent—providing access to choices related to modifying characters (refer to Figure 1.25).

The way characters display onscreen or print in documents, including qualities such as size, spacing, and shape, is determined by the font. When you open a Blank document, you are opening the Normal template with an Office theme and the Normal style. The Office theme with Normal Style includes the following default settings: Calibri font, 11-point font size, and black font color. These settings remain in effect unless you change them. Some formatting commands, such as Bold and Italic, are called ***toggle commands***. They act somewhat like a light switch that you can turn on and off. Once you have applied bold formatting to text, the Bold command is highlighted on the ribbon when that text is selected. To undo bold formatting, select the bold formatted text and click Bold again.

Use the Mini Toolbar

You have learned that you can always use commands on the Home tab of the ribbon to change selected text within a document, worksheet, or presentation. Although using the ribbon to select commands is simple enough, the ***Mini Toolbar*** provides another convenient way to accomplish some of the same formatting changes. When you select or right-click any amount of text within a worksheet, document, or presentation, the Mini Toolbar displays (see Figure 1.26) along with the shortcut menu. The Mini Toolbar provides access to the most common formatting selections, as well as access to styles and list options. Unlike the QAT, you cannot add or remove options from the Mini Toolbar. To temporarily remove the Mini Toolbar from view, press Esc. You can permanently disable the Mini Toolbar so that it does not display in any open file when text is selected by selecting Options on the File tab. Ensure the General tab is selected and deselect *Show Mini Toolbar on selection* in the User Interface options section.

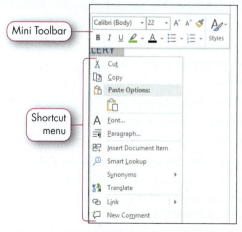

FIGURE 1.26 The Mini Toolbar and Shortcut Menu

Relocating Text

On occasion, you may want to relocate a section of text from one area of a Word document to another. Or suppose that you have included text on a PowerPoint slide that you believe would be more appropriate on a different slide. Or perhaps an Excel formula should be copied from one cell to another because both cells should show totals in a similar manner. In all these instances, you would use the cut, copy, and paste features found in the Clipboard group on the Home tab. The **Office Clipboard** is an area of memory reserved to temporarily hold selections that have been cut or copied and enables you to paste the selections to another location.

STEP 4 ## Cut, Copy, and Paste Text

To *cut* means to remove a selection from the original location and place it in the Office Clipboard. To *copy* means to duplicate a selection from the original location and place a copy in the Office Clipboard. To *paste* means to place a cut or copied selection into another location in a document. It is important to understand that cut or copied text remains in the Office Clipboard even after you paste it to another location. The Office Clipboard can hold up to 24 items at one time.

To cut or copy text, and paste to a new location, complete the following steps:

1. Select the text you want to cut or copy.
2. Click the appropriate command in the Clipboard group either to cut or copy the selection.
3. Click the location where you want the cut or copied text to be placed. The location can be in the current file or in another open file within most Office applications.
4. Click Paste in the Clipboard group on the Home tab.

You can paste the same item multiple times, because it will remain in the Office Clipboard until you power down your computer or until the Office Clipboard exceeds 24 items. It is best practice to complete the paste process as soon after you have cut or copied text.

In addition to using the commands in the Clipboard group, you can also cut, copy, and paste by using the Mini Toolbar, a shortcut menu (right-clicking), or by keyboard shortcuts. These methods are listed in Table 1.3.

TABLE 1.3	Cut, Copy, and Paste Options
Command	**Actions**
Cut	• Click Cut in Clipboard group. • Right-click selection and select Cut. • Press Ctrl+X.
Copy	• Click Copy in Clipboard group. • Right-click selection and select Copy. • Press Ctrl+C.
Paste	• Click in destination location and select Paste in Clipboard group. • Click in destination location and press Ctrl+V. • Right-click in destination location and select one of the choices under Paste Options in the shortcut menu. • Click Clipboard Dialog Box Launcher to open Clipboard pane. Click in destination location. With Clipboard pane open, click the arrow beside the intended selection and select Paste.

Use the Office Clipboard

When you cut or copy selections, they are placed in the Office Clipboard. Regardless of which Office application you are using, you can view the Office Clipboard by clicking the Clipboard Dialog Box Launcher, as shown in Figure 1.27.

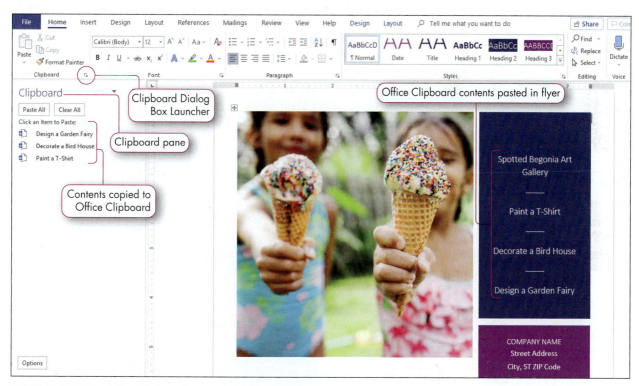

FIGURE 1.27 The Office Clipboard

Unless you specify otherwise when beginning a paste operation, the most recently added item to the Office Clipboard is pasted. If you know you will be cutting or copying and then pasting several items, rather than doing each individually, you can cut or copy all the items to the Office Clipboard, and then paste each or all Office Clipboard items to the new location. This is especially helpful if you are pasting the Office Clipboard items to a different Office file. Just open the new file, display the Clipboard pane, and select the item in the list to paste it into the document. The Office Clipboard also stores graphics that have been cut or copied. You can delete items from the Office Clipboard by clicking the arrow next to the selection in the Clipboard pane and selecting Delete. You can remove all items from the Office Clipboard by clicking Clear All. The Options button at the bottom of the Clipboard pane enables you to control when and where the Office Clipboard is displayed. Close the Clipboard pane by clicking the Close button in the top-right corner of the pane or by clicking the arrow in the title bar of the Clipboard pane and selecting Close.

Reviewing a Document

As you create or edit a file, and certainly as you finalize a file, you should make sure no spelling or grammatical errors exist. It is important that you carefully review your document for any spelling or punctuation errors, as well as any poor word choices before you send it along to someone else to read. Word, Excel, and PowerPoint all provide standard tools for proofreading, including a spelling and grammar checker and a thesaurus.

STEP 5 Check Spelling and Grammar

Word and PowerPoint automatically check your spelling and grammar as you type. If a word is unrecognized, it is flagged as misspelled or grammatically incorrect. Misspellings are identified with a red wavy underline, and grammatical or word-usage errors (such as using *bear* instead of *bare*) have a blue double underline. Excel does not check spelling as you type, so it is important to run the spelling checker in Excel. Excel's spelling checker will review charts, pivot tables, and textual data entered in cells.

Although spelling and grammar is checked along the way, you may find it more efficient to use the spelling and grammar feature when you are finished with the document. The Check Document command is found on the Review tab in the Proofing group in Word. In Excel and PowerPoint the Spelling command is on the Review tab in the Proofing group. When it is selected, the Editor pane will open on the right. For each error, you are offered one or more suggestions as a correction. You can select a suggestion and click Change, or if it is an error that is made more than one time throughout the document, you can select Change All (see Figure 1.28). If an appropriate suggestion is not made, you can always enter a correction manually.

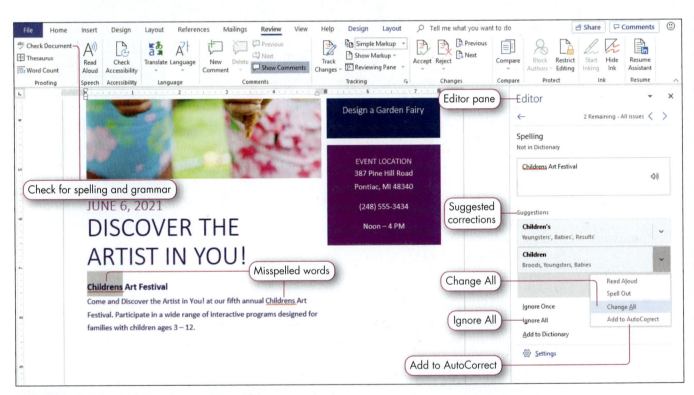

FIGURE 1.28 Using the Editor Pane to Correct Spelling

It is important to understand that the spelling and grammar check is not always correct, so you still need to proof a document thoroughly and review the errors carefully. For example, you might have a word that is truly misspelled in its context, but perhaps is still a valid word in the dictionary. Spell check might not pick it up as a misspelled word, but a careful read through would probably pick it up. There are times when the spelling and grammar check will indicate a word is misspelled and it really is not. This often happens with names or proper nouns or with new technical terms that may not be in the application's dictionary. In these instances, you can choose to Ignore, Ignore All, or Add. Choosing Ignore will skip the word without changing it. If you know there are multiple instances of that word throughout the document, you can choose Ignore All, and it will skip all instances of the word. Finally, if it is a word that is spelled correctly and that you use it often, you can choose to Add it to the dictionary, so it will not be flagged as an error in future spell checks.

If you right-click a word or phrase that is identified as a potential error, you will see a shortcut menu similar to that shown in Figure 1.29. The top of the shortcut menu will identify the type of error, whether it is spelling or grammar. A pane opens next to the shortcut menu with a list of options to correct the misspelling. These would be the same options that would display in the Editor pane if you ran the Spelling & Grammar command from the ribbon. Click on any option to insert it into the document. Similarly, you have the choices to Add to Dictionary or Ignore All. Each alternative also has options to Read Aloud or Add to AutoCorrect.

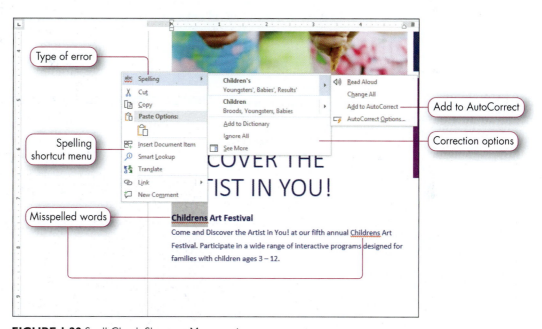

FIGURE 1.29 Spell Check Shortcut Menu options

You can use AutoCorrect to correct common typing errors, misspelled words, and capitalization errors, as well as to insert symbols (see Figure 1.30). There is a standard list of common errors and suggested replacements that is used in Excel, Word, and PowerPoint. So, if you type a word that is found in the Replace column, it will automatically be replaced with the replacement in the With column. For example, if you typed *accross* it would automatically correct to *across*. If you typed (tm) it would automatically change to the trademark symbol ™. You can add or delete terms and manage AutoCorrect by selecting Options from the File tab, and then in the Options dialog box, select Proofing and then click AutoCorrect Options.

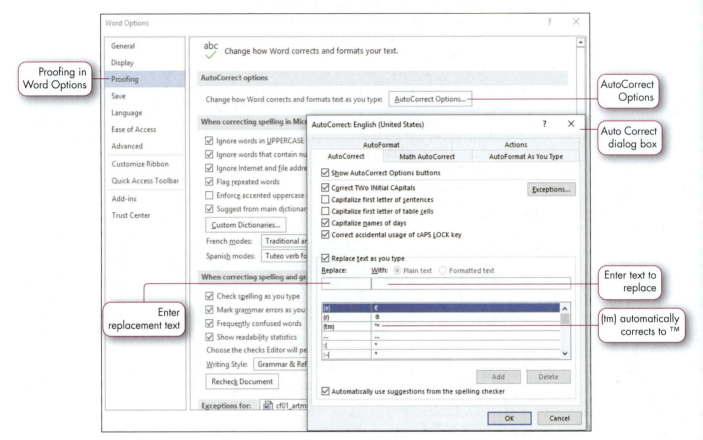

FIGURE 1.30 Proofing and AutoCorrect

Working with Pictures

Documents, worksheets, and presentations can include much more than just words and numbers. You can add energy and additional description to a project by including pictures and other graphic elements. A ***picture*** is just that—a digital photo. A picture can also be considered an illustration. Illustrations can also be shapes, icons, SmartArt, and Charts. While each of these types of illustrative objects have definitive differences, they are all handled basically the same when it comes to inserting and resizing. For the purposes of simplicity, the following discussion focuses on pictures, but the same information can be applied to any illustrative object you include in your document, worksheet, or presentation.

STEP 6 **Insert Pictures**

In Word, Excel, and PowerPoint, you can insert pictures from your own library of digital photos you have saved on your hard drive, OneDrive, or another storage medium. If you want a wider variety of pictures to choose from, you can search directly inside the Office program you are using for an online picture using Bing. Pictures and Online Pictures are found on the Insert tab.

When the picture is inserted into a document, the Picture Tools Format tab displays. You can use these tools to modify the picture as needed.

> **TIP: CREATIVE COMMONS LICENSE**
> The Bing search filters are set to use the Creative Commons license system so the results display images that have been given a Creative Commons license. These are images and drawings that can be used more freely than images found directly on websites. Because there are different levels of Creative Commons licenses, you should read the Creative Commons license for each image you use to avoid copyright infringement.

STEP 7 Modify a Picture

Once you add a picture to your document, you may need to resize or adjust it. Before you make any changes to a picture, you must first select it. When the picture is selected, eight sizing handles display on the corners and in the middle of each edge (see Figure 1.31) and the Picture Tools tab displays on the ribbon. To adjust the size while maintaining the proportions, place your pointer on one of the corner sizing handles, and while holding the left mouse button down, drag the pointer on an angle upward or downward to increase or decrease the size, respectively. If you use one of the center edge sizing handles, you will

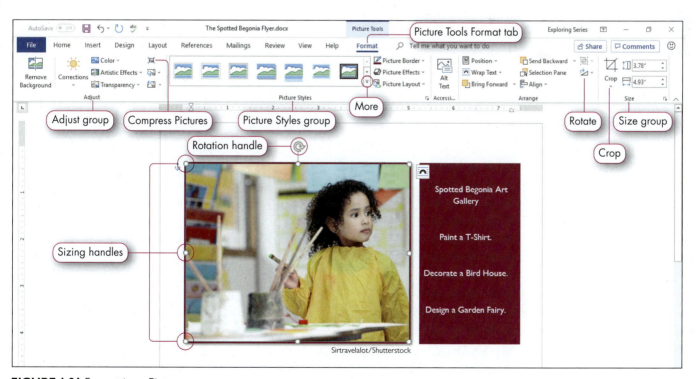

FIGURE 1.31 Formatting a Picture

stretch or shrink the picture out of proportion. In addition to sizing handles, a rotation handle displays at the top of the selected image. Use this to turn the image. For more precise controls, use the Size and Rotate commands on the Picture Tools Format tab. When a picture is selected, the Picture Tools Format tab includes options for modifying a picture. You can apply a picture style or effect, as well as add a picture border, from selections in the Picture Styles group. Click More to view a gallery of picture styles. As you point to a style, the style is shown in Live Preview, but the style is not applied until you select it. Options in the Adjust group simplify changing a color scheme, applying creative artistic effects, and even adjusting the brightness, contrast, and sharpness of an image (refer to Figure 1.31).

If a picture contains areas that are not necessary, you can crop it, which is the process of trimming edges that you do not want to display. The Crop tool is located on the Picture Tools Format tab (refer to Figure 1.31). Even though cropping enables you to adjust the amount of a picture that displays, it does not actually delete the portions that are cropped out. Therefore, you can later recover parts of the picture, if necessary. Cropping a picture does not reduce the file size of the picture or the document in which it displays. If you want to permanently remove the cropped portions of a figure and reduce the file size, you must compress the picture. Compress Pictures is found in the Adjust group on the Picture Tools Format tab (refer to Figure 1.31).

Quick Concepts

5. Discuss the differences between themes and templates. *p. 25*

6. Discuss several ways text can be modified. *p. 27*

7. Explain how the Office Clipboard is used when relocating text. *p. 31*

8. Explain how to review a document for spelling and grammar. *p. 32*

9. Explain why it is important to use the corner sizing handles of a picture when resizing. *p. 35*

Hands-On Exercises

 Watch the Video for this Hands-On Exercise!

Skills covered: Open a Template • Apply a Theme • Select Text • Format Text • Cut, Copy, and Paste Text • Check Spelling and Grammar • Insert a Picture • Modify a Picture

2 Format Document Content

As the administrative assistant for the Spotted Begonia Art Gallery, you want to create a flyer to announce the *Discover the Artist in You!* Children's Art Festival. You decide to use a template to help you get started more quickly and to take advantage of having a professionally formatted document without knowing much about Word. You will modify the flyer created with the template by adding and formatting your own content and changing out the photo.

STEP 1 OPEN A TEMPLATE

To facilitate making a nice-looking flyer, you review the templates that are available in Microsoft Word. You search for flyers and finally choose one that is appropriate for the event, knowing that you will be able to replace the photo with your own. Refer to Figure 1.32 as you complete Step 1.

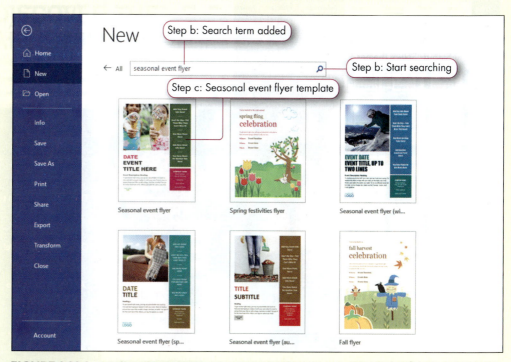

FIGURE 1.32 Search for a Template

a. Ensure Word is open. Click **File** and click **New**.

b. Type the search term **seasonal event flyer** in the *Search for online templates* box to search for event flyer templates. Click **Start searching**.

Your search results in a selection of event flyer templates.

c. Locate the Seasonal event flyer template as shown in Figure 1.32 and click to select it.

The template displays in a preview.

Hands-On Exercise 2   37

Use the Page Setup Dialog Box

Page Orientation settings for Word and Excel are found in the Layout (or Page Layout) tab in the Page Setup group. The Page Setup group contains Margins and Orientation settings as well as other commonly used page options for each Office application. Some are unique to Excel, and others are more applicable to Word. Other less common settings are available in the Page Setup dialog box only, displayed when you click the Page Setup Dialog Box Launcher. The Page Setup dialog box includes options for customizing margins, selecting page orientation, centering horizontally or vertically, printing gridlines, and creating headers and footers. Figure 1.41 shows both the Excel and Word Page Setup dialog boxes.

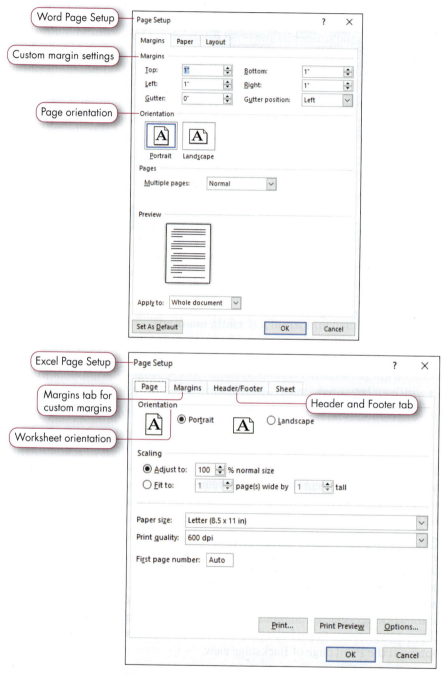

FIGURE 1.41 Page Setup Dialog Boxes in Word and Excel

Although PowerPoint slides are generally set to landscape orientation, you can change to portrait orientation by accessing the Slide Size controls on the Design tab and selecting Custom Slide Size. When choosing to print Notes Pages, Outline, or Handouts, the page orientation can be changed in Print Settings in Backstage view.

STEP 3 ▸ Creating a Header and a Footer

The purpose of including a header or footer is to better identify the document and give it a professional appearance. A **header** is a section in the top margin of a document. A **footer** is a section in the bottom margin of a document. Generally, page numbers, dates, author's name, or file name are included in Word documents or PowerPoint presentations. Excel worksheets might include the name of a worksheet tab, as well. Company logos are often displayed in a header or footer. Contents in a header or footer will appear on each page of the document, so you only have to specify the content once, after which it displays automatically on all pages. Although you can type the text yourself at the top or bottom of every page, it is time-consuming, and the possibility of making a mistake is great.

Header and footer commands are found on the Insert tab. In Word, you can choose from a predefined gallery of headers and footers as shown in Figure 1.42. To create your own unformatted header or footer, select Edit Header (or Edit Footer) at the bottom of the gallery. You can only add footers to PowerPoint slides (see Figure 1.42). You can apply footers to an individual slide or to all slides. To add date and time or a slide number, check each option to apply. Check the Footer option to add in your own content. In PowerPoint, the location of a footer will depend on the template or theme applied to the presentation. For some templates and themes, the footer will display on the side of the slide rather than at the bottom. Headers and footers are available for PowerPoint Notes and Handouts. Select the Notes and Handouts tab in the Header and Footer dialog box and enter in the content

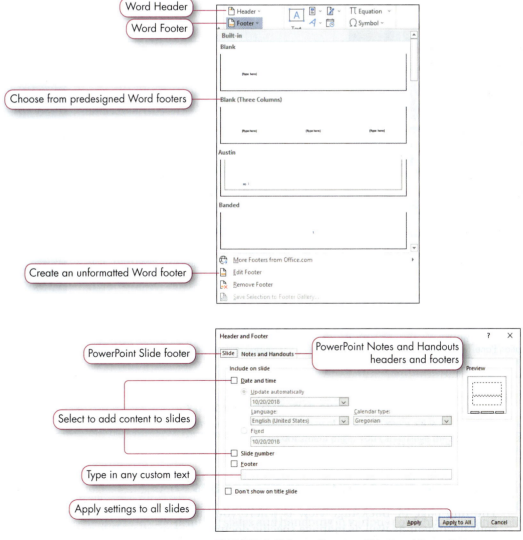

FIGURE 1.42 Insert Footer in Word and PowerPoint

ENTER DOCUMENT PROPERTIES

You add document properties, which will help you locate the file in the future when performing a search of your files. Refer to Figure 1.48 as you complete Step 4.

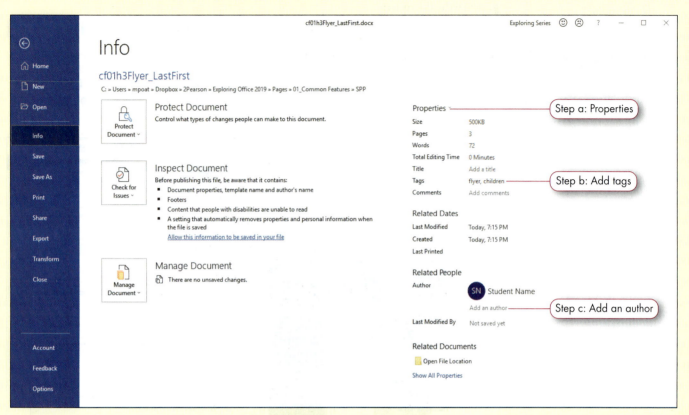

FIGURE 1.48 Enter Document Properties

a. Click the **File tab** and click Info on the Backstage Navigation Pane. Locate Properties at the top of the right section of Backstage view.

b. Click the **Add a tag box** and type **flyer, children**.

> **MAC TROUBLESHOOTING:** On a Mac, to add a tag click the File menu and select Properties. Click the Summary tab and enter text in the Keywords box.

You added tag properties to the flyer.

c. Click the **Add an Author box** and type your first and last name.

You added an Author property to the flyer.

d. Click **Save** in the Backstage Navigation Pane.

You have reviewed and almost finalized the flyer. You want to look at how it will appear when printed. You also want to look over Print Settings to ensure they are correct. Refer to Figure 1.49 as you complete Step 5.

FIGURE 1.49 Backstage Print View

a. Click **Print** in the Backstage Navigation Pane.

It is always a good idea before printing to use Print Preview to check how a file will look when printed.

b. Click **Print All Pages arrow** and select **Print Current Page**.

You notice that the template created extra pages. You only want to print the current page.

c. Select the **1** in the Copies box and type **15**.

The orientation and custom margins settings match what was done previously. Even though you will not print the document now, the print settings will be saved when you save the document.

d. Click the **Back arrow**.

e. Save and close the file. Based on your instructor's directions, submit the following:

cf01h1Letter_LastFirst
cf01h3Flyer_LastFirst

Chapter Objectives Review

After reading this chapter, you have accomplished the following objectives:

1. Start an Office application.
- Use your Microsoft account: Your Microsoft account connects you to all of Microsoft's Internet-based resources.
- Use OneDrive: OneDrive is an app used to store, access, and share files and folders on the Internet. OneDrive is the default storage location for Microsoft Office files. OneDrive is incorporated directly in File Explorer.

2. Work with files.
- Create a new file: You can create a document as a blank document or from a template.
- Save a file: Saving a file enables you to open it later for additional updates or reference. Files are saved to a storage medium such as a hard drive, CD, flash drive, or to OneDrive.
- Open a saved file: You can open an existing file using the Open dialog box. Recently saved files can be accessed using the Recent documents list.

3. Use common interface components.
- Use the ribbon: The ribbon, the long bar located just beneath the title bar containing tabs, groups, and commands, is the command center of Office applications.
- Use a dialog box and gallery: Some commands are not on the ribbon. To access these commands, you need to open a dialog box with a Dialog Box Launcher. A gallery displays additional formatting and design options for a command. Galleries are accessed by clicking More at the bottom of a gallery scroll bar
- Customize the ribbon: You can personalize the ribbon by creating your own tabs and custom groups with commands you want to use. You can create a custom group and add to any of the default tabs.
- Use and Customize the Quick Access Toolbar: The Quick Access Toolbar, located at the top-left corner of any Office application window, provides one-click access to commonly executed tasks, such as saving a file or undoing recent actions.
- You can add additional commands to the QAT.
- Use a Shortcut menu: When you right-click selected text or objects, a context-sensitive menu displays with commands and options relating to the selected text or object.
- Use keyboard shortcuts: Keyboard shortcuts are keyboard equivalents for software commands. Universal keyboard shortcuts in Office include Ctrl+C (Copy), Ctrl+X (Cut), Ctrl+V (Paste), and Ctrl+Z (Undo). Not all commands have a keyboard shortcut. If one exists, it will display in the command ScreenTip.

4. Get help.
- Use the Tell me box: The Tell me box not only links to online resources and technical support but also provides quick access to commands.

- Use the Help tab: The Help tab includes resources for written and video tutorials and training, a means to contact Microsoft Support, and a way to share feedback. What's New displays a webpage that discusses all newly added features organized by release date.
- Use Enhanced ScreenTips: An Enhanced ScreenTip describes a command and provides a keyboard shortcut, if applicable.

5. Install add-ins.
- Add-ins are custom programs or additional commands that extend the functionality of a Microsoft Office program.

6. Use templates and apply themes.
- Open a template: Templates are a convenient way to save time when designing a document. A gallery of template options displays when you start any application. You can also access a template when you start a new document, worksheet, presentation, or database.
- Apply a theme: Themes are a collection of design choices that include colors, fonts, and special effects used to give a consistent look to a document, workbook, or presentation.

7. Modify text.
- Select text: Text can be selected by a variety of methods. You can drag to highlight text and select individual words or groups of text with shortcuts.
- Format text: You can change the font, font color, size, and many other attributes.
- Use the Mini Toolbar: The Mini Toolbar provides instant access to common formatting commands after text is selected.

8. Relocate text.
- Cut, copy, and paste text: To cut means to remove a selection from the original location and place it in the Office Clipboard. To copy means to duplicate a selection from the original location and place a copy in the Office Clipboard. To paste means to place a cut or copied selection into another location.
- Use the Office Clipboard: When you cut or copy selections, they are placed in the Office Clipboard. You can paste the same item multiple times; it will remain in the Office Clipboard until you exit all Office applications or until the Office Clipboard exceeds 24 items.

9. Review a document.
- Check spelling and grammar: As you type, Office applications check and mark spelling and grammar errors (Word only) for later correction. The Thesaurus enables you to search for synonyms. Use AutoCorrect to correct common typing errors and misspelled words and to insert symbols.

10. Work with pictures.

- Insert a picture: You can insert pictures from your own library of digital photos saved on your hard drive, OneDrive, or another storage medium, or you can initiate a Bing search for online pictures directly inside the Office program you are using.
- Modify a picture: To resize a picture, drag a corner-sizing handle; never resize a picture by dragging a center sizing handle. You can apply a picture style or effect, as well as add a picture border, from selections in the Picture Styles group.

11. Change document views.

- Change document views using the ribbon: The View tab offers views specific to the individual application. A view is how a file will be seen onscreen.
- Change document views using the status bar: In addition to information relative to the open file, the Status bar provides access to View and Zoom level options.

12. Change the page layout.

- Change margins: A margin is the area of blank space that displays to the left, right, top, and bottom of a document or worksheet.

- Change page orientation: Documents and worksheets can be displayed in different page orientations. Portrait orientation is taller than it is wide; landscape orientation is wider than it is tall.
- Use the Page Setup dialog box: The Page Setup dialog box includes options for customizing margins, selecting page orientation, centering horizontally or vertically, printing gridlines, and creating headers and footers.

13. Create a header and a footer.

- A header displays at the top of each page.
- A footer displays at the bottom of each page.

14. Configure Document Properties.

- View and edit document properties: Information that identifies a document, such as the author, title, or tags can be added to the document's properties. Those data elements are saved with the document as metadata, but do not appear in the document as it displays onscreen or is printed.

15. Preview and print a file.

- It is important to preview your file before printing.
- Print options can be set in Backstage view and include page orientation, the number of copies, and the specific pages to print.

Key Terms Matching

Match the key terms with their definitions. Write the key term letter by the appropriate numbered definition.

a. Add-in
b. Backstage view
c. Cloud storage
d. Footer
e. Format Painter
f. Group
g. Header
h. Margin
i. Microsoft Access
j. Microsoft Office

k. Mini Toolbar
l. Office Clipboard
m. OneDrive
n. Quick Access Toolbar
o. Ribbon
p. Status bar
q. Tag
r. Tell me box
s. Template
t. Theme

1. _____ A productivity software suite including a set of software applications, each one specializing in a type of output. **p. 4**

2. _____ The long bar located just beneath the title bar containing tabs, groups, and commands. **p. 9**

3. _____ A custom program or additional command that extends the functionality of a Microsoft Office program. **p. 17**

4. _____ A collection of design choices that includes colors, fonts, and special effects used to give a consistent look to a document, workbook, or presentation. **p. 25**

5. _____ A data element or metadata that is added as a document property. **p. 51**

6. _____ A component of Office that provides a concise collection of commands related to an open file and includes save and print options. **p. 6**

7. _____ A tool that displays near selected text that contains formatting commands. **p. 29**

8. _____ Relational database software used to store data and convert it into information. **p. 4**

9. _____ A feature in a document that consists of one or more lines at the bottom of each page. **p. 49**

10. _____ A predesigned file that incorporates formatting elements, such as a theme and layouts, and may include content that can be modified. **p. 25**

11. _____ A feature that enables you to search for help and information about a command or task you want to perform and will also present you with a shortcut directly to that command. **p. 15**

12. _____ A tool that copies all formatting from one area to another. **p. 17**

13. _____ Stores up to 24 cut or copied selections for use later in your computing session. **p. 30**

14. _____ A task-oriented section of a ribbon tab that contains related commands. **p. 9**

15. _____ An online app used to store, access, and share files and folders. **p. 6**

16. _____ Provides handy access to commonly executed tasks, such as saving a file and undoing recent actions. **p. 13**

17. _____ The long bar at the bottom of the screen that houses the Zoom slider and various View buttons. **p. 46**

18. _____ The area of blank space that displays to the left, right, top, and bottom of a document or worksheet **p. 47**

19. _____ A technology used to store files and to work with programs that are stored in a central location on the Internet. **p. 6**

20. _____ A feature in a document that consists of one or more lines at the top of each page. **p. 49**

Multiple Choice

1. In Word or PowerPoint, a quick way to select an entire paragraph is to:

   (a) place the pointer at the left of the line, in the margin area, and click.

   (b) triple-click inside the paragraph.

   (c) double-click at the beginning of the paragraph.

   (d) press Ctrl+C inside the paragraph.

2. When you want to copy the format of a selection but not the content, you should:

   (a) double-click Copy in the Clipboard group.

   (b) right-click the selection and click Copy.

   (c) click Copy Format in the Clipboard group.

   (d) click Format Painter in the Clipboard group.

3. Which of the following is *not* a benefit of using One Drive?

   (a) Save your folders and files to the cloud.

   (b) Share your files and folders with others.

   (c) Hold video conferences with others.

   (d) Simultaneously work on the same document with others.

4. What does a red wavy underline in a document or presentation mean?

   (a) A word is misspelled or not recognized by the Office dictionary.

   (b) A grammatical mistake exists.

   (c) An apparent formatting error was made.

   (d) A word has been replaced with a synonym.

5. Which of the following is *true* about headers and footers?

   (a) They can be inserted from the Layout tab.

   (b) Headers and footers only appear on the last page of a document.

   (c) Headers appear at the top of every page in a document.

   (d) Only page numbers can be included in a header or footer.

6. You can get help when working with an Office application in which one of the following areas?

   (a) The Tell me box

   (b) The Status bar

   (c) Backstage view

   (d) The Quick Access Toolbar

7. To access commands that are not on the ribbon, you need to open which of the following?

   (a) Gallery

   (b) Dialog box

   (c) Shortcut menu

   (d) Mini Toolbar

8. To create a document without knowing much about the software, you should use which of the following?

   (a) Theme

   (b) Live Preview

   (c) Template

   (d) Design Style

9. Which is the preferred method for resizing a picture so that it keeps its proportions?

   (a) Use the rotation handle

   (b) Use a corner-sizing handle

   (c) Use a side-sizing handle

   (d) Use the controls in the Adjust group

10. Which is *not* a description of a tag in a Word document?

    (a) A data element

    (b) Document metadata

    (c) Keyword

    (d) Document title

Practice Exercises

1 Designing Webpages

You have been asked to make a presentation at the next Montgomery County, PA Chamber of Commerce meeting. With the Chamber's continued emphasis on growing the local economy, many small businesses are interested in establishing a Web presence. The business owners would like to know more about how webpages are designed. In preparation for the presentation, you will proofread and edit your PowerPoint file. You decide to insert an image to enhance your presentation and use an add-in to include a map and contact information for the Chamber of Commerce. Refer to Figure 1.50 as you complete this exercise.

FIGURE 1.50 Designing Webpages Presentation

a. Open the PowerPoint presentation *cf01p1Design*.

b. Click the **File tab**, click **Save As**, and then save the file as **cf01p1Design_LastFirst**.

c. Click the **Design tab** and click **More** in the Themes group. Scroll through the themes to find and select **Retrospect theme**. Select the **third Variant** in the Variants group. Close the Design Ideas pane if it opens.

d. Click **Slide 2** in the Slides pane on the left. Double-click to select **Resources** on the slide title. Use the Mini Toolbar to click the **Font Color arrow**. Select **Orange, Accent 2** in the Theme Colors group. Click **Bold** on the Mini Toolbar.

e. Click **Slide 3** in the Slides pane. Click the **Pictures icon** in the left content placeholder. Browse to the student data files, locate and select *cf01p1Website.jpg*, and then click **Insert**. Close the Design Ideas pane if it opens.

f. Select the picture. Click the **Format tab** and click **More** in the Picture Styles group to open the Pictures Style Gallery. Click the **Reflected Perspective Right**. Click the **Height box** in the Size group and type **4**. Press **Enter**. Place the pointer over the image to display a 4-headed arrow and drag to position the image so it is centered vertically in the open space.

g. Click the **Home tab** and click the **Clipboard Dialog Box Launcher**. Click **Slide 7** and select all the placeholder content. Right-click the selected text and click **Cut** from the shortcut menu.

> **TROUBLESHOOTING:** If there is content in the Office Clipboard, click Clear All to remove all previously cut or copied items from the Office Clipboard.

> **MAC TROUBLESHOOTING:** On a Mac, select the text and press Control+X. Click Slide 4 and press Control+V. Repeat for Step h. Skip to Step j.

h. Click **Slide 5** and select all the placeholder content. Press **Ctrl+X**.

i. Click **Slide 4** and click the **content placeholder**. Click **Paste All** in the Office Clipboard. Close the Office Clipboard.

j. Click **Slide Sorter** on the status bar. Click **Slide 5** and press **Delete**. Click **Slide 6** and press **Delete**. Drag **Slide 2** to the right of **Slide 5**. Click the **View tab** and click **Normal**.

k. Click **Slide 6** in the Slides pane. Click the **Insert tab**, point to **My Add-ins** in the Add-ins group, and read the Enhanced Screen Tip to find out more about Add-ins. Click **My Add-ins**, click the **Store tab**, and then in the search box, type **map**. Press **Enter**.

l. Click **Add** to add OfficeMaps - Insert maps quick and easy!

m. Click Open OfficeMaps on the Insert tab. Click in the Enter a location box and type the address shown on Slide 6. Click Insert Map. Close the OfficeMaps pane.

n. Select the map, click the **Height box** in the Size group, and type **4**. Press **Enter**. Position the map attractively in the slide.

o. Click **Slide 1**. Click **Header & Footer** in the Text group on the Insert tab. Click the **Slide number check box** to select it. Click the **Footer box** to select it and type **Business Owners Association Presentation**. Click **Don't show on title slide check box** to select it. Click **Apply to All**.

p. Click the **Review tab** and click **Spelling** in the Proofing group. In the Spelling pane, click **Change** or **Ignore** to make changes as needed. The words *KompoZer* and *Nvu* are not misspelled, so you should ignore them when they are flagged. Click **OK** when you have finished checking spelling.

q. Click the **File tab**. Click the **Add a Tag box** and type **business, BOA, web design**.

r. Click **Print**. Click the **Full Page Slides arrow** and select **6 Slides Horizontal** to see a preview of all the slides as a handout.

> **MAC TROUBLESHOOTING:** Click the File menu, click Print, and then click Show Details. In the Print dialog box, click the Layout arrow and select Handouts (6 slides per page).

s. Click the **Portrait Orientation arrow** and select **Landscape Orientation**. Click the **Back arrow**.

t. Save and close the file. Based on your instructor's directions, submit cf01p1Design_LastFirst.

2 Upscale Bakery

You have always been interested in baking and have worked in the field for several years. You now have an opportunity to devote yourself full time to your career as the CEO of a company dedicated to baking cupcakes and pastries. One of the first steps in getting the business off the ground is developing a business plan so that you can request financial support. You will use Word to develop your business plan. Refer to Figure 1.51 as you complete this exercise.

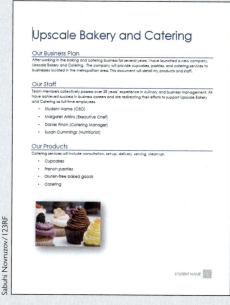

FIGURE 1.51 Upscale Bakery Business Plan

a. Open the Word document *cf01p2Business*. Click the **File tab**, click **Save As**, and save the file as **cf01p2Business_LastFirst**.

b. Click the **Design tab**, click **Themes**, and then select **Slice**.

c. Select the paragraphs beginning with *Our Staff* and ending with *(Nutritionist)*. Click the **Home tab** and click **Cut** in the Clipboard group. Click to the left of *Our Products* and click **Paste**.

d. Select the text **Your name** in the first bullet in the *Our Staff* section and replace it with your first and last names. Select the entire bullet list in the *Our Staff* section. On the Mini Toolbar, click the **Font Size arrow** and select **11**.

e. Click **Format Painter** in the Clipboard group. Drag the Format Painter pointer across all four *Our Products* bullets to change the bullets' font size to 11 pt.

f. Click the **Tell me box** and type **footer**. Click **Add a Footer**, scroll to locate the **Integral footer**, and click to add it to the page. Keep the footer open.

g. Right-click the **page number box** in the footer. Click the **Shading arrow** in the Paragraph group on the Home tab and select **White Background 1 Darker 50%**. Click **Close Header and Footer** on the Header & Footer Tools Design tab.

h. Triple-click to select the last line in the document, which says *Insert and position picture here*, and press **Ctrl+X**. Click the **Insert tab** and click **Online Pictures** in the Illustrations group.

i. Click in the **Bing Image search box**, type **Cupcakes**, and then press **Enter**.

j. Select any **cupcake image** and click **Insert**. Do not deselect the image.

k. Ensure the Picture Tools Format tab is active, and in the Picture Styles group, select the **Drop Shadow Rectangle**.

> **TROUBLESHOOTING:** If you are unable to find a cupcake image in Bing, you can use *cf01p2Cupcake* from the student data files.

l. Click the **Size Dialog Box Launcher** and ensure that Lock aspect ratio is selected. Click **OK**. Click the **Shape width box** in the Size group and change the width to **2.5**.

m. Click outside the picture.

n. Press **Ctrl+Home**. Click **Customize Quick Access Toolbar** and select **Spelling & Grammar** (ignore if present). Click **Spelling & Grammar** from the QAT. Correct the spelling error and click **OK**.

o. Click the **View tab** and select **Draft** in the Views group. Click **Print Layout** in the Views group and click **One Page** in the Zoom group.

p. Click the **Layout tab** and click **Margins** in the Page Setup group. Change to **Moderate Margins**.

q. Click the **File tab**. In the Properties section, click in Add a tag box and add the tag **business plan**. Click **Add an author** and add your first and last name to the Author property. Right-click the **current author** (should say Exploring Series) and click **Remove Person**.

r. Click **Print** in Backstage view. Notice the author name has changed in the footer. Change the number of copies to **2**. Click the **Back arrow**.

s. Save and close the file. Based on your instructor's directions, submit cf01p2Business_LastFirst.

Mid-Level Exercises

1   Reference Letter

You are an instructor at a local community college. A student asked you to provide her with a letter of reference for a job application. You have used Word to prepare the letter, but now you want to make a few changes before it is finalized.

a. Open the Word document *cf01m1RefLetter* and save it as **cf01m1RefLetter_LastFirst**.

b. Change the theme to **Gallery**. Point to Colors in the Document Formatting group and read the Enhanced ScreenTip. Click **Colors** and select **Red**.

c. Insert a **Blank footer**. Type **410 Wellington Parkway, Huntsville, AL 35611**. Center the footer. Close the footer.

d. Place the insertion point at the end of Professor Smith's name in the signature line. Press **Enter** twice. Insert a picture from your files using *cf01m1College.png*. Resize the image to **1"** tall. Click **Color** in the Adjust group and select **Dark Red, Accent color 1 Light**. Click **Center** in the Paragraph group on Home tab.

e. Press **Ctrl+Home**. Select the **date** and point to several font sizes on the Mini Toolbar. Use Live Preview to view them. Click **12**.

f. Right-click the word **talented** in the second paragraph starting with *Stacy is a* and click **Synonyms** from the shortcut menu. Replace *talented* with **gifted**.

g. Move the last paragraph—beginning with *In my opinion*—to position it before the second paragraph—beginning with *Stacy is a gifted*.

h. Press **Ctrl+Home**. Use Spelling & Grammar to correct all errors. Make any spelling and grammar changes that are suggested. Stacy's last name is spelled correctly.

i. Change the margins to **Narrow**.

j. Customize the QAT to add **Print Preview and Print**. Preview the document as it will appear when printed. Stay in Backstage view.

k. Click **Info** in Backstage view. Add the tag **reference** to the Properties for the file in Backstage view.

l. Save and close the file. Based on your instructor's directions, submit cf01m1RefLetter_LastFirst.

2   Medical Monitoring

You are enrolled in a Health Informatics study program in which you learn to manage databases related to health fields. For a class project, your instructor requires that you monitor your blood pressure, recording your findings in an Excel worksheet. You have recorded the week's data and will now make a few changes before printing the worksheet for submission.

a. Open the Excel workbook *cf01m2Tracker* and save it as **cf01m2Tracker_LastFirst**.

b. Change the theme to **Crop**.

c. Click in the cell to the right of *Name* and type your first and last names. Press **Enter**.

d. Select **cells H1, I1, J1,** and **K1**. Cut the selected cells and paste to **cell C2**. Click **cell A1**.

e. Press **Ctrl+A**. Use Live Preview to see how different fonts will look. Change the font of the worksheet to **Arial**.

f. Add the Spelling feature to the QAT and check the spelling for the worksheet to ensure that there are no errors.

g. Select **cells E22, F22,** and **G22**. You want to increase the decimal places for the values in cells so that each value shows one place to the right of the decimal. Use **Increase Decimal** as the search term in the Tell me box. Click **Insert Decimal** in the results to increase the decimal place to **1**.

h. Press **Ctrl+Home** and insert an **Online Picture** of your choice related to blood pressure. Resize and position the picture so that it displays in an attractive manner. Apply the **Drop Shadow Rectangle** picture style to the image.

i. Insert a footer. Use the Page Number header and footer element in the center section. Use the File Name header and footer element in the right section of the footer. Click in a cell on the worksheet. Return to Normal view.

j. Change the orientation to **Landscape**. Change the page margins so Left and Right are **1.5"** and Top and Bottom and **1"**. Center on page both vertically and horizontally. Close the dialog box.

k. Add **blood pressure** as a tag and adjust print settings to print two copies. You will not actually print two copies unless directed by your instructor.

l. Save and close the file. Based on your instructor's directions, submit cf01m2Tracker_LastFirst.

Running Case

New Castle County Technical Services

New Castle County Technical Services (NCCTS) provides technical support for companies in the greater New Castle County, Delaware, area. The company has been in operation since 2011 and has grown to become one of the leading technical service companies in the area. NCCTS has prided itself on providing great service at reasonable costs, but as you begin to review the budget for next year and the rates your competitors are charging, you are realizing that it may be time to increase some rates. You have prepared a worksheet with suggested rates and will include those rates in a memo to the CFO. You will format the worksheet, copy the data to the Office Clipboard, and use the Office Clipboard to paste the information into a memo. You will then modify the formatting of the memo, check the spelling, and ensure the document is ready for distribution before sending it on to the CFO.

a. Open the Excel workbook *cf01r1NCCTSRates* and save as **cf01r1NCCTSRates_LastFirst**.

b. Select **cells A4:C4**. Click **More** in the Styles group on the Home tab and select **Heading 2**.

c. Select **cells A5:C5**. Press **Ctrl** and select cells **A7:C7**. Change the font color to **Red** in Standard Colors.

d. Select **cells A5:C10** and increase the font size to **12**.

e. Select cells **A4:C10**. Open the **Office Clipboard**. Clear the Office clipboard if items display. Click **Copy** in the Clipboard group. Keep Excel open.

f. Open the Word document *cf01r1NCCTSMemo* and save it as **cf01r1NCCTSMemo_LastFirst**.

g. Change Your Name in the From: line to your own name.

h. Press **Ctrl+Home**. Insert image *cf01r1Logo.jpg*. Resize the height to **1"**.

i. Change the document theme to **Retrospect**.

j. Place insertion point in the blank line above the paragraph beginning with *Please*.

k. Open Office Clipboard and click the item in the Office Clipboard that was copied from the NCCTS Rates workbook. Clear then close the **Office Clipboard**.

l. Check the spelling. Correct all grammar and spelling mistakes.

m. Increase left and right margins to **1.5"**.

n. Insert a footer and click **Edit Footer**. Click **Document Info** in the Insert group on the Header and Footer Tools Design tab. Click **File Name**. Click **Close Header and Footer**.

o. Enter **2022**, **rates** as tags.

p. Save and close the files. Based on your instructor's directions, submit the following files:
cf01r1NCCTSMemo_LastFirst
cf01r1NCCTSRates_LastFirst

Disaster Recovery

Resume Enhancement

You are applying for a new position and you have asked a friend to look at your resume. She has a better eye for details than you do, so you want her to let you know about any content or formatting errors. She has left some instructions pointing out where you can improve the resume. Open the Word document *cf01d1Resume* and save it as **cf01d1Resume_LastFirst**. Add your name, address, phone and email in the placeholders at the top of the document. Change the theme of the resume to Office. Bold all the job titles and dates held. Italicize all company names and locations. Use Format Painter to copy the formatting of the bullets in the Software Intern description and apply them to the bullets in the other job description. Bold the name of the university and location. Apply italics to the degree and date. Change the margins to Narrow. Add resume as a tag. Check the spelling and grammar. Save and close the file. Based on your instructor's directions, submit cf01d1Resume_LastFirst.

Capstone Exercise

Social Media Privacy

You have been asked to create a presentation about protecting privacy on social media sites. You have given the first draft of your presentation to a colleague to review. She has come up with several suggestions that you need to incorporate before you present.

Open and Save Files

You will open, review, and save a PowerPoint presentation.

1. Open the PowerPoint presentation *cf01c1SocialMedia* and save it as **cf01c1SocialMedia_LastFirst**.

Apply a Theme and Change the View

You generally develop a presentation using a blank theme, and then when most of the content is on the slides, you add a different theme to provide some interest.

2. Apply the **Quotable theme** to the presentation and use the **Purple variant**.
3. Change to **Slide Sorter view**. Drag **Slide 2** to become **Slide 3** and drag **Slide 8** to become **Slide 6**.
4. Return to **Normal view**.

Select Text, Move Text, and Format Text

You make some changes to the order of text and change some word choices.

5. Click **Slide 5** and cut the second bullet. Paste it so it is the first bullet.
6. Right-click the second use of **regularly** in the first bullet to find a synonym. Change the word to **often**.
7. Double-click **location** in the fourth bullet. Drag it so it comes after *Disable* and add a space between the two words. Delete the word **of** so the bullet reads *Disable location sharing*.
8. Use the Mini Toolbar to format **Never** in the fifth bullet in italics.

Insert and Modify a Picture

You think Slide 2 has too much empty space and needs a picture. You insert a picture and add a style to give it a professional look.

9. Click **Slide 2** and insert the picture *cf01c1Sharing.jpg* from your data files.
10. Resize the picture height to **4.5"**.
11. Apply the **Rounded Diagonal Corner, White Picture Style**.

Use the Tell me Box

You also want to center the picture on Slide 2 vertically. You use the Tell Me box to help with this. You also need help to change a bulleted list on Slide 5 to SmartArt because many of your slides use SmartArt. You know that there is a way to convert text to SmartArt, but you cannot remember where it is. You use the Tell me box to help you with this function, too.

12. Ensure the picture on Slide 2 is still selected. Type **Align** in the Tell me box. Click **Align Objects** and select **Align Middle**.
13. Select the bulleted text on **Slide 5**. Use the Tell me box to search **SmartArt**.
14. Click the first instance of Convert text to SmartArt from your search and click **More SmartArt Graphics** to convert the text to a **Lined List**.

Insert Header and Footer

You want to give the audience printed handouts of your presentation, so you add a header and footer to the handouts, with page numbers and information to identify you and the topic.

15. Add **page numbers** to all Handouts.
16. Add **Social Media Privacy** as a Header in all Handouts.
17. Add **your name** as a Footer in all Handouts.

Customize the Quick Access Toolbar

You know to review the presentation for spelling errors. Because you run spell check regularly, you add a button on the QAT. You also add a button to preview and print your presentation for added convenience.

18. Add **Spelling** to the QAT.
19. Add **Print Preview and Print** to the QAT.

Check Spelling and Change View

Before you call the presentation complete, you will correct any spelling errors and view the presentation as a slide show.

20. Press **Ctrl+Home** and check the spelling.
21. View the slide show. Click after reviewing the last slide to return to the presentation.

Get to Know Word

Text format and paragraph fill

Drop cap

Heading style

Pull quote

SmartArt

Image

Columns

Table

Bulleted list

Shape and shading

Watermark

Style applied Center-aligned

Wrapped text

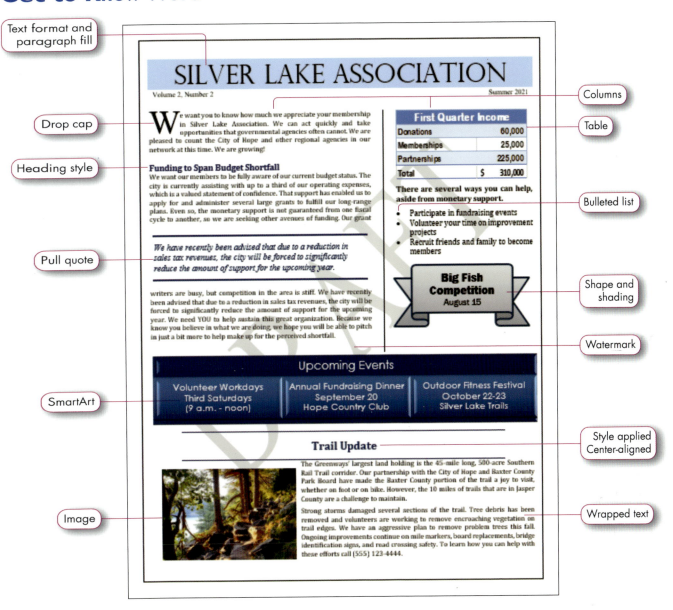

SILVER LAKE ASSOCIATION

Volume 2, Number 2   Summer 2021

We want you to know how much we appreciate your membership in Silver Lake Association. We can act quickly and take opportunities that governmental agencies often cannot. We are pleased to count the City of Hope and other regional agencies in our network at this time. We are growing!

Funding to Span Budget Shortfall
We want our members to be fully aware of our current budget status. The city is currently assisting with up to a third of our operating expenses, which is a valued statement of confidence. That support has enabled us to apply for and administer several large grants to fulfill our long-range plans. Even so, the monetary support is not guaranteed from one fiscal cycle to another, so we are seeking other avenues of funding. Our grant

We have recently been advised that due to a reduction in sales tax revenues, the city will be forced to significantly reduce the amount of support for the upcoming year.

writers are busy, but competition in the area is stiff. We have recently been advised that due to a reduction in sales tax revenues, the city will be forced to significantly reduce the amount of support for the upcoming year. We need YOU to help sustain this great organization. Because we know you believe in what we are doing, we hope you will be able to pitch in just a bit more to help make up for the perceived shortfall.

First Quarter Income	
Donations	60,000
Memberships	25,000
Partnerships	225,000
Total	$ 310,000

There are several ways you can help, aside from monetary support.

- Participate in fundraising events
- Volunteer your time on improvement projects
- Recruit friends and family to become members

Big Fish Competition
August 15

Upcoming Events

| Volunteer Workdays Third Saturdays (9 a.m. - noon) | Annual Fundraising Dinner September 20 Hope Country Club | Outdoor Fitness Festival October 22-23 Silver Lake Trails |

Trail Update

The Greenways' largest land holding is the 45-mile long, 500-acre Southern Rail Trail corridor. Our partnership with the City of Hope and Baxter County Park Board have made the Baxter County portion of the trail a joy to visit, whether on foot or on bike. However, the 10 miles of trails that are in Jasper County are a challenge to maintain.

Strong storms damaged several sections of the trail. Tree debris has been removed and volunteers are working to remove encroaching vegetation on trail edges. We have an aggressive plan to remove problem trees this fall. Ongoing improvements continue on mile markers, board replacements, bridge identification signs, and road crossing safety. To learn how you can help with these efforts call (555) 123-4444.

Other Word Features

3D Models

Rotate and turn objects in 360 degree directions to present an object from all angles - or to show just the right angle.

Table of Contents

Table of Contents:

Apply styles to document headers and create a Table of Contents that updates easily when content changes.

Works Cited:

Insert references to sources used in the body of a document. Create Works Cited to list the references in applied writing style. Easily updated when references change.

Works Cited

Hovet, Theodore R. "Once Upon a Time: Sarah Orne Jewett's 'A White Heron' as a Fairy Tale." *Studies in Short Fiction* 25 Sept. 2011: 63-68.

Jewett, Sarah Orne. "A White Heron." Literature, The American Tradition in. Ed. George Perkins and Barbara Perkins. Vol. 2. New York: McGraw-Hill, 2009. 531-537.

Use Word on Windows PCs and Macs

To Do This:	In Word for Windows	In Word for Mac
Format Fonts	Font Dialog Box Launcher	Format Menu, select Font
Format Paragraphs	Paragraph Dialog Box Launcher	Format Menu, select Paragraph
Modify Styles	Styles Dialog Box Launcher	Format Menu, select Styles
Copy text or object	Ctrl+C	Command+C
Paste text or object	Ctrl+V	Command+V
Move to the top of a document	Ctrl+Home	Command+Home or Command+fn+←
Move to the end of a document	Ctrl+End	Command+End or Command+fn+→
Select to the end of a line	Shift+→	Shift+End or Command+Shift+→
Select an entire document	Ctrl+A	Command+A

Use Print Preview, Change Print Layout, and Adjust Document Properties

You want to print handouts of the presentation so that 3 slides will appear on one page.

22. Click the **Print Preview and Print command** on the QAT to preview the document as it will appear when printed.

23. Change Full Page Slides to **3 Slides**.

> **MAC TROUBLESHOOTING:** Click the File menu and click Print. Click Show Details. Click Layout and choose Handouts (3 slides per page).

24. Change the Page Orientation to **Landscape**.

25. Adjust the print settings to print **two** copies. You will not actually print two copies unless directed by your instructor.

26. Change document properties to add **social media** as a tag and change the author name to your own.

27. Save and close the file. Based on your instructor's directions, submit cf01c1SocialMedia_LastFirst.

Introduction to Word

LEARNING OUTCOME   You will develop a document using features of Microsoft Word.

OBJECTIVES & SKILLS: After you read this chapter, you will be able to:

CASE STUDY | Swan Creek National Wildlife Refuge

You are fascinated with wildlife in its natural habitat. For that reason, you are excited to work with Swan Creek National Wildlife Refuge, assigned the task of promoting the refuge's educational outreach programs. Emily Traynom, Swan Creek's site director, is concerned that children in the city have little opportunity to interact with nature. She fears that a generation of children will mature into adults with little appreciation of the role of our country's natural resources in the overall balance of nature. Her passion is encouraging students to visit Swan Creek and become actively involved in environmental activities.

Ms. Traynom envisions summer day camps where children explore the wildlife refuge and participate in learning activities. She asked you to use your expertise in Microsoft Word to produce documents such as flyers, brochures, memos, contracts, and letters. You will design and produce an article about a series of summer camps available to children from fifth through eighth grades. From a rough draft, you will create an attractive document for distribution to schools.

Organizing a Document

Nd3000/Shutterstock

Emily Traynom, Director
Swan Creek National Wildlife Refuge
89667 Mill Creek Road
Hastings, PA 19092

May 23, 2021

RE: Summer Day Camp Program at Swan Creek

As an educator in our comunity, you are sure to be interested in an opportunity for your students to learn at Swan Creek National Wildlife Refuge this summer. I hope you will encourage your students who are rising 5th through 8th graders to join us for a few days this summer. The day camp program, which is described on the following page, is an effort to instill an appreciation for our environment, all in an engaging and fun atmosphere. Funded through a grant from the Nature Federation, the program is free to campers; however, space is limited, so please encourage early registration.

I, or a member of my staff, will be happy to visit your classroom to promote the refuge and to answer questions or accept registration for the summer day camp program. Feel free to copy and distribute the article on the following page. We hope to hear from you soon and look forward to working with your students this summer!

Swan Creek National Wildlife Refuge

What: Swan Creek National Wildlife Refuge Day Camp

When: Week-Long Day Camps from June 15-August 6, 2021

Where: Swan Creek National Wildlife Refuge (at the headquarters)

Open to: 5th through 8th Grade Students

When was the last time you spent an afternoon absorbed in nature, experiencing sights and sounds you could never enjoy in the city? Did you know there are 38 different types of birds native to our area, all of which you can find at Swan Creek National Wildlife Refuge? The refuge backwaters are home to beavers, mallard ducks, geese, largemouth bass, and slider turtles, among many other inhabitants. What better way to spend a few days this summer than with us at the refuge, experiencing nature at its finest?

Swan Creek National Wildlife Refuge is offering a series of week-long day camps this summer, designed for children who are rising fifth through eighth graders. The series of wildlife camps will begin on June 15, with the last camp ending on August 6. Children will participate in informative seminars and nature observations led by wildlife rangers. On nature hikes through the refuge, camp participants will explore a native forest comprised of trees and forestry indigenous to the area. Other activities include hiking along the raised boardwalk through the sunken forest, identifying wildlife from the refuge observation center, and participating in nature photography classes. The first 50 campers to register will receive a Striker™ backpack, compliments of Swan Creek!

Explore nature

Learn to identify native plants and wildlife

Take digital photos

Participate in nature seminars

Enjoy relaxing days at the refuge

For further information, or to register, please contact:

Melinda Gifford, Events Coordinator

(660) 555-5578

mgifford@scnwf.org

U.S. Fish and Wildlife Service   w01h3Refuge_LastFirst.docx

FIGURE 1.1 Swan Creek Documents

CASE STUDY | Swan Creek National Wildlife Refuge

Starting Files	Files to be Submitted
Blank document **w01h1Camps** **w01h2Letter** **w01h3NewEmployee**	**w01h2Flyer_LastFirst** **w01h3NewEmployee_LastFirst** **w01h3Refuge_LastFirst**

MyLab IT Grader An alternate version of this project is available as a MyLab IT Grader Assessment

Introduction to Word Processing

Word processing software, often called a word processor, is one of the most commonly used types of software in homes, schools, and businesses. People around the world—students, office assistants, managers, and professionals in all fields—use word processing programs such as ***Microsoft Word*** for a variety of tasks. You can create letters, reports, research papers, newsletters, brochures, and all sorts of documents with Word. You can even create and send email, produce webpages, post to social media sites, and update blogs with Word. Figure 1.2 shows examples of documents created in Word. If a project requires collaboration online or between offices, Word facilitates sharing documents, tracking changes, viewing comments, and efficiently producing a document to which several authors can contribute. By using Word to develop a research paper, you can create citations, a bibliography, a table of contents, a cover page, an index, and other reference pages. To enhance a document, you can change colors, add interesting styles of text, insert graphics, and use tables to present data. With emphasis on saving documents to the cloud, Word enables you to share these documents with others or access them from any device. Word is a comprehensive word processing solution, to say the least.

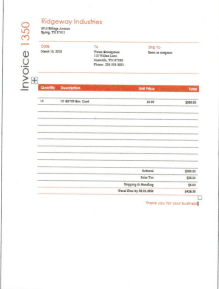
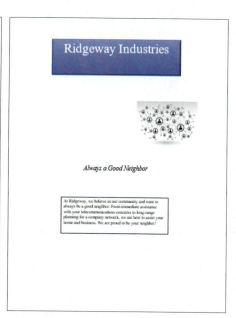

FIGURE 1.2 Sample Word Processing Documents

Communicating through the written word is an important, in fact, vital, task for any business or organization. Word processing software, such as Word, simplifies the technical task of preparing documents, but a word processor does not replace the writer. Be careful when phrasing a document so you are sure it is appropriate for the intended audience. Always remember that once you distribute a document, either on paper or electronically, you cannot retract the words. Therefore, you should never send a document that you have not carefully checked several times to be sure it conveys your message in the best way possible. Also, you cannot depend completely on a word processor to identify all spelling and grammatical errors, so be sure to closely proofread every document you create. Although several word processors, including Word, provide predesigned documents (called templates) that include basic layouts for various tasks, it is ultimately up to you to compose well-worded documents. The role of business communication, including the written word, in the success or failure of a business cannot be overemphasized.

In this section, you will explore Word's interface, learn how to create a document, explore the use of templates, and perform basic editing operations. You will learn to adjust document settings and to modify document properties. Using Word options, you will explore ways to customize Word to suit your preferences.

Beginning and Editing a Document

When you open Word, your screen will be similar to Figure 1.3, although it may vary a bit depending upon whether Office has recently updated. You can create a blank document, or you can select from several types of templates. In addition, you can open a previously created document, perhaps selecting from the list of recent files, and then edit and print a document as desired.

FIGURE 1.3 Word Document Options

STEP 1 Create a Document

To create a blank document, click Blank document when Word opens. As you type text, the **word wrap** feature automatically pushes words to the next line when you reach the right margin, creating what is known as a soft return. The location of automatically generated soft returns changes as text is inserted or deleted, or as page features or settings, such as objects or margins are added or changed. Such soft returns cannot be deleted.

Although word wrap is convenient, you may occasionally want to control when one line ends and another begins, such as at the end of a paragraph or a major section. Or perhaps you are typing several lines of an address or bulleted lines. In those cases, you can indicate that a line should end before text reaches the right margin. To do so, you can either insert a hard return or a soft return. When you press Enter, Word inserts a hard return. As a hard return is entered, a new paragraph begins, with any associated paragraph spacing separating the two paragraphs. In the case of multiple address lines, bulleted text, or text associated with objects such as SmartArt, however, you might want to avoid the paragraph space that results from a hard return. You can insert a manual soft return, or line break, when you press Shift+Enter at the end of any line of text. A new line begins after the soft return, but without any associated paragraph spacing. Manual soft returns, as opposed to the automatic soft returns generated by Word when the right margin is reached, are considered characters and can be deleted. Hard returns are also nonprinting characters that can be removed.

Actions such as a hard return, manual soft return, or even a tab or space are included in a document as nonprinting characters that are only visible when you make a point to display them. To show nonprinting characters, click Show/Hide ¶ on the Home tab (see Figure 1.4). The display of nonprinting characters can assist you with troubleshooting a document and modifying its appearance before printing or distributing. For example, if lines in a document end awkwardly, some not even extending to the right margin, you can check for the presence of poorly placed, or perhaps unnecessary, hard returns (if nonprinting characters are displayed). Deleting the hard returns might realign the document so that lines end in better fashion. Just as you delete any other character by pressing Backspace or Delete (depending on whether the insertion point is positioned to the right or left of the item to remove), you can delete a nonprinting character. To turn off the display of nonprinting characters, click Show/Hide again.

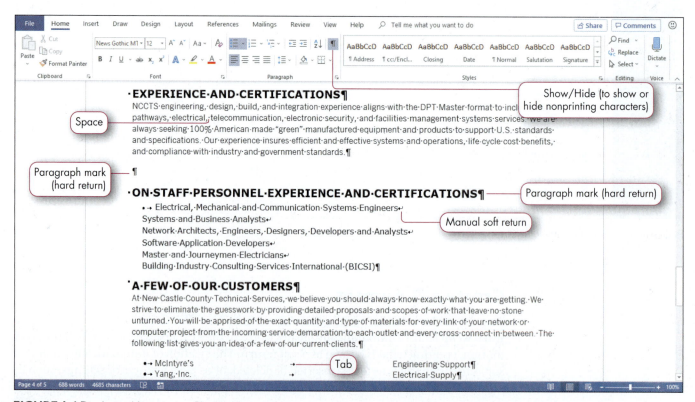

FIGURE 1.4 Displaying Nonprinting Characters

As you work with Word, you must understand that Word's definition of a paragraph and your definition are not likely to be the same. You would probably define a paragraph as a related set of sentences, which is correct in a literary sense. When the subject or direction of thought changes, a new paragraph begins. However, Word defines a paragraph as text that ends in a hard return. Even a blank line, created by pressing Enter, is considered a paragraph. Therefore, as a Word student, you will consider every line that ends in a hard return a paragraph. When you press Enter, a paragraph mark is displayed in the document if you choose to show nonprinting characters (refer to Figure 1.4).

Reuse Text

You might find occasion to reuse text from a previously created document. For example, a memo to employees describing new insurance benefits might borrow all wording from another document describing the same benefits to company retirees. Word facilitates the addition of all text from a saved document to any location within a document that is being developed. Inserting text in that way can save development time, as existing text is inserted without the need to type it again and can also avoid typing errors that are likely to occur if text is typed instead of inserted.

Inserting text from a previously saved document into one that is currently open incorporates all text from the saved document, unlike the copy and paste procedure that is often used to acquire only a portion of text from another document. Text that is copied and pasted must be drawn from a currently open document, whereas text that is reused is retrieved from a saved document without the need to first open it. If the intention is to include all text from a saved file into one that is being created, you will find that inserting text is an efficient way to accomplish that.

To insert text from another document, complete the following steps:

1. Position the insertion point where the inserted text is to be placed.
2. Click the Insert tab. Click the Object arrow (see Figure 1.5).
3. Click Text from File.
4. Navigate to the location of the source document and double-click the file name.

FIGURE 1.5 Inserting Text from Another File

Use a Template

Developing a new document related to a specific scenario or with precise or elaborate formatting can be difficult. With that in mind, the developers of Word have included a library of **templates** from which you can select a predesigned document. You can then modify the document to suit your needs. Various types of templates are displayed when you first open Word, or when you click the File tab and click New. In addition to local templates—those that are available offline with a typical Word installation—Microsoft provides many more online. All online templates are displayed or searchable within Word, as shown in Figure 1.6. Microsoft continually updates content in the template library, so you are assured of having access to all the latest templates each time you open Word.

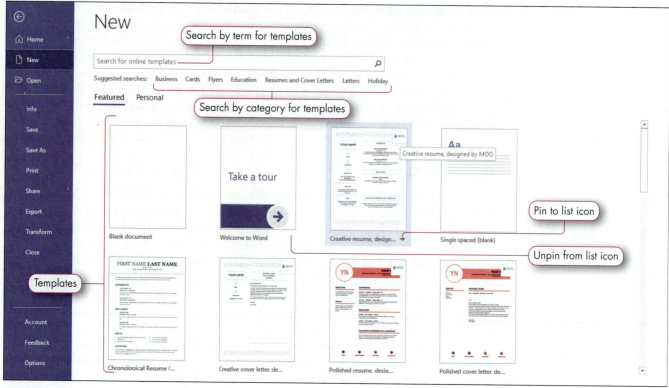

FIGURE 1.6 Working with Templates

Some templates are likely to become your favorites. Because you will want quick access to those templates, you can pin them to the top of the templates menu so they will always be available. Having pinned a template, you can also unpin it when it is no longer necessary. To pin a template, either right-click a favorite template and then pin it to the list or point to a template and click the horizontal Pin to list icon (refer to Figure 1.6). Unpin a template by completing the same steps but choosing to unpin.

STEP 2 Add Text and Navigate a Document

The *insertion point* indicates where the text you type will be placed. It is shown as a blinking vertical line in a Word document. It is important to remain aware of the location of the insertion point and to know how to move it to control where text is typed. Most often, you will move the insertion point by moving the I-bar pointer $\boxed{\text{I}}$ and clicking the desired location. You can also position the insertion point in other ways, including the use of arrow keys on the keyboard or by using shortcuts such as Ctrl+Home (to move to the beginning of the document) and Ctrl+End (to move to the end). In addition, you can tap a touchscreen with a finger or stylus to reposition the insertion point.

If a document contains more text than will display onscreen at one time, click the horizontal or vertical scroll arrows (or drag a scroll bar) to view different parts of the document. An alternative is to press the Page Up or Page Down keys. Then, when the text you want to see displays, position the insertion point and continue editing the document. Be aware that using the scroll bar or scroll arrows to move the display does not reposition the insertion point. It merely enables you to see different parts of the document, leaving the insertion point where it was last positioned. Only when you click or tap in the document, or use a keyboard shortcut, is the insertion point moved.

Review Spelling and Grammar

It is important to create a document that is free of spelling and grammatical errors. One of the easiest ways to lose credibility with readers is to allow such errors to occur. Choose words that are appropriate and that best convey your intentions in writing or editing a document. Word provides tools on the Review tab that simplify the tasks of reviewing a document for errors, identifying proper wording, and providing insight into unfamiliar words.

A word considered by Word to be misspelled is underlined with a red wavy line. A possible grammatical mistake or word usage error is underlined in blue. Both types of errors are shown in Figure 1.7. To correct possible grammatical or word usage errors in a document, right-click an underlined error and complete one of the following steps:

- Select the correct spelling from one or more options that may be displayed.
- Ignore the misspelled word.
- Add the word to the Office dictionary so it will be recognized as a valid term.

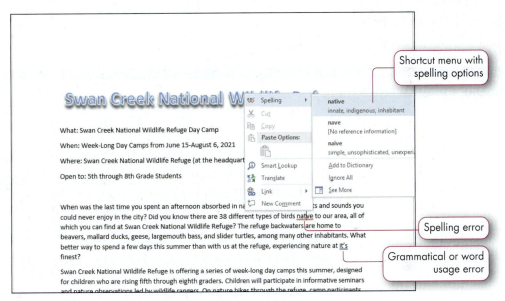

FIGURE 1.7 Correcting Spelling and Grammatical Errors

Correcting each error individually by right-clicking can become time-consuming, especially if the mistakes are many. In that case, Word can check an entire document, pausing at each identified error so that you can determine whether to correct or ignore the problem. To check an entire document for spelling, grammatical, and writing errors, use the Review tab to check the document (see Figure 1.8). Review each error as it is displayed, selecting an identified correction or ignoring the error if it is correct (as might be the case with a name or medical term). If a correct spelling is not displayed, and a word is misspelled, you can manually make the correction.

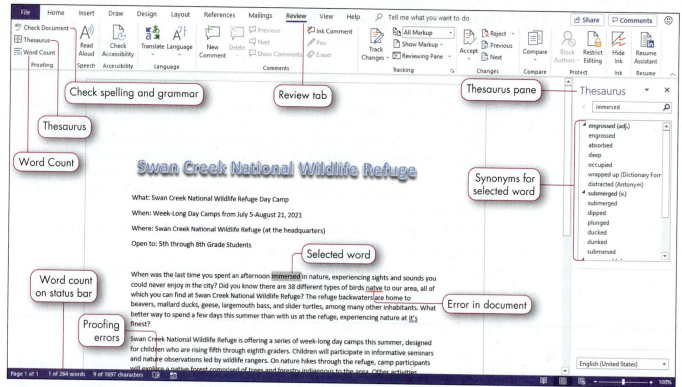

FIGURE 1.8 Options for Proofing a Document

As an alternative to identifying errors, check the Proofing errors icon on the status bar (refer to Figure 1.8). By default, Word automatically checks the entire open document for spelling, grammatical, and word usage errors, displaying ⌨ on the status bar if errors are found. Click the Proofing errors icon and choose a category of error (Spelling or Grammar) to either change or ignore all errors, one at a time. If, instead, you see a check mark on the Proofing errors icon, the document appears to be error free. The document in Figure 1.8 contains at least one error, as indicated by the Proofing errors icon on the status bar.

Never depend completely on Word to catch all errors; always proofread a document yourself. For example, typing the word *fee* when you meant to type *free* is not an error that Word would typically catch, because *fee* is not actually misspelled and might not be flagged as a word usage error, depending upon the sentence context.

Words do not always come easily. Occasionally, you might want to find a synonym (a word with the same meaning as another) for a particular word. Word provides a handy ***thesaurus*** for just such an occasion. In addition to providing synonyms, Word's thesaurus also includes antonyms (words with the opposite meaning) for a selected word, if any are available. To identify a synonym, select a word in a document and choose Thesaurus on the Review tab (refer to Figure 1.8). Point to a synonym and click the arrow that displays to insert the word. You can also right-click a selected word and point to Synonyms on the shortcut menu. Select a synonym from a subsequent list of words or click Thesaurus to open the Thesaurus pane for more options.

You can identify a synonym for a word that is not in the current document. In that case, open the thesaurus, type the word for which you want a synonym in the Thesaurus pane, and begin a search. The Thesaurus pane is shown in Figure 1.8. Select from the list presented. If a dictionary is installed, the Thesaurus pane also displays a definition of a selected or typed search term.

Especially when editing or collaborating on a document created by someone else, you might come across a word with which you are unfamiliar. Select Smart Lookup on the References tab to peruse additional information in the Smart Lookup pane related to a selected word (see Figure 1.9).

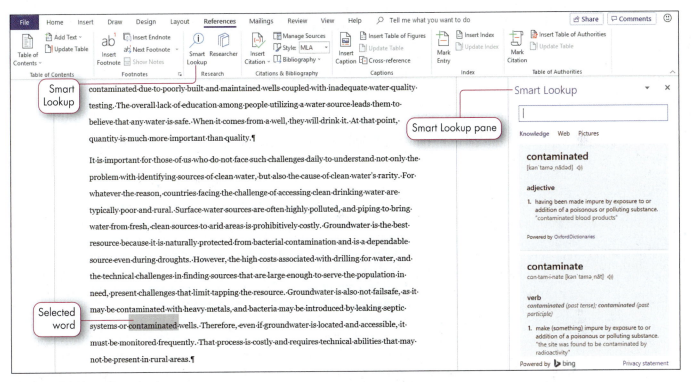

FIGURE 1.9 Using Smart Lookup

Customizing Word

As installed, Word is immediately useful. However, you might find options that you would prefer to customize so that your Word installation is personalized and effective. You might prefer to change the default location to which documents are saved, or maybe you prefer a particular theme or background. These and other options are available for customization within Word.

Explore Word Options

By default, certain Word settings are determined and in place when you begin a Word document. For example, unless you specify otherwise, Word will automatically check spelling as you type. Similarly, the Mini Toolbar will automatically display when text is selected. Although those and other settings are most likely what you will prefer, there may be occasions when you want to change them. When you change Word options, you change them for all documents—not just the currently open file. To modify Word options, click the File tab and click Options. Then select from categories of options, as shown in Figure 1.10.

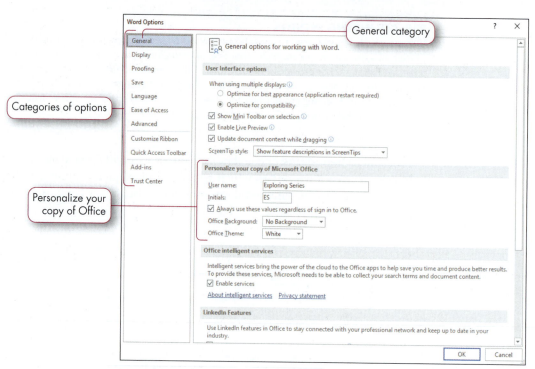

FIGURE 1.10 Accessing Word Options

Although you can choose from many options as you customize your Word installation, you are likely to find a few that are more useful or more commonly accessed than others. The General category (refer to Figure 1.10) provides options to personalize Word by associating a particular name and initials. In the same area, you can select a background and theme for the Word interface. The Save category enables you to change the location where files are saved by default or to adjust the time between automatic saves. Other settings in other categories facilitate additional customization.

The *AutoCorrect* option in the Proofing category includes a standard list of typical misspellings and grammatical errors. As you type text in a Word document, you might notice that some items are automatically corrected, such as the automatic replacement of "teh" with "the." Because the mistake is so common, it is included in the standard set of AutoCorrect entries. AutoCorrect also corrects various capitalization errors and facilitates the inclusion of certain symbols. For example, typing (c) in a document automatically results in the copyright symbol of © because those keystrokes are included in AutoCorrect's standard set of replacements. You can check the list of automatic corrections or changes when you click AutoCorrect Options in the Proofing category in Word Options (see Figure 1.11).

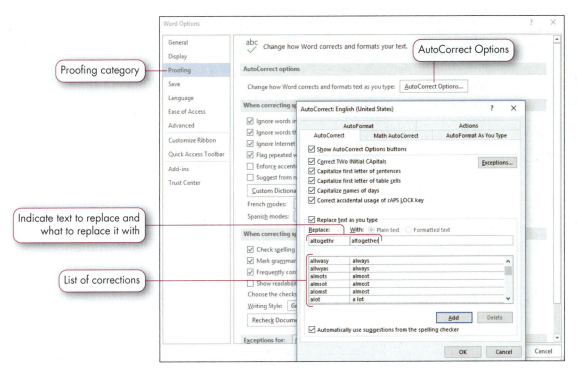

FIGURE 1.11 AutoCorrect Options

In the same dialog box (refer to Figure 1.11), you can customize AutoCorrect entries to include words or names that you often misspell or changes that you choose to make based on text typed. You might even consider using AutoCorrect to simplify the production of documents by replacing abbreviations with whole words. For example, you could include an entry that replaces an abbreviation for your company with the entire company name. That way, whenever you type the initials for a lengthy law firm name, for example, Word could automatically display the entire law firm name. To add AutoCorrect entries, indicate what to replace and what to replace it with in the AutoCorrect dialog box.

> **TIP: SETTING WORD OPTIONS**
> Word options that you change will remain in effect until you change them again, even after Word is closed and reopened. Keep in mind that if you are working in a school computer lab, you might not have permission to change options permanently.

Quick Concepts

1. Explain how the way you are likely to define a paragraph and the way Word defines a paragraph can differ. ***p. 75***

2. Describe the process of reusing text from another document and compare the process to that of copying and pasting text. Provide an example of when reusing text would be preferable to copying and pasting. ***p. 75***

3. Describe an advantage of using Word templates to begin document production. ***p. 75***

4. Explain why a document might still contain spelling or word usage errors even after Word has checked a document for errors. Provide an example of an error that Word might not identify. ***p. 78***

Hands-On Exercises

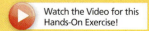

Skills covered: Create a Document • Reuse Text • Add Text and Navigate a Document • Review Spelling and Grammar

1 Introduction to Word Processing

As an office assistant working with the wildlife refuge, you prepare a document publicizing the summer day camps at Swan Creek. Your supervisor provided a few paragraphs that you modify, creating an article for distribution to schools in the area.

STEP 1 CREATE A DOCUMENT AND REUSE TEXT

As you create a new document, you insert text provided by your supervisor and save the document for later editing. Refer to Figure 1.12 as you complete Step 1.

FIGURE 1.12 Beginning a Document

a. Open Word. Click **Blank document**. Click **Save** on the Quick Access Toolbar. In the right pane, click the location where you save your files, or click **Browse** and navigate to the location. Change the file name to **w01h1Refuge_LastFirst**. Click **Save**.

   When you save files, use your last and first names. For example, as the Word author, I would name my document "w01h1Refuge_HoganLynn."

> **TROUBLESHOOTING:** If you make any major mistakes in this exercise, you can close the file without saving, open a blank document, and then start this exercise over.

b. Click the **Insert tab** and click the **Object arrow** in the Text group. Click **Text from File**. Navigate to your student data files for this chapter and double-click *w01h1Camps*. Press **Ctrl+Home** to move the insertion point to the beginning of the document.

c. Click **Save** on the Quick Access Toolbar.

   This saves the document without changing the name or the location where it is saved.

d. Click the **File tab** and click **Close**.

Although Ms. Traynom provided you with a good start, you add a bit more detail to the wildlife refuge article. Refer to Figure 1.13 as you complete Step 2.

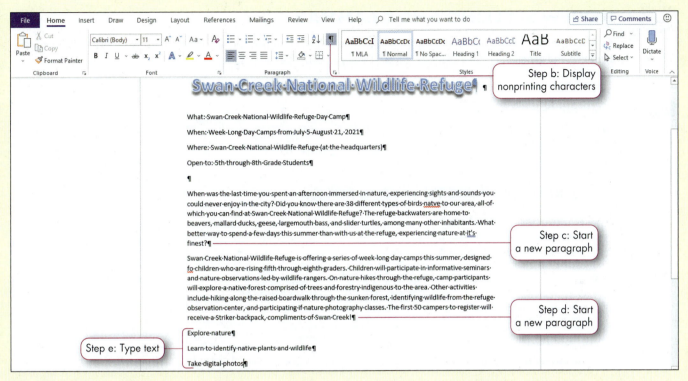

FIGURE 1.13 Editing a Document

a. Click the **File tab**. In the Recent list, click **w01h1Refuge_LastFirst**.

b. Click **Show/Hide** in the Paragraph group on the Home tab to display nonprinting formatting marks (unless they are already displayed).

c. Click after the sentence ending in *finest?*—immediately after the question mark and before the nonprinting space character (that is not shown in Figure 1.13) at the end of the fourth sentence in the body text. Press **Enter**. Press **Delete**.

> **TROUBLESHOOTING:** There will be no space before Swan if you clicked after the space instead of before it when you pressed Enter. In that case, there is no space to delete, so leave the text as is.

d. Scroll down and click after *Creek!*—immediately after the exclamation point after the second body paragraph—and press **Enter**.

e. Type the following text, pressing **Enter** at the end of each line:

explore nature

learn to identify native plants and wildlife

take digital photos

participate in nature seminars

enjoy relaxing days at the refuge

As you type each line, the first letter is automatically capitalized.

f. Press **Ctrl+End**. Press **Delete**.

The final paragraph mark is deleted and the second blank page is removed.

g. Save the document.

STEP 3 ## REVIEW SPELLING AND GRAMMAR

As you continue to develop the article, you check for spelling, grammar, and word usage mistakes. You also identify a synonym and get a definition. Refer to Figure 1.14 as you complete Step 3.

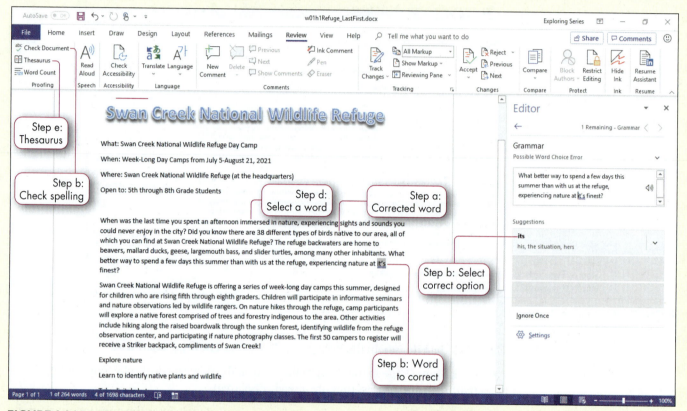

FIGURE 1.14 Proofing a Document

a. Press **Ctrl+Home**. Right-click the red underlined word **natve** in the second line of the first body paragraph in the document. Click **native** on the shortcut menu.

b. Click the **Review tab** and click **Check Document** (or Spelling & Grammar) in the Proofing group. Click **Spelling** in the Editor pane, if shown. As an error is displayed, click to select the correct option. The word *fo* should be **for**. Click **Grammar** in the Editor pane. The word *birds* is not possessive, so ignore the suggested error. The word *it's* should not include an apostrophe, so click the correct option (refer to Figure 1.14). Click **OK** when the check is complete. Close the Editor pane.

c. Read through the document. At least one error in the document is not identified as a spelling or word usage error by Word. Identify and correct the error. The error is a word that is not misspelled but is misused. It is located near the end of the second body paragraph.

d. Select the word *immersed* in the first sentence of the first body paragraph. Click the **References tab**. Click **Smart Lookup** in the Research group.

A definition is shown in the Smart Lookup pane.

> **TROUBLESHOOTING:** If the Smart Lookup pane has not been used before, you may have to respond to a privacy prompt before the Smart Lookup pane will open.

e. Close the Smart Lookup pane. With the word *immersed* still selected, click the **Review tab** and click **Thesaurus** in the Proofing group. Point to the word *absorbed*, click the arrow at the right, and then select **Insert**.

> **TROUBLESHOOTING:** If you click the word *absorbed* instead of the arrow at the right, you will see related word choices, but the word will not be inserted. Click the back arrow at the top of the Thesaurus pane, and repeat Step e.

f. Close the Thesaurus pane.

g. Save the document. Keep the document open if you plan to continue with the next Hands-On Exercise. If not, close the document and exit Word.

Document Organization

Most often, the reason for creating a document is for others to read; therefore, the document should be designed to meet the needs of the reading audience. It should not only be well worded and structured, but also might include features that better identify it, such as headers, footers, and watermarks. In addition, adjusting margins and changing page orientation might better suit a document's purpose and improve its readability. Depending on its purpose, a document might need to fit on one page, or it could be very lengthy.

Before printing or saving a document, review it to ensure that it is attractive and appropriately organized. Word has various views, including Read Mode, Print Layout, Web Layout, Outline, and Draft, that you can use to get a good feel for the way the entire document looks, regardless of its length. The view selected can also give a snapshot of overall document organization, so you can be assured that the document is well structured and makes all points. Using options on the View tab on the ribbon, you can display a document in various ways, showing all pages, only one page, or zooming to a larger view, among other selections.

In this section, you will explore features that improve readability, and you will learn to change the view of a document.

Using Features That Improve Readability

Choosing your words carefully will result in a well-worded document. However, no matter how well worded, a document that is not organized in an attractive manner so that it is easy to read and understand is not likely to impress an audience. Consider not only the content, but also how a document will look when printed or displayed. Special features that can improve readability, such as headers, footers, and symbols, are located on Word's Insert tab. Other settings, such as margins, page orientation, and paper size, are found on the Layout tab. The Design tab provides access to watermarks, which can help convey the purpose or originator of a document.

STEP 1 Insert Headers and Footers

Headers and *footers* are sections of text that appear in the top or bottom margin of a document. Although headers and footers typically contain such information as a page number, date, or document title, they can also contain graphics, multiple paragraphs, and fields. Typically, the purpose of including a header or footer is to better identify the document. As a header, you might include an organization name or a class number so that each page identifies the document's origin or purpose. A page number is a typical footer, although it could just as easily be included as a header. You can specify that a header or footer does not appear on the first page, as might be the case if a document includes a title page, or you might create a different header or footer for odd and even pages. If a document is divided into sections, each section could include a different header or footer.

One advantage of using headers and footers is that you specify the content only once, after which it displays automatically on all pages. Although you can type the text yourself at the top or bottom of every page, it is time-consuming, and the possibility of making a mistake is great. Insert a header or footer by making selections on the Insert tab. You can select from a gallery of predefined header or footer styles that include graphics, borders, color, and text areas (see Figure 1.15). However, if you plan to design a simple unformatted header, you can select Edit Header and then type and align text as you like. Alternatively, to begin a simple unformatted header or footer, you can double-click in the top or bottom margin.

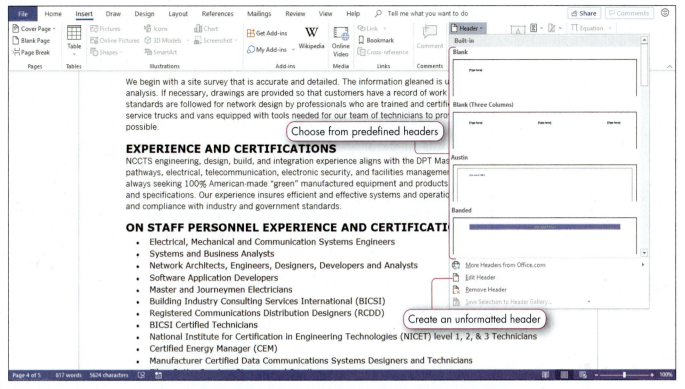

FIGURE 1.15 Inserting a Header

A header or footer can be formatted like any other text. It can be left-, center-, or right-aligned and formatted in any font or font size. When working with a header or footer, the main body text of the document is grayed out temporarily. When you return to the document, the body text is active, with the header or footer text dimmed.

Word provides fields, such as author, date, and file name, that you can include in headers and footers. Some header and footer fields, such as page numbers, will change from one page to the next. Other fields, such as author name and date, will remain constant. Regardless, selecting fields (instead of typing the actual data) simplifies the task of creating headers and footers. Some of the most frequently accessed fields, such as Date & Time and Page Number, are available on the Header & Footer Tools Design contextual tab as separate commands (see Figure 1.16). Others, including Author, File Name, and Document Title, are available when you click Document Info in the Insert group. Depending on the field selected, you might have to indicate a specific format and/or placement. For example, you could display the date as Monday, August 16, 2021, or you might direct that a page number is centered. Document Info also includes a Field option, which provides access to a complete list of fields from which to choose (see Figure 1.16). The same fields are available when you click Quick Parts in the Insert group and click Field.

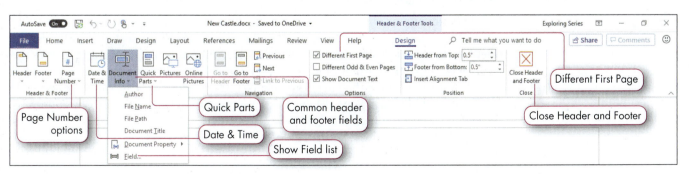

FIGURE 1.16 Header and Footer Fields and Options

STEP 2 ## Adjust Margins

Although a 1″ margin all around the document is the default setting, you might want to change a document's margins to improve appearance and readability. Also, depending on the purpose of a document, certain margin settings may be required for formal papers and publications. To change margins, you have two options. You can select from predefined margin settings using Margins on the Layout tab, or create custom margins by clicking Custom Margins (see Figure 1.17). You can also change the margins using File tab print options.

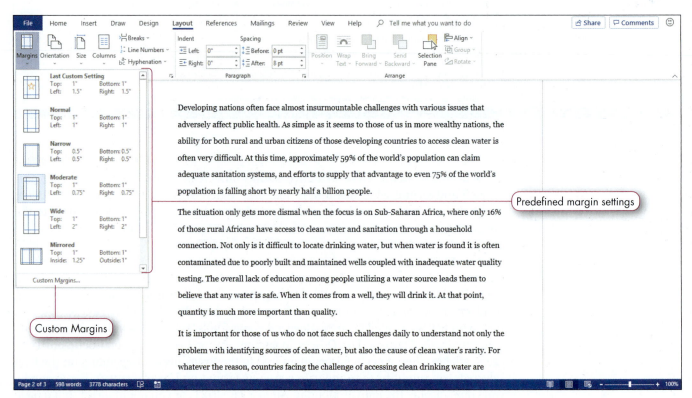

FIGURE 1.17 Setting Margins

STEP 3 ## Change Page Orientation

Some documents are better suited for portrait orientation, whereas others are more attractive in landscape. For example, certificates are typically designed in landscape orientation, in which a document is shown wider than it is tall; letters and memos are more often in portrait orientation. You can change page orientation on the Layout tab or on the Margins tab in the Page Setup dialog box (see Figure 1.18), which is accessible when you click the Page Setup Dialog Box Launcher on the Layout tab. Print options on the File tab also enable you to adjust page orientation.

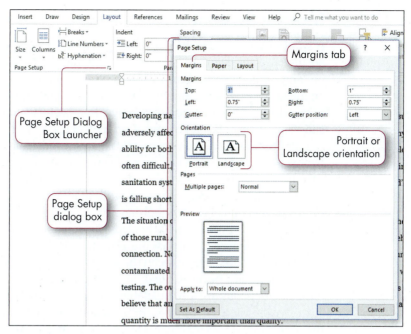

FIGURE 1.18 Changing Page Orientation

Insert a Watermark

A ***watermark***, which is text or a graphic that displays behind text on a page, is often used to include a very light, washed-out logo for a company within a document, or to indicate the status of a document. For example, a watermark displaying *Draft* indicates that a document is not in final form. The document shown in Figure 1.19 contains a watermark. Watermarks do not display on a document that is saved as a webpage, nor will they display in Word's Web Layout view (discussed later in this chapter).

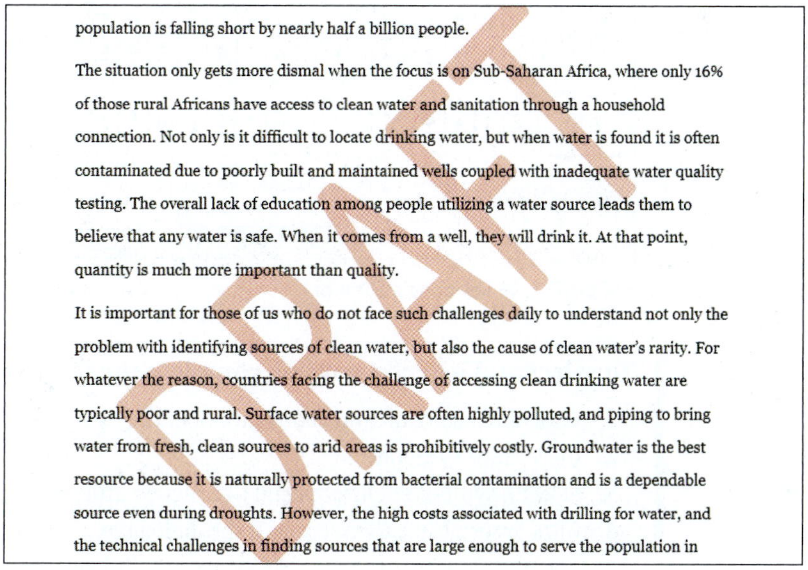

> population is falling short by nearly half a billion people.
>
> The situation only gets more dismal when the focus is on Sub-Saharan Africa, where only 16% of those rural Africans have access to clean water and sanitation through a household connection. Not only is it difficult to locate drinking water, but when water is found it is often contaminated due to poorly built and maintained wells coupled with inadequate water quality testing. The overall lack of education among people utilizing a water source leads them to believe that any water is safe. When it comes from a well, they will drink it. At that point, quantity is much more important than quality.
>
> It is important for those of us who do not face such challenges daily to understand not only the problem with identifying sources of clean water, but also the cause of clean water's rarity. For whatever the reason, countries facing the challenge of accessing clean drinking water are typically poor and rural. Surface water sources are often highly polluted, and piping to bring water from fresh, clean sources to arid areas is prohibitively costly. Groundwater is the best resource because it is naturally protected from bacterial contamination and is a dependable source even during droughts. However, the high costs associated with drilling for water, and the technical challenges in finding sources that are large enough to serve the population in

FIGURE 1.19 Using a Watermark

Insert a watermark by selecting Watermark in the Page Background group on the Design tab. Select from predesigned styles or click Custom Watermark to create your own, selecting text, color, and transparency settings. You can even identify a picture as a watermark if you like. To remove a watermark, follow the same steps, choosing to remove a watermark.

STEP 5 — Insert a Symbol

A **symbol** is text, a graphic, or a foreign language character that can be inserted into a document. Some symbols, such as $ and #, are located on the keyboard; however, others are only available from Word's collection of symbols. Symbols such as © and ™ can be an integral part of a document; in fact, those particular symbols are necessary to properly acknowledge a source or product. Because they are typically not located on the keyboard, you can access them in Word's library of symbols or use a shortcut key combination, if available.

Some symbols serve a very practical purpose. For example, it is unlikely you will want a hyphenated word to be divided between lines in a document. In that case, instead of typing a simple hyphen between words, you can insert a nonbreaking hyphen, which is available as a symbol. That special-purpose symbol, along with others, is located in the Special Characters section of the Symbol dialog box. Similarly, you can insert a nonbreaking space when you do not want words divided between lines. For example, a person's first name on one line followed by the last name on the next line is not a very attractive placement. Instead, make the space between the words a nonbreaking space by inserting the symbol, so the names are never divided. Mathematical symbols, foreign currency marks, and popular emoticons are also available in Word's symbol library.

A typical Microsoft Office installation includes a wide variety of fonts. Depending upon the font selected (normal text is shown in Figure 1.20), your symbol choices will vary. Fonts such as Wingdings, Webdings, and Symbol contain a wealth of special symbols, many of which are actually pictures.

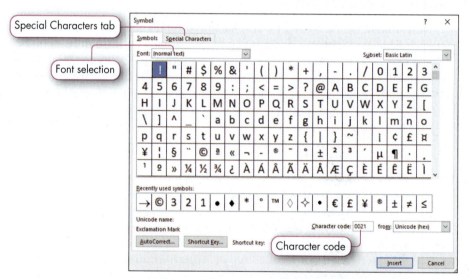

FIGURE 1.20 Selecting a Symbol

To select and insert a symbol, complete the following steps:

1. Click the Insert tab and click Symbol in the Symbols group.
2. Click More Symbols.
3. Select a symbol or click Special Characters and select from the list.
4. Click Insert. Click Close to close the dialog box.

Each symbol is assigned a character code. If you know the character code, you can type the code (refer to Figure 1.20) instead of searching for the symbol itself.

> **TIP: USING SYMBOL SHORTCUTS**
> Some symbols, such as © and ™, are included in Word's list of AutoCorrect entries. When you type (c), Word will automatically "correct" it to display ©. Type (tm), and Word shows ™.

Viewing a Document in Different Ways

Developing a document is a creative process. As you create, edit, or review a project, you will want to view the document in various ways. Word provides a view that enables you to see a document as it will print, as well as views that maximize typing space by removing page features. You might review a document in a magazine-type format for ease of reading, or perhaps a hierarchical view of headings and subheadings would help you better understand and proof the structure of a document. The ability to zoom in on text and objects can make a document easier to proofread, while viewing a document page by page helps you manage page flow—perhaps drawing attention to awkward page endings or beginnings. Taking advantage of the various views and view settings in Word, you will find it easy to create attractive, well-worded, and error-free documents.

Select a Document View

When you begin a new document, you see the top, bottom, left, and right margins. This default document view is called *Print Layout view*. You can choose to view a document differently, which is something you might do if you are at a different step in its production. For example, as you type or edit a document, you might prefer *Draft view*, which provides the most typing space possible without regard to margins and special page features. *Outline view* displays a document in hierarchical fashion, clearly delineating levels of heading detail. If a document is destined for the Web, you can view it in *Web Layout view*.

Designed to make a document easy to read and to facilitate access across multiple devices, *Read Mode* presents a document in a left to right flow, automatically splitting text into columns, for a magazine-like appearance. Text often displays in a two-page format. Text adjusts to fit any size screen, flowing easily from page to page with a simple flick of a finger (if using a tablet or touch-sensitive device) or click of the mouse. Users of touch-based devices can rotate the device between landscape and portrait modes, with the screen always divided into equally sized columns. When in Read Mode (see Figure 1.21), the ribbon is removed from view. Instead, you have access to only three menu items: File, Tools, and View. One of the most exciting features of Read Mode is object zooming. Simply double-click an object, such as a table, chart, picture, or video, to zoom in. Press Esc to leave Read Mode.

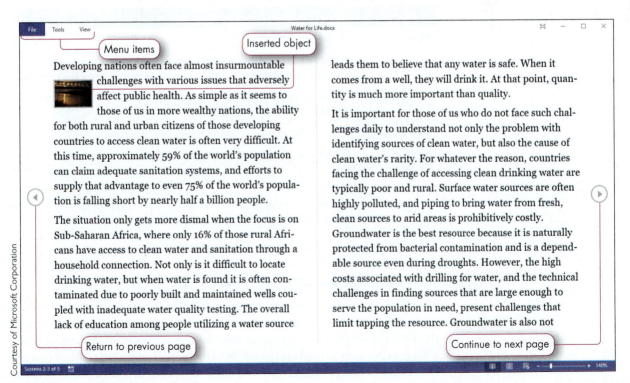

FIGURE 1.21 Read Mode

To change a document's view, click the View tab and select a view from the Views group (see Figure 1.22). Although slightly more limited in choice, the status bar also provides views to choose from (Read Mode, Print Layout, and Web Layout). Word views are summarized in Table 1.1.

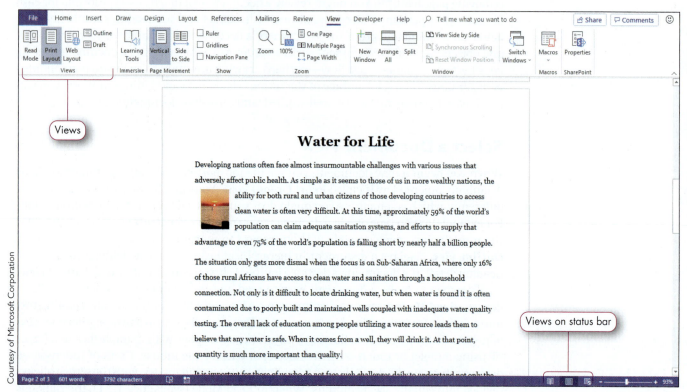

FIGURE 1.22 Word Views

TABLE 1.1	Word Views
View	**Appearance**
Read Mode	Primarily used for reading, with a document shown in pages, much like a magazine. The ribbon is hidden, with only a limited number of menu selections shown.
Print Layout	Shows margins, headers, footers, graphics, and other page features—much like a document will look when printed.
Web Layout	Shows a document as it would appear on a webpage.
Outline	Shows level of organization and detail. You can collapse or expand detail to show only what is necessary. Often used as a springboard for a table of contents or a PowerPoint summary.
Draft	Provides the most space possible for typing. It does not show margins, headers, or other features, but it does include the ribbon.

STEP 6 **Change the Zoom Setting**

Regardless of the view selected, you can use Word's zoom feature to enlarge or reduce the view of text. Unlike zooming in on an object in Read Mode, the zoom feature available on the View tab enables you to enlarge text, not objects or videos. Enlarging text might make a document easier to read and proofread. However, changing the size of text onscreen does not actually change the font size of a document. Zooming in or out is simply a temporary change to the way a document appears onscreen. The View tab includes options that change the onscreen size of a document (see Figure 1.23). You can also enlarge or reduce the view of text by dragging the Zoom slider on the status bar. Click Zoom In and Zoom Out on the status bar to change the view incrementally by 10% for each click.

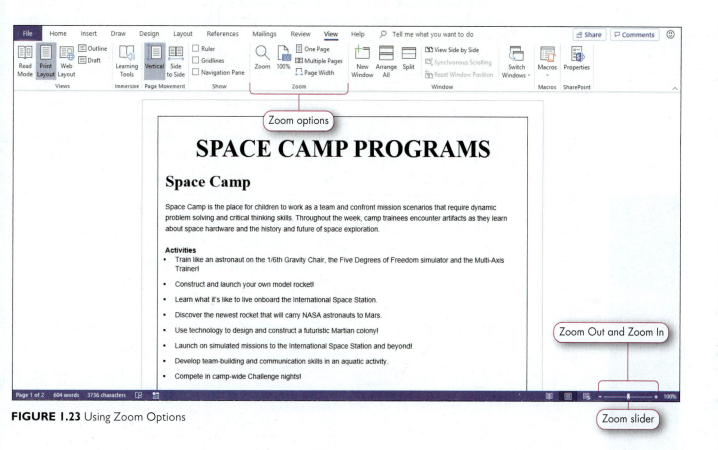

FIGURE 1.23 Using Zoom Options

Use the Zoom command on the View tab to select a percentage of zoom or to indicate a preset width (page width, text width, or whole page). Preset widths are also available as individual options in the Zoom group on the View tab (refer to Figure 1.23).

Preview a Document and Manage Page Flow

Document lengths can vary greatly. A research paper might span 20 pages, whereas a memo is seldom more than a few pages (most often, only one). Obviously, it is easier to view a memo onscreen than an entire research paper. Even so, Word enables you to get a good feel for the way a document will look when printed or distributed, regardless of document length.

Before printing, it is a good idea to view a document in its entirety. One way to do that is to click the File tab and click Print. A document is shown one page at a time in Print Preview (see Figure 1.24). You can use the Next Page or Previous Page navigation arrows to proceed forward or backward in pages. You can also view a document by using options on the View tab (refer to Figure 1.23). Clicking One Page provides a snapshot of the current page, while Multiple Pages shows pages of a multiple-page document side by side (and on separate rows, in the case of more than two pages).

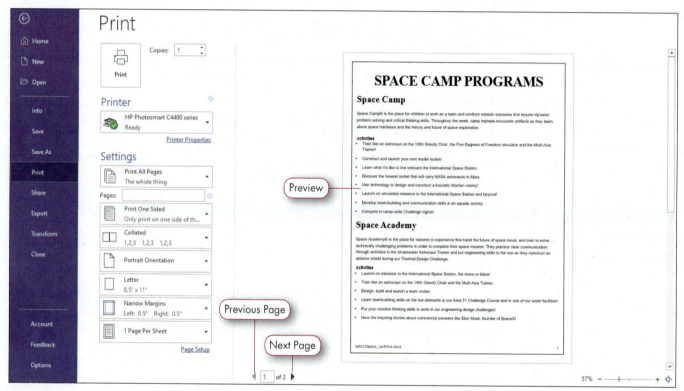

FIGURE 1.24 Previewing a Document

Occasionally, a page will end poorly—perhaps with a heading shown alone at the bottom of a page or with a paragraph split awkwardly between pages. Or perhaps it is necessary to begin a new page after a table of contents, so that other pages follow in the order they should. In those cases, you must manage page flow by forcing a page break where it would not normally occur. To insert a page break, you can use the shortcut Ctrl+Enter or click the Layout tab, click Breaks, and then select Page. Alternatively, click the Insert tab and click Page Break in the Pages group.

With nonprinting characters shown, you will see the Page Break designation (see Figure 1.25). To remove a page break, click the Page Break indicator and press Delete.

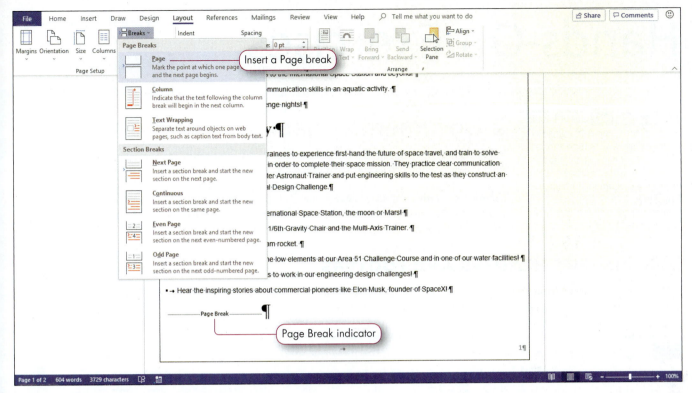

FIGURE 1.25 Inserting a Page Break

Quick Concepts

5. Provide an example of a header or footer whose value changes from one page to the next. ***p. 87***

6. Describe a document that would benefit from the use of a watermark. Explain why that is the case. ***p. 89***

7. Explain how, without using a hard or soft return, you might ensure that a person's first name and last name are never separated between lines in a document. ***p. 90***

8. Provide an explanation of why Read Mode would be used and how it differs from Print Layout view. ***p. 91***

9. Describe a situation in which inserting a page break would be beneficial. ***p. 94***

Hands-On Exercises

MyLab IT HOE2 Sim Training

▶ Watch the Video for this Hands-On Exercise!

Skills covered: Insert Headers and Footers • Adjust Margins • Change Page Orientation • Insert a Watermark • Insert a Symbol • Change the Zoom Setting • Preview a Document • Manage Page Flow

2 Document Organization

You are almost ready to submit a draft of the summer day camp article to your supervisor for approval. After inserting a footer to identify the document as originating with the U.S. Fish and Wildlife Service, you adjust the margins and determine the best page orientation for the document. By inserting symbols, you control how words are divided between lines and you give credit through a trademark indication. Next, you insert a watermark to indicate it is a draft document. Finally, you review the document for overall appearance and page flow.

STEP 1 INSERT HEADERS AND FOOTERS

You insert a footer to identify the article as a publication of the U.S. Fish and Wildlife Service. The footer also includes the file name. Refer to Figure 1.26 as you complete Step 1.

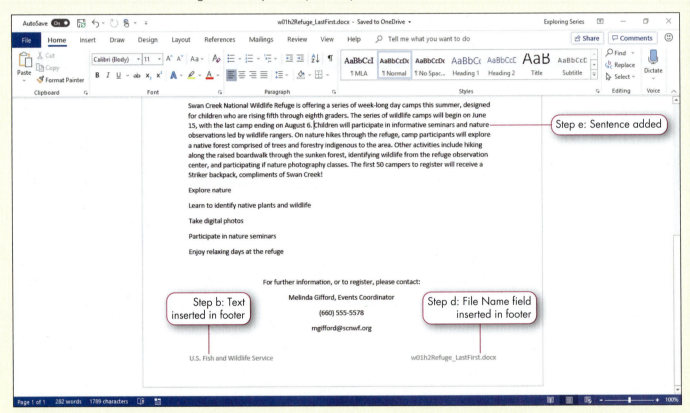

FIGURE 1.26 Designing a Footer

a. Open *w01h1Refuge_LastFirst* if you closed it at the end of Hands-On Exercise 1 and save it as **w01h2Refuge_LastFirst**, changing h1 to h2.

b. Click the **Insert tab**, click **Footer** in the Header & Footer group, and then select **Edit Footer**. Type **U.S. Fish and Wildlife Service**.

> **TROUBLESHOOTING:** If you selected a predefined footer instead of clicking Edit Footer, click Undo on the Quick Access Toolbar and repeat Step b.

c. Click **Insert Alignment Tab** in the Position group on the Header & Footer Tools Design tab. Click **Right** and click **OK**. The Header & Footer Tools Design tab includes several commands in the Position group that facilitate the placement of a header or footer. One of those commands, Insert Alignment Tab, enables you to align text at the right side of an existing header or footer.

> **MAC TROUBLESHOOTING:** The Insert Alignment Tab option is not available on a Mac. You can use tabs to position the footer near the right margin.

d. Click **Document Info** in the Insert group and select **File Name**. Click **Close Header and Footer** in the Close group.

e. Click after the first sentence of the second body paragraph, ending with *through eighth graders.* Be sure to click after the period ending the sentence. Press **Spacebar** and type the following sentence: **The series of wildlife camps will begin on June 15, with the last camp ending on August 6.**

f. Save the document.

STEP 2 ADJUST MARGINS

The article fits on one page, but you anticipate adding text. You suspect that with narrower margins, you might be able to add text while making sure the article requires only one page. You experiment with a few margin settings. Refer to Figure 1.27 as you complete Step 2.

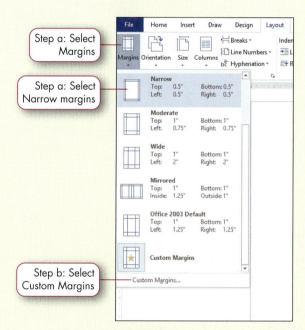

FIGURE 1.27 Working with Margins

a. Click the **Layout tab**, click **Margins** in the Page Setup group, and then select **Narrow**.

At a glance, you determine the right and left margins are too narrow, so you adjust them.

b. Click **Margins** and select **Custom Margins**. Adjust the Left and Right margins to **1″** and click **OK**.

c. Click the **View tab** and click **One Page** in the Zoom group.

The document appears to be well positioned on the page, with room for a small amount of additional text, if necessary.

d. Save the document.

Ms. Traynom asked you to prepare an abbreviated version of the article, retaining only the most pertinent information. You prepare and save the shortened version, but you also retain the lengthier version. The shortened article provides a snapshot of the summer activity in an at-a-glance format. Refer to Figure 1.28 as you complete Step 3.

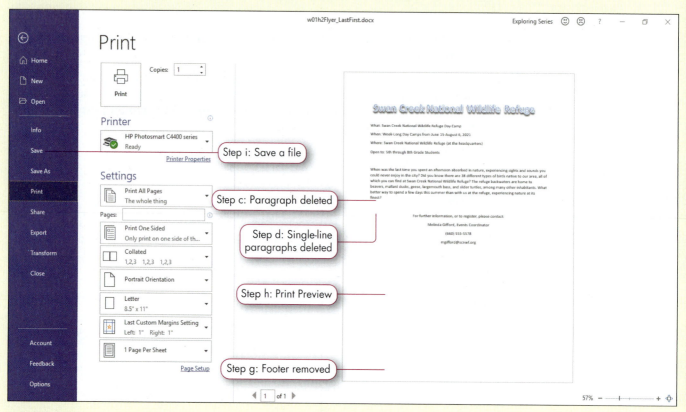

FIGURE 1.28 Previewing a Document

a. Click **100%** in the Zoom group on the View tab.

b. Ensure that nonprinting characters display. If they do not, click **Show/Hide** in the Paragraph group on the Home tab.

c. Triple-click in the second body paragraph, beginning with *Swan Creek National Wildlife Refuge is offering*, to select the entire paragraph and press **Delete** to remove the paragraph.

d. Delete the single-line paragraphs near the end of the document, beginning with *Explore nature* and ending with *Enjoy relaxing days at the refuge*.

e. Click the **File tab** and click **Save As**. Save the file as **w01h2Flyer_LastFirst**.

   Because the document is a shortened version of the original, you save it with a different name.

f. Click the **Layout tab** and click **Orientation** in the Page Setup group. Click **Landscape**. Click the **View tab** and click **One Page**. Click **Undo** on the Quick Access Toolbar.

   You had suspected the shortened document would be more attractive in landscape orientation. However, since the appearance did not improve, you return to portrait orientation.

g. Select **100%**. Scroll down and double-click in the footer area. Select both footer entries and press **Delete** to remove the footer text. Double-click in the document to close the footer.

   The flyer does not require a footer so you remove it.

h. Click the **File tab** and click **Print**. Check the document preview to confirm that the footer is removed.

i. **Save** the document. Click the **File tab** and click **Close**.

You close the flyer without exiting Word. You will submit this file to your instructor at the end of the last Hands-On Exercise.

INSERT A WATERMARK

You open the original article so you can add the finishing touches, making sure to identify it as a draft and not the final copy. To do so, you insert a DRAFT watermark, which can be removed after your supervisor has approved the document for distribution. Refer to Figure 1.29 as you complete Step 4.

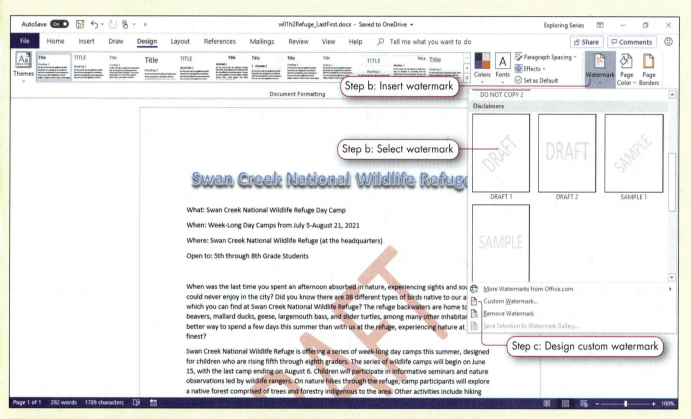

FIGURE 1.29 Inserting a Watermark

a. Click the **File tab**. Select **w01h2Refuge_LastFirst** in the list of Recent Documents.

b. Click the **Design tab** and click **Watermark** in the Page Background group. Scroll through the gallery of watermarks and select **DRAFT 1** (under Disclaimers). The word DRAFT in an angular arrangement displays in the watermark choice.

c. Click **Watermark** again and select **Custom Watermark**. Click the **Color arrow** in the Printed Watermark dialog box and click **Red** (under Standard Colors). Click **OK**.

The watermark is not as visible as you would like, so you change the color.

> **MAC TROUBLESHOOTING:** Select the Text option for a watermark. Ensure DRAFT displays. To slant the watermark, change the orientation to Diagonal.

d. Save the document.

The article you are preparing will be placed in numerous public venues, primarily schools. Given the widespread distribution of the document, you must consider any legality, such as appropriate recognition of name brands or proprietary mentions, by inserting a trademark symbol. You also ensure that words flow as they should, with no awkward or unintended breaks between words that should remain together. Refer to Figure 1.30 as you complete Step 5.

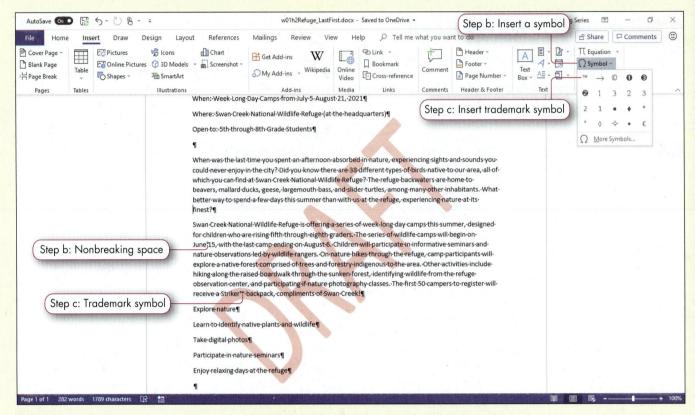

FIGURE 1.30 Working with Symbols

a. Click after the word *June* on the second line in the second body paragraph. Make sure you have placed the insertion point before the space following the word *June*. Press **Delete** to remove the space.

b. Click the **Insert tab** and click **Symbol** in the Symbols group. Click **More Symbols**. Click the **Special Characters tab**. Click **Nonbreaking Space**. Click **Insert** and click **Close**.

Regardless of where the line ends, you want to make sure the phrase June 15 is not separated, with the month on one line and the day on the following line. Therefore, you insert a nonbreaking space.

c. Click after the word *Striker* in the last sentence of the same paragraph. Make sure you have placed the insertion point before the space following the word *Striker*. Click **Symbol** in the Symbols group and click the **Trademark symbol** shown in the list of symbols.

You use the Trademark symbol to indicate that Striker is a brand name.

> **TROUBLESHOOTING:** If you do not find the Trademark symbol in the list of symbols, click More Symbols, click Special Characters, and click the Trademark symbol. Click Insert and click Close.

d. Save the document.

CHANGE THE ZOOM SETTING, PREVIEW A DOCUMENT, AND MANAGE PAGE FLOW

Ms. Traynom provided you with a cover letter to include with the article. You incorporate the letter text into the article as the first page, remove the footer from the first page, proofread the document, and ensure that both pages are attractively designed. Refer to Figure 1.31 as you complete Step 6.

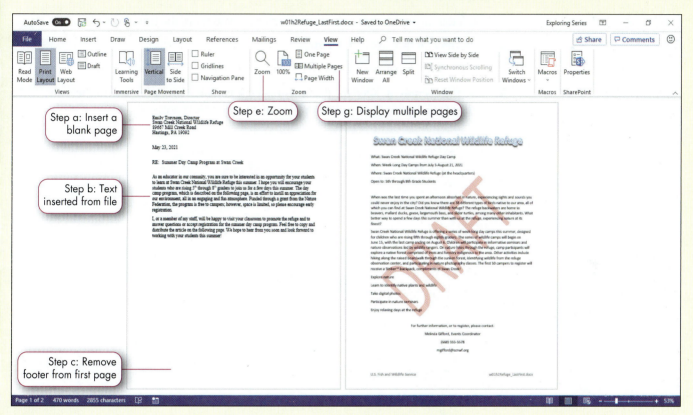

FIGURE 1.31 Modifying and Previewing a Multi-Page Document

a. Press **Ctrl+Home** to position the insertion point at the top of the article. Press **Ctrl+Enter** to insert a blank page at the top. Press **Ctrl+Home** to move to the top of the new page.

Note that both the watermark and the footer display on the new page. That is because those features are designed to appear by default on all pages of a document.

b. Click the **Object arrow** in the Text group on the Insert tab. Click **Text from File**. Navigate to *w01h2Letter* in your student data files and double-click the file name.

You insert text from a previously saved letter as the first page of this document.

c. Double-click in the footer area of the first page. Click **Different First Page** in the Options group of the Header & Footer Tools Design tab.

You indicate that the watermark and footer are not to appear on the first page but will remain on all others.

d. Click **Close Header and Footer** in the Close group.

e. Press **Ctrl+Home**. Click the **View tab** and click **Zoom** in the Zoom group. Click in the **Percent box** and change the Zoom to **125%**. Click **OK**.

f. Scroll through the letter on the first page, proofreading for spelling and grammatical errors. Right-click any underlined error and either correct or ignore it. Manually correct any errors that Word has not flagged. Press **Ctrl+Home**.

g. Click **Multiple Pages** in the Zoom group.

h. Click the **File tab** and click **Print**. Click **Next Page** (the arrow that follows 1 of 2 at the bottom of the screen) to view the article. Click **Previous Page** to return to the letter.

i. Click **Back** ⬅ to return to the document. Click **100%** in the Zoom group. Ensure the insertion point is at the top of the document, and press **Enter** three times to move the text down the page.

The letter appears to be too high on the page, so you move the text down a bit.

j. Click the **File tab** and click **Print**.

The first page is better situated on the page with additional space at the top.

k. Save the document. Keep the document open if you plan to continue with the next Hands-On Exercise. If not, close the document and exit Word.

Document Settings and Properties

After you organize your document and make formatting changes, you save the document in its final form and prepare it for use by others. You can take advantage of features in Word that enable you to manipulate the file in a variety of ways, including ensuring that people with different abilities are able to read and edit the document. You might also choose to include information about the file that does not display in the document, such as a title, author name, subject, and keywords. Such information further identifies the file and can be used as a basis on which to search for or categorize a document later. As you develop a document, you have the option to save the file so that you can access it later, and you should consider methods of document retrieval so that important documents are always available.

In this section, you will explore ways to prepare a document for distribution, including ensuring that a document is as readable as possible, converting a file created in an earlier version to Office 2019, checking for sensitive information included in a file, ensuring adequate document retrieval if a document is lost or corrupted, and working with print options. In addition, you will learn to customize and print document properties.

Modifying Document Properties

Occasionally, you might want to include information to identify a document, such as author, document title, or general comments. Those data elements, or ***document properties***, are saved with the document, but do not appear in the document as it displays onscreen or is printed. Standard document properties that you can assign include author, company, and subject, among others. Such document properties can be useful in categorizing documents and finding them later as the result of a search. For example, suppose you apply a tag of *Computer Applications 225* to all documents you create that are associated with that particular college class. Later, you can use that keyword as a search term, locating all associated documents. Some properties are automatically updated, such as file size and file creation date, while others are optionally created or denoted by the document creator.

If you change the author, or add a title or comments, that information is saved with the file. Comments are notes to yourself or other authors, documenting a process or intention, and they are especially helpful when several authors are collaborating. You can also include tags, or keywords, to help organize and locate document files; however, tags are not saved with the document file. Instead, they are managed by the operating system, making them available across applications. The use of tags facilitates identifying files that are related, albeit from different applications—perhaps identifying related PowerPoint presentations and Word documents.

STEP 1 ### Customize Document Properties

For statistical information related to the current document, display Backstage view, which is shown when you access the File tab and ensure that Info is selected. Data such as file size, number of pages, and total words are displayed in the right pane on the Info window (see Figure 1.32). You can modify some document information in this view, such as adding a title, tags, or comments. Additional document information can identify a document by author, subject, or title. Tags can assist in organizing files and locating them later. For more possibilities, click Properties and then Advanced Properties (see Figure 1.32). You can then navigate through the file's dialog box, clicking the Summary tab to add or modify properties.

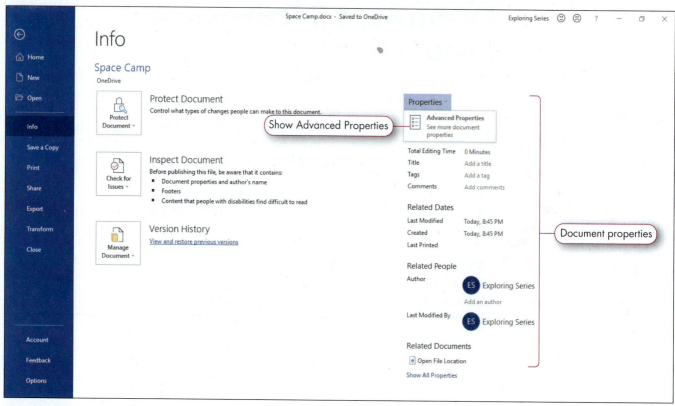

FIGURE 1.32 Working with Document Properties

Although standard document properties, such as title, author, and comments, are helpful in organizing documents by category, you can create your own custom document properties, as well. Suppose you want to identify a document by date assigned, or perhaps as a part of a particular project. Such properties are not considered standard property fields but can be created.

> **To create a custom property, complete the following steps:**
> 1. Click the File tab.
> 2. Ensure that Info is selected. Click Properties.
> 3. Click Advanced Properties.
> 4. Click the Custom tab. Scroll through existing fields or create a custom field, assigning a field type and value.

Print Document Properties

Document properties that were either automatically assigned or that you indicate serve the purpose of identifying and categorizing a document. Because they are not shown onscreen when you open the associated document, you might want to print them for later reference or to include as documentation of the file. From Backstage view (shown when you click File and then click Print), click Print All Pages and then select Document Info (see Figure 1.33). Although the Print Preview pane continues to show the document contents, only document properties will be printed at that point.

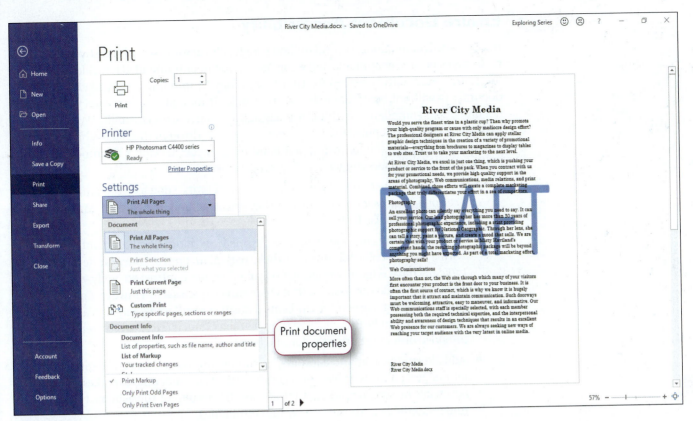

FIGURE 1.33 Printing Document Properties

> **TIP: PRINTING DOCUMENT PROPERTIES WITH ALL DOCUMENTS**
> To print the summary information of document properties with every document that you print, shown as a final page, click the File tab and click Options. Click Display. In the Printing options section, select Print document properties.

Preparing a Document for Distribution

There will be occasions when you want to distribute a document to someone else. Whether it is a report to submit to your instructor or a memo on which you collaborated, most likely the document is something that will be shared with others. Regardless of how you plan to develop, save, and distribute a document, you will not want to chance losing your work because you did not save it properly or failed to make a backup copy. Inevitably, files are lost, systems crash, or a virus compromises a disk. So, the importance of saving work frequently and ensuring that backup copies exist cannot be overemphasized.

A document developed for wide distribution should be readable by people of varying ability levels, even those who are visually challenged or who deal with other disabilities. To assist with that task, Word includes an *Accessibility Checker* that locates elements that might cause difficulty for people with disabilities. As you develop a document for such an audience, keep in mind the possible need to use simple language, ensure that font is sufficiently large, provide enough contrast between font color and background color, and provide other types of appropriate document organization.

As Word versions and updates continue to evolve, there is a chance that someone who needs to read your document is working with an installation that is not compatible with yours, or perhaps the person is not working with Word at all. You can eliminate that source of frustration by saving a document in a compatible format before distributing it.

Ensure Document Accessibility

In the United States alone, several million people rely on some sort of assistive technology to access electronic documents and webpages. If documents intended for wide distribution are not created with the need for that technology in mind, it is very likely that those documents will not be readable by many people. It may also be necessary to produce documents in compliance with federal legislation related to accessibility. Word provides assistance with development of accessible documents through the Accessibility Checker, but you should keep the following points in mind as you develop a document so that a check will likely find few suggestions for improvement.

- Use appropriate font style and size. Sans serif fonts, such as Arial and Verdana, are good choices for readability as they are clean and uncluttered. Make sure the font size is at least 12 pt.

- Use contrasting colors and do not rely solely on color to make a point. Readers with a level of color-blindness or those with glaucoma or macular degeneration typically have difficulty reading text that does not contrast strongly with the background. Do not assume that color choice necessarily conveys a message. For example, using a green X to indicate a positive result and a red X as a negative indicator might be less effective than a green Y and a red N, which represent the intended outcome both by color and by letter.

- Add alternative text and captions. Including alternative text and captions for images, pictures, tables, and various objects in a document makes them accessible by screen readers. In that way, the content of those items is understandable to those with certain disabilities.

- Construct simple tables with header rows. When developing a Word table, be sure to use only one row for a header, clearly formatted differently from remaining table text. Do not merge or split table cells and do not leave any rows or columns blank.

- Use meaningful hyperlink text. Do not create hyperlinks with such text as "Click here," as a person using assistive technology might navigate a document by skipping from hyperlink to hyperlink, without access to surrounding text that would provide meaning to such hyperlinks. Instead, make sure a hyperlink provides clear description of the link destination.

- Use built-in formatting styles, especially in the development of headings and lists. Headings that are defined using Word's built-in heading styles enable users to quickly skip through a document by navigating from one heading to another. Use bulleted or numbered lists where appropriate to clearly identify items as included in groups.

Before a document is distributed, run the Accessibility Checker so that questionable areas are first identified and corrected. Select Check Accessibility on the Review tab. As an alternative, you can also choose Check for Issues from the Info group on the File tab and indicate that you want to check accessibility. The Accessibility Checker pane (see Figure 1.34) displays errors (content that is difficult or impossible for those with disabilities), warnings (content that is challenging for those with disabilities), and tips (suggestions for better organization or presentation).

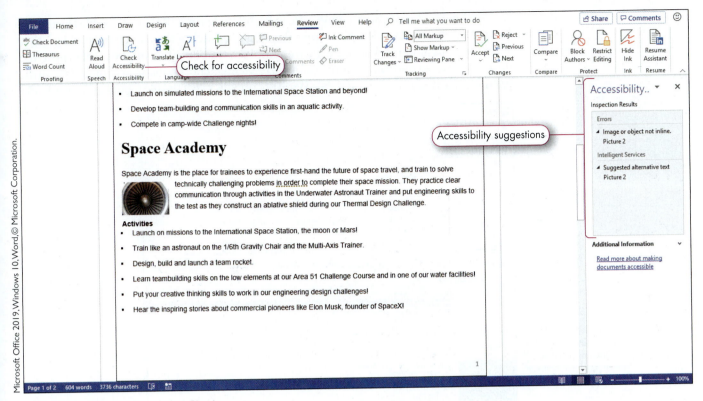

FIGURE 1.34 Using Accessibility Checker

Ensure Document Compatibility

Office 365, a subscription plan that is preferred by many Word users, ensures that Word is continually updated with the most recent additions and software improvements. Whereas historically Microsoft relied solely on major updates—called versions—of its Microsoft Office software for purchase every few years, there is currently less reliance on that form of development and distribution. When that was the norm, however, each new software version was likely to incorporate a different type of file, so that users of early versions might not be able to open files created by newer software installations. While such a challenge is becoming much less likely, you should be aware of the possibility and should understand how to check a document for compatibility before distributing it to those with less up-to-date software installations. From the Info group on the File tab, select Check for Issues and then click Check Compatibility.

You might also consider saving a file in Rich Text Format (RTF) or Portable Document Format (PDF), which adds even more flexibility, as such a file can be opened by other software in addition to Word. Be aware, however, that doing so might compromise the document somewhat because other software types might not be able to accommodate all the current Word features. As you save a Word document, select the file type (see Figure 1.35).

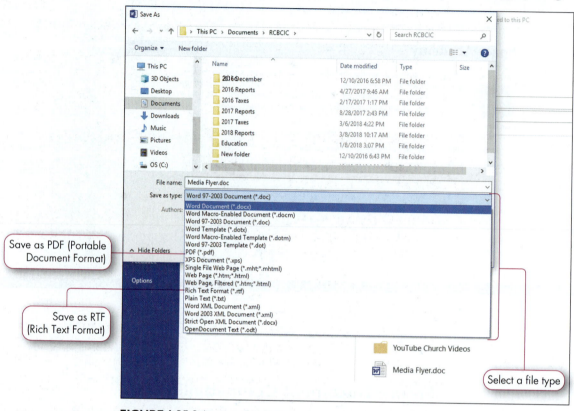

FIGURE 1.35 Selecting a File Type

Occasionally, you might receive a Word document that was created in a much earlier Word version. In that case, the words *Compatibility Mode* are included in the title bar, advising you that some of Word's features may not be available or viewable in the document (see Figure 1.36). While in Compatibility Mode, you might not be able to use new and enhanced Word features; by keeping the file in Compatibility Mode, you ensure that people with earlier Word versions will still have full editing capability when they receive the document. Word simplifies the process of converting a Word document to the newest version. Click the File tab and click Convert (only shown if the file is not in the newest format). Click OK.

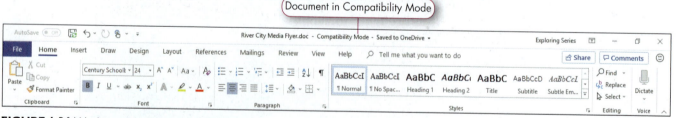

FIGURE 1.36 Working with Compatibility Mode

STEP 3 Understand Document Retrieval

It is inevitable that you will, at some point, lose access to a document before you have saved it, or possibly after you have made a significant amount of progress since the last save. Perhaps the problem is a power disruption or an unexplainable failure that causes Word to become unresponsive. In these instances, the immediate need is to get your document back, without having lost too much content. In a proactive mode, you might have configured

Word to create an automatic backup copy so that you can retrieve most, if not all, of what you have typed. If you are using OneDrive to save the document, you will find that the document was automatically saved and readily available. Even if you have not yet saved a document at all, it is likely that Word can recover much of the document. Obviously, Word is well equipped to address many situations related to recovering documents. Even so, the best practice is to save a document often as you are creating it, perhaps even configuring Word to automatically create a backup copy, so that you are less likely to have to depend on Word's safety nets related to recovering files.

A possible scenario is one in which you close a document without saving it. You may fear that it is gone forever, but that may not be the case. A link to recover unsaved documents is shown at the bottom of the list of recent documents when you click the File tab and click Open, or when you manage documents from the Info selection on the File tab.

To locate an unsaved document, complete the following steps:

1. Click the File tab and ensure that Info is selected.
2. Click Manage Document.
3. Select Recover Unsaved Documents.
4. Recovered documents are temporarily saved with an ASD extension. If the file you seek is shown, open it and then save it as a Word file, changing the type to Word Document during the save operation.

If you save a document to OneDrive, you do not have to be quite as conscientious about saving often because an open document is automatically saved every few seconds. The **AutoSave** feature is applicable to files saved to OneDrive, OneDrive for Business, and SharePoint Online. If you prefer to save files on local storage, such as a flash drive or a folder on a hard drive, Word provides support through its **AutoRecover** feature, in which you can prescribe an interval of time at which a file should automatically be saved. Word can then recover a document, losing only those changes that might have occurred between saves. Word will be able to recover a previous version of your document when you restart the program, with any files that are recovered shown. By default, file information is saved every 10 minutes (see Figure 1.37), but you can adjust the setting so that the AutoRecover process occurs more or less frequently. You can access controls to adjust the time interval through selections in the Word Options dialog box.

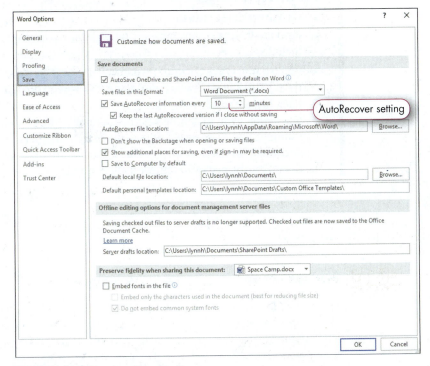

FIGURE I.37 The AutoRecover Feature

You can also configure Word to create a backup copy each time a document is saved. Although the setting to always create a backup copy is not enabled by default, you can enable it from Word Options in the Advanced category. Even so, creating frequent backup copies can slow your system and may not be altogether necessary, given the excellent File History facility provided by Windows 10. Click the File tab and click Options. Click Advanced. Scroll to the Save group and select Always create backup copy. A backup copy is saved in the same folder as the original, but includes a slightly different file name and the WBK extension, which represents a Word Backup file.

STEP 4 ## Run the Document Inspector

Before you send or give a document to another person, you should run the *Document Inspector* to reveal any hidden or personal data in the file. For privacy or security reasons, you might want to remove certain items contained in the document such as author name, comments made by one or more people who have access to the document, or document server locations. Word's Document Inspector will check for and enable you to remove various types of identifying information, including:

- Comments, revisions, versions, and annotations
- Document properties and personal information
- Custom XML data
- Headers, footers, and watermarks
- Invisible content
- Hidden text

Because some information removed by the Document Inspector cannot be recovered with the Undo command, you should save a copy of your original document, using a different name, prior to inspecting the document.

> **To inspect a document, complete the following steps:**
>
> 1. Click the File tab and ensure that Info is selected.
> 2. Click Check for Issues.
> 3. Click Inspect Document.
> 4. Respond if a dialog box appears, by clicking Yes if you have not saved the file and want to do so.
> 5. Confirm the types of content you want to check in the Document Inspector dialog box (see Figure 1.38). Deselect any categories you do not want to check.
> 6. Click Inspect to begin the process. When the check is complete, Word lists the results and enables you to choose whether to remove the content from the document. For example, if you are distributing a document to others, you might want to remove all document properties and personal information. In that case, you can instruct the Document Inspector to remove such content.

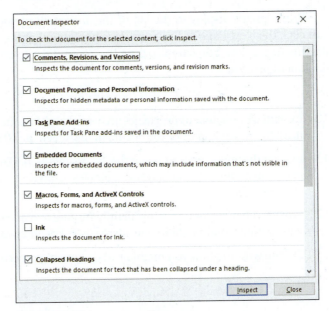

FIGURE 1.38 Inspecting a Document

Select Print Options

Although by default, Word prints one copy of an entire document, you might find it necessary to print multiple copies, or only a few pages. Those settings and others are available when you click the File tab and click Print. The Print settings shown in Figure 1.39 enable you to select the number of copies, the pages or range of pages to print, the printer to use, whether to collate pages, whether to print on only one side of the paper, and how many pages to print per sheet. In addition, you can adjust page orientation, paper size, and even customize a document's margins—all by paying attention to print options. Please note that the wording of some print options will vary, depending on whether you have previously selected the option and indicated a custom setting.

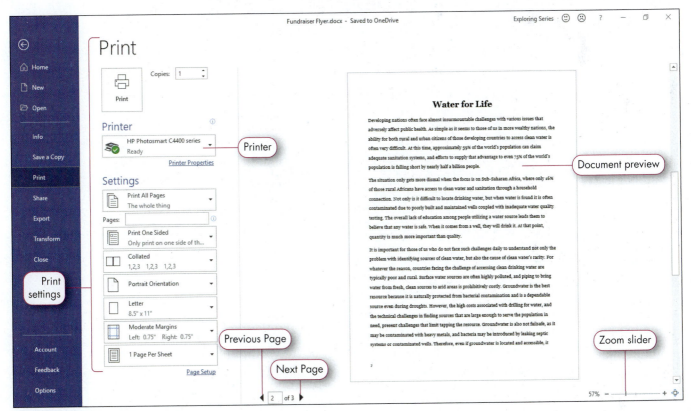

FIGURE 1.39 Word Print Settings

Print options display to the left of the document preview (refer to Figure 1.39). You can click the Next Page or Previous Page navigation arrows to move among pages in the document preview. You can also drag the Zoom slider to enlarge or reduce the size of the document preview.

Quick Concepts

10. Explain why document properties are useful in a document, even though they are not actually shown as part of the document onscreen. *p. 103*

11. Explain the importance of using the Accessibility Checker for a document that you plan to distribute. Provide several examples of suggestions that might occur during the check. *p. 106*

12. Provide rationale for removing identifying data in a document, such as comments or author name, that might be considered useful in other cases. *p. 110*

13. Explain why and how you might print document properties. *p. 104*

Hands-On Exercises

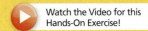
Skills covered: Customize Document Properties • Print Document Properties • Ensure Document Accessibility • Ensure Document Compatibility • Understand Document Retrieval • Run the Document Inspector • Select Print Options

3 Document Settings and Properties

As the office assistant for Swan Creek National Wildlife Refuge, you are responsible for the security, management, and backup of the organization's documents. The article promoting the summer day camps is ready for final approval. Before that happens, however, you will check it one last time, making sure it is saved in a format that others can read. You will also ensure that you have sufficient backup copies. You also want to include appropriate document properties for additional identification, and you will consider print options. Privacy and security are to be considered as well, so you check for identifiers that should be removed before distributing the document. To ensure that the document is readable by as many people as possible, you will check for accessibility.

STEP 1 CUSTOMIZE AND PRINT DOCUMENT PROPERTIES

You assign document properties to the summer camp document to identify its author and purpose. You also create an additional property to record a project identifier. Finally, you prepare to print document properties. Refer to Figure 1.40 as you complete Step 1.

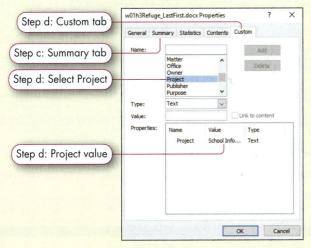

FIGURE 1.40 Customizing Document Properties

a. Open *w01h2Refuge_LastFirst* if you closed it at the end of Hands-On Exercise 2 and save it as **w01h3Refuge_LastFirst**, changing h2 to h3.

b. Click the **File tab**, ensure that Info is selected, click **Properties** in the right pane, and then click **Advanced Properties**.

The Properties dialog box displays.

c. Click the **Summary tab**. Ensure that the Author box contains your name. Click in the **Comments box** and type **Summer Camp Information**.

d. Create a custom property by completing the following steps:

- Click the **Custom tab** and scroll to select **Project** in the Name list.
- Type **School Information** in the Value box, and click **Add**.
- Click **OK** to close the dialog box.

You want to catalog the documents you create for Swan Creek National Wildlife Refuge, and one way to do that is to assign a project identifier using the custom properties that are stored with each document. Because you set up a custom field, you can later perform searches and find all documents in that Project category.

e. Click **Print**, click **Print All Pages**, and then click **Document Info**. Click **Print** if directed to do so by your instructor. Otherwise, continue without printing by clicking **Back**.

STEP 2 # ENSURE DOCUMENT ACCESSIBILITY AND COMPATIBILITY

Because the document will be distributed in schools as well as electronically, you check the document for accessibility by those with disabilities. You also convert a document created in an earlier Word version to ensure currency. Refer to Figure 1.41 as you complete Step 2.

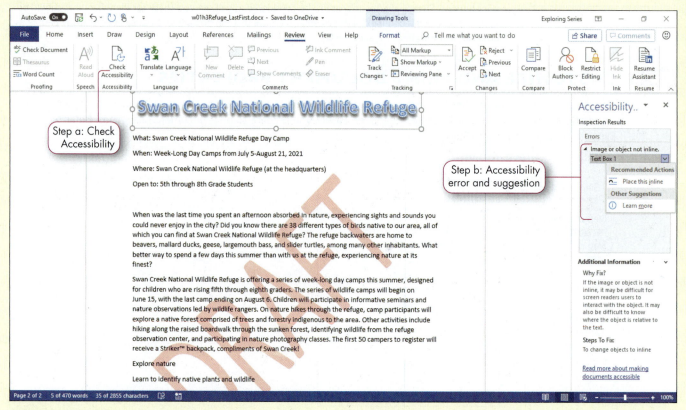

FIGURE 1.41 Check for Accessibility

a. Press **Ctrl+Home** to ensure the insertion point is at the beginning of the document. Click the **Review tab**. Click **Check Accessibility** in the Accessibility group, or alternatively click the File tab, click Check for Issues, and click Check Accessibility.

b. Click **Image or object not inline** in the Accessibility Checker pane, point to Text Box 1, and click the arrow to the right. Click **Place this inline**.

The memo heading is adjusted as it relates to surrounding text. Although other errors may be displayed in the Accessibility Checker pane, you will not address them at this point.

> **TROUBLESHOOTING:** If the adjustment for accessibility results in additional space at the end of the document, perhaps forcing it to another page, delete the extra space to return the display to two pages.

c. Close the Accessibility Checker pane. Save and close w01h3Refuge_LastFirst.

The personnel director has prepared a draft of a memo introducing a new employee. He asked you to proof the document and prepare it for printing. However, he created and saved the memo using an earlier version of Word.

d. Open *w01h3NewEmployee* from the student data files.

The title bar displays *Compatibility Mode* following the file name *w01h3NewEmployee*, indicating that it is not a file saved with a recent installation of Word.

e. Click the **File tab**, ensure that Info is selected, and click **Convert** (beside Compatibility Mode). A message box displays explaining the consequences of upgrading the document. Click **OK**.

The file is converted to the newest Word format. The Compatibility Mode designation is removed from the title bar.

f. Save the document as **w01h3NewEmployee_LastFirst**.

STEP 3 ▶ UNDERSTAND DOCUMENT RETRIEVAL

The timeline for preparing for the summer day camps is short. Given the time spent in developing the article, you know that if it were lost, recreating it in a timely fashion would be difficult. In fact, it is critical to ensure appropriate backups and recovery plans for all files for which you are responsible at Swan Creek. You explore document retrieval options on your computer to verify that files are saved periodically and that backups are automatically created. Refer to Figure 1.42 as you complete Step 3.

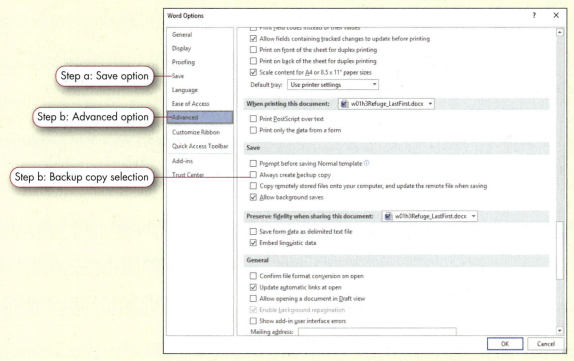

FIGURE 1.42 Exploring Document Retrieval and Recovery Options

a. Click the **File tab** and click **Options**. Click **Save** in the left pane of the Word Options dialog box. If *Save AutoRecover information every* is checked, note the number of minutes between saves.

b. Click **Advanced** in the left pane. Scroll to the Save area and determine whether *Always create backup copy* is selected.

You do not select the setting at this time because you are likely to be in a school computer lab.

c. Click **Cancel**. Close the document.

Before distributing the article, you run the Document Inspector to identify any information that should first be removed. You also prepare to print the document. Refer to Figure 1.43 as you complete Step 4.

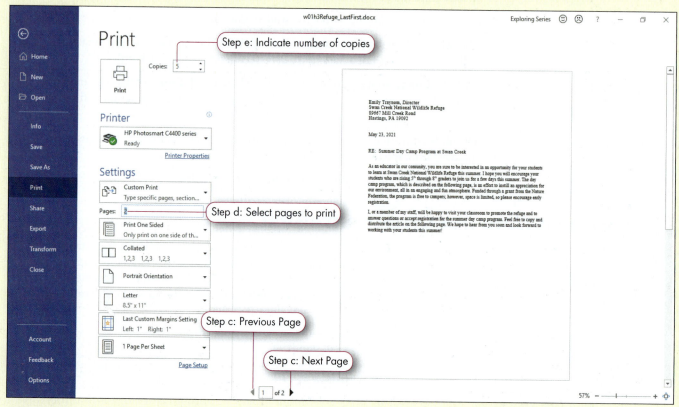

FIGURE 1.43 Working with Print Options

a. Open *w01h3Refuge_LastFirst*. Click the **File tab**, ensure that Info is selected, and click **Check for Issues** (beside Inspect Document). Click **Inspect Document**. Click **Inspect**.

You check for document areas that might display sensitive information. The inspection suggests that the category of Document Properties and Personal Information contains identifying data, as does that of Headers, Footers, and Watermarks, and Custom XML Data.

b. Click **Remove All** beside Document Properties and Personal Information. Click **Close**.

You determine that it would be best to remove all document properties, but you leave headers, footers, and watermarks.

c. Click **Print**. Click **Next Page** to view the next page. Click **Previous Page** to return to the first page.

d. Click in the **Pages box** below Print All Pages. Type **2**.

You indicate that you want to print page 2 only.

e. Click the **Copies up arrow** repeatedly to print five copies.

You indicate that you want to print five copies of page 2.

f. Press **Esc** to return to the document without printing.

g. Save and close the file. Based on your instructor's directions, submit the following:

w01h2Flyer_LastFirst

w01h3Refuge_LastFirst

w01h3NewEmployee_LastFirst

Chapter Objectives Review

After reading this chapter, you have accomplished the following objectives:

1. Begin and edit a document.

- Create a document: Begin a blank document when Word opens and type text.
- Reuse text: Text from previously created documents can be inserted in another document.
- Use a template: Predesigned documents save time by providing a starting point.
- Add text and navigate a document: The insertion point indicates where the text you type will be placed. Use scroll bars or keyboard shortcuts to move around in a document.
- Review spelling and grammar: Use the Review tab to make sure all documents are free of spelling and grammatical errors.

2. Customize Word.

- Explore Word options: Word options are global settings you can select, such as whether to check spelling automatically, or where to save a file by default.

3. Use features that improve readability.

- Insert headers and footers: Headers and footers provide information, such as page number and organization name, in the top and bottom margins of a document.
- Adjust margins: You can change margins, selecting predefined settings or creating your own.
- Change page orientation: Select Landscape to show a document that is wider than it is tall, or Portrait to show a document taller than it is wide.
- Insert a watermark: A watermark is text or a graphic that displays behind text to identify such items as a document's purpose, owner, or status.
- Insert a symbol: A symbol is typically a character or graphic that is not found on the keyboard, such as ©.

4. View a document in different ways.

- Select a document view: A view is the way a document displays onscreen; available Word views include Print Layout, Read Mode, Outline, Web Layout, and Draft.

- Change the zoom setting: By changing the zoom setting, you can enlarge or reduce text size onscreen.
- Preview a document and manage page flow: Forcing a page break is useful to divide document sections (for example, to separate a cover page from other report pages), or to better manage page flow so that pages do not end awkwardly.

5. Modify document properties.

- Customize document properties: Document properties are items you can add to a document to further describe it, such as author, keywords, and comments.
- Print document properties: Because document properties are not shown onscreen when you open the associated document, you might consider printing them for later reference or to include as documentation of the file.

6. Prepare a document for distribution.

- Ensure document accessibility: The Accessibility Checker helps ensure that documents are readable by people with disabilities.
- Ensure document compatibility: Word includes features that assist with converting documents from earlier file formats and saving files so they are easily accessible.
- Understand document retrieval: Word's AutoSave, AutoRecover, and backup features address file recovery and help ensure that documents are not irretrievably lost.
- Run the Document Inspector: Word's Document Inspector reveals any hidden or personal data in a file and enables you to remove sensitive information.
- Select print options: Using Word's print options, you can specify the pages to print, the number of copies, and various other print selections.

Key Terms Matching

Match the key terms with their definitions. Write the key term letter by the appropriate numbered definition.

a. Accessibility Checker
b. AutoCorrect
c. AutoRecover
d. AutoSave
e. Document Inspector
f. Document property
g. Draft view
h. Header or footer
i. Insertion point
j. Microsoft Word

k. Outline view
l. Print Layout view
m. Read Mode
n. Symbol
o. Template
p. Thesaurus
q. Watermark
r. Web Layout view
s. Word processing software
t. Word wrap

1. _____ Text or graphic that displays behind text. **p. 89**

2. _____ A structural view of a document or presentation that can be collapsed or expanded as necessary. **p. 91**

3. _____ The feature that automatically moves words to the next line if they do not fit on the current line. **p. 73**

4. _____ The feature that enables Word to recover a previous version of a document. **p. 109**

5. _____ The tool that checks for document readability by people with disabilities. **p. 105**

6. _____ A computer application, such as Microsoft Word, used primarily with text to create, edit, and format documents. **p. 72**

7. _____ A view in which text reflows to screen-sized pages to make it easier to read. **p. 91**

8. _____ The feature that saves documents automatically so they can be retrieved later. **p. 109**

9. _____ The word processing application included in the Microsoft Office software suite. **p. 72**

10. _____ A predesigned document that may include formats that can be modified. **p. 75**

11. _____ A view that closely resembles the way a document will look when printed. **p. 91**

12. _____ A character or graphic not normally included on a keyboard. **p. 90**

13. _____ A feature that checks for and removes certain hidden and personal information from a document. **p. 110**

14. _____ Information that displays at the top or bottom of each document page. **p. 86**

15. _____ A view that shows a great deal of document space, but no margins, headers, footers, or other special features. **p. 91**

16. _____ A blinking bar that indicates where text that you next type will appear. **p. 76**

17. _____ A tool that enables you to find a synonym for a selected word. **p. 78**

18. _____ A feature that corrects standard misspellings and word errors as they are typed. **p. 80**

19. _____ A view that displays a document as it would appear on a webpage. **p. 91**

20. _____ A data element that is saved with a document but does not appear in the document as it is shown onscreen or is printed. **p. 103**

Multiple Choice

1. Which of the following is a reason to use the Accessibility Checker?

   (a) To ensure compatibility with earlier Word versions.
   (b) To comply with federal legislation related to disabilities.
   (c) To provide access to appropriate document properties.
   (d) To ensure that any headers and footers are visible to everyone.

2. The Document Inspector is useful when you want to:

   (a) troubleshoot a document, identifying and adjusting nonprinting characters.
   (b) check the document for spelling and grammatical errors.
   (c) adjust page layout.
   (d) reveal any hidden or personal data in the file so that it can be removed, if necessary.

3. To keep a first name and last name, such as Susan Barksdale, from being separated between lines of a document, where the word Susan might display on one line, with Barksdale on the next, you could:

   (a) insert a nonbreaking hyphen symbol after the word Susan.
   (b) insert a hard return after Barksdale.
   (c) insert a soft return between Susan and Barksdale.
   (d) insert a nonbreaking space symbol between Susan and Barksdale.

4. To rely on AutoSave to automatically save a document, you must first:

   (a) check the AutoSave setting in Word Options.
   (b) ensure that Word is set to make an automatic backup every few minutes.
   (c) save the document to local storage, such as a flash drive.
   (d) save the document using OneDrive, OneDrive for Business, or SharePoint Online.

5. One reason to use a header or footer is because:

   (a) the header or footer becomes a document property that can be used to search for the document later.
   (b) you only have to specify the content once, after which it displays automatically on all pages.
   (c) most writing style guides require both headers and footers.
   (d) headers and footers are required for all professional documents.

6. Suppose you find that a heading within a report is displayed at the end of a page, with remaining text in that section placed on the next page. To keep the heading with the text, you would position the insertion point before the heading and then:

   (a) press Ctrl+Enter.
   (b) click the Layout tab, click Breaks, and then select Line Numbers.
   (c) insert an automatic soft return.
   (d) press Ctrl+Page Down.

7. In which of the following situations would you consider inserting a soft return instead of a hard return?

   (a) At the end of a single line of an address, with more address lines to follow.
   (b) At the end of a paragraph.
   (c) At the end of a page.
   (d) After words that you prefer not to divide, such as a month name and the date.

8. One reason to display nonprinting characters is to:

   (a) simplify the process of converting a document to an earlier Word version.
   (b) enable document properties to be added to a document.
   (c) assist with troubleshooting a document and modifying its appearance.
   (d) enable spell checking on the document.

9. You want to include all text from another document, which is not currently open, in the document in which you are working. How would you do that?

   (a) Open the document with text to use and append it to the current document.
   (b) Include the file name of the closed file as a header on the last page of the current document.
   (c) Use the Text from File option to reuse text from the closed document at the current location in the open document.
   (d) Create a custom document property listing the file name of the document from which you want to include text and then insert it as an object.

10. To identify a document as a draft, and not in final form, which of the following would you mostly likely add to the document?

    (a) Symbol
    (b) Watermark
    (c) Template
    (d) Document property

1 River City Media

Having recently graduated from college with a marketing degree, you are employed by River City Media as a marketing specialist. River City Media provides promotional material in a variety of ways, including print, Web communications, photography, and news releases. It is your job to promote River City Media so that it attracts a large number of new and recurring contacts seeking support with the marketing of products and services. One of your first tasks is updating printed material that describes the specific services that River City Media offers to prospective clients. You modify a brief description of services, first converting the document from an earlier version of Word, in which it was originally saved, to the most current. Refer to Figure 1.44 as you complete this exercise.

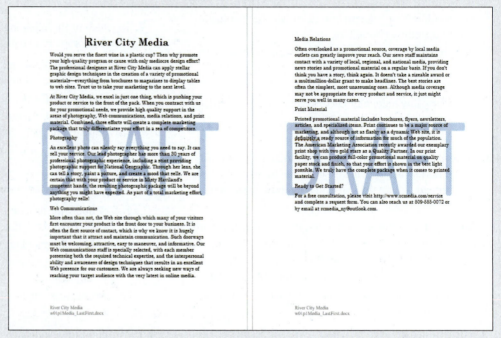

FIGURE 1.44 River City Media Draft

a. Open the *w01p1Media* document. The words *Compatibility Mode* in the title bar inform you the document was created in an earlier version of Word.

b. Click the **File tab**, and click **Save As**. Change the file name to **w01p1Media_LastFirst**. Click in the **Save as type box** and select **Word Document**. Click **Save**. If you are presented with a dialog box letting you know the document will be upgraded to the newest file format, click **OK**.

c. Ensure that nonprinting characters are displayed by clicking **Show/Hide** in the Paragraph group on the Home tab. Press **Ctrl+Home** to ensure that the insertion point is at the beginning of the document. Check the document for errors:

   • Click the **Review tab** and check for spelling errors. Correct any identified errors.
   • Check for grammatical errors. Correct any identified errors, but ignore any that are flagged for clarity and conciseness.
   • Read the document again, checking for errors the spelling check might have missed.

d. Double-click to select the word **maneuver** in the paragraph under the *Web Communications* heading. Click the **References tab** and click **Smart Lookup** in the Research group. Scroll through the Smart Lookup pane to view information related to the selected word. Close the Smart Lookup pane.

e. Double-click **capable** in the paragraph under the *Photography* heading. Click the **Review tab** and click **Thesaurus** in the Proofing group. Locate and insert the word **competent**. Close the Thesaurus pane.

f. Make the following edits in the document:
- Select the words **When they are** from the second body paragraph on the first page and press **Delete**.
- Capitalize the word *Combined* in the same sentence.
- Rearrange the words *We at River City Media* in the same paragraph, so they read **At River City Media, we** (including a comma after the word *Media*).

g. Click after the word **materials** in the first body paragraph on the first page. Delete the following hyphen. Click the **Insert tab** and click **Symbol** in the Symbols group. Click **More Symbols**. Click the **Special Characters tab**. Ensure that Em Dash is selected. Click **Insert** and click **Close**. Click after the word **National** in the paragraph under the *Photography* heading and delete the following space. Press **Ctrl+Shift+Space** to insert a nonbreaking space, ensuring that the magazine title will not be divided between lines. Similarly, insert a nonbreaking space between *Misty* and *Haviland* so the photographer's name will not be divided between lines.

h. Click the **Design tab** and click **Watermark** in the Page Background group. Scroll through the watermarks and click **Draft 2**. Click **Watermark**, click **Custom Watermark**, and then click the **Semitransparent check box** to deselect it. Click **Color**, select **Blue Accent 5** (first row, ninth column under Theme Colors), and then click **OK**.

> **MAC TROUBLESHOOTING:** Select the Text option for a watermark. Ensure Draft displays as the watermark text and transparency is set to 0%.

i. Set up a footer:
- Click the **Insert tab** and click **Footer** in the Header & Footer group.
- Click **Edit Footer**. Type **River City Media** and press **Enter**.
- Click **Document Info** on the Header & Footer Tools Design tab and select **File Name**.
- Click **Close Header and Footer** (or double-click in the body of the document).

j. Adjust the left and right margins:
- Click the **Layout tab** and click **Margins** in the Page Setup Group.
- Click **Custom Margins**.
- Change the left and right margins to **1.5″**. Click **OK**.
- Click the **View tab** and click **Multiple Pages** in the Zoom group to see how the text is lining up on the pages.

k. Click before the *Media Relations* heading at the bottom of the first page and press **Ctrl+Enter** to insert a page break.

l. Press **Ctrl+Home**. Click **Read Mode** in the Views group. Click the arrow on the right to move from one page to the next. Press **Esc** to return to the previous document view. Click **100%** in the Zoom group. Save the document.

m. Click the **File tab** and click **Info**. Click **Check for Issues**. Click **Inspect Document** and click **Inspect**. Click **Remove All** beside Document Properties and Personal Information and click **Close**.

n. Save and close the file. Based on your instructor's directions, submit w01p1Media_LastFirst.

2 Freshwater Research

You work with the Office of Media Relations at Tarrant State University. Several faculty researchers have been involved with a study on freshwater analysis, with their findings receiving national recognition. The university plans to post a news release describing the successful research. You will work with a draft of the press release, ensuring that it is properly formatted and readable by all. Refer to Figure 1.45 as you complete this exercise.

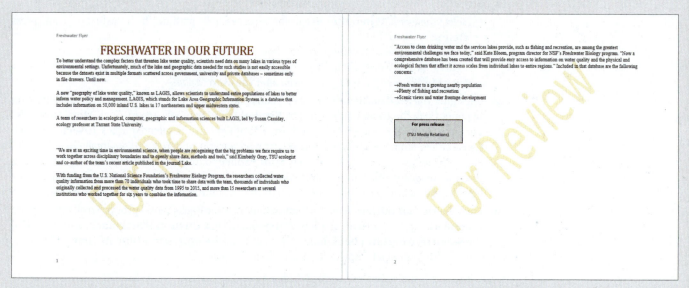

FIGURE 1.45 Freshwater Analysis Document

a. Open *w01p2Lake* and save it as **w01p2Lake_LastFirst**.

b. Press **Ctrl+End** to move the insertion point to the end of the document. Press **Enter**. Click the **Insert tab** and click the **Object arrow** in the Text group. Click **Text from File**. Locate and double-click *w01p2Article*.

c. Click the **Home tab** and click **Show/Hide** to display nonprinting characters. Select the year **1990** in the fifth body paragraph. Change the year to **1995**.

d. Click the **Layout tab**, click **Orientation** in the Page Setup group, and then click **Landscape**. Click the **View tab** and click **Multiple Pages** to view all document pages, noting the poorly situated second page. Return the view to **100%**.

e. Adjust the margins:
- Click the **Layout tab**. Click **Margins** in the Page Setup group.
- Click **Custom Margins**.
- Change the left and right margins to **1.5″**. Click **OK**.

f. Place the insertion point after the word *population* on the second page. Press **Shift+Enter** to insert a soft return. Type **Plenty of fishing and recreation**. (Do not type the period.) Press **Shift+Enter**. Type **Scenic views and water frontage development**. (Do not type the period.)

g. Insert symbols:
- Place the insertion point before *Fresh water to a growing nearby population*.
- Click the **Insert tab** and click **Symbol** in the Symbols group.
- Click **More Symbols**.
- Change the font in the dialog box to **Symbol**. Locate the **right arrow symbol**, or click in the Character Code box and type **174**.
- Click **Insert**. Click **Close**.
- Repeat the process for the remaining two lines of text. Note that you can now select the right arrow symbol from the list of recent symbols shown when you click **Symbol** in the Symbols group.

h. Click before the quotation mark that begins the last body paragraph on the first page (beginning with *Access to clean drinking water*). Click the **Layout tab** and click **Breaks** in the Page Setup group. Click **Page**. Click the **View tab** and click **Multiple Pages** to see how text appears on all pages. Return the view to **100%**.

i. Insert a footer:

- Click the **Insert tab** and click **Footer** in the Header & Footer group.
- Click **Edit Footer**.
- Click **Page Number** in the Header & Footer group, point to **Current Position**, and then click **Plain Number**.
- Double-click in the current page of the document to close the footer.

j. Click the **File tab** and click **Info**. Click **Properties** and click **Advanced Properties**. Click in the **Comments box** and type **Freshwater Flyer**. Click **OK**. Click **Back** to return to the document.

k. Double-click in the **Header area** (top margin). Click **Document Info** in the Insert group, point to **Document Property**, and then click **Comments**. Close the header.

l. Press **Ctrl+Home**. Click the **Review tab** and check spelling. Correct any identified errors, if they are actual errors. There are no misspelled names. Click **OK** when the spelling check is complete. Close the Editor pane.

m. Insert a watermark:

- Click the **Design tab** and click **Watermark** in the Page Background group.
- Click **Custom Watermark**.
- Click to select **Text watermark**. Type **For Review** in the Text box, replacing any existing text.
- Click **Color** and click **Orange** (third selection in Standard Colors).
- Click **OK**.

> **MAC TROUBLESHOOTING:** Select the Text option for a watermark. To slant the watermark, change the orientation to Diagonal.

n. Click the **Review tab**. Click **Check Accessibility** in the Accessibility group. Click **Image or object not inline. (1)** in the Accessibility Checker pane. Point to the Text Box problem shown in the Accessibility Checker pane and click the arrow. Click **Place this inline**. Alternatively, you can follow the directions shown at the bottom of the Accessibility Checker pane. Close the Accessibility Checker pane.

o. Save and close the file. Based on your instructor's directions, submit w01p2Lake_LastFirst.

Mid-Level Exercises

1 Water for Life

MyLab IT Grader

The student organization of which you are a member has selected the supply of clean drinking water to developing nations as a fundraising cause for the current semester. You will design an informational handout that will introduce the current situation and encourage others to become involved with the effort. You begin with a draft and format the document so that it is attractive and informative.

a. Open *w01m1Water* and save it as **w01m1Water_LastFirst**.

b. Change the orientation to **Portrait**. Display nonprinting characters if they are not already shown. Delete the first two lines (*Water for Life* and *Changing Lives Daily*).

c. Change the margin setting to **Moderate**. Preview the document in **Multiple Pages**. Return the view to **100%**.

d. Place the insertion point at the beginning of the document and insert a page break. Place the insertion point at the beginning of the new page. Insert text from *w01m1Cover*. Preview the new page as **One Page**.

e. Return the view to 100%. Insert an unformatted footer containing a page number. The page number should be in the **Current Position** and as a **Plain Number**. Ensure that the footer does not show on the first page. Close the footer.

f. Click after the word *that* in the first line of the second page. Press **Spacebar** and type **adversely**. Ensure that a space precedes and follows the word. Select the words *As long as* in the second paragraph on the second page. Replace the selected words with the word **When**.

g. Select the word **reliable** in the third paragraph on the second page. Use the thesaurus and identify a synonym beginning with the letter *d*. Replace the selected word with the synonym. Close the Thesaurus pane.

h. Modify the watermark so that it displays **DRAFT** in a diagonal fashion. Ensure that the watermark is colored **Red** (second color in Standard Colors).

i. Open Document Properties and add **Flyer for Water for Life** in the Comments section.

j. Insert an unformatted header. Click **Quick Parts** in the Insert group on the Header & Footer Tools Design tab and insert the Comments document property. The header should be left aligned.

k. Check spelling and correct any errors that are found.

l. Run the Accessibility Checker. Correct any problems identified.

m. Save and close the file. Based on your instructor's directions, submit w01m1Water_LastFirst.

2 Backyard Bonanza

MyLab IT Grader

With a degree in horticulture, you have recently been employed to work with Backyard Bonanza, a local outdoor living business specializing in garden gifts, statuary, outdoor fireplaces, landscaping materials, and pavers. The first Friday of each month, Backyard Bonanza participates in a downtown event in which vendors, artists, and musicians set up areas to perform or display products. To encourage those passing by to visit the store, you prepare a document describing a few do-it-yourself backyard projects—all of which can be completed with the help of products sold at Backyard Bonanza. The document is well underway, but you modify it slightly, making sure it is attractive and ready for distribution at the next event.

a. Open *w01m2Backyard*. The document was originally saved in an earlier version of Word, so you should save it as a Word Document with the file name of **w01m2Backyard_LastFirst**. Agree that the upgrade should proceed, if asked.

b. Display nonprinting characters. Preview the document in Multiple Pages to get a feel for the text flow. Change the orientation to **Portrait**.

c. Return to 100% view. Add a page number footer. The page number should be placed at the **Bottom of Page** with the **Plain Number 2** selection. Close the footer.

d. Insert text from *w01m2Fish* at the end of the document.

e. Scroll to the top of page 2. Change the word *Create* to **Build**.

f. Check the document for spelling and grammatical errors. The word *Delite* is not misspelled as it is a brand name. Because there is no correct suggestion for the misuse of the word *layer*, you will need to manually change it. (Hint: You can ignore the error and return to manually correct the mistake, or you can correct the mistake during the spell check and resume the check afterward.) Proofread the document to identify and correct errors that Word might have missed.

g. Preview the document and note the small amount of text on page 3. Change margins to **Narrow**.

h. Insert a page break so that *Build a Backyard Fish Pond* begins on a new page.

i. View the document in Read Mode. Return to Print Layout view.

j. Click after the word *noticed* on page 2 and before the comma in the third sentence of the first body paragraph of directions. Remove the comma and the following space, and insert an **Em Dash**. On page 1, click after the words *Paving Delite*, but before the closing parenthesis (in the first paragraph of directions under *What to do:*). Insert a trademark symbol.

k. Add a watermark with the text **Backyard Bonanza** shown in **Red**. The watermark should be horizontal and semitransparent. Save the document before completing the next step.

l. Run the Document Inspector to identify any information that should be removed before the document is distributed. Remove all document properties and personal information.

m. Save and close the file. Based on your instructor's directions, submit w01m2Backyard_LastFirst.

Running Case

New Castle County Technical Services

New Castle County Technical Services (NCCTS) provides technical services to clients in the greater New Castle County, Delaware area. Founded in 2011, the company is rapidly expanding to include technical security systems, network infrastructure cabling, and basic troubleshooting services. With that growth comes the need to promote the company and to provide clear written communication to employees and clients. Microsoft Word is used exclusively in the development and distribution of documents, including an "About New Castle" summary that will be available both in print and online. You will begin development of the document in this case and continue working with it in subsequent Word chapters.

a. Open *w01r1NewCastle* and save it as **w01r1NewCastle_LastFirst**. Display nonprinting characters. Place the insertion point at the end of the document and insert a page break.

b. Ensure that the insertion point is at the top of the second page. Insert text from *w01r1News*. Preview the document in Multiple Pages. Return to 100% view. Add a left-aligned unformatted footer with the words **New Castle County Technical Services**. On the same line in the footer, but right-aligned, insert a File Name field. Ensure that the footer does not display on the first page. Close the footer.

c. Replace the hyphen after the word *off* in the first sentence of the second body paragraph in the Company Background section with a nonbreaking hyphen. Replace the hyphen after the word *the* in the phrase *off-the-shelf* with a nonbreaking hyphen.

d. Select the words *set up* in the first paragraph on the third page. Change the selected words to **equipped**, ensuring that a space precedes and follows the newly inserted word.

e. Place the insertion point at the end of the first body paragraph on page 1, after the period following the word *offer*. Press **Spacebar** and type **We are proud to include the following new services, added to our inventory this past March.** (Include the period.) Press **Enter**. Type **Desktop troubleshooting**. (Do not type the period.) Insert a soft return. Type **Software training support**. (Do not type the period.)

f.   Place the insertion point before the word *We* at the beginning of the first body paragraph on the fourth page (under the *A FEW OF OUR CUSTOMERS* heading). Type **At New Castle County Technical Services,** and press **Spacebar**. Ensure that a comma follows **New Castle County Technical Services**. Change the following word **We** to lowercase, as in *we*.

g.   Include a watermark using the *DRAFT 1* selection. Color the watermark **Blue** (eighth color from the left in Standard Colors).

h.   Change the page orientation to **Landscape**. Preview the document in Multiple Pages. Note that the first two pages of the document are poorly situated in that orientation, but remaining pages are attractive. You will correct the view of the first pages in a future exercise. Return the view to 100%

i.   Check the document for spelling and grammatical errors. Ignore all possible misspellings of company names, but correct any other spelling errors. If grammatical errors are shown, correct them as well. If Clarity and Conciseness concerns are shown, check but ignore any occurrence.

j.   Run the Accessibility Checker. Note the comments related to the picture in the first paragraph of the Company Background section. You may also see a warning flagging hard-to-read text contrast, although you will not address that issue at this time. You could correct the issues, but because the picture is not necessary, click the picture of the keyboard and press **Delete** to remove it. Close the Accessibility Checker pane.

k.   Open Document Properties, selecting **Advanced Properties** to display the dialog box. Add a Company name of **New Castle County Technical Services**. (Do not type the period.)

l.   Save and close the file. Based on your instructor's directions, submit w01r1NewCastle_LastFirst.

Disaster Recovery

Logo Policy

Open *w01d1Policy* and save it as **w01d1Policy_LastFirst**. The document was started by an office assistant, but was not finished. You must complete the document, ensuring that it is error free and attractive. The current header includes a page number at the top right. Remove the page number from the header and create a footer with a centered page number instead. Adjust the font size of any headings throughout the document to ensure consistency and suggest hierarchy. Remove the word *copyright* anywhere it appears in the document and replace it with the copyright symbol. Show nonprinting characters and remove any unnecessary or improperly placed paragraph marks. The AMT Brand section should include only three bulleted items (One name, One voice, and One look). Use solid round black bullets. Insert hard returns where necessary to better space paragraphs. The hyphenated word *non-Association,* in the Improper Use paragraph, should not be divided between lines, so replace the hyphen wherever it occurs in that paragraph with a nonbreaking hyphen. Change the orientation to Landscape. Modify the document properties to include yourself as the author, deleting any other author. Check spelling and grammar, correcting any mistakes. Ensure that all pages begin and end attractively, with no headings standing alone at the end of a page. Insert a page break where necessary. Check spelling and grammar, correcting any mistakes, but ignoring any clarity and conciseness flags. Finally, use a watermark to indicate that the document is not in final form. Save and close the document. Based on your instructor's directions, submit w01d1Policy_LastFirst.

Capstone Exercise

Space Camp

You are serving as a summer intern at the Space Center. One of the most popular programs offered at the Center is the Space Camp Experience, which is a collection of exploratory programs designed for various age groups. You are using Word to prepare a two-page flyer to promote the camps. In the process, you will apply various formatting and readability features, and will ensure an error-free and informative document.

Inserting Text, Editing a Document, and Changing Margins

Inserting text from another document can save time in creating a document, so you insert text to begin the Space Camp flyer. You also edit the document to ensure attractive arrangement of text. By adjusting margins, you improve readability.

1. Open *w01c1Space* and save it as **w01c1Space_LastFirst**.
2. Display nonprinting characters. In the blank paragraph above *Adult Space Academy* on the second page, insert text from *w01c1Family*.
3. Remove the two blank paragraphs after the Family Space Camp section.
4. Preview the document in **Multiple Pages**. Note the poor placement of the text box on the second page. Remove the five blank paragraphs before the text box so that it moves up the page to better position.
5. Change margins to **Narrow**. Insert a page break before the Family Space Camp heading at the bottom of the first page. Return to 100% view.

Changing Document View, Previewing a Document, Inserting Symbols, and Inserting a Footer

The document contains several sections that are identified by headers. In Outline view, you are able to rearrange sections for better document flow. Because the document contains multiple pages, previewing it in another way facilitates understanding of document layout across pages. A page number footer identifies each page and a symbol is used to ensure that words are not awkwardly divided.

6. Change the view to **Outline**. Click the arrow beside Show Level in the Outline Tools group and click Level 1 to show only major headings. Click + beside *Space Camp* and drag the heading to position it above *Space Academy*. Click **Close Outline View** in the Close group.

7. Preview the document in **Multiple Pages**. Remove the page break on the first page along with the blank paragraph that precedes the Space Academy heading. Insert a page break before the Family Space Camp heading. Return the view to **100%**.
8. Replace the hyphen following the Word *three* in the paragraph below The Adult Space Academy heading with a nonbreaking hyphen.
9. Insert a left-aligned footer with the **File Name** inserted as a field. On the same line, insert a right-aligned footer showing a **Plain Number** page number.

Including a Watermark, Checking Spelling and Grammar, Working with Document Properties, and Checking Accessibility

A watermark is included, identifying the document as a copy. All documents should be checked for spelling and grammatical errors before distribution, so you identify and correct any errors. Document properties are modified so that the document is identified by subject, and text is checked for accessibility by those with disabilities.

10. Insert a horizontal blue watermark with the word **Copy**.
11. Open Document Properties and add **Space Camp Flyer** as the Subject.
12. Check the document for spelling and grammatical errors. Correct any errors, but ignore any clarity and conciseness flags. Use the thesaurus to identify a synonym for the word *exciting* in the first paragraph under the Adult Space Academy heading. The synonym you select should begin with the letter *t*. Change the word *an* that precedes the newly inserted synonym to *a* so that it is grammatically correct.
13. Check for accessibility and correct the error related to alignment of a text box. Disregard other flags at this time.
14. Save and close the document. Based on your instructor's directions, submit w01c1Space_LastFirst.

Document Presentation

LEARNING OUTCOME   You will modify a Word document with formatting, styles, and objects.

OBJECTIVES & SKILLS: After you read this chapter, you will be able to:

CASE STUDY | Phillips Studio L Photography

Having recently opened your own photography studio, you are engaged in marketing the business. Not only do you hope to attract customers from the local community who want photos of special events, but you will also offer classes in basic photography for interested amateur photographers. In addition, you have designed a website to promote the business and to provide details on upcoming events and classes. The business is not large enough yet to employ an office staff, so much of the work of developing promotional material falls on you.

Among other projects, you are currently developing material to include in a quarterly mailing to people who have expressed an interest in upcoming studio events. You have prepared a rough draft of a newsletter describing photography basics—a document that must be formatted and properly organized before it is distributed to people on your mailing list. You will modify the document to ensure attractive line and paragraph spacing, and you will format text to draw attention to pertinent points. Formatted in columns, the document will be easy to read. The newsletter is somewhat informal, and you will make appropriate use of colors, borders, and pictures so that it is well received by your audience.

CHAPTER 2

Editing and Formatting

Nd3000/Shutterstock

FIGURE 2.1 Phillips Studio L Photography Document

CASE STUDY | Phillips Studio L Photography

Starting Files	File to be Submitted
w02h1Studio	w02h3Studio_LastFirst
w02h3Kayak.jpg	
w02h3Float.jpg	

MyLab IT Grader An alternate version of this project is available as a MyLab IT Grader Assessment

Text and Paragraph Formatting

When you format text, you change the way it looks. Your goal in designing a document is to ensure that it is well received and understood by an audience of readers. Seldom will your first attempt at designing a document be the only time you work with it. Inevitably, you will identify text that should be reworded or emphasized differently, paragraphs that might be more attractive in another alignment, or the need to bold, underline, or use italics to call attention to selected text. As you develop a document, or after reopening a previously completed document, you can make all these modifications and more. That process is called *formatting*.

In this section, you will learn to change font and font size, and format text with character attributes, such as bold, underline, and italics. At the paragraph level, you will adjust paragraph and line spacing, set tab stops, change alignment, and apply bullets and numbering.

Applying Font Attributes

A *font* is a combination of typeface and type style. The font you select should reinforce the message of the text without calling attention to itself, and it should be consistent with the information you want to convey. For example, a paper prepared for a professional purpose, such as a resume, should have a standard font, such as Times New Roman, instead of one that looks casual or frilly, such as *Freestyle Script* or *Gigi*. Additionally, more than one font might need to be used to distinguish the purpose of the text, such as paragraph headings, body text, captions, etc., but you will want to minimize the variety of fonts in a document to maintain a professional look. Typically, you should use three or fewer fonts within a document. Word provides default font styles for each of these purposes: Calibri Light is used for headings and Calibri for the body of the text. However, Word enables you to format text in a variety of ways. Not only can you change a font type, but you can also change the font size and apply text attributes, such as bold, italic, or underline, to selected text or to text that you are about to type. Several of the most commonly used text formatting commands are in the Font group on the Home tab.

STEP 1 Select Font Options

A definitive characteristic of any font is the presence or absence of serifs, thin lines that begin and end the main strokes of each letter. A *serif font* contains a thin line or extension at the top and bottom of the primary strokes on characters. Times New Roman is an example of a serif font. A *sans serif font* (*sans* from the French word meaning *without*) does not contain the thin lines on characters. Calibri is a sans serif font.

Serifs help the eye connect one letter with the next and generally are used with large amounts of text. The paragraphs in this book, for example, are set in a serif font. Body text of newspapers and magazines is usually formatted in a serif font, as well. A sans serif font, such as Calibri, Arial, or Verdana, is more effective with smaller amounts of text such as titles, headlines, corporate logos, and webpages. For example, the heading *Select Font Options*, at the beginning of this section, is set in a sans serif font. Web developers often prefer a sans serif font because the extra strokes that begin and end letters in a serif font can blur or fade into a webpage, making it difficult to read. Examples of serif and sans serif fonts are shown in Figure 2.2.

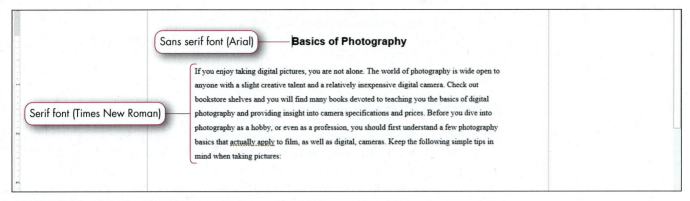

FIGURE 2.2 Serif and Sans Serif Fonts

When you begin a new, blank document, if you do not like the default font for the headings and body text of the document, you can change the fonts for the current document to something that you like. To change the font for selected text, a heading, or for a document you are beginning, click the Font arrow and select a font from those displayed (see Figure 2.3). Each font shown is a sample of the actual font. With text selected, you can point to any font in the list, without clicking, to see a preview of the way the selected text will look in that font. *Live Preview* enables you to select text and see the effects without finalizing the selection.

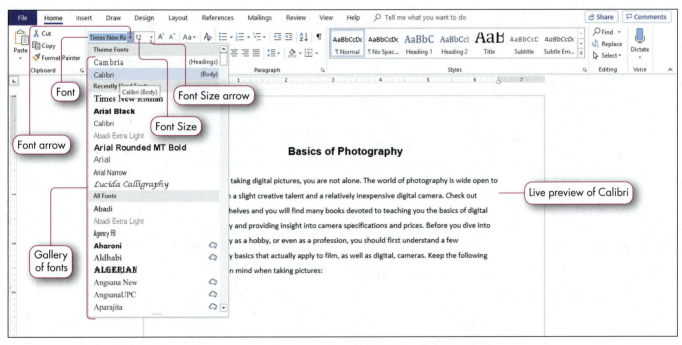

FIGURE 2.3 Select a Font and Font Size

You can also change font size when you click the Font Size arrow (refer to Figure 2.3) and select a point size. Each point size is equivalent to 1/72 of an inch; therefore, the larger the point size, the larger the font. A document often contains various sizes of the same font. For example, a document that includes levels of headings and subheadings might have major headings formatted in a larger point size than lesser headings. The default font size for the body text in a Word document is 11 pt while the default font size for Heading 1 is 16 pt.

Change Text Appearance

Commonly accessed commands related to font settings are on the Home tab in the Font group (see Figure 2.4). There are features that enable you to bold, underline, and italicize text; apply text highlighting; change font color; and work with various text effects and other formatting options from commands in the Font group. For even more choices, click the Font Dialog Box Launcher in the Font group and select from additional formatting commands available in the Font dialog box (see Figure 2.5). With text selected, you will see the Mini Toolbar when you move the pointer near the selection, making it more convenient to quickly select a format (instead of locating it on the ribbon or using a keyboard shortcut). Toggle the same command to turn off the formatting effect.

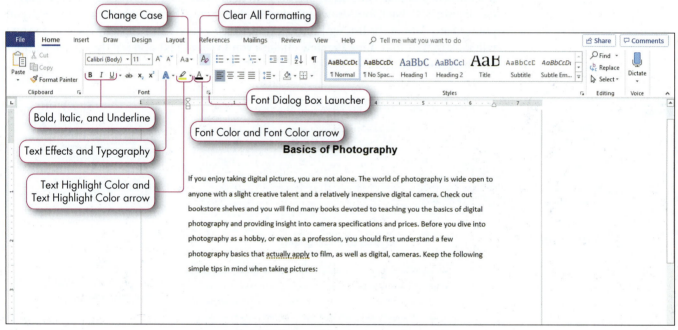

FIGURE 2.4 Font Commands

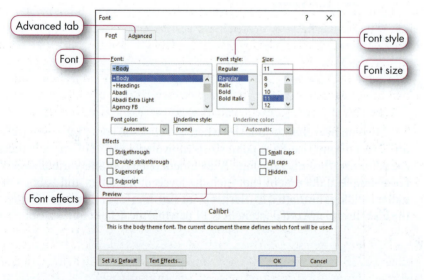

FIGURE 2.5 Font Dialog Box

Word includes a variety of text effects that enable you to add a shadow, outline, reflection, or glow to text. The Text Effects and Typography gallery (see Figure 2.6) provides access to those effects as well as to WordArt styles, number styles, ligatures, and stylistic sets that you can apply to text.

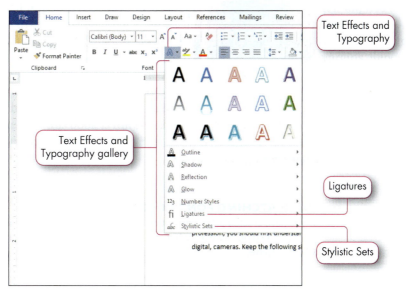

FIGURE 2.6 Text Effects and Typography Gallery

A ligature is two letters that are crafted together into a single character, or glyph. For example, you often see the letters *f* and *i* bound together in a ligature. A stylistic set is a collection of letter styles that you can apply to OpenType fonts. Some fonts include more stylistic sets than others. Stylistic sets and ligatures are often used in the preparation of formal documents such as wedding invitations.

> **TIP: ADVANCED FONT SETTINGS**
> If you intend to use a ligature and/or stylistic set, you may select it via the Advanced tab in the Font dialog box (refer to Figure 2.5). However, the ligatures and stylistic sets are also readily available in the Text Effects and Typography gallery as shown in Figure 2.6.

As a student, you are likely to highlight important parts of textbooks, magazine articles, and other documents. You probably use a highlighting marker to shade the parts of text that you want to remember or to which you want to draw attention. Word provides an equivalent tool with which you can highlight text you want to stand out or to locate easily—the Text Highlight Color command, located in the Font group on the Home tab (refer to Figure 2.4). This highlighting tool can be toggled on to highlight multiple parts of a document, or you can select specific text and apply the highlighter. To highlight text after selecting it, select Text Highlight Color or click the Text Highlight Color arrow and choose another color. You can remove highlights in the same manner, except that you will select No Color.

When creating a document, you must consider when and how to apply capitalization. Titles and headings typically capitalize each key word, but some headings may occasionally be in all capital letters, and sentences begin with a capital letter. Use the Change Case option in the Font group on the Home tab to quickly change the capitalization of selected document text (refer to Figure 2.4).

By default, text color is black. For a bit of interest, or to draw attention to text within a document, you can change the font color of previously typed text or of text that you are about to type. Click the Font Color arrow (refer to Figure 2.4) and select from a gallery of colors. For even more choices, click More Colors and select from a variety of hues or shades. As shown in Figure 2.7, you can click the Custom tab in the Colors dialog box and select a color hue by dragging along a hue continuum.

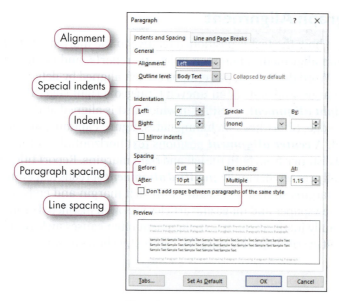

FIGURE 2.10 Paragraph Dialog Box

Select Line and Paragraph Spacing

Paragraph spacing is the amount of space between paragraphs, measured in points. (Recall that one point is 1/72 of an inch.) Paragraph spacing is a good way to differentiate between paragraphs, especially if the beginning of each paragraph is not clearly identified by an indented line. In such a case, paragraph spacing identifies where one paragraph ends and another begins. Spacing used to separate paragraphs usually comes after each affected paragraph, although you can specify that it is placed before the affected paragraph. Use the Paragraph dialog box to select paragraph spacing (refer to Figure 2.10).

To change paragraph spacing, complete one of the following steps:

• Click Line and Paragraph Spacing in the Paragraph group on the Home tab (see Figure 2.11). Click to Add Space Before Paragraph (or to Add Space After Paragraph).
• Click the Paragraph Dialog Box Launcher in the Paragraph group on the Home tab. Type a number to indicate the amount of Spacing Before or After in the respective areas (refer to Figure 2.10) or click the spin arrows to adjust the spacing. Click OK.
• Change the Before or After spacing in the Paragraph group on the Layout tab (see Figure 2.12).

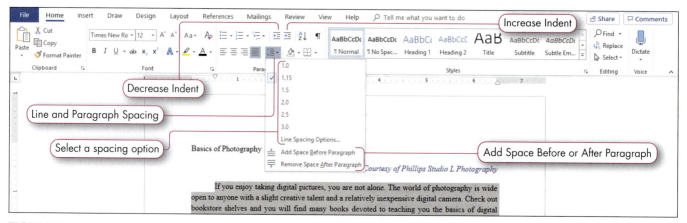

FIGURE 2.11 Spacing Options

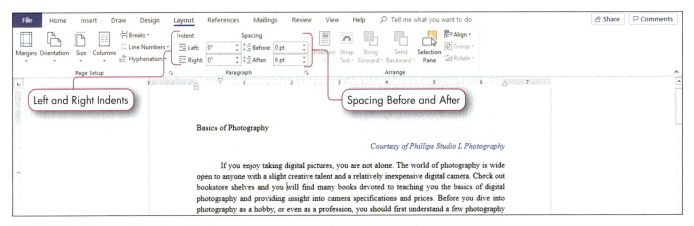

FIGURE 2.12 Paragraph Spacing and Indents

Just as paragraph spacing is the amount of space between paragraphs, **line spacing** is the amount of space between lines. Typically, line spacing is determined before beginning a document, such as when you know that a research paper should be double-spaced, so you identify that setting before typing. Of course, you can change line spacing of a current paragraph or selected text at any point as well.

You can change line spacing using either the Paragraph dialog box or the Line and Paragraph Spacing option in the Paragraph group on the Home tab. The most common line spacing options are single, double, 1.15, or 1.5 lines. Word provides those options and more. From the Paragraph dialog box (refer to Figure 2.10), you can select Exactly, At Least, or Multiple. To specify an exact point size for spacing, select Exactly. If you select At Least, you will indicate a minimum line spacing size while allowing Word to adjust the height, if necessary, to accommodate such features as drop caps (oversized letters that sometimes begin paragraphs). The Multiple setting enables you to select a line spacing interval other than single, double, 1.15, or 1.5 lines.

Select Indents

An **indent** is a setting associated with how part of a paragraph is distanced from the margin. One of the most common indents is a **first line indent**, in which the first line of each paragraph is set off from the left margin. For instance, your English instructor might require that the first line of each paragraph in a writing assignment is indented 0.5″ from the left margin, which is a typical first line indent. If you have ever prepared a bibliography for a research paper, you have most likely specified a **hanging indent**, where the first line of a source begins at the left margin, but all other lines in the source are indented. Indenting an entire paragraph from the left margin is a **left indent**, while indenting an entire paragraph from the right margin is a **right indent**. A lengthy quote is often set apart by indenting from both the left and right margins.

Using the Paragraph dialog box (refer to Figure 2.10), you can select an indent setting for one or more paragraphs. First line and hanging indents are considered special indents.

f. Click **Shadow** in the Setting section. Scroll through the Style box and select the seventh style—**double line**. Click **OK**. Do not deselect the text. Click the **Shading arrow** and select **Blue, Accent 1, Lighter 60%** (third row, fifth column). Click anywhere to deselect the text.

Studio hours are bordered and shaded.

g. Save the document.

CREATE BULLETED AND NUMBERED LISTS

At several points in the newsletter, you include either a list of items or a sequence of steps. You will add bullets to the lists and number the steps. Refer to Figure 2.23 as you complete Step 4.

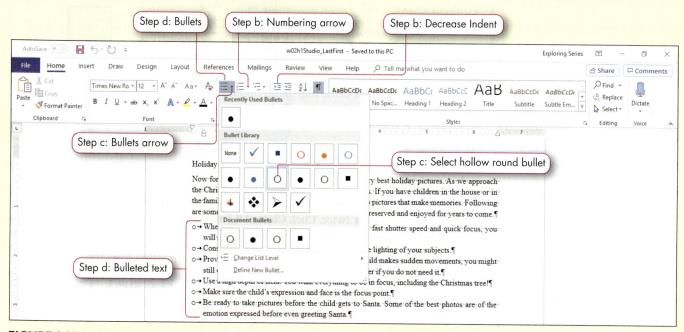

FIGURE 2.23 Add Bullets and Numbers

a. Press **Ctrl+Home**. Select the five boldfaced paragraphs, beginning with *Compose with Care* and ending with *Be Bold*.

b. Click the **Numbering arrow** and select the **Number Alignment** showing each number followed by a right parenthesis. Click **Decrease Indent** in the Paragraph group to move the numbered items to the left margin. Click anywhere to deselect the text.

c. Scroll to the second page and select the four paragraphs following the sentence *Depth of field is determined by several factors*, beginning with *Aperture/F-Stop* and ending with *Point of View*. Click the **Bullets arrow** and select the **hollow round bullet**. Decrease the indent to move the selected text to the left margin. Deselect the text.

d. Press **Ctrl+End** and select the six paragraphs above the last paragraph of text, beginning with *Where kids are involved*, and ending with *even greeting Santa*. Click **Bullets** to apply a hollow round bullet to the selected paragraphs. Decrease the indent so the bullets begin at the left margin.

Clicking Bullets applied the most recently selected bullet style to selected text. You did not have to click the Bullets arrow and select from the Bullet Library.

e. Save the document. Keep the document open if you plan to continue with the next Hands-On Exercise. If not, close the document, and exit Word.

Document Appearance

The overall appearance and organization of a document is the first opportunity to effectively convey your message to readers. You should ensure that a document is formatted attractively with coordinated and consistent style elements. Not only should a document be organized by topic, but also it should be organized by design, so that it is easy to read and that topics of the same level of emphasis are similar in appearance. Major headings are typically formatted identically, with subheadings formatted to indicate a subordinate relationship—in a smaller font, for example. Word includes tools on the Design tab that enable you to create a polished and professional-looking document. You will find options for creating a themed document, with color-coordinated design elements, as well as *style sets*, which are predefined combinations of font, style, color, and font size that can be applied to selected text. Organizing a document into sections enables you to combine diverse units into a whole, formatting sections independently of one another.

In this section, you will explore document formatting options, including themes and style sets. In addition, you will learn to create and apply styles. You will work with sections and columns, learning to organize and format sections independently of one another to create an attractive document that conveys your message.

Formatting a Document

A *document theme* is a set of coordinating fonts, colors, and special effects that are combined into a package to provide a stylish appearance in a Word document. Applying a theme enables you to visually coordinate various page elements. In some cases, adding a page border or page background can also yield a more attractive and effective document. All these design options are available on the Design tab. When formatting a document, you should always keep in mind the document's purpose and its intended audience. Whereas a newsletter might use more color and playful text and design effects, a legal document should be more conservative. With the broad range of document formatting options available in Word, you can be as playful or conservative as necessary.

> **TIP: APPLY DOCUMENT THEME**
> Themes are similar across the Office applications. If a Word document includes a table from Excel, both the Word and Excel files can be formatted with the same document theme, so the effects are consistent across the two applications.

STEP 1 ▸ Select a Document Theme

When you open a new blank Word document, it is based on the default Office theme. However, you can select and change the entire theme of the document or just customize the theme fonts, colors, or effects using the Design tab, where you will find a wide selection related to themes, colors, fonts, effects, watermarks, page background, and even page borders (see Figure 2.24). You can choose from a variety of document themes, theme colors, theme fonts, and theme effects, which are in the Document Formatting group. Point to each theme in the Themes gallery to display a preview of the effect on the document and select to change the document theme. Depending on document features and color selections already in place, you might not see an immediate change when previewing a theme.

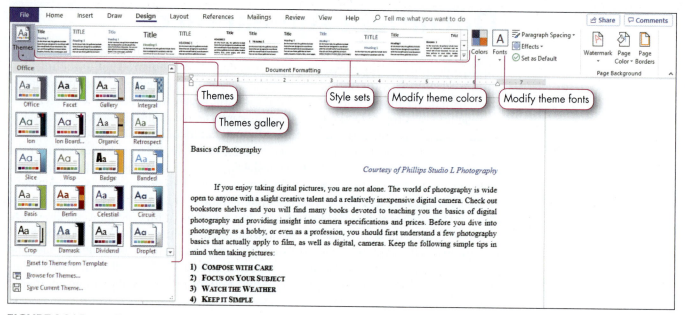

FIGURE 2.24 Design Tab

Modifying a theme color or theme font may be necessary for color coordination and/or to give the document a consistent, professional look. Similarly, you may modify the theme colors or fonts by selecting from a group of coordinated colors or font selections summarized and identified by a unique name. Theme fonts can be applied to headings or body text.

If your document contains objects, you may utilize theme effects to instantly change the general look of the objects in the document. Selections in the theme gallery use lines, borders, fills, and visual effects, such as shading and shadow, to give the objects a unique look, thus drawing attention to the selected item. With the object selected, point to each option in the effects gallery to display a preview of the effect on the object and select to apply the theme effect. You may also add a watermark, page color, or a page border using the tools in the Page Background group.

Work with Sections

As you consider ways to organize a document, you might find it necessary to vary the layout of a document within a page or between pages and incorporate sections into a document with each section arranged or formatted independently of others. For instance, a headline of an article might center horizontally across the width of a page, while remaining article text is divided into columns (see Figure 2.25). In this case, the headline should be situated in one section, while article text resides in another. By arranging text in columns, you can easily create an attractive newsletter or brochure. The Layout tab facilitates the use of sections and formatting in columns. Or, a cover page can be a section by itself that might be centered vertically, while all other pages in the same document are aligned at the top. A ***section*** is a part of a document that contains its own page format settings, such as those for margins, columns, and orientation. To have text on the same page accommodating both single column and two-column text, break it into sections. So that sections can be managed separately, you must indicate with section breaks where one section ends and another begins. A ***section break*** is a marker that divides a document into sections. Word stores the formatting characteristics of each section within the section break at the end of a section. Section breaks are often used to change page orientation, add columns to selected text within a document, and add page borders to selected text within a document.

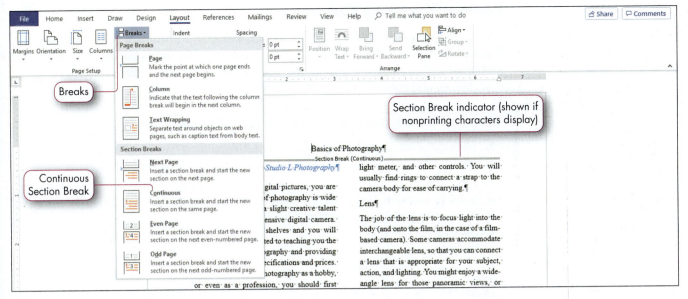

FIGURE 2.25 Select and Display a Section Break

There are four types of section breaks, as shown in Table 2.2. The most common type of section break is the Next Page, which manually forces the text to start at the top of a new page. If you want to format content in a newsletter, then a Continuous section break would be ideal. Even Page and Odd Page section breaks are often used in assembling a book.

TABLE 2.2	Section Breaks	
Type	**Text that follows . . .**	**Use to . . .**
Next Page	must begin at the top of the next page.	force a chapter to start at the top of a page.
Continuous	can continue on the same page.	format text in the middle of the page into columns.
Even Page	must begin at the top of the next even-numbered page.	force a chapter to begin at the top of an even-numbered page.
Odd Page	must begin at the top of the next odd-numbered page.	force a chapter to begin at the top of an odd-numbered page.

To place a section break in a document, complete the following steps:

1. Click at the location where the section break should occur.
2. Click the Layout tab. Click Breaks in the Page Setup group.
3. Select a section break type (refer to Table 2.2). If nonprinting characters are displayed, you will see a section break (refer to Figure 2.25).

If you delete a section break, you also delete the formatting for that section, causing the text above the break to assume the formatting characteristics of the following section. To delete a section break, click the section break indicator (refer to Figure 2.25) and press Delete.

Format Text into Columns

One reason to create a section in a document is to display a portion of the text in columns. Newsletters are often formatted with text in columns. **Columns** format a document or section of a document into side-by-side vertical blocks in which the text flows down the first column and continues at the top of the next column.

To format text into columns, complete the following steps:

1. Click at the location where you want to start formatting the text into columns.
2. Click the Layout tab and click Columns in the Page Setup group.
3. Specify the number of columns or select More Columns to display the Columns dialog box. The Columns dialog box (see Figure 2.26) provides options for setting the number of columns and spacing between columns.
4. Click OK.

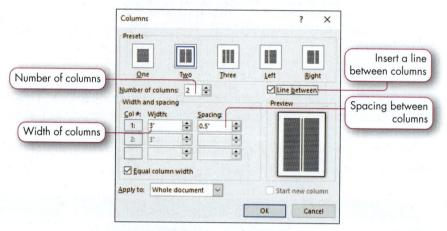

FIGURE 2.26 Columns Dialog Box

Having created a two-column document, you should preview the document to ensure an attractive arrangement of columns. Try to avoid columns that end awkwardly, such as a column heading at the bottom of one column with remaining text continuing at the top of the next column. In addition, columns should be somewhat balanced, if possible, so that one column is not far lengthier than the next. To remedy these kinds of issues, use a column break, which enables you to choose where a column ends. To insert a column break at a specified location in the document, use the Layout tab, select Breaks in the Page Setup group, and then click Column in the Page Breaks section. With nonprinting characters displayed, you will see the Column Break indicator at the location where one column ends and the next begins.

Applying Styles

A characteristic of a professional document is uniform formatting. As you complete reports, assignments, and other projects, you probably apply the same text, paragraph, table, and list formatting for similar elements. Instead of formatting document elements individually, you can apply a style for each element to save time in designing titles, headings, and paragraphs. A **style** is a named collection of formatting characteristics. Styles automate the formatting process and provide a consistent appearance to a document so all major headings look the same, with uniform subheadings. Even paragraphs can be styled to lend consistency to a document. In addition, if styles are appropriately assigned, Word can automatically generate reference pages such as a table of contents and indexes. Although document themes provide a quick way to change the overall color and fonts of a document, styles are more effective when you want to change text formatting quickly and uniformly.

By default, the Normal style is applied to new Word documents. Normal style is a paragraph style with specific font and paragraph formatting, and the features that are set as default are: Calibri (Body) font, 11 pt font size, left alignment, 0 pt Spacing Before, 8 pt Spacing After, and 1.08 Multiple Line spacing. If that style is not appropriate for a document you are developing, you can select another style from Word's Style gallery. The most frequently accessed styles are shown in the Styles group on the Home tab (see Figure 2.27).

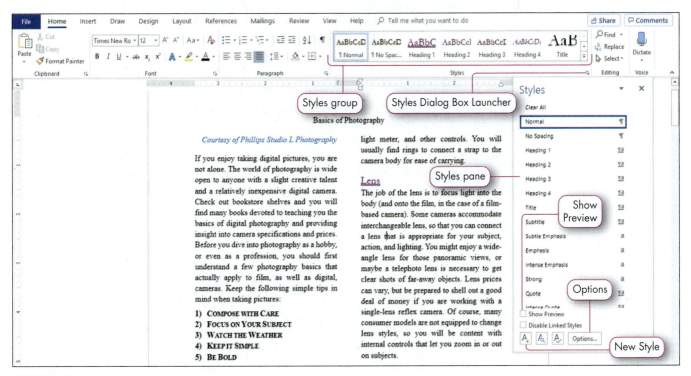

FIGURE 2.27 Styles

STEP 2 ▶ Select and Modify Styles

Some styles are considered either character or paragraph styles. Examples of character styles include Emphasis, Quote, Book Title, and List Paragraph, while headings are examples of paragraph styles. A character style formats one or more selected characters within a paragraph, often applying font formats found in the Font group on the Home tab. A paragraph style changes the entire paragraph in which the insertion point is located or changes multiple selected paragraphs. A paragraph style typically includes paragraph formats found in the Paragraph group on the Home tab, such as alignment, line spacing, indents, tabs, and borders. Other styles are neither character nor paragraph but are instead linked styles in which both character and paragraph formatting are included. A linked style applies formatting dependent upon the text selected. For example, when the insertion point is located within a paragraph, but no text is selected, a linked style applies both font characteristics (such as bold or italic) and paragraph formats (such as paragraph and line spacing) to the entire paragraph. However, if text is selected within a paragraph when a linked style is applied, the style will apply font formatting only.

To apply a style to selected text or to an existing paragraph, complete the following steps:

1. Select the text or place the insertion point within the paragraph.
2. Complete one of the following steps:
   - Click a style in the Styles group on the Home tab.
   - Click More for more styles.
   - Click the Styles Dialog Box Launcher (refer to Figure 2.27) to display the Styles pane for more choices.
3. Click to select a style.

Modifying a style, or even creating a new style, affects only the current document, by default. However, you can cause the style to be available to all documents that are based on the current template when you select *New documents based on this template* in the Modify Style dialog box (see Figure 2.28). Unless you make that selection, however, the changes are not carried over to new documents you create or to others that you open. As an example, the specifications for the Title style are shown in Figure 2.28.

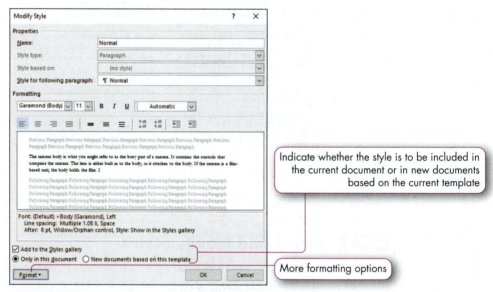

FIGURE 2.28 Modify a Style

To modify a style, complete the following steps:

1. Click the Styles Dialog Box Launcher in the Styles group to open the Styles pane showing all available styles.
2. Point to a style in the Styles pane and click the arrow on the right.
3. Click Modify. The Modify Style dialog box displays (refer to Figure 2.28).
4. Change any font and paragraph formatting or click Format for even more choices.
5. Click Add to the Styles gallery if the style is one you are likely to use often.
6. Indicate whether the style should be available only in the current document, or in new documents based on the current template.
7. Click OK.

On a Mac, to modify a style, complete the following steps:

1. Click the Format menu and select Style.
2. Click Modify in the Style dialog box.
3. Change any font and paragraph settings you want to modify in the Modify Style dialog box. Click Format for more choices.
4. Click Add to template to add a new style to the template the current document is based on. For a single use, do not click this option.
5. Click Add to Quick Style list to add the new style to the Quick Style list that displays on the Home tab.
6. Click OK.

Word provides a gallery of styles from which you can choose. The styles gallery contains a variety of styles that are conveniently located and frequently used. Therefore, you can apply a specific style from the Styles gallery or manage the contents of the gallery by adding or deleting styles that you need or do not need. If a style does not fit with your document design, you can modify almost any component of the style. For example, you might format a Heading 1 style with Black font color instead of the default Blue. When a style is modified, the changes will automatically be applied to all document elements formatted with that style, or you can create your own style. It is possible to store any type of character or paragraph formatting within a style. For example, having formatted a major report heading with various settings, such as font type, color, and size, you can create a style from the heading, calling it Major_Heading. The next time you type a major heading, apply the Major_Heading style so that the two headings are identical in format. Subsequent major headings can be formatted in the same way. If you later decide to modify the Major_Heading style, all text based on that style will automatically adjust as well.

STEP 3 ▶ Use a Style Set

A style set is a combination of title, heading, and paragraph styles that are designed to work together. Using a style set, you can format all elements in a document at one time. Style sets are on the Design tab in the Document Formatting group (refer to Figure 2.24). Click a style set to apply the format combination to the document.

Create a New Style from Text

Having applied several formatting characteristics to text, you can repeat that formatting on other selections that are similar in purpose. For example, suppose you format a page title with a specific font size, font color, and bordering. Subsequent page titles should be formatted identically. To copy formatting from one selection to another, you can certainly use Format Painter. A better alternative is to create a new style from the selection and apply the new style to additional text. For example, you can select the formatted page title and create a new style based on the formatting of the selected text. Then select the next title to which the formatting should be applied and choose the newly created style name from the Styles group or from the Styles pane. You may also check your styles by clicking Style Inspector in the Styles task pane.

Once a style is created, it remains available in both the current document and in other documents based on the same template, if you indicate that preference when you create the style. That way, the same formatting changes can be applied repeatedly in various documents or positions within the same document, even after a document is closed and reopened. Further, styles that indicate a hierarchy (such as Heading 1, Heading 2) can be used to prepare a table of contents or outline.

To create a new style from existing text, complete the following steps:

1. Select text the new style will be based upon.
2. Click More in the Style group.
3. Click Create a Style.
4. Type a name for the new style. Do not use the name of an existing style.
5. Click OK.

On a Mac, to create a new style from existing text, complete the following steps:

1. Select the text the new style will be based upon or click in a paragraph containing paragraph characteristics you want to include in a new style.
2. Click Styles Pane on the Home tab.
3. Click New Style and type a name for the new style. The name must be unique and cannot be the name of an existing style.

STEP 4 ## Use Outline View

One benefit of applying styles to headings in a long document is the ability to use those headings to view the document in Outline view, making it easier to review and modify the organization of a long document. Outline view in Word displays a document in various levels of detail, according to heading styles applied in a document. Figure 2.29 shows Outline view of a document in which major headings were formatted in Heading 1 style, with subheadings in Headings 2 and 3 styles. You can modify the heading styles to suit your preference. To select a level to view, perhaps only first-level headings, click All Levels (beside Show Level) and select a level. You can display the document in Outline view by clicking the View tab and clicking Outline in the Views group.

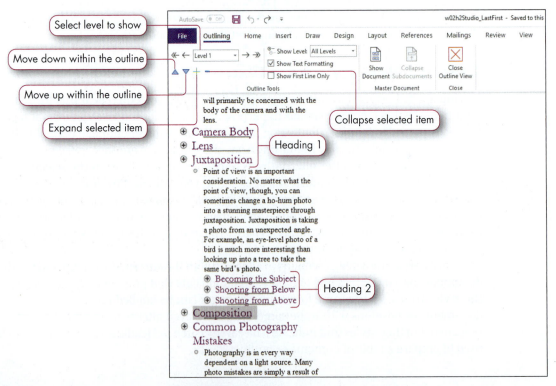

FIGURE 2.29 Outline View

Use Outline view to glimpse or confirm a document's structure. Especially when developing lengthy reports, you will want to make sure headings are shown at the correct level of detail. A document shown in Outline view can also be easily converted to a PowerPoint presentation, with Heading 1 becoming the slide titles, and lower levels becoming bullets on each slide. Also, a table of contents is automatically generated when you select Table of Contents on the References tab.

To collapse or expand a single heading, click the heading in Outline view and click the plus sign (to expand) or the minus sign (to collapse) on the ribbon. For example, having clicked text formatted as Heading 1, click + to show any lower-level headings associated with the particular heading (refer to Figure 2.29). Text other than that associated with the selected heading will remain unaffected. As shown in Figure 2.29, you can move a heading (along with all associated subheadings) up or down in the document. In Outline view, you can also drag the plus or minus sign beside a heading to move the entire group, including all sublevels, to another location.

You can quickly move through and restructure a document in Outline view. Using Outline view to move through a lengthy document can save a great deal of time because it is not necessary to page through a document looking for a particular section heading. To restructure a document in Outline view, drag and drop a heading to reposition it within a document or use Move Up or Move Down. If subheadings are associated, they will move with the heading as well.

Change the view to Print Layout, and when the levels are collapsed so that body text does not display, you can select a heading to move quickly to that section. In Print Layout view, you can collapse everything except the section with which you want to work. Point to a heading and click the small triangle that displays beside the heading (see Figure 2.30) to collapse or expand the following body text and sublevels. Collapsing text in that manner is a handy way to provide your readers with a summary. The document will expand, and the insertion point will be in the section identified by the heading you selected.

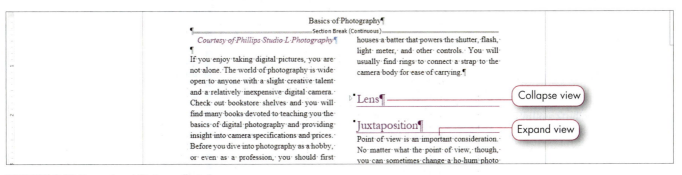

FIGURE 2.30 Expand and Collapse Detail

Quick Concepts

5. Describe why a document may need to be divided into two or more sections. *p. 150*

6. Describe a situation where it would be appropriate to insert a column break into a Word document. *p. 152*

7. Explain the benefit of using styles when formatting several different areas of text. *p. 152*

8. Discuss how the concept of styles relates to Outline view. *p. 156*

Objects

An ***object*** is an item that can be individually selected and manipulated within a document. Objects, such as pictures, icons, clip art, tables, and other graphic types, are often included in documents to add interest or convey a point (see Figure 2.36). Newsletters typically include pictures and other decorative elements to liven up what might otherwise be a somewhat mundane document. As you work with a document, you can search for appropriate pictures and graphics online—all without ever leaving your document workspace.

FIGURE 2.36 Word Objects

One thing all objects have in common is that they can be selected and worked with independently of surrounding text. You can resize them, add special effects, and move them to other locations within the document. Word includes convenient text wrapping controls so that you can adjust the way text wraps around an object. With Live Layout and alignment guides, you can line up pictures and other diagrams with existing text.

In this section, you will explore the use of objects in a Word document. Specifically, you will learn to include pictures, searching for them online as well as obtaining them from your own storage device. You will create text boxes and learn to create impressive text displays with WordArt.

Inserting and Formatting Objects

Objects such as pictures, icons, and illustrations can be selected from the Web or a storage device. When you select an image using Bing Search on Microsoft Word, the image is set to use the Creative Commons license system, which enables you to use the image more freely than other online images. It is important that you read the Creative Commons license on copyright infringement before using the image. You can also create other objects, such as WordArt, text boxes, screenshots, charts, and tables. A ***text box*** is a bordered area you can use to draw attention to specific text. When you insert an object, it is automatically selected so that you can manipulate it independently of surrounding text. An additional tab displays on the ribbon with options related to the selected object, making it easy to quickly modify and enhance an object.

A *picture* is a graphic image, such as a drawing or photograph. You can insert pictures in a document from your own library of digital pictures you have saved, or you can access abundant picture resources from the Internet. For instance, you can use Bing Search in Word to conduct a Web search to locate picture possibilities. Once incorporated into your document, a picture can be resized and modified with special borders and artistic effects. Other options enable you to easily align a picture with surrounding text, rotate or crop it if necessary, and even recolor it so it coordinates with an existing color scheme.

To insert an online picture, complete the following steps:

1. Click to place the insertion point in the document in the location where the picture is to be inserted.
2. Click the Insert tab and click Online Pictures in the Illustrations group (see Figure 2.37).
3. Complete one of the following steps:
   - **Use Bing Search:**
     1. Click in the Bing Search box.
     2. Type a search term (for example, type *school* to identify school-related images), and press Enter.
     3. Ensure that the *Creative Commons only* check box is selected if you choose to use only Creative Commons approved images.
     4. Review any relevant licensing information and select an image.
     5. Click Insert.
     6. Select and delete any additional text boxes from the online picture.
   - **Use OneDrive:**
     1. Click the Bing arrow and select OneDrive.
     2. Navigate to the folder containing the picture you want to insert.
     3. Click the picture and click Insert.

There are several hundreds of icons available online to users, and these icons can be searched and inserted similarly to any image by selecting Icons in the Illustrations group (see Figure 2.37). You may enhance the icons by changing the icon's fill or outline, or add a special visual effect such as glow or reflection to match the rest of the document using the formatting options provided on the Graphics tab.

Microsoft has made it so much easier for users to find and insert permission-approved images from the Internet. For instance, Pickit Images is a quick and convenient add-in app that contains images that you are legally allowed to use for any purpose. However, PickIt requires a fee after a brief free trial period. If you believe you will use this resource quite often, it may be a good idea to add it to your ribbon by clicking Store in the Add-ins group of the Insert tab and then selecting Pickit Free Images.

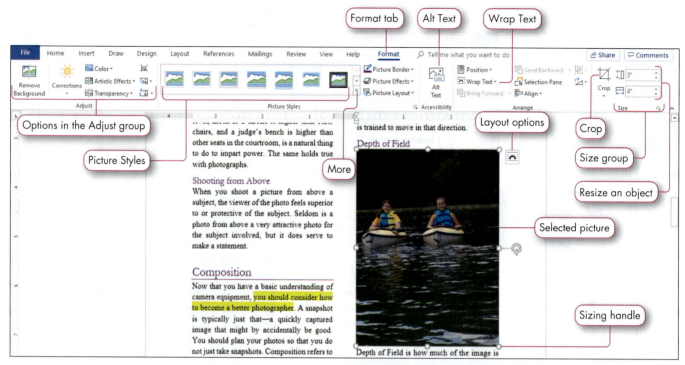

FIGURE 2.39 Picture Tools Format Tab

TABLE 2.3	Text Wrap Options
Type	**Effect**
In Line with Text	The image is part of the line of text in which it is inserted. Typically, text wraps above and below the object.
Square	Text wraps on all sides of an object, following an invisible square.
Tight	Text follows the shape of the object, but it does not overlap the object.
Through	Text follows the shape of the object, filling any open spaces in the shape.
Top and Bottom	Text flows above and below the borders of the object.
Behind Text	The object is positioned behind text. Both the object and text are visible (unless the fill color exactly matches the text color).
In Front of Text	The object is positioned in front of text, often obscuring the text.

Word has a feature that simplifies text wrapping around an object—Layout Options. Located next to a selected object, the Layout Options control (see Figure 2.40) includes the same selections shown in Table 2.3. The close proximity of the control to the selected object streamlines adjusting text wrapping.

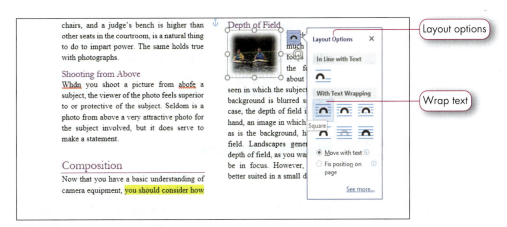

FIGURE 2.40 Text Wrap Options

Word has two interesting features to assist you as you wrap text: Live Layout and alignment guides. **Live Layout** enables you to watch text flow around an object as you move it, so you can position the object exactly as you want it. **Alignment guides** are horizontal or vertical green bars that display as you drag an object, so you can line up an object with text or with another object. The green alignment guide shown in Figure 2.41 helps align the picture object with paragraph text.

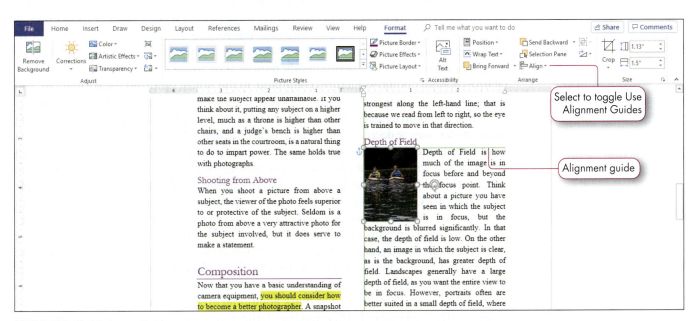

FIGURE 2.41 Alignment Guides

> **TIP: TURNING OFF THE ALIGNMENT GUIDES**
> If you decide that you do not need to use the alignment guides anymore, you can manually turn off this feature by selecting the alignment guides in the Align command and clicking Delete.

Often, a picture is inserted in a size that is too large or too small for your purposes. There are two ways to shrink the picture to fit it in a smaller space or enlarge it to fill some white space. To resize a picture, you can drag a *sizing handle*, which is a dot on each corner and in the center of each side of the selected object. When you drag the corner sizing handles, the image will be resized proportionally. Resizing a picture by dragging a center sizing handle is generally not recommended, as doing so distorts the picture. You can also resize a picture with more precise measurements by adjusting settings in the Size group of the Format tab (refer to Figure 2.39).

You can move a text box by dragging it from one area to another. Similar to a picture, you will want to control how the text flows around the text box. When you select or confirm a text wrapping option, text will wrap automatically around the text box as you move it. Position the pointer on a border of the text box so it appears as a small, four-headed arrow. Drag to reposition the text box. As you drag the box, green alignment guides assist in positioning it neatly. The Format tab includes a Position command in the Arrange group that enables you to align the text box in various ways within existing text. You can even indicate the exact height and width of a text box using the Format tab (see Figure 2.44).

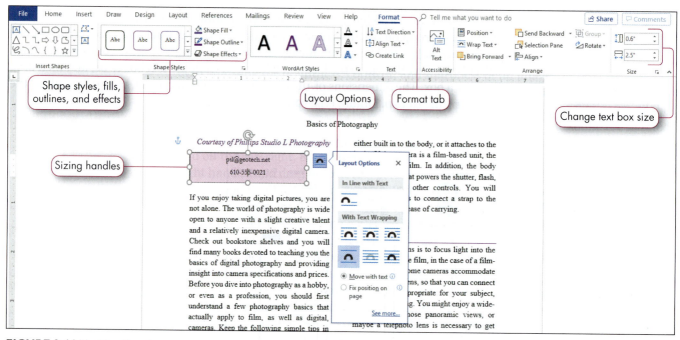

FIGURE 2.44 Modify a Text Box

Like a picture, a text box can be resized using the Size dialog box for precise sizing, or by using the sizing handles. Unlike a picture that can become distorted when using the center sizing handles, the center sizing handles are best used to modify the height or width of a text box. When these are used, the text inside repositions, but does not get distorted.

The text inside the text box can also be formatted. Before formatting text in a text box, select the text to be affected. To do so, drag to select the text to be formatted. Or, if you want to select all text, you can click the dashed border surrounding the text box (when the pointer is a small four-headed arrow). The dashed line should become solid, indicating that all text is selected. Once the text is selected, you may select an alignment option on the Home tab to left-align, right-align, center, or justify text. At that point, any formatting selections you make related to text are applied to all text in the text box.

STEP 5 Insert WordArt

WordArt is a feature that modifies text to include special effects, including colors, shadows, gradients, and 3-D effects (see Figure 2.45). It is a quick way to format text so that it is vibrant and eye-catching. Of course, WordArt is not appropriate for all documents, especially more conservative business correspondence, but it can give life to newsletters, flyers, and other more informal projects, especially when applied to headings and titles. WordArt is well suited for single lines, such as document headings, where the larger print and text design draws attention and adds style to a document title. However, it is not appropriate for body text, because a WordArt object is managed independently of

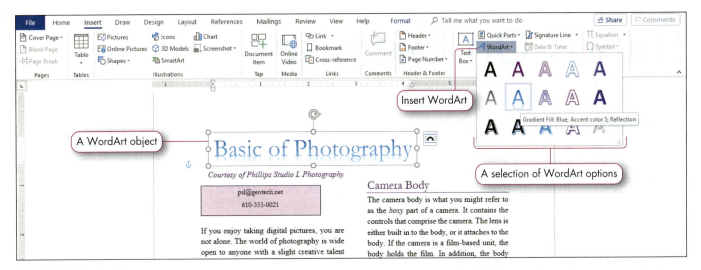

FIGURE 2.45 WordArt

surrounding text and cannot be formatted as a document (with specific margins, headers, footers, etc.). Instead, styles and headings are would be more appropriately used to format body text. In addition, if WordArt were incorporated into body text, the more ornate text design would adversely affect the readability of the document.

You can format existing text as WordArt, or you can insert new WordArt text into a document by selecting WordArt in the Text group on the Insert tab. WordArt is considered an object; as such, the preceding discussion related to positioning pictures and text boxes applies to WordArt as well. Also, Live Layout and alignment guides are available to facilitate ease of positioning, and you can select a text wrapping style with layout options. You may also use the options in the WordArt Styles group to add fills, outline colors, and effects to the WordArt text itself.

> **To insert new text as WordArt, complete the following steps:**
>
> 1. Place the insertion point at the point where WordArt will be added.
> 2. Click the Insert tab.
> 3. Click WordArt in the Text group.
> 4. Select a WordArt style.
> 5. Type text.

Depending on the purpose of a document and its intended audience, objects such as pictures, text boxes, and WordArt can help convey a message and add interest. As you learn to incorporate objects visually within a document so that they appear to flow seamlessly within existing text, you will find it easy to create attractive, informative documents that contain an element of design apart from simple text.

Quick Concepts

9. Describe how you would determine the type of text wrapping to use when positioning a picture in a document. *p. 168*

10. Describe two methods to modify the height and width of a picture. *p. 169*

11. Explain how a text box differs from simple shaded text. *p. 170*

12. Explain why WordArt is most often used to format headings or titles, and not text in the body of a document. *p. 172*

Mid-Level Exercises

1 Mount Vernon Balloon Festival

As chair of the Mount Vernon Hot Balloon Festival, you are responsible for promoting the upcoming event. You started a document providing details on the festival. You plan to distribute the document both in print and online. First, you must format the document to make it more attractive and well designed. You will use styles, bullets, and line and paragraph spacing to coordinate various parts of the document. In addition, you will add interest by including objects, such as pictures and WordArt.

a. Open *w02m1Festival* and save it as **w02m1Festival_LastFirst**.

b. Change the document theme to **Organic**. Select the first paragraph in the document, *Mount Vernon Hot Air Balloon Festival*. Insert WordArt, selecting **Fill: Black, Text color 1; Outline: White, Background color 1; Hard Shadow: Orange, Accent color 5** (third row, second column). Change the font size of the WordArt object to **24**.

c. Wrap text around the WordArt object as **Top and Bottom**. Format the WordArt object with Shape Style **Subtle Effect – Teal, Accent 2** (fourth row, third column). Visually center the WordArt object on the first paragraph of the document.

d. Select the second paragraph in the document, *See the Canyon From The Top!* Center and bold the text and apply a font color of **Teal, Accent 2**.

e. Select the remaining text on page 1, beginning with *May 28-29, 2022* and ending with *on the festival grounds*. Format the selected text into two columns with a line in between and equal column width. Change the font of the columned text on page 1 to **Century Schoolbook**. Insert a page break (not a section break) on page 3 after the sentence ending with *inflate balloons on the festival grounds*.

f. Check spelling and grammar—the word *Ballumination* is not misspelled (for the purposes of this document). Also, ignore *From* and *The* in the second paragraph on page 1.

g. Click in the third paragraph on page 1—*May 28-29, 2022*—and right align it. Select all columned text, including the line containing festival dates, and select a line spacing of **1.5** and paragraph spacing after of **6 pt**. Insert a column break before the paragraph beginning with *And don't forget the dogs!*

h. Click to place the insertion point before the paragraph beginning *As for the kids*. Insert an online picture from Bing Search relating to hot air balloons. Note: Alternatively, you can search for an image in a Web browser, and then download and insert a relevant image from the results. Select and delete any additional text boxes from the online picture. Size the picture with a width of **1″**. Select **Square text wrapping** and a picture style of **Reflected Bevel, White**. Position the picture so that it is on the left side of the paragraph beginning with *As for the kids*, but still in the right column.

i. Select the picture and recolor it with **Teal, Accent color 2 Light**. Choose the **Paint Brush Artistic effect**.

j. Scroll to page 3 and select the heading, *When is the best time to see balloons?* Bold the selection and change the font color to **Teal, Accent 2**. Do not deselect the heading. Open the Styles pane and create a new style named **Questions**. Apply the **Questions style** to other questions (headings) on page 3.

k. Scroll to page 4 and apply **solid round bullets** to the first nine paragraphs on the page. Decrease the indent so the bullets begin at the left margin. With the bulleted items selected, click the **Bullets arrow** and click **Define New Bullet**. Click **Font** and change the font color to **Teal, Accent 2**. Click **OK**. Click **OK** again.

l. Insert a page break (not a section break) before the heading *How can I plan for the best experience?* on page 3.

m. Select the schedule of items under the heading *Saturday (5/28/2022)*, beginning with *6:00 AM* and ending with *Balloon Glow*. Set a left tab at **1″** and another left tab with a dot leader at **3″**. Press **Tab** to move selected paragraphs to the left tab, and then move the activities to the 3″ tab stop. Select the schedule of items under *Sunday (5/29/2022)*, set a left tab at **1″** and another left tab with a dot leader at **3″**. Press **Tab** to move selected paragraphs to the left tab and move the activities to the 3″ tab stop.

n. Save and close the file. Based on your instructor's directions, submit w02m1Festival_LastFirst.

CREATIVE CASE

You are the office manager for Dr. Lockwood, a general dentist for children, who periodically conducts informational sessions for his young patients. You have written a letter to children in the neighborhood reminding them about the upcoming monthly session, but you want to make the letter more professional looking. You decide to use paragraph formatting such as alignment, paragraph spacing, borders and shading, and bullets that describe some of the fun activities of the day. You also want to add Dr. Lockwood's email address and an appropriate image to the letter.

a. Open the document *w02m2Dentist* and save it as **w02m2Dentist_LastFirst**.

b. Change the capitalization of the recipient *ms. nancy lancaster* and her address so that each word is capitalized and the state abbreviation displays in uppercase. Also capitalize her first name in the salutation. Change Dr. Lockwood's name to your full name in the signature block. Type your email address (or a fictitious email address) on the next line below your name.

c. Show nonprinting characters, if they are not already displayed. Apply **Justify alignment** to body paragraphs beginning with *On behalf* and ending with *September 11*.

d. Select the paragraph mark under the first body paragraph and create a bulleted list, selecting a bullet of your choice. Type the following items in the bulleted list. Do not press Enter after the last item in the list.

Finding hidden toothbrushes in the dental office

Participating in the dental crossword puzzle challenge

Writing a convincing letter to the tooth fairy

Digging through the dental treasure chest

e. Select text from the salutation *Dear Nancy*: through the last paragraph that ends with *seeing you on September 11*. Set **12 pt Spacing After paragraph**. Remove the paragraph mark just after the *Dear Nancy* paragraph.

f. Select *Dr. Lockwood Pediatric Dentistry Office* in the first paragraph and apply **small caps**.

g. Select the italicized lines of text that give date, time, and location of the meeting. Remove the italics, do not deselect the text, and then complete the following:

- Increase left and right indents to **1.25** and set **0 pt Spacing After paragraph**.
- Apply a **double-line box border** with the color **Purple, Accent 4**, and a line width of **3/4 pt**. Shade selected text with the **Purple, Accent 4, Lighter 40% shading color**.
- Delete the extra tab formatting marks to the left of the lines containing *September 4, 2021*; *4:00 p.m.*; and *Dr. Lockwood Pediatric Dentistry Office* to align them with other text in the bordered area.

h. Remove the paragraph mark before the paragraph that begins with *Please call our office*.

i. Click the paragraph containing the text *Funville, VA 23000* and set **6 pt Spacing After** the paragraph. Click the paragraph containing *Sincerely* and set **6 pt Spacing Before** the paragraph. Add **6 pt Spacing Before** the paragraph beginning with the text *Dr. Lockwood is pleased to let you know*.

j. Select the entire document and change the font to **12 pt Bookman Old Style**.

k. Move to the beginning of the document. Search online for a picture related to **tooth**. Insert the picture, and select and delete any additional text boxes from the online picture.

l. Apply a **Square text wrap** and position the picture in the top-right corner of the document, just below the header area. Resize the graphic to **1.1″** high. Apply the **Beveled Oval, Black Picture Style** (second row, third column) and choose the **Chalk Sketch Artistic Effect**.

m. Move to the end of the document. Insert a **Next Page section break**. Change the orientation to **Landscape**. Change Paragraph Spacing After to **6 pt**. Change the font size to **14**.

n. Move to Section 2 and center the first paragraph. Type **Wellington Water Park & Slide Fun Day!** Press **Enter** and type **September 11, 2021**. Press **Enter** and change the alignment to **Left**. Change the font size to **12**.

o. Set a left tab at **2″** and a right tab at **7″**. Type the following text, with the first column at the 2″ tab and the next column at the 7″ tab. Do not press Enter after typing the last line.

Check-in	**9:00**
Wave pool	**9:30-11:00**
Lunch at the pavilion	**11:00-12:00**
Bungee	**12:00-2:00**
Water slide	**2:00-3:00**
Parent pickup at the gate	**3:00-3:30**

p. Select **Wellington Water Park & Slide Fun Day!** on page 2 and insert WordArt with the style **Gradient Fill: Purple, Accent color 4; Outline: Purple, Accent 4** (second row, third column). Wrap text around the WordArt object at **Top and Bottom**, change the font size of the WordArt object to **24**, and drag to center the object horizontally on the first paragraph.

q. Select the tabbed text, beginning with *Check-in* and ending with *3:00-3:30*. Modify the 7″ right tab to include a dot leader.

r. Check spelling and grammar, correcting any errors and ignoring those that are not errors. Turn off the nonprinting characters feature.

s. Save and close the file. Based on your instructor's directions, submit w02m2Dentist_LastFirst.

Running Case

New Castle County Technical Services

New Castle County Technical Services (NCCTS) provides technical services to clients in the greater New Castle County, Delaware area. Founded in 2011, the company is rapidly expanding to include technical security systems, network infrastructure cabling, and basic troubleshooting services. With that growth comes the need to promote the company and to provide clear written communication to employees and clients. Microsoft Word is used exclusively in the development and distribution of documents, including an "About New Castle" summary that will be available both in print and online. You made a few changes to the document and you are now ready to make this into a professional-looking business document in this exercise.

a. Open *w02r1NewCastle* and save it as **w02r1NewCastle_LastFirst**.

b. Change the document theme to **Facet**, theme colors to **Grayscale**, and theme fonts to **Office**. Show nonprinting characters.

c. Select the first paragraph on page 3 of the document, *About New Castle, Inc.* Insert WordArt, selecting **Fill: Gray, Accent color 3; Sharp Bevel** (second row, fifth column). Ensure that the font size of the WordArt object is **36**.

d. Wrap text around the WordArt object as **Top and Bottom**. Format the WordArt object with Shape Style **Subtle Effect – Light Gray, Accent 2** (fourth row, third column). Visually center the WordArt object on the first paragraph of the document.

e. Place the insertion point in front of the *On Staff Personnel Experience and Certifications* heading on page 4 and insert a page break. Select all the bullets in this section, beginning with *Electrical, Mechanical* and ending with *CompTIA Security+, A+, Server+, Network+*, and format the selected text into two columns with a line in between. Change the font of the columned text to **Century Schoolbook**.

f. Click to place the insertion point before the *Experience and Certifications* heading on page 4. Insert the *w02r1Digital* file from your student data folder. Size the picture with a height of **2″**. Select **Top and Bottom text wrapping** and a picture style of **Reflected Rounded Rectangle**. Position the picture so that it is right below the *Experience and Certifications* heading.

g. Select the picture and recolor it to coordinate with the gray theme of the document. Choose the **Cement Artistic effect**. Delete the blank page if needed.

h. Scroll to page 4, select the 14 bullets right below the *On Staff Personnel Experience and Certifications* heading, and then change the bullets to a **diamond shape**. With the bulleted items selected, click the **Bullets arrow** and click **Define New Bullet**. Change the font color to **Light Gray, Accent 1 Darker 50%**. Open the Styles pane and create a new style named **GrayDiamond**.

i. Select the three sub-items in the last bullet and apply the **square bullet** to them.

j. Scroll to the last page, and select and remove the bullets from the list of 6 companies in the *A Few of Our Customers* section. Delete all the tab stops between company information and time frame information. Set a left tab at **1″** and a right tab with a dot leader at **5″**. Press **Tab** once to move selected paragraphs to the left tab and move the time frame information of each clients to the 5″ tab stop.

k. Save and close the file. Based on your instructor's directions, submit w02r1NewCastle_LastFirst.

Disaster Recovery

Fundraising Letter

Each year, you update a letter to several community partners soliciting support for an auction. The auction raises funds for your organization, and your letter should impress your supporters. Open *w02d1Auction* and notice how unprofessional and unorganized the document looks so far. You must make changes immediately to improve the appearance. Consider replacing much of the formatting that is in place now and instead use columns for auction items, apply bullets to draw attention to the list of forms, page borders, and pictures or images—and that is just for starters! Save your work as **w02d1Auction_LastFirst** and close the file. Based on your instructor's directions, submit w02d1Auction_LastFirst.

Sam's Gym

You are the newly hired membership director of Sam's Gym and one of your responsibilities is to put together a membership package providing essential information to the new members. You quickly collected information from various sources and wrote a draft about the gym and its services. Now you are ready to format the draft to enhance readability and highlight important information. You will use skills from this chapter to format multiple levels of headings, arrange and space text, and insert graphics.

Applying Styles

This document is ready for enhancements, and the Styles feature is a good tool that enables you to add them quickly and easily.

1. Open *w02c1SamGym* and save it as **w02c1SamGym_LastFirst**.

2. Change the document theme to **Integral**, theme colors to **Median**, and theme fonts to **Cambria**.

3. Press **Ctrl+Home**. Create a paragraph style named **Title_Page_1** with these formats: **22 pt** font size and **Ice Blue, Accent 1, Darker 25%** font color (fifth row, fifth column). Ensure that this style is applied to the first paragraph of the document, *Sam's Gym* (including the colon).

4. Select the second paragraph, *Membership Information*, change the font size to **16**, and then apply a font color of **Ice Blue, Accent 1, Darker 25%**.

5. Place the insertion point after the colon in the line *Updated by:* and type your first and last names. Change the capitalization for your name to **Small caps**.

6. Select the remainder of the text in the document, starting with *Introduction* and ending with *MEMBERSHIP FEES*. Justify the alignment of selected text and change line spacing to **1.15**. Place the insertion point on the left side of the *Introduction* paragraph and insert a page break (not a section break).

7. Apply **Heading 1 style** to *Introduction* and *Facility Description* on page 2, *Activities* on page 3, and *Membership Fees* on page 4. Apply **Heading 2 style** to paragraph headings, including *Operational Hours, Holiday Hours, Childcare Hours, Group Exercise Class Description*, and *Individual Training Packages*.

8. Modify the Heading 2 style to use the **Dark Red font color**.

Formatting the Paragraphs

Next, you will apply paragraph formatting to the document. These format options will further increase the readability and attractiveness of your document.

9. Select the second body paragraph in the *Mission Statement* section, which begins with *Mission Statement* and ends with *individual training programs*, and apply these formats: **1″ left** and **right indents**, **6 pt** spacing after the paragraph, **boxed double-line**, **3/4 pt** border using the color **Dark Red**, and the shading color **Ice Blue, Accent 1, Lighter 80%**. Delete the blank paragraph above the *Facility Description* heading.

10. Select the nine holidays listed in the *Holiday Hours* section and display them in two columns with a line between the columns.

11. Apply a bulleted list format to the 6 paragraphs in the *Group Exercise Class Description* section on page 3 starting with *Gentle Strength* and ending with *low impact Zumba moves*. Use the symbol of a **diamond**.

12. Apply a **bulleted list format** for the 10-item list in the second paragraph of the *Group Exercise Class Description* section on page 3 starting with *Barre* and ending with *music while burning calories*. Use the symbol of a **solid round circle**.

13. Apply the **numbered list format (1., 2., 3.)** to the four types of packages in the *Individual Training Packages* section.

14. Apply a **1″ left tab** and a **4″ right tab** with a dot leader to the three schedule items in the *Childcare Hours* section on page 3.

Inserting Graphics

To put the finishing touches on your document, you will add graphics that enhance the explanations given in some paragraphs.

15. Insert the picture file *w02c1Gym.jpg* at the beginning of the paragraph that contains *Welcome to Sam's Gym* in the *Introduction* section. Change the height of the picture to **2″**. Change text wrapping to **Top and Bottom**, and apply the **Center Shadow Rectangle Picture Style** and the **Film Grain Artistic Effect**. Position the picture so that it appears below the *Introduction* heading.

16. Insert the picture file *w02c1Swimming.jpg* at the blank paragraph below the paragraph beginning with *The gym is founded by Sam* in the *Facility Description* section. Change the height of the picture to **2.1″** and text wrapping to **Top and Bottom**. Apply the **Simple Frame, White Picture Style** (first row, first column) to the graphic. Position the picture so that it displays below the *Facility Description* paragraph and ensure that it stays at the bottom of page 2.

17. Insert an online picture from Bing Search using the search word **yoga** at the beginning of the *Group Exercise Class Description* heading. Delete additional text boxes from the online picture. Change the height of the picture to **2.5″** and text wrapping to **Top and Bottom**. Apply the **Reflected Bevel, White Picture Style**. Position the picture so that it is below the *Group Exercise Class Description* heading.

18. Check spelling and grammar, correcting any errors and ignoring those that are not errors, and review the entire document.

19. Display the document in Outline view. Collapse all paragraphs so only lines formatted as Heading 1 or Heading 2 display. Move the *Membership Fees* section to above the *Activities* section and delete the soft return above the *Operational Hours* heading. Close Outline view.

20. Save and close the file. Based on your instructor's directions, submit w02c1SamGym_LastFirst.

LEARNING OUTCOMES
You will demonstrate how tables are used to organize and present information. You will apply mail merge to create personalized letters.

OBJECTIVES & SKILLS: After you read this chapter, you will be able to:

CASE STUDY | Traylor University Economic Impact Study

As director of marketing and research for Traylor University, a mid-sized university in northwest Nebraska, you have been involved with an economic impact study during the past year. The study is designed to measure as closely as possible the contribution of the university to the local and state economy. An evaluation of data led university researchers to conclude that Traylor University serves as a critical economic driver in the local community and, to a lesser extent, the state of Nebraska. It is your job to summarize those findings and see that they are accurately reflected in the final report.

Your assistant has prepared a draft of an executive summary that you will present to the board of trustees, outlining the major findings and conclusions. The best way to present some of the data analysis will be through tables, which your assistant is not very familiar with, so you will take responsibility for that phase of the summary preparation. You will send an executive summary, along with a cover letter, to community and university leaders. You will use Word's mail merge feature to prepare personalized letters.

CHAPTER 3

Working with Tables and Mail Merge

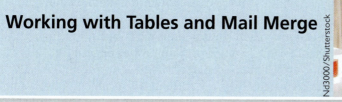

Nd3000/Shutterstock

FIGURE 3.1 Traylor University Documents

CASE STUDY | Traylor University Economic Impact Study

Starting Files	Files to be Submitted
w03h1Traylor w03h2KeyFindings w03h2Text w03h3Letter w03h3Trustees.xlsx	w03h2Traylor_LastFirst w03h3Merged_LastFirst

MyLab IT Grader An alternate version of this project is available as a MyLab IT Grader Assessment

Tables

A *table* is a grid of columns and rows that organizes data. As shown in Figure 3.2, a table is typically configured with headings in the first row and related data in the following rows. The intersection of each column and row is a *cell*, in which you can type data. A table is an excellent format in which to summarize numeric data because you can easily align numbers and even include formulas to sum or average numbers in a column or row. Text can be included in a table as well. Although you can use tabs to align text in columns in a Word document, you might find it quicker to create a table than to set tabs, and you have more control over format and design when using a table.

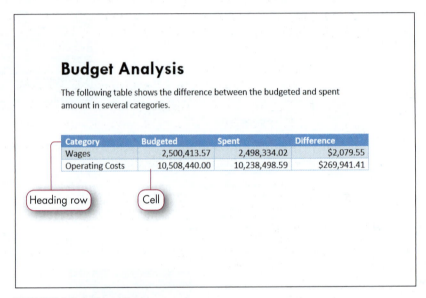

FIGURE 3.2 A Word Table

Word's Table feature is a comprehensive but easy-to-use tool, enabling you to insert a table, add and remove rows and columns, format table elements, include formulas to summarize numbers in a table, and customize borders and shading. You can always change a table, or format it differently, even after it is developed.

In this section, you will learn to insert a table. After positioning the table within a document, you will explore inserting and deleting columns and rows, merging and splitting cells, and adjusting row height and column width. Using table styles, you will modify the appearance of a table, and you will adjust table position and alignment.

Inserting a Table

Inserting a table in a document is an easy task. You can either create a table with uniformly spaced rows and columns, or you can draw a table with the pointer, creating rows and columns of varying heights and widths. Regardless of how a table is created, you can always change table settings so that rows and columns better fit the data included in the table.

When you create a table, you specify the number of columns and rows that should be included. For example, the table shown in Figure 3.2 is a 4×3 table, which means it contains four columns and three rows.

STEP 1 Create or Draw a Table

A table is an object; as such, it can be selected and manipulated independently of surrounding text. You can insert a table in a few ways, beginning by clicking the Insert tab and clicking Table. At that point, you can select from three different methods of creating tables:

- Drag to select the number of columns or rows to include in the table, as shown in Figure 3.3. Click in the bottom-right cell of the selection.
- Click Insert Table to display the Insert Table dialog box, where you can indicate the number of rows and columns you want to include. Click OK.
- Click Quick Tables to insert a predesigned table, including such items as calendars, tabular lists, and matrices.

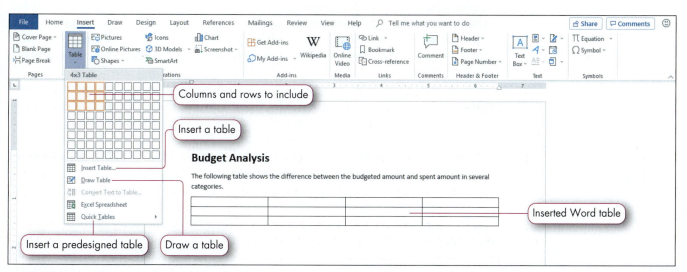

FIGURE 3.3 Inserting a Table

Instead of inserting a table by indicating the number of columns or rows to include, as described in the previous set of steps, you can draw a table. You might choose to draw a table if you know that rows and/or columns should have varying heights or widths. It is sometimes easier to draw rows and columns of varying dimensions when a table is created rather than to modify the dimensions later, as would be necessary if you use the Insert Table feature to create evenly distributed columns and rows.

> **To draw a table, complete the following steps:**
>
> 1. Click the Insert tab and click Table in the Tables group.
> 2. Click Draw Table (refer to Figure 3.3). As you move the pointer over the document, it resembles a pencil.
> 3. Drag a rectangle and then draw horizontal and vertical lines to create rows and columns within the rectangular table space.
> 4. Press Esc when the table is complete.

After the table structure is created, you can enter characters, numbers, or graphics in cells, moving from one cell to another when you press Tab or a directional arrow key. You can also click a cell to move to it. As you type text in a cell, it is automatically left-aligned, although you can adjust alignment with options on the Table Tools Layout tab or on the Home tab. If typed text requires more space than is available, the text will wrap and the row height will adjust when it reaches the right edge of the cell. To force text to a new line in a cell (before reaching the right cell border), press Enter. You can instead insert a soft return by pressing Shift+Enter, which forces text to a new line in a cell, but without any additional paragraph spacing.

Insert and Delete Rows and Columns

If a table structure needs to be modified, you can insert or delete columns and rows. For example, suppose you have inserted a table and typed text in cells. As you enter data into a table and complete the last row, you find that an additional row is required. Press Tab to begin a new row. Continue entering data and pressing Tab to create new rows until the table is complete.

Occasionally, you will want to insert a row above or below an existing row, when the row is not the last row in the table. You might even want to insert a column to the left or right of a column in a table. You can insert rows or columns by clicking an **insert control** that displays when you point to the edge of a row or column gridline, as shown in Figure 3.4. To insert several rows or columns, drag to select the number of rows or columns to insert, and click the insert control.

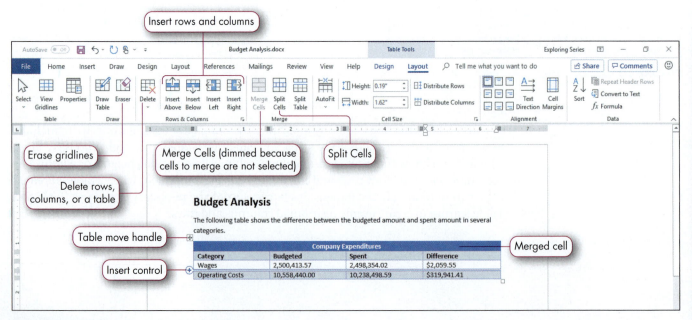

FIGURE 3.4 Working with Rows and Columns

Although it is convenient to use the insert control to insert rows and columns, the Table Tools Layout tab includes more comprehensive options that enable you to insert both columns and rows. Select from options in the Rows & Columns group (refer to Figure 3.4) to insert rows or columns. You can also delete rows or columns.

When you delete a table, you remove the entire table, including all table contents. Although you can select contents and delete them, the table structure remains as an empty set of rows and columns. The key to deleting a table is to first select the table by clicking the table move handle in the top left corner of the table (refer to Figure 3.4). At that point, you can complete any of the following options:

- Right-click the selected table and select Delete Table from the shortcut menu.
- Click Delete in the Rows & Columns group on the Table Tools Layout tab and select Delete Table.
- Press Backspace.

STEP 2 Merge and Split Cells

The first row of the table shown in Figure 3.4 is a merged cell. When several cells are combined into one, the new cell is considered a merged cell. If you want to place a title across the top of a table or center a label over columns or rows of data, you can merge cells. After selecting cells to merge, use Merge Cells on the Table Tools Layout tab to complete the merge. Once cells are merged, you can align data in the merged cells and change the font size to create a table title. You can also erase one or more gridlines within the table. The Eraser tool on the Table Tools Layout tab enables you to remove gridlines (refer to Figure 3.4). Click the Eraser tool and click any table gridline to erase it. Press Esc or click the Eraser tool again to toggle off the eraser.

Conversely, you might want to split a single cell into multiple cells. You can split a selected row or column to provide additional detail in separate cells. Splitting cells is an option on the Table Tools Layout tab (refer to Figure 3.4).

Change Row Height and Column Width

An inserted table is a grid of evenly spaced columns and rows. As mentioned earlier, text automatically wraps within a cell and the row height adjusts to accommodate the entry. Row height is the vertical distance from the top to the bottom of a row, whereas column width is the horizontal space from the left to the right edge of a column. You can manually adjust row height or column width to modify the appearance of a table, perhaps making it more readable or more attractive. Increasing row height can better fit a header that has been enlarged for emphasis. You can increase column width to display a wide area of text, such as a first and last name, to prevent wrapping of text in a cell.

A simple, but not very precise way to change row height or column width is to position the pointer on a border so that it displays as ⊪, which is a line with double pointed arrows, and drag to increase or reduce height or width. For more precision, you can use ribbon commands to adjust row height or column width. After selecting a row or column to be adjusted, change the height or width in the Cell Size group on the Table Tools Layout tab. Alternatively, you can right-click the selected row or column and select Table Properties on the shortcut menu. You can then work with selections from the Column tab or Row tab in the dialog box, as shown in Figure 3.5.

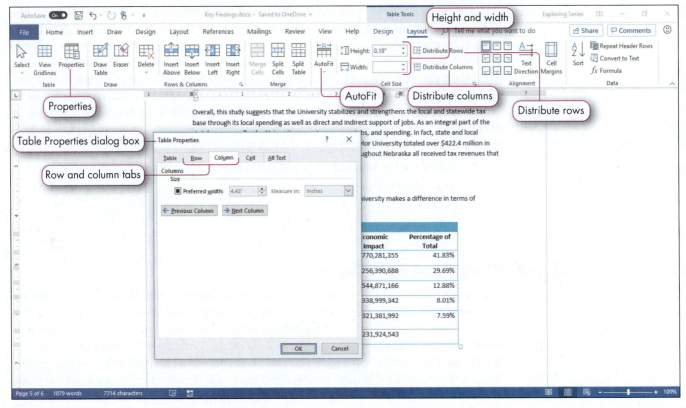

FIGURE 3.5 Changing Row Height and Column Width

You can evenly distribute selected columns and rows to ensure that they are the same height and/or width. Select the columns and rows and click Distribute Rows (or Distribute Columns) in the Cell Size group on the Table Tools Layout tab (refer to Figure 3.5). Distributing rows and columns ensures uniformity within a table.

Instead of adjusting individual columns and rows, you can format a table with column and row dimensions that accommodate all cell entries. The feature, called AutoFit, automatically adjusts rows and columns. After clicking in any cell, select AutoFit on the Table Tools Layout tab (refer to Figure 3.5) and choose to AutoFit Contents.

Formatting a Table

After a table is inserted in a document, you can enhance its appearance by applying coordinated colors, borders, shading, and other design elements. Just as you format other document text by boldfacing, italicizing, or otherwise modifying it, you can format text within a table. You can also align text within cells by selecting an alignment from the Alignment group on the Table Tools Layout tab. Lists or series within cells can be bulleted or numbered, and you can indent table text. A table can be positioned and moved to any location on a page.

STEP 3 · Apply and Modify Table Styles

Word provides several predesigned *table styles* that contain borders, shading, font sizes, and other attributes that enhance the readability of a document. Use a table style when you want to create a color-coordinated, professional document or when you do not want to design your own custom borders and shading.

> **TIP: USING TABLE STYLES**
> When you apply a table style or manually modify table shading and color selections, the color choices are associated with the theme in use. Therefore, if you change the document theme, the color selections applied through a table style or manual selections are likely to also change.

As shown in Figure 3.6, the Table Styles gallery provides styles for Plain, List, and Grid tables, although the size of each gallery prohibits all three groups from displaying at once. Select a style from the Table Styles group on the Table Tools Design tab. In Live Preview, the result of a style selection will show as you point to a style in the gallery.

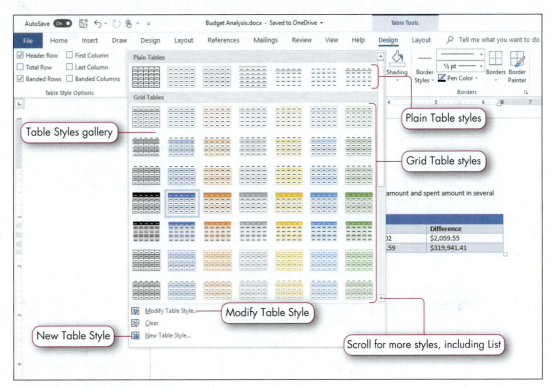

FIGURE 3.6 Working with Table Styles

After choosing a table style, you can modify it, as shown in Figure 3.6. As you modify a table style, you can apply changes to the entire table or to elements such as the header row. In that way, you can adjust a style so that it better suits your purposes. If you have modified a table style and want to make the style available for use in other documents, select New Table Style at the bottom of the Table Styles gallery. Otherwise, choose to save the changes for use only in the current document.

Adjust Table Position and Alignment

Table alignment refers to the horizontal position of a table between the left and right document margins. When you insert a table, it aligns at the left margin, although you can change the alignment, choosing to center the table or align it at the right margin. Right-click any cell and choose Table Properties (or select Properties from the Table Tools Layout tab) to display the Table Properties dialog box shown in Figure 3.7. You can also select alignment options on the ribbon.

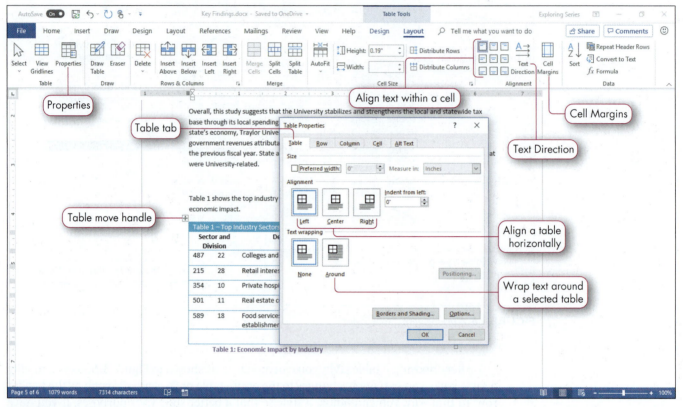

FIGURE 3.7 Adjusting Table and Text Alignment

Move a table to any location within the document when you drag the table move handle. As you move the table, a dashed border displays, indicating the position of the table. Release the mouse button to position the table.

Text within cells can be aligned using alignment options on the Table Tools Layout tab. You can align cell contents both vertically and horizontally within the current cell, as indicated in Figure 3.7. Especially when working with a small table that does not require much document space, you might find it useful to wrap text around the table so that the table is better incorporated visually into the document, much as you would do when wrapping text around a picture or object in a document. Figure 3.7 illustrates the use of text wrapping with a table. Text will wrap on the right side of a left-aligned table, on both sides of a centered table, and on the left side of a right-aligned table. If you select None in the Text Wrapping section, text is prevented from wrapping, ensuring that text displays only above and below a table.

Format Table Text

Text within a cell can be formatted just as any other text in a document. Select text to format and apply one or more font attributes such as font type, font size, underline, boldface, or italics.

By default, text within a cell is oriented horizontally so that it reads from left to right. On occasion, you might want to change that direction. Lengthy column headings can be oriented vertically, so that they require less space. Or perhaps a table includes a row of cells repeating a telephone number, with each cell designed to be ripped from the bottom of a printed document. Such cells are often in a vertical format for ease of removal. Cycle through Text Direction options on the Table Tools Layout tab (refer to Figure 3.7) to rotate text in the current cell.

The Cell Margins command in the Alignment group enables you to adjust the amount of white space inside a cell as well as spacing between cells. With additional empty space shown between typed entries, a table can appear more open and readable. Other times, you will want to remove extra space created by cell margins such as when preparing a photo layout in a Word table in which you do not want to display any space at all between photos.

Quick Concepts

1. Explain why it is sometimes beneficial to merge cells in a table, as well as when it might be best to split cells. *p. 199*

2. Describe a table that would be best designed by drawing instead of inserting. *p. 197*

3. Describe a situation in which you would want to increase cell margins. Also provide an example of when reducing cell margins would be beneficial. *p. 203*

Hands-On Exercises

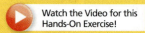
Skills covered: Create or Draw a Table • Insert and Delete Rows and Columns • Merge and Split Cells • Change Row Height and Column Width • Apply and Modify Table Styles • Adjust Table Position and Alignment • Format Table Text

1 Tables

The executive summary is the first section of the economic impact report for Traylor University. Although the summary is already well organized, the data analysis part of the summary needs some attention. Specifically, you develop tables to organize major findings.

STEP 1 CREATE A TABLE AND INSERT AND DELETE ROWS AND COLUMNS

You modify a couple of tables to summarize study findings, including those tables in the executive summary. As you develop or edit the tables, you find it necessary to insert rows to accommodate additional data and to delete columns that are not actually required. Refer to Figure 3.8 as you complete Step 1.

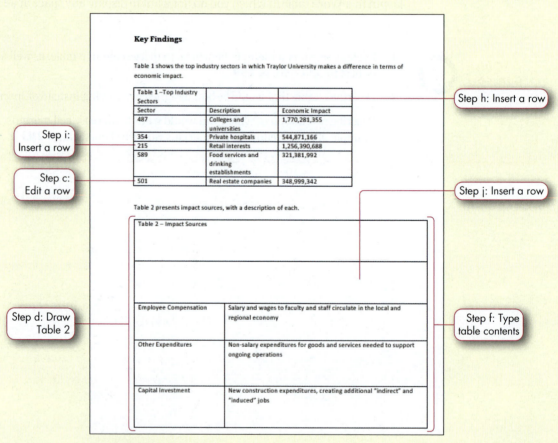

FIGURE 3.8 Report Tables

a. Open *w03h1Traylor* and save it as **w03h1Traylor_LastFirst**.

> **TROUBLESHOOTING:** If you make any major mistakes in this exercise, you can close the file, open *w03h1Traylor* again and then start this exercise over.

b. Click the **View tab** and ensure that Ruler is selected in the Show group. Ensure that non-printing characters are shown. Move to the last page of the document and click in the first cell on the last row of the table.

c. Type the following text on the last row, tabbing between cells. Do not press Tab after the last entry.

501	Real estate companies	Land	348,999,342

You completed the entry of data in a table to indicate community and state interests that are positively impacted by the presence of Traylor University.

> **TROUBLESHOOTING:** If you press Tab after the last entry, a new row is created. Click Undo. If the insertion point moves to a new line within a cell instead of advancing to another cell or row, you pressed Enter instead of Tab between entries. Press Backspace and press Tab. Do not press Tab if you are in the last cell on the last row.

d. Press **Ctrl+End** to position the insertion point at the end of the document. Click the **Insert tab**, click **Table** in the Tables group, and then click **Draw Table**. The pointer displays as [icon]. Drag a box approximately six inches wide and four inches tall, using the vertical and horizontal rulers as guides. Draw one vertical gridline at two inches from the left to create two columns—the first column approximately two inches wide, and the second at four inches wide. Draw three horizontal gridlines to divide the table into four approximately evenly spaced rows of about one inch each. Press **Esc** or click **Draw Table** in the Draw group on the Table Tools Layout tab to toggle the tool off.

> **TROUBLESHOOTING:** It is possible that the lines you draw to form the table are in a color or style other than black. That occurs if someone using the same computer previously selected a different pen color. For this exercise, it will not matter what color the table borders are.

It is OK if the row height is not identical for each row. Simply approximate the required height for each.

e. Click **Eraser** in the Draw group and click to erase the vertical gridline in the first row, so that the row includes only one column. Click **Eraser** to toggle off the eraser.

> **TROUBLESHOOTING:** If you make any mistakes while erasing gridlines, press Esc. Click Undo to undo your actions.

f. Ensure the insertion point is in the first row, type **Table 2 - Impact Sources**. (Do not type the period.) Press **Tab** and complete the table as follows (do not press Tab at the end of the last entry):

Employee Compensation	Salary and wages to faculty and staff circulate in the local and regional economy
Other Expenditures	Non-salary expenditures for goods and services needed to support ongoing operations
Capital Investment	New construction expenditures, creating additional "indirect" and "induced" jobs

Text you type will wrap within some cells. You will resize the columns later, so leave the text as it appears.

g. Position the pointer just above the *Category* column in Table 1, so that the pointer resembles [↓]. Click to select the column. Click **Delete** in the Rows & Columns group on the Table Tools Layout tab and select **Delete Columns**.

h. Click anywhere in **row 1** of Table 1. Click **Insert Above** in the Rows & Columns group. Click in the **first cell** in the new row and type **Table 1 - Top Industry Sectors**. (Do not type the period.)

Text will wrap within the first cell.

APPLY AND MODIFY TABLE STYLES, ADJUST TABLE POSITION AND ALIGNMENT, AND FORMAT TABLE TEXT

The tables included in the Key Findings section are complete with respect to content, but you realize that they could be far more attractive with a bit of color and appropriate shading. You explore Word's gallery of table styles. You also bold and center column headings and explore aligning the tables horizontally on the page. Refer to Figure 3.10 as you complete Step 3.

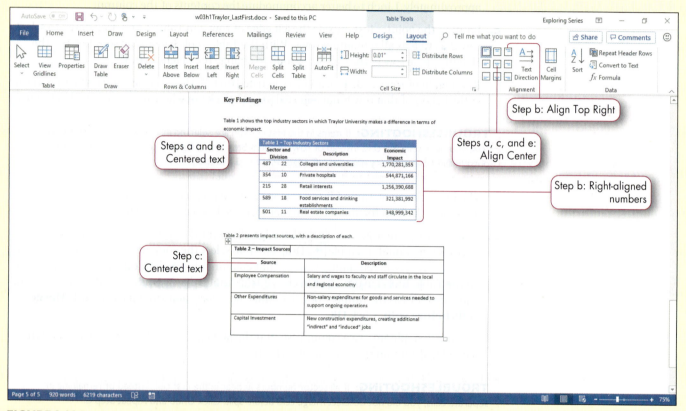

FIGURE 3.10 Formatting and Aligning a Table

a. Select the **second row** in Table 1. Click **Align Center** in the Alignment group on the Table Tools Layout tab.

Text in row 2 is centered both vertically and horizontally within each cell.

b. Select the cells containing numbers in the rightmost column of Table 1 (beginning with 1,770,281,355 and ending with 348,999,342). Click **Align Top Right** in the Alignment group. Click anywhere to deselect the cells. Position the pointer on the right border of the rightmost column of Table 1 so that it resembles ⊣⊢. Drag to the left to reduce the column so that the width is approximately **1″**, better accommodating the contents of the column.

c. Select the **second row** in Table 2, containing column headings. Click **Align Center** in the Alignment group. With the column headings selected, click the **Home tab** and click **Bold** in the Font group. Bold the contents of row 1 in Table 2.

d. Bold the contents of the first two rows in Table 1. Click anywhere in Table 1, click the **Table Tools Design tab**, and click **More** in the Table Styles group. Scroll through the gallery and select **List Table 3 - Accent 1** (row 3, column 2 under List Tables). You must scroll through the list of styles to locate the List Tables area.

The table style removed some of the formatting from Table 1, applying color-coordinated font color, shading, and a colored border. The style also removed the inside vertical borders.

e. Click the **First Column check box** in the Table Style Options group to deselect it. Click the **Table Tools Layout tab**. Select the **second row** in Table 1 (containing column headings) and click **Align Center** in the Alignment group.

f. Click the **View tab** and click **One Page** in the Zoom group to view the current page. Note that the tables are not centered on the page horizontally. Click **100%** in the Zoom group.

g. Right-click anywhere in **Table 1** and select **Table Properties**. Click **Center** in the Alignment group of the Table tab in the Table Properties dialog box to center the table horizontally. Click **OK**. Repeat this technique to center Table 2 horizontally. Click **One Page** in the Zoom group to view the effects of the realignment. Click **100%**.

h. Save the document. Keep the document open if you plan to continue with the next Hands-On Exercise. If not, close the document, and exit Word.

As an example, the expression =C12+C15*1.8 is evaluated as follows: Multiply cell C15 by 1.8 and add the result to cell C12. If, however, you wanted the addition to be performed first, you would enclose that calculation in parentheses. Because the use of parentheses has a higher order of operation than multiplication, that addition would be done first, and the result would be multiplied by 1.8.

> **TIP: UPDATING A FORMULA**
> Unlike Microsoft Excel, a formula in a table is not automatically updated when the contents of cells referenced by the formula change. However, you can manually update a formula. Right-click the cell containing the formula and select Update Field. On a Mac, you must first select the value and then update the field.

Common equations, such as the area of a circle, and more complex equations, such as the quadratic formula, are available to be incorporated into a document or table. The Equation command on the Insert tab provides a list of equations and enables you to create your own. The formula is created in a placeholder, so you can manage it independently of surrounding text. Most math symbols and operators are not located on the keyboard; however, you can create a formula so that it seamlessly integrates with surrounding text by making selections from the Symbols group on the Insert tab or the Equation Tools Design tab, shown when you click the Insert tab and select Equation from the Symbols group.

Use a Function

Word provides *functions*, which are built-in formulas, to simplify the task of performing basic calculations. A function uses values in a table to produce a result. For example, the SUM function totals values in a series of cells, whereas the COUNT function identifies the number of entries in a series of cells. The total scholarship amount, that is included in the Total row shown in Figure 3.11, is calculated with a SUM function, which adds the values in the column above. In most cases, a function provides an alternative to what would otherwise be a much lengthier calculation.

To determine a final scholarship amount in the Total row of the table shown in Figure 3.11, you could click in the cell underneath the last scholarship award amount and add all cells individually in the fourth column, as in =D2+D3+D4+D5+D6, continuing to list cells in the range through D13. A *range* is a series of adjacent cells. Although the formula would produce a final total, the formula would be extremely lengthy. Imagine the formula length in a more realistic situation in which hundreds of students received a scholarship! A much more efficient approach would be to use a SUM function, in which you indicate, by position, the series of cells to total. For example, the function to produce a total scholarship amount is =SUM(ABOVE). Similarly, a function to produce an average scholarship amount is =AVERAGE(ABOVE). In fact, you can select from various table functions, as shown in Table 3.1. The positional information within parentheses is referred to as an *argument*. Positional information indicates the position of the data being calculated. You can use positional notation of ABOVE, BELOW, LEFT, or RIGHT as arguments. An argument of ABOVE indicates that data to be summarized is located above the cell containing the function. Although not a comprehensive list, the functions shown in Table 3.1 are commonly used. Note that an argument will be included within parentheses in each function.

TABLE 3.1	Table Functions
Function	**Action**
=SUM(argument)	Totals a series of cells
=AVERAGE(argument)	Averages a series of cells
=COUNT(argument)	Counts the number of entries in a series of cells
=MAX(argument)	Displays the largest number in a series of cells
=MIN(argument)	Displays the smallest number in a series of cells

To place a formula or function in a table cell, complete the following steps:

1. Click in the cell that is to contain the result of the calculation. For example, click in cell D14 of the table shown in Figure 3.11 to include a function totaling all scholarship amounts.
2. Click Formula in the Data group on the Table Tools Layout tab.
3. Type a formula or edit the suggested function. Alternatively, you can click the Paste function, select a function, and then type an argument. Click OK.

> **TIP: COMBINING ARGUMENTS**
>
> Combine arguments in a function to indicate cells to include. For example, =SUM(ABOVE,BELOW) totals numeric cells above and below the current cell. =SUM(LEFT,ABOVE) totals numeric cells to the left and above the current cell, whereas =SUM(RIGHT,BELOW) totals numeric cells to the right and below the current cell. Combine any two arguments, separated by a comma, to indicate cells to include.

STEP 2 · Sort Data in a Table

Columns of text, dates, or numbers in a Word table can be sorted alphabetically, chronologically, or numerically. The table shown in Figure 3.11 is sorted alphabetically in ascending order by student name. It might be beneficial to sort the data in Figure 3.11 by date, so that scholarship awards are shown in chronological order. Or you could sort table rows numerically by award amount, with highest awards shown first, followed in descending order by lesser award amounts. You might even want to sort awards alphabetically by major, with scholarship award amounts within programs of study shown in order from low to high. Such a sort uses a primary category (major, in this case) and a secondary category (award amount). You can sort a Word table by up to three categories.

A table is often designed so that the first row contains column headings. Those column headings, also called a header row, serve as categories that you can sort by. As you conduct a sort, described in the following steps, you should first indicate whether the table has a header row. In doing so, you can then select one or more sort categories. Even if a table has no header row, you can select rows to sort and indicate which column to sort by.

To sort table rows, complete the following steps:

1. Click anywhere in the table (or click in the column to sort by).
2. Click Sort in the Data group on the Table Tools Layout tab.
3. Specify whether the table includes a header row.
4. Indicate or confirm the primary category, or column, to sort by (along with the sort order, either ascending or descending), as shown in Figure 3.13.
5. Select any other sort columns and indicate or confirm the sort order. Click OK.

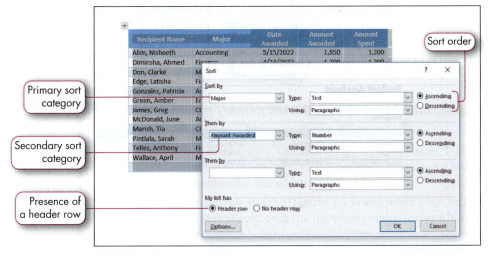

FIGURE 3.13 Sorting a Table

As shown in Figure 3.15, the Design tab also includes options for selecting shading. *Shading* applies color or a pattern to the background of a cell or group of cells. You might want to apply shading to a header row to emphasize it, setting it apart from the rows beneath. Apply shading to selected areas by choosing from options on the Table Tools Design tab. The Shading option provides various color selections, whereas the Borders option enables you to open the Borders and Shading dialog box, from which you click the Shading tab for shading choices.

TIP: USING BORDER SAMPLER

After applying a custom border or border style to one or more borders in a table, you can copy the selection to other table borders. You can easily accomplish this task using Border Sampler. Click the Border Styles arrow (refer to Figure 3.15) and click Border Sampler. The pointer becomes an eyedropper tool; click a table border that you want to copy. The pointer automatically switches to the Border Painter tool, as indicated by the ink pen designation or a paintbrush, if using a Mac, so you can brush another border to apply the border selection.

STEP 4 ▶ **Convert Text to a Table and Convert a Table to Text**

Suppose you are working with a list of items organized into two areas, with each item separated from the next by a comma, tab, or a paragraph marker. For example, you develop a list of items in a sale along with each respective price, with the items and prices separated by a tab. You know that if the areas, or columns, were organized as a table, you could easily apply a table style, sort rows, and even use formulas to summarize numeric information. In that case, you can convert text to a table.

To convert text to a table, complete the following steps:

1. Select text to be converted.
2. Click the Insert tab and click Table in the Tables group.
3. Click Convert Text to Table.
4. Select options from the Convert Text to Table dialog box (see Figure 3.16), including the number of columns and rows to include.
5. Click OK.

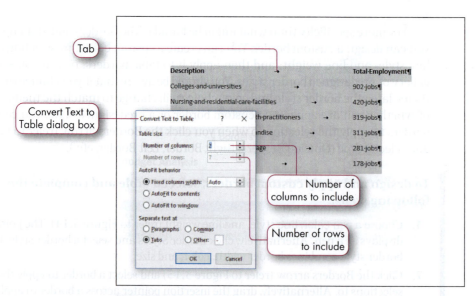

FIGURE 3.16 Converting Text to a Table

Conversely, you might identify a need to convert table text to plain text, removing special table features, and then organizing columns into simple tabbed columns.

To convert a table to text, complete the following steps:

1. Click anywhere in the table.
2. Click Convert to Text in the Data group on the Table Tools Layout tab.
3. Indicate how table text is to be divided in the Convert Table to Text dialog box (see Figure 3.17).
4. Click OK.

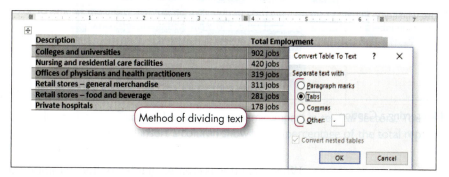

FIGURE 3.17 Converting a Table to Text

Include a Table Caption

A **caption**, such as *Table 1*, is a numbered item of text that identifies a table, figure, or other object in a Word document. A particular writing style may be required for class papers or published works. This style will prescribe a standard set of guidelines, including the usage of captions. A caption is often used to cite a table that came from a research source. A caption typically includes a label, such as the word *Figure* or *Table*, followed by a sequential number that can be automatically updated with the addition of new tables or captioned objects.

To include a table caption, complete the following steps:

1. Click a cell in the table.
2. Click the References tab and click Insert Caption in the Captions group. The Caption dialog box displays, as shown in Figure 3.18. Because you are providing a caption to a table, the word *Table* displays in the Label box, although that can be changed to *Figure* or *Equation*. Depending on the wording of the caption, you might find that a label is unnecessary or even redundant. In that case, select the check box to exclude the label from the caption.
3. Click the Position arrow and indicate a caption position—above or below the table.
4. Click Numbering to select a numbering style (1, 2, 3, or A, B, C, for example).
5. Click OK to close the dialog box.

STEP 1 Use an Excel Worksheet as a Data Source

An Excel worksheet organizes data in columns and rows, and it can be used to develop a data source that can be merged with a main document during a mail merge. With only a bit of introduction, you can learn to enter data in an Excel worksheet, designing columns and rows of data so that a lengthy address list can be easily maintained. With many columns and rows available in a single worksheet, Excel can store a huge number of records, making them available as you create a mail merge document. Figure 3.24 shows an Excel worksheet that can be used as a data source. Note the header row, with records beneath.

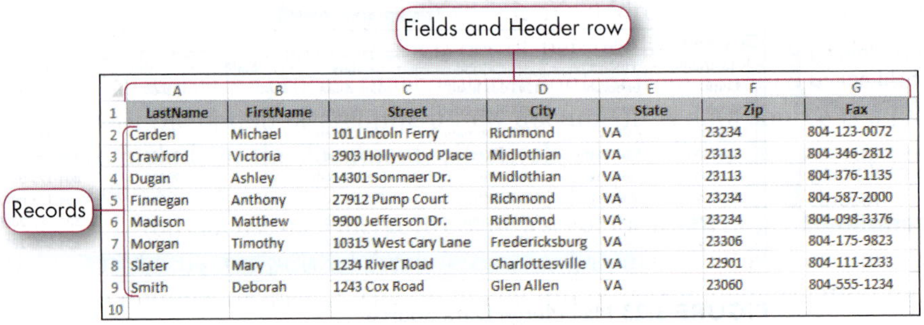

	A	B	C	D	E	F	G
1	LastName	FirstName	Street	City	State	Zip	Fax
2	Carden	Michael	101 Lincoln Ferry	Richmond	VA	23234	804-123-0072
3	Crawford	Victoria	3903 Hollywood Place	Midlothian	VA	23113	804-346-2812
4	Dugan	Ashley	14301 Sonmaer Dr.	Midlothian	VA	23113	804-376-1135
5	Finnegan	Anthony	27912 Pump Court	Richmond	VA	23234	804-587-2000
6	Madison	Matthew	9900 Jefferson Dr.	Richmond	VA	23234	804-098-3376
7	Morgan	Timothy	10315 West Cary Lane	Fredericksburg	VA	23306	804-175-9823
8	Slater	Mary	1234 River Road	Charlottesville	VA	22901	804-111-2233
9	Smith	Deborah	1243 Cox Road	Glen Allen	VA	23060	804-555-1234
10							

FIGURE 3.24 Excel Worksheet

Use an Access Database as a Data Source

As a database program, Microsoft Access is designed to manage large amounts of data. An Access database typically contains one or more tables; each table is a collection of related records that contains fields of information. Access enables you to query a table, which is the process of filtering records to show only those that meet certain search criteria. For example, you might want to view only the records of employees who work in the Accounting department. If you want to send a personalized communication, such as a letter or email, to all employees in the Accounting department, you could use the query as a basis for a mail merge. An Access table is well suited for use as a mail merge data source, due to its datasheet design (approximating an Excel worksheet) and its propensity for filtering records. Figure 3.23 shows a sample Access table that could be used as a data source.

Use a Word Table or an Outlook List as a Data Source

Because a Word table is organized in rows and columns, it is ideal for use as a data source in a mail merge. The first row in the Word table should include descriptive headers, with each subsequent row including a record from which data can be extracted during a mail merge process. The document used in a mail merge must contain a single table.

To merge a main document with an existing data source, click Select Recipients in the Start Mail Merge group on the Mailings tab. Click Use Existing List (see Figure 3.25). Navigate to the Excel, Access, or Word data source and double-click the file.

You can also use a list of Outlook contacts as a data source, which is especially helpful when you have bulk mail to send to your contacts. If you have an Outlook account, you can access basic information included with your contacts, including name, email address, mailing address, and phone number. Select Outlook Contacts as a data source when you begin the process of selecting recipients on the Mailings tab.

FIGURE 3.25 Selecting an Existing List

Edit a Data Source

Before merging a data source with the main document, you can rearrange records in the data source so that output from a mail merge is arranged accordingly. For example, you can sort the data source in alphabetical order by last name so that letters are arranged alphabetically or so that mailing labels print in order by last name. Or perhaps data in the data source should be updated, as might be the case if a recipient's address has changed. In addition, you could consider filtering a data source to limit the mail merge output based on criteria. You might, for example, want to print letters to send to clients in a specific region or state. Select Edit Recipient List on the Mailings tab and work with the dialog box shown in Figure 3.26 to edit, sort, filter, or otherwise modify the data source before including its contents in the main document during the mail merge process.

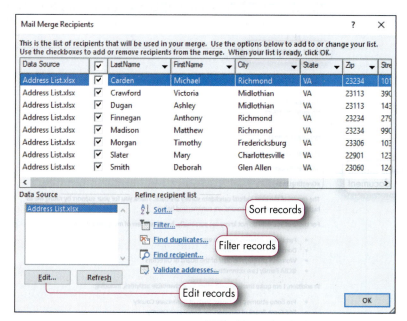

FIGURE 3.26 Editing and Sorting a Data Source

The same data source can be used to create multiple sets of form documents. You could, for example, create a marketing campaign in which you send an initial letter to the entire list, and then send follow-up letters at periodic intervals to the same mailing list. Alternatively, you could filter the original mailing list to include only a subset of names, such as the individuals who responded to the initial letter.

Although the body of the letter will be the same for all recipients, you create merge fields to accommodate variable data, including each recipient's name and address. Refer to Figure 3.30 as you complete Step 3.

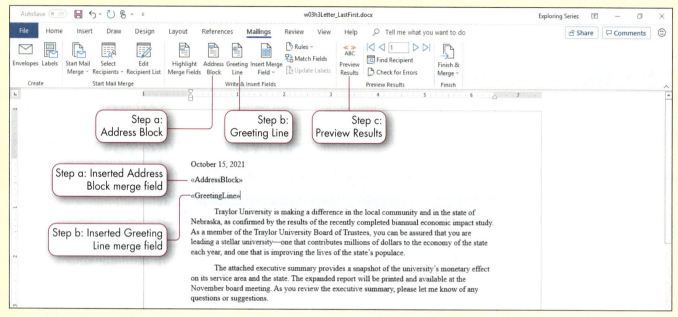

FIGURE 3.30 Inserting Merge Fields

a. Click after *2021* in the first line of the document. Press **Enter** twice. Click **Address Block** in the Write & Insert Fields group. Note the address in the Preview area. Ensure that *Insert recipient's name in this format*, *Insert company name*, and *Insert postal address* are selected. Click **OK**.

   The AddressBlock merge field is inserted, with double chevrons on each side, indicating its status.

> **MAC TROUBLESHOOTING:** Because the Address Block and Greeting Line selections may not be available, click Insert Merge Field and choose fields that comprise the address block and greeting line—Title, First Name, Last Name, etc., ensuring that a space is shown between fields where necessary.

b. Press **Enter**. Click **Greeting Line**. Click **OK**.

   A salutation is added, using the Greeting Line placeholder.

> **TROUBLESHOOTING:** If you make a mistake when entering merge fields, you can backspace or otherwise delete a field.

c. Click **Preview Results** in the Preview Results group.

d. Select the first four lines of the address block, from Ms. Rebecca Hardin through Suite 10. Click the **Layout tab** and remove any paragraph spacing shown in the Paragraph group.

Now that you have inserted merge fields into the form letter, the letter is complete. You will merge the main document with the data source so that each letter is personally addressed and ready to be printed. Refer to Figure 3.31 as you complete Step 4.

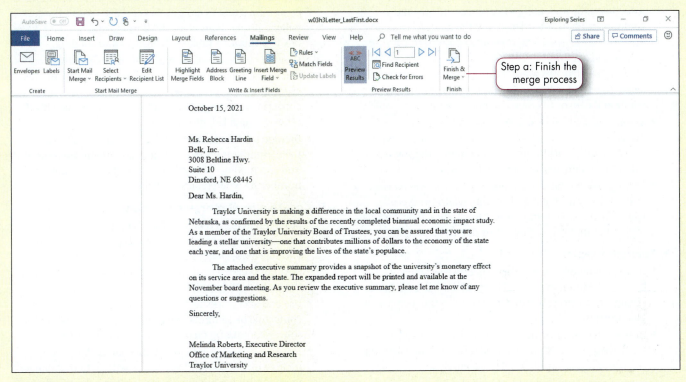

FIGURE 3.31 Completing a Mail Merge

a. Click the **Mailings tab**. Click **Finish & Merge** in the Finish group. Click **Edit Individual Documents**. Ensure that *All* is selected in the *Merge to New Document* dialog box and click **OK**.

Scroll through the letters, noting that each address and salutation is unique to the recipient. The main document and data source were merged to create a new document titled *Letters1*. You will save the document.

b. Save the document as **w03h3Merged_LastFirst** and close the document. Save and close w03h3Letter_LastFirst. Based on your instructor's directions, submit the following:

w03h2Traylor_LastFirst

w03h3Merged_LastFirst

Chapter Objectives Review

1. Insert a table.

- Create or draw a table: You can include a table in a document by indicating the number of rows and columns, enabling Word to create the table, or you can draw the table, designing rows and columns of varying height and width.
- Insert and delete rows and columns: You can insert or delete rows and columns in a table to accommodate additional data or to otherwise update a table.
- Merge and split cells: As you update a table, you can merge cells in a row or column, accommodating text that is to be aligned within the row or column, and you can split cells within an existing row or column as well.
- Change row height and column width: You can increase or decrease row height and column width in several ways—using selections on the Table Tools Layout tab, as well as manually dragging column or row borders.

2. Format a table.

- Apply and modify table styles: Apply predesigned color, borders, and shading to a table by selecting a table style. Modify an existing style to adjust settings that better suit your purposes.
- Adjust table position and alignment: A table can be aligned horizontally on a page; in addition, you can align cell contents within each cell horizontally and vertically.
- Format table text: Format text included in a cell just as you would format text outside a table, with bold, italics, underlining, etc. You can also apply paragraph formatting, such as alignment, bullets, and numbering.

3. Manage table data.

- Calculate using table formulas or functions: Numeric data in a table can be summarized through the use of formulas or functions. Formulas refer to table cells as a column and row, such as cell A1.
- Use a formula: A formula includes table cells and mathematical operators to calculate data in a table.
- Use a function: A function is a simplified formula, such as SUM or AVERAGE, that can be included in a table cell.
- Sort data in a table: You can sort table columns in ascending or descending order, including up to three sort categories. For example, you can sort a table by department name, and then by employee name within department.
- Include a recurring table header: When table rows are divided between pages, you can repeat header rows so that they display at the top of table rows on a new page.

4. Enhance table data.

- Include borders and shading: Use borders and shading to customize a table's design. You can use Word's Borders gallery, Border Painter, or the Borders and Shading dialog box to enhance a table with borders and shading.
- Convert text to a table and convert a table to text: You can convert text that is arranged in columns, with tabs separating columns, to a table. Conversely, you can convert text arranged in a table into text that is tabbed or otherwise divided into columns.
- Include a table caption: A table caption identifies a table, numbering each table in a document sequentially. You can modify the caption style and update caption numbering when tables are deleted.

5. Create a mail merge document.

- Select or create a recipient list: To prepare a form letter or other document type so that it is personalized with variable data, such as recipient name and address, you select or create a recipient list that will be merged with the main document.
- Use an Excel worksheet as a data source: A worksheet, comprised of columns and rows, can be used as a data source containing records used in a mail merge.
- Use an Access database as a data source: An Access table or query, containing records with data that can be merged with a main document, is often used as a data source for a mail merge.
- Use a Word table or an Outlook list as a data source: A Word table is often used as a data source, with data merged into a main document. Similarly, Outlook contacts can be incorporated into a main document during a mail merge.
- Edit a data source: Records in a data source can be sorted or filtered before they are merged with the main document. In addition, you can update records, and add or delete them.

6. Complete a Mail Merge.

- Insert merge fields: Merge fields are placeholders in a main document to accommodate variable data obtained from a data source.
- Complete a merge: As you complete a mail merge procedure, you update a main document with variable data from a data source, resulting in a new document that is a combination of the two.

Key Terms Matching

Match the key terms with their definitions. Write the key term letter by the appropriate numbered definition.

a. Argument
b. Border
c. Border Painter
d. Caption
e. Cell
f. Data source
g. Form letter
h. Formula
i. Function
j. Insert control

k. Mail Merge
l. Main document
m. Merge field
n. Order of operations
o. Range
p. Record
q. Shading
r. Table
s. Table alignment
t. Table style

1. _____ The position of a table between the left and right document margins. **p. 202**

2. _____ A descriptive title for a table. **p. 217**

3. _____ A document used in a mail merge process with standard information that you personalize with recipient information. **p. 226**

4. _____ A line that surrounds a Word table, cell, row, or column. **p. 214**

5. _____ A named collection of color, font, and border design that can be applied to a table. **p. 200**

6. _____ A background color that displays behind text in a table, cell, row, or column. **p. 216**

7. _____ A combination of cell references, operators, and values used to perform a calculation. **p. 211**

8. _____ The intersection of a column and row in a table. **p. 196**

9. _____ A process that combines content from a main document and a data source. **p. 226**

10. _____ Contains the information that stays the same for all recipients in a mail merge. **p. 226**

11. _____ An indicator that displays between rows or columns in a table, enabling you to insert one or more rows or columns. **p. 198**

12. _____ Organizes information in a series of rows and columns. **p. 196**

13. _____ A list of information that is merged with a main document during a mail merge procedure. **p. 227**

14. _____ Determines the sequence by which operations are calculated in an expression. **p. 211**

15. _____ Serves as a placeholder for the variable data that will be inserted into the main document during a mail merge procedure. **p. 230**

16. _____ A pre-built formula that simplifies creating a complex calculation. **p. 212**

17. _____ Feature that enables you to choose border formatting and click on any table border to apply the formatting. **p. 214**

18. _____ A positional reference contained in parentheses within a function. **p. 212**

19. _____ A group of related fields representing one entity, such as a person, place, or event. **p. 227**

20. _____ A series of adjacent cells. **p. 212**

Research Paper Basics

Researching a topic and preparing a research paper are common components of most college degrees. Although Word cannot replace the researcher, it can provide a great deal of support for properly citing sources and adhering to specific style manuals. A ***style manual***, or style guide, is a set of rules and standards for writing documents. In addition, Word assists with preparing footnotes and endnotes and preparing a bibliography. Although the research and wording of a research paper are up to you, Word is an excellent tool in the production of an attractive, well-supported document.

In this section, you will explore the use of Word features that support the preparation of a research paper. Specifically, you will learn how to use style manuals, create source references and insert citations, develop a bibliography, and work with footnotes and endnotes.

Using a Writing Style and Acknowledging Sources

As you write a research paper, you will develop content that supports your topic. The wording you use and the way you present your argument are up to you; however, you will be expected to adhere to a prescribed set of rules regarding page design and the citing of sources. Those rules are spelled out in a style guide that you can refer to as you develop a research paper. A style guide prescribes such settings as margins, line and paragraph spacing, the use of footnotes and endnotes, the way sources are cited, and the preparation of a bibliography.

It is common practice to use a variety of ***sources*** to supplement your own thoughts when writing a paper, report, legal brief, or other type of research-based document. In fact, the word *research* implies that you are seeking information from other sources to support or explore your topic when writing a research paper. Properly citing or giving credit to your sources of information ensures that you avoid plagiarizing. Merriam-Webster's Collegiate Dictionary's[1] definition of ***plagiarizing*** is "to steal and pass off (the ideas or words of another) as one's own." Not limited to failure to cite sources, plagiarism includes buying a paper that is already written or asking (or paying) someone else to write a paper for you. In addition to written words, plagiarism applies to spoken words, multimedia works, or graphics. Plagiarism has serious moral and ethical implications and is typically considered as academic dishonesty in a college or university.

STEP 1 ▶ Select a Writing Style

When assigning a research paper, your instructor will identify the preferred ***writing style***. The choice of writing style is often a matter of the academic discipline in which the research is conducted. A writing style provides a set of rules that results in standardized documents that present citations in the same manner and that include the same general page characteristics. In that way, research documents contain similar page features and settings, so a reader can focus on the content of a paper without the distraction of varying page setups. However, a style manual does not require specific wording within a research paper and it will not assist with developing your topic or conducting research.

The humanities disciplines, including English, foreign languages, philosophy, religion, art, architecture, and literature, favor the ***MLA (Modern Language Association)*** style, which has been in existence for more than 50 years. Brief parenthetical (synonymous with

---

[1] By permission. From Merriam-Webster's Collegiate Dictionary, 11th edition © 2019 by Merriam-Webster, Inc. (www.Merriam-Webster.com).

in-text) citations throughout a paper identify sources of information, with those sources arranged alphabetically in a Works Cited page. MLA style is used in many countries around the world, including the United States, Brazil, China, India, and Japan. Current MLA guidelines are published in the *MLA Handbook for Writers of Research Papers* and the *MLA Style Manual and Guide to Scholarly Publishing.*

Such disciplines as business, economics, communication, and social sciences promote the use of **APA (American Psychological Association)** writing style. Developed in 1929, APA attempts to simplify the expression of scientific ideas and experiment reports in a consistent manner. Its focus is on the communication of experiments, literature reviews, and statistics. The *Publication Manual of the American Psychological Association* provides current rules and guidelines associated with the writing style.

The **Chicago writing style** is an excellent choice for those who are preparing papers and books for publication. In fact, it is one of the most trusted resources within the book publishing industry. True to its name, the Chicago writing style was developed at the University of Chicago in 1906. It is currently in its 17th edition. The style is often referred to as CMS or CMOS. Often associated with the Chicago writing style, the Turabian writing style originated as a subset of Chicago. The dissertation secretary at the University of Chicago, Kate Turabian, narrowed the Chicago writing style to focus on writing papers. To do so, she omitted much of the information that is relevant for publishing. Currently, Turabian style is used mainly for the development of papers in the field of history. As you start working on your research paper, you may ensure the correct writing style is designated to your Word document from the Citations & Bibliography group on the References tab (see Figure 4.2).

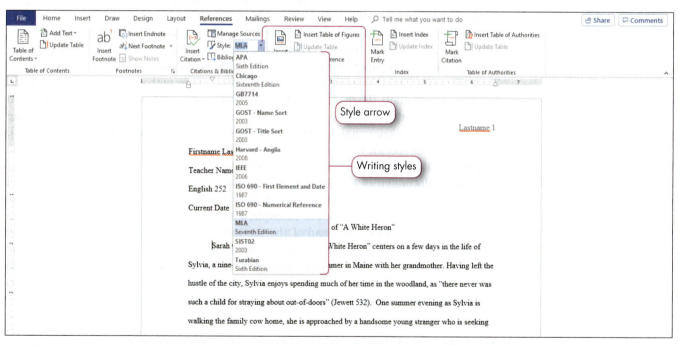

FIGURE 4.2 Select a Writing Style

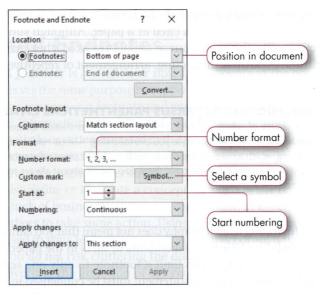

FIGURE 4.8 Footnote and Endnote Dialog Box

You can remove note text and replace it with alternate wording, just as you would adjust wording in a document. If you plan to change the format of a single note, instead of affecting all footnotes or endnotes in a document, you can select the note text and apply different formatting—perhaps italicizing or bolding words. More often, you might want to adjust the format of every footnote or endnote in a document. Footnotes are formatted in Footnote Text style and endnotes are formatted in Endnote Text style. Those styles include a specific font type, font size, and paragraph spacing, and can also be accessed from the Styles pane.

> **To modify the style of either a footnote or endnote, complete the following steps:**
>
> 1. Right-click a footnote or endnote and select Style.
> 2. Click Modify in the Style dialog box.
> 3. Adjust the font and alignment settings or click Format for more selections.
> 4. Click OK repeatedly to accept the settings and return to the document.

Exploring Special Features

Although writing a research paper is a typical requirement of a college class, it is not the only type of paper you are likely to write. In the workplace, you might be asked to contribute to technical reports, grant proposals, and other types of business documents. Those reports are not likely to be as strictly bound to writing style rules as are reports written for academic purposes. In fact, you might find it necessary to include special features such as a table of contents, an index, and even a cover page to properly document a paper and make it easier to navigate. Such features are not usually included in a college research report or required by academic writing style guides, but they are common components of papers, chapters, and articles to be published or distributed.

STEP 4 ▸ Create a Table of Contents

For a long, written report or research paper, a **_table of contents_** lists headings and subheadings in the order they appear in the document, along with the page numbers on which the entries begin. The key to enabling Word to create a table of contents is to apply heading styles to headings in the document at appropriate levels. You can apply built-in styles, Heading 1 through Heading 9, or identify your own custom styles to use when generating the table of contents. For example, if you apply Heading 1 style to major headings, Heading 2 style to subordinate headings, and lower-level heading styles to remaining headings as appropriate, Word can create an accurate table of contents. The table of contents is displayed on a separate section of the document.

To insert a predefined table of contents, complete the following steps:

1. Ensure that headings in the document are formatted with heading styles according to level.
2. Click the References tab.
3. Click Table of Contents in the Table of Contents group.
4. Select an Automatic table style to create a formatted table of contents that can be updated when heading text or positioning changes (or select Manual Table to create a table of contents that is not updated when changes occur).

For more flexibility as you design a table of contents, you can choose Table of Contents (on the References tab) and select Custom Table of Contents. From the Table of Contents dialog box, select options related to page numbering and alignment, general format, level of headings to show, and leader style (the characters that lead the reader's eye from a heading to its page number).

A table of contents is inserted as a field. When you click a table of contents, the entire table is shown as an entity that you can update or remove. As shown in Figure 4.9, controls at the top of the selection enable you to update, modify, or remove a table of contents. As you make changes to a document, especially if those changes affect the number, positioning, or sequencing of headings, you will want to update any associated table of contents. You will indicate whether you want to update page numbers only or the entire table.

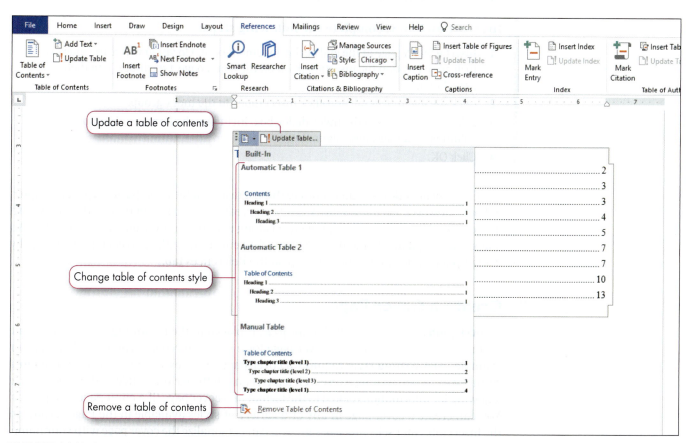

FIGURE 4.9 Update a Table of Contents

Hands-On Exercises

Skills covered: Select a Writing Style • Format a Research Paper • Create a Source and Include a Citation • Share and Search for a Source • Create a Bibliography • Create Footnotes • Modify Footnotes • Create a Table of Contents • Create an Index • Create a Cover Page

1 Research Paper Basics

You have completed a draft of an analysis of the short story "A White Heron." As a requirement for the literature class in which you are enrolled, you must format the paper according to MLA style, including citations and a bibliography. In addition to the literature analysis, you have also completed a marketing plan for a fictional company, required for a business management class. The instructor of that class, Mr. Carpenter, asked you to consider submitting the paper for inclusion in a collection of sample papers produced by the School of Business at your university. For that project, you will include a table of contents, an index, and a cover page.

STEP 1 SELECT A WRITING STYLE, FORMAT A RESEARCH PAPER, CREATE A SOURCE, AND INCLUDE A CITATION

You will format the analysis of "A White Heron" in MLA style and include citations where appropriate. Refer to Figure 4.10 as you complete Step 1.

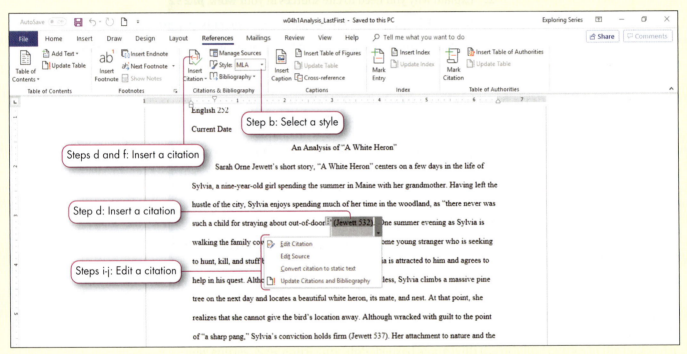

FIGURE 4.10 Add Sources and Insert Citations

a. Open *w04h1Analysis* and save it as **w04h1Analysis_LastFirst**.

> **TROUBLESHOOTING:** If you make any major mistakes in this exercise, you can close the file, open *w04h1Analysis* again, and then start this exercise over.

b. Click the **References tab** and click the **Style arrow** in the Citations & Bibliography group. Select **MLA Seventh Edition**. Apply the following MLA style settings to the whole document:

- Text is **left** aligned.
- Line spacing is **2.0** (or double).
- Paragraph spacing Before and After is **0**.

- Font is **Times New Roman** at **12 pt** size.
- Margins are 1" at the top, bottom, left, and right.
- First line of all body paragraphs are indented 0.5".
- Report title is centered.

c. Insert a right-aligned header that includes your last name, followed by a space and a plain page number. Make sure the page number is inserted as a field, not simply typed. Format the header as **Times New Roman 12 pt**.

d. Place the insertion point after the ending quotation mark and before the ending period in Jewett's notation in the first body paragraph (ending in *straying about out-of-doors*). Click the **References tab** and click **Insert Citation** in the Citations & Bibliography group. Click **Add New Source**. Click the **Type of Source arrow** and click **Book Section**. Complete the citation as follows, but do not click OK after completing the source.

Author: **Jewett, Sarah Orne**

Title: **A White Heron**

Book Title: **The American Tradition in Literature**

Year: **2009**

Pages: **531–537**

City: **New York**

Publisher: **McGraw-Hill**

e. Click to select **Show All Bibliography Fields**. Scroll down and click in the **Editor box** and type **Perkins, George**. Click **Edit** beside Editor. Type **Perkins** in the Last box. Click in the **First box** and type **Barbara**. Click **Add** and click **OK**. Click in the **Volume box** and type **2**. Click **OK**.

You have added a source related to a section of a book in which the short story is printed.

f. Click after the word *firm* and before the ending period in Jewett's notation (that ends in *Sylvia's conviction holds firm*) in the first paragraph. Click **Insert Citation** in the Citations & Bibliography group and click **Jewett, Sarah Orne** to insert a citation to the same source as that created earlier.

> **MAC TROUBLESHOOTING:** Click Citations on the References tab, double-click the citation in the Citations pane, and then close the pane.

g. Place the insertion point after the ending quotation mark and before the ending period in Hovet's notation in the second body paragraph (ending in *functions that are also present in "A White Heron"*). Add a new source, selecting **Article in a Periodical** as the source and type:

Author: **Hovet, Theodore R.**

Title: **Once Upon a Time: Sarah Orne Jewett's 'A White Heron' as a Fairy Tale**

Periodical Title: **Studies in Short Fiction**

Year: **2011**

Month: **Sept.**

Day: **25**

Pages: **63–68**

You have to use single quotes for the title of the source because double quotes will be added around the full title in the Bibliography.

h. Click to select **Show All Bibliography Fields**, set the Volume to **15** and the Issue to **1**, and then click **OK**.

STEP 1 ▶ Use Track Changes

When Track Changes is not active, any change you make to a document is untraceable, and no one will know what you have changed unless he or she compares your revised document with the previous version. When Track Changes is active, it applies ***revision marks***, which indicate where a person added, deleted, or formatted text. You can use the predefined settings in Track Changes, or you may change the track changes format using the Advanced Track Changes Options dialog box (see Figure 4.16).

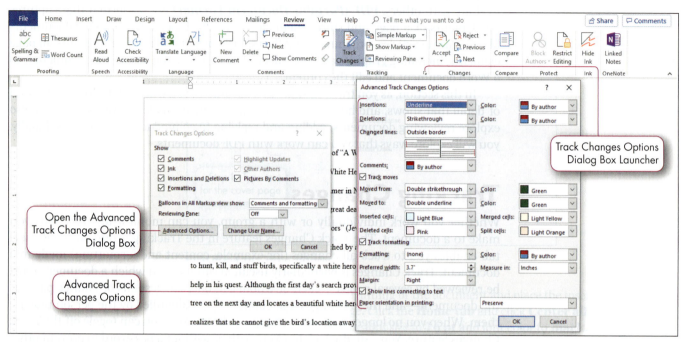

FIGURE 4.16 Format Track Changes

Accept and Reject Changes

As you complete the revisions in a document, you will review all comments and act on them or otherwise reply to the reviewer. You also can view all edits, including changes in wording and formatting. You can move through the document and review each individual change using Previous or Next. The Accept or Reject features in the Changes group enable you to accept or reject all changes, or you can be more specific with respect to which changes to accept or reject (see Figure 4.17). The options in the Accept/Reject features include Accept/Reject and Move to Next; Accept/Reject This Change; Accept/Reject All Changes Shown; Accept/Reject All Changes; and Accept/Reject All Changes and Stop Tracking. For instance, to review with the option of accepting or rejecting individual changes, you can use Accept and Reject. To accept or reject individual changes, the pointer must be in an edited area in the document. Before submitting a final document, ensure that all changes have been accepted and track changes turned off to produce a clean copy. You can use the Accept/Reject All option or you can turn off tracking at the same time by using the Accept/Reject All Changes and Stop Tracking option.

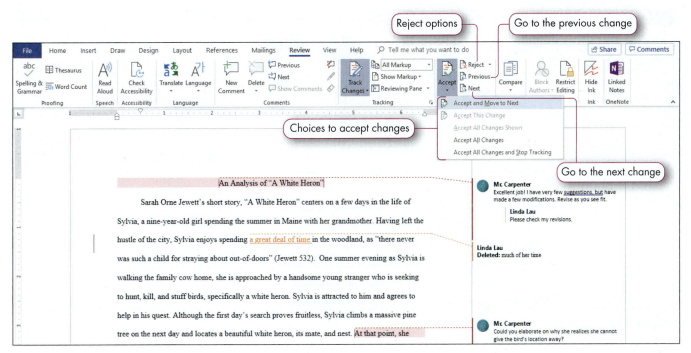

FIGURE 4.17 Accept or Reject Changes

Reviewing a Document

In today's organizational environment, teams of people with diverse backgrounds, skills, and knowledge prepare documents. Team members work together while planning, developing, writing, and editing important documents. A large part of that process is reviewing work begun or submitted by others. No doubt you have focused on a document of your own so completely that you easily overlooked obvious mistakes or alternative wording. A reviewer, bringing a fresh perspective, can often catch mistakes, perhaps even suggest ways to improve readability. In reviewing a document, you will most often find ways to change wording or otherwise edit the format, and you might find an opportunity to provide **comments** related to the content. Although comments are most often directed to the attention of another author or editor, you can even include comments to remind yourself of a necessary action.

STEP 2 Use Markup

Markup is a way of viewing tracked changes. If a lot of changes have been made, they may become distracting as you read through an entire document. Therefore, you can use markup to customize how track changes are displayed. The Show Markup feature (see Figure 4.18) enables readers to view document revisions organized by the type of revisions (such as comments, insertions, deletions, and formatting), how the revisions are shown, as well as by reviewer. There are four markup views that modify how one sees changes made to a document: Simple Markup, All Markup, No Markup, and Original. You can toggle each selection on or off to view the types of markups that you want to see. **Simple Markup** is a clutter-free way to display tracked changes (see Figure 4.19). In Simple Markup, a vertical red bar displays on the left side of any paragraph in which edits have occurred, but the revisions are hidden (see Figure 4.19). Toggle the red bar to display the full changes or to remove them from view.

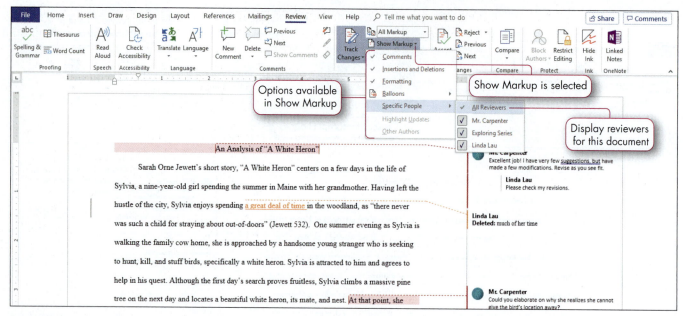

FIGURE 4.18 Show Markup

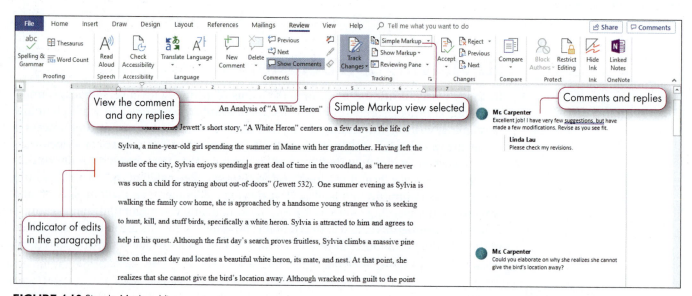

FIGURE 4.19 Simple Markup View

The document in Figure 4.20 is shown with **All Markup** in the Tracking group selected. This view shows the document with all the revisions, markups, and comments using the formats predefined in Track Changes Options. **No Markup** provides a completely clean view of a document, temporarily hiding all comments and revisions, and displays the document as it would if all changes were applied and does not show any of the markups or comments. It enables you to preview the document before accepting the changes. Although no revisions or comments show, keep in mind that they are only hidden. To remove them permanently, you have to accept or reject the changes. Lastly, **Original Markup** displays the document in its original form, as it was before any changes were applied.

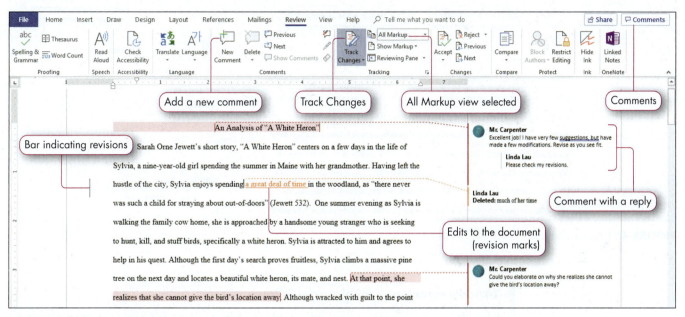

FIGURE 4.20 All Markup View

One of the benefits of Track Changes is that you can filter the changes by reviewer, thereby enabling you to review, accept, or reject individual or all changes recommended by a specific person. You can also use Track Changes Options to select types of revision and to change the settings for track changes and balloons.

Add a Comment

Besides tracking changes and changing the markup view, the Review tab has a Comments group that provides commands to add new comments, delete existing comments, or navigate through the document and review each individual comment using Previous or Next (see Figure 4.21). Comments can also be added using the comment icon on the right side of the window above the ribbon, which displays onscreen no matter what ribbon tab is currently selected. A comment works like a sticky note on a hard copy, enabling you to attach notes or information to various parts of your document. It is also a good way to ask the writer a question, to express concern about a particular sentence, or to remind yourself of a necessary action.

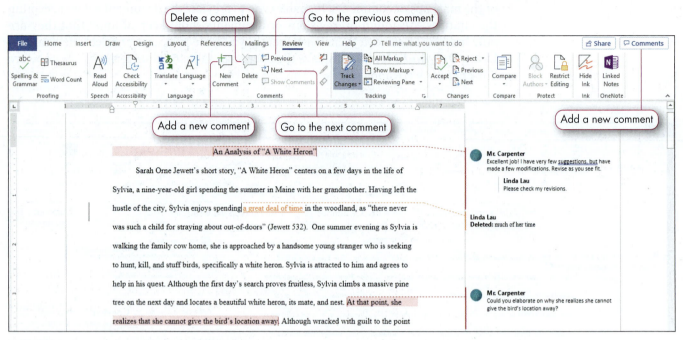

FIGURE 4.21 Add a Comment

If you do not select anything prior to clicking New Comment, the comment is assigned to the word or object closest to the insertion point.

TIP: CONFIRMING THE USER NAME

Before you use the Comments feature, make sure your name appears as you want it to display in any comments. To do so, click the File tab and click Options. In the General section, confirm that your name and initials display as the user. Word uses that information to identify the person who uses collaboration tools, such as Comments. If you are in a lab environment, you might not have permission to modify settings or change the user name; however, you should be able to change those settings on a home computer.

View Comments

Any comment is displayed on the right side of the document in a ***comment balloon***. A comment balloon displays as a boxed note in the margin and when selected highlights the text to which the comment is applied. You can also choose to display revisions in balloons. Font and paragraph options of the comment balloon can be changed using Styles or the shortcut menu.

Comments can be viewed in both Simple Markup and All Markup views, but not in No Markup and Original views. Print Layout is the most common means of viewing a document, but even in other views (e.g., Read Mode and Web Layout), comments display similarly, except in Draft view, where they appear as tags embedded in the document. However, when you point to the embedded tags, the comments show.

Reply to Comments

Replying to a comment is a feature that helps provide a "conversation" around a comment. Move the pointer over the comment and click Reply to type a response (see Figure 4.22). The response will be placed within the original comment balloon. All replies to original comments are indented beneath the original, with the commenter identified by name, making it easy to follow the progression of a comment through its replies. After you have addressed a comment and clicked Resolve, the comment is grayed out. However, you can still reopen the comment again by clicking Reopen on the right of Reply.

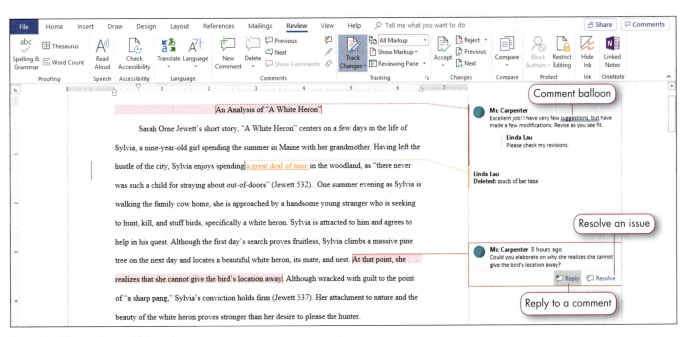

FIGURE 4.22 Reply to a Comment

Online Document Collaboration

With its continuing commitment to incorporate collaboration features, Microsoft is simplifying how people in any location can work together in groups to complete projects. The global marketplace and Web 2.0 technologies create a dynamic in which collaboration on projects is the norm, rather than the exception. Marketing proposals, company reports, and all sorts of other documents are often prepared by a group of people working with a shared documents folder, in which all can contribute to the shared documents at any time. Similarly, group projects that are assigned as part of a class requirement may more easily be completed by sharing documents online for review and completion. Recognizing the proliferation of devices that students and professionals use to collaborate on projects, including personal computers and mobile devices, the Office suite has become a complete, cross-platform, cross-device solution for working collaboration. Individuals can work from anywhere and on almost any device. The key to such sharing is online accessibility.

In this section, you will learn how to use OneDrive with File Explorer. You will also learn how to use Word Online. Further, you will explore the various options of sharing your documents and collaborating with your peers in real time using Word and Word Online.

Using OneDrive

Word facilitates document saving and sharing through *OneDrive*, which is a Web-based storage site and sharing utility. Saving a document to OneDrive is sometimes referred to as "saving to the cloud," because the document is saved and stored online (in the cloud) but it is also made available to work offline through File Explorer.

When you use OneDrive as a storage location, you can retrieve documents from any Internet-connected device and share documents with others. You may also want to use OneDrive as a location for backing up documents. Documents saved to OneDrive will not be lost if your hard drive crashes or your flash drive is lost or damaged. OneDrive has ample free storage available to users, making it a viable alternative to a local drive. Another advantage of using OneDrive is the AutoSave feature, which is enabled when you save your files to OneDrive. With AutoSave on, any document saved to OneDrive is automatically saved every few seconds. You can see the auto-saving status in the file name at the top of the window. The AutoSave default is On, but if you do not want to save your work continually you can turn AutoSave off manually by toggling the AutoSave icon on the Quick Access Toolbar. If you accidentally saved changes through AutoSave, you can revert to and restore any older versions of the file and make the older version the current one. Click the file name at the top of the window to see all versions in the Version History pane, open the version that you want, and click Restore to keep the chosen version.

> **TIP: ONEDRIVE FOR MOBILE DEVICES**
> You can download a OneDrive app on your mobile device that enables you to easily access your OneDrive files from the mobile device and upload videos and pictures to OneDrive.

STEP 1 ▸ Use OneDrive with File Explorer

Windows 10 incorporates OneDrive into File Explorer, so you can see and easily access files stored on OneDrive. Moreover, files in the OneDrive folder are available offline, so you can access and work with files stored on OneDrive even when you do not have access to the Internet. When access to the Internet becomes available, any changes made to the files will sync to OneDrive. Because there is a OneDrive folder in File Explorer, you can save directly to OneDrive in a similar fashion as you would save to any other storage device. Files and folders can be moved and copied between OneDrive and other storage locations on your computer as shown in Figure 4.27. You can also delete files from OneDrive as easily as you can from any other folder in File Explorer.

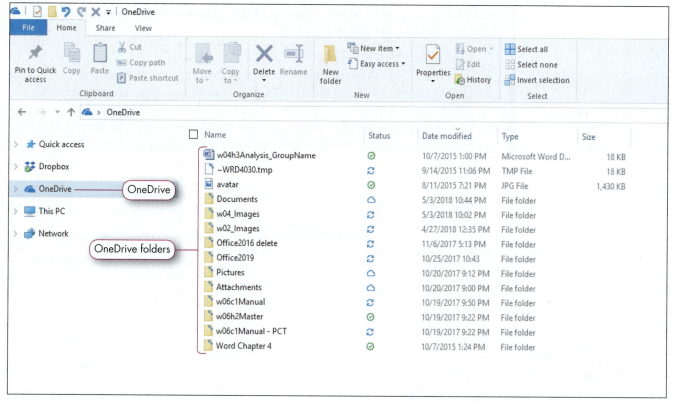

FIGURE 4.27 OneDrive in File Explorer

You can select which folders to sync between the online storage and your computer, and which folders are available only online. Using this feature can help manage storage space on your computing device and save time by only syncing those files that you modify and use most often. You can manage the syncing options through OneDrive settings, found by clicking the OneDrive icon in the Notification area on the taskbar, as shown in Figure 4.28.

FIGURE 4.28 OneDrive Icon

To choose and sync files and folders between OneDrive and File Explorer, complete the following steps:

1. Sign in to Windows with a Microsoft account and enable OneDrive to display the OneDrive icon in the notification area at the far right of the taskbar (refer to Figure 4.28).
2. Click the OneDrive icon, click More Options (three vertical dots), and then click Settings.
3. Click the Account tab in the Microsoft OneDrive dialog box and select Choose folders.
4. Complete one of the following substeps in the Choose folders dialog box:
   - Check the *Make all files available* box to make all your OneDrive files available on your computer.
   - Check the boxes for the folders you want to sync under *Or make these folders visible* (see Figure 4.29). Only checked folders will sync.
5. Click OK to sync the files and folders.
6. Close the OneDrive dialog box.

On a Mac, to choose and sync files and folders between OneDrive and Finder, complete the following steps:

1. Ensure OneDrive is installed on your Mac.
2. Start OneDrive from Launchpad and complete the setup process by signing in.
3. Click More Options (three vertical dots), click Preferences, click Account, and then click Choose Folders.
4. Choose to sync everything, individual folders, or individual files, and then click OK. New items you add to the OneDrive folder on your Mac will sync to OneDrive.

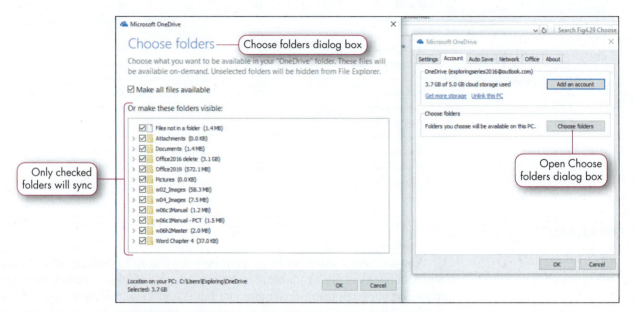

FIGURE 4.29 Choose and Sync Folders between OneDrive and File Explorer

---

TIP: USING A MICROSOFT ACCOUNT

To use Microsoft services such as OneDrive, you must have a Microsoft account. If you use Outlook, Hotmail, OneDrive, Office Online, Skype, or Xbox Live, Windows Live, or if you had a Windows Phone, you already have a Microsoft account. If you do not have an account, you can create one at signup.live.com.

Sharing Documents

OneDrive also is a means of online collaboration. Because a document saved in OneDrive is stored online, you can share the document with others who have access to the Internet. Also, sharing via OneDrive removes the hassles of version control, which is a problem created by passing around versions of the same document via email. To use the share feature, the document must be saved to OneDrive and you must also be connected to the Internet.

When viewing a list of files in OneDrive, you can right-click a file and click Share to open a Share dialog box from which you can select a method of sharing (Get a link, Email, or share through a social media site such as Facebook or LinkedIn) and stipulate editing privileges. You can also set an expiration date or a password to manage the accessibility of a document (see Figure 4.30). Alternatively, you can also share files directly from Word or Word Online. After saving a document to OneDrive or if you are working with Word or Word Online, you can share your document with others in several ways. You can share a document through a link or as an attachment via email. As you share a document, you can indicate whether those you share with can edit the document or simply view it.

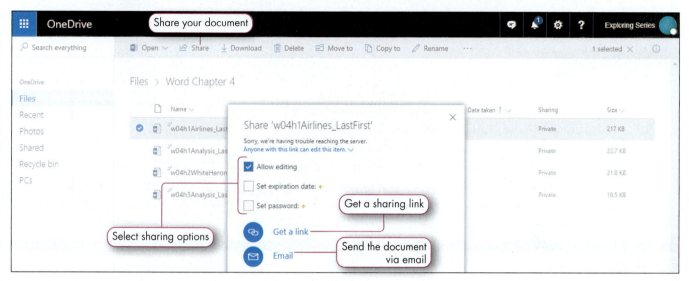

FIGURE 4.30 Share a document on OneDrive

Invite Others to Share

You can invite others to share a document with you by sending them a link to your file using Word or Word Online. You choose whether your invitee can edit or only view the document. Those invited to share receive an email with a link to work on the document. When the link is selected, the document opens in Word Online. If multiple people have been invited to share, everyone can be in the document and make changes at the same time. Because you are working in real time, all changes are synced so all users will be able to see changes in a matter of seconds.

To share a Word document already saved to OneDrive, complete the following steps:

1. Open the document that you have saved to your OneDrive folder on File Explorer in Word.
2. Complete one of the following substeps:
   - Click the File tab and click Share.
   - Click Share at the top-right corner of the Word window.
3. Complete one of the following substeps (see Figure 4.31):
   - Type the email addresses of invitees in the Invite people box in the Share pane. Separate each name or email address with a semicolon.
   - Click *Search the Address Book for contacts* on the right of the Invite people box and find your recipient(s).
4. Indicate whether the recipient(s) can edit or only view the shared document.
5. Type a message (optional).
6. Click Send.

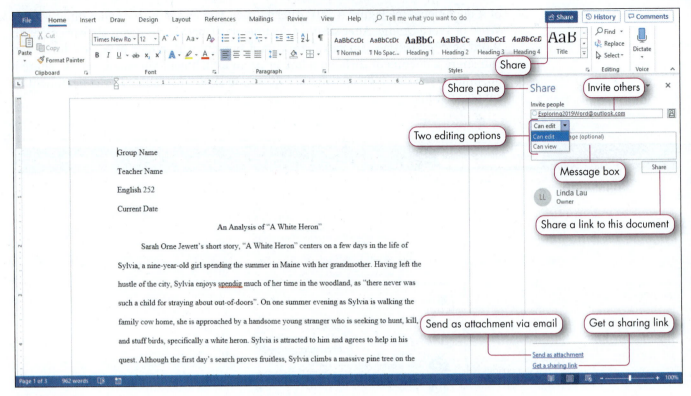

FIGURE 4.31 Invite Others

Share a Document Link

Another way to share your document with your recipients is to generate a sharing link. A sharing link can either grant editing privileges or limit access to view only. Once a link is generated, it is copied and can be pasted to an email message, into another document, or made available in a website or blog. The document opens in Word Online when the link is clicked and all changes made to the document are made in real time and synced simultaneously.

> **To get a sharing link to a OneDrive document, complete the following steps:**
>
> 1. Open the document that you have saved to your OneDrive folder on File Explorer in Word.
> 2. Complete one of the following substeps:
>   - Click the File tab and click Share.
>   - Click Share at the top-right corner of the window.
> 3. Click Get a sharing link at the bottom of the Share pane (refer to Figure 4.31).
> 4. Complete one of the following substeps (see Figure 4.32):
>   - Click *Create an edit link* under Edit link if you want anyone with the link to edit the shared document.
>   - Click *Create a view-only link* under View-only link if you want anyone with the link to view but not edit the shared document.
> 5. Click Copy and distribute the generated link to intended recipients using your preferred email service provider.

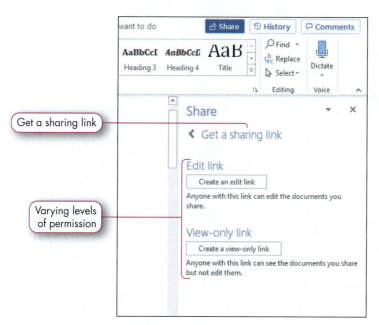

FIGURE 4.32 Share a Document Link

Send as an Attachment

If working in Word, an additional option is to share a document as an email attachment. Using this method, recipients receive a copy of the full document. However, recipients cannot make edits or to view the document online. When you share a document as an email attachment, choose one of the following two formats (see Figure 4.33) and a new email message will open in your default email account:

- Send a copy: In this option, the recipient gets a copy of the original Word document to review. This could be a problem for large files with photos and images, or database files, because there might be some file size limitations with some email accounts. Further, the recipients must have the appropriate application to open and view the attached document.

- Send a PDF: The recipient gets a PDF attachment of the original Word document. The PDF file preserves all layout, formatting, fonts, and images. This is a recommended option if revisions are not expected.

Because email recipients receive a copy of the document, if they want to make changes, the changes must be saved and the revised version emailed back to the primary author. If revisions are received from multiple people, the primary author needs to consolidate all the changes onto one document, which can be a daunting task. Therefore, distributing documents as email attachments is acceptable, but is the least collaborative, most noninteractive method of working together.

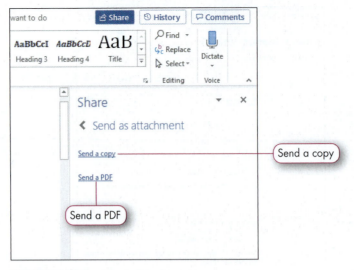

FIGURE 4.33 Send as an Attachment

Collaborating with Word and Word Online

Imagine gathering around a conference table to work on a document with others. The group shares ideas and comments on content, working to produce a collaborative document that is representative of the group's best effort. Now expand that view to include co-authors who are widespread geographically instead of gathered in a conference room. Because the far-flung group members are all online at the same time, they can view a document and collaborate on content, although not simultaneously, ultimately producing a document to which all attendees have had the opportunity to contribute. Whether your goal is to present a document for discussion (but no editing) or to seek input from a group, you will appreciate the ease with which documents saved to OneDrive and opened in Word or Word Online facilitate that task.

After you have saved a document to OneDrive and shared it with others, you are ready to collaborate in real time. As mentioned above, if a recipient was granted editing privileges to a shared document via a link or an email invitation, when the link is selected, the document opens in Word Online. At any point, you can switch to Word to continue working with a shared document. Because Word Online is somewhat limited, you might find that you need to edit a document in Word to access a feature not found in Word Online. For example, you might want to add a bibliography or check a document in Outline view. The option to edit in Word is available with the same collaborative features as with Word Online. Any document saved to OneDrive and shared with editing privileges has real-time, collaborative functionality.

STEP 2 ⟩ **Use Word Online**

Word Online is a Web-based version of Word that enables you to edit and format a document online. As a component of Office Online, which also includes Excel Online, PowerPoint Online, and OneNote Online, Word Online is free and is available when you sign in to OneDrive.com. Using Word Online you can begin a new document, open a document previously saved in OneDrive, or open a document shared with you. The document opens in a browser window with a selection of commands. Because it is Web-based, you are not required to purchase or install software on your computer to use Word Online. Using Word Online, you can create and edit Word documents from any Internet-connected computer, and across any platform. Word Online is similar to Word, but with fewer features.

To create a new document in Word Online, complete the following steps:

1. Log in to your Microsoft account at OneDrive.com.
2. Click New (see Figure 4.34). A menu displays enabling you to create a Folder, or a new Word, Excel, PowerPoint, OneNote file, an Excel survey, or a Plain text document.
3. Click and select Word document.
4. Click the default file name, *Document1*, on the title bar and type a file name.
5. Type content in the document, and it is automatically saved to OneDrive.
6. For additional functionality, click Open in Word.

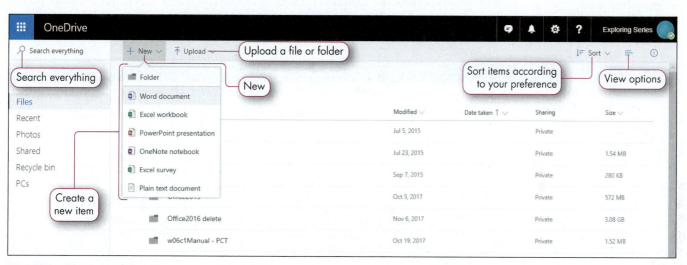

FIGURE 4.34 Create a New Document in Word Online

There are three views in the Document Views group on the View tab: Editing, Reading, and Immersive Reader. By default, all new documents open in Editing View. Editing View enables you to make changes to a document. Click Open in Word to switch to the fully featured version of Word. Reading View shows the document as it will print and enables the addition of comments. You cannot edit in Reading View. To make changes to the document, click Edit Document, and choose Edit in Word or Edit in Browser using Word Online (see Figure 4.35). **Immersive Reader** is another document view that is an add-in learning tool designed to help readers pronounce words correctly, read quickly and accurately, and understand what is read.

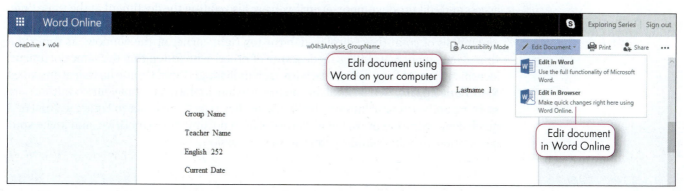

FIGURE 4.35 Use Word Online

Word Online has the familiar look and feel of Microsoft Word; however, you will note that the ribbon in Word Online has fewer tabs than the ribbon in Word installed on your computer (see Figure 4.36). In addition, there are also limited, but sufficient, functionality using the Insert, Page Layout, Review, and View tabs that are similar to Word. As you work with Word Online, you will find some other differences and limitations. For example, Dialog Box Launchers are not present for some groups, and certain features such as nonprinting characters, hidden text, Citations and Bibliography, Table of Contents, Cover Page, and Index are not supported. An important advantage of Word and Word Online is it enables authors to collaborate online and author and edit in real-time. Word Online has a new feature called *Simplified Ribbon*, which displays a two-line instead of the classic three-line view to provide more space for users to focus on their work and to collaborate with others. Unlike the installed version of Word, Track Changes is not a feature on the Review tab in Word Online.

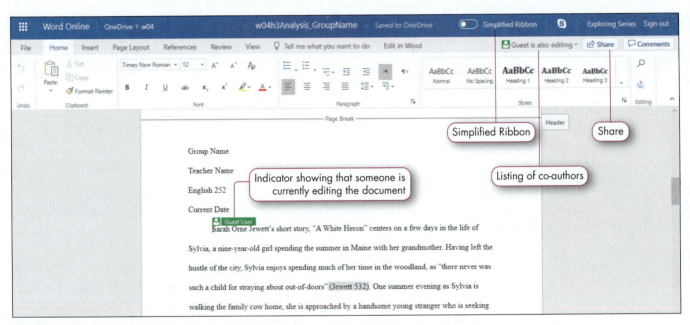

FIGURE 4.36 Notification of Co-Authors

Co-authoring a document is simple, with no specific commands required to begin editing. Simply open a shared document from OneDrive and use either Word or Word Online to modify the document. Of course, the document must be shared in such a way that editing by other authors is permitted. When you save or upload a Word document to OneDrive, anyone with whom you share the document (with editing privileges) can access and edit the document, even if you are also editing the document at the same time. This simultaneous editing is also called ***real-time co-authoring***. You will see pictures and initials of co-authors displayed in the top right corner of the window. As you edit a shared document, you will be made aware of others who are editing the same document, identified by color flags associated with each individual. Word Online has a feature called ***Real Time Typing***, which enables you to see where in the document your co-authors are working and any contributions they make as they type them (refer to Figure 4.36). For a quick demonstration of this new feature, save a document to OneDrive, and invite your peers to join you in a simultaneous authoring session.

Quick Concepts

9. As you save a document to OneDrive, you will most likely also want to have a copy on your computer for backup purposes. Explain how you can make sure that as you modify one copy, the other is also updated. *p. 284*

10. Both Word and Word Online enable you to create and edit a document. Explain when one might be preferred over the other. *p. 290*

11. Describe the advantages of online collaboration. *p. 290*

12. Editing View and Reading View of Word Online serve different purposes. Describe some extra features of Editing View. *p. 291*

b. Click **Edit Document** and select **Edit in Browser** to start editing the shared document. Type the Group Name assigned by the instructor to replace Student Name on the first line of the document.

c. Divide the following tasks among group members, with each task completed by only one team member (unless there are fewer team members than tasks; in that case, assign the tasks as appropriate). As each group member completes a task, it is automatically saved. These tasks can be done simultaneously and you will see indicators showing that someone is currently editing the document as well.

- Task 1: Remove the word *On* from the fourth sentence of the first paragraph and the sentence should begin with the word **One**.
- Task 2: Change the highlighted word *facets* in the second sentence of the second paragraph to **components**.
- Task 3: Change the highlighted word *killing* in the first paragraph of page 3 to **revealing**.
- Task 4: Change the word *helpful* to **interesting** in the last paragraph of the document.

d. Click the **Home tab**, click **Text Highlight Color**, and then toggle the following areas in the document to remove the yellow highlights:

- The word *components* in the second sentence of the second paragraph on page 1.
- The word *revealing* in the first paragraph of page 3.
- The word *interesting* in the last paragraph of the document.

e. Check the document for spelling errors. All authors' names are correctly spelled, so ignore flagged errors of names. The essay begins with a capital *A*, so ignore the apparent grammatical error. Correct any misspelled words. Group members will see an onscreen message informing them of an edit.

f. Click **Open in Word** to open the document in Word on your computer.

You want to insert a cover page but this feature is not available on Word Online, so you will open the document in Word on your computer.

g. Scroll to the top of the document. Click the **Insert tab**, click **Cover Page** in the Pages group, and then select **Banded**. Type **Analysis of "A White Heron"** as the document title and your full name as the author. Remove any content controls that you are not using and delete the *An Analysis of "A White Heron"* title on the next page.

h. Close the browser. Save and close the file. Based on your instructor's directions, submit the following:

w04h1Airlines_LastFirst

w04h2Entry_LastFirst.pdf

w04h2WhiteHeron_LastFirst

w04h3Analysis_GroupName

After reading this chapter, you have accomplished the following objectives:

1. Use a writing style and acknowledge sources.

- Select a writing style: A research paper is typically written to adhere to a particular writing style, often dictated by the academic discipline.
- Format a research paper: Research papers share a set of common formatting features to maintain consistency and help to make the document look more professional.
- Create a source and include a citation: Each source consulted for a paper must be cited, according to the rules of a writing style.
- Share and search for a source: Sources are included in a Master List, available to all documents created on the same computer, and a Current List, available to the current document.
- Create a bibliography: A bibliography, also known as works cited or references, lists all sources used in the preparation of a paper.

2. Create and modify footnotes and endnotes.

- Create footnotes and endnotes: Footnotes (located at the bottom of a page) and endnotes (located at the end of a paper) enable you to expand on a statement or provide a citation.
- Modify footnotes and endnotes: You can change the format or style of footnotes and endnotes, or delete them.

3. Explore special features.

- Create a table of contents: If headings are formatted in a heading style, Word can prepare a table of contents, listing headings and associated page numbers.
- Create an index: Mark entries for inclusion in an index, which is an alphabetical listing of marked topics and associated page numbers.
- Create a cover page: Some writing styles require a cover page, which you can create as the first page, listing a report title and other identifying information.

4. Track changes.

- Use Track Changes: With Track Changes active, all edits in a document are traceable so you can see what has been changed.
- Accept and reject changes: With Track Changes active, you can evaluate each edit made, accepting or rejecting it.

5. Review a document.

- Use markup: Markup views enable you to customize how tracked changes are displayed in a document. There are four markup views: Simple Markup, All Markup, No Markup, and Original.
- Add a comment: A comment is located in a comment balloon in the margin of a report, providing a note to the author.
- View comments: Comments are viewed in comment balloons in the document.
- Reply to comments: Replying to comments creates a conversation around the comment with the reply placed within the original comment balloon.
- Work with a PDF document: Documents are saved in PDF format to preserve the layout, format fonts, and images of the original Word document.
- Reflow is a Word feature that converts a PDF document into an editable Word document.

6. Use OneDrive.

- Use OneDrive with File Explorer: Windows 10 incorporates OneDrive into File Explorer to simplify the process of organizing and managing OneDrive folders (and contents), as well as ensuring that files are synchronized.

7. Share documents.

- Invite others to share: Use Word and Word Online to share documents through links, with varying levels of permission.
- Share a document link: Word will generate a sharing link with varying levels of permission and send the link to recipients in a separate email.
- Send as an attachment: Send an email to recipients with an attached document, either in PDF or the original format.

8. Collaborate with Word and Word Online.

- Use Word Online: Word Online is a Web-based version of Word that enables you to create, edit, and format a document online without having to install Word on your computer.

Practice Exercises

1 Live. Work. Dine. Shop.

You are the assistant publicity manager of a construction company building a community where residents can live, work, dine, and shop within the community without having to get into a car. You and a team of colleagues are designing promotional materials for this project. You conducted your research online for such communities in other states and wrote a promotional article. You will share your research with your team members online so that they can contribute, comment, and collaborate with you before submitting it to your manager for final approval. Refer to Figure 4.39 as you complete this exercise.

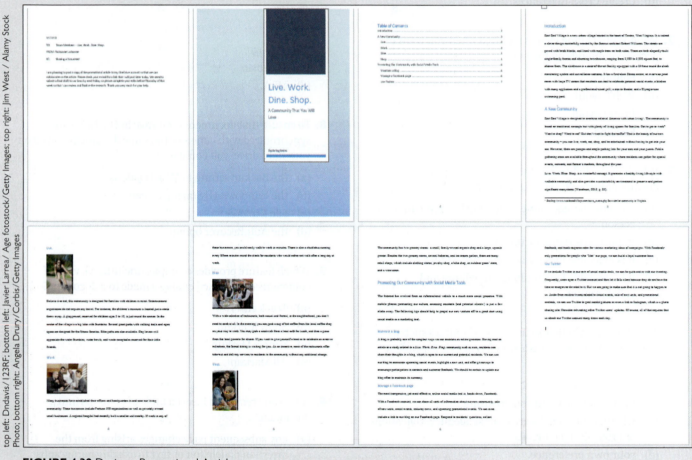

FIGURE 4.39 Design a Promotional Article

a. Open *w04p1Live* and save it as **w04p1Live_LastFirst**.

b. Apply the following formatting to the whole document:
   - Document is double spaced.
   - Font is Times New Roman 12 pt size.
   - No paragraph spacing before or after any paragraph.
   - Margins are 1"at the top, bottom, left, and right.
   - Alignment is left.

c. Press **Ctrl+Home**. Click the **Insert tab**, click **Cover Page**, and then select **Facet**. Complete the cover page by completing the following:
   - Click **Document title** and type **Live. Work. Dine. Shop.** (include the periods).
   - Click **Document subtitle** and type **A Community That You Will Love**.
   - Remove the current author (unless the current author shows your first and last names) and type your first and last names.
   - Right-click the **Abstract paragraph** at the top of the page and click **Remove Content Control**.

d. Click the **Review tab**. Click the **Track Changes arrow** and click **Track Changes**. All of your edits will be marked as you work. Change the view to **All Markup**. Make the following changes to the document:

- Change the *Promotion* heading on page 5 to **Promoting Our Community Using Social Media Tools**.
- Scroll to page 5 and select the heading **Maintain a blog**. Click the **Review tab** and click **New Comment**. Type **Susie, do you like what I wrote in this section?**

e. Insert a page break at the beginning of the cover page and move to the beginning of the new page. Open the PDF file *w04p1Invite.pdf* in Word, then copy and paste all the text to the first page of the *w04p1Live_LastFirst* document. Replace Firstname Lastname with your first and last names. Because Track Changes is on, the text you inserted is colored to indicate it is a new edit.

f. Scroll through the document, noting the edits that were tracked. On page 6, you will see the comment you made earlier. Press **Ctrl+Home** to move to the beginning of the document. Click the **Review tab** and change the Display for Review in the Tracking group to **No Markup**. Scroll through the document to note that revision marks (indicating edits) do not display. Move to the beginning of the document and select **Simple Markup**. Scroll through the document once more. Click a bar beside an edited paragraph to display the edits. Click the bar again to remove them from view.

g. Check the document for spelling errors. All names of people and websites are correctly spelled. Scroll to page 6 and click the **comment balloon** beside the *Maintain a blog* section. Click **Reply** in the expanded markup balloon. Type **I will review the document and give you my suggestions on Monday afternoon.** (include the period). Close the comment balloon.

h. Click after the period at the end of the first sentence on page 4, under the *A New Community* heading. The sentence ends with *urban living*. Click the **References tab** and click **Insert Footnote** in the Footnotes group. Type **See http://www.westbroadvillage.com/news_events. php for a similar community in Virginia.** (include the period). Right-click the **hyperlink** in the footnote and click **Remove Hyperlink**.

i. Click the **Review tab** and change the view to **No Markup**. Right-click the footnote at the bottom of page 3 and click **Style**. Click **Modify**. Change the font to **Times New Roman** and the font size to **10**. Click **OK** and click **Close**.

j. Move to the top of page 3 (beginning with the *Introduction* heading) and insert a page break at the top of the page. Move to the top of the new page (page 3). Click the **References tab**, click **Table of Contents** in the Table of Contents group, and then click **Automatic Table 2**.

k. Double-click the *Conclusion* link and press **Ctrl+Click**. Delete the Conclusion section (removing the heading and the paragraph below the heading). Scroll to page 3 and click **Table of Contents**. Click **Update Table** in the content control and select **Update entire table**. Click **OK**. Note that the Conclusion section is no longer included in the table of contents.

l. Click the **Review tab** and change the view to **Simple Markup**. Click the **Accept arrow** and click **Accept All Changes and Stop Tracking**. Scroll through the document and note that edits are no longer marked.

m. Click before the period in the last sentence in the second paragraph in the *A New Community* section that ends *protect significant ecosystems*. Click the **References tab** and click the **Style arrow** in the Citations & Bibliography group. Select **APA Sixth Edition**. Click **Insert Citation** in the Citations & Bibliography group and click **Add New Source**. Add the following source from a Journal Article and click **OK**:

Author: **Woodman, Jennifer Lynn**

Title: **Protecting Ecosystems**

Journal Name: **Journal of Ecosystems Studies**

Year: **2015**

Pages: **23–30**

Volume: **6**

Issue: **4**

(Hint: Click *Show All Bibliography Fields* to enter the volume and issue.)

n. Click the **citation** you just created, click the **Citation Options arrow**, and then click **Edit Citation**. Type **23** in the Pages box. Click **OK**.

o. Sign in to your Microsoft account and save the document to your OneDrive folder on File Explorer. Click **Share** at the top right corner, enter your own email address, and ensure the **Can edit option** is selected in the Share pane. Type an optional message and click **Share**.

p. Open your email with the shared link and click **View in OneDrive**. Scroll through the document on Word Online. Click **Edit Document** and select **Edit in Browser**. Select *MEMO* at the top of the letter. Click **Comments** and click **New Comment**. Type **I have completed my research for this project. Please review this document and make any edits you feel necessary.** (include the period). Click **Post**. Close the Comments pane. Click **Open in Word**.

q. Click the **File tab**, click **Export**, and then select **Create PDF/XPS**. Leave the file name as w04p1Live_LastFirst and ensure that the type is PDF. Click **Publish** to save the document as a PDF file. Scroll through the PDF file and note that the edits and the comment were saved as part of the PDF document.

r. Close all open files, saving a file if prompted to do so. Based on your instructor's directions, submit the following:

w04p1Live_LastFirst

w04p1Live_LastFirst.pdf

2 DREAM Act Letter

You are a partner in a law firm that deals with a large number of potential DREAM Act beneficiaries. The DREAM Act (Development, Relief, and Education for Alien Minors) provides conditional permanent residency to undocumented residents under certain conditions (good moral character, completion of U.S. high school degree, arrival in the United States as minors, etc.). Supporters of the Act contend that it provides social and economic benefits, whereas opponents label it as an amnesty program that rewards illegal immigration. Your law firm has partnered with leading law professors across the country to encourage the U.S. Executive Branch (Office of the President) to explore various options related to wise administration of the DREAM Act. In a letter to the president, you outline your position. Because it is of a legal nature, the letter makes broad use of footnotes and in-text references. Because the letter is to be signed and supported by law professors across the country, you will share the letter online, making it possible for others to edit and approve of the wording. Refer to Figure 4.40 as you complete this exercise.

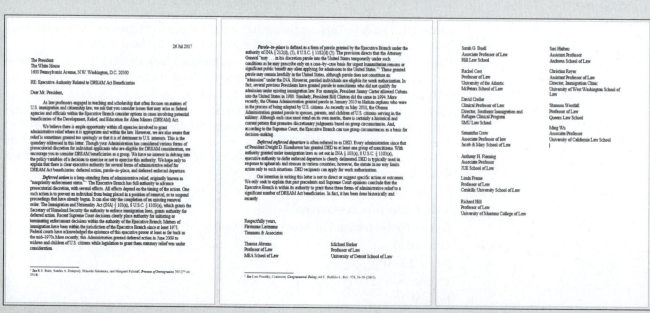

FIGURE 4.40 Format the DREAM Act Letter

a. Open *w04p2Law* and save as **w04p2Law_LastFirst**.

b. Scroll through the document and change *Firstname Lastname* in the closing to your first and last names. Add two blank paragraphs above *Respectfully yours*. Check the document for spelling errors. All names are spelled correctly. The word *parol* should be spelled parole. The word *nonpriority* is not misspelled. Select the text in the document from *As law professors engaged in teaching and scholarship* through *historically and recently*. Ensure the paragraph spacing After is **6 pt**. Deselect the text. Change the margin setting to **Normal**.

c. Scroll down and select the text from *Theresa Abroms* through the end of the document. Format the selected text in two columns. Deselect the text. Ensure that *Rachel Cost* and her information are in the same column by adding a **hard return** in front of her name. Scroll to the last page and place the insertion point to the left of *Sari Haibau*. Click **Breaks** in the Page Setup group on the Layout tab. Click **Column**.

d. Place the insertion point after the ending quotation mark that ends the first sentence in the third body paragraph on page 1. Click the **References tab** and click **Insert Footnote** in the Footnotes group. Type *See* **R.S. Bane, Sandra A. Dempsey, Minoshi Satomura, and Margaret Falstaff,** *Process of Immigration* **785 (7th ed. 2014).** (include the period). Note: the word *See* is italicized in the footnote.

e. Scroll to page 2 and place the insertion point after the quotation mark that ends the second sentence in the paragraph that begins *Parole-in-place is defined*. Click the **Footnotes Dialog Box Launcher** in the Footnotes group and click **Insert**. Type *See* **Lani Parosky, Comment,** *Congressional Policy*, **64 U. Buffalo L. Rev. 578, 56–58 (2003).** (include the period). Note: the word *See* is italicized in the footnote.

f. Sign in to your Microsoft account and save the document to your OneDrive folder on File Explorer. Click **Share** at the top right corner, enter your own email address, and ensure the **Can edit option** is selected in the Share pane. Type an optional message and click **Share**.

g. Open your email with the shared link and click **View in OneDrive**. Scroll through the document and note that Word Online shows a placeholder for the footnotes you created. However, you cannot edit or work with footnotes in Word Online because it is limited in features. Point to a footnote placeholder to read a comment to the effect that you must open Word to work with footnotes.

h. Click **Edit Document** and select **Edit in Browser**. Click the **Review tab**, ensure that **Show Comments** in the Comments group is enabled, and review the comment on the Comments pane.

i. Select *The President* at the top of the letter. Click **New Comment** in the Comment pane. Type **Please review this document very carefully and pay attention to all the names and their associations. Also, please make any edits you feel necessary.** (include the period). Click **Post**. Close the Comments pane.

j. Click **Open in Word**. Click the **Track Changes arrow** in the Tracking group and click **Track Changes**. Click **Reviewing Pane** (not the Reviewing Pane arrow). Reverse the words *to* and *not* in the second body paragraph on page 1. Note the changes in the Reviewing Pane as well as the vertical bar on the right side of the affected paragraph indicating that edits have been made. Click the **vertical bar** to view the changes. Click it again to return to Simple Markup. Close the Reviewing (Revisions) Pane.

k. Ensure that w04p2Law_LastFirst.docx is displayed, click the **Review tab**, click the **Accept arrow** in the Changes group, and then click **Accept All Changes and Stop Tracking**.

l. Save the document. Click **Share** at the top right corner and click **Send as attachment** at the bottom of the Share pane. Click **Send a PDF**. Type your own email address when your default email account opens. Type an optional subject and send the email. Open your own email and download the PDF file to your computer. Open the PDF file and review the whole document for any last-minute revisions.

m. Save and close both files. Based on your instructor's directions, submit the following:

w04p2Law_LastFirst

w04p2Law_LastFirst.pdf

Mid-Level Exercises

1 WWW Web Services Agency

You work as a Web designer at WWW Web Services Agency and have been asked to provide some basic information to be used in a senior citizens' workshop. You want to provide the basic elements of good Web design and format the document professionally. Use the basic information you have already prepared in a Word document and revise it to include elements appropriate for a research-oriented paper.

a. Open *w04m1Web* and save as **w04m1Web_LastFirst**. Delete the square brackets and change the author name to your own name.

b. Apply the following formatting to the whole document:
- Alignment is left.
- Document is double-spaced.
- The font is Times New Roman 12 pt.
- Paragraph spacing before or after any paragraph is 0.
- Margins are 1" at the top, bottom, left, and right.

c. Change citation style to **APA Sixth Edition**. Place the insertion point at the end of the Proximity paragraph (after the period) on the second page of the document. The paragraph ends with *indicates less proximity*. Insert the following footnote: **Max Rebaza, Effective Websites, Chicago: Windy City Publishing, Inc. (2018)**. Do not include the period.

d. Insert a table of contents on a new page after the cover page. Use a style of your choice.

e. Add a bibliography to the document by inserting citation sources from the footnotes already in place. Because you will not use in-text citations, you will use the Source Manager to create the sources. To add new sources, complete the following steps:
- Click the **References tab** and click **Manage Sources** in the Citations & Bibliography group.
- Add a source for the footnote you created in Step c (a Book). Click **New** in the Source Manager dialog box and add the source to both the Current List and the Master List.
- Create citation sources for the two additional sources identified in the document footnotes. The footnote on the fourth page is from an article in a periodical (issue 7) and the footnote on the fifth page cites a journal article.

f. Change the citation style to **Chicago.** Insert a bibliography at the end of the document on a separate page. Select **Bibliography**. Apply **Heading 2 style** to the Bibliography heading and center the heading. Double space the bibliography and ensure that there is no paragraph spacing before or after. Update the table of contents to include this new addition and change the font for Bibliography to **Times New Roman**.

g. Mark all occurrences of *Web*, *content*, and *site* as index entries. Cross-reference *Web pages* with *Web sites*. Create an index on a separate page after the bibliography using the **Formal format**.

h. Check the document for spelling errors. All names are spelled correctly.

i. Begin to track changes. Select the heading **Proximity and Balance** on the third page. Add a new comment, typing **This section seems incomplete. Please check and add content.** (include the period)

j. Add the following sentence as the second sentence in the Contrast and Focus section: **You are most likely familiar with the concept of contrast when working with pictures in an image editor.**

k. Sign in to your Microsoft account and save the document to your OneDrive folder on File Explorer. Click **Share** at the top right corner and click **Get a sharing link** at the bottom of the Share pane. Click **Copy** to create an edit link.

l. Scroll to the end of the document, press **Enter**, and then paste the link.

m. Click the **File tab**, click **Export**, and then select **Create PDF/XPS**. Leave the file name as w04m1Web_LastFirst and ensure that the type is PDF. Click **Publish** to save the document as a PDF file. Scroll through the PDF file and note that the edits and the comment were saved as part of the PDF document.

n. Close all files and based on your instructor's directions, submit the following:
w04m1Web_LastFirst
w04m1Web_LastFirst.pdf

You want to study for a semester in a foreign country. For the application process, you need to write a proposal describing the program that you are interested in. You conducted online research, found a foreign university that appealed to you, and developed a list of activities that you will participate in while away. Now you want to format the Word document to enhance the readability and to include a cover page, table of contents, and index, before submitting it to your academic advisor for discussion.

a. Open *w04m2StudyAbroad* and save it as **w04m2StudyAbroad_LastFirst**.

b. Turn on **Track Changes** so any further changes will be flagged.

c. Apply **Heading 1 style** to section headings that display in all capital letters. Apply **Heading 2 style** (scroll to locate the style) to section headings that display alone on a line in title case (the first letter of each word is capitalized). Format the program fees' items in the *Included in the Tuition* section as a bulleted list.

d. Sign in to your Microsoft account and save the document to your OneDrive folder on File Explorer. Click **Share** at the top right corner, enter your own email address, and then ensure the **Can edit option** is selected in the Share pane. Type an optional message and click **Share**. Open your email with the shared link and click **View in OneDrive**. Scroll through the document on Word Online. Click **Edit Document** and select **Edit in Browser**. Click the **Review tab** and ensure that **Show Comments** in the Comments group is enabled.

e. Type the following reply to the first comment in the document (you will insert the cover page and TOC in a later step): **I have changed this heading to Heading 1, and inserted a cover page and a TOC before this heading.** (include the period). Type the following reply to the third comment: **I have formatted these items as a bulleted list.** (include the period). Close the Comments pane.

f. Click **Open in Word**. Change the citation style to **APA Sixth Edition**. Insert a footnote on page 1 at the end of the first sentence in the first paragraph (after the period), which ends with *Strasbourg, France*. Type the following for the footnote: **EU Studies Program in Strasbourg, France. http://www.eustudiesprogram.eu/resources/eustudies-web.pdf**. Change the number format for footnotes to **a, b, c** in the Footnotes dialog box. (Click **Apply**, not Insert.) Locate the endnote at the end of the document and convert it to a footnote.

g. Create a footer for the document consisting of the title **Study Abroad**, followed by a space and a page number. If the page number already displays as a footer, adjust it so that it follows Study Abroad. Left align the footer in the footer area. Do not display the footer on the first page.

h. Create a cover page of your choosing. Delete any placeholders that you are not using.

i. Create a page specifically for the table of contents right after the cover page and generate a table of contents.

j. Mark all occurrences of the following text for inclusion in the index: Alsace, Black Forest, Classes, European Union, France, Grand Île, and Rhine valley. Cross-reference *Strasbourg* with *France* and *European Union* with *EU*. On a separate page at the end of the document, create the index in **Classic format** and accept all default settings. Accept all changes to the document and turn off Track Changes.

k. Click **Share** at the top right corner and click **Send as attachment** at the bottom of the Share pane. Click **Send a PDF**. Type your own email address when your default email account opens. Type an optional subject and send the email. Open your own email and download the PDF file to your computer. Open the PDF file and review the whole document for any last-minute revisions.

l. Save and close both files. Based on your instructor's directions, submit the following:

w04m2StudyAbroad_LastFirst

w04m2StudyAbroad_LastFirst.pdf

Running Case

New Castle County Technical Services

New Castle County Technical Services (NCCTS) provides technical services to clients in the greater New Castle County, Delaware, area. Founded in 2011, the company is rapidly expanding to include technical security systems, network infrastructure cabling, and basic troubleshooting services. With that growth comes the need to promote the company and to provide clear written communication to employees and clients. Microsoft Word is used exclusively in the development and distribution of documents, including an "About New Castle" summary that will be available both in print and online. You made a few changes to the document and you are now ready to make this into a professional-looking business document in this exercise.

a. Sign in to your Microsoft account. Open *w04r1NewCastle* and save it as **w04r1NewCastle_LastFirst** to your OneDrive folder on File Explorer.

b. Accept the following formatting changes in the document and turn off Track Changes.
   • Font is Times New Roman.
   • Margins are 1" at the top, bottom, left, and right.
   • Alignment is left.

c. Click **Share** at the top right corner, enter your own email address, and then ensure the **Can edit option** is selected in the Share pane. Type an optional message and click **Share**.

d. Open your email with the shared link and click **View in OneDrive**. Scroll through the document on Word Online. Click **Edit Document** and select **Edit in Browser**. Click the **Review tab** and ensure that **Show Comments** in the Comments group is enabled. Select the date at the top of the letter. Click **New Comment** in the Comment pane and type **I have accepted all the formatting changes.** (include the period). Click **Post**.

e. Address the comment in the *Active Accounts* section of the document by typing the following sentence as the third sentence in the paragraph: **It is not surprising to see that network security and cloud integration have a larger increase than IT consulting and disaster recovery.** (include the period) Click **Reply** and click **Resolve** to close the comment since you have taken action on the item. Close the Comments pane.

f. Click **Open in Word**. Insert a footnote on page 6 at the end of the second sentence in the first paragraph (after the period), which ends with *of the past two years*. Type the following for the footnote: **Information for the past five years can be made available upon direct request from the company.** (include the period). Change the number format for footnotes to **1, 2, 3** in the Footnotes dialog box. (Click **Apply**, not Insert.) Use a style to change the font to **Times New Roman, 11 pt size**.

g. Create the **Integral cover page**. Change the document title to **About New Castle** and change the author name to your own name. Delete any placeholders that you are not using.

h. Create a page specifically for the table of contents right after the cover page and generate a table of contents using the **Automatic Table 2 style**.

i. Mark all occurrences of the following text for inclusion in the index: *computer, certification, network, NCCTS, training support,* and *troubleshooting*. Cross-reference *New Castle* with *Technical Services*. On a separate page at the end of the document, create the index in **Classic format**.

j. Click **Share** at the top right corner and click **Send as attachment** at the bottom of the Share pane. Click **Send a PDF**. Type your own email address when your default email account opens. Type an optional subject and send the email. Open your own email and download the PDF file to your computer. Open the PDF file and review the whole document for any last-minute revisions.

k. Save and close both files. Based on your instructor's directions, submit the following:
   w04r1NewCastle_LastFirst
   w04r1NewCastle_LastFirst.pdf

Disaster Recovery

Computer History

You are preparing a brief history of computers for inclusion in a group project. Another student began the project but ran out of time and needs your help. You need to turn the draft into a professional-looking document by applying formatting based on the APA writing style and including proper citations of the sources used in your research. Adding a cover page, a table of contents, and an index to the research paper will also help to enhance the document. Open *w04d1Computers* and save it as **w04d1Computers_LastFirst**. Turn on Track Changes and respond to all comments left for you by the previous student, and then mark the comments as resolved when you are done. Save and close the file. Based on your instructor's directions, submit w04d1Computers_LastFirst.

Capstone Exercise

Funding a College Education

Funding a college education can be an expensive and daunting task for parents. Being a recent college graduate provides you with first-hand experience on how to finance a four-year education. Upon graduation, you and a fellow student created a consulting business to educate parents on college funding and help them maneuver the maze of scholarships and federal funding. To get things started, your business partner has written a draft of the comprehensive guide to college funding and is ready for you to review it.

Use Word Online, and Apply Formatting

Your business partner sent you the guide in PDF format, so you will open and save it in Word. To apply consistency throughout the draft document, you will format the document in the APA style.

1. Sign in to your Microsoft account. Open *w04c1College* and save it as **w04c1College_LastFirst** to your OneDrive folder on File Explorer.

2. Use Word Online to apply the following formatting to the whole document:

   - Document is double-spaced.
   - Font is Times New Roman 12 pt size.
   - No paragraph spacing before or after any paragraph.
   - Margins are 1" at the top, bottom, left, and right.
   - Alignment is left.

Track Revisions

The document you received has several changes and comments made by your partner. You will review the tracked changes and make a few of your own.

3. Ensure that the markup view is All Markup. In the first paragraph on the first page, reject the addition of the words *2- or*. Reject the *Click here for more* change in the FAFSA section. Accept all other tracked changes in the document and stop tracking.

4. Review and act on the three comments about formatting all headings to the correct heading styles as per the comments left by your business partner. Reply to these comments by typing **I have made the style replacement** and mark them as Resolved.

Credit Sources

You are now ready to add the citations for resources that your partner used when assembling this guide. However, because these features are not available on Word Online, you need to use Word on your computer to perform the rest of the tasks.

5. Select **APA Sixth Edition style**. Click before the period ending in the sentence *More information on how* to complete the FASFA is available online in the FAFSA section. Insert the following website citation:

   Name of Webpage: **How to Complete the FAFSA**

   Name of Website: **Collegeboard**

   Year: **2018**

   Month: **May**

   Day: **03**

   URL: **https://bigfuture.collegeboard. gov/pay-for-college/financial-aid-101/ how-to-complete-the-fafsa**

6. Click before the period ending in the sentence *grants and scholarships, federal loans, and work-study* on page 1 in the FAFSA section. Insert the following website citation:

   Name of Webpage: **FAFSA**

   Name of Website: **fafsa**

   Year: **2018**

   Month: **May**

   Day: **03**

   URL: **https://fafsa.edu.gov**

7. Insert a footnote on page 2 before the period in the sentence ending *for the academic year of 2017-2018*: **The amount of Pell Grant award changes every year. For more information, please consult the Department of Education.** (include the period). Change the number format for footnotes to **a, b, c** in the Footnotes dialog box. (Click **Apply**, not Insert.) Use style to change the font to **Times New Roman, 11 pt size**.

8. Delete the reminder comment at the bottom of the last page. Insert a blank page at the end of the report and insert a bibliography in APA style on the blank page with the title **Works Cited**. Double space the bibliography, with no paragraph spacing and a font of **Times New Roman 12 pt**. Center the *Works Cited* title, apply **12 pt**, but **not bold** formatting. Ensure that all text in the bibliography is formatted to **Black, Text 1 font color**.

Insert a Cover Page, a Table of Contents, Page Number, and Index

To put the finishing touches on your document, you add a cover page, a table of contents, page number, and an index to the document.

9. Insert the **Retrospect cover page**. Change the author name to your own name and delete any placeholders that you are not using. Address the first comment and delete the comment, the title, and the blank paragraphs.

10. Create a page specifically for the table of contents right after the cover page using the **Automatic Table 1** style.

11. Display a centered page number, using **Plain Number 2 format,** in the footer of the document. Do not display the page number footer on the first page. Numbering begins with page 1 on the Table of Contents page.

12. Mark all occurrences of *scholarship*, *grant*, and *FAFSA* as index entries. Cross-reference *college* with *university*. Create an index on a separate page after the bibliography using the **Formal format**. Use all other default settings.

Share the Document and Create a PDF Document

13. Sign in to your Microsoft account, save the document to your OneDrive folder on File Explorer, and then get a sharing link. Scroll to the end of the document, insert a blank paragraph, and then paste the link.

14. Create a PDF document with the same name.

15. Close all files and based on your instructor's directions, submit the following:

w04c1College_LastFirst

w04c1College_LastFirst.pdf

Excel

Introduction to Excel

LEARNING OUTCOME You will create and format a basic Excel worksheet.

OBJECTIVES & SKILLS: After you read this chapter, you will be able to:

CASE STUDY | Celebrity Musician's Souvenir Shop

Melissa Rogers, the merchandise manager for Celebrity Musician's Souvenir Shop, asked you to calculate the retail price, sale price, and profit analysis for selected items on sale for the upcoming concert. Using markup rates that Melissa provided, you will calculate the retail price—the amount the souvenir shop charges its customers for the products. In addition, you will calculate sale prices based on discount rates. Finally, you will calculate the profit margin to determine the percentage of the final sale price over the cost.

Creating and Formatting a Worksheet

Yanlev/123RF

After you create the initial pricing spreadsheet, you will be able to change values and see that the formulas update the results automatically. In addition, you will insert data for additional sale items or delete an item based on the manager's decision. After inserting formulas, you will format the data in the worksheet to have a professional appearance.

J6 ▾ : × ✓ fx =(H6-C6)/H6

	A	C	D	E	F	G	H	I	J	K	L
1				Celebrity Musician's Souvenir Shop							
2				9/1/2021							
3											
4	Product	Cost	Markup Rate	Markup Amount	Retail Price	Percent Off	Sale Price	Profit Amount	Profit Margin		
5	Apparel										
6	Hat	$ 7.95	109.5%	$ 8.71	$ 16.66	15%	$ 14.16	$ 6.21	43.8%		
7	Hoodie	$ 27.25	125.0%	$ 34.06	$ 61.31	20%	$ 49.05	$ 21.80	44.4%		
8	T-shirt	$ 7.10	315.5%	$ 22.40	$ 29.50	10%	$ 26.55	$ 19.45	73.3%		
9	Souvenirs										
10	Mug	$ 5.00	200.0%	$ 10.00	$ 15.00	15%	$ 12.75	$ 7.75	60.8%		
11	Souvenir Program	$ 9.95	101.0%	$ 10.05	$ 20.00	25%	$ 15.00	$ 5.05	33.7%		
12	Travel Mug	$ 7.00	200.0%	$ 14.00	$ 21.00	15%	$ 17.85	$ 10.85	60.8%		
13											

September | Formulas | (+)

Ready ⊞ ▦ ▣ ─── + 160%

	Product	Cost	Markup Rate	Markup Amount	Retail Price	Percent Off	Sale Price	Profit Amount	Profit Margin
4	Product	Cost	Markup Rate	Markup Amount	Retail Price	Percent Off	Sale Price	Profit Amount	Profit Margin
5	Apparel								
6	Hat	7.95	1.095	=C6*D6	=C6+E6	0.15	=F6*(1-G6)	=H6-C6	=(H6-C6)/H6
7	Hoodie	27.25	1.25	=C7*D7	=C7+E7	0.2	=F7*(1-G7)	=H7-C7	=(H7-C7)/H7
8	T-shirt	7.1	3.155	=C8*D8	=C8+E8	0.1	=F8*(1-G8)	=H8-C8	=(H8-C8)/H8
9	Souvenirs								
10	Mug	5	2	=C10*D10	=C10+E10	0.15	=F10*(1-G10)	=H10-C10	=(H10-C10)/H10
11	Souvenir Program	9.95	1.01	=C11*D11	=C11+E11	0.25	=F11*(1-G11)	=H11-C11	=(H11-C11)/H11
12	Travel Mug	7	2	=C12*D12	=C12+E12	0.15	=F12*(1-G12)	=H12-C12	=(H12-C12)/H12
13									
14									
15									
16									

September | Formulas | (+)

Ready ⊞ ▦ ▣ ─── + 130%

FIGURE 1.1 Completed Souvenir Shop Worksheet

CASE STUDY | Celebrity Musician's Souvenir Shop

Starting File	File to be Submitted
e01h1Souvenirs	e01h5Souvenirs_LastFirst

MyLab IT Grader An alternate version of this project is available as a MyLab IT Grader Assessment

Introduction to Spreadsheets

Organizing, calculating, and evaluating quantitative data are important skills required today for personal and managerial decision making. You track expenses for your household budget, maintain a savings plan, and determine what amount you can afford for a house or car payment. Retail managers create and analyze their organizations' annual budgets, sales projections, and inventory records.

A *spreadsheet* is an electronic file that contains a grid of columns and rows to organize related data and to display results of calculations, enabling interpretation of quantitative data for decision making. When you make changes, the formula results recalculate automatically and accurately.

In this section, you will learn how to design spreadsheets. You will also explore the Excel window. Then, you will enter text, values, and dates in a spreadsheet. In addition, you will correct spelling errors and find and replace data.

Exploring the Excel Window

In Excel, a *worksheet* is a spreadsheet that usually contains descriptive labels, numeric values, formulas, functions, and charts. A *workbook* is a collection of one or more related worksheets contained within a single file. Storing multiple worksheets within one workbook helps organize related data together in one file and enables you to perform calculations among the worksheets. For example, you can create a budget workbook of 13 worksheets, one for each month to store income and expenses and a final worksheet to calculate totals across the entire year.

Identify Excel Window Elements

Figure 1.2 identifies elements in the Excel window, and Table 1.1 lists and describes the Excel window elements.

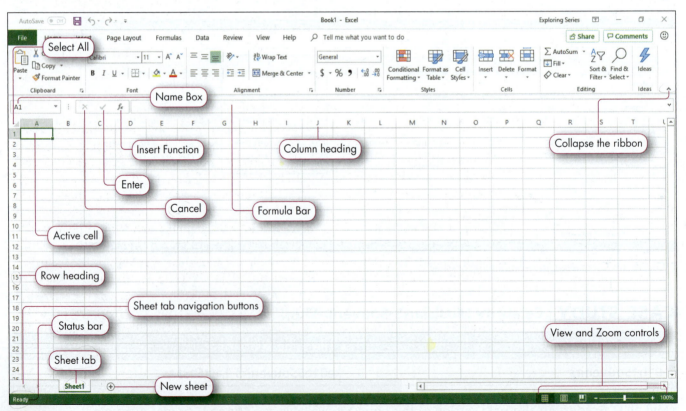

FIGURE 1.2 Excel Window

TABLE 1.1 Excel Elements

Element		Description
Name Box		A rectangular area located below the ribbon that displays the address (or name) of the active cell, selected chart, or selected table. Use the Name Box to go to a cell, chart, or table; select a range; or assign a name to one or more cells.
Cancel	☒	A command to the left of the Formula Bar used to cancel data being entered or edited into the active cell. As you enter or edit data in a cell, the Cancel command changes from gray to red when you position the pointer over it.
Enter	☑	A command to the left of the Formula Bar used to accept data typed in the active cell and keep the current cell active. As you enter or edit data in a cell, the Enter command changes from gray to blue when you position the pointer over it.
Insert Function	fx	A command that displays the Insert Function dialog box to search for and select a function to insert into the active cell. The Insert Function command changes from gray to green when you position the pointer over it.
Formula Bar		A bar below the ribbon and to the right of the Insert Function command that shows the contents (text, value, date, formula, or function) stored in the active cell. You enter or edit cell contents here.
Select All	◢	The triangle at the intersection of the row and column headings in the top-left corner of the worksheet used to select everything contained in the active worksheet.
Column heading		The letter above each column in a worksheet.
Row heading		The number to the left of a row in a worksheet.
Active cell		The currently selected cell in a worksheet. It is indicated by a dark green border.
Sheet tab		A label that looks like a file folder tab, located between the bottom of the worksheet and the status bar, that shows the name of a worksheet contained in the workbook. When you create a new Excel workbook, the default worksheet is named Sheet1.
New sheet	⊕	Button used to insert a new worksheet to the right of the current worksheet.
Sheet tab scroll buttons	◀ ▶	Buttons to the left of the sheet tabs used to scroll through sheet tabs; not all the sheet tabs are displayed at the same time. Use the left scroll button to scroll through sheets to the left; use the right scroll button to scroll through sheets to the right.
View controls	▦ ▣ ▥	Buttons on the right side of the status bar that control how a worksheet displays. **Normal view**, the default, displays the worksheet without showing margins, headers, footers, and page breaks. **Page Layout view** displays margins, header and footer area, and a ruler. **Page Break Preview** displays page breaks within the worksheet.

Identify Columns, Rows, and Cells

A worksheet contains columns and rows, with each column and row assigned a heading. Columns are assigned alphabetic headings from columns A to Z, continuing from AA to AZ, and then from BA to BZ until XFD, which is the last of the possible 16,384 columns. Rows have numeric headings ranging from 1 to 1,048,576. Depending on your screen resolution, you may see more or fewer columns and rows than what are shown in the figures in this book.

The intersection of a column and a row is a *cell*; a total of more than 17 billion cells are available in a worksheet. Each cell has a *cell address*, a unique identifier starting with its column letter and then its row number. For example, the cell at the intersection of column C and row 6 is cell C6 (see Figure 1.3). The active cell is the current cell. Excel displays a dark green border around the active cell in the worksheet, and the Name Box shows the cell address of the active cell, which is C6 in Figure 1.3. The contents of the active cell, or the formula used to calculate the results of the active cell, appear in the Formula Bar. Cell references are useful in formulas or in navigation.

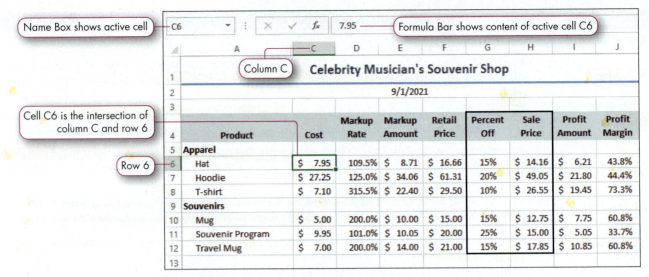

FIGURE 1.3 Columns, Rows, and Cells

Navigate in and Among Worksheets

To move to a new cell, use the pointer or the arrow keys on the keyboard. If you work in a large worksheet, use the vertical and horizontal scroll bars to display another area of the worksheet and click in the desired cell to make it the active cell.

The worksheet that is currently displayed is called the *active sheet*. The sheet tab for the active sheet is bold green with a green horizontal line below the tab name. Use the sheet tabs at the bottom of the workbook window (above the status bar) to display the contents of another worksheet within the workbook. Once a sheet is the active sheet, you can then navigate within that worksheet.

The keyboard contains several keys that can be used in isolation or in combination with other keys to navigate in a worksheet. Table 1.2 lists the keyboard navigation methods.

TABLE 1.2	Keystrokes and Actions	
PC Keystroke	**Mac Keystroke**	**Used to**
▲	↑	Move up one cell in the same column.
▼	↓	Move down one cell in the same column.
◀	←	Move left one cell in the same row.
▶	→	Move right one cell in the same row.
Tab	Tab	Move right one cell in the same row.
Page Up	fn ↑	Move the active cell up one screen.
Page Down	fn ↓	Move the active cell down one screen.
Home	fn ←	Move the active cell to column A of the current row.
Ctrl+Home	Control fn ←	Make cell A1 the active cell.
Ctrl+End	Control fn →	Make the lower right active corner of the worksheet—the intersection of the last column and row that contains data—the active cell. Does not move to cell XFD1048576 unless that cell contains data.
Ctrl+Page Down	Option ↓	Move to the next sheet on the right side of the active sheet.
Ctrl+Page Up	Option ↑	Move to the next sheet on the left side of the active sheet.
F5 or Ctrl+G		Open the Go To dialog box to enter any cell address.

Go To is a helpful navigation feature when working in large workbooks. Use Go To to navigate to a specific cell, particularly when that cell is not visible onscreen or is many columns or rows away. For example, you might want to go to the cell containing the profit margin for the Travel Mug in the Souvenir Shop workbook. Use the Go To dialog box or the Go To Special dialog box.

To use the Go To dialog box, complete the following steps:

1. Click Find & Select in the Editing group on the Home tab.
2. Select Go To on the menu to open the Go To dialog box (see Figure 1.4).
3. Select a range name from the Go to list, or type a cell address (such as B5) or a range such as B5:B10 in the Reference box.
4. Click OK.

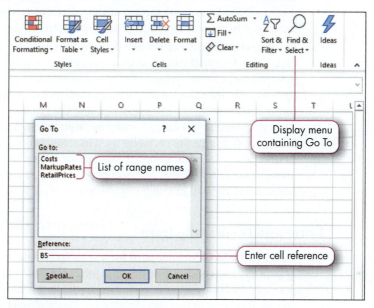

FIGURE 1.4 Go To Dialog Box

If you enter a specific cell address in the Go To dialog box, Excel will make it the active cell. If you select a range name from the list or if you type a range address (such as G5:G12) in the Go To dialog box, Excel will select the entire range defined by the name or addresses. For more specific options, select the Go To Special option. The Go To Special dialog box opens so that you can go to a cell containing comments, constants, formulas, blanks, and so on. Use Help to learn more about the options in this dialog box.

> **TIP: USING THE NAME BOX**
> You can enter a cell address, such as G12, in the Name Box and press Enter to go to that cell.

Entering and Editing Cell Data

You should plan the structure of a worksheet before you start entering data. Using the Souvenir Shop case presented at the beginning of the chapter as an example, use the following steps to plan the worksheet design, enter and format data, and complete the workbook. Refer to Figure 1.1 for the completed workbook.

Plan the Worksheet Design

1. **State the purpose of the worksheet.** The purpose of the Souvenir Shop worksheet is to store data about products on sale and to calculate the retail price based on the markup, the sales price based on a discount rate, and the profit margin.

2. **Decide what outputs are required to achieve the purpose of the worksheet.** Outputs are the calculated results. For the Souvenir Shop worksheet, the outputs include columns to calculate the retail price (i.e., the original price you charge your customers), the sale price (the price you charge when the product is on sale), and the profit margin. Some worksheets contain an *output area*, the range of cells in the worksheet to contain formulas dependent on the values in the input area.

3. **Decide what input values are required to achieve the desired output.** Input values are the initial values, such as variables and assumptions. You would change these values to see what type of effects different values have on the end results. For the Souvenir Shop worksheet, the input values include the costs Souvenir Shop pays the manufacturers, the markup rates, and the proposed discount rates for the sale. In some worksheets, you should create an *input area*, a range of cells in the worksheet to store and change the variables used in calculations. For example, if you use the same Markup Rate and same Percent Off for all products, it would be easier to create an input area at the top of the worksheet. Then you could change the values in one location rather than in several locations.

Enter and Format the Data

4. **Enter the labels, values, and formulas in Excel.** Use the design plan (steps 2–3) as you enter labels, input values, and formulas. In the Souvenir Shop worksheet, descriptive labels (the product names) in the first column indicate that the values on a specific row pertain to a specific product. Descriptive labels at the top of each column, such as Cost and Retail Price, describe the values in the respective column. Enter the values and formulas. Change some values to test that your formulas produce correct results. If necessary, correct any errors in the formulas to produce correct results. For the Souvenir Shop worksheet, change some of the original costs and markup rates to ensure the calculated retail price, selling price, and profit margin percentage results update correctly.

5. **Format the numeric values in the worksheet.** Align decimal points in columns of numbers and add number formats and styles. In the Souvenir Shop worksheet, you will use Accounting Number Format and the Percent Style to format the numerical data. Adjust the number of decimal places based on the data.

6. **Format the descriptive titles and labels.** Add bold and color to headings so that they stand out. Apply other formatting to headings and descriptive labels to achieve a professional appearance. In the Souvenir Shop worksheet, you will center the main title over all the columns, bold and center column labels over the columns, and apply other formatting.

Complete the Workbook

7. **Document the workbook as thoroughly as possible.** Include the current date, your name as the workbook author, assumptions, and purpose of the workbook. Some people provide this documentation in a separate worksheet within the workbook. You can also add some documentation in the Properties section when you click the File tab.

8. **Save and share the completed workbook.** Preview and prepare printouts for distribution in meetings, send an electronic copy of the workbook to those who need it, or upload the workbook to a shared network drive or in the cloud.

> **TIP: TEMPLATES AND THEMES**
>
> To save time designing a workbook, consider using an Excel template that contains some of the text, formulas, and formatting. You can then enter specific values and text, and customize the worksheet. You can apply a theme to a workbook to provide a consistent appearance with a unique set of fonts, colors, and other visual effects on worksheet data, shapes, charts, and objects. The Page Layout tab contains commands to change Themes, Colors, Fonts, and Effects.

STEP 1 Enter Text

Text is any combination of letters, numbers, symbols, and spaces not used in calculations. Excel treats phone numbers, such as 617-555-1234 as text entries. You enter text for a worksheet title to describe the contents of the worksheet, as row and column labels to describe data, and as cell data. In Figure 1.5, the cells in column A contain text, such as Class. Text aligns at the left side of the cell by default.

As soon as you begin typing text into a cell, the ***AutoComplete*** feature searches for and automatically displays any other text in the same column that matches the letters you type. The left side of Figure 1.5 shows Spreadsheet Apps was typed in cell A3. When you start to type *Sp* in cell A4, AutoComplete displays *Spreadsheet Apps* because a text entry in the same column already starts with *Sp*. Press Enter to accept the repeated label, or continue typing to enter a different label, such as Spanish II. When you press Enter, the next cell down in the same column becomes the active cell. However, if you press Ctrl+Enter or click Enter (the check mark between the Name Box and the Formula Bar) after entering data in a cell, the cell remains the active cell.

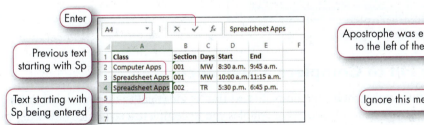

FIGURE 1.5 Entering Text

> **TIP: ENTER A NUMBER AS TEXT**
>
> If you want to enter a numeric value as text, type an apostrophe and the number, such as '002. The right side of Figure 1.5 shows that '002 was entered in cell B4 to start the text with a 0. Otherwise, Excel would have eliminated the zeros in the class section number. Ignore the error message that displays when you intentionally use an apostrophe to enter a number that is not actually a value.

Check the Spelling in a Worksheet

Unlike Word, which displays a red wavy line below misspelled words, Excel does not display any visual indicators for potentially misspelled words. After entering and editing text in a worksheet, you should use the Spelling tool to detect and correct misspelled words.

To check the spelling of text in a worksheet, complete the following steps:

1. Make cell A1 the active cell. If you want to check the spelling in several worksheets, click the first sheet tab and hold Shift to select the last sheet tab; otherwise, only the active sheet will be checked.

2. Click the Review tab and click Spelling in the Proofing group to open the Spelling dialog box (see Figure 1.6). The Spelling dialog box opens, and the potentially misspelled word is displayed in the Not in Dictionary box. The Suggestions box contains a list of potentially correct words.

3. Select the correct word in the Suggestions box and click Change. If the correct word is not listed, click Cancel and correct the misspelled word manually. Start Spelling again to check the rest of the worksheet. If the word is spelled correctly but is not in the dictionary, click Ignore Once to ignore the current occurrence or click Ignore All to ignore all occurrences of the word. You can also click Add to Dictionary to add the word to the dictionary.

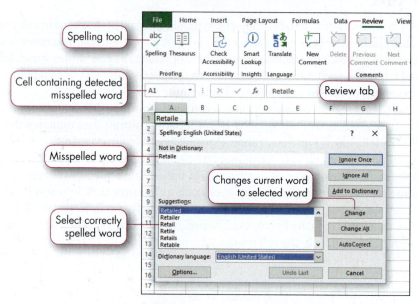

FIGURE 1.6 Spelling Dialog Box

STEP 2 ## Use Auto Fill to Complete a Sequence

Although AutoComplete helps to complete text that is identical to another label in the same column, **Auto Fill** is a feature that enables you to complete a sequence of words or values and is implemented by using the **fill handle** (a small green square in the bottom-right corner of the active cell). For example, if you enter January in a cell, use Auto Fill to fill in the rest of the months in adjacent cells so that you do not have to type the rest of the month names. Auto Fill can help you complete other sequences, such as quarters (Qtr 1, etc.), weekdays, and weekday abbreviations after you type the first item in the sequence. Figure 1.7 shows the results of filling in months, abbreviated months, quarters, weekdays, abbreviated weekdays, numeric series, and increments of 5.

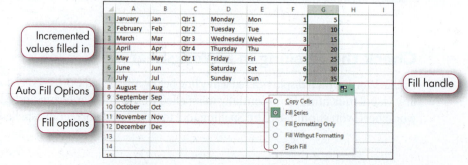

FIGURE 1.7 Auto Fill Examples

To use Auto Fill to complete a text or numeric series, complete the following steps:

1. Type the first text, such as January, in the starting cell or type the first value, such as 1 (refer to Figure 1.7).
2. Make sure the original text or value is the active cell.
3. Point to the fill handle until the pointer changes to a thin black plus sign.
4. Drag the fill handle to repeat the content in other cells (e.g., through cell A12).

Immediately after you use Auto Fill, Excel displays Auto Fill Options in the bottom-right corner of the filled data (refer to Figure 1.7). Click Auto Fill Options to display several fill options: Copy Cells, Fill Series, Fill Formatting Only, Fill Without Formatting, or Flash Fill. The menu will also include other options, depending on the cell content: Fill Months for completing months; Fill Weekdays for completing weekdays; and Fill Days, Fill Weekdays, Fill Months, Fill Years to complete dates. Select Fill Formatting Only when you want to copy the formats but not complete a sequence. Select Fill Without Formatting when you want to complete the sequence but do not want to format the rest of the sequence. For example, if the first cell contains a top border, use Fill Without Formatting to prevent Auto Fill from formatting the rest of the cells with a top border.

For a single value, Auto Fill will copy that value. Use Auto Fill Options and select Fill Series to change the numbers to be in sequential order, starting with the original value you typed. For nonconsecutive numeric sequences, you must specify the first two values in sequence. To use Auto Fill to fill a sequence of number patterns (such as 5, 10, 15, 20, as shown in Figure 1.7), type the first two numbers in the sequence of adjoining cells, select those two cells, and then drag the fill handle to fill in the rest of the sequence.

> **TIP: FLASH FILL**
>
> Flash Fill is a similar feature to Auto Fill in that it can quickly fill in data for you; however, **Flash Fill** is a feature that uses data in previous columns as you type in a new label as a pattern in an adjoining column to determine what to fill in. For example, in Figure 1.8 column M contains a list of first and last names (such as Penny Sumpter in cell M2), but you want to have a column of just first names. To do this, type Penny's name in cell N2, click Fill in the Editing group on the Home tab and select Flash Fill to fill in the rest of column N with people's first names based on the data entered in column M. After you use Flash Fill, the status bar displays *Flash Fill Changed Cells: 3*, where 3 indicates the number of cells filled in.

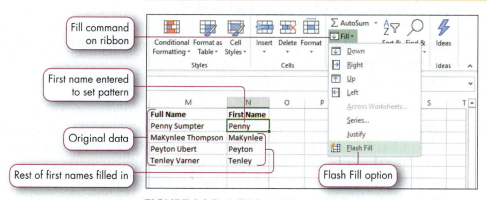

FIGURE 1.8 Flash Fill Examples

STEP 3 ## Enter Values

Values are numbers that represent a quantity or a measurable amount. Excel usually distinguishes between text and value data based on what you enter. The primary difference between text and value entries is that value entries can be the basis of calculations, whereas text cannot. In Figure 1.3, the data below the Cost, Markup Rate, and Percent Off labels are values. Values align at the right side of the cell by default. After entering values, align decimal places and apply formatting by adding characters, such as $ or %. Entering values is the same process as entering text: Type the value in a cell and click Enter or press Enter.

Enter Dates and Times

You can enter dates and times in a variety of formats. You should enter a static date to document when you create or modify a workbook or to document the specific point in time when the data were accurate, such as on a balance sheet or income statement. Later, you will learn how to use formulas to enter dates that update to the current date. In Figure 1.9, the data in column A contains the date 9/1/2021, but in different formats. Dates are values, so they align at the right side of a cell. The data in column C contains the time 2:30 PM, but in different formats.

	A	B	C	D
1	9/1/2021		2:30 PM	
2	Wednesday, September 1, 2021		2:30:00 PM	
3	9/1		14:30	
4	9/1/21		14:30:00	
5	09/01/21			
6	1-Sep			
7	1-Sep-21			
8	September 1, 2021			
9				

FIGURE 1.9 Date and Time Examples

Excel displays dates differently from the way it stores dates. Excel stores dates as serial numbers starting at 1 for January 1, 1900. For example, 9/1/2021 is stored as 44440, and 10/1/2021 is stored as 44470. Because Excel stores dates as serial numbers, you can create formulas to calculate the number of days between dates. When you subtract 9/1/2021 from 10/1/2021, the result is 30 days.

Edit and Clear Cell Contents

After entering data in a cell, you may want to change it. For example, you may want to edit a label to make it more descriptive, such as changing a label from Ceramic Mug to Souvenir Mug, or changing a value from 500 to 5000. There are several methods to edit cell contents:

- Double-click the cell.
- Click in the Formula Bar.
- Press F2.

You may want to clear or delete the contents in a cell if you no longer require data in a cell. To delete the contents of the active cell but keep the formatting, press Delete. If you want to clear the content and formatting or clear other settings, use the Clear command in the Editing group on the Home tab (see Figure 1.10).

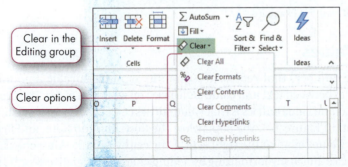

FIGURE 1.10 Clear Options

Find and Replace Data

When you work with a large dataset in Excel or a workbook with multiple worksheets, you can search through it to find a value or specific label. For example, you can search through the Souvenir Shop worksheet to find all occurrences of 0.15. Use the Find & Select tool to find data and select data.

To find data, complete the following steps:

1. Click Find & Select in the Editing group on the Home tab.
2. Select Find to open the Find and Replace dialog box.
3. Enter data you want to find in the Find what box.
4. Click Options if you want to specify conditions. The dialog box expands to display options to narrow the search (see Figure 1.11).
   - Click Format to specify a number, alignment, font, fill, or border format.
   - Click the Within arrow to specify where to find the data: within the current sheet or within the entire workbook.
   - Click the Match case check box to select it to identify cells that contain the same capitalization style as the data you entered.
5. Click Find All or Find Next to locate the data with the conditions you specified.

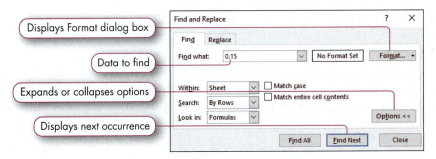

FIGURE 1.11 Find Options

> **MAC TIP:** The Mac version of Excel does not have a Find All option.

If you click Find All, the dialog box will list the workbook, sheet, cell, and exact value. The bottom of the dialog box specifies the number of cells where the data is found, such as 37 cell(s) found. In the worksheet, Excel makes the first occurrence it finds as the active cell. If you click Find Next, Excel makes the next occurrence it finds as the active cell. The dialog box does not display a list of the other occurrences.

Instead of just finding data, you may want to find and replace it. For example, you can search to find all occurrences of the 0.15 discount rate and replace those occurrences with a 0.17 discount rate.

To find and replace data, compete the following steps:

1. Click Find & Select in the Editing group on the Home tab.
2. Select Replace to open the Find and Replace dialog box.
3. Enter data you want to find in the Find what box and enter the replacement data in the Replace with box (see Figure 1.12).
4. Click Options if you want to specify conditions. You can specify specific formatting for both the data to find and the data to replace.
5. Click Replace All to replace all occurrences, click Replace to replace the current occurrence only, click Find All, or click Find Next to review the data before replacing it.

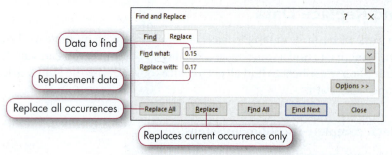

Data to find

Replacement data

Replace all occurrences

Replaces current occurrence only

FIGURE 1.12 Find and Replace Options

Quick Concepts

1. Describe two situations in which you could create workbooks to store and calculate data. **p. 312**

2. Describe how Excel indicates which cell is the active cell. **p. 313**

3. List the steps you should perform before entering data into a worksheet. **p. 316**

4. Explain the difference between Auto Fill and Flash Fill. **pp. 318–319**

Hands-On Exercises

MyLab IT HOE1 Sim Training

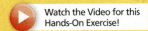 Watch the Video for this Hands-On Exercise!

Skills covered: Go to a Cell • Enter Text • Check the Spelling in a Worksheet • Use Auto Fill to Complete a Sequence • Enter Values • Enter a Date • Clear Cell Contents • Find and Replace Data

1 Introduction to Spreadsheets

As the assistant manager of the Celebrity Musician's Souvenir Shop, you will create a worksheet that shows the cost (the amount Souvenir Shop pays its suppliers), the markup percentage (the percentage over cost), and the retail selling price. You also will list the discount percentage (such as 25% off) for each product, the sale price, and the profit margin percentage.

STEP 1 ENTER TEXT AND CHECK THE SPELLING IN A WORKSHEET

Now that you have planned the Souvenir Shop worksheet, you are ready to enter the rest of the product names in the first column. Although you should check the spelling as a final step before distributing a workbook, it is also a good practice to check spelling after entering or editing a lot of text. Refer to Figure 1.13 as you complete Step 1.

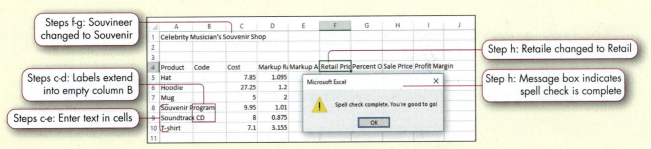

FIGURE 1.13 Text Entered in Cells

a. Open *e01h1Souvenirs* and save it as **e01h1Souvenirs_LastFirst**.

When you save files, use your last and first names. For example, as the Excel author, I would name my workbook "e01h1Souvenirs_MulberyKeith."

> **TROUBLESHOOTING:** If you make any major mistakes in this exercise, you can close the file, open *e01h1Souvenirs* again, and then start this exercise over.

b. Press **Ctrl+G**, type **A8** in the Reference box, and then click **OK**.

You used the Go To dialog box to make cell A8 the active cell.

c. Type **Souvenir Program** and press **Enter**.

Cell A9 becomes the active cell. The text Souvenir Program does not completely fit in cell A8, and some of the text displays in cell B8. However, the text is stored only in cell A8. If you make cell B8 the active cell, the Formula Bar is empty, indicating that nothing is stored in that cell.

d. Type **Soundtrack CD** in **cell A9** and press **Enter**.

When you start typing S in cell A9, AutoComplete displays a ScreenTip suggesting a previous text entry starting with S—Souvenir Program—but keep typing Soundtrack CD instead.

e. Type **T-shirt** in **cell A10** and press **Enter**.

You just entered the product labels to describe the data in each row.

f. Press **Ctrl+Home** to make **cell A1** the active cell, click the **Review tab**, and then click **Spelling** in the Proofing group.

The Spelling dialog box opens, indicating that *Souvineer* is not in the dictionary. *Souvenir*, the first word in the Suggestions box, is the correct word.

g. Click **Change** to change the misspelled word to Souvenir.

Retaile is detected as not being in the dictionary.

h. Select **Retail**, the third word in the Suggestions box, click **Change.** Correct any other misspelled words and click **OK** when prompted.

i. Click **Save** on the Quick Access Toolbar.

If your file is saved on OneDrive, it will be automatically saved if AutoSave is On. Otherwise, you should manually save your workbook periodically. That way if your system unexpectedly shuts down, you will not lose your work.

STEP 2 ▸ USE AUTO FILL TO COMPLETE A SEQUENCE

Product codes help to identify products with a unique number. Therefore, you will assign a product code for each product on sale at the Souvenir Shop. You will assign consecutive numbers 101 to 106. After typing the first code number, you will use Auto Fill to complete the rest of the series. Refer to Figures 1.14 and 1.15 as you complete Step 2.

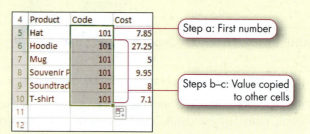

FIGURE 1.14 Auto Fill Copied Original Value

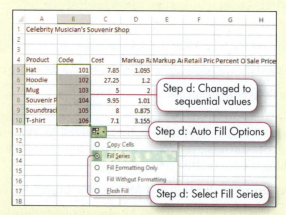

FIGURE 1.15 Auto Fill Sequence

a. Click **cell B5**, type **101**, and then press **Ctrl+Enter**.

Pressing Ctrl+Enter or clicking Enter to the left of the Formula Bar keeps cell B5 the active cell.

b. Position the pointer on the fill handle in the bottom-right corner of **cell B5**.

The pointer looks like a black plus sign when you point to a fill handle.

c. Double-click the **cell B5 fill handle**.

Excel copies 101 as the item number for the rest of the products. Excel stops inserting item numbers in column B when it detects the last label in cell A10 (refer to Figure 1.14). The product names no longer overlap into column B after you enter data into cells B8 and B9. The data in cells A8 and A9 are hidden and will fully display if the column width is adjusted.

d. Click **Auto Fill Options** and select **Fill Series**. Save the workbook.

Excel changes the duplicate values to continue sequentially in a series of numbers.

STEP 3 ⟩ ENTER VALUES, ENTER DATES, AND CLEAR CONTENTS

Now that you have entered the descriptive labels and item numbers, you will enter the percentage off as a decimal value for each product. You want to provide a date to indicate when the sale starts. Refer to Figure 1.16 as you complete Step 3.

	A	B	C	D	E	F	G	H	I	J
1	Celebrity Musician's Souvenir Shop									
2	9/1/2021		Step e: Date				Steps a–b: Percentage Off values			
3										
4	Product	Code	Cost	Markup Ra	Markup Aɪ	Retail Priɕ	Percent O	Sale Price	Profit Margin	
5	Hat	101	7.85	1.095			0.15			
6	Hoodie	102	27.25	1.2			0.2			
7	Mug	103	5	2			0.05			
8	Souvenir P	104	9.95	1.01			0.25			
9	Soundtracl	105	8	0.875			0.3			
10	T-shirt	106	7.1	3.155			0.05			
11										

FIGURE 1.16 Values and a Date Entered in Cells

a. Click **cell G5**, type **0.15**, and then press **Enter**.

Although you could have entered .15 without the 0, in this book, 0 will be shown before the decimal point to clearly indicate a decimal value. However, you can type just the decimal value such as .15 and get the same results. You entered the percentage off rate as a decimal (0.15) instead of a percentage (15%). You will apply Percent Style later, but now you will concentrate on data entry.

b. Type the remaining values in **cells G6** through **G10** as shown in Figure 1.16.

To improve your productivity, use the number keypad (if available) on the right side of your keyboard. It is much faster to type values and press Enter on the number keypad rather than to use the numbers at the top of the keyboard. Make sure Num Lock is active before using the number keypad to enter values.

c. Click **cell A2**, type **9/1**, and then press **Enter**.

Because you entered 9/1 without a preceding =, Excel treats 9/1 as a date rather than dividing 9 by 1. The date aligns on the right cell margin by default. Excel displays 1-Sep instead of 9/1.

d. Click **cell A2**, click the **Home tab**, click **Clear** in the Editing group, and then select **Clear Formats**.

The date formatting is cleared, and the date displays as the serial number. Later in this chapter, you will learn how to apply different date formats. For now, you will type the date differently.

e. Type **9/1/2021** in **cell A2** and press **Ctrl+Enter**. Save the workbook.

When you retype the date, Excel detects the data entry is a date and displays the date rather than the serial number. The date now displays as 9/1/2021 instead of 44440.

> **TROUBLESHOOTING:** If you did not use Clear Formats and typed 9/1/2021 in cell A2, Excel retains the previous date format and displays 1-Sep again. Repeat Step d, ensuring that you select Clear Formats, and then repeat Step e.

STEP 4 FIND AND REPLACE DATA

To motivate the Souvenir Shop customers to buy more products, you want to change the percentage off from 5% (0.05) to 10% (0.10). Although the Souvenir Shop worksheet contains a small dataset, where you could easily find the 0.05 rate, you will use the Find and Replace feature so that you do not miss any occurrences. Refer to Figure 1.17 as you complete Step 4.

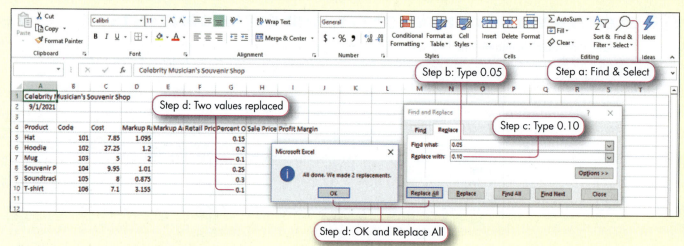

FIGURE 1.17 Data Replaced in the Worksheet

a. Go to **cell A1**, click **Find & Select** in the Editing group on the Home tab, and then select **Replace**.

The Find and Replace dialog box opens with the Replace tab options displayed.

> **MAC TROUBLESHOOTING:** Click Edit, point to Find, and then click Find.

b. Type **0.05** in the Find what box.

You want to find all occurrences of the 0.05 rate.

> **TROUBLESHOOTING:** Make sure you include the decimal place and 0 in the correct location to avoid finding and replacing the wrong rate.

c. Press **Tab** and type **0.10** in the Replace with box.

You want the replacement value to be 0.10.

d. Click **Replace All** and click **OK** when prompted. Click **Close** in the Find and Replace dialog box.

Excel found two occurrences of 0.05 and replaced them with 0.10.

e. Save the workbook. Keep the workbook open if you plan to continue with the next Hands-On Exercise. If not, close the workbook, and exit Excel.

Mathematical Operations and Formulas

A *formula* combines cell references, arithmetic operations, values, and/or functions used in a calculation. Formulas transform static numbers into meaningful results that update as values change. In the Souvenir Shop product sales worksheet, you will create formulas to calculate the retail price, sale price, and profit margin (refer to Figure 1.1).

In this section, you will learn how to use mathematical operations in Excel formulas. You will refresh your memory of the mathematical order of operations and learn how to construct formulas using cell references so that when the value of an input cell changes, the result of the formula changes without you having to modify the formula.

Creating Formulas

Formulas help you analyze how results change as the input data changes. You can change the value of your assumptions or inputs and explore the results quickly and accurately. For example, if the vendor increases the cost of the souvenir mugs, how does that affect your retail selling price?

STEP 1 ▸ Use Cell References in Formulas

Use cell references instead of values in formulas where possible so if the value of the cell changes, the results of the formulas will update and reflect the change in input. You may include values in an input area—such as dates, salary, or costs—that you will need to reference in formulas. Referencing these cells in your formulas, instead of typing the value of the cell to which you are referring, keeps your formulas accurate if you change values to perform a what-if analysis.

To enter a formula in the active cell, type = followed by the arithmetic expression, using cell references instead of values. If you type B2+B3 without the equal sign, Excel does not recognize that you entered a formula and stores the "formula" as text. You can enter cell references in uppercase, such as =B2+B3, or lowercase, such as =b2+b3. Excel changes the cell references to uppercase automatically.

> **TIP: EXCEL INTELLISENSE FORMULA AUTOCOMPLETE**
> When you start typing a cell reference immediately after the equal sign (such as =B), Excel Intellisense Formula AutoComplete displays a list of functions that start with that letter. Keep typing the cell reference (such as =B4) and complete the rest of the formula.

Figure 1.18 shows a worksheet containing input values and results of formulas. For example, cell E2 contains the formula =B2+B3. Excel uses 10, the value stored in cell B2, and adds it to 2, the value stored in cell B3. The result of 12 displays in cell E2 instead of the actual formula. The Formula Bar displays the formula contained in the active cell.

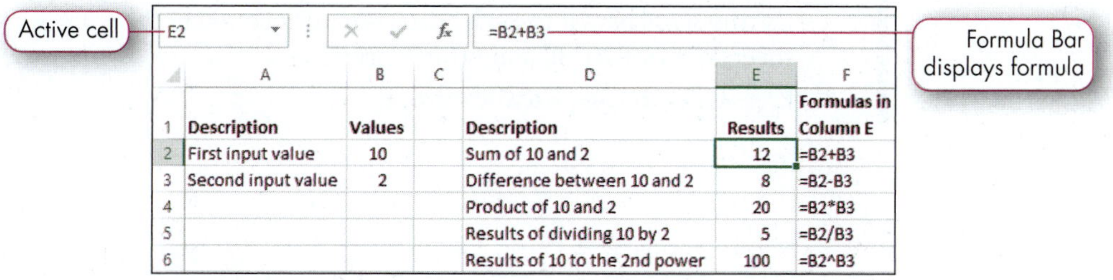

	A	B	C	D	E	F
1	Description	Values		Description	Results	Formulas in Column E
2	First input value	10		Sum of 10 and 2	12	=B2+B3
3	Second input value	2		Difference between 10 and 2	8	=B2-B3
4				Product of 10 and 2	20	=B2*B3
5				Results of dividing 10 by 2	5	=B2/B3
6				Results of 10 to the 2nd power	100	=B2^B3

Active cell — E2 ... fx =B2+B3 ... Formula Bar displays formula

FIGURE 1.18 Formula Results

In Figure 1.18, cell B2 contains 10, and cell B3 contains 2. Cell E2 contains =B2+B3 but shows the result 12. If you change the value of cell B3 to 5, cell E2 displays the new result, which is 15. However, if you had typed actual values in the formula, =10+2, the formula would still show a result of 12, and you would have to edit the formula to =10+5, even though the value in cell B3 was changed to 5. Using values in formulas can cause problems if you forget to edit the formula or if you create a typographical error when editing the formula. Where possible, design worksheets in such a way as to be able to place those values that might change as input values. Referencing cells with input values in formulas instead of using the values themselves will avoid having to modify the formulas if an input value changes later.

> **TIP: WHEN TO USE A VALUE IN A FORMULA**
> Use cell references instead of actual values in formulas, unless the value will never change. For example, if you want to calculate how many total months are in a specified number of years, enter a formula such as =B5*12, where B5 contains the number of years. You might want to change the number of years; therefore, type that value in cell B5. However, every year always has 12 months, so you can use the value 12 in the formula.

Copy a Formula

After you enter a formula in a cell, duplicate the formula without retyping the formula for other cells that require a similar formula. Previously, you learned about the Auto Fill feature that enables you to use the fill handle to fill in a series of values, months, quarters, and weekdays. You can also drag the fill handle to copy the formula in the active cell to adjacent cells down a column or across a row, depending on how the data are organized. Cell references in copied formulas adjust based on their relative locations to the original formula.

Use Semi-Selection to Create a Formula

To decrease typing time and ensure accuracy, use *semi-selection*, a process of selecting a cell or range of cells for entering cell references as you create formulas. Semi-selection is often called *pointing* because you use the pointer to select cells as you build the formula. Some people prefer using the semi-selection method instead of typing a formula so that they can make sure they use the correct cell references as they build the formula.

To use the semi-selection technique to create a formula, complete the following steps:

1. Type = to start a formula.
2. Click the cell that contains the value to use in the formula. A moving marquee appears around the cell you select, and Excel displays the cell reference in the formula.
3. Type a mathematical operator.
4. Continue clicking cells, selecting ranges, and typing operators to finish the formula. Use the scroll bars if the cell is in a remote location in the worksheet or click a worksheet tab to see a cell in another worksheet.
5. Press Enter to complete the formula.

The ***order of operations*** (also called *order of precedence*) is a set of rules that control the sequence in which arithmetic operations are performed, which affects the result of the calculation. Excel performs mathematical calculations left to right in this order: **P**arentheses, **E**xponentiation, **M**ultiplication or **D**ivision, and finally **A**ddition or **S**ubtraction. Some people remember the order of operations with the phrase ***Please Excuse My Dear Aunt Sally***.

Table 1.3 lists the primary order of operations. Use Help to learn about the complete order of operations.

TABLE 1.3	Order of Operations	
Order	**Description**	**Symbols**
1	Parentheses	( )
2	Exponentiation	^
3	Multiplication and Division	* and / (respectively)
4	Addition and Subtraction	+ and − (respectively)

Use parentheses to make sure a lower-order operation occurs first. For example, if you want to add the values stored in cells A1 and A2 and multiply that result by the value stored in cell A3, enclose parentheses around the addition operation: =(A1+A2)*A3. Without parentheses, =A1+A2*A3, the first calculation multiplies the values stored in A2 and A3. That result is then added to the value stored in cell A1, because multiplication has a higher order of operation than addition.

Figure 1.19 shows formulas, the sequence in which calculations occur, description of the calculations, and the formula results. The highlighted results are the final formula results. This figure illustrates the arithmetic symbols and the how parentheses affect the formula results.

	A	B	C	D	E	F
1	**Input**		**Formula**	**Sequence**	**Description**	**Result**
2	2		=A2+A3*A4+A5	1	3 (cell A3) * 4 (cell A4)	12
3	3			2	2 (cell A2) + 12 (order 1)	14
4	4			3	14 (order 2) + 5 (cell A5)	19
5	5					
6			=(A2+A3)*(A4+A5)	1	2 (cell A2) + 3 (cell A3)	5
7				2	4 (cell A4) + 5 (cell A5)	9
8				3	5 (order 1) * 9 (order 2)	45
9						
10			=A2/A3+A4*A5	1	2 (cell A2) / 3 (cell A3)	0.666667
11				2	4 (cell A4) * 5 (cell A5)	20
12				3	0.666667 (order 1) + 20 (order 2)	20.66667
13						
14			=A2/(A3+A4)*A5	1	3 (cell A3) + 4 (cell A4)	7
15				2	2 (cell A2) / 7 (order 1)	0.285714
16				3	0.285714 (order 2) * 5 (cell A5)	1.428571
17						
18			=A2^2+A3*A4%	1	4 (cell A4) is converted to percentage	0.04
19				2	2 (cell A2) to the power of 2	4
20				3	3 (cell A3) * 0.04 (order 1)	0.12
21				4	4 (order 2) + 0.12 (order 3)	4.12

FIGURE 1.19 Formula Results Based on Order of Operations

Display Cell Formulas

Excel shows the result of the formula in the cell (see the top half of Figure 1.20); however, you can display the formulas instead of the calculated results in the cells (see the bottom half of Figure 1.20). Displaying the cell formulas may help you double-check all your formulas at one time or troubleshoot a problem with a formula instead of looking at each formula individually. To display cell formulas, press Ctrl and the grave accent (`) key between the Tab and Esc keys or click Show Formulas in the Formula Auditing group on the Formulas tab. Repeat the process to hide formulas and display results again.

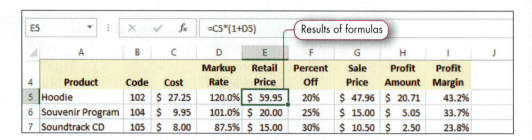

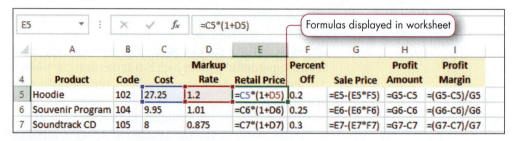

FIGURE 1.20 Formulas and Formula Results

Quick Concepts

5. Describe the importance of the order of operations. Provide an example where the outcome is affected using and not using parentheses. **p. 329**

6. Explain why you should use cell references instead of typing values in formulas. **p. 327**

7. Explain when it would be useful to display formulas instead of formula results in a worksheet. **p. 330**

Hands-On Exercises

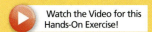

2 Mathematical Operations and Formulas

In Hands-On Exercise 1, you created the Souvenir Shop worksheet by entering text, values, and a date for items on sale. Now you will insert formulas to calculate the missing results—specifically, the retail (before sale) price, sale price, and profit margin. You will use cell references in your formulas, so when you change a referenced value, the formula results will update automatically.

STEP 1 ▶ USE CELL REFERENCES IN A FORMULA, COPY A FORMULA, AND USE SEMI-SELECTION TO CREATE A FORMULA

The first formula you create will calculate the markup amount. The markup is based on the cost and markup rate. After you enter the formula for the first product, you will copy the formula down the column to calculate the markup amount for the other products. Then, you will use the semi-selection method to calculate the retail price, which is the price you charge customers. It is the sum of the cost and the markup amount. Refer to Figure 1.21 as you complete Step 1.

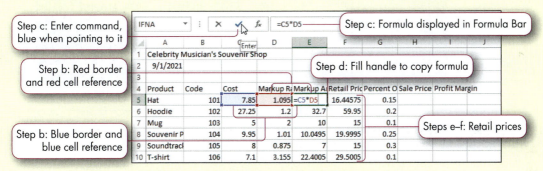

FIGURE 1.21 Markup Amount and Retail Price Formulas

a. Open *e01h1Souvenirs_LastFirst* if you closed it at the end of Hands-On Exercise 1 and save it as **e01h2Souvenirs_LastFirst**, changing h1 to h2.

b. Click **cell E5** and type **=C5*D5**, but do not press Enter.

Note the cell references in the formula match colored borders around the cells. This helps to identify cells as you construct your formulas (refer to Figure 1.21).

c. Click **Enter** to enter the formula.

Multiplying 7.85 (the cost in cell C5) by 1.095 (the markup rate in cell D5) equals 8.59575. You are marking up the hat by $8.60 over your cost. View the formula in the Formula Bar to check it for accuracy.

TROUBLESHOOTING: If the result is not correct, with cell E5 active, check the Formula Bar to make sure the formula contains the correct cell references and the asterisk for multiplication. Correct any errors.

d. Position the pointer on the **cell E5 fill handle**. When the pointer changes from a white plus sign to a thin black plus sign, double-click the **fill handle**.

Excel copies the Markup Amount formula down the column for the remaining products. Excel stops copying the formula when it detects the last row in the dataset.

e. Click **cell F5**. Type **=**, click **cell C5**, type **+**, click **cell E5**, and click **Enter**.

You used the semi-selection method to add 7.85 (the cost) plus 8.59575 (the markup amount) to equal 16.44575 (the retail price).

f. Double-click the **cell F5 fill handle** and save the workbook.

Excel copies the Retail Price formula through cell F10.

APPLY THE ORDER OF OPERATIONS

The products are on sale this week, so you want to calculate the sale prices. For example, the hat is on sale for 15% off the retail price. After calculating the sale price, you will calculate the profit margin. The formulas you create will apply the order of operations. Refer to Figure 1.22 as you complete Step 2.

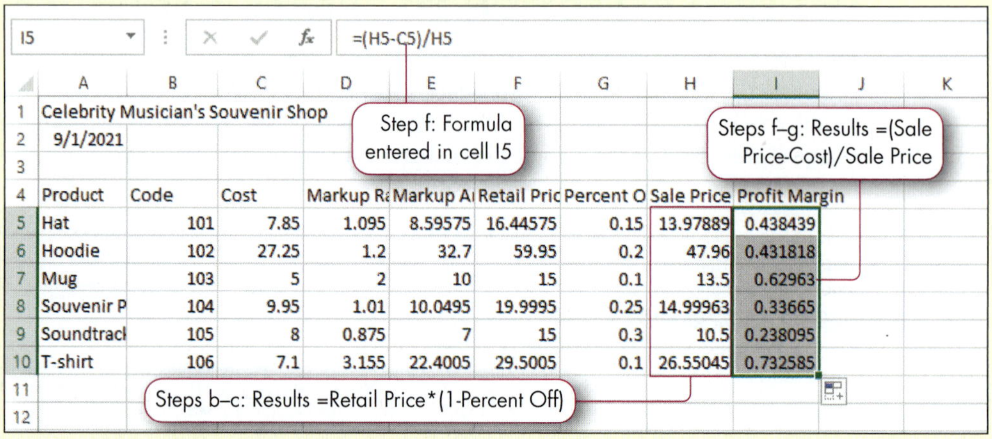

	A	B	C	D	E	F	G	H	I	J	K
1	Celebrity Musician's Souvenir Shop										
2	9/1/2021										
3											
4	Product	Code	Cost	Markup Ra	Markup A	Retail Pric	Percent O	Sale Price	Profit Margin		
5	Hat	101	7.85	1.095	8.59575	16.44575	0.15	13.97889	0.438439		
6	Hoodie	102	27.25	1.2	32.7	59.95	0.2	47.96	0.431818		
7	Mug	103	5	2	10	15	0.1	13.5	0.62963		
8	Souvenir P	104	9.95	1.01	10.0495	19.9995	0.25	14.99963	0.33665		
9	Soundtrack	105	8	0.875	7	15	0.3	10.5	0.238095		
10	T-shirt	106	7.1	3.155	22.4005	29.5005	0.1	26.55045	0.732585		

I5 formula: =(H5-C5)/H5

Step f: Formula entered in cell I5

Steps f–g: Results =(Sale Price-Cost)/Sale Price

Steps b–c: Results =Retail Price*(1-Percent Off)

FIGURE 1.22 Sale Price and Profit Margin Formulas

a. Click **cell H5**.

b. Type **=F5*(1-G5)** and press **Ctrl+Enter** to keep the current cell as the active cell.

The result is 13.97889. The formula first subtracts 0.15 (the percentage off) from 1, which is 0.85. Then Excel multiplies 16.44575 (the value in cell F5) by 0.85 to get 13.97889 (the retail price).

> **TROUBLESHOOTING:** If your result is different, check the formula for correct cell references, mathematical operators, and parentheses.

c. Double-click the **cell H5 fill handle** to copy the formula down column H.

d. Click **cell H6** and view the Formula Bar.

The original formula was =F5*(1-G5). The copied formula in cell H6 is adjusted to =F6*(1-G6) so that it calculates the sales price based on the data in row 6.

e. Click **cell I5**.

f. Type **=(H5-C5)/H5** and click **Enter**.

Profit margin is (Sale Price – Cost)/Sale Price. The Souvenir Shop paid $7.85 for the hat and sells it for $13.98. The $6.13 profit is divided by the $13.98 sale price, which gives a profit margin of 0.438484, which will be formatted later as a percentage (43.8%).

g. Double-click the **cell I5 fill handle** to copy the formula down the column. Save the workbook.

You want to display the formulas in the worksheet to check for accuracy. In addition, you want to see how the prices and profit margins are affected when you change three original values. For example, the supplier might notify you that the cost to you will increase. Refer to Figures 1.23 and 1.24 as you complete Step 3.

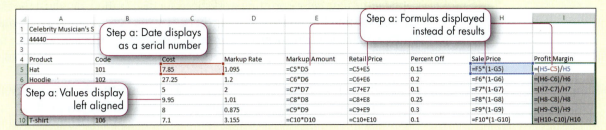

FIGURE 1.23 Formulas Displayed in the Worksheet

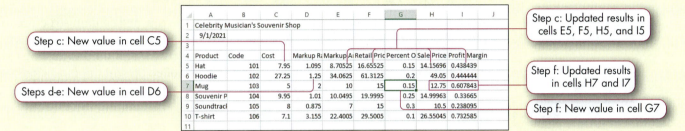

FIGURE 1.24 Results of Changed Values

a. Press **Ctrl+`** (the grave accent mark).

The workbook displays the formulas rather than the formula results (refer to Figure 1.23). This is helpful when you want to review several formulas at one time.

b. Click the **Formulas tab** and click **Show Formulas** in the Formula Auditing group.

Alternatively, you can press Ctrl+`. The workbook now displays the formula results in the cells again.

c. Click **cell C5**, type **7.95**, and then press **Enter**.

The results of the markup amount, retail price, sale price, and profit margin formulas change based on the new cost.

d. Click **cell D6** and press **F2**.

The insertion point blinks to the right of 1.2.

e. Type **5** and press **Enter**.

You added 5, so the new markup rate is 1.25. The results of the markup amount, retail price, sale price, and profit margin formulas change based on the new markup rate.

f. Click **cell G7**, type **0.15**, and then press **Ctrl+Enter**.

The results of the sale price and profit margin formulas change based on the new percentage off rate. Note that the retail price did not change because that formula is not based on the markup rate.

g. Save the workbook. Keep the workbook open if you plan to continue with the next Hands-On Exercise. If not, close the workbook, and exit Excel.

Worksheet Structure and Clipboard Tasks

Although you plan worksheets before entering data, you can insert a new row to accommodate new data, delete a column that you no longer want, hide a column of confidential data before printing worksheets for distribution, or adjust the size of columns and rows so that the data fit better. Furthermore, you may decide to move data to a different location in the same worksheet, or even to a different worksheet. In some instances, you will create a copy of data entered so that you can explore different values and compare the results of the original dataset and the copied and edited dataset.

In this section, you will learn how to make changes to columns and rows. You will also learn how to select ranges, move data to another location, copy data to another range, and use the Paste Special feature.

Managing Columns and Rows

As you enter and edit worksheet data, you can adjust the row and column structure to accommodate new data or remove unnecessary data. You can add rows and columns to add new data and delete data, columns, and rows that you no longer need. Adjusting the height and width of rows and columns, respectively, can often present the data better.

STEP 1 Insert Cells, Columns, and Rows

After you construct a worksheet, you can insert cells, columns, or rows to accommodate new data. For example, you can insert a new column to perform calculations or insert a new row to list a new product. To insert a new column or row, make a cell the active cell on that column or row, use the Insert arrow in the Cells group on the Home tab (see Figure 1.25), and then select Insert Sheet Columns or Insert Sheet Rows. Alternatively, you can use a shortcut menu: Right-click the column (letter) or row (number) heading and select Insert from the shortcut menu. Excel inserts a new blank column to the left of the current column and moves the remaining columns to the right. When you insert a new row, Excel moves the remaining rows down.

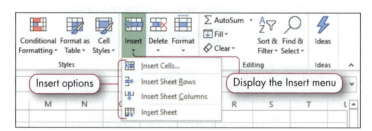

FIGURE 1.25 Insert Menu

Inserting a cell is helpful when you realize that you left out an entry after you have entered a lot of data. Instead of inserting a new row or column, you just want to move the existing content down or over to enter the missing value. You can insert a single cell in a row or column. When you insert cells, rows, and columns, cell addresses in formulas adjust automatically.

If you click Insert in the Cells group, the default action inserts a cell at the current location, which moves existing data down *in that column only*. For more options for inserting cells, use the Insert arrow in the Cells group on the Home tab and select Insert Cells to display the Insert dialog box (see Figure 1.26). You can then insert cells and shift existing cells to the right or down.

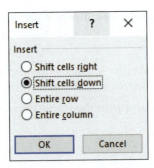

FIGURE 1.26 Insert Dialog Box

STEP 2 ## Delete Cells, Columns, and Rows

If you no longer require data in a cell, column, or row, you should delete it. For example, you can delete a row containing a product you no longer carry. In these situations, you are deleting the entire cell, column, or row, not just the contents of the cell to leave empty cells. As with inserting new cells, columns, or rows, any affected formulas adjust the cell references automatically.

To delete a column or row, select the column or row heading for the column or row you want to delete and use Delete in the Cells group on the Home tab. Alternatively, make any cell within the column or row you want to delete the active cell, click the Delete arrow in the Cells group on the Home tab (see Figure 1.27), and then select Delete Sheet Columns or Delete Sheet Rows. Another alternative is to right-click the column letter or row number for the column or row you want to delete and select Delete from the shortcut menu.

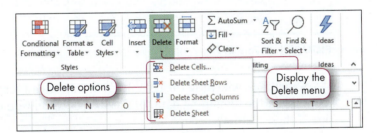

FIGURE 1.27 Delete Menu

Clicking Delete in the Cells group immediately deletes the active cell, which moves existing data up in that column only. To delete a cell or range of cells, select Delete Cells to display the Delete dialog box (see Figure 1.28). Select the option to shift cells left or up.

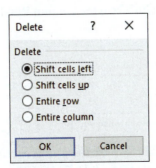

FIGURE 1.28 Delete Dialog Box

STEP 3 ## Adjust Column Width

After you enter data in a column, you often will adjust the *column width*—the horizontal measurement of a column in a table or a worksheet. For example, in the worksheet you created in Hands-On Exercises 1 and 2, the labels in column A displayed into column B when those adjacent cells were empty. However, after you typed values in column B, the labels in column A appeared cut off. You should widen column A to show the full name of your products. Excel provides two ways to widen a column to accommodate the longest text or value in a column:

- Point to the right vertical border of the column heading. When the pointer displays as a two-headed arrow, double-click the border.
- Click Format in the Cells group on the Home tab (see Figure 1.29) and select AutoFit Column Width.

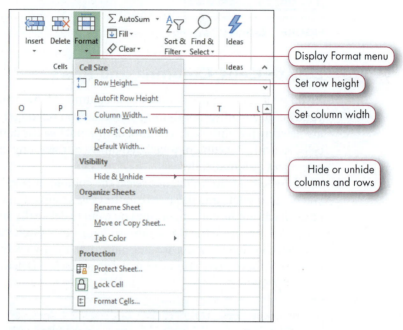

FIGURE 1.29 Format Menu

Sometimes, widening the column to fit the longest text or value makes the column too wide for the remaining data. In those cases, specify an exact column width by using one of these methods:

- Drag the vertical border to the left to decrease the column width or to the right to increase the column width. As you drag the vertical border, Excel displays a Screen-Tip specifying the width (see Figure 1.30) from 0 to 255 characters and in pixels.
- Click Format in the Cells group on the Home tab (refer to Figure 1.29), select Column Width, type a value that represents the maximum number of characters to display in the Column width box in the Column Width dialog box, and then click OK.

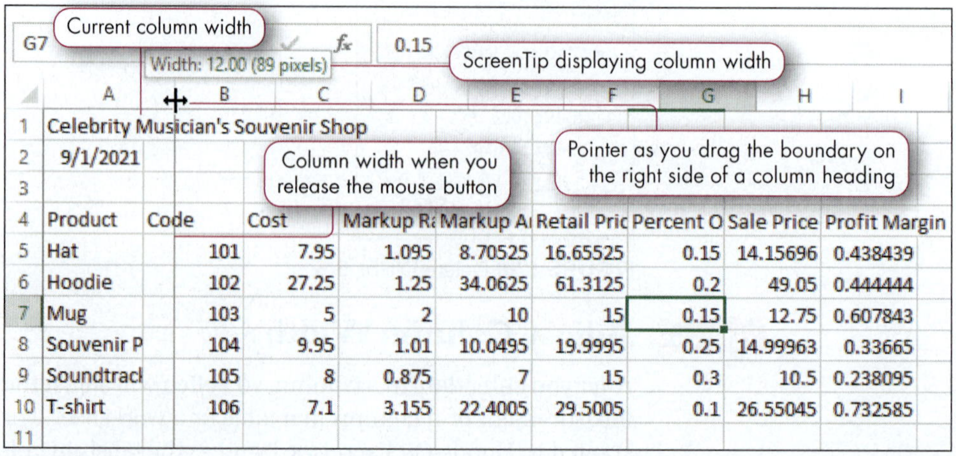

	A	B	C	D	E	F	G	H	I
1	Celebrity Musician's Souvenir Shop								
2	9/1/2021								
3									
4	Product	Code	Cost	Markup R;	Markup A	Retail Pric	Percent O	Sale Price	Profit Margin
5	Hat	101	7.95	1.095	8.70525	16.65525	0.15	14.15696	0.438439
6	Hoodie	102	27.25	1.25	34.0625	61.3125	0.2	49.05	0.444444
7	Mug	103	5	2	10	15	0.15	12.75	0.607843
8	Souvenir P	104	9.95	1.01	10.0495	19.9995	0.25	14.99963	0.33665
9	Soundtrack	105	8	0.875	7	15	0.3	10.5	0.238095
10	T-shirt	106	7.1	3.155	22.4005	29.5005	0.1	26.55045	0.732585
11									

G7 — fx 0.15 — Width: 12.00 (89 pixels) — Current column width — ScreenTip displaying column width — Column width when you release the mouse button — Pointer as you drag the boundary on the right side of a column heading

FIGURE 1.30 Increasing Column Width

> **TIP: POUND SIGNS DISPLAYED**
> When a column is too narrow for text, the text appears cut off. However, if the column is too narrow for numbers or dates, the cell displays a series of pound signs (######) rather than part of the number or date.

Adjust Row Height

You can adjust the ***row height***—the vertical measurement of the row—similarly to how you change column width by double-clicking the border between row numbers or by selecting Row Height or AutoFit Row Height from the Format menu (refer to Figure 1.29). In Excel, row height is a value between 0 and 409 based on point size (abbreviated as *pt*) and pixels. Whether you are measuring font sizes or row heights, one point size is equal to 1/72 of an inch, The row height should be taller than the font size. For example, with an 11 pt font size, the default row height is 15.

> **TIP: MULTIPLE COLUMN WIDTHS AND ROW HEIGHTS**
> You can set the size for more than one column or row at a time to make the selected columns or rows the same size. Drag across the column or row headings for the area you want to format, and set the size using any method. To select nonadjacent columns or rows, press and hold Ctrl while you click the column or row headings; then adjust column widths or row heights.

Hide and Unhide Columns and Rows

Sometimes a worksheet might contain data that you do not want to display, such as employee IDs or birthdates, or assumptions, or internal notes. You can hide columns or rows that contain the sensitive data before printing a copy to distribute or displaying the worksheet on a screen during a meeting.

However, the column or row is not deleted. If you hide column B, you will see columns A and C side by side. If you hide row 3, you will see rows 2 and 4 together. Figure 1.31 shows that column B and row 3 are hidden. Excel displays a double line between column headings or row headings to indicate that columns or rows are hidden.

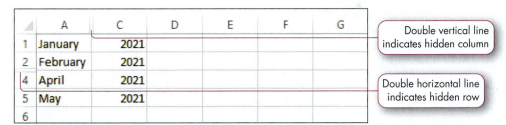

FIGURE 1.31 Hidden Columns and Rows

> **To hide a column or row, complete the following steps:**
> 1. Select a cell or cells in the column or row you want to hide.
> 2. Click Format in the Cells group on the Home tab (refer to Figure 1.29).
> 3. Point to Hide & Unhide.
> 4. Select Hide Columns or Hide Rows, depending on what you want to hide.

Alternatively, you can right-click the column or row heading(s) you want to hide and select Hide. You can hide multiple columns or multiple rows at the same time. To select adjacent columns (such as columns B through E) or adjacent rows (such as rows 2 through 4), drag across the adjacent column or row headings and use the Hide command. To hide nonadjacent columns or rows, press and hold Ctrl while you click the desired column or row headings, and then use the Hide command. To unhide, select the columns or rows on both sides of the hidden column or row and select Unhide Columns or Unhide Rows, respectively.

Selecting, Moving, Copying, and Pasting Data

You may already know the basics of selecting, cutting, copying, and pasting data in other programs, such as Word. The overall process is the same in Excel. However, some of the techniques differ slightly as you work with cells, columns, and rows of data in Excel.

STEP 4 ## Select a Range

A *range* refers to a group of adjacent or contiguous cells in a worksheet. A range may be as small as a single cell or as large as the entire worksheet. It may consist of a row or part of a row, a column or part of a column, or multiple rows or columns, but the range will always be a rectangular shape, as you must select the same number of cells in each row or column for the entire range. A range is specified by indicating the top-left and bottom-right cells in the selection. For example, in Figure 1.32, the date is a single-cell range in cell A2, the Mug product data are stored in the range A7:H7, the cost values are stored in the range C5:C10, and the sales prices and profit margins are stored in range G5:H10. A *nonadjacent range* contains multiple ranges, such as D5:D10 and F5:F10, that are not positioned in a contiguous cluster in the worksheet. At times, you will select nonadjacent ranges so that you can apply the same formatting at the same time, such as formatting the nonadjacent range D5:D10 and F5:F10 with Percent Style.

Table 1.4 lists methods to select ranges, including nonadjacent ranges.

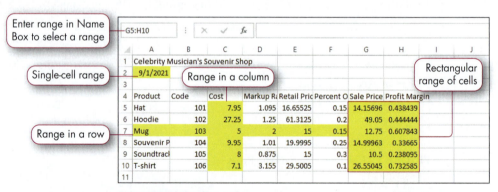

FIGURE 1.32 Sample Ranges

TABLE 1.4	Selecting Ranges
To Select	**Do This**
A range	Drag until you select the entire range. Alternatively, click the first cell in the range, press and hold Shift, and click the last cell in the range.
An entire column	Click the column heading.
Column of data (current cell to last cell containing data in the column)	Press Ctrl+Shift+down arrow. (On a Mac, press Shift+Command+arrow.)
An entire row	Click the row heading.
Row of data (current cell to last cell on the row containing data)	Press Ctl+Shift+right arrow. (On a Mac, press Shift+Command+arrow.)
Current range containing data, including headings	Click in the range of data and press Ctrl+A. (On a Mac, press Command+A.)
All cells in a worksheet	Click Select All or press Ctrl+A twice.
Nonadjacent range	Select the first range, press and hold Ctrl, and select additional range(s).

A green border surrounds a selected range. Any command you execute will affect the entire range. The range remains selected until you select another range or click in any cell in the worksheet.

Move a Range

You can move cell contents from one range to another. For example, you can move an input area from the right side of the worksheet to above the output range. When you move a range containing text and values, the text and values do not change. However, any formulas that refer to cells in that range will update to reflect the new cell addresses.

To move a range, complete the following steps:

1. Select the range.
2. Click Cut in the Clipboard group (see Figure 1.33). Unlike cutting data in other Microsoft Office applications, the data you cut in Excel remain in their locations until you paste them elsewhere. A moving dashed green border surrounds the selected range and the status bar displays *Select destination and press ENTER or choose Paste.*
3. Ensure the destination range—the range where you want to move the data—is the same size or greater than the size of the cut range.
4. Click in the top-left corner of the destination range and click Paste (see Figure 1.33). If any cells within the destination range contain data, Excel overwrites that data when you use the Paste command.

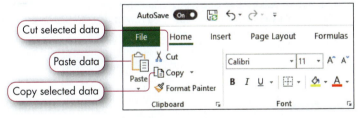

FIGURE 1.33 Cut, Copy, Paste

Cut selected data

Paste data

Copy selected data

STEP 5 ## Copy and Paste a Range

You may want to copy cell contents from one range to another. When you copy a range, the original data remain in their original locations. For example, you can copy your January budget to another worksheet to use as a model for creating your February budget. Cell references in copied formulas adjust based on their relative locations to the original data. Furthermore, you want to copy formulas from one range to another range. In this situation, where you cannot use the fill handle, you will use the Copy and Paste functions to copy the formula.

The process for copying a range is similar to moving a range. Instead of using the Cut command, use the Copy command after selecting the range. Then, when you use the Paste command, Excel overwrites any data if any cells within the destination range contain data. Figure 1.34 shows a selected range (A4:H10) and a copy of the range (J4:Q10). The original range still has the moving dashed green border, and the pasted copied range is selected with a solid green border. Press Esc to turn off the moving dashed border.

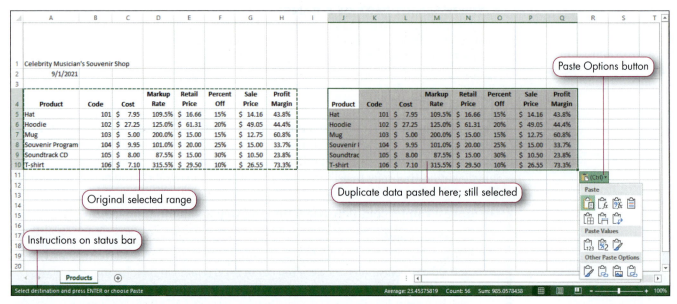

FIGURE 1.34 Copied and Pasted Range

TIP: INSERT COPIED CELLS

Instead of inserting a blank column or row, cutting, and then pasting the data in the new column or row, you can simplify the process. Select the data and click Cut. Right-click the upper-left cell where you want the data to be moved, select Insert Copied Cells, and then select Shift Cells Right when copying a column of data or Shift Cells Down when copying a row of data. Excel inserts a column or row and pastes the data at the same time without overwriting existing data.

TIP: COPY AS PICTURE

Click the Copy arrow in the Clipboard group to select Copy as Picture. This option copies an image of the selected data. When you use Paste, the copied data becomes an object that can be modified like other pictures. It is like taking a screenshot of a selected range. However, when you copy the data as an image, you cannot edit individual cell data in the image.

STEP 6 > **Use Paste Options**

Sometimes you want to paste data in a different format than they are in the Clipboard. For example, you can preserve the results of calculations before changing the original data by pasting the data as values. Immediately after you click Paste, the **Paste Options button** displays near the bottom-right corner of the pasted data. Click the arrow to select a different result for the pasted data (refer to Figure 1.34).

Instead of using the Paste Options button, the Paste arrow in the Clipboard group contains many different paste options. To display more information about a paste option, point to it on the Paste gallery (see Figure 1.35).

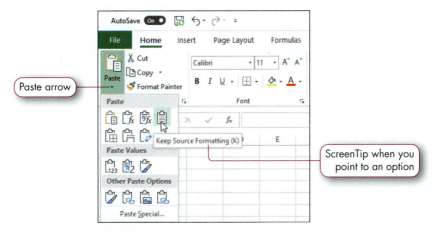

FIGURE 1.35 Paste Options

Table 1.5 lists and describes some of the options in the Paste gallery that opens when you click the Paste arrow in the Clipboard group or the Paste Options button that displays immediately after you use Paste. Paste options enable you to paste content or attributes, such as a formula or format.

TABLE 1.5	Paste Options	
Icon	**Option Name**	**Paste Description**
	Paste	Cell contents and all formatting from copied cells.
	Formulas	Formulas, but no formatting, from copied cells.
	Formulas & Number Formatting	Formulas and number formatting, such as Currency, but no font formatting, such as font color, fill color, or borders.
	Keep Source Formatting	Cell contents and formatting from copied cells.
	No Borders	Cell contents, number formatting, and text formatting except borders.
	Keep Source Column Widths	Cell contents, number and text formatting, and the column width of the source data when pasting in another column.
	Transpose	Transposes data from rows to columns and columns to rows.
	Values	Unformatted values that are the results of formulas, not the actual formulas.
	Values & Number Formatting	Values that are the results of formulas, not the actual formulas; preserves number formatting but not text formatting.
	Values & Source Formatting	Values that are the results of formulas, not the actual formulas; preserves number and text formatting.
	Formatting	Number and text formatting only from the copied cells; no cell contents.
	Paste Link	Creates a reference to the source cells (such as =$G$15), not the cell contents; preserves number formatting but not text formatting.
	Picture	Creates a picture image of the copied data; pasted data is not editable.
	Linked Picture	Creates a picture with a reference to the copied cells; if the original cell content changes, so does the picture.
	Paste Special	Opens the Paste Special dialog box (see Figure 1.36).

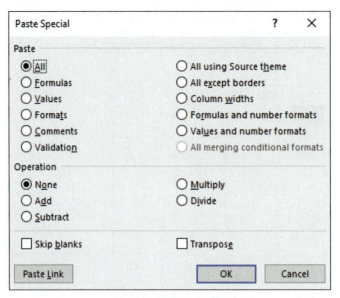

FIGURE 1.36 Paste Special Dialog Box

TIP: TRANSPOSING COLUMNS AND ROWS

You can transpose the columns and rows so that the data in the first column appear as column labels across the first row, or the column labels in the first row appear in the first column. Figure 1.37 shows the original data with the months in column A and the utility costs in columns B, C, and D. In the transposed data, the months are shown in the first row, and each row contains utility information. The original formats (bold and right-aligned) are copied in the transposed data.

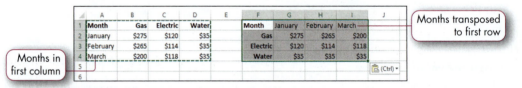

Months in first column

Months transposed to first row

FIGURE 1.37 Transposed Data

TIP: COPY EXCEL DATA TO OTHER PROGRAMS

You can copy Excel data and use it in other applications, such as in a Word document or in a PowerPoint presentation. For example, you can perform statistical analyses in Excel and copy the data into a research paper in Word. Alternatively, you can create a budget in Excel and copy the data into a PowerPoint slide show for a meeting. After selecting and copying a range in Excel, you must decide how you want the data to appear in the destination application. Use the Paste arrow in the destination application to see a gallery of options or to select the Paste Special option. For example, you can paste the Excel data as a worksheet object, as unformatted text, or in another format.

Quick Concepts

8. Give an example of when you would delete a column versus when you would hide a column. ***pp. 335, 337***

9. When should you adjust column widths instead of using the default width? ***p. 335***

10. Discuss how you would use a paste option. ***pp. 340–342***

Hands-On Exercises

MyLab IT HOE3 Sim Training

▶ Watch the Video for this Hands-On Exercise!

Skills covered: Insert a Column • Insert and Delete Rows • Adjust Column Width • Adjust Row Height • Hide a Column • Select a Range • Move a Range • Copy and Paste a Range • Use Paste Options

3 Worksheet Structure and Clipboard Tasks

You want to insert a column to calculate the amount of markup and delete a row containing data you no longer require. You also want to adjust column widths to display the labels in the columns. In addition, Melissa asked you to enter data for a new product. Because it is almost identical to an existing product, you will copy the original data and edit the copied data to save time. You also want to experiment with the Paste Special option to see the results of using it in the Souvenir Shop workbook.

STEP 1 ▶ INSERT A COLUMN

You decide to add a column to display the profit. Because profit is a dollar amount, you want to keep the profit column close to another column of dollar amounts. Therefore, you will insert a new column before the profit margin column. Refer to Figure 1.38 as you complete Step 1.

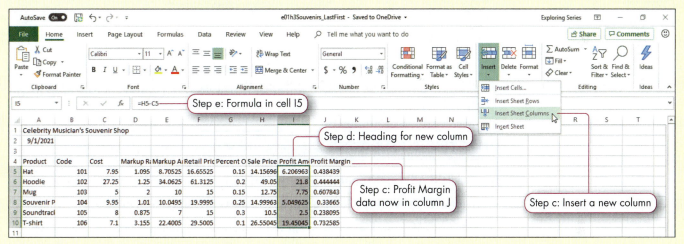

FIGURE 1.38 Profit Amount Column Inserted

a. Open *e01h2Souvenirs_LastFirst* if you closed it at the end of Hands-On Exercise 2 and save it as **e01h3Souvenirs_LastFirst**, changing h2 to h3.

b. Click any cell in **column I**.

You want to insert a column between the Sale Price and Profit Margin columns.

c. Click the **Insert arrow** in the Cells group on the Home tab and select **Insert Sheet Columns**.

You inserted a new blank column I. The contents in the original column I are now in column J.

d. Click **cell I4**, type **Profit Amount**, and then press **Enter**.

e. Ensure the active cell is **cell I5**. Enter the formula **=H5-C5**. Double-click the **cell I5 fill handle**. Save the workbook.

You calculated the profit amount by subtracting the original cost from the sale price and then copied the formula down the column. The profit for the soundtrack CD is $2.50.

STEP 2 INSERT AND DELETE ROWS

You decide to insert new rows for product information and category names. Furthermore, you decided not to include the Soundtrack CD for this week's list of sale items, so you want to delete the row containing that data. Refer to Figure 1.39 as you complete Step 2.

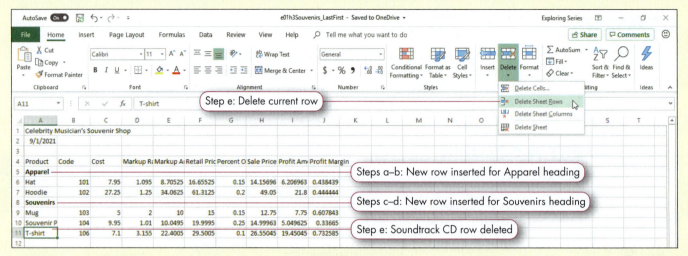

FIGURE 1.39 Category Rows Inserted and the Soundtrack CD Row Deleted

a. Right-click the **row 5 heading** and select **Insert** from the shortcut menu.

You inserted a new blank row 5, which is selected. The original rows of data move down a row each.

> **MAC TROUBLESHOOTING:** Use Control+click when instructed to right-click in the instructions.

b. Click **cell A5**. Type **Apparel** and press **Ctrl+Enter**. Click **Bold** in the Font group.

c. Right-click the **row 8 heading** and select **Insert** from the shortcut menu.

You inserted a new blank row 8. The data that was originally on row 8 is now on row 9.

d. Click **cell A8**. Type **Souvenirs** and press **Ctrl+Enter**. Click **Bold** in the Font group.

You typed and applied bold formatting to the category name Souvenirs above the list of souvenir products.

e. Click **cell A11**, click the **Delete arrow** in the Cells group, and then select **Delete Sheet Rows**. Save the workbook.

The Soundtrack CD row is deleted, and the remaining row moves up one row.

> **TROUBLESHOOTING:** If you accidentally delete the wrong row or accidentally select Delete Sheet Columns instead of Delete Sheet Rows, click Undo on the Quick Access Toolbar to restore the deleted row or column. Then complete Step e again.

ADJUST COLUMN WIDTH, ADJUST ROW HEIGHT, AND HIDE A COLUMN

As you review your worksheet, you notice that the text in column A appears cut off. You will increase the width of that column to display the entire product names. In addition, you want to make row 1 taller so that the title stands out. Finally, you decide to hide the column containing the codes because the managers are more interested in the monetary values than the codes. Refer to Figure 1.40 as you complete Step 3.

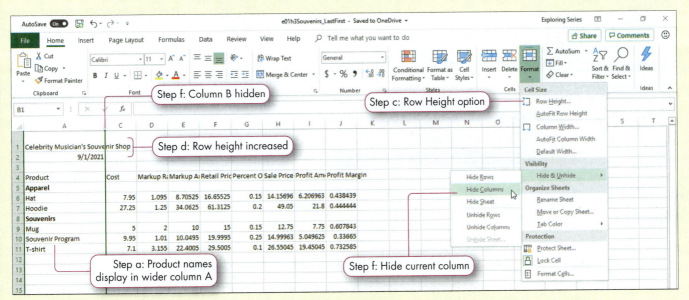

FIGURE 1.40 Column Width and Row Height Changed; Codes Column Hidden

a. Point to the **right border** of column A. When the pointer looks like a double-headed arrow with a solid black vertical line, double-click the **border**.

Excel increased the width of column A based on the cell containing the longest content (the title in cell A1). You decide to adjust the column width to the longest product name instead.

b. Point to the **right border** of column A until the double-headed arrow appears. Drag the border to the left until the ScreenTip displays **Width: 23.00 (166 pixels)**. Release the mouse button.

You decreased the column width to 23 for column A. The longest product name is visible. You will adjust the other column widths after you apply formats to the column headings in Hands-On Exercise 4.

c. Click **cell A1**. Click **Format** in the Cells group and select **Row Height**.

The Row Height dialog box opens so that you can adjust the height of the current row.

d. Type **30** in the Row height box and click **OK**.

You increased the height of the row that contains the worksheet title so that it is more prominent.

e. Click the **column B heading**.

f. Click **Format** in the Cells group, point to **Hide & Unhide**, and then select **Hide Columns**. Save the workbook.

Excel hides column B, the column containing the Codes. You see a gap in column heading letters A and C, indicating column B is hidden instead of deleted.

You want to move the T-shirt product to be immediately after the Hoodie product. Before moving the T-shirt row, you will insert a blank row between the Hoodie and Souvenirs. Refer to Figure 1.41 as you complete Step 4.

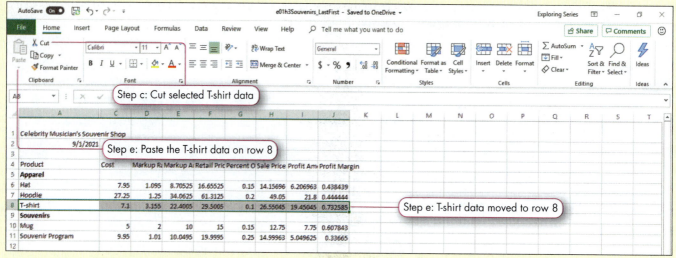

FIGURE 1.41 T-shirt Row Moved

a. Right-click the **row 8 heading** and select **Insert** from the menu.

You inserted a blank row so that you can move the T-shirt data to be between the Hoodie and Souvenirs rows.

b. Select the **range A12:J12**.

You selected the range of cells containing the T-shirt data.

c. Click **Cut** in the Clipboard group.

A moving dashed green border outlines the selected range. The status bar displays the message *Select destination and press ENTER or choose Paste*.

d. Click **cell A8**.

This is the first cell in the destination range. If you cut and paste a row without inserting a new row first, Excel will overwrite the original row of data, which is why you inserted a new row in step a.

e. Click **Paste** in the Clipboard group and save the workbook.

The T-shirt product data is now located on row 8.

In addition to selling ceramic mugs, Melissa ordered travel mugs. She asked you to enter the data for the new product. Because most of the data is the same as the current mug, you will copy the original mug data, edit the product name, and change the cost to reflect the cost of the second type of mug. Refer to Figure 1.42 as you complete Step 5.

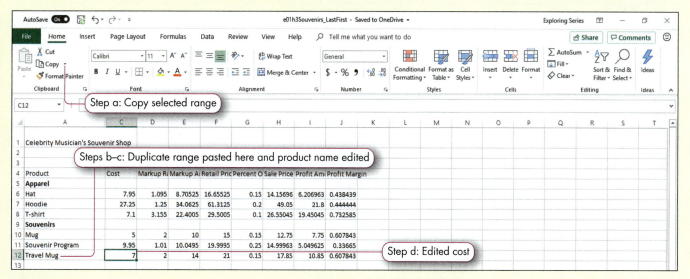

FIGURE 1.42 Mug Data Copied and Edited

a. Select the **range A10:J10** and click **Copy** in the Clipboard group.

You copied the row containing the Mug product data to the Clipboard.

b. Click **cell A12**, click **Paste** in the Clipboard group, and then press **Esc**.

The pasted range is selected in row 12.

c. Click **cell A12**, press **F2** to activate Edit Mode, press **Home**, type **Travel**, press **Spacebar**, and then press **Enter**.

You edited the product name to display Travel Mug.

d. Change the value in **cell C12** to **7**. Save the workbook.

The formulas calculate the results based on the $7 cost for the Travel Mug.

During your lunch break, you want to experiment with some of the Paste options. Particularly, you are interested in pasting Formulas and Value & Source Formatting. First, you will apply bold and a font color to the title to help you test these Paste options. Refer to Figure 1.43 as you complete Step 6.

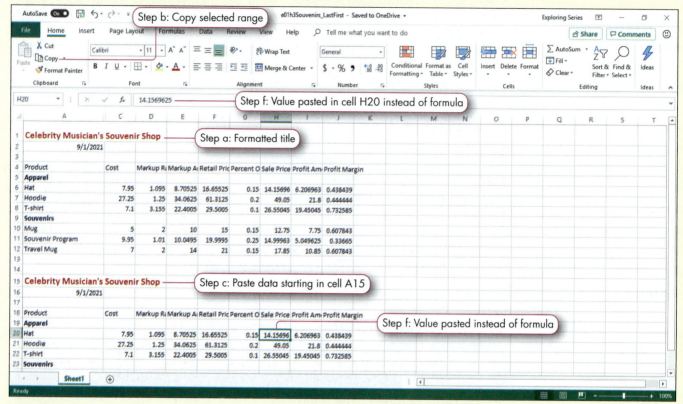

FIGURE 1.43 Results of Paste Options

a. Click **cell A1**. Click the **Font Size arrow** in the Font group and select **14**, click **Bold**, click the **Font Color arrow**, and then select **Dark Red** in the Standard Colors section.

b. Select the **range A1:J12** and click **Copy** in the Clipboard group.

c. Click **cell A15**, the top-left corner of the destination range.

d. Click the **Paste arrow** in the Clipboard group and point to **Formulas**, the second icon from the left in the Paste group.

   Without clicking the command, Excel shows you a preview of what that option would do. The pasted copy would not contain the font formatting you applied to the title or the bold on the two category names. In addition, the pasted date would appear as a serial number. The formulas would be maintained.

e. Position the pointer over **Values & Source Formatting**, the first icon from the right in the Paste Values group.

   This option would preserve the formatting, but it would convert the formulas into the current value results.

f. Click **Values & Source Formatting** and press **Esc**. Click **cell H6** to see a formula and click **cell H20**.

   Cell H6 contains a formula, but in the pasted version, the equivalent cell H20 has converted the formula result into an actual value. If you were to change the original cost in cell C20, the contents of cell H20 would not change. In a working environment, this is useful only if you want to capture the exact value in a point in time before making changes to the original data.

g. Save the workbook. Keep the workbook open if you plan to continue with the next Hands-On Exercise. If not, close the workbook, and exit Excel.

Worksheet Formatting

After entering data and formulas, you should format the worksheet. A professionally formatted worksheet—through adding appropriate symbols, aligning decimals, and using fonts and colors to make data stand out—makes finding and analyzing data easy. You can apply different formats to accentuate meaningful details or to draw attention to specific ranges in a worksheet.

In this section, you will learn to apply a cell style, different alignment options, including horizontal and vertical alignment, text wrapping, and indent options. In addition, you will learn how to format different types of values.

Applying Cell Styles, Cell Alignment, and Font Options

Visual clues, created by formatting changes, can differentiate parts of the worksheet. For example, the title may be centered in 16 pt size; column labels may be bold, centered, and Dark Blue font; and input cells may be formatted differently from output cells. The Font group on the Home tab contains the Font, Font Size, Bold, Italic, Underline, and Font Color commands. In addition to these commands, you will use other options in the Font, Alignment, and Styles groups to format data in a worksheet.

STEP 1 ▸ Apply Cell Styles

You can apply formats individually, or you can apply a group of formats by selecting a cell style. A *cell style* is a collection of format characteristics that provides a consistent appearance within a worksheet and among similar workbooks. A cell style controls the following formats: font, font color, font size, borders, fill colors, alignment, and number formatting. When you click Cell Styles in the Styles group on the Home tab, the Cell Styles gallery displays (see Figure 1.44). Position the pointer over a style name to see a Live Preview of how the style will affect the selected cell or range. The gallery provides a variety of built-in styles to apply to cells in your worksheet to make it easy to apply consistent formatting.

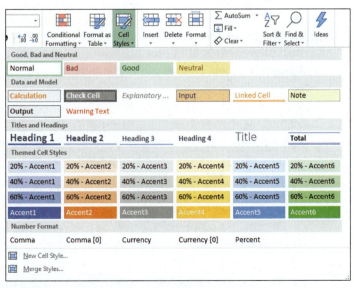

FIGURE 1.44 Cell Styles

Merge Cells

Often, a worksheet title is centered over the columns of data in the worksheet. Use Merge and Center to combine selected cells together into one cell. When the cells are merged horizontally, only data in the far-left cell are merged. When cells are merged vertically, only data in the top-left cell is maintained. Any other data in the merged cells are deleted.

You can use Merge and Center to center main titles over the columns of data in the worksheet, and you can merge and center category titles over groups of related columns. You can also merge cells on adjacent rows. Table 1.6 lists the four options when you click the Merge & Center arrow.

TABLE 1.6	Merge Options
Option	**Results**
Merge & Center	Merges selected cells and centers data into one cell.
Merge Across	Merges the selected cells but keeps text left aligned or values right aligned.
Merge Cells	Merges a range of cells and keeps original alignment.
Unmerge Cells	Separates a merged cell into multiple cells again.

STEP 2 Change Cell Alignment

Alignment refers to how data are positioned in the boundaries of a cell. Each type of data has a default alignment. ***Horizontal alignment*** specifies the position of data between the left and right cell margins. Text aligns at the left cell margin, and dates and values align at the right cell margin. You should change the alignment of cell contents to improve the appearance of data within the cells. For example, you can apply center horizontal alignment to center column labels over the values in a column. ***Vertical alignment*** specifies the position of data between the top and bottom cell margins. Bottom Align is the default vertical alignment. While this alignment is not noticeable with the default row height, if you increase the row height to accommodate text in another cell on that row, data might not appear aligned properly across the row. In that situation, consider applying Top Align or Middle Align to see if that improves readability.

The Alignment group on the Home tab contains the vertical and horizontal alignment options. The vertical and horizontal alignments applied to the active cell display with a green background on the ribbon. In Figure 1.45, cell I4 is formatted with Bottom Align vertical alignment and Center horizontal alignment, as indicated by the light green background of those commands on the ribbon.

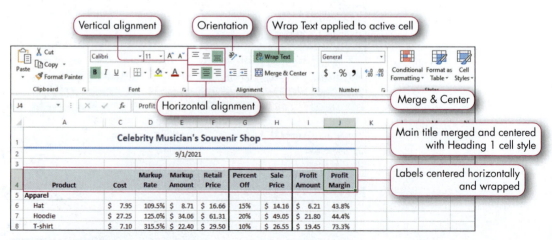

FIGURE 1.45 Cell Style and Alignment Settings Applied

The Format Cells dialog box contains options for changing horizontal and vertical alignment, text wrapping, merging cells, and rotating data in cells. In addition, you can shrink data to fit within the cell and change the text direction in the cell. To open the Format Cells dialog box, click the Dialog Box Launcher in the Alignment group on the Home tab.

> **MAC TIP:** Office for Mac does not have Dialog Box Launchers. Instead, use the Format menu.

> **TIP: CHANGE TEXT ORIENTATION**
> People sometimes rotate headings in cells. More text may fit when it is rotated at an angle, rotated up, or rotated down. To rotate data in a cell, click Orientation in the Alignment group on the Home tab and select an option, such as Angle Clockwise.

Wrap Text

Use **wrap text** to word-wrap data on multiple lines within a cell by adjusting the row height to fit the cell contents within the column width. Excel wraps the text on two or more lines within the cell. In Figure 1.45, the Markup Rate and Percent Off labels on row 4 are examples of wrapped text. The Wrap Text option is in the Alignment group on the Home tab. Wrap Text has a light green background because the text is wrapped in the active cell I4.

> **TIP: LINE BREAK IN A CELL**
> If a long text label does not fit well in a cell even after you have applied wrap text, you can insert a line break to display the text label on multiple lines within the cell. To insert a line break while you are typing a label, press Alt+Enter where you want to start the next line of text within the cell. On a Mac, press Option+Enter.

STEP 3 ## Increase and Decrease Indent

Cell content is left-aligned or right-aligned based on the default data type. However, you can **indent** the cell contents to offset the data from its current alignment. For example, text is left-aligned, but you can indent it to offset it from the left side. Indenting helps others see the hierarchical structure of data. Accountants often indent the word Totals in financial statements so that it stands out from a list of items above the total row. Values are right-aligned by default, but you can indent a value to offset it from the right side of the cell. In Figure 1.46, the specific products (Hat, Hoodie, T-shirt, Mug, Souvenir Program, and Travel Mug) are indented. Use the Increase Indent or Decrease Indent in the Alignment group to adjust the indent of data in a cell.

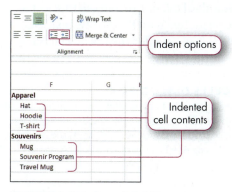

FIGURE 1.46 Indented Cell Contents

STEP 4 Apply Borders and Fill Color

A worksheet with a lot of text and numbers will be hard to read without some formatting to help emphasize headings, important data, input and output areas, etc. You can apply a border or fill color to accentuate data in a worksheet. A **border** is a line that surrounds a cell or a range of cells. Use borders to offset some data from the rest of the worksheet data. Borders are applied by using the Border command in the Font group on the Home tab. The Border arrow displays different options, and for more control, select More Borders to display the Format Cells dialog box with additional border options. In Figure 1.47, a border surrounds the range G4:H12. To remove a border, select No Border from the Borders menu.

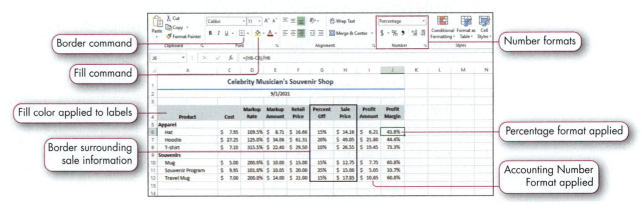

FIGURE 1.47 Borders, Fill Color, and Number Formats

Add some color to your worksheets to emphasize data or headers by applying a fill color. **Fill color** is a background color that displays behind data in a cell so that the data stand out. Choose a fill color that contrasts with the font color. For example, if the font color is Black, Text 1, select White or Yellow fill color. If the font color is White, Background 1, select a dark fill color such as Dark Blue. The color palette contains two sections: Theme Colors and Standard Colors. The Theme Colors section displays variations of colors that match the current theme applied in the worksheet. The Standard Colors section contains basic colors that do not change with the theme. When you click the Fill Color arrow in the Font group on the Home tab, a color palette displays. If you want to remove a fill color, select No Fill from the bottom of the palette. Select More Colors to open the Colors dialog box and use the Standard tab or Custom tab to select a color. In Figure 1.47, the column labels in row 4 are formatted with Blue-Gray, Text 2, Lighter 80% fill color to complement the Blue-Gray, Text 2 font color for the title in cell A1.

Applying Number Formats

Values have no special formatting when you enter data. However, you can apply *number formats*, settings that control how a value is displayed in a cell. The default number format is General, which displays values as you originally enter them. General number format does not align decimal points in a column or include symbols, such as dollar signs, percent signs, or commas. Applying number formats provides context for the values, such as displaying currency symbols for monetary values and percent signs for percentages, and make the data easier to read.

STEP 5 Apply a Number Format

The Number group on the Home tab contains commands for applying Accounting Number Format, Percent Style, and Comma Style numbering formats. The *Accounting Number Format* and *Currency format* both display the dollar sign, commas for every three digits on the left side of the decimal point, align decimal points, and display two digits to the right of the decimal point; however, the placement of the dollar sign differs. In Accounting Number Format, the dollar sign aligns on the left side of the cell; in Currency format, the dollar sign is immediately to the left of the value. You can click the Accounting Number Format arrow and select other denominations, such as English pounds or euros. For other number formats, click the Number Format arrow and select the numbering format you want to use. Figure 1.47 shows the Accounting Number Format applied to the ranges C6:C12, E6:F12, and H6:I12. Percent Style is applied to the ranges D6:D12, G6:G12, and J6:J12.

Applying a different number format changes the way the number displays in a cell, but the format does not change the stored value. If, for example, you enter 123.456 into a cell and format the cell with the Currency number type, the value shows as $123.46 onscreen where the value is rounded to the nearest cent, but Excel uses the full value 123.456 when performing calculations.

Table 1.7 lists and describes the primary number formats in Excel. Figure 1.48 shows different number formats applied to the value 1234.567 and the special Zip+4 and phone number formats.

TABLE 1.7	Number Formats
Format Style	**Display**
General	The default number format.
Number	A number with or without the comma separator and with any number of decimal places. Negative numbers can be displayed with parentheses and/or red.
Currency format	A number, the dollar sign immediately to the left of the number, a comma for every three digits on the left side of the decimal point, and two digits to the right of the decimal point. Negative values are preceded by a minus sign. Zero displays as $0.00.
Accounting Number Format	A number, the dollar sign on the left side of the cell, a comma for every three digits on the left side of the decimal point, and two digits to the right of the decimal point. Negative values are enclosed in parentheses by default. Zero displays as a dollar sign and a hyphen.
Comma Style	The *Comma Style* formats with a comma for every three digits on the left side of the decimal point and displays two digits to the right of the decimal point.
Date	A serial number formatted as a date.
Time	A number formatted for time.
Percent Style	The *Percent Style* formats a value as if it was multiplied by 100 and with a percent symbol.
Fraction	A number formatted as a fraction.
Scientific	A number as a decimal fraction followed by a whole number exponent of 10; for example, the number 12345 would display as 1.23E+04.
Text	Treats data as text, even if it contains numbers.
Special	A number with editing characters, such as the parentheses and hyphen in a phone number, hyphen in a Zip Code+4, and the hyphens in a Social Security number.
Custom	Predefined customized number formats or special symbols to create your own customized number format.

	A	B	C	D	E	F
1	General	1234.567		Original Value	9171234567	
2	Number	1234.57		Phone Number Format	(917) 123-4567	
3	Currency	. $1,234.57				
4	Accounting	$ 1,234.57		Original Value	102821234	
5	Comma	1,234.57		Zip + 4 Number Format	10282-1234	
6	Percent	123457%				

FIGURE 1.48 Number Formats

TIP: CUSTOM NUMBER FORMATS
You can create a custom format if the built-in formats do not meet your needs by accessing the Custom Format options in the Format Cells dialog box. Select Custom in the Category list (see Figure 1.49) and select the custom format. Use Help to learn how to create custom number formats.

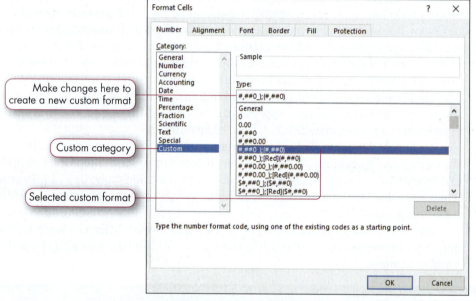

FIGURE 1.49 Custom Number Formats

Increase and Decrease Decimal Places

After applying a number format, you will usually adjust the number of decimal places that display. For example, if you have an entire column of monetary values formatted in Accounting Number Format, Excel displays two decimal places by default. If the entire column of values contains whole dollar values and no cents, displaying .00 down the column looks cluttered. Decrease the number of decimal places to show whole numbers only. By default, Percent Style displays percentages as whole numbers. However, for greater precision, you can increase the number of decimal places displayed to one or two. Use Increase Decimal or Decrease Decimal in the Number group on the Home tab to adjust the number of decimal points for a value.

TIP: FORMAT PAINTER
Use Format Painter in the Clipboard group on the Home tab to copy formats (alignment, fill color, border, number format, text wrapping, and number formats) to other cells in the workbook.

Quick Concepts

11. Discuss when you would use Merge and Center in a worksheet. **p. 350**

12. Explain why you would wrap text in a cell. **p. 351**

13. Explain why you would increase the number of decimal places for values formatted with Percent Style. **p. 354**

Hands-On Exercises

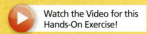
Skills covered: Apply a Cell
Style • Merge Cells • Change Cell
Alignment • Wrap Text • Increase
Indent • Apply a Border • Apply
Fill Color • Apply Number
Formats • Increase and Decrease
Decimal Places

4 Worksheet Formatting

In the first three Hands-On Exercises, you entered data about products on sale, created formulas to calculate markup and profit, and inserted new rows and columns. You are ready to format the Souvenir Shop worksheet. Specifically, you will apply a cell style, merge and center the title, align text, format values, and apply other formatting to enhance the readability of the worksheet.

STEP 1 APPLY A CELL STYLE AND MERGE CELLS

To make the title stand out, you want to apply a cell style and center it over all the data columns. You will use the Merge & Center command to merge cells and center the title at the same time. Refer to Figure 1.50 as you complete Step 1.

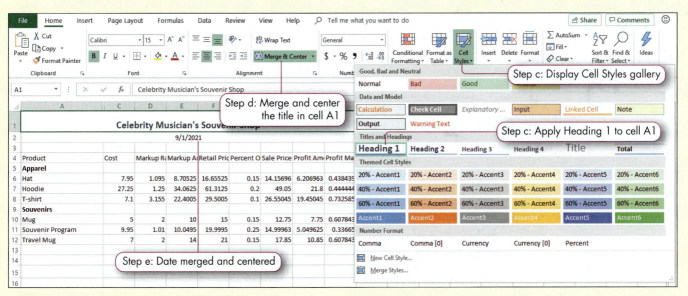

FIGURE 1.50 Cell Style Applied and Cells Merged

a. Open *e01h3Souvenirs_LastFirst* if you closed it at the end of Hands-On Exercise 3 and save it as **e01h4Souvenirs_LastFirst**, changing h3 to h4.

b. Select the **range A15:J26** and press **Delete**.

You maintained a copy of your Paste Special results in the e01h3Souvenirs_LastFirst workbook, but you do not need it to continue.

c. Select the **range A1:J1**, click **Cell Styles** in the Styles group on the Home tab, and then click **Heading 1** from the gallery.

You applied the Heading 1 style to the range A1:J1. This style formats the contents with 15-pt font size, Blue-Gray, Text 2 font color, and a thick blue bottom border.

d. Click **Merge & Center** in the Alignment group.

Excel merges cells in the range A1:J1 into one cell and centers the title horizontally within the merged cell, which is cell A1.

> **TROUBLESHOOTING:** If you merge too many or not enough cells, unmerge the cells and start again. To unmerge cells, click in the merged cell. The Merge & Center command is shaded in green when the active cell is merged. Click Merge & Center to unmerge the cell. Then select the correct range to merge and use Merge & Center again.

e. Select the **range A2:J2**. Click **Merge & Center** in the Alignment group. Save the workbook.

> **TROUBLESHOOTING:** If you try to merge and center data in the range A1:I2, Excel will keep the top-left data only and delete the date. To merge separate data on separate rows, you must merge and center data separately.

CHANGE CELL ALIGNMENT AND WRAP TEXT

You want to center the title vertically between the top and bottom cell margins. In addition, you will center the column labels horizontally between the left and right cell margins and wrap the text in the column labels to avoid columns that are too wide for the data (such as Profit Margin). Refer to Figure 1.51 as you complete Step 2.

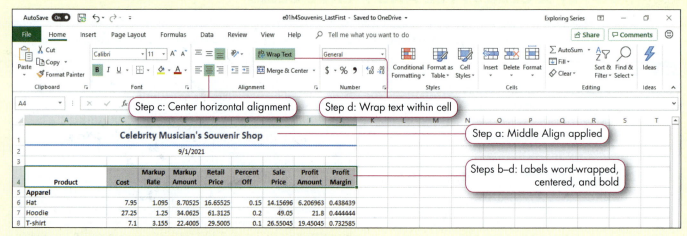

FIGURE 1.51 Alignment Options Applied to the Title and Column Labels

a. Click **cell A1**, which contains the title, and click **Middle Align** in the Alignment group.

Middle Align vertically centers data between the top and bottom edges of the cell.

b. Select the **range A4:J4** to select the column labels.

c. Click **Center** in the Alignment group and click **Bold** in the Font group to format the selected column labels.

The column labels are centered horizontally between the left and right edges of each cell.

d. Click **Wrap Text** in the Alignment group. Save the workbook.

The multiple-word column labels (such as Markup Rate and Profit Margin) are now visible on two lines within each cell.

INCREASE INDENT

You decide to indent the labels within each category to better display which products are in the Apparel and Souvenirs categories. Refer to Figure 1.52 as you complete Step 3.

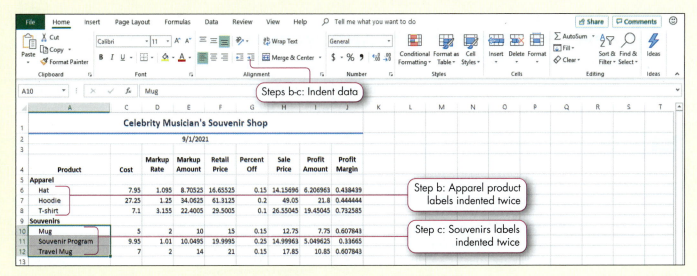

FIGURE 1.52 Product Names Indented

a. Select the **range A6:A8**, the cells containing Apparel products labels.

b. Click **Increase Indent** in the Alignment group twice.

The three selected product names are indented below the Apparel heading.

c. Select the **range A10:A12** and click **Increase Indent** twice. Save the workbook.

The three selected product names are indented below the Souvenirs heading.

APPLY A BORDER AND FILL COLOR

You want to apply a light blue-gray fill color to highlight the column labels. In addition, you want to emphasize the percentage off and sale prices by applying a border around that range. Refer to Figure 1.53 as you complete Step 4.

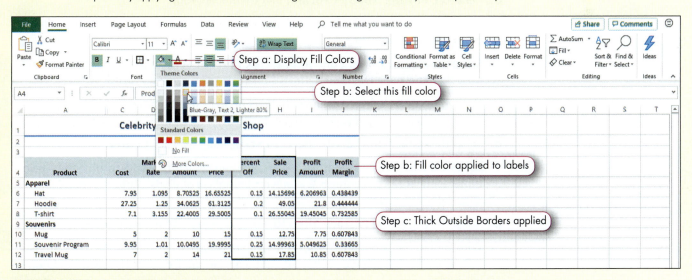

FIGURE 1.53 Border and Fill Color Applied

a. Select the **range A4:J4** and click the **Fill Color arrow** in the Font group.

b. Click **Blue-Gray, Text 2, Lighter 80%** in the Theme Colors section (second row, fourth column).

You applied a fill color that complements the Heading 1 cell style applied to the title.

c. Select the **range G4:H12**, click the **Border arrow** in the Font group, and then select **Thick Outside Borders**. Click **cell A4**. Save the workbook.

You applied a border around the selected cells.

APPLY NUMBER FORMATS AND INCREASE AND DECREASE DECIMAL PLACES

You want to format the values to improve readability and look more professional. You will apply number formats and adjust the number of decimal points displayed. Refer to Figure 1.54 as you complete Step 5.

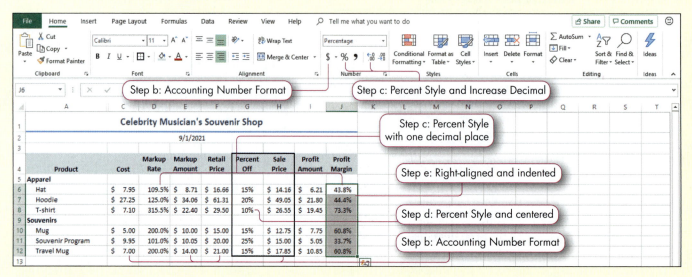

FIGURE 1.54 Number Formats and Decimal Places

a. Select the **ranges C6:C12, E6:F12, and H6:I12**.

To apply the same format to nonadjacent ranges, hold Ctrl while selecting each range.

b. Click **Accounting Number Format** in the Number group.

Accounting Number Format aligns dollar signs on the left side of the cell and aligns values on the decimal point.

c. Select the **ranges D6:D12 and J6:J12**, click **Percent Style** in the Number group, and then click **Increase Decimal** in the Number group.

You formatted the selected values with Percent Style and displayed one decimal place to avoid misleading your readers by displaying the values as whole percentages.

d. Select the **range G6:G12**, click **Percent Style**, and then click **Center**.

Because all the percentages are two digits, you can center the values to align them below the heading. If the percentages had different numbers of digits, centering would not align values correctly.

e. Select the **range J6:J12**, click **Align Right**, and then click **Increase Indent**.

With values, you want to keep the decimal points aligned, but you can then use Increase Indent to adjust the indent so that the values appear more centered below the column labels.

f. Save the workbook. Keep the workbook open if you plan to continue with the next Hands-On Exercise. If not, close the workbook, and exit Excel.

Worksheet Management, Page Setup, and Printing

When you start a new blank workbook in Excel, the workbook contains one worksheet named Sheet1. However, you can add additional worksheets. The individual worksheets are saved under one workbook file name. Having multiple worksheets in one workbook is helpful to keep related items together. After creating and formatting worksheets, consider if you will use these for your own purposes or if you will distribute the workbook electronically or as printouts to other people. If you plan to distribute a workbook to others, you should set up the worksheets so that they can print attractively and meaningfully on a printout.

In this section, you will copy, move, and rename worksheets. You will also select options on the Page Layout tab; specifically, you will use the Page Setup, Scale to Fit, and Sheet Options groups. After selecting page setup options, you will learn how to print the worksheet.

Managing Worksheets

Creating a multiple-worksheet workbook takes some planning and maintenance. Worksheet tab names should reflect the contents of the respective worksheets. In addition, you can insert, copy, move, and delete worksheets within the workbook. You can even apply background color to the worksheet tabs so that they stand out onscreen. Figure 1.55 shows a workbook in which the sheet tabs have been renamed, colors have been applied to worksheet tabs, and a worksheet tab has been right-clicked so that the shortcut menu displays.

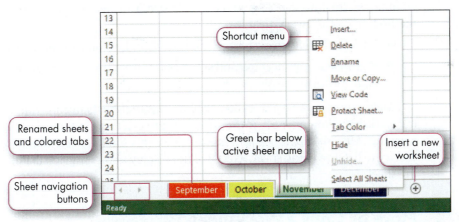

FIGURE 1.55 Worksheet Tabs

If a color has been applied to the sheet tab, the tab shows in the full color when it is not active. When that sheet is active, the sheet tab color is a gradient of the selected color. Regardless of whether a tab color has been applied, the active sheet tab has a green horizontal bar below the sheet name, and the sheet name is bold and green.

> **TIP: USING OTHER SHORTCUT MENUS**
> Right-click a sheet tab scroll arrow to display a list of worksheets. You can then make another worksheet active by selecting the name from the menu. Press Ctrl and click the left sheet tab scroll button to display the first sheet tab. Press Ctrl and click the right sheet tab scroll button to display the last sheet tab.

Insert and Delete a Worksheet

Sometimes you want more than one worksheet in the workbook. For example, you can create one worksheet for each month to track your monthly income and expenses for one year. When tax time comes around, you have all your data stored in one workbook file. Adding worksheets within one workbook enables you to save related sheets of data together. Excel provides several methods to insert a new sheet; choose one of these methods:

- Click New sheet to the right of the last worksheet tab to insert a sheet to the right of the active sheet.
- Click the Insert arrow in the Cells group on the Home tab and select Insert Sheet to insert a sheet to the left of the active sheet.
- Right-click any sheet tab, select Insert from the shortcut menu (refer to Figure 1.55), click Worksheet in the Insert dialog box, and then click OK to insert a sheet to the left of the active sheet. You can also use the Insert dialog box to insert worksheets based on Microsoft Office templates, such as the Cashflow analysis template. The inserted worksheets contain formatted text, default values, and formulas to save you time in planning and setting up worksheets.
- Press Shift+F11.

> **MAC TIP:** Use the shortcut menu to insert a sheet. A dialog box does not open.

When you insert a new blank worksheet, the default name is Sheet with a number, such as Sheet2. The next sheet would be Sheet3, and so on. Even if you rename or delete worksheets, the additional sheet names will continue incrementing the number.

If you no longer require the data in a worksheet, delete the worksheet. Doing so will eliminate extra data in a file and reduce file size. You can choose either of the following methods to delete a worksheet:

- Click the Delete arrow in the Cells group on the Home tab and select Delete Sheet.
- Right-click any sheet tab and select Delete from the shortcut menu (refer to Figure 1.55).

Make sure you save a workbook before deleting sheets in case you decide you want the worksheet data after all. If the sheet you are deleting contains data, Excel displays a warning: *Microsoft Excel will permanently delete this sheet. Do you want to continue?* When you try to delete a blank sheet, Excel will not display a warning; it will immediately delete the sheet.

STEP 1 ▷ Move or Copy a Worksheet

After creating a worksheet, you can copy it to use as a template or starting point for similar data. For example, if you create a worksheet for your September budget, you can copy the worksheet and easily edit the data on the copied worksheet to enter data for your October budget. Copying the entire worksheet saves you a lot of time in entering and formatting the new worksheet, and it preserves the column widths and row heights. You can rearrange the sheet tabs to be in a different sequence by moving a worksheet within the workbook. You can also move a worksheet to a new workbook or to another workbook that is open. For example, you can move worksheets created by different sales representatives into a consolidated sales workbook.

To copy or move a worksheet, complete the following steps:

1. Right-click the sheet tab of the worksheet you want to copy or click Format in the Cells group on the Home tab.
2. Select Move or Copy from the shortcut menu or Move or Copy Sheet from the ribbon menu to display the Move or Copy dialog box (see Figure 1.56).
3. Click the To book arrow. The list options include (new book), the name of the current workbook, and the names of other open workbooks. The default option is the current workbook. Select which book you want to contain the original or copy of the active worksheet.
4. Select a sheet in the Before sheet list, which displays the names of the worksheets in the workbook you selected in Step 3. If you selected (new book), no worksheets are listed. If you select the current workbook or another open workbook, the list displays the names of the worksheets in left-to-right sequence in that workbook. The default selected sheet is the first sheet in the respective workbook.
5. Click the Create a copy check box to select it if you want to make a copy of it. By default, the check box is not selected; leave the check box empty if you want to move the worksheet.
6. Click OK.

FIGURE 1.56 Move or Copy Dialog Box

TIP: DRAGGING TO COPY OR MOVE SHEETS

You can also move a worksheet within the existing workbook by clicking and dragging the sheet tab to the left or right of other sheet tabs. As you drag a sheet tab, the pointer resembles a piece of paper. A triangle displays between sheet tabs to indicate where the sheet will be placed when you release the mouse button. To copy a worksheet, press and hold Ctrl as you drag a sheet tab. A plus sign displays on the pointer to indicate that you are copying the sheet.

When you copy a worksheet within the same workbook, the tab for the copied sheet contains the name of the original sheet and a number. For example, if you copy a sheet named Sales, the copied sheet name is Sales (2). However, if you copy a worksheet to a new book or another open workbook, the copied sheet name is identical to the original sheet name.

Rename a Worksheet

The default worksheet name Sheet1 does not describe the contents of the worksheet. It is good practice to rename worksheet tabs to reflect the sheet contents. Although you can

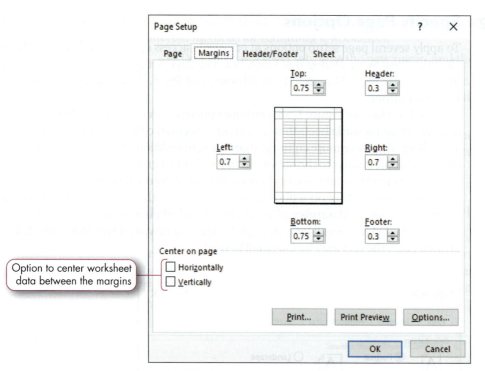

FIGURE 1.59 Page Setup Dialog Box: Margins Tab

Option to center worksheet data between the margins

STEP 3 **Create a Header or Footer**

Use headers and footers to provide additional information about the worksheet. You can include your name, the date the worksheet was prepared, and page numbers, for example. You can insert a header or footer by using Header & Footer in the Text group on the Insert tab or by using Page Layout in the Workbook Views group on the Views tab. When you use the Header & Footer command, Excel displays the worksheet in Page Layout view with left, center, and right sections. The insertion point is in the center section, and the Header & Footer Tools Design contextual tab displays (see Figure 1.60). Enter text or insert data from the Header & Footer Elements group on the tab. If you display the worksheet in Page Layout view from the View tab, click in the *Add header* area to display the contextual tab.

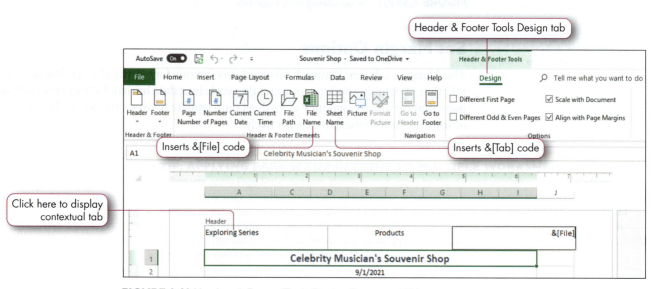

Header & Footer Tools Design tab

Inserts &[File] code

Inserts &[Tab] code

Click here to display contextual tab

FIGURE 1.60 Headers & Footer Tools Design Contextual Tab

To hide the header or footer and display the worksheet in Normal view, make any cell the active cell and use Normal in the Workbook Views group on the View tab or click Normal on the status bar. You can also create a header by clicking Page Layout in the Workbook Views group to display the header area.

Another way to insert a header or footer is to use the Header/Footer tab in the Page Setup dialog box (see Figure 1.61). This method is efficient when you want to insert headers or footers and select other page setup options from within the dialog box. Use the Header or Footer arrows to choose from several preformatted entries, or use Custom Header or Custom Footer to display the Header or the Footer dialog box, respectively, to insert text and other objects.

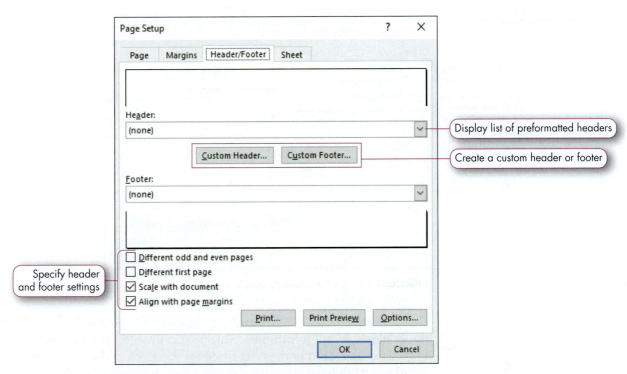

FIGURE 1.61 Page Setup Dialog Box: Header/Footer Tab

You can create different headers or footers on different pages, such as one header with the file name on odd-numbered pages and a header containing the date on even-numbered pages. Select the *Different odd and even pages* check box in the Page Setup dialog box (refer to Figure 1.61).

You can have a different header or footer on the first page from the rest of the printed pages, or you might not want a header or footer to show up on the first page but want the header or footer to display on the remaining pages. Select the *Different first page* check box in the Page Setup dialog box to specify a different first page header or footer.

> **TIP: DIFFERENT PAGE SETUP OPTIONS AND HEADERS**
> If you applied different orientation, scaling, and margins to different worksheets, do not group the worksheets to create headers or footers. Doing so would apply identical page settings to all the grouped worksheets. When you have different settings for different worksheets, create the headers or footers individually on each sheet.

Select Sheet Options

The Sheet tab (see Figure 1.62) contains options for setting the print area, print titles, print options, and page order. Some of these options are also located in the Sheet Options group on the Page Layout tab.

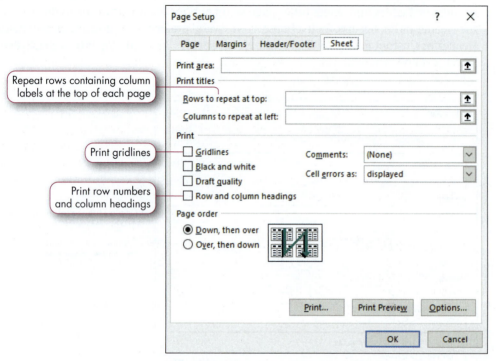

Repeat rows containing column labels at the top of each page

Print gridlines

Print row numbers and column headings

FIGURE 1.62 Page Setup Dialog Box: Sheet Tab

By default, Excel displays gridlines onscreen to show you each cell's margins, but the gridlines do not print unless you specifically select the Gridlines check box in the Page Setup dialog box or the Print Gridlines check box in the Sheet Options group on the Page Layout tab. In addition, Excel displays row and column headings onscreen. However, these headings do not print unless you click the *Row and column headings* check box in the Page Setup dialog box or click the Print Headings check box in the Sheet Options group on the Page Layout tab. For most worksheets, you do not need to print gridlines and row/column headings; however, when you want to display and print cell formulas instead of formula results, consider printing the gridlines and row/column headings. Doing so will help you analyze your formulas. The gridlines help you see the cell boundaries, and the headings help you identify what data are in each cell. Displaying gridlines helps separate data on a printout to increase readability.

> **TIP: REPEATING ROWS AND COLUMNS (TITLES)**
>
> If worksheet contains too many rows to print on one page, click Print Titles in the Page Setup group to open the Page Setup dialog box with the Sheet tab options displayed. Select the *Rows to repeat at top* box and select the row(s) containing column labels. The rows containing the descriptive column labels will repeat at the top of each printed page so that you can easily know what data is in each column. Likewise, if the worksheet has too many columns to print across on one page, select the *Columns to repeat at left* box and select the column(s) so that the row labels will display on the left side of each printed page.

Previewing and Printing a Worksheet

Backstage view displays print options and the worksheet in print preview mode. Print preview used before printing enables you to see if the data are balanced on the page or if data will print on multiple pages.

You can specify the number of copies to print and which printer to use to print the worksheet. The first option in the Settings area specifies what to print. The default option is Print Active Sheets. You can choose other options, such as Print Entire Workbook or Print Selection, or specify which pages to print. For example, you can select a range and display the print options to print only that range, or you can print only page 1 if it contains summary data.

The bottom of the Print window indicates how many pages will print. If the worksheet data flows just a little onto a second page, you can set smaller margins or adjust the scaling so that the data fits on one page. If the worksheet data fits on several pages, make sure the row and/or column labels repeat at the top and left of each printed page. You can also adjust column widths to improve the readability of the data and preview how the worksheet will print. A link to open the Page Setup dialog box is at the bottom of the print settings for easy access to make any of these adjustments.

> **TIP: PRINTING MULTIPLE WORKSHEETS**
> To print more than one worksheet at a time, select the sheets you want to print. To select adjacent sheets, click the first sheet tab, press and hold Shift, and then click the last sheet tab. To select nonadjacent sheets, press Ctrl as you click each sheet tab. When you display the Print options, Print Active Sheets is one of the default settings. If you want to print all worksheets within the workbook, change the setting to Print Entire Workbook.

Quick Concepts

14. Why would you insert several worksheets of data in one workbook instead of creating a separate workbook for each worksheet? *p. 360*

15. Why would you select a *Center on page* option in the Margins tab within the Page Setup dialog box if you have already set the margins? *p. 363*

16. List at least five elements you can insert in a header or footer. *p. 364*

17. Why would you want to print gridlines and row and column headings? *p. 366*

Hands-On Exercises

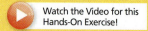
Skills covered: Copy a
Worksheet • Move a Worksheet •
Rename a Worksheet • Set
Page Orientation • Select Scaling
Options • Set Margin Options •
Create a Header or Footer •
View in Print Preview • Print a
Worksheet

5 Worksheet Management, Page Setup, and Printing

You are ready to complete the Souvenirs Shop worksheet. You want to copy the existing worksheet so that you display the results on the original sheet and display formulas on the duplicate sheet. Before printing the worksheet for your supervisor, you want to make sure the data will appear professional when printed. You will adjust some page setup options to put the finishing touches on the worksheet.

STEP 1 COPY, MOVE, AND RENAME A WORKSHEET

You want to copy the worksheet, move it to the right side of the original worksheet, and rename the duplicate worksheet so that you can show formulas on the duplicate sheet. Refer to Figure 1.63 as you complete Step 1.

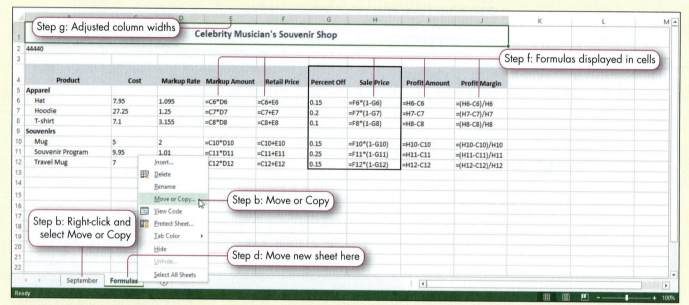

FIGURE 1.63 Two Worksheets

a. Open *e01h4Souvenirs_LastFirst* if you closed it at the end of Hands-On Exercise 4 and save it as **e01h5Souvenirs_LastFirst**, changing h4 to h5.

b. Right-click the **Sheet1 tab** at the bottom of the worksheet and select **Move or Copy**.

The Move or Copy dialog box opens so that you can move the existing worksheet or make a copy of it.

> **MAC TROUBLESHOOTING:** Press Control and click the Sheet1 tab.

c. Click the **Create a copy check box** to select it and click **OK**.

The duplicate worksheet is named Sheet1 (2) and is placed to the left of the original worksheet.

d. Drag the **Sheet1 (2) worksheet tab** to the right of the Sheet1 worksheet tab.

The duplicate worksheet is now on the right side of the original worksheet.

e. Double-click the **Sheet1 sheet tab**, type **September**, and then press **Enter**. Rename Sheet1 (2) as **Formulas**.

You renamed the original worksheet as September to reflect the September sales data, and you renamed the duplicate worksheet as Formulas to indicate that you will keep the formulas displayed on that sheet.

f. Press **Ctrl+`** to display the formulas in the Formulas worksheet.

g. Change these column widths in the Formulas sheet:

- Column A: **12.00**
- Columns C and D: **6.00**
- Columns E, F, H, I, and J: **7.00**
- Column G: **5.00**

You reduced the column widths so that the data will fit on a printout better.

h. Save the workbook.

SET PAGE ORIENTATION, SCALING, AND MARGIN OPTIONS

Because the worksheet has several columns, you decide to print it in landscape orientation. You want to set a 1″ top margin and center the data between the left and right margins. Furthermore, you want to make sure the data fits on one page on each sheet. Currently, if you were to print the Formulas worksheet, the data would print on two pages. Refer to Figure 1.64 as you complete Step 2.

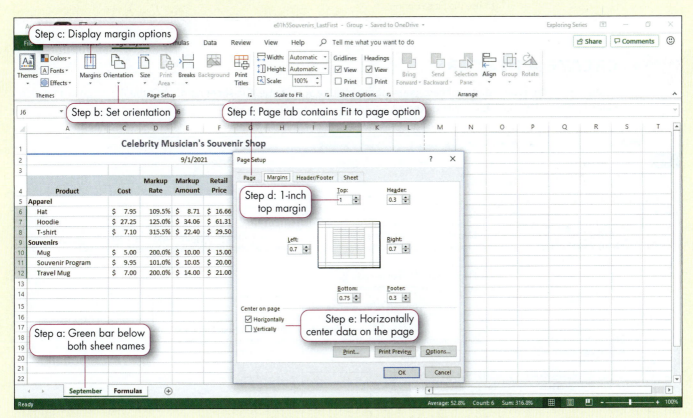

FIGURE 1.64 Page Setup Options Applied

a. Click the **September sheet tab**, press and hold **Ctrl**, and then click the **Formulas sheet tab**.

Both sheets are grouped and active, as indicated by the solid green bar below both sheet tab names. Anything you do on one sheet affects both sheets.

b. Click the **Page Layout tab**, click **Orientation** in the Page Setup group, and then select **Landscape** from the list.

Because both worksheets are active, both worksheets are formatted in landscape orientation.

c. Click **Margins** in the Page Setup group on the Page Layout tab and select **Custom Margins**.

The Page Setup dialog box opens with the Margins tab options displayed.

d. Click the **Top spin arrow** to display **1**.

Because both worksheets are grouped, the 1" top margin is set for both worksheets.

e. Click the **Horizontally check box** in the Center on page section to select it. Click **OK**.

Because both worksheets are grouped, the data on each worksheet are centered between the left and right margins.

f. Right-click the **Formulas sheet tab** and select **Ungroup Sheets**. With the Formulas sheet active, click the **Page Setup Dialog Box Launcher** in the Scale to Fit group, click **Fit to** in the Scaling section, and then click **OK**. Save the workbook.

The data on the September sheet fit on one page; however, the data on the Formulas sheet did not, so you used the Fit to option ensuring that the Formulas sheet data fits on one page.

> **TROUBLESHOOTING:** If you leave both sheets selected and use the Fit to option, the Fit to setting will apply to only the September sheet. Make sure that the Formulas sheet is active (not grouped) to use the Fit to option.

STEP 3 ## CREATE A HEADER

To document the grouped worksheets, you want to include your name, the sheet name, and the file name in a header. Refer to Figure 1.65 as you complete Step 3.

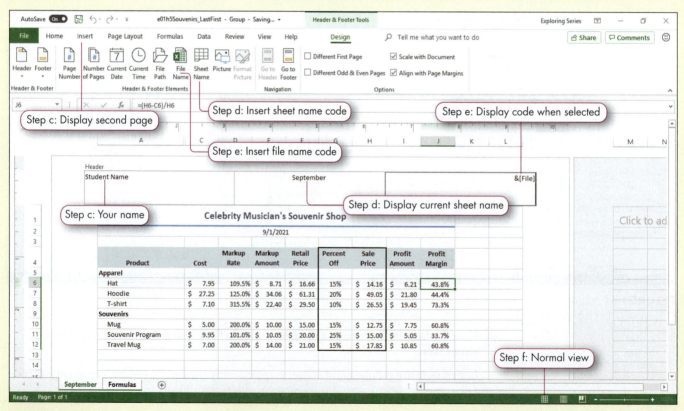

FIGURE 1.65 Header in Souvenir Shop Workbook

a. Click the **September sheet tab**, press and hold **Ctrl**, and then click the **Formulas sheet tab**.

b. Click the **Insert tab**, click **Text**, and then click **Header & Footer** in the Text group.

Excel displays the Header & Footer Tools Design contextual tab. The worksheet displays in Page Layout view, which displays the header area, margin space, and ruler. The insertion point is active in the center section of the header.

c. Click in the **left section** of the header and type your name.

d. Click in the **center section** of the header and click **Sheet Name** in the Header & Footer Elements group on the Design tab.

Excel inserts the code &[Tab]. This code displays the name of the worksheet. If you change the worksheet tab name, the header will reflect the new sheet name.

e. Click in the **right section** of the header and click **File Name** in the Header & Footer Elements group on the Design tab.

Excel inserts the code &[File]. This code displays the name of the file. Notice that &[Tab] in the center section now displays the current tab name, September. Because the worksheets were selected when you created the header, a header will display on both worksheets. The file name will be the same; however, the sheet names will be different.

f. Click in any cell in the worksheet and click **Normal** on the status bar.

Normal view displays the worksheet but does not display the header or margins.

g. Click **cell A1**, click the **Review tab**, and then click **Spelling** in the Proofing group. Correct all errors, if any, and click **OK** when prompted with the message, *Spell check complete. You're good to go!* Leave the worksheets grouped. Save the workbook.

You should always check the spelling immediately before distributing a workbook.

STEP 4 ▸ VIEW IN PRINT PREVIEW AND PRINT

Before printing the worksheets, you should preview it. Doing so helps you detect margin problems and other issues, such as a single row or column of data flowing onto a new page. Refer to Figure 1.66 as you complete Step 4.

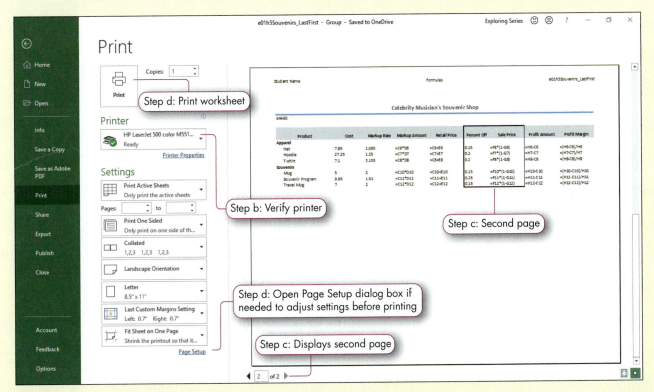

FIGURE 1.66 Worksheet in Print Preview

a. Click the **File tab** and click **Print**.

The Print Preview window displays options and a preview of the worksheet.

b. Verify the Printer box displays the printer that you want to use to print your worksheet, and verify the last Settings option displays Fit Sheet on One Page.

The bottom of the Print Preview window shows 1 of 2, indicating two pages will print.

c. Click **Next Page** to see the second page.

d. Click the **Back arrow** and save the workbook.

Although you did not print the worksheets, all the print options are saved.

e. Save and close the file. Exit Excel. Based on your instructor's directions, submit e01h5Souvenirs_LastFirst.

> **TROUBLESHOOTING:** Once the file is closed, the Formulas sheet may not display the formulas when you open the workbook again. If that happens, press Ctrl+` again.

Chapter Objectives Review

After reading this chapter, you have accomplished the following objectives:

1. Explore the Excel window.

- A worksheet is a single spreadsheet containing data. A workbook is a collection of one or more related worksheets contained in a single file.
- Identify Excel window elements: The Name Box displays the name of the current cell. The Formula Bar displays the contents of the current cell. The active cell is the current cell. A sheet tab shows the name of the worksheet.
- Identify columns, rows, and cells: Columns have alphabetical headings, such as A, B, C; rows have numbers, such as 1, 2, 3. A cell is the intersection of a column and row and is indicated with a column letter and a row number.
- Navigate in and among worksheets: Use the arrow keys to navigate within a sheet, or use the Go To command to go to a specific cell. Click a sheet tab to display the contents on another worksheet.

2. Enter and edit cell data.

- You should plan the worksheet design by stating the purpose, deciding what output you want, and then identifying what input values are required. Next, you enter and format data in a worksheet. Finally, you document, save, and then share a workbook.
- Enter text: Text may contain letters, numbers, symbols, and spaces. Text aligns at the left side of a cell.
- Check the spelling in a worksheet: After entering or editing text, check the spelling in the worksheet to identify and correct misspelled words.
- Use Auto Fill to complete a sequence: Auto Fill can automatically fill in sequences, such as month names or values, after you enter the first label or value. Double-click the fill handle to fill in the sequence.
- Enter values: Values are numbers that represent a quantity. Values align at the right side of a cell by default.
- Enter dates and times: Excel stores dates and times as serial numbers so that you can calculate the number of days between dates or times.
- Edit and clear cell contents: You can edit the contents of a cell to correct errors or to make labels more descriptive. Use the Clear option to clear the cell contents and/or formats.
- Find and replace data: Use Find to locate data within a worksheet. Use Find and Replace to find specific data and replace it with other data.

3. Create formulas.

- A formula is used to perform a calculation. The formula results display in the cell.
- Use cell references in formulas: Use references, such as =B5+B6, instead of values within formulas.
- Copy a formula: Double-click the fill handle to copy a formula down a column.

- Use semi-selection to create a formula: When building a formula, click a cell containing a value to enter that cell reference in the formula.
- Apply the order of operations: The most commonly used operators are performed in this sequence: Parentheses, exponentiation, multiplication, division, addition, and subtraction.
- Display cell formulas: Displaying cell formulas instead of formula results is helpful when you want to review several formulas for accuracy. You can display formulas by pressing Ctrl+`.

4. Manage columns and rows.

- Insert cells, columns, and rows: Insert a cell to move the remaining cells down or to the right in a specific column or row to enter missing data. Rows or columns can be inserted, moving the remaining rows or columns down or to the right, respectively.
- Delete cells, columns, and rows: Delete cells, columns, and rows you no longer want.
- Adjust column width: Double-click between the column headings to widen a column based on the longest item in that column, or drag the border between column headings to increase or decrease a column width.
- Adjust row height: Drag the border between row headings to increase or decrease the height of a row.
- Hide and unhide columns and rows: Hiding rows and columns protects confidential data from being displayed.

5. Select, move, copy, and paste data.

- Select a range: A range is a single cell or a rectangular block of cells. After selecting a range, you can copy, move, or format the cells in the range.
- Move a range: After selecting a range, cut it from its location. Then select the top-left corner of the destination range to make it the active cell and paste the range there.
- Copy and paste a range: You can copy a range within a worksheet, to another sheet within the workbook, or to a different workbook.
- Use Paste Options: Use the Paste Options button or the Paste arrow to specify how the data are pasted into the worksheet.

6. Apply cell styles, cell alignment, and font options.

- Apply cell styles: Cell styles contain a collection of formatting, such as font, font color, font size, fill, and borders. You can apply an Excel cell style to save formatting time.
- Merge cells: You can merge multiple cells into one cell. The Merge & Center command merges cells and then horizontally centers data between the left and right sides of the combined cell.

- Change cell alignment: You can change how data aligns between the top and bottom edges of the cell and between the left and right sides of the cell.
- Wrap text: Use the Wrap Text option to display text on multiple lines in order to avoid having extra-wide columns.
- Increase and decrease indent: To indicate hierarchy of data or to offset a label, increase or decrease how much the data are indented in a cell.
- Apply borders and fill color: Borders and fill colors help improve readability of worksheets. Borders are lines that surround one or more edges of a cell or range. Fill is a background color that displays behind the data in a cell.

7. Apply number formats.
- Apply a number format: The default number format is General, which does not apply any particular format to values. Apply appropriate formats to values to display the data with the correct symbols and decimal alignment. For example, Accounting Number Format is a common number format for monetary values.
- Increase and decrease decimal places: After applying a number format, you can increase or decrease the number of decimal places displayed.

8. Manage worksheets.
- Insert and delete a worksheet: You can insert new worksheets to include related data within one workbook, or you can delete extra worksheets you do not want.
- Move or copy a worksheet: Drag a sheet tab to rearrange the worksheets. You can copy a worksheet within a workbook or to another workbook.
- Rename a worksheet: The default worksheet tab name is Sheet1, but you should change the name to describe the contents of the worksheet.

9. Select page setup options.
- The Page Layout tab on the ribbon contains options for setting margins, selecting orientation, specifying page size, selecting the print area, and applying other settings.
- Specify page options: Page options include orientation, paper size, and scaling. The default orientation is portrait, but you can select landscape orientation for worksheets containing a lot of columns. Use scaling options to increase or decrease the magnification of data on a printout.
- Set margin options: You can set the left, right, top, and bottom margins. In addition, you can center worksheet data horizontally and vertically on a page.
- Create a header or footer: Insert a header or footer to display documentation, such as your name, date, time, and worksheet tab name. A header displays at the top of the page, and a footer displays at the bottom of a printout.
- Select sheet options: Sheet options control the print area, print titles, print options, and page order. You can specify that row of column headings repeat at the top of each printed page and the row headings repeat on the left side of each printed page.

10. Preview and print a worksheet.
- Before printing a worksheet, display a preview to ensure the data will print correctly. The Print Preview enables you to see if margins are correct or if isolated rows or columns will print on separate pages.
- After making appropriate adjustments, print the worksheet.

Key Terms Matching

Match the key terms with their definitions. Write the key term letter by the appropriate numbered definition.

a. Alignment
b. Auto Fill
c. Cell
d. Column width
e. Fill color
f. Fill handle
g. Formula
h. Formula Bar
i. Input area
j. Name Box

k. Order of operations
l. Output area
m. Range
n. Row height
o. Sheet tab
p. Text
q. Value
r. Workbook
s. Worksheet
t. Wrap text

1. _____ A spreadsheet that contains formulas, functions, values, text, and visual aids. **p. 312**

2. _____ A file containing related worksheets. **p. 312**

3. _____ A range of cells containing values for variables used in formulas. **p. 316**

4. _____ A range of cells containing results based on manipulating the variables. **p. 316**

5. _____ Identifies the address of the current cell. **p. 313**

6. _____ Displays the content (text, value, date, or formula) in the active cell. **p. 313**

7. _____ Displays the name of a worksheet within a workbook. **p. 313**

8. _____ The intersection of a column and a row. **p. 313**

9. _____ Includes letters, numbers, symbols, and spaces. **p. 317**

10. _____ A number that represents a quantity or an amount. **p. 319**

11. _____ Rules that control the sequence in which Excel performs arithmetic operations. **p. 329**

12. _____ Enables you to copy the contents of a cell or cell range or to continue a sequence by dragging the fill handle over an adjacent cell or range of cells. **p. 318**

13. _____ A small green square at the bottom-right corner of a cell. **p. 318**

14. _____ The horizontal measurement of a column. **p. 335**

15. _____ The vertical measurement of a row. **p. 337**

16. _____ A rectangular group of cells. **p. 338**

17. _____ The position of data between the cell margins. **p. 350**

18. _____ Formatting that enables a label to appear on multiple lines within the current cell. **p. 351**

19. _____ The background color appearing behind data in a cell. **p. 352**

20. _____ A combination of cell references, operators, values, and/or functions used to perform a calculation. **p. 327**

Multiple Choice

1. Cell A5 is the active cell. You want to make cell B10 the active cell. Which of the following is *not* a method for going to cell B10?

   (a) Use the Go To dialog box.
   (b) Type B10 in the Name Box and press Enter.
   (c) Use the scroll arrows on the keyboard.
   (d) Type B10 in the Formula Bar and press Enter.

2. Which step is *not* part of planning a worksheet design?

   (a) Decide what input values are required.
   (b) Enter labels, values, and formulas.
   (c) State the purpose of the worksheet.
   (d) Decide what outputs are required to achieve the purpose.

3. Cell A2 contains the regular price $100. Cell B2 contains the discount rate 15%. Cell C3 contains =A2*(1-B2) to calculate the sale price of $85. Which of the following formulas produces the same result?

   (a) =A2*(B2-1)
   (b) =A2-(A2*B2)
   (c) =A2*B2-1
   (d) =A2*1-B2

4. What should you do if you see pound signs (###) instead of values or results of formulas?

   (a) Increase the column width.
   (b) Increase the zoom percentage.
   (c) Delete the column.
   (d) Adjust the row height.

5. You just copied a range of data containing formulas. However, you want to preserve the formula results and the original number and text formatting in the pasted range. Which paste option would you select?

   (a) Formulas
   (b) Keep Source Formatting
   (c) Values & Source Formatting
   (d) Values & Number Formatting

6. The label *Souvenir Shop* is in cell A1, and *April Sales Report* is in cell B1. You select the range A1:E1 and click Merge & Center. What is the result?

   (a) Souvenir Shop is centered over the range A1:E1, and April Sales Report is moved to cell F1.
   (b) Excel does not let you merge and center a range of cells where those cells each contain data.

   (c) Souvenir Shop is combined with April Sales Report. The new combined label is then centered over the range A1:E1.
   (d) Souvenir Shop is centered over the range A1:E1, and April Sales Report is deleted.

7. What number format places a dollar sign on the left side of the cell, includes commas to separate thousands, displays two decimal places, and displays zero values as hyphens?

   (a) Currency Format
   (b) Monetary Number Format
   (c) Dollars and Cents Format
   (d) Accounting Number Format

8. You want to copy the March worksheet to use it to enter data for April. After you right-click the March sheet tab and select Move or Copy, you click OK in the Move or Copy dialog box without changing any settings. What happens?

   (a) A copy of the March sheet is inserted to the right of the original March sheet. The new sheet is named April automatically.
   (b) A copy of the March sheet is inserted to the left of the original March sheet. The new sheet is named March (1).
   (c) The March sheet is moved to the left of the first sheet tab. The worksheet is not copied.
   (d) The March sheet is moved to a new workbook named Book1. The March sheet no longer exists in the original workbook.

9. The Header & Footer Tools tab contains commands that insert codes into a header or footer. These codes enable the header or footer text to change automatically. You can insert a code for all of the following *except*:

   (a) Your Name.
   (b) File Name.
   (c) Sheet Name.
   (d) Page Number.

10. Assume that the data on a worksheet consume a whole printed page and two columns on a second page. You can do all of the following *except* what to force the data to print all on one page?

   (a) Decrease the Scale value
   (b) Increase the left and right margins
   (c) Decrease column widths
   (d) Decrease the font size

1 Mathematics and Formatting

You want to apply the skills you learned in this chapter. First, you will use Auto Fill to fill in a sequence of values in the input area and check the spelling in the worksheet to correct errors. You will copy the input and transpose the data vertically to improve readability and move the output range to the right side of the input area. You will adjust the worksheet by deleting an unnecessary row, adjusting column and row heights. Using input and output areas, you want to create several formulas with different arithmetic operators and explore the order of operations. Furthermore, you will copy a worksheet from another workbook, apply cell styles and alignment settings to improve the formatting, and then apply different number formats to compare the formatted values. Finally, you will apply page setup options to finalize your workbook. Refer to Figure 1.67 as you complete this exercise.

FIGURE 1.67 Math Review Worksheet

Left worksheet (Calculations tab):

	A	B	C	D	E
1	Excel Formulas and Order of Precedence				
2					
3	Input Area:			Output Area:	
4	First Value	2		Sum of 1st and 2nd values	6
5	Second Value	4		Difference between 4th and 1st values	6
6	Third Value	6		Product of 2nd and 3rd values	24
7	Fourth Value	8		Quotient of 3rd and 1st values	3
8				2nd value to the power of 3rd value	4096
9				1st value added to product of 2nd and 4th values and difference between sum and 3rd value	28
10				Product of sum of 1st and 2nd and difference between 4th and 3rd values	12
11				Product of 1st and 2nd added to product of 3rd and 4th values	56

Right worksheet (Number Formats tab):

	A Original Values	B Accounting	C Currency	D Comma	E Number
2	12.3	$ 12.30	$12.30	12.30	12.30
3	12.34	$ 12.34	$12.34	12.34	12.34
4	123.456	$ 123.46	$123.46	123.46	123.46
5	1234.5	$1,234.50	$1,234.50	1,234.50	1234.50

a. Open *e01p1Math* and save it as **e01p1Math_LastFirst**.

b. Click **cell C5**, type **0**, and then press **Ctrl+Enter**. Use Auto Fill to complete the series by doing the following:
   - Drag the **cell C5 fill handle** to **cell G5** to fill in the range with 0.
   - Click **Auto Fill Options** and select **Fill Series** to fill the series from 0 to 4.

c. Press **Ctrl+Home** to navigate to cell A1, click **Find & Select** in the Editing group on the Home tab, and then select **Replace**.
   - Type **Number** in the Find what box and type **Value** in the Replace with box.
   - Click **Replace All**, click **OK** in the message box, and then click **Close** in the dialog box.

d. Click the **Review tab**, click **Spelling** in the Proofing group, and then do the following:
   - Click **Change** when prompted to change Formules to Formulas.
   - Click **Change** when prompted to change Presedence to Precedence.
   - Click **OK** when prompted with *Spell check complete. You're good to go!*

e. Use copy and paste to transpose the input range from being organized horizontally to being organized vertically by doing the following:
   - Select the **range C4:G5**, click the **Home tab**, and then click **Copy** in the Clipboard group.
   - Click **cell A4**, click the **Paste arrow** in the Clipboard group, and then click **Transpose**.
   - Press **Esc**, select the **range C4:G5**, and then press **Delete**.

f. Select the **range A10:A19** (the output range), click **Cut** in the Clipboard group, click **cell D3**, and then click **Paste** to move the output range.

g. Click **cell A4**, click the **Delete arrow** in the Cells group, and then select **Delete Sheet Rows** to delete the Starting Value row.

h. Click **cell A5**, click **Format** in the Cells group, and then select **Column Width**. Type **12.6** in the Column width box and click **OK**. Click **cell D5** and set the column width to **36**.

i. Click **cell D9**, click **Format** in the Cells group, select **Row Height**, type **45** in the Row height box, and then click **OK**. Select the **range D10:D11** and set the row height to **30**.

j. Click **cell E4**. Type **=B4+B5** and press **Enter**. Excel adds the value in cell B4 (1) to the value in cell B5 (2). The result (3) displays in cell E4, as described by the label in cell D4.

k. Enter the following formulas:
  - Cell E5: **=B7-B4**
  - Cell E6: **=B5*B6**
  - Cell E7: **=B6/B4**
  - Cell E8: **=B5^B6**

l. Type **=B4+B5*B7-B6** in **cell E9**. Calculate the answer: 2*4=8; 1+8=9; 9-3=6. Multiplication occurs first, followed by addition, and finally subtraction.

m. Type **=(B4+B5)*(B7-B6)** in **cell E10**. Calculate the answer: 1+2=3; 4-3=1; 3*1=3. This formula is almost identical to the previous formula; however, calculations in parentheses occur before the multiplication.

n. Type **=(B4*B5)+(B6*B7)** in **cell E11**. Calculate the answer: 1*2=2; 3*4=12; 2+12=14. Although multiplication would have occurred first without the parentheses, the parentheses help improve the readability of the formula.

o. Enter **2** in **cell B4**, **4** in **cell B5**, **6** in **cell B6**, and **8** in **cell B7**. Refer to Figure 1.67 to compare the updated formula results.

p. Double-click the **Sheet 1 tab**, type **Calculations**, and then press **Enter** to rename the sheet tab.

q. Open *e01p1Values*. Copy the worksheet to your *e01p1Math_LastFirst* workbook by doing the following:
  - Right-click the **Number Formats sheet tab** and select **Move or Copy**.
  - Click the **To book arrow** and select **e01p1Math_LastFirst.xlsx**.
  - Select **(move to end)**, click the **Create a copy check box** to select it, and then click **OK**.
  - Close the e01p1Values workbook without saving it.

r. Format the headings on row 1 of the Numbers Format worksheet by doing the following:
  - Select the **range A1:E1**, click **Wrap Text** in the Alignment group, and then click **Center**.
  - Click the **Fill Color arrow** in the Font group and select **Light Gray, Background 2** (the third color from the left on the first row).

s. Select the **range A2:A5**, click **Cell Styles** in the Styles group, and then click **Input**. Select the **range B2:E5** and apply the **Output cell style**.

t. Apply number formatting by doing the following:
  - Select the **range B2:B5** and click **Accounting Number Format** in the Number group.
  - Select the **range C2:C5**, click the **Number Format arrow**, and then select **Currency**.
  - Select the **range D2:D5** and click **Comma Style** in the Number group.
  - Select the **range E2:E5**, click the **Number Format arrow**, and then select **Number**.

u. Right-click the **Calculations sheet tab** and select **Select All Sheets** to group the sheets. Apply Page Setup options by doing the following:
  - Click the **Page Layout tab**, click **Margins** in the Page Setup group, select **Custom Margins**, click the **Top spin arrow** to display **1**, and then click the **Horizontally check box** to select it.
  - Click the **Header/Footer tab** within the Page Setup dialog box and click **Custom Footer**. Type your name in the Left section box, click **Insert Sheet Name** in the Center section box, click **Insert File Name** in the Right section box, and then click **OK**. Click **OK** to close the Page Setup dialog box.

v. Click the **File tab** and click **Print**. Verify that each worksheet will print on one page. Press **Esc** to close the Print Preview, and right-click the **Calculations sheet tab** and click **Ungroup Sheets**.

w. Save and close the file. Exit Excel. Based on your instructor's directions, submit e01p1Math_LastFirst.

FROM SCRATCH

You want to create a calendar for October 2021. The calendar will enable you to practice alignment settings, including center, merge and center, and indents. In addition, you will adjust column widths and increase row height to create cells large enough to enter important information, such as birthdays. You will create a formula and use Auto Fill to complete the days of the week and the days within each week. To improve the appearance of the calendar, you will add fill colors, font colors, and borders. Refer to Figure 1.68 as you complete this exercise.

FIGURE 1.68 Calendar

a. Start Excel and create a new blank workbook. Save the workbook as **e01p2October_LastFirst**.

b. Type **'October 2021** (be sure to include the apostrophe before October) in **cell A1** and click **Enter** on the left side of the Formula Bar.

c. Format the title:
- Select the **range A1:G1** and click **Merge & Center** in the Alignment group.
- Change the font size to **48**.
- Click the **Fill Color arrow** and click **Orange, Accent 2** in the Theme Colors section of the color palette.
- Click **Middle Align** in the Alignment group.

d. Complete the days of the week:
- Type **Sunday** in **cell A2** and click **Enter** to the left side of the Formula Bar.
- Drag the **cell A2 fill handle** across the row through **cell G2** to use Auto Fill to complete the rest of the weekdays.
- Ensure that the **range A2:G2** is selected. Click the **Fill Color arrow** and select **Orange, Accent 2, Lighter 60%** in the Theme Colors section of the color palette.
- Click **Bold** in the Font group, click the **Font Size arrow**, and then select **14** to format the selected range.
- Click **Middle Align** and click **Center** in the Alignment group to format the selected range.

e. Complete the days of the month:
- Type **1** in **cell F3** and type **2 in cell G3**. Type **3** in **cell A4** and press **Ctrl+Enter**. Drag the **cell A4 fill handle** across the row through **cell G4**.
- Click **Auto Fill Options** near the bottom-right corner of the copied data and select **Fill Series** to change the numbers to 3 through 9.
- Type **=A4+7** in **cell A5** and press **Ctrl+Enter**. Usually you avoid numbers in formulas, but the number of days in a week is always 7. Drag the **cell A5 fill handle** down through **cell A8** to get the date for each Sunday in October.

- Keep the **range A5:A8** selected and drag the fill handle across through **cell G8**. This action copies the formulas to fill in the days in the month.
- Select the **range B8:G8** and press **Delete** to delete the extra days 32 through 37 because October has only 31 days.

f. Format the columns and rows:

- Select **columns A:G**. Click **Format** in the Cells group, select **Column Width**, type **16** in the Column width box, and then click **OK**.
- Select **row 2**. Click **Format** in the Cells group, select **Row Height**, type **30**, and then click **OK**.
- Select **rows 3:8**. Set the row height to **75**.

g. Apply borders around the cells:

- Select the **range A1:G8**. Click the **Borders arrow** in the Font group and select **More Borders** to display the Format Cells dialog box with the Border tab selected.
- Click the **Color arrow** and select **Orange, Accent 2**.
- Click **Outline** and **Inside** in the Presets section. Click **OK**. This action applies an orange border inside and outside the selected range.

h. Clear the border formatting around cells that do not have days:

- Select the **range B8:G8**.
- Click **Clear** in the Editing group and select **Clear All**. This action removes the borders around the cells after the last day of the month.

i. Format the days in the month:

- Select the **range A3:G8**. Click **Top Align** and **Align Left** in the Alignment group.
- Click **Increase Indent** in the Alignment group to offset the days from the border.
- Click **Bold** in the Font group, click the **Font Size arrow**, and then select **12**.

j. Double-click the **Sheet1 tab**, type **October**, and then press **Enter**.

k. Click in any cell in the worksheet, click the **Page Layout tab**, and then do the following:

- Click **Orientation** in the Page Setup group and select **Landscape**.
- Click **Margins** in the Page Setup group and select **Custom Margins**. Click the **Top margin spin arrow** to display **0.5**, click the **Bottom margin spin arrow** to display **0.5**, click the **Horizontally check box** to select it in the *Center on page* section, and then click **OK**.

l. Click the **Insert tab** and click **Header & Footer** in the Text group and do the following:

- Click **Go to Footer** in the Navigation group. Click in the **left side** of the footer and type your name.
- Click in the **center** of the footer and click **Sheet Name** in the Header & Footer Elements group on the Design tab.
- Click in the **right side** of the footer and click **File Name** in the Header & Footer Elements group on the Design tab.
- Click in any cell in the workbook, press **Ctrl+Home**, and then click **Normal** on the status bar.

m. Save and close the file. Exit Excel. Based on your instructor's directions, submit e01p2October_LastFirst.

Mid-Level Exercises

1 Guest House Rental Rates

ANALYSIS CASE

You manage a beach guesthouse in Ft. Lauderdale containing three types of rental units. Prices are based on off-peak and peak times of the year. You want to calculate the maximum daily revenue for each rental type, assuming all units are rented. In addition, you will calculate the discount rate for off-peak rental times. Finally, you will improve the appearance of the worksheet by applying font, alignment, and number formats.

a. Open *e01m1Rentals* and save it as **e01m1Rentals_LastFirst**.

b. Apply the **Heading 1 cell style** to the **range A1:G1** and the **20% - Accent1 cell style** to the **range A2:G2**.

c. Merge and center *Peak Rentals* in the **range C4:D4**, over the two columns of peak rental data. Apply **Dark Red fill color** and **White, Background 1 font color**.

d. Merge and center *Off-Peak Rentals* in the **range E4:G4** over the three columns of off-peak rental data. Apply **Blue fill color** and **White, Background 1 font color**.

e. Center horizontally and wrap the headings on row 5. Set the width of columns D and F to **10.0**. Horizontally center the data in the **range B6:B8**.

f. Create and copy the following formulas:
  - **Cell D6:** Calculate the Peak Rentals Maximum Revenue by multiplying the number of units (No. Units) by the Peak Rentals Daily Rate. Copy the formula from **cell D6** to the **range D7:D8**.
  - **Cell F6:** Calculate the Off-Peak Rentals Maximum Revenue by multiplying the number of units (No. Units) by the Off-Peak Rentals Daily Rate. Copy the formula from **cell F6** to the **range F7:F8**.
  - **Cell G6:** Calculate the Off-Peak Rentals Discount Rate by dividing the Off-Peak Rentals Daily Rate by the Peak Rentals Daily Rate (to get the off-peak percent of the peak rate) and then subtracting that from 1 (which represents 100%). For example, the off-peak daily rate for the studio apartment is .226075 (22.6%) off the peak daily rate. Copy the formula from **cell G6** to the **range G7:G8**.

g. Format the monetary values in the **range C6:F8** with **Accounting Number Format**. Format the **range G6:G8** with **Percent Style** with one decimal place.

h. Apply **Blue, Accent 1, Lighter 80% fill color** to the **range E5:G8**.

i. Select the **range C5:D8**, click the **Fill Color arrow** and select **More Colors**. Create a custom color with these settings: **Red 242**, **Green 220**, and **Blue 219**.

j. Answer the four questions below the worksheet data. Enter the answer to question 1 in **cell A15**, question 2 in **cell A18**, question 3 in **cell A21**, and question 4 in **cell A24**. If you change any values to answer the questions, change the values back to the original values.

k. Check the spelling in the worksheet and correct any errors in your answers.

l. Create a copy of the Rental Rates worksheet, place the new sheet to the right side of the original worksheet, and rename the new sheet **Formulas**. Display cell formulas on the Formulas sheet.

m. Select the two worksheet tabs and do the following:
  - Select landscape orientation.
  - Set **1"** top, bottom, left, and right margins. Center the data horizontally on the page.
  - Insert a footer with your name on the left side, the sheet name code in the center, and the file name code on the right side.
  - Apply the setting to fit to one page.

n. Click the **Formulas sheet tab** and set options to print gridlines and headings. Adjust the column widths to display all data.

o. Save and close the file. Exit Excel. Based on your instructor's directions, submit e01m1Rentals_LastFirst.

2 Real Estate Sales Report

You are a real estate agent in Indianapolis. You track the real estate properties you list for clients. You want to analyze sales for selected properties. Yesterday, you prepared a workbook with a worksheet for recent sales data and another worksheet listing several properties. You want to calculate the number of days that the houses were on the market and their sales percentage of the list price. In one situation, the house was involved in a bidding war between two families who really wanted the house; therefore, the sale price exceeded the list price.

a. Open *e01m2Sales* and save it as **e01m2Sales_LastFirst**.

b. Delete the row that has incomplete sales data. The owners took their house off the market.

c. Type **2021-001** in **cell A5** and use Auto Fill to complete the series to assign a property ID to each property.

d. Calculate the number of days each house was on the market in **cell C5** by subtracting the date listed from the date sold. Copy the formula to the **range C6:C12**.

e. Format list prices and sold prices with **Accounting Number Format** with zero decimal places.

f. Calculate the sales price percentage of the list price in **cell H5** by dividing the sold price by the list price. Format the percentages with two decimal places. Copy the formula to the **range H6:H12**. The second house was listed for $500,250, but it sold for only $400,125. Therefore, the sale percentage of the list price is 79.99%.

g. Center horizontally and wrap the headings on row 4.

h. Insert a new column between the Date Sold and List Price columns. Do the following:
   - Move the Days on Market **range C4:C12** to the **range F4:F12**.
   - Delete the empty column C.

i. Edit the list date of the 41 Chestnut Circle house to be **4/22/2021**. Edit the list price of the house on Amsterdam Drive to be **$355,000**.

j. Select the property rows and set a **25 row height** and apply **Middle Align**.

k. Apply the **All Borders border style** to the **range A4:H12**. Adjust column widths as necessary.

l. Apply **Align Right** and increase indent twice the values in the **range E5:E12**.

m. Delete the Properties worksheet.

n. Insert a new worksheet and name it **Formulas**.

o. Click the **Select All button** to select all data on the Houses Sold worksheet and copy it to the Formulas worksheet.

p. Select the worksheet tabs and do the following:
   - Set landscape orientation.
   - Center the page horizontally and vertically between the margins.
   - Insert a footer with your name on the left side, the sheet tab code in the center, and the file name code on the right side.

q. Complete the following steps on the Formulas worksheet:
   - Hide the Date Listed and Date Sold columns.
   - Display cell formulas.
   - Set options to print gridlines and row and column headings.
   - Adjust column widths.

r. Display the Houses Sold worksheet and apply **120% scaling**.

s. Save and close the file. Exit Excel. Based on your instructor's directions, submit e01m2Sales_LastFirst.

New Castle County Technical Services

New Castle County Technical Services (NCCTS) provides technical support for companies in the greater New Castle County, Delaware, area. You downloaded a dataset from the company database that contains a list of call cases closed during March. You want to calculate the number of days between the start and end dates and the amount owed per transaction. Then you will format the worksheet.

a. Open *e01r1NCCTS* and save it as **e01r1NCCTS_LastFirst**.

b. Insert a row above the first row and do the following:
   - Type **Billing Hours and Amounts** in **cell A1**.
   - Apply the **Orange, Accent2 cell style**.
   - Merge and center the title in the **range A1:K1**.
   - Bold the title and change the font size to **16 pt**.

c. Select the **range A2:K2**, apply the **40% - Accent2 cell style**, bold, and merge and center.

d. Find *Virus Detection* and replace it with **Virus Removal** throughout the worksheet.

e. Apply these formats to the **range A4:K4**: bold, wrap text, center horizontally, and **Orange, Accent 2, Lighter 60% fill color**.

f. Hide columns C and D that contain the RepID and CallTypeID.

g. Create and copy the following formulas:
   - **Cell J5**: Calculate the number of days each case was opened by subtracting the Opened Date from the Closed Date. Copy the formula to the **range J6:J36**.
   - **Cell K5**: Calculate the amount billed for each transaction by multiplying the Rate by the Hours Logged. Copy the formula to the **range K6:K36**.

h. Apply these number formats:
   - Apply the **Accounting Number Format** with **zero** decimal places to the **range F5:F36**.
   - Apply **Accounting Number Format** to the **range K5:K36**.
   - Apply **Comma Style** to the **range G5:G36**.

i. Set a width of **28** for column E.

j. Cut the **range G4:G36** (Hours Logged), right-click **cell K4**, and then select **Insert Cut Cells**.

k. Rename the sheet tab as **March Hours**. Change the sheet tab color to **Orange, Accent 2**.

l. Set **0.4"** left and right margins and center the worksheet data horizontally on the page. Set **90% scaling**.

m. Insert a footer with your name on the left side, the sheet name code in the center, and the file name code on the right side.

n. Save and close the file. Exit Excel. Based on your instructor's directions, submit e01r1NCCTS_LastFirst.

Disaster Recovery

Net Proceeds from House Sale

Daryl Patterson is a real estate agent. He wants his clients to have a realistic expectation of how much money they will receive when they sell their houses. Sellers know they pay a commission to the agent and pay off their existing mortgages; however, many sellers forget to consider they might have to pay some of the buyer's closing costs, title insurance, and prorated property taxes.

Daryl created a worksheet to enter values in an input area to calculate the estimated deductions at closing and calculate the estimated net proceeds the seller will receive; however, the worksheet contains errors. Open *e01d1Proceeds* and save it as **e01d1Proceeds_LastFirst**. Review the font formatting and alignment for consistency. Use the New Comment command in the Comments group on the Review tab to insert a comment in a cell. As you identify the errors, insert comments in the respective cells to explain the errors. Correct the errors, including formatting errors.

In the Output Area, the only entered value should be the title insurance policy. The other numbers should be results of formulas or a reference to a cell in the Input Area. The commission and closing costs are amounts based on the sale price and respective rates. The prorated property tax is the product of the annual property taxes and the months to prorate the taxes out of the entire year. The estimated net proceeds is calculated as the difference between the sale price and the total estimated deductions.

Apply Landscape orientation, 115% scaling, 1.5" top margin, and center horizontally. Insert your name on the left side of the header, the sheet name code in the center, and the file name code on the right side. Save and close the file. Exit Excel. Based on your instructor's directions, submit e01d1Proceeds_LastFirst.

Theatre Ticket Sales

You work in the accounting division at Sugarhouse District Theatre, where touring Broadway plays and musicals are performed. You started a worksheet that lists the number of seats in each section (orchestra and the tiers) and the number of seats sold for a specific performance date. You will calculate the percentage of sold and unsold seats and gross revenue by section. You will format the worksheet to improve readability and copy the final worksheet to use as a template to enter data for the next day's performance.

Format the Title and Enter the Date

Your first task is to format the title by centering it over the data columns, enlarging the font size, and applying a different font color. Next, you will enter and format the performance date on the next row.

1. Open *e01c1TicketSales* and save it as **e01c1TicketSales_LastFirst**.

2. Merge and center the title over the **range A1:G1**, change the font size to **20**, and then apply **Purple font color**.

3. Type **4/16/2021** in **cell A2**, then apply the **Long Date number format**, apply the **Note cell style**, and then merge and center the date over the **range A2:G2**.

Format Seating Labels

Previously, you entered section labels Orchestra Front and Tiers to identify the seating sections. You will insert a new row for Orchestra Back, indent the specific seating sections to distinguish these labels from the main labels, and adjust the column width.

4. Insert a new row above row 9, between Right and Left. The new row is row 9. Copy the data from **cell A5** to **cell A9** and change the data in **cell A9** from Front to **Back**.

5. Indent twice the data in the **ranges A6:A8**, **A10:A12**, and **A14:A17**.

6. Change the width of **column A** to **18**.

Format Labels, Replace Text, and Checking Spelling

Previously, you applied Lavender fill and bold to the label in cell A4. You will use Format Painter to copy the formats to the other column labels on row 4. Then you will apply other alignment settings to the labels, replace *Purchased* with *Sold*, and check the spelling in the worksheet.

7. Use Format Painter to copy the formats in **cell A4** to the **range B4:G4**.

8. Wrap text and horizontally center the labels in the **range A4:G4** and set the height of row 4 to **30**.

9. Find all occurrences of *Purchased* and replace them with **Sold**.

10. Check the spelling in the worksheet and correct all spelling errors.

Insert Formulas and Apply Number Formats

You are ready to enter formulas in the last three columns to calculate the percentage of seats sold at the performance, percentage of unsold seats (i.e., empty), and the gross revenue for the sold seats.

11. Calculate the Percentage Sold in **cell E6** by dividing the Seats Sold by the Seats in Section. Copy the formula to the **range E7:E17**. Delete the formula in **cells E9** and **E13** because those are empty rows.

12. Calculate the Percentage Not Sold in **cell F6** by subtracting the Percentage Sold from 1. Copy the formula to the **range F7:F17**. Delete the formula in **cells F9** and **F13** because those are empty rows.

13. Calculate the Gross Revenue in **cell G6** by multiplying the Seats Sold by the Price Per Seat. Copy the formula to the range **G7:G17**. Delete the formula in **cells G9** and **G13** because those are empty rows.

14. Apply **Accounting Number Format** with zero decimal places to the **ranges D6:D17** and **G6:G17**.

15. Apply **Percentage Style** with one decimal place to the **range E6:F17**.

Move a Column, Adjust Alignment, and Add Borders

After reviewing the data, you decide to move the Price Per Seat to be to the left of the Gross Revenue data. In addition, you decide to center the values in the Seats in Section and Seats Sold columns.

16. Insert a new column G. Select and move the **range D4:D17** to the **range G4:G17**. Delete the empty column D.

17. Center horizontally the data in the **range B6:C17**.

18. Apply **Align Right** and indent twice the data in the **range D6:E17**.

19. Apply **Outside Borders** to the **range A4:G4**, the **range A5:G8, A9:G12**, and **A13:G17** one range at a time.

Format the Worksheet

To finalize the worksheet, you are ready to set a larger top margin, center the worksheet between the left and right margins, and insert a footer. Finally, you will rename the sheet tab, copy the worksheet, and delete some data to use a template for the next performance.

20. Set a **1"** top margin and center the worksheet horizontally between the left and right margins.

21. Insert a footer with your name on the left side, the sheet name code in the center, and the file name code on the right side.

22. Rename Sheet1 as **4-16-2021**.

23. Copy the worksheet, place the duplicate to the right, and rename it as **4-17-2021**.

24. Change the date in **cell A2** to **4/17/2021**. Keep the Long Date Format. Delete the values in the **range C6:C17**.

25. Save and close the file. Exit Excel. Based on your instructor's directions, submit e01c1TicketSales_LastFirst.

Excel

Formulas and Functions

LEARNING OUTCOME You will apply formulas and functions to calculate and analyze data.

OBJECTIVES & SKILLS: After you read this chapter, you will be able to:

CASE STUDY | Townsend Mortgage Company

You are an assistant to Erica Matheson, a mortgage broker at the Townsend Mortgage Company. Erica spends her days reviewing mortgage rates and trends, meeting with clients, and preparing paperwork. She relies on your expertise in using Excel to help analyze mortgage data.

Today, Erica provided you with sample mortgage data: loan number, house cost, down payment, mortgage rate, and the length of the loan in years. She has asked you to perform some basic calculations so that she can check the output provided by her system to verify that it is calculating results correctly. She wants you to calculate the amount financed, the periodic interest rate, the total number of payment periods, the percentage of the house cost financed, and the payoff year for each loan. In addition, you will calculate totals, averages, and other basic statistics.

Furthermore, she has asked you to complete another worksheet that uses functions to look up interest rates from a separate table, calculate the monthly payments, and determine how much (if any) the borrower will have to pay for private mortgage insurance (PMI).

Performing Quantitative Analysis

	A	B	C	D	E	F	G	H	I	J	K	L
1	**Townsend Mortgage Company**											
2												
3		**Input Area**										
4	Today's Date:		4/3/2021									
5	Pmts Per Year:		12									
6												
7	Loan #	House Cost		Down Payment	Amount Financed	Mortgage Rate	Rate Per Period	Years	# of Pmt Periods	% Financed	Date Financed	Payoff Year
8	452786	$	400,000	$ 80,000	$ 320,000	3.625%	0.302%	25	300	80.0%	5/1/2018	2043
9	453000	$	425,000	$ 60,000	$ 365,000	3.940%	0.328%	30	360	85.9%	11/3/2018	2048
10	453025	$	175,500	$ 30,000	$ 145,500	3.550%	0.296%	25	300	82.9%	4/10/2019	2044
11	452600	$	265,950	$ 58,000	$ 207,950	2.500%	0.208%	15	180	78.2%	10/14/2019	2034
12	452638	$	329,750	$ 65,000	$ 264,750	3.250%	0.271%	30	360	80.3%	2/4/2020	2050
13												
14		**Summary Statistics**										
15	Statistics	House Cost		Down Payment	Amount Financed							
16	Total	$	1,596,200	$ 293,000	$ 1,303,200							
17	Average	$	319,240	$ 58,600	$ 260,640							
18	Median	$	329,750	$ 60,000	$ 264,750							
19	Lowest	$	175,500	$ 30,000	$ 145,500							
20	Highest	$	425,000	$ 80,000	$ 365,000							
21	# of Mortgages		5	5	5							

FIGURE 2.1 Townsend Mortgage Company Worksheet

CASE STUDY | Townsend Mortgage Company

Starting File	File to be Submitted
e02h1Loans	**e02h3Loans_LastFirst**

MyLab IT Grader An alternate version of this project is available as a MyLab IT Grader Assessment

Formula Basics

When you increase your understanding of formulas, you can construct robust workbooks that perform a variety of calculations for quantitative analysis. Your ability to build sophisticated workbooks and to interpret the results increases your value to any organization. By now, you should be able to create simple formulas using cell references and mathematical operators and use the order of operations to control the sequence of calculations in formulas.

In this section, you will create formulas in which cell addresses change or remain fixed when you copy them.

Using Relative, Absolute, and Mixed Cell References in Formulas

When you copy a formula, Excel either adjusts or preserves the cell references in the copied formula based on how the cell references appear in the original formula. Excel uses three different ways to refer to a cell in a formula: relative, absolute, and mixed. Relative references change when a formula is copied. For example, if a formula containing the cell A1 is copied down one row in the column, the reference would become A2. In contrast, absolute references remain constant, no matter where they are copied. Mixed references are a combination of both absolute and relative, where part of the cell reference will change and part will remain constant.

When you create a formula that you will copy to other cells, ask yourself the following question: Do the cell references contain constant or variable values? In other words, should the cell reference adjust or always refer to the same cell location, regardless of where the copied formula is located?

STEP 1 Use a Relative Cell Reference

A *relative cell reference* is the default method of referencing in Excel. It indicates a cell's relative location on a worksheet, such as five rows up and one column to the left, from the original cell containing the formula. When you copy a formula containing a relative cell reference, the cells referred to in the copied formula change relative to the position of the copied formula. Regardless of where you paste the formula, the cell references in the copied formula maintain the same relative distance from the cell containing the copied formula, as the cell references the relative location to the original formula cell.

In Figure 2.2, the formulas in column G contain relative cell references. When you copy the original formula =D2-E2 from cell F2 down one row to cell F3, the copied formula changes to =D3-E3. Because you copy the formula to the next row in the column, the column letters in the formula stay the same, but the row numbers change to reflect the row to which you copied the formula. Using relative referencing is an effective time saving tool.

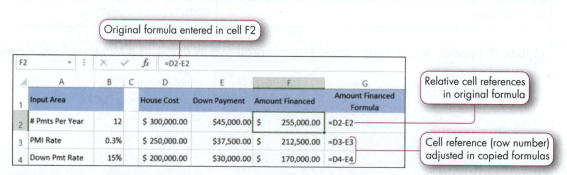

FIGURE 2.2 Relative Cell References

Use an Absolute Cell Reference

In many calculations, there are times in which a value should remain constant, such as an interest rate or payoff date. In these situations, absolute cell references are needed. An *absolute cell reference* provides a constant reference to a specific cell. When you copy a formula containing an absolute cell reference, the absolute cell reference in the copied formula does not change, regardless of where you copy the formula. An absolute cell reference is designated with a dollar sign before both the column letter and row number, such as $B$4.

In Figure 2.3, the down payment is calculated by multiplying the house cost by the 15% down payment rate. Each down payment calculation uses a different purchase price and constant down payment rate; therefore, an absolute reference is required for the down payment rate. Cell E2 contains =D2*$B$4 ($300,000*15.0%) to calculate the first borrower's down payment. When you copy the formula down to the next row, the copied formula in cell E3 is =D3*$B$4. The relative cell reference D2 changes to D3 (for the next house cost), and the absolute cell reference $B$4 remains the same to refer to the constant 15.0% down payment rate in cell B4. This formula ensures that the cell reference to the house cost changes for each row but that the house cost is always multiplied by the rate in cell B4.

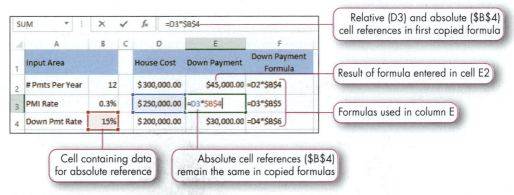

FIGURE 2.3 Relative and Absolute Cell References

TIP: INPUT AREA AND ABSOLUTE CELL REFERENCES

In Figure 2.3, values that can be modified, such as the down payment rate, are put in an input area. Generally, formulas use absolute references to the cells in the input area. For example, B4 is an absolute cell reference in all the down payment calculations. If the value in B4 is modified, Excel recalculates the amount of down payment for all the down payment formulas. By using cell references from an input area, you can perform what-if analyses very easily.

When utilizing the fill handle to copy a formula, if an error or unexpected result occurs, a good starting point for troubleshooting is checking cell references in the formula to determine if an absolute reference is needed. Figure 2.4 shows what happens if the down payment formula used a relative reference to cell B4. If the original formula in cell E2 is =D2*B4, the copied formula becomes =D3*B5 in cell E3. The relative cell reference to B4 changes to B5 when you copy the formula. Because cell B5 is empty, the $350,000 house cost in cell D3 is multiplied by 0, giving a $0 down payment, which is not a valid down payment amount.

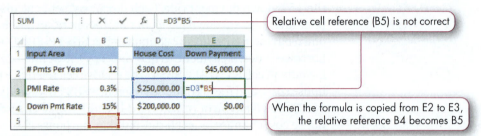

FIGURE 2.4 Error in Formula

> **TIP: THE F4 KEY**
> When using Windows, the function F4 key toggles through relative, absolute, and mixed references. Click a cell reference within a formula on the Formula Bar and press F4 to change it. For example, click in B4 in the formula =D2*B4. Press F4 and the relative cell reference (B4) changes to an absolute cell reference ($B$4). Press F4 again and $B$4 becomes a mixed reference (B$4); press F4 again and it becomes another mixed reference ($B4). Press F4 a fourth time and the cell reference returns to the original relative reference (B4). Note to laptop users: Many laptops assign shared functions to the F4 key. If your keyboard has two functions assigned to the F4 key, the Fn key and the F4 key must be pressed to toggle references.

STEP 3 ▶ Use a Mixed Cell Reference

A *mixed cell reference* combines an absolute cell reference with a relative cell reference. When you copy a formula containing a mixed cell reference, either the column letter or the row number that has the absolute reference remains fixed while the other part of the cell reference that is relative changes in the copied formula. $B4 and B$4 are examples of mixed cell references. In the reference $B4, the column B is absolute, and the row number is relative; when you copy the formula, the column letter B does not change, but the row number will change. In the reference B$4, the column letter B changes, but the row number, 4, does not change. To create a mixed reference, type the dollar sign to the left of the part of the cell reference you want to be absolute.

In the down payment formula, you can change the formula in cell E2 to be =D2*B$4. Because you are copying down the same column, only the row reference 4 must be absolute; the column letter stays the same. Figure 2.5 shows the copied formula =D3*B$4 in cell E3. In situations where you can use either absolute or mixed references, consider using mixed references to shorten the length of the formula.

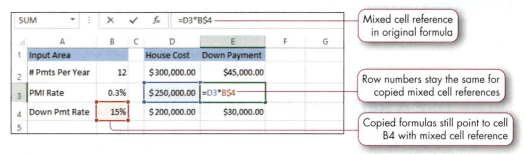

FIGURE 2.5 Relative and Mixed Cell References

MAC TIP: TOGGLING REFERENCES ON A MAC

For Apple users, the F4 key is reserved to launch the macOS dashboard. When using Excel on a Mac, the shortcut to toggle between relative, absolute, and mixed cell references is Command+T.

Quick Concepts

1. Describe what happens when you copy a formula containing a relative cell reference one row down. **p. 390**

2. Explain why you would use an absolute reference in a formula. **p. 391**

3. Describe the benefits of using a mixed reference. **p. 392**

Before finalizing the worksheet, you will insert the current date to document when the data was created. You will use the TODAY function to display the current date. Refer to Figure 2.18 as you complete Step 5.

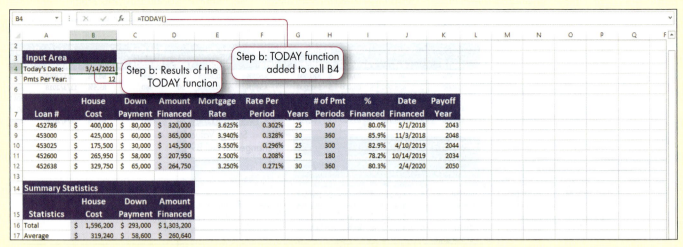

FIGURE 2.18 Insert the Current Date with the TODAY Function

a. Click **cell B4**, the cell to contain the current date.

b. Click **Date & Time** in the Function Library group, select **TODAY** to display the Function Arguments dialog box, and then click **OK** to close the dialog box.

The Function Arguments dialog box opens, although no arguments are necessary for this function. Excel displays TODAY() in the Edit formula bar, and inserts the current date in Short Date format, such as 3/14/2021, based on the computer system's date.

c. Click the **Format arrow** from the Cells group on the Home tab and select **AutoFit Column Width**.

d. Save the workbook. Keep the workbook open if you plan to continue with the next Hands-On Exercise. If not, close the workbook and exit Excel.

Logical, Lookup, and Financial Functions

As you prepare complex spreadsheets using functions, you will frequently use functions from three categories: lookup and reference, logical, and finance. Lookup and reference functions are useful when looking up a value in a list to identify the applicable value. Financial functions are useful to anyone who plans to take out a loan or invest money. Logical functions compare two or more situations and return results based on the comparison.

In this section, you will learn how to use the lookup, logical, and financial functions.

Using Lookup Functions

You can use lookup and reference functions to quickly find data associated with a specified value. For example, when you order merchandise on a website, the webserver looks up the shipping costs based on weight and distance; or at the end of a semester, your professor uses your average, such as 88%, as a reference to assign a letter grade, such as B+. There are numerous lookup functions in Excel that can be used to identify and return information based, in part, on how the data is organized.

STEP 1 ### Use the VLOOKUP Function

The *VLOOKUP function* accepts a value, looks for the value in the left column of a specified table array, and then returns another value located in the same row from a specified column. This is similar to a menu in which the item is in the left most column and the corresponding price is in the right column. Use VLOOKUP to search for exact matches or for the nearest value that is less than or equal to the search value, such as assigning a B grade for a class average between 80% and 89%. The VLOOKUP function has the following three required arguments and one optional argument: (1) lookup_value, (2) table_array, (3) col_index_num, and (4) range_lookup.

=VLOOKUP(lookup_value,table_array,col_index_num,[range_lookup])

Figure 2.19 shows a partial gradebook that contains a vertical lookup table, as well as the final scores and letter grades. The function in cell F3 is =VLOOKUP(E3,$A$3:$B$7,2). The data shown in Figure 2.19 is a small sample; however, the true value of VLOOKUP can be found in large datasets. When working with large datasets, it is time consuming and also error prone to look up information manually. Using VLOOKUP can quickly retrieve data no matter the size of the dataset.

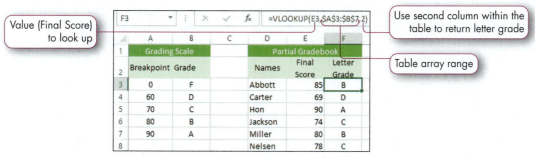

FIGURE 2.19 VLOOKUP Function for Gradebook

- The ***lookup value*** is the cell reference that contains the value to look up. The lookup value for the first student is cell E3, which contains 85.
- The ***table array*** is the range that contains the lookup table: $A$3:$B$7. The table array range must be absolute, and the value you want to look up must be located in the first column and cannot include column labels for the lookup table.
- The ***column index number*** is the column number in the lookup table that contains the return values. In this example, the column index number is 2, which corresponds to the letter grades in column B.

TIP: USING VALUES IN FORMULAS

You know to avoid using values in formulas because the input values in a worksheet cell might change. However, as shown in Figure 2.19, the value 2 is used in the col_index_number argument of the VLOOKUP function. The 2 refers to a particular column within the lookup table.

- The optional ***range_lookup*** determines how the VLOOKUP function handles lookup values that are not an exact match for the data in the table array. By default, the range_lookup is set to TRUE, which is appropriate to look up values in a range such as numeric grades in a gradebook and matching them to a letter grade. Omitting the optional argument or typing TRUE in it enables the VLOOKUP function to find the nearest value that is less than or equal in the table to the lookup value.

To look up an exact match, enter FALSE in the range_lookup argument. For example, if you are looking up product numbers, you must find an exact match to display the price. The function returns a value for the first lookup value that exactly matches the first column of the table array. If no exact match is found, the function returns #N/A.

Here is how the VLOOKUP function works:

1. The first argument of the function evaluates the value to be located in the left column of the table array.
2. Excel searches the first column of the table array until it (a) finds an exact match or (b) identifies the correct range if an exact match is not required.
3. If Excel finds an exact match, it moves across the table to the column designated by the column index number on that same row, and returns the value stored in that cell. If the last argument is TRUE or omitted, then Excel is looking for an approximate value (not an exact value). In Figure 2.19, the VLOOKUP function assigns letter grades based on final scores. Excel identifies the lookup value (85 in cell E3) and compares it to the values in the first column of the table array (range A3:B7). The last argument is omitted, so Excel tries to find 85. Excel detects that 85 is greater than 80 but is not greater than 90. Therefore, it stays on the 80 row. Excel looks at the second column (column index number of 2) and returns the letter grade of B. The B grade is then displayed in cell F3.

Create the Lookup Table

A **lookup table** is a range containing a table array of values. A table array is a range containing a table of values and text from which data can be retrieved. The table should contain at least two rows and two columns, not including headings. Figure 2.20 illustrates a college directory with three columns. The first column contains professors' names. You look up a professor's name in the first column to see his or her office (second column) and phone extension (third column).

Name	Office	Extension
Brazil, Estivan	GT 218b	7243
Fiedler, Zazilia	CS 417	7860
Lam, Kaitlyn	SC 124a	7031
Rodriquez, Lisa	GT 304	7592
Yeung, Braden	CS 414	7314

FIGURE 2.20 College Directory Lookup Table Analogy

It is important to plan the table so that it conforms to the way in which Excel can utilize the data in it. If the values you look up are exact values (i.e., range lookup = False), you can arrange the first column in any order. However, to look up an approximate value in a range (i.e., range lookup = True), such as the range 80–89, you must arrange data from the lowest to the highest value and include only the lowest value in the range (such as 80 is the lowest value for the range of a B grade) instead of the complete range (as demonstrated in Table 2.2). The lowest value for a category or in a series is the **breakpoint**. Table 2.3 shows how to construct the lookup table in Excel. The first column contains the breakpoints—such as 60, 70, 80, and 90—or the lowest values to achieve a particular grade. The lookup table contains one or more additional columns of related data to retrieve.

TABLE 2.2	Grading Scale
Range	**Grade**
90–100	A
80–89	B
70–79	C
60–69	D
Below 60	F

TABLE 2.3	Table Array
Range	**Grade**
0	F
60	D
70	C
80	B
90	A

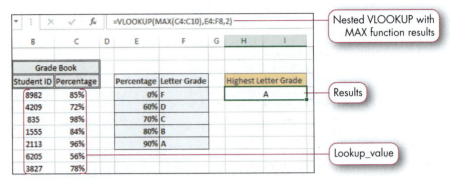

FIGURE 2.21 MAX Function Nested in VLOOKUP Function

Use the HLOOKUP Function

Lookup functions are not limited to only retrieving data from tables that are arranged in vertical tables. In situations in which data is better organized horizontally, you can design a lookup table where the first row contains the values for the basis of the lookup or the breakpoints, and additional rows contain data to be retrieved. This data must be arranged in ascending order from left to right. With a horizontal lookup table, use the *HLOOKUP function*. Table 2.4 shows the previous grades arranged horizontally for use with HLOOKUP.

TABLE 2.4	Horizontal Lookup Table				
Range	0	60	70	80	90
Grade	F	D	C	B	A

The syntax is similar to the syntax of the VLOOKUP function, except the third argument is row_index_num instead of col_index_num.

=HLOOKUP(lookup_value,table_array,row_index_num,[range_lookup])

Using the PMT Function

Excel contains several financial functions to enable you to perform calculations with monetary values. If you take out a loan to purchase a car, you need to know the monthly payment to determine if you can afford the car. The monthly payment depends on the price of the car, the down payment amount, and the terms of the loan. The decision is made easier by developing the worksheet in Figure 2.22 and by changing the various input values as indicated.

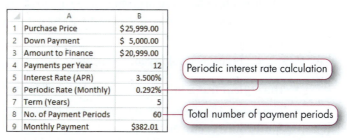

	A	B
1	Purchase Price	$25,999.00
2	Down Payment	$ 5,000.00
3	Amount to Finance	$20,999.00
4	Payments per Year	12
5	Interest Rate (APR)	3.500%
6	Periodic Rate (Monthly)	0.292%
7	Term (Years)	5
8	No. of Payment Periods	60
9	Monthly Payment	$382.01

Periodic interest rate calculation

Total number of payment periods

FIGURE 2.22 Car Loan assumptions

Creating a loan model enables you to evaluate options. You realize that the purchase of a $25,999 car might be prohibitive if you cannot afford the monthly payment of $382.01. Purchasing a less expensive car, coming up with a substantial down payment, taking out a longer-term loan, or finding a better interest rate can decrease your monthly payments.

The *PMT function* calculates payments for a loan with a fixed amount at a fixed periodic rate for a fixed time period. The PMT function uses three required arguments and two optional arguments: rate, nper, pv, fv, and type.

`=PMT(rate,nper,pv,[fv],[type])`

- The *rate* is the interest rate per payment period. Because the PMT function calculates a periodic (i.e., monthly) payment, the units of each of the arguments must be converted to that same periodic unit. Bank rates are usually given as annual rates, so the annual rate must be converted to the periodic rate—in this case, a monthly rate so the annual rate should be divided by 12. A quarterly payment would require the annual rate to be divided by 4. However, instead of calculating the periodic interest rate within the PMT function, you can calculate it in a separate cell and refer to that cell in the PMT function, as is done in cell B6 of Figure 2.22.

- The *nper* is the total number of payment periods. The term of a loan is usually stated in years; however, you need to convert the number of years to the number of periodic payments. For monthly payments, you make 12 payments per year. To calculate the nper, multiply the number of years by the number of payments in one year. You can either calculate the number of payment periods in the PMT function, or calculate the number of payment periods in cell B8 and use that calculated value in the PMT function.

- The *pv* is the present value of the loan. The result of the PMT function is a negative value because it represents your debt. However, you can display the result as a positive value by typing a minus sign in front of the present value cell reference in the PMT function.

TIP: FINANCIAL FUNCTIONS AND NEGATIVE VALUES

When utilizing the PMT and other financial functions in Excel, the results are often displayed as negative numbers. This happens because Excel understands accounting cash flow and the negative value represents a debt or outgoing monetary stream. It is important to understand why this happens and to understand in some situations this should be a positive number. This can be manipulated by changing the pv argument of the PMT function between positive and negative values or by adding a minus sign in front of the PMT function.

Using the IF Function

The most common logical function is the **IF function**, which tests specified criteria to see if it is true or false, then returns one value when a condition is met, or is true, and returns another value when the condition is not met, or is false. For example, a company gives a $500 bonus to employees who sold over $10,000 in merchandise in a week, but no bonus to employees who did not sell over $10,000 in merchandise. Figure 2.23 shows a worksheet containing the sales data for three representatives and their bonuses, if any.

The IF function has three arguments: (1) a condition that is tested to determine if it is either true or false, (2) the resulting value if the condition is true, and (3) the resulting value if the condition is false.

=IF(logical_test,[value_if_true],[value_if_false])

- The **logical test** is any value or expression that can be evaluated to TRUE or FALSE.
- The **value_if_true** is the value returned if the Logical_test is TRUE; if omitted, the word TRUE is returned.
- The **value_if_false** is the value returned if Logical_test is FALSE; if omitted, the word FALSE is returned.

FIGURE 2.23 Function to Calculate Bonus

You might find it helpful to create two flowcharts to illustrate an IF function. First, construct a flowchart that uses words and numbers to illustrate the condition and results. For example, the left flowchart in Figure 2.24 tests to see if sales are greater than $10,000, and the $500 bonus if the condition is true or $0 if the condition is false. Then, create a second flowchart—similar to the one on the right side of Figure 2.24—that replaces the words and values with actual cell references. Creating these flowcharts can help you construct the IF function that is used in cell F2 in Figure 2.23.

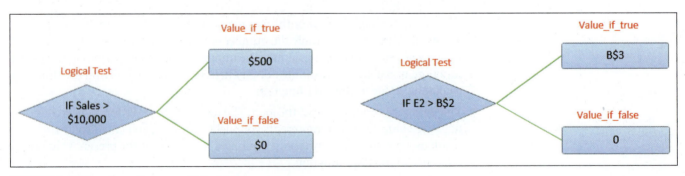

FIGURE 2.24 Flowcharts Illustrating IF Function

Design the Logical Test

The first argument for the IF function is the logical test. The logical test requires a comparison between at least two variables, such as the sales amount and the sales goal needed to receive a bonus. The comparison results are a true or false outcome. Either the sales amount meets the sales goal (true) or it does not meet the sales goal (false). Table 2.5 lists and describes in more detail the logical operators to make the comparison in the logical test.

In Figure 2.23, cell F2 contains an IF function where the logical test is E2>B$2, which determines if Tiffany's sales in cell E2 are greater than the sales goal in cell B2. Copying the function down the column will compare each sales representative's sales with the $10,000 value in cell B2.

TABLE 2.5 Comparison Operators

Operator	Description
=	Equal to
<>	Not equal to
<	Less than
>	Greater than
<=	Less than or equal to
>=	Greater than or equal to

Design the Value_If_True and Value_If_False Arguments

The second and third arguments of an IF function are value_if_true and value_if_false. When Excel evaluates the logical test, the result is either true or false. If the logical test is true, the value_if_true argument executes. If the logical test is false, the value_if_false argument executes. Only one of these two arguments is executed; both arguments cannot be executed, because the logical test is either true or false but not both. The value_if_true and value_if_false arguments can contain text, cell references, formulas, or constants.

In Figure 2.23, cell F2 contains an IF function in which the value_if_true argument is B$3 and the value_if_false argument is 0. Because the logical test (E2>B$2) is true—that is, Tiffany's sales of $11,000 are greater than the $10,000 goal—the value_if_true argument is executed, and the result displays $500, the value that is stored in cell B3. Jose's sales of $10,000 are *not* greater than $10,000, and Rex's sales of $9,000 are *not* greater than $10,000; therefore, the value_if_false argument is executed and returns no bonus in cells F3 and F4.

> **TIP: AT LEAST TWO POSSIBLE RIGHT ANSWERS**
> In many situations, the IF function can have at least two constructions to produce the desired result. Since the logical test is a comparative expression, it can be written two ways. For example, comparing whether E2 is greater than B2 can be written using greater than (E2>B2), or the reverse can also be compared to see if B2 is less than E2 (B2<E2). Depending on the logical test, the value if true and value if false arguments will switch.

Figure 2.25 illustrates several IF functions, how they are evaluated, and their results. The input area contains values that are used in the logical tests and results. You can create this worksheet with the input area and IF functions to develop your understanding of how IF functions work.

⊿	A	B	C
1	Input Values		
2	$ 1,000.00		
3	$ 2,000.00		
4	10%		
5	5%		
6	$ 250.00		
7			
8	IF Function	Evaluation	Result
9	=IF(A2=A3,A4,A5)	$1,000 is equal to $2,000: FALSE	5%
10	=IF(A2<A3,A4,A5)	$1,000 is less than $2,000: TRUE	10%
11	=IF(A2<>A3,"Not Equal","Equal")	$1,000 and $2,000 are not equal: TRUE	Not Equal
12	=IF(A2>A3,A2*A4,A2*A5)	$1,000 is greater than $2,000: FALSE	$ 50.00
13	=IF(A2>A3,A2*A4,MAX(A2*A5,A6))	$1,000 is greater than $2,000: FALSE	$ 250.00
14	=IF(A2*A4=A3*A5,A6,0)	$100 (A2*A4) is equal to $100 (A3*A5): TRUE	$ 250.00
15			

FIGURE 2.25 Sample IF Functions

- **Cell A9.** The logical test A2=A3 compares the values in cells A2 and A3 to see if they are equal. Because $1,000 is not equal to $2,000, the logical test is false. The value_if_false argument is executed, which displays 5%, the value stored in cell A5.

- **Cell A10.** The logical test A2<A3 determines if the value in cell A2 is less than the value in A3. Because $1,000 is less than $2,000, the logical test is true. The value_if_true argument is executed, which displays the value stored in cell A4, which is 10%.

- **Cell A11.** The logical test A2<>A3 determines if the values in cells A2 and A3 are not equal. Because $1,000 and $2,000 are not equal, the logical test is true. The value_if_true argument is executed, which displays the text Not Equal.

- **Cell A12.** The logical test A2>A3 is false. The value_if_false argument is executed, which multiplies the value in cell A2 ($1,000) by the value in cell A5 (5%) and displays $50. The parentheses in the value_if_true (A2*A4) and value_if_false (A2*A5) arguments are optional. They are not required but may help you read the function arguments better.

- **Cell A13.** The logical test A2>A3 is false. The value_if_false argument, which contains a nested MAX function, is executed. The MAX function, MAX(A2*A5,A6), multiplies the values in cells A2 ($1,000) and A5 (5%) and returns the higher of the product ($50) and the value stored in cell A6 ($250).

- **Cell A14.** The logical test A2*A4=A3*A5 is true. The contents of cell A2 ($1,000) are multiplied by the contents of cell A4 (10%) for a result of $100. That result is then compared to the result of A3*A5, which is also $100. Because the logical test is true, the function returns the value of cell A6 ($250).

TIP: USE TEXT IN AN IF FUNCTION

You can use text within a formula. For example, you can build a logical test comparing the contents of cell A1 to specific text, such as A1="Input Values". The IF function in cell A11 in Figure 2.25 uses "Not Equal" and "Equal" in the value_if_true and value_if_false arguments. When you use text in a formula or function, you must enclose the text in quotation marks. However, do not use quotation marks around formulas, cell references, or values.

Quick Concepts

8. Describe a situation in which an IF statement could be used. *p. 414*

9. Describe how you should structure a vertical lookup table if you need to look up values in a range. *p. 411*

10. Explain why the PMT function often produces negative results. *p. 413*

Hands-On Exercises

Skills covered: Use the VLOOKUP Function • Use the PMT Function • Use the IF Function

3 Logical, Lookup, and Financial Functions

Erica wants you to complete another model that she might use for future mortgage data analysis. As you study the model, you realize you need to incorporate logical, lookup, and financial functions.

STEP 1 USE THE VLOOKUP FUNCTION

Rates vary based on the number of years to pay off the loan. Erica created a lookup table for three common mortgage terms and she entered the current APR for each item. The lookup table will provide efficiency later when the rates change. You will use the VLOOKUP function to display the correct rate for each customer based on the number of years of their respective loans. Refer to Figure 2.26 as you complete Step 1.

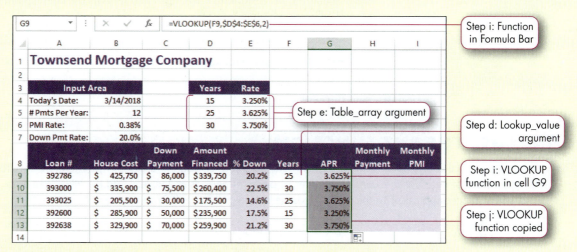

FIGURE 2.26 VLOOKUP Function to Determine APR

a. Open *e02h2Loans_LastFirst* if you closed it at the end of Hands-On Exercise 2 and save it as **e02h3Loans_LastFirst**, changing h2 to h3.

b. Click the **Payment Info worksheet tab** to display the worksheet containing the data to complete. Click **cell G9**, the cell that will store the APR for the first customer.

c. Click the **Formulas tab**, click **Lookup & Reference** in the Function Library group, and then select **VLOOKUP**.

The Function Arguments dialog box opens.

d. Ensure that the insertion point is in the Lookup_value box, click the **Collapse Dialog Box**, click **cell F9** to enter F9 in the Lookup_value box, and then click the **Expand Dialog Box** to return to Function Arguments dialog box.

Cell F9 contains the value you need to look up in the table: 25 years.

e. Press **Tab**, click **Collapse Dialog Box** to the right of the Table_array box, select the **range D4:E6**, and then click **Expand Dialog Box** to return to the Function Arguments dialog box.

This is the range that contains that data for the lookup table. The Years values in the table are arranged from lowest to highest.

Anticipate what will happen if you copy the formula down the column. What do you need to do to ensure that the cell references always point to the exact location of the table? If your answer is to make the table array cell references absolute, then you answered correctly.

f. Select the **range D4:E6** and press **F4** to make the range references absolute.

The Table_array box now contains $D$4:$E$6.

g. Press **Tab** and type **2** in the Col_index_num box.

The second column of the lookup table contains the Rates that you want to return and display in the cells containing the formulas.

h. Press **Tab** and type **False** in the Range_lookup box.

To ensure an exact match to look up in the table, you enter *False* in the optional argument.

i. Click **OK**.

The VLOOKUP function uses the first loan's term in years (25) to find an exact match in the first column of the lookup table, and then returns the corresponding rate from the second column, which is 3.625%.

j. Copy the formula down the column.

Spot-check the results to make sure the function returned the correct APR based on the number of years.

k. Save the workbook.

USE THE PMT FUNCTION

The worksheet now has all the necessary data for you to calculate the monthly payment for each loan: the APR, the number of years for the loan, the number of payment periods in one year, and the initial loan amount. You will use the PMT function to calculate the monthly payment. Refer to Figure 2.27 as you complete Step 2.

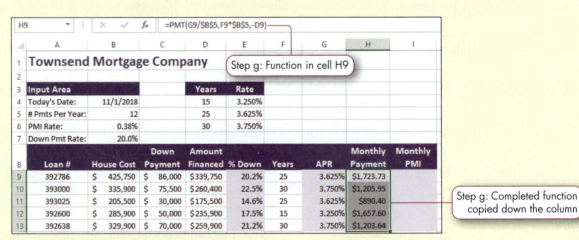

FIGURE 2.27 PMT Function to Calculate Monthly Payment

a. Click **cell H9**, the cell that will store the payment for the first customer.

b. Click **Financial** in the Function Library group, scroll through the list, and then select **PMT**.

The Function Arguments dialog box opens.

c. Enter **G9/B5** in the Rate box.

Think about what will happen if you copy the formula. The argument will be G10/B6 for the next customer. Are those cell references correct? G10 does contain the APR for the next customer, but B6 does not contain the correct number of payments in one year. Therefore, you need to make B5 an absolute cell reference because the number of payments per year does not vary.

d. Press **F4** to make the reference to cell B5 absolute.

e. Press **Tab** and type **F9*$B$5** in the Nper box.

You calculate the nper by multiplying the number of years by the number of payments in one year. You must make B5 an absolute cell reference so that it does not change when you copy the formula down the column.

f. Press **Tab** and type **-D9** in the Pv box.

The bottom of the dialog box indicates that the monthly payment is 1723.73008, or $1,723.73.

TROUBLESHOOTING: If the payment displays as a negative value, you probably forgot to type the minus sign in front of the D9 reference in the Pv box. Edit the function and type the minus sign in the correct place.

---

g. Click **OK**. Copy the formula down the column.

h. Save the workbook.

STEP 3 USE THE IF FUNCTION

Lenders often want borrowers to have a 20% down payment. If borrowers do not put in 20% of the cost of the house as a down payment, they pay a private mortgage insurance (PMI) fee. PMI serves to protect lenders from absorbing loss if the borrower defaults on the loan, and it enables borrowers with less cash to secure a loan. The PMI fee is about 0.38% of the amount financed. Some borrowers pay PMI for a few months or years until the outstanding balance owed is less than 80% of the appraised value of the property. The worksheet contains the necessary values in the input area. You use the IF function to determine which borrowers must pay PMI and how much they will pay. Refer to Figure 2.28 as you complete Step 3.

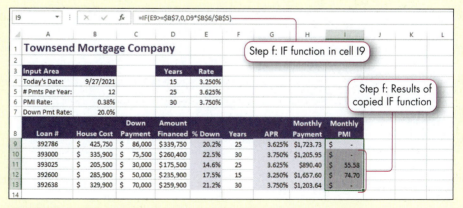

FIGURE 2.28 IF Function to Calculate Monthly PMI

a. Click **cell I9**, the cell that will store the PMI, if any, for the first customer.

b. Click **Logical** in the Function Library group and select **IF**.

The Function Arguments dialog box opens. You will enter the three arguments.

c. Type **E9>=$B$7** in the Logical_test box.

The logical test compares the down payment percentage to see if it is at least 20%, the threshold stored in B7. The customer's percentage cell reference is relative so that it will change when you copy it down the column; however, cell B7 must be absolute because it contains a value that should remain constant when the formula is copied to other cells.

d. Press **Tab** and type **0** in the Value_if_true box.

If the customer makes a down payment that is at least 20% of the purchase price, the customer does not pay PMI, so a value of 0 will display whenever the logical test is true. The first customer paid more than 20% of the purchase price, so he or she does not have to pay PMI.

e. Press **Tab** and type **D9*$B$6/$B$5** in the Value_if_false box.

If the logical test is false, the customer must pay PMI, which is calculated by multiplying the amount financed (D9) by the periodic PMI rate (the result of dividing the yearly PMI (B6) by the number of payments per year (B5)).

f. Click **OK** and copy the formula down the column.

The first, second, and fifth customers paid at least 20% of the purchase price, so they do not have to pay PMI. The third and fourth customers must pay PMI because their respective down payments were less than 20% of the purchase price.

> **TROUBLESHOOTING:** If the results are not as you expected, check the logical operators. People often mistype < and > or forget to type = for >= situations. Also check for the appropriate use of absolute or mixed cell references. Correct any errors in the original formula and copy the formula again.

g. Set the worksheets to print on one page and return to Normal View. Add a footer with your name on the left, sheet code in the middle, and the file name code on the right.

h. Save and close the file. Based on your instructor's directions, submit e02h3Loans_LastFirst.

Chapter Objectives Review

After reading this chapter, you have accomplished the following objectives:

1. Use relative, absolute, and mixed cell references in formulas.

- Use a relative cell address: A relative reference indicates a cell's location relative to the formula cell. When you copy the formula, the relative cell reference changes.
- Use an absolute cell reference: An absolute reference is a permanent pointer to a particular cell, indicated with $ before the column letter and the row number, such as $B$5. When you copy the formula, the absolute cell reference does not change.
- Use a mixed cell reference: A mixed reference contains part absolute and part relative reference, such as $B5 or B$5. Either the column or the row reference changes, while the other remains constant when you copy the formula.

2. Insert a function.

- A function is a predefined formula that performs a calculation. It contains the function name and arguments. Formula AutoComplete, function ScreenTips, and the Insert Function dialog box enable you to select and create functions. The Function Arguments dialog box guides you through the entering requirements for each argument.

3. Insert basic math and statistics functions.

- Use the SUM function: The SUM function calculates the total of a range of values. The syntax is =SUM(number1,[number2], . . .).
- Use the AVERAGE: The AVERAGE function calculates the arithmetic mean of values in a range.
- Use the MEDIAN function: The MEDIAN function identifies the midpoint value in a set of values.
- Use the MIN and MAX functions: The MIN function identifies the lowest value in a range, whereas the MAX function identifies the highest value in a range.
- Use the COUNT functions: The COUNT function tallies the number of cells in a range that contain values, whereas the COUNTBLANK function tallies the number of blank cells in a range, and COUNTA tallies the number of cells that are not empty.

- Perform calculations with Quick Analysis tools: With the Quick Analysis tools you can apply formatting, create charts or tables, and insert basic functions.

4. Use date functions.

- Use the TODAY function: The TODAY function displays the current date.
- Use the NOW function: The NOW function displays the current date and time.

5. Use lookup functions.

- Use the VLOOKUP function: The VLOOKUP function contains the required arguments lookup_value, table_array, and col_index_num and one optional argument, range_lookup.
- Create the lookup table: Design the lookup table using exact values or the breakpoints for ranges. If using breakpoints, the breakpoints must be in ascending order.
- Use the HLOOKUP function: The HLOOKUP function looks up values by row (horizontally) rather than by column (vertically).

6. Use the PMT function.

- The PMT function calculates periodic payments for a loan with a fixed interest rate and a fixed term. The PMT function requires the periodic interest rate, the total number of payment periods, and the original value of the loan.

7. Use the IF function.

- Design the logical test: The IF function is a logical function that evaluates a logical test using logical operators, such as <, >, and =, and returns one value if the condition is true and another value if the condition is false.
- Design the value_if_true and value_if_false arguments: The arguments can contain cell references, text, or calculations. If a logical test is true, Excel executes the value_if_true argument. If a logical test is false, Excel executes the value_if_false argument.
- You can nest or embed other functions inside one or more of the arguments of an IF function to create more complex formulas.

Key Terms Matching

Match the key terms with their definitions. Write the key term letter by the appropriate numbered definition.

a. Absolute cell reference	**k.** Mixed cell reference
b. Argument	**l.** NOW function
c. AVERAGE function	**m.** PMT function
d. COUNT function	**n.** Relative cell reference
e. IF function	**o.** ROUND function
f. Logical test	**p.** SUM function
g. Lookup table	**q.** Syntax
h. MAX function	**r.** TODAY function
i. MEDIAN function	**s.** VLOOKUP function
j. MIN function	

1. _____ A set of rules that governs the structure and components for properly entering a function. **p. 409**

2. _____ Displays the current date. **p. 403**

3. _____ Indicates a cell's specific location; the cell reference does not change when you copy the formula. **p. 391**

4. _____ An input, such as a cell reference or value, needed to complete a function. **p. 397**

5. _____ Identifies the highest value in a range. **p. 402**

6. _____ Tallies the number of cells in a range that contain values. **p. 402**

7. _____ Looks up a value in a vertical lookup table and returns a related result from the lookup table. **p. 409**

8. _____ A range that contains data for the basis of the lookup and data to be retrieved. **p. 411**

9. _____ Calculates the arithmetic mean, or average, of values in a range. **p. 401**

10. _____ Identifies the midpoint value in a set of values. **p. 401**

11. _____ Displays the current date and time. **p. 403**

12. _____ Evaluates a condition and returns one value if the condition is true and a different value if the condition is false. **p. 414**

13. _____ Calculates the total of values contained in one or more cells. **p. 400**

14. _____ Calculates the periodic payment for a loan with a fixed interest rate and fixed term. **p. 413**

15. _____ Indicates a cell's location from the cell containing the formula; the cell reference changes when the formula is copied. **p. 390**

16. _____ Contains both an absolute and a relative cell reference in a formula; the absolute part does not change but the relative part does when you copy the formula. **p. 392**

17. _____ An expression that evaluates to true or false. **p. 414**

18. _____ Displays the lowest value in a range. **p. 402**

19. _____ Rounds a number to a specified number of digits. **p. 402**

Multiple Choice

1. If cell E15 contains the function =PMT(B$15/12,C7*12,-D8), what type of cell reference is B$15?

   (a) Relative reference
   (b) Absolute reference
   (c) Mixed reference
   (d) Syntax

2. What function would most efficiently accomplish the same thing as =(B5+C5+D5+E5+F5)?

   (a) =SUM(B5:F5)
   (b) =AVERAGE(B5:F5)
   (c) =MEDIAN(B5:F5)
   (d) =COUNT(B5:F5)

3. When you start to type =AV, what feature displays a list of functions and defined names?

   (a) Function ScreenTip
   (b) Formula AutoComplete
   (c) Insert Function dialog box
   (d) Function Arguments dialog box

4. A formula containing the entry =J$7 is copied to a cell three columns to the right and four rows down. How will the entry display in its new location?

   (a) =M$7
   (b) =J$7
   (c) =M11
   (d) =J$11

5. Which of the following functions should be used to insert the current date and time in a cell?

   (a) =TODAY()
   (b) =CURRENT()
   (c) =NOW()
   (d) =DATE

6. Which of the following is *not* a comparison operator?

   (a) <
   (b) >
   (c) &
   (d) <>

7. Which of the following is *not* true about the VLOOKUP function?

   (a) The col_index_num argument cannot be 1.
   (b) The lookup table must be in descending order.
   (c) The default match type is approximate.
   (d) The match type must be false when completing an exact match.

8. The function =PMT(C5,C7,-C3) is stored in cell C15. What must be stored in cell C5?

   (a) APR
   (b) Periodic interest rate
   (c) Loan amount
   (d) Number of payment periods

9. Which of the following is *not* an appropriate use of the MAX function?

   (a) =MAX(B3:B45)
   (b) =MAX(F1:G10)
   (c) =MAX(A8:A15,D8:D15)
   (d) =MAX(D15-C15)

10. What is the keyboard shortcut to create an absolute reference?

    (a) F2
    (b) F3
    (c) F4
    (d) Alt

Practice Exercises

1 Hamilton Heights Auto Sales

You are the primary loan manager for Hamilton Heights Auto Sales, an auto sales company located in Missouri. To most efficiently manage the auto loans your company finances, you have decided to create a spreadsheet to perform several calculations. You will insert the current date, calculate down payment and interest rates based on credit score, calculate periodic payment amounts, and complete the project with basic summary information. Refer to Figure 2.29 as you complete this exercise.

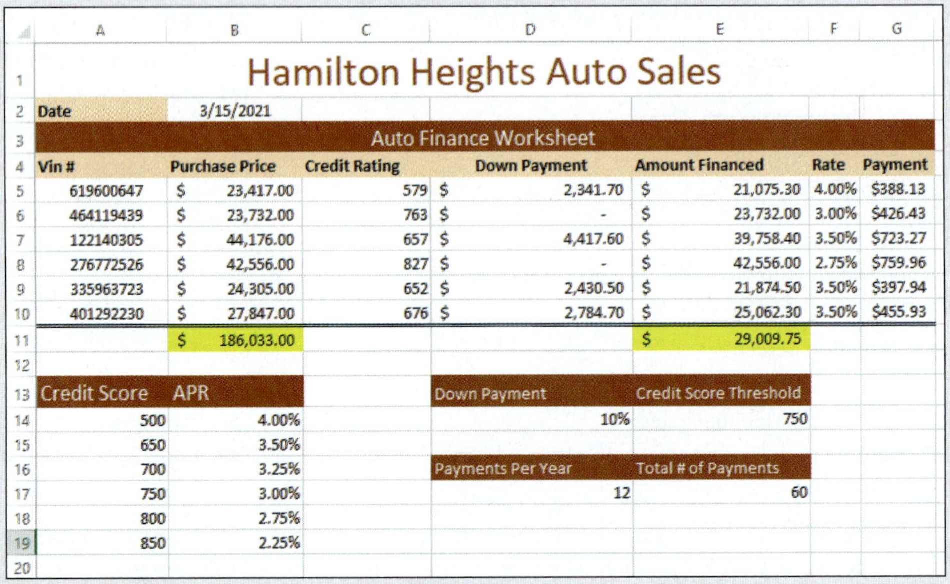

	A	B	C	D	E	F	G
1	Hamilton Heights Auto Sales						
2	Date	3/15/2021					
3	Auto Finance Worksheet						
4	Vin #	Purchase Price	Credit Rating	Down Payment	Amount Financed	Rate	Payment
5	619600647	$ 23,417.00	579	$ 2,341.70	$ 21,075.30	4.00%	$388.13
6	464119439	$ 23,732.00	763	$ -	$ 23,732.00	3.00%	$426.43
7	122140305	$ 44,176.00	657	$ 4,417.60	$ 39,758.40	3.50%	$723.27
8	276772526	$ 42,556.00	827	$ -	$ 42,556.00	2.75%	$759.96
9	335963723	$ 24,305.00	652	$ 2,430.50	$ 21,874.50	3.50%	$397.94
10	401292230	$ 27,847.00	676	$ 2,784.70	$ 25,062.30	3.50%	$455.93
11		$ 186,033.00			$ 29,009.75		
12							
13	Credit Score	APR		Down Payment	Credit Score Threshold		
14	500	4.00%		10%	750		
15	650	3.50%					
16	700	3.25%		Payments Per Year	Total # of Payments		
17	750	3.00%		12	60		
18	800	2.75%					
19	850	2.25%					
20							

FIGURE 2.29 Hamilton Heights Auto Sales

a. Open *e02p1AutoSales* and save it as **e02p1AutoSales_LastFirst**.

b. Click **cell B2**, click the **Formulas tab**, click **Date & Time** in the Function Library group, select **NOW**, and then click **OK** (**Done** on a Mac) to enter today's date in the cell.

c. Click **cell D5**, ensure the Formulas tab is displayed, click **Logical** in the Function Library group, and select **IF**.

d. Type **C5<=$E$14** in the Logical_test box, type **$D$14*B5** in the Value_if_true box, type **0** in the Value_if_false box, and then click **OK**.

This uses the IF function to calculate the required down payment based on credit score. If the customer has a credit score higher than 750 a down payment is not required. All clients with credits scores lower than 750 must pay a required 10% down payment in advance.

e. Double-click the fill handle to copy the contents of **cell D5** down the column, click **Auto Fill Options** to the lower-right of the copied cells, and then select **Fill Without Formatting** to ensure that the **Bottom Double border** remains applied to cell D10.

f. Calculate the Amount Financed by doing the following:
- Click **cell E5** and type **=B5-D5**.
- Use **cell E5's fill handle** to copy the function down the column.
- Apply **Bottom Double border** to cell E10.

g. Calculate the Rate by doing the following:
- Click **cell F5**. Click **Lookup & Reference** in the Function Library group on the Formula tab, and select **VLOOKUP**.
- Type **C5** in the Lookup_value box, type **$A$14:$B$19** in the Table_array box, type **2** in the Col_index_num box, and then click **OK**.
- Double-click **cell F5's fill handle** to copy the function down the column.
- Click **Auto Fill Options**, and select **Fill Without Formatting**.

h. Calculate the required periodic payment by doing the following:
- Click **cell G5**, click **Financial** in the Function Library Group, scroll down, and then select **PMT**.
- Type **F5/$D$17** in the Rate box, type **$E$17** in the Nper box, type **–E5** in the Pv box, and then click **OK**.
- Double-click **cell G5's** fill handle to copy the function down the column.
- Click the **Auto Fill Options button**, and select **Fill Without Formatting**.

i. Select the **range B5:B10**, click the **Quick Analysis button**, click **Totals**, and then select **Sum** from the Quick Analysis Gallery. (On a Mac, select the range B5:B10 and click AutoSum on the ribbon.)

j. Click **cell E11** and type **=AVERAGE(E5:E10)** to calculate the average amount financed.

k. Create a footer with your name on the left side, the sheet name code in the center, and the file name on the right side.

l. Save and close the workbook. Based on your instructor's directions, submit e02p1AutoSales_LastFirst.

2 | Garten Realty

As the accounting manager for Garten Realty, you have the task of calculating monthly salaries including performance bonuses for the company's sales agents. Sales agents receive a base salary and a bonus based on the amount of sales generated. The bonus award is a percentage of the amount of sales generated and is calculated using a graduated scale based on years of service with the company. Refer to Figure 2.30 as you complete this exercise.

	A	B	C	D	E	F
1			Garten Realty			
2						
3	**Inputs and Constants**				**Bonus Data**	
4	Date:	3/15/2018		Sales	<3 Years of Service	>=3 Years of Service
5	Number of Agents	7		$ 50,000.00	1%	2%
6				$ 500,000.00	2%	4%
7				$ 1,000,000.00	4%	6%
8						
9	**Agent ID**	**Years of Service**	**Base Annual Salary**	**Total sales generated**	**Bonus**	**Monthly Take Home**
10	73822278	1	$ 68,621.00	$ 50,000.00	$ 500.00	$ 6,218.42
11	92261130	2	$ 65,411.00	$ 60,000.00	$ 600.00	$ 6,050.92
12	24697518	9	$ 68,308.00	$ 84,000.00	$ 1,680.00	$ 7,372.33
13	78235598	9	$ 68,855.00	$ 101,000.00	$ 2,020.00	$ 7,757.92
14	41061578	10	$ 47,316.00	$ 175,000.00	$ 3,500.00	$ 7,443.00
15	88306993	18	$ 43,441.00	$ 500,000.00	$ 20,000.00	$ 23,620.08
16	58569982	20	$ 64,665.00	$ 750,000.00	$ 30,000.00	$ 35,388.75
17						
18	**Statistics**					
19	Lowest Bonus	$ 500.00				
20	Average Bonus	$ 8,328.57				
21	Highest Bonus	$ 30,000.00				

Bonus_Calculation

FIGURE 2.30 Garten Realty

a. Open *e02p2Realty* and save it as **e02p2Realty_LastFirst**.

b. Click **cell B4**, click the **Formulas tab**, click **Date & Time** in the Function Library group, select **TODAY**, and then click **OK** to enter today's date in the cell.

c. Click **cell B5**, click the **AutoSum arrow** in the Function Library group, and then select **Count Numbers**. Select the **range A10:A16** and press **Enter**.

d. Click **cell E10**, type **=VLOOKUP(D10,$D$5:$F$7,IF(B10<3,2,3),TRUE)*D10**, press **Ctrl+Enter**, and then double-click the **fill handle**.

This nested function uses the IF function nested within the VLOOKUP function to determine which values should be used from the lookup table. The IF function is required because there are two different bonus values based on years of service.

e. Calculate each employee's monthly take-home pay by doing the following:

- Click **cell F10** and type **=C10/12+E10**.
- Press **Ctrl+Enter** and double-click the **cell F10 fill handle**.

f. Calculate basic summary statistics by doing the following:

- Click **cell B19**, click the **Formulas tab**, click the **AutoSum arrow**, and then select **MIN**.
- Select the **range E10:E16** and press **Enter**.
- Click **cell B20**, click the **AutoSum arrow**, select **AVERAGE**, select the **range E10:E16**, and then press **Enter**.
- Click **cell B21**, click the **AutoSum arrow**, select **MAX**, select the **range E10:E16**, and then press **Enter**.

g. Create a footer with your name on the left side, the sheet name in the center, and the file name code on the right side.

h. Save and close the workbook. Based on your instructor's directions, submit e02p2Realty_LastFirst.

Mid-Level Exercises

1 | Metropolitan Zoo Gift Shop Weekly Payroll

MyLab IT Grader

As manager of the gift shop at the Metropolitan Zoo, you are responsible for managing the weekly payroll. Your assistant developed a partial worksheet, but you will enter the formulas to calculate the regular pay, overtime pay, gross pay, taxable pay, withholding tax, FICA, and net pay. In addition, you want to include total pay columns and calculate some basic statistics. As you construct formulas, make sure you use absolute and relative cell references correctly in formulas.

a. Open the *e02m1Payroll* workbook and save it as **e02m1Payroll_LastFirst**.

b. Study the worksheet structure and read the business rules in the Notes section.

c. Use IF functions to calculate the regular pay and overtime pay based on a regular 40-hour work-week in **cells E5** and **F5**. Pay overtime only for overtime hours. Calculate the gross pay in **cell G5** based on the regular and overtime pay. Abram's regular pay is $398. With eight overtime hours, Abram's overtime pay is $119.40.

d. Create a formula in **cell H5** to calculate the taxable pay. Multiply the number of dependents by the deduction per dependent and subtract that from the gross pay. With two dependents, Abram's taxable pay is $417.40.

e. Insert a VLOOKUP function in **cell I5** to identify and calculate the federal withholding tax. With a taxable pay of $417.40, Abram's tax rate is 25% and the withholding tax is $104.35. The VLOOKUP function returns the applicable tax rate, which you must then multiply by the taxable pay.

f. Calculate FICA in **cell J5** based on gross pay and the FICA rate, and calculate the net pay in **cell K5**.

g. Copy all formulas down their respective columns.

h. Use Quick Analysis tools to calculate the total regular pay, overtime pay, gross pay, taxable pay, withholding tax, FICA, and net pay on **row 17**. (On a Mac, this step must be completed using the AutoSum feature on the ribbon).

i. Apply **Accounting Number Format** to the **range C5:C16**. Apply **Accounting Number Format** to the first row of monetary data and to the total row. Apply the **Comma style** to the monetary values for the other employees. Underline the last employee's monetary values and use the Format Cells dialog box to apply Top and Double Bottom borders for the totals.

j. Insert appropriate functions to calculate the average, highest, and lowest values in the Summary Statistics area (the **range I21:K23**) of the worksheet. Format the # of hours calculations as **Number format** with one decimal and the remaining calculations with **Accounting Number Format**.

k. Insert a footer with your name on the left side, the sheet name in the center, and the file name code on the right side of both worksheets.

l. Save and close the workbook. Based on your instructor's directions, submit e02m1Payroll_LastFirst.

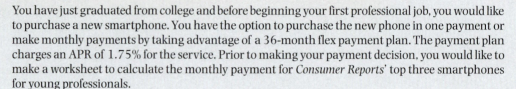

FROM SCRATCH

You have just graduated from college and before beginning your first professional job, you would like to purchase a new smartphone. You have the option to purchase the new phone in one payment or make monthly payments by taking advantage of a 36-month flex payment plan. The payment plan charges an APR of 1.75% for the service. Prior to making your payment decision, you would like to make a worksheet to calculate the monthly payment for *Consumer Reports'* top three smartphones for young professionals.

a. Start a new Excel workbook, save it as **e02m2SmartPhone_LastFirst**, and then rename Sheet1 **FlexPay**.

b. Type **Flex Pay Calculator** in cell A1. Apply **bold, 20 pt** font size, **Blue, Accent 1**, font color.

c. Type **Inputs** in **cell A2**. Apply **Thick Outside Borders** to the **range A2:C2**.

d. Type **APR** and **# of payments** in the **range A3:A4**, and adjust the column width as needed.

e. Type **1.75%** in **cell B3** and **36** in **cell B4**. Type **Outputs** in **cell A6**. Select the **range A6:C6** and apply **Thick Outside Borders**.

f. Type **Model** in **cell A7**, **Price** in **cell B7**, and **Payment** in **cell C7**. Next enter the price information listed below in the range A8:B10. Adjust the column width as needed and apply **Currency Number Format** to the **range B8:C10**.

Model	Price
iPhone X	949.00
Samsung Galaxy	799.00
LG V30	650.00

g. Use the PMT function in **cell C8** to calculate the monthly flex payment for the first option. Be sure to use the appropriate absolute, relative, or mixed cell references. Next use the fill handle to copy the function down, completing the **range C8:C10**.

h. Type **Highest payment**, **Average payment**, and **Lowest payment** in the **range A12:A14**. Resize column A as needed.

i. Use the MAX function in **cell B12** to calculate the highest flex payment, in **cell B13** use the AVERAGE function to calculate the average flex payment, and in **cell B14** use the MIN function to calculate the lowest flex payment.

j. Insert a footer with your name on the left side, the sheet name in the center, and the file name code on the right side of the worksheet.

k. Save and close the workbook. Based on your instructor's directions, submit e02m2SmartPhone_LastFirst.

Running Case

New Castle County Technical Services

New Castle County Technical Services (NCCTS) provides technical support services for a number of companies in New Castle County, Delaware. You previously downloaded a dataset from the company's database that contains a list of call cases that were closed during March, formatted the worksheet, and calculated the number of days each case was open and the amount owed per transaction. Since then, you added two worksheets, one for your customer list and one for the rates. In the March Hours worksheet, you inserted new columns to look up customer names and rates from the respective worksheets. You want to use this data to enter summary statistics to complete billing analysis for March.

a. Open *e02r1NCCTS* and save it as **e02r1NCCTS_LastFirst**.

b. Insert a **VLOOKUP** function in **cell C5**, to return the customer name based on the customer ID in column B and the lookup table in the Customers worksheet.

c. Copy the function from cell C5 to the **range C6:C36**.

d. Insert a **VLOOKUP** function in **cell F5** to look up Rates for CallTypeID in column D using the lookup table in the Rates worksheet. Copy the function from cell F5 to the **range F6:F36**.

e. Insert an IF function in **cell K5** to calculate the amount billed. If the hours logged is less than or equal to 10 (cell O12), multiply the rate by the hours worked. Otherwise multiply the rate by the hours worked and add a $100 premium (cell O13) to the bill. Copy the function from cell K5 to the **range K6:K36**.

f. Insert a function in **cell O5** to calculate the total hours logged in column J.

g. Insert a function in **cell O6** to calculate the total amount billed in column K.

h. Insert a function in **cell O7** to calculate the average days required to complete a service request (column I).

i. Insert a function in **cell O8** to calculate the fewest days open in column I.

j. Insert a function in **cell O9** to calculate the most days open in column I.

k. Insert a function in **cell E2** to add the current date and time to the worksheet.

l. Insert a footer with your name on the left side, the sheet name in the center, and the file name code on the right side of the worksheet. Return to Normal view.

m. Save and close the workbook. Based on your instructor's directions, submit e02r1NCCTS_LastFirst.

Disaster Recovery

Auto Finance

After many years of service your automobile has been diagnosed with a cracked engine block. It has been determined that the damage is too costly to repair so you have decided to purchase a new vehicle. Before purchasing the car, you want to create a worksheet to estimate the monthly payment based on the purchase price, APR, down payment, and years. Your monthly budget is $500 and you will used conditional logic to automatically determine if you can afford the cars you are evaluating. After completing the calculations for the first car option in row 12, you used the fill handle to copy the functions down completing the worksheet. Unfortunately, after using the fill handle you receive errors in your calculations. You need to locate and repair the errors in order to complete the worksheet. Open the workbook *e02d1CarLoan* and save it as **e02d1CarLoan_LastFirst**. Review the formula in cell B12. Add the appropriate mixed cell reference for the down payment located in cell D4 and use the fill handle to copy the formula down completing the column. Review the formula in cell C12. Add the appropriate mixed cell references for the APR and years financed located in cells D5 and D6. Next use the fill handle to copy the formula down completing the column. Include a footer with your name on the left side, the date in the center, and the file name on the right side. Save and close the workbook. Based on your instructor's directions, submit e02d1CarLoan_LastFirst.

Capstone Exercise

W.C. Hicks Appliances

You are an account manager for W.C. Hicks Appliances, a local appliance store that also provides financing, delivery, and installation. As part of your daily tasks, you create an Excel workbook that reports sales, payment plan information, and summary statistics.

Insert Current Date

In order to ensure proper documentation you want to insert the current date and time.

1. Open the *e02c1Appliances* workbook and save it as **e02c1Appliances_LastFirst**.
2. Insert a function in **cell B2** to display the current date and format as a **Long Date**.
3. Set column B's width to **Autofit**.

Create Item Lookup

Your first task is to use a lookup function based on the data in the range A18:C23 to determine the name of the item purchased and the corresponding price based on the provided SKU number.

4. Insert a function in **cell C5** to display the item named based on the provided inventory lookup information.
5. Copy the function from **cell C5** down through **C13** to complete column C.
6. Set column C's width to **12.5**.
7. Insert a function in **cell E5** to display the item price based on the provided inventory lookup information.
8. Copy the function from **cell E5** down through **E13** to complete column E.
9. Apply **Currency Number Format** to **column E**.

Determine Delivery Fee

You will calculate the total due for each customer's order. The total is the purchase price plus an optional $75.00 delivery charge.

10. Insert an IF function in **cell F5** to calculate the total due. If the customer has chosen home delivery, there is an additional delivery charge located in **cell B25**. Be sure to use appropriate relative and absolute cell references.

11. Copy the function from **cell F5** down through **F13** to complete column Gra F.
12. Apply **Currency format** to **column F**.

Calculate the Monthly Payment

Your next step is to calculate the periodic payment for each customer's purchase. The payments are based on the years financed in column G and the annual interest rate in cell B26. All accounts are paid on a monthly basis.

13. Insert the function in **cell H5** to calculate the first customer's monthly payment, using appropriate relative and absolute cell references.
14. Copy the formula down the column.
15. Insert a function in **cell H14** to calculate the total of all monthly payments in column H.
16. Apply **Currency Number Format** to **column H**.

Finalize the Workbook

You perform some basic statistical calculations and finalize the workbook with formatting and page setup options.

17. Insert a function in **cell H18** to calculate the total number of orders.
18. Insert a function in **cell H19** to calculate the lowest monthly payment in column H.
19. Insert a function in **cell H20** to calculate the average monthly payment in column H.
20. Insert a function in **cell H21** to calculate the highest monthly payment in column H.
21. Insert a function in **cell H22** to calculate the median monthly payment in column H.
22. Apply **Currency format** to the **range H19:H22**.
23. Insert a footer with your name on the left side, the sheet name in the center, and the file name on the right side.
24. Save and close the workbook. Based on your instructor's directions, submit e02c1Appliances_ LastFirst.

Charts

You will create charts and insert sparklines to represent data visually.

OBJECTIVES & SKILLS: After you read this chapter, you will be able to:

CASE STUDY | Computer Job Outlook

You are an academic advisor for the School of Computing at a university in Seattle, Washington. You will visit high schools over the next few weeks to discuss the computing programs at the university and to inform students about the job outlook in the computing industry. Your assistant, Doug Demers, researched growing computer-related jobs in the *Occupational Outlook Handbook* published by the Bureau of Labor Statistics on the U.S. Department of Labor's website. Doug listed computer-related jobs that require a bachelor's degree, the number of those jobs in 2016, the projected number of jobs by 2026, the growth in percentage increase and number of jobs, and the 2017 median pay.

To prepare for your presentation to encourage students to select a computing major in your School of Computing, you will create several charts that depict the job growth in the computer industry. Each chart will provide different perspectives on the data. After you complete the charts, you will be able to use them in a variety of formats, such as presentations, fliers, and brochures.

CHAPTER 3

Depicting Data Visually

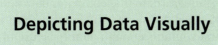

Yanlev/123RF

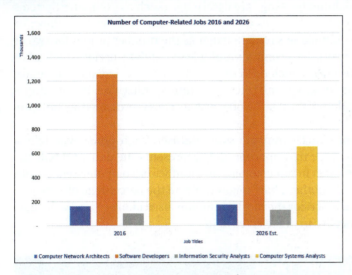

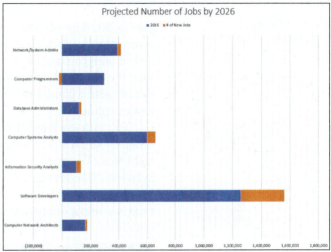

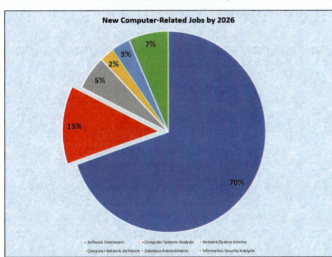

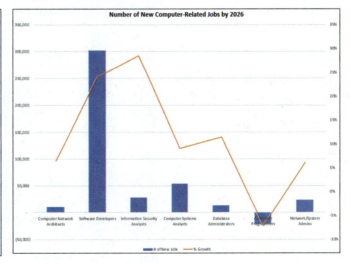

FIGURE 3.1 Computer-Related Jobs Outlook

CASE STUDY | Computer Job Outlook

Starting File	File to be Submitted
e03h1Jobs	e03h3Jobs_LastFirst

MyLab IT Grader An alternate version of this project is available as a MyLab IT Grader Assessment

Chart Basics

A *chart* is a visual representation of numeric data that compares data and reveals trends or patterns to help people make informed decisions. An effective chart depicts data in a clear, easy-to-interpret manner and contains enough data to be useful without being overwhelming.

Review the structure of the worksheet—the column labels, the row labels, the quantitative data, and the calculated values. Before creating a chart, make sure the values or units in each column or row are consistent (such as number of jobs for a specific year) and that the row and column headings are descriptive (such as Computer Systems Analysts). Identify if the worksheet contains a single set of data (such as the number of jobs in 2026 by job title) or multiple sets of data (such as the number of jobs for two or more years by job title). If the worksheet contains multiple sets of data, decide which set or sets of data you want to focus on and include in the chart. As you review the data, make sure the dataset does not include any blank rows or columns. Otherwise, if you select a dataset with a blank row or column, the chart would display gaps represented by the blank row or column.

You can create different charts from the same dataset; each chart type tells a different story. Select a chart type that appropriately represents the data and tells the right story. For example, one chart might compare the number of computer-related jobs between 2016 and 2026, and another chart might indicate the percentage of new jobs by job title. Table 3.1 lists and describes the most commonly used chart types. Each chart type provides a unique perspective to the selected data.

TABLE 3.1	Common Chart Types	
Chart	**Chart Type**	**Description**
	Column chart	Displays values in vertical columns where the height represents the value; the taller the column, the larger the value. Categories display along the horizontal (category) axis.
	Bar chart	Displays values in horizontal bars where the length represents the value; the longer the bar, the larger the value. Categories display along the vertical (category) axis.
	Pie chart	Shows proportion of individual data points to the total or whole of all those data points.
	Line chart	Displays category data on the horizontal axis and value data on the vertical axis. Appropriate to show continuous data to depict trends over time, such as months, years, or decades.
	Combo	Combines two chart types (such as column and line) to plot different data types (such as values and percentages).

In this section, you will select the data source, use different methods for creating a chart, move and size a chart, and prepare a chart for distribution.

STEP 1 Creating a Basic Chart

After reviewing the data in a worksheet and deciding what story to represent, you are ready to create a chart. First, you select the data to be included in the chart, and then you select the type of chart to create. After the chart is created, you can move the chart, adjust the size of the chart, and prepare it for distribution.

Select the Data Source

The first step to creating a chart is to identify the range that contains the data you want to include in the chart. It is important that you decide the range first to ensure the chart contains the necessary values and text. After you identify the data source, select the values and text headings needed to create the chart. However, do not select worksheet titles or subtitles; doing so would add meaningless data to the chart.

> **TIP: SELECTING NONADJACENT RANGES FOR THE DATA SOURCE**
> The values and text that you want to use as the data source may be in nonadjacent ranges. It is impor-
> tant that you select the same start and end points for both ranges. For example, if you select the range
> A4:A7, you would need to select a range with the same row numbers, such as C4:C7. To select non-
> adjacent ranges as the data source, select the first range and press and hold Ctrl while you select the
> nonadjacent range. On a Mac, press Command.

Figure 3.2 shows worksheet data and the resulting chart. The range A4:C7 was selected as the data source to create the chart. An individual value in a cell that is plotted in a chart is a ***data point.*** The value 654,900 in cell C5 is a data point for the estimated number of Computer Systems Analysts in 2026. A ***data series*** is a group of related data points typically originated in columns in a worksheet that are plotted in a chart. For example, the values 654,900, 415,300, and 273,600 show the number of estimated jobs in the 2026 data series. Each data series is represented by a different color on the chart. For example, the 2016 data series is blue, and the 2026 data series is orange. Furthermore, the text row headings, such as Computer Systems Analysts, are used as categories.

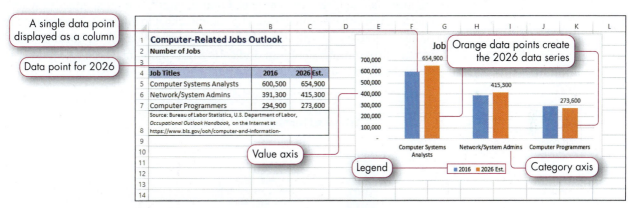

FIGURE 3.2 Dataset and Chart

Data are plotted on two axes. The ***x-axis***, also known as the *horizontal axis*, is the horizontal border that provides a frame of reference for measuring data left to right in a chart. The ***y-axis***, also known as the *vertical axis*, is the vertical border that provides a frame of reference for measuring data up and down in a chart. Excel refers to chart axes as the category axis and the value axis. The ***category axis*** is the axis that displays descriptive labels for the data points plotted in a chart. In Figure 3.2, the category axis displays on the x-axis using the text row headings. The ***value axis*** is the axis that displays incremental numbers to identify the approximate values of data points in a chart. In Figure 3.2, the value axis displays on the y-axis using increments for the number of jobs.

If you change the underlying data used in a chart, the chart automatically changes to reflect the new data. For example, if you change the value in cell C5 from 654,900 to 800,000, the 2026 column for Computer Systems Analysts becomes taller to reflect the higher value in the worksheet.

Use the Insert Tab to Create a Chart

The Charts group on the Insert tab contains commands for creating a variety of charts (see Figure 3.3). When you click a command, a gallery displays specific chart subtypes. For example, selecting Column or Bar Chart displays a gallery of 2-D and 3-D column and bar charts, such as clustered column, stacked column, and 100% stacked column. You should select the specific chart type that best achieves the purpose of the selected data source.

FIGURE 3.3 Charts Group on the Insert Tab

Create a Column Chart

A *column chart* compares values across categories, such as job titles, using vertical columns where the height represents the value of an individual data point. The taller the column is, the larger the value is. Column charts are most effective when they are limited to seven or fewer categories. The column chart in Figure 3.4 compares the number of projected jobs by job title. The Computer Systems Analysts column is taller than the Computer Programmers column, indicating that more jobs are projected for Computer Systems Analysts than Computer Programmers.

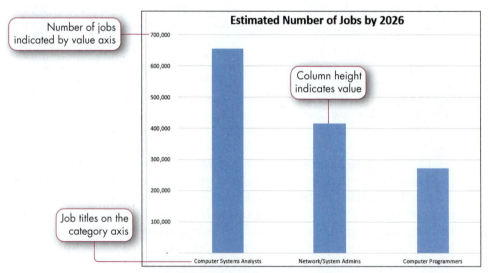

FIGURE 3.4 Column Chart

A *clustered column chart* compares groups or clusters of columns set side by side. The clustered column chart facilitates quick comparisons across data series, and it is effective for comparing several data points among categories. Figure 3.5 shows a clustered column chart where each yearly data series is assigned a color. This chart makes it easy to compare the predicted job growth from 2016 to 2026 for each job title, and then to compare the trends among job titles. The legend displays at the bottom of the chart to identify the color assigned to each data series in a chart. In this case, blue represents the 2016 data series, and orange represents the 2026 data series.

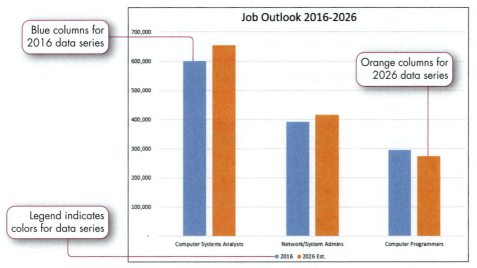

FIGURE 3.5 Clustered Column Chart

> **TIP: SELECTING HEADINGS FOR MULTIPLE DATA SERIES**
> When you create a chart that contains more than one data series, you must include the row and column headings. If you select only the values, Excel will display Series 1 and Series 2 in the legend. In that case, you would not know which color represents what data series.

A **stacked column chart** shows the relationship of individual data points to the whole category by stacking data in segments on top of each other in a column. Only one stacked column displays for each category. Each segment within the stacked column is color-coded for one data series. Use the stacked column chart to compare total values across categories, as well as to display the individual values. Figure 3.6 shows a stacked column chart in which a single column represents each year, and each column stacks color-coded data-point segments representing the different jobs. The stacked column chart compares the total number of computer-related jobs for each year. The height of each color-coded data point shows the relative contribution of each job to the total number of jobs for that year.

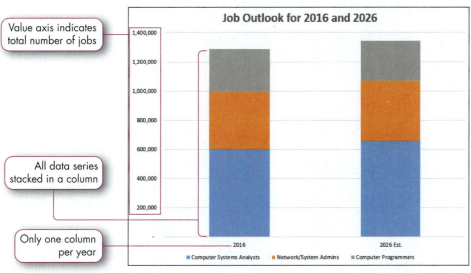

FIGURE 3.6 Stacked Column Chart

When you create a stacked column chart, make sure data are additive: Each column represents a sum of the data for each segment. Figure 3.6 correctly uses years as the category axis and the jobs as data series. For each year, Excel sums the number of jobs, and the columns display the total number of jobs. For example, the estimated total number of the three computer-related jobs in 2026 is about 1,344,000. Figure 3.7 shows a meaningless stacked column chart because the yearly number of jobs by job title is *not* additive. Adding the number of current actual jobs to the number of estimated jobs in the future does not make sense. It is incorrect to state that about 1,255,400 Computer Systems Analysts jobs exist; therefore, it is important to ensure the chart reflects a logical interpretation of data.

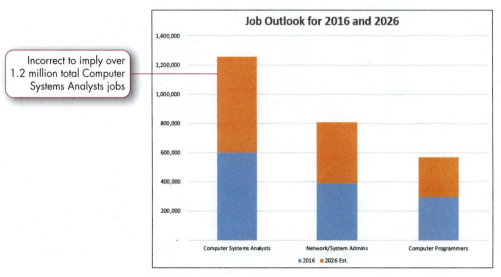

FIGURE 3.7 Incorrectly Constructed Stacked Column Chart

A **100% stacked column chart** converts individual data points (values) into percentages of the total value. Similar to a stacked column chart, each data series is a different color of the stack, though with a 100% stacked column chart, the data series is represented as a percentage of the whole, not as a discrete value. The total of each column is 100%. For example, the chart in Figure 3.8 illustrates that Computer Systems Analysts account for 47–49% of the computer-related jobs in both 2016 and 2026.

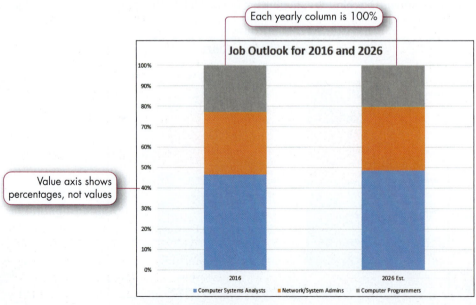

FIGURE 3.8 100% Stacked Column Chart

Move a Chart

When you create a chart, Excel displays the chart in the worksheet where the data is located, often on top of existing worksheet data. Therefore, you should move the chart so that it does not cover up data. With the chart selected, you can use the Cut and Paste commands to move the chart to a different location in the worksheet, or you can drag the chart to a different location. Before dragging a chart, point to the chart area to display the Chart Area ScreenTip, and when the pointer includes the white arrowhead and a four-headed arrow, drag the chart to the new location.

Instead of keeping the chart on the same worksheet as the data source, you can place the chart in a separate worksheet, called a ***chart sheet***. A chart sheet contains a single full-size chart only; you cannot enter data and formulas on a chart sheet. Moving a chart to its own sheet enlarges the chart so that you can easily see the different components of the chart.

To move a chart to a new sheet, complete the following steps:

1. Select the chart.
2. Click the Design tab and click Move Chart in the Location group (or right-click the chart and select Move Chart) to open the Move Chart dialog box (see Figure 3.9).
3. Select *New sheet* to move the chart to its own sheet and type a name for the chart sheet.
4. Click OK.

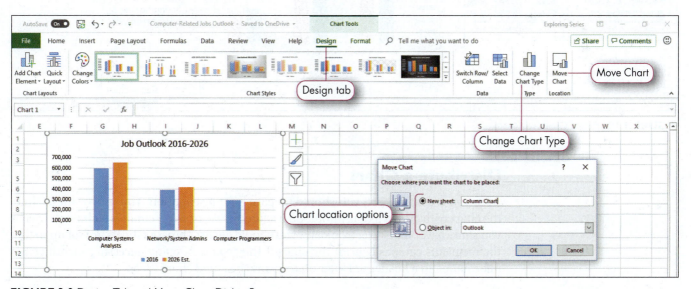

FIGURE 3.9 Design Tab and Move Chart Dialog Box

You can also move the chart as an object to another sheet within the same workbook or to a sheet within another open workbook. For example, you could move all charts to one worksheet to provide a visual summary of the data of key points contained in the workbook. To move a chart to another worksheet, click *Object in* within the Move Chart dialog box and select a worksheet to which you want to move the chart. After you move the chart to that worksheet, you can move it to a different location on that sheet.

Size a Chart

After moving a chart within a worksheet, you can adjust the size of the chart to fit in a range or to ensure the chart is appropriately sized. With the chart selected, you can set height and width of the chart using a *sizing handle*, which is one of eight circles that display around the four corners and outside middle edges of a chart when you select it. Use a middle sizing handle to change either the height or the width of the chart; use a corner-sizing handle to change both the height and width at the same time. When you position the pointer on a sizing handle, the pointer changes to a two-headed arrow so that you can drag the sizing handle to change the size the chart. Press and hold Shift as you drag a corner sizing handle to change the height and width proportionately.

One concern about using sizing handles to adjust the chart size is that the chart may become distorted if you later adjust row height, column width, or insert or delete rows or columns. If you anticipate making these types of changes, use the Shape Height and Shape Width settings in the Size group on the Format tab (see Figure 3.10) instead to change the size of the chart. Setting the height and width on the Format tab ensures the chart dimensions do not change if you adjust column widths or row heights or insert or delete columns or rows in the worksheet.

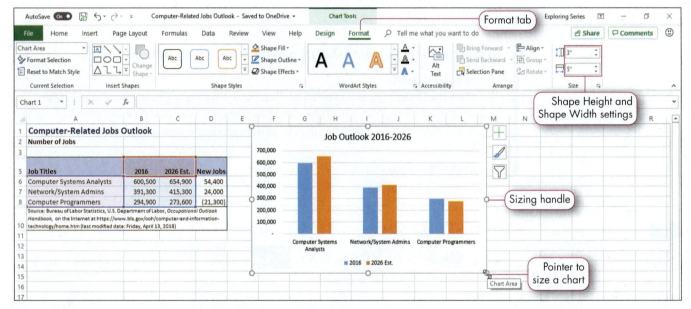

FIGURE 3.10 Sizing a Chart

Distribute a Chart

After you create a chart, you should prepare it for distribution. You may want to share the chart with others as a printout, on a shared drive, or as an email attachment. Even if you share a workbook electronically, you should ensure the worksheets are set up so that the recipients can easily print the chart if they want. Add any necessary identification information in a header or footer on the worksheet and chart sheets.

> **TIP: GROUPING SHEETS TO INSERT HEADERS AND FOOTERS**
> If you insert footers in a workbook containing both regular worksheets and chart sheets, you cannot group all sheets together and insert headers or footers. You can group all chart sheets together to insert a header or footer; then group all regular worksheets together to insert a header or footer.

Follow these guidelines to print a chart:

- If the data and chart are on the same worksheet, but you want to print only the data or only the chart, select the data or the chart, and then display the Print Preview window. Select the Print Selection setting to print spreadsheet data or ensure Print Selected Chart is selected to print the chart.

- To print both the data and chart, display the Print Preview window to ensure the data and chart fit appropriately on a page. Adjust the margins and scaling if needed to achieve the desired printout.

- If the chart is on a chart sheet, the chart is the only item on that worksheet. When you display Print Preview, the chart displays as a full-page chart within the margins.

Using Other Methods to Create Charts

The chart commands in the Chart group on the Insert tab are helpful when you know the exact type of chart you want to create. However, if you are unsure which type of chart would effectively represent the data, you can use the Recommended Charts command or Quick Analysis to review potential charts to depict the selected data source. In addition, you can change the chart type after creating the chart if you decide that another chart type will better depict the data.

STEP 2 Create a Recommended Chart

Use the Recommended Charts command in the Charts group on the Insert tab to display the Insert Chart dialog box (see Figure 3.11). This dialog box contains two tabs: Recommended Charts and All Charts. Excel analyzes the selected data and displays thumbnails of recommended charts. Click a thumbnail to see a larger visualization of how the selected data would look in that chart type. The dialog box displays a message indicating the purpose of the selected chart. When you click OK within the dialog box, Excel creates the type of chart you selected in the dialog box.

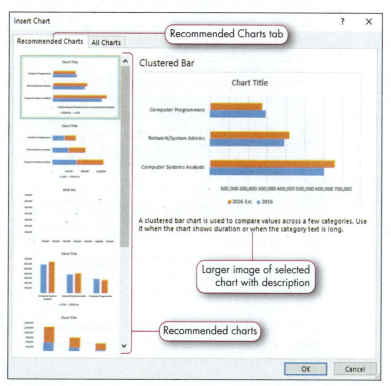

FIGURE 3.11 Insert Chart Dialog Box: Recommended Charts

Change the Chart Type

After you create a chart, you may decide that the data would be better represented by a different type of chart. For example, you might decide a bar chart would display the labels better than a column chart, or you might want to change a clustered bar chart to a stacked bar chart to provide a different perspective for the data. Use the Change Chart Type command to change a chart to a different type of chart. The Change Chart Type dialog box opens, which is similar to the Insert Chart dialog box that contains the Recommended Charts and All Charts tabs.

To change the type of an existing chart, complete the following steps:

1. Select the chart and click the Design tab.
2. Click Change Chart Type in the Type group to open the Change Chart Type dialog box.
3. Click a chart type on the left side of the Change Chart Type dialog box.
4. Click a chart subtype on the right side of the dialog box and click OK.

STEP 3 › ## Create a Chart with Quick Analysis

Recall that when you select a range of adjacent cells (such as the range A5:C12) and position the pointer over that selected range, Excel displays Quick Analysis in the bottom-right corner of the selected area (see Figure 3.12). Quick Analysis does not display when you select nonadjacent ranges, such as ranges A6:A12 and D6:D12.

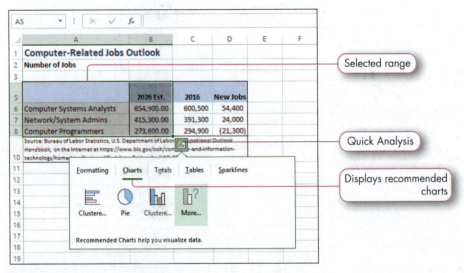

FIGURE 3.12 Quick Analysis Tool

Previously, you used the Quick Analysis tool to insert basic functions for a selected range. Another feature of Quick Analysis is that you can quickly create charts. Similar to Recommended Charts, you can use Quick Analysis to display recommended charts based on the data you selected. The thumbnails of recommended charts change based on the data you select.

To create a chart using Quick Analysis, complete the following steps:

1. Select the data and click Quick Analysis.
2. Click Charts in the Quick Analysis gallery.
3. Point to each recommended chart thumbnail to see a preview of the type of chart that would be created from the selected data.
4. Click the thumbnail of the chart you want to create.

> **MAC TIP:** Quick Analysis is not available for Mac users. Use Recommended Charts or create a chart by using the Insert tab.

Create a Chart with Ideas

Similar to Quick Analysis and Recommended Charts, the new **Ideas feature** provides intelligent analysis of a dataset to recommend potentially useful charts. With the active cell in a dataset or with a range selected, click Ideas in the Ideas group on the Home tab. Ideas analyzes the data and provides visualizations of the data in a task pane. A **task pane** is a window of options specific to a feature in an Office application. The task pane name and options change based on the selected range, object, or feature. For Ideas to work best, the dataset should have single-row, unique headers, no blank cells within the header row and no blank columns or rows within the dataset. Figure 3.13 shows the Ideas task pane with recommended charts using a dataset.

> **MAC TIP:** Ideas may not be available for Mac users.

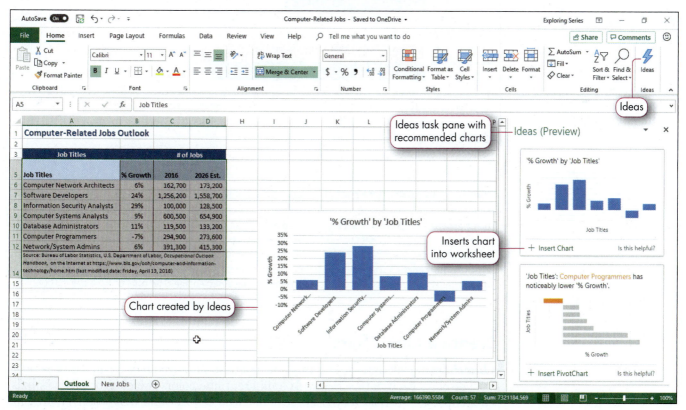

FIGURE 3.13 Charts Recommended by Ideas

Creating Other Charts

Column, bar, line, and pie charts are some of the most common chart types. Other frequently created charts include combo charts, X Y (scatter) charts, and area charts. For people who study the stock market, stock charts are useful.

Create a Bar Chart

A **bar chart** is similar to a column chart in that it compares values across categories. Unlike a column chart that displays values in vertical columns, a bar chart displays values using horizontal bars. The horizontal axis displays values, and the vertical axis displays categories (see Figure 3.14). Bar charts and column charts tell a similar story: they both compare categories of data. A bar chart is preferable when category names are long, such as *Computer Network Architects*. A bar chart displays category names in an easy-to-read format, whereas a column chart might display category names at an awkward angle or in a smaller font size. The overall decision between a column and a bar chart may come down to the fact that different data may look better with one chart type than the other.

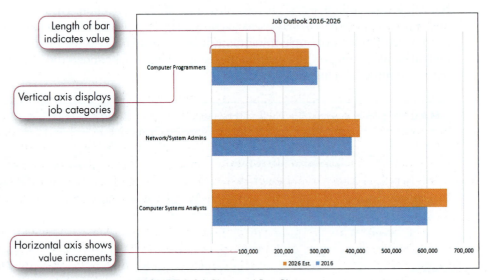

FIGURE 3.14 Clustered Bar Chart

TIP: CLUSTERED, STACKED, AND 100% BAR CHARTS
Similar to column charts, you can create different types of bar charts. A **clustered bar chart** compares groups—or clusters—of bars displayed horizontally in groups. A **stacked bar chart** shows the relationship of individual data points to the whole category. A stacked bar chart displays only one bar for each category. Each category within the stacked bar is color-coded for one data series. A **100% stacked bar chart** converts individual data points (values) into percentages of the total value. Each data series is a different color of the stack, representing a percentage. The total of each bar is 100%.

Create a Line Chart

A **line chart** displays lines connecting data points to show trends over equal time periods. Excel displays each data series with a different line color. The category axis (x-axis) represents time, such as 10-year increments, whereas the value axis (y-axis) represents a value, such as money or quantity. A line chart enables you to detect trends because the line continues to the next data point. To show each data point, choose the Line with Markers chart type. Figure 3.15 shows a line chart indicating the number of majors from 2010 to 2025 (estimated) at five-year increments. The number of Arts majors remains relatively constant, but the number of Technology majors increases significantly over time, especially between the years 2015 and 2025.

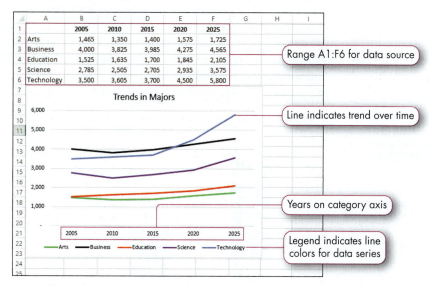

FIGURE 3.15 Line Chart

Create a Pie Chart

A *pie chart* shows each data point as a proportion to the whole data series. The pie chart displays as a circle, or "pie," where the entire pie represents the total value of the data series. Each slice represents a single data point. The larger the slice, the larger percentage that data point contributes to the whole. Use a pie chart when you want to convey percentages for up to seven data points in a data series. Including more than seven data points in a pie chart makes the chart look too cluttered or hard to interpret. Unlike column, bar, and line charts that typically chart multiple data series, pie charts represent a single data series only.

The pie chart in Figure 3.16 divides the pie representing the estimated number of new jobs into three slices, one for each job title. The size of each slice is proportional to the percentage of total computer-related jobs depicted in the worksheet for that year. For example, for the three jobs listed, Computer Systems Analysts account for 49% of the estimated total number of computer-related jobs in 2026. Excel creates a legend to indicate which color represents which pie slice.

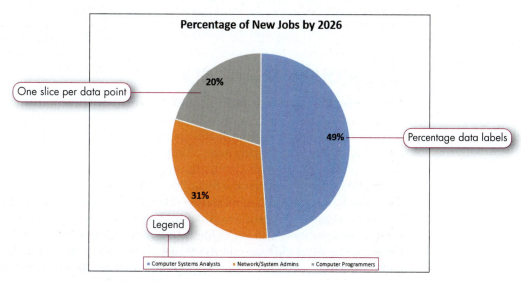

FIGURE 3.16 Pie Chart

Create a Combo Chart

A *combo chart* is a chart that combines two chart types, such as column and line charts. This type of chart is useful to show two different but related data types, such as quantities and percentages. Several types of combo charts are available. A combo chart can share the same axis or have a secondary axis. For example, Figure 3.17 shows a combo chart called *clustered column-line on its secondary axis* that combines a clustered column chart and a line chart to show the number of new jobs in columns and the percentage growth of new jobs in a line within the same chart (see Figure 3.17).

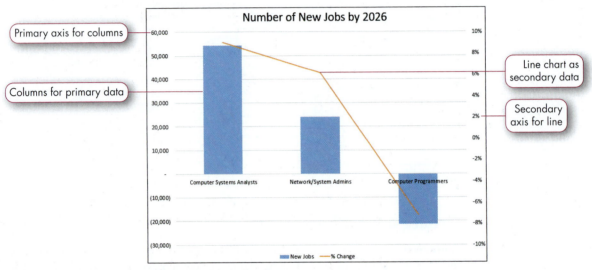

FIGURE 3.17 Combo Chart

When a combo chart has a primary and secondary axis, the primary axis displays on the left side, and the secondary axis displays on the right side. In Figure 3.17, the primary axis on the left side indicates the number of jobs, and the secondary axis on the right side indicates the percentage of new jobs. Combining two chart types (column and line) gives you a better understanding of the data. For example, you know that the 55,000 new Computer Systems Analysts jobs (indicated by the blue column) is about a 9% increase between 2016 and 2026 (indicated by the line).

For more control in designing a combo chart, you can create custom dual-axis combo charts. This method enables you to specify the chart type for each series and specify which series is displayed on the secondary axis. To create a custom combo chart, click Combo in the Charts group on the Insert tab and select Create Custom Combo Chart. The Insert Chart dialog box opens with Combo selected on the left side and the specific options for selecting the chart type and secondary axis on the right side of the dialog box.

Create Other Types of Charts

An *X Y (scatter) chart* shows a relationship between two numeric variables using their X and Y coordinates. Excel plots one variable on the horizontal x-axis and the other variable on the vertical y-axis. Scatter charts are often used to represent data in educational, scientific, and medical experiments. Figure 3.18 shows the relationship between the number of minutes students view a training video and their test scores. The more minutes of a video a student watches, the higher the test score.

A *stock chart* shows fluctuations in stock prices. Excel has four stock subtypes: High-Low-Close, Open-High-Low-Close, Volume-High-Low-Close, and Volume-Open-High-Low-Close. The High-Low-Close stock chart marks a stock's trading range on a given day with a vertical line from the lowest to the highest stock prices. Rectangles mark the opening and closing prices. Table 3.2 lists and describes some of the other types of charts you can create in Excel.

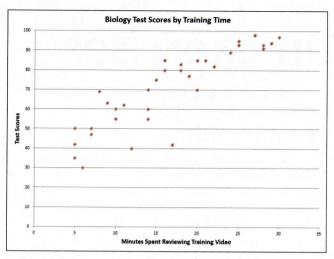

FIGURE 3.18 *X Y* (Scatter) Chart

Chart	Chart Type	Description
TABLE 3.2	**Other Chart Types**	
	**Area chart**	Similar to a line chart in that it shows trends over time; however, the area chart displays colors between the lines to help illustrate the magnitude of changes.
	Surface chart	Represents numeric data and numeric categories. Displays trends using two dimensions on a continuous curve.
	Radar chart	Uses each category as a spoke radiating from the center point to the outer edges of the chart. Each spoke represents each data series, and lines connect the data points between spokes, similar to a spider web. A radar chart compares aggregate values for several data series. For example, a worksheet could contain the number of specific jobs for 2018, 2019, 2020, and 2021. Each year would be a data series containing the individual data points (number of specific jobs) for that year. The radar chart would aggregate the total number of jobs per year for all four data series.
	Histogram	A histogram is similar to a column chart. The category axis shows bin ranges (intervals) where data is aggregated into bins, and the vertical axis shows frequencies. For example, your professor might want to show the number (frequency) of students who earned a score within each grade interval, such as 60–69, 70–79, 80–89, and 90–100.

Quick Concepts

1. Explain the importance of selecting row and column headings when selecting the data source for a chart. *p. 435*

2. Explain when you would create a bar chart instead of a column chart. *p. 444*

3. Explain why a professor would create a pie chart instead of a column chart to show overall class results for a test. *p. 445*

4. Describe the purpose of a combo chart. *p. 446*

Hands-On Exercises

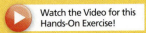

Skills covered: Select a Data Source • Use the Insert Tab to Create a Chart • Create a Column Chart • Move a Chart • Size a Chart • Create a Recommended Chart • Create a Bar Chart • Change the Chart Type • Create a Chart with Quick Analysis • Create a Pie Chart • Create a Combo Chart

1 Chart Basics

Doug Demers, your assistant, gathered data about seven computer-related jobs from the *Occupational Outlook Handbook* online. He organized the data into a structured worksheet that contains the job titles, the number of jobs in 2016, the projected number of jobs by 2026, and other data. Now you are ready to transform the data into charts to detect the trends.

STEP 1 CREATE A BASIC CHART

You want to compare the number of jobs in 2016 to the projected number of jobs in 2026 for the four highest-paid computer-related jobs. You decide to create a clustered column chart to depict this data. After you create this chart, you will move it to the right of the data and adjust its size. Refer to Figure 3.19 as you complete Step 1.

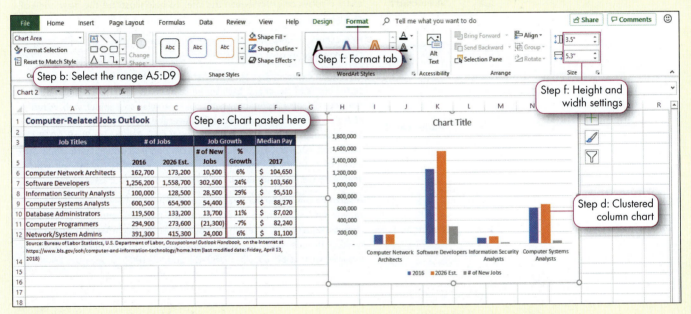

FIGURE 3.19 Clustered Column Chart

a. Open *e03h1Jobs* and save it as **e03h1Jobs_LastFirst**.

> **TROUBLESHOOTING:** If you make any major mistakes in this exercise, you can close the file, open *e03h1Jobs* again, and then start this exercise over.

b. Select the **range A5:D9** on the Outlook sheet.

> You selected the job titles, the number of jobs in 2016, the projected number of jobs in 2026, and the number of estimated new jobs between 2016 and 2026 for the four highest-paid computer jobs listed. Because you are selecting three data series (three columns of numeric data), you must also select the column headings on row 5.

c. Click the **Insert tab** and click **Insert Column or Bar Chart** in the Charts group.

A gallery of column and bar charts displays. The thumbnails provide a visual of the different chart types.

d. Point to **Clustered Column** (the first thumbnail in the 2-D Column group) and click **Clustered Column**.

When you point to a thumbnail, Excel displays a ScreenTip describing what the chart does and when to use it. When you click the thumbnail, Excel inserts a chart in the middle of the worksheet. With the newly created chart selected, the Chart Tools Design and Format tabs display on the ribbon, and sizing handles display around the chart.

e. Click the **Home tab**, click **Cut** in the Clipboard group, click **cell H1**, and then click **Paste**.

You moved the chart from its original location so that the top-left corner is in cell H1.

f. Click the **Format tab**, click in the **Shape Height box** in the Size group, type **3.5**, and then press **Enter**. Click in the **Shape Width box** in the Size group, type **5.3**, and then press **Enter**.

You adjusted the height and width of the chart to make it easier to read. Save the workbook.

STEP 2 ## CREATE A RECOMMENDED CHART AND CHANGE THE CHART TYPE

You want to review potential charts to depict the number of jobs in 2016 and the number of new jobs that will be created by 2026. To help you decide which type of chart to create, you will use the Recommended Chart command to see different chart options. After creating a clustered bar chart, you decide to change it to a stacked bar chart to show the total number of jobs in 2026. Finally, you will move the bar chart to its own chart sheet. Refer to Figure 3.20 as you complete Step 2.

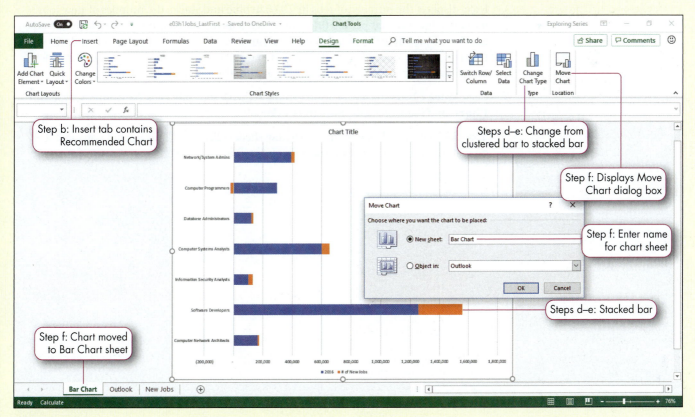

FIGURE 3.20 Stacked Bar Chart on Chart Sheet

a. Select the **range A5:B12**, press and hold **Ctrl**, and then select the **range D5:D12**.

You used Ctrl to select nonadjacent ranges: the job title labels, the number of jobs in 2016, and the number of new jobs. Because you selected nonadjacent ranges, each range must contain the same number of cells. For example, A5:A12, B5:B12, and D5:D12 are parallel ranges. Even though cell A5 is blank, you must include it to have a parallel range with the other two selected ranges that include cells on row 5.

> **TROUBLESHOOTING:** If you do not select parallel ranges, the chart you are about to create will not display correctly. Before continuing, make sure that both ranges A5:B12 and D5:D12 are selected. If not, deselect the ranges and select the correct ranges.

b. Click the **Insert tab** and click **Recommended Charts** in the Charts group.

The Insert Chart dialog box opens, displaying recommended charts based on the data you selected. The first recommended chart is a clustered bar chart. The right side of the dialog box shows how your data will be depicted with the selected chart type.

c. Click **OK**.

Excel inserts a clustered bar chart in the worksheet. You decide that clustered bars do not convey the story you want. You want to display the number of estimated new jobs in addition to the number of jobs in 2016 to show the total estimated number of jobs in 2026. Therefore, you decide to change from a clustered bar chart to a stacked bar chart.

d. Click **Change Chart Type** in the Type group on the Design tab.

The Change Chart Type dialog box opens. The left side of the dialog box lists all chart types. The top-right side displays thumbnails of various bar charts, and the lower section displays a sample of the selected chart. On a Mac, clicking Change Chart Type displays a menu.

e. Click **Stacked Bar** in the top center of the dialog box and click **OK**. Save the workbook.

Excel displays the number of jobs in 2016 in blue and stacks the number of new jobs in orange into one bar per job title. This chart tells the story of how the total projected number of jobs in 2026 is calculated: the number of existing jobs in 2016 and the number of new jobs. Because the estimated number of jobs is expected to decrease for Computer Programmers, the orange displays to the left of the blue bar.

f. Click **Move Chart** in the Location group on the Design tab, click **New sheet**, type **Bar Chart**, and then click **OK**. Save the workbook.

You moved the stacked bar chart to a new sheet called Bar Chart so that you can focus on just the chart. The chart is the only object in a chart sheet.

You decide to create a pie chart that depicts the percentage of new jobs by job title calculated from the total number of new jobs created for six job titles. You will use Quick Analysis because it is a simple way to create a standard pie chart. Because the number of programmers is expected to decrease, you will exclude that data from the pie chart. Refer to Figure 3.21 as you complete Step 4.

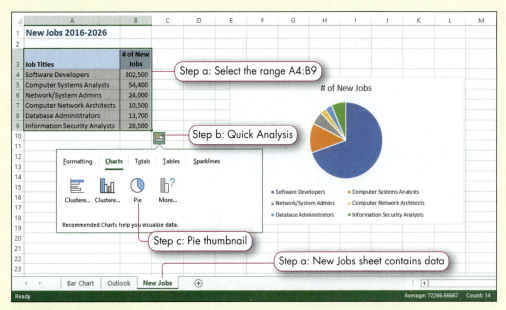

FIGURE 3.21 Pie Chart

a. Click the **New Jobs sheet tab** and select the **range A4:B9**.

While you must select column headings when creating column and bar charts for multi data series, you do not select column headings when selecting data for a pie chart.

b. Click **Quick Analysis** at the bottom-right corner of the selected range and click **Charts**.

> **MAC TROUBLESHOOTING:** Quick Analysis is not available on Excel for Mac. Click the Insert tab, click Pie, click the first option below 2-D Pie and skip Step c.

The Quick Analysis gallery displays recommended charts based on the selected range.

c. Click **Pie**.

Each slice of the pie indicates the percentage of new jobs created by category. The pie chart clearly shows that Software Developers will account for over 50% of the new jobs created between 2016 and 2026.

d. Click **Move Chart** in the Location group on the Design tab, click **New sheet**, type **Pie Chart**, and then click **OK**. Save the workbook.

Excel creates a new sheet called Pie Chart between the Outlook and New Jobs sheets.

You want to create a chart that shows the number of new jobs and the percentage of new jobs. Because the two data types are different, you will create a combo chart. Although the number of new jobs is higher for software developers, the percentage increase is higher for information security analysts. Refer to Figure 3.22 as you complete Step 5.

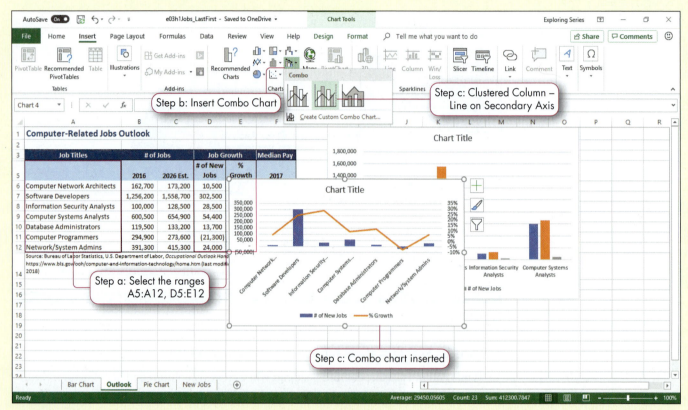

FIGURE 3.22 Combo Chart

a. Click the **Outlook sheet tab**, select the **range A5:A12**, press and hold **Ctrl**, then select the **range D5:E12**.

You selected the job titles, number of new jobs, and percent growth data.

b. Click the **Insert tab** and click **Insert Combo Chart** in the Charts group.

The Combo Chart gallery of thumbnails displays.

c. Click the **Clustered Column – Line on Secondary Axis thumbnail**, which is the middle thumbnail.

Excel creates a combo chart based on the thumbnail you selected. The number of new jobs displays in blue columns, and the percentage growth displays as an orange line. Because the number of programming jobs is expected to decline, the orange line drops below 0.

d. Click **Move Chart** in the Location group on the Design tab, click **New sheet**, type **Combo Chart**, and then click **OK**.

e. Save the workbook. Keep the workbook open if you plan to continue with the next Hands-On Exercise. If not, close the workbook, and exit Excel.

Chart Elements

After creating a chart, you should add appropriate chart elements. A ***chart element*** is a component that completes or helps clarify the chart. Some chart elements, such as chart titles, should be included in every chart. Other elements are optional. When you point to a chart element, Excel displays a ScreenTip with the element name. Table 3.3 describes the chart elements, and Figure 3.23 illustrates several chart elements.

TABLE 3.3	Chart Elements
Element	**Description**
Axis title	Label that describes the category or value axes, such as In Millions of Dollars, to clarify the axis.
Chart area	Container for the entire chart and its elements.
Chart title	Heading that describes the entire chart.
Data label	Descriptive label that shows the exact value or name of a data point.
Data table	Grid that contains the data source values and labels; useful when the chart is on a different sheet from the data source.
Error bars	Visuals that indicate the standard error amount, a percentage, or a standard deviation for a data point or marker.
Gridlines	Horizontal or vertical lines that extend from the tick marks on the value axis across the plot area to guide the reader's eyes across the chart to identify values.
Legend	Box that contains a key to identify the color or pattern assigned to each data series.
Plot area	Region containing the graphical representation of the values in the data series; surrounded by two axes.
Trendline	Line that depicts trends or helps forecast future data, such as estimating future sales or number of births in a region. Add a trendline to column, bar, line, stock, scatter, and bubble charts. Excel analyzes the trends and displays a line indicating future values.

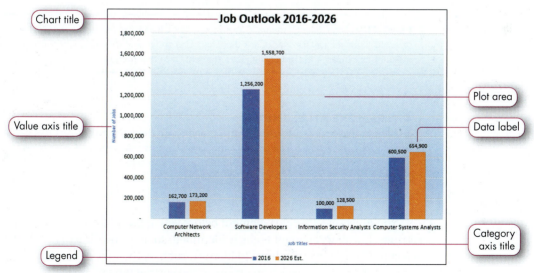

FIGURE 3.23 Chart Elements

In this section, you will learn how to add, edit, and format chart elements. Specifically, you will type a chart title, add axis titles, add data labels, and position the legend. Furthermore, you will learn how to format these elements as well as format axes, position the legend, and add gridlines. Finally, you will learn how to format the chart area, plot area, data series, and a data point.

Adding and Formatting Chart Elements

When you create a chart, one or more elements may display by default. For example, when you created the charts in Hands-On Exercise 1, Excel displayed a placeholder for the chart title and displayed a legend so that you know which color represents each data series. After you create a chart, you usually add elements to enhance the chart. Adding descriptive labels and a meaningful title provide information for the reader to comprehend the chart without knowing or seeing the underlying data. Finally, you can format the chart elements to improve the appearance of the chart.

When a chart is selected, two contextual tabs display: Design and Format. In addition, three icons display to the right of the chart. The top icon is Chart Elements, and when clicked displays a menu so that you can conveniently add or hide chart elements (see Figure 3.24). Click a check box to select and display that element. When you point to the right side of a chart element name on the menu, a triangle displays. Click the triangle to display a submenu specific for that chart element. Click Chart Elements again to hide the menu. Another way to add a chart element is to use the Add Chart Elements command in the Chart Layouts group on the Design tab.

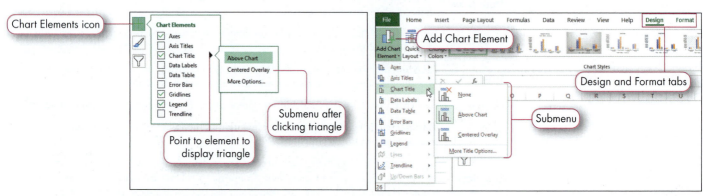

FIGURE 3.24 Add Chart Elements

> **MAC TIP:** The Chart Elements, Chart Styles, and Chart Filters icons do not display next to a selected chart in Excel for Mac. Click the Chart Design tab and click Add Chart Elements to display a menu of chart elements. Select the chart element from that menu.

> **TIP: REMOVE AN ELEMENT**
> To remove an element, click Chart Elements and click a check box to deselect that element. Alternatively, use Add Chart Element in the Chart Layouts group on the Chart Tools Design tab, point to the element name, and then select None. You can also select a chart element and press Delete to remove it.

You must select a chart element before you apply additional formatting or change its settings. If a chart element is easily identified, such as the Chart Title, click the element to select it. If the element is hard to identify, such as the Plot Area, use the Chart Elements arrow in the Current Selection group on the Format tab and select the chart element from the list.

The Chart Elements menu includes a More option. When you select that option or when you double-click a chart element, a task pane displays on the right side of the screen. The task pane name and options change based on the selected chart element. Figure 3.25 shows the components of a task pane.

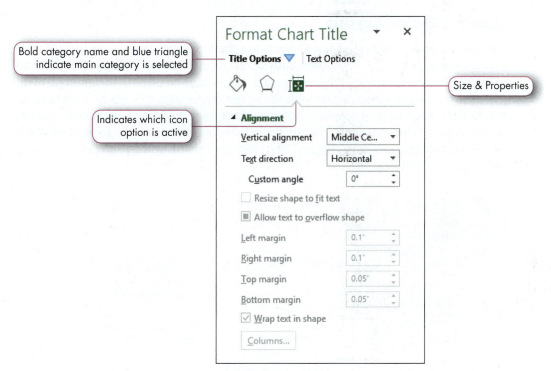

Bold category name and blue triangle indicate main category is selected

Indicates which icon option is active

Size & Properties

FIGURE 3.25 Format Chart Title Task Pane

TIP: ALTERNATIVE FOR OPENING FORMAT TASK PANES
Another way to display a task pane is to right-click the chart element and choose Format Element, where Element is the specific chart element, such as Format Chart Title. If you do not close a task pane after formatting a particular element, such as gridlines, and then click another chart element, the task pane will change so that you can format that chart element.

The top of a task pane displays the name of the task pane, such as Format Chart Title. Task panes contain a hierarchy of categories and subcategories to organize the options and settings. For example, category names such as Title Options and Text Options display below the task pane title. When you select a category, the category name is bold so that you know what category of options is displayed in the task pane.

Icons display below the category names. For example, Fill & Line, Effects, and Size & Properties icons display below the Title Options category name. A thin horizontal gray line separates the icons from the options. The line contains a partial triangle that points to the icon that is active to indicate which options are displayed. Figure 3.25 shows the triangle is pointing to Size & Properties. When you click an icon, the task pane displays specific options. For example, the Size & Properties options include vertical alignment and text direction.

After you select a chart element, you can format the chart element using commands in the Font group on the Home tab. For example, you can apply bold, increase the font size, and change the font color.

TIP: CHANGE THE FONT COLOR FOR CHART ELEMENTS
The default font color for the chart title, axes, axes titles, and legend is Black, Text 1, Lighter 35%. If you want these elements to stand out, change the color to Black, Text 1 or another solid color to improve the contrast, making it easier to read.

Apply a Quick Layout

Use Quick Layout to apply predefined layouts to a chart. Specifically, you can apply a layout to add several chart elements conveniently at one time. Select Quick Layout in the Chart Layouts group on the Design tab (see Figure 3.26). When you point to a thumbnail in the gallery, Excel displays a ScreenTip with the layout name, such as Layout 3, and a list of what chart elements are included. Each layout contains predefined chart elements and their positions. When you apply a layout, your chart does not retain any custom formatting that you might have previously applied. The chart is formatted with the predefined settings of the layout you select.

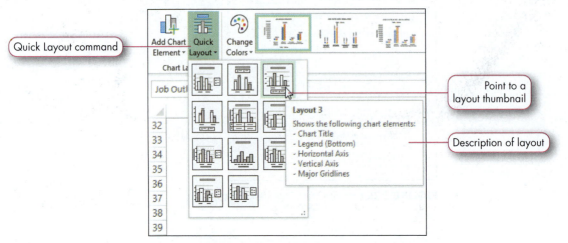

FIGURE 3.26 Quick Layout Gallery

STEP 1 Edit, Position, and Format Chart Titles

Excel includes the placeholder text *Chart Title* above a newly created chart. To give the chart a more meaningful or descriptive title, select the default chart title, type a descriptive title, and press Enter. For example, Houses Sold is too generic, but Houses Sold in Seattle in 2021 indicates the what (Houses), the where (Seattle), and the when (2021).

By default, the chart title displays centered above the plot area. Although this is a standard location for the chart, you can position the chart title elsewhere in the chart area by using the Chart Elements icon. Selecting Centered Overlay centers the chart title over the top of the plot area and increases the height of the plot area. However, only use this location if the overlay title does not hide data points in the plot area. You can also remove the chart title if you position the title immediately below the data source and plan to print both the data source and chart. Refer to Figure 3.24 to identify the chart title options. Use the Home tab to format the chart title.

> **TIP: LINKING A CHART TITLE OR AN AXIS TITLE TO A CELL**
> Instead of typing text directly in the Chart Title or Axis Title placeholder, you can link the title to a label in a cell. Click the Chart Title or Axis Title placeholder, type = in the Formula Bar, click the cell containing the label you want for the title, and then press Enter. The sheet name and cell reference, such as =Outlook!$A$1, displays in the Formula Bar. If you change the worksheet label, Excel will also change the chart title.

STEP 2 Add and Format Axis Titles

Axis titles help people understand charts by adding a brief description of the value or category axis. For example, if the values are abbreviated as 7 instead of 7,000,000, you should indicate the unit of measurement on the value axis as In Millions. To further clarify the labels on the category axis, include a category axis title, such as Job Titles. You can add the following types of axis titles:

- **Primary Horizontal:** Displays a title for the primary horizontal axis.
- **Primary Vertical:** Displays a title for the primary vertical axis.
- **Secondary Horizontal:** Displays a title for the secondary horizontal axis in a combo chart.
- **Secondary Vertical:** Displays a title for the secondary vertical axis in a combo chart.

The horizontal axis title displays below the category labels, and the rotated vertical axis title displays on the left side of the value axis. After adding an axis title, select the title, type the text for the title, and then press Enter similar to editing text for a chart title. Use the Home tab to format axis titles. If you want to further customize an axis title, use the Format Axis Title task pane.

Format the Axes

Based on the data source values and structure, Excel determines the start, incremental, and end values that display on the value axis when you create the chart. However, you can adjust the value axis so that the numbers displayed are simplified or fit better on the chart. For example, when working with large values such as 4,567,890, the value axis displays increments, such as 4,000,000 and 5,000,000. You can simplify the value axis by displaying values in millions, so that the values on the axis are 4 and 5 with the word Millions placed by the value axis to indicate the units.

Double-click the axis to open the Format Axis task pane (see Figure 3.27). Use the Axis Options to specify the bounds, units, display units, labels, and number formatting for an axis. Table 3.4 lists and describes some of the axis options. In addition, you can use the Home tab to format the axis.

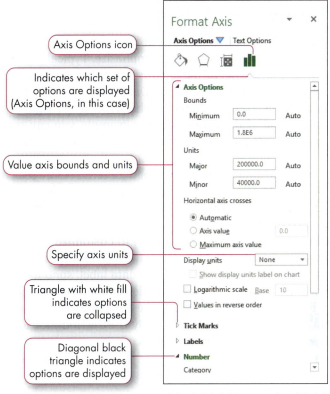
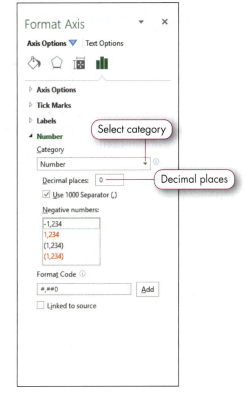

FIGURE 3.27 Format Axis Task Pane

well balanced after you position the legend. Use the Format Legend task pane to customize and format the legend. Use the Home tab to format the legend. For example, select a larger font size and Black, Text 1 font color so that the legend is easier to read.

Add and Format Gridlines

Gridlines are horizontal or vertical lines that span across the plot area of the chart to help people identify the values plotted by the visual elements, such as a column. Excel displays horizontal gridlines for column, line, scatter, surface, and bubble charts and vertical gridlines for bar charts. Use either Chart Elements or Add Chart Elements in the Chart Layouts group on the Design tab to add gridlines.

Format gridlines by double-clicking a gridline to open the Format Major Gridlines task pane. You can change the line type, color, and width of the gridlines so that the gridlines help guide the reader's eye across the column, bar, line, and combo chart.

STEP 4 ## Format the Chart Area, Plot Area, and Data Series

Apply multiple settings, such as fill colors and borders, at once using the Format task pane for an element. To open a chart element's task pane, double-click the chart element. Figure 3.29 displays the Format Plot Area, Format Chart Area, and Format Data Series task panes with different fill options selected to display the different options that result. All three task panes include the same fill and border elements. For example, you change the fill color of a data series from blue to green to complement the green used in the worksheet data. After you select a fill option, such as *Gradient fill*, the remaining options change in the task pane.

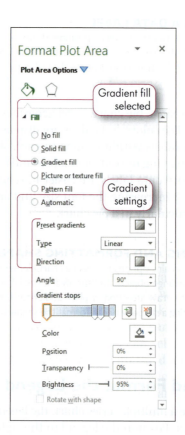
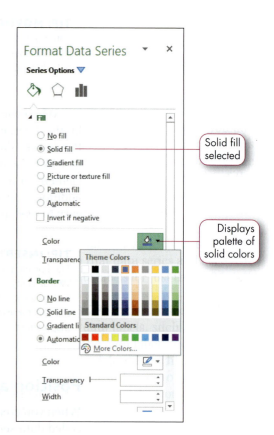

FIGURE 3.29 Format Task Panes

Include Alt Text

It is a good practice to apply some features that are accessibility compliant for people who have disabilities, such as vision or cognitive impairments, that may prevent them from seeing or comprehending the visual aid. In addition to assigning a meaningful name to a chart, you should provide **Alt Text**, also known as *alternative text*, which is a description that displays when a pointer moves over the chart or image. A screen reader can read the description to the user to help them understand the chart. To add Alt Text, click Alt Text in the Accessibility group on the Format tab. Alternatively, right-click the chart and select Edit Alt Text. The Alt Text task pane displays (see Figure 3.30). Enter a description of the chart in the text box and close the task pane.

FIGURE 3.30 Alt Text Task Pane

Format a Data Point

Earlier in this chapter, you learned that a data point reflects a value in a single cell in a worksheet. You can select that single data point in a chart and format it differently from the rest of the data series. Select the data point you want to format, display the Format Data Point task pane, and make the changes you want.

In a pie chart, you can focus a person's attention on a particular slice by separating one or more slices from the rest of the chart in an **exploded pie chart**. Figure 3.31 shows the Computer Network Architects slice is exploded 14%. You can explode a pie slice by selecting the slice and dragging it away from the pie.

d. Click the **Pie Chart sheet tab**, select the **Chart Title placeholder**, type **New Computer-Related Jobs by 2026** in the Formula Bar, and then press **Enter**.

e. Click the **Home tab**, click **Bold**, click the **Font Size arrow** and select **18**, and then click the **Font Color arrow** and select **Black, Text 1**.

You formatted the pie chart title so that it stands out.

f. Click the **Bar Chart sheet tab**, select the **Chart Title placeholder**, type **Projected Number of Jobs by 2026** in the Formula Bar, and then press **Enter**. Click **Bold**, click the **Font Size arrow**, and then select **18**. Click the **Font Color arrow** and click **Black, Text 1** font color to the chart title.

g. Click the **Outlook sheet tab**, select the **Chart Title placeholder**, type **Number of Computer-Related Jobs 2016 and 2026**, and then press **Enter**.

h. Click **Bold**, click the **Font Color arrow**, and then select **Dark Blue** in the Standard Colors section. Save the workbook.

You formatted the bar chart title to have a similar font color as the worksheet title.

STEP 2 **ADD AND FORMAT AXIS TITLES AND FORMAT THE AXES**

For the column chart, you want to add and format a title to describe the job titles on the category axis. In addition, you want to simplify the value axis values to avoid displaying *,000* for each increment and add the title *Thousands*. Refer to Figure 3.33 as you complete Step 2.

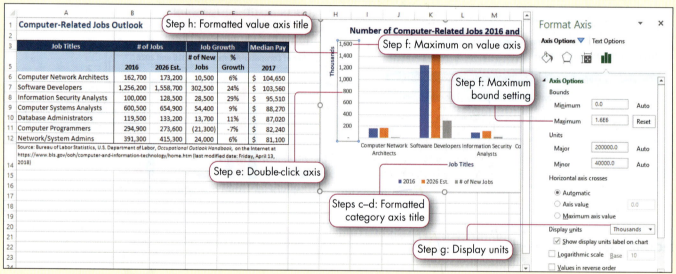

FIGURE 3.33 Formatted Axis Titles and Axes

a. Select the column chart on the Outlook worksheet and click **Chart Elements** to the right of the chart.

Excel displays the Chart Elements menu.

> **MAC TROUBLESHOOTING:** Click the Chart Design tab and click Add Chart Elements.

b. Point to **Axis Titles**, click the **Axis Titles arrow**, and then click the **Primary Horizontal check box** to select it. Click **Chart Elements** to close the menu.

Excel displays Axis Title below the horizontal axis.

c. Ensure that the Axis Title placeholder is selected, type **Job Titles**, and then press **Enter**.

d. Click the **Home tab**, click the **Font Color arrow**, and then click **Dark Blue** in the Standard Colors section.

e. Point to the **vertical axis**. When you see the ScreenTip, *Vertical (Value) Axis*, double-click the values on the vertical axis.

The Format Axis task pane opens for you to format the value axis.

f. Select **1.8E6** in the Maximum Bounds box, type **1.6E6**, and then press **Enter**.

You changed the maximum value on the value axis from 1,800,000 to 1,600,000.

g. Click the **Display units arrow** and select **Thousands**.

> **TROUBLESHOOTING:** If the Display units setting is not shown, click the Axis Options icon, and click Axis Options to display the options.

The axis now displays values such as 1,600 instead of 1,600,000. The title *Thousands* displays in the top-left corner of the value axis.

h. Click the **Home tab**, select the value axis title **Thousands**, and then apply **Dark Blue** font color in the Font group. Close the task pane. Save the workbook.

STEP 3 ADD AND FORMAT DATA LABELS

The pie chart includes a legend to identify which color represents each computer-related job; however, it does not include numeric labels to help you interpret what percentage of all computer-related jobs will be hired for each position. You want to insert and format percentage value labels. Refer to Figure 3.34 as you complete Step 3.

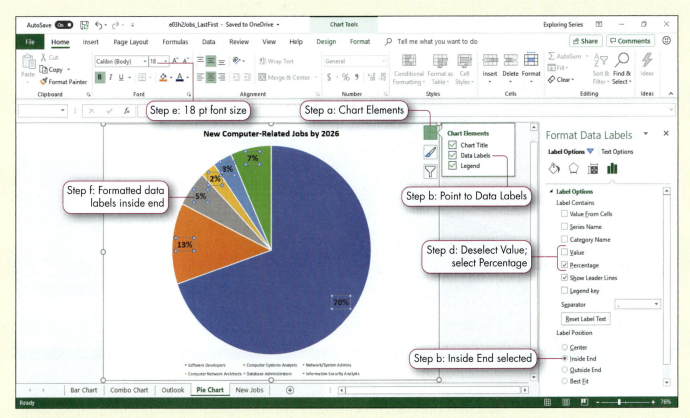

FIGURE 3.34 Formatted Data Labels

a. Click the **Pie Chart sheet tab** and click **Chart Elements**. (On a Mac, click Add Chart Element on the Chart Design tab.)

b. Click the **Data Labels arrow** and select **Inside End**. Close the Chart Elements menu.

   You added data labels to the pie slices. The default data labels show the number of new jobs in the pie slices.

c. Right-click one of the data labels and select **Format Data Labels** to open the Format Data Labels task pane.

d. Click **Label Options**, click the **Percentage check box** to select it, and then click the **Value check box** to deselect it. Close the Format Data Labels task pane.

   Typically, pie chart data labels show percentages instead of values.

e. Click **Bold** and change the font size to **18**. Save the workbook.

STEP 4 FORMAT THE CHART AREA, ADD ALT TEXT, AND FORMAT A DATA POINT

You want to apply a texture fill to the chart area to create a softer appearance around the chart. In addition, you want to change the fill color and explode for the Computer Systems Analysts slice. Refer to Figure 3.35 as you complete Step 4.

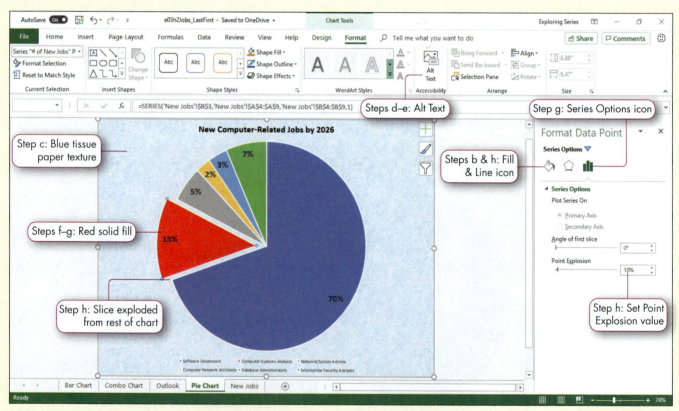

FIGURE 3.35 Formatted Chart Area and Data Point

a. Point to the **chart area** (the white space in the chart) and double-click when you see the Chart Area ScreenTip.

b. Click the **Fill & Line icon** in the Format Chart Area task pane and click **Fill**.

   The task pane displays different fill options.

c. Click **Picture or texture fill**, click the **Texture arrow**, and then click **Blue tissue paper** (fourth row, second column).

The chart area now has the blue tissue paper texture fill.

d. Click the **Format tab** and click **Alt Text** in the Accessibility group.

The Alt Text task pane displays.

> **MAC TROUBLESHOOTING:** Double-click the chart and click Edit Alt Text.

e. Type **Displays the percentage of new computer jobs by job title.** (including the period) in the text box. Close the Alt Text task pane.

You entered a description of the chart.

f. Click the **13% Computer Systems Analyst slice** (which is currently filled with Orange, Accent 2 color), pause, and then click the **Computer Systems Analyst slice** again to select just that data point (slice).

The first click selects all slices of the pie. The second click selects only the Computer Systems Analyst slice so that you can format that data point. Because you did not close the Format Chart Area task pane after Step c, Excel changes the task pane from Format Chart Area to Format Data Point when you select a data point.

g. Click the **Fill & Line icon**, click **Solid fill**, click the **Color arrow**, and then click **Red** in the Standard Colors section.

You changed the fill color from Orange, Accent 2 to Red.

h. Click the **Series Options icon** in the Format Data Point task pane and click the **Point Explosion increment** to **10%**. Close the task pane.

The Computer Systems Analyst slide is now exploded 10% to emphasize that slice.

i. Save the workbook. Keep the workbook open if you plan to continue with the next Hands-On Exercise. If not, close the workbook and exit Excel.

Chart Design and Sparklines

After you add and format chart elements, consider experimenting with other features to enhance a chart. The Chart Tools Design tab contains the Chart Styles and Data groups. These groups contain options to apply a different style or color scheme to a chart or manipulate the data that are used to build a chart. You can also use Chart Styles and Chart Filters to the right of a chart to change the design of a chart. Furthermore, as an alternative to regular charts, you can insert sparklines into cells to provide a quick visualization of a trend in a series of values.

In this section, you will learn how to apply chart styles and colors, filter chart data, and insert and customize miniature charts (sparklines) within individual cells.

STEP 1 ▶ Applying a Chart Style and Colors

After you create a chart and include the chart elements you want, you can change the appearance of the chart by applying a different chart style. A ***chart style*** is a collection of formatting that controls the colors of the chart area, plot area, and data series, as well as the font and font size of the titles. The colors and font attributes are based on the colors defined by the theme applied to the workbook. Selecting a different chart style can save you time from individually applying different colors to the various chart elements.

Figure 3.36 shows the options when you click Chart Styles to the right of the chart, and Figure 3.37 shows the Chart Styles gallery that displays from Chart Styles on the Design tab. The styles in the Chart Styles gallery reflect what is available for the currently selected chart, such as a pie chart. If you select a different type of chart, the gallery will display styles for that type of chart.

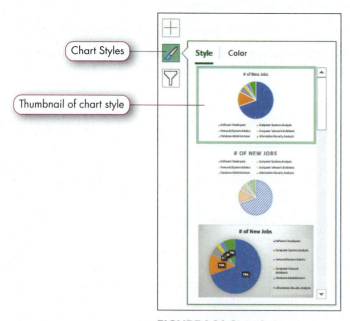

FIGURE 3.36 Chart Styles

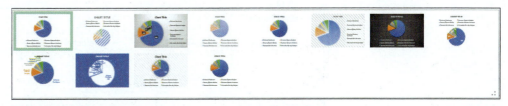

FIGURE 3.37 Chart Styles Gallery

Use Change Colors in the Chart Style group on the Design tab to select a different set of predefined colorful or monochromatic combinations of the colors defined by the workbook theme. The colorful set includes different colors, whereas the monochromatic colors displays different shades of the same color.

> **TIP: CHANGING THE WORKBOOK THEME**
> Explore how different themes impact the colors and formats in your charts by changing the workbook theme. Use Themes on the Page Layout tab to apply a different theme to the workbook, which controls the Change Colors palette and the colors, fonts, and other formatting applied to your charts. You can also customize a workbook theme to use the exact colors you want for the worksheet data as well as the chart elements.

Save a Chart as a Template

You can save a chart as a template to be able to create other charts with those chart elements, formats, and colors. Right-click the chart and select Save as Template from the menu. Enter a name for the chart template and save it. The chart template is available when you display the Insert Chart or the Change Chart Type dialog box and select Templates. If you use the chart template to create a chart in another workbook, Excel uses the chart template colors, not the workbook theme colors.

Modifying the Data Source

The data source is the range of worksheet cells that are used to construct a chart. Although you should select the data source carefully before creating a chart, you may decide to alter that data source after you create and format the chart. The Data group on the Design tab is useful for adjusting the data source. Furthermore, you can apply filters to display or hide a data series without adjusting the entire data source.

STEP 2 ## Change the Data Source

Use the Select Data command in the Data group on the Design tab to open the Select Data Source dialog box (see Figure 3.38). This dialog box is a way to filter which categories and data series are visible in your chart. Furthermore, this dialog box enables you to change the source data range, as well as add, edit, or remove data that is being used to create the chart. Specifically, use this dialog box to add any category labels you forgot to include when you selected the original data source before creating the chart or use this dialog box to remove a data series. For example, you can use this dialog box to remove the 2016 data series or the Software Developers category from being included in the chart.

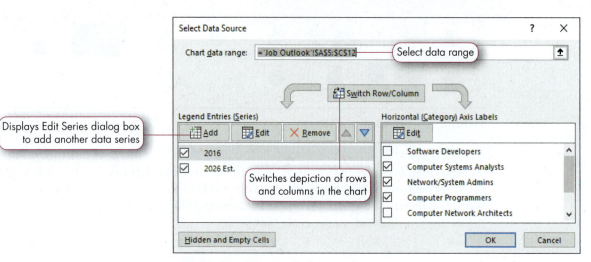

FIGURE 3.38 Select Data Source Dialog Box

Switch Row and Column Data

Recall earlier in the chapter that you learned that data in rows are used to create categories, and data in columns create data series. You can switch data used to create the horizontal axis and the legend to give a different perspective and to change the focus on the data. For example, after displaying years as data series to compare different years for categories, you can switch the data to show years on the category axis to compare job titles within the same year. In Figure 3.39, the chart on the left uses the job titles to build the category axis and the years to build the data series and legend. The chart on the right shows the results after switching the data: the job titles build the data series and legend, and the years display on the category axis. The Switch Row/Column command in the Data group on the Design tab switches how the rows and columns are depicted in the selected chart, or you can switch rows and columns from within the Select Data Source dialog box.

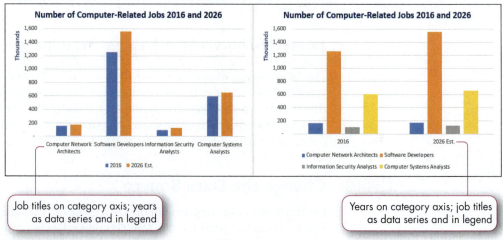

FIGURE 3.39 Original Chart and Chart with Switched Rows/Columns

Apply Chart Filters

A **chart filter** controls which data series and categories are visible in a chart. By default, all the data you selected to create the chart are used to construct the data series and categories. However, you can apply a chart filter to focus on particular data. For example, filter the chart to focus on just one job title at a time. Use Chart Filters to the right of the chart to display the options (see Figure 3.40). A check mark indicates the data series or categories currently displayed in the chart. Use the check boxes to select (display) or deselect (hide) a data series or a category.

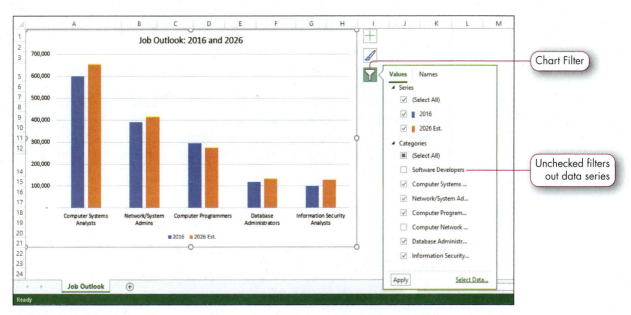

FIGURE 3.40 Chart Filter Options

> **MAC TIP:** The Chart Filters feature is not available on a Mac.

Creating and Customizing Sparklines

A *sparkline* is a small line, column, or win/loss chart contained in a single cell. The purpose of a sparkline is to present a simple visual illustration of data. Unlike a regular chart, a sparkline does not include any of the standard chart labels, such as a chart title, axis label, axis titles, legend, or data labels. Inserting sparklines next to data helps to create a visual "dashboard" to help you understand the data quickly without having to look at a full-scale chart.

Figure 3.41 shows three sample sparklines: line, column, and win/loss. The line sparkline shows trends over time, such as each student's trends in test scores. The column sparkline compares data, such as test averages for a class. The win/loss sparkline depicts the team's trends of wins and losses.

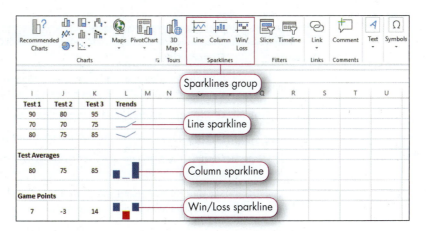

FIGURE 3.41 Sample Sparklines

STEP 3 Insert a Sparkline

Before creating a sparkline, identify the data range you want to depict (such as A2:C2 for the first person's test score) and where you want to place the sparkline (such as cell D2).

To insert a sparkline, complete the following steps:

1. Click the Insert tab.
2. Click Line, Column, or Win/Loss in the Sparklines group. The Create Sparklines dialog box opens (see Figure 3.42).
3. Type in the Data Range box or select the range of cell references containing the values you want to chart with the sparkline.
4. Enter or select the range where you want the sparkline to display in the Location Range box and click OK. The default cell location is the active cell unless you change it.

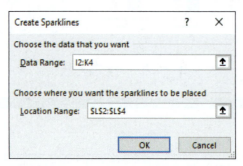

FIGURE 3.42 Create Sparklines Dialog Box

Customize a Sparkline

After you insert a sparkline, the Sparkline Tools Design tab displays (see Figure 3.43), with options to customize the sparkline. Table 3.5 lists and describes the groups on the Sparkline Tools Design tab.

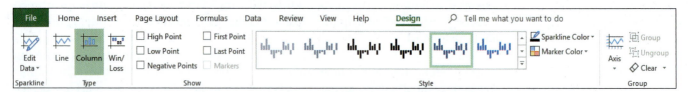

FIGURE 3.43 Sparkline Tools Design Tab

TABLE 3.5	Sparkline Tools Design Tab
Group	**Description**
Sparkline	Edits the location and data source for a group or individual data point that generates a group of sparklines or an individual sparkline.
Type	Changes the selected sparkline type (line, column, win/loss).
Show	Displays points, such as the high points, or markers within a sparkline.
Style	Changes the sparkline style, similar to a chart style, changes the sparkline color, or changes the marker color.
Group	Specifies the horizontal and vertical axis settings, groups objects together, ungroups objects, and clears sparklines.

Quick Concepts

8. Describe the relationship of a workbook theme, chart styles, and chart colors. *p. 459*
9. Explain why you would switch rows and columns in a chart. *p. 470*
10. Describe the purpose of inserting sparklines in a worksheet. *p. 471*

Hands-On Exercises

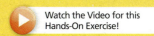
Skills covered: Apply a Chart
Style • Change the Data Source •
Switch Row and Column Data •
Insert a Sparkline • Customize
Sparklines

3 Chart Design and Sparklines

Now that you have completed the pie chart, you want to focus again on the bar chart. You are not satisfied with the overall design and want to try a different chart style. In addition, you want to include sparklines to show trends for all jobs between 2016 and 2026.

STEP 1 APPLY A CHART STYLE

You want to give more contrast to the bar chart. Therefore, you will apply the Style 2 chart style. That style changes the category axis labels to all capital letters and displays data labels inside each segment of each bar. Refer to Figure 3.44 as you complete Step 1.

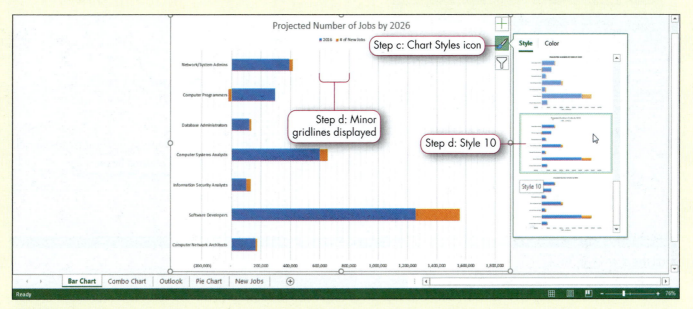

FIGURE 3.44 Chart Style Applied

a. Open *e03h2Jobs_LastFirst* if you closed it at the end of the Hands-On Exercise 2, and save it as **e03h3Jobs_LastFirst**, changing h2 to h3.

b. Click the **Bar Chart sheet tab**.

c. Click **Chart Styles** to the right of the chart.

The gallery of chart styles opens.

> **MAC TROUBLESHOOTING:** Click the Design tab and click More in the Chart Styles group.

d. Scroll through the gallery and point to **Style 10**. When you see the ScreenTip that identifies *Style 10*, click **Style 10**. Click **Chart Styles** to close the gallery. Save the workbook.

Excel applies the Style 10 chart style to the chart, which displays the minor gridlines in light gray between the major gridlines displayed in dark gray. The chart title font changes and is no longer bold using Style 10.

CHANGE THE DATA SOURCE AND SWITCH ROW AND COLUMN DATA

When you first created the clustered column chart, you included the number of new jobs as well as the number of 2016 jobs and the projected number of 2026 jobs. However, you decide that the number of new jobs is implied by comparing the 2016 to the 2026 jobs. Therefore, you want to change the data source to exclude the number of new jobs. In addition, you want to switch the data series from years to job titles for a different perspective. Refer to Figure 3.45 as you complete Step 2.

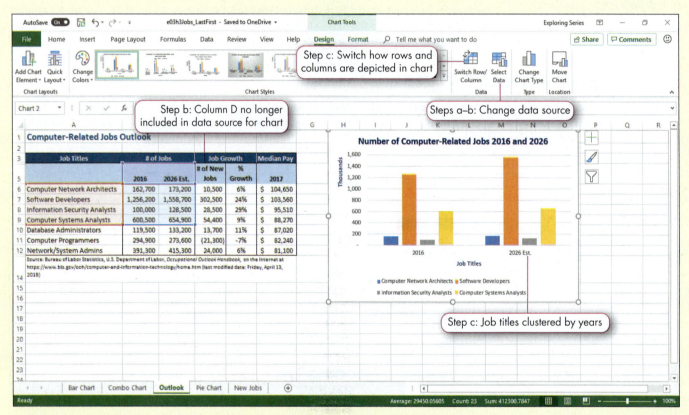

FIGURE 3.45 Chart Filters

a. Click the **Outlook sheet tab**, select the **column chart**, click the **Design tab**, and then click **Select Data**.

The Select Data Source dialog box opens.

b. Change D to **C** in =Outlook!$A$5:$D$9 in the Chart data range box and click **OK**.

The number of new jobs (gray) data series no longer displays in the clustered column chart.

c. Click **Switch Row/Column** in the Data group on the Design tab. Save the workbook.

The columns are arranged by clustering data series for each year rather than clustering the two years for each job title. The legend shows the color coding for the job titles data series.

INSERT AND CUSTOMIZE SPARKLINES

You want to insert sparklines to show the trends between 2016 and 2026. After inserting the sparklines, you want to display the high points to show that all jobs will have major increases by 2026. Refer to Figure 3.46 as you complete Step 3.

FIGURE 3.46 Sparkline Tools Design Tab

a. Click **cell D6** on the Outlook sheet, click the **Insert arrow** in the Cells group, and then select **Insert Sheet Columns**. Type **Trends** in **cell D5**.

You inserted a new column so that you can place the sparklines close to the data you want to visualize.

b. Select the **range B6:C12**, click the **Insert tab**, and then click **Line** in the Sparklines group.

The selected range is entered in the Data Range box in the Create Sparklines dialog box.

> **MAC TROUBLESHOOTING:** Click Sparklines and click Line.

c. Select the **range D6:D12** to enter that range in the Location Range box. Click **OK**.

Excel inserts sparklines in the range D6:D12 with each sparkline representing data on its respective row. The Sparkline Tools Design tab displays.

d. Click the **Markers check box** in the Show group to select it and click **Dark Blue, Sparkline Style Dark #4** in the Style group.

e. Click **Marker Color** in the Style group, point to **Markers**, and then select **Dark Red** in the Standard Colors section.

f. Click **Axis** in the Group group and click **Same for All Sparklines** in the Vertical Axis Minimum Value Options section. Click **Axis** again and click **Same for All Sparklines** in the Vertical Axis Maximum Value Options section.

Because the sparklines look identical in trends, you changed the axis settings to set the minimum and maximum values as relative to the sparkline values in the entire selected range of rows rather than the default setting that bases the minimum and maximum for each row.

g. Save and close the file. Based on your instructor's directions, submit e03h3Jobs_LastFirst.

Chapter Objectives Review

After reading this chapter, you have accomplished the following objectives:

1. Create a basic chart.

- Select the data source: Select row and column headings to create column and bar charts. To select a nonadjacent range, press and hold Ctrl while selecting the ranges. Each value is a data point, and several related data points create a data series in a chart. A legend displays a key to identify the color for each data series. The category axis displays categories of data, and the value axis displays increments of the values used in the chart.

- Use the Insert tab to create a chart: Use commands in the Charts group to create charts. When you click a command, a menu displays specific chart types. Excel creates the selected chart using the data you selected.

- Create a column chart: A clustered column chart compares groups of side-by-side columns where the height of the column indicates its value. The taller the column, the larger the value. A stacked column chart shows relationships of individual data points to the whole. The row headings display on the category axis, and the value axis displays incremental numbers based on the values contained in the columns.

- Move a chart: Use the Cut and Paste commands to move a selected chart to a different area within a worksheet. Use Move Chart in the Location group on the Design tab to display the Move Chart dialog box. Select New sheet and enter a name to move the chart to a chart sheet. The chart is the only object on that sheet.

- Size a chart: If a chart is on a regular worksheet, you can adjust the chart size by dragging a sizing handle or specifying exact measurements in the Size group on the Format tab. Use the Size group on the Format tab to ensure the chart size does not change if you adjust row height, adjust column widths, or add or delete columns or rows.

- Distribute a chart: Before distributing a chart, ensure the worksheets are set up so that recipients can easily print the chart. To print a chart with its data series, the chart needs to be on the same worksheet as the data source. To ensure both the data and the chart print, make sure the chart is not selected. If the chart is on its own sheet or if you select the chart on a worksheet containing other data, the chart will print as a full-size chart.

2. Use other methods to create charts.

- Create a recommended chart: Use the Recommended Charts command in the Charts group on the Insert tab to display the Insert Chart dialog box. Excel displays a gallery of recommended charts based on the selected data. The dialog box displays a message indicating the purpose of the selected chart.

- Change the chart type: After creating a chart, you can change it to a different type by clicking Change Chart Type in the Type group on the Design tab.

- Create a chart with Quick Analysis: When you select a range of adjacent cells and position the pointer over that selected range, Excel displays Quick Analysis near the bottom-right corner of the selected area. Quick Analysis displays thumbnails of recommended charts based on the data you selected so that you can create a chart quickly.

- Create a chart with Ideas: The Ideas feature provides intelligent analysis of a dataset to recommend potentially useful charts. The Ideas task pane displays thumbnails of charts. Click Insert Chart to insert a recommended chart.

3. Create other charts.

- Create a bar chart: A bar chart compares values across categories using horizontal bars where the width of the bar indicates its value. The wider the bar, the larger the value. A stacked bar chart shows relationships of individual data points to the whole.

- Create a line chart: A line chart compares trends over time. Values are displayed on the value axis, and time periods are displayed on the category axis.

- Create a pie chart: A pie chart indicates the proportion to the whole for one data series. The size of the slice indicates the size of the value. The larger the pie slice, the larger the value.

- Create a combo chart: A combo chart combines elements of two chart types, such as column and line, to depict different data, such as individual data points compared to averages or percentages.

- Create other types of charts: An X Y (scatter) chart shows a relationship between two numeric variables. A stock chart shows fluctuations in prices of stock, such as between the opening and closing prices on a specific day.

4. Add and format chart elements.

- Click Chart Elements to the top-right of the selected chart to add elements. Chart elements include a chart title, axis titles, data labels, legend, gridlines, chart area, plot area, data series, and data point.

- Apply a Quick Layout: Applying a layout adds several chart elements conveniently at one time. Each layout specifies which chart elements are displayed and their locations.

- Edit, position, and format chart titles: The default chart title is Chart Title, but you should edit it to provide a descriptive title for the chart. Apply font formats, such as bold, font size, and font color, to the chart title. Position the chart title above the chart, centered and overlaid, or in other locations.

- Add and format axis titles: Display titles for the value and category axes to help describe the axes better. Use the Format Axis Title task pane to customize the axis title. When you click an icon at the top of the task pane, specific options display related to that category.

- Format the axes: Use the Format Axis task pane to set the minimum and maximum bounds, set the major and minor intervals on the value axis, change the unit of display for the value axis, display major and minor tick marks, specify location of the interval labels on the axis, and format numbers.
- Add, position, and format data labels: Data labels provide exact values for a data series. Select the position of the data labels and the content of the data labels. Use the Format Data Labels task pane to customize and format data labels.
- Position and format the legend: Position the legend to the right, top, bottom, or left of the plot area. Change the font size to adjust the label sizes within the legend.
- Add and format gridlines: Gridlines help the reader read across a column chart. Use the Format Major Gridlines task pane to change the line type, color, and width of the gridlines.
- Format the chart area, plot area, and data series: The Format task panes enable you to apply fill colors, select border colors, and apply other settings.
- Include Alt Text: Alternative text is used by a screen reader to help people understand the content of an object, such as a chart. Click Alt Text in the Accessibility group on the Design tab to display the Alt Text task pane. Enter a description of the chart in the text box within the task pane.
- Format a data point: Format a single data point, such as changing the fill color for a single pie slice or specifying the percentage to explode a slice in a pie chart.

5. Apply a chart style and colors.
- A chart style feature applies predetermined formatting, such as the background color and the data series color.
- Save a chart as a template: You can save a chart as a template to be able to create other charts with those chart elements, formats, and colors. The chart template is available when you display the Insert Chart or Change Chart Type dialog box and select Templates.

6. Modify the data source.
- Change the data source: Use the Select Data Source dialog box to filter chart data and change the range of data being used to create the chart.
- Switch row and column data: You can switch the way data is used to create a chart by switching data series and categories.
- Apply chart filters: Use the Select Data Source dialog box to modify the ranges used for the data series. When you deselect a series, Excel removes that series from the chart.

7. Create and customize sparklines.
- Insert a sparkline: A sparkline is a miniature chart in a cell representing a single data series. The Sparklines group on the Insert tab contains commands to insert a line, column, or win/loss sparkline.
- Customize a sparkline: Change the data source, location, and style. Display markers and change line or marker colors.

Key Terms Matching

Match the key terms with their definitions. Write the key term letter by the appropriate numbered definition.

a. Axis title
b. Bar chart
c. Category axis
d. Chart area
e. Chart title
f. Clustered column chart
g. Combo chart
h. Data label
i. Data point
j. Data series

k. Gridline
l. Legend
m. Line chart
n. Pie chart
o. Plot area
p. Sizing handle
q. Sparkline
r. Task pane
s. Value axis
t. X Y (scatter) chart

1. _____ A chart that groups columns side by side to compare data points among categories. **p. 436**

2. _____ A miniature chart contained in a single cell. **p. 471**

3. _____ A chart that shows trends over time in which the value axis indicates quantities and the horizontal axis indicates time. **p. 444**

4. _____ The label that describes the entire chart. **p. 453**

5. _____ The label that describes either the category axis or the value axis. **p. 453**

6. _____ The key that identifies the color or pattern fill assigned to each data series in a chart. **p. 453**

7. _____ A chart that compares categories of data horizontally. **p. 444**

8. _____ A chart that shows each data point in proportion to the whole data series. **p. 445**

9. _____ A numeric value that describes a single value on a chart. **p. 435**

10. _____ A chart that contains two chart types, such as column and line, to depict two types of data, such as individual data points and percentages. **p. 446**

11. _____ A circle that enables you to adjust the height or width of a selected chart. **p. 440**

12. _____ A horizontal or vertical line that extends from the horizontal or vertical axis through the plot area. **p. 453**

13. _____ A chart that shows the relationship between two variables. **p. 446**

14. _____ A group of related data points that display in row(s) or column(s) in a worksheet. **p. 435**

15. _____ A window that contains options specific to a selected text, an object or a feature, such as options to format and customize chart elements. **p. 443**

16. _____ A chart element that contains descriptive labels for the data points plotted in a chart. **p. 435**

17. _____ The section of a chart that contains graphical representation of the values in a data series. **p. 453**

18. _____ A container for the entire chart and all of its elements. **p. 453**

19. _____ An identifier that shows the exact value of a data point in a chart. **p. 453**

20. _____ The chart element that displays incremental numbers to identify approximate values, such as dollars or units, of data points in a chart. **p. 435**

Multiple Choice

1. Which type of chart is the *least* appropriate for depicting yearly rainfall totals for five cities for four years?

   (a) Pie chart

   (b) Line chart

   (c) Column chart

   (d) Bar chart

2. Why would Series 1 and Series 2 display in a chart legend?

   (a) The data are contained in one column.

   (b) The data are contained only in one row.

   (c) Column headings were not selected when creating a chart.

   (d) The selected headings are in non-adjacent cells to the values.

3. You moved a chart to its own chart sheet. What chart element can you add to provide a grid that contains a copy of the data source at the bottom of the chart?

   (a) Axis title

   (b) Data table

   (c) Gridlines

   (d) Error bars

4. You want to create a single chart that shows the proportion of yearly sales for five divisions for each year for five years. Which type of chart can accommodate your needs?

   (a) Pie chart

   (b) Surface chart

   (c) Clustered column chart

   (d) 100% stacked column chart

5. A combo chart displays the number of new jobs on the primary value axis, percentage growth on the secondary value axis, job titles in the category axis, "New Job Growth by 2026" as the chart title, but no legend. Which is the *least important* title to include in the chart?

   (a) The chart title *New Job Growth by 2026*

   (b) The primary value axis title *Number of New Jobs*

   (c) The category axis *Job Titles*

   (d) The secondary value axis title *Percentage Growth*

6. The value axis currently shows increments such as 50,000 and 100,000. What option would you select to display the values in increments of 50 and 100?

   (a) Show Axis in Thousands

   (b) More Primary Vertical Axis Title Options

   (c) Show Axis in Millions

   (d) Show Right to Left Axis

7. If you want to show exact values for a data series in a bar chart, which chart element should you display?

   (a) Chart title

   (b) Legend

   (c) Value axis title

   (d) Data labels

8. You applied a chart style to a clustered column chart. However, you want to experiment with other settings to change the colors used in the chart without individually changing colors. Which of the following *does not* apply changes to the entire chart?

   (a) Change the workbook theme.

   (b) Change colors in the Format Data Series task pane.

   (c) Select a color set from the Change Colors palette.

   (d) Change the colors for the workbook theme.

9. Currently, a column chart shows values on the value axis, years on the category axis, and state names in the legend. What should you do if you want to organize data with the states on the category axis and the years shown in the legend?

   (a) Click Switch Row/Column in the Data group on the Design tab.

   (b) Change the chart type to a clustered column chart.

   (c) Click Layout 2 in the Chart Layouts group on the Design tab and apply a different chart style.

   (d) Click Legend in the Labels group on the Layout tab and select Show Legend at Bottom.

10. You created a worksheet that tracks data for a basketball team. The range B10:F10 contains the difference in final points between your team and the other team. What is the recommended sparkline to create to represent this data?

    (a) Line

    (b) Column

    (c) Win/Loss

    (d) Plus/Minus

Practice Exercises

1 Loza Family Utility Expenses

Your cousin, Alexander Loza, wants to analyze her family's utility expenses for 2021. She gave you her files for the electric, gas, and water bills for the year. You created a worksheet that lists the individual expenses per month, along with yearly totals per utility type and monthly totals. You will create some charts to depict the data. Refer to Figure 3.47 as you complete this exercise.

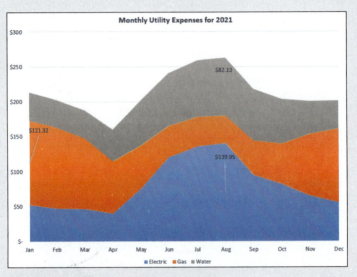

FIGURE 3.47 Loza Family Utility Expenses

a. Open *e03p1Utilities* and save it as **e03p1Utilities_LastFirst**.

b. Select the **range A4:E17**, click **Quick Analysis**, click **Charts**, and then select **Clustered Column**. If Quick Analysis displays two Clustered Column thumbnails, select the thumbnail that shows monthly totals in columns (not as a line).

> **MAC TROUBLESHOOTING:** Quick Analysis is not available on a Mac. Click the Insert tab and click Clustered Column.

c. Click **Chart Filters** to the right of the chart and do the following:
   - Click the **Monthly Totals check box** to deselect it in the Series group
   - Scroll through the Categories group and click the **Yearly Totals check box** to deselect it.
   - Click **Apply** to remove totals from the chart. Click **Chart Filters** to close the menu.

> **MAC TROUBLESHOOTING:** Chart Filters is not available on a Mac.

d. Point to the **chart area**. When you see the Chart Area ScreenTip, drag the chart so that the top-left corner of the chart is in **cell A21**.

e. Click the **Format tab** and change the size by doing the following:
   - Click in the **Shape Height box** in the Size group, type **3.5"**, and then press **Enter**.
   - Click in the **Shape Width box** in the Size group, type **6"**, and then press **Enter**.

f. Click the **Design tab**, click **Quick Layout** in the Chart Layouts group, and then click **Layout 3**.

g. Select the **Chart Title placeholder**, type **Monthly Utility Expenses for 2021**, and then press **Enter**.

h. Click the chart and click **Style 6** in the Chart Styles group.

i. Click the **Home tab**, click **Copy** on the Clipboard group, click **cell A39**, and then click **Paste**. With the second chart selected, do the following:

- Click the **Design tab**, click **Change Chart Type** in the Type group, click **Line** on the left side of the dialog box, select **Line with Markers** in the top-center section, and then click **OK**.
- Click the **Electric data series line** to select it and click the **highest marker (August)** to select only that marker. Click **Chart Elements** and click the **Data Labels check box** to select it.

> **MAC TROUBLESHOOTING:** Click Add Chart Element, point to Data Labels, and then select Above.

- Double-click the **data label** to display the Format Data Labels task pane. Make sure Label Options is bold, click the **Label Options icon**, scroll through the task pane and click **Number**, scroll down, click the **Category arrow**, and then select **Accounting**.
- Click the **Gas data series line** to select it and click the **highest marker (January)** to select only that marker. With the Chart Elements menu displayed, click the **Data Labels check box** to select it.
- Click the **Water data series line** to select it and click the highest marker (August) to select only that marker. With the Chart Elements menu displayed, click the **Data Labels check box** to select it. Click **Chart Elements** to close the menu.
- Double-click the **Water data label** to display the Format Data Labels task pane. Make sure Label Options is bold, click the **Label Options icon**, scroll through the task pane and click **Number**, scroll down, click the **Category arrow**, and then select **Accounting**.
- Select the chart, copy it, and then paste it in **cell A57**.

j. Ensure that the third chart is selected and do the following:

- Click the **Design tab**, click **Change Chart Type** in the Type group, select **Area** on the left side, select **Stacked Area** in the top-center section of the dialog box, and then click **OK**.

> **MAC TROUBLESHOOTING:** Point to Line, scroll down if necessary, and then under 2-D Area, click Stacked Area.

- Click **Move Chart** in the Location group, click **New sheet**, type **Area Chart**, and then click **OK**.
- Select each data label and change the font size to **12**. Move each data label up closer to the top of the respective shaded area. Each label now has a line pointing to where the label had been originally. Apply **Accounting Number Format** to any data labels that did not retain this format.
- Select the **value axis** and change the font size to **12**.
- Right-click the **value axis** and select **Format Axis**. Scroll down in the Format Axis task pane, click **Number**, click in the **Decimal places box**, and then type **0**. Close the Format Axis task pane.
- Change the font size to **12** for the category axis and the legend.

k. Click the **Expenses sheet tab**, select the **line chart**, and do the following:

- Click the **Design tab**, click **Move Chart** in the Location group, click **New sheet**, type **Line Chart**, and then click **OK**.
- Change the font size to **12** for the value axis, category axis, data labels, and legend.
- Apply **Accounting Number Format** to any data labels that did not retain this format.
- Format the vertical axis with zero decimal places.
- Right-click the **chart area**, select **Format Chart Area**, click **Fill**, click **Gradient fill**, click the **Preset gradients arrow**, and then select **Light Gradient – Accent 1**. Close the Format Chart Area task pane.

l. Click the **Expenses sheet**, click the chart area of the **column chart**, click the **Format tab**, and then click **Alt Text** in the Accessibility group. Type **The chart compares the electric, gas, and water bills for each month in 2021.** (including the period) in the text box in the Alt Text task pane. Enter the same Alt Text for the other two charts.

Mid-Level Exercises

1 Airport Passenger Counts

ANALYSIS CASE

As an analyst for the airline industry, you track the number of passengers at the top six major U.S. airports: Atlanta (ATL), Chicago (ORD), Los Angeles (LAX), Dallas/Fort Worth (DFW), Denver (DEN), and New York (JFK). You researched passenger data and created a worksheet that lists the number of total yearly passengers at the top six airports. To prepare for an upcoming meeting, you will create a clustered column chart to compare the number of passengers at each airport. Then, you will create a line chart that compares trends over time. Next, you will create a bar chart to compare the passenger count for the latest year of data available and then emphasize the airport with the largest number of passenger traffic. Finally, you want to insert sparklines to visually represent trends in passengers at each airport over the ten-year period. You can then refer to the sparklines and clustered column chart to answer critical-thinking questions.

a. Open *e03m1Airports* and save it as **e03m1Airports_LastFirst**.

b. Use Quick Analysis to create a clustered column chart for the **range A4:L10**. Cut the chart and paste it in **cell A15**.

c. Customize the column chart by doing the following:
   - Type **Passengers by Top U.S. Airports** as the chart title
   - Swap the data on the category axis and in the legend.
   - Set a **3.5" height** and **11.4" width**.
   - Apply the **Style 7 chart style**.

d. Adjust the value axis by doing the following:
   - Change the display units to **Millions** for the value axis.
   - Edit the axis title to display **Millions of Passengers**.

e. Display data labels above the columns for the 2016 data series only.

f. Apply the **Light Gradient - Accent 1 fill color** to the chart area.

g. Add Alt Text **The column chart displays the number of passengers in millions for the top six airports from 2006 to 2016.** (including the period).

h. Use the Page Layout tab to change the workbook theme to **Slice**.

i. Create a recommended clustered bar chart for the **range A5:A10 and L5:L10** and move the chart to a chart sheet named **Bar Chart**.

j. Customize the bar chart by doing the following:
   - Change the chart color to **Monochromatic Palette 7**.
   - Enter **Passengers at Top 6 U.S. Airports in 2016** as the chart title.
   - Apply the **Style 5 chart style**.
   - Add Alt Text **Atlanta had the most passengers in 2016.** (including the period).

k. Modify the axes by doing the following:
   - Change the font size to **10** for the category axis and value axis.
   - Change the value axis Maximum Bound to **1.1E8**. (The Minimum Bound will change automatically.)

l. Format a data point and add gridlines by doing the following:
   - Format the Atlanta data point with solid **Dark Blue fill color**.
   - Add **Primary Minor Vertical gridlines**.

m. Create a line chart using **the range A4:L10** in the Passengers worksheet and move the chart to a chart sheet named **Line Chart**.

n. Add a chart title **Passengers at U.S. Airports 2006-2016** and bold the title.

o. Customize the line chart by doing the following:
   - Set the **Minimum Bound** at **4.0E7** for the value axis. The Maximum Bound should change to 1.1E8 automatically.
   - Display the value axis in **Millions**. Add a value axis title **In Millions**.
   - Change the font size to **10** for the value axis and category axis.
   - Move the legend to the top.

- Filter the chart by deselecting the odd-numbered years.
- Add the Alt Text **The line chart displays trends for top six U.S. airports from 2006 to 2016 at two-year intervals.** (including the period).

p. Display the Passenger worksheet and insert **Line sparklines** in the **range M5:M10** to illustrate the data in the **range B5:L10**. This should insert a sparkline to represent yearly data for each airport.

q. Customize the sparklines by doing the following:
- Show the high and low points in each sparkline.
- Apply **Black, Text 1 color** to the high point marker in each sparkline.

r. Display the Questions worksheet. Read the question in cell B2 and type the answer in **cell A2**. Read the rest of the questions in column B and type the correct answers in column A in the respective cells.

s. Group the Bar Chart and Line Chart sheets and insert a footer with your name on the left side, the sheet name code in the center, and the file name code on the right on all worksheets. Group the Passenger and Questions sheets and insert a footer with the same data. Change to Normal view.

t. Set the page formats for the Passenger worksheet:
- Select **Legal paper size** and **Landscape orientation**.
- Set **0.3"** left and right margins.
- Scale to fit to 1 page.

u. Save and close the file. Based on your instructor's directions, submit e03m1Airports_LastFirst.

---

2 **Grade Analysis**   **MyLab IT Grader**

You are a teaching assistant for Dr. Elizabeth Croghan's BUS 101 Introduction to Business class. You have maintained her gradebook all semester, entering three test scores for each student and calculating the final average. You created a section called Final Grade Distribution that contains calculations to identify the number of students who earned an A, B, C, D, or F. Dr. Croghan wants you to create a chart that shows the percentage of students who earn each letter grade. Therefore, you decide to create and format a pie chart. You will also create a bar chart to show a sample of the students' test scores. Furthermore, Dr. Croghan wants to see if a correlation exists between attendance and students' final grades; therefore, you will create a scatter chart depicting each student's percentage of attendance with his or her respective final grade average.

a. Open *e03m2Grades* and save it as **e03m2Grades_LastFirst**.

b. Use the Insert tab to create a pie chart from the Final Grade Distribution data located below the student data in the **range F35:G39** and move the pie chart to its own sheet named **Final Grade Distribution**.

c. Customize the pie chart with these specifications:
- Apply the **Style 12 chart style**.
- Type **BUS 101 Final Grades: Fall 2021** for the chart title.
- Explode the A grade slice by **7%**.
- Change the F grade slice to **Dark Red**.
- Remove the legend.
- Add Alt Text **The pie chart shows the percentage of the class that earned each letter grade. Most students earned B and C grades.** (including the period).

d. Add data labels and customize the labels with these specifications:
- Display these data labels: **Percentage** and **Category Name** in the Inside End position. Remove other data labels.
- Change the font size to **20** and apply **Black, Text 1 font color**.

e. Create a clustered bar chart using the **ranges A5:D5** and **A18:D23** in the Grades worksheet and move the bar chart to its own sheet named **Sample Student Scores**.

Capstone Exercise

Fitness Gym

You and a business partner opened a fitness gym three years ago. Your partner oversees managing the operations of the gym, ensuring the right equipment is on hand, maintenance is conducted, and the appropriate classes are being offered with the right trainers and staff. You oversee managing the business aspects, such as marketing, finance, and general personnel issues. The business is nearing the end of its third year. You have put together the financials, and now you want to show the data more visually because you know it will make more sense to your business partner that way. You want to create charts and insert sparklines that show the trends to discuss with your partner.

Create and Move a Basic Chart

You want to focus on just the expenses for the current year. Creating a pie chart will help your partner visualize the breakdown of all operating expenses for that year. After you create the chart, you will move it to a new chart sheet and add a meaningful title.

1. Open *e03c1Gym* and save as *e03c1Gym_LastFirst*.
2. Insert a 2-D pie chart using the **ranges A11:A19** and **D11:D19** on the Income worksheet and move the chart to a new chart sheet named **Expenses**. Move it to the right of the Membership sheet.
3. Change the chart title to **Expenses for Year 3** and change the font size to **20**.

Create a Chart and Apply Filter

Seeing how Payroll and Cost of Sales make up most of the expenses, you want to create a chart to focus on the other expenses. You create a clustered bar chart, filter out Payroll and Cost of Sales, add a title and move the chart to the Summary worksheet.

4. Insert a clustered bar chart using the **ranges A4:D4** and **A11:D19** on the Income worksheet. Move the chart as an object on the Summary worksheet. Cut the chart and paste it in **cell I1**.
5. Change the chart title to **Expenses (Without Payroll and Cost of Sales)**.
6. Select the category axis and use the Format Axis task pane to display categories in reverse order.
7. Apply a chart filter to remove Payroll and Cost of Sales.
8. Change the Maximum Bound to **25000**.

Add and Format Chart Elements

You decide to format the pie chart with data labels and remove the legend because there are too many categories for the legend to be effective. In addition, you want to add a gradient fill color to the chart area.

9. Display the Expenses sheet and remove the legend.

10. Add **Percentage** and **Category Name data labels** and choose **Best Fit** position for the labels. Change the data labels font size to **10**.
11. Explode the Education & Training slice by **12%**.
12. Add the **Light Gradient – Accent 2 fill color** to the chart area.

Create and Modify a Column Chart

You create another chart showing the Balance sheet items. You change the chart to a clustered column and switch the row and column data to focus on each balance sheet item. You move the chart to the Summary worksheet and give it a meaningful title.

13. Insert a stacked column chart using the **ranges A4:D4, A10:D10, A15:D15**, and **A16:D16** on the Balance sheet.
14. Change the chart type to **Clustered Column** and switch the rows and columns in the chart.
15. Change the title to **3-Year Balance Sheet**.
16. Move the column chart to the Summary worksheet. Cut the chart and paste it in **cell A1**.

Create and Format a Line Chart

You create one last chart to show the trend in Memberships. You modify the vertical axis and insert an axis title and move the legend. You change the chart style to add data points and change the chart color. You move the chart to the Summary worksheet.

17. Insert a line chart using the **range I3:L15** on the Membership worksheet.
18. Adjust the vertical axis so the Minimum Bound is **200** and display a vertical axis title **# of Memberships**.
19. Apply **Chart Style 4** and change colors to **Monochromatic Palette 8**.
20. Move the legend to the top of the chart and add the chart title **3-Year Membership Trends**.
21. Move chart to the Summary worksheet. Cut the chart and paste it in **cell A17**.

Add Alt Text

You remember that you should add Alt Text for each chart as a best practice for accessibility.

22. Display the pie chart and add Alt Text **Displays percentage of expenses for Year 3.** (including the period).
23. Display the column chart and add Alt Text **Displays total assets, total liabilities, and retained earnings.** (including the period).

24. Display the bar chart and add Alt Text **Displays expenses for three years without payroll or cost of sales.** (including the period).

25. Display the line chart and add Alt Text **Displays monthly trends in memberships for three years.** (including the period).

Insert Sparklines

Finally, you add sparklines to the Daily Attendance Trends. You add high points to emphasize which time of day is the most popular for your membership.

26. Select **range B16:F16** on the Membership worksheet. Insert **Column Sparklines** using data from the **range B6:F14**.

27. Display the **high points** for the sparklines.

28. Insert a footer with your name on the left side, the sheet name in the center, and the file name code on the right side of the Membership, Expenses, and Summary sheets. Return to Normal view.

29. Save and close the file. Based on your instructor's directions, submit e03c1Gym_LastFirst.

Excel

Datasets and Tables

LEARNING OUTCOME

You will demonstrate how to manage and analyze large sets of data.

OBJECTIVES & SKILLS: After you read this chapter, you will be able to:

CASE STUDY | Reid Furniture Store

Vicki Reid owns Reid Furniture Store in Portland, Oregon. She divided her store into four departments: Living room, Bedroom, Dining room, and Appliances. All merchandise is categorized into one of these four departments for inventory records and sales. Vicki has four sales representatives: Chantalle Desmarais, Jade Gallagher, Sebastian Gruenewald, and Ambrose Sardelis. The sales system tracks which sales representative processed each transaction.

The business has grown rapidly, and Vicki hired you to analyze the sales data to increase future profits. For example, which department generates the most sales? Who is the leading salesperson? Do most customers purchase or finance? Are sales promotions necessary to promote business, or will customers pay the full price?

You downloaded March 2021 data from the sales system into an Excel workbook. Because the dataset is large, you will convert the data into a table, sort, filter, and utilize conditional formatting to complete your analysis.

Managing Large Volumes of Data

Reid Furniture Store

	A	B	C	D	E	F	G	H	I	J
1	Reid Furniture Store									
2	Monthly Transactions:			March 2021						
3	Down Payment Requirement:			25%						
4										
5	Trans_No	Operator	Sales_First	Sales_Last	Date	Department	Furniture	Pay_Type	Trans_Type	Amount
6	2021-001	KRM	Sebastian	Gruenewald	3/1/2021	Bedroom	Mattress	Finance	Promotion	2,788
7	2021-002	RKM	Sebastian	Gruenewald	3/1/2021	Bedroom	Mattress	Finance	Promotion	3,245
8	2021-003	MAP	Jade	Gallagher	3/1/2021	Living Room	Sofa, Loveseat, Chair Package	Finance	Promotion	10,000
9	2021-004	MAP	Jade	Gallagher	3/1/2021	Living Room	End Tables	Finance	Promotion	1,000
10	2021-005	MAP	Jade	Gallagher	3/1/2021	Appliances	Washer and Dryer	Finance	Promotion	2,750
11	2021-006	COK	Ambrose	Sardelis	3/1/2021	Living Room	Sofa, Loveseat, Chair Package	Finance	Promotion	12,000
12	2021-006	COK	Ambrose	Sardelis	3/1/2021	Living Room	Sofa, Loveseat, Chair Package	Finance	Promotion	12,000
13	2021-007	MAP	Jade	Gallagher	3/1/2021	Dining Room	Dining Room Table	Finance	Promotion	3,240
14	2021-008	COK	Chantalle	Desmarais	3/1/2021	Dining Room	Dining Room Table	Finance	Promotion	4,080
15	2021-009	KRM	Sebastian	Gruenewald	3/1/2021	Appliances	Washer and Dryer	Finance	Promotion	2,750
16	2021-010	MAP	Jade	Gallagher	3/2/2021	Dining Room	Dining Room Table and Chairs	Finance	Standard	6,780
17	2021-011	COK	Chantalle	Desmarais	3/2/2021	Dining Room	Dining Room Table and Chairs	Finance	Standard	10,000
18	2021-012	KRM	Ambrose	Sardelis	3/2/2021	Appliances	Washer	Paid in Full	Promotion	1,100
19	2021-013	COK	Chantalle	Desmarais	3/3/2021	Living Room	Recliners	Finance	Standard	2,430
20	2021-014	COK	Jade	Gallagher	3/3/2021	Dining Room	Dining Room Table and Chairs	Paid in Full	Standard	4,550
21	2021-015	MAP	Chantalle	Desmarais	3/3/2021	Living Room	Sofa, Loveseat, Chair Package	Finance	Standard	6,784
22	2021-016	MAP	Jade	Gallagher	3/4/2021	Appliances	Dishwasher	Paid in Full	Standard	640
23	2021-017	MAP	Jade	Gallagher	3/4/2021	Appliances	Refrigerator, Oven, Microwave Combo	Finance	Promotion	8,490
24	2021-018	KRM	Sebastian	Gruenewald	3/4/2021	Appliances	Refrigerator, Oven, Microwave Combo	Finance	Promotion	6,780
25	2021-018	KRM	Sebastian	Gruenewald	3/4/2021	Appliances	Refrigerator, Oven, Microwave Combo	Finance	Promotion	6,780

Page 1 Page 4

Reid Furniture

	A	B	C	D	E	F	G	H	I	J	K
1	Reid Furniture										
2	Monthly Transactions:			March 2021							
3	Down Payment Requirement:			25%							
4											
5	Trans_No	Date	Sales_First	Sales_Last	Department	Furniture		Pay_Type	Trans_Type	Amou	Down_Pa	Owe
6	2021-001	3/1/2021	Sebastian	Gruenewald	Bedroom	Mattress		Finance	Promotion	2,788	697.00	2,091.00
7	2021-002	3/1/2021	Sebastian	Gruenewald	Bedroom	Mattress		Finance	Promotion	3,245	811.25	2,433.75
8	2021-003	3/1/2021	Jade	Gallagher	Living Room	Sofa, Loveseat, Chair Package		Finance	Promotion	10,000	2,500.00	7,500.00
9	2021-004	3/1/2021	Jade	Gallagher	Living Room	End Tables		Finance	Promotion	1,000	250.00	750.00
10	2021-005	3/1/2021	Jade	Gallagher	Appliances	Washer and Dryer		Finance	Promotion	2,750	687.50	2,062.50
11	2021-006	3/1/2021	Ambrose	Sardelis	Living Room	Sofa, Loveseat, Chair Package		Finance	Promotion	12,000	3,000.00	9,000.00
12	2021-007	3/1/2021	Jade	Gallagher	Dining Room	Dining Room Table		Finance	Promotion	3,240	810.00	2,430.00
13	2021-008	3/1/2021	Chantalle	Desmarais	Dining Room	Dining Room Table		Finance	Promotion	4,080	1,020.00	3,060.00
14	2021-009	3/1/2021	Sebastian	Gruenewald	Appliances	Washer and Dryer		Finance	Promotion	2,750	687.50	2,062.50
15	2021-010	3/2/2021	Jade	Gallagher	Dining Room	Dining Room Table and Chairs		Finance	Standard	6,780	1,695.00	5,085.00
16	2021-011	3/2/2021	Chantalle	Desmarais	Dining Room	Dining Room Table and Chairs		Finance	Standard	10,000	2,500.00	7,500.00
17	2021-012	3/2/2021	Ambrose	Sardelis	Appliances	Washer		Paid in Full	Promotion	1,100	1,100.00	-
18	2021-013	3/3/2021	Chantalle	Desmarais	Living Room	Recliners		Finance	Standard	2,430	607.50	1,822.50
19	2021-014	3/3/2021	Jade	Gallagher	Dining Room	Dining Room Table and Chairs		Paid in Full	Standard	4,550	4,550.00	-
20	2021-015	3/3/2021	Chantalle	Desmarais	Living Room	Sofa, Loveseat, Chair Package		Finance	Standard	6,784	1,696.00	5,088.00
21	2021-016	3/4/2021	Jade	Gallagher	Appliances	Dishwasher		Paid in Full	Standard	640	640.00	-
22	2021-017	3/4/2021	Jade	Gallagher	Appliances	Refrigerator, Oven, Microwave Combo		Finance	Promotion	8,490	2,122.50	6,367.50
23	2021-018	3/4/2021	Sebastian	Gruenewald	Appliances	Refrigerator, Oven, Microwave Combo		Finance	Promotion	6,780	1,695.00	5,085.00
24	2021-019	3/5/2021	Jade	Gallagher	Living Room	Sofa		Paid in Full	Standard	2,500	2,500.00	
25	2021-020	3/5/2021	Jade	Gallagher	Living Room	End Tables		Paid in Full	Standard	950	950.00	

March Totals **March Individual**

FIGURE 4.1 Managing Large Datasets

CASE STUDY | Reid Furniture Store

Starting File	File to be Submitted
e04h1Reid	**e04h4Reid_LastFirst**

MyLab IT Grader An alternate version of this project is available as a MyLab IT Grader Assessment

Large Datasets

So far, you have worked with worksheets that contain small datasets, a collection of structured, related data in a limited number of columns and rows. In reality, you will probably work with large datasets consisting of hundreds or thousands of rows and columns of data. When you work with small datasets, you can usually view most or all of the data without scrolling. When you work with large datasets, you probably will not be able to see the entire dataset onscreen even on a large, widescreen monitor set at high resolution. Figure 4.2 shows Reid Furniture Store's March 2021 sales transactions. Because it contains a lot of transactions, the entire dataset is not visible. You could decrease the zoom level to display more transactions; however, doing so decreases the text size onscreen, making it hard to read the data.

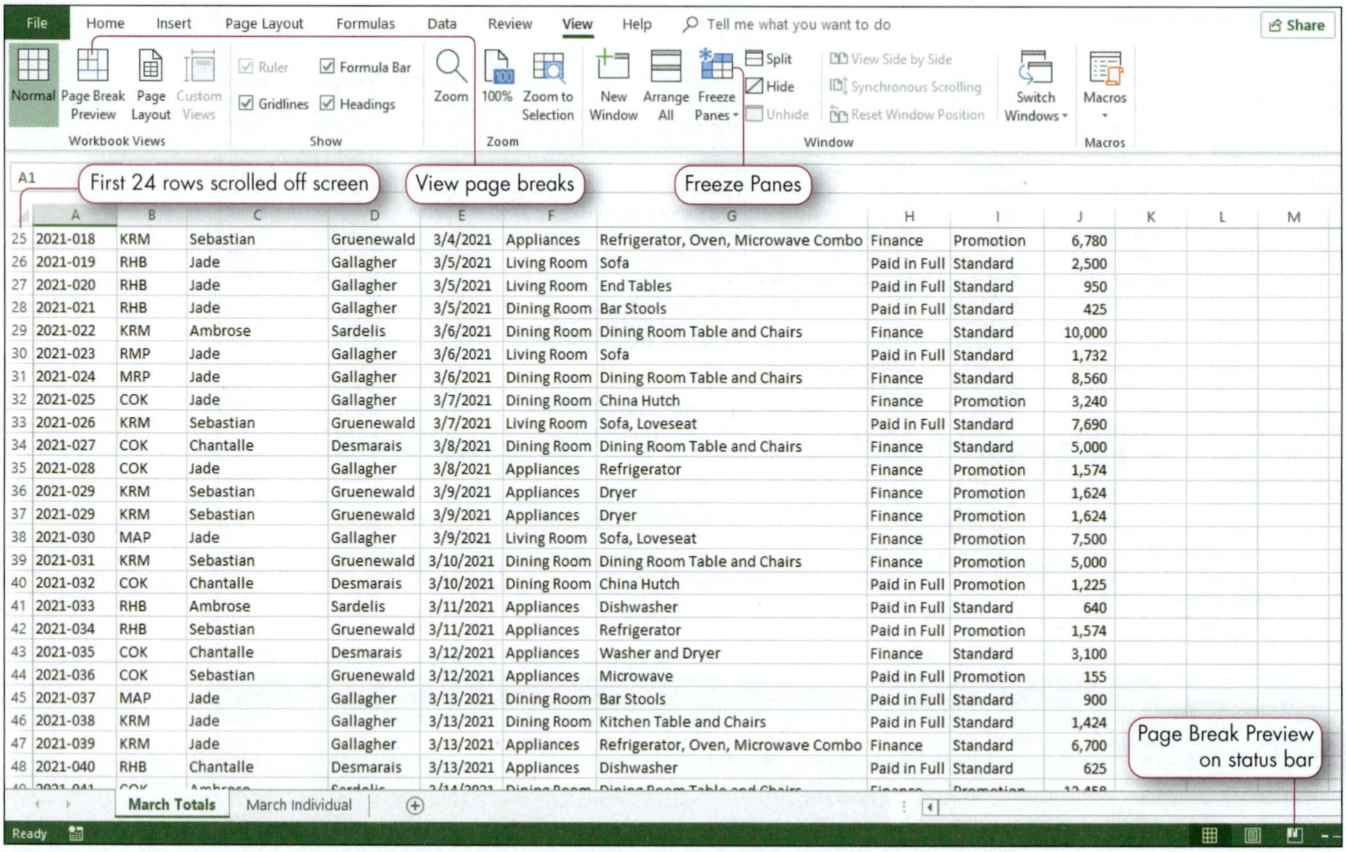

FIGURE 4.2 Large Dataset

As you work with larger datasets, realize that the data will not always fit on one page when it is printed. It will be helpful to keep the column and row labels always in view, even as you scroll throughout the dataset. You will want to preview the automatic page breaks and probably insert some manual page breaks in more desirable locations, or you might want to print only a selected range within the large dataset to distribute to others.

In this section, you will learn how to keep labels onscreen as you scroll through a large dataset. In addition, you will learn how to manage page breaks, print only a range instead of an entire worksheet, print row headings on the left and print column labels at the top of each page of a large dataset.

> **TIP: GO TO A SPECIFIC CELL**
> You can navigate through a large worksheet by using the Go To command. Click Find & Select in the Editing group on the Home tab and select Go To (or press F5 or Ctrl+G) to display the Go To dialog box, enter the cell address in the Reference box, and then press Enter to go to the cell. You can also click in the Name Box, type the cell reference, and then press Enter to go to a specific cell. (On a Mac, click the Edit menu, point to Find, and then select Go To).

STEP 1 Freezing Rows and Columns

When you scroll to parts of a dataset not initially visible, some rows and columns, such as headings, disappear from view. When the row and column labels scroll off the screen, it is hard to remember what each column or row represents. You can keep labels onscreen by freezing them. ***Freezing*** is the process of keeping rows and/or columns visible onscreen at all times even when you scroll through a large dataset. Table 4.1 describes the three freeze options.

TABLE 4.1 Freeze Options

Option	Description
Freeze Panes	Keeps both rows and columns above and to the left of the active cell visible as you scroll through a worksheet.
Freeze Top Row	Keeps only the top row visible as you scroll through a worksheet.
Freeze First Column	Keeps only the first column visible as you scroll through a worksheet.

To freeze one or more rows and columns, use the Freeze Panes option. Before selecting this option, make the active cell one row below and one column to the right of the rows and columns you want to freeze. For example, to freeze the first five rows and the first column, make cell B6 the active cell before clicking the Freeze Panes option. As Figure 4.3 shows, Excel displays a horizontal line below the last frozen row (row 5) and a vertical line to the right of the last frozen column (column F). Unfrozen rows (such as rows 6–20) are no longer visible as you scroll down.

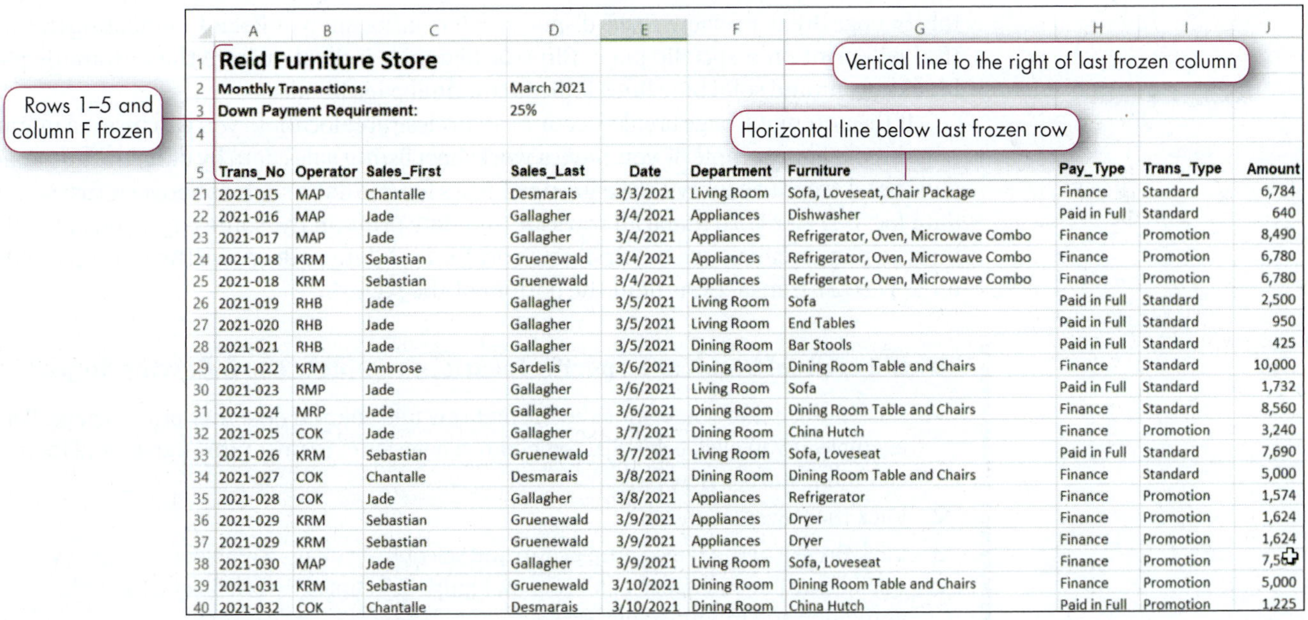

	A	B	C	D	E	F	G	H	I	J
5	Trans_No	Operator	Sales_First	Sales_Last	Date	Department	Furniture	Pay_Type	Trans_Type	Amount
21	2021-015	MAP	Chantalle	Desmarais	3/3/2021	Living Room	Sofa, Loveseat, Chair Package	Finance	Standard	6,784
22	2021-016	MAP	Jade	Gallagher	3/4/2021	Appliances	Dishwasher	Paid in Full	Standard	640
23	2021-017	MAP	Jade	Gallagher	3/4/2021	Appliances	Refrigerator, Oven, Microwave Combo	Finance	Promotion	8,490
24	2021-018	KRM	Sebastian	Gruenewald	3/4/2021	Appliances	Refrigerator, Oven, Microwave Combo	Finance	Promotion	6,780
25	2021-018	KRM	Sebastian	Gruenewald	3/4/2021	Appliances	Refrigerator, Oven, Microwave Combo	Finance	Promotion	6,780
26	2021-019	RHB	Jade	Gallagher	3/5/2021	Living Room	Sofa	Paid in Full	Standard	2,500
27	2021-020	RHB	Jade	Gallagher	3/5/2021	Living Room	End Tables	Paid in Full	Standard	950
28	2021-021	RHB	Jade	Gallagher	3/5/2021	Dining Room	Bar Stools	Paid in Full	Standard	425
29	2021-022	KRM	Ambrose	Sardelis	3/6/2021	Dining Room	Dining Room Table and Chairs	Finance	Standard	10,000
30	2021-023	RMP	Jade	Gallagher	3/6/2021	Living Room	Sofa	Paid in Full	Standard	1,732
31	2021-024	MRP	Jade	Gallagher	3/6/2021	Dining Room	Dining Room Table and Chairs	Finance	Standard	8,560
32	2021-025	COK	Jade	Gallagher	3/7/2021	Dining Room	China Hutch	Finance	Promotion	3,240
33	2021-026	KRM	Sebastian	Gruenewald	3/7/2021	Living Room	Sofa, Loveseat	Paid in Full	Standard	7,690
34	2021-027	COK	Chantalle	Desmarais	3/8/2021	Dining Room	Dining Room Table and Chairs	Finance	Standard	5,000
35	2021-028	COK	Jade	Gallagher	3/8/2021	Appliances	Refrigerator	Finance	Promotion	1,574
36	2021-029	KRM	Sebastian	Gruenewald	3/9/2021	Appliances	Dryer	Finance	Promotion	1,624
37	2021-029	KRM	Sebastian	Gruenewald	3/9/2021	Appliances	Dryer	Finance	Promotion	1,624
38	2021-030	MAP	Jade	Gallagher	3/9/2021	Living Room	Sofa, Loveseat	Finance	Promotion	7,5[illegible]
39	2021-031	KRM	Sebastian	Gruenewald	3/10/2021	Dining Room	Dining Room Table and Chairs	Finance	Promotion	5,000
40	2021-032	COK	Chantalle	Desmarais	3/10/2021	Dining Room	China Hutch	Paid in Full	Promotion	1,225

FIGURE 4.3 Freeze Panes Set

To unlock the rows and columns from remaining onscreen as you scroll, click Freeze Panes in the Window group and select Unfreeze Panes. After you unfreeze the panes, the Freeze Panes option displays on the menu instead of Unfreeze Panes.

When you freeze panes and press Ctrl+Home, the first unfrozen cell is the active cell instead of cell A1. For example, with column F and rows 1 through 5 frozen in Figure 4.3, pressing Ctrl+Home makes cell G6 the active cell. If you want to edit a cell in the frozen area, click the particular cell to make it active and edit the data.

Printing Large Datasets

For a large dataset, some columns and rows may print on several pages. Analyzing the data on individual printed pages is difficult when each page does not contain column and row labels. To prevent wasting paper, always use Print Preview. Doing so enables you to adjust page settings until you are satisfied with how the data will print.

The Page Layout tab (see Figure 4.4) contains options to prepare large datasets to print. Previously, you changed the page orientation, set different margins, and adjusted the scaling. In addition, you can manage page breaks, set the print area, and print titles using the Page Layout tab.

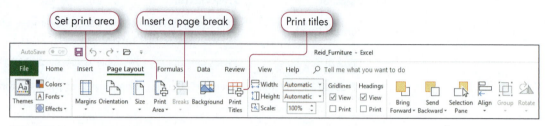

FIGURE 4.4 Page Setup Options

STEP 2 Display and Change Page Breaks

Based on the paper size, orientation, margins, and other settings, Excel identifies how much data can print on a page. Then it displays a ***page break***, indicating where data will start on another printed page. To identify where these automatic page breaks will occur, click Page Break Preview on the status bar or in the Workbook Views group on the View tab. In Page Break Preview, Excel displays watermarks, such as Page 1, indicating the area that will print on a specific page. Blue dashed lines indicate where the automatic page breaks occur and solid blue lines indicate manual page breaks.

If the automatic page breaks occur in an undesirable location, you can insert a manual page break. For example, if you have a worksheet listing sales data by date, the automatic page break might occur within a group of rows for one date, such as between two rows of data for 3/1/2021. To make all rows for that date print on the same page, you can either insert a page break above the first data row for that date or decrease the margins so that all 3/1/2021 transactions fit at the bottom of the page.

> **To set a manual break at a specific location, complete the following steps:**
>
> 1. Click the cell that you want to be the first row and column on a new printed page. For example, if you click cell D50, you create a page for columns A through C, and then column D starts a new page.
> 2. Click the Page Layout tab.
> 3. Click Breaks in the Page Setup group and select Insert Page Break. Excel displays a solid blue line in Page Break Preview. Figure 4.5 shows a worksheet with both automatic and manual page breaks.

An alternative method is to use the pointer to adjust a page break by pointing to the page break line to see the two-headed arrow and dragging the line to the location where you want the page break to occur. If you want to remove a manual page break, click below the horizontal line indicating the page break or to the right of the vertical page break, click Breaks in the page Setup group and click Remove Page Break. You can also reset all page breaks by using the Breaks command in the Page Setup group.

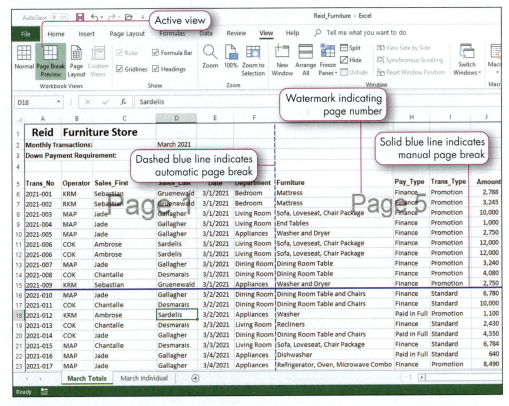

FIGURE 4.5 Page Breaks in Page Break Preview

Set and Clear a Print Area

The default Print settings send an entire dataset on the active worksheet to the printer. However, you might want to print only part of the worksheet data. If you display the worksheet in Page Break view, you can identify which page(s) you want to print. Then click the File tab and select Print. Under Settings, type the number(s) of the page(s) you want to print. For example, to print page 2 only, type 2 in the Pages text box and in the *to* text box.

You can further restrict what is printed by setting the ***print area***, which is the range of cells that will print. For example, you might want to print only an input area or just the transactions that occurred on a particular date. Begin by selecting the range you want to print, click the Page Layout tab, and then click Print Area in the Page Setup group. Next use the Set Print Area command to set the print area you want.

In Page Break Preview, the print area has a white background and solid blue border; the rest of the worksheet has a gray background (see Figure 4.6). In Normal view or Page Layout view, the print area is surrounded by thin gray lines.

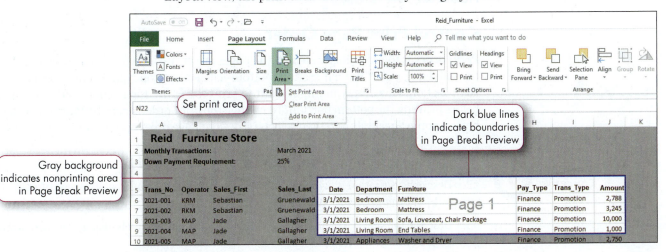

FIGURE 4.6 Print Area in Page Break Preview

To add print areas where each print area will print on a separate page, select the range you want to print, click Print Area, and then select Add to Print Area. You can clear the print area by clicking Print Area in the Page Setup group and selecting Clear Print Area.

> **TIP: PRINT A SELECTION**
> Another way to print part of a worksheet is to select the range you want to print. Click the File tab and click Print. Click the first arrow in the Settings section and select Print Selection. This provides additional flexibility compared to using a defined print area in situations in which you may be required to print materials outside a consistent range of cells.

STEP 4 ## Print Titles

When you print large datasets, it is helpful if every page contains descriptive column and row labels. When you click Print Titles in the Page Setup group on the Page Layout tab, Excel opens the Page Setup dialog box with the Sheet tab active so that you can select which row(s) and/or column(s) to repeat on each page of a printout (see Figure 4.7).

To repeat rows or columns at the top or left of each page when printed, select the row(s) that contain the labels or titles (such as row 5) in the *Rows to repeat at top* box to display $5:$5. To print the row labels at the left side of each page, select the column(s) that contain the labels or titles (such as column A) in the *Columns to repeat at left* box to display AA.

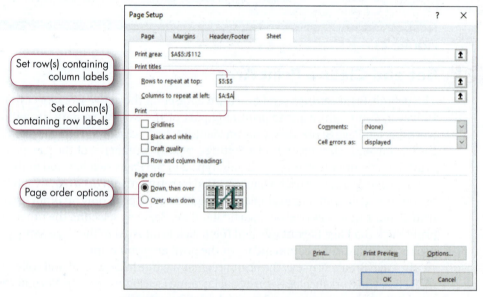

FIGURE 4.7 Sheet Tab Options

Control Print Page Order

Print order is the sequence in which the pages are printed. By default, the pages print in the following order: top-left section, bottom-left section, top-right section, and bottom-right section. However, you might want to print the entire top portion of the worksheet before printing the bottom portion. To change the print order, open the Page Setup dialog box, click the Sheet tab, and then select the desired Page order option (refer to Figure 4.7).

Quick Concepts

1. Explain the purpose of freezing panes in a worksheet. **p. 493**

2. Describe a situation in which you would want to insert page breaks instead of using the automatic page breaks. **p. 494**

3. Describe the steps you should take to ensure that column labels display on each printed page of a large dataset. **p. 496**

Hands-On Exercises

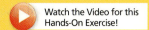

Skills covered: Freeze
Rows and Columns • Display and
Change Page Breaks • Set and
Clear a Print Area • Print Titles

1 Large Datasets

You want to review the large dataset that shows the March transactions for Reid Furniture Store. You will view the data and adjust some page setup options so that you can print necessary labels on each page.

STEP 1 FREEZE ROWS AND COLUMNS

Before printing the March transaction dataset, you want to view the data. The dataset contains more rows than will display onscreen at the same time. You decide to freeze the column and row labels to stay onscreen as you scroll through the transactions. Refer to Figure 4.8 as you complete Step 1.

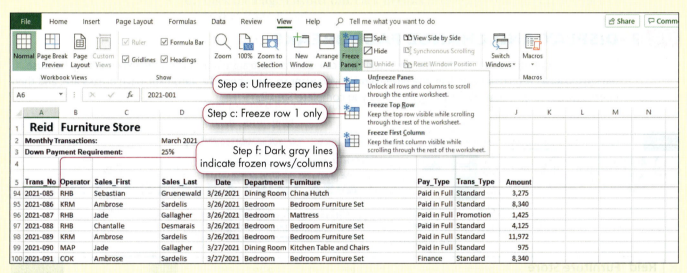

FIGURE 4.8 Freeze Panes Activated

    a. Open *e04h1Reid* and save it as **e04h1Reid_LastFirst**. Ensure the March Totals worksheet is active.

> **TROUBLESHOOTING:** If you make any major mistakes in this exercise, you can close the file, open *e04h1Reid* again, and then start this exercise over.

    The workbook contains two worksheets: March Totals (for Hands-On Exercises 1–3) and March Individual (for Hands-On Exercise 4).

    b. Press **Page Down** five times to scroll through the dataset, note the column headers are not visible. Press **Ctrl+Home** to go back to the top of the worksheet.

    After you press Page Down, the column labels in row 5 scroll off the screen, making it challenging to remember what type of data are in some columns.

    c. Click the **View tab**, click **Freeze Panes** in the Window group, and then select **Freeze Top Row**.

    A dark gray horizontal line displays between rows 1 and 2.

    d. Press **Page Down** to scroll down through the worksheet.

    As rows scroll off the top of the Excel window, the first row remains frozen onscreen. The title by itself is not helpful; you need to freeze the column labels as well.

Excel Tables

All organizations maintain lists of data. Businesses maintain inventory lists, educational institutions maintain lists of students and faculty, and governmental entities maintain lists of contracts. Although more complicated related data should be stored in a database management program, such as Access, you can manage basic data structure in Excel tables. A *table* is a structured range that contains related data organized in a method that increases the capability to manage and analyze information.

In this section, you will learn table terminology and rules for structuring data. You will create a table from existing data, manage records and fields, and remove duplicates. You will then apply a table style to format the table.

Exploring the Benefits of Data Tables

When dealing with large datasets it is imperative that documents are strategically organized to maintain data integrity and ease of use. Thus far you have worked with the manipulation of data ranges, and while you can use many tools in Excel to analyze simple data ranges, tables provide many additional analytical and time saving benefits. Using tables in Excel can help create and maintain data structure. *Data structure* is the organization method used to manage multiple data points within a dataset. For example, a dataset of students may include names, grades, contact information, and intended majors of study. The data structure of this dataset would define how the information is stored, organized, and accessed. Although you can manage and analyze data structure as a range in Excel, a table provides many advantages:

- Column headings remain onscreen without having to use Freeze Panes.
- Table styles easily format table rows and columns with complementary fill colors.
- Calculated columns enable you to create and edit formulas that copy down the columns automatically.
- A calculated total row enables you to implement a variety of summary functions.
- You can use structured references instead of cell references in formulas.

Designing and Creating Tables

The Reid furniture data is entered in the worksheet as a range. Converting the range into a table will help further manipulate the data. A table is a group of related data organized in a series of rows and columns that is managed independently from any other data on the worksheet. Once a data range is converted into a table, each column represents a *field*, which is an individual piece of data, such as last names or quantities sold. Each field should represent the smallest possible unit of data. For example, instead of a Name field, separate name data into First Name and Last Name fields. Instead of one large address field, separate address data into Street Address, City, State, and ZIP Code fields. Separating data into the smallest units possible enables you to manipulate the data in a variety of ways for output.

> **TIP: FLASH FILL**
> Flash Fill can be used to separate data such as first and last names across columns. To use Flash Fill to split data, enter the first name or value in the first column to the right of the original content. In the next row, type the first few letters of the next name and press Enter.

Each row in a table represents a *record*, which is a collection of related data about one entity. For example, all data related to one particular transaction form a record in the Reid Furniture Store worksheet.

You should plan the structure before creating a table. The more thoroughly you plan, the fewer changes you will have to make to gain information from the data in the table after you create it. To help plan your table, follow these guidelines:

- Enter field (column) names on the top row of the table.
- Keep field names short, descriptive, and unique. No two field names should be identical.
- Format the field names so that they stand out from the data.
- Enter data for each record on a row below the field names.
- Do not leave blank rows between records or between the field names and the first record.
- Delete any blank columns between fields in the dataset.
- Make sure each record has something unique, such as a transaction number or ID.
- Insert at least one blank row and one blank column between the table and other data, such as the main titles. When you need multiple tables in one workbook, a best practice is to place each table on a separate worksheet.

STEP 1 ▸ Create a Table

By taking the time to create an organized data structure, you will ensure that the data can be used to identify specific information easily, is efficient to manage, and is scalable. When your worksheet data is structured correctly, you can easily create a table.

To create a table from existing data, complete the following steps:

1. Click within the existing range of data.
2. Click the Insert tab and click Table in the Tables group. The Create Table dialog box opens (see Figure 4.12), prompting you to enter the range of data.
   - Select the range for the *Where is the data for your table* box if Excel does not correctly predict the range.
   - Click the *My table has headers* check box if the existing range contains column labels.
3. Click OK to create the table.

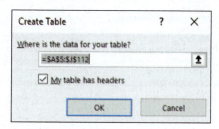

FIGURE 4.12 Create Table Dialog Box

If the results are not what you expect, an existing table can be converted back into a range. To convert a table back to a range, click within the table range, click the Table Tools Design tab, click Convert to Range in the Tools group, and then click Yes in the message box asking, *Do you want to convert the table to a normal range.*

> **TIP: QUICK ANALYSIS TABLE CREATION**
> You can also create a table by selecting a range, clicking the Quick Analysis button, clicking Tables (see Figure 4.13) in the Quick Analysis gallery, and then selecting Table. While Quick Analysis is efficient for tasks such as creating a chart, it may take more time to create a table because you must select the entire range first. Some people find that it is faster to create a table on the Insert tab. The Quick Analysis feature is only available for PC. (On a Mac, use the Insert tab to create a table.)

FIGURE 4.13 Quick Analysis Gallery

After you create a table, the Table Tools Design tab displays. Excel applies the default Table Style Medium 2 style to the table and each cell in the header row has filter arrows (see Figure 4.14).

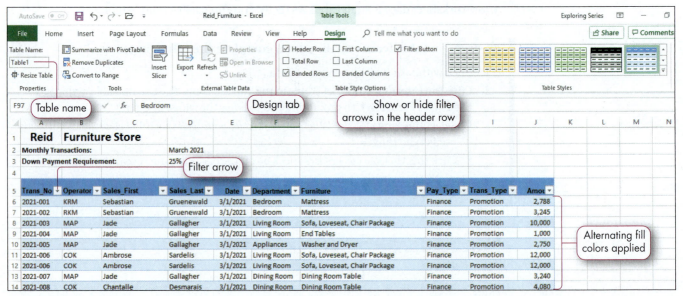

FIGURE 4.14 Excel Table in Default Format

Instead of converting a range to a table, you can create a table structure first and add data to it later. Select an empty range and follow the previously listed steps to create the range for the table. The default column headings are Column1, Column2, and so on. Click each default column heading and type a descriptive label. Then enter the data into each row of the newly created table.

STEP 2 · Rename a Table

By default, when a table is created, Excel assigns a name automatically. For example, the first table created in a worksheet will be named Table1 (refer to figure 4.14). The default nomenclature does not provide descriptive information and, as a best practice, you should change the default name to something more meaningful. Not only does changing the name provide clarification, it also is a good practice for accessibility compliance. The name of the table can be changed using the Table Name box in the Properties group on the Table Tools Design tab. Once a name has been assigned to a table, it can be used when building functions in place of the traditional absolute references.

STEP 3 > Add and Delete Fields

After creating a table, you can insert new fields. For example, you might want to add a field for product numbers to the Reid Furniture Store transaction table. To insert a new column in a table, select any data cell in a field that will be to the right of the new field. Then use the Insert Table Columns to the Left feature located on the Home tab in the Cells group.

If you want to add a field at the end of the right side of a table, click in the cell to the right of the last field name and type a label. Excel will extend the table to include that field and will format the cell as a field name.

You can also delete a field if you no longer need any data for that particular field. Although deleting records and fields is easy, you must make sure not to delete data erroneously. To delete a field in a table, select a cell in the field you want to delete and use the Delete Table Columns feature located on the Home tab in the Cells group. If you accidentally delete data, click Undo immediately.

STEP 4 > Add, Edit, and Delete Records

After you begin storing data in your newly created table, you can add new records, such as a new client or a new item to an inventory table. One of the advantages to using tables in Excel is you can easily add, edit, or delete records within the dataset.

To add a record to a table, complete the following steps:

1. Click a cell in the record below which you want the new record inserted. If you want to add a new record below the last record, click the row containing the last record.
2. Click the Home tab and click the Insert arrow in the Cells group.
3. Select Insert Table Rows Above to insert a row above the current row or select Insert Table Row Below if the current row is the last one and you want a row below it.

You can also add a record to the end of a table by clicking in the row immediately below the table and typing. Excel will extend the table to include that row as a record in the table and will apply consistent formatting.

You might want to change data for a record. For example, when a client moves, you will change the client's address. You edit data in a table the same way you edit data in a regular worksheet cell.

Finally, you can delete records. For example, if you maintain an inventory of artwork in your house and sell a piece of art, delete that record from the table. To delete a record first select the record you want to remove. Next use the Delete Table Rows feature located on the Home tab in the Cells group to remove the entire row.

STEP 5 > Remove Duplicate Rows

Due to clerical issues or human error, a table might contain duplicate records, which can give false results when totaling or performing other calculations on the dataset. For a small table, you might be able to scan the data to detect duplicate records and delete them manually. For large tables, it is more difficult and less time efficient to identify duplicate records by simply scanning the table with the eye. The Remove Duplicates command launches the Remove Duplicates dialog box (see Figure 4.15) which enables you to automatically locate and remove all duplicates. This feature is located on the Design tab. To remove duplicate records, select any cell in the table, click the Design tab, and click Remove Duplicates in the Tools group. Select the columns with duplicate values in the Remove Duplicates dialog box and click OK.

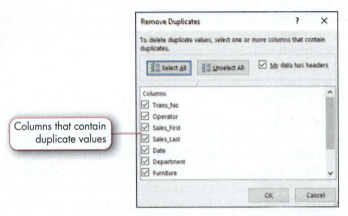

FIGURE 4.15 Remove Duplicates Dialog Box

Applying a Table Style

When you create a table, it is automatically formatted with the default table style of alternating colored rows and bold format for the header row. A ***Table style*** controls the fill color of the header row (the row containing field names) and rows of records. In addition, table styles specify heading formats and border lines. You can change the table style to complement your organization's color scheme or to emphasize data in the header rows or columns. Click More in the Table Styles group to display the Table Styles gallery (see Figure 4.16). On a PC to see how a table style will format your table using Live Preview, point to a style in the Table Styles gallery. After you identify a style you want, select it to apply it to the table. (Note: Live Preview is unavailable on a Mac).

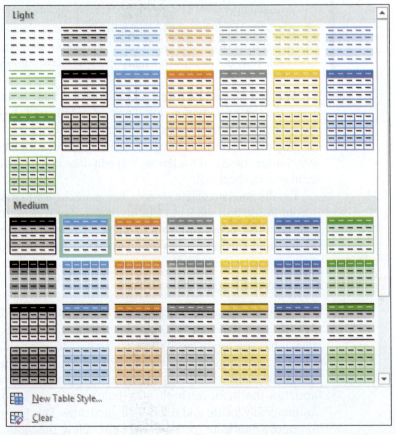

FIGURE 4.16 Table Styles Gallery

After you select a table style, you can control what the style formats. The Table Style Options group contains check boxes to select specific format actions in a table. Table 4.2 lists the options and the effect of each check box. Avoid over-formatting the table. Applying too many formatting effects may obscure the message you want to present with the data. Be sure to apply only formatting and options that best reflect the data. For example, add a total row only when you want to summarize key performance indicators in the data.

TABLE 4.2	Table Style Options
Check Box	**Action**
Header Row	Displays the header row (field names) when selected; removes field names when deselected. Header Row formatting takes priority over column formats.
Total Row	Displays a total row when selected. Total Row formatting takes priority over column formats.
First Column	Applies a different format to the first column so that the row headings stand out. First Column formatting takes priority over Banded Rows formatting.
Last Column	Applies a different format to the last column so that the last column of data stands out; effective for aggregated data, such as grand totals per row. Last Column formatting takes priority over Banded Rows formatting.
Banded Rows	Displays alternate fill colors for even and odd rows to help distinguish records.
Banded Columns	Displays alternate fill colors for even and odd columns to help distinguish fields.
Filter Button	Displays a filter button on the right side of each field name in the header row.

Quick Concepts

4. List at least four guidelines for planning a table in Excel. ***pp. 502–503***

5. Discuss two reasons why you would convert a range of data into an Excel table. ***p. 502***

6. Describe a situation in which it would be beneficial to add a total row. ***p. 502***

Hands-On Exercises

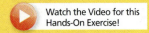
MyLab IT HOE2 Sim Training

Watch the Video for this
Hands-On Exercise!

Skills covered: Create a
Table • Rename a Table • Add
and Delete Fields • Add, Edit, and
Delete Records • Remove Duplicate
Rows • Apply a Table Style

2 Excel Tables

You want to convert the March Totals data to a table. As you review the table, you will delete the
unnecessary Operator field, add two new fields, insert a missing furniture sale transaction, and remove
duplicate transactions. Finally, you will enhance the table appearance by applying a table style.

STEP 1 CREATE A TABLE

Although Reid Furniture Store's March transaction data are organized in an Excel worksheet, you know that you will
have additional functionality if you convert the range to a table. Refer to Figure 4.17 as you complete Step 1.

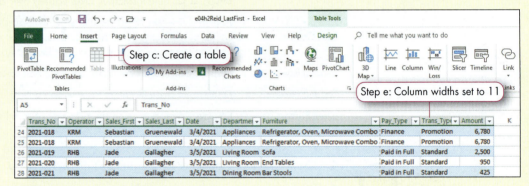

FIGURE 4.17 Range Converted to a Table

a. Open *e04h1Reid_LastFirst* if you closed it at the end of Hands-On Exercise 1, and save it
as **e04h2Reid_LastFirst**, changing h1 to h2.

b. Unfreeze the panes and scroll through the data.

With a regular range of data, column labels scroll off the top of the screen if you do not
freeze panes. When you scroll within a table, the table's header row remains onscreen by
moving up to where the Excel column (letter) headings usually display. Note that it will
not retain the bold formatting when scrolling.

c. Click in any cell within the transactional data, click the **Insert tab**, and then click **Table**
in the Tables group.

The Create Table dialog box opens. The *Where is the data for your table?* box displays
=$A$5:$J$112. Keep the *My table has headers* check box selected so that the headings on
the fifth row become the field names for the table.

d. Click **OK** and click **cell A5**.

Excel creates a table from the data range and displays the Design tab, filter arrows, and
alternating fill colors for the records.

e. **Ctrl** and click the field names, **Sales_First**, **Sales_Last**, **Department**, **Pay_Type**, and
Trans_Type. Click the **Home tab**, click **Format** in the Cells group, and then select
Column Width. Type 11 in the column width box and click **OK**.

f. Save the workbook.

RENAME THE TABLE

After creating the table, you will change the name from the default *Table 2* to a more descriptive title that meets your business standards. Refer to Figure 4.18 as you complete Step 2.

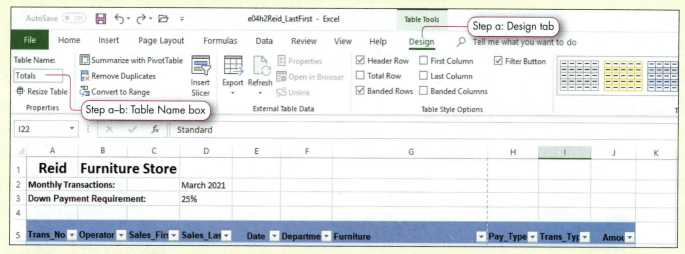

FIGURE 4.18 Rename the Table

a. Click the Design tab and click the **Table Name box** in the Properties group.

b. Type **Totals** in the Table Name box and press **Enter**.

You have given the table a custom name.

ADD AND DELETE FIELDS

The original range included a column for the data entry operators' initials. You will delete this column because you do not need it for your analysis. In addition, you want to add a field to display down payment amounts in the future. Refer to Figure 4.19 as you complete Step 3.

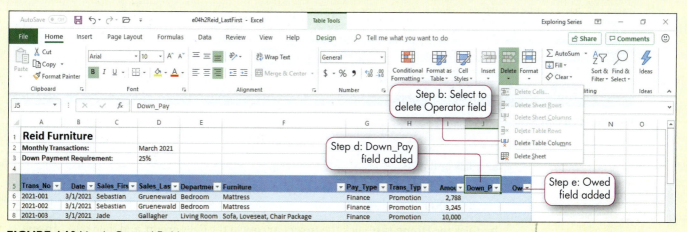

FIGURE 4.19 Newly Created Fields

a. Click any cell containing a value in the Operator column.

You need to make a cell active in the field you want to remove.

b. Click the **Home tab**, click the **Delete arrow** in the Cells group, and then select **Delete Table Columns**.

Excel deletes the Operator column and may adjust the width of other columns.

c. Set the widths of columns E, F, and G to **AutoFit**. Click **cell J5**, the first blank cell on the right side of the field names.

d. Type **Down_Pay** and press **Enter**.

Excel extends the table formatting to column J automatically. A filter arrow displays for the newly created field name, and alternating fill colors appear in the rows below the field name.

e. Click **cell K5**, type **Owed**, and then press **Enter**. Save the workbook.

STEP 4 ▶ ADD RECORDS

As you review the March transaction table, you notice that two transactions are missing: 2021-068 and 2021-104. After finding the paper invoices, you are ready to add records with the missing transaction data. Refer to Figure 4.20 as you complete Step 4.

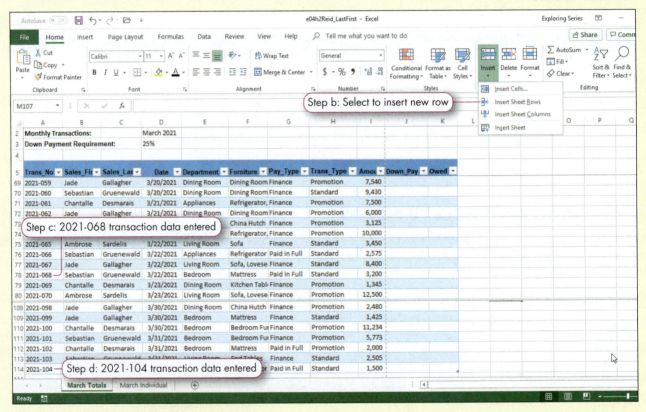

FIGURE 4.20 Missing Records Added

a. Click **cell A78**.

The missing record 2021-068 needs to be inserted between 2021-067 on row 77 and 2021-069 on row 78.

b. Click the **Home tab**, click the **Insert arrow** in the Cells group, and then select **Insert Table Rows Above**.

Excel inserts a new table row on row 78, between the 2021-067 and 2021-069 transactions.

c. Enter the following data in the respective fields on the newly created row:

2021-068, Sebastian, Gruenewald, 3/22/2021, Bedroom, Mattress, Paid in Full, Standard, 3200

d. Click **cell A114** and enter the following data in the respective fields:

2021-104, **Ambrose**, **Sardelis**, **3/31/2021**, **Appliances**, **Refrigerator**, **Paid in Full**, **Standard**, **1500**

When you start typing 2021-104 in the row below the last record, Excel immediately includes and formats row 114 as part of the table. Review Figure 4.20 to ensure that you inserted the records in the correct locations. In the figure, rows 81–109 are hidden to display both new records in one screenshot.

e. Save the workbook.

STEP 5 **REMOVE DUPLICATE ROWS**

You noticed that the 2021-006 transaction is duplicated on rows 11 and 12 and that the 2021-018 transaction is duplicated on rows 24 and 25. You think the table may contain other duplicate rows. To avoid having to look at the entire table row by row, you will have Excel find and remove the duplicate rows for you. Refer to Figure 4.21 as you complete Step 5.

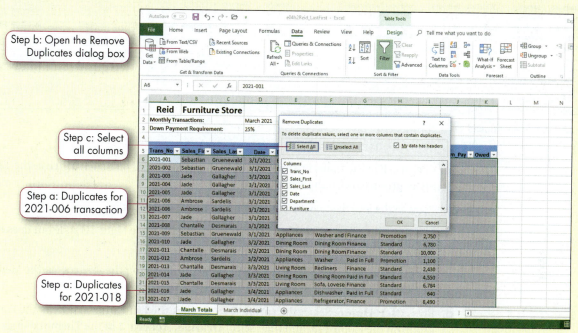

FIGURE 4.21 Remove Duplicate Records

a. Click a cell in the table. Scroll to see rows 11 and 12. Click the **Design tab**.

The records on rows 11 and 12 are identical. Rows 24 and 25 are also duplicates. You need to remove the extra rows.

b. Click **Remove Duplicates** in the Tools group.

The Remove Duplicates dialog box opens.

c. Ensure Select All is selected, ensure the *My data has headers* check box is selected, and then click **OK**.

Excel displays a message box indicating 5 *duplicate records found and removed; 104 unique values remain.*

d. Click **OK** in the message box. Click **cell A109** to view the last record in the table. Save the workbook.

Transaction 2021-104 is located on row 109 after the duplicate records are removed.

STEP 6 › APPLY A TABLE STYLE

Now that you have finalized the fields and added missing records to the March transaction table, you want to apply a table style to format the table. Refer to Figure 4.22 as you complete Step 6.

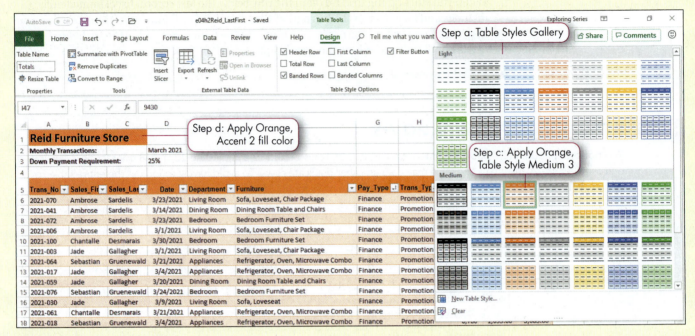

FIGURE 4.22 Table Style Applied

a. Click a cell in the table. Ensure the Design tab is displayed and click **More** in the Table Styles group to open the Table Styles gallery.

b. Point to the fourth style on the second row in the Light section.

Live Preview shows the table with the Orange, Table Style Light 10 style but does not apply it.

c. Select **Orange, Table Style Medium 3**, the third style on the first row in the Medium section.

d. Press **Ctrl+Home**. Select the **range A1:C1**, click the **Fill Color arrow** in the Font group on the Home tab, and then select **Orange, Accent 2** in the Theme colors.

You applied a fill color for the title to match the fill color of the field names on the header row in the table.

e. Save the workbook. Keep the workbook open if you plan to continue with the next Hands-On Exercise. If not, close the workbook, and exit Excel.

Table Manipulation

Along with maintaining data structure, tables have a variety of options to enhance and manipulate data, in addition to managing fields, adding records, and applying table styles. You can build formulas and functions, arrange records in different sequences to get different perspectives on the data, and restrict the onscreen appearance of data using filtering. For example, you can arrange the transactions by sales representative. Furthermore, you can display only particular records instead of the entire dataset to focus on a subset of the data. For example, you might want to focus on the financed transactions.

In this section, you will learn how to create structured references, and how to sort records by text, numbers, and dates in a table. In addition, you will learn how to filter data based on conditions you set.

STEP 1 Creating Structured References in Formulas

Your experience in building formulas involves using cell references, such as =SUM(B1:B15) or =H6*$B$3. Cell references in formulas help to identify where the content is on a worksheet but do not tell the user what the content represents. An advantage to Excel tables is that they use structured references to clearly indicate which type of data is used in the calculations. A ***structured reference*** is a tag, or the use of a table element such as a field heading, as a reference in a formula. As shown in Figure 4.23, structured references in formulas clearly indicate which type of data is used in the calculations.

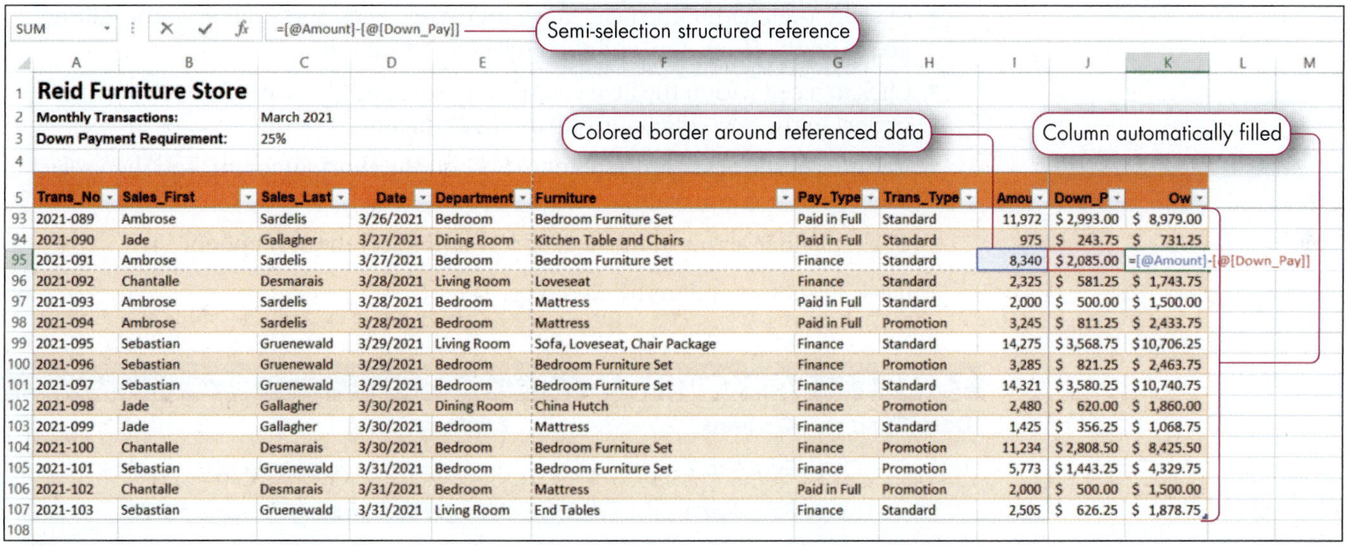

	A	B	C	D	E	F	G	H	I	J	K
1	Reid Furniture Store										
2	Monthly Transactions:		March 2021								
3	Down Payment Requirement:		25%								
4											
5	Trans_No	Sales_First	Sales_Last	Date	Department	Furniture	Pay_Type	Trans_Type	Amou	Down_P	Ow
93	2021-089	Ambrose	Sardelis	3/26/2021	Bedroom	Bedroom Furniture Set	Paid in Full	Standard	11,972	$ 2,993.00	$ 8,979.00
94	2021-090	Jade	Gallagher	3/27/2021	Dining Room	Kitchen Table and Chairs	Paid in Full	Standard	975	$ 243.75	$ 731.25
95	2021-091	Ambrose	Sardelis	3/27/2021	Bedroom	Bedroom Furniture Set	Finance	Standard	8,340	$ 2,085.00	=[@Amount]-[@[Down_Pay]]
96	2021-092	Chantalle	Desmarais	3/28/2021	Living Room	Loveseat	Finance	Standard	2,325	$ 581.25	$ 1,743.75
97	2021-093	Ambrose	Sardelis	3/28/2021	Bedroom	Mattress	Paid in Full	Standard	2,000	$ 500.00	$ 1,500.00
98	2021-094	Ambrose	Sardelis	3/28/2021	Bedroom	Mattress	Paid in Full	Promotion	3,245	$ 811.25	$ 2,433.75
99	2021-095	Sebastian	Gruenewald	3/29/2021	Living Room	Sofa, Loveseat, Chair Package	Finance	Standard	14,275	$ 3,568.75	$ 10,706.25
100	2021-096	Sebastian	Gruenewald	3/29/2021	Bedroom	Bedroom Furniture Set	Finance	Promotion	3,285	$ 821.25	$ 2,463.75
101	2021-097	Sebastian	Gruenewald	3/29/2021	Bedroom	Bedroom Furniture Set	Finance	Standard	14,321	$ 3,580.25	$ 10,740.75
102	2021-098	Jade	Gallagher	3/30/2021	Dining Room	China Hutch	Finance	Promotion	2,480	$ 620.00	$ 1,860.00
103	2021-099	Jade	Gallagher	3/30/2021	Bedroom	Mattress	Finance	Standard	1,425	$ 356.25	$ 1,068.75
104	2021-100	Chantalle	Desmarais	3/30/2021	Bedroom	Bedroom Furniture Set	Finance	Promotion	11,234	$ 2,808.50	$ 8,425.50
105	2021-101	Sebastian	Gruenewald	3/31/2021	Bedroom	Bedroom Furniture Set	Finance	Promotion	5,773	$ 1,443.25	$ 4,329.75
106	2021-102	Chantalle	Desmarais	3/31/2021	Bedroom	Mattress	Paid in Full	Promotion	2,000	$ 500.00	$ 1,500.00
107	2021-103	Sebastian	Gruenewald	3/31/2021	Living Room	End Tables	Finance	Standard	2,505	$ 626.25	$ 1,878.75
108											

FIGURE 4.23 Structured Reference

When creating a formula in a table using structured references, field headings are set off by brackets around column headings or field names, such as =[Amount]–[Down_Pay]. The use of field headings without row references in a structured formula is called an ***unqualified reference***. After you type the equal sign to begin the formula, type an opening bracket, and then Formula AutoComplete displays a list of field headings. Type or double-click the column name from the list and type the closing bracket. Excel displays a colored border around the referenced column that coordinates with the structured reference in the formula, similar to Excel identifying cell references and their worksheet placement. When you enter a formula using structured references, Excel copies the formula down the rest of the table column automatically, compared to typing references in formulas and using the fill handle to copy the formula down a column.

You can also use the semi-selection process to create a formula. As you click cells to enter a formula in a table, Excel builds a formula like this: =[@Amount]–[@Down_Pay], where the @ indicates the current row. If you use the semi-selection process to create a formula outside the table, the formula includes the table and field names, such as =Table1[@Amount]–Table1[@Down_Pay]. Table1 is the name of the table; Amount and Down_Pay are field names. This structured formula that includes references with a table name is called a ***fully qualified structured reference***. When you build formulas *within* a table, you can use either unqualified or fully qualified structured references. If you need to use table data in a formula *outside* the table boundaries, you must use fully qualified structured references.

Sorting Data

Sometimes if you rearrange the order of records, a new perspective is gained making the information easier to understand. In Figure 4.23, the March data is arranged by transaction number. You might want to arrange the transactions so that all of the transactions for a particular sales representative are together. **Sorting** is the process of arranging records by the value of one or more fields within a table. Sorting is not limited to data within tables; normal data ranges can be sorted as well.

STEP 2 ▸ ## Sort One Field

You can sort data in a table or a regular range in a worksheet. For example, you could sort by transaction date or department. You can sort by only one field using any of the following steps:

- Click in a cell within the field you want to sort, click Sort & Filter in the Editing group on the Home tab, and then select a sort option.
- Click in a cell within the field you want to sort and click Sort A to Z, Sort Z to A, or Sort in the Sort & Filter group on the Data tab.
- Right-click the field to sort, point to Sort on the shortcut menu, and then select the type of sort you want.
- Click the filter arrow in the header row and select the sort option.

Table 4.3 lists sort options by data type.

TABLE 4.3	Sort Options	
Data Type	**Options**	**Explanation**
Text	Sort A to Z	Arranges data in alphabetic order
	Sort Z to A	Arranges data in reverse alphabetic order
Dates	Sort Oldest to Newest	Displays data in chronological order, from oldest to newest
	Sort Newest to Oldest	Displays data in reverse chronological order, from newest to oldest
Values	Sort Smallest to Largest	Arranges values from the smallest value to the largest
	Sort Largest to Smallest	Arranges values from the largest value to the smallest
Color	Sort by Cell Color	Arranges data together for cells containing a particular fill color
	Sort by Font Color	Arranges data together for cells containing a particular font color

Sort Multiple Fields

After sorting by one field, if a second sort is applied, the original sort will be removed. However, at times, sorting by only one field does not yield the desired outcome. Using multiple level sorts enables like records in the primary sort to be further organized by additional sort levels. Always check the data to determine how many levels of sorting to apply. If your table contains several people with the same last name but different first names, you would first sort by the Last Name field, then sort by First Name field. All the people with the last name Desmarais would be grouped together and further sorted by first name, such as Amanda and then Bradley. Excel enables you to sort data on 64 different levels.

To perform a multiple level sort, complete the following steps:

1. Click in any cell in the table.
2. Click Sort in the Sort & Filter group on the Data tab to display the Sort dialog box.
3. Select the primary sort level by clicking the Sort by arrow, selecting the field to sort by, clicking the Order arrow, and then selecting the sort order from the list.
4. Click Add Level (On a Mac, click the plus icon), select the second sort level by clicking the Then by arrow, select the column to sort by, click the Order arrow, and then select the sort order from the list.
5. Continue to click Add Level and add sort levels until you have entered all sort levels (see Figure 4.24). Click OK.

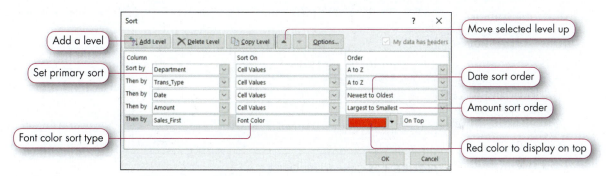

FIGURE 4.24 Sort Dialog Box

STEP **4** **Create a Custom Sort**

When sorting, Excel arranges data in alphabetic or numeric order. For example, days of the week are sorted alphabetically: Friday, Monday, Saturday, Sunday, Thursday, Tuesday, and Wednesday. However, if you want to sort the days of the week in the traditional sequence of Sunday to Saturday, then you would create a custom sort.

To create a custom sort sequence, complete the following steps:

1. Click Sort in the Sort & Filter group on the Data tab.
2. Click the Order arrow and select Custom List to display the Custom Lists dialog box (see Figure 4.25).
3. Select an existing sort sequence in the Custom lists box or select NEW LIST.
4. Type the entries in the sort sequence in the List entries box. Enter a comma between entries.
5. Click Add and click OK.

On a Mac, to create a custom sort sequence, complete the following steps:

1. Click the Excel menu.
2. Select Preferences and select Custom Lists in the Formulas and Lists group.
3. Enter the new list in the List entries box and click Add.
4. Close the Custom List dialog box.

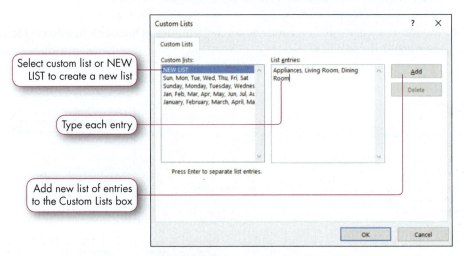

FIGURE 4.25 Custom Lists Dialog Box

Filtering Data

To display only a subset of the data available, for example, the data to show transactions for only a particular sales representative, you would apply a filter to achieve the desired results. In Excel, you can filter using various criteria such as date, value, text, and color. *Filtering* is the process of displaying only those records that meet certain conditions. When a filter is applied, the filter arrow displays a filter icon, indicating which field is filtered. Excel displays the row numbers in blue, indicating that you applied a filter. The missing row numbers indicate hidden rows of data. When you remove the filter, all the records display again.

To apply a filter, complete the following steps:

1. Click any cell in the range of data to be filtered.
2. Click the Data tab and click Filter in the Sort & Filter group to display the filter arrows (this step can be skipped if the data is in a table).
3. Click the filter arrow for the column you want to filter.
4. Deselect the Select All check box and select the check boxes for the text you want to remain visible in the dataset. Click OK.

Clear Filters

Filtering is nondestructive; you can remove the filters from one or more fields to expand the dataset again. To remove only one filter and keep the other filters, click the filter arrow for the field from which you want to clear the filter and select Clear Filter From. All filters can be removed by clicking Clear in the Sort & Filter group on the Data tab. As an alternate method, click Sort & Filter in the Editing group on the Home tab and select Clear.

STEP 5 ▶ **Apply Text Filters**

When you apply a filter to a text field, the filter menu displays each unique text item. You can select one or more text items from the list to be filtered. Once completed, only the selected text will be displayed. You can also select Text Filters to see a submenu of additional options, such as Begins With, Ends with, and Contains.

For example, Figure 4.26 shows the Sales_Last filter menu with two names selected. Excel displays records for these two reps only. The records for the other sales reps are hidden but not deleted.

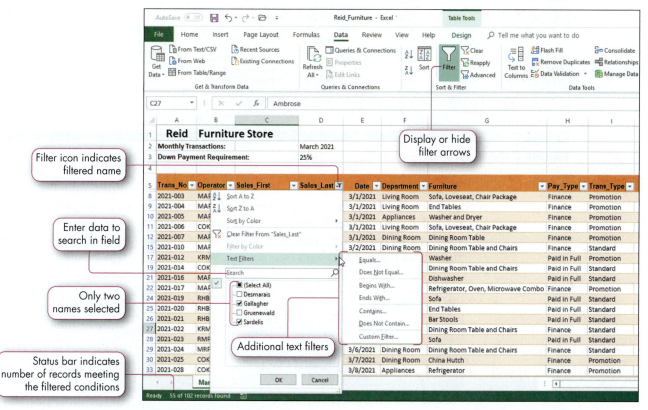

FIGURE 4.26 Filtered Text

STEP 6 ▶ **Apply Number Filters**

Excel contains a variety of number filters that enable you to display specific numbers, or a range of numbers such as above average or top 10 values. When you filter a field of numbers, you can select specific numbers. Or, you might want to filter numbers by a range, such as numbers greater than $5,000 or numbers between $4,000 and $5,000. If the field contains a large number of unique entries, you can click in the Search box and enter a value to display all matching records. For example, if you enter $7, the list will display only values that start with $7. The filter submenu enables you to set a variety of number filters. In Figure 4.27, the amounts are filtered to show only those that are above the average amount. In this example, Excel calculates the average amount as $4,512. Only records above that amount display.

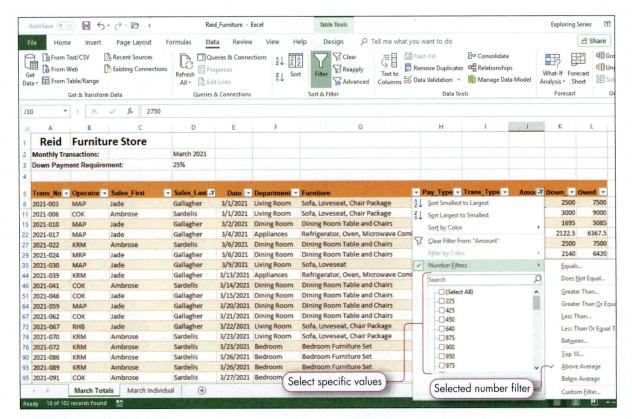

FIGURE 4.27 Filtered Numbers

The Top 10 option enables you to specify the top records. Although the option name is Top 10, you can specify the number or percentage of records to display. For example, you can filter the list to display only the top five or the bottom 7%. Figure 4.28 shows the Top 10 AutoFilter dialog box.

FIGURE 4.28 AutoFilter Dialog Box

STEP 7 **Apply Date Filters**

When you filter a field of dates, you can select specific dates or a date range, such as dates after 3/15/2021 or dates between 3/1/2021 and 3/7/2021. The submenu enables you to set a variety of date filters such as week, month, quarter, and year. For more specific date options, point to Date Filters, point to All Dates in the Period, and then select a period, such as Quarter 2 or October. Figure 4.29 shows the Date Filters menu.

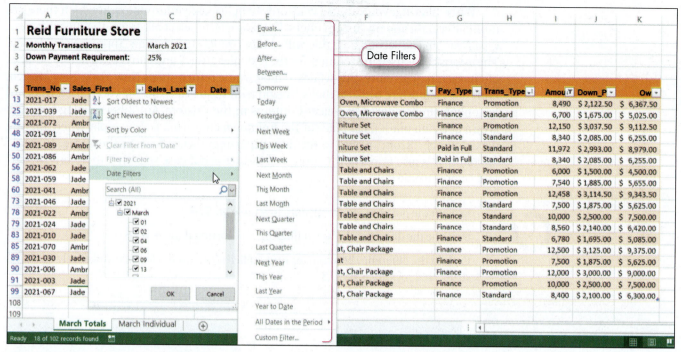

FIGURE 4.29 Date Filters

Apply a Custom Filter

Suppose as the manager of a furniture store, you are only interested in marketing directly to people who spent between $500 and $1,000 in the last month. To quickly identify the required data, you could use a custom AutoFilter. If you select options such as Greater Than or Between, Excel displays the Custom AutoFilter dialog box (see Figure 4.30). You can also select Custom Filter from the menu to display this dialog box, which is designed for more complex filtering requirements.

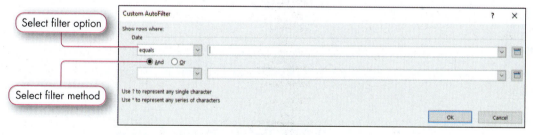

FIGURE 4.30 Custom AutoFilter Dialog Box

The dialog box indicates the column being filtered. To set the filters, click the arrows to select the comparison type, such as equals or contains. Click the arrow on the right to select a specific text, value, or date entry, or type the data yourself. For ranges of dates or values, click And, and then specify the comparison operator and value or date for the next condition row. For text, click Or. For example, if you want both Gallagher and Desmarais, you must select Or because each data entry contains either Gallagher or Desmarais but not both at the same time.

When filtering, you can use wildcards to help locate information in which there are multiple criteria and no custom filters. For example, to select all states starting with New, type *New* * in the second box; this will obtain results such as New York or New Mexico. The asterisk (*) is used in exchange for the text after "New" and can represent any number of characters. Therefore, this wildcard filter would return states New York, New Mexico, and New Hampshire because they all begin with the word "New." If you want a wildcard for only a single character, select Contains in the Custom Autofilters dialog box, and type a question mark (?) in place of the unknown character. For example, when filtering departments, "R?om" would return any department with *Room* in the name, as would "Room*." It is also important to note this feature is not case sensitive, therefore "R?om" and "r?om" would both return *Room*.

Quick Concepts

7. Explain the purpose of sorting data in a table. ***p. 514***

8. Describe the difference between filtering and sorting data. ***p. 516***

9. Explain the difference between an unqualified structured reference and a fully qualified structured reference. ***p. 513***

Hands-On Exercises

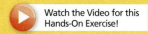
Skills covered: Create a Structured Reference in a Formula • Sort One Field • Sort Multiple Fields • Create a Custom Sort • Apply Text Filters • Apply Number Filters • Apply Date Filters

3 Table Manipulation

You want to start analyzing the March transactions for Reid Furniture Store by calculating the totals owed, then sorting and filtering data in a variety of ways to help you understand the transactions better.

STEP 1 CREATE A STRUCTURED REFERENCE IN A FORMULA

First, you want to calculate the down payment owed by each customer. You will then calculate the total amount owed by subtracting the down payment from the total down payment. You will use structured references to complete these tasks. Refer to Figure 4.31 as you complete Step 1.

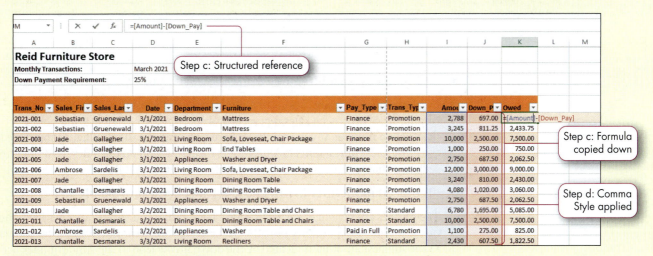

FIGURE 4.31 Create a Structured Reference

a. Open *e04h2Reid_LastFirst* if you closed it at the end of Hands-On Exercise 2. Save it as **e04h3Reid_LastFirst**, changing h2 to h3.

b. Click **cell J6**. Type **=** click **cell I6**, type *. Click **cell D3**, press **F4**, and then press **Enter**.

The down payment required is 25% of the total purchase price. Structured reference format is used for Amount to create the formula that calculates the customer's down payment. Since the percentage in cell D3 (25%) is a constant it is entered as an absolute reference. Excel then copies the formula down the column.

c. Click **cell K6**. Enter the formula **=[Amount]-[Down_Pay]** and press **Enter**.

The formula calculates the total value owed for the transaction and copies the formula down the column.

d. Select the **range J6:K109** and apply the **Comma Style Number Format**.

e. Save the workbook.

You want to compare the number of transactions by sales rep, so you will sort the data by the Sales_Last field. After reviewing the transactions by sales reps, you want to arrange the transactions to show the one with the largest purchase first and the smallest purchase last. Refer to Figure 4.32 as you complete Step 2.

Step a: Sort alphabetically by last name

Step b: Sort amount from largest to smallest

	Trans_N	Sales_Fir	Sales_Las	Date	Department	Furniture	Pay_Type	Trans_Typ	Amou	Down_P	Ow
5											
6	2021-073	Chantalle	Desmarais	3/24/2021	Living Room	Sofa, Loveseat, Chair Package	Finance	Standard	17,500	4,375.00	13,125.00
7	2021-097	Sebastian	Gruenewald	3/29/2021	Bedroom	Bedroom Furniture Set	Finance	Standard	14,321	3,580.25	10,740.75
8	2021-095	Sebastian	Gruenewald	3/29/2021	Living Room	Sofa, Loveseat, Chair Package	Finance	Standard	14,275	3,568.75	10,706.25
9	2021-056	Chantalle	Desmarais	3/19/2021	Living Room	Sofa, Loveseat, Chair Package	Finance	Standard	12,500	3,125.00	9,375.00
10	2021-070	Ambrose	Sardelis	3/23/2021	Living Room	Sofa, Loveseat, Chair Package	Finance	Promotion	12,500	3,125.00	9,375.00
11	2021-041	Ambrose	Sardelis	3/14/2021	Dining Room	Dining Room Table and Chairs	Finance	Promotion	12,458	3,114.50	9,343.50
12	2021-072	Ambrose	Sardelis	3/23/2021	Bedroom	Bedroom Furniture Set	Finance	Promotion	12,150	3,037.50	9,112.50
13	2021-006	Ambrose	Sardelis	3/1/2021	Living Room	Sofa, Loveseat, Chair Package	Finance	Promotion	12,000	3,000.00	9,000.00
14	2021-089	Ambrose	Sardelis	3/26/2021	Bedroom	Bedroom Furniture Set	Paid in Full	Standard	11,972	2,993.00	8,979.00
15	2021-100	Chantalle	Desmarais	3/30/2021	Bedroom	Bedroom Furniture Set	Finance	Promotion	11,234	2,808.50	8,425.50
16	2021-011	Chantalle	Desmarais	3/2/2021	Dining Room	Dining Room Table and Chairs	Finance	Standard	10,000	2,500.00	7,500.00
17	2021-003	Jade	Gallagher	3/1/2021	Living Room	Sofa, Loveseat, Chair Package	Finance	Promotion	10,000	2,500.00	7,500.00
18	2021-064	Sebastian	Gruenewald	3/21/2021	Appliances	Refrigerator, Oven, Microwave Combo	Finance	Promotion	10,000	2,500.00	7,500.00
19	2021-022	Ambrose	Sardelis	3/6/2021	Dining Room	Dining Room Table and Chairs	Finance	Standard	10,000	2,500.00	7,500.00

FIGURE 4.32 Sorted Data

a. Click the **Sales_Last filter arrow** and select **Sort A to Z**.

Excel arranges the transactions in alphabetic order by last name, starting with Desmarais. Within each sales rep, records display in their original sequence by transaction number. If you scan the records, you can see that Gallagher completed the most sales transactions in March. The up arrow icon on the Sales_Last filter arrow indicates that records are sorted in alphabetic order by that field.

b. Click the **Amount filter arrow** and select **Sort Largest to Smallest**.

The records are no longer sorted by Sales_Last. When you sort by another field, the previous sort is not saved. In this case, the transactions are arranged from the largest amount to the smallest amount, indicated by the down arrow icon in the Amount filter arrow.

c. Save the workbook.

You want to review the transactions by payment type (financed or paid in full). Within each payment type, you further want to compare the transaction type (Promotion or Standard). Finally, you want to compare costs within the sorted records by displaying the highest costs first. You will use the Sort dialog box to perform a three-level sort. Refer to Figure 4.33 as you complete Step 3.

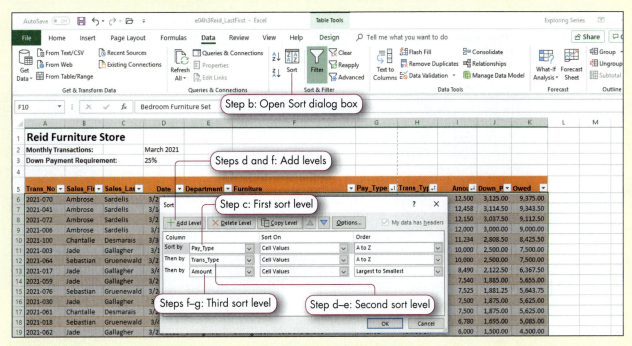

FIGURE 4.33 Three-Level Sort

a. Click inside the table and click the **Data tab**.

   Both the Data and Home tabs contain commands to open the Sort dialog box.

b. Click **Sort** in the Sort & Filter group to open the Sort dialog box.

c. Click the **Sort by arrow** and select **Pay_Type**. Click the **Order arrow** and select **A to Z**.

   You start by specifying the column for the primary sort. In this case, you want to sort the records first by the payment type column.

d. Click **Add Level**.

   The Sort dialog box adds the Then by row, which adds a secondary sort.

e. Click the **Then by arrow** and select **Trans_Type**.

   The default order is A to Z, which will sort in alphabetic order by Trans_Type. Excel will first sort the records by the Pay_Type (Finance or Paid in Full). Within each Pay_Type, Excel will further sort records by Trans_Type (Promotion or Standard).

f. Click **Add Level** to add another Then by row. Click the second **Then by arrow** and select **Amount**.

g. Click the **Order arrow** for the Amount sort and select **Largest to Smallest**.

   Within the Pay_Type and Trans_Type sorts, this will arrange the records with the largest amount first in descending order to the smallest amount.

h. Click **OK** and scroll through the records. Save the workbook.

   Most customers finance their purchases instead of paying in full. For the financed transactions, more than half were promotional sales. For merchandise paid in full, a majority of the transactions were standard sales, indicating that people with money do not necessarily wait for a promotional sale to purchase merchandise.

For the month of March, you want to closely monitor sales of the Dining Room and Living Room departments. After completing the prior sort, you will add an additional level to create a custom sort of the department's data. Refer to Figure 4.34 as you complete Step 4.

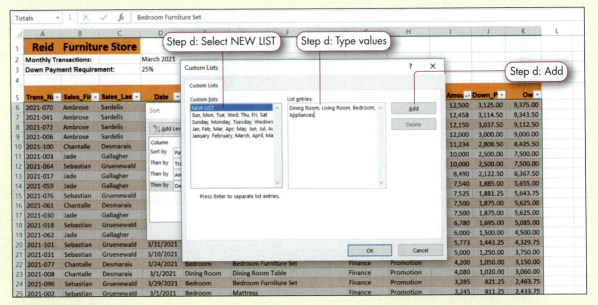

FIGURE 4.34 Custom Sort

a. Click inside the table and click **Sort** in the Sort & Filter group to open the Sort dialog box.

The Sort dialog box will open with the prior sort criteria displayed.

b. Click the last Then by (Amount) in the Sort dialog box created in the prior step and click **Add Level**.

c. Click the Then by arrow and select **Department**. Click the **Order arrow** and select **Custom List**.

This will open the Custom Lists dialog box, enabling you to manually specify the sort order.

MAC TROUBLESHOOTING: Click the Excel menu and select Preferences. Click Custom Lists in the Formulas and Lists section.

d. Click **NEW LIST** in the Custom lists box, click the **List entries box**, and then type **Dining Room, Living Room, Bedroom, Appliances**. Click **Add**, click **OK**, and then click **OK** again to complete to return to the worksheet.

After completing the custom list, the data in column E will be sorted by Dining room, Living Room, Bedroom, and Appliances as the last step within the custom sort.

e. Save the workbook.

You will filter the table to focus on Jade Gallagher's sales. You notice that she sells more merchandise from the Dining room department, so you will filter out the other departments. Refer to Figure 4.35 as you complete Step 5.

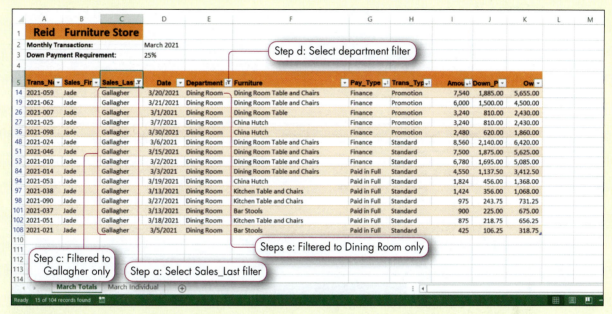

FIGURE 4.35 Apply Text Filters

a. Click the **Sales_Last filter arrow**.

The (Select All) check box is selected.

b. Click the **(Select All) check box** to deselect all last names.

c. Click the **Gallagher check box** to select it and click **OK**.

The status bar indicates that 33 out of 104 records meet the filtering condition. The Sales_Last filter arrow includes a funnel icon, indicating that this column is filtered.

d. Click the **Department filter arrow**.

e. Click the **(Select All) check box** to deselect all departments, click the **Dining Room check box** to focus on that department, and then click **OK**. Save the workbook.

The remaining 15 records show Gallagher's dining room sales for the month. The Department filter arrow includes a funnel icon, indicating that this column is also filtered.

Vicki is considering giving a bonus to employees who sold high-end dining room furniture during a specific time period (3/16/2021 to 3/31/2021). You want to determine if Jade Gallagher qualifies for this bonus. In particular, you are interested in how much gross revenue she generated for dining room furniture that cost at least $5,000 or more. Refer to Figure 4.36 as you complete Step 6.

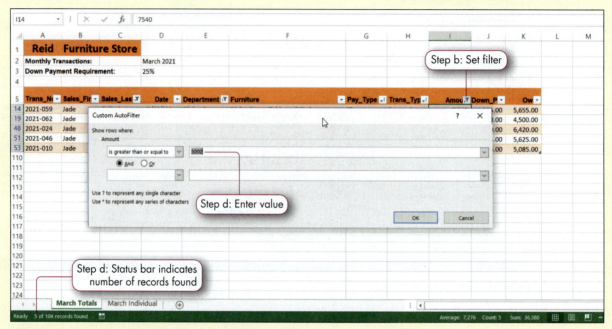

FIGURE 4.36 Filtered to Amounts Greater Than or Equal to $5,000

a. Select the **range I14:I108** of the filtered list and view the status bar.

The average transaction amount is $3,754 with 15 transactions (i.e., 15 filtered records).

b. Click the **Amount filter arrow**.

c. Point to **Number Filters** and select **Greater Than** Or **Equal To**.

The Custom AutoFilter dialog box opens.

d. Type **5000** in the box to the right of *is greater than or equal to* and click **OK**. Save the workbook.

When typing numbers, you can type raw numbers such as 5000 or formatted numbers such as $5,000. Out of Gallagher's original 15 dining room transactions, only five transactions (one-third of her sales) were valued at $5,000 or more.

Finally, you want to study Jade Gallagher's sales records for the last half of the month. You will add a date filter to identify those sales records. Refer to Figure 4.37 as you complete Step 7.

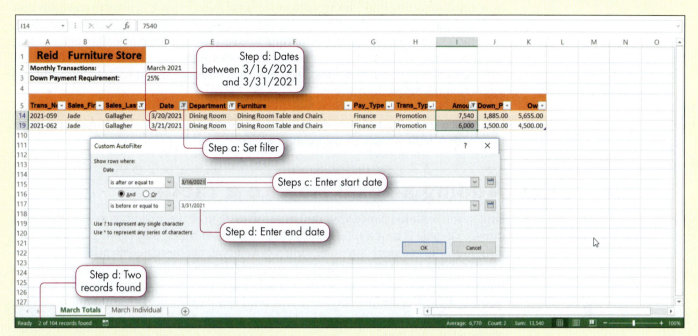

FIGURE 4.37 Filtered by Dates Between 3/16/2021 and 3/31/2021

a. Click the **Date filter arrow**.

b. Point to **Date Filters** and select **Between**.

The Custom AutoFilter dialog box opens. The default comparisons are *is after or equal to* and *is before or equal to*, ready for you to enter the date specifications.

c. Type **3/16/2021** in the box on the right side of *is after or equal to*.

You specified the starting date of the range of dates to include. You will keep the *And* option selected.

d. Type **3/31/2021** in the box on the right side of *is before or equal to*. Click **OK**.

Gallagher had only two dining room sales greater than $5,000 during the last half of March.

e. Save the workbook. Keep the workbook open if you plan to continue with the next Hands-On Exercise. If not, close the workbook, and exit Excel.

Table Aggregation and Conditional Formatting

In addition to sorting and filtering tables to analyze data, you might want to add fields that provide data aggregation such as Average or the total amount purchased. Furthermore, you might want to apply special formatting to cells that contain particular values or text using conditional formatting. For example, a sales manager might want to highlight employees that have reached their sales goal, or a professor might want to highlight test scores that fall below the average.

In this section, you will learn how to add a total row to a table along with learning about the five conditional formatting categories and how to apply conditional formatting to a range of values based on a condition you set.

STEP 1 ## Adding a Total Row to a Table

Earlier, you explored converting ranges to tables. One of the advantages of converting a range to a table is that a total row could be added. At times, aggregating data provides insightful information. For regular ranges of data, you use basic statistical functions, such as SUM, AVERAGE, MIN, and MAX, to provide summary analysis for a dataset. An Excel table provides the advantage of being able to display a total row automatically without creating the aggregate function yourself. A *total row* displays below the last row of records in an Excel table and enables you to display summary statistics, such as a sum of values displayed in a column.

> **To display and use the total row in a table, complete the following steps:**
>
> 1. Click any cell in the table.
> 2. Click the Design tab.
> 3. Click Total Row in the Table Style Options group. Excel displays the total row below the last record in the table. Excel displays Total in the first column of the total row.
> 4. Click a cell in the total row, click that cell's total row arrow, and then select the function result that you want. Excel calculates the summary statistics for values, but if the field is text, the only summary statistic that can be calculated is Count.
> 5. Click in the empty cell to add a summary statistic to another column for that field in the total row and click the arrow to select a function. Select None to remove the function.

Figure 4.38 shows the active total row with totals applied to the Amount, Down_Pay, and Owed fields. A list of functions displays to change the function for the last field.

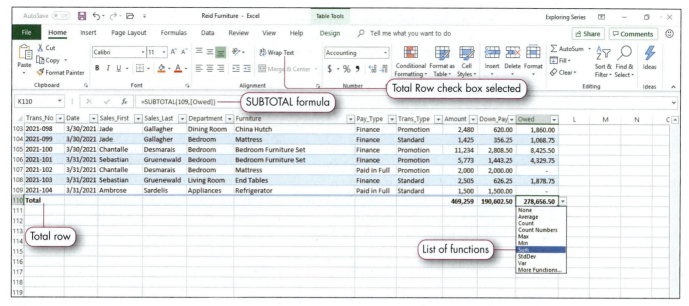

FIGURE 4.38 Total Row

The calculations on the total row use the SUBTOTAL function. The ***SUBTOTAL function*** calculates an aggregate value, such as totals or averages, for displayed values in a range, table, or database. If you click in a calculated total row cell, the SUBTOTAL function displays in the Formula Bar. The function for the total row looks like this: =SUBTOTAL(function_num,ref1). The function_num argument is a number that represents a function (see Table 4.4). The ref1 argument indicates the range of values to calculate. The SUBTOTAL function used to total the values in the Owed field would be =SUBTOTAL(109,[Owed]), where the number 109 represents the SUM function, and [Owed] represents the Owed field. A benefit of the SUBTOTAL function is that it subtotals data for filtered records, so you have an accurate total for the visible records.

=SUBTOTAL(function_num,ref1, . . .)

TABLE 4.4 Subtotal Function Numbers

Function	Function Number	Table Number
AVERAGE	1	101
COUNT	2	102
COUNTA	3	103
MAX	4	104
MIN	5	105
PRODUCT	6	106
STDEV.S	7	107
STDEV.P	8	108
SUM	9	109
VAR.S	10	110
VAR.P	11	111

TIP: FILTERING DATA AND SUBTOTALS

If you filter the data and display the total row, the SUBTOTAL function's 109 argument ensures that only the displayed data are summed; data for hidden rows are not calculated in the aggregate function.

Applying Conditional Formatting

Conditional formatting enables you and your audience understand a dataset better because it adds a visual element to the cells. ***Conditional formatting*** applies formatting to any set of data to highlight or emphasize cells that meet specific conditions. The term is called *conditional* because the formatting displays only when a condition is met. This is similar logic to the IF function you have used. Remember with an IF function, you create a logical test that is evaluated. If the logical or conditional test is true, the function produces one result. If the logical or conditional test is false, the function produces another result. With conditional formatting, if the condition is true, Excel formats the cell automatically based on that condition; if the condition is false, Excel does not format the cell. If you change a value in a conditionally formatted cell, Excel examines the new value to see if it should apply the conditional format.

Table 4.5 lists and describes a number of different conditional formats that can be applied.

TABLE 4.5	Conditional Formatting Options
Options	**Description**
Highlight Cells Rules	Highlights cells with a fill color, font color, or border (such as Light Red Fill with Dark Red Text) if values are greater than, less than, between two values, equal to a value, or duplicate values; text that contains particular characters; or dates when a date meets a particular condition, such as *In the last 7 days*.
Top/Bottom Rules	Formats cells with values in the top 10 items, top 10%, bottom 10 items, bottom 10%, above average, or below average. You can change the exact values to format the top or bottom items or percentages, such as top 5 or bottom 15%.
Data Bars	Applies a gradient or solid fill bar in which the width of the bar represents the current cell's value compared relatively to other cells' values.
Color Scales	Formats different cells with different colors, assigning one color to the lowest group of values and another color to the highest group of values, with gradient colors to other values.
Icon Sets	Inserts an icon from an icon palette in each cell to indicate values compared to each other.

Another way to apply conditional formatting is with Quick Analysis. When you select a range and click the Quick Analysis button, the Formatting options display in the Quick Analysis gallery. Point to a thumbnail and Live Preview will show how it will affect the selected range (see Figure 4.39). You can also apply conditional formatting by clicking Conditional Formatting in the Styles group on the Home tab. Table 4.6 describes the conditional formatting options in the Quick Analysis gallery.

MAC TROUBLESHOOTING: Quick Analysis is not available for Mac users. Conditional Formatting can be applied by clicking the Home tab and selecting Conditional Formatting.

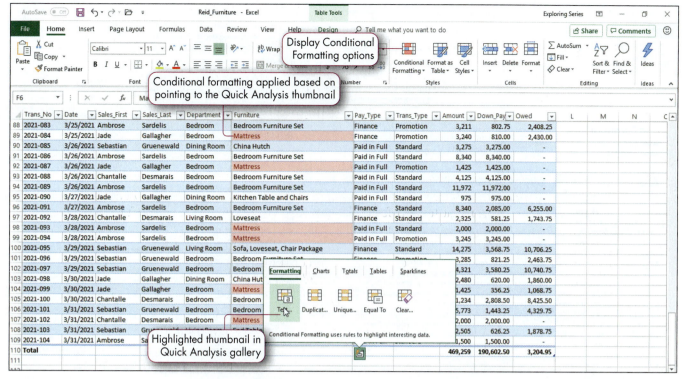

FIGURE 4.39 Quick Analysis Gallery to Apply Conditional Formatting

TABLE 4.6	Conditional Formatting Options in Quick Analysis Gallery
Options	**Description**
Text Contains	Formats cells that contain the text in the first selected cell. In Figure 4.39, the first selected cell contains Mattress. If a cell contains Mattress and Springs, Excel would format that cell also because it contains Mattress.
Duplicate Values	Formats cells that are duplicated in the selected range.
Unique Values	Formats cells that are unique; that is, no other cell in the selected range contains the same data.
Equal To	Formats cells that are exactly like the data contained in the first selected cell.
Clear Format	Removes the conditional formatting from the selected range.

STEP 2 ## Apply a Highlight Cells Rules

The Highlight Cells Rules category enables you to apply a highlight to cells that meet a condition, such as cells containing values greater than a particular value. This option contains predefined combinations of fill colors, font colors, and/or borders. For example, suppose you are a sales manager who developed a worksheet containing the sales for each day of a month. You are interested in sales between $5,000 and $10,000. You can apply a conditional format to cells that contain values within the desired range. To apply this conditional formatting, select Highlight Cells Rules, and then select Between. In the Between dialog box (see Figure 4.40), type 5000 in the first value box and 10000 in the second value box, select the type of conditional formatting, such as Light Red Fill with Dark Red Text, and then click OK to apply the formats. The results are displayed in Figure 4.41.

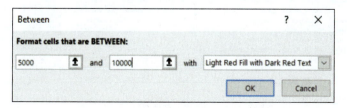

FIGURE 4.40 Between Dialog Box

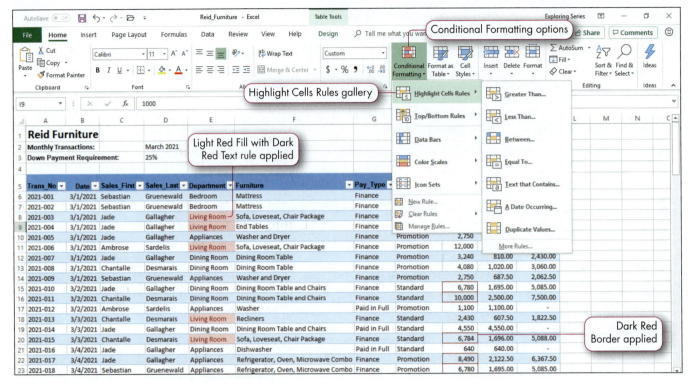

FIGURE 4.41 Conditional Formatting Highlight Cells Rules

STEP 3 Specify Top/Bottom Rules

If you wanted to identify the top five sales to reward the sales associates or want to identify the bottom 15% of sales for more focused marketing, the Top/Bottom Rules category enables you to specify the top or bottom number, top or bottom percentage, or values that are above or below the average value in a specified range. In Figure 4.42, the Amount column is conditionally formatted to highlight the top five amounts. (The data has been sorted so the top 5 display at the top of the table.) Although the menu option is Top 10 Items, you can specify the exact number of items to format.

	Trans_No	Date	Sales_First	Sales_Last	Department	Furniture	Pay_Type	Trans_Type	Amou	Down_Pa	Owe
59	2021-054	3/19/2021	Jade	Gallagher	Appliances	Refrigerator, Oven Combo	Paid in Full	Standard	3,280	3,280.00	-
60	2021-055	3/19/2021	Chantalle	Desmarais	Dining Room	Kitchen Table and Ch			1,172	1,172.00	-
61	2021-056	3/19/2021	Chantalle	Desmarais	Living Room	Sofa, Loveseat, Chai			12,500	3,125.00	9,375.00
62	2021-057	3/20/2021	Ambrose	Sardelis	Dining Room	Kitchen Table and Ch			975	975.00	-
63	2021-058	3/20/2021	Sebastian	Gruenewald	Appliances	Microwave			125	125.00	-
64	2021-059	3/20/2021	Jade	Gallagher	Dining Room	Dining Room Table a			7,540	1,885.00	5,655.00
65	2021-060	3/20/2021	Sebastian	Gruenewald	Dining Room	Dining Room Table a			9,430	2,357.50	7,072.50
66	2021-061	3/21/2021	Chantalle	Desmarais	Appliances	Refrigerator, Oven, Microwave Combo	Finance	Promotion	7,500	1,875.00	5,625.00
67	2021-062	3/21/2021	Jade	Gallagher	Dining Room	Dining Room Table and Chairs	Finance	Promotion	6,000	1,500.00	4,500.00
68	2021-063	3/21/2021	Chantalle	Desmarais	Dining Room	China Hutch	Finance	Promotion	3,125	781.25	2,343.75
69	2021-064	3/21/2021	Sebastian	Gruenewald	Appliances	Refrigerator, Oven, Microwave Combo	Finance	Promotion	10,000	2,500.00	7,500.00
70	2021-065	3/22/2021	Ambrose	Sardelis	Living Room	Sofa	Finance	Standard	3,450	862.50	2,587.50
71	2021-066	3/22/2021	Sebastian	Gruenewald	Appliances	Refrigerator	Paid in Full	Standard	2,575	2,575.00	-
72	2021-067	3/22/2021	Jade	Gallagher	Living Room	Sofa, Loveseat, Chair Package	Finance	Standard	8,400	2,100.00	6,300.00
73	2021-068	3/22/2021	Sebastian	Gruenewald	Bedroom	Mattress	Paid in Full	Standard	3,200	3,200.00	-
74	2021-069	3/23/2021	Chantalle	Desmarais	Dining Room	Kitchen Table and Chairs	Finance	Promotion	1,345	336.25	1,008.75
75	2021-070	3/23/2021	Ambrose	Sardelis	Living Room	Sofa, Loveseat, Chair Package	Finance	Promotion	12,500	3,125.00	9,375.00
76	2021-071	3/23/2021	Ambrose	Sardelis	Appliances	Dishwasher	Paid in Full	Standard	450	450.00	-
77	2021-072	3/23/2021	Ambrose	Sardelis	Bedroom	Bedroom Furniture Set	Finance	Promotion	12,150	3,037.50	9,112.50

FIGURE 4.42 Top 10 Items Dialog Box

Data bars apply a gradient or solid fill bar in which the width of the bar represents the current cell's value compared relatively to other cells' values (see Figure 4.43). The width of the data bar represents the value in a cell, with a wider bar representing a higher value and a narrower bar a lower value. Excel locates the largest value and displays the widest data bar in that cell. Excel then finds the smallest value and displays the smallest data bar in that cell. Excel sizes the data bars for the remaining cells based on their values relative to the high and low values in the column. If you change the values, Excel updates the data bar widths. Excel uses the same color for each data bar, but each bar differs in size based on the value in the respective cells.

Color scales format cells with different colors based on the relative value of a cell compared to other selected cells. You can apply a two- or three-color scale. This scale assists in comparing a range of cells using gradations of those colors. The shade of the color represents higher or lower values. In Figure 4.43, for example, the red color scales display for the lowest values, the green color displays for the highest values, and gradients of yellow and orange represent the middle range of values in the Down_Pay column. Use color scales to understand variation in the data to identify trends, for example, to view good stock returns and weak stock returns.

Icon sets are symbols or signs that classify data into three, four, or five categories, based on the values in a range. Excel determines categories of value ranges and assigns an icon to each range. In Figure 4.43, a three-icon set was applied to the Owed column. Excel divided the range of values between the lowest value of $0 and the highest value of $13,125 into thirds. The red diamond icon displays for the cells containing values in the lowest third ($0 to $4,375), the yellow triangle icon displays for cells containing the values in the middle third ($4,376 to $8,750), and the green circle icon displays for cells containing values in the top third ($8,751 to $13,125). Most purchases fall into the lowest third.

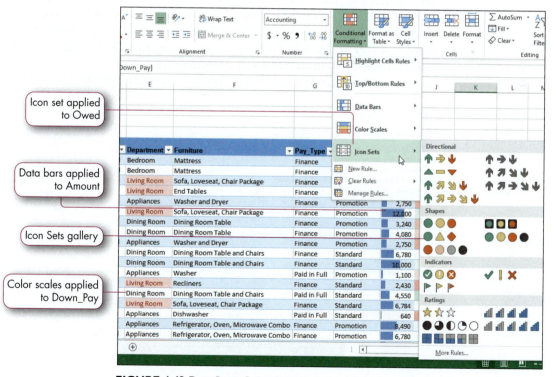

FIGURE 4.43 Data Bars, Color Scales, and Icon Sets

STEP 5 Creating a New Conditional Formatting Rule

The default conditional formatting categories provide a variety of options. Excel also enables you to create your own rules to specify different fill colors, borders, or other formatting if you do not want the default settings. Excel provides three ways to create a new rule:

- Click Conditional Formatting in the Styles group and select New Rule.
- Click Conditional Formatting in the Styles group, select Manage Rules to open the Conditional Formatting Rules Manager dialog box, and then click New Rule. (On a Mac, click the **+** icon to add a new rule.)
- Click Conditional Formatting in the Styles group, select a rule category such as Highlight Cells Rules, and then select More Rules.

When creating a new rule, the New Formatting Rule dialog box opens (see Figure 4.44) so that you can define the conditional formatting rule. First, select a rule type, such as *Format all cells based on their values*. The *Edit the Rule Description* section changes, based on the rule type you select. With the default rule type selected, you can specify the format style (2-Color Scale, 3-Color Scale, Data Bar, or Icon Sets). You can then specify the minimum and maximum values, the fill colors for color sets or data bars, or the icons for icon sets. After you edit the rule description, click OK to save the new conditional format.

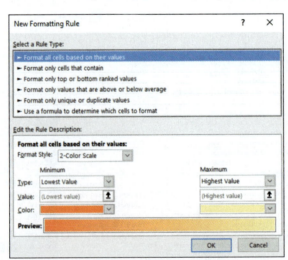

FIGURE 4.44 New Formatting Rule Dialog Box

If you select any rule type except the *Format all cells based on their values* rule, the dialog box contains a Format button. When you click Format, the Format Cells dialog box opens so that you can specify number, font, border, and fill formats to apply to your rule. (On a Mac, to access the Format Cells dialog box, select Classic in the Style box, click Format with, and then select Custom Format.)

Manage Rules

Periodically, conditional formatting rules may need to be updated, moved, or completely deleted. To edit or delete any conditional formatting rule that has been applied to data, use the features in the Manage Rules dialog box. To display the manage rules dialog box, click Conditional Formatting in the Styles group and select Manage rules (see Figure 4.45). You can display rules for data in a table, worksheet, or a selection of cells. To modify a setting of a conditional formatting rule, click Edit Rule. Use Delete Rule to remove conditional formats. You can also delete or clear rules from a worksheet, table, or selection by using Clear Rules in the Conditional Formatting command on the Home tab.

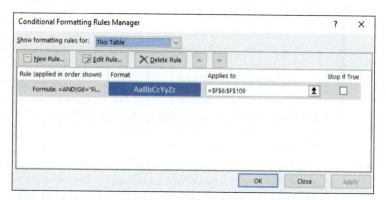

FIGURE 4.45 Conditional Formatting Rules Manager Dialog Box

Use Formulas in Conditional Formatting

Suppose you want to format merchandise amounts of financed items *and* amounts that are $10,000 or more. You can use a formula to create a conditional formatting rule to complete the task. Figure 4.46 shows the Edit Formatting Rule dialog box and the corresponding conditional formatting applied to cells.

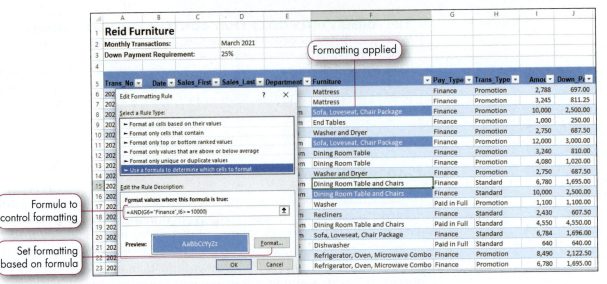

Formatting applied

Formula to control formatting

Set formatting based on formula

FIGURE 4.46 Formula Rule Created and Applied

To create a formula-based conditional formatting rule, complete the following steps:

1. Select the data range.
2. Click the Home tab, click Conditional Formatting in the Styles group, and then click New Rule.
3. Select *Use a formula to determine which cells to format* and type the formula, using cell references in the first row, in the *Format values where this formula is true* box.
4. Click Format, select the desired formatting to be applied, and then click OK.

Once complete, Excel applies the general formula to the selected range, substituting the appropriate cell reference as it makes the comparisons. In the Figure 4.45 example, =AND(G6="Finance",I6>=10000) requires that the text in the Pay_Type column (column G) contain Finance and the Amount column (column I) contain a value that is greater than or equal to $10,000. The AND function requires that both logical tests be met to apply the conditional formatting. A minimum of two logical tests are required; however, you can include additional logical tests. Note that *all* logical tests must be true to apply the conditional formatting.

Quick Concepts

10. Describe the ways in which How is conditional formatting similar to an IF function. **p. 530**

11. Describe a situation in which you would use conditional formatting. **p. 530**

12. Describe how is data bar conditional formatting helpful when reviewing a column of data. **p. 533**

Hands-On Exercises

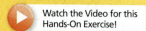
Skills covered: Add a Total
Row • Apply Highlight Cells
Rules • Specify Top/Bottom
Rules • Display Data Bars, Color
Scales, and Icon Sets • Create a
New Conditional Formatting Rule •
Use Formulas in Conditional
Formatting • Manage Rules

4 Table Aggregation and Conditional Formatting

Vicki Reid wants to review the transactions with you. She is interested in Sebastian Gruenewald's sales record and the three highest transaction amounts. In addition, she wants to compare the down payment amounts visually. Finally, she wants you to analyze the amounts owed for sales completed by Sebastian.

STEP 1 ► ADD A TOTAL ROW

You want to see the monthly totals for the Amount, Down_Pay, and Owed columns. You will add a total row to calculate the values. Refer to Figure 4.47 as you complete Step 1.

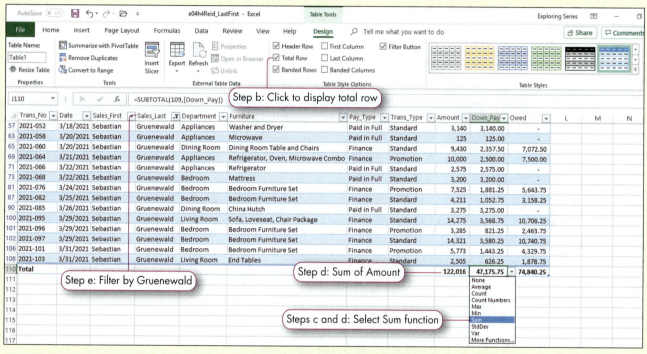

FIGURE 4.47 Add a Total Row

a. Open *e04h3Reid_LastFirst* if you closed it at the end of Hands-On Exercise 3. Save the workbook as **e04h4Reid_LastFirst**, changing h3 to h4.

b. Select the **March Individual worksheet**, click any cell inside the table, click the **Design tab**, and then click **Total Row** in the Table Style Options group.

Excel displays the total row after the last record. It sums the last field of values automatically. The total amount customers owe is 278,656.50.

c. Click the **Down_Pay cell** in row 110, click the **Total arrow**, and then select **Sum**.

You added a total to the Down_Pay field. The total amount of down payment collected is 190,602.50. The formula displays as =SUBTOTAL(109,[Down_Pay]) in the Formula Bar.

d. Click the **Amount cell** in row 110, click the **Total arrow**, and then select **Sum**.

You added a total to the Amount column. The total amount of merchandise sales is $469,259. The formula displays as =SUBTOTAL(109,[Amount]) in the Formula Bar.

e. Click the **Sales_Last filter arrow**, click the **Select All check box**, and then deselect the values. Click the **Gruenewald check box** to select it and click **OK**.

The total row values change to display the totals for only Gruenewald: $122,016 (Amount), 47,175.75 (Down_Pay), and 74,840.25 (Owed). This is an advantage of using the total row, which uses the SUBTOTAL function, as opposed to if you had inserted the SUM function manually. The SUM function would provide a total for all data in the column, not just the filtered data.

f. Click the **Data tab** and click **Clear** in the Sort & Filter group to remove all filters.

g. Save the workbook.

STEP 2 · APPLY HIGHLIGHT CELLS RULES

You want to identify Sebastian's sales for March without filtering the data. You will set a conditional format to apply a fill and font color so cells that document appliance sales stand out. Refer to Figure 4.48 as you complete Step 2.

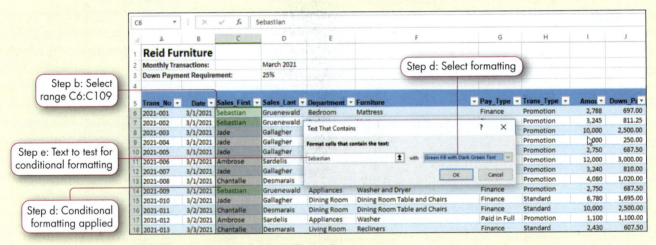

FIGURE 4.48 Highlight Cell Rules Dialog Box

a. Select the **range C6:C109**.

b. Click **Conditional Formatting** in the Styles group, point to **Highlight Cells Rules**, and then select **Text that Contains**.

The Text that Contains dialog box opens. (On a Mac, the New Formatting Rule box opens.)

c. Type **Sebastian** in the box, click the **with arrow**, and then select **Green Fill with Dark Green Text**. Click **OK**. Deselect the range and save the workbook.

Excel formats only cells that contain Sebastian with the fill and font color.

SPECIFY TOP/BOTTOM RULES

Vicki is now interested in identifying the highest three sales transactions in March. Instead of sorting the records, you will use the Top/Bottom Rules conditional formatting. Refer to Figure 4.49 as you complete Step 3.

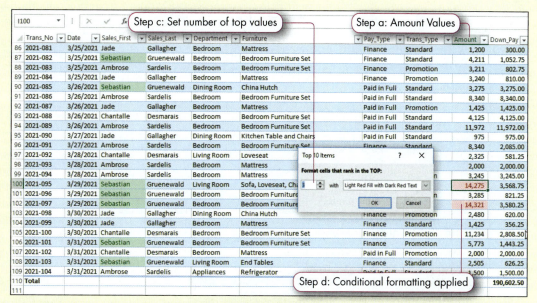

FIGURE 4.49 Top Three Amounts Conditionally Formatted

    a. Select the **range I6:I109**, the range containing the amounts.

    b. Click **Conditional Formatting** in the Styles group, point to **Top/Bottom Rules**, and then select **Top 10 Items**.

        The Top 10 Items dialog box opens.

    c. Click the arrow to display **3** and click **OK**.

    d. Scroll through the worksheet to see the top three amounts. Save the workbook.

Vicki wants to compare all of the down payments. Data bars will add visual references that will enable her to quickly evaluate the data. Refer to Figure 4.50 as you complete Step 4.

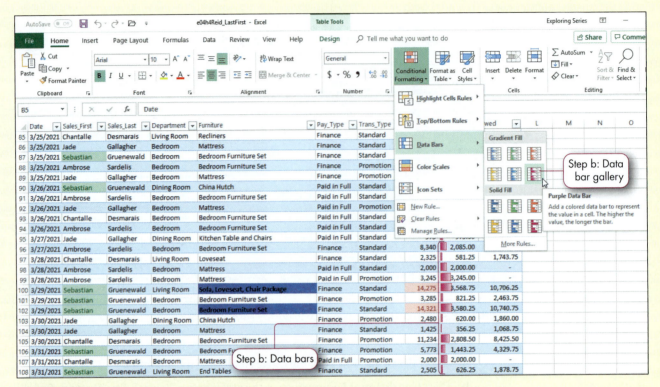

FIGURE 4.50 Data Bars Conditional Formatting

a. Select the **range J6:J109**, which contains the down payment amounts.

Excel displays a data bar in each cell. Note that one customer paid the full purchase price up front. In this case the down payment was 100% of the purchase price therefore the data bar fills the entire cell and the amount owed is 0.

b. Click **Conditional Formatting** in the Styles group, point to **Data Bars**, and then select **Purple Data Bar** in the Gradient Fill section. Scroll through the list and save the workbook.

Vicki's next request is to analyze the amounts owed by Sebastian's customers. In particular, she wants to highlight the merchandise for which more than $5,000 is owed. To do this, you realize you need to create a custom rule that evaluates both the Sales_First column and the Owed column. Refer to Figure 4.51 as you complete Step 5.

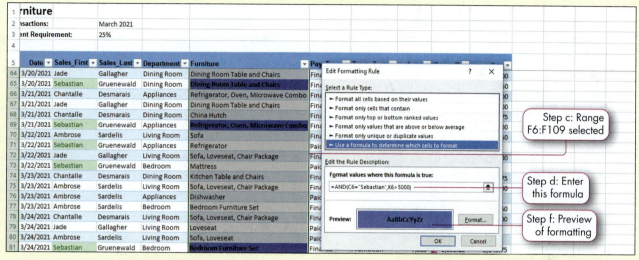

FIGURE 4.51 Custom Rule Created

a. Select the **range F6:F109**, which contains the furniture merchandise.

b. Click **Conditional Formatting** in the Styles group and select **New Rule**.

The New Formatting Rule dialog box opens.

c. Select **Use a formula to determine which cells to format**.

> **MAC TROUBLESHOOTING:** On a Mac, select Classic from the Style box and select Use a formula to determine which cells to format.

d. Type **=AND(C6="Sebastian",K6>5000)** in the *Format values where this formula is true* box.

Because you are comparing the contents of cell C6 to text, you must enclose the text within quotation marks.

e. Click **Format** in the New Formatting Rule dialog box to open the Format Cells dialog box. On a Mac, select Custom Format in the Format with box to display the Format Cells dialog box.

f. Click the **Font tab** and click **Bold** in the Font style list. Click the **Border tab**, click the **Color arrow**, select **Blue, Accent 5**, and then click **Outline**. Click the **Fill tab**, click **Blue, Accent 5 background color** (the second color from the right on the first row), and then click **OK**.

Figure 4.51 shows the Edit Formatting Rule dialog box, but the options are similar to the New Formatting Rule dialog box.

g. Click **OK** in the New Formatting Rule dialog box and scroll through the list to see which amounts owed are greater than $5,000 for Sebastian only.

> **TROUBLESHOOTING:** If the results seem incorrect, click Conditional Formatting and select Manage Rules. Edit the rule you just created and make any corrections to the formula.

h. Save and close the file. Based on your instructor's directions, submit e04h4Reid_LastFirst.

Chapter Objectives Review

After reading this chapter, you have accomplished the following objectives:

1. Freeze rows and columns.
- The Freeze Panes setting freezes the row(s) above and the column(s) to the left of the active cell. When you scroll, those rows and columns remain onscreen.
- Use Unfreeze Panes to clear the frozen rows and columns.

2. Print large datasets.
- Display and change page breaks: Display the data in Page Break Preview to see the automatic page breaks. Dashed blue lines indicate automatic page breaks. You can insert manual page breaks, indicated by solid blue lines.
- Set and clear a print area: If you do not want to print an entire worksheet, select a range and set a print area.
- Print titles: Select rows to repeat at top and/or columns to repeat at left to print the column and row labels on every page of a printout of a large dataset.
- Control print page order: You can control the sequence in which the pages will print.

3. Explore the benefits of data tables.
- A table is a structured range that contains related data. Tables have several benefits over regular ranges. The column labels, called field names, display on the first row of a table. Each row is a complete set of data for one record.

4. Design and create tables.
- Plan a table before you create it. Create unique field names on the first row of the table and enter data below the field names, avoiding blank rows.
- Create a table: You can create a table from existing data. Excel applies Table Style formatting and assigns a name, such as Table1, to the table. When the active cell is within a table, the Table Tools Design tab displays.
- Rename a table: When a table is created, Excel assigns a generic name and enables you to edit the default to a more suitable name.
- Add and delete fields: You can insert and delete table rows and columns to adjust the structure of a table.
- Add, edit, and delete records: You can add table rows, edit records, and delete table rows.
- Remove duplicate rows: Use the Remove Duplicates dialog box to remove duplicate records in a table. Excel will display a dialog box telling you how many records are deleted.

5. Apply a table style.
- Table styles control the fill color of the header row and records within the table.

6. Create structured references in formulas.
- Structured references use tags as field headings that can be used in formulas in place of cell references.

7. Sort data.
- Sort one field: You can sort text in alphabetic or reverse alphabetic order, values from smallest to largest or largest to smallest, and dates from oldest to newest or newest to

oldest. Click the filter arrow and select the sort method from the list.
- Sort multiple fields: Open the Sort dialog box and add column levels and sort orders.
- Create a custom sort: You can create a custom sort for unique data, such as ensuring that the months sort in sequential order rather than alphabetic order.

8. Filter data.
- Filtering is the process of specifying conditions for displaying records in a table. Only records that meet those conditions display; the other records are hidden.
- Clear filters: If you do not need filters, you can clear the filters.
- Apply text filters: A text filter can find exact text, text that does not equal a condition, text that begins with a particular letter, and so forth.
- Apply number filters: A number filter can find exact values, values that do not equal a particular value, values greater than or equal to a value, and so on.
- Apply date filters: You can set filters to find dates before or after a certain date, between two dates, yesterday, next month, and so forth.
- Apply a custom filter: You can create a custom AutoFilter to filter values by options such as Greater Than, Less Than, or Before.

9. Add a total row to a table.
- You can display a total row after the last record. You can add totals or select a different function, such as Average.

10. Apply conditional formatting.
- After selecting text, click Formatting in the Quick Analysis gallery to apply a conditional format.
- Apply a highlight cells rule: This rule highlights cell contents with a fill color, font color, and/or border color where the contents match a particular condition.
- Specify top/bottom rules: These rules enable you to highlight the top or bottom x number of items or percentage of items.
- Display data bars, color scales, and icon sets: Data bars compare values within the selected range. Color scales indicate values that occur within particular ranges. Icon sets display icons representing a number's relative value compared to other numbers in the range.

11. Create a new conditional formatting rule.
- You can create conditional format rules. The New Formatting Rule dialog box enables you to select a rule type.
- Manage rules: Use the Conditional Formatting Rules Manager dialog box to edit and delete rules.
- Use formulas in conditional formatting: You can create rules based on content in multiple columns.

Match the key terms with their definitions. Write the key term letter by the appropriate numbered definition.

a. Color scale
b. Conditional formatting
c. Data bar
d. Data Structure
e. Field
f. Filtering
g. Freezing
h. Fully qualified structured reference
i. Icon set
j. Page break

k. Print area
l. Print order
m. Record
n. Sorting
o. Structured reference
p. SUBTOTAL function
q. Table
r. Table style
s. Total Row
t. Unqualified reference

1. _____ A conditional format that displays a horizontal gradient or solid fill indicating the cell's relative value compared to other selected cells. **p. 533**

2. _____ The process of listing records or text in a specific sequence, such as alphabetically by last name. **p. 514**

3. _____ The process of specifying conditions to display only those records that meet those conditions. **p. 516**

4. _____ A set of rules that applies specific formatting to highlight or emphasize cells that meet specifications. **p. 530**

5. _____ A group of related fields representing one entity, such as data for one person, place, event, or concept. **p. 502**

6. _____ The rules that control the fill color of the header row, columns, and records in a table. **p. 506**

7. _____ An indication of where data will start on another printed page. **p. 494**

8. _____ A table row that appears below the last row of records in an Excel table and displays summary or aggregate statistics, such as a sum or an average. **p. 528**

9. _____ A conditional format that displays a particular color based on the relative value of the cell contents to the other selected cells. **p. 533**

10. _____ The sequence in which the pages are printed. **p. 496**

11. _____ A tag or use of a table element, such as a field label, as a reference in a formula. **p. 513**

12. _____ Symbols or signs that classify data into three, four, or five categories, based on the values in a range. **p. 533**

13. _____ The range of cells within a worksheet that will print. **p. 495**

14. _____ A predefined formula that calculates an aggregate value, such as totals, for values in a range, a table, or a database. **p. 529**

15. _____ An individual piece of data in a table, such as first name, last name, address, and phone number. **p. 528**

16. _____ A structure that organizes data in a series of records (rows), with each record made up of a number of fields (columns). **p. 513**

17. _____ The process of keeping rows and/or columns visible onscreen at all times, even when you scroll through a large dataset. **p. 493**

18. _____ The organization method used to manage multiple data points within a dataset. **p. 502**

19. _____ The use of headings without row references in a structured formula. **p. 513**

20. _____ A structured formula that includes references, for table name. **p. 513**

Multiple Choice

1. You have a large dataset that will print on several pages. You want to ensure that related records print on the same page with column and row labels visible and that confidential information is not printed. You should apply all of the following page setup options *except* which one to accomplish this task?

   (a) Set a print area.
   (b) Print titles.
   (c) Adjust page breaks.
   (d) Change the print page order.

2. You are working with a large worksheet. Your row headings are in column A. Which command(s) should be used to see the row headings and the distant information in columns X, Y, and Z?

   (a) Freeze Panes command
   (b) Hide Rows command
   (c) New Window command and cascade the windows
   (d) Split Rows command

3. Which statement is *not* a recommended guideline for designing and creating an Excel table?

   (a) Avoid naming two fields with the same name.
   (b) Ensure that no blank columns separate data columns within the table.
   (c) Leave one blank row between records in the table.
   (d) Include field names on the first row of the table.

4. Which of the following characters are wildcards in Excel? (Check all that apply.)

   (a) *
   (b) #
   (c) &
   (d) $

5. What should you do to ensure that records in a table are unique?

   (a) Do nothing; a logical reason probably exists to keep identical records.
   (b) Use the Remove Duplicates command.
   (c) Look at each row yourself and manually delete duplicate records.
   (d) Filter the data to show only unique records.

6. Which Conditional Formatting rule is best suited to highlight sales value greater than $5,000?

   (a) Equals
   (b) Between
   (c) Greater Than
   (d) Less Than

7. Which date filter option enables you to restrict the view to only dates between April 1, 2021, and April 30, 2021?

   (a) Equals
   (b) Before
   (c) After
   (d) Between

8. Which of the following is a fully qualified structured reference?

   (a) =[Purchase_Price]-[Down_Payment]
   (b) =Sales[@Purchase_Price]-Sales[@Down_Payment]
   (c) =Purchase_Price-Down_Payment
   (d) =[Sales]Purchase_Price-[Sales]Down_Payment

9. Which of the following is *not* an aggregate function that can be applied in a total row?

   (a) MAX
   (b) AVERAGE
   (c) COUNT
   (d) VLOOKUP

10. If you would like to set a conditional formatting rule based on the function =AND(G6="Finance", H7<7000), which formatting rule type is needed?

    (a) Format all cells based on their values.
    (b) Format only cells that contain.
    (c) Use a formula to determine which cells to format.
    (d) Format only values that are above or below average.

Practice Exercises

1 Institute for Study Abroad

You are an administrative assistant for the local university's Institute for Study Abroad. The institute for study abroad is responsible for the coordination and management of all students that plan to study overseas. As part of your duties, you have been asked to enhance a preexisting worksheet by creating an Excel table, applying filters, conditional formatting, adding tuition calculations, and making the document printer friendly. Refer to Figure 4.52 as you complete this exercise.

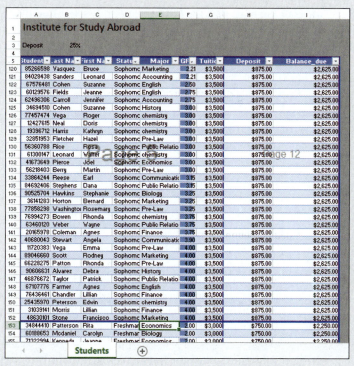

FIGURE 4.52 Institute for Study Abroad

a. Open *e04p1StudyAbroad* and save it as **e04p1StudyAbroad_LastFirst**.

b. Select the **range A5:G209**. Click the **Insert tab**, click **Table** in the Tables group. Be sure to click *My table has headers* and click **OK** in the Create Table dialog box.

c. Type **Students** in the Table Name box in the Properties group.

d. Click **cell A1** and click **cell A6**. Click the **View tab**, click **Freeze Panes** in the Window group, and then select Freeze Panes.

e. Click the **Data tab** and click **Remove Duplicates** in the Data Tools group. Click **OK** and then click **OK** again.

   Four Duplicate values should be found and removed.

f. Click **cell H5**, type **Deposit**, and then press **Enter**. Click **cell I5**, type **Balance_due**, and then press **Enter**.

g. Click **cell H6**, type **=$B$3*[Tuition]**, and then press **Enter**.

h. Click **cell I6**, type **=[Tuition]-[Deposit]**, and then press **Enter**.

i. Select the **range H5:I205**. Click the **Home tab**, click **Format** in the cells group, and then select **AutoFit Column Width**.

j. Click **Currency Number Format** in the Numbers group.

k. Select the **range F6:F205**. Click the **Quick Analysis box** located at the bottom of the selection, and select **Data Bars** in the Formatting group. (On a Mac, click the Home tab, click Conditional Formatting, and then select Data Bars.)

l. Click the **Design tab** and click **Total Row** in the Table Style Options group.

m. Select the **range A6:A205**. Click the **Home tab**, click **Conditional Formatting** in the Styles group, and then select **New Rule**. Click **Use a formula to determine which cells to format** and type **=AND(D6="Senior", F6<=2)**.

n. Click **Format**, click the **Fill tab**, and then select **Red** (last row, second from the left). Click **OK** and click **OK** again to apply the conditional formatting.

o. Click **cell F6**, click the **Data tab**, and then click **Sort** in the Sort & Filter group. Click the **Column arrow** and select **Status**. Click the **Order arrow** and select **Custom list**. Click **NEW LIST** in the Custom lists box and click the List entries box. Type **Senior, Junior, Sophomore, Freshman** in the List entries box.

MAC TROUBLESHOOTING: Click the Excel menu and select Preferences. Click Custom Lists in the Formulas and Lists section.

---

p. Click **OK** to return to the Sort dialog box. Click **Add Level**, click the **Then by arrow**, and then select **GPA**. Click **OK**.

q. Prepare the Students worksheet for printing by doing the following:
- Select the **range A5:I206**, click the **Page Layout tab**, click **Print Area** in the Page Setup group, and then select **Set Print Area**.
- Click **Print Titles** in the Page Setup group, click the **Rows to repeat at top Collapse Dialog Box**, click the **row 5 header**, and then click **Expand Dialog Box**. Click **OK**.
- Click the **View tab** and click **Page Break Preview** in the Workbook Views group. Click the **Page Layout tab**. Click the row that contains the first student with Junior status (row 58), click **Breaks** in the Page Setup group, and then click Insert Page Break. Repeat the last step to add page breaks at each change in status (rows 110 and 153).

r. Save and close the file. Based on your instructor's directions, submit e04p1StudyAbroad_LastFirst.

2 | Sunny Popcorn, Inc.

You are a financial analyst for Sunny Popcorn, Inc., and have been given the task of compiling a workbook to detail weekly sales information. The current information provides detailed sales rep information, flavors ordered, account type, and volume ordered. The owners are specifically interested in local sales that are generating at least $150.00 a week. To complete the document you will sort, filter, use table tools, and apply conditional formatting. Refer to Figure 4.53 as you complete this exercise.

FIGURE 4.53 Sunny Popcorn Inc.

a. Open *e04p2Popcorn* and save it as **e04p2Popcorn_LastFirst**.

b. Click **cell C7**, ensure the Home tab is displayed, click the **Sort & Filter arrow** in the Editing group, and then select **Sort A to Z**.

c. Click the **Insert tab**, click **Table** in the Tables group, and then click **OK** in the Create Table dialog box.

d. Click **Orange, Table Style Medium 3** in the Table Styles group on the Design tab.

e. Click **cell G7**, type **=[Price per lb]*[Volume in lbs]*$B$3** and then press **Enter**.

f. Click **cell H7**, type **=[Price per lb]*[Volume in lbs]-[Deposit]** and then press **Enter**

g. Select the **range G7:H106**, click the **Home tab**, and then click **Currency Number Format** in the Number group.

h. Click the **Design tab** and click **Total Row** in the Table Style Options group.

i. Click the **Deposit Total Row arrow**, ensure **Sum** is selected, click the **Volume in lbs Total Row arrow**, and then select **Average**.

j. Click the **filter arrow** of the Account type column, click the **Select All check box** to deselect it, click **Local**, and then click **OK**. Click the **filter arrow** of Amount Due, select **Number Filters**, and then select Above Average.

k. Select the **range H11:H106**, click **Quick Analysis**, and then select **Greater Than**. Type **150.00** in the Format cells that are GREATER THAN box, select **Green Fill with Dark Green Text**, and then click **OK**. (On a Mac, click the Home tab, click Conditional Formatting, and then click **Highlight Cells Rules**. Select **Greater Than** and enter the parameters.)

> **MAC TROUBLESHOOTING:** Quick Analysis is not available for Mac. In order to apply conditional formatting click the Home tab and click Conditional Formatting.

l. Select the **range E11:E106**, click **Quick Analysis**, and then select **Data Bars**.

m. Click the **Page Layout tab**, click the **Scale box** in the Scale to Fit group, and then type **85%**. (On a Mac, click the Page Layout tab, click Page Setup, and then adjust the scale to 85%.)

n. Create a footer with your name on the left side, the sheet name code in the center, and the file name code on the right side.

o. Save and close the file. Based on your instructor's directions, submit e04p2Popcorn_LastFirst.

Mid-Level Exercises

1 Crafton's Pet Supplies

You are the inventory manager for Crafton's Pet Supplies. You are currently performing an analysis to determine inventory levels, as well as the total value of inventory on hand. Your last steps will be to check the report for duplicate entries and format for printing.

a. Open *e04m1Inventory* and save it as **e04m1Inventory_LastFirst**.

b. Freeze the panes so that the column labels do not scroll offscreen.

c. Convert the data to a table and name the table **Inventory2021**.

d. Apply **Red**, **Table Style Medium 3** to the table.

e. Sort the table by Warehouse (A to Z), then Department, and then by Unit Price (smallest to largest). Create a custom sort order for Department so that it appears in this sequence: Food & Health, Collars & Leashes, Toys, Clothes, Training, and Grooming.

f. Remove duplicate records from the table. Excel should find and remove one duplicate record.

g. Create an unqualified structured reference in column G to determine the value of the inventory on hand. To calculate the inventory on hand, multiply the **Unit Price** and the **Amount on Hand.**

h. Apply a **Total Row** to the Inventory2021 table; set the Amount on Hand to Average. Format the results to display with two decimal points.

i. Create a new conditional formatting rule that displays any Inventory Value for the Food & Health department with a value of $30,000 or more as **Red, Accent 2 fill color** with **White, Background 1** font color. There will be two qualifying entries.

j. Ensure the warehouse information is not broken up between pages when printed. Add a page break to make sure that each warehouse prints on its own consecutive page.

k. Set the worksheet to **Landscape orientation** and repeat row 1 labels on all pages.

l. Display the Inventory sheet in Page Break Preview.

m. Insert a footer with your name on the left side, the sheet name code in the center, and the file name code on the right side.

n. Save and close the file. Based on your instructor's directions, submit e04m1Inventory_LastFirst.

2 Riverwood Realty

You work as a real estate agent for Riverwood Realty, an independent real estate agency in Utah. As part of your end of year reports, you compile a list of homes that have sold in your sales region. To complete the report, you will create an Excel table, apply Filters, Sort, perform basic calculations using unqualified structured references, and then prepare the document to print.

a. Open *e04m2Homes* and save it as **e04m2Homes_LastFirst**.

b. Freeze the panes so that the column labels do not scroll offscreen.

c. Convert the data to a table and name the table Sales.

d. Apply **Purple, Table Style Dark 10** to the table.

e. Remove duplicate records from the table. Excel should find and remove eight duplicate records.

f. Add a new column in column I named **Days on Market**. Use unqualified structured references to calculate the days on market (Sale date – list date) in column I. Set column I's width to **18**.

g. Apply a **Total Row** to the Sales table; set the selling price and Days on Market totals to Average with one decimal point.

h. Use Quick Analysis to apply Top 10% conditional formatting to column F. On a Mac Quick Analysis is not available. Click the Home tab, click Conditional Formatting, click Top/Bottom Rules, and then select Top 10%.

i. Apply **3 Traffic Lights (Unrimmed)** conditional formatting icon set to column I. Set the icon to display green for homes that sold within 45 days, yellow for 46 to 90, and red to homes that took more than 90 days to sell.

j. Filter the data to only display sales by the **Selling Agent Hernandez**.

k. Sort the table in **Ascending order** by City (Column C).

l. Set the **range A1:I83** as the print area.

m. Save and close the file. Based on your instructor's directions, submit e04m2Homes_LastFirst.

Running Case

New Castle County Technical Services

New Castle County Technical Services (NCCTS) provides technical support services for a number of companies in New Castle County, Delaware. You previously created charts to depict summary data by service type, customer, and days open. Since then, you copied the charts as pictures to replace the actual charts so changes you make to the dataset will not alter the charts. However, you have a backup of the original charts in case you need to change them later. Now, you will sort the main dataset for analysis and prepare it to be printed on two pages. You will apply conditional formatting to highlight transactions that took more than 9 days to close and display data bars for the amount billed to give a quick visual for transaction amounts. You will also filter a copy of the dataset to set filters to further analyze the transactions. Finally, you will convert the summary sections into tables.

a. Open *e04r1NCCTS* and save it as **e04r1NCCTS_LastFirst**.

b. Freeze the fourth row and second column so that they do not scroll off the window on the March Hours worksheet.

c. Sort the data on the March Hours worksheet in alphabetic order by Call Type and within call type by Amount Billed from largest to smallest.

d. Apply conditional formatting that highlights over 9 days open in Light Red Fill with Dark Red Text.

e. Apply solid fill **Orange Data Bar** conditional formatting to the Amount Billed values.

f. Display the March Filtered worksheet and set a filter to display transactions with an Opened Date in March.

g. Set another filter to display transactions with an Amount Billed greater than or equal to $400.

h. Display the Summary Statistics worksheet. Create a table for the Summary Statistics by Customer dataset. As you create the table, adjust the table range to start on row 2.

i. Assign the name **Customer_Stats** to the table.

j. Apply **Orange, Table Style Medium 3**.

k. Add a total row to display the sum of the Total Amount Billed column to the table.

l. Select the **range A1:D20** in the Summary Stats worksheet and set it as a print area.

m. Create a table for the Summary Statistics by Call Type dataset below the first dataset. As you create the table, adjust the table range to start on row 27.

n. Assign the name **CallType_Stats** to the table.

o. Apply **Orange, Table Style Medium 3**.

p. Add a total row to display the sum of the Total Amount Billed column to the table.

q. Click **cell D27** and insert a table column to the left. Type **Hours per Day** in **cell D27**.

r. Insert a structured reference in a formula in **cell D28** that divides the Total Days Open by the Total Hours Logged.

s. Use Format Painter to copy the fill formatting from **cell D26** to **cell E26**.

t. Insert a footer with your name on the left side, the sheet name in the center, and the file name code on the right side of Summary Charts and Summary Statistics worksheets. Return to Normal view.

u. Save and close the workbook. Based on your instructor's directions, submit e04r1NCCTS_LastFirst.

Disaster Recovery

Dairy Farm

You are the product manager for Schaefer Dairy farm, a local organic farm that produces dairy products. Current inventory information is stored in an Excel worksheet and conditional formatting is used to indicate when a product has expired and should be discarded. Unfortunately, the conditional formatting rule that was created to indicate a product should be discarded has stopped working. You need to examine the existing conditional formatting rule and repair the error in order to identify the expired products. All products have a shelf life of 30 days.

Open *e04d1Dairy* and save it as **e04d1Dairy_LastFirst**. Review the shelf-life information referenced in cell D3. Note the 30-day shelf life was erroneously changed to 300. Enter the correct input to reflect the actual shelf life. Next, edit the custom conditional formatting rule applied to **column B** to reflect the correct shelf life referenced in cell D3. Rename the table **Products** and add a total row that calculates the total value of inventory in column D and counts the total number of products in column E.

Save and close the file. Based on your instructor's directions, submit e04d1Dairy_LastFirst.

IT Department Analysis

You have been hired as a student assistant in the IT department of your university. As part of your responsibilities, you have been asked to enhance the Excel workbook used to analyze the department's performance. The workbook contains records of all support issues resolved over the past year. You will convert the data to a table, format the table, sort and filter the table, insert calculations to evaluate key performance indicators, and then prepare the worksheet for printing

Prepare the Large Worksheet as a Table

You will freeze the panes so that labels remain onscreen. You also want to convert the data to a table so that you can apply table options.

1. Open the *e04c1TechSupport* workbook and save it as **e04c1TechSupport_LastFirst**.
2. Freeze Panes so the first row containing column headings (Row 5) on the SupportCalls worksheet will remain static when scrolling.
3. Convert the data to a table, name the table **SupportCalls**, and then apply the **Gold, Table Style Medium 12**.
4. Remove duplicate records.

Add a Structured Reference and a Total Row

To help the IT analyze productivity, you will use unqualified structured references to add a calculation to the table. You will also add a total row to provide basic summary data.

5. Add a new column to the table named **Duration**.
6. Create a formula using unqualified structured references to calculate the days required to resolve the incident (Date Resolved – Date created) and apply General Number Format.
7. Add a total row to display the Average days required to resolve an issue.

Sort and Filter the Table

To help the IT manager analyze the effectiveness of each support technician, you will create a custom sort to display Agents in alphabetic order, then by problem description, and then by incident duration.

8. Sort the table by Agent Name in alphabetic order, add a second level to sort by description, and then create a custom sort order as follows: Won't power on, Virus, Printing Issues, Software Update, Forgotten Password. Add a third level to sort by duration smallest to largest.
9. Filter the table to only display closed incidents as indicated in the status column.

Apply Conditional Formatting

The IT department has a 30-day threshold to resolve all technical incidents. You will use conditional formatting to identify issues that lasted or exceeded 30 days to resolve.

10. Use Quick Analysis to apply **Data Bars** conditional formatting to the column that contains duration. (On a Mac, click the Home tab and use Conditional Formatting to apply **Data Bars** to the column that contains the data.)
11. Create a conditional format that applies **Red fill** and White Background 1 font color to the incidents (column A) that required 30 or more days to resolve.

Prepare the Worksheet for Printing

The final report will be distributed in print for your end-of-the-year meeting. You will set page breaks and repeating column headings before printing.

12. Select **Landscape orientation** for all sheets and set appropriate margins so that the data will print on one page. Set the print scale to **85%**.
13. Change page breaks so agent information is not split between pages.
14. Set row 5 to repeat on each page that is printed.
15. Add a footer with your name on the left side, the sheet name code in the center, and the file name code on the right side.
16. Save and close the file. Based on your instructor's directions, submit e04c1TechSupport_LastFirst.

Access

Introduction to Access

LEARNING OUTCOME You will demonstrate understanding of relational database concepts.

OBJECTIVES & SKILLS: After you read this chapter, you will be able to:

CASE STUDY | Managing a Business in the Global Economy

Northwind Traders is an international gourmet food distributor that imports and exports specialty foods from around the world. Keeping track of customers, vendors, orders, and inventory is a critical task. The owners of Northwind have just purchased an order-processing database created with Microsoft Access 2019 to help manage their customers, suppliers, products, and orders.

You have been hired to learn, use, and manage the database. Northwind's owners are willing to provide training about their business and Access. They expect the learning process to take about three months. After three months, your job will be to support the order-processing team as well as to provide detail and summary reports to the sales force as needed. Your new job at Northwind Traders will be a challenge, but it is also a good opportunity to make a great contribution to a global company. Are you up to the task?

CHAPTER 1

Navigating an Access Database

Sfio Cracho/Shutterstock

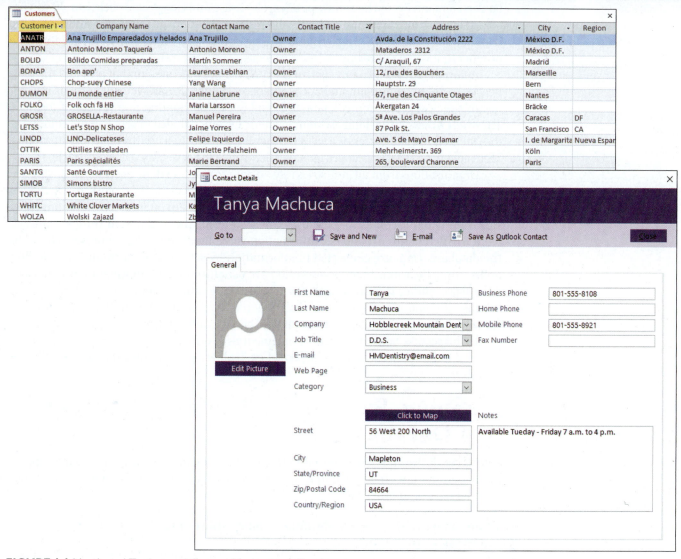

FIGURE 1.1 Northwind Traders and Contact Management Databases

CASE STUDY | Managing a Business in the Global Economy

Starting File	Files to be Submitted
a01h1Traders	a01h1Traders_LastFirst_*CurrentDate* a01h2Traders_LastFirst a01h3Contacts_LastFirst

MyLab IT Grader An alternate version of this project is available as a MyLab IT Grader Assessment

Databases Are Everywhere!

A *database* is a collection of data organized as meaningful information that can be accessed, managed, stored, queried, sorted, and reported. You participate in data collection and are exposed to databases on a regular basis. Your college or university stores your personal and registration data. When you registered for this course, your data was entered into a database. If you have a bank account, a Social Security card, a medical history, or if you have ever booked a flight with an airline, your information is stored in a database.

You use databases online without realizing it, such as when you shop or check your bank statement. Even when you type a search phrase into Google and click Search, you are using Google's massive database with all of its stored webpage references and keywords. Look for something on Amazon, and you are searching Amazon's database to find a product that you want to buy.

A *database management system (DBMS)* is a software system that provides the tools needed to create, maintain, and use a database. Database management systems make it possible to access and control data and display the information in a variety of formats. *Microsoft Access* is the database management system included in professional editions of the Office 2019 suite. Access is a valuable decision-making tool used by many organizations. More advanced DBMS packages include Microsoft SQL Server, MySQL, and Oracle.

Organizations from all industries rely on data to conduct daily operations. Businesses maintain and analyze data about their customers, employees, orders, volunteers, activities, and facilities. Data and information are two terms that are often used interchangeably. However, when it comes to databases, the two terms mean different things. Data are what is entered into a database. Information is the finished product that is produced by the database. Data are converted to information by selecting, performing calculations, and sorting. Decisions in an organization are usually based on information produced by a database, rather than raw data. For example, the number 55 is just an item of data, because it could mean anything. Only when a label is attached to it (for example, as someone's age) does it take on meaning and become information.

In this section, you will learn the fundamentals of organizing data in a database, explore Access database objects and the purpose of each object, and examine the Access interface.

STEP 1   Opening, Saving, and Enabling Content in a Database

As you work through the material in this book, you will frequently be asked to open a database, save it with a new name, and enable content. You can also start by creating a new database if appropriate.

> **To open an existing Access database and enable content, complete the following steps:**
>
> 1. Start Access. Backstage view displays. (Note: If Access is already open, click the File tab to display Backstage view).
> 2. Click Open Other Files.
> 3. Click Browse to open the Open dialog box.
> 4. Locate and select the database and click Open.
> 5. Click Enable Content on the message bar (see Figure 1.2). Access will close and reopen the database, and the security warning disappears and will not display again for this database.

If you have been provided a database, open the file to get started. When you open any database for the first time, you will be presented with a warning that it might contain harmful code. By enabling the content, the database file will be trusted on the computer you are working on. All content from this publisher and associated with this book can be trusted.

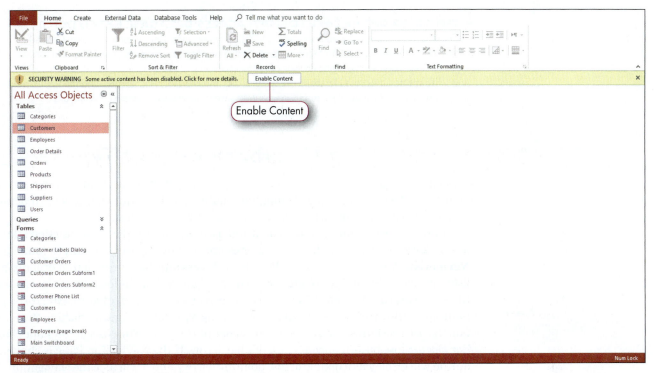

FIGURE 1.2 Access Security Warning

The File tab gives you access to the Save As command. Most assignments will have you save the starting database file with a new name. The name given to the file should help describe the purpose of the database. On the File tab, select Save As and ensure *Save Database As* is selected (see Figure 1.3). The saving process is similar to that of any other program except that in Access you have the option to save objects within the database. After you have named the file an appropriate name, click Save.

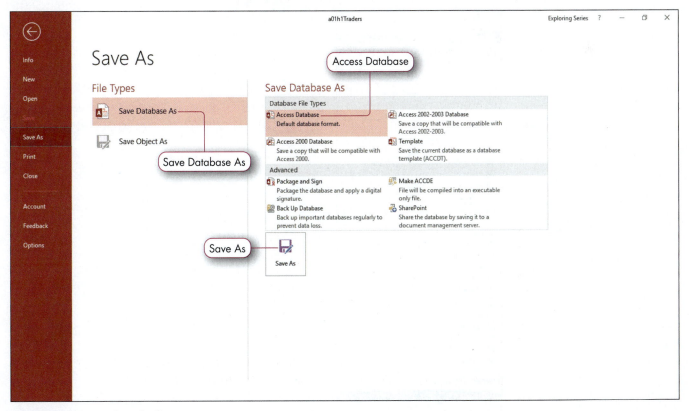

FIGURE 1.3 Access Save As Options

STEP 2 ## Recognizing Database Object Types

Databases must be carefully managed to keep information accurate. Data need to be changed, added, and deleted. Managing a database also requires that you understand when data are saved and when you need to use the Save commands.

In Access, each component created and used to make the database function is known as an ***object***. Objects include tables, queries, forms, and reports, and can be found in the ***Navigation Pane***. The Navigation Pane is an Access interface element that organizes and lists the objects in an Access database. The Navigation Pane is located on the left side of the screen and displays all objects. You can open any object by double-clicking the object's name in the list. You can toggle the display of the Navigation Pane by clicking the Shutter Bar Open/Close button at the top-right corner of the pane. The Navigation Pane Shutter Bar Open/Close button appears as a double arrow. If the Navigation Pane is shown, the button will display as a double arrow pointing left $\ll$, and it will hide the Navigation Pane when clicked. If the Navigation Pane is hidden, the button displays as a double arrow pointing right $\gg$, and it will show the Navigation Pane when clicked. You can collapse the contents of an object group by clicking the group heading or the double arrows to the right of the group heading. To expand the contents of an object group that has been hidden, click the heading again or click the double arrows to the right of the group heading again. To change the way objects are grouped in the Navigation Pane, click the Object list arrow ⊙ on the Navigation Pane title bar and select your preferred configuration of the available options. See Figure 1.4 to see the features of the Navigation Pane.

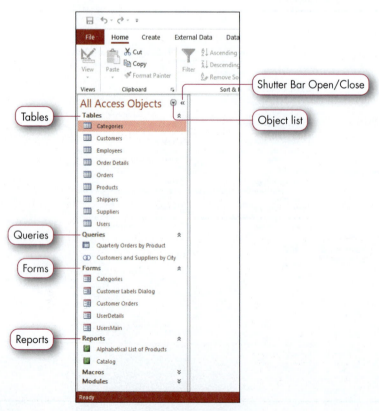

FIGURE 1.4 Navigation Pane Features

Most databases contain multiple tables. By default, the objects display in groups by object type in the Navigation Pane. In other words, you will see a list of tables, followed by queries, followed by forms, followed by reports. The purpose of each of these objects is described below.

Tables are where all data are stored in your database and, thus, can be said to be the foundation of each database. Tables organize data into columns and rows. Each column represents a ***field***, a category of information we store in a table. For example, in the Northwind database, a table containing customer information would include fields such as Customer ID, Company Name, and City. Each row in a table contains a ***record***, a complete set of all the fields about one person, place, event, or concept. A customer record, for example, would contain all the fields about a single customer, including the Customer ID, the Company Name, Contact Name, Contact Title, Address, City, etc. Figure 1.5 shows both fields and records. The ***primary key*** is a field (or combination of fields) that uniquely identifies each record in a table. Common primary keys are driver's license number, government ID number (such as a Social Security number), passport number, and student ID. Many of these primary keys are generated by a database. Your college or university's database likely assigns a unique identifier to a student as soon as they apply, for example.

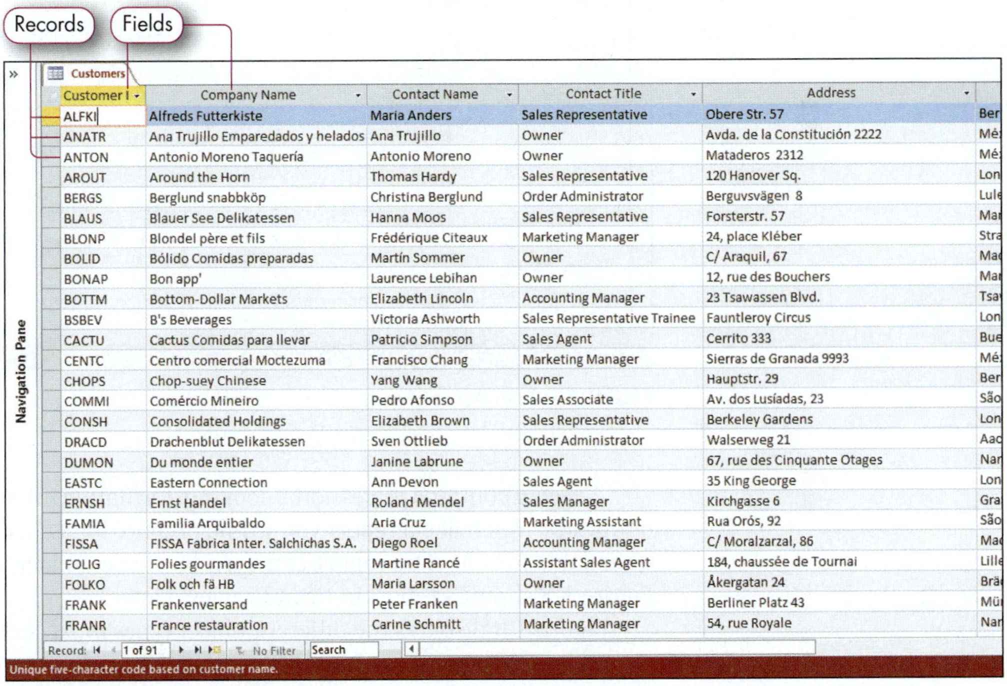

Customer I	Company Name	Contact Name	Contact Title	Address	
ALFKI	Alfreds Futterkiste	Maria Anders	Sales Representative	Obere Str. 57	Ber
ANATR	Ana Trujillo Emparedados y helados	Ana Trujillo	Owner	Avda. de la Constitución 2222	Mé
ANTON	Antonio Moreno Taquería	Antonio Moreno	Owner	Mataderos 2312	Mé
AROUT	Around the Horn	Thomas Hardy	Sales Representative	120 Hanover Sq.	Lon
BERGS	Berglund snabbköp	Christina Berglund	Order Administrator	Berguvsvägen 8	Lul
BLAUS	Blauer See Delikatessen	Hanna Moos	Sales Representative	Forsterstr. 57	Ma
BLONP	Blondel père et fils	Frédérique Citeaux	Marketing Manager	24, place Kléber	Str
BOLID	Bólido Comidas preparadas	Martín Sommer	Owner	C/ Araquil, 67	Ma
BONAP	Bon app'	Laurence Lebihan	Owner	12, rue des Bouchers	Ma
BOTTM	Bottom-Dollar Markets	Elizabeth Lincoln	Accounting Manager	23 Tsawassen Blvd.	Tsa
BSBEV	B's Beverages	Victoria Ashworth	Sales Representative Trainee	Fauntleroy Circus	Lon
CACTU	Cactus Comidas para llevar	Patricio Simpson	Sales Agent	Cerrito 333	Bue
CENTC	Centro comercial Moctezuma	Francisco Chang	Marketing Manager	Sierras de Granada 9993	Mé
CHOPS	Chop-suey Chinese	Yang Wang	Owner	Hauptstr. 29	Ber
COMMI	Comércio Mineiro	Pedro Afonso	Sales Associate	Av. dos Lusíadas, 23	São
CONSH	Consolidated Holdings	Elizabeth Brown	Sales Representative	Berkeley Gardens	Lon
DRACD	Drachenblut Delikatessen	Sven Ottlieb	Order Administrator	Walserweg 21	Aac
DUMON	Du monde entier	Janine Labrune	Owner	67, rue des Cinquante Otages	Nar
EASTC	Eastern Connection	Ann Devon	Sales Agent	35 King George	Lon
ERNSH	Ernst Handel	Roland Mendel	Sales Manager	Kirchgasse 6	Gra
FAMIA	Familia Arquibaldo	Aria Cruz	Marketing Assistant	Rua Orós, 92	São
FISSA	FISSA Fabrica Inter. Salchichas S.A.	Diego Roel	Accounting Manager	C/ Moralzarzal, 86	Ma
FOLIG	Folies gourmandes	Martine Rancé	Assistant Sales Agent	184, chaussée de Tournai	Lill
FOLKO	Folk och fä HB	Maria Larsson	Owner	Åkergatan 24	Brä
FRANK	Frankenversand	Peter Franken	Marketing Manager	Berliner Platz 43	Mü
FRANR	France restauration	Carine Schmitt	Marketing Manager	54, rue Royale	Nar

FIGURE 1.5 An Access Table

A ***query*** (or queries, plural) is a question you ask about the data in your database. Notice the word query is similar to the word inquiry, which means "question." It produces a subset of data that provides information about the question you have asked. For example, a query may display a list of which customers live in a specific town or a list of children registered for a specific after-school program. You can double-click a query in the Navigation Pane and you will notice the interface is similar to that of a table, as shown in Figure 1.6.

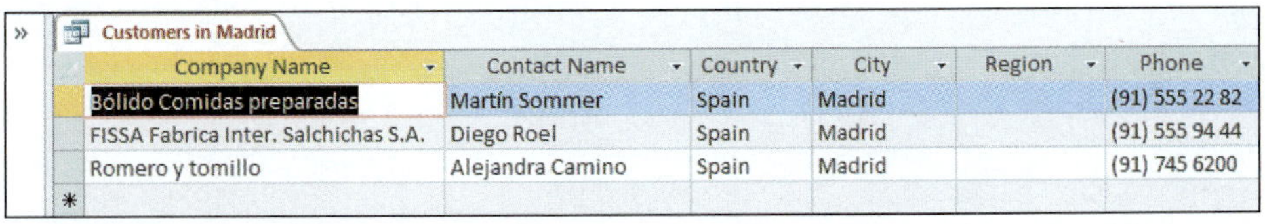

Company Name	Contact Name	Country	City	Region	Phone
Bólido Comidas preparadas	Martín Sommer	Spain	Madrid		(91) 555 22 82
FISSA Fabrica Inter. Salchichas S.A.	Diego Roel	Spain	Madrid		(91) 555 94 44
Romero y tomillo	Alejandra Camino	Spain	Madrid		(91) 745 6200

FIGURE 1.6 An Access Query

A *form* allows simplified entry and modification of data. Much like entering data on a paper form, a database form enables you to add, modify, and delete table data. Most forms display one record at a time, which helps prevent data entry errors. Forms are typically utilized by the users of the database, while the database designer creates and edits the form structure. Figure 1.7 shows a form. Notice a single record is displayed.

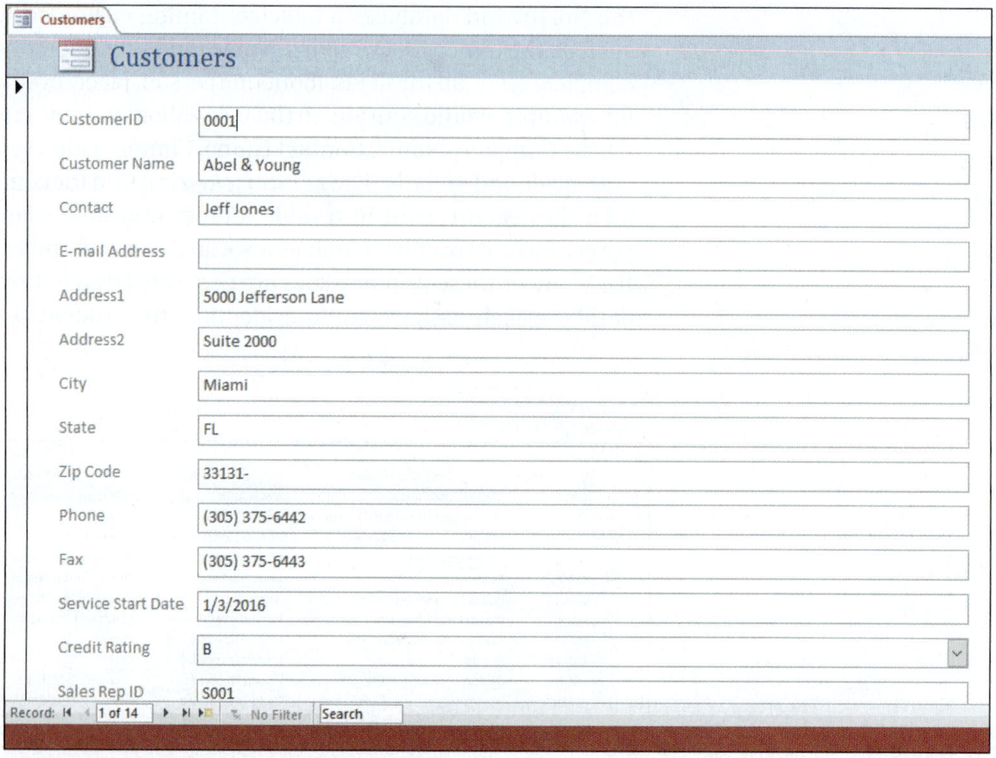

FIGURE 1.7 An Access Form

A *report* contains professional-looking, formatted information from underlying tables or queries. Much like a report you would prepare for a class, a report puts the results into a readable format. The report can then be viewed onscreen, saved to a file, or printed. Figure 1.8 shows a report in Print Preview view.

Figure 1.9 displays the different object types in Access with the foundation object—the table—in the center of the illustration. The purpose each object serves is explained underneath the object name. The flow of information between objects is indicated by single-arrowhead arrows if the flow is one direction only. Two-arrowhead arrows indicate that the flow goes both directions. For example, you can use forms to view, add, delete, or modify data from tables.

Customer Contacts

Contact Name	Company Name	Contact Title	Phone	City	Region	Country
Alejandra Camino	Romero y tomillo	Accounting Manager	(91) 745 6200	Madrid		Spain
Alexander Feuer	Morgenstern Gesundkost	Marketing Assistant	0342-023176	Leipzig		Germany
Ana Trujillo	Ana Trujillo Emparedados y helados	Owner	(5) 555-4729	México D.F.		Mexico
Anabela Domingues	Tradição Hipermercados	Sales Representative	(11) 555-2167	São Paulo	SP	Brazil
André Fonseca	Gourmet Lanchonetes	Sales Associate	(11) 555-9482	Campinas	SP	Brazil
Ann Devon	Eastern Connection	Sales Agent	(171) 555-0297	London		UK
Annette Roulet	La maison d'Asie	Sales Manager	61.77.61.10	Toulouse		France
Antonio Moreno	Antonio Moreno Taquería	Owner	(5) 555-3932	México D.F.		Mexico
Aria Cruz	Familia Arquibaldo	Marketing Assistant	(11) 555-9857	São Paulo	SP	Brazil
Art Braunschweiger	Split Rail Beer & Ale	Sales Manager	(307) 555-4680	Lander	WY	USA
Bernardo Batista	Que Delícia	Accounting Manager	(21) 555-4252	Rio de Janeiro	RJ	Brazil
Carine Schmitt	France restauration	Marketing Manager	40.32.21.21	Nantes		France
Carlos González	LILA-Supermercado	Accounting Manager	(9) 331-6954	Barquisimeto	Lara	Venezuela
Carlos Hernández	HILARIÓN-Abastos	Sales Representative	(5) 555-1340	San Cristóbal	Táchira	Venezuela
Catherine Dewey	Maison Dewey	Sales Agent	(02) 201 24 67	Bruxelles		Belgium
Christina Berglund	Berglund snabbköp	Order Administrator	0921-12 34 65	Luleå		Sweden
Daniel Tonini	La corne d'abondance	Sales Representative	30.59.84.10	Versailles		France

Page: 1 ▶ ▶| No Filter

FIGURE 1.8 An Access Report

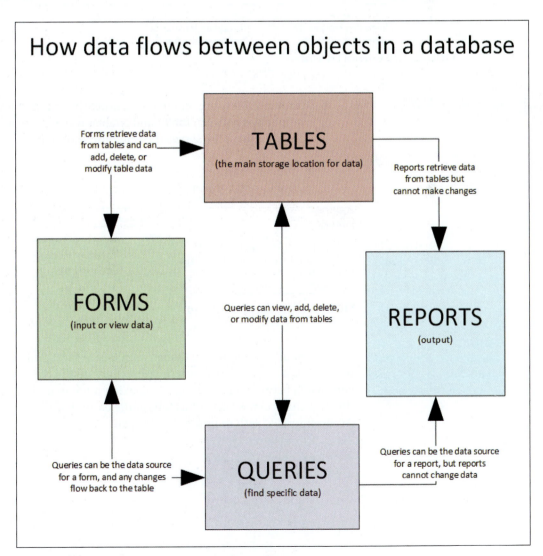

FIGURE 1.9 Flow of Information between Object Types

Two other object types, macros and modules, are rarely used by beginning Access users. A **macro** object is a stored series of commands that carry out an action. Macros are often used to automate tasks. A **module** is an advanced object written using the VBA (Visual Basic for Applications) programming language. Modules provide more functionality than macros but are not generally required for even intermediate users.

Examine the Access Interface

While Access includes the standard elements of the Microsoft Office applications interface such as the title bar, the ribbon, the Home tab, the File tab, and scroll bars, it also includes elements unique to Access.

The Access ribbon has six tabs that always display, as well as tabs that appear only when particular objects are open. The two tabs that are unique to Access are:

- External Data tab: Contains all the operations used to facilitate data import and export (see Figure 1.10).

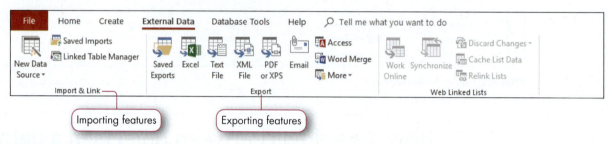

FIGURE 1.10 External Data Tab

- Database Tools tab: Contains the feature that enables users to create relationships between tables and enables use of more advanced features of Access. Figure 1.11 shows the Database Tools tab.

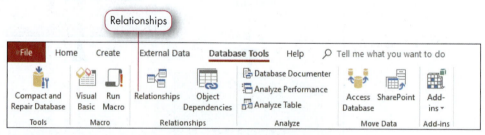

FIGURE 1.11 Database Tools Tab

By default, Access uses a tabbed objects interface. That means that each object that is open has its own tab beneath the ribbon and to the right of the Navigation Pane. You can switch between open objects by clicking a tab to make that object active, similar to the way an Excel worksheet has tabs at the bottom of the screen. Figure 1.12 shows the Access interface with multiple objects open.

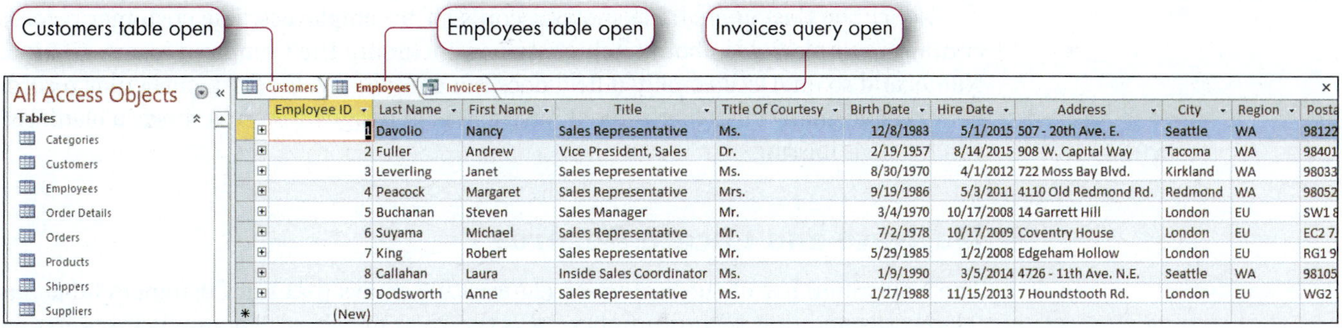

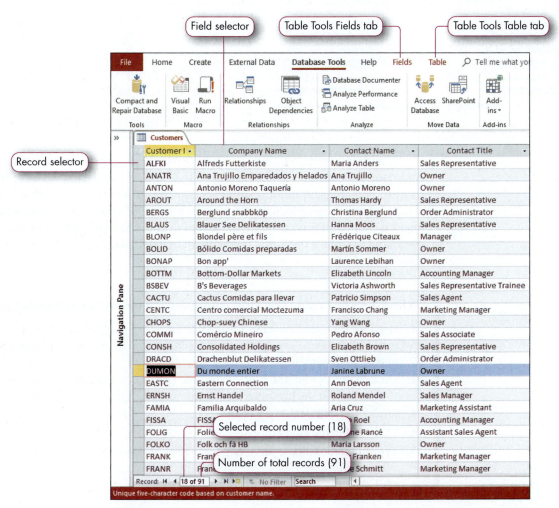

FIGURE 1.12 Access Database with Multiple Objects Open

Explore Table Datasheet View

Access provides two different ways to view a table: Datasheet view and Design view. When you open a table, Datasheet view displays by default. *Datasheet view* is a grid containing fields (columns) and records (rows). You can view, add, edit, and delete records in Datasheet view. Figure 1.13 shows the Customers table in Datasheet view. Each row contains a record for a specific customer. The record selector, or row heading (when clicked), is used to select the entire record. Each column represents a field, or one attribute about a customer.

FIGURE 1.13 Datasheet View for Customers Table

Notice the Customers table shows records for 91 employees. The customer records contain multiple fields about each customer, including the Company Name, Contact Name, and so on. Occasionally a field does not contain a value for a particular record. For example, many customers do not have a Region assigned. Access shows a blank cell when data is missing.

Navigate and Locate Records

The Navigation bar at the bottom of Figure 1.14 shows that the Customers table has 91 records and that record number 18 is the current record. The navigation arrows enable you to go to the first record, the previous record, the next record, or the last record. Click the right arrow with a yellow asterisk to add a new (blank) record. Navigation works for more than just tables. Navigation arrows are also available in queries and forms.

FIGURE 1.14 Navigation Arrows in a Table

In addition to navigating, you also have access to the Find command. The Find command is located in the Find group on the Home tab and can be used to locate specific records. You can search for a single field or the entire record, match all or part of the selected field(s), move forward or back in a table, or specify a case-sensitive search. A Replace command is on the ribbon located next to the Find command. You can use this command to replace the found text with an updated value.

To find a record using the Find command, complete the following steps:

1. Open the table that contains the data you are searching for. Note that if you want to search a query, form, or report, you can follow the same steps, except open the appropriate object instead of the table.
2. Click any cell within the field you want to search. For example, if you want to search the City field in the Customers table, as shown in Figure 1.15, click any City value.
3. Ensure the Home tab is selected.
4. Click Find in the Find group.
5. Type the value you are searching for in the Find What box. Note that the entry is not case sensitive.
6. Click Find Next to find the next matching value.

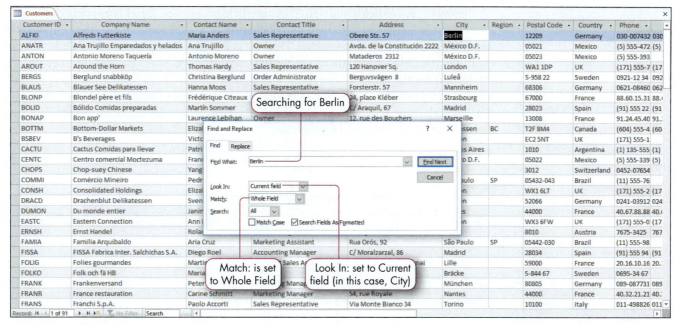

FIGURE 1.15 The Find and Replace Dialog Box

Explore Table Design View

Design view gives you a detailed view of the table's structure and is used to create and modify a table's design by specifying the fields it will contain, the fields' data types, and their associated properties. Recall a table opens in Datasheet view by default. You switch between Datasheet and Design views by clicking View in the Views group on the Home tab (see Figure 1.16).

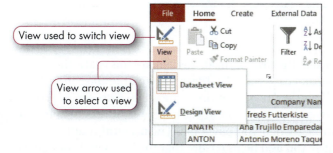

FIGURE 1.16 View Button

View is a two-part command. Clicking the top part of the command toggles between Design and Datasheet view. Clicking the command arrow opens a menu from which you can select the view you want. Either way of performing this task is correct.

Figure 1.17 shows Design view for the Orders table. In the top portion, each row contains the field name, the data type, and an optional description for each field in the table. The fields listed in Design view correspond to the fields (or column headings) in Datasheet view. In the bottom portion, the Field Properties pane contains the properties (details) for a field.

Data types define the type of data that will be stored in a field, such as short text, numeric, currency, date/time, etc. Defining the type of data is important because Access will behave a specific way based on the type of data the field contains. Each field's data type determines the type of input accepted. For example, if you want to store the hire date of an employee, you would input a field name and select the Date/Time data type. Data types will be discussed further in a later chapter.

Next to the data type is Description, where a description of the field can be added. Some field names are obvious such as Student First Name. Other fields may require a bit more detail to better understand the values the field will capture.

Below the list of fields and data types are field properties. A ***field property*** defines the characteristics of a field in more detail. Field properties are displayed for the field selected and change as each field is selected. Figure 1.17 shows field properties for Order ID. For example, the field OrderDate has a Date/Time data type, then you can further choose the format for the date. A ShortDate format will display dates in the following format: mm/dd/yyyy or 4/19/2018. Furthermore, you can choose whether the field is required or not. Though some changes can be made to the field properties in Datasheet view, Design view gives you access to more properties.

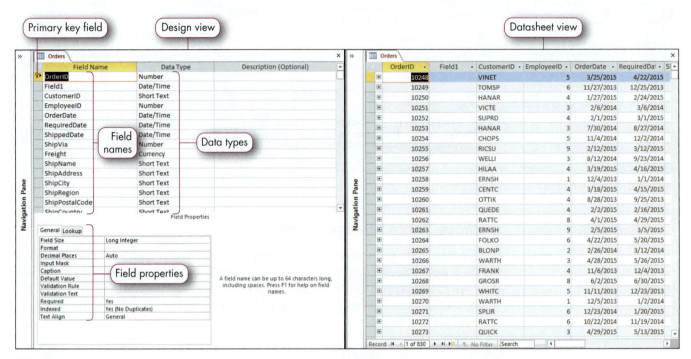

FIGURE 1.17 Orders Table Design and Datasheet View

Notice the key icon next to the OrderID field; this denotes this field is the primary key in the Orders table; it ensures that each record in the table is unique and can be distinguished from every other record. If you had two orders from the same customer, you could tell they are different because there are two separate OrderIDs. This is the reason many companies ask for your account number when you pay a bill. The account number, similar to an OrderID, uniquely identifies you and helps ensure that the payment is not applied to the wrong customer.

Rename and Describe Tables

To make a table easy to use, Access includes a few properties you can modify. Tables default to a name of Table 1 (or Table 2, etc.) if you do not specify otherwise. As you can imagine, this would make it very difficult to determine the contents of the table. Therefore, it is important to give a table a name that clearly defines the data it contains. It is simple to rename a table and give it a more descriptive name.

To rename a table, complete the following steps:

1. Verify that the table is closed. If it is not closed, right-click the table tab and select Close. A table cannot be renamed while it is open.
2. Right-click the table name in the Navigation Pane.
3. Select Rename from the shortcut menu.
4. Type the new name over the selected text and press Enter.

Tables also include a description, which provides documentation about the contents of a table. For example, most table names in the Northwind database are straightforward. However, the database comes with predefined descriptions for most tables to explain the purpose of each field. This can provide a user with additional clarification regarding the purpose of a table if they know where to look. By default, descriptions are not shown unless you right-click the table and select Table Properties. If you are working with a complex database, adding descriptions can be extremely helpful for new users. Figure 1.18 shows a table description.

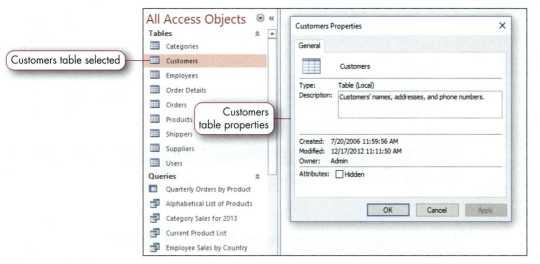

FIGURE 1.18 Previewing a Table Description

> **TIP: SHOWING OBJECT DETAILS**
>
> Most users will not need to see a description frequently. However, if necessary, you can change the Navigation Pane to display details by default. The details include the creation date, modification date, and description of the object. You may need to increase the size of the Navigation Pane to see the full description, so this works better on wider screens.
>
> To show object details, right-click All Access Objects in the Navigation Pane and click View By. Select Details to display the full details. Resize the Navigation Pane so you can view the complete descriptions. Figure 1.19 shows a view of objects with descriptions.

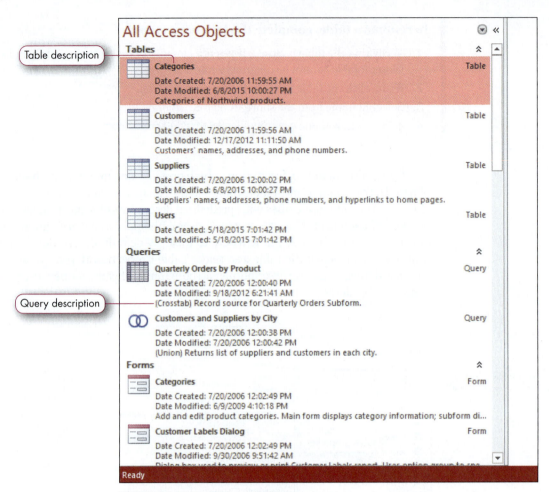

Table description

Query description

FIGURE 1.19 Detail View of Objects

Understand Relationships between Tables

A **relationship** is a connection between two tables using a common field. The benefit of a relationship is the ability to efficiently combine data from related tables to create queries, forms, and reports. If you are using an existing database, relationships are likely created already. The design of the Latte database, which contains multiple tables, is illustrated in Figure 1.20. The diagram shows the relationships that were created between tables using join lines. Join lines enable you to create a relationship between two tables using a common field. For example, the Customers table is joined to the Orders table using the common field CustomerID. These table connections enable you to query the database for information stored in multiple tables. This feature gives the manager the ability to ask questions like, "What orders are there for Katie's Casual Wear?" In this case, the name of the customer (Katie's Casual Wear) is stored in the Customers table, but the orders are stored in the Orders table. Notice in Figure 1.21, a plus sign ⊞ displays to the left of each Customer. If you click the plus sign, a subdatasheet will display with a list of related records from a related table. If there is not a plus sign, then a related record does not exist. Figure 1.21 is the Datasheet view of the Customers table. Because of the relationship with the Orders table, you can see what orders are associated with each customer by clicking the plus sign ⊞ next to each customer.

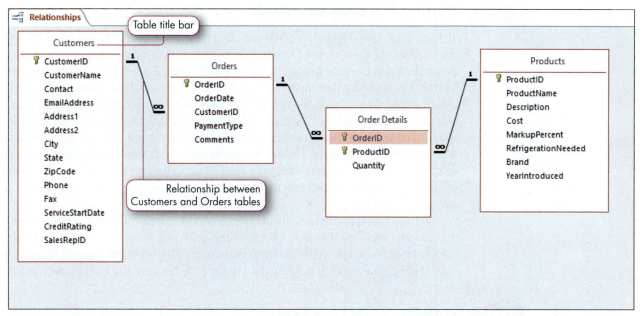

FIGURE 1.20 Database Relationships

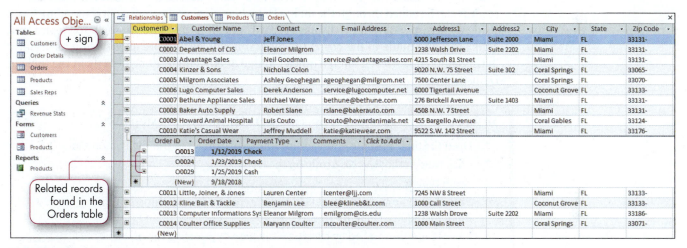

FIGURE 1.21 Related Tables

Relationships will be discussed further in the next chapter. However, you can view the existing relationships in any database to familiarize yourself with the way tables work together. To view existing database relationships, click Relationships in the Relationships group on the Database Tools tab. Then, reposition tables by dragging the table's title bar (as shown in Figure 1.20) to a new location so all relationships are visible. This is not required but doing so may make the relationships easier to follow. Save and close the relationships window when you are finished.

Modifying, Adding, and Saving Data

Data in a database will be always changing. You should expect new records to be added or current records to be modified. If you are working with a Customer database, you would expect new customers to be added constantly. If you are dealing with a university database, new students will be added, some will graduate, and others will transfer from one program of study to another.

STEP 3 Modify Records in a Table

To keep databases current, records are often modified. A record can be modified through the table's Datasheet view or through a corresponding form. You must locate the record first which can be done using Find which you learned about previously. After you have located the record, click in the cell for the field you want to update and type the new information. As you edit the record you may notice a pencil symbol to the left of the record you are editing (see Figure 1.22). The pencil indicates that the data in that record is being edited and that changes have not yet been saved. The pencil icon disappears when you move to another record. Access saves data automatically as soon as you move from one record to another. This may seem counterintuitive at first because other Office applications, such as Word and Excel, do not save changes automatically unless they are stored in OneDrive.

Editing data is done similarly in queries and forms. Recall that reports cannot change data, so changes to data cannot be done there. To edit a record in a query or form, open the query or form, tab to the field you want to modify, and type the new data. When you start typing, you erase all existing data in the field because the entire field is selected.

STEP 4 Add Records to a Table

Often it is necessary to add new records to a table such as a new student record. New records can be added through the table's Datasheet view or through a corresponding form. Using a corresponding form displays records one at a time and can help to ensure that edits are being made to the correct record. You will learn more about using forms later in this chapter. However, often a quick change or edit can be done directly in the table in Datasheet view.

To add a new record to a table, complete the following steps:

1. Open the table in Datasheet view by double-clicking it in the Navigation Pane.
2. Click New in the Records group on the Home tab.
3. Begin typing.
4. Press Tab to move to the next field and enter data. Repeat this step until you have input all required data for this record.
5. Move to another record by clicking elsewhere or pressing Tab in the last field in a record. As soon as you move to another record, Access automatically saves the changes to the record you created or changed.

If you are unable to type in a field, then you have selected a field with a data type of AutoNumber, which Access assigns for you. If this is the case, click in a different field and begin typing. The asterisk record indicator changes to a pencil symbol to show that you are in editing mode (see Figure 1.22).

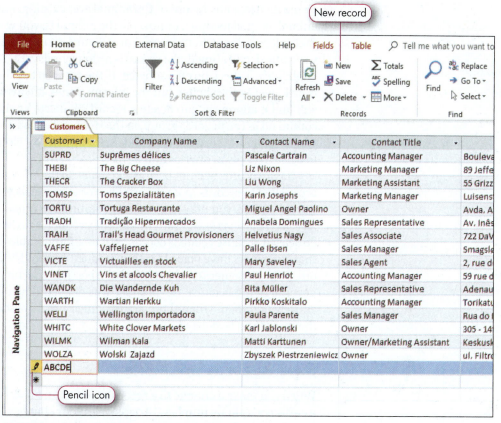

FIGURE 1.22 Adding a Record Using a Table

As with most of Microsoft Office applications, there are several ways to perform the same task. There are many ways to facilitate moving around a datasheet as you navigate from record to record. In addition to using commands on the ribbon, you can use keyboard shortcuts. See Table 1.1 for a list of some shortcuts you can use when performing data entry.

TABLE 1.1	Keyboard Shortcuts for Entering Data
Keystroke	**Result**
Up arrow (↑)	Moves insertion point up one row.
Down arrow (↓)	Moves insertion point down one row.
Left arrow (←)	Moves insertion point left one field in the same row.
Right arrow (→)	Moves insertion point right one field in the same row.
Tab or Enter	Moves insertion point right one field in the same row.
Shift+Tab	Moves insertion point left one field in the same row.
Home	Moves insertion point to the first field in the current row.
End	Moves insertion point to the last field in the current row.
Esc	Cancels any changes made in the current field while in Edit mode.
Ctrl+Z	Undo. Reverses the last unsaved edit.

STEP 5 ## Delete Records from a Table

Deciding to delete records is not a simple decision. Many times, deleting records is a bad idea. Say you are working in the database for an animal shelter. After an animal has been adopted, you may be tempted to delete the animal from the database. However, you would then lose any record of the animal ever existing, and if the owner calls asking if the animal has had its shots, or how old the animal is, you would no longer be able to provide that information. Often, instead of deleting information, it would be better to create a yes/no field indicating that a record is no longer relevant. For example, the shelter database might have a check box for adopted. If the adopted box displays a checkmark, the animal is no longer at the shelter, but the information is still available. That said, sometimes you will find it appropriate to delete a record. To delete a record from a table, use the Delete command in the Records group on the Home tab. Read any warning that might pop up. If you are comfortable with the deletion, then click Yes. Note that you can take similar steps to delete records in queries and forms.

Some records will not permit you to delete them, even if you wanted to, because they are related to records in another table. For example, if you try to delete a product from a store database, you may get a message stating *You cannot delete this record because another table has related records*. Even though the product is no longer available for sale, it cannot be deleted because related records exist in another table. In this case, there may be orders that customers have placed for that product. It would be best to know about outstanding orders, so customers can be notified of a possible alternative product rather than an order never arriving because the product was deleted. The order can be modified or deleted entirely and then, when there are no longer orders associated with the related product, the record can be deleted.

Save Records in a Table

When you make a change to a record's content in an Access table (for example, changing a customer's phone number), Access saves your changes as soon as you move to a different record. You will only be prompted to save if you make changes to the design of the table (such as changing the font or background color).

The Save function in Access works differently than in the other Office applications. Access works primarily from storage (i.e., the hard drive). As you enter and update the data in an Access database, the changes are automatically saved to the storage location you specified when you saved the database. If a power failure occurs, you will lose only the changes to the record that you are currently editing.

> **TIP: UNDO WORKS DIFFERENTLY**
> You can click Undo to reverse the most recent change (the phone number you just modified, for example) to a single record immediately after making changes to that record. However, unlike other Office programs that enable multiple Undo steps, you cannot use Undo to reverse multiple edits in Access. Undo (and Redo) are found on the Quick Access Toolbar.

STEP 6 Using Database Utilities

Database administrators spend a lot of time maintaining databases. Software utility programs make this process simpler. As Access is a database management utility, there are a few tools that can be used to protect, maintain, and improve the performance of a database.

Back Up a Database

Back Up Database is a utility that creates a duplicate copy of the entire database to protect data from loss or damage. Imagine what would happen to a firm that loses track of orders placed, a charity that loses the list of donor contributions, or a hospital that loses the digital records of its patients. Making backups is especially important when you have multiple users working with the database. Mistakes can be made, and records can unintentionally be deleted. When you use the Back Up Database utility, Access provides a file name for the backup that uses the same file name as the database you are backing up, an underscore, and the current date. This makes it easy for you to keep track of backups by the date they were created.

Keep in mind, backing up a database on the same storage device as the original database can leave you with no protection in the event of hardware failure. Backups are typically stored on a separate device, such as an external hard drive or network drive.

> **To back up a database, complete the following steps:**
> 1. Click the File tab.
> 2. Click Save As.
> 3. Click Back Up Database under the Advanced group (see Figure 1.23).
> 4. Click Save As. Revise the location and file name if you want to change either and click Save.

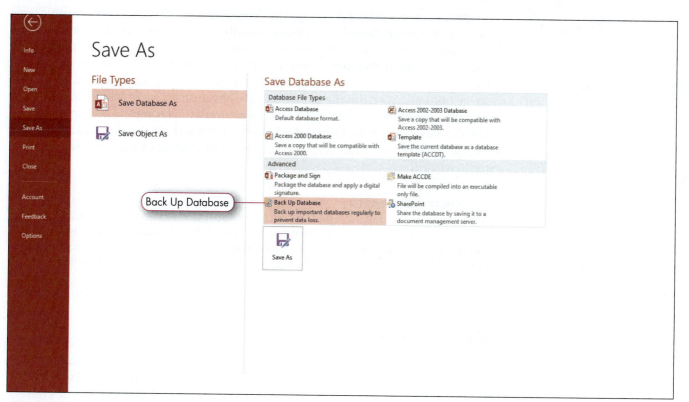

FIGURE 1.23 Back Up Database Option

> **TIP: RESTORE A DATABASE FROM A BACKUP**
> In the case of a total database failure, you can use a backup as the new database. If just particular information is missing, you can recover information to an existing database. To do so, open the database that has lost or corrupted information, delete the corrupted object from the current database and import the missing object from the backup.

To delete the corrupted object from the current database and import the missing object from the backup, complete the following steps:

1. Click the External Data tab, and click New Data Source in the Import & Link group. Select From Database and then click Access.
2. Click Browse, select the backup file, and click Open.
3. Ensure the option to Import tables, queries, forms, reports, macros, and modules into the current database is selected, and click OK.
4. Click the tab related to the object you want to restore (Tables, Queries, Forms, Reports, Macros, or Modules).
5. Click the object to select it and click OK.
6. Click Close to close the Get External Data – Access Database dialog box. The object is now restored to the current database.

Compact and Repair a Database

Occasionally Access databases experience corruption. Database corruption occurs when the data are stored improperly, resulting in the loss of data or database functionality. With everyday use, databases may become corrupt, so Access provides the ***Compact and Repair Database*** utility. Compact and Repair Database reduces the size of a database and fixes any errors that may exist in the file. Compact and Repair Database is in the Info options on the File tab. If you have any unsaved design changes, you will be prompted to save before the compact and repair process can complete. Alternatively, you can have Access perform a Compact and Repair automatically by clicking the Compact on Close check box under Application Options in the Options for the current database pane to select it.

> **TIP: SPLIT DATABASES**
> Another utility built into Access is the Database Splitter tool, which puts the tables in one file (the back-end database), and the queries, forms, and reports in a second file (the front-end). This way, each user can create their own queries, forms, and reports without potentially changing an object someone else needs. The Split Database option is found on the Database Tools tab. Click Access Database in the Move Data group.

Print Information

Though Access is primarily designed to store data electronically, you can produce a printed copy of your data. Reports are database objects that are specifically designed to be printed and distributed, but occasionally it is necessary to print out the Datasheet view of a table or query to check results. Each object in the database prints individually, so you would select the object you want to print from the Navigation Pane, and access the print commands from the File tab. It is good practice to preview your work before printing a document. This way, if you notice an error, you can fix it and not waste paper.

Quick Concepts

1. Describe each of the four main types of objects in an Access database. ***pp. 557–558***
2. Discuss the difference between Datasheet view and Design view in a table. ***pp. 561, 563***
3. Explain why it is important to define data types in Access. ***p. 563***
4. Explain the purpose of using the compact and repair utility. ***p. 572***

Hands-On Exercises

Skills covered: Open a Database • Save a Database with a New Name • Enable Content in a Database • Examine the Access Interface • Explore Table Datasheet View • Navigate Through Records • Explore Table Design View • Understand Relationships between Tables • Add Records in a Table • Modify Records in a Table • Delete Records from a Table • Back Up a Database • Print Information

1 Databases Are Everywhere!

Northwind purchases food items from suppliers around the world and sells them to restaurants and specialty food shops. Northwind depends on the data stored in its Access database to process orders and make daily decisions. You will open the Northwind database, examine the Access interface, review the existing objects in the database, and explore Access views. You will add, edit, and delete records using both tables and forms. Finally, you will back up the database.

STEP 1 OPEN, SAVE, AND ENABLE CONTENT IN A DATABASE

As you begin your job, you first will become familiar with the Northwind database. This database will help you learn the fundamentals of working with database files. Refer to Figure 1.24 as you complete Step 1.

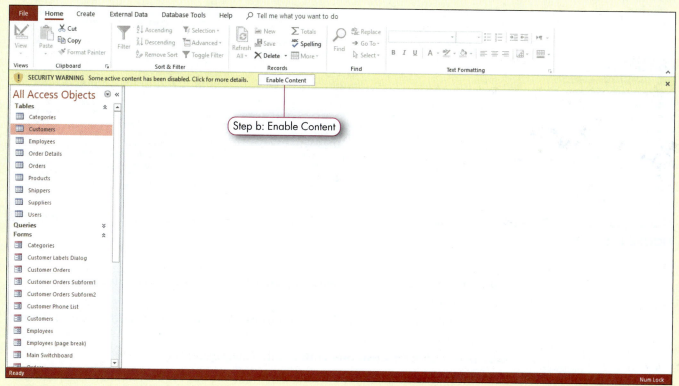

FIGURE 1.24 Northwind Database

a. Start your computer. Click **Start**, and click **Access** from the list of applications. Click **Open Other Files** and click **Browse**. Navigate to the location of your student files. Double-click *a01h1Traders*. Click the **File tab**, click **Save As**, and then click **Access Database**. Click **Save As** and save the file as **a01h1Traders_LastFirst**.

When you save files, use your last and first names. For example, as the Access author, I would save my database as "a01h1Traders_RutledgeAmy".

The Security Warning message bar displays below the ribbon, indicating that some database content is disabled.

b. Click **Enable Content** on the Security Warning message bar.

When you open an Access file, you should enable the content.

STEP 2 RECOGNIZE DATABASE OBJECT TYPES

Now that you have opened the Northwind database, you should examine the Navigation Pane, objects, and views to become familiar with these fundamental Access features. Refer to Figure 1.25 as you complete Step 2.

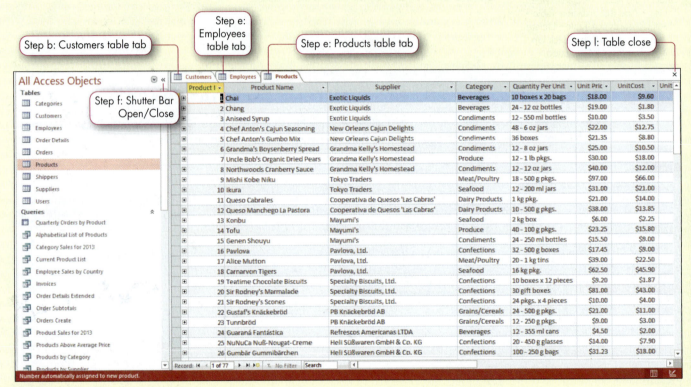

FIGURE 1.25 Northwind Objects

a. Scroll through the Navigation Pane and notice the Access objects listed under each expanded group.

The Tables group and the Forms group are expanded, displaying all the table and form objects.

b. Double-click the **Customers table** in the Navigation Pane.

The Customers table opens in Datasheet view, showing the data contained in the table. The Customers tab displays below the ribbon indicating the table object is open. Each customer's record displays on a table row. The columns of the table display the fields that comprise the records.

c. Click the **View arrow** and select **Design view**, in the Views group on the Home tab.

The view of the Customers table switches to Design view. The top portion of Design view displays and the field names match the field headings previously seen in Datasheet view. Additionally, the field's data type, and an optional description of what the field should contain can be seen. The bottom portion of Design view displays the field properties (details) for the selected field.

d. Click the **View arrow** and select **Datasheet view** in the Views group on the Home tab again.

Your view returns to Datasheet view, which shows the data stored in the table.

e. Double-click **Employees** in the Tables group of the Navigation Pane. Double-click **Products** from the same location.

The Employees and Products tables open. The tabs for three table objects display below the ribbon: Customers, Employees, and Products.

f. Click **Shutter Bar Open/Close** ⟪ on the title bar of the Navigation Pane to hide the Navigation Pane. Click ⟫ again to show the Navigation Pane.

The Navigation Pane collapses and expands to enable you to view more in the open object window, or to view your database objects.

g. Scroll down in the Navigation Pane and locate Reports.

The Reports group is expanded, and all report objects are displayed.

h. Scroll up until you see Forms. Click **Forms** in the Navigation Pane.

The Forms group collapses and individual form objects no longer display.

i. Click the **Database Tools tab** and click **Relationships** in the Relationships group.

j. Examine the join lines showing the relationships that connect the various tables. For example, the Orders table is connected to the Order Details table using the OrderID field as the common field.

k. Click **Relationship Report** in the Tools group. The report opens in a new tab. Right-click on the tab and select **Save** and click **OK**.

The report is now saved in the Reports section on the Navigation Pane.

l. Click **Close** ✕ the at the top right of the report to close the Relationships Report. Click **Close** ✕ the at the top right of the tab to close the Relationships window. Click **Close** ✕ the at the top right of the table to close the Products table.

STEP 3 ## MODIFY RECORDS IN A TABLE

You want to learn to edit the data in the Northwind database, because data can change. For example, employees will change their address when they move, and customers will change their order data from time to time. Refer to Figure 1.26 as you complete Step 3.

FIGURE 1.26 Northwind Employees Table

a. Click the **Employees tab** to view the Employees table.

b. Double-click **Peacock** (the value of the Last Name field in the fourth row); the entire name highlights. Type your last name to replace Peacock.

The pencil symbol in the record selector box indicates that the record is being edited but has not yet been saved.

c. Press **Tab** to move to the next field in the fourth row. Replace **Margaret** with your first name and press **Tab**.

You have made changes to two fields in the same record.

d. Click **Undo** on the Quick Access Toolbar.

Your first and last names revert to Margaret Peacock because you have not yet left the record.

e. Type your first and last names again to replace Margaret Peacock. Press **Tab**.

You should now be in the title field, and the title, Sales Representative, is selected. The record has not been saved, as indicated by the pencil symbol in the record selector box.

f. Click anywhere in the third row where Janet Leverling's data are stored.

The pencil symbol disappears, indicating that your changes have been saved.

g. Click the **Address field** in the first row, Nancy Davolio's record. Select the entire address and type **4004 East Morningside Dr.** Click anywhere on the second record, Andrew Fuller's record.

h. Click **Undo**.

Nancy Davolio's address reverts to 507 - 20th Ave. E. However, the Undo command is now faded. You can no longer undo the change that you made replacing Margaret Peacock's name with your own.

i. Click **Close** ✕ at the top right of the table to close the Employees table.

The Employees table closes. You are not prompted to save your changes; they have already been saved for you because Access works in storage, not memory. If you reopen the Employees table, you will see your name in place of Margaret Peacock's name.

STEP 4 **ADD RECORDS TO A TABLE**

You have been asked to add information about a new line of products to the Northwind database. You add records to the Products table through the Products Form. The two objects are directly connected. Refer to Figure 1.27 as you complete Step 4.

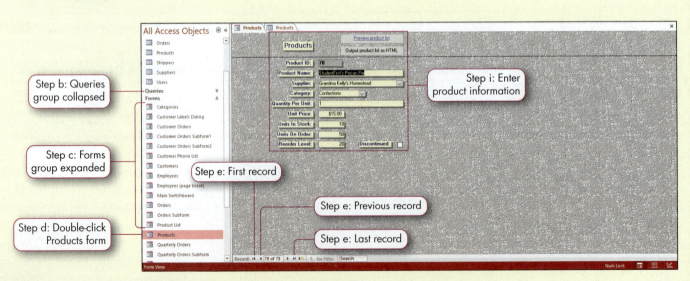

FIGURE 1.27 Adding Data Using Products Form

a. Right-click the **Customers tab** and click **Close All**.

b. Click the **Queries group** in the Navigation Pane to collapse it. Click the **Reports group** in the Navigation Pane to collapse it as well.

c. Click the **Forms group** in the Navigation Pane to expand the list of available forms.

d. Double-click the **Products form** to open it.

e. Click the Next record arrow in the Navigation bar at the bottom of the form window. Click **Last record**, click **Previous record**, and then click **First record**.

f. Click **Find** in the Find group on the Home tab, type **Grandma** in the Find What box, click the **Match arrow**, and then select **Any Part of Field**. Click **Find Next**.

You should see the data for Grandma's Boysenberry Spread. Selecting the Any Part of Field option will return a match even if it is contained as part of a word.

g. Click **Cancel** to close the Find dialog box.

h. Click **New** in the Records group on the Home tab.

i. Type the following information for a new product. Click, or press **Tab**, to move into the next cell. Notice as soon as you begin typing, Access will assign a ProductID to this product.

Field Name	Value to Type
Product Name	***Your name's* Pecan Pie** (replacing Your name with your first name) For example, as the Access author, my Product name would be Amy's Pecan Pie.
Supplier	**Grandma Kelly's Homestead** (click the arrow to select from the list of Suppliers)
Category	**Confections** (click the arrow to select from the list of Categories)
Quantity Per Unit	I
Unit Price	**15.00**
Units In Stock	**18**
Units On Order	**50**
Reorder Level	**20**
Discontinued	**No** (Ensure the checkbox is unchecked)

The Products form and Products table are linked so the new record was added to the Products table.

j. Click anywhere on the **Pecan Pie record** you just typed. Click the **File tab**, select **Print**, and then click **Print Preview**.

The first four records display in the Print Preview.

k. Click **Last Page** in the Navigation bar and click **Previous Page** to show the new record you entered.

The beginning of the Pecan Pie record is now visible. The record continues to the next page.

l. Click **Close Print Preview** in the Close Preview group.

m. Close the Products form.

To help you understand how Access stores data, you verify that the new product is in the Products table. You also attempt to delete a record. Refer to Figure 1.28 as you complete Step 5.

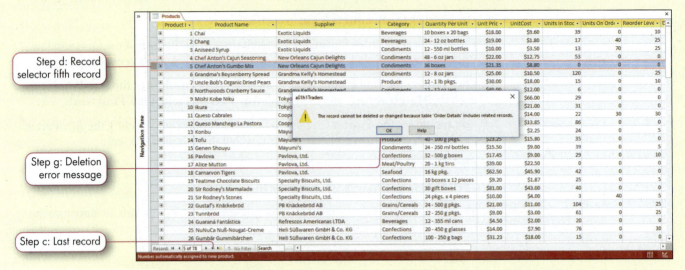

Step d: Record selector fifth record

Step g: Deletion error message

Step c: Last record

The record cannot be deleted or changed because table 'Order Details' includes related records.

OK   Help

FIGURE 1.28 Deleting Data

a. Click the **Forms group** in the Navigation Pane to collapse it. Expand the **Tables group**.

b. Double-click the **Products table** to open it.

c. Click **Last record** in the Navigation bar.

The Pecan Pie record you entered in the Products form is listed as the last record in the Products table. The Products form was created from the Products table. Your newly created record, Pecan Pie, is stored in the Products table even though you added it using the form.

d. Navigate to the fifth record in the table and place the pointer in the record, Chef Anton's Gumbo Mix.

e. Scroll right using the horizontal scroll bar until you see the Discontinued field.

The check mark in the Discontinued check box tells you that this product has been discontinued.

f. Click the **record selector** to the left of the fifth record.

A border surrounds the record and the record is shaded, indicating it is selected.

g. Click **Delete** in the Records group and read the error message.

The error message tells you that you cannot delete this record because the table "Order Details" has related records. (Customers ordered this product in the past.) Even though the product is now discontinued and no stock remains, it cannot be deleted from the Products table because related records exist in the Order Details table.

h. Click **OK**.

i. Navigate to the last record and click the **record selector**.

The Pecan Pie record you added earlier is displayed.

j. Click **Delete** in the Records group. Read the warning.

The warning box tells you that this action cannot be undone. Although this product can be deleted because it was just entered and no orders were created for it, you do not want to delete the record.

k. Click **No**. You do not want to delete this record. Close the Products table.

> **TROUBLESHOOTING:** If you clicked Yes and deleted the record, return to Step 4d. Re-open the form and re-enter the information for this record. This will be important later in this lesson.

STEP 6 USE DATABASE UTILITIES

You will protect the Northwind database by using the Back Up Database utility. Refer to Figure 1.29 as you complete Step 6.

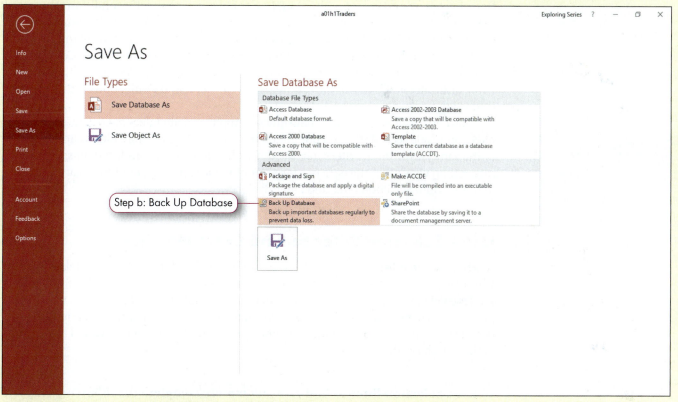

FIGURE 1.29 Backing Up a Database

a. Click the **File tab** and click **Save As**.

b. Double-click **Back Up Database** under the Advanced section to open the Save As dialog box.

The backup utility assigns the default name by adding a date to your file name.

c. Verify that the Save in folder displays the location where you want your file saved and click **Save**. You will submit this file to your instructor at the end of the last Hands-On Exercise.

You just created a backup of the database after completing Hands-On Exercise 1. The original database file remains onscreen.

d. Keep the database open if you plan to continue with the next Hands-On Exercise. If not, close the database and exit Access.

Filters and Sorts

Access provides many tools that you can use to change the order of information and to identify and extract only the data needed. You can find specific information, such as which suppliers are in Denton, TX, or which customers have placed orders in the last seven days. There may be other times you simply want to sort information rather than extract information.

In this section, you will learn how to use filters to create subsets of information that match one or more criteria. Next, you will learn how to organize data by sorting on single or multiple categories. Finally, you will learn how to locate records in a table based on criteria.

Working with Filters

Suppose you wanted to see a list of the products in the Confections category in the Northwind database. To obtain this list, you would open the Products table in Datasheet view and create a filter. A *filter* enables you to specify conditions that need to be met in order to display the desired records. These conditions are known as criteria (or criterion, singular) and are a number, a text phrase, or an expression (such as >50) used to select records from a table. Therefore, to view a list of all Confections, you would apply a filter to the Products table, displaying only records with a Category value of Confections. In this case, Category is the field, and Confections is the criterion that is applied to the field.

You can use filters to analyze data quickly. Applying a filter does not delete any records; filters only hide records that do not match the criteria. One or more filters can be applied to the same set of data. Filters narrow down the data so you can focus on specific data rather than view all of the data in a large set of records. Two types of filters are discussed in this section: Selection filter and Filter By Form.

STEP 1 ▶ Use a Selection Filter to Find Exact Matches

A *Selection filter* displays in Datasheet view only the records that exactly match a criterion you select. Access uses the current selection as the criterion. For example, if you filter a Job Title field and you select "equals Owner," you would only find customers who have a Job Title of Owner (but not any other variation such as Co-Owner). Selection filters are not case sensitive, so any variation of capitalization (OWNER, owner) would also display in the search results.

To use a Selection filter to find an exact match, complete the following steps:

1. Click in any field in Datasheet view that contains the criterion on which you want to filter.
2. Click Selection in the Sort & Filter group on the Home tab.
3. Select Equals "criterion" from the list of options (*criterion* will be replaced by the value of the field).

Figure 1.30 displays a Customers table with 91 records. The records in the table are displayed in sequence according to the Job title. The Navigation bar at the bottom indicates that the active record is the second 34th row in the table. Owner in the Job Title field is selected.

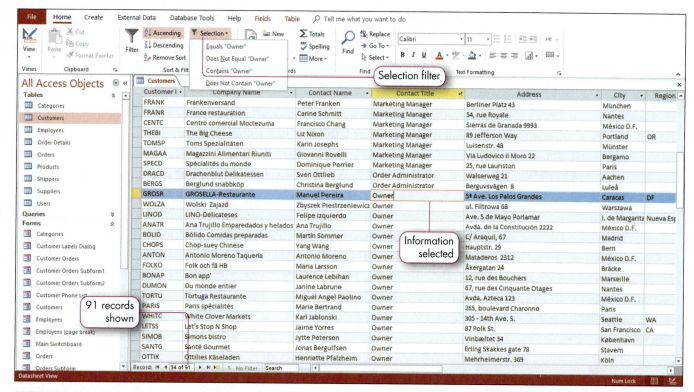

FIGURE 1.30 Unfiltered Customers Table

Figure 1.31 displays a filtered view of the Customers table, showing records with the job title Owner. The Navigation bar shows that this is a filtered list containing 17 records matching the criterion. The Customers table still contains the original 91 records, but only 17 records are visible with the filter applied.

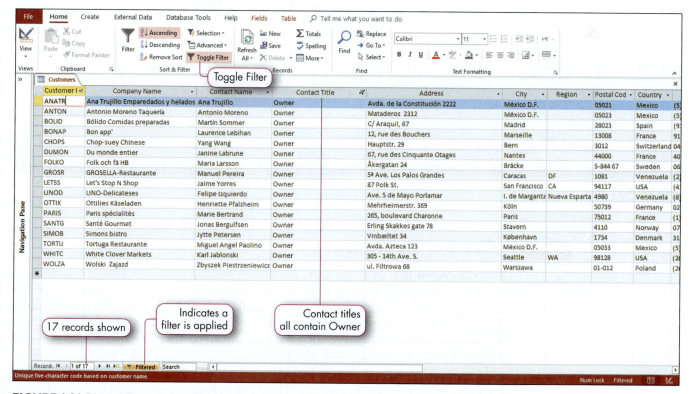

FIGURE 1.31 Filtered Customers Table

You can use the Toggle Filter command (refer to Figure 1.31) to remove the filter and display all the records in the table. When you save and close the filtered table and reopen it, all of the records will be visible again. After reopening the table, you can click Toggle Filter again to display the results of the last saved filter. If you no longer want to keep the filter, you can click Advanced in the Sort & Filter group and click Clear All Filters.

Only one filter can be applied at a time. Therefore, when you apply another filter to a dataset that is already filtered, the first filter will be removed.

STEP 2 ## Use a Selection Filter to Find Records Containing a Value

A Selection filter is used to find records that contain a criterion. Access uses the current selection as the criterion. For example, if you filter a title field using "contains Manager," it would find Manager, as well as any titles containing Manager (such as Accounting Managers, Marketing Managers, etc,). As with the exact match, this is not case sensitive, as shown in the results in Figure 1.32. The steps to locating values containing certain text is similar to the steps to find exact matches except you select *Contains* from the list of options presented. Your results will show all records containing a partial or full match.

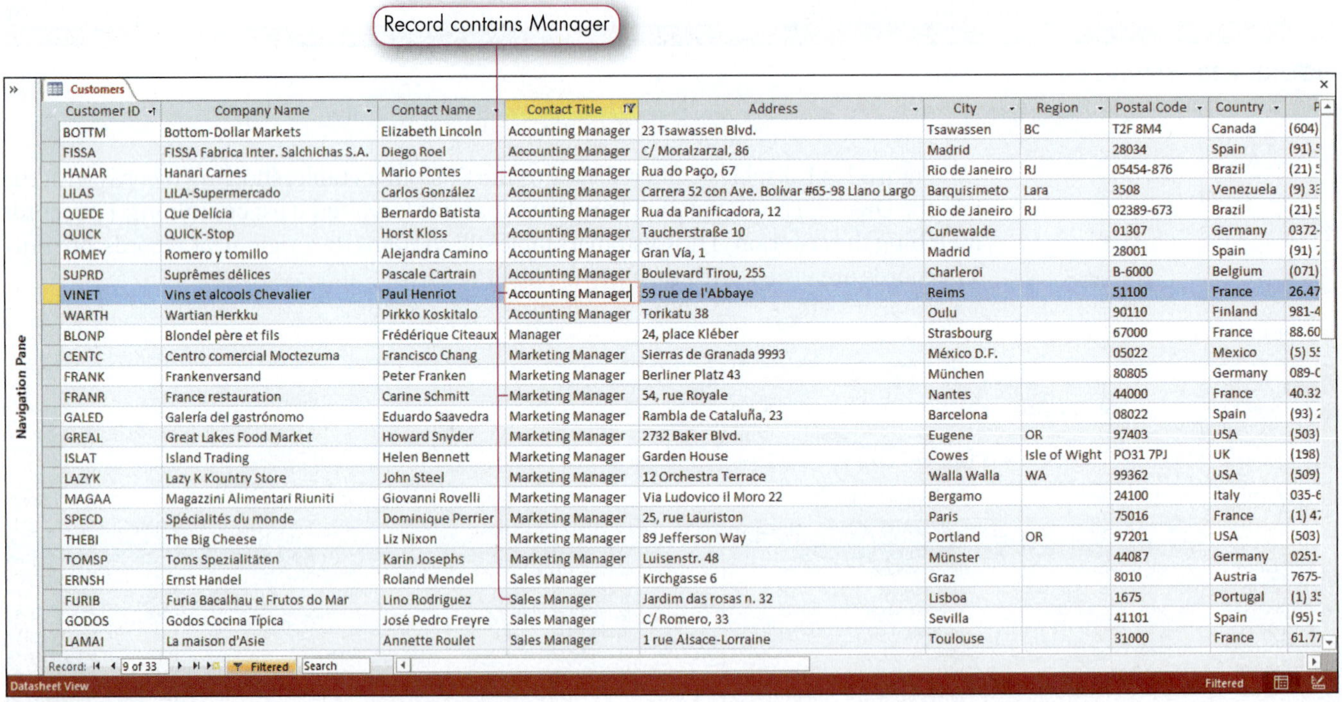

Record contains Manager

Customer ID	Company Name	Contact Name	Contact Title	Address	City	Region	Postal Code	Country	P
BOTTM	Bottom-Dollar Markets	Elizabeth Lincoln	Accounting Manager	23 Tsawassen Blvd.	Tsawassen	BC	T2F 8M4	Canada	(604)
FISSA	FISSA Fabrica Inter. Salchichas S.A.	Diego Roel	Accounting Manager	C/ Moralzarzal, 86	Madrid		28034	Spain	(91) 5
HANAR	Hanari Carnes	Mario Pontes	Accounting Manager	Rua do Paço, 67	Rio de Janeiro	RJ	05454-876	Brazil	(21) 5
LILAS	LILA-Supermercado	Carlos González	Accounting Manager	Carrera 52 con Ave. Bolívar #65-98 Llano Largo	Barquisimeto	Lara	3508	Venezuela	(9) 33
QUEDE	Que Delícia	Bernardo Batista	Accounting Manager	Rua da Panificadora, 12	Rio de Janeiro	RJ	02389-673	Brazil	(21) 5
QUICK	QUICK-Stop	Horst Kloss	Accounting Manager	Taucherstraße 10	Cunewalde		01307	Germany	0372-
ROMEY	Romero y tomillo	Alejandra Camino	Accounting Manager	Gran Vía, 1	Madrid		28001	Spain	(91) 7
SUPRD	Suprêmes délices	Pascale Cartrain	Accounting Manager	Boulevard Tirou, 255	Charleroi		B-6000	Belgium	(071)
VINET	Vins et alcools Chevalier	Paul Henriot	Accounting Manager	59 rue de l'Abbaye	Reims		51100	France	26.47
WARTH	Wartian Herkku	Pirkko Koskitalo	Accounting Manager	Torikatu 38	Oulu		90110	Finland	981-4
BLONP	Blondel père et fils	Frédérique Citeaux	Manager	24, place Kléber	Strasbourg		67000	France	88.60
CENTC	Centro comercial Moctezuma	Francisco Chang	Marketing Manager	Sierras de Granada 9993	México D.F.		05022	Mexico	(5) 55
FRANK	Frankenversand	Peter Franken	Marketing Manager	Berliner Platz 43	München		80805	Germany	089-0
FRANR	France restauration	Carine Schmitt	Marketing Manager	54, rue Royale	Nantes		44000	France	40.32
GALED	Galería del gastrónomo	Eduardo Saavedra	Marketing Manager	Rambla de Cataluña, 23	Barcelona		08022	Spain	(93) 2
GREAL	Great Lakes Food Market	Howard Snyder	Marketing Manager	2732 Baker Blvd.	Eugene	OR	97403	USA	(503)
ISLAT	Island Trading	Helen Bennett	Marketing Manager	Garden House	Cowes	Isle of Wight	PO31 7PJ	UK	(198)
LAZYK	Lazy K Kountry Store	John Steel	Marketing Manager	12 Orchestra Terrace	Walla Walla	WA	99362	USA	(509)
MAGAA	Magazzini Alimentari Riuniti	Giovanni Rovelli	Marketing Manager	Via Ludovico il Moro 22	Bergamo		24100	Italy	035-6
SPECD	Spécialités du monde	Dominique Perrier	Marketing Manager	25, rue Lauriston	Paris		75016	France	(1) 47
THEBI	The Big Cheese	Liz Nixon	Marketing Manager	89 Jefferson Way	Portland	OR	97201	USA	(503)
TOMSP	Toms Spezialitäten	Karin Josephs	Marketing Manager	Luisenstr. 48	Münster		44087	Germany	0251-
ERNSH	Ernst Handel	Roland Mendel	Sales Manager	Kirchgasse 6	Graz		8010	Austria	7675-
FURIB	Furia Bacalhau e Frutos do Mar	Lino Rodriguez	Sales Manager	Jardim das rosas n. 32	Lisboa		1675	Portugal	(1) 35
GODOS	Godos Cocina Típica	José Pedro Freyre	Sales Manager	C/ Romero, 33	Sevilla		41101	Spain	(95) 5
LAMAI	La maison d'Asie	Annette Roulet	Sales Manager	1 rue Alsace-Lorraine	Toulouse		31000	France	61.77

Record: 9 of 33 ▶ ▶▶ Filtered Search

Datasheet View — Filtered

FIGURE 1.32 Finding Records Containing a Value

STEP 3 ## Use Filter By Form

Filter By Form is a more versatile method of selecting data because it enables you to display records based on multiple criteria. When you use Filter By Form, all of the records are hidden, and Access creates a blank form. On this form, you see only field names with an arrow in the first field. Clicking the arrow displays the data in the field. For example, in the Customers table, clicking the arrow for the Contact Title field will display a list of unique titles from which to choose. By choosing Sales Manager, the form will filter for all records that have Sales Manager as the Contact Title. Because Filter By Form allows for multiple filter fields you could also choose another field such as Country.

To apply the filter and view the results, click Toggle. Choosing Austria would result in two records that have Sales Manager as the Contact Title and where the person is also from Austria. Both criteria must be met in the same record for them to appear in the result. If a person has the title of Sales Manager but is not from the country of Austria, they will not be found in the filtered results. Figure 1.33 shows Filter By Form with these two criteria chosen.

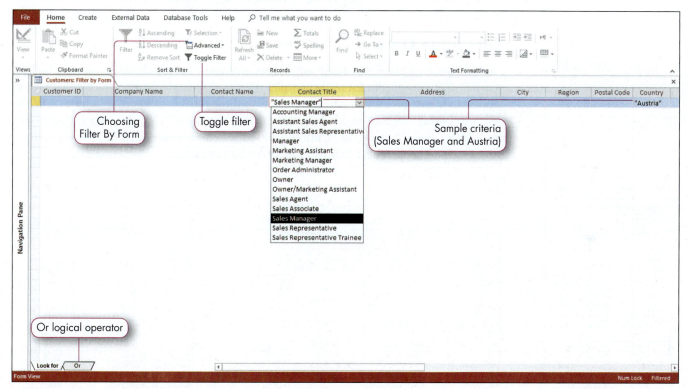

FIGURE 1.33 Filter By Form in a Table

An advantage of Filter By Form is that you can use a comparison operator such as equal (=), not equal (<>), greater than (>), less than (<), greater than or equal to (>=), and less than or equal to (<=). For example, you can locate employees with a Hire date after a specific date such as 2015. To add this criterion, you would click in the field and type the operator followed by the date, in this case you would type >1/1/2015 in the Hire date field.

Another advantage of using this filter method is that you can specify an OR logical operator. As previously discussed, using Filter By Form that displays a record in the results if ALL the criteria are true. However, if you use the OR operator, a record is included if at least one criterion is true. Figure 1.33 shows the location of the OR operator on the Filter by Form page.

To use Filter By Form, complete the following steps:

1. Open the table in Datasheet view and click Advanced in the Sort & Filter group on the Home tab.
2. Click Filter By Form.
3. Click in the field you want to use as a criterion. Click the arrow to select the criterion from existing data.
4. Add additional criterion and comparison operators as required.
5. Click Toggle Filter in the Sort & Filter group on the Home tab to apply the filter.

Performing Sorts

You can change the order of information by sorting one or more fields. A *sort* lists records in a specific sequence, such as alphabetically by last name or by ascending EmployeeID. Sorting adds organization to data and makes the records easier to visualize and understand. Records are not necessarily added in a specific order so sorting by Employee Last Name for example may be more beneficial than viewing the data sorted by an autonumber. Sorting does not change the order of the data in the database, only the way the data are viewed.

Sort Table Data

Ascending sorts a list of text data in alphabetical order or a numeric list in lowest to highest order. Descending sorts a list of text data in reverse alphabetical order or a numeric list in highest to lowest order. You can equate this to these terms outside of a database. When you are coming down from a high place (such as the top of a ladder), you are said to be descending, and when you are climbing a ladder, you are ascending. Figure 1.34 shows the Customers table sorted in ascending order by city name.

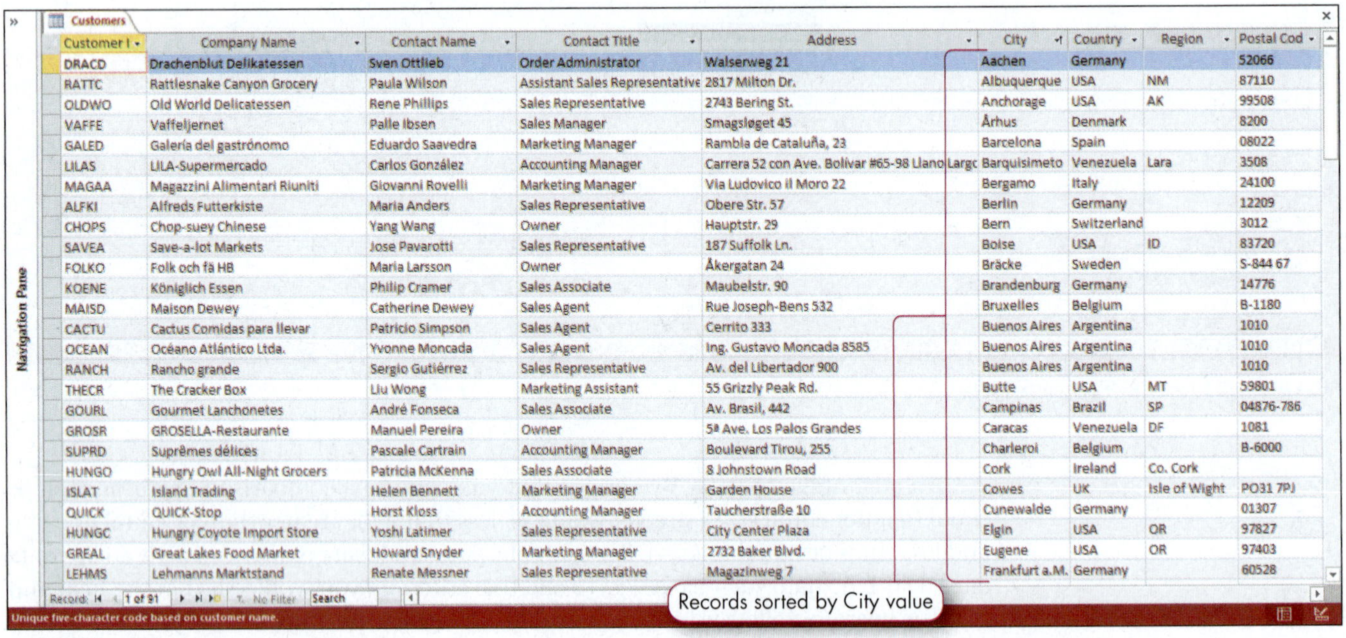

Customer I	Company Name	Contact Name	Contact Title	Address	City	Country	Region	Postal Cod
DRACD	Drachenblut Delikatessen	Sven Ottlieb	Order Administrator	Walserweg 21	Aachen	Germany		52066
RATTC	Rattlesnake Canyon Grocery	Paula Wilson	Assistant Sales Representative	2817 Milton Dr.	Albuquerque	USA	NM	87110
OLDWO	Old World Delicatessen	Rene Phillips	Sales Representative	2743 Bering St.	Anchorage	USA	AK	99508
VAFFE	Vaffeljernet	Palle Ibsen	Sales Manager	Smagsløget 45	Århus	Denmark		8200
GALED	Galería del gastrónomo	Eduardo Saavedra	Marketing Manager	Rambla de Cataluña, 23	Barcelona	Spain		08022
LILAS	LILA-Supermercado	Carlos González	Accounting Manager	Carrera 52 con Ave. Bolívar #65-98 Llano Largo	Barquisimeto	Venezuela	Lara	3508
MAGAA	Magazzini Alimentari Riuniti	Giovanni Rovelli	Marketing Manager	Via Ludovico il Moro 22	Bergamo	Italy		24100
ALFKI	Alfreds Futterkiste	Maria Anders	Sales Representative	Obere Str. 57	Berlin	Germany		12209
CHOPS	Chop-suey Chinese	Yang Wang	Owner	Hauptstr. 29	Bern	Switzerland		3012
SAVEA	Save-a-lot Markets	Jose Pavarotti	Sales Representative	187 Suffolk Ln.	Boise	USA	ID	83720
FOLKO	Folk och fä HB	Maria Larsson	Owner	Åkergatan 24	Bräcke	Sweden		S-844 67
KOENE	Königlich Essen	Philip Cramer	Sales Associate	Maubelstr. 90	Brandenburg	Germany		14776
MAISD	Maison Dewey	Catherine Dewey	Sales Agent	Rue Joseph-Bens 532	Bruxelles	Belgium		B-1180
CACTU	Cactus Comidas para llevar	Patricio Simpson	Sales Agent	Cerrito 333	Buenos Aires	Argentina		1010
OCEAN	Océano Atlántico Ltda.	Yvonne Moncada	Sales Agent	Ing. Gustavo Moncada 8585	Buenos Aires	Argentina		1010
RANCH	Rancho grande	Sergio Gutiérrez	Sales Representative	Av. del Libertador 900	Buenos Aires	Argentina		1010
THECR	The Cracker Box	Liu Wong	Marketing Assistant	55 Grizzly Peak Rd.	Butte	USA	MT	59801
GOURL	Gourmet Lanchonetes	André Fonseca	Sales Associate	Av. Brasil, 442	Campinas	Brazil	SP	04876-786
GROSR	GROSELLA-Restaurante	Manuel Pereira	Owner	5ª Ave. Los Palos Grandes	Caracas	Venezuela	DF	1081
SUPRD	Suprêmes délices	Pascale Cartrain	Accounting Manager	Boulevard Tirou, 255	Charleroi	Belgium		B-6000
HUNGO	Hungry Owl All-Night Grocers	Patricia McKenna	Sales Associate	8 Johnstown Road	Cork	Ireland	Co. Cork	
ISLAT	Island Trading	Helen Bennett	Marketing Manager	Garden House	Cowes	UK	Isle of Wight	PO31 7PJ
QUICK	QUICK-Stop	Horst Kloss	Accounting Manager	Taucherstraße 10	Cunewalde	Germany		01307
HUNGC	Hungry Coyote Import Store	Yoshi Latimer	Sales Representative	City Center Plaza	Elgin	USA	OR	97827
GREAL	Great Lakes Food Market	Howard Snyder	Marketing Manager	2732 Baker Blvd.	Eugene	USA	OR	97403
LEHMS	Lehmanns Marktstand	Renate Messner	Sales Representative	Magazinweg 7	Frankfurt a.M.	Germany		60528

Record: 1 of 91 — No Filter — Search

Unique five-character code based on customer name.

Records sorted by City value

FIGURE 1.34 Sorted Customers Table

To sort data in a table by one criterion, select the field that you want to use to sort the records. Then, select Ascending or Descending in the Sort & Filter group on the Home tab.

Access can sort records by more than one field, for example, sorting by City and State. When sorting by multiple criteria, Access first sorts in order of fields from left to right. It is important to understand that to sort by multiple fields, you must arrange your columns in the order you want them sorted by. So, for example, in most databases, State fields are usually added to the right (after) the City fields; however, if you want to first sort by State, and then by Cities listed in alphabetical order within each state, the order of the fields will need to change so the State field is to the left of the City field. In this case you would move the State field. To move a field, click the column heading and hold down the left mouse button. A thick line displays to the left of the column. Drag the field to the appropriate position and release the mouse button.

Once the column has been moved, you can perform a sort by selecting the field to the left, sorting, and then doing the same for the secondary sort column.

5. Explain the purpose of creating a filter. ***p. 580***

6. Explain the difference between a Selection filter and a Filter By Form. ***pp. 580, 582***

7. Discuss the benefits of sorting records in a table. ***p. 584***

Hands-On Exercises

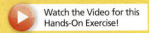

MyLab IT HOE2 Sim Training

Watch the Video for this
Hands-On Exercise!

Skills covered: Use a Selection
Filter to Find Exact Matches • Use
a Selection Filter to Find Records
Containing a Value • Use Filter By
Form • Sort Table Data

2 Filters and Sorts

The sales manager at Northwind Traders wants quick answers to her questions about customer orders.
You use the Access database to filter tables to answer these questions and sort the records based on the
manager's requirements.

STEP 1 USE A SELECTION FILTER TO FIND EXACT MATCHES

The sales manager asks for a list of customers who live in London. You use a Selection filter with an equal condition to
locate these customers. Refer to Figure 1.35 as you complete Step 1.

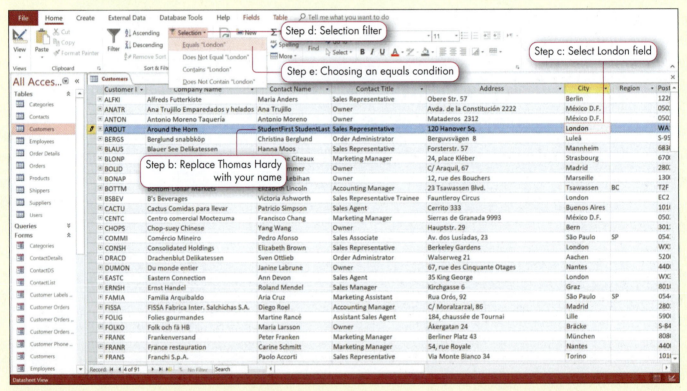

FIGURE 1.35 Filtering the Customers Table

a. Open the *a01h1Traders_LastFirst* database if you closed it at the end of Hands-On Exercise 1,
and save it as **a01h2Traders_LastFirst**, changing h1 to h2. Click **Enable Content**.

b. Double-click the **Customers table** in the Navigation Pane, navigate to record **4**, and
then replace **Thomas Hardy** with your name in the Contact Name field.

c. Scroll right until the City field is visible. The fourth record has a value of London in the
City field. Click the **London field** to select it.

d. Click **Selection** in the Sort & Filter group on the Home tab.

e. Select **Equals "London"** from the menu. Six records are displayed.

The Navigation bar display shows that six records that meet the London criterion are available. The other records in the Customers table are hidden. The Filtered icon also displays on the Navigation bar and column heading, indicating that the Customers table has been filtered.

f. Click **Toggle Filter** in the Sort & Filter group to remove the filter.

g. Click **Toggle Filter** again to reset the filter.

STEP 2 ## USE A SELECTION FILTER TO FIND RECORDS CONTAINING A VALUE

The sales manager asks you to narrow the list of London customers so that it displays only records that contain the title Sales Representatives. To accomplish this task, you add a second layer of filtering using a Selection filter. Refer to Figure 1.36 as you complete Step 2.

FIGURE 1.36 Filtered Customers

a. Click in any field value in the Contact Title field that contains the value **Sales Representative**.

b. Click **Selection** in the Sort & Filter group, select **Contains "Sales Representative,"** and then compare your results to those shown in Figure 1.36.

Three records match the criteria you set. You have applied a second layer of filtering to the customers in London. The second layer further restricts the display to only those customers who have the words Sales Representative contained in their titles. Because you chose Contains as your filter, any representatives with the phrase Sales Representative appear. This includes Victoria Ashworth, who is a Sales Representative Trainee.

> **TROUBLESHOOTING:** If you do not see the record for Victoria Ashworth, you selected Equals "Sales Representative" instead of Contains "Sales Representative." Repeat Steps a and b, making sure you select Contains "Sales Representative."

c. Close the Customers table. Click **Yes** when prompted to save the design changes to the Customers table.

You are asked to provide a list of records that do not match just one set of criteria. You will provide a list of all extended prices less than $50 for a specific sales representative. Use Filter By Form to provide the information when two or more criteria are necessary. You also preview the results in Print Preview to see how the list would print. Refer to Figure 1.37 as you complete Step 3.

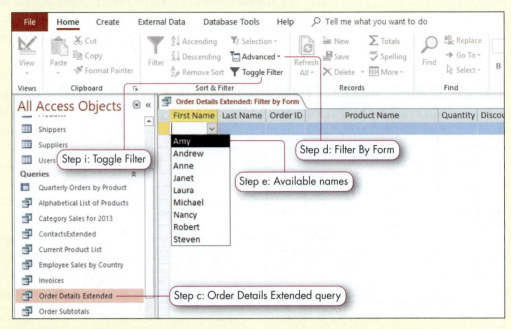

FIGURE 1.37 Using Filter By Form

a. Click the **Tables group** in the Navigation Pane to collapse the listed tables.

b. Click the **Queries group** in the Navigation Pane to expand the list of available queries.

c. Locate and double-click **Order Details Extended** to open it.

   This query contains information about orders. It has fields containing information about the sales person, the Order ID, the product name, the unit price, quantity ordered, the discount given, and an extended price. The extended price is a field used to total order information.

d. Click **Advanced** in the Sort & Filter group and select **Filter By Form** from the list. The first field, First Name, is active by default.

   All of the records are now hidden, and you see only field names and an arrow in the first field. Although you are applying Filter By Form to a query, you can use the same process as applying Filter By Form to a table. You are able to input more than one criterion using Filter By Form.

e. Click the **First Name arrow**.

   A list of all available first names displays. Your name should be on the list. Figure 1.38 shows *Amy Rutledge*, which replaced Margaret Peacock in Hands-On Exercise 1.

> **TROUBLESHOOTING:** If you do not see your name and you do see Margaret on the list, you probably skipped steps in Hands-On Exercise 1. Close the query without saving changes, return to the first Hands-On Exercise, and then rework it, making sure not to omit any steps. Then you can return to this location and work the remainder of this Hands-On Exercise.

f. Select your first name from the list.

g. Click in the first row under the Last Name field to reveal the arrow. Locate and select your last name by clicking it.

h. Scroll right until you see the Extended Price field. Click in the first row under the Extended Price field and type **<50**.

This will select all of the items ordered where the total price was less than 50.

i. Click **Toggle Filter** in the Sort & Filter group.

You have specified which records to include and have executed the filtering by clicking Toggle Filter.

j. Click the **File tab**, click **Print**, and then click **Print Preview**.

You instructed Access to preview the filtered query results. The preview displays the query title as a heading. The current filter is applied, as well as page numbers.

k. Click **Close Print Preview** in the Close Preview group.

l. Close the Order Details Extended query. Click **Yes** when prompted to save your changes.

STEP 4 **PERFORM SORTS**

The Sales Manager is pleased with your work; however, she would like some of the information displayed in a different order. You will now sort the records in the Customers table using the manager's new criteria. Refer to Figure 1.38 as you complete Step 4.

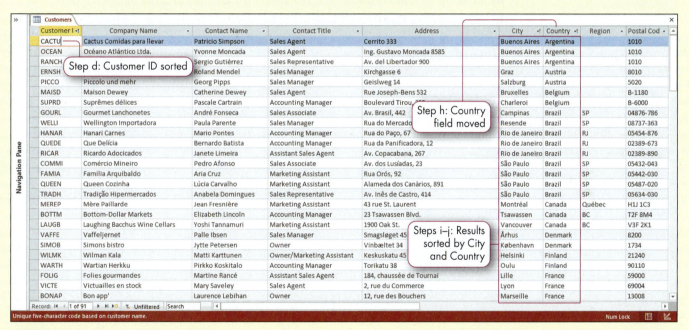

FIGURE 1.38 Updated Customers Table

a. Click the **Queries group** in the Navigation Pane to collapse the listed queries.

b. Click the **Tables group** in the Navigation Pane to expand the list of available tables and double-click the **Customers table** to open it.

This table contains information about customers. The table is sorted in alphabetical order by CustomerID.

c. Click **Shutter Bar Open/Close** in the Navigation Pane to hide the Navigation Pane.

It will be easier to locate fields in the Customer table if the Navigation Pane is hidden.

d. Click any entry in the Customer ID field. Click **Descending** in the Sort & Filter group on the Home tab.

Sorting in descending order on a text field produces a reverse alphabetical order.

e. Scroll right until you can see both the Country and City fields.

f. Click the **Country column heading**.

The entire field is selected.

g. Click the **Country column heading** again and hold down the **left mouse button**.

A thick line displays on the left edge of the Country field.

h. Ensure that you see the thick line on the edge of the Country field. Drag the **Country field** to the left until the thick line moves between the City and Region fields. Release the mouse button and the Country field position moves to the right of the City field.

You moved the Country field next to the City field so that you can easily sort the table based on both fields.

i. Click any city name in the City field and click **Ascending** in the Sort & Filter group.

The City field displays the cities in alphabetical order.

j. Click any country name in the Country field and click **Ascending** in the Sort & Filter group.

The countries are sorted in alphabetical order. The cities within each country also are sorted alphabetically. For example, the customer in Graz, Austria, is listed before the customer in Salzburg, Austria.

k. Close the Customers table. Click **Yes** to save the changes to the design of the table.

l. Click **Shutter Bar Open/Close** in the Navigation Pane to show the Navigation Pane.

m. Close the database. You will submit this file to your instructor at the end of the last Hands-On Exercise.

Access Database Creation

Now that you have examined the fundamentals of an Access database and explored the power of databases, it is time to create one! A lot of careful thought should go into designing a database. Businesses may use a database only to keep track of customers, or they may use a database for much more, such as orders and inventory tracking. Databases can range from a simple table or two to complex business applications with many tables, forms, reports, etc. that become the core of the business operations. Depending on the purpose of the database, its size, and how many people will use it, one of two methods may be used to create a database.

In this section, you explore the benefits of creating a database from a blank database, which enables you to design it to your specific requirements. Additionally, you will learn how to create a database from a template to save time by having tables, forms, reports, etc. already available to modify to your specifications.

Creating a Database

When you first start Access, you can create a database using one of two methods:

- Create a blank database
- Create a database from a template (note: there will be many templates shown)

Creating a blank database enables you to create a database specific to your requirements. Rather than starting from scratch by creating a blank database, you can use a template to create a new database. An Access ***template*** is a predefined database that includes professionally designed tables, forms, reports, and other objects that you can use to jumpstart the creation of your database.

Figure 1.39 shows the options for creating a blank database and multiple templates from which you can select the method for which you want to create a database.

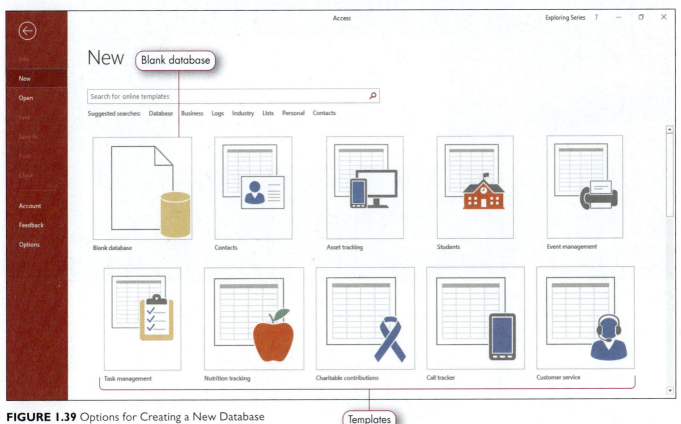

FIGURE 1.39 Options for Creating a New Database

Create a Blank Database

Often, if you are migrating data from Excel to Access, you would start by creating a blank database. At that point, you could import your existing structure and data into a new table. Another time you might use a blank database is when you are starting a project and want to design your own tables.

When you create a blank database, Access opens to a blank table in Datasheet view where you can add fields or data. You can also refine the table in Design view. You would then create additional tables and objects as necessary. Obviously, this task requires some level of Access knowledge, so unless you have requirements to follow, you may be better served using a template.

To create a blank database, complete the following steps:

1. Open Access. (If Access is already open, click the File tab and click New.)
2. Click Blank database.
3. Type the file name for the file in the text box, click Browse to navigate to the folder where you want to store the database file, and then click OK.
4. Click Create (see Figure 1.40).
5. Type data in the empty table that displays.

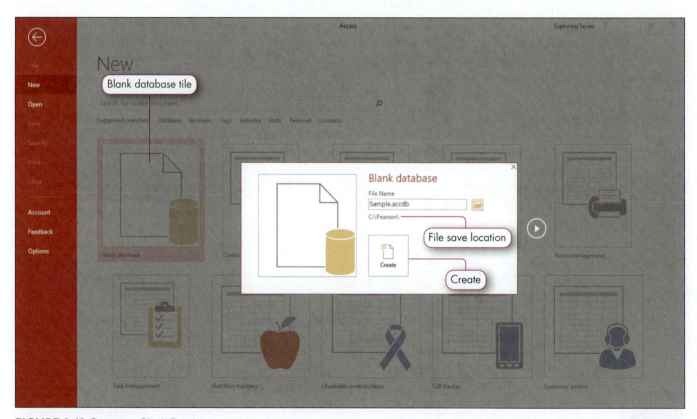

FIGURE 1.40 Creating a Blank Database

STEP 1 **Create a Database Using a Template**

Using a template to start a database saves you a great deal of creation time. Working with a database template can also help a new Access user become familiar with database design. Database templates are available from Backstage view, where you can select from a variety of templates or search online for more templates.

> **To create a database from a template, complete the following steps:**
>
> 1. Open Access. (If Access is already open, click the File tab and click New.)
> 2. Click the desktop database template you want to use or use the search box at the top of the page to find templates for a specific purpose. Figure 1.41 shows some examples of templates.
> 3. Type the file name for the file in the text box, click Browse to navigate to the folder where you want to store the database file, and then click OK.
> 4. Click Create to download the template. The database will be created and will open.
> 5. Click Enable Content in the Security Warning message bar.

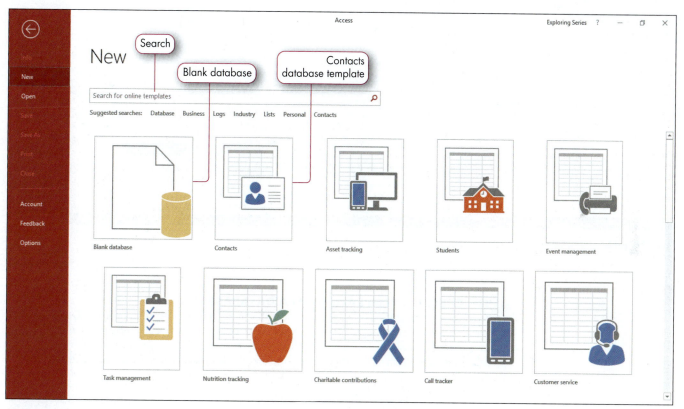

FIGURE 1.41 Database Templates

After the database opens, you may see a Welcome page that includes a video you can use to learn more about the database. When finished reviewing the learning materials, close the Welcome page to view the database. Figure 1.42 displays the Welcome page included with the Task management template. Because you downloaded a template, some objects will have already been created. You can work with these objects just as you did in the first two sections of this chapter. Edit any object to meet your requirements.

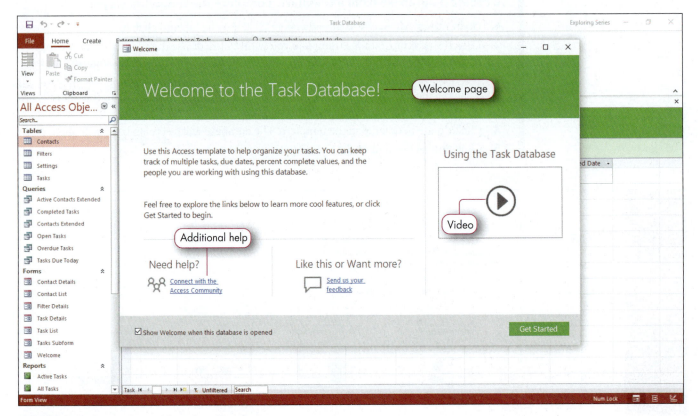

FIGURE 1.42 Getting Started Page for a Template

> **TIP: CREATE A TEMPLATE FROM A DATABASE**
> If you have a database you may want to reuse in the future, you can save it as a template. Doing so will enable you to create new databases with the same tables, queries, forms, and reports as the one you have created. You can also reuse just specific objects within the database such as a form or report. To create a template from an existing database, use the File tab option of Save As and select Template as the file type.

Explore and Customize a Database Template

Once a database template has been downloaded, you can use it as you would use any Access database. Figure 1.43 shows the Contact Details form from the Contact management database template.

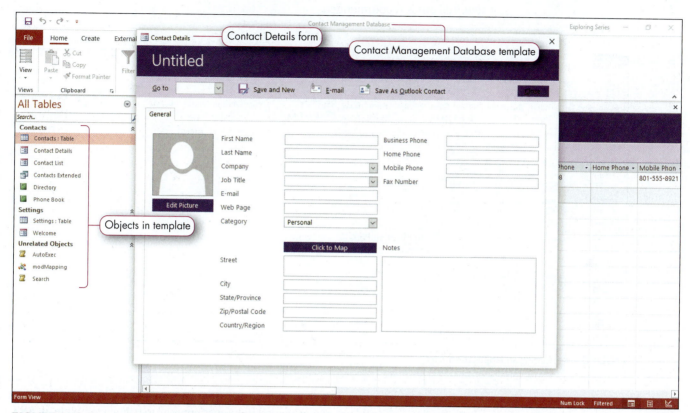

FIGURE 1.43 Contact Management Database

One of the reasons to use a template is so you do not have to create any of the objects. Therefore, you will notice each template comes with a varying number of predefined queries, forms, and reports. Familiarize yourself with the unique features of a template; because they are professionally designed, they are typically well thought out. Review the objects listed in the Navigation Pane. After you are familiar with the database design, you can enter your data using a table or form.

Create a Table Using an Application Part

An *application part* enables you to add a set of common Access components to an existing database, such as a table, a form, and a report for a related task. These are provided by Microsoft and offer components (for example, a Contacts table) you can add to an existing database, rather than creating an entirely new database, as shown in Figure 1.44. Using the pre-built application parts can save time and effort. A Contacts application part for example has a Contacts table with typical fields such as Last Name, First Name, Address, etc. Along with the table you will find there are also some queries, forms, and reports that would be useful for the Contacts table.

To add an application part to a database, click Application Parts in the Templates group on the Create tab. A list of options displays, with Quick Start options such as Contacts, Tasks, Issues, and Comments. Once you have made an option selection from the list, you will respond to the dialog boxes to complete the process of setting up the application part. After it is created, you will see the new components displayed in the Navigation Pane. You may be prompted to create a relationship between your tables. Setting up a relationship is not required but is recommended.

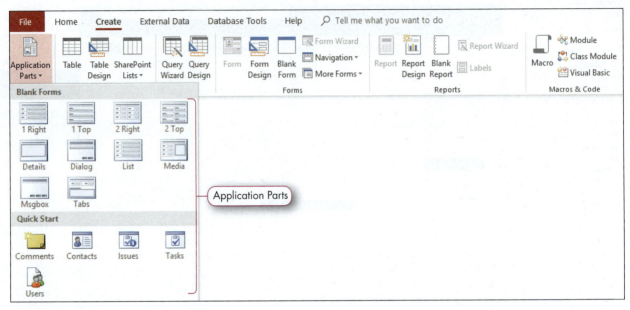

FIGURE 1.44 Adding an Application Part

 **Quick Concepts**

8. Explain why you would use a new blank database as opposed to using a template. *p. 591*

9. Discuss two benefits of using a template to create a database. *pp. 593, 595*

10. Explain the purpose of using an application part. *p. 595*

Hands-On Exercises

MyLab IT HOE3 Sim Training

▶ Watch the Video for this Hands-On Exercise!

Skills covered: Create a Database Using a Template • Explore and Customize a Database Template

3 Access Database Creation

After working with the Northwind database on the job, you decide to use Access to create a personal contact database. Rather than start from a blank table, you use an Access Contacts template to make your database creation simpler. You explore the template objects and customize the database to suit your needs.

<table><tr><td>STEP 1</td></tr></table> ### CREATE A DATABASE USING A TEMPLATE

You locate an Access template that you can use to create your personal contact database. This template not only enables you to store names, addresses, telephone numbers, and other information, but also helps you categorize your contacts, send email messages, and create maps of addresses. You download and save the template. Refer to Figure 1.45 as you complete Step 1.

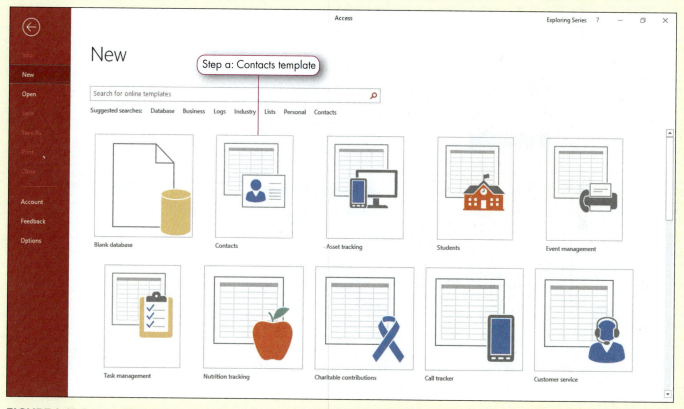

FIGURE 1.45 Contacts Template

a. Open Access. Click the **Contacts** template.

> **TROUBLESHOOTING:** If the Contacts template is not visible, type contacts in the search box at the top of the screen and click the magnifying glass. Note there may be slight differences to the name, so look for the template matching the icon above.

b. Click **Browse** to navigate to the folder where you are saving your files, type **a01h3Contacts_LastFirst** as the file name, and then click **OK**.

c. Click **Create** to download the template.

d. Click **Enable Content** on the Security Warning message bar.

e. Click the **Show Welcome when this database is opened check box** to deselect it. Close the Welcome to the Contacts Database page.

The database displays the Contact List form.

STEP 2 ## EXPLORE AND CUSTOMIZE A DATABASE TEMPLATE

Because the database opens in the Contact List form, you decide to begin by entering a contact in the form. You then explore the objects created by the template so that you understand the organization of the database. Refer to Figure 1.46 as you complete Step 2.

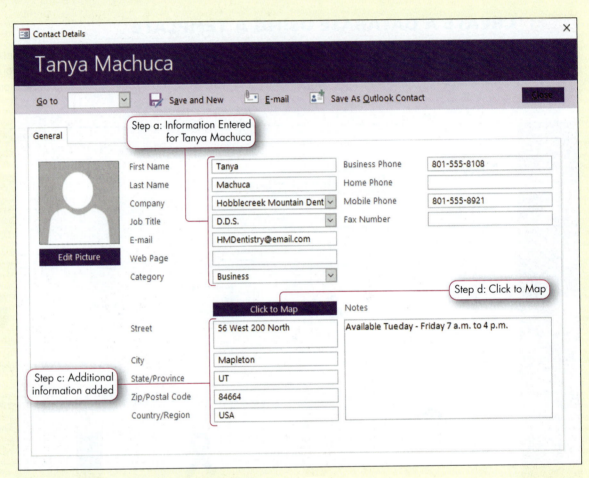

FIGURE 1.46 Contact Details for Tanya Machuca

a. Click in the **First Name field** of the first record. Type the following information, pressing **Tab** between each entry. Do not press Tab after entering the ZIP/Postal Code.

Field Name	Value to Type
First Name	**Tanya**
Last Name	**Machuca**
Company	**Hobblecreek Mountain Dentistry**
Job Title	**D.D.S.**
Category	**Business** (select from list)
Email	**HMDentistry@email.com**
Business Phone	**801-555-8108**
Home Phone	(leave blank)
Mobile Phone	**801-555-8921**
Zip/Postal Code	**84664**

b. Scroll back to the left if necessary to see the first field. Click **Open** in the first field of Dr. Machuca's record.

Open is a hyperlink to a different form in the database. The Contact Details form opens, displaying Dr. Machuca's information. More fields are available for you to use to store information. (Note that this form could also be opened from the Navigation Pane.)

c. Type the following additional information to the record:

Field Name	Value to Type
Street	**56 West 200 North**
City	**Mapleton**
State/Province	**UT**
Country/Region	**USA**
Notes	**Available Tuesday - Friday 7 a.m. to 4 p.m.**

d. Click the **Click to Map hyperlink** to view a map to Dr. Machuca's office.

Bing displays a map to the address in the record. You can get directions, locate nearby businesses, and use many other options.

> **TROUBLESHOOTING:** You may be prompted to choose an application. Select any Web browser such as Microsoft Edge from the list.

e. Close the map. Click **Close** in the top right of the form to save and close the Contact Details form.

The record is saved.

f. Click **New Contact** beneath the Contact List title bar.

The Contact Details form opens to a blank record.

g. Type the following information for a new record, pressing **Tab** to move between fields. Some fields will be blank.

Field Name	Value to Type
First Name	**Rowan**
Last Name	**Westmoreland**
Company	**Phoenix Aesthetics**
Job Title	**Aesthetician**
Email	**Rowan55W5@email.com**
Category	**Personal**
Street	**425 North Main Street**
City	**Springville**
State/Province	**UT**
Zip/Postal Code	**84663**
Mobile Phone	**801-555-2221**
Notes	**Recommended by Michelle**

h. Click **Close**.

i. Double-click the **Contacts table** in the Navigation Pane.

The information you entered using the Contact List form and the Contact Details form displays in the Contacts table.

j. Double-click the **Phone Book report** in the Navigation Pane.

The Phone Book report opens displaying the contact name and phone information organized by category.

k. Double-click the **Directory report** in the Navigation Pane.

The Directory report opens, displaying a full alphabetical contact list. The Directory report was designed to display more fields than the Phone Book, but it is not organized by category.

l. Click **All Access Objects** on the Navigation Pane and select **Tables and Related Views**.

You can now see the objects that are based on the Contacts table.

m. Right-click the **Directory report tab** and select **Close All**.

n. Close the database and exit Access. Based on your instructor's directions, submit the following:

a01h1Traders_LastFirst_*CurrentDate*

a01h2Traders_LastFirst

a01h3Contacts_LastFirst

Chapter Objectives Review

After reading this chapter, you have accomplished the following objectives:

1. Open, save, and enable content in a database.

- A database is a collection of data organized as meaningful information that can be accessed, managed, stored, queried, sorted, and reported. A database management system (DBMS) is a software system that provides the tools to create, maintain, and use a database. Access is the database management system found in business versions of Microsoft Office. A database is opened from the File tab.
- When a database is first opened, Access displays a message bar with a security warning. Click Enable Content if you trust the database's source.

2. Recognize database object types.

- Examine the Access interface: The DBMS manages objects. Common object types are Tables, Queries, Forms, Reports. Objects are organized and listed in the Navigation Pane. Access also uses a Tabbed objects interface in which each object that is open has its own tab.
- Explore table Datasheet view: Datasheet view is a grid containing fields (columns) and records (rows).
- Navigate and locate records: Navigation arrows enable you to move through records, with arrows for the first, previous, next, and last records, as well as one to add a new record.
- Explore table Design view: Design view gives you a detailed view of the table's structure and is used to create and modify a table's design by specifying the fields it will contain, the fields' data types, and their associated properties.
- Rename and describe tables: Tables can be renamed as necessary and a description can be added. The description gives the user more information about what an object does.
- Understand relationships between tables: A relationship is a connection between two tables using a common field. The benefit of a relationship is the ability to efficiently combine data from related tables to create queries, forms, and reports.

3. Modify, add, and save data.

- Access works primarily from storage. Records can be added, modified, or deleted in the database, and as the information is entered, it is automatically saved. Undo cannot reverse edits made to multiple records.
- Modify records in a table: A pencil symbol displays in the record selector box to indicate when you are in editing mode. Moving to another record saves the changes.
- Add records in a table: New records can be added through the table's Datasheet view or through a corresponding form. To add a new record to a table, click New in the Records group on the Home tab and begin

typing the values in the field for the new record. Press Tab to move to subsequent fields.
- Delete records from a table: To delete a record, click the record selector and click Delete in the Records group on the Home tab.
- Save records in a table: Access saves your changes as soon as you move to a different record.

4. Use database utilities.

- Back up a database: The Back Up Database utility creates a duplicate copy of the database. This may enable users to recover from failure.
- Compact and Repair a database: The Compact and Repair utility reduces the size of a database and fixes any errors that may exist in the file.
- Print information: Access can create a print copy of your data. Previewing before printing is a good practice to avoid wasting paper.

5. Work with filters.

- Filters enable the display of desired records that meet specific criteria.
- Use a selection filter to find exact matches: A selection filter can be used to find exact matches.
- Use a selection filter to find records containing a value: A selection filter can find partial matches, for example, find values containing a certain phrase.
- Use Filter By Form: Filter By Form displays records based on multiple criteria and enables the user to apply logical operators and use comparison operators.

6. Perform sorts.

- Sort table data: Sorting changes the order of information, and information may be sorted by one or more fields. Data can be sorted ascending (low to high) or descending (high to low).

7. Create a database.

- Create a blank database: Creating a blank database enables you to create a database specific to your requirements.
- Create a database using a template: A template is a predefined database that includes professionally designed tables, forms, reports, and other objects that you can use to jumpstart the creation of your database.
- Explore database objects and customize a database template: After you create a database using a template, explore it and become familiar with the contents.
- Create a table using an application part: If you require a certain type of table (such as Contacts) you can add them using an application part.

Practice Exercises

1 Replacement Parts

As a recent hire at Replacement Parts, you are tasked with performing updates to the customer database. You have been asked to open the company's database, save it with a new name, and then modify, add, and delete records. You will then back up the database, apply filters and sorts, and use an application part to add a new table that will be used to track customer shipping and receiving complaints. Refer to Figure 1.47 as you complete the exercise.

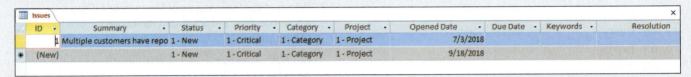

FIGURE 1.47 Issues Table Added to Replacement Parts Database

a. Start your computer. Click **Start**, and click **Access** from the list of applications. Click **Open Other Files** and click **Browse**. Navigate to the location of your student files. Double-click to open the *a01p1Replace* file. Click the **File tab**, click **Save As**. Click **Access Database**, and click **Save As**. Save the database as **a01p1Replace_LastFirst**. Click **Enable Content** on the message bar.

b. Locate the Navigation Pane. Double-click the **Manufacturers table** to open the table in Datasheet view. Locate record 800552 (Haas). Click the **ManufacturerName field** for the record. Change the name from Haas to **Haas International**. For the same record, click the **CountryOfOrigin field** and change the CountryOfOrigin from Germany to **Austria**.

c. Locate the last (blank) record. Click the **MfgID field**. Type **801411** and press **Tab**. In the ManufacturerName field type **Bolshoy Fine China** and press **Tab**. In the CountryOfOrigin field type **Russia** and press **Tab**. In the EmployeeID field type **817080** and press **Tab**. Type the following new records:

MfgID	ManufacturerName	CountryofOrigin	EmplolyeeID
801422	Tejada and Sons	Dominican Republic	816680
801433	Lubitz UK	England	817580

d. Locate the sixth record, with MfgID **800661** (John Bradshaw). Right-click on the **row indicator** for the record and select **Delete Record**. Click **Yes** to delete the record.

e. Click **Close** ☒ the at the top right of the table to close the Manufacturers table.

f. Click the **File tab**, click **Save As**, and then double-click **Back Up Database**. Accept the default backup file name and click **Save**.

g. Double-click the **Customers table** in the Navigation Pane to open the table in Datasheet view.

h. Click the **State field** for the first record (Diego Martinez). Click **Selection** in the Sort & Filter group and select **Equals "OR"** to display the two customers in Oregon. Close the table. Click Close ☒ at the top right of the Customers table tab. Click **Yes** when prompted to save the changes to the table.

i. Double-click the **Employees table** to open the table in Datasheet view.

j. Click the **plus sign** next to Alfonso Torres. Notice he is assigned as the representative for the manufacturer Antarah. Click the **minus sign** next to Alfonso Torres to close the subdatasheet.

k. Click **Advanced** in the Sort & Filter group on the Home tab and select **Filter By Form**. Click in the **Salary field**. Type **>60000** and click **Toggle Filter** in the Sort & Filter group on the Home tab to apply the filter. Six employees are displayed. Click Close ☒ at the top right of the Employees table tab. Click **Yes** when prompted to save the changes to the table.

l. Double-click the **Manufacturers table** to open the table in Datasheet view.

m. Click any value in the **ManufacturerName** field. Click **Ascending** in the Sort & Filter group to sort the table by the name of the manufacturer. Click Close ☒ at the top right of the Manufacturers table tab. Click **Yes** when prompted to save the changes to the table.

n. Click **Application Parts** in the Templates group on the Create tab. Select **Issues**. Select the option for "There is no relationship." Click **Create**.

o. Double-click the **Issues table** to open the table in Datasheet view.

p. Click in the Summary field and type **Multiple customers have reported damaged goods received in Denton, Texas.** (include the period). Leave all other fields as the default values. Click Close ☒ at the top right of the Issues table tab. Click **Yes** when prompted to save the changes to the table.

q. Close the database and exit Access. Based on your instructor's directions, submit the following:

a01p1Replace_LastFirst

a01p1Replace_LastFirst_*CurrentDate*

2 Custom Coffee

The Custom Coffee Company provides coffee, tea, and snacks to offices in Miami. Custom Coffee also supplies and maintains the equipment for brewing the beverages. To improve customer service, the owner recently had an Access database created to keep track of customers, orders, and products. This database will replace the Excel spreadsheets currently maintained by the office manager. The company hired you to verify and input all the Excel data into the Access database. Refer to Figure 1.48 as you complete the exercise.

Product ID	ProductName	Description	Cost	MarkupPercent	RefrigerationNeeded	Brand	Click to Add
2	Coffee - Hazelnut	24/Case, Pre-Ground 1.75 Oz Bags	$23.00	1	No	Premium	
4	Coffee - Assorted Flavors	18/Case. Pre-Ground 1.75 Oz Bags	$23.00	0.5	No	House	
26	Robusto Chai Tea Latte K-Cups	40/Box	$26.00	0.75	No	Premium	
27	Robusto French Roast K-Cups	40/Box	$28.00	1	No	Premium	

FIGURE 1.48 Filtered Products Table

a. Start your computer. Click **Start** and click **Access** from the list of applications. Click **Open Other Files** and click **Browse**. Navigate to the location of your student files. Double-click to open the *a01p2Coffee* file. Click the **File tab**, click **Save As**. Click **Access Database**, and then click **Save As**. Save the database as **a01p2Coffee_LastFirst**. Click **Enable Content** on the message bar.

b. Click the **Database Tools tab** and click **Relationships** in the Relationships group. Review the table relationships. Notice the join line between the Customers and Orders tables. Click **Relationship Report** in the Tools group on the Relationship Tools Design tab. Right-click the **Relationships** for a01p2Coffee_LastFirst tab, and click **Save**. Click **OK** to save the report with the default name.

c. Click Close ☒ at the top right of the Relationships Report tab. Click Close ☒ at the top right of the Relationships tab. Click **No** if prompted to save the changes to the relationships.

d. Double-click the **Sales Reps table** in the Navigation Pane to open it in Datasheet view. For rep number 2, replace **YourFirstName** and **YourLastName** with your first and last names. Close the table by clicking **Close** on the right side of the Sales Reps window.

e. Double-click the **Customers table** to open it in Datasheet view. Click **New** in the Records group. Add a new record by typing the following information; press **Tab** after each field. The first field is an autonumber data type, therefore you will begin by adding data to the Customer Name field. Input masks will add the correct formatting to the Phone and Sales Rep ID fields.

Customer Name:	**Budrow Driving School**
Contact:	**Eric Cameron**
Address 1:	**1 Clausen Blvd**
Address 2:	**Floor 2**
City:	**Chesterton**
State:	**IN**
Zip Code:	**46304**
Phone:	**8575556661**
Credit Rating:	**A**
Sales Rep ID:	**2**

Notice the pencil symbol in the record selector for the new row. Press **Tab**. The pencil symbol disappears, and the new customer is automatically saved to the table.

f. Click the **City field** for the last record (Chesterton). Click **Selection** in the Sort & Filter group and select **Equals "Chesterton"** to display the three customers located in the town of Chesterton.

g. Save and close the table. Click **Yes** if prompted to save the changes to the table.

h. Double-click the **Products table** to open it in Datasheet view. Click **New** in the Records group. Add a new record by typing the following information:

Product ID:	**26**
ProductName:	**Robusto Chai Tea Latte K-Cups**
Description:	**40/Box**
Cost:	**26**
MarkupPercent:	**.75**
RefrigerationNeeded	**No**
Brand	**Premium**

i. Add a second product using the following information:

Product ID:	**27**
ProductName:	**Robusto French Roast K-Cups**
Description:	**40/Box**
Cost:	**28**
MarkupPercent:	**1**
RefrigerationNeeded	**No**
Brand	**Premium**

j. Click **Advanced** in the Sort & Filter group and select **Filter By Form**. Type **>=23** in the Cost field and click **Toggle Filter** in the Sort & Filter group.

k. Save and close the table.

l. Click the **File tab**, click **Save As**, and then double-click **Back Up Database**. Accept the default backup file name and click **Save.**

m. Click **Application Parts** in the Templates group on the Create tab. Select **Issues**. Click **Next** to accept the default relationship. Select "**CustomerName**" as the Field from "Customers," select **Sort Ascending** from Sort this field, and then type **Customer** as the name for the lookup column. Click **Create**.

n. Double-click the **Issues table** to open it in Datasheet view.

o. Click the **Customer field** for the first record. Click the **arrow** and select **Advantage Sales**. Click in the **Summary field** and type **Customer reports French roast coffee delivered instead of decaf.** Leave all other fields as the default values.

p. Close the table. Close the database and exit Access. Based on your instructor's directions, submit the following:

a01p2Coffee_LastFirst

a01p2Coffee_LastFirst_*CurrentDate*

3 Healthy Living

FROM SCRATCH

You and two friends from your gym have decided to use Access to help you reach your weight goals. You will use the Access Nutrition template to help you get organized. Refer to Figure 1.49 as you complete this exercise.

ID	TipDescription	TipCategory	Click to Add
150	Walk, jog, skate, or cycle.	Activity	
147	Replace a coffee break with a brisk 10-minute walk. Ask a friend to go with yo	Activity	
146	Get off the bus or subway one stop early and walk or skate the rest of the way	Activity	
141	Walk, skate, or cycle more, and drive less.	Activity	
139	Walk the dog—don't just watch the dog walk.	Activity	
138	Walk up and down the soccer or softball field sidelines while watching the kid	Activity	
135	Join a walking group in the neighborhood or at the local shopping mall. Recruit	Activity	
*	(New)		

FIGURE 1.49 Filtered Tips Table

a. Start your computer. Click **Start**, and click **Access** from the list of applications. Click the **Nutrition tracking template** in Backstage view.

> **TROUBLESHOOTING:** If the Nutrition tracking template is not visible, type nutrition in the search box at the top of the screen and click the magnifying glass. Note there may be slight differences to the name, so look for the template matching the image above.

b. Type **a01p3Nutrition_LastFirst** in the File name box. Click **Browse**. Navigate to the location where you are saving your files in the File New Database dialog box, click **OK** to close the dialog box, and then click **Create** to create the new database.

c. Click **Enable Content** on the message bar. A form titled *Today at a glance* is already open. Close the form.

d. Double-click the **My Profile table** in the Navigation Pane to open it in Datasheet view.

e. Click **record selector**, click **Delete** in the Records group. Click **Yes** to delete the existing record.

f. Click **New** in the Records group. Type the following information in as a new record, pressing **Tab** between each field:

Sex:	Male
Height:	64
Weight:	190
Age:	28
Lifestyle:	Lightly active
Goal:	Lose weight

g. Click **New** in the Records group. Type the following information, pressing **Tab** between each field:

Sex:	Male
Height:	69
Weight:	140
Age:	20
Lifestyle:	Moderately active
Goal:	Gain weight

h. Click **New** in the Records group. Type the following information, pressing **Tab** between each field:

Sex:	Female
Height:	66
Weight:	140
Age:	23
Lifestyle:	Moderately active
Goal:	Maintain my weight

i. Close the table by clicking **Close** on the right side of the My Profile window.

j. Double-click the **Foods table**. Click **Advanced** in the Sort and Filter group and select **Filter By Form**.

k. Click the **Calories field** for the first record. Type **<200** in the Calories field and **>=10** in the Fiber [grams] field. Click **Toggle Filter** in the Sort & Filter group.

l. Save and close the table by clicking **Close** on the right side of the Foods window and clicking **Yes** when asked if you want to save the changes.

m. Double-click the **Tips table** to open it in Datasheet view.

n. Click in the first **TipCategory**. Click **Ascending** in the Sort & Filter group to sort the tips in alphabetical order.

o. Place the pointer over the word **Walk** in the fifth record (ID #138) and drag to select it. Make sure you do not highlight the space after the word Walk when you select the text. Click **Selection** in the Sort & Filter group and select **Contains "Walk"**.

p. Save and close the table by clicking **Close** on the right side of the Tips window and clicking **Yes** when asked if you want to save the changes.

q. Click the **File tab**, click **Save As**, and then double-click **Back Up Database**. Use the default backup file name.

r. Close the database and exit Access. Based on your instructor's directions, submit the following:

a01p3Nutrition_LastFirst
a01p3Nutrition _LastFirst_*CurrentDate*

Mid-Level Exercises

1   Home Sales

An independent real estate firm that specializes in home sales needs to create a database in which to store its records. In the following project, you will open a database containing information about the properties the real estate firm has listed. You will work with a table in which to store agent information, and then sort the table. You create a relationship between two tables and enforce referential integrity. You also apply filters, sort a table, and save the results.

a. Open the *a01m1HomeSales* file and save the database as **a01m1HomeSales_LastFirst**. Click **Enable Content** on the Security Warning message bar.

b. Open the **Agents table** in Datasheet view and add the following records letting Access assign the AgentID:

FirstName	LastName	Title
Guillaume	Picard	Broker
Keith	Martin	Agent
Usa-chan	Yang	Agent
Steven	Dougherty	Agent in Training
Rajesh	Khanna	Agent in Training
Juan	Rosario	President

c. Add yourself as a new Agent member, allowing Access assign the AgentID. Type your **first name** in the FirstName field and your **last name** in the LastName field. Type **Agent** for your Title.

d. Sort the Agents table by the LastName field in ascending order.

e. Apply a selection filter so that everyone with a title other than *Agent in Training* displays. Save the changes to the table design and close the Agents table.

f. Open the Properties table in Design View. Change the data type for the specified fields as follows:

Field Name	Data Type
iDateListed	Date/Time
ListPrice	Currency
SqFeet	Number
Beds	Number
Baths	Number
AgentID	Number

Save the changes to the design of the table. Access will alert you that some of the data in the table may be lost due to changing the data type of the fields listed above. Click **Yes** then view the table in Datasheet View.

g. Sort the records in the Properties table by the **ListPrice field** from largest to smallest.

h. Use **Filter by Form** to create a filter that will identify all properties with a ListPrice less than $300,000 with 2 bedrooms. Apply the filter and preview the filtered table. Save the changes and close the table.

i. Back up the database. Accept the default file name.

j. Add an **Issue application part** to the database. Change the relationship so there is One 'Agents' to many 'Issues.'. Click **Next**. Select the **AgentID** field from 'Agents', choose the **Sort Ascending** option, and name the lookup column **Agent**. Click **Create**.

k. Open the **IssueNew form** in Form view.

l. Select the Summary field and type **Merrydale property listed twice**. Click **Save & Close** to close the form.

m. Close the database and exit Access. Based on your instructor's directions, submit the following:

a01m1HomeSales_LastFirst
a01m1HomeSales_LastFirst_*CurrentDate*

Capstone Exercise

Lending for Small Businesses

You are employed as a technical supervisor at a lending firm for small business loans. You will work with a form that is used to store loan officer information, add records, and sort tables.

Modify Data in a Table

You will open an original database file and save the database with a new name. You will then demonstrate modifying, adding, and deleting information by using tables and forms.

1. Open the *a01c1Loans* file and save the database as **a01c1Loans_LastFirst**.

2. Open the **Loan Officers table** in Datasheet view. Update the database with the information below and close the table.

First Name	Last Name	Email Address	Phone Ext	Title
John	Badman	john_badman@loanofficer.com	x1757	Loan Officer
Stan	Dupp	stan_dupp@loanofficer.com	x6720	Senior Loan Officer
Herb	Avore	herb_avore@loanofficer.com	x2487	Loan Officer
Polly	Esther	polly_esther@loanofficer.com	x8116	Senior Loan Officer
Strawberry	Fields	strawberry_fields@loanofficer.com	x3219	Loan Officer
Ann	Serdifone	ann_serdifone@loanofficer.com	x5962	Managing Loan Officer

3. Close the Loan Officers table.

4. Open the **Loans table** in Datasheet view. Add a new record with the following information:

OfficerID:	5
MemberID:	15
LoanAmount:	7000
Term:	36 months
InterestRate:	15.41%
Payment:	244.07
Grade:	D
IssueDate:	12/15/18
LoanStatus:	Late (31-120 days)

5. Open the **Maintain Members form**. In record 3 (for *Brynn Anderson*, MemberID 13), add a new loan to the subform:

OfficerID:	5
LoanAmount:	17000
Term:	36 months
InterestRate:	4.35%
Payment:	300.45
Grade:	B
IssueDate:	9/1/18
LoanStatus:	Fully Paid

6. Use the Navigation bar to search for MemberID **16**, and edit the subform so that the InterestRate is **0.1254** instead of 0.1899 for the LoanID *47*.

7. Close the Maintain Members form.

Sort a Table and Use Filter By Form

You will sort the Loan table and apply a filter to display only publishers located in New York.

8. Sort the records in the Loans table by the **IssueDate** field in descending order (newest to oldest).

9. Locate the loans that have a rate of less than **11%** (**<0.11**) and a term of **36 months**. Use the Filter By Form to apply the filters and preview the filtered table.

10. Close the table and save the changes.

Apply a Selection Filter and Sort a Query

You are interested in quickly filtering the data in the Loans, Officers, and Members query based on a specific loan officer. You then sort the filtered results to view the loans by loan status.

11. Open the **Loans, Officers, and Members query** in Datasheet view.

12. Use a Selection filter to show only the loans managed by the loan officer whose name is **John Badman**.

13. Sort the query by **LoanStatus** in alphabetical order. Save and close the query.

Back Up a Database and Add an Application Part

You will demonstrate adding an application part to the manager to show how tables are created. You will first back the database up to reinforce the importance of backing up the data.

14. Create a backup copy of your database, accepting the default file name.

15. Add a Comments application part, selecting the option **One 'Loans' to many 'Comments.'** Select the **LoanStatus field** for the Field from Loans and **Sort Ascending** for Sort this field. Name the lookup column **Status**.

16. Close the database and exit Access. Based on your instructor's directions, submit the following:

    a01c1Loans_LastFirst
    a01c1Loans_LastFirst_CurrentDate

Tables and Queries in Relational Databases

LEARNING OUTCOMES

You will create and modify tables for data input and organization.
You will develop queries to extract and present data.

OBJECTIVES & SKILLS: After you read this chapter, you will be able to:

CASE STUDY | Bank Internship

You have started an internship at Commonwealth Federal Bank in Wilmington, Delaware. The bank is considering converting its existing records into an Access application. To analyze whether that would be advantageous, the manager asks you to create a sample Access database made up of customers, accounts, and the bank's respective branches.

Designing Databases and Extracting Information

As you begin, you realize that some of the data are contained in external Excel and Access files that you will import directly into the new database. Importing from Excel and Access is fairly straightforward and will help to avoid common errors that are associated with data entry. Once the data have been imported, you will use queries to view the records in ways that are relevant to the bank's usage.

Once the new database is created and the data are entered, you will extract information about the customers, accounts, and branches by creating and running queries. The value of that information depends entirely on the quality of the underlying data—the tables. This chapter uses the bank database to present the basic principles of table and query design.

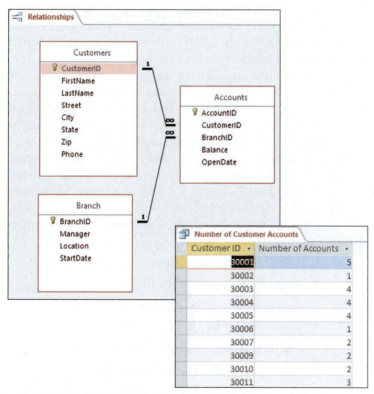

FIGURE 2.1 Bank Database

CASE STUDY | Bank Internship

Starting Files	File to be Submitted
Blank database **a02h2Accounts** **a02h2Customers.xlsx**	**a02h4Bank_LastFirst**

MyLab IT Grader An alternate version of this project is available as a MyLab IT Grader Assessment

Table Design, Creation, and Modification

A successful and usable database design begins with the tables. Because tables store all the data, they provide the basis for all the activities you perform in a database. If the tables are not designed properly, the database will not function as expected. Whether you are experienced in designing tables or are a new database designer, the process should not be done haphazardly. You should follow a systematic approach when creating tables for a database.

In this section, you will learn the essentials of good table design. After developing and analyzing the table design on paper, you will implement that design in Access. In addition, you will learn to create and refine tables by changing the properties of various fields.

Designing a Table

A table is a collection of records, with each record made up of a number of fields. During the table design process, consider the specific fields you will need in each table; list the proposed fields with their table names, and determine what type of data each field will store (numbers, dates, pictures, etc.). The order of the fields within the table and the specific field names are not as significant at this stage, as they can be modified later. What is important is that the tables contain all necessary fields so that the database can produce the required information later.

For example, consider the design process necessary to create a database for a bank. Typically, your bank has your name, address, phone number, and Social Security number. It also knows which accounts you have (checking, savings, money market), your account balances, and if you have a credit card with that bank. Additionally, your bank keeps information about its branches around the city or state. If you think about the data your bank maintains, you can make a list of the categories of data needed to store that information. These categories for the bank—customers, accounts, branches—become the tables in the bank's database. A bank's customer list is an example of a table; it contains a record for each bank customer.

After the tables have been identified, plan for the necessary fields using these six guidelines, which are discussed in detail in the following paragraphs:

- Include the necessary data.
- Design for now and for the future.
- Store data in their smallest parts.
- Determine primary keys.
- Link tables using common fields.
- Design to accommodate calculations.

Figure 2.2 shows a customer table and two other tables found in a sample bank database. It also lists fields that would be needed in each table.

Include Necessary Data

A good way to determine what data (inputs) are necessary in tables is to consider the output you will need from your database. You will probably need to create professional-looking reports for others, so begin by creating a rough draft of the reports you will need. Then design tables that contain the fields necessary to create those reports. In other words, ask yourself what information will be expected from the database (outputs) and determine the data required (inputs) to produce that information. Defining and organizing good data input will result in better output from your database. Consider, for example, the tables and fields in Figure 2.2. Is there required information that could not be generated from those tables?

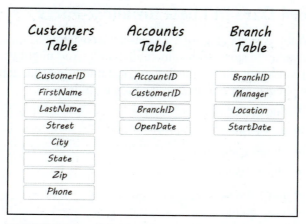

FIGURE 2.2 Rough Draft of Tables and Fields in a Sample Bank Database

- You will be able to determine how long a customer has banked with the branch because the date he or she opened the account is stored in the Accounts table, which will eventually connect to the Customers and Branch tables.

- You will be able to determine which branch a customer uses because the Accounts table includes both the CustomerID and the BranchID. The Accounts table will eventually connect to both the Customers and Branch tables, making it possible to gather this information.

- You will not be able to generate the monthly bank statement. To generate a customer bank statement (showing all deposits and withdrawals for the month), you would need to add an additional table—to track activity for each account.

- You will not be able to email a customer because the Customers table does not contain an email field at this time. If additional fields are required, such as a cell phone number, email address, or an emergency contact, you will want to include them in this stage of the design process. However, it is possible to add missing fields later.

Design for Now and for the Future

As the information requirements of an organization evolve over time, the database that stores and organizes the data must change as well. When designing a database, try to anticipate future needs and build in the flexibility to satisfy those demands. For example, you may also decide to create additional fields for future use (such as an email or customer photo field). However, additional fields will also require more storage space, which you will need to consider, especially when working with larger databases. Good database design must balance the data collection needs of the organization with the cost associated with collection and storage. Plans must also include the frequency and cost necessary to modify and update the database.

In the Customers table, for example, you would store each customer's name, address, and home phone number. You would also want to store additional phone numbers for many customers—a cell phone number, and perhaps a work number. As a database designer, you will design the tables to accommodate multiple entries for similar data.

Store Data in Their Smallest Parts

The table design in Figure 2.2 separates a customer's name into two fields (FirstName and LastName) to store each value individually. You might think it is simpler to use a single field consisting of both the first and last name, but that approach is too limiting. Consider a list of customer names stored as single values:

- Sue Grater
- Rick Grater
- Nancy Gallagher
- Harry Weigner
- Barb Shank
- Pete Shank

The first problem in this approach is the lack of flexibility: You could not easily create a salutation for a letter using the form *Dear Sue* or *Dear Ms. Gallagher* because the first and last names are not stored or retrievable individually.

A second difficulty is that the list of customers cannot be easily displayed in alphabetical order by last name because the last name begins in the middle of the value. The most common way to sort names is by the last name, which you can do more efficiently if the last name is stored as a separate field.

You may need to select customer records for a particular state or zip code, which will be easier if you store the data as separate fields. The customer's city, state, and zip code should always be stored as individual fields, along with any other values that you may want to sort by or retrieve separately.

Determine Primary Keys

When designing your database tables, it is important to determine the primary key. Recall that the primary key is the field whose values will uniquely identify each record in a table. For example, in Figure 2.2, the CustomerID field will uniquely identify each customer in the database. If you have two customers with the same first and last names, such as John Williams, how would you be able to distinguish one from the other when entering records? In a Customers table, the CustomerID values can be typed individually, or you could have a system that assigns these unique values automatically. Either way, each record should have its own unique primary key field value.

Plan for Common Fields Between Tables

As you create the tables and fields for the database, keep in mind that some tables will be joined in relationships using common fields. Creating relationships will enable you to extract data from more than one table when creating queries, forms, and reports. For example, you will be able to determine which customers have which accounts by joining the Customers and Accounts tables. CustomerID in the Customers table will join to the CustomerID field in the Accounts table. It may make sense to you to name the common fields the same way in each table, although that is not a firm requirement in Access. Draw a *join line* between common fields to indicate how the tables will be related, as shown in Figure 2.3. You will create join lines between tables when you learn to create table relationships later in the chapter.

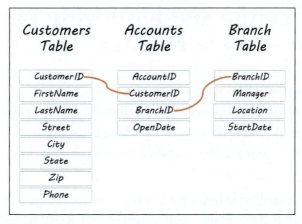

FIGURE 2.3 Determine Relationships Using Common Fields

Avoid *data redundancy*, which is the unnecessary storing of duplicate data in two or more tables. Having redundant or duplicate data in multiple tables can lead to serious errors. Suppose the customer address is stored in both the Customers and Accounts tables. If a customer moved to a new address, it is possible that the address would be updated in only one of the two tables. The result would be inconsistent and unreliable information. Depending on which table you would use to check an address, either the new or the old one might be given to someone requesting the information. Storing the address in only one table is more reliable; if it changes, it only needs to be updated one time (in the Customers table) and can be referenced again and again from that table. In the case of the bank database, each customer's address will only be stored one time. CustomerID in the Customers table will join to the CustomerID field in the Accounts table. Because of this relationship, the address will be retrievable when required by other objects created in the database.

> **TIP: COMMON FIELD NAMES AND DATA TYPES**
> Although it may make sense to name the common fields the same way between tables, it is not a requirement in Access. For example, you could use CustomerID in one table and CustomerNumber in another to identify your customers. However, the data types of the fields should match, so if you are using the Short Text data type in one table, use the same data type for the common field in the related table.

Design to Accommodate Calculations

A calculated field produces a value from an expression or function that references one or more existing fields. Calculated fields are frequently created in database objects with numeric data, such as a monthly interest field that multiplies the balance in a customer's account by 1% each month (Balance*.01). You can also create calculated fields using date/time data. For example, if you want to store the length of time a customer has had an account, you can create a calculated field that subtracts the opening date from today's date. The result will be the number of days each customer has been an account holder.

A person's age is another example of a calculated field using date arithmetic—the date of birth is subtracted from today's date and the result is divided by 365 (or 365.25 to account for leap years). It might seem easier to store a person's age as a number rather than the birth date to avoid using a calculated field, but that would be a mistake because age changes over time and the field would need to be updated each time it changes. You can use date arithmetic to subtract one date from another to find out the number of days, months, or years that have elapsed between them.

Access enables you to store calculated fields in a table using the calculated data type and to include those fields in queries, forms, and reports. However, many Access users prefer to create calculated fields in their query designs rather than in the tables themselves.

Creating and Modifying Tables and Working with Data

Tables can be created in a new blank database or in an existing database by using any of the following methods:

- Enter field names and table data directly in Datasheet view.
- Type field names in rows in Design view and enter the data in Datasheet view.
- Import data from another database or application, such as Excel.
- Use a template.

Regardless of how a table is first created, you can always modify it later to include a new field or to change an existing field. Changes to existing fields should be handled with caution. Generally, we think about Datasheet view as the "front end" of the table, where data can be entered, edited, and viewed, although it is possible to create and modify a table using the datasheet. For more sophisticated options, you can switch to Design view of the table, which can be considered the "back end" of the table. More design changes can be made in Design view; however, you will need to return to Datasheet view to enter, edit, or view data. Figure 2.4 shows a table created by entering fields in Design view.

When you add a field to a table, the field must be given an appropriate name to identify the data it stores. The field name should be descriptive of the data and can be up to 64 characters in length, including letters, numbers, and spaces. Field names cannot begin with a leading blank space. Database developers sometimes use Pascal Case notation for field names. Instead of spaces in multiword field names, you can use uppercase letters to distinguish the first letter of each new word, for example, ProductCost or LastName (some developers use Camel Case, which is similar to Pascal Case, where the first letter of the first word is lowercase). It is sometimes preferable to avoid spaces in field names because spaces can cause naming conflicts with other applications that may use these fields, such as Microsoft Visual Basic for Applications. As mentioned previously, fields can be added, deleted, or renamed either in Design view or Datasheet view.

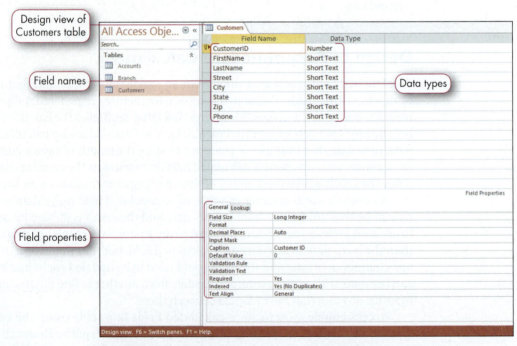

FIGURE 2.4 Customers Table Created in Design View

To rename a field, select the field name you want to change, type the new field name, press Enter, and then save the table. To delete a field from a table, use one of the following methods:

- In Datasheet view, select the field and press Delete. Click Yes in the message box.
- In Design view, click the record selector of the field you want to delete, and click Delete Rows in the tools group on the design tab. Click Yes in the message box that displays to confirm that you want to permanently delete the field and the data in it.

> **TIP: HIDE FIELDS IN AN ACCESS DATASHEET**
>
> At times, not all fields in a datasheet need to be displayed at once. You may only need to view or modify certain fields and not others. To hide a field in a datasheet, right-click the column selector that displays the field name and from the shortcut menu, select Hide Fields. To make the field visible again, right-click any column selector, select Unhide Fields, and then select the appropriate column's check box.

Determine Data Type

Every field in a table has an assigned *data type* that determines the type of data that can be entered and the operations that can be performed on that data. Table 2.1 lists the data types, their uses, and examples of each. Data types are important when creating and joining common fields in tables. The data types of the common fields must match (with a few minor exceptions). For example, if CustomerID is a Number field in one table, but a Short Text value in another, you will need to change the data type in one or the other to avoid a data type mismatch. You can change a data type after you have entered data into your table but do so with caution. In some cases, changing data types is inconsequential; for example, you may want to convert a number to a currency value. This type of change would only affect the formatting displayed with the values, not the underlying values themselves. Other types of changes could become more problematic. In any case, when designing tables, choose the initial data type carefully, and be sure to back up your database before changing data types.

> **TIP: KEYBOARD SHORTCUT FOR DATA TYPES**
>
> You also can type the first letter of the data type, such as d for Date/Time, s for Short Text, or n for Number. To use the keyboard shortcut, click in the field name and press Tab to advance to the Data Type column. Next, type the first letter of the data type.

TABLE 2.1 Data Types and Uses

Data Type	Description	Example
Short Text	Stores alphanumeric data, such as a customer's name or address. It can contain alphabetic characters, numbers, and/or special characters (e.g., an apostrophe in O'Malley). Social Security numbers, telephone numbers, and postal codes should be designated as text fields because they are not used in calculations and often contain special characters such as hyphens and parentheses. A short text field can hold up to 255 characters.	2184 Walnut Street
Long Text	Lengthy text or combinations of text and numbers, such as several sentences or paragraphs; used to hold descriptive data. Long text controls can display up to 64,000 characters.	A description of product packaging
Number	Contains a value that can be used in a calculation, such as the number of credits a course is worth. The contents are restricted to numbers, a decimal point, and a plus or minus sign.	12
Large Number	Used for storing very large numeric values in a database, allowing a greater range for calculations. Enabling this data type makes your database incompatible with versions of Access prior to 2016.	9,223,372,036,854,775,807
Date/Time	Stores dates or times that can be used in date or time arithmetic.	10/31/2018 1:30:00 AM
Currency	Used for fields that contain monetary values.	$1,200
AutoNumber	A special data type used to assign the next consecutive number each time you add a record. The value of an AutoNumber field is unique for each record in the table.	1, 2, 3
Yes/No	Only one of two values can be stored, such as Yes or No, True or False, or On or Off (also known as a Boolean). For example, is a student on the Dean's list: Yes or No.	Yes
OLE Object	Contains an object created by another application. OLE objects include pictures and sounds.	JPG image
Hyperlink	Stores a Web address (URL) or the path to a folder or file. Hyperlink fields can be clicked to retrieve a webpage or to launch a file stored locally.	http://www.irs.gov
Attachment	Used to store one or multiple images, spreadsheet files, documents, and other types of supported files in records.	An Excel workbook
Calculated	The results of an expression that references one or more existing fields.	[Price]*.05
Lookup Wizard	Creates a field that enables you to choose a value from another table or from a list of values by using a list box or a combo box.	Accounts table with a CustomerID field that looks up the customer from the records in the Customers table

STEP 2 ▶ **Set a Table's Primary Key**

The primary key is the field (or possibly a combination of fields) that uniquely identifies each record in a table. Access does not require that each table have a primary key. However, a good database design usually includes a primary key in each table. You should select unique and infrequently changing data for the primary key. For example, a credit card number may seem to be unique, but would not make a good primary key because it is subject to change when a new card is issued due to fraudulent activity.

You probably would not use a person's name as the primary key, because several people could have the same name. A value like CustomerID, as shown in the Customers table in Figure 2.5, is unique and is a better choice for the primary key. When no field seems to stand out as a primary key as a natural choice, you can create a primary key field with the AutoNumber data type. The **AutoNumber** data type is a number that automatically increments each time a record is added, starting with 1. The next added record would be 2, and so forth.

FIGURE 2.5 Customers Table with a Natural Choice for the Primary Key

Figure 2.6 depicts a Speakers table, where no unique field can be identified from the data itself. In this case, you can identify the SpeakerID field with an AutoNumber data type. Access automatically numbers each speaker record sequentially with a unique ID as each record is added.

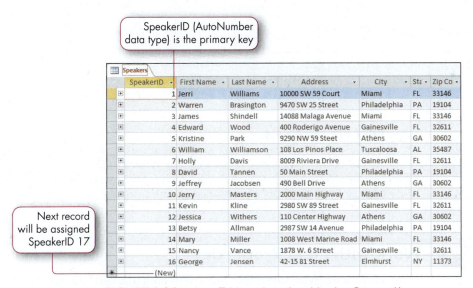

FIGURE 2.6 Speakers Table with an AutoNumber Primary Key

Explore a Foreign Key

Recall that part of good database planning is to plan for common fields between tables that will be joined in relationships. This is necessary so that data from different tables can be combined into meaningful queries and reports. One of the common fields will be the primary key in one table; the other common field in the related table is denoted as the ***foreign key***. The CustomerID is the primary key (identified with a primary key icon) in the Customers table and uniquely identifies each customer in the database. CustomerID also displays as a foreign key in the related Accounts table to establish which customer owns the account(s). A CustomerID can be entered only one time in the Customers table (to avoid data redundancy), but it may be entered multiple times in the Accounts table because one customer may own several accounts (checking, savings, credit card, etc.). Therefore, CustomerID is the primary key in the Customers table and a foreign key in the Accounts table, as shown in Figure 2.7.

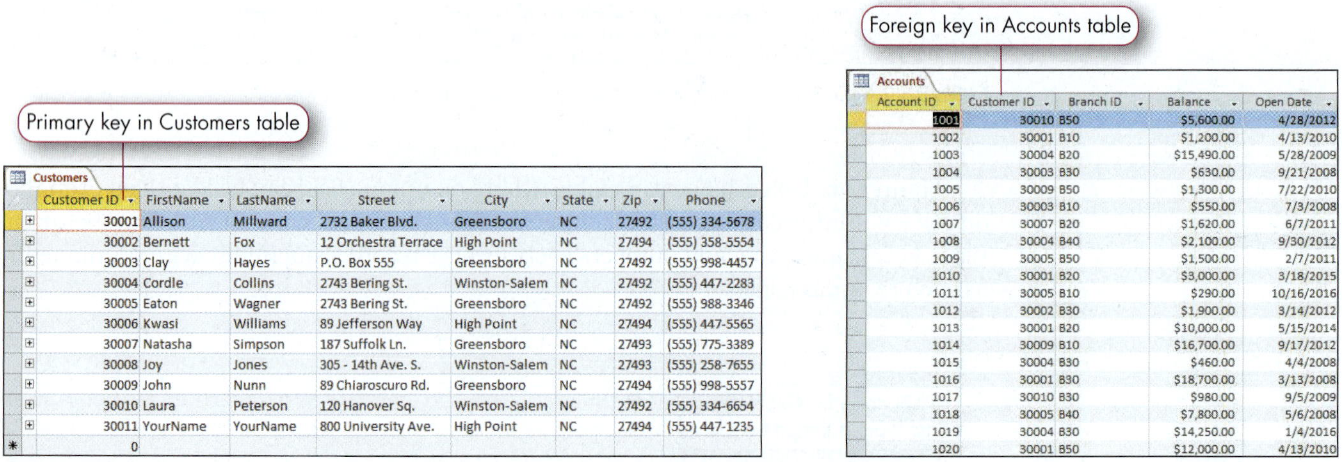

Customers

Customer ID	FirstName	LastName	Street	City	State	Zip	Phone
30001	Allison	Millward	2732 Baker Blvd.	Greensboro	NC	27492	(555) 334-5678
30002	Bernett	Fox	12 Orchestra Terrace	High Point	NC	27494	(555) 358-5554
30003	Clay	Hayes	P.O. Box 555	Greensboro	NC	27492	(555) 998-4457
30004	Cordle	Collins	2743 Bering St.	Winston-Salem	NC	27492	(555) 447-2283
30005	Eaton	Wagner	2743 Bering St.	Greensboro	NC	27492	(555) 988-3346
30006	Kwasi	Williams	89 Jefferson Way	High Point	NC	27494	(555) 447-5565
30007	Natasha	Simpson	187 Suffolk Ln.	Greensboro	NC	27493	(555) 775-3389
30008	Joy	Jones	305 - 14th Ave. S.	Winston-Salem	NC	27493	(555) 258-7655
30009	John	Nunn	89 Chiaroscuro Rd.	Greensboro	NC	27494	(555) 998-5557
30010	Laura	Peterson	120 Hanover Sq.	Winston-Salem	NC	27492	(555) 334-6654
30011	YourName	YourName	800 University Ave.	High Point	NC	27494	(555) 447-1235
0							

Accounts

Account ID	Customer ID	Branch ID	Balance	Open Date
1001	30010	B50	$5,600.00	4/28/2012
1002	30001	B10	$1,200.00	4/13/2010
1003	30004	B20	$15,490.00	5/28/2009
1004	30003	B30	$630.00	9/21/2008
1005	30009	B50	$1,300.00	7/22/2010
1006	30003	B10	$550.00	7/3/2008
1007	30007	B20	$1,620.00	6/7/2011
1008	30004	B40	$2,100.00	9/30/2012
1009	30005	B50	$1,500.00	2/7/2011
1010	30001	B20	$3,000.00	3/18/2015
1011	30005	B10	$290.00	10/16/2016
1012	30002	B30	$1,900.00	3/14/2012
1013	30001	B20	$10,000.00	5/15/2014
1014	30009	B10	$16,700.00	9/17/2012
1015	30004	B30	$460.00	4/4/2008
1016	30001	B30	$18,700.00	3/13/2008
1017	30010	B30	$980.00	9/5/2009
1018	30005	B40	$7,800.00	5/6/2008
1019	30004	B30	$14,250.00	1/4/2016
1020	30001	B50	$12,000.00	4/13/2010

FIGURE 2.7 Two Tables Illustrating Primary and Foreign Keys

> **TIP: BEST FIT COLUMNS**
>
> If a field name is cut off in Datasheet view, you can adjust the column width by positioning the pointer on the vertical border on the right side of the column. When the pointer displays as a two-headed arrow, double-click the border. You can also click More in the Records group on the Home tab, select Field Width, and then click Best Fit in the Column Width dialog box.

STEP 3 Work with Field Properties

While a field's data type determines the type of data that can be entered and the operations that can be performed on that data, its ***field properties*** determine how the field is formatted and behaves. The field properties are set to default values according to the data type, but you can modify them as required. Field properties are commonly set in Design view, as shown in Figure 2.4; however, certain properties can be set in Datasheet view on the Table Tools Fields tab. Common properties are defined in Table 2.2.

TABLE 2.2 Common Access Table Properties and Descriptions

Property	Description
Field Size	Determines the maximum number of characters of a text field or the format of a number field. If you shorten a field size and save the change, a warning dialog box opens to indicate that "Some data may be lost" because the new field size is able to store less data.
Format	Changes the way a field is displayed or printed but does not affect the stored value.
Input Mask	Simplifies data entry by providing literal characters that are typed for every entry, such as hyphens in a Social Security number or slashes in a date. It also imposes data validation by ensuring that data entered conform to the mask.
Caption	Enables an alternate (or more readable) name to be displayed other than the field name; alternate name displays in datasheets, forms, and reports.
Default Value	Enters automatically a predetermined value for a field each time a new record is added to the table. For example, if most customers live in Los Angeles, the default value for the City field could be set to Los Angeles to save data entry time and promote accurate data entry.
Validation Rule	Requires data entered to conform to a specified rule.
Validation Text	Specifies the error message that is displayed when the validation rule is violated.
Required	Indicates that a value for this field must be entered. Primary key fields always require data entry.
Allow Zero Length	Allows entry of zero length text strings in a Hyperlink, or Short or Long Text fields.
Indexed	Increases the efficiency of a search on the designated field. When a primary key is set on a field, an index is automatically created by Access for that field. If you create a unique index on any field, Yes (No Duplicates), you cannot duplicate a value in that field.
Expression	Used for calculated fields only. Specifies the expression you want Access to evaluate and store.
Result Type	Used for calculated fields only. Specifies the format for the calculated field results.

Field Size is a commonly changed field property. The field size determines the amount of space a field uses in the database. A field with a Short Text data type can store up to 255 characters; however, you can limit the characters by reducing the field size property. For example, you might limit the State field to only two characters because state abbreviations are two letters. When setting field sizes, anticipate any future requirements of the database that might necessitate larger values to be stored. If you shorten a field size and save the change, a warning dialog box opens to indicate that "Some data may be lost" because the new field size is able to store less data. If your table contained State values that were longer than two characters earlier, this type of change could truncate the data in that field. Use caution when shortening field sizes and ensure that your data is backed up before making such changes.

You can set the ***Caption property*** to create a label that is more understandable than a field name. While Pascal Case is preferred for field names, adding a space between words is often more readable. When a caption is set, it displays at the top of a table or query column in Datasheet view (instead of the actual field name), and when the field is used in a report or form. For example, a field named CustomerID could have the caption *Customer Number*.

Set the ***Validation Rule*** property to restrict data entry in a field to ensure that correct data are entered. The validation rule checks the data entered when the user exits the field. If the value entered violates the validation rule, an error message displays and prevents the invalid data from being entered into the field. For example, if you set a rule on a date field that the date entered must be on or after today, and a date in the past is entered in the field, an error message will display. You can customize the error message (validation text) when you set the validation rule.

The ***Input Mask*** property simplifies data entry by providing literal characters that are typed for every entry, such as hyphens in a Social Security number or dashes in a phone number. Input masks ensure that data in fields such as these are consistently entered and formatted.

STEP 4 ## Create a New Field in Design View

At times, it may be necessary to add table fields that were not included in the original design process. While it is possible to add fields in Datasheet view (using the Click to Add arrow at the top of an empty column), Design view, as shown in Figure 2.4, offers more flexibility in setting field properties.

To add a new field in Design view, complete the following steps:

1. Click in the first empty field row in the top pane of the table's Design view.
2. Enter the Field Name, Data Type, and Description (optional), and set the Field Properties.
3. Click the row selector, and then click and drag the new field to place it in a different position in the table.
4. Click Save on the Quick Access Toolbar and switch to Datasheet view to enter or modify data.

STEP 5 ## Modify the Table in Datasheet View

Whereas Design view is commonly used to create and modify the table structure by enabling you to add and edit fields and set field properties, Datasheet view is used to add, edit, and delete records. In a Customers table, you might find that frequent data updates are common. New customers need to be added, and at times, customers may need to be deleted. If a customer changes his/her address, telephone number, or email address, the existing record will be edited. You may notice that when you call customer service representatives, they often ask you to update your personal information; up-to-date data produces the best possible information in a database.

Quick Concepts

1. Explain why it is important to "Plan for common fields" when designing database tables. ***p. 618***

2. Consider why it is important to set a primary key in a table. ***p. 618***

3. Discuss how the Validation Rule field property helps to control data entry and why that is important. ***p. 625***

Hands-On Exercises

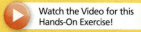

Skills covered: Design a Table • Create a Table in Datasheet View • Delete a Field • Set a Table's Primary Key • Work with Field Properties • Create a New Field in Design View • Modify the Table in Datasheet View

1 Table Design, Creation, and Modification

Creating a sample database as an intern for Commonwealth Federal Bank will be a great opportunity for you to showcase your database design and Access skills.

STEP 1 CREATE A TABLE IN DATASHEET VIEW

You create a new database and a table to store information about the bank's branches. You enter the data for the first record (BranchID, Manager, and Location). You examine the design of the table and realize that the BranchID field is a better unique identifier, making the ID field redundant. You delete the ID field. Refer to Figure 2.8 as you complete Step 1.

FIGURE 2.8 Create the Branch Table in Datasheet View

a. Start Access and click **Blank database**.

b. Type **a02h1Bank_LastFirst** in the File Name box.

c. Click **Browse** to find the folder location where you will store the database and click **OK**. Click **Create** to create the new database.

Access will create the new database named a02h1Bank_LastFirst and a new table, Table1, will automatically open in Datasheet view. There is already an ID field in the table by default that uses the AutoNumber data type.

d. Click **Click to Add** and select **Short Text** as the Data type.

Click to Add changes to Field1. Field1 is selected to make it easier to change the field name.

e. Type **BranchID** and press **Tab**.

A list of data types for the third column opens so that you can select the data type for the third column.

f. Select **Short Text** in the Click to Add list, type **Manager**, and then press **Tab**.

g. Select **Short Text** in the Click to Add list and type **Location**.

h. Click in the **first column** (the ID field) next to the New Record asterisk, press **Tab**, and then type the data for the new table as shown in Figure 2.8, letting Access assign the ID field for each new record (using the AutoNumber data type). Replace *YourLastName* with your own last name.

i. Click **Save** on the Quick Access Toolbar. Type **Branch** in the Save As dialog box and click **OK**.

Entering field names, data types, and data directly in Datasheet view provides a simplified way to create the table initially.

j. Click **View** in the Views group on the Home tab to switch to Design view of the Branch table.

The field name for each of the four fields displays along with the data type.

k. Ensure that the ID field is selected, click **Delete Rows** in the Tools group on the Design tab. Click **Yes** to both warning messages.

Access responds with a warning that you are about to permanently delete a field and a second warning that the field is the primary key. You delete the field because you will set the BranchID field as the primary key.

STEP 2 ▶ SET A TABLE'S PRIMARY KEY

You determine that BranchID is a better choice as the table's primary key field. Rather than the sequential auto-numbering that Access uses by default for the key field, it is better to use the actual branch numbers. In this step, you will make the BranchID field the primary key field. Refer to Figure 2.9 as you complete Step 2.

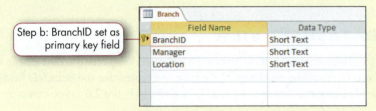

Step b: BranchID set as primary key field

FIGURE 2.9 Branch Table in Design View

a. Ensure that the BranchID field is selected, as shown in Figure 2.9.

b. Click **Primary Key** in the Tools group on the Design tab.

You set BranchID as the primary key. The Indexed property in the Field Properties section at the bottom of the design window displays Yes (No Duplicates). When a primary key is set on a field, an index is automatically created by Access for that field to speed up searching through it.

c. Click **Save** on the Quick Access Toolbar to save the table.

STEP 3 ▶ WORK WITH FIELD PROPERTIES

You will modify the table design further to comply with the bank's specifications. Refer to Figure 2.10 as you complete Step 3.

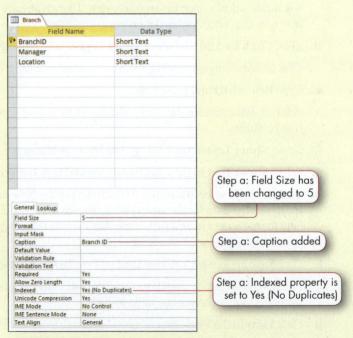

Step a: Field Size has been changed to 5

Step a: Caption added

Step a: Indexed property is set to Yes (No Duplicates)

FIGURE 2.10 Changes to the Field Properties of the Branch Table in Design View

a. Click in the **BranchID field name**; modify the BranchID field properties by completing the following steps:

- Click in the **Field Size box** in the Field Properties pane and change 255 to **5**.
- Click in the **Caption box** and type **Branch ID**. Make sure Branch and ID have a space between them.
  A caption provides a more descriptive field name. It will display as the column heading in Datasheet view.
- Check the Indexed property; confirm it is Yes (No Duplicates).
- Check the Required property; confirm it is Yes. A primary key field always requires a value to be entered.

b. Click the **Manager field name**; modify the Manager field properties by completing the following steps:

- Click in the **Field Size box** in the Field Properties pane and change 255 to **30**.
- Click in the **Caption box** and type **Manager's Name**.

c. Click the **Location field name** and modify the following Location field properties by completing the following steps:

- Click in the **Field Size box** in the Field Properties pane and change 255 to **30**.
- Click in the **Caption box** and type **Branch Location**.

STEP 4 **CREATE A NEW FIELD IN DESIGN VIEW**

You notice that a date field is missing from your new table. Modify the table to add the new field. Refer to Figure 2.11 as you complete Step 4.

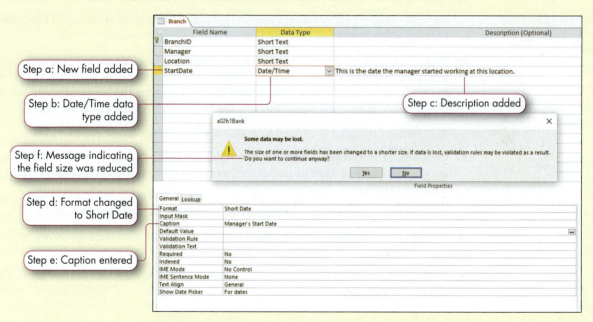

FIGURE 2.11 Adding a New Field to the Branch Table in Design View

a. Click in the **first blank field row** below the Location field name and type **StartDate**.

You added a new field to the table.

b. Press **Tab** to move to the Data Type column. Click the **Data Type arrow** and select **Date/Time**.

c. Press **Tab** to move to the Description column and type **This is the date the manager started working at this location.**

d. Click in the **Format box** in the Field Properties pane, click the **arrow**, and then select **Short Date** from the list of date formats.

e. Click in the **Caption box** and type **Manager's Start Date**.

f. Click **Save** on the Quick Access Toolbar.

A warning dialog box opens to indicate that "Some data may be lost" because the size of the BranchID, Manager, and Location field properties were shortened (in the previous step). It asks if you want to continue anyway. Always read the Access warning! In this case, you can click Yes to continue because you know that the existing and anticipated data values are no longer than the new field sizes.

g. Click **Yes** in the warning box.

STEP 5 ## MODIFY THE TABLE IN DATASHEET VIEW

As you work with the new sample, you will modify tables in the bank database by adding and modifying records. Refer to Figure 2.12 as you complete Step 5.

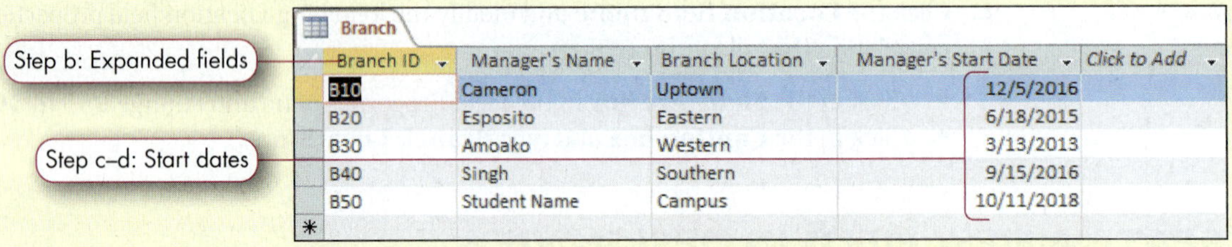

FIGURE 2.12 Start Dates Added to the Branch Table

a. Right-click the **Branch tab** and select **Datasheet View** from the shortcut menu.

The table displays in Datasheet view. The field captions display at the top of the columns, but they are cut off.

b. Position the pointer over the border between Branch ID and Manager's Name so that it becomes a double-headed arrow and double-click the border. Repeat the process for the border between Manager's Name and Branch Location, the border between Branch Location and Manager's Start Date, and the border after Manager's Start Date.

The columns contract or expand to display the best fit for each field name.

c. Click inside the **Manager's Start Date** in the first record and click the **Date Picker** 🗐 next to the date field. Use the navigation arrows to find and select **December 5, 2016** from the calendar.

You can also enter the dates by typing them directly into the StartDate field.

d. Type the start date directly in each field for the rest of the managers, as shown in Figure 2.12.

e. Click the **Close** at the top-right corner of the Branch datasheet, below the ribbon. Click **Yes** to save the changes.

> **TROUBLESHOOTING:** If you accidentally click Close at the top of the ribbon, you will exit Access completely. To start again, launch Access and click the first file in the Recent list.

f. Double-click the **Branch table** in the Navigation Pane to open the table.

g. Click the **File tab**, click **Print**, and then click **Print Preview**.

Occasionally, users will print an Access table. However, database developers usually create reports to print table data.

h. Click **Close Print Preview** in the Close Preview group and close the Branch table.

i. Keep the database open if you plan to continue with the Hands-On Exercise. If not, close the database and exit Access.

Multiple-Table Databases

In Figure 2.2, the sample bank database contains three tables—Customers, Accounts, and Branch. You created one table, the Branch table, in the previous section using Datasheet view and modified the table fields in Design view. You will create the two remaining tables using different methods—by importing data from external sources.

In this section, you will learn how to import data from Excel and Access to populate the bank database. You will modify tables, create indexes, create relationships between tables, and enforce referential integrity.

Importing Data from External Sources

Often in organizations, files that can be used to create tables or add records to existing tables in databases are stored in external sources. Common sources are Excel spreadsheets, other Access databases, other file types (such as text files), and online sources. If data can be imported and are compatible with an existing database, it can save a great deal of data entry effort. Often, the data stored in external sources can be more efficiently managed in an Access database. Data can be imported as a new table in a database or added to an existing table (appended). Importing data copies records to your database and so will increase the file size, sometimes dramatically. It is also possible to link your database to an external source so that you can use the data that it contains without having to copy it into your own database file.

STEP 1 Import Excel Data

Access provides a wizard that guides you through the process of importing data from Excel. The process is relatively simple when the data are well-organized in the Excel worksheet, with column headings that will import as field names in the Access table.

To import an Excel spreadsheet to Access, complete the following steps:

1. Click the External Data tab.
2. Click New Data Source in the Import & Link group, point to From File, and then select Excel. The Get External Data – Excel Spreadsheet dialog box opens, as shown in Figure 2.13.
3. Click Browse to locate the Excel file you want to import, click the file to select it, and then click Open to specify this file as the source of the data.
4. Ensure the *Import the source data* option is selected and click OK. The Import Spreadsheet Wizard launches.
5. Select the worksheet from the list of worksheets shown at the top of the dialog box, as shown in Figure 2.14, and then click Next.
6. Ensure the *First Row Contains Column Headings* check box is selected and click Next, as shown in Figure 2.15. The column headings of the Excel spreadsheet will become the field names in the Access table.
7. Change the field options for the imported data, as shown in Figure 2.16, and click Next.
8. Click the *Choose my own primary key* option if the imported data have a field that is acceptable as a primary key, as shown in Figure 2.17, and click Next. Access will set the value in the first column of the spreadsheet (for example, AID) as the primary key field of the table. You can also allow Access to set the primary key if there is no value that is eligible to be a key field, or to set no primary key at all (not recommended).
9. Type the new table name in the Import to Table box, as shown in Figure 2.18, and click Finish.
10. Click Close when prompted to Save Import Steps.

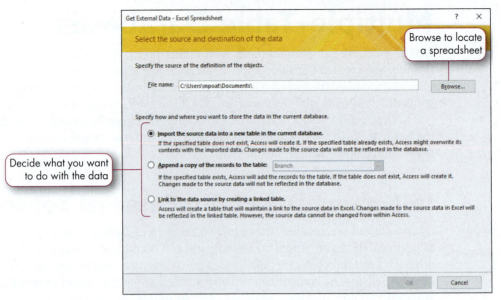

FIGURE 2.13 Import Excel Data

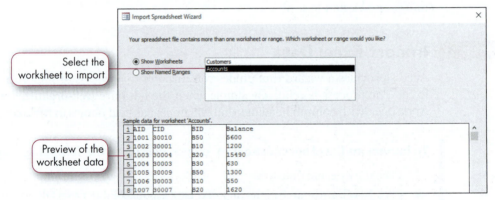

FIGURE 2.14 Available Worksheets and Preview of Data

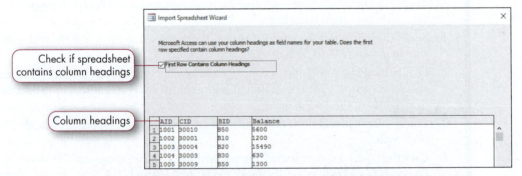

FIGURE 2.15 Excel Column Headings Become Access Field Names

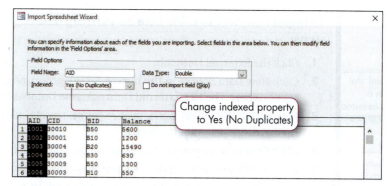

FIGURE 2.16 Change Field Options for Imported Data

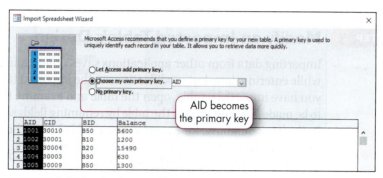

FIGURE 2.17 Set the Primary Key

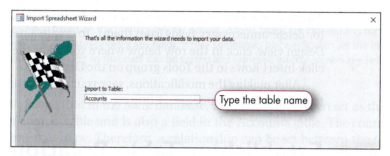

FIGURE 2.18 Enter a Table Name

> **TIP: LINKING TO EXTERNAL DATA**
> At times you might need to include a table in your database that already exists in another database. Instead of importing the data from this external source, you can create a link to it from within your database, and the table remains in the original database. You will be able to use the linked data as usual, but you will not be able to modify the original table's design. You can also link to existing spreadsheets from your database without having to copy a large amount of data into your file.

STEP 2 **Import Access Data**

A wizard can also guide you as you import data from Access databases. If there is an object in an external database (such as a table) that contains valuable data or suits another purpose in your application, there is no need to recreate it entirely. You can import an existing table's design only or a table with usable data. Likewise, if there is an existing form or report that will complement your data, you may not need to create it from scratch. You can import tables, queries, forms, reports, pages, macros, and modules from other databases. You can also modify the design of objects that are imported into your database to adapt them to your own application.

would not want to delete a customer from the Customers table if he or she has active accounts in the Accounts table. If you were to delete a customer with active accounts, those account records would then become "orphaned," as they would no longer relate to a valid CustomerID in the Customers table. Referential integrity helps to guarantee consistency between related tables.

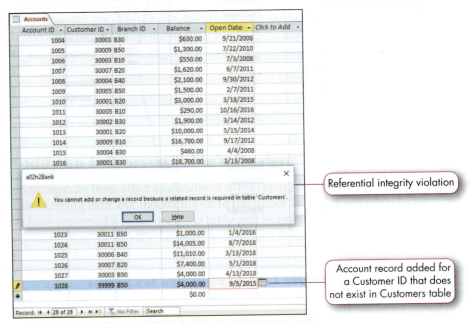

FIGURE 2.20 Error Message for Referential Integrity Violation

---

TIP: COMMON ERROR MESSAGES WHEN ENFORCING REFERENTIAL INEGRITY

When you set referential integrity between tables, common error messages can occur. For example, adding a value in a foreign key that does not exist as a primary key value produces an error, as shown in Figure 2.20. Common fields are not required to have the same names (although they often do), but they must have the same data type. If a CustomerID is a Number field in one table, but a Short Text value in another, you will need to change the data type in one or the other. Changing data types in tables can sometimes cause you to lose data, so setting data types carefully in the design process is a good strategy for avoiding this issue.

Set Cascade Options

When you create a relationship in Access and click the Enforce Referential Integrity check box, Access presents two additional options: Cascade Update Related Fields and Cascade Delete Related Records (see Figure 2.21). Select the ***Cascade Update Related Fields*** option so when the primary key value is modified in a primary table, Access will automatically update all foreign key values in a related table. If a CustomerID is updated for some reason, all of the matching CustomerID values in the Accounts table will update automatically. This option can save a great deal of data entry time and assures accuracy in the data updates.

Select the ***Cascade Delete Related Records*** option so when a record containing a primary key value is deleted in a primary table, Access will automatically delete all records in related tables that match the primary key. If one branch of a bank closes and its record is deleted from the Branch table, any account that is associated with this branch would then be deleted. Access will give a warning first to enable you to avoid the action of deleting records inadvertently.

Setting the Cascade Update and Cascade Delete options really depends on the business rules of an organization, and they should be set with caution. For example, if a branch of a bank closes, do you really want the accounts at that branch to be deleted? Another option might be to assign them to a different branch of the bank. Always ensure that your database is backed up; even though a warning message is displayed, it is still feasible to inadvertently delete valuable records from a database.

Establish a One-to-Many Relationship

Figure 2.21 also shows that the relationship that will be created is a one-to-many relationship. Access provides three different relationships for joining tables: one-to-one, one-to-many, and many-to-many. The most common type by far is the one-to-many relationship. A *one-to-many relationship* is established when the primary key value in the primary table can match many of the foreign key values in the related table.

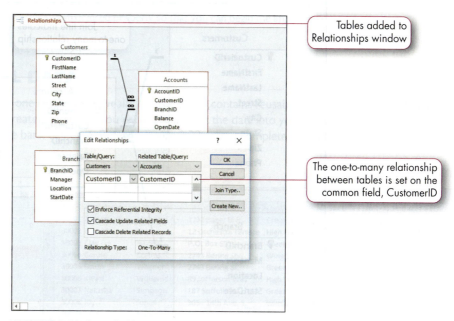

FIGURE 2.21 Cascade Update and Delete Options

For example, a bank customer will be added to the Customers table one time only. The primary key value, which is the CustomerID number, might be 1585. That same customer could set up a checking, a savings, and a credit card account. With each account, the CustomerID (1585) is required and, therefore, will occur three times in the Accounts table. The value is entered one time in the Customers table and three times in the Accounts table. The relationship between Customers and Accounts is described as one-to-many. Table 2.3 lists and describes all three types of relationships you can create between Access tables.

TABLE 2.3	Relationship Types
Relationship Type	**Description**
One-to-Many	The primary key table must have only one occurrence of each value. For example, each customer must have a unique identification number in the Customers table. The foreign key field in the related table may have repeating values. One customer can have many different account numbers.
One-to-One	Two different tables use the same primary key. Exactly one record exists in the second table for each record in the first table. Sometimes security issues require a single table to be split into two related tables. For example, in an organization's database anyone in the company might be able to access the Employee table and find the employee's office number, department assignment, or telephone extension. However, only a few people need to have access to the employee's network login password, salary, Social Security number, performance review, or marital status, which would be stored in a second table. Tables containing this information would use the same unique identifier to identify each employee.
Many-to-Many	This is an artificially constructed relationship allowing many matching records in each direction between tables. It requires construction of a third table called a junction table. For example, a database might have a table for employees and one for projects. Several employees might be assigned to one project, but one employee might also be assigned to many different projects. To create the junction table that connects the employees to their projects, a third table containing the primary key of each would be created.

Figure 2.30 shows the Design of a sample query with four fields, with a criterion set for one field. The results of the query display in Datasheet view, as shown in Figure 2.31.

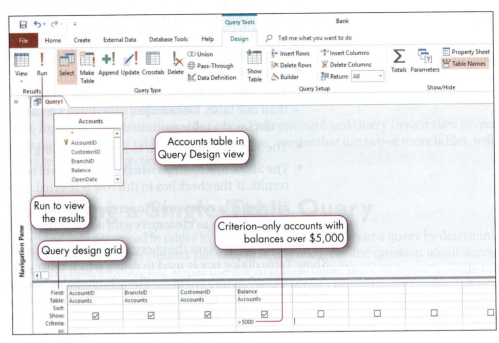

FIGURE 2.30 Query Design View with Sample Criterion

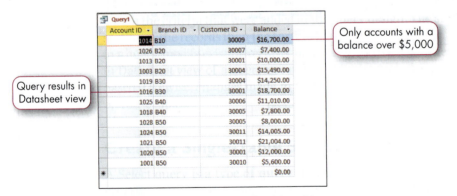

FIGURE 2.31 Query Results in Datasheet View

Should you need to fine-tune the query, switch back to Design view, make a change, and then run the query again to view the results. After you are satisfied with the results, you can save and name the query so it becomes a permanent part of the database and can be used later. Each time you run a query, the results will update based on the current data in the underlying table(s).

TIP: EXAMINE THE RECORDS

Be sure to examine the records returned in the query results. Verify that the records in the query results match the criteria that you specified in Design view. If the results are not what you anticipated, return to Design view, and check your criteria. If your criteria are inaccurate, your query may not return any results at all. Unexpected results can also occur from inaccurate data, so troubleshooting your queries is a skill that you will acquire as your experience progresses.

Using the Query Wizard

The **Simple Query Wizard** guides you through query design with a step-by-step process. The wizard is helpful for creating basic queries that do not require criteria. Any further modifications to the query after it has been created will be done in Design View. Launch the Query Wizard in the Queries group on the Create tab (see Figure 2.32). Select Simple Query Wizard in the New Query dialog box, as shown in Figure 2.33. In the first step of the Simple Query Wizard dialog box, you specify the tables or queries and fields required in your query. When you select a table from the Tables/Queries arrow (queries can also be based on other queries), a list of the table's fields displays in the Available Fields list box (see Figure 2.34).

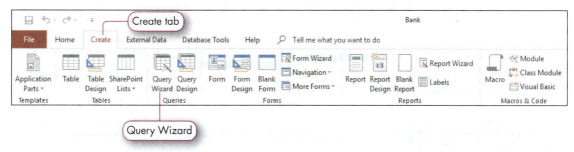

FIGURE 2.32 Launching the Query Wizard

FIGURE 2.33 Simple Query Wizard

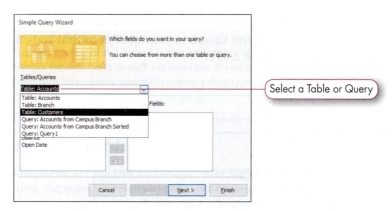

FIGURE 2.34 Specify Which Tables or Queries to Use

The wildcard characters stand in for the unknown characters. Wildcard characters can be placed in the beginning, middle, or end of a text string. There are several wildcards that you can use to produce different results. Table 2.5 shows more query criterion examples that use wildcards.

TABLE 2.5	Query Criteria Using Wildcards		
Character	**Description**	**Example**	**Result**
*	Matches any number of characters in the same position as the asterisk	Sm*	Small, Smiley, Smith, Smithson
?	Matches a single character in the same position as the question mark	H?ll	Hall, Hill, Hull
[ ]	Matches any single character within the brackets	F[ae]ll	Fall and Fell, but not Fill or Full
[!]	Matches any character not in the brackets	F[!ae]ll	Fill and Full, but not Fall or Fell

Use Comparison Operators in Queries

Comparison operators, such as equal (=), not equal (<>), greater than (>), less than (<), greater than or equal to (>=), and less than or equal to (<=), can be used in query criteria. Comparison operators enable you to limit the query results to only those records that meet the criteria. For example, if you only want to display accounts that have a balance greater than $5,000, you would type >5000 in the Criteria row of the Balance field. Table 2.6 shows more comparison operator examples. As an alternative to comparison operators, you can use the BETWEEN operator in criteria to specify inclusive values in a range. For example, to display accounts that have a balance of greater than or equal to (>=) 1000 and less than or equal to (<=) 5000, you can set the criteria as BETWEEN 1000 AND 5000.

TABLE 2.6	Comparison Operators in Queries
Expression	**Example**
=10	Equals 10
<>10	Not equal to 10
>10	Greater than 10
>=10	Greater than or equal to 10
<10	Less than 10
<=10	Less than or equal to 10

> **TIP: FINDING VALUES IN A DATE RANGE**
> To find the values contained within a date range, use the greater than (>) and less than (<) comparison operators. For example, to find the values of dates on or after January 1, 2019, and on or before December 31, 2019, use the criterion >=1/1/2019 and <=12/31/2019. You can also use the BETWEEN operator to find the same inclusive dates, for example, BETWEEN 1/1/2019 and 12/31/2019.

Work with Null

Sometimes finding missing (blank) values is an important part of making a decision. For example, if you need to know which orders have been completed but not shipped, you would create a query to find the orders with a missing (blank) ShipDate. The term that Access uses for a blank field is null (or not null for a populated field). Table 2.7 provides two examples of when to use the null criterion in a query.

TABLE 2.7 Establishing Null Criteria Expressions

Expression	Description	Example
Is Null	Used to find blank fields	For a SalesRepID field in the Customers table when the customer has not been assigned to a sales representative.
Is Not Null	Used to find fields with data	For a ShipDate field; a value has been entered to indicate that the order was shipped to the customer.

Establish AND, OR, and NOT Criteria

Recall the earlier question, "Which customers currently have an account with a balance over $5,000?" This question was answered by creating a query with a single criterion. At times, questions are more focused and require queries with more than one criterion. For example, you may need to know "Which customers from the Eastern branch currently have an account with a balance over $5,000?" To answer this question, you specify two criteria in different fields using the **AND condition**. This means that the query results will display only records that match *all* criteria. When the criteria are in the same row of the query design grid, Access interprets this as an AND condition. When you want to test two criteria in the same field, you can also use the AND logical operator as shown in Table 2.8.

When you have multiple criteria and you need to satisfy only one, not all the criteria, use the **OR condition**. The query results will display records that match any of the specified criteria. You can use the OR logical operator, and type the expression into the Criteria row, separating the criteria with the OR keyword. Table 2.8 shows an example of an OR condition created using this method. You can also type the first criterion in the Criteria row and type the next criterion in the Or row of the same field (to test for different values in the same field) or in a different field in the design grid (see Figure 2.38). The NOT logical operator returns all records except the specified criteria. For example, "Not Eastern" would return all accounts except those opened at the Eastern branch.

FIGURE 2.38 Query Design Views Showing the AND, OR, and NOT Operators

Hands-On Exercises

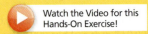

Skills covered: Create a Single-Table Query • Use the Simple Query Wizard • Use Query Design View • Specify Query Criteria • Specify Query Sort Order • Run a Query • Copy and Modify a Query • Change Query Data

3 Single-Table Queries

The tables and table relationships have been created, and some data have been entered in the bank database. Now, you begin the process of analyzing the bank data using queries. You decide to begin with the Accounts table.

STEP 1 USE THE QUERY WIZARD

You decide to start with the Query Wizard, knowing you can always alter the design of the query later in Design view. You will display the results in Datasheet view. Refer to Figure 2.40 as you complete Step 1.

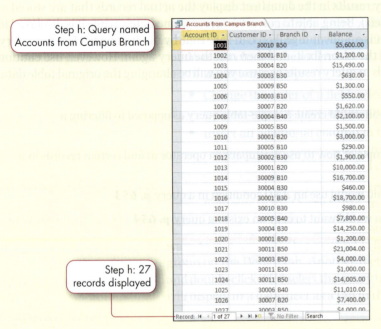

Step h: Query named Accounts from Campus Branch

Step h: 27 records displayed

FIGURE 2.40 Query Results Before Criteria Are Applied

a. Open *a02h2Bank_LastFirst* if you closed it at the end of Hands-On Exercise 2, and save it as **a02h3Bank_LastFirst**, changing h2 to h3.

b. Click the **Create tab** and click **Query Wizard** in the Queries group.

The New Query dialog box opens. Simple Query Wizard is selected by default.

c. Click **OK**.

d. Verify that Table: Accounts is selected in the Tables/Queries box.

e. Click **AccountID** in the Available Fields list and click **Add One Field** `>` to move it to the Selected Fields list. Repeat the process with **CustomerID**, **BranchID**, and **Balance**.

The four fields should now display in the Selected Fields list box.

f. Click **Next**.

g. Confirm that Detail (shows every field of every record) is selected and click **Next**.

h. Name the query **Accounts from Campus Branch**. Click **Finish**.

This query name describes the data in the query results. Your query should have four fields: AccountID, CustomerID, BranchID, and Balance. The Navigation bar indicates that 27 records are present in the query results.

STEP 2 **SPECIFY QUERY CRITERIA, SPECIFY SORT ORDER, AND RUN THE QUERY**

You decide to modify your query to analyze accounts specifically for the Campus branch. Refer to Figure 2.41 as you complete Step 2.

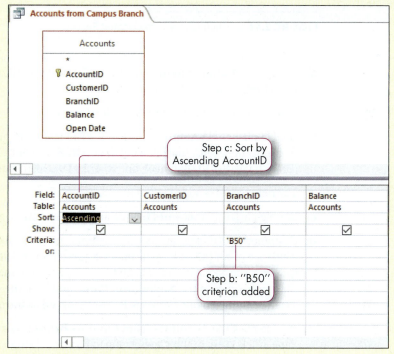

FIGURE 2.41 Enter Criteria and Add Sort Order

a. Click the **Home tab** and click **View** in the Views group.

The Accounts from Campus Branch query opens in Design view. You have created and named this query to view only those accounts at the Campus branch. However, other branches' accounts also display. You need to limit the query results to only the records for the branch of interest.

b. Click in the **Criteria row** (fifth row) in the BranchID column of the query design grid, type **B50**, and then press **Enter**.

B50 is the BranchID for the Campus branch. Access criteria are not case sensitive; therefore, b50 and B50 will produce the same results. Access adds quotation marks around text criteria after you press Enter, or you can type them yourself.

c. Click in the **Sort row** (third row) in the AccountID column and select **Ascending**.

d. Click **Run** in the Results group.

You decide to modify a value directly in the query datasheet and add a new record using the Accounts table. To create a second query that sorts the records in a different way, you copy and modify the existing query. Refer to Figure 2.42 as you complete Step 3.

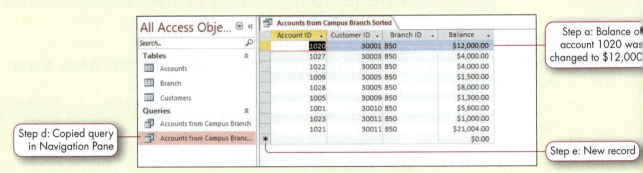

Step a: Balance of account 1020 was changed to $12,000

Step d: Copied query in Navigation Pane

Step e: New record

FIGURE 2.42 Modified Query with Updated Records

a. Click in the **Balance field** in the record for account 1020. Change $1,200 to **$12,000**. Press **Enter**. Save and close the query.

You modified the record directly in the query results.

b. Double-click the **Accounts table** in the Navigation Pane. Add a new record to the Accounts table with the following data: **1028** (Account ID), **30005** (Customer ID), **B50** (Branch ID), **8000** (Balance), and **8/4/2019** (Open Date). Press **Tab**.

The new record is added to the Accounts table.

c. Double-click the **Accounts from Campus Branch query** in the Navigation Pane.

d. Customer 30005 now shows two accounts: one with a balance of $1,500 and one with a balance of $8,000. Close the query. Right-click the **Accounts from Campus Branch query** in the Navigation Pane, and from the shortcut menu, select **Copy**. Right-click in the empty space in the **Navigation Pane**, and from the shortcut menu, select **Paste**. Type **Accounts from Campus Branch Sorted** as the query name. Click **OK**.

e. Double-click the **Accounts from Campus Branch Sorted** query in the Navigation Pane. Click **View** in the Views group to return to Design view of the duplicate query.

f. Click in the **Sort row** of the AccountID field, click the **arrow**, and then select **(not sorted)**. Click in the **Sort row** of the CustomerID field and select **Ascending**. Click in the **Sort row** of the Balance field and select **Ascending**.

g. Click **Run** in the Results group.

Customer 30005 now shows two accounts with the two balances sorted in ascending order. The record for Account ID 1028 was added in the underlying Accounts table, and the query updates automatically to display it with the others. All other customers with more than one Campus branch account are listed in ascending order by balance.

h. Save the query. Close the Accounts from Campus Branch Sorted query and close the Accounts table.

i. Keep the database open if you plan to continue with the next Hands-On Exercise. If not, close the database and exit Access.

Multitable Queries

Multitable queries contain two or more tables and enable you to take advantage of the relationships that have been established in your database. When you extract information from a database with a query, often you will need to pull data from multiple tables. One table may contain the core information that you want, while another table may contain the related data that make the query provide the complete results. The query will then combine data from both tables into one datasheet.

For example, the sample bank database contains three tables: Customers, Accounts, and Branch. You connected the tables through relationships in order to store data efficiently and to enforce consistent data entry between them. The Customers table provides the information for the owners of the accounts. However, the Accounts table includes the balances of each account—the key financial information. Recall that these two tables were joined by the CustomerID field. Because the Accounts table only contains a CustomerID but no personal data, if you want to include information such as the customer's name in your query results, both the Customers and Accounts tables are needed to provide the information that you want.

In this section, you will learn different ways to create and modify multitable queries. As you acquire these new skills, you will realize the power of using related tables in your database.

Creating a Multitable Query

There are several ways to create multitable queries. One method is to add tables to an existing query; another way is to copy an existing query and add to it. You can also create a multitable query from scratch either using the Query Wizard or the Query Design tool.

STEP 1 ▶ ### Add Additional Tables and Fields to an Existing Query

One way to create a multitable query is to add additional tables and fields to an existing query. For example, you may want to add branch or customer data to a query that already includes account information.

> **To add tables to an existing query, complete the following steps:**
>
> 1. Open the existing query in Design view.
> 2. Drag additional tables from the Navigation Pane directly into the top pane of the query design window.
> 3. Add fields, criteria, and sorting options in the query design grid.
> 4. Run and save the query.

The Branch and Customers tables were added to the Accounts from Campus Branch query, as shown in Figure 2.43. The join lines between tables indicate that relationships were previously set in the Relationships window. With the additional tables and fields available, you can now add the customer's name (from Customers) and the branch location name (from Branch) rather than using CustomerID and BranchID in your results. The datasheet will contain more readily identifiable information than ID numbers for customers and locations.

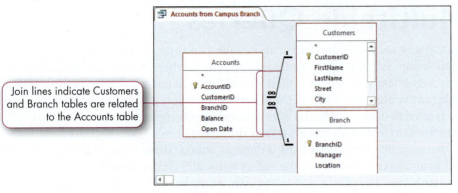

Join lines indicate Customers and Branch tables are related to the Accounts table

FIGURE 2.43 Two Additional Tables Added to a Query

STEP 2 ### Create a Multitable Query from Scratch

Creating a multitable query from scratch is similar to creating a single-table query except that you are adding two or more tables to the query design grid. However, choosing the right tables and managing the relationships in the query might require some additional skills. First, you should only use related tables in a multitable query. Related tables are tables that are joined in a relationship using a common field. Once tables are joined by a common field, you can pull related data from each to create complete and usable information in queries. Using Figure 2.43 as a guide, creating a query with the Accounts and Branch tables would be acceptable, as would using Accounts and Customers tables, or Accounts, Branch, and Customers tables. All three scenarios include related tables. However, creating a query with only the Branch and Customers tables would not be acceptable because these tables are not directly related to one another (in other words, they do not have a common field).

To create a multitable query, complete the following steps:

1. Click the Create tab.
2. Click Query Design in the Queries group.
3. Add the tables you want in your query from the Show Table dialog box. Close the Show Table dialog box.
4. Drag the fields you want to display from the tables to the query design grid (or alternatively, double-click the field names); then add criteria and sorting options.
5. Click Run in the Results group on the Design tab to display the results in Datasheet view.

> **TIP: PRINT THE RELATIONSHIP REPORT TO HELP CREATE A MULTITABLE QUERY**
> When you create a multitable query, you only include related tables. As a guide, when the Relationships window is open, you can print the Relationship Report. Click the Database Tools tab and click Relationship Report in the Tools group on the Relationship Tools Design tab. This report will provide a diagram that displays the tables, fields, and relationships in your database. A Relationship Report is also very useful when you need to understand a database that is unfamiliar to you. The report is exportable to other formats such as Word if you want to share it with colleagues.

STEP 3 ## Modifying a Multitable Query

After creating a multitable query, you may find that you did not include all the fields you needed or that you included fields that are unnecessary to the results. To modify multitable queries, use the same techniques you learned for single-table queries.

- To add tables, use the Show Table dialog box in the Query Setup group on the Query Tools Design tab (or drag the tables into the top pane of the query design from the Navigation Pane).
- To remove tables, select the unwanted tables and press Delete.

- To add fields, double-click the fields you want to include.
- To remove fields, click the column selector of each field and press Delete.

Join lines between related tables should display automatically in a query if the relationships were previously established, as shown in Figure 2.43.

Add and Delete Fields in a Multitable Query

In Figure 2.44, the design grid and fields from all three tables display. Figure 2.44 shows that Location (from the Branch table) replaced BranchID and LastName (from the Customers table) replaced CustomerID to make the results more useful. BranchID was deleted from the query; therefore, the "B50" criterion was removed as well. "Campus" was added to the Location field's Criteria row to extract the names of the branches rather than their BranchID numbers. The results of the revised query are shown in Figure 2.45.

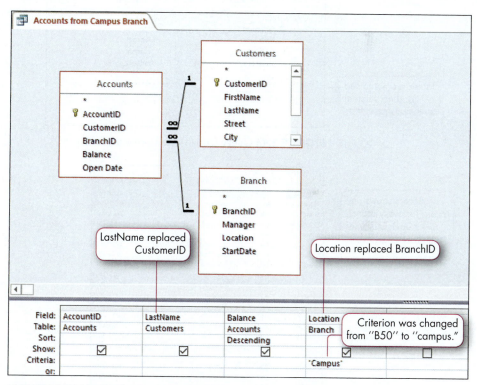

FIGURE 2.44 Modify the Query Design

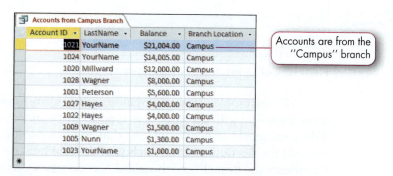

FIGURE 2.45 Datasheet View of a Multitable Query

Add Join Lines in a Multitable Query

Over time, your databases may grow, and additional tables might be added. Occasionally, new tables are added to the database but not to the Relationships window. When queries are created with the newly added tables, join lines will not be established. When this happens, you can create temporary join lines in the query design window. These join lines will provide a temporary relationship between tables (for that query only) and enable Access to interpret the query properly. It may be that you are not planning to save the query in your database or even make the additional table a permanent object. However, if you plan to extract data from related tables repeatedly, it is preferable to create a permanent relationship between the tables in the Relationships window.

In Figure 2.46, two tables are added to a new query's design, but no join line connects them. The results of the query will be unpredictable and will display more records than expected. The Customers table contains 11 records, and the Branch table contains 5 records. Because Access does not know how to interpret the unrelated tables, the results will show 55 records—every possible combination of customer and branch (11 × 5). See Figure 2.47.

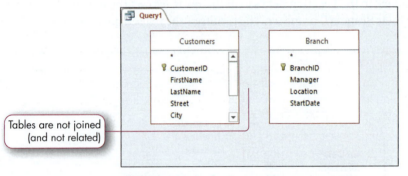

FIGURE 2.46 Query Design with Unrelated Tables

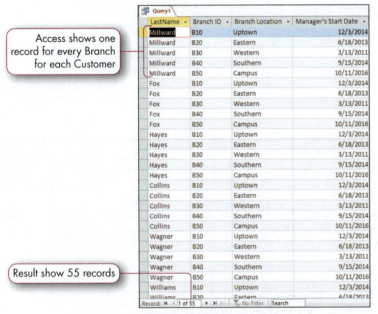

FIGURE 2.47 Query Results Using Unrelated Tables

To fix this problem, you can create join lines using existing tables if the tables contain a common field with the same data type. In this example, in which there is no common field, you can add an additional table that provides join lines between all three tables. You can add the Accounts table, which provides join lines between the two existing tables, Customers and Branch, and the added Accounts table. As soon as the third table is added to the query design, the join lines display automatically.

STEP 4 # Use a Total Row to Summarize Data in a Query

You can get valuable information from your database using a multitable query. For example, if you want to know how many accounts each customer has, you would create a new query and add both the Customers and Accounts tables to Design view. After you verify that the join lines are correct, you add the CustomerID field from the Customers table and the AccountID field from the Accounts table to the query design grid. When you initially run the query, the results show duplicates in the CustomerID column because some customers have multiple accounts. Suppose that you want to display a single row for each Customer ID in the query, with a count of how many accounts each customer has. To summarize information this way, you can add a Total row to the query, create one group (or effectively one record) for each customer and use a function to count the number of accounts each customer has.

To summarize this information (how many accounts each customer has), in Design view, select Totals in the Show/Hide group on the Query Tools Design tab. The Total row displays. Both fields show the Group By option in the Total row. The Total row enables you to summarize records by using functions such as Sum, Average, Count, etc. Before selecting a function that will summarize the values for each group, you must determine which field will represent your groupings. In this case, you will group the records by the Customer ID field and use the Count function to count the number of accounts per group.

With Group By selected in the Customer ID field, click in the Total row of the AccountID field, select Count from the list of functions, and then run the query again. This time the results show one row for each customer and the number of accounts for each customer, as shown in Figure 2.48. There are additional ways of aggregating data in queries, which will be covered in a later chapter.

Customer ID	CountOfAccountID
30001	5
30002	1
30003	4
30004	4
30005	4
30006	1
30007	2
30009	2
30010	2
30011	3

FIGURE 2.48 Datasheet Results with the Count of Accounts per Customer

Quick Concepts

12. Discuss the advantage of creating a multitable query. ***p. 659***

13. Explain a situation where you would use a Total row in a query. ***p. 663***

14. Consider what happens when you create a query with tables that have no common field. ***p. 662***

Hands-On Exercises

4 Multitable Queries

In order to evaluate the sample set of data further, you will create queries that are based on multiple tables rather than on a single table. To create a multitable query, you decide to open an existing query, add additional tables and fields to it, and then save the query.

STEP 1 ADD ADDITIONAL TABLES AND FIELDS TO A QUERY

The previous query was based on the Accounts table, but now you want to add information to the query from the Branch and Customers tables. You will add the Branch and Customers tables along with some additional fields from these tables to the query. Refer to Figure 2.49 as you complete Step 1.

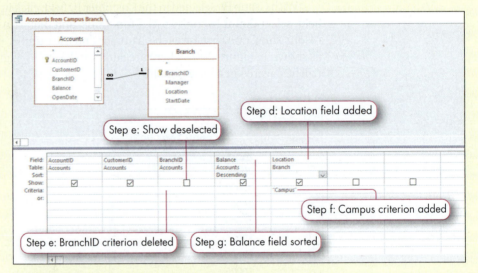

FIGURE 2.49 Add Tables to an Existing Query

a. Open *a02h3Bank_LastFirst* if you closed it at the end of Hands-On Exercise 3, and save it as **a02h4Bank_LastFirst**, changing h3 to h4.

b. Right-click the **Accounts from Campus Branch query** in the Navigation Pane and select **Design View** from the shortcut menu.

c. Drag the **Branch table** from the Navigation Pane to the top pane of the query design window to the right of the Accounts table.

   A join line connects the Branch table to the Accounts table. The tables in the query inherit the relationship created earlier in the Relationships window.

d. Drag the **Location field** from the Branch table to the first empty column in the design grid.

   The Location field should be positioned to the right of the Balance field.

e. Click the **Show check box** below the BranchID field to deselect it and hide this field from the results.

   The BranchID field is no longer needed in the results because the Location field provides the branch name instead. Because you deselected the BranchID Show check box, the BranchID field will not display the next time the query is run.

f. Delete the B50 criterion in the BranchID column.

g. Type **Campus** as a criterion in the Location field and press **Enter**.

Access adds quotation marks around Campus for you because Campus is a text criterion. You are substituting the Location criterion (Campus) in place of the BranchID criterion (B50).

h. Click in the AccountID field **Sort row**, click the **arrow**, and then select **not sorted**. Click in the **Sort row** of the Balance field. Click the **arrow** and select **Descending**.

i. Click **Run** in the Results group.

The BranchID field does not display in Datasheet view because you hid the field in Step e. Only Campus accounts display in the datasheet (10 records). Next, you will add the Customers LastName field to, and delete the CustomerID field from, the query.

j. Save the changes to the query design.

k. Click **View** in the Views group to return to Design view. Point to the column selector at the top of the BranchID field, and when an arrow displays, click to select it. Press **Delete**.

The BranchID field has been removed from the query design grid.

l. Drag the **Customers table** from the Navigation Pane to the top pane of the query design window and reposition the tables so that the join lines are not blocked (see Figure 2.49).

The join lines automatically connect the Customers table to the Accounts table (similar to Step c above).

m. Drag the **LastName field** in the Customers table to the second column in the design grid.

The LastName field should be positioned to the right of the AccountID field.

n. Click the **column selector** in the CustomerID field to select it. Press **Delete**.

The CustomerID field is no longer needed in the results because you added the LastName field instead.

o. Click **Run** in the Results group.

The last names of the customers now display in the results.

p. Save and close the query.

STEP 2 ## CREATE A MULTITABLE QUERY FROM SCRATCH

You realize that another query is needed to show those customers with account balances of $1,000 or less. You create the query and view the results in Datasheet view. Refer to Figure 2.50 as you complete Step 2.

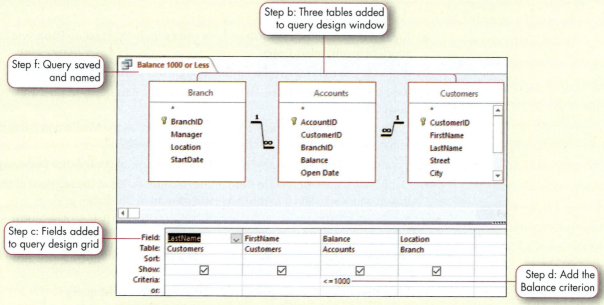

FIGURE 2.50 Create a Multitable Query

a. Click the **Create tab** and click **Query Design** in the Queries group.

b. Double-click the **Branch table name** in the Show Table dialog box. Double-click **Accounts** and **Customers** so that all three are added to Design view. Click **Close** in the Show Table dialog box.

Three tables are added to the query. The join lines were set earlier in the Relationships window.

c. Double-click the following fields to add them to the query design grid: **LastName**, **FirstName**, **Balance**, and **Location**.

d. Type **<=1000** in the Criteria row of the Balance column.

e. Click **Run** in the Results group to see the query results.

Six records that have a balance of $1,000 or less display.

f. Click **Save** on the Quick Access Toolbar and type **Balance 1000 or Less** as the Query Name in the Save As dialog box. Click **OK**.

g. Close the query.

STEP 3 ▶ MODIFY A MULTITABLE QUERY

You decide to make additional changes to the Balance 1000 or Less query you just created. You will create a copy of the existing query and modify the criteria to display the accounts that were opened on or after January 1, 2011, with balances of $2,000 or less. Refer to Figure 2.51 as you complete Step 3.

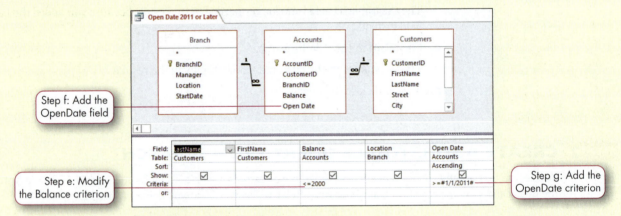

Step f: Add the OpenDate field

Step e: Modify the Balance criterion

Step g: Add the OpenDate criterion

FIGURE 2.51 Query Using the And Condition

a. Right-click the **Balance 1000 or Less query** in the Navigation Pane, and from the shortcut menu, select **Copy**.

b. Right-click in the empty space of the **Navigation Pane** and select **Paste**.

c. Type the name **Open Date 2011 or Later** for the new query in the Paste As dialog box and click **OK**.

d. Double-click the **Open Date 2011 or Later** query in the Navigation Pane. Click **View** in the Views group to switch the query to Design view.

e. Type **<=2000** in place of <=1000 in the Criteria row of the Balance field and press **Enter**.

f. Double-click the **Open Date field** in the Accounts table in the top pane of the query design window to add it to the first blank column in the design grid.

g. Type **>=1/1/2011** in the Criteria row of the Open Date field and press **Enter** to extract only accounts that have been opened since January 1, 2011.

After you type the expression and move to a different column, Access will add the # symbols around the date automatically.

h. Click **Run** in the Results group to display the results of the query.

Five records display in the query results.

i. Click **View** in the Views group to return to Design view of the duplicate query.

j. Click in the **Sort row** of the Open Date field and select **Ascending**.

k. Click **Run** in the Results group.

The records are sorted from the earliest open date on or after January 1, 2011, to the most recent open date.

l. Save and close the query.

STEP 4 ## USE A TOTAL ROW TO SUMMARIZE DATA IN A QUERY

You will to create a query that displays the number of accounts each customer has opened. You create a query using a Total row to summarize the number of accounts per customer. Refer to Figure 2.52 as you complete Step 4.

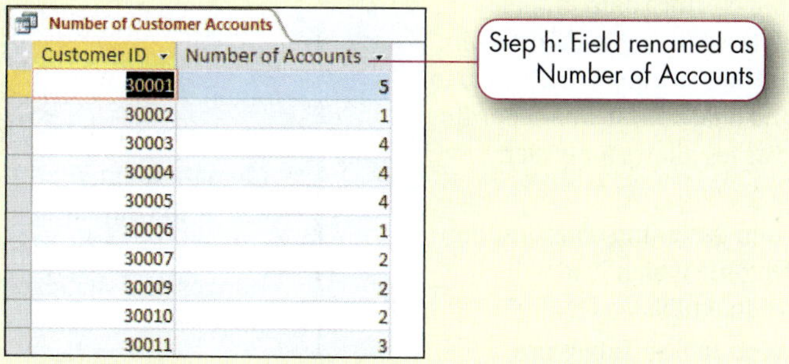

FIGURE 2.52 Number of Accounts per Customer

a. Click the **Create tab** and click **Query Design** in the Queries group.

b. Add the **Accounts table** and the **Customers table** to the top pane of the query design window. Click **Close** in the Show Table dialog box.

c. Double-click the **CustomerID** in the Customers table in the top pane of the query design window to add it to the first blank column in the design grid and double-click the **AccountID** in the Accounts table to add it to the second column.

d. Click **Run** in the Results group.

The results show there are 28 records. Every account for every customer is displayed in its own record. You want only the total number of accounts a customer has, so you modify the query to group the records by the CustomerID and summarize the AccountIDs using a function.

e. Click **View** in the Views group to return to Design view of the query.

f. Click **Totals** in the Show/Hide group.

Both columns show the Group By option in the Total row.

g. Click **Group By** in the Total row of the AccountID field and select **Count**.

The Count function will count the number of Account IDs per customer. You will give the AccountID field a more identifiable description to display in the results.

h. Modify the AccountID field to read **Number of Accounts: AccountID**.

You typed a descriptive name followed by a colon that will display Number of Accounts in the datasheet when you run the query.

i. Click **Run** in the Results group. Resize the columns of the datasheet to fully display the results.

The results show one row for each customer and the number of accounts each customer has opened since the database was created.

j. Click **Save** on the Quick Access Toolbar and type **Number of Customer Accounts** as the query name. Click **OK**. Close the query.

k. Close the database and exit Access. Based on your instructor's directions, submit a02h4Bank_LastFirst.

Chapter Objectives Review

After reading this chapter, you have accomplished the following objectives:

1. Design a table.

- Include necessary data: Consider the output requirements when creating your table design. Determine the data (input) required to produce the expected information (output) later.
- Design for now and for the future: When designing a database, anticipate the future needs of the system and build in the flexibility to satisfy those demands.
- Store data in their smallest parts: Store data in their smallest parts for more flexibility. Storing a full name in a Name field is more limiting than storing a first name in a separate FirstName field and a last name in a separate LastName field. Separating values allows for easier sorting/filtering of records.
- Determine primary keys: When designing your database tables, it is important to determine which field will uniquely identify each record in a table.
- Plan for common fields between tables: Tables are joined in relationships using common fields. You are not required to name the common fields with the same name, but make sure they have the same data type.
- Design to accommodate calculations: Calculated fields are frequently created with numeric data. You can use date arithmetic to subtract one date from another to find the number of days, months, or years that have elapsed between them.

2. Create and modify tables and work with data.

- You can create tables in Datasheet view or Design view. Alternatively, you can import data from another database or an application such as Excel to create tables in an Access database.
- Determine data type: Data type assignments determine the type of data that can be entered and the operations that can be performed on that data. Access recognizes 13 data types.
- Set a table's primary key: The primary key is the field that uniquely identifies each record in a table.
- Explore a foreign key: A foreign key is a field in one table that is also the primary key of another table. A CustomerID might be the primary key field in a Customers table and the foreign key field in a related Accounts table.
- Work with field properties: Field properties determine how the field looks and behaves. Examples of field properties are the Field Size property and the Caption property.
- Create a new field in Design view: It may be necessary to add table fields that were not included in the original design process. While it is possible to add fields in Datasheet view, Design view offers more flexibility.
- Modify the table in Datasheet view: Datasheet view is used to add, edit, and delete records. Design view is used

to create and modify the table structure by enabling you to add and edit fields and set field properties. You cannot work with records in Design view.

3. Import data from external sources.

- Import Excel data: You can import data from other applications such as an Excel spreadsheet.
- Import Access data: You can import data from another database by using the Import Wizard.
- Modify an imported table's design: After importing a table, examine the design and make necessary modifications. Use Design view to modify the field names, data types, field sizes, and other properties.
- Add data to an imported table: After you have imported a table into your database, you may want to add new fields to the tables. After making the modifications, save your changes and switch back to Datasheet view to add new data or modify existing records.

4. Establish table relationships.

- Relationships enable you to extract records from more than one table and help to avoid data redundancy. Use the Show Table dialog box to add tables to the Relationships window. Drag a field name from one table to the corresponding field name in another table to join the tables.
- Enforce and test referential integrity: Referential integrity enforces rules in a database that are used to preserve relationships between tables when records are changed.
- Set cascade options: The Cascade Update Related Fields option ensures that when the primary key is modified in a primary table, Access will automatically update all foreign key values in a related table. The Cascade Delete Related Records option ensures that when the primary key is deleted in a primary table, Access will automatically delete all records in related tables that reference the primary key.
- Establish a one-to-many relationship: A one-to-many relationship is established when the primary key value in the primary table can match many of the foreign key values in the related table. One-to-one and many-to-many are also relationship possibilities, but one-to-many relationships are the most common.

5. Create a single-table query.

- Create a single-table select query: A single-table select query uses fields from one table to display only those records that match certain criteria.
- Use Query Design view: Use Query Design view to create and modify a query. The top pane of the query design window contains tables with their respective field names and displays the join lines between tables. The bottom pane, known as the query design grid, contains columns and rows that you use to build and control the query results.

6. Use the Query Wizard.

- The Simple Query Wizard is an alternative method for creating queries. It enables you to follow a series of prompts to select tables and fields from lists. The last step of the wizard prompts you to save and name the query.

7. Specify query criteria.

- Different data types require different syntax. Date fields are enclosed in pound signs and text fields in quotations. Numeric and currency fields require no delimiters.
- Use wildcards: Wildcards are special characters that can represent one or more characters in a text value. A question mark is a wildcard that stands for a single character in the same position as the question mark, while an asterisk is a wildcard that stands for any number of characters in the same position as the asterisk.
- Use comparison operators in queries: Comparison operators such as equal, not equal, greater than, less than, greater than or equal to, and less than or equal to can be used in the criteria of a query to limit the query results to only those records that meet the criteria.
- Work with null: Access uses the term null for a blank field. Null criteria can be used to find missing information.
- Establish AND, OR, and NOT criteria: The AND, OR, and NOT conditions are used when queries require logical criteria. The AND condition returns only records that meet all criteria. The OR condition returns records meeting any of the specified criteria. The NOT logical operator returns all records except the specified criteria.

8. Specify query sort order and run a query.

- The query sort order determines the order of records in a query's Datasheet view. You can change the order of records by specifying the sort order in Design view.
- The sort order is determined from the order of the fields from left to right. Move the field columns to position them in left to right sort order.

- To obtain the results for a query, run the query. To run the query, click Run in the Results group in Design view. Another method is to locate the query in the Navigation Pane and double-click it. A similar method is to select the query and press Enter.

9. Copy and modify a query.

- To save time, after specifying tables, fields, and conditions for one query, copy the query, rename it, and then modify the fields and criteria in the copied query.
- Change query data: You can correct an error immediately while data are displayed in the query datasheet. Use caution when editing records in query results because you will be changing the original table data.

10. Create a multitable query.

- Add additional tables and fields to an existing query: Open the Navigation Pane and drag the tables from the Navigation Pane directly into the top pane of the query design window.
- Create a multitable query from scratch: Multitable queries contain two or more tables enabling you to take advantage of the relationships that have been set in your database.

11. Modify a multitable query.

- Add and delete fields in a multitable query: Multitable queries may need to be modified. Add fields by double-clicking the field name in the table you want; remove fields by clicking the column selector and pressing Delete.
- Add join lines in a multitable query: If the tables have a common field, create join lines by dragging the field name of one common field onto the field name of the other table. Or you can add an additional table that will provide a join between all three tables. Multitable queries inherit the relationships that have been set in the Relationships window.
- Use a Total row to summarize data in a query: Use the Total Row options of a field such as Group By and Count to aggregate and summarize values in queries.

Key Terms Matching

Match the key terms with their definitions. Write the key term letter by the appropriate numbered definition.

a. AND condition
b. AutoNumber
c. Caption property
d. Cascade Delete Related Records
e. Cascade Update Related Fields
f. Comparison operator
g. Criteria row
h. Data redundancy
i. Data type
j. Field property

k. Foreign key
l. Input mask
m. Join line
n. One-to-many relationship
o. OR condition
p. Query
q. Referential integrity
r. Simple Query Wizard
s. Validation rule
t. Wildcard

1. _____ Connects two tables together by their common field in the Relationships window. **p. 619**

2. _____ The unnecessary storing of duplicate data in two or more tables. **p. 619**

3. _____ Determines the type of data that can be entered and the operations that can be performed on that data. **p. 621**

4. _____ A number that automatically increments each time a record is added. **p. 622**

5. _____ A field in one table that is also the primary key of another table. **p. 623**

6. _____ Characteristic of a field that determines how it looks and behaves. **p. 624**

7. _____ Used to create a more understandable label than a field name label that displays in the top row in Datasheet view and in forms and reports. **p. 625**

8. _____ Checks the data for allowable value when the user exits the field. **p. 625**

9. _____ Simplifies data entry by providing literal characters that are typed for every entry. **p. 625**

10. _____ Rules in a database that are used to preserve relationships between tables when records are added, deleted, or changed. **p. 635**

11. _____ An option that directs Access to automatically update all foreign key values in a related table when the primary key value is modified in a primary table. **p. 636**

12. _____ When the primary key value is deleted in a primary table, Access will automatically delete all foreign key values in a related table. **p. 636**

13. _____ When the primary key value in the primary table can match many of the foreign key values in the related table. **p. 637**

14. _____ Enables you to ask questions about the data stored in a database and provides answers to the questions in a datasheet. **p. 646**

15. _____ A row in the Query Design grid that determines which records will be selected. **p. 647**

16. _____ Provides a step-by-step guide to help you through the query design process. **p. 649**

17. _____ Special character that can represent one or more characters in the criterion of a query. **p. 651**

18. _____ Uses greater than (>), less than (<), greater than or equal to (>=), and less than or equal to (<=), etc. to limit query results that meet these criteria. **p. 652**

19. _____ Returns only records that meet all criteria. **p. 653**

20. _____ Returns records meeting any of the specified criteria. **p. 653**

Multiple Choice

1. All of the following are suggested guidelines for table design *except*:
   (a) include all necessary data.
   (b) store data in their smallest parts.
   (c) avoid date arithmetic.
   (d) link tables using common fields.

2. Which of the following determines the amount of space a field uses in the database?
   (a) Field size
   (b) Data type
   (c) Caption property
   (d) Normalization

3. When entering, deleting, or editing data:
   (a) the table must be in Design view.
   (b) the table must be in Datasheet view.
   (c) the table can be in either Datasheet or Design view.
   (d) data can only be entered in a form.

4. With respect to importing data into Access, which of the following statements is *true*?
   (a) The Import Wizard works only for Excel files.
   (b) The Import Wizard is found on the Create tab.
   (c) You can assign a primary key while you are importing Excel data.
   (d) Imported table designs cannot be modified in Access.

5. The main reason to set a validation rule in Access is to:
   (a) limit the entry of incorrect values in a table.
   (b) make it possible to delete records.
   (c) keep your database safe from unauthorized users.
   (d) keep redundant data from being entered in a table.

6. An illustration of a one-to-many relationship would be:
   (a) an employee listed in the Employees table earns a raise, so the Salaries table must be updated.
   (b) a customer may have more than one account in an accounts table.
   (c) each employee in an Employees table has a matching entry in the Salaries table.
   (d) an employee leaves the company so that when he is deleted from the Employees table, his salary data will be deleted from the Salaries table.

7. A query's specifications as to which records to include must be entered on the:
   (a) table row of the query design grid.
   (b) show row of the query design grid.
   (c) sort row of the query design grid.
   (d) Criteria row of the query design grid.

8. When adding date criteria to the Query Design view, the dates you enter will be delimited by:
   (a) parentheses.
   (b) pound signs.
   (c) quotes.
   (d) at signs.

9. It is more efficient to make a copy of an existing query rather than to create a new query when which of the following is *true*?
   (a) The existing query contains only one table.
   (b) The existing query and the new query use the same tables and fields.
   (c) The existing query and the new query have the exact same criteria.
   (d) The original query is no longer being used.

10. Which of the following is *true* for the Query Wizard?
    (a) No criteria can be added as you step through the Wizard.
    (b) You can only select related tables as a source.
    (c) Fields with different data types are not allowed.
    (d) You are required to summarize the data.

Practice Exercises

1 Philadelphia Bookstore

FROM SCRATCH

Tom and Erin Mullaney own and operate a bookstore in Philadelphia, Pennsylvania. Erin asked you to help her create an Access database to store the publishers and the books that they sell. The data for the publishers and books are currently stored in Excel worksheets that you decide to import into a new database. You determine that a third table—for authors—is also required. Your task is to create and populate the three tables, set the table relationships, and enforce referential integrity. You will then create queries to extract information from the tables. Refer to Figure 2.53 as you complete this exercise.

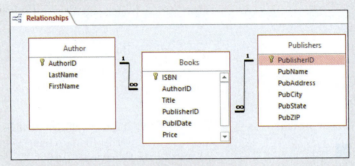

FIGURE 2.53 Books Relationships Window

a. Open Access and click **Blank database**. Type **a02p1Books_LastFirst** in the File Name box. Click **Browse** to navigate to the location where you are saving your files in the File New Database dialog box, click **OK** to close the dialog box, and then click **Create** to create the new database.

b. Type **11** in the Click to Add column in the new Table1 and click **Click to Add**. The field name becomes Field1 and *Click to Add* now displays as the third column. In the third column, type **Beschloss** and press **Tab**. Repeat the process for the fourth column; type **Michael R.** and press **Tab** two times. The insertion point returns to the first column where (New) is selected.

c. Press **Tab**. Access will automatically increment the ID field. Type the rest of the data using the following table. These data will become the records of the Author table.

ID	Field1	Field2	Field3
1	11	**Beschloss**	**Michael R.**
(New)	12	**Turow**	**Scott**
	13	**Rice**	**Anne**
	14	**King**	**Stephen**
	15	**Connelly**	**Michael**
	16	**Rice**	**Luanne**
	17	*your last name*	*your first name*

d. Click **Save** on the Quick Access Toolbar. Type **Author** in the Save As dialog box and click **OK**.

e. Click **View** in the Views group to switch to Design view of the Author table.

f. Select **Field1**—in the second row—in the top portion of the table design and type **AuthorID** to rename the field. In the Field Properties section in the lower pane of the table design, type **Author ID** in the Caption box and verify that Long Integer displays for the Field Size property.

g. Select **Field2** and type **LastName** to rename the field. In the Field Properties section in the bottom portion of Design view, type **Author's Last Name** in the Caption box and type **20** as the field size.

h. Select **Field3** and type **FirstName** to rename the field. In the Field Properties section in the bottom portion of the table design, type **Author's First Name** as the caption and type **15** as the field size.

i. Click the **ID field row selector** (which displays the primary key) to select the row and click **Delete Rows** in the Tools group. Click **Yes** two times to confirm both messages.

j. Click the **AuthorID row selector** and select **Primary Key** in the Tools group to set the primary key.

k. Click **Save** on the Quick Access Toolbar to save the design changes. Click **Yes** to the *Some data may be lost* message. You will not lose any data because of the field size changes you made. Close the table.

l. Click the **External Data tab**, click **New Data Source**, point to **From File** in the Import & Link group, and then select **Excel** to launch the Get External Data – Excel Spreadsheet dialog box. Verify that the *Import the source data into a new table in the current database* option is selected, click **Browse**, and then navigate to your student data folder. Select the *a02p1Books.xlsx* workbook, click **Open**, and then click **OK**. This workbook contains two worksheets. Follow the steps below:

- Select the **Publishers worksheet** and click **Next**.
- Click the **First Row Contains Column Headings check box** to select it and click **Next**.
- Ensure that the PubID field is selected, click the **Indexed arrow**, select **Yes (No Duplicates)**, and then click **Next**.
- Click the **Choose my own primary key arrow**, ensure that PubID is selected, and then click **Next**.
- Accept the name Publishers for the table name, click **Finish**, and then click **Close** without saving the import steps.

m. Use the Import Wizard again to import the Books worksheet from the *a02p1Books.xlsx* workbook into the Access database. Follow the steps below:

- Ensure that the Books worksheet is selected and click **Next**.
- Ensure that the **First Row Contains Column Headings check box** is selected and click **Next**.
- Click the **ISBN column**, click the **Indexed arrow**, set the Indexed property box to **Yes (No Duplicates)**, and then click **Next**.
- Click the **Choose my own primary key arrow**, select **ISBN** as the primary key field, and then click **Next**.
- Accept the name Books as the table name. Click **Finish** and click **Close** without saving the import steps.

n. Right-click the **Books table** in the Navigation Pane and select **Design View**. Make the following changes:

- Click the **PubID field** and change the name to **PublisherID**.
- Set the caption property to **Publisher ID.**
- Change the PublisherID Field Size property to **2**.
- Click the **ISBN field** and change the Field Size property to **13**.
- Change the AuthorCode field name to **AuthorID**.
- Change the AuthorID Field Size property to **Long Integer**.
- Click the **ISBN field row selector** (which displays the primary key) to select the row. Click and drag to move the row up to the first position in the table design. You want the primary key field to display in the first column of the table.
- Click **Save** on the Quick Access Toolbar to save the design changes to the Books table. Click **Yes** to the *Some data may be lost* warning. You will not lose any data because of the field size changes you made.
- Close the table.

o. Right-click the **Publishers table** in the Navigation Pane and select **Design View**. Make the following changes:

- Click the **PubID field** and change the name to **PublisherID**.
- Change the PublisherID Field Size property to **2**.
- Change the Caption property to **Publisher's ID**.
- Change the Field Size property to **50** for the PubName and PubAddress fields.
- Change the Pub Address field name to **PubAddress** (remove the space).
- Change the PubCity Field Size property to **30**.

- Change the PubState Field Size property to **2**.
- Change the Pub ZIP field name to **PubZIP** (remove the space).
- Click **Save** on the Quick Access Toolbar to save the design changes to the Publishers table.
- Click **Yes** to the *Some data may be lost* warning. You will not lose any data because of the field size changes you made. Close the Publishers table.

p. Click the **Database Tools tab** and click **Relationships** in the Relationships group. Click **Show Table**, if the Show Table dialog box does not open automatically. Follow the steps below:
- Double-click each **table name** in the Show Table dialog box to add it to the Relationships window and close the Show Table dialog box.
- Drag the **AuthorID field** from the Author table onto the AuthorID field in the Books table.
- Click the **Enforce Referential Integrity** and **Cascade Update Related Fields check boxes** in the Edit Relationships dialog box to select them. Click **Create** to create a one-to-many relationship between the Author and Books tables.
- Drag the **PublisherID field** from the Publishers table onto the PublisherID field in the Books table.
- Click the **Enforce Referential Integrity** and **Cascade Update Related Fields check boxes** in the Edit Relationships dialog box to select them. Click **Create** to create a one-to-many relationship between the Publishers and Books tables.
- Click **Save** on the Quick Access Toolbar to save the changes to the Relationships window, then in the Relationships group, click **Close**.

q. Click **Query Wizard** in the Queries group on the Create tab. With Simple Query Wizard selected, click **OK**. Follow the steps below:
- Ensure that the **Publishers table** is selected and double-click to add **PubName**, **PubCity**, and **PubState** to the Selected Fields list. Click **Next** and click **Finish**. In Datasheet view, double-click the **border** to the right of each column to set the column widths to Best Fit to view the results. Click **Save** on the Quick Access Toolbar. Close the query.

r. Right-click the **Publishers Query** in the Navigation Pane, and from the shortcut menu, select **Copy**. Right-click in the **Navigation Pane**, and from the shortcut menu, select **Paste**. Type **New York Publishers Query** as the query name. Click **OK**. Follow the steps below:
- Open the New York Publishers Query. Click **View** in the Views group on the Home tab to switch to Design view of the query. Click and drag the **Books table** from the Navigation Pane into the top pane of the query design window.
- Select the **Books table**, double-click **Title** and **PublDate** to add the fields to the query design grid.
- Click in the **Criteria row** of the PubState field and type **NY**. Click the **Sort cell** of the PublDate field, click the arrow, and then select **Descending**.
- Click **Run** in the Results group (12 records display in the Datasheet sorted by PublDate in descending order). Double-click the border to the right of each column to set the column widths to Best Fit to view the results.
- Save and close the query.

s. Right-click the **New York Publishers Query** in the Navigation Pane, and from the shortcut menu, select **Copy**. Right-click in the **Navigation Pane**, and from the shortcut menu, select **Paste**. Type **Summary by Publisher** as the query name. Click **OK**.

t. Open the query. Click **View** in the Views group on the Home tab to switch to Design view of the query.

u. Click in the **Criteria row** of the PubState field and delete "NY". Click the **Sort cell** of the PubName field, click the **arrow**, and then select **Ascending**.

v. Click the gray **column selector** at the top of the PubCity field and press **Delete**. Delete the **PubState** and **PublDate** fields from the query. There are now two fields remaining in the query, PubName and Title.

w. Click **Totals** in the Show/Hide group on the Query Tools Design tab. Click in the **Total row** of the Title field, click the **arrow**, and then select **Count**. The records will be grouped by the publisher's name and the titles for each publisher will be summarized.

x. Modify the field name of the Title column as **Title Count: Title** to make the field name more identifiable.

y. Click **Run** in the Results group (8 records display in the Datasheet). The results display the title count for each publisher.

z. Save and close the query.

aa. Close the database and exit Access. Based on your instructor's directions, submit a02p1Books_LastFirst.

2 Employee Salary Analysis

The Morgan Insurance Company offers a full range of insurance services. They store the firm's employee data in an Access database. This file contains each employee's name and address, job performance, salary, and title, but the data need to be imported into a different existing database. A database file containing two of the tables (Location and Titles) already exists; your job is to import the employee data from Access to create the third table. Once imported, you will modify field properties and set new relationships. The owner of the company, Victor Reed, is concerned that some of the Atlanta and Boston salaries may be below the guidelines published by the national office. He asks that you investigate the salaries of the two offices and create a separate query for each city. Refer to Figure 2.54 as you complete this exercise.

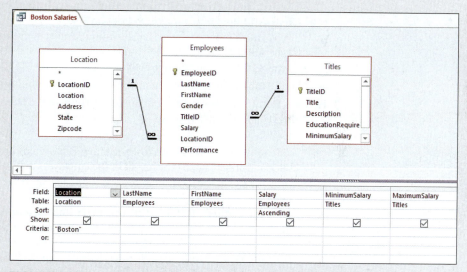

FIGURE 2.54 Boston Salaries Query Design

a. Open *a02p2Insurance* and save it as **a02p2Insurance_LastFirst**. Double-click the **Location table** and review the data to become familiar with the field names and the type of information stored in the table. Review the Titles table. Double-click the **border** to the right of the TitleID column to set the column width to Best Fit. Save the table. Close both tables.

b. Click the **External Data tab**, click **New Data Source**, point to **From Database**, and then select **Access** in the Import & Link group. Complete the following steps:
- Click **Browse** and navigate to the *a02p2Employees* database in your student data folder. Select the file, click **Open**.
- Click **OK** in the Get External Data – Access Database dialog box.
- Select the **Employees table** in the Import Objects dialog box and click **OK**.
- Click **Close** without saving the import steps.

c. Double-click the **Employees table** in the Navigation Pane, then click **View** in the Views group on the Home tab to switch to Design view of the Employees table. Make the following changes:

- Ensure that the EmployeeID field is selected and click **Primary Key** in the Tools group on the Table Tools Design tab.
- Click the **LastName field** and change the Field Size property to **20**.
- Change the Caption property to **Last Name**.
- Click the **FirstName field** and change the Field Size property to **20**.
- Change the Caption property to **First Name**.
- Click the **LocationID field** and change the Field Size property to **3**.
- Change the Caption property to **Location ID**.
- Click the **TitleID field** and change the Field Size property to **3**.
- Change the Caption property to **Title ID**.
- Change the Salary field data type to **Currency**.
- Save the design changes. Click **Yes** to the *Some data may be lost* warning.

d. Click **View** in the Views group to view the Employees table in Datasheet view and examine the data. Click any record in the Title ID column and click **Ascending** in the Sort & Filter group on the Home tab.

e. Double-click the **Titles table** in the Navigation Pane to open it in Datasheet view. Notice that the T04 title is not in the list.

f. Add a new record in the first blank record at the bottom of the Titles table. Use the following data:
- Type **T04** in the TitleID field.
- Type **Senior Account Rep** in the Title field.
- Type **A marketing position requiring a technical background and at least three years of experience** in the Description field.
- Type **Four year degree** in the Education Requirements field.
- Type **45000** in the Minimum Salary field.
- Type **85000** in the Maximum Salary field.

g. Close all tables. Click **Yes** if you are prompted to save changes to the Employees table.

h. Click **Relationships** in the Relationships group on the **Database Tools tab** and Click **Show Table**. Follow the steps below:
- Double-click each of the three **table names** in the Show Table dialog box to add it to the Relationships window and close the Show Table dialog box.
- Click and drag to adjust the height of the Employees table so that all fields display in each one.
- Drag the **LocationID field** in the Location table onto the LocationID field in the Employees table.
- Click the **Enforce Referential Integrity** and **Cascade Update Related Fields check boxes** in the Edit Relationships dialog box to select them. Click **Create** to create a one-to-many relationship between the Location and Employees tables.
- Drag the **TitleID field** in the Titles table onto the TitleID field in the Employees table (move the field lists by clicking and dragging their title bars as needed so that they do not overlap).
- Click the **Enforce Referential Integrity** and **Cascade Update Related Fields check boxes** in the Edit Relationships dialog box to select them. Click **Create** to create a one-to-many relationship between the Titles and Employees tables.
- Click **Save** on the Quick Access Toolbar to save the changes to the Relationships window and close the Relationships window.

i. Click the **Create tab** and click the **Query Wizard** in the Queries group. Follow the steps below:
- Select **Simple Query Wizard** and click **OK**.
- Select **Table: Employees** in the Tables/Queries box.
- Double-click **LastName** in the Available Fields list to move it to the Selected Fields list.
- Double-click **FirstName** in the Available Fields list to move it to the Selected Fields list.
- Double-click **LocationID** in the Available Fields list to move it to the Selected Fields list.
- Click **Next**.
- Type **Employees Location** as the query title and click **Finish**.

- Click **View** in the Views group on the Home tab to switch to Design view of the query. Click and drag the **Titles table** from the Navigation Pane into the top pane of the query design window.
- Double-click **Title** in the Titles table to add the field to the query design grid.
- Click the **Sort cell** of the LocationID field, click the **arrow**, and then click **Ascending**.
- Click **Run** in the Results group (311 records display in the Datasheet sorted by LocationID in ascending order). Double-click the **border** to the right of each column to set the column widths to Best Fit.
- Click **View** in the Views group on the Home tab to switch to Design view of the query.
- Click the gray **column selector** at the top of the **LastName field** and press **Delete**. Delete the **FirstName field** from the query. There are now two fields remaining in the query, LocationID and Title.
- Click **Totals** in the Show/Hide group on the Query Tools Design tab. Click in the **Total row** of the Title field, click the **arrow**, and then select **Count**. The records will be grouped by the location and the titles for each location will be summarized.
- Modify the field name of the Title column as **Count by Title: Title** to make the field name more identifiable.
- Click **Run** in the Results group (11 records display in the Datasheet). The results display the title count for each active location.
- Save and close the query.

j. Click **Query Design** in the Queries group on the Create tab. Follow the steps below:
- Add **Location**, **Employees**, and **Titles tables** to the top pane of the query window.
- Double-click **Location** in the Location table to move it to the first field in the query design grid.
- Double-click **LastName**, **FirstName**, and **Salary** in the Employees table to add the next three fields.
- Double-click **MinimumSalary** and **MaximumSalary** in the Titles table to add the next two fields.
- Save the query as **Atlanta Salaries** and run the query.

k. Click **View** in the Views group on the Home tab to switch to Design view of the Atlanta Salaries query. Follow the steps below:
- Click in the **Criteria row** of the Location field, and type **Atlanta**. Click the **Sort cell** of the Salary field, click the **arrow**, and then select **Ascending**.
- Click **Run** in the Results group. Review the data to determine if any of the Atlanta employees have a salary less than the minimum or greater than the maximum when compared to the published salary range. You notice that several salaries fall below the minimum value specified by the company. These salaries will be investigated and updated later.
- Save and close the query.

l. Right-click the **Atlanta Salaries query** in the Navigation Pane and from the shortcut menu, select **Copy**. Right-click a blank area in the **Navigation Pane** and select **Paste**. In the Paste As dialog box, type **Boston Salaries** for the query name. Click **OK**.

m. Right-click the **Boston Salaries query** in the Navigation Pane and select **Design View**. In the Criteria row of the Location field, replace Atlanta with **Boston**. Follow the steps below:
- Click **Run** in the Results group. Review the data to determine if any of the Boston employees have a salary less than the minimum or greater than the maximum when compared to the published salary range. You notice that several salaries fall below the minimum value specified by the company.
- Modify some data that were incorrectly entered in the data that you imported. In the query results, for the first employee, Frank Cusack, change the salary to **$48,700.00**; for Brian Beamer, **$45,900.00**; for Lorna Weber, **$45,700.00**; for Penny Pfleger, **$45,800.00**.
- Save and close the query.

n. Close the database and exit Access. Based on your instructor's directions, submit a02p2Insurance_LastFirst.

f. Create a relationship between the Service and Orders tables using the ServiceID field, ensuring that you enforce referential integrity and cascade update related fields. Save and close the Relationships window.

g. Create a new query in Design view using **Location**, **Members**, **Orders**, and **Service tables**. Add the following fields to the query (in this order): **ServiceDate** from the Orders table; **City** from the Location table, **NoInParty** from Orders table; **ServiceName** from the Service table; and **FirstName** and **LastName** from the Members table. Set the criteria in city field to limit the output to **Denver**.

h. Display only service dates from 7/1/2017 to 6/30/2018 (Hint: Use the Between operator).

i. Set the NoInParty criterion to **2**. Sort the results in ascending order by the ServiceDate. Run and save the query with the name **Denver Rooms 2 Guests**.

j. Use Design view to change the order of the query fields so that they display as FirstName, LastName, ServiceDate, City, NoInParty, and ServiceName. Run, save the changes to the query, and close the query.

k. Copy the **Denver Rooms 2 Guests query** and paste it in the **Navigation Pane**, renaming the new query **Chicago Rooms 2 Guests**.

l. Open the Chicago Rooms 2 Guests query in Design view and change the City criterion from Denver to **Chicago**. Run the query and save the changes. Close the query.

m. Close the database and exit Access. Based on your instructor's directions, submit a02m2Hotel_LastFirst.

Running Case

New Castle County Technical Services

New Castle County Technical Services (NCCTS) provides technical support for several companies in the greater New Castle County, Delaware area. Once you have completed the changes to the database tables and set the appropriate relationships, you will be ready to extract information by creating queries.

a. Open the database *a02r1NCCTS* and save it as **a02r1NCCTS_LastFirst**.

b. Open the Call Types table in Design view. Before you create your queries, you want to modify some of the table properties:
  - Set the caption of the HourlyRate field to **Hourly Rate**.
  - View the table in Datasheet view and save the changes when prompted.

c. Close the table.

d. Make the following additional changes to the tables:
  - Open the Calls table in Design view. Set the caption of the HoursLogged field to **Hours Logged**.
  - Set the caption of the OpenedDate field to **Opened Date**.
  - Set the caption of the ClosedDate field to **Closed Date**.
  - Set the caption of the CustomerSatisfaction field to **Customer Satisfaction**.
  - View the table in Datasheet view and save the changes when prompted. You will not lose any data by making this change, so click **Yes** in the message box when prompted. Close the table.
  - Open the Customers table in Design view. Set the field size of CompanyName to **50** and the caption to **Company Name**. View the table in Datasheet view and save the changes when prompted. You will not lose any data by making this change, so click **Yes** in the message box when prompted. Close the table.

- Open the Reps table in Design view. Set the caption of the RepFirst field to **Rep First Name**. Set the caption of the RepLast field to **Rep Last Name**. View the table in Datasheet view and save the changes when prompted. Close the table.

e. Open the Relationships window. Create a join line between the Call Types and Calls tables, ensuring that you enforce referential integrity and cascade update related fields. Set a relationship between Reps and Calls and between Customers and Calls using the same options. Save and close the Relationships window.

f. Create a multitable query, following the steps below:
   - Add the following fields (in this order): **CallID** (from Calls), **Description** (from Call Types), **CompanyName** (from Customers), and **RepFirst** and **RepLast** (from Reps).
   - Run the query, and then modify it to add **HoursLogged** (from Calls).
   - Sort the query by HoursLogged in ascending order. Set the criteria of the HoursLogged field to **Is Not Null** and run the query again.
   - Modify the criteria of the HoursLogged field to **>=5** and **<=10**, the Description to **Disaster Recovery**, and the RepFirst to **Barbara** (do not enter RepLast criterion).
   - Save the query as **Complex Disaster Recovery Calls_Barbara**. Run and close the query.

g. Create a copy of the **Complex Disaster Recovery Calls_Barbara query** and modify it following the steps below:
   - Save the copy of the query as **Complex Network Installation Calls_Barbara**.
   - Modify the query so that the description displays Barbara's network installation calls that logged between 5 and 10 hours.
   - Save, run, and then close the query.

h. Close the database and exit Access. Based on your instructor's directions, submit a02r1NCCTS_LastFirst.

Disaster Recovery

May Beverage Sales

If criteria in a query are inaccurate, the query may not return any results at all. Unexpected results can also occur from inaccurate data, so troubleshooting queries is a skill that you can put to work in your organization. A coworker explained that he was having difficulty with queries that were not returning correct results and asked you to help diagnose the problem. Open *a02d1Traders* and save it as **a02d1Traders_LastFirst**. It contains two queries, *May 2019 Orders of Beverages and Confections* and *2019 Beverage Sales by Ship Country*. He also asked for your help in adding the CompanyName from the Customers table to the last column of the *2019 Beverage Sales by Ship Country* query. You will correct the errors in the criteria of both queries and add the extra field to one of them.

The May 2019 Orders of Beverages and Confections query is supposed to contain only information for orders shipped in May 2019. You find other shipped dates included in the results. Change the criteria to exclude the other dates. Run and save the query. Close the query.

The 2019 Beverage Sales by Ship Country query returns no results. Check the criteria in all fields and modify so that the correct results are returned. Add the **CompanyName** from the Customers table to the last column of the *2019 Beverage Sales by Ship Country* query. Run and save the query. Close the query.

Close the database and exit Access. Based on your instructor's directions, submit a02d1Traders_LastFirst.

To calculate the monthly installment with a 20% surcharge you would enter as an expression the following formula: Balance*1.2/12. You cannot exactly type that formula as it appears in the preceding sentence – a few modifications will need to be made. To input an expression in a way Access can understand, first add a new calculated field by clicking the field row. Then, to begin entering the expression, double-click the Balance field in the table above, to add the Balance field to the expression. You might notice that as you type the rest of the expression, Access adds brackets [ ] around field names as shown in Figure 3.4. In addition, Access assigns a default column heading of Expr1: to the start of the expression. The resulting expression in Access is: Expr1: [Balance]*1.2/12.

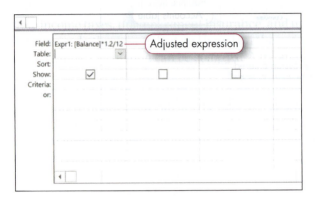

FIGURE 3.4 Modified Expression

When you run the query, the column heading will be *Expr1*. To rename this column MonthlyPayment, delete *Expr1* and type a name such as MonthlyPayment, making certain to leave the colon in place. The column is renamed MonthlyPayment in Figure 3.5. Alternatively, you can include the field name when you start to build the expression, followed by a colon, and then enter the expression.

FIGURE 3.5 Expression Renamed

The query results, as shown in Figure 3.6, display a decimal number in the MonthlyPayment column. Notice that the results are not easy to read and should be formatted. Sometimes a column will result in cells that are filled with pound signs #### rather than numbers as you would have expected. The pound signs represent that the column is too narrow to display the results properly. To fix this issue, double-click the outer edge of the column to widen it and view the numbers. You will learn more about formatting the results in the next section.

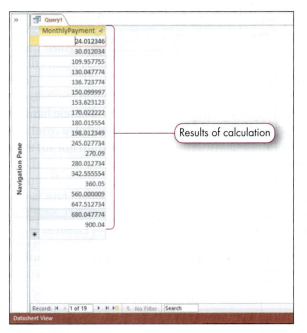

FIGURE 3.6 Unformatted Results

As you create expressions in a calculated field, you may find one or more of the following elements in the calculated field:

- Arithmetic operator (for example: *, /, +, or −)
- *Constant*, a value that does not change (such as a person's birthdate)
- Function (built-in calculations like Pmt)
- Identifier (the names of fields – such as *Balance* from the example above, controls, or properties)

To see the entire calculated field expression in Design view, right-click the Field row and select Zoom. A dialog box (the Zoom box) will open to enable you to easily see and edit the entire contents of the cell, as shown in Figure 3.7. Once you have finished modifying a field, click Close in the top-right corner of the Zoom box.

Recovering from Common Errors

When creating calculated fields, a number of common errors can occur. Learning how to recognize errors and recover from issues is important. Some common types of errors:

Syntax Error: Forgetting the Colon

A correct formula looks like this: MonthlyPayment: [Balance]*1.2/12

If you forget the colon, you will get an invalid syntax error, indicating something is wrong with the way the formula is written, as shown in Figure 3.9.

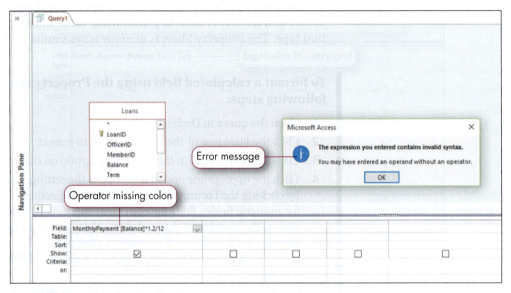

FIGURE 3.9 Syntax Error Warning

Syntax Error: Spelling Error

If you mistype the field name as *Baalance*, you will get an error when you run the query that prompts you to give a value for *Baalance* as shown in Figure 3.10.

Access cannot complete the calculation because the database does not recognize a field named *Baalance*. Correct the misspelling, and the calculation is made.

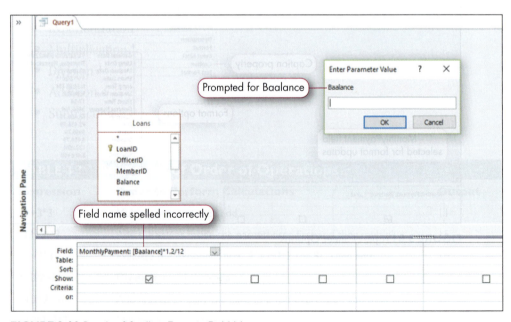

FIGURE 3.10 Result of Spelling Error in Field Name

Syntax Error: Order of Operations Error

If you do not check your formulas, you may get incorrect results. For example, the following would not produce the expected output:

NewMonthlyBalance: [Balance] + 100/12

If you want addition to be done before division, you must remember the parentheses:

NewMonthlyBalance: ([Balance] + 100)/12

Verifying Calculated Results

After the query runs, review the field values and calculated values in Datasheet view to make sure the results make sense. As noted above, you might have forgotten to add in parentheses causing the wrong order of operations to be conducted. In a real-world scenario, you will not be given step-by-step directions and instead will apply critical thinking skills to your work. Access will calculate exactly what you tell it to calculate, even if you make logical errors in the calculation.

Assume you are calculating a car payment for a $10,000 car, with monthly payments for 5 years. If your results indicated that the monthly payment is $1,000, you should ask yourself, "Does it make sense for me to pay $1,000 every month for five years to finance a $10,000 car?"

You can verify results with a calculator. Alternatively, you could check the results in Excel by copying and pasting the data into a worksheet, conducting the calculations in Excel, and then comparing the answers to the query results in Access. The Access calculated field, the calculator, and the Excel calculations should all return identical results.

Quick Concepts

1. Discuss the four types of elements that can appear as part of an expression in Access. *p. 689*

2. Briefly describe the order of operations. Give an example of how the order of operations makes a difference in a calculation. *p. 690*

3. Explain how Access responds when you spell a field name incorrectly in a query. *p. 692*

Hands-On Exercises

Skills covered: Build Expressions • Format Fields • Recognize and Correct Common Errors • Evaluate Results

1 Calculated Fields and Expressions

Using the data from the homes for sale lists that Don and Matt acquired, you can help them target properties that meet their criteria. As you examine the data, you discover other ways to analyze the properties. You create several queries and present your results to the two investors for their comments.

STEP 1 **BUILD EXPRESSIONS**

You begin your analysis by creating a query using the Properties and Agents tables from the Property database. The Properties table contains all the properties the investors will evaluate; the Agents table contains a list of real estate agents who represent the properties' sellers. In this exercise, you will add requested fields and only show properties that have not been sold. You will then build an expression to calculate the price per square foot for each property. Refer to Figure 3.11 as you complete Step 1.

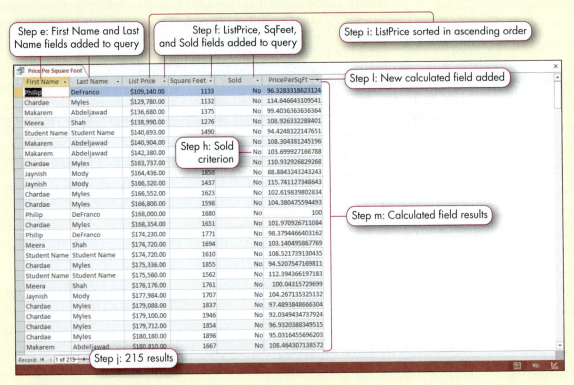

FIGURE 3.11 Modified Expression

a. Open *a03h1Property*. Save the database as **a03h1Property_LastFirst**.

> **TROUBLESHOOTING:** If you make any major mistakes in this exercise, you can close the file, open *a03h1Property* again, and then start this exercise over.

b. Open the Agents table and replace the name *Student Name* with your name. Close the table.

c. Click the **Create tab** and click **Query Design** in the Queries group to create a new query.

The Show Table dialog box opens so you can specify the table(s) and/or queries to include in the query design.

d. Select the **Agents table** and click **Add**. Select the **Properties table** and click **Add**. Click **Close** to close the Show Table dialog box.

e. Double-click the **FirstName** and **LastName fields** in the Agents table to add them to the query.

f. Double-click the **ListPrice**, **SqFeet**, and **Sold fields** in the Properties table to add them to the query.

g. Click **Run** in the Results group to display the results in Datasheet view.

A total of 303 properties display in the results.

h. Switch to Design view. Type **No** in the Criteria row of the Sold field.

> **TROUBLESHOOTING:** As you begin typing *No* the designer will popup a suggestion of "Now()." Press Esc to close the dialog box.

i. Click the **Sort row** in the ListPrice field. Click the **arrow** and select **Ascending**.

j. Click **Run** in the Results group to display the results.

The 215 unsold properties display in the datasheet, with the least expensive houses displayed first.

k. Click **Save** on the Quick Access Toolbar and type **Price Per Square Foot** as the Query Name in the Save As dialog box. Click **OK**.

l. Switch to Design view. Click the **Field row** of the first blank column of the query design grid. Right-click and select **Zoom** to show the Zoom box. Type **PricePerSqFt: ListPrice/SqFeet** and click **OK**.

Access inserts square brackets around the fields for you. The new field divides the values in the ListPrice field by the values in the SqFeet field.

m. Click **Run** in the Results group to view the results. Adjust column widths as necessary.

The new calculated field, PricePerSqFt, is displayed. Compare your results to those shown in Figure 3.11.

> **TROUBLESHOOTING:** If you see pound signs (#####) in an Access column, double-click the vertical line between column headings to increase the width.

> **TROUBLESHOOTING:** If, when you run the query, you are prompted for a parameter value, cancel and return to Design view. Ensure that you have entered the correct spelling for the field name from Step l in the first row of a blank column.

n. Save the changes to the query.

Don and Matt want the calculated field formatted with two decimal places. You will change the format to Currency and add a caption to the calculated field. Refer to Figure 3.12 as you complete Step 2.

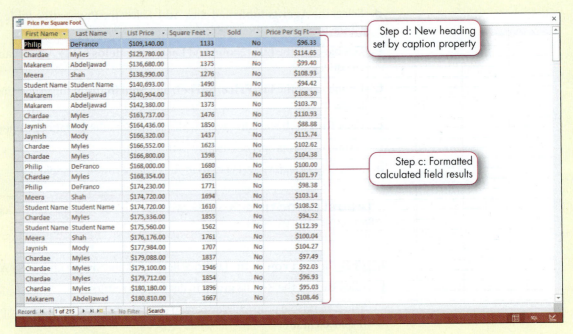

FIGURE 3.12 Formatted Field

a. Ensure the Price Per Square Foot query is open in Design view.

b. Click the **PricePerSqFt calculated field cell**. Click **Property Sheet** in the Show/Hide group on the Design tab.

The Property Sheet displays.

c. Click the **Format property**. Click the **Format property arrow** and select **Currency**.

d. Click the **Caption property** and type **Price Per Sq Ft**. (Do not include the period.) Press **Enter**. Close the Property Sheet.

e. Click **Run** to view your changes.

The calculated field values are formatted as Currency, and the column heading displays Price Per Sq Ft instead of PricePerSqFt.

f. Compare your result to Figure 3.12. Save the changes to the query.

A few errors arise as you test a new calculated field. You check the spelling of the field names in the calculated fields because that is a common mistake. You decide to verify your data prior to showing it to the investors. You use the estimation method to check your calculations. Refer to Figure 3.13 as you complete Step 3.

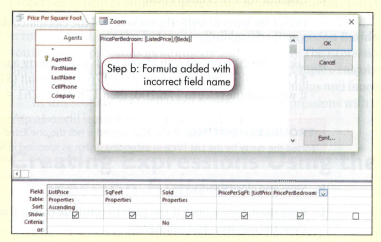

FIGURE 3.13 Incorrect Expression

a. Switch to Design view of the Price Per Square Foot query. Scroll to the first blank column of the query design grid and click the **Field row**.

b. Right-click and select **Zoom** to display the Zoom box. Type **PricePerBedroom: [ListedPrice]/[Beds]**. Your formula should match Figure 3.13. Click **OK** in the Zoom dialog box.

You are intentionally misspelling the field name for the ListPrice (as ListedPrice which does not exist as a field in the database) to see how Access will respond.

c. Click **Property Sheet** in the Show/Hide group of the Design tab. Click the **Format property**. From the menu, select **Currency**. Click the **Caption box** and type **Price Per Bedroom**. Press **Enter**. Close the Property Sheet.

d. Click **Run** in the Results group.

You should see the Enter Parameter Value dialog box. Access does not recognize ListedPrice in the tables defined for this query in the first record. When Access does not recognize a field name, it will ask you to supply a value.

e. Type **100000** in the first parameter box. Press **Enter**.

The query has the necessary information to run and returns the results in Datasheet view.

f. Examine the results of the calculation for Price Per Bedroom.

All the records display 50000 because you entered the value 100000 into the parameter box. Because Access could not recognize the field name and use individual values for the field, to run the query, you supplied the constant value 100000, which Access used for the calculation in each record. The value was treated as a constant and gave the same results for all records.

g. Return to Design view. Display the Zoom box. Change the formula to **PricePerBedroom: [ListPrice]/[Beds]**. Click **OK**.

You corrected the error in the field name, ListPrice.

To add conditions to an existing totals query, complete the following steps:

1. Double-click the field you want to limit by to add it to the design grid. The location of this field is not important, as it will not be displayed.
2. Select Where from the menu in the Total row.
3. Enter the condition.
4. Run the query.

Figure 3.28 shows a query with a condition added, and Figure 3.29 shows the results. In Figure 3.28, the Yes condition was added to the Sold field to so only Properties that were sold are added to the Aggregate query. Compare this to Figure 3.27 to see the change in results.

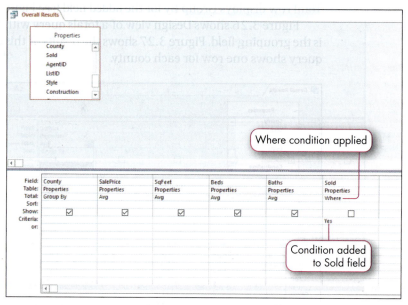

FIGURE 3.28 Totals Query with Condition Design View

County	AvgOfSalePrice	AvgOfSqFeet	AvgOfBeds	AvgOfBaths
Bergen	$220,431.12	2223.11764705882	3.29411764705882	1.73529411764706
Essex	$284,091.38	2829.53846153846	3.96153846153846	1.94230769230769
Hudson	$243,285.50	2432.25	3	1.75
Mercer	$341,085.67	3440.55555555556	4.55555555555556	2
Morris	$322,404.05	3233.42857142857	4.33333333333333	1.9047619047619
Passaic	$219,325.20	2171.4	2.8	1.8
Sussex	$269,411.17	2610	3.83333333333333	2

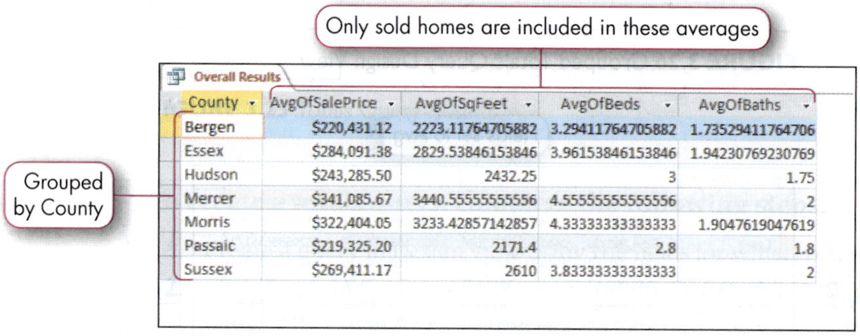

FIGURE 3.29 Totals Query with Condition Results

TIP: MULTIPLE GROUPING LEVELS

At times, you may want to add multiple grouping fields. For example, instead of grouping by state, you might want to group by city. However, if you group by city, customers with the same city name in different states would be grouped together. For example, all 50 states have a location named Greenville. If you grouped by city, all customers with a city of Greenville, regardless of state, would appear as a group. This is probably not your intent. Instead, you probably would want to see results by city and state and, thus would want to add both fields to a query and select Group By.

Calculated fields can also have aggregate functions applied to them. For example, you may want to calculate mortgage payments and see the average of your calculation (see Figure 3.30). The results of the query will resemble Figure 3.31. Note that you can also use any of the other methods shown earlier, so you can add grouping (as shown in the figures below) and format the field as required.

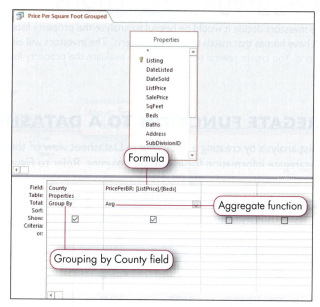

FIGURE 3.30 Adding Calculated Field to Totals Query

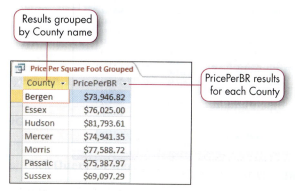

FIGURE 3.31 Calculated Field Results

7. Discuss the purpose of using aggregate functions. *p. 708*

8. Explain when you would use a Total row and when you would use a totals query. *p. 708*

9. Explain what is meant by a query that is "grouped by" state. *p. 711*

Create Basic Forms to Simplify Data Management

Most Access database applications use forms rather than tables for data entry and for viewing information. A *form* is a database object used to view, add, or edit data in a table. Three main reasons exist for using forms rather than tables for working with data:

- You are less likely to edit the wrong record by mistake, which is easy to do in a large table containing many records.
- You can create a form that displays data from more than one table simultaneously.
- You can create customized Access forms to resemble the paper (or other types of) forms that users employ in their data entry processes.

When you are adding or editing data using a table with many records, you may select and edit the wrong record accidentally. A form is less likely to allow this type of error because many form types restrict entry to one record at a time. This enables you to focus on working with a single record rather than viewing many records at the same time.

Some forms require more than one table as their basis. For example, you may want to view a customer's details (name, address, email, phone, etc.) as well as all the orders the customer placed at the same time. This would require using data from both the Customers and the Orders tables (when there is a relationship set between them) in one form. Such a form enables a user to view two sources at the same time and make changes—additions, edits, or deletions—to one or both sources of data. When a change is made in the form, the data in the underlying table (or tables) are affected. A form is really a mirror image of the data in the tables and simply presents a user-friendly interface for users of the database.

Access forms can be designed to emulate the paper documents already used by an organization. When paper forms are currently used to collect data, it is a good idea to customize the electronic forms to resemble the paper forms. This will make the data entry process more efficient and ease the transition from paper to electronic form.

In this section, you will learn the basics of form design. You will discover multiple methods to create and modify Access forms.

STEP 1 Creating Forms Using Form Tools

Access provides a variety of options for creating forms. You will eventually develop a preference for one or two types of form layouts, but keep in mind that you have a good variety of options, if needed. You will want your forms to balance ease of use with the power to be effective.

Access provides 14 different tools for creating forms. You can find these options in the Forms group on the Create tab. The Forms group contains four of the most common form tools (Form, Form Design, Blank Form, and Form Wizard), a list of Navigation forms, and More Forms. The Navigation list provides six templates to create a user interface for a database; the More Forms list provides four additional form tools (Multiple Items, Datasheet, Split Form, and Modal Dialog).

A list of many of the Form tools available in Access is found in Table 4.1. Some tools will not be covered in detail, because they are not commonly used or because they are beyond the scope of this chapter (for example, Form Design, Blank Form, and Modal Dialog Form). Use Microsoft Access Help to find more information about Form tools that are not covered in this chapter.

TABLE 4.1	Form Tools in Access
Form Tool	**Use**
Form	Creates a form with a stacked layout that displays all the fields in the record source.
Form Design	Creates a new blank form in Design view.
Blank Form	Creates a new blank form in Layout view.
Form Wizard	Creates a custom form based on your answers to a series of step-by-step questions.
Navigation	Creates handy user-interface forms that enable users to switch between various forms and reports in a database. Six different Navigation form layouts are available from the list.
Split Form	Creates a two-part form with a stacked layout in one section and a tabular layout in the other.
Multiple Items	Creates a tabular layout form that includes all the fields from the record source.
Datasheet	Creates a form that resembles the datasheet of a table or query.
Modal Dialog	Creates a custom dialog box that requires user input that is needed for a database object.

> **TIP: USABILITY TESTING**
> After a database object (such as a form) is finalized, it should be tested by both the database designer and the end users. The designer should be certain that the form meets any requirements the users have given him or her. The designer should also browse through the records to make sure the values in all records (and not just the first record) display correctly. After testing is completed by both the designer and end users, the form should be modified and tested again before it is deployed with the database.

Ideally, a form should simplify data entry and editing. Creating a form is a collaborative process between the database designer and the end users. This process continues throughout the life of the form because the data management needs of an organization may change over time. Forms designed long ago to collect data for a new customer account may not include an email or a website field; both the customer table and its associated form would have to be modified to include these fields. The designer needs to strike a balance between collecting the data required for use by the database and cluttering the form with extraneous fields. The database users generally offer good opinions about which fields should be on a form and how the form should behave. If you listen to their suggestions, your forms will function more effectively, the users' work will be easier, and the data will contain fewer data-entry errors.

Similar to designing a table, you can make a sketch in advance to determine which fields are required in a form and what the order of the fields should be. Your form design should be approved by the client or users for whom you are building it before actual development begins.

Identify a Record Source

Before you create a form, you must identify the record source. A **record source** (or data source) is the table or query that supplies the records for a form or report. Use a table if you want to include all the records from a single table. Create a query first and use it as the record source if you want to filter the records in the source table, combine records from two or more related tables, or if you do not want to display all fields from the table(s) on your form. For example, if you want to create a form that displays customers from a single state only, you should base the form on a query.

may end up with hundreds of pages of printouts. A form with a stacked layout and 1,000 records could print thousands of pages unless you select the Selected Record(s) option in the Print dialog box. The Selected Record(s) option, as shown in Figure 4.11, will only print the current record (or selected records).

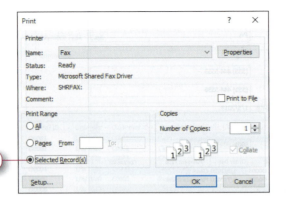

Selected Record(s) option

FIGURE 4.11 Print Selected Records Using a Form

TIP: POSITION A FORM WHEN PRINTING
If it becomes necessary to print a form, you can set the page margins to position the form on the printed sheet. To set the page margins, click the File tab, click Print, and then click Print Preview. Click Margins in the Page Size group of the Print Preview tab, and then select one of the predefined margin settings.

Modifying Forms

As previously mentioned, Access provides different views for a form; most forms display Layout, Form, and Design views. As you work with the form tools to create and modify forms, you will need to switch between the three form views in Access. Much of your design work can be done in Layout view; sometimes, you will need to switch to Design view to use a more advanced feature, such as changing the order of the fields as you press Tab to move from one to the next, or to use an option that is otherwise unavailable. Users of the form will typically only work in Form view; there is little reason for a user to switch to Layout or Design view, and these views can be disabled by the database designer to protect the integrity of the form. Modifications to the form should ideally be done only by a designated designer.

STEP 2 ▸ Edit Data in Form View

Use Form view to add, edit, and delete data in a form; the layout and design of the form cannot be changed in this view. The Navigation bar at the bottom of the form displays buttons to move between records, and you can click the New (blank) record button to add a new record. You can move from one field to another field by pressing Tab or clicking a field. Form view provides tools like those in Datasheet view of a table for finding, sorting, and filtering records. Using the Find command is a convenient way of locating a specific record when the record needs to be viewed, modified, or deleted.

STEP 3 ▸ Use Layout View to Modify Form Design

Use Layout view to modify the form design while viewing the data. The data are not editable in this view. You use Layout view to add or delete fields in a form, change the order of fields, modify field or form properties (such as which views are available), change the widths of controls, and enhance a form by adding a theme or styling. Reviewing the data in Layout view makes it easier to move and size controls and to ensure that all data are visible in Form view. You can move controls in Layout view by dragging and dropping them into a new location. It is good practice to toggle back and forth between Layout view and Form view when making changes to the form's design.

Forms have a good number of options that you can use in your design process. In Layout view, under the Form Layout Tools tab, you have access to three contextual tabs on the ribbon that provide a number of tools for modifying forms as follows:

- Design tab: To make changes to the design of the form, such as applying themes, inserting headers and footers, and additional controls.
- Arrange tab: To change the layout of a form, to move fields up or down, or to control margins.
- Format tab: To work with different fonts, font sizes, and colors; to add or remove bolding, italics, or underlining; to adjust text alignment; or to add a background image.

Similarly, in Design view, the Form Design Tools tabs are available (Design, Arrange, and Format) with many of the same options you will find in Layout view.

Adjust Column Widths in a Form

When column widths are adjusted in a form with a stacked layout, all field sizes will increase and decrease in size together. Therefore, it is best to make sure that the columns are wide enough to accommodate the widest value in each field. For example, if a form contains information such as a customer's first name, last name, address, city, state, ZIP, phone, and email address, you will need to make sure the longest address and the longest email address are completely visible (because those fields are likely to contain the longest data values). To increase or decrease column widths in a form with a stacked layout, display the form in (Stacked) Layout view and click the text box control of the first field to select it. Point to the right border of the control until the pointer turns into a double-headed arrow. Drag the right edge of the control to the left or right until you arrive at the required width.

You will notice that all field sizes change as you change the width of the first field. All fields that are included in the layout will have a standard width. If you want to resize one specific field, remove that field from the layout control. Select the field and the label to be removed, right-click, click Layout, and then select Remove Layout. If you remove a field from the layout control, it stays on the form but can be moved and resized more freely.

It is also possible to resize form fields by setting a specific width or height using the Property sheet. In Layout view or Design view of the form, select Property Sheet in the Tools group on the Design tab. Use the Width and Height boxes to set specific values by typing them.

Add and Delete Form Fields

There will be instances when you will want to add or delete form fields. At times, new fields may be added to tables and then incorporated into forms. At other times, you may decide that while a field is present in a table, it is not necessary to display it to users in a form.

To add a field to a form, complete the following steps:

1. Display the form in (Stacked) Layout view and click Add Existing Fields in the Tools group on the Design tab. In the Field List pane, you will see a list of fields from the table (record source), as shown in Figure 4.12. For a multiple-table form, click the plus sign (+) to the left of the appropriate table to expand it and locate the desired field(s).
2. Click and drag the desired field to the precise location on the form, using the shaded line as a guide for positioning the new field. Alternatively, double-click a field to add it to the form; the field will be added below the selected field. The other fields will automatically adjust to make room for the new field.

1. Switch to Design view (the Remove Layout option on the ribbon is only available in Design view) and click any one of the controls that is currently part of the layout.
2. Click Select Layout in the Rows & Columns group on the Arrange tab.
3. Click Remove Layout in the Table group.
4. Switch to Layout view. Drag and drop the control(s) to a different location on the form.

The Rows & Columns group also contains commands that enable you to insert rows and columns in a form's layout. In a form with a stacked layout, you may want to separate some controls from the rest of the fields or create some empty space so that fields can be added or repositioned. For example, you can select a control and click Insert Below. This will create an empty row (or space) below the selected control. This group also contains the Select Layout, Select Column, and Select Row commands, which you can use to select the entire layout or a single column or row in a layout. In Figure 4.14, three empty rows have been inserted above the Cost field.

FIGURE 4.14 Rows Inserted in a Form Layout

TIP: APPLY A BACKGROUND IMAGE TO A FORM

To apply a background image to a form, open the form in Layout or Design view, and then click Background Image in the Background group on the Format tab. Next, click Browse to locate the image you want to apply to the form. Once the image has been applied to the form, you can change the properties of the image so that the image displays correctly. You can use the same technique to add a background image to a report.

Sorting Records in a Form

When a form is created using a Form tool, the sort order of the records in the form is initially dependent on the sort order of the record source—the underlying table or query. Tables are usually sorted by the primary key, whereas queries can be sorted in a variety of ways. No matter how the records are initially sorted, you can modify the sort order in a form so that it is different from the sort order of the underlying table or query. The sort options for a form are shown in Figure 4.15.

FIGURE 4.15 Adding and Removing Sort Order

You can easily sort on a single field, in ascending or descending order. Open the form in Form view and select the field by which you want to sort. Click Ascending or Descending in the Sort & Filter group on the Home tab.

If you want to sort on multiple fields, you would create a query with a more advanced sort order, and base the form on the query. For example, you might want to sort your records first by a state name, and within each group of state records, sort them by city. Open the query in Design view, add the sort settings you want, save the query, and then use the query as the record source of the form. To remove the sort order in a form, open the form in Form view, and then click Remove Sort in the Sort & Filter group on the Home tab.

Quick Concepts

1. Explain how a form simplifies data entry (when compared to entering data into a table). ***p. 732***

2. Discuss the benefit of creating a Navigation form for users of a database. ***p. 738***

3. Consider how to determine the record source of a form. ***p. 733***

4. Explain the advantage of creating a form with a subform. ***p. 737***

5. Discuss the best strategy for creating a form that sorts by more than one field. ***p. 745***

f. Save the form as **Revenue by Order Item**. Close the form.

g. Open the **Sales Reps form** in Layout view. Notice that the form is not attractively organized.

h. Click **Select All** in the Selection group on the Format tab (alternatively press Ctrl+A).

All 14 controls are selected in the form.

i. Click **Tabular** in the Table group on the Arrange tab.

The controls are lined up horizontally across the top of the form.

j. Click **Stacked** in the Table group on the Arrange tab.

The controls are lined up vertically and the form is much easier to read.

k. Click the first **Sales Rep ID text box** and click the **Format tab**. Click **Shape Fill** in the Control Formatting group. Select **Blue, Accent 1, Lighter 60%** under Theme Colors.

l. Switch to Form view. Save and close the form.

m. Open the **Customer Information form** in Form view. Click **Next record** in the Navigation bar at the bottom several times to advance through the records.

Note that the customers are in Customer ID order.

n. Click **First record** in the Navigation bar to return to the customer *McAfee, Rand, & Karahalis*.

o. Click in the **Customer Name text box** and click **Ascending** in the Sort & Filter group on the Home tab.

Advantage Sales displays (Customer ID C0003) because it is the first customer name in alphabetical order, as shown in Figure 4.19.

p. Click **Next record** in the Navigation bar at the bottom of the form to advance through the records.

The records are now in Customer Name order, whereas in the original Customers table, they are sorted by the primary key field, CustomerID.

q. Save and close the Customer Information form.

r. Keep the database open if you plan to continue with the next Hands-On Exercise. If not, close the database, and exit Access.

Create Basic Reports to Present Information

By now, you know how to plan a database, create tables, establish relationships between tables, enter data into tables, and extract data using queries. In the previous section of this chapter, you learned how to create and modify several types of data-entry forms. Next, you will learn how to create professional reports using the report-generating tools in Access.

A *report* is a document that displays meaningful information from a database to its users. Access reports can be printed, viewed onscreen, or even saved as files, such as Word documents. A report is designed for output of information only based on data from tables or queries in your database (record sources); you cannot use reports to change data in your database.

The following are all examples of reports that might be created in Access:

- A contacts list sorted by last name and then by first name
- A customer report grouped by orders for each customer
- An employee list grouped by department
- A monthly statement from a bank
- A transcript of a student and his/her grades
- A set of mailing labels

Reports are used to help the reader understand and analyze information. For example, in a report you can group the customers together for each sales rep and highlight the customers who have not placed an order in six months. This is an example of using a list of customers from the Customers table together with sales rep data in the database as an effective business analysis tool. To increase business, the sales reps could contact their customers who have not ordered in the past six months and review the findings with the sales manager. A sales report could be run each month to see if the strategy has helped to produce any new business.

Before you create a report in Access, you should consider the following questions:

- What is the purpose of the report?
- Who will use the report?
- Which tables, queries, and fields are needed for the report?
- How will the report be distributed? Will users view the report directly from the Access database, or will they receive it through email, fax, or the Internet?
- Will the results be converted to Word, Excel, HTML, or another format?

In the Forms section of this chapter, you learned that it is helpful to talk to users and design a form before you begin to create it in Access. The same applies to creating an Access report. Users can give you solid input and creating a design in advance of working in Access will help you determine which report tool to use to create the report. Interview end users of a report (employer, customer, organization for whom you are creating the report) to determine which records and fields need to be included as well as any formatting or readability concerns they may have. Once you agree on the basic format of the report, you can begin to consider how to handle the execution of it in Access.

The next step in planning your report is to create or identify an optimal record source. You may use one or more tables, queries, or a combination of tables and queries as the report's record source. Sometimes, a single table contains all the records you need for the report. Other times, you will incorporate several tables. When data from multiple related tables are needed to create a report, you can first create a single query (with criteria, if necessary) and then base the report on that query. Multiple tables used in a query must be related, as indicated with join lines. Make sure that whatever record source you decide to use, you will be able to access all the data required for the report.

Reports can contain text and numeric data as well as formatting, calculated fields, graphics, and so forth. For example, you can add a company logo to the report header. Be sure that you have appropriate permission to use any company logo, graphic, or photo in your reports to avoid inappropriate or illegal use of an asset.

In this section, you will create reports in Access by first identifying a record source, then designing the report, and finally choosing a Report tool. You will learn how to modify a report by adding and deleting fields, resizing columns, and sorting records. You will also learn about the report sections, the report views, and controls on reports.

STEP 1 Creating Reports Using Report Tools

Access provides five different report tools for creating reports. The report tools are located on the Create tab in the Reports group, as shown in Figure 4.20. The most common of the tools, the Report tool, is used to instantly create a tabular report based on a selected table or query. Table 4.3 provides a summary of the five report tools and their usages. Once you create a report using one of the report tools, you can perform modifications in either Layout view or Design view.

FIGURE 4.20 Reports Group on the Create Tab

TABLE 4.3	Report Tools and Their Usages
Report Tool	**Usage**
Report	Create a tabular report that displays all the fields in the selected record source (table or query).
Report Design	Create a new blank report in Design view. Add fields and controls manually. This tool is used by advanced users who want to create a report from scratch with no help from Access.
Blank Report	Create a new blank report in Layout view. Drag and drop to add fields and controls manually.
Report Wizard	Answer a series of step-by-step questions, and Access will design a custom report for you.
Labels	Select a preformatted label template and create printable labels.

Use the Report Tool

The easiest way to create a report is with the Report tool. The **Report tool** is used to create a tabular report based on the selected table or query. Select a table or query in the Navigation Pane and click Report in the Reports group on the Create tab.

Access creates a tabular layout report instantly. Notice that this type of report displays data horizontally in columns across the page, as shown in Figure 4.21.

FIGURE 4.21 Tabular Report Created with the Report Tool

If you prefer, you can display a report using a stacked layout, which displays fields in a vertical column. This type of report is less common because it would result in longer printouts. The number of pages depends on the number of records in the record source.

Use the Report Wizard

The **Report Wizard** prompts you for input in a series of steps to generate a customized report. The wizard enables you to make certain customizations quickly and easily without having to be an expert in report design.

Select the report's record source (table or query) in the Navigation Pane and click Report Wizard in the Reports group on the Create tab. The wizard opens with the selected table or query (the record source) displayed in the first dialog box. Click the Tables/Queries list arrow to display a list of available tables or queries, if you want to choose a different record source. Select the fields you want to include in the report. You can select an available field and click ⟩ to add a single field to the Selected Fields list, ⟩⟩ to select all fields, ⟨ to remove a field, and ⟨⟨ to remove all fields from the report (see Figure 4.22). Set the fields, then advance to the next screen.

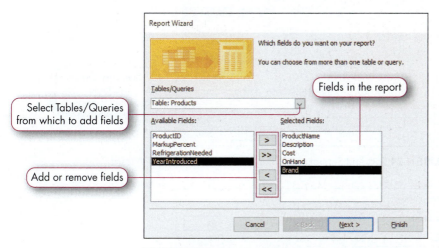

FIGURE 4.22 Selecting Fields in the Report Wizard

Apply the grouping levels, as shown in Figure 4.23. Grouping enables you to organize and summarize the data in a report, based on values in a field. For example, you can group products by their brand name and average the cost of products in each group. To group records in a report, select the field you want to group by and click Add One Field ⟩ to add the new group. If you need a second or third grouping level, add those field names in order. The order in which you select the groups determines the order of display in the report. In Figure 4.23, the products are grouped by the Brand field. Once you have selected the appropriate options, advance to the next step. For a basic report, you would not select any grouping fields and instead just skip this screen.

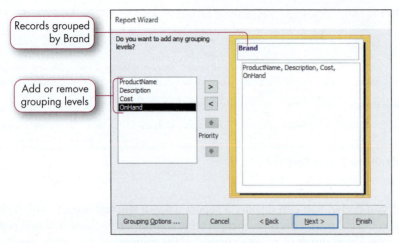

Records grouped by Brand

Add or remove grouping levels

FIGURE 4.23 Grouping Options in the Report Wizard

Apply the sorting and summary options in the next dialog box. Figure 4.24 displays the sort options for a grouped report. You can click Summary Options if you want to apply aggregating functions (e.g., Sum, Average, Minimum, and Maximum) and to specify whether you want to see detailed records on the report or only the aggregated results (see Figure 4.25). You can also choose to calculate values as percentages of totals in your report results. If no grouping is specified in your report, the summary options are not available. In Figure 4.25, no summary options are selected. Click OK to return to the Report Wizard.

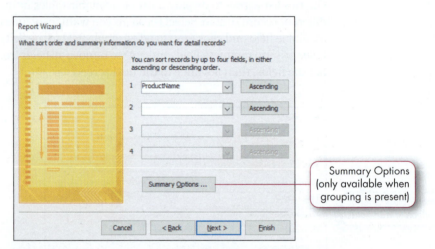

Summary Options (only available when grouping is present)

FIGURE 4.24 Sort and Summarize Grouped Data in the Report Wizard

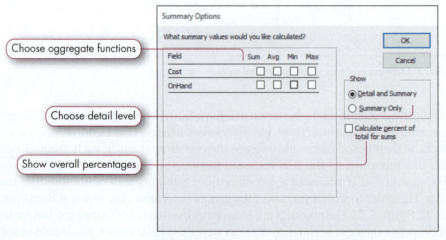

Choose aggregate functions

Choose detail level

Show overall percentages

FIGURE 4.25 Summary Options Dialog Box

In the next dialog box, select the layout as shown in Figure 4.26, to determine the report's appearance. In a grouped report, you will be prompted to select the layout from three options:

- Stepped Layout will display column headings at the top of the page and keep the grouping field(s) in their own row.
- Block Layout will include the grouping field(s) in line with the data, saving some space when printing. It has one set of column headings at the top of each page.
- Outline Layout will display the grouping field(s) on their own separate rows and has column headings inside each group. This leads to a longer report when printing but may help make the report easier to read.

Clicking any of these layouts will give you a general preview in the preview area. In a report without grouping, the layouts are Columnar, Tabular, and Justified. You can determine how the data fit on a page by selecting Portrait or Landscape.

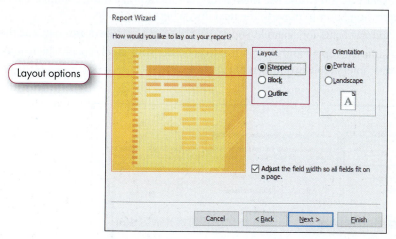

FIGURE 4.26 Layout Options for Grouped Data in the Report Wizard

Finish the wizard by giving the report a name. Your grouped report will resemble Figure 4.27.

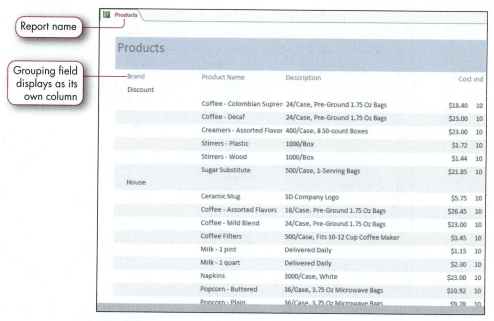

FIGURE 4.27 Grouped Report

Use the Label Wizard

The *Label Wizard* enables you to easily create mailing labels, name tags, and other specialized tags. A mailing label report is a specialized report that you can create and print with name-brand labels, such as Avery and many others. If you purchase a store brand label from an office supply store, it will generally state the comparable manufacturer and product number; the wizard provides a long list of both manufacturers and label sizes.

To use the Label Wizard, complete the following steps:

1. Select the table or query that you will use as the record source for the report.
2. Click Labels in the Reports group on the Create tab.
3. Select the manufacturer, product number, unit of measure, label type, and then click Next.
4. Select the font and color options and click Next.
5. Add the fields to the prototype label, as shown in Figure 4.28. You add the fields exactly as you would like them to display, including adding commas, spacing, and pressing Enter to move to the next line, where applicable.
6. Add sort fields, for example, you may want to sort by state or zip code, and then click Next.
7. Name the report and click Finish to generate your label report. The results using the Customers table are shown in Figure 4.29.

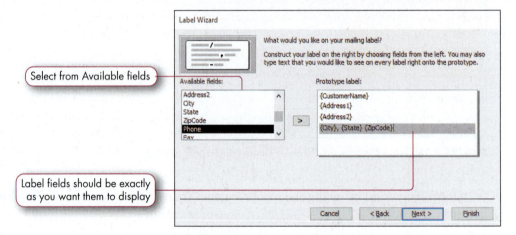

Select from Available fields

Label fields should be exactly as you want them to display

FIGURE 4.28 Create a Customers Prototype Label

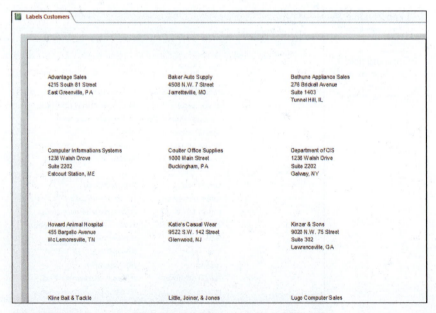

FIGURE 4.29 Customer Mailing Labels Created by Label Wizard

Using Report Views

As you work with the report tools to create and modify reports, you might need to switch between the four report views in Access—Report, Layout, Design, and Print Preview. Report view and Print Preview are generally used only for viewing or printing the report. To make modifications to a report, use Layout view and Design view. Most of the design work can be done in Layout view, but sometimes Design view is necessary to apply a more advanced feature, such as setting the tab order of the controls. Click the View arrow in the Views group and select the view to switch between the four views (alternatively, right-click the report tab and select the desired view from the shortcut menu).

View a Report in Report View

Report view enables you to view a report onscreen in a continuous page layout. However, because the data cannot be changed in Report view, it is simply a way of viewing the information without having to worry about accidentally moving a control. You can also use Report view to filter data if you only want to view a selected group of records.

STEP 2 Use Print Preview and Export a Report

Print Preview enables you to see exactly what the report will look like when it is printed. You cannot modify the design of the report or the data in Print Preview. By default, Print Preview will display all the pages in the report. Figure 4.29 displays the mailing labels report in Print Preview.

From Print Preview, you have the option to export and save the report to a different file type, such as Word. This is a useful option if you plan to share a report electronically but do not want to distribute the entire database. Alternatively, you can share a report with an individual or group who does not have Access installed on their computer or is not conversant with Access. In the Data group, on the Print Preview tab, you will find several eligible file types, as shown in Figure 4.30. Select the option in the Data group and follow the onscreen prompts to export your report. Commonly used formats include Excel, Word, and Portable Document Format (PDF).

Portable Document Format (PDF) is a file type that was created for exchanging documents independently of software applications and operating system environments. In other words, you can email a report in PDF format to users running various operating systems, and they can open it even if they do not have Microsoft Access installed. PDF files open in Adobe Reader, a free downloadable program; recent versions of Windows have a Reader program that displays PDF files as well. The Reader app can be downloaded from the Microsoft store for free if it is not installed on your system.

Because databases contain a great deal of information, Access reports can become very long, requiring many pages to print. At times, reports can be formatted incorrectly, or blank pages might print in between each page of information. Be sure to troubleshoot your reports before sending them to the printer, or to recipients via email.

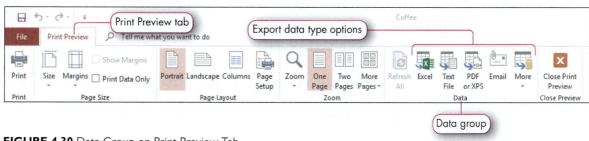

FIGURE 4.30 Data Group on Print Preview Tab

Use Layout View to Modify a Report

Use Layout view to modify the report's design while still viewing the data. You should use Layout view to add or delete fields in the report, modify field properties, change the column widths, group, sort, and summarize data. The Page Setup tab presents options for setting the page size, orientation, and margins. Although you will be able to view your modifications along with the data in Layout view, you will still need to check the report in Print Preview to evaluate all the changes before printing it.

STEP 3 Modifying a Report

After you create a report by using one of the report tools, you may want to modify it. Some of the common changes you make in reports are adding and deleting controls, changing the arrangement, widths, and formatting of controls, and modifying the title. From either Layout or Design view, there are four tabs available for report modification:

- Design: Use this tab to make changes to the design of the report, such as adding fields, grouping and sorting records, changing themes, and inserting additional controls.
- Arrange: Use this tab to change the layout of a report, to move fields up and down, and to control margins and spacing.
- Format: Use this tab to work with fonts, font sizes, and colors; add or remove bolding, italics, or underlining; adjust text alignment; or add a background image or color.
- Page Setup: Use this tab to change paper size, margins, or page orientation or to format reports into multiple columns.

Change the Report Layout

When you use one of the report tools to create a new report, Access will add a layout control to help align the fields. Layout controls in reports work similarly to layout controls in forms. The layout control provides guides to help keep controls aligned horizontally and vertically and give your report a neat appearance. The Arrange tab displays in both Layout view and Design view and contains commands for working with the layout of a report. Some key commands on the Arrange tab from Layout view are highlighted in Figure 4.31.

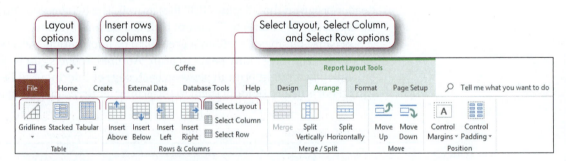

FIGURE 4.31 Report Layout Tools Arrange Tab

The Table group contains commands that enable you to add gridlines to a report's layout and to change a report's layout from stacked to tabular (and vice versa). The Remove Layout command is available in Design view only.

The Rows & Columns group contains commands that enable you to insert rows and columns inside a report's layout. In a report with a stacked layout, you may want to separate some controls from the rest of the fields or create some empty space so that fields can be added or repositioned. For example, you can select a control and click Insert Below. This will create an empty row (or space) below the selected control. This group also contains the Select Layout, Select Column, and Select Row commands, which you can use to select the entire layout, or a single column or row in a layout.

The Merge/Split group contains commands that enable you to merge and split the controls on a report. There are times when you might want to deviate from the basic row and column formats that the report tools create. For example, you can make a label such as *Product Name* display in two controls (Product and Name), with one positioned below the other rather than in one single control.

The Move group contains commands to move a field up or down in a stacked layout. Moving controls up or down in a report may cause unexpected results; you can always click Undo if you need to reverse your changes.

The Position group contains commands to control the margins and the padding (the spacing between controls) in a report. The preset margin settings are convenient to use; make sure that if you change the margins, you preview the report to view the result.

Remove a Report Layout Control

If you want to have more control over the location of the fields, you can remove the layout control and position the controls manually on the report.

You can add a layout control to a report by first selecting all the controls you want to include in the layout. To select multiple controls, click the first control, press and hold Ctrl, and then click the additional controls you want to include. Press Ctrl+A to select all the controls on a form. Click Tabular or Stacked in the Table group.

Modify Report Controls

The Format tab contains a series of commands that enable you to change the font, display, and alignment of the controls on a report, as shown in Figure 4.32. The formatting tools in Access are like those in other Microsoft Office applications. To format report controls, open the report in Layout view (or Design view) and select the control(s) you want to format. Click the Format tab and click the formatting tools as desired.

To change the sorting in a report, complete the following steps:

1. Open the report in Layout or Design view and click Group & Sort in the Grouping & Totals group on the Design tab.

2. Click *Add a sort* and select the field by which you want to sort. The default sort order is ascending.

3. Add another sort by clicking *Add a sort* again. For example, you could sort first by Brand and then by ProductName, as shown in Figure 4.34.

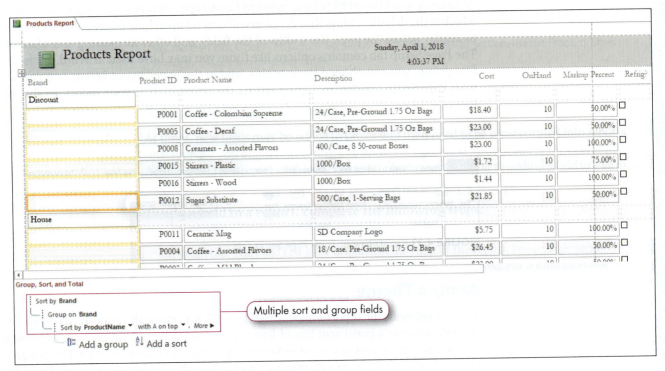

FIGURE 4.34 Report in Layout View with Two Sort Fields

Quick Concepts

6. Discuss the difference between Report view and Print Preview. **p. 759**

7. Explain why it is beneficial to save a report in the PDF format. **p. 759**

8. Consider the advantage of viewing your reports in Layout view. **p. 760**

9. Discuss an example for which you would remove a report layout control while modifying a report. **p. 760**

10. Describe how sorting records in a report can be helpful. **p. 763**

Hands-On Exercises

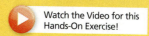
Skills covered: Use the Report Tool • Use the Report Wizard • Use Print Preview • Export a Report • Add a Field to a Report • Remove a Field from a Report • Adjust Column Widths in a Report • Change Orientation • Apply a Theme • Sort and Group Records in a Report

2 Create Basic Reports to Present Information

You create a products report using the Access Report tool to help Ryung stay on top of the key information for her business. You will modify the column widths so that they all fit across one page. You will also use the Report Wizard to create additional reports that Ryung requires.

STEP 1 CREATING REPORTS USING REPORT TOOLS

You use the Report tool to create an Access report to help Ryung manage her product information. This report is especially useful for determining which products she needs to order to fill upcoming orders. You also use the Report Wizard to determine sales by city. Refer to Figure 4.35 as you complete Step 1.

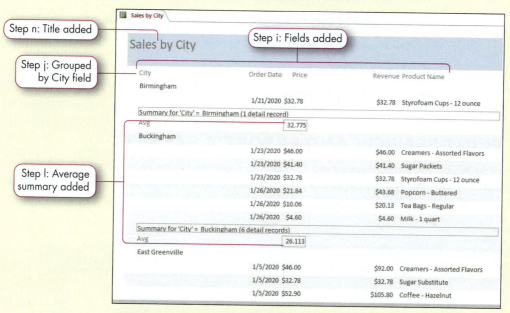

FIGURE 4.35 Sales by City Report

a. Open *a04h1Coffee_LastFirst* if you closed it at the end of Hands-On Exercise 1 and save it as **a04h2Coffee_LastFirst**, changing h1 to h2.

b. Select the **Products table** in the Navigation Pane. Click the **Create tab** and click **Report** in the Reports group.

   Access creates a new tabular layout report based on the Products table. The report opens in Layout view, ready for editing.

c. Click the **Products title** at the top of the report to select it, click again on **Products**, and then change the title to **Products Report**. Press **Enter** to accept the change.

d. Right-click the **Products report tab** and select **Print Preview**.

   The report is too wide for the page; you will close Print Preview and change the orientation to Landscape.

e. Click **Close Print Preview** in the Close Preview group to return to Layout view.

f. Click the **Page Setup tab** and click **Landscape** in the Page Layout group.

   The report changes to Landscape orientation. Most of the columns now fit across one page. You will make further revisions to the report later so that it fits on one page.

g. Save the report as **Products Report**. Close the report.

h. Select the **Revenue query** in the Navigation Pane. Click the **Create tab** and click **Report Wizard** in the Reports group.

   The Report Wizard launches.

i. Click the **City field** and click **Add One Field** [>] to add the City field to the report. Repeat the same process for the **OrderDate**, **Price**, **Revenue**, and **ProductName fields**. Click **Next**.

j. Ensure that City is selected, click **Add One Field** [>] to add grouping by city. Click **Next**.

k. Click the **arrow** in the first sort box and select **OrderDate**. Accept the default sort order as Ascending. Click **Summary Options**.

l. Click the **Avg check box** in the Price row to summarize the Price field. Click **OK**.

m. Click **Next**. Click **Next** again to accept the default layout.

n. Type **Sales by City** for the title of the report. Click **Finish**.

   The report is displayed in Print Preview mode.

o. Click **Close Print Preview**.

p. Save and close the report.

STEP 2 USE PRINT PREVIEW AND EXPORT A REPORT

The Products Report you created looks good according to Ryung. However, Access does not run on her smart device, and she wants to have a copy of the report saved in PDF format so she can review it outside of the office. You will export a copy of the report to PDF format for her. Refer to Figure 4.36 as you complete Step 2.

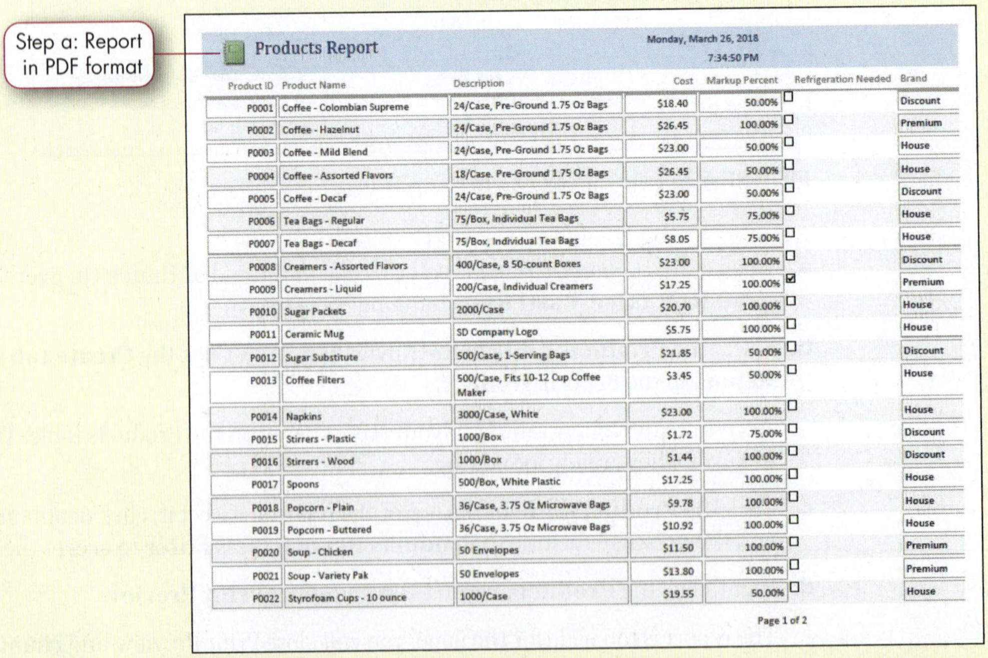

Products Report

Monday, March 26, 2018
7:34:50 PM

Product ID	Product Name	Description	Cost	Markup Percent	Refrigeration Needed	Brand
P0001	Coffee - Colombian Supreme	24/Case, Pre-Ground 1.75 Oz Bags	$18.40	50.00%	☐	Discount
P0002	Coffee - Hazelnut	24/Case, Pre-Ground 1.75 Oz Bags	$26.45	100.00%	☐	Premium
P0003	Coffee - Mild Blend	24/Case, Pre-Ground 1.75 Oz Bags	$23.00	50.00%	☐	House
P0004	Coffee - Assorted Flavors	18/Case. Pre-Ground 1.75 Oz Bags	$26.45	50.00%	☐	House
P0005	Coffee - Decaf	24/Case, Pre-Ground 1.75 Oz Bags	$23.00	50.00%	☐	Discount
P0006	Tea Bags - Regular	75/Box, Individual Tea Bags	$5.75	75.00%	☐	House
P0007	Tea Bags - Decaf	75/Box, Individual Tea Bags	$8.05	75.00%	☐	House
P0008	Creamers - Assorted Flavors	400/Case, 8 50-count Boxes	$23.00	100.00%	☐	Discount
P0009	Creamers - Liquid	200/Case, Individual Creamers	$17.25	100.00%	☑	Premium
P0010	Sugar Packets	2000/Case	$20.70	100.00%	☐	House
P0011	Ceramic Mug	SD Company Logo	$5.75	100.00%	☐	House
P0012	Sugar Substitute	500/Case, 1-Serving Bags	$21.85	50.00%	☐	Discount
P0013	Coffee Filters	500/Case, Fits 10-12 Cup Coffee Maker	$3.45	50.00%	☐	House
P0014	Napkins	3000/Case, White	$23.00	100.00%	☐	House
P0015	Stirrers - Plastic	1000/Box	$1.72	75.00%	☐	Discount
P0016	Stirrers - Wood	1000/Box	$1.44	100.00%	☐	Discount
P0017	Spoons	500/Box, White Plastic	$17.25	100.00%	☐	House
P0018	Popcorn - Plain	36/Case, 3.75 Oz Microwave Bags	$9.78	100.00%	☐	House
P0019	Popcorn - Buttered	36/Case, 3.75 Oz Microwave Bags	$10.92	100.00%	☐	House
P0020	Soup - Chicken	50 Envelopes	$11.50	100.00%	☐	Premium
P0021	Soup - Variety Pak	50 Envelopes	$13.80	100.00%	☐	Premium
P0022	Styrofoam Cups - 10 ounce	1000/Case	$19.55	50.00%	☐	House

Page 1 of 2

FIGURE 4.36 Products Report Saved in PDF Format

a. Open the Products Report, click the **File tab**, click **Print**, and then select **Print Preview**. Click **PDF or XPS** in the Data group on the Print Preview tab. Navigate to where you are saving your files, type the file name **a04h2Products_LastFirst**, ensure that *Open file after publishing* is selected, and then click **Publish**.

   Windows will open the report in your system's default PDF viewer, which may be Adobe Reader or the Windows Reader app. Close the reader window.

b. Ensure that you return to the Access window, and in the Export – PDF dialog box, click **Close** when prompted to save the export steps.

c. Click **Close Print Preview** and close the report.

STEP 3 MODIFYING A REPORT

Ryung realized the Products table is missing a field that she requires for her reports. She asked you to add the field to the table and update the report to include the new field. She also wants to make sure the report fits nicely across one landscape page. She also asked you to show her some sample color schemes. Refer to Figure 4.37 as you complete Step 3.

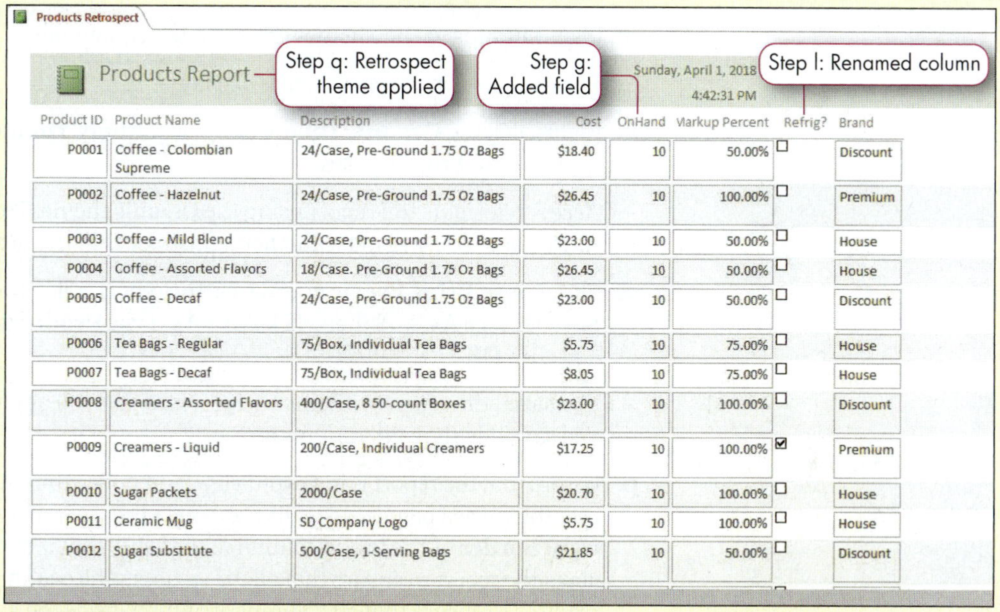

Product ID	Product Name	Description	Cost	OnHand	Markup Percent	Refrig?	Brand
P0001	Coffee - Colombian Supreme	24/Case, Pre-Ground 1.75 Oz Bags	$18.40	10	50.00%	☐	Discount
P0002	Coffee - Hazelnut	24/Case, Pre-Ground 1.75 Oz Bags	$26.45	10	100.00%	☐	Premium
P0003	Coffee - Mild Blend	24/Case, Pre-Ground 1.75 Oz Bags	$23.00	10	50.00%	☐	House
P0004	Coffee - Assorted Flavors	18/Case. Pre-Ground 1.75 Oz Bags	$26.45	10	50.00%	☐	House
P0005	Coffee - Decaf	24/Case, Pre-Ground 1.75 Oz Bags	$23.00	10	50.00%	☐	Discount
P0006	Tea Bags - Regular	75/Box, Individual Tea Bags	$5.75	10	75.00%	☐	House
P0007	Tea Bags - Decaf	75/Box, Individual Tea Bags	$8.05	10	75.00%	☐	House
P0008	Creamers - Assorted Flavors	400/Case, 8 50-count Boxes	$23.00	10	100.00%	☐	Discount
P0009	Creamers - Liquid	200/Case, Individual Creamers	$17.25	10	100.00%	☑	Premium
P0010	Sugar Packets	2000/Case	$20.70	10	100.00%	☐	House
P0011	Ceramic Mug	SD Company Logo	$5.75	10	100.00%	☐	House
P0012	Sugar Substitute	500/Case, 1-Serving Bags	$21.85	10	50.00%	☐	Discount

FIGURE 4.37 Products Retrospect Report

a. Right-click the **Products table** and select **Design View**.

   You need to add the OnHand field to the Products table.

b. Click in the **MarkupPercent field** and click **Insert Rows** in the Tools group on the Design tab.

   A new blank row displays above the MarkupPercent field.

c. Type **OnHand** in the Field Name box and select **Number** as the Data Type.

d. Save the table. Click **View** in the Views group to switch to Datasheet view.

   The new OnHand column contains no data. Next, you will add some sample data to the new field for testing purposes only.

e. Type the number **10** for each item's OnHand value. Close the Products table.

f. Right-click **Products Report** in the Navigation Pane and select **Layout View**. Click **Add Existing Fields** in the Tools group on the Design tab to open the Field List pane, if necessary.

g. Drag the **OnHand field** from the Field List pane between the Cost and MarkupPercent fields. Close the Field List pane.

Because of the tabular layout control, Access adjusts all the columns to make room for the new OnHand field.

h. Display the report in Print Preview.

The report is still too wide for a single page.

i. Click **Close Print Preview**. Ensure that you are in Layout view.

j. Scroll to and click anywhere in the **Year Introduced column**. Click the **Arrange tab** and click **Select Column** in the Rows & Columns group. Press **Delete** to remove the column.

The Year Introduced column is removed from the report.

k. Scroll to and click the **ProductID column heading** and drag the right border to the left until the Product ID heading still fits, but any extra white space is removed.

l. Scroll to and click the **Refrigeration Needed column heading** and rename the column **Refrig?**. Adjust the width of the *Refrig?* column heading so that any extra white space is removed.

m. Click **Themes** in the Themes group on the Design tab.

The available predefined themes display.

n. Right-click the **Organic theme** and select **Apply Theme to This Object Only**. Display the report in Print Preview.

Access reformats the report using the Organic theme. The report is still too wide for a single page. You will make further adjustments in the next steps.

o. Click **Close Print Preview** and save the report. Click the **File tab**, select **Save As**, select **Save Object As**, and then click **Save As**. Type **Products Organic** as the report name and click **OK**.

You saved the report with one theme. Now, you will apply a second theme to the report and save it with a different name.

p. Ensure that the report is in Layout view. You notice that the Brand column is extending over the dashed page break to its right and needs to be resized to fit on the page. Drag the **right border** of the Brand column to the left so that it fits inside the page break. Scroll down the report to ensure that all the values in the column are visible. Narrow columns as required to ensure that all columns are fitting inside the dashed page break. Save the report.

q. Click **Themes** in the Themes group to apply a different theme. Right-click the **Retrospect theme** and select **Apply Theme to This Object Only**. Display the report in Print Preview.

If you do not apply the theme to this object only, all database objects will adopt the Retrospect theme.

r. Click **Close Print Preview**. Click the **File tab**, select **Save As**, select **Save Object As**, and then click **Save As**. Type **Products Retrospect** as the report name and click **OK**. Close the report.

You will be able to show Ryung two product reports with different themes applied.

Ryung wants the Products Report records to be sorted and grouped by Brand. You will change the sort order, group the records, and preview the report to see the results. Refer to Figure 4.38 as you complete Step 4.

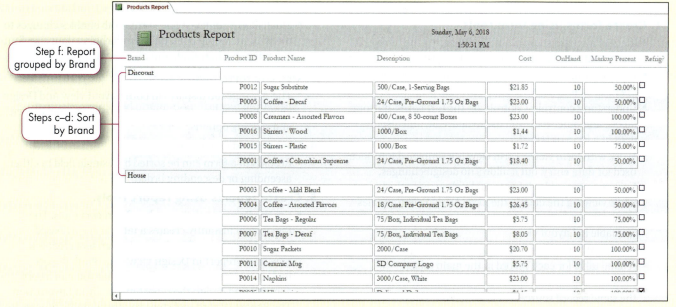

FIGURE 4.38 Products Report Grouped by Brand

a. Open **Products Report** in Layout view.

b. Click **Group & Sort** in the Grouping & Totals group on the Design tab.

   The *Add a group* and *Add a sort* options display at the bottom of the report in the Group, Sort, and Total pane.

> **TROUBLESHOOTING:** If the options do not display, the Group, Sort, and Total pane may have been open. If the pane is closed after selecting the command, try clicking Group & Sort again.

c. Click **Add a sort**.

   A new Sort bar displays at the bottom of the report.

d. Select **Brand** from the list.

   The report is now sorted by Brand in ascending order (with the Discount brand at the top).

e. Click **Add a group**.

f. Select **Brand** from the list.

   The report is now grouped by Brand.

g. View the report in Report view. Save and close the report.

h. Close the database and exit Access. Based on your instructor's directions, submit the following:

   a04h2Coffee_LastFirst

   a04h2Products_LastFirst.pdf

Key Terms Matching

Match the key terms with their definitions. Write the key term letter by the appropriate numbered definition.

a. Control
b. Design view
c. Form
d. Form tool
e. Form view
f. Label Wizard
g. Layout control
h. Layout view
i. Multiple Items form
j. Navigation form

k. Portable Document Format (PDF)
l. Print Preview
m. Record source
n. Report
o. Report tool
p. Report view
q. Report Wizard
r. Split form
s. Stacked layout
t. Tabular layout

1. _____ A database object that is used to add data into, or edit data in, an underlying table. **p. 732**

2. _____ Used to create data entry forms for customers, employees, products, and other tables. **p. 734**

3. _____ The table or query that supplies the records for a form or report. **p. 733**

4. _____ Arrangement that displays fields in a vertical column. **p. 734**

5. _____ Arrangement that displays fields horizontally across the screen or page. **p. 734**

6. _____ A text box, button, label, or other tool you use to add, edit, and display the data in a form or report. **p. 734**

7. _____ Provides guides to help keep controls aligned horizontally and vertically and give your form or report a uniform appearance. **p. 734**

8. _____ A simplified user interface primarily used for data entry; does not allow you to make changes to the layout. **p. 735**

9. _____ Enables users to make changes to a layout while viewing the data in the form or report. **p. 736**

10. _____ Enables you to change advanced design settings you cannot see in Layout view, such as removing a layout control. **p. 736**

11. _____ Combines two views of the same record source—one section is displayed in a stacked layout and the other section is displayed in a tabular layout. **p. 737**

12. _____ Displays multiple records in a tabular layout like a table's Datasheet view, with more customization options. **p. 738**

13. _____ User interface that allows users to switch between various forms and reports in a database. **p. 738**

14. _____ A database document that outputs meaningful information to its readers. **p. 753**

15. _____ Used to instantly create a tabular report based on the table or query currently selected. **p. 754**

16. _____ Prompts you for input and then uses your answers to generate a customized report. **p. 755**

17. _____ Enables you to easily create mailing labels, name tags, and other specialized tags. **p. 758**

18. _____ Enables you to determine what a printed report will look like in a continuous page layout. **p. 759**

19. _____ Enables you to see exactly what the report will look like when it is printed. **p. 759**

20. _____ A file type that was created for exchanging documents independent of software applications and operating system environment. **p. 759**

Multiple Choice

1. A form or report can be made from one or more tables or a query. The object(s) that is the underlying basis for a form or a report is the:

(a) control source.

(b) record source.

(c) grouped object.

(d) Multiple Items form.

2. Which of the following statements is *false*?

(a) Both forms and reports can use tabular and stacked layouts.

(b) A stacked layout displays data in a vertical column.

(c) A tabular layout displays data horizontally.

(d) Stacked layouts are more common for reports because they use less paper when printed.

3. To summarize data in a report and override the sort order of the record source you would use:

(a) a text box.

(b) a button on a report.

(c) the Group, Sort, and Total pane.

(d) a label on a report.

4. The view you can use to export a report to a different format is:

(a) Layout view.

(b) Form view.

(c) Design view.

(d) Print Preview.

5. Which of the following views provides you with the option to view data while making design and layout changes?

(a) Design view

(b) Layout view

(c) Form view/Report view

(d) Print Preview

6. Which of the following statements about reports is *false*?

(a) Reports can be saved to a file (such as a Word document) on your computer.

(b) Reports are primarily used to modify data.

(c) Reports can produce output in several ways, including mailing labels.

(d) Reports can be created simply by using the Report tool.

7. Create a _____ form as a user interface that enables you to switch between forms and reports in a database.

(a) Stacked

(b) Multiple items

(c) Split

(d) Navigation

8. If you need to send a report to a user who does not have Microsoft Office available, which of the following file formats would be the best choice to ensure it can be opened?

(a) Word

(b) Excel

(c) Reader

(d) Portable Document Format (PDF)

9. Which of the following statements is *false*?

(a) Reports are generally used for printing, emailing, or viewing data on the screen.

(b) Themes are the predefined sets of colors, fonts, and graphics.

(c) Forms are used for viewing but not inputting data.

(d) Forms and reports both include controls, such as text boxes, that can be resized.

10. Which of the following statements is *true*?

(a) You can add grouping and sorting to records in a report that vary from the underlying record source.

(b) You can sort records in reports but not in forms.

(c) The default sort order for a field is descending.

(d) You can either group or sort records (but not both).

Practice Exercises

1 Salary Analysis

The Human Resources department of the Comfort Insurance Agency has initiated its annual employee performance reviews. You will create forms for them to perform data entry using the Form tool, a split form, and a multiple items form. You will create a report to display locations, and a report displaying employee salary increases grouped by location. Additionally, you will export the salary increases report as a PDF file. Refer to Figure 4.39 as you complete this exercise.

Employee Compensation

Location YearHired	LastName	FirstName	Salary	2020Increase	2020Raise
L01					
2019	Abrams	Wendy	$47,500.00	3.00%	$1,425.00
2015	Anderson	Vicki	$47,900.00	4.00%	$1,916.00
2019	Bichette	Susan	$61,500.00	4.00%	$2,460.00
2017	Block	Leonard	$26,200.00	3.00%	$786.00
2018	Brown	Patricia	$25,000.00	5.00%	$1,250.00
2016	Brumbaugh	Paige	$49,300.00	3.00%	$1,479.00
2018	Daniels	Phil	$42,600.00	3.00%	$1,278.00
2017	Davis	Martha	$51,900.00	4.00%	$2,076.00
2016	Drubin	Lolly	$37,000.00	3.00%	$1,110.00
2015	Gander	John	$38,400.00	3.00%	$1,152.00
2017	Grippando	Joan	$26,100.00	3.00%	$783.00
2019	Harrison	Jenifer	$44,800.00	3.00%	$1,344.00
2018	Imber	Elise	$63,700.00	4.00%	$2,548.00
2019	Johnshon	Billy	$22,800.00	5.00%	$1,140.00
2019	Johnson	Debbie	$39,700.00	3.00%	$1,191.00
2019	McCammon	Johnny	$43,100.00	4.00%	$1,724.00
2015	Mills	Jack	$44,600.00	3.00%	$1,338.00

FIGURE 4.39 Employee Compensation Report

a. Open *a04p1Insurance*. Save the database as **a04p1Insurance_LastFirst**.

b. Click the **Locations table** in the Navigation Pane. Click **Form** in the Forms group on the Create tab.

c. Click the **View arrow** in the Views group on the Home tab and select **Design View**. Click anywhere in the **Table.Employees subform control** and press **Delete**. Switch to Layout view.

d. Ensure that the LocationID text box containing *L01* in Record 1 is selected. Drag the **right border** to the left to resize the column to approximately half of its original width (to about 3.4"). The other text boxes will resize as well.

e. Change the font size of the Location text box control (containing *Atlanta*) to **14** and change the Background Color to **Blue, Accent 1, Lighter 60%**.

f. Click **Select Row** in the Rows & Columns group on the Arrange tab. Click **Move Up** in the Move group until Location displays above LocationID.

g. Save the form as **Locations Data Entry**.

h. Delete the **LocationID field**. Delete the **Office Phone label**. Move the **Office Phone field** to the row immediately below the Location field.

i. Click **Add Existing Fields** in the Tools group on the Form Layout Tools Design tab. Click and drag to add **LocationID** back to the form from the Field List pane, immediately below the Address field. Close the Field List pane.

j. Switch to Form view, and then save and close the form.

k. Click the **Titles table** in the Navigation Pane. Click **More Forms** in the Forms group on the Create tab to create a Multiple Items form based on the Titles table. Resize the width of the Title field to approximately **1"** and the EducationRequired field to approximately **1.5"** so that all fields are visible onscreen without scrolling.

l. Click the **File tab**, click **Print**, and then select **Print Preview**. Click **Landscape** in the Page Layout group. Click **Close Print Preview** in the Close Preview group.

m. Save the form as **Job Titles Multiple Items**. Close the form.

n. Click the **Employees table** in the Navigation Pane. Click **More Forms** in the Forms group on the Create tab to create a Split Form based on the Employees table. Switch to Form view.

o. Select the bottom pane of the form, scroll down and click in the record for **EmployeeID 22** (Denise Smith). In the top pane of the form, select the existing Performance value (*Average*), and replace it with **Good**. Press Tab two times to save the record.

p. Save the form as **Employees Split Form**. Close the form.

q. Click the **Locations table** in the Navigation Pane. Click **Report** in the Reports group on the Create tab.

r. Click and drag the **right border** of each label to the left to reduce the column widths until there are no controls on the right side of the vertical dashed line (page break). Drag the control containing the page number to the left so that it is inside the page break.

s. Display the report in Report view. Verify that the report is only one page wide in Report view. Save the report as **Locations** and close the report.

t. Click the **Employees Query** in the Navigation Pane. Click **Report Wizard** in the Reports group on the Create tab. Respond to the prompts as follows:
- Add all the fields to the Selected Fields list. Click **HireDate** and remove the field from the Selected Fields. Remove **YearHired** from the Selected Fields. Click **Next**.
- Accept grouping by Location. Click **Next**.
- Select **LastName** for the first sort order, and **FirstName** for the second (ascending order for both). Click **Summary Options**.
- Click **Sum** for Salary, and **Avg** for 2020Increase. Click **OK**. Click **Next**.
- Accept the Stepped layout. Change Orientation to **Landscape**. Click **Next**.
- Type **Employee Compensation** for the title of the report. Click **Finish**.

u. Click **Close Print Preview**. Switch to Layout view.

v. Adjust the widths of the controls so that all the data values are visible and the columns all fit within the vertical dashed border (page break). Some of the text boxes and labels will need to be relocated; select the control to be moved and click and drag it to a new location but keep them in the same order.

w. Click **Themes** in the Themes group on the Design tab. Right-click the **Slice theme** and select **Apply Theme to This Object Only**. Adjust the label widths and report title so that they are fully visible. Scroll to the bottom of the report and move any text boxes, such as the page number control, so that they are inside the page break. Resize all text boxes and labels so that their values are fully visible.

x. Click and drag **YearHired** from the Field List into the report layout. Drag and drop the column into the space immediately to the right of the Location column. Close the Field List. Display the report in Print Preview. Compare your report to Figure 4.39. Make adjustments as required.

y. Export the report as a PDF file named **a04p1Employee_Compensation_LastFirst**. Close the reader window. Do not save the export steps.

z. Save and close the Employee Compensation report.

aa. Click the **Create tab**, click **Navigation** in the Forms group, and then select **Horizontal Tabs**.

ab. Drag the **Job Titles Multiple Items form icon** from the Navigation Pane onto the **[Add New] tab** at the top of the form.

ac. Drag the **Employee Compensation report icon** from the Navigation Pane onto the **[Add New] tab** at the top of the form. Click the **Job Titles Multiple Items tab** and click the **Employee Compensation tab**.

ad. Save the Navigation form with the default name and close all open objects.

ae. Close the database and exit Access. Based on your instructor's directions, submit the following:

a04p1Insurance_LastFirst

a04p1Employee Compensation_LastFirst.pdf

Financial Management Prospects

You are working as a customer service representative for a financial management firm. Your task is to contact a list of prospective customers and introduce yourself and the services of your company. You will create a form to view, add, and update data for one customer at a time. After creating the form, you will customize it and add sorting. You will also create a report to display all the information on one screen, for viewing purposes. Refer to Figure 4.40 as you complete this exercise.

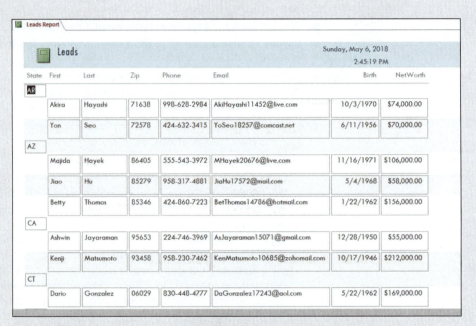

FIGURE 4.40 Grouped and Sorted Leads Report

a. Open *a04p2Prospects*. Save the database as **a04p2Prospects_LastFirst**.

b. Click the **Leads table** in the Navigation Pane. Click **Form** in the Forms group on the Create tab.

c. Select the **LeadID text box** of Record 1 and drag the right border to the left to resize the column to approximately half of its original width (to about 3.4"). The other text boxes will resize as well.

d. Change the title of the form to **New Leads**.

e. Change the font size of the NetWorth text box control to **14** and change the Background Color to **Blue, Accent 5, Lighter 60%**.

f. Click **Select Row** in the Rows & Columns group on the Arrange tab. Click **Move Up** in the Move group until NetWorth displays above First.

> **TROUBLESHOOTING:** If the text box and the label do not move together, click Undo, ensure that both controls are selected, and then follow the instructions in Step f.

g. Save the form as **Leads Form**. Switch to Form view.

h. Navigate to Record 63. Enter **your name** in both the first and last fields. Leave the Email field blank.

i. Click in the **Last field** and click **Ascending** in the Sort & Filter group on the Home tab.
   Farrah Aaron should be the first record displayed unless your last name appears before hers alphabetically.

j. Save and close the form.

k. Click the **Leads table** in the Navigation Pane. Click **More Forms** in the Forms group on the Create tab and select **Split Form**.

l. Modify the form title to read **Leads-Split Form**. Save the form as **Leads-Split Form** and close the form.

m. Click the **Leads table**. Click **Report** in the Reports group on the Create tab.

A new report is created based on the Leads table.

n. Make the fields as narrow as possible to remove any extra white space in them. Change the report's orientation to **Landscape**.

o. Delete the **LeadID**, **Address**, and **City** columns from the report.

p. Click Group & Sort in the Grouping & Totals group on the Design tab. Group the records by **State** and sort them by **LastName** in ascending order. Close the Group, Sort, and Total pane.

q. Click **Themes** in the Themes group on the Design tab. Right-click the **Integral theme** and select **Apply Theme to This Object Only**. At the bottom of the report, change the font size of the control that displays the total to **10**. Move any text boxes, such as the page number control, so that they are inside the page break.

r. Export the report as a PDF file named **a04p2LeadsReport_LastFirst**. Close the reader window. Do not save the export steps.

s. Save the report as **Leads Report**. Close the report.

t. Click the **Create tab**, click **Navigation** in the Forms group, and then select **Vertical Tabs, Left**.

u. Drag the **Leads Form form icon** from the Navigation Pane onto the **[Add New] tab** at the left of the form.

v. Drag the **Leads Report report icon** from the Navigation Pane onto the second **[Add New] tab** at the left of the form. Click the **Leads Form tab** and click the **Leads Report tab**.

w. Save the Navigation form with the default name and close all open objects.

x. Close the database and exit Access. Based on your instructor's directions, submit the following:

a04p2LeadsReport_LastFirst

a04p2Prospects_LastFirst.pdf

Mid-Level Exercises

1 Hotel Chain

ANALYSIS CASE

You are the general manager of a large hotel chain. You track revenue by categories, such as conference room rentals and weddings. You want to create a report that shows which locations are earning the most revenue in each category. You will also create a report to show you details of your three newest areas: St. Paul, St. Louis, and Seattle.

a. Open *a04m1Rewards*. Save the database as **a04m1Rewards_LastFirst**.

b. Select the **Members table** and create a Multiple Items form. Save the form as **Maintain Members**.

c. Change the MemNumber label to **MemID** and use the Property Sheet to reduce the MemNumber column width to **0.6"**.

d. Change the widths of the LastName, FirstName, City, and Phone fields to **1.25"**; change the width of the State and Zip fields to **0.75"**; and change the width of the Address field to **1.75"**. Delete the form icon (the picture next to the title of the form) in the Form Header.

e. Change the sorting on the MemberSince control so that the members who joined most recently are displayed first.

f. Click the **LastName field**. Change the Control Padding to **Wide**. (Hint: Search **Control Padding** in the *Tell me* box.)

g. Save and close the form.

h. Select the **Revenue query** and create a report using the Report Wizard. Include all fields in the report and add grouping first by **City** and then by **ServiceName**. Add a **Sum** to the Revenue field and click the **Summary Only option**. Select **Outline Layout** and name the report **Revenue by City and Service**.

i. Scroll through all the pages to check the layout of the report while in Print Preview mode. Close Print Preview. Switch to Layout view and delete the **NumInParty** and **PerPersonCharge** controls.

j. Select the result of the aggregate sum function for the city's revenue. Change the font size to **12**, change the font color to **Dark Blue, Text 2**, and change the background color of the control to **Yellow**.

k. Change the sort on the report, so that it sorts by city in descending order—that is, so that the last city alphabetically (St. Paul) is displayed first.

l. Examine the data in the report to determine which city (of these three: St. Paul, St. Louis, or Seattle) has the highest Sum of event revenue. You will use this information to modify a query. Save and close the report. Modify the Totals by Service query so the criteria for the City field is the city you determined had the highest sum of event revenue (St. Paul, St. Louis, or Seattle). Run, save, and close the query.

m. Create a report using the Report tool based on the Totals by Service query. Name the report **Targeted City**. Close the report.

n. Close the database and exit Access. Based on your instructor's directions, submit a04m1Rewards_LastFirst.

2 Benefit Auction

FROM SCRATCH

You are helping to organize a benefit auction to raise money for families who lost their homes in a natural disaster. The information for the auction is currently stored in an Excel spreadsheet, but you have volunteered to import it into Access. You will create a database that will store the data from Excel in Access. You will create a form to manage the data-entry process. You also create two reports: one that lists the items collected in each category and one for labels so you can send the donors a thank-you letter after the auction.

a. Open Access and create a new database named **a04m2Auction_LastFirst**.

b. Switch to Design view. Type **Items** in the Save As dialog box and click **OK**.

c. Change the ID Field Name to **ItemID**. Add a second field named **Description**. Accept **Short Text** as the data type for the Description field and change the field size to **50**.

d. Enter the remaining field names in the table (in this order): **DateOfDonation**, **Category**, **Price**, **DonorName**, **DonorAddress1**, and **DonorAddress2**. Change the data type of the DateOfDonation field to **Date/Time** and the Price field to **Currency**. Accept **Short Text** as the data type for the remaining fields.

e. Open Excel and open the file *a04m2Items.xlsx*. Examine the length of the Category, DonorAddress1, and DonorAddress2 columns. Return to Access. Change the field size for the Category to **15**, DonorAddress1 to **25**, and DonorAddress2 to **30**. Save the table, and switch to Datasheet view.

f. Copy and paste the 26 rows from the Excel spreadsheet into the Items table. To paste the rows, locate the * to the left of the first blank row, click the **Record Selector**, right-click the **Record Selector**, and then from the shortcut menu, select **Paste**. AutoFit all the column widths so all data are visible. Save and close the table. Close the workbook and exit Excel.

> **TROUBLESHOOTING:** Once you have pasted the data, ensure that your chosen field sizes did not cause you to lose data. If so, update the field sizes, delete the records you pasted to the table, and then repeat Step f.

g. Verify that the Items table is selected in the Navigation Pane. Create a new form using the Form tool.

h. Select all of the fields and labels in the Detail section of the form. Change the layout of the form to a **Tabular Layout**. With all of the fields selected, switch to Design view and use the Property Sheet to set their widths to **1.3"**. Then change the width of the ItemID, Category, and Price columns to **0.75"**.

i. Add conditional formatting so that each Price that is **greater than 90** has a font color of **Green** (in the first row, under Standard Colors). (Hint: Search **Conditional Formatting** in the *Tell me* box.)

j. Save the form as **Auction Items Form**.

k. Switch to Form view and create a new record. Enter **iPad** as the Description; **12/31/2018** as the DateOfDonation; **House** as the Category; **$400** as the Price; **Staples** as the DonorName; **500 Market St** as the DonorAddress1; and **Brick, NJ 08723** as the DonorAddress2.

l. Add a sort to the form, so that the lowest priced items display first. Save and close the form.

m. Select the **Items table** in the Navigation Pane, and create a report using the Report Wizard. Include all fields except the two donor address fields, group by Category, include the Sum of Price as a Summary Option, accept the default layout, and then save the report as **Auction Items by Category**.

n. Switch to Layout view. Resize the **DateOfDonation control** so that the left edge of the control aligns with the left edge of the column label. Select the **Price** and **Sum of Price controls** and increase the width to **0.75"**. Select any value in the **DonorName column** and drag the left edge of the controls to the right to decrease the width of the column. Resize the **Grand Total control** so that its value displays. Preview the report to verify the column widths are correct.

o. Switch to Layout view and sort the report so the least expensive item is displayed first in each group. Save and close the report.

p. Select the **Items table** in the Navigation Pane. Create mailing labels based on the Avery 5660 template. (Hint: Search **Labels** in the *Tell me* box and click the **Labels** tool in the results.) Place **DonorName** on the first line, **DonorAddress1** on the second line, and **DonorAddress2** on the third line. Sort the labels by **DonorName**. Name the report **Donor Labels**. After you create the labels, display them in Print Preview mode to verify that all values will fit onto the label template. Close the label report.

q. Close the database and exit Access. Based on your instructor's directions, submit a04m2Auction_LastFirst.

Running Case

New Castle County Technical Services

New Castle County Technical Services (NCCTS) provides technical support for a number of companies in the greater New Castle County, Delaware, area. Now that you have completed the database tables, set the appropriate relationships, and created queries, you are ready to create a form and a report.

a. Open the database *a04r1NCCTS* and save it as **a04r1NCCTS_LastFirst**.
b. Create a split form based on the Calls table.
c. Add the **Description field** by dragging and dropping it immediately below the CallTypeID. (Hint: Click Show all tables in the Field List pane and locate the field by expanding the Call Types table.) Close the Field List pane. Switch to Form view and ensure that the records are sorted by CallID in ascending order.
d. Save the form as **Calls Data Entry** and close the form.
e. Use the Report tool to create a basic report based on the Customer Happiness query.
f. Sort the records by the **Avg Rating field** in ascending order.
g. Apply the **Integral theme** to this report only.
h. Change the title of the report to **Customer Satisfaction Ratings** and format the background color of the control to **Medium Gray** (under Standard Colors).
i. Set the font color of the title control to **Blue, Accent 2**, the font size to **20**, and the alignment to **Center**. Click the default logo in the report header and press **Delete**.
j. Switch to Report view. Save the report as **Customer Satisfaction Survey** and close the report.
k. Close the database and exit Access. Based on your instructor's directions, submit a04r1NCCTS_LastFirst.

Disaster Recovery

Properties by City

A co-worker is having difficulty with an Access report and asked for your assistance. He was trying to fix the report and seems to have made things worse. Open the *a04d1Sales* database and save the file as **a04d1Sales_LastFirst**. Open the Properties Report in Report view. The report columns do not fit across one page. In addition, there is a big gap between two fields, and he moved the Beds and Baths fields so they are basically on top of one another. Add all the fields to a tabular layout. Group the records first by City in ascending order, and then by Beds in descending order. Within each group, sort the report by ListPrice in ascending order. Change the report to Landscape orientation and adjust the column widths so they all fit across one page (inside the dashed vertical page break). Apply the Organic theme to this report only, and switch to Report view. Save the new report as **Properties by City**, close the report, and then delete the original **Properties Report** from the database (right-click the report in the Navigation Pane, and from the shortcut menu, select **Delete**). Close the database and exit Access. Based on your instructor's directions, submit a04d1Sales_LastFirst.

Foodies Forms and Reports

You will create a form so that users of the database can enter and edit suppliers of products to your business easily. You create an attractive report that groups the products that you purchase by their suppliers and export it to PDF format for easy distribution. Finally, you create a Navigation form so that database users can switch between major objects in the database readily.

Create and Customize a Form

You will create a form to manage the data in the Suppliers table. Use the Form tool to create the form and modify the form as required. You will also remove the layout control from the form so that the controls can be repositioned freely.

1. Open the *a04c1Foodies* database and save it as **a04c1Foodies_LastFirst**.

2. Select the **Suppliers table** as the record source for a form. Use the Form tool to create a new form with a stacked layout.

3. Change the form's title to **Enter/Edit Suppliers**.

4. Reduce the width of the text box controls to approximately half of their original size (about 3.4").

5. Delete the **Products subform** control from the form.

6. View the form and the data in Form view. Sort the records by **CompanyName** in ascending order.

7. Set the background color of the CompanyName text box to **Blue, Accent 1, Lighter 80%** and set the font size to **14**.

8. Save the form as **Edit Suppliers**.

9. Open the Edit Suppliers form in Design view. Select all controls in the form and remove the layout.

10. View the form in Layout view. Delete the **Contact Title label** from the form and move the text box up and to the right of ContactName so that their top edges are aligned.

11. Delete the **Country label** from the form and move the text box up and to the right of PostalCode so that their top edges are aligned. Move the **Phone** and **Fax labels** and text boxes up to below PostalCode so that they close in the white space, keeping the spacing close to that of the rest of the controls.

12. View the form in Print Preview and set the orientation to **Landscape**.

13. Switch to Form view, and then save and close the form.

Create a Report

You will create a report based on the Company by Product List query. You decide to use the Report Wizard to accomplish this task. You are planning to email a copy of the report to your business partner, who is not conversant in Access, so you will export the report as a PDF file prior to sending it.

14. Select the **Company by Product List query** in the Navigation Pane as the record source for the report.

15. Activate the Report Wizard and use the following options as you proceed through the wizard steps:

    - Select all the available fields for the report.
    - View the data by Suppliers.
    - Accept the default grouping levels and click **Next**.
    - Use **ProductName** as the primary sort field in ascending order.
    - Accept the Stepped and Portrait options.
    - Save the report as **Products by Suppliers**.
    - Switch to Layout view and apply the **Organic theme** to this report only.
    - Set the width of the **ProductCost label** to approximately 0.8" so that the entire text of the label is visible.

16. Switch to Report view to determine whether all the columns fit across the page. Switch to Layout view and drag the left edge of the **ProductName text box** to the left so that the column width is wide enough to display the values in the field (approximately 2.5").

17. Delete the **ContactName label** and **text box** from the report. Drag the right edge of the **CompanyName text box** to the right so that the column width is wide enough to display the values in the field (approximately 2.6"). Save the report.

18. Switch to Print Preview and export the report as a PDF file named **a04c1ProductsbySuppliers_LastFirstpdf**.

19. Close the reader program that displays the PDF report and return to Access. Close Print Preview. Save and close the report.

Add an Additional Field to the Query and the Report

You realize that the Country field was not included in the query that is the record source for your report. You add the field to the query and modify the report in Layout view to include the missing field.

20. Open the **Company by Product List query** in Design view.

21. Add the **Country field** from the Suppliers table to the query design grid, after the ProductCost field. Run, save, and close the query.

22. Open the Products by Suppliers report in Layout view. Add the **Country field** from the Field List pane by dragging it into the report layout. Click the selection handle at the top of the Country column and move

the column immediately to the left of the Phone field. Resize the Country text box so that the column width is wide enough to display the values in the field (approximately .75"). Switch to Print Preview, and then save and close the report.

Create a Navigation Form

You will create a Navigation form so that users can switch between objects in the database readily.

23. Create a **Vertical Tabs, Left** Navigation form.

24. Drag the **Edit Suppliers form icon** from the Navigation Pane onto the **[Add New] tab** at the left of the form.

25. Drag the **Products by Suppliers report icon** from the Navigation Pane onto the second **[Add New] tab** at the left of the form. Save the Navigation form with the default name and close all open objects.

26. Close the database and exit Access. Based on your instructor's directions, submit the following:

a04c1Foodies_LastFirst

a04c1ProductsbySuppliers_LastFirst.pdf

Get to Know PowerPoint

Slide Design Elements

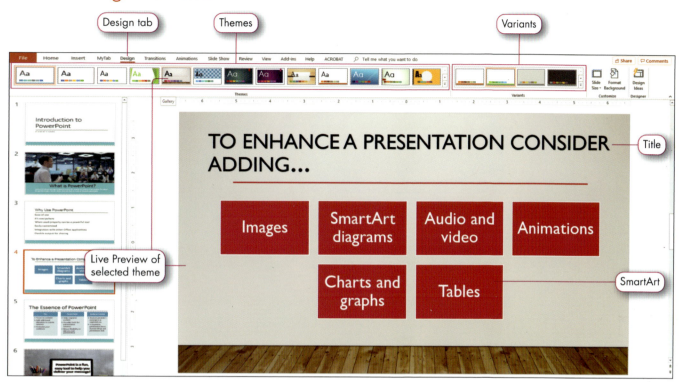

Design Ideas

Slide Views and Panes

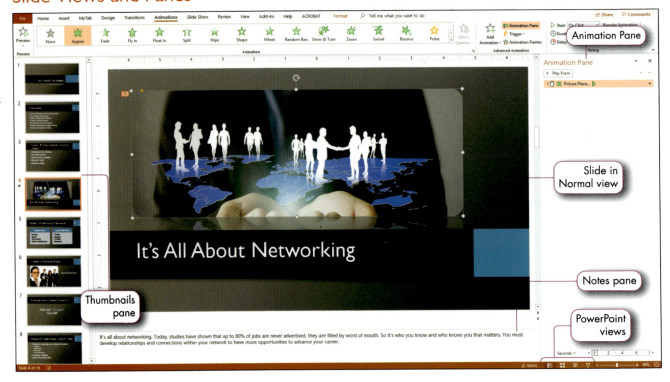

Transition and Animation

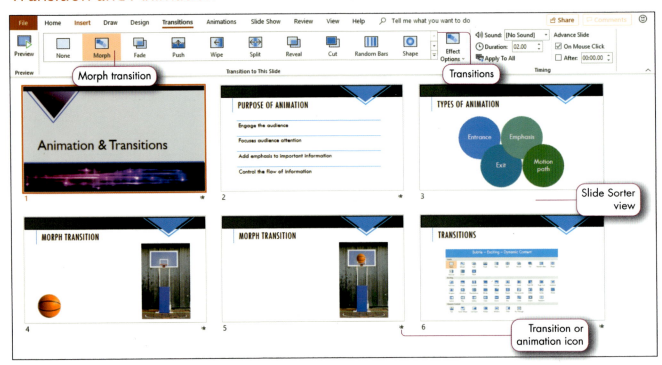

Introduction to PowerPoint

LEARNING OUTCOME

You will plan, create, modify, navigate, and print a basic presentation.

OBJECTIVES & SKILLS: After you read this chapter, you will be able to:

CASE STUDY | University Career Center Presentation

You are a career counselor in the Career & Employment Services (CES) at the college. You are responsible for providing personalized and innovative career services to your students. The mission of CES is to assist students so they can create meaningful lives and careers in alignment with their personal goals. The college career counselors will be giving presentations to students on job search strategies throughout the year. The director has asked you to put together a PowerPoint presentation that can be used by all counselors. This presentation will incorporate basic career guidance principles and setup so that it can be tweaked by each counselor as needed for specific careers. You have made great progress on the presentation content but recognize that further changes are necessary to help make the presentation more engaging.

CHAPTER 1

Creating a Basic Presentation

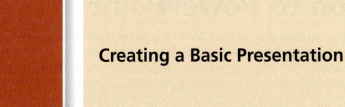

Sfio Cracho/Shutterstock

Violetkaipa/Shutterstock

Kurhan/Shutterstock

FIGURE 1.1 Employment Search Strategies Presentation

CASE STUDY | University Career Center Presentation

Starting Files	File to be Submitted
Blank Presentation p01h1Jobs p01h2Networking.jpg p01h2StandOut.jpg	p01h3JobSearch_LastFirst

MyLab IT Grader An alternate version of this project is available as a MyLab IT Grader Assessment

Introduction to PowerPoint

PowerPoint is the leading presentation software used across the globe. It includes tools you can use to create dynamic, engaging, and professional-looking presentations.

A **PowerPoint presentation**, also referred to as a **slide show**, is a collection of **slides**. Slides contain the information you want to communicate to your audience. This information can include text, bulleted lists, images, tables, charts, SmartArt, video, and audio. The slides are often referred to as a **deck** of slides because of how easily they can be shuffled around like a deck of cards.

Figure 1.2 shows the first four slides of a PowerPoint presentation with various layouts and content inserted. Learning the skills presented in this text will enable you to create your own polished and professional presentations.

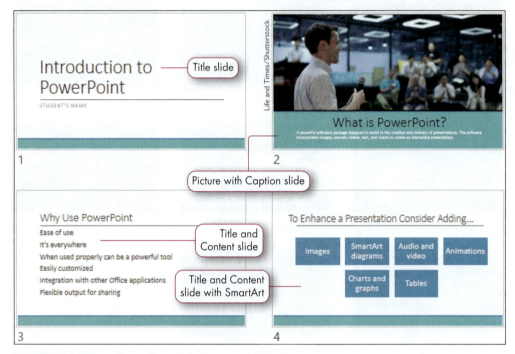

FIGURE 1.2 Various PowerPoint Slide Layouts and Content

In this section, you will learn about the planning stage of developing a presentation, explore ways to create a new presentation, add a theme and change the variant, create a title slide, add new slides, and reuse slides from another presentation. In addition, you will work with views to assist you with rearranging and deleting slides.

Planning and Preparing a Presentation

Whether used in business, the classroom, or for personal use, creating effective presentations takes time and planning to get your message across in an engaging way. Planning is considered the key to a successful presentation. It is recommended that for each hour of your presentation, at least four hours should be set aside for planning.

Plan a Presentation

As you plan for your presentation, you will determine the purpose of your presentation. Is it to inform, educate, or persuade the audience? An informative presentation could notify the audience about a change in policy or procedure. An educational presentation could teach an audience about a skill or subject. Sales presentations are often persuasive calls to action to encourage the purchase of a product, but they can also be used to sell an idea or process. Another type of presentation, a goodwill presentation, can be used to recognize an employee or acknowledge an organization. PowerPoint is even used to create banners.

It will be important to know whom the intended audience is and their needs. Will it be a live audience or a *kiosk* setting, an interactive computer terminal available for public use, such as on campus, at a mall, or a trade show? Researching the audience will enable you to customize the presentations to their needs.

Next, you will consider the content needed for the presentation. Keep the following in mind as you prepare your content.

- Ensure that all content is relevant and points to the desired outcome, whether that is persuading, informing, or entertaining the audience. What is the message you want the audience to remember?

- How much do you already know about the topic, and how much do you need to research and gather?

- What is the logical flow?

- What visuals should be included to support key ideas and engage the audience?

- Will there be handouts?

Once you know who your audience is and how you want to communicate, you are ready to start preparing your presentation. Many presenters like to begin by brainstorming their ideas, narrowing down their ideas into an outline, and then arranging them into a storyboard. A *storyboard* is a visual plan for a presentation that helps map out the direction of a presentation. Another method that individuals use to map out their presentation is sticky notes to lay out the main ideas and supporting data to see the entire presentation at once. Regardless of how you want to approach the preparation of your presentation, planning will be the key to your success. You cannot build a dynamic and engaging presentation without good preparation.

STEP 1 Creating a New Presentation and Adding a Title Slide

When you first open PowerPoint, you are presented with a list of recently opened presentations. In addition, there are presentation thumbnails offering the ability to open a blank presentation, a QuickStarter, or presentations based on specific design templates.

Create a New Presentation

There are several options for creating a new presentation. You can start from a blank presentation, create a presentation based on a built-in theme, search for online templates and themes, or use QuickStarter. Figure 1.3 shows the various options.

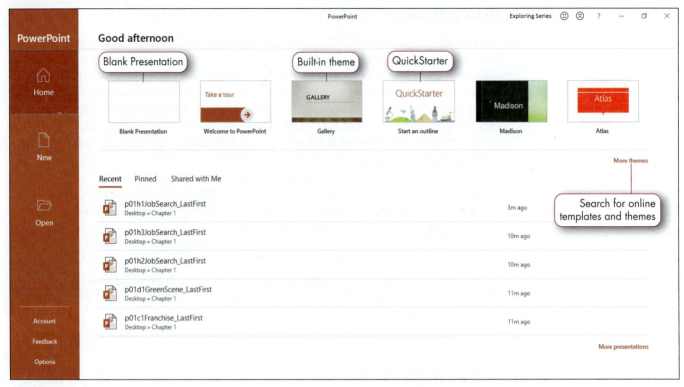

FIGURE 1.3 New Presentation

To create a blank presentation, click Blank Presentation on the Home screen that displays when you launch the application. A blank presentation opens with one slide, the title slide. A blank presentation has a theme applied, the default Office theme.

A **theme** has a predetermined set of colors, fonts, and effects that provide a unified look to a presentation. If you want to begin creating a presentation with a theme already applied, you can choose from a variety of themes that will quickly give your presentation a consistent and professional look. To begin a presentation with a built-in theme, click the **thumbnail** (slide miniature) in the right pane. A new presentation with the applied theme opens with one slide, the title slide.

Searching for online templates and themes is another option for creating a new presentation. A **template** has consistent fonts, colors, and other design elements similar to a theme, but it also can include suggested content.

To create a presentation from a template, in the Search for online templates and themes box, type a key word or phrase and click Start searching. Click the thumbnail of the template you want to use and click Create. A new presentation with the template will open. Alternatively, you can click one of the search option categories below the search box to narrow down the search.

One of the newest features of PowerPoint is QuickStarter. **QuickStarter** creates a collection of slides to provide research and design suggestions based on a presentation topic. QuickStarter builds an outline with suggested sections, talking points, and properly attributed Creative Commons images to get you started. Although it does not create a finished presentation, it gives you a jump start on your content. Figure 1.4 shows a search for Bicycle Safety.

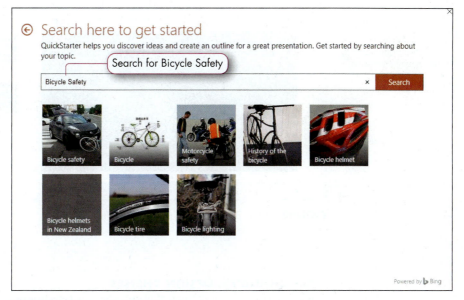

FIGURE 1.4 Search in QuickStarter

To create a presentation using QuickStarter, complete the following steps:

1. Start PowerPoint.
2. Click the Start an Outline (QuickStarter) thumbnail in the right pane.
3. Type a topic in the search bar and click Search. QuickStarter displays possible presentation topics.
4. Select a topic. All topics are selected by default; deselect the topics you do not want to include and click Next.
5. Choose a slide layout in the Pick a look screen and click Create.

Add a Theme and Variant

A PowerPoint theme is the base of your presentation. If you want an effective presentation, it is important to choose the right one to appeal to the audience and match the content of the presentation. Recall that a theme has a predetermined set of colors, fonts, and effects. PowerPoint has several themes from which to choose. You can select a built-in theme when completed. To add or change a theme, choose from the Themes gallery on the Design tab.

To apply a different color variation to your theme, you can select a variant. A *variant* offers four different color options for each theme. Figure 1.5 shows the Ion Boardroom theme with the four variant options available when creating a new presentation.

FIGURE 1.5 Ion Boardroom Theme and Variant Options

> **TIP: CHANGING DESIGN THEMES**
> Themes can change the location of placeholders, so a title may be positioned to the left or the bottom of a slide depending on the theme. Therefore, it is recommended that you choose a slide theme at the beginning of creating your presentation to avoid having to move and rearrange slide content.

Create a Title Slide

A title slide is the first slide in a presentation. The title slide typically includes the name of the presentation and the name of the presenter. It can also include a company logo, company name, or any other information that is important to be introduced to the audience on the title slide.

The title slide, as shown in Figure 1.6, includes two text placeholders: the title placeholder and a subtitle placeholder. ***Placeholders*** are objects on a slide that are enclosed by dotted borders. Placeholders hold specific content, such as text, images, charts, tables, SmartArt, or videos. Placeholders determine the position of objects on the slide. The theme will determine the font type, font color, and font size in the placeholders. You can always change these font choices by using the font commands on the Home tab.

To add text to the title and subtitle placeholders, click within the placeholder and type the text into the placeholder. By default, PowerPoint automatically fits text in a placeholder.

FIGURE 1.6 Title Slide with Title and Subtitle Placeholders

Adding Presentation Content

Once you have added a title slide, the next step is to add additional content to the presentation. You can add content on new slides or bring in content from other presentations or other applications such as Word.

STEP 2 Add New Slides

To add new slides to a presentation, you use the New Slide button on the Home tab. The New Slide button has two parts: New Slide button (top part) and New Slide arrow (bottom part). By default, when you click the New Slide button, it will insert a new slide with the layout of the current slide. The exception to this rule occurs after a slide formatted with the Title Slide layout, where the next slide will always be a slide with the Title and Content layout. The Title and Content layout is the most common layout used because it provides simple incorporation of text, images, SmartArt, video, tables, and charts into the content section of the slide. Clicking the New Slide arrow will display the Layout gallery for the theme, enabling you to select a different layout.

After inserting a new slide, click inside a placeholder to add the content. Clicking on the border of the placeholder changes the border to a solid line and displays *sizing handles*, white circles that display on the sides and corners of the placeholder, and the *rotation handle*, a circular arrow at the top of the placeholder. With the border selected, you can resize, move, rotate, or delete the placeholder. If the placeholder contains text, clicking on the border selects all of the text within the placeholder, and any formatting changes you make will be applied to all of the text in the placeholder.

> **TIP: UNUSED PLACEHOLDERS**
> It is recommended that you delete any unused placeholders on a slide, although unused placeholders do not show in Slide Show view. This makes for a cleaner slide design and removes clutter from the slide.

STEP 3 Create Bulleted and Numbered Lists

Bullets and numbering enable you to organize text in lists. By default, when you type text into a placeholder, a bullet is placed at the beginning of each paragraph, automatically creating a bulleted list. You can convert a bulleted list to a numbered list by selecting the bulleted list and clicking the Numbering command in the Paragraph group on the Home tab. Use the same technique to convert a numbered list to a bulleted list.

Use a *numbered list* if the list is a sequence of steps. The numerical sequence in a numbered list is automatically updated to accommodate additions or deletions, which means that if you add or remove items, the list is renumbered. If the list is not of a sequential nature, but is a simple itemization of points, use a *bulleted list*.

Although a bulleted list is the default layout for text content on a slide, it is good to keep in mind that bulleted text should be kept to a minimum and should only represent the key points. Often slides are text heavy with slide after slide of bullet points. If your slides contain a great deal of text, the audience is reading your slides, and they are not listening to you, the speaker. Often the concepts of "Less is More" and "Keep it Simple" are good approaches when you are designing your presentation and adding key concepts.

Here are some suggestions for reducing the amount of bullet points on your slides:

- Cut down your content to the essentials only. Use main ideas instead of full sentences.

- Use multiple slides to split up content. Splitting your content across several slides enables your audience to focus on one main idea at a time.

- Represent content visually. PowerPoint has a lot of tools to assist you with visually representing bullet points in a more interesting way.

Reuse Slides from Another Presentation

Co-workers often share presentation content as they create presentations for the workplace, and the Reuse Slides feature makes this convenient. If you want to add slides that exist in another presentation, you can import them without opening the presentation. The Reuse Slides feature saves considerable time, as you do not have to copy and paste slides from another presentation. The imported slides display in a pane on the right so that you can select the slides you want to import into your existing presentation.

To reuse existing slides into a presentation, complete the following steps:

1. Click the New Slide arrow in the Slides group on the Home tab.
2. Select Reuse Slides at the bottom of the gallery.
3. Click Browse and navigate to the folder containing the presentation that has the slides you want to use.
4. Click Open.
5. Select each slide individually or right-click any slide and click Insert All Slides to add all slides from the presentation.
6. Close the Reuse Slides pane.

On a Mac, to reuse slides, complete the following steps:

1. Click the New Slide arrow on the Home tab under Slides and click Reuse Slides.
2. Navigate to the folder where the presentation you want to use is located in the Finder window, select the presentation, and then click OK. Copies of all slides are inserted into the presentation. If you only need some of them, you can remove them by selecting them in the Thumbnails pane and pressing Delete.

By default, when you insert a slide into a presentation, it takes on the formatting of the open presentation. If you want to retain the formatting of the original presentation, click the Keep source formatting check box at the bottom of the Reuse Slides pane to select it as shown in Figure 1.7.

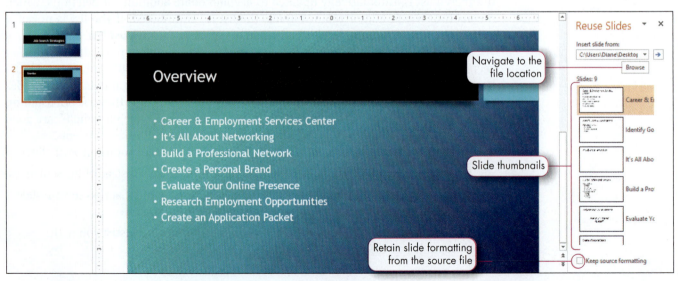

FIGURE 1.7 Reuse Slides Pane

Import a Word Outline

Outlines created using Outline view in Microsoft Word can be imported to quickly create a PowerPoint presentation or to add to existing content. With Word documents, PowerPoint uses heading styles to determine slide heading levels. Each paragraph formatted with the Heading 1 style becomes the title of a new slide, each Heading 2 paragraph becomes the first level of bulleted text on the slide, and so on.

> **To create a presentation from a Word outline, complete the following steps:**
>
> 1. Click the New Slide arrow in the Slides group on the Home tab.
> 2. Select Slides from Outline at the bottom of the gallery.
> 3. Find and select the Word document in the Insert Outline dialog box, and click Insert.
> 4. Select the newly imported slides and click Reset in the Slides group. This resets all of the imported fonts, font styles, and font colors on the selected slides to the default setting of the template.

STEP 4 ▸

Viewing, Rearranging, and Deleting Slides

As you develop your presentation, you navigate between slides, rearrange, or delete slides. The various views available in PowerPoint will make it easier to complete these tasks.

Use Views

When you create a new presentation or open an existing presentation, the presentation will open in the default **Normal view**. All views are found on the View tab, and the most frequently used views are on the right side of the status bar as shown in Figure 1.8. The view you use depends on the task with which you are working.

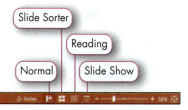

FIGURE 1.8 View Options on the Status Bar

There are three main areas in Normal view as shown in Figure 1.9. The pane on the left displays the slide thumbnails. The large Slide pane on the right is the main workspace and displays the current slide. The pane at the bottom is the Notes pane, where you add speaker notes for that slide. Normal view is where you will work most frequently while creating your presentation.

FIGURE 1.9 Normal View (Default PowerPoint View)

While in Normal view, you can reduce the size of the thumbnail pane. Doing so will expand the workspace so you can see more details while editing content. To hide the thumbnail pane, drag the border that separates the thumbnail and Slide pane to the left until you see the word Thumbnails display. To restore the view, click the arrow at the top of the collapsed thumbnail pane, or click the View tab and click Normal in the Presentation Views group. You can also widen the thumbnail pane to show more detail by dragging the border to the right between the thumbnails and the Slide pane.

In addition to Normal view, PowerPoint offers other views to enable you to work efficiently when creating slides.

- *Outline view*: Use this view when you want to enter text into your presentation using an outline rather than entering the text in the placeholder on the slide. This view can be accessed using the View tab.

- *Slide Sorter view*: This view displays thumbnails of your slides, which enables you to view multiple slides simultaneously. This view is helpful when you want to change the order of your slides or to delete one or more slides. This view is available both on the status bar and the View tab.

- *Notes Page view*: This view shows one slide at a time along with the notes associated with the slide. Use this view for entering and editing large amounts of text you want to place in the notes section. This view is available on the View tab only.

- *Reading View*: Use this view to display your presentation full screen, one slide at a time. It contains some simple controls to assist viewing the presentation.

- *Slide Show view*: When you present your slide show, you use Slide Show view. Slide Show view displays your presentation full screen, one slide at a time to your audience. This view can be accessed on the Slide Show tab or on the status bar.

> **TIP: KEYBOARD SHORTCUT TO SWITCH TO SLIDE SHOW VIEW**
> You will often switch to Slide Show view so that you can get a feel for how the presentation will be seen by the audience. Pressing F5 on your keyboard is a quick way to do this. This keyboard shortcut will start at the beginning of your presentation in Slide Show view. If you want to start viewing on the current slide, click Slide Show on the status bar.

Rearrange Slides

There are times when you will want to rearrange your slides. If the slides you want to move are close to each other, you can "drag and drop" them in Normal view. Click on the thumbnail of the slide in the left pane and drag the slide to the new location. Release the mouse button and the slide will be placed in the new location.

If you have a lot of slides to move and rearrange, or if the slide and its new location are not easily seen in the thumbnail pane, it is easier to do this in Slide Sorter view as you can see more slides in this view. In Slide Sorter view, move the pointer over the slide thumbnail of the slide you want to move and drag to the new location.

> **TIP: MOVING MULTIPLE SLIDES**
> To move multiple slides, hold down Ctrl while you select each slide you want to move and drag them to the new location.

Delete Slides

There will be times when you will want to delete slides from a presentation. Slides can be deleted in Normal view, Slide Sorter view, and Outline view. In Normal view, select the slide in the thumbnail pane, and press Delete on the keyboard. You can also right-click the slide to be deleted and select Delete Slide on the shortcut menu.

Quick Concepts

1. Discuss the importance of knowing who your audience is when creating a presentation. *p. 787*

2. Explain the difference between a theme and a template. *p. 788*

3. Describe the main advantage for using each of the following views: Normal view, Notes Page view, Slide Sorter view, and Slide Show view. *p. 794*

4. Discuss why you might want to reuse slides from another presentation. *p. 792*

Hands-On Exercises

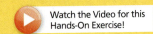

Skills covered: Create a New Presentation • Add a Theme and Variant • Create a Title Slide • Add New Slides • Create Bulleted and Numbered Lists • Reuse Slides from Another Presentation • Use Views • Rearrange Slides • Delete Slides

1 Introduction to PowerPoint

As a career counselor in Career & Employment Services at the college, you have been asked to put together a presentation on job search strategies that can be shared with other counselors for career counseling sessions throughout the year.

STEP 1 ▶ CREATE A NEW PRESENTATION AND ADD A TITLE SLIDE

You will begin to build the presentation by creating a new presentation with the Berlin theme. You will change the theme variant and create the title slide. Refer to Figure 1.10 as you complete Step 1.

FIGURE 1.10 Title Slide with Berlin Theme and Variant Applied

a. Open PowerPoint. Select the **Berlin theme**. Select the second theme variant, the **Blue variant**, and click **Create**.

b. Save the file as **p01h1JobSearch_LastFirst**. When you save files, use your last and first names. For example, as the PowerPoint author, I would name my presentation "p01h1JobSearch_KosharekDiane."

> **TROUBLESHOOTING:** If you make any major mistakes in this exercise, you can close the file, open a new blank presentation again, and then start this exercise over.

c. Click in the **title placeholder** on the Title Slide and type **Job Search Strategies**.

d. Click in the **subtitle placeholder** and type **Career & Employment Services**.

e. Save the presentation.

You continue building your presentation by adding a second slide with the Title and Content layout. After adding a title to the slide, you create a bulleted list of the topics the presentation will cover. Refer to Figure 1.11 as you complete Step 2.

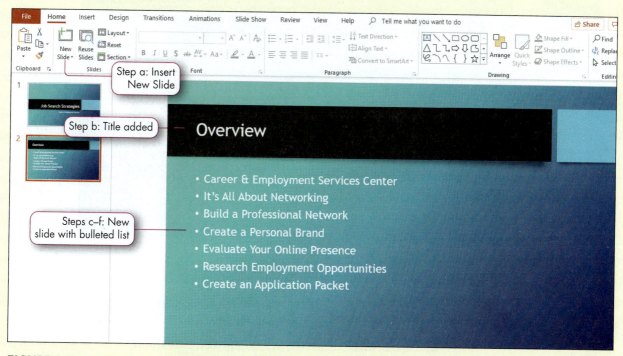

FIGURE 1.11 New Slide with Bulleted List

a. Click **New Slide** in the Slides group on the Home tab.

Because you clicked the top half of New Slide, the new slide uses the Title and Content layout, which is the default slide layout after a Title Slide layout. The new slide contains two placeholders: one for the title and one for body text.

b. Click in the **title placeholder** and type **Overview**.

c. Click in the **content placeholder** below the title placeholder. Type **Career & Employment Services Center** and press **Enter**.

d. Type **It's All About Networking** and press **Enter**.

By default, the list level is the same as the previous level.

e. Type **Build a Professional Network** and press **Enter**.

f. Add the remaining bullet points as listed below, pressing **Enter** after each to move to the next bullet point.

Create a Personal Brand

Evaluate Your Online Presence

Research Employment Opportunities

Create an Application Packet

All bullet points are at the same list level.

g. Save the presentation.

A colleague has content you want to add to your presentation. You will use the Reuse Slides feature to add the slides to your presentation. Refer to Figure 1.12 as you complete Step 3.

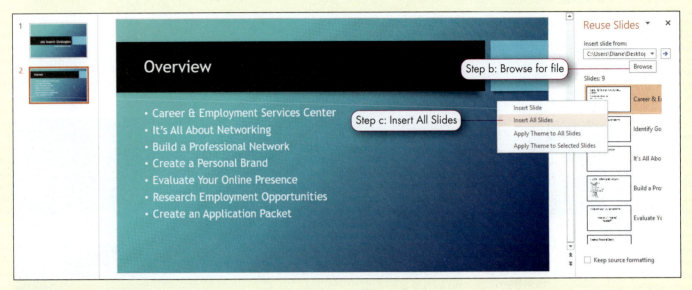

FIGURE 1.12 Reuse Slides pane

a. Ensure you are on Slide 2. Click the **New Slide arrow** in the Slides group on the Home tab and select **Reuse Slides** at the bottom on the New Slides gallery.

b. Click **Browse**, locate *p01h1Jobs*, and then click **Open**.

> **TROUBLESHOOTING:** If you do not see the *p01h1Jobs* file, click Files of type and select All PowerPoint Presentations.

c. Right-click the **first slide**, *Career & Employment Services Center*, in the Reuse Slides pane, and select **Insert All Slides**.

The slides will be added to the presentation after the current slide, Slide 2.

d. Close the Reuse Slides pane.

e. Save the presentation.

While viewing your presentation, you realize that you want to rearrange the slides to allow for a more logical flow. You delete a slide that you have decided will not fit well into your presentation. Refer to Figure 1.13 as you complete Step 4.

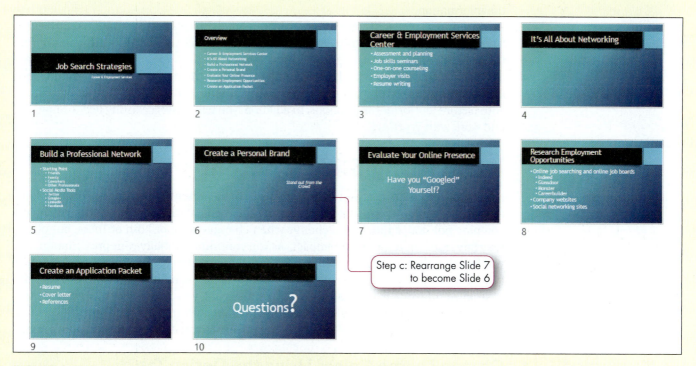

FIGURE 1.13 Content in Slide Sorter View After Rearranging and Deleting Slides

a. Click the **View tab** and click **Slide Sorter** in the Presentation Views group. Change the magnification to make all slides visible.

Note that each slide in the presentation is numbered and has a slide thumbnail.

b. Click **Slide 4** and press **Delete**.

The slides are renumbered to adjust to the deleted slide.

c. Select **Slide 7** and drag it between Slides 5 and 6 so it becomes Slide 6.

After you reposition the slide, the slides will be renumbered.

d. Double-click **Slide 1**.

Your presentation returns to Normal view.

e. Save the presentation. Keep the presentation open if you plan to continue with the next Hands-On Exercise. If not, close the presentation and exit PowerPoint.

Modify a Basic Presentation

As you continue to build your presentation, you will want to make modifications that will enhance the presentation. You can change theme colors and fonts that you feel are more appropriate for the presentation as well as change slide layouts to better showcase the information.

The impact of visual content is well documented. Images and illustrations can be used to convey emotion or illustrate your point. Adding SmartArt and WordArt can improve the presentation's appearance and design.

In this section, you will change theme colors and theme fonts, explore slide layouts, insert pictures stored on your computer or from online using Bing, as well as experiment with picture tool formatting options. In addition, you will convert existing text to SmartArt and work with WordArt.

Formatting Slide Content

If you found a theme that you initially applied to the presentation, but the colors or fonts are not working for your topic, you can change them. With some of the theme choices you may not notice much of a change when changing one or both of these, but others may have more of a significant impact. As you continue to modify your presentation, you will find that there are times when a different slide layout may showcase the information in a better way. Multiple slide layouts are available for each of the themes. You can also customize a layout if you cannot find exactly what you need. Slides often need text formatting changes to better emphasize important information. You can use the text formatting tools on the Home tab in the Font group to assist you when formatting text.

STEP 1 Change Theme Colors Using the Design Tab

Each theme has its own set of coordinating colors. However, in some instances, you might want to choose a different set of colors for that theme. Perhaps you would like the colors to better match a corporate logo, or to offer better contrast, or to coordinate better with selected images.

To change the theme colors, click More in the Variants group on the Design tab and click Colors. There are numerous color combinations available. Select the color theme in the gallery, as shown in Figure 1.14.

FIGURE 1.14 Design Tab with Theme Colors Gallery Open

Change Theme Fonts Using the Design Tab

Theme fonts include two settings, one for headings and another for body text. The headings font applies to all title placeholders, and the body font applies to text in all other placeholders, including default text in charts, tables, SmartArt, and individual text boxes. Using these two fonts for most text helps establish a consistent look throughout a presentation. If you would like a different set of fonts from those that were applied with the selected theme, you can choose from the built-in theme font sets. Various font combinations are available that are designed to work well together.

To change theme fonts, click More in the Variants group on the Design tab and click Fonts. Select the theme fonts from the gallery, as shown in Figure 1.15.

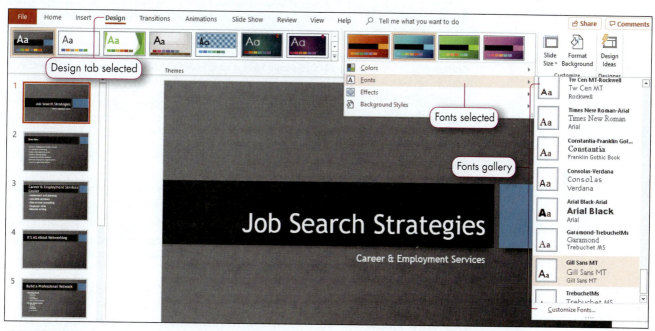

FIGURE 1.15 Design Tab with Theme Fonts Gallery Open

STEP 2 ▶ Change Slide Layouts

PowerPoint provides a set of predefined *slide layouts*. Slide layouts determine the position of placeholders on a slide, and each slide layout is defined by the type and placement of placeholders. When you click the New Slide arrow on the Home tab, a gallery of layouts is displayed. Figure 1.16 shows the Layout gallery available when you select the Blank presentation with the Office theme. Table 1.1 describes some of the most common slide layouts. The number and type of layouts will vary depending on the theme or template chosen when creating a presentation.

FIGURE 1.16 Layout Gallery for the Office Theme

TABLE 1.1	Common Layout Options
Slide Layout	**Description**
Title Slide	Title Slide layout includes a placeholder for a title and a placeholder for a subtitle.
Title and Content	Title and Content layout includes title and content placeholders. The default formatting for text entered in a content placeholder is a bulleted list. In addition, content icons are used to insert objects such as a table, chart, SmartArt graphic, picture, online picture, or video.
Section Header	Section Header layout is used to divide the presentation into sections or main topics similar to how a tabbed page separates sections in a notebook.
Two Content	Two Content layout includes a title placeholder and two side-by-side content placeholders. Often this layout is used to put text on one side of the slide and graphic content on the other side.
Comparison	Comparison layout includes a title placeholder and side-by-side content placeholders used to make a comparison between two topics or sets of data. Above each content placeholder is a heading placeholder.
Title Only	Title Only layout includes just a title placeholder. This layout is often used to insert any type of object such as shapes, WordArt, pictures, charts, etc. without the restrictions of additional placeholders.
Blank	Blank layout contains no placeholders, making it ideal for content that will cover the entire slide, such as a picture.
Content with Caption	Content with Caption layout includes placeholders for a title and for text on the left side. The right side includes a placeholder for content such as a chart or picture.
Picture with Caption	Picture with Caption layout includes a large placeholder for a picture. To the left of the picture placeholder is a placeholder for a caption and a placeholder for descriptive text.

Format Text

When you create a new presentation, the text formatting is determined by the theme applied. Recall that even a blank presentation has a theme, the Office theme. Themes include a default font, font size, and font color for text in the placeholders. However, there may be times when you want to format text so it stands out from the rest. To apply formatting to text, the text must be selected. If you want to apply formatting to all text in a placeholder, click the border of the placeholder so that the border changes to a solid line, which indicates the entire contents of the placeholder are selected. Use the commands in the Font group on the Home tab to apply formatting to the text.

As you format text, keep in mind the following text design guidelines:

- Avoid using underlined text. Underlined text is harder to read, and it is generally assumed that underlined text is a hyperlink.
- Avoid using all capital letters. In addition to being difficult to read, words and phrases in all caps are considered to be "yelling" at the audience.
- Use italics and bold sparingly. Too much emphasis using italics and bold is confusing and makes it difficult to determine what is important.
- Be consistent in capitalization in title placeholders and punctuation in content placeholders.
- Avoid leaving a single word hanging on a line of its own. Modify the placeholder size or press Shift+Enter to create a soft break so that more than one word is on a line.

Inserting and Modifying Pictures

Pictures can be used to add meaning to your message. Often, visually representing an idea or key point is more effective than using words. You can insert pictures from your own library of digital photos that are saved on your hard drive, OneDrive, or another storage medium, or you can insert an online picture using Bing.

PowerPoint supports many graphic file formats. Table 1.2 lists the most commonly used file formats for images.

TABLE 1.2	Types of Graphic File Formats Supported by PowerPoint	
File Format	**Extension**	**Description**
Bitmap	.bmp	**Device Independent Bitmap** A representation consisting of rows and columns of dots. The value of each dot is stored in one or more bits of data. Uncompressed and creates large file size.
GIF File	.gif	**Graphics Interchange Format** Limited to 256 colors. Effective for scanned images such as illustrations rather than for color photographs. Good for line drawings and black-and-white images. Supports transparent backgrounds.
JPEG File Interchange Format	.jpg, .jpeg	**Joint Photographic Experts Group** Supports 16 million colors and is optimized for photographs and complex graphics. Format of choice for most photographs on the Web. Uses lossy compression.
PICT File	.pict, .pic, .pct	**Macintosh PICT** Holds both vector and bitmap images. PICT supports eight colors; PICT2 supports 16 million colors.
PNG File	.png	**Portable Network Graphics** Supports 16 million colors. Approved as a standard by the World Wide Web Consortium (W3C). Intended to replace .gif format. Uses lossy compression.
TIFF File	.tif, .tiff	**Tagged Image File Format** Best file format for storing bitmapped images on personal computers. Can be any resolution. Lossless image storage creates large file sizes. Not widely supported by browsers.
Windows Metafile	.wmf	**Windows Metafile** A Windows 16-bit file format.

Once you have inserted pictures, you may want to enhance their appearance on a slide by resizing, cropping, or adding a picture style. PowerPoint has tools available using the Picture Tools Format tab to accomplish this.

STEP 3 Insert Pictures

There are two ways to add a picture that you have saved to a storage device or location. One way is to use the icon in a content placeholder that is available on the Title and Content and other slide layouts.

> **To add a picture to a slide using a placeholder, complete the following steps:**
>
> 1. Select a layout with a placeholder that includes a Pictures icon.
> 2. Click the Pictures icon to open the Insert Picture dialog box.
> 3. Navigate to the location of your picture files and select the picture you want to use.
> 4. Click Insert.

Figure 1.17 shows an example of a placeholder with a Pictures icon. When you insert a picture in this manner, the picture is centered within the placeholder frame and is sometimes cropped to fit within the placeholder. This effect can cause unwanted results, such as the tops of heads cropped off. If this situation occurs, undo the insertion, enlarge the placeholder, and then repeat the steps for inserting an image to see if this fixes the problem.

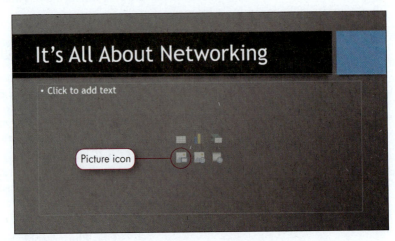

FIGURE 1.17 Example of Content Placeholder with Pictures Icon

Another way to insert a picture is to click Pictures on the Insert tab. The advantage of this method is that your picture comes in at full size rather than centered and cropped in a placeholder, and you do not need a picture placeholder. You can then resize the picture to fit the desired area.

To add a picture using the Insert tab, complete the following steps:

1. Click the Insert tab.
2. Click Pictures in the Images group.
3. Navigate to the location of your picture files and select the picture you want to use.
4. Click Insert.

Add an Online Picture

When you add an online picture, you use Bing. The images available through Bing comply with the Creative Commons license system. Read the Creative Commons license for each image you use to ensure you have the proper permission to avoid copyright infringement.

Keep in mind that legal rights to use images you find on the Internet are a gray area for many reasons. Most search engines do not have reliable filters to distinguish between copyrighted and non-copyrighted images. It is difficult to know whether the image you want to use is in its original form or copied from another site. Therefore, it is recommended that you use Creative Commons and follow their licensing agreements to be safe when using Internet resources for images.

A *copyright* provides legal protection to a written or artistic work, including pictures, drawings, poetry, novels, songs, movies, computer software, and architecture. The owner of the copyright may sell or give up a portion of his or her rights; for example, an author may give distribution rights to a publisher and/or grant movie rights to a studio. *Infringement of copyright* occurs any time a right held by the copyright owner is used without permission of the owner. Anything on the Internet should be considered copyrighted unless the site specifically says it is in the *public domain*, in which case the author is giving everyone the right to freely reproduce and distribute the material, thereby making the work owned by the public at large. A work also may enter the public domain when the copyright has expired. Facts themselves are not covered by copyright, so you can use statistical data without fear of infringement. Images are protected unless the owner gives his or her permission for downloading.

To add an online picture, complete the following steps:

1. Click the Insert tab.
2. Click Online Pictures in the Images group.
3. Type a search term in the search box and press Enter.
4. Select the picture you want to use in the list of results and click Insert.

STEP 4 ## Resize and Position a Picture

You can resize a picture by dragging the sizing handles on a selected picture. Click and drag the corner sizing handles until the picture is the size you want. The corner sizing handles will resize a picture while preserving its original aspect ratio. If you use the side, top, or bottom sizing handles, the image will become distorted.

To resize a picture to an exact size, select the picture. On the Picture Tools Format tab in the Size group, click in the Shape Height or Shape Width box and type the new size.

You may want to position a picture or object on a slide in an exact location. Using the Position function gives you very precise control of where your slide objects are located.

To position a picture in an exact location on a slide, complete the following steps:

1. Click the Dialog Box Launcher in the Size group on the Picture Tools Format tab to open the Format Picture pane.
2. Click the Position arrow in the Format Picture pane.
3. Click inside the Vertical position box and set the position you want. By default, you measure from the top-left corner, but if you want, choose another option in the From list.
4. Click inside the Horizontal position box and set the position you want. By default, you measure from the top-left corner, but if you want, choose another option in the From list.

On a Mac, to position a picture in an exact location on a slide, complete the following steps:

1. Click the Format menu and select Format Object to open the Format Picture pane.
2. Click the Size & Proportion tab and click Position.
3. Continue with Steps 3 and 4 in the PC step box above.

Crop a Picture

Cropping a picture using the Crop tool enables you to eliminate unwanted portions of an image. You can crop it manually to any size you want, to a preset ratio that enables you to crop a picture with an exact measurement and fit it into a predefined space, or to a shape. Figure 1.18 shows a picture with the area to be cropped from view displayed in gray.

FIGURE 1.18 Use Crop to Remove Unwanted Portions of an Image

To crop a picture, complete the following steps:

1. Select the picture.
2. Click the Picture Tools Format tab.
3. Click Crop in the Size group.
4. Point to a cropping handle and drag inward to eliminate the portion of the image you do not want to view. Use a corner cropping handle to crop in two directions at once.
5. Repeat Step 4 for the remaining sides of the picture.
6. Click Crop again to toggle it off.

When you crop a picture, the cropped portion does not display on the slide, but it is not removed from the presentation file. This is helpful in case you decide later to reset the picture to its original state. When you crop an image, because the unwanted portions of the image are not deleted, the file size is not reduced. Use the Compress Pictures feature on the Picture Tools Format tab to reduce the file size of the image, or all images at once, to reduce the file size of the presentation.

> **TIP: COMPRESSING PICTURES**
> When you add pictures to your PowerPoint presentation, the presentation file size increases significantly. The Compress Pictures feature enables you to reduce file sizes by permanently deleting any cropped areas of a selected picture and by changing the resolution of pictures.

Apply Picture Styles

PowerPoint offers a variety of styles that can be used to apply borders and other formatting to pictures to give your images a more visually appealing style. You can apply styles with different borders, border weights, shadows, and reflections as well as different shapes such as rounded rectangles and ovals. When you click on a picture, the picture styles on the Picture Tools Format tab becomes available. Figure 1.19 shows four of the possible picture styles.

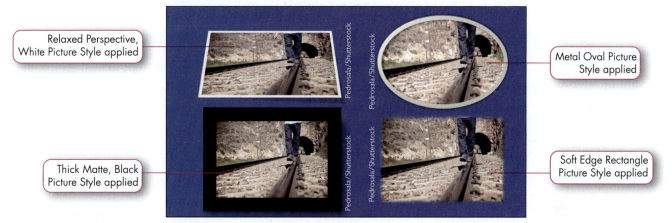

FIGURE 1.19 Picture Style Applications

To apply a picture style, complete the following steps:

1. Select the picture.
2. Click More in the Picture Styles group to open the gallery and point to a style to see a Live Preview, or click the style to apply it to the picture.
3. Apply additional image changes by completing one or more of the following steps:
   - Click Picture Border in the Picture Styles group to select the border color, weight, or dash style.
   - Use Picture Effects to select from Preset, Shadow, Reflection, Glow, Soft Edges, Bevel, and 3-D Rotation effects.
   - Select Picture Layout to apply your picture to a SmartArt graphic.

TIP: CONSISTENCY IN PICTURE STYLES
When you add multiple pictures to your PowerPoint presentation, your pictures should maintain consistency in their formatting, unless there is a reason for making them display differently.

Using SmartArt and WordArt

Bullet points are an effective way of highlighting key points that are being made in a presentation. However, a presentation with just bullet points can lead to audience fatigue and boredom. To break up the visual boredom, and to add an extra means of communicating your message, you can use SmartArt graphics. *SmartArt* enables you to communicate information visually with graphics instead of just using text. There are a variety of styles to choose from in order to illustrate different ideas. You can create the following types:

- List—Shows nonsequential information
- Process—Displays steps in a process
- Cycle—Shows a continual process
- Hierarchy—Displays a decision tree, organizational chart, or pedigree
- Relationship—Illustrates connections
- Matrix—Shows how parts relate to a whole
- Pyramid—Shows proportional relationships with the largest component on the top or bottom
- Picture—Includes a placeholder for pictures within the graphic
- Office.com—Additional layouts available online

Sometimes it is useful to emphasize a word or short phrase. Although you could use bold, or change the font size or color, those modifications may not provide the additional emphasis you require. In these instances, you can call attention to text on a slide by using *WordArt*. You can apply WordArt formatting to existing text or insert a text box with WordArt formatting applied. The WordArt feature modifies text to include special effects, such as color, shadow, gradient, and 3-D appearance.

STEP 5 ## Convert Text to SmartArt

After putting your words on a slide in bullet points or lists, you may realize that the content might be more interesting when put into a SmartArt graphic. Instead of creating a SmartArt graphic from scratch, you can convert text to a SmartArt graphic by selecting the placeholder containing the text and clicking Convert to SmartArt Graphic in the Paragraph group on the Home tab. You can also select the text, right-click the placeholder, and then select Convert to SmartArt. When the gallery opens, click the layout for the SmartArt graphic, or if you do not see a layout that will work, click More SmartArt Graphics as shown in Figure 1.20 to open the Choose a SmartArt Graphic dialog box for additional choices.

In a later chapter you will learn alternative ways to create and insert SmartArt graphics into your presentations. In addition, you will learn other modification techniques for the inserted SmartArt graphics.

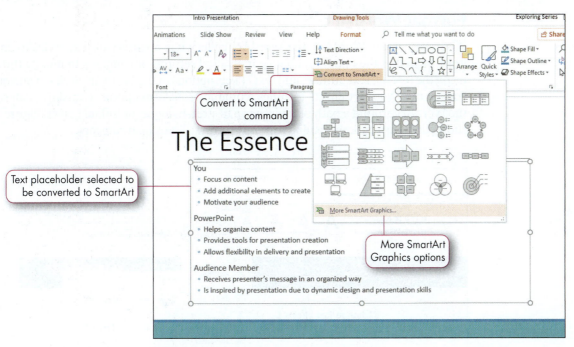

FIGURE 1.20 Convert Text to SmartArt

STEP 6 ▸ Create WordArt

When you create WordArt, the WordArt gallery has a variety of text styles to choose from, as well as the option to change individual settings or elements to modify the style using the text fill, text outline, and text effects options in the WordArt Styles group on the Format tab. Color choices are dependent upon the theme you select. WordArt can be anywhere in your presentation. For example, you can apply WordArt formatting to a slide title or body text. Using WordArt sparingly and keeping the design simple on your slides can create impact. Using too much WordArt, adding complex designs, and adding lots of effects will distract from the slides' appearance and readability, rather than enhance them.

You can create WordArt by clicking WordArt in the Text group on the Insert tab. When the gallery opens, choose a style and type the text in the WordArt placeholder. Additionally, you can convert existing text to WordArt by selecting the text to convert, clicking More in the WordArt Styles group on the Format tab, and then selecting the desired style from the WordArt gallery as shown in Figure 1.21.

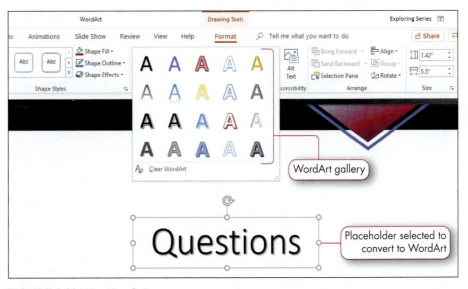

FIGURE 1.21 WordArt Gallery

Format WordArt

When you create WordArt, the WordArt gallery has a variety of text styles to choose from, as well as the option to change individual settings or elements to modify the style using the text fill, text outline, and text effects options in the WordArt Styles group on the Format tab. WordArt Effects includes a unique Transform option. Transform can rotate the WordArt around a path or add a warp to stretch, angle, or inflate letters. Figure 1.22 shows the Warp options available in the WordArt Transform category.

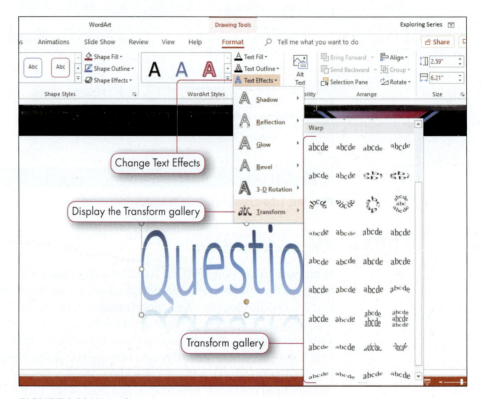

FIGURE 1.22 Warp Options

Quick Concepts

5. Explain why you would change theme colors or theme fonts. ***p. 800***

6. Discuss why it might be necessary to change the layout of a slide. ***p. 801***

7. Describe the text design guidelines and why they are important. ***p. 802***

8. Discuss some of the issues with inserting online images and permissions. ***p. 804***

9. Explain how converting simple text to SmartArt can improve a slide. ***p. 808***

Hands-On Exercises

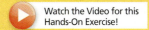

Skills covered: Change Theme Colors • Change Theme Fonts • Change Slide Layouts • Format Text • Insert Pictures • Crop a Picture • Resize and Position a Picture • Apply Picture Styles • Convert List to SmartArt • Create WordArt • Format WordArt

2 Modify a Basic Presentation

To strengthen the message of your presentation, you decide to modify the basic presentation with pictures, WordArt, and SmartArt. Although you like the theme you have chosen, you feel that the colors and fonts are not right, so you decide to change these without changing the overall presentation appearance.

STEP 1 CHANGE THEME COLORS AND THEME FONTS

To make the theme of the presentation fit better with the colors of the college, you change the theme colors. You also decide to change the theme font to one you have used in the past and you know projects well on the screen to large audiences. Refer to Figure 1.23 as you complete Step 1.

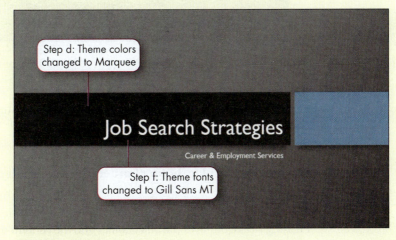

Step d: Theme colors changed to Marquee

Step f: Theme fonts changed to Gill Sans MT

FIGURE 1.23 Changed Theme Colors and Fonts

a. Open *p01h1JobSearch* if you closed it at the end of Hands-On Exercise 1, and save it as **p01h2JobSearch_LastFirst**, changing h1 to h2.

b. Click the **Design tab** and click **More** in the Variants group.

c. Click **Colors**.

   A gallery of theme colors displays showing theme color choices.

d. Scroll down the list of color themes and select **Marquee**.

   The presentation changes to apply the new color theme to the presentation.

e. Click **More** in the Variants groups and click **Fonts**.

f. Scroll down the list and select **Gill Sans MT**.

   PowerPoint applies the new fonts to the presentation.

g. Save the presentation.

You continue modifying the presentation by changing the layout of one of the slides to a layout that will work better for the image you are adding. You will make some minor adjustments to content on the slide to make the title placeholder work. For consistency and appearance, you also decide to make some formatting changes to text on other slides in the presentation. Refer to Figure 1.24 as you complete Step 2.

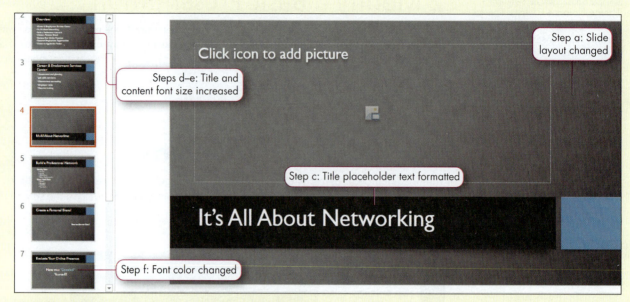

FIGURE 1.24 New Slide Layout and Content Formatted

a. Click **Slide 4**. In the Slides group on the Home tab, click the **Layout arrow**, and then select **Panoramic Picture with Caption**.

The slide layout changes to the new layout.

b. Click the **subtitle placeholder border** (last placeholder on the slide) and press **Delete** on the keyboard.

The dotted line border becomes a solid line, which indicates the placeholder is selected. Pressing Delete removes the placeholder and the content of that placeholder.

c. Click the **title placeholder border** with the text *It's All About Networking*. Click the **Shape Height box** in the Size group on the Format tab. Type **0.9"** and press **Enter**.

d. Click **Slide 2** and click the **title placeholder border**. In the Font group on the Home tab, click the **Font Size arrow** and select **54** from the font size menu.

The font size for the title text is changed to 54 pt.

e. Click the **content placeholder border.** In the Font group, click **Increase Font Size** twice.

The font size for the body placeholder text will increase to 32 pt.

f. Click **Slide 7**. Select the text **Googled** including the quotation marks. Click the **Font Color arrow** and select **Aqua, Accent 1, Lighter 40%**.

g. Save the presentation.

You have found two images that you feel will enhance the presentation and better portray your message. You want to insert them into the presentation. Refer to Figure 1.25 as you complete Step 3.

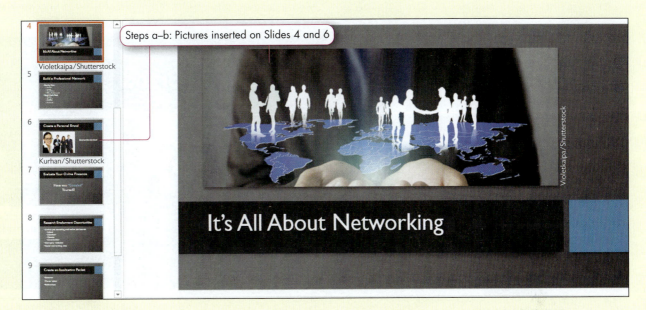

FIGURE 1.25 Inserted Pictures

a. Click **Slide 4**. Click the **Pictures icon** in the content placeholder, navigate to the folder containing your student data files, and then select the *p01h2Networking.jpg* picture file. Click **Insert**.

The picture will be inserted into the content placeholder.

b. Click **Slide 6**. Click the **Pictures icon** in the left placeholder, navigate to the folder containing your student data files, and then select the *p01h2StandOut.jpg* picture file. Click **Insert**.

c. Save the presentation.

The inserted images are a definite improvement to your presentation but need some adjustments. You will crop, resize, and apply styles to the images. Refer to Figure 1.26 as you complete Step 4.

FIGURE 1.26 Formatted Pictures

a. Click the **View tab** and ensure that the Ruler is selected in the Show group.

Activating the ruler will make it easier for you to determine the area to crop.

b. Select the picture on **Slide 6**. Click the **Format tab** and click **Crop** in the Size group.

c. Drag the middle right crop handle to the left until the horizontal ruler reaches approximately the **+.25"** mark.

d. Click **Crop** in the Size group again to crop the area from view and to turn off the Crop feature.

e. Ensure that the picture is selected. In the Size group, change the Shape Width to **7"**.

The photo better fills out the space on the slide.

f. Click **More** in the Picture Styles group.

The picture styles gallery opens.

g. Point to the styles and see how each style impacts the image. Select **Reflected Rounded Rectangle**.

A reflection is added to the bottom of the image and the shape of the image is changed to a rounded rectangle.

h. Click **Slide 4**. Select the image and add the **Reflected Rounded Rectangle Picture Style** by repeating Steps f–g above.

To add consistency to your presentation, you added the same picture style to both images.

i. Save the presentation.

CONVERT A LIST TO A SMARTART GRAPHIC

To illustrate your information in a better way, you decide to convert a bulleted list to SmartArt. This will better showcase your information. Refer to Figure 1.27 as you complete Step 5.

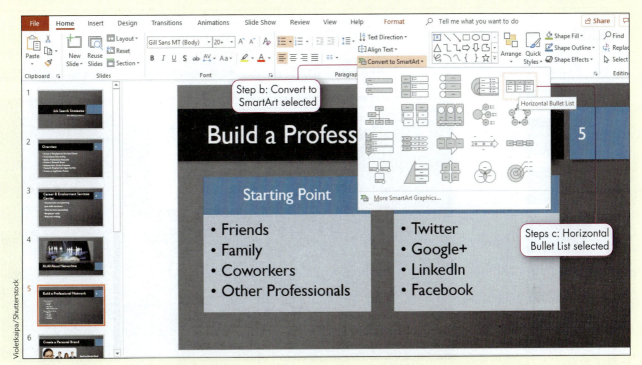

FIGURE 1.27 Convert to SmartArt Graphic

a. Click **Slide 5**. Select the **bulleted text placeholder border**.

b. Click the **Home tab**. Click **Convert to SmartArt** in the Paragraph group.

The gallery displays layouts that are designed to show list information, which is what you want.

c. Click **Horizontal Bullet List**.

The bulleted list is converted to the SmartArt graphic.

d. Save the presentation.

On the last slide, you decide to apply WordArt to add an interesting text effect to text on the slide. Refer to Figure 1.28 as you complete Step 6.

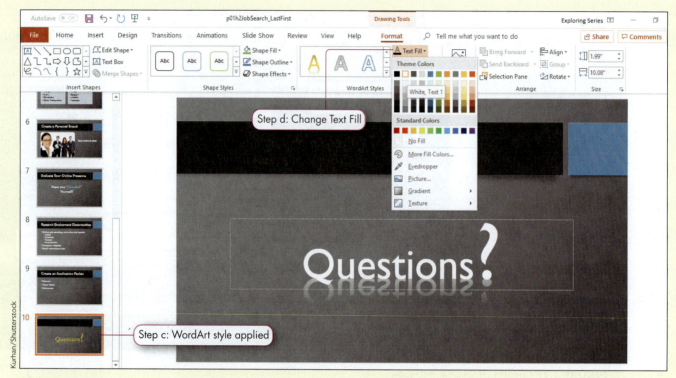

FIGURE 1.28 WordArt Applied to Text

a. Click **Slide 10** and click the **content placeholder border**.

b. Click the **Format tab** and click **More** in the WordArt Styles group.

The gallery displays several preset text effects to choose from. Point to a style to see a Live Preview applied to the text.

c. Select **Gradient Fill: Gold, Accent color 5; Reflection**.

The WordArt style is applied to the text.

d. Click the **Text Fill arrow** and select **White, Text 1** in the WordArt Styles group.

e. Save the presentation. Keep the presentation open if you plan to continue with the next Hands-On Exercise. If not, close the presentation and exit PowerPoint.

Configure and Run a Presentation

After you create the presentation, there are still important things to do before you are ready to distribute or present your presentation. You will need to add some finishing touches to the presentation such as including speaker notes, checking spelling, and adjusting printing options. You can also add identifying information to slides or audience handouts by inserting headers and footers and slide numbers. After all those adjustments, you should look at the handouts in Print Preview and run the presentation in Slide Show and Presenter view to ensure it looks the way you want when distributed and during the presentation.

In this section, you will add speaker notes, insert headers and footers, and check the presentation for spelling errors. You will finish by learning about the Presenter view and exploring printing options for slides and handouts.

Configuring a Presentation for Distribution

With PowerPoint you can add notes to your slides, often referred to as *speaker notes*, to assist you with preparing or delivering your presentation. Headers and footers are used to add identifying information such as the name of the author, the date, the name of the presentation, or slide numbers. After you create the presentation, check it carefully for spelling errors, incorrect word usage, and inconsistent capitalization. Nothing is more embarrassing or can make you appear more unprofessional than a misspelled word enlarged on a big screen.

STEP 1 Add Speaker Notes

You can enter and view your speaker notes using the Notes pane or Notes Page view. If you have a lot of speaker notes to add to your slides, you will want to use the Notes Page view. If you have just a few notes to add, rather than change your view to Notes Page view, you can change Normal view from a two-paned view to a three-paned view as shown in Figure 1.29. To display the Notes pane, click Notes on the status bar. The Notes pane displays below the Slide pane. Drag the splitter bar between the Slide pane and the Notes pane up to expand the Notes pane. The notes will not be displayed to the audience during the presentation, but you can view them in Presenter view, or print them for reference as you deliver the presentation.

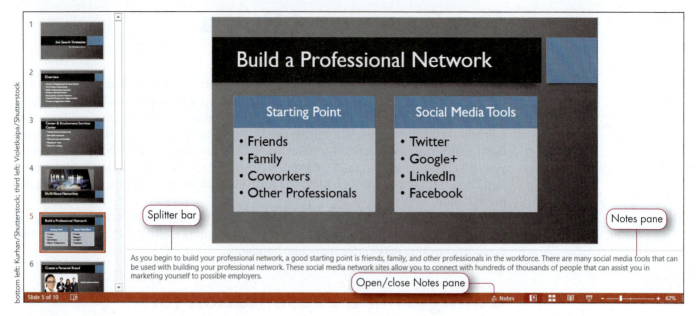

FIGURE 1.29 Normal View with Speaker Notes

> **TIP: FORMAT A SPEAKER NOTE**
> You can apply simple formatting to notes (bold, italics, bullets) in Notes pane. These will show when you use Presenter view and can help guide you to particular comments to emphasize while presenting.

STEP 2 **Insert a Header or Footer**

Only a footer can be added to slides, but both headers and footers can be added to handouts and notes pages. As the theme controls the placement of these elements, you may find headers and footers in various locations.

As a default, no information is included in the header and footer. You can apply a footer to all slides, the current slide, or omit the footer from the title slide by selecting *Don't show on title slide* in the Header and Footer dialog box. Headers and footers can also be customized with font color, type, and size.

> **To insert text in a header or footer, complete the following steps:**
>
> 1. Click the Insert tab.
> 2. Click Header & Footer in the Text group.
> 3. Click the Slide tab or the Notes and Handouts tab.
> 4. Select options and enter text.
> 5. Click Apply to All to add the information to all slides or pages, or if you are adding the footer to a single slide, click Apply.

You can set date and time options in the Header and Footer dialog box as shown in Figure 1.30 to Update automatically or to Fixed. Click Update automatically if you want the date to always be current. Once you select Update automatically, you can select the date format you prefer. Alternatively, you can choose the option to enter a fixed date to preserve the original date, which can enable you to keep track of versions.

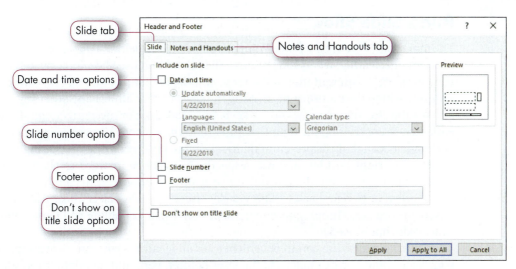

Slide tab

Notes and Handouts tab

Date and time options

Slide number option

Footer option

Don't show on title slide option

FIGURE 1.30 Header and Footer Dialog Box

STEP 3 Check Spelling

To check your presentation for spelling or typographical errors, click the Spelling command in the Proofing group on the Review tab. The Spelling pane displays on the right side of the window. For each error in your presentation, PowerPoint will offer one or more suggestions. Select a suggestion and click Change to correct the error.

The spelling checker is not always correct. It may flag a person's name as being incorrect when it is correct because the name is not part of the built-in dictionary in PowerPoint. In these instances, you can choose to Ignore Once, which will skip the word without changing it; Ignore All, which will not change the word and will skip all instances of the word in the presentation; or Add, which will add the word to the dictionary, so it will not come up as an error in the future.

> **TIP: PROOFING OPTIONS**
> The Spelling feature, by default, does not catch contextual errors like *to*, *too*, and *two*, but you can set the proofing options to help you find and fix this type of error. To modify the proofing options, click File and click Options. Click Proofing in the PowerPoint Options dialog box and click Frequently confused words. With this option selected, the spelling checker will flag contextual mistakes with a red wavy underline. To correct the error, right-click the flagged word and select the proper word choice.

Presenting and Distributing a Slide Show

After creating and proofing the presentation, you will want to view it so you can see how it will appear to your audience. PowerPoint has several ways to do this. You learned about two ways in the Use Views section—Slide Show view and Reading View.

Presenter view is another way to view the presentation. Presenter view requires the use of two monitors when presenting but can be accessed with just one monitor to see how it works.

PowerPoint has several ways to print and preview slides, handouts, notes, and outlines. A printed copy of a PowerPoint presentation can be used as speaker notes for reference during the presentation, for audience handouts or a study guide, or to deliver the presentation if there is an equipment failure. A printout of a single slide with text on it can be used as a poster or banner.

Run a Slide Show

The main goal of creating a PowerPoint presentation is to deliver a message to an audience. As mentioned earlier, when you present a slide show, you use Slide Show view. Slide Show view displays the presentation full screen, one slide at a time. You advance from slide to slide by clicking the mouse or by pressing the spacebar (or almost any other key). You can also use the directional arrows on the keyboard to advance or reverse through slides. If it is easier to use controls on the monitor rather than the keyboard, hover the pointer over the bottom-left corner of the presentation to reveal the onscreen controls (see Figure 1.31).

Use the right and left arrows, respectively, to move forward to the next slide or backward to a previous slide. If during your presentation you need to jump to a slide out of order, or to refer back to a previously discussed slide, select Show All Slides in the onscreen controls. Thumbnails of each slide will display, enabling you to navigate to the exact slide that is needed.

PowerPoint also has some convenient tools and features you can use while presenting your slide show. For example, use the laser pointer, pen, and highlighter tools from the onscreen controls, or by pressing Ctrl+P to draw attention to specific areas of interest on a slide. You can magnify a part of the slide to enlarge hard to read details. For example, if you have a table of data that you would like to enlarge during the presentation, click the magnifying glass from the onscreen controls, and then click the section of the table data you want to magnify. To revert back to the standard view, press Esc or click the magnifying glass icon again.

After the last slide is presented, the presentation will end with a dark screen. Click the mouse or press the spacebar to return to Normal view. If you want to exit the presentation before the last slide is reached, press Esc or click More Slide Show Options in the onscreen controls and select End Show.

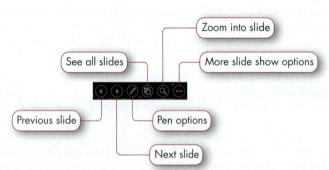

FIGURE 1.31 Onscreen Controls in Slide Show View

Use Presenter View

Presenter view is a valuable view that enables you to deliver a presentation using two monitors simultaneously. Typically, one monitor is a projector that delivers the full screen presentation to the audience; the other monitor is a laptop or computer that displays the presentation for the presenter to refer to in Presenter view. Presenter view includes a slide, a thumbnail image of the next slide, and any speaker notes you have created. Presenter view can be accessed from the Monitors group on the Slide Show tab.

If you want to see what Presenter view looks like or would like to practice using Presenter view until you have access to a second monitor, you can switch to Presenter view from Slide Show view by clicking More slide show options from the onscreen controls in the lower left corner of the slide, and selecting Show Presenter View. Alternatively, you can press Alt+F5 on the keyboard while in Normal view to start Presenter view. Figure 1.32 shows Presenter view.

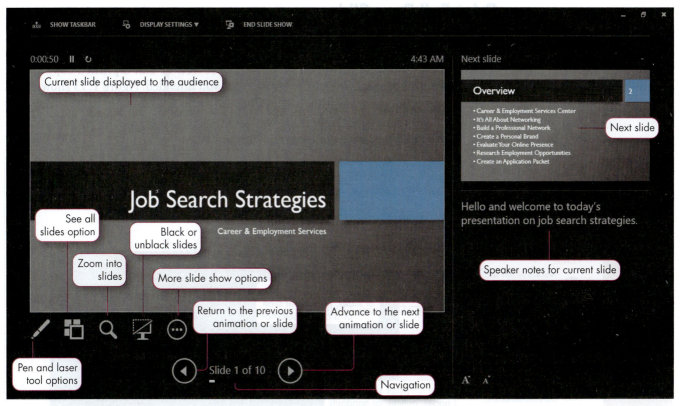

FIGURE 1.32 Presenter View

STEP 5 Print Handouts

Handouts can be used as a reference for you or for the audience. You can print the handouts with one, two, three, four, six, or nine slides per page. Printing three slides per page is a popular option because it places thumbnails of the slides on the left side of the printout and lines on which the audience can write on the right side of the printout. Which handout option you choose will be dependent on what your intended purpose is for the handout. Figure 1.34 shows the option set to Handouts and the Slides per page option set to 6.

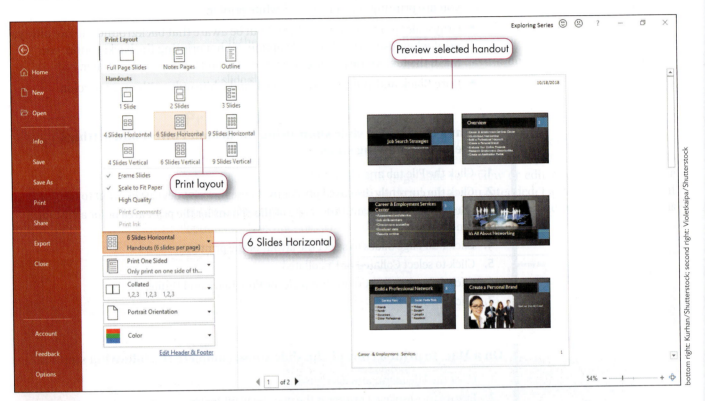

FIGURE 1.34 Setting Print Options for Handouts

Print Notes Pages

If you include charts, technical information, or references in a speaker note, print a notes page if you want the audience to have a copy. To print a specific notes page, change the print layout to Notes Pages and click the Print All Slides arrow. Click Custom Range and enter the specific slide numbers to print.

Print Outlines

You can print your presentation as an outline made up of the slide titles and main text from each of your slides if you want to deal with only a few pages while presenting. The outline generally gives you enough detail to keep you on track with your presentation but does not display speaker notes.

Quick Concepts

10. Discuss the purpose of a speaker note. **p. 817**

11. Compare the Update automatically and Fixed date options for slide footers. Give an example of when each would be used. **p. 818**

12. Discuss the printing options for handouts in PowerPoint. **p. 824**

Hands-On Exercises

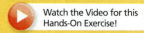
Skills covered: Add a Speaker Note • Insert a Header, Footer, and Slide Numbers • Check Spelling • Use Presenter View • Print Handouts

3 Configure and Run a Presentation

To add the final touches to your presentation, you add speaker notes to three of your slides, create a slide footer and a Notes and Handouts header and footer, and check the presentation for errors on your slides and in your notes. You will work with Presenter view practicing the various ways to move around in a presentation. Finally, you work with print options to set up the presentation to print three slides per page.

STEP 1 ADD SPEAKER NOTES

The slides that you imported into the presentation using the Reuse Slides feature have notes already included. You add speaker notes to the three slides that do not have notes to remind you of what you want to say during your presentation. Refer to Figure 1.35 as you complete Step 1.

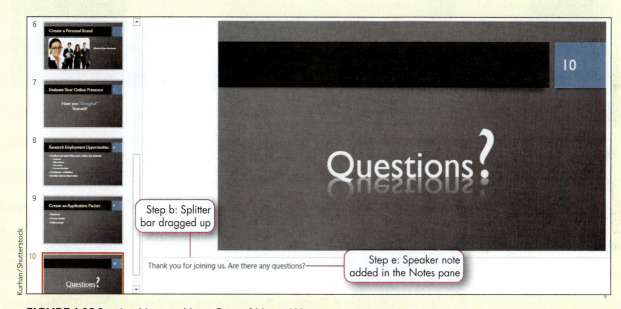

Kurhan/Shutterstock

FIGURE 1.35 Speaker Notes in Notes Pane of Normal View

a. Open *p01h2JobSearch_LastFirst* if you closed it after the last Hands-On Exercise and save it as **p01h3JobSearch_LastFirst**, changing h2 to h3.

b. Click **Slide 3**. In Normal view, expand the Notes pane by clicking **Notes** on the status bar. Drag the splitter bar up to see all of the notes. Review the notes. Continue to review the notes for Slides 4–9.

c. Click **Slide 1**. Type **Hello and welcome to today's presentation on job search strategies.** including the period in the Notes pane.

d. Click **Slide 2**, and in the Notes pane type **Listed are the topics we will be discussing in today's presentation.**

e. Click **Slide 10**, and in the Notes pane type **Thank you for joining us. Are there any questions?**

f. Save the presentation.

You add information to the Notes and Handouts footer and a slide number to all the slides with the exception of the title slide. Refer to Figure 1.36 as you complete Step 2.

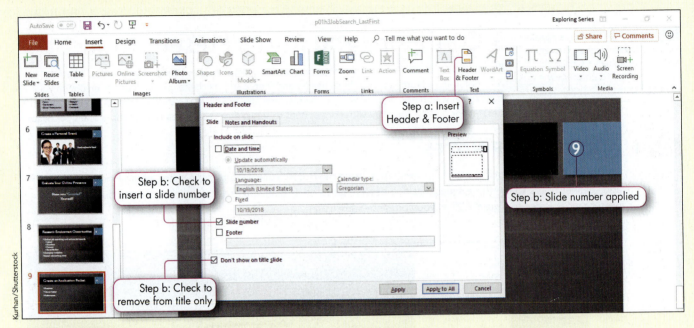

FIGURE 1.36 Slide Footer Options

a. Click the **Insert tab** and click **Header & Footer** in the Text group.

The Header and Footer dialog box opens with the Slide tab active.

b. Click the **Slide number check box** to select it. Click **Don't show on title slide** and click **Apply to All**.

The slide number will display on all slides except the title slide. Note the position of the slide number on the slide. The theme determined the location of the slide number on the slide.

c. Click **Header & Footer** in the Text group, click the **Notes and Handouts tab**, and then click **Footer**. Type **Career & Employment Services** in the footer box and click **Apply to All**.

The footer will be added to the notes and handouts when printed or viewed in Print Preview.

d. Save the presentation.

CHECK SPELLING

It is important to proofread your presentation to ensure you did not make any errors in spelling or grammar. Although you intend for the speaker notes to be just for you, you want to ensure there are no spelling errors in case you distribute the presentation after all. In this step you will check the spelling of your presentation and notes. Refer to Figure 1.37 as you complete Step 3.

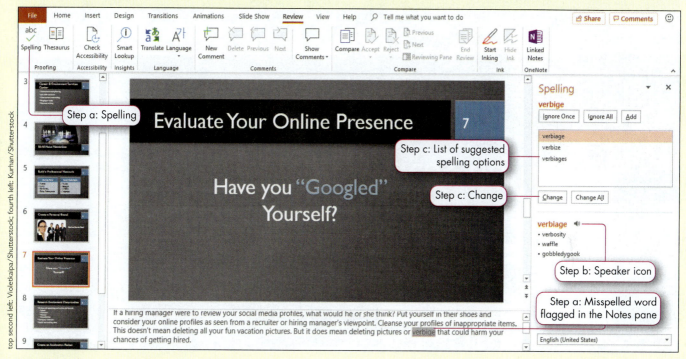

FIGURE 1.37 Spelling Task Pane with Misspelled Word in Notes Pane

a. Click **Slide 1**. Click the **Review tab** and click **Spelling** in the Proofing group.

The spelling pane opens on the right of Slide 7 with the flagged word "verbige" highlighted in the Notes pane.

b. Click the **speaker icon** in the Spelling task pane. The word "verbiage" is pronounced.

c. Click **verbiage** in the list of suggested corrections and click **Change**.

The word is corrected and the next slide containing a possible spelling error is displayed. Slide 8 displays with the word "Careerbuilder" flagged.

d. Click **CareerBuilder** in the list of suggested corrections and click **Change**.

This is the last error in the presentation. A dialog box will display indicating that the spell check is complete.

e. Click **OK** in the Microsoft PowerPoint dialog box.

f. Save the presentation.

You will use Presenter view when you present your slide show to an audience. You will switch to Presenter view to familiarize yourself with this view and the tools available. Refer to Figure 1.38 as you complete Step 4.

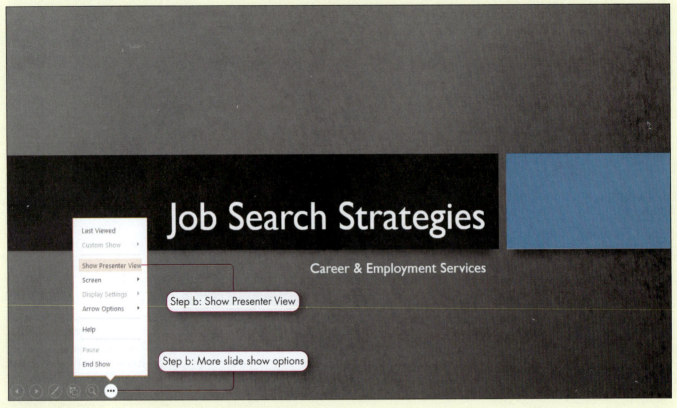

FIGURE 1.38 Switch to Presenter View from Slide Show View

a. Click **Slide 1**. Click **Slide Show** on the status bar.

Slide 1 displays on the screen in Slide Show view.

b. Move the pointer to display the buttons in the lower left-hand corner of the slide. Click **More slide show options** to open the menu and select **Show Presenter View**.

The presentation will change to Presenter view.

c. Click **See all slides** below the current slide on the control bar.

The screen changes to show thumbnails of all the slides in the presentation.

d. Click the **Slide 7 thumbnail**.

The presentation will return to Presenter view and display Slide 7.

e. Click **Advance to next slide** on the control bar.

The presentation moves to Slide 8, which is the next slide.

f. Press **Spacebar** twice.

The presentation displays the last slide, Slide 10. Pressing the spacebar is another way to advance slides.

g. Press **Esc** on the keyboard to return the presentation to Normal view.

h. Save the presentation.

To enable your audience to follow along, you create handouts. You choose a handout option with space for them to take notes on during the presentation and to have as a reference for the future. Refer to Figure 1.39 as you complete Step 5.

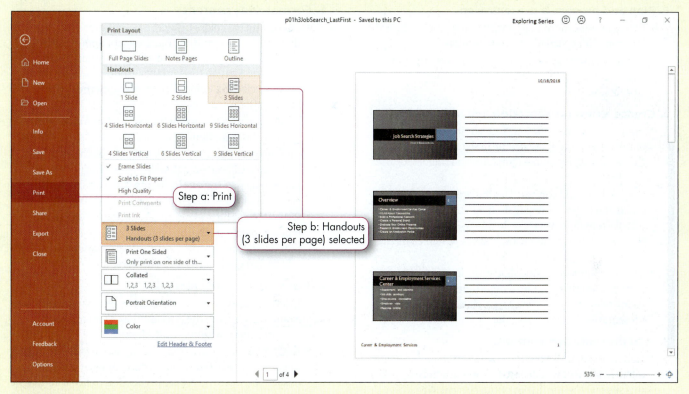

FIGURE 1.39 Audience Handouts

a. Click **File** and click **Print**.

b. Click **Full Page Slides** and select **3 Slides** in the Handouts section.

> **TROUBLESHOOTING:** If you have previously selected a different print layout, Full Page Slides will be changed to that layout. Click the arrow next to the displayed layout option to select a different layout.

> **MAC TROUBLESHOOTING:** Click the Layout arrow and select Handouts (3 slides per page).

c. Click **Print** to print the presentation if requested by your instructor.

d. Save and close the file. Based on your instructor's directions, submit the following:

   p01h3JobSearch_LastFirst.

Chapter Objectives Review

After reading this chapter, you have accomplished the following objectives:

1. Plan and prepare a presentation.

- Plan a presentation: Determine the purpose, audience, and content needed for the presentation.
- Begin by brainstorming your ideas, narrowing them down into an outline, and arranging them in a storyboard.

2. Create a new presentation and add a title slide.

- Create a new presentation: You can start from a blank presentation, create one based on a built-in theme, search for online templates and themes, or use QuickStarter.
- Add a theme and variant: Themes provide you with a quick and easy way to add design to the presentation for a consistent look. Variants modify the theme by offering the same theme design with different design elements such as colors, fonts, and effects.
- Create a title slide: A title slide is the first slide in the presentation that contains important information to be introduced to the audience such as the name of the presentation and the presenter.

3. Add presentation content.

- Add new slides: Use the New Slide button on the Home tab to insert a new slide into the presentation. By default, this slide will be the layout of the current slide.
- Each slide should represent a key concept in your presentation. Be mindful that "less is more" so the audience can focus on the speaker rather than reading the slides.
- Create bulleted and numbered lists: Bullets and numbering enable you to organize text in lists.
- Reuse slides from another presentation: The Reuse Slides feature saves time by importing slides that exist in another presentation to your current presentation.
- Import a Word outline: Outlines created using Outline view in Microsoft Word can be imported to quickly create a PowerPoint presentation or to add to existing content.

4. View, rearrange, and delete slides.

- Use views: PowerPoint offers additional views to help you work efficiently when creating slides such as Outline view, Slide Sorter view, Notes Page view, Reading view, and Slide Show view.
- Rearrange slides: When you want to rearrange the order of your slides, "drag and drop" them in Normal view or move around many slides in Slide Sorter view.
- Delete slides: When you want to delete slides in a presentation, you can select the slide and press Delete on the keyboard, or right-click the slide to be deleted and on the shortcut menu select Delete Slide.

5. Format slide content.

- Change theme colors using the Design tab: If you find that the theme's built-in colors are not appropriate for the presentation, you can apply new theme colors by clicking More in the Variants group on the Design tab and selecting Colors. There are numerous color combinations available.
- Change theme fonts using the Design tab: You can choose from the built-in theme fonts or create a custom font set.
- Change slide layouts: PowerPoint provides a set of predefined slide layouts that determine the position of the placeholders in various locations. You can customize the elements of the slide layout to better fit your presentation.
- Format text: The presentation is formatted with a style of text based on a theme, but you can change this style so that it better fits the needs of the presentation. Recall the text design guidelines for the best result.

6. Insert and modify pictures.

- Insert pictures: Insert a previously saved picture directly from your files into the presentation. You can insert a picture with or without a placeholder.
- Add an online picture: When using pictures found online, read the Creative Commons license for each image to ensure you have the proper permission to avoid copyright infringement.
- Resize and position a picture: You can resize a picture by dragging the sizing handles on the selected picture or using the Format Picture task pane.
- Crop a picture: Cropping a picture enables you to eliminate unwanted portions of an image.
- Apply Picture Styles: You can apply styles and other formatting to pictures such as different borders, border weights, shadows, and reflections as well as different shapes.

7. Use SmartArt and WordArt.

- Convert text to SmartArt: The SmartArt feature enables you to create a visual representation of the information.
- Create WordArt: Call attention to text on a slide by using WordArt, which uses special effects based on text rather than a shape.
- Format WordArt: The WordArt gallery has a variety of text styles to choose from, as well as the option to change individual settings or elements to modify the style using the text fill, text outline, and text effects options.

8. Configure a presentation for distribution.

- Add speaker notes: Speaker notes assist you with preparing or delivering your presentation. Enter and view your speaker notes using the Notes pane or the Notes Page view.

- Insert a header or footer: Headers and footers are used for identifying information on the slide or on handouts and notes pages. Header and footer locations vary depending on the theme applied. Slide numbers are also inserted in the header or footer.
- Check spelling: Check spelling for possible misspelling on the slides and notes sections for the presentation. If a word is flagged as misspelled, you have the option to change, ignore, ignore all, or add to the dictionary.

9. Present and distribute a slide show.

- Run a slide show: Use Slide Show view to run a presentation. Use the keyboard or onscreen controls to advance through the presentation. Onscreen controls also enable you to use a pen or highlighter to mark up a slide during the presentation.
- Use Presenter view: The Presenter view enables the presenter to deliver a presentation by using two monitors simultaneously. One view displays the presentation to the audience, whereas the other displays the presentation for the presenter, including any speaker notes that may have been added.
- Various controls help the presenter navigate through the presentation. These controls include moving to different slides, viewing all slides, pointing to or writing on the slides, and hiding or unhiding slides.
- Print full page slides: Print full page slides for use as a backup or when the slides contain a great deal of detail the audience needs to examine.
- Print handouts: Handouts print miniatures of the slides using 1, 2, 3, 4, 6, or 9 slide thumbnails per page. Handouts are useful to an audience.
- Print notes pages: The Notes Page option prints a single thumbnail of a slide with its associated notes.
- Print outlines: Outline view prints the titles and main points of the presentation in outline format.

Key Terms Matching

Match the key terms with their definitions. Write the key term letter by the appropriate numbered definition.

a. Bulleted list
b. Copyright
c. Cropping
d. Deck
e. Normal view
f. Numbered list
g. Placeholder
h. Presenter view
i. Public domain
j. QuickStarter

k. Rotation handle
l. Sizing handles
m. Slide
n. Slide layout
o. Slide show
p. Speaker notes
q. Storyboard
r. Theme
s. Thumbnail
t. Variant

1. _____ Defines containers, positioning, and formatting for all of the content that displays on a slide. **p. 801**

2. _____ The default PowerPoint view, containing three panes that provide maximum flexibility in working with the presentation. **p. 793**

3. _____ A container that holds content. **p. 790**

4. _____ The most basic element of PowerPoint, analogous to a page in a Word document. **p. 786**

5. _____ White circles that display on the sides and corners of a placeholder; enables the user to adjust the height and width of the object. **p. 791**

6. _____ The process of reducing an image size by eliminating unwanted portions of an image or other graphical object. **p. 805**

7. _____ The rights to a literary work or property owned by the public at large. **p. 804**

8. _____ Slides are often referred to as because of how easily they can be shuffled around. **p. 786**

9. _____ Used if the speaker needs to enter and edit text for reference in the presentation. **p. 817**

10. _____ A view that delivers a presentation on two monitors simultaneously. **p. 821**

11. _____ A variation of the theme you have chosen, using different color options. **p. 789**

12. _____ The legal protection afforded to a written or artistic work. **p. 804**

13. _____ A slide miniature. **p. 788**

14. _____ A graphic element that itemizes and separates paragraph text to increase readability. **p. 791**

15. _____ A collection of slides. **p. 786**

16. _____ A visual plan that helps you plan the direction of your presentation slides. **p. 787**

17. _____ A collection of formatting choices that includes colors, fonts, and special effects. **p. 788**

18. _____ A circular arrow at the top of the placeholder used to change the angle of the placeholder. **p. 791**

19. _____ Sequences items in a list by displaying a successive number beside each item. **p. 791**

20. _____ Builds an outline with suggested sections, talking points, and properly attributed Creative Commons images. **p. 788**

Multiple Choice

1. Which of the following terms describes a visual planning tool that is used to map out the direction of a presentation?

   (a) Theme

   (b) Storyboard

   (c) Variant

   (d) SmartArt

2. Which of the following statements is *not* accurate about placeholders?

   (a) Placeholders may be resized.

   (b) All of the content contained in a placeholder is selected when the border of the placeholder is double-clicked.

   (c) Placeholder positions are determined by the slide layout and may not be changed.

   (d) Placeholders can contain text, pictures, tables, and more.

3. Which of the following is *false* about headers and footers?

   (a) Headers and footers can be customized with font color, type, and size.

   (b) Only a footer can be added to slides, but both headers and footers can be added to handouts and notes pages.

   (c) Slide header or footer information can be different for handouts and notes pages.

   (d) As a default, information is displayed in the header and footer.

4. Which print method provides lined space for note taking by the audience?

   (a) Handout, 6 Slides Horizontal

   (b) Outline

   (c) Notes Pages

   (d) Handout, 3 Slides

5. Which of the following components are contained in Normal view?

   (a) Slide Sorter pane, Slides tab, and Reading pane

   (b) Slides pane and View pane

   (c) Slides tab, Slide pane, and Reading pane

   (d) Thumbnails, Slide pane, and Notes pane

6. What view is the best choice if you want to reorder the slides in a presentation?

   (a) Slide Sorter view

   (b) Presenter view

   (c) Reading view

   (d) Slide Show view

7. Which of the following layouts is most commonly used when introducing the topic of the presentation and the speaker?

   (a) Blank

   (b) Title Slide

   (c) Comparison

   (d) 3 column

8. Which is *not* a way to reduce bullet points on your slides?

   (a) Use multiple slides to split up content.

   (b) Display 10 lines of bullet points.

   (c) Cut content down to essentials only using main ideas instead of full sentences.

   (d) Represent content visually.

9. SmartArt is used to:

   (a) apply borders and other formatting to pictures.

   (b) create a visual representation of information.

   (c) eliminate unwanted portions of an image.

   (d) add special effects based on text rather than shape.

10. Which of the following is considered copyright infringement?

   (a) A copyrighted poem used without the permission of the author

   (b) An image denoted as public domain

   (c) Facts

   (d) Work with expired copyright

Practice Exercises

1 Stress Management for Students

FROM SCRATCH The slide show you create in this practice exercise covers concepts and skills that will enable you to understand your stress as a college student. You create a title slide, an introduction slide, and reuse slides from another presentation. You will then add and format images, SmartArt, and WordArt to enhance your presentation. Finally, you print your slides to use as a reference. Refer to Figure 1.40 as you complete the exercise.

FIGURE 1.40 Managing Your Stress

a. Start PowerPoint and click **New**.

b. Click the **Integral theme** and change the variant to the the second variant in the second row. Click **Create**.

c. Save the presentation as **p01p1ManageStress_LastFirst**.

d. Click in the **title placeholder** and type **Stress Relief**. Click in the **subtitle placeholder** and type **your name**.

e. Click the **New Slide arrow** in the Slides group on the Home tab to create a new slide (Slide 2) using the **Title and Content layout**. Type **Fast Facts on Stress** in the title placeholder. In the content placeholder, type the following bullet points pressing **Enter** after each to move to the next bullet point:

   • **Stress helps the body prepare to face danger**
   • **Symptoms can be both physical and psychological**
   • **Short-term stress can be helpful**
   • **Long-term stress is linked to various health conditions**
   • **Prepare for stress by learning some self-management tips**

f. Click the **New Slide arrow** and select **Reuse Slides** to open the Reuse Slides pane. Click **Browse**, select *p01p1Stress*, and then click **Open**.

g. Right-click the first slide in the Reuse Slides pane and select **Insert All Slides** to insert all of the slides into the presentation. Close the Reuse Slides pane.

h. Click the **View tab** and click **Slide Sorter**.

i. Click **Slide 3** and press **Delete**.

j. Click **Slide 6**, press **Ctrl** on the keyboard, and then click **Slide 7**. Drag the slides between Slides 2 and 3 so they become Slides 3 and 4.

k. Click **Normal** to return to the default view and select **Slide 1**.

l. Click the **Design tab**, click **More** in the Variants group, and then select **Colors**. Select the **Blue Warm** color theme.

m. Click **Slide 3**. Click the **Layout arrow** in the Slides group on the Home tab and select **Picture with Caption**.

n. Click **Slide 2**. Click the **title placeholder border** in the Font group on the Home tab, click the **Font Size arrow**, and then select **66**.

o. Click the **content placeholder border** and click **Increase Font Size** in the Font group three times to increase the font size to **32**.

p. Click **Slide 4** and select the text **new skills**. In the Font group, click the **Font Color arrow**, and select **Light Blue, Text 2, Darker 25%**.

q. Click **Slide 3**. Click **Pictures** in the content placeholder, locate the *p01p1Balance.jpg* picture file from your student data files, and then click **Insert**. With the picture selected, click **More** in the Picture Styles group on the Format tab, and then select **Soft Edge Rectangle**.

r. Select the picture on **Slide 8**. Click the **Format tab** and click **Crop** in the Size group. Drag the middle bottom crop handle up until it is slightly below the words *Take 5*. Click **Crop** in the Size group again to crop the area from view. In the Size group, change the width to **9.6"**.

s. Ensure the picture is still selected, click **More** in the Pictures Styles group, and then select **Soft Edge Rectangle**.

t. Type the following in the Notes pane for Slide 6: **If you are experiencing any of these items, you may be experiencing too much stress.**

u. Click **Slide 5**. Select the **bulleted text placeholder border**. Click on the **Home tab**, click **Convert to SmartArt** in the Paragraph group, and then select **Horizontal Bullet List**.

v. Click **Slide 3** and select the **title placeholder border** on the left. Click the **Format tab**, click **More** in the WordArt Styles group, and then select **Gradient Fill: Teal, Accent color 5; Reflection**. In the WordArt Styles group, click the **Text Fill arrow** and select **White, Text 1**. Click the **Home tab**, click the **Font Size arrow** in the Font group, and then select **88**.

w. Click the **Review tab** and click **Spelling**. Correct any errors.

x. Click the **Insert tab** and click **Header & Footer** in the Text group. Click the **Notes and Handouts tab**, and click **Footer**. Type **Managing Stress** in the footer box and click **Apply to All**.

y. Click the **File tab**, click **Print**, and then click **Full Page Slides**. Select **6 Slides Horizontal** and click **Print** if your instructor asks you to submit printed slides.

z. Save and close the presentation. Close PowerPoint. Based on your instructor's directions, submit p01p1ManageStress_LastFirst.

2 Introduction to PowerPoint

FROM SCRATCH You have been asked to put together a brief presentation introducing PowerPoint to a group of individuals who are new to PowerPoint and its use as presentation software. You have been given a basic presentation to enhance and modify. Refer to Figure 1.41 as you complete this exercise.

FIGURE 1.41 Introduction to PowerPoint

a. Start PowerPoint and click **Blank Presentation**.

b. Save the presentation as **p01p2PowerPointIntro_LastFirst**.

c. Click in the **title placeholder** and type **Introduction to PowerPoint**. Click in the **subtitle placeholder** and type **your name**.

d. Click the **Design tab** and click **More** in the Themes group. Select **Retrospect** and change the variant to the **second** one (white with green).

e. Click **More** in the Variants group, and select **Colors**. In the Colors gallery, select **Blue Green**.

f. Click the **New Slide arrow** in the Slides group on the Home tab to create a new slide (Slide 2) using the **Title and Content layout** for the first main point of the slide show. Type **Why Use PowerPoint** in the title placeholder and type the following bulleted text in the content placeholder:

- **Ease of use**
- **It's everywhere**
- **When used properly can be a powerful tool**
- **Easily customized**
- **Integration with other Office applications**
- **Flexible output for sharing**

g. Click the **New Slide arrow** and select **Reuse Slides** to open the Reuse Slides pane. Click **Browse**, select *p01p2Intro*, and then click **Open**.

h. Click **Slides 2**, **3**, **4**, and **6** in the Reuse Slides pane to add these slides to the presentation.

i. Click the **Keep source formatting check box** to select it and click **Slide 5**. Close the Reuse Slides pane.

j. Click the **View tab** and click **Slide Sorter view**.

k. Move **Slide 3** so that it becomes Slide 2. Move **Slide 7** so it becomes Slide 6.

l. Click **Normal view** to return to the default view and select **Slide 2**. Click the **Layout arrow** in the Slides group on the Home tab and select **Picture with Caption**.

m. Click the bottom placeholder and type **A powerful software package designed to assist in the creation and delivery of presentations. The software incorporates images, sounds, videos, text, and charts to create an interactive presentation.**

n. Click the **content placeholder border** and increase the font size to **18 pt**.

o. Click the **Pictures icon** in the content placeholder, locate the image *p01p2Speaker.jpg*, and then click **Insert**. With the picture selected, click **More** in the Picture Styles group on the Format tab, and then select **Simple Frame, Black**.

p. Type the following in the Notes pane for Slide 1: **Welcome to Introduction to PowerPoint**.

q. Click **Slide 5** and select the **bulleted text placeholder border**. On the Home tab, click **Convert to SmartArt** in the Paragraph group. Select **Horizontal Bullet List**.

r. Click **Slide 4** and select the **bulleted text placeholder border**. On the Home tab, click **Convert to SmartArt** in the Paragraph group, click **More SmartArt Graphics** at the bottom of the gallery, and then select **Basic Block List**.

s. Click **Slide 3** and select the **bulleted text placeholder border**. On the Home tab, click the **Font Size arrow** in the Font group and select **32**.

t. Click **Slide 7** and select the **content placeholder border**. In the WordArt styles group, on the Format tab, click **More**, and select **Fill: Black, Text color 1; Shadow**. In the WordArt Styles group, click the **Text Effects arrow**, select **Transform**, and then select **Square** in the Warp group.

u. Click the **Review tab** and click **Spelling** in the Proofing group. Correct any errors.

v. Click the **Insert tab** and click **Header & Footer** in the Text group. Click the **Notes and Handouts tab** and click **Footer**. Type **Introduction to PowerPoint** in the footer box, and click **Apply to All**.

w. Save and close the presentation. Close PowerPoint. Based on your instructor's directions, submit p01p2PowerPointIntro_LastFirst.

1 Time Management

FROM SCRATCH

You belong to a student organization on campus that has asked you to put together a presentation on time management. You created a presentation with some basic content for a school project you will use as a starting point. You want to modify the presentation to make it more appealing and better portray the message.

a. Start a new presentation. Apply the **Gallery theme** and change the variant to the **second** (gray) variant. Save the presentation as **p01m1TimeManagement_LastFirst**.

b. Change the theme colors to **Aspect** and the theme fonts to **Corbel**.

c. Add the title **Time Management** in the title placeholder. Type **Use Your Time Wisely** in the subtitle placeholder.

d. Click the **New Slide arrow** in the Slides group on the Home tab and select **Reuse Slides**.

e. Browse to locate the *p01m1Time* presentation from the student data files in the Reuse Slides pane.

f. Insert all slides in the Reuse Slides pane. Close the Reuse Slides pane.

g. Change the view to Slide Sorter view and delete Slide 2.

h. Move Slide 3 so that it becomes Slide 2. Double-click **Slide 2** to return to Normal view.

i. Click **Slide 5**. Click **New Slide** in the Slides group on the Home tab.
   - Change the slide layout of the inserted slide to **Content with Caption**.
   - Click inside the **top placeholder** on the left side and type **What's Stealing Your Time?** Increase the font size of the text to **44** and apply **Bold**.
   - Click inside the bottom placeholder on the left side and type **Identify aspects of your personal management that need to improve!** Increase the font size of the text to **24**.
   - Click the **Pictures icon** in the right placeholder, locate the image *p01m1Steal.jpg* from your student data files, and then click **Insert**. Change the Shape Width of the image to **6.3"**. Apply the **Bevel Perspective Left, White Picture Style**. Change the Picture Border to **Tan, Background 2**. Set the horizontal position of the image to **4.8"** from Top Left Corner and the vertical position to **1.5"** from the Top Left Corner.

j. Click **Slide 4** and change the layout to **Title and Content**.
   - Click the **Pictures icon**, locate the image *p01m1TimeMarches.jpg* from your student data files, and then click **Insert**.
   - Crop the top and bottom of the image so that most of the white area is removed. Change the Shape Width of the image to **7.9"**. Apply the **Moderate Frame, White Picture Style**. Change the Picture Border to **Tan, Background 2**. Set the Horizontal position of the image to **2.7"** from Top Left Corner and the Vertical position to **2.5"** from the Top Left Corner.

k. Click **Slide 5** and convert the list in the body placeholder to a **Vertical Box List SmartArt graphic**.

l. Click **Slide 3** and convert the list in the body placeholder to a **Basic Block List SmartArt graphic**.

m. Use the spelling checker on the presentation and correct all errors.

n. Type the following speaker note on Slide 6: **To better manage your time it will become important to identify aspects of your personal management that may need to improve.**

o. Save and close the file. Close PowerPoint. Based on your instructor's directions, submit p01m1TimeManagement_LastFirst.

FROM SCRATCH You have been asked to put together a promotional presentation on the company you work for, Peddle and Paddle. The company has a presentation it has used in the past that you have been asked to modify.

a. Start a new presentation. Apply the **Wood Type theme**. Save the presentation as **p01m2OutdoorAdventures_LastFirst**.

b. Add the title **Peddle and Paddle** in the title placeholder. Type **The Ultimate Outdoor Adventure** in the subtitle placeholder.

c. Click the **New Slide arrow** in the Slides group on the Home tab and select **Reuse Slides**.

d. Browse to locate the *p01m2Adventure* presentation from the student data files in the Reuse Slides pane.

e. Insert all slides in the Reuse Slides pane. Close the Reuse Slides pane.

f. Change the view to Slide Sorter view and delete Slide 2.

g. Select **Slide 6** and move it so it becomes Slide 4.

h. Double-click **Slide 4** to return to Normal view.

i. Click **Slide 5** and insert the *p01m2Peddle.jpg* image. Change the height to **5.8"**. Set the Horizontal position of the image to **3.4"** from Top Left Corner and the Vertical position to **1.25"** from the Top Left Corner.

j. Click **Slide 6** and insert the *p01m2Paddle.jpg* image. Change the height to **5.8"**. Set the Horizontal position of the image to **3.4"** from Top Left Corner and the Vertical position to **1.25"** from the Top Left Corner.

k. Add **Reflected Perspective Right** picture style to the images on both Slides 5 and 6.

l. Click **Slide 4** and convert the list to a **Basic Block List SmartArt graphic**. In the SmartArt Styles group on the Design tab, change the style to **Intense Effect**.

m. Select the text **Book Your Adventure Soon!** on the last slide. Format the text as WordArt **Fill: Black, Text color 1; Shadow**.

n. Click **Slide 2**. Change the font size of the text in the placeholder to **80**.

o. Add the slide number to each of the slides with the exception of the title slide.

p. Review the presentation and correct errors as needed.

q. Save and close the file. Close PowerPoint. Based on your instructor's directions, submit p01m2OutdoorAdventures_LastFirst.

New Castle County Technical Services

New Castle County Technical Services (NCCTS) provides technical support for a number of companies in the greater New Castle County, Delaware area. As a trainer in the Human Resources department, you have been asked to provide a training seminar for managers. Team members have mentioned that they would like to improve their skills on designing and delivering more effective presentations that are not strictly bullet points. In this exercise you will begin enhancing the presentation that will be used for training employees.

a. Open *p01r1Guidelines* and save the presentation as **p01r1Guidelines_LastFirst**.

b. Change the theme fonts to **Gill Sans MT**.

c. Replace Student Name in the bottom placeholder on the title page by typing your **first** and **last name**.

d. Click **Slide 1** and click the **New Slide arrow** in the Slides group on the Home tab to create a new slide (Slide 2) using the **Title and Content layout**. Type **Overview** in the title placeholder and type the following bulleted text in the content placeholder:
   - **Prepare**
   - **Design**
   - **Bullet Points**
   - **Font & Font Size**
   - **Images**

e. Change the slide layout to **Section Header** for Slides 7–9.

f. Click **Slide 14** and click the **Pictures icon** in the placeholder. Browse to insert the *p01r1Roatan.jpg* image.

g. Apply the **Drop Shadow Rectangle Picture Style** to the image.

h. Click **Slide 2** and convert the list to a **Basic Block List SmartArt graphic**. In the SmartArt Styles group on the Design tab, change the style to **Intense Effect**.

i. Click **Slide 15** and convert the list to a **Lined List SmartArt graphic**.

j. Click **Slide 16** and select **Questions** on the last slide. Format the text as **WordArt Gradient Fill: Blue, Accent color 5; Reflection**.

k. Click the **Text Effects arrow** in the WordArt Styles group, select **Transform**, and then select **Chevron: Up** in the Warp group.

l. Click **Slide 7**, click the **New Slide arrow** in the Slides group on the Home tab, and then select **Reuse Slides**.

m. Browse to locate the *p01r1Guide* presentation from the student data files in the Reuse Slides pane. Right-click the **first slide** in the Reuse Slides pane and select **Insert All Slides** to insert all of the slides into the presentation. Close the Reuse Slides pane.

n. Click the **View tab** and click **Slide Sorter view**.

o. Click **Slide 11**, press **Ctrl**, and then click **Slide 12**. Move the slides between Slides 13 and 14 so the rearranged slides become Slides 12 and 13, respectively.

p. Double-click **Slide 1** to return to Normal view.

q. Type the following in the Notes pane for Slide 1: **Welcome to Presentation Guidelines.**

r. Click the **Review tab** and click **Spelling**. Correct any errors.

s. Click the **Insert tab** and click **Header & Footer** in the Text group. Click the **Notes and Handouts tab** and click **Footer**. Type **Presentation Guidelines** in the footer box and click **Apply to All**.

t. Save and close the presentation. Close PowerPoint. Based on your instructor's directions, submit p01r1Guidelines_LastFirst.pptx.

Disaster Recovery

Polishing a Business Presentation

A neighbor created a slide show to present to a local business explaining his company's services. He asked you to refine the slide show so it has a more professional appearance. Open *p01d1GreenScene* and save the file as **p01d1GreenScene_LastFirst**. View the slide show. On the title slide you notice that the text is difficult to read due to lack of contrast with the background and could use the logo *p01d1Logo.jpg* picture file inserted, resized, and positioned on the slide. Converting the bulleted text on Slides 2 and 4 to a SmartArt will better represent the information in an attractive way. Although the images in the presentation are of good quality, various picture styles have been applied throughout the presentation. To ensure consistency you apply the same picture style to each of the images. In addition, cropping the image on Slide 5 and removing portions of leaves will focus the attention on what's important. The placement will also need to be adjusted so that it does not cover any of the text. On the last slide, the slide layout does not work for the inserted logo as it crops it off, so you will change the slide layout to one that better works for this information. Also, on the last slide, you think that the text "Call Today!" should have a WordArt style applied. Finalize the presentation by adding speaker notes to the slides where they are missing, capitalization and spelling errors corrected, placeholders resized and moved as needed, font sizes adjusted as you see fit, unused placeholders deleted, and header and footer information added. Include slide numbers on each slide but the title slide. Create a handout header with your name and the current date. Include a handout footer with your instructor's name and your course name. Review the presentation to ensure there are no errors by viewing each slide in Slide Show view and then in Presenter View. Save and close the file. Close PowerPoint. Based on your instructor's directions, submit p01d1GreenScene_LastFirst.

Capstone Exercise

Want to Waffle

Want to Waffle is a successful mobile food business. The company was started by two culinary students and their families to finance the students' college education. A year later they own three food trucks that sell breakfast waffles, waffle sandwiches, and dessert waffles. Street-food lovers line up around the block when the food trucks park in their neighborhood. The truck locations are advertised via Twitter and on Facebook, so waffle lovers can follow the trucks from place to place. The business has increased its revenue and profits, and the owners are looking to expand their operation by offering franchises. They need to prepare a presentation for an important meeting with financiers.

Create a Title Slide

You add your name to the title slide, change the theme variant, and modify the theme colors and fonts.

1. Open *p01c1Franchise* and save it as **p01c1Franchise_LastFirst**.
2. Change the theme variant to the **second** one (orange variant).
3. Change the theme color to **Yellow** and the theme font to **Candara**.
4. Replace YOUR NAME in the subtitle placeholder on Slide 1 with your **first** and **last name**.

Add Content

You add the information about your business, adding new slides and reusing slides from another presentation.

5. Create a new slide after Slide 1 using the **Panoramic Picture with Caption layout**. Type the following in the middle placeholder: **Interested in Bringing Waffle Love to Your Town?** In the bottom placeholder type **The opportunity can be yours!**
6. Select the text **Waffle Love** in the middle placeholder and change the font size to **36 pt**, apply **Shadow**, and change the font color to **Gold, Accent 1**.
7. Click **Slide 2**. Use the Reuse Slides option to insert all of the slides from *p01c1Waffles*.
8. Add the following speaker note to Slide 1: **We have a great opportunity for you to join our growing waffle family.**
9. View the presentation in Slide Sorter view.
10. Delete Slide 3.
11. Move Slide 5 (*92% Increase in Sales*) so that it becomes Slide 4.

12. Create a Notes and Handouts header with your name and a footer with the following: **Franchise Information**. Include the date and time updated automatically. Apply to all.

Pictures, SmartArt, and WordArt

You want to include pictures to inspire interest in the franchise. You also want to enhance the presentation by adding SmartArt and WordArt.

13. Click **Slide 1**. Insert the *p01c1WaffleTexture.jpg* image file. Crop the image by dragging the middle bottom crop handle up until approximately 25 percent of the image is remaining. Change the width of the cropped image to **13.3"**. Apply the **Drop Shadow Rectangle Picture Style**. Set the Horizontal position of the image to **0"** from Top Left Corner and the Vertical position to **0"** from the Top Left Corner.
14. Click the **Pictures icon** on Slide 2 and insert the *p01c1DessertWaffle.jpg* image file. Apply the **Simple Frame, White Picture Style**.
15. Click the **Pictures icon** on Slide 8 and insert the *p01c1Waffle.jpg* image file. Change the width of the image to **7.3"**. Apply the **Simple Frame, White Picture Style**. Set the Horizontal position of the image to **5.4"** from Top Left Corner and the Vertical position to **1.6"** from the Top Left Corner.
16. Click **Slide 7**, and convert the list to the **Step Up Process SmartArt graphic**.
17. Select the text **Why We're HOT** in the title placeholder on Slide 3. Apply the **Fill: Gold, Accent color 1; Shadow WordArt Style** to the text. Increase the font size of the WordArt to **60 pt**.

Navigate and Print

You review the presentation in Slide Show and Presenter views to check the spelling and layout of the objects on the slide. You notice a spelling error on a slide and realize you did not check the spelling in the presentation before running the slide show.

18. Change the presentation to Slide Show view and navigate through the presentation.
19. Change to Presenter view and navigate through the presentation. Return to Normal view.
20. Check spelling and fix errors.
21. Save and close the presentation. Close PowerPoint. Based on your instructor's directions, submit p01c1Franchise_LastFirst.

Effective Presentation Development

LEARNING OUTCOME You will apply design concepts while adding shapes, animation, and multimedia to create a professional-quality presentation.

OBJECTIVES & SKILLS: After you read this chapter, you will be able to:

CASE STUDY | The Summerfield Music School

The Summerfield Music School provides music education opportunities for local area students. The school fills a gap for several local school districts that cannot fund music classes for their own schools. The director of the school asked you to create a slide show that he can use to tell the community about the services available at the school and the yearly music festival held each spring.

You create a presentation to inform the public about the school's services using standard design guidelines. You include shapes, multimedia, animations, and transitions in the presentation.

FIGURE 2.1 Summerfield Music School Presentation

CASE STUDY | The Summerfield Music School

Starting Files	File to be Submitted
p02h1Music **p02h4Music_Media folder**	**p02h4Music_LastFirst**

MyLab IT Grader An alternate version of this project is available as a MyLab IT Grader Assessment

Slide Show Design

As you begin to develop a presentation, there are key questions to ask:

- Who is my audience?
- What is the purpose of my presentation?
- What message do I need to convey?
- What is the best way to convey the message to my audience?
- What venue will be used to deliver the presentation?

Demographic information should influence how you put your message together and how the presentation is designed. In making design choices, you will evaluate many elements when considering the visual design of your presentation. The primary design elements are background, color, images, and text but may also include shapes, multimedia, and animation. All elements used will work together to convey the presentation's intended purpose and message in a way that the audience can easily grasp. Additionally, consideration must be given to basic design principles and best practices while using the elements.

In this section, you will learn about some basic design principles that are used to create PowerPoint presentations. Then you will explore how PowerPoint enables you to create a well-designed presentation.

Examining Slide Show Design Principles

Presentation design principles are more than a set of rules on how to put content onto a slide. Good presentation design encompasses planning, creating, and delivering the presentation. When applied to a presentation, universally accepted design principles can increase its appeal and professionalism.

The goal in using design principles is to develop a presentation where the presenter creates a relationship with the audience instead of reading the slides to the audience or where the audience reads the slides for themselves while ignoring the presenter. Ideally, the presentation functions as a visual aid that reinforces the presenter's message to the audience. The audience will respect the presenter and understand the message more when they are involved in a well-planned and well-designed presentation. Figure 2.2 shows a depiction of the relationships formed during a presentation.

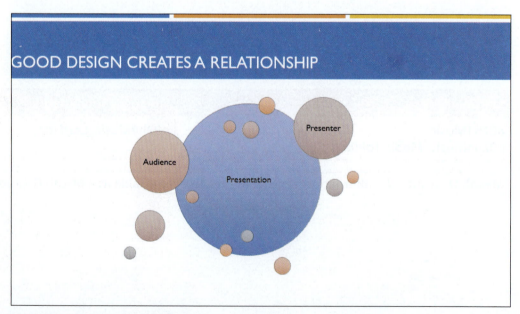

FIGURE 2.2 Presentation Relationships

STEP 1   Understand Media-Specific Design Principles

Good design principles are media-specific and venue-specific. They may be applied in specific ways to the various types of modern communications: print media such as flyers or brochures, audio media such as narrations, video media such as recorded lectures, or a visual medium such as a slide show. The medium dictates the need and importance of the design principle to be applied.

For example, font choices can impact the meaning and professionalism of your presentation. It is recommended that you use no more than three fonts per presentation, but using two, one for the titles and one for the body text, is more common. It is important that you plan the font choice used in the presentation. Ensure the font size is appropriate for how it will be viewed onscreen. Larger font sizes are needed for a presentation delivered to a large room, but smaller font sizes are acceptable for presentations delivered online for a webinar.

In addition, the choice of font type can be determined by how the presentation will be delivered in order to improve readability. For example, if a presentation is to be delivered through a projection device, consider using sans serif fonts such as Calibri or Arial. Sans serif fonts do not have serifs or extra tails at the end of the letters and are easier to read when projected at a distance from your eye. If your presentation will be delivered as a printout or will be seen online through a monitor, consider using serif fonts such as Times New Roman or Bookman. Serif fonts have serifs or extra tails on the end of each letter. This font type makes it easier to follow along a line of text when viewed in closer proximity.

STEP 2   Plan Design Elements

Other design principles, such as recommendations for background, colors, images, and text, may be applied to specific elements on slides in a PowerPoint presentation. Each of these elements helps to determine the overall appeal and professionalism of your presentation, so applying design principles to these elements should be appropriate for the specific audience. For example, a presentation to elementary students might use bright, primary colors and cartoon-like images. For an adult audience, use photographs and data representations to reflect professional content. A sales presentation may feature more images of the device or service being offered, whereas a results-oriented presentation may be filled with charts and tables. Once you have determined the goal of the presentation and nature of the audience, then you can determine which elements will best fit. As always, you should strive to be consistent with your choices.

One of the first considerations is the background selection. When selecting a background, keep in mind that this is the surface on which all other visual elements are placed. The background should never compete with the content of the slide. A simple background conveys your message more clearly.

Use white space to open up the design. Empty space, or white space, on a slide can be very powerful. Presenters often try and spread out the content to fill the slide. Putting too much text and too many images can drown out the key points on your slides. When used strategically, the white space will inform your audience instantly where to look. Apart from making your layout easier to follow, it also offers the eye a visual resting place.

Color use is also an important part of the background selection and the overall design process. It sets the overall tone for your presentation. There should be good contrast between the background color and the rest of the slide objects. Keep in mind that colors can be emotionally charged. For example, using red for a presentation on heart attacks or blue when presenting about water conservation trigger associations with the topic being presented. Colors can also have different meanings for different cultures, for example the color white in the United States often symbolizes purity, whereas in Asia it is often associated with death and mourning. When you are making a presentation for an organization or business, you may be told what colors to use to convey the organization's message and brand.

Images and shapes are very important in creating a professional presentation. Use images only in one style such as all photographs or all line art throughout the presentation. Use high-quality images that support the message of the presentation. The inclusion of inappropriate or cartoon-like graphics can undermine the professionalism of the presenter. Images should either support the slide content or be the focal point of the slide. If you do not take your own images, you can find professional stock images online, but be mindful of the copyright clearance on them. Some images are free to use without restriction. Others may require a fee to be paid before use.

Use caution when adding animation and transitions to your presentation. Although PowerPoint provides many options for animation and transitions, overusing these features can distract your audience and make your presentation look unprofessional. The most important thing to remember when using animations in PowerPoint is to keep it simple. Animations can really make a presentation powerful if used in the right way and with purpose. But regardless, the choice of animation or transitions effects should usually be subtle and professional.

STEP 3 **Apply Design Principles**

The main design principles used in presentations are contrast, alignment, repetition, and proximity. These design principles are the foundation of most graphic design, but they apply to slide design as well. Keeping in mind these four principles when planning and creating a presentation will lead to more effective presentations.

You create contrast by making striking or strong differences in the colors used. Contrast means difference—difference in color, font size, space, and so forth. Contrast is relatively simple to achieve because almost any design element can be contrasted with another. Contrast can be provided through color choices (dark or light, warm or cool), font size (large and small), font style (serif or sans serif), line thickness (thin or thick), graphic sizes (big or small), text direction (horizontal or vertical), and white space (empty or filled). Contrast is used to create interest or grab the audience's attention. It adds emphasis and directs focus. It also aids in readability and supports accessibility compliance. Figure 2.3 shows some examples of contrast.

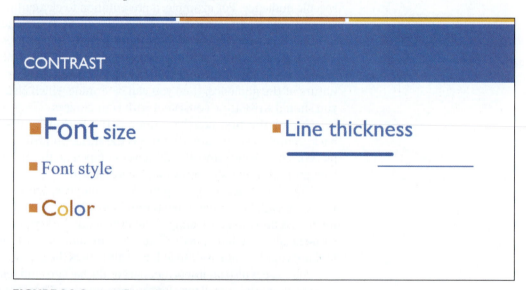

FIGURE 2.3 Contrast Examples

You utilize alignment and repetition when choosing and manipulating the images and shapes used in the presentation. Alignment means that there is organized placement of titles and body text as well as other objects on the slide. Alignment keeps the focus on the intended message and slide focal point because it creates order and unifies the presentation.

Do not randomly place objects on a slide; every object should be meaningfully placed and usually align with the edge of another object, and each object should be balanced within the white space of a slide. You should strive to create a visual line between elements. Break the slide (visually or by using the guidelines) into nine squares using four lines like a tic-tac-toe board. Place points of interest on one of the guidelines or at the intersection with another. Use the bottom or top thirds for creating "horizon" lines. Figure 2.4 shows an example of proper alignment.

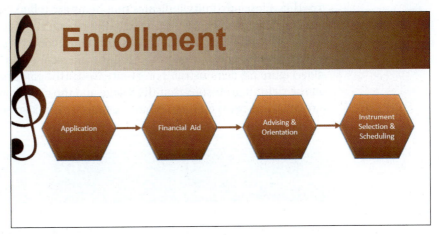

FIGURE 2.4 Alignment Example

Whereas alignment applies to individual slides, repetition applies to the entire presentation. Repetition is the use of the same design principles throughout the presentation and the reuse of elements for an overall cohesiveness. Repetition creates unity, ensuring all slides in a presentation belong together. Using unified design elements creates a professional look. Visual repetition creates a harmony among the elements of the slide and among the slides in the slide show. It gives the audience a sense of order while adding visual interest.

Repetition can be applied to anything the audience would recognize, including shapes, images, fonts, colors, bullets, lines, alignment, and spacing. It is not necessarily about strictly enforcing a repetitive design to each slide, but the placement of some objects, such as the title slide placeholder, can be modified to create interest. PowerPoint themes repeat colors, background designs, and text placeholder placements while still allowing for slight variances. This balance between repetition and modification becomes more obvious when looking at the variety of slide element placements shown in different slide layouts. The title placement shown in the slide layouts in Figure 2.5 demonstrates PowerPoint's use of repetition in the various layouts available for the Dividend theme.

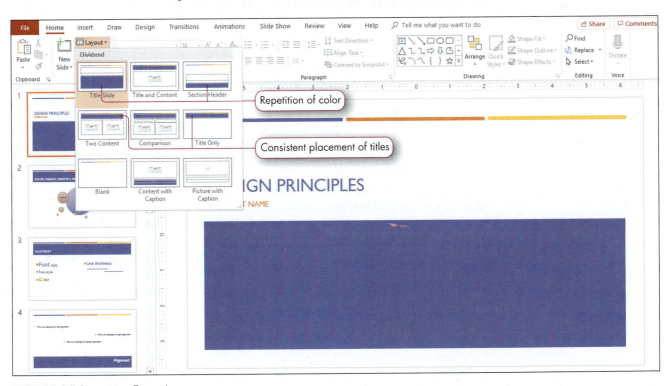

FIGURE 2.5 Repetition Example

You can utilize proximity by visually connecting or aligning related objects on a slide. Proximity is the relative placement of objects on a slide, ensuring related objects are placed together. Close proximity indicates that items are related, whereas distance between two objects indicates they are not related. For example, an image and its caption on a slide should have proximity to each other to create a cohesive group and imply a relationship between them. This helps to organize the message while helping the eye move over the slide. Figure 2.6 demonstrates proximity. Notice the placement of the caption for the image on the right. It is obvious that the image and the caption belong as a group, and there is a relationship between them. That relationship is not so clear for the image on the left.

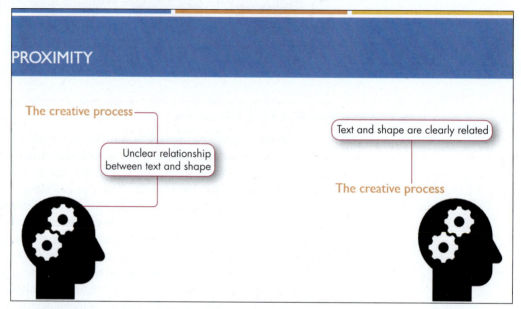

FIGURE 2.6 Proximity Example

Remember that these design principles are guidelines. For example, although using all capital letters implies someone is shouting, certain themes break this premise by featuring all capital letters in headings and titles. You may choose to avoid applying one or more of the principles, but you should be aware of the principles and carefully consider why you are not following them as you plan your presentation. Planning the design principles in each of the elements used in your presentation will create a presentation that delivers its message in a way the audience will easily receive.

Use Designer

Designer helps you convey a message and automatically generates design ideas. **Designer** is an intelligent tool that aids you in designing a PowerPoint presentation. Designer is only available to Office 365 subscribers. It can help you match the content with a layout that will highlight your ideas. Because Designer uses an intelligent agent, it remembers your choices and then adds suggestions that align with your previous choices.

The first time you use Designer, you will be asked for permission to get design ideas. The Microsoft Privacy Statement is available for you to read before you make your decision. If you agree, click *Turn on* to begin using Designer. Once you have consented to the privacy statement, you access Designer through Design Ideas in the Designer group on the Design tab. Figure 2.7 shows the Design Ideas pane. To turn off Designer, click the File tab. Click Options, click General, and then click the check box *Automatically show me design ideas* to deselect it.

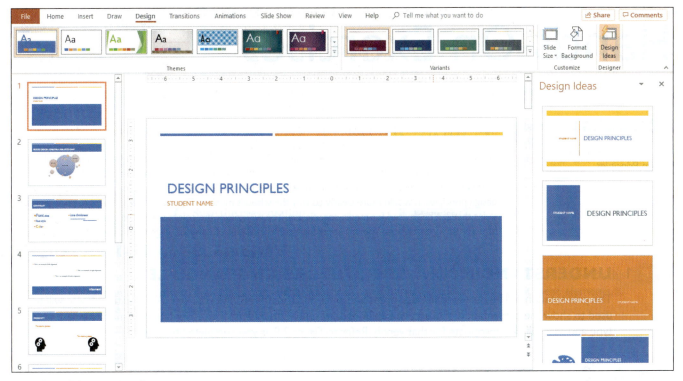

FIGURE 2.7 Design Ideas Pane

When you add an image to your slide, Designer provides suggestions on how to integrate the image with the content by showing you many layouts. When the Design Ideas pane opens, several slide thumbnails display with interesting arrangements of slide content. You can choose one or close the pane if the ideas do not fit your needs.

If you are not getting any Designer suggestions, make sure that you are connected to the Internet. Designer accesses the Internet for its design ideas. If you are using themes, make sure that it is a PowerPoint theme. Presentations can be edited by more than one person at a time. Keep in mind that if two or more people are editing the same slide, Designer will not give you any suggestions. When using a slide with pictures, be sure to use the Title layout or the Title + Content layout with Designer. You are limited to a maximum of four images per slide to receive design ideas.

Quick Concepts

1. Describe the key questions you should ask yourself to inform the design choices for the presentation. ***p. 844***

2. Explain the importance of having unified design elements in a presentation. ***p. 844***

3. Describe why it is important to use contrast for presentation objects. ***p. 846***

4. Explain the benefits of using Designer. ***p. 848***

5. Describe situations where Designer may not work. ***p. 849***

The changes that you have made in the presentation are beginning to give it a more professional look so that it will convey the message well. After reviewing the Summerfield Music School presentation, you decide to work with alignment and proximity to improve the design of the presentation. Refer to Figure 2.10 as you complete Step 3.

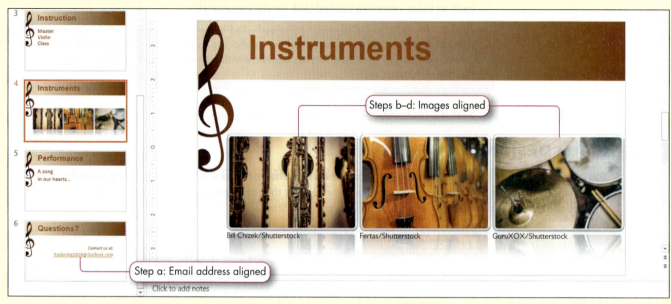

FIGURE 2.10 Design Principles Applied

a. Click **Slide 6**. Select the email address and click **Align Right** in the Paragraph group on the Home tab. Select *Contact us at:* and change the size to **44**.

   The email address now aligns with *Contact us at:* and the two lines are in proximity with each other. Increasing the font size of that phrase makes the email address really stand out.

b. Click **Slide 4**. Right-click the **brass instruments image** and select **Format Picture**. Select **Size & Properties**. Expand the Size section, if necessary. Click to ensure the **Lock aspect ratio check box** is deselected and ensure the image height is **2.77"** and width is **4.0"**. Expand the Position section, if necessary. Position the image horizontally at **0.96"** from the Top Left Corner and vertically at **3.39"** from the Top Left Corner.

> **MAC TROUBLESHOOTING:** On a Mac, select the image. Click Format Pane in the Picture Format tab. In the Format Picture pane, click the Size & Properties tab. Click Size and Position to expand the menu options.

c. Click the **violin image**. Click to ensure the **Lock aspect ratio check box** in the Size section is deselected. Ensure the image height is **2.77"** and width is **4.0"**. Position the image horizontally at **5.11"** from the Top Left Corner and vertically at **3.39"** from the Top Left Corner.

d. Click the **drums image** and ensure **Lock aspect ratio** is not selected. Ensure the image height is **2.77"** and width is **4.0"**. Position the image horizontally at **9.26"** from the Top Left Corner and vertically at **3.39"** from the Top Left Corner. Close the Format Picture pane.

   The three shapes now are aligned to one another and demonstrate proximity as related instruments used in Summerfield Music School curriculum.

e. Save the presentation. Keep the presentation open if you plan to continue with the next Hands-On Exercise. If not, close the presentation, and exit PowerPoint.

Shapes

PowerPoint is used as a visual communication tool that can convey both messages and data. Bulleted text is a common part of a presentation, but a visual element can often provide additional clarity to the idea being presented or even be enough to convey the entire idea. One type of visual element is a **shape**, a geometric or non-geometric object used to create an illustration or to highlight or provide information. For example, you can add text inside a shape to convey a message and call attention to it. Or you can also combine shapes to create complex images. Although there is a shape for virtually every need, the use of shapes should conform to the design principles stated earlier.

The simple, tasteful use of shapes is a powerful way to convey a message while adding interest to your presentation. Shapes can be used to present complex data or knowledge in an easily understood visual representation. Shapes can also convey relationships. Contrasting shapes makes it easy for your audience to see the difference among slide elements. These differences may be size, color, shade, proximity, or the shape itself. Figure 2.11 shows a PowerPoint slide using shapes to convey relationships.

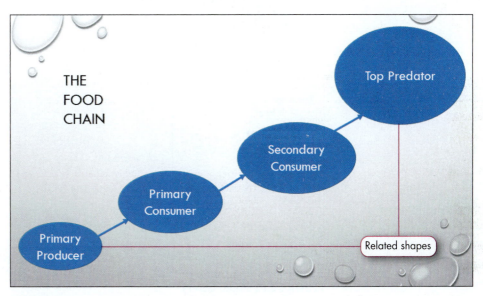

FIGURE 2.11 Using Shapes to Convey Relationships

In this section, you will create and modify various shapes and text boxes. You will also connect shapes and text boxes. Finally, you will learn how to apply styles to shapes and text boxes and to change fills, outlines, and effects.

Creating Shapes

PowerPoint includes robust drawing tools you can use to create shapes. In addition to using the drawing tools, you can enhance shapes by adding effects such as a preset effect, a shadow, a reflection, a glow, a soft edge, a bevel, or a 3-D rotation. Using these visual effects makes it easy for you to create professional-looking graphics to enhance your presentation.

STEP 1 **Create a Shape**

As you develop a presentation, a shape can be added to help convey any message, from arrows to point out something or to imply progress, to basic geometric figures that contain text or are used in diagrams. After you create a shape, text may also be added to a shape by clicking inside the shape and typing, or by pasting text into the shape. You can modify a shape by applying fills, outlines, and special effects to add interest or to create repetition across the presentation. These effects are accessible through style galleries. Figure 2.12 shows the Shapes gallery and the many shapes from which you can choose. Notice the most recently used shapes are at the top of the list so you can conveniently reuse them.

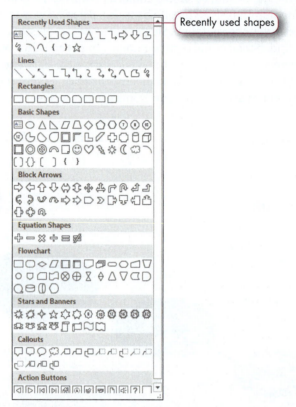

FIGURE 2.12 Shapes Gallery

To create a shape, complete the following steps:

1. Click the Insert tab.
2. Click Shapes in the Illustrations group.
3. Select the shape you want from the Shapes gallery.
4. Click the position in which to place the shape, or drag the cross-hair pointer to control the approximate size of the shape.

To resize the shape, drag any of the sizing handles that surround the shape when it is selected. Sizing handles are a series of circles on the outside border of a selected object that enable the user to adjust the height and width of the object. The sizing handles on the corners are used to resize the shape proportionately. Sizing handles on the sides are used to modify either the height or width.

In addition to sizing handles, some shapes have an adjustment handle, represented by a yellow circle. The **adjustment handle** can be dragged to change the structure of the shape. For example, an adjustment handle located at the base of a **callout** shape can be dragged in any direction to change where the callout connects to another shape or object. A callout is an example of a shape that can be used to add text and is often used in cartooning. Keep in mind that not all shapes have an adjustment handle. Figure 2.13 shows a callout with the sizing handles and the adjustment handle.

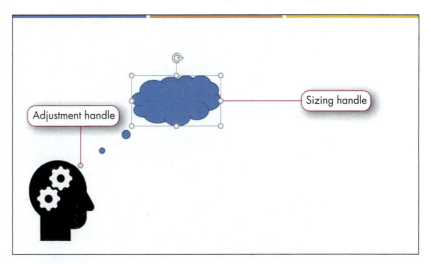

FIGURE 2.13 Sizing and Adjustment Handles

The Shapes command deactivates the selected shape after you draw it once, forcing you to reselect the shape each time you want to use it. By activating *Lock Drawing Mode*, you can add several shapes of the same type on the slide without selecting the shape each time. For any shape in the Shapes gallery, you can select Lock Drawing Mode by right clicking a shape and selecting it in the shortcut menu. After creating the first shape, you can click or drag to create additional shapes of the same type. Press Esc to release Lock Drawing Mode after you complete drawing the shapes you want.

Create a Text Box

You can add a *text box*, a shape object that provides space for text, to a slide. For example, you can use a text box to add a quote to a slide that is separate from the slide content placeholder. You can add a text box by clicking Text Box in the Text group on the Insert tab. You can also add a text box through the Shapes gallery. Text inside a text box can be formatted just as text in placeholders is formatted using standard formatting tools. You can add a border, fill, shadow, or 3-D effect to the text in a text box.

Although a text box is a shape, it differs from a rectangle shape in that a text box does not exist unless there is text inside. But a rectangle shape can exist with or without text. The size of a text box expands and contracts depending on the quantity of text inside, but a rectangle remains the same size and must be manually adjusted to accommodate text.

STEP 2 Draw Lines and Connectors

Lines are shapes that can be used to point to information, to connect shapes on a slide, or to divide a slide into sections. Lines are used often in slide design. You can easily draw a straight line by selecting Line in the Lines category of the Shapes gallery. Position the pointer on the slide where you want the line to begin and drag to create the line. If you hold Shift as you drag, you constrain the line to create a perfectly horizontal, vertical, or any multiple of a 45-degree angle line.

You can create curved lines and arcs. These may take a little practice to get the curve you want. The Curve option is found in the Lines category of the Shapes gallery. After clicking the slide at the location where you want to start the curve, you click again wherever the peaks or valleys of the curve occur. Then click and move the pointer to shape the curve in the pattern you want. As you click while creating the curve, you set a point for the curve to bend around. Double-click when you have finished drawing the curve. To draw a shape that looks like it was drawn by hand, select the Scribble shape.

Lines also can be used to connect two shapes or placeholders. **Connectors** are lines with connection points at each end that stay connected to the shapes to which they are attached. If you move a shape that is joined to another shape using a connector line, the line moves with it, extending or shortening as necessary to maintain the connection.

Connectors can be straight, elbow (to create angled lines), or curved. When you choose a connector and drag it close to the shape, solid dots display on the shape edge indicating where a connection can be made. Once a connection is made, the connection point changes to green.

To connect shapes with connector lines, complete the following steps:

1. Create the shapes you want to connect.
2. Select a line from the Lines category of the Shape gallery.
3. Move the pointer over a shape to display the connection points.
4. Click one of the connection points to connect the line and drag to the next shape, releasing the mouse button at another connection point.

Shapes can be used to depict a process or sequential steps similar to a flow chart. For example, you could use a series of shapes to illustrate the sequence to follow when implementing a new product. Connector lines could then join the shapes through the sequence to demonstrate the order in which the sequence should be followed to accomplish the goal.

Terminal points, or the start and end points, are shown in oval shapes. Process points, or steps, are shown in rectangular shapes. Decision points are shown in diamond shapes. Colored shapes are optional, but if used, apply consistency when you select the colors to convey a consistent message. Each shape in a flow chart has a label to which you can add text. Figure 2.14 shows an example of shapes being used in a flow chart.

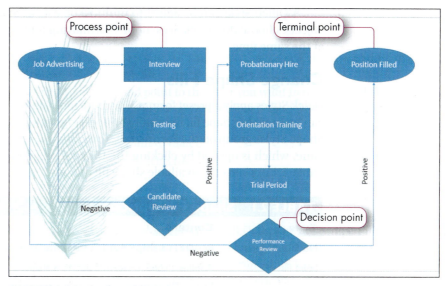

FIGURE 2.14 Shapes in a Flow Chart

Formatting Shapes

After you have added shapes to your presentation, you can modify them in several ways. You can use a tool to adjust the overall style of shapes. You can modify shape characteristics individually such as the fill or interior of the shape. You can change the outline of the shape to make it stand out from the background. You can also modify the shape effect so that the shape displays with a shadow or reflection or even as a 3-D object.

STEP 3 ## Apply Quick Styles and Customize Shapes

You can add a professional look to your shapes by applying a Quick Style. A ***Quick Style*** is a combination of different formats that can be selected from the Shape Styles gallery and applied to a shape or other objects such as text boxes or images. Options in the gallery include edges, shadows, line styles, gradients, and 3-D effects. Figure 2.15 shows the Shape Styles gallery and several shapes with a variety of Quick Styles applied to them.

Quick Styles are available on the Format tab in the Shape Styles group or on the Home tab in the Drawing group. You can preview the styles as you move the pointer over the various styles. When you see the effect you want, click that Quick Style to apply it.

FIGURE 2.15 Shape Styles Gallery

FIGURE 2.18 Shape Filled with a Picture

A *texture fill*, such as canvas, denim, marble, or cork, can add depth or interest to an object or give a shape a "real-life" effect. The process of applying a texture fill is the same as applying a color fill. The distinction with texture fills is that the textures can be tiled. Tiled textures have seamless edges so that you cannot tell where one tile ends and another begins. You can also adjust the transparency of a texture fill.

You can fill shapes with a *gradient fill*, a blend of two or more colors. When you select Gradient from the Shape Fill gallery, a gallery of options opens, enabling you to select no Gradient, Light Variations, or Dark Variations that blend the current color with white or black in linear or radial gradients. Figure 2.19 shows the gradient options for a selected object.

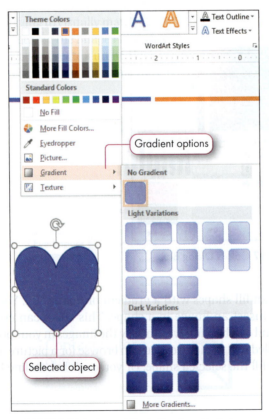

FIGURE 2.19 Light and Dark Gradient Variations

To create a custom gradient, select More Gradients at the bottom of the Gradients gallery to open the Format Shape pane. The Gradient fill option provides access to the Preset gradients gallery as well as means to customize a gradient. The trick to creating a gradient fill is managing the gradient stops where two adjacent colors blend. You can use between 2 and 10 stops, with two or three being the norm. Figure 2.20 shows a custom gradient created in the Format Shape pane.

FIGURE 2.20 Creating a Custom Gradient

To create a custom gradient, complete the following steps:

1. Click the shape you want to fill, click the Shape Fill arrow in the Shape Styles group on the Format tab, and then point to Gradient. Select More Gradients to open the Format Shape pane.
2. Select Gradient fill.
3. Click the first gradient stop. Click the Color arrow and select the color from one of the color categories.
4. Click the next gradient stop. Click the Color arrow and select the color from one of the color categories.
5. Drag each gradient stop until you create the blend you want.
6. Click *Add gradient stop* to add an additional stop and color and repeat to set additional gradient stops.
7. Click a gradient stop and click *Remove gradient stop* to remove a color.

TIP: TEXT BOX READABLITY
You can add fills, textures, and gradients to text boxes using the Shape Styles gallery. However, care should be taken to ensure readability. Make sure there is enough contrast between the text and the background and that the background's overall pattern will not detract from the words.

To customize an effect, click More in the Shape Styles group and click Effects on the Shape Options tab. The Format Shape Effects pane opens where you can define many effect options such as color, transparency, or size. Figure 2.23 displays some of the Format Shape options.

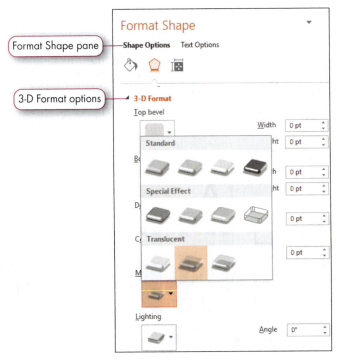

FIGURE 2.23 3-D Shape Options

6. Explain how shapes can be used to convey relationships. **p. 853**

7. Describe the value of using connector lines when creating a sequence or process. **p. 856**

8. Explain why you should be cautious when applying a fill to a text box. **p. 861**

Hands-On Exercises

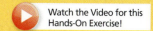
Skills covered: Create a Shape • Create a Text Box • Draw Lines and Connectors • Apply Quick Styles and Customize Shapes • Change Shape Fills • Change Shape Outlines • Change Shape Effects

2 Shapes

Now that you have used design principles to improve the Summerfield Music School presentation, you decide that there should be more content added to better convey the message of the presentation to potential students and their parents. As you add new slides, you are careful to ensure the new design elements match the existing design elements.

STEP 1 ▶ CREATE A SHAPE

According to the school's director, one of the first questions he gets when speaking to groups is about the enrollment process at the school. You use a series of shapes to depict the enrollment process. Then you will add a shape to hold additional content. Refer to Figure 2.24 as you complete Step 1.

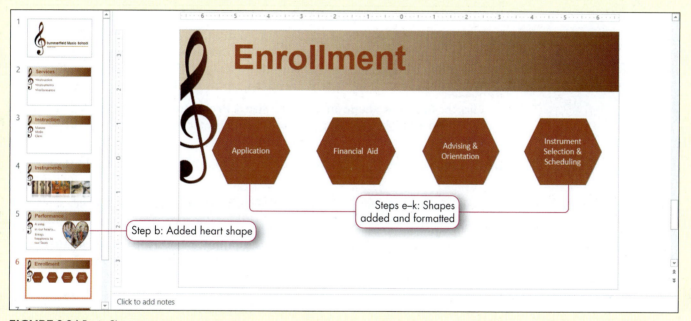

FIGURE 2.24 Basic Shapes

a. Open *p02h1Music_LastFirst*, and save it as **p02h2Music_LastFirst**, changing h1 to h2.

b. Click **Slide 5** in the Slides pane and click the **Insert tab**. Click **Shapes** in the Illustrations group. Select the **Heart** in the Basic Shapes group and click in the **right content placeholder**.

   The heart is a perfect 1" square and is too small for its intended use. It also has a solid fill. You will change both of these in a later step.

c. Click between Slides 5 and 6 in the Slides pane. Click the **Home tab** and click the **New Slide arrow**. Select **Title and Content**.

d. Type **Enrollment** in the Title placeholder of the new Slide 6. Select *Enrollment* and change the font to **Arial**. Change the font size to **72**. Change the font color to **Brown, Accent 1**.

e. Click the **Insert tab** and click the **Shapes arrow** in the Illustrations group. Select the **Hexagon shape** in the Basic Shapes category. Position the pointer in the **content placeholder** and click to create the shape.

f. Set the height of the shape to **1.94"** and the width to **2.35"** in the Size group. Click the **Dialog Box Launcher** in the Size group. Ensure the Position section is expanded in the Format Shape pane. Set the Horizontal position to **0.99"** from the Top Left Corner and the Vertical position to **2.53"** from the Top Left Corner. Close the Format Shape pane.

> **MAC TROUBLESHOOTING:** Select the shape, click the Format Pane on the Shape Format tab. Click the Size & Properties icon.

g. Click the **Insert tab** and click the **Shapes arrow** in the Illustrations group. Right-click the **Hexagon shape**. Select **Lock Drawing Mode**. Click the slide three times. Press **Esc** to get out of Lock Drawing Mode.

> **MAC TROUBLESHOOTING:** Lock Drawing Mode is not available for Mac users. Instead, create the shape once, then, with the shape selected, press Command+D three times.

h. Click the first new shape and click and hold **Shift** while clicking the other two new shapes. Click the **Size Dialog Box Launcher** to open the Format Shape pane. Set the height for all three shapes to **1.94"** and the width to **2.35"** in the Size section. Set Vertical position to **2.53"** from the Top Left Corner. Press **Esc**.

i. Click the **first new shape** and click the **Size & Properties tab.** Set the Horizontal position to **4.16"** from the Top Left Corner. Click the second new shape and set the Horizontal position to **7.34"** from the Top Left Corner.

j. Click the third new shape. Set the Horizontal position to **10.46"** from the Top Left Corner.

You created three additional shapes and aligned them in a row across the slide similarly to the images on Slide 4.

k. Click inside the first hexagon and type the text **Application**. Type **Financial Aid** in the second hexagon. Type **Advising & Orientation** in the third hexagon. Type **Instrument Selection & Scheduling** in the last hexagon.

The text you typed becomes part of the shapes.

l. Save the presentation.

To continue developing the depiction of the enrollment process, you create line arrows to connect the shapes. These additional shapes will help convey the order of steps taken during the enrollment process. Refer to Figure 2.25 as you complete Step 2.

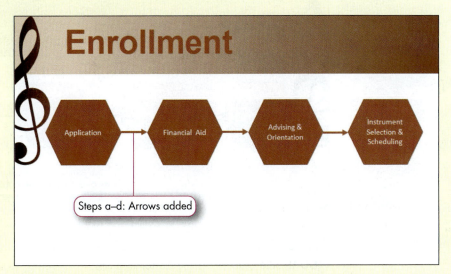

FIGURE 2.25 Connector Lines Applied

a. Click **Shapes** in the Illustrations group on the Insert tab, select **Line Arrow** in the Lines category, move the cross-hair pointer over the right-side center point of the first hexagon, and then drag over to the left-side center point of the second hexagon.

The shape's handles display when a line is selected and the cross-hair pointer is moved onto the shape. An arrow is placed between the first and second hexagons. The default line weight is thin at 0.5 pt.

b. Click **Shape Outline** in the Shape Styles group. Point to **Weight** and click **4½ pt**.

The increase in the connector's weight makes a clearer message for the direction of the enrollment process.

c. Click **Copy** in the Clipboard group on the Home tab. Click **Paste** in the Clipboard group Drag the new line arrow to connect the second and third hexagons.

The line arrow is already formatted and just needs to be placed in the correct location.

d. Repeat to connect the third and fourth hexagons.

e. Save the presentation.

You decide to add some visual interest to the new shapes so you work with Quick Styles to modify shape fills for the shapes. Refer to Figure 2.26 as you complete Step 3.

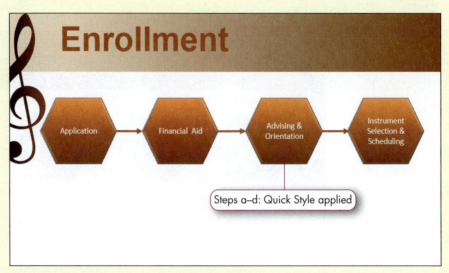

FIGURE 2.26 Quick Styles and Customized Fills

a. Click the **last shape** in the row, which is labeled *Instrument Selection & Scheduling* on the right side of the slide.

b. Click the **Format tab** and click **More** in the Shape Styles group.

The Quick Style gallery opens.

c. Move the pointer over the Quick Styles and note the changes in fill, outline, and effects to the shape as you do so. After you have reviewed several options in Live Preview, select **Gradient Fill – Brown, Accent 1, No Outline** (fifth row, second column) in the Presets section. Click in an empty area to deselect the shape.

Live Preview shows the effects on the object as you move the pointer over the Quick Style options.

d. Press **Ctrl** and click the three remaining shapes and add the same Quick Style to the shapes. Press **Esc**.

You apply a gradient fill to more than one shape at a time.

e. Save the presentation.

CHANGE SHAPE EFFECTS

PowerPoint provides many shape effects that you can use for emphasis. You apply effects to the shapes used in the presentation. Refer to Figure 2.27 as you complete Step 4.

FIGURE 2.27 Shape Effects

a. Ensure that all of the hexagons on Slide 6 are selected. Click the **Format tab**, click the **Shape Effects arrow** in the Shape Styles group, point to **Preset**, and then select **Preset 3**.

Preset 3 combines a bevel type, a depth, contours, and a surface effect.

b. Click the **Shape Outline arrow** in the Shape Styles group. Select **Blue** in the Standard Colors category.

A blue outline is applied to the shapes.

c. Click **Slide 5** and click the **Heart shape** in the right content placeholder. Size the heart to a height of **5.5"** and a width of **5.5"**. Position it horizontally at **7.45"** from Top Left Corner and vertically **1.75"** from Top Left Corner.

d. Click **Shape Fill** in the Shape Styles group and select **Picture**. Click **From a File** and navigate to where you have your files stored. Click *p02h2Children.jpg* in the p02h4Music_Media folder and click **Insert**.

e. Begin a new paragraph after the ellipse in the left content placeholder and type **Brings happiness to our faces**.

f. Click the **Review tab** and click **Spelling**. Correct any errors.

g. Save the presentation. Keep the presentation open if you plan to continue with the next Hands-On Exercise. If not, close the presentation, and exit PowerPoint.

Animations and Transitions

To engage the audience's interest or to keep their attention focused on specific slide objects, you can use an animation or transition in the presentation. An ***animation*** is motion that you can apply to text and objects. A ***transition*** is a visual effect that takes place when you move from one slide to the next during a presentation. Carefully plan animations and transitions to ensure that they enhance the message of the slide or control how the message is delivered. Used indiscriminately, animations and transitions can detract from the message of the presentation.

Well-planned animations function as intentional communication tools that enhance the message. You should identify places in your presentation where an animation will help you make your point by providing emphasis or where you want more control on how the message is delivered. For example, your audience will likely read any information as soon as it is presented, so use animations to create a pace for the information to be revealed. This will help the audience appropriately absorb and process the information.

In this section, you will learn about applying animations to objects and slides, and will explore how to control animations. You will also learn about applying transitions.

Applying Animation to Slide Content

Virtually anything on a slide can be animated: text, shapes, images, charts, and SmartArt. Animations control how objects and text come onto a slide, what they do while on a slide, and how objects and text leave the slide. When applied to slide objects, animations can show action and purpose for these objects. For example, if you plan for two shapes to use the Fade entrance animation, it could be used to indicate a change or shift in rank between the two. On special and rare occasions, and with limitations, you could add animations that create emphasis such as Pulse or Grow/Shrink. Table 2.2 shows PowerPoint's four animation types. Each of these animation types has properties, effects, and timing that can be modified.

TABLE 2.2	PowerPoint Animation Types
Type	**Content**
Entrance	Controls how an object moves onto or displays on a slide
Emphasis	Draws attention to an object already on a slide
Exit	Controls how an object leaves or disappears from a slide
Motion Paths	Controls the movement of an object from one position to another along a predetermined path

STEP 1 ### Apply Animation to an Object

To apply an animation to an object, select the object you want to animate, and display the Animation gallery by clicking the Animations tab and click More in the Animation group.

The slide in Figure 2.28 shows an animation added to a quote. The quote has the number 0 on the left to show that it will play After Previous. The Expand animation in the gallery is shaded to show that it is the selected animation. Click Preview in the Preview group to see the animation on the slide play. You can also see animations play in Reading View and in Slide Show view. Slides that include a transition display a star icon beneath the slide when viewed in Slide Sorter view or beneath the slide number on the Slides tab in Normal view.

The Animation Painter feature (see Figure 2.28) enables you to copy an animation from one object to another. It works similarly to the Format Painter. The Animation Painter picks up the animation from the first object and applies it to another object on the same slide or a different slide. And just like with the Format Painter, if you double-click the Animation Painter, you can apply the animation to multiple objects. To turn off the Animation Painter, press Esc on the keyboard. The Animation Painter is in the Advanced Animation group on the Animations tab.

FIGURE 2.28 Animation Gallery

Apply Multiple Animations to an Object

Multiple animations can be applied to an object. For example, you use a rectangle to outline a particular area of a table that is on a slide. You use the Fade animation to bring the rectangle onto the table. When you are finished talking about that set of data, then you use the Fade animation to have the rectangle exit the slide. This would keep your audience engaged while they focus on the message of the slide.

The management of multiple animations must be carefully planned. You can control the timing of the animations as well as the trigger that starts the animation sequence. In addition, keep in mind that a complex set of animations can quickly become a distraction, especially when too many animations are applied to one object or slide. This type of overuse of animation can result in diminishing the message of the object or slide.

To add multiple animations to an object, select the object and choose an animation from the Animation gallery on the Animations tab. Then, click Add Animation in the Advanced Animation group, and select another animation to add it. You can repeat the process to add additional animations to the object. Click Preview to see that the animations applied to the slide work the way you intended. Figure 2.29 shows multiple animations applied to a shape.

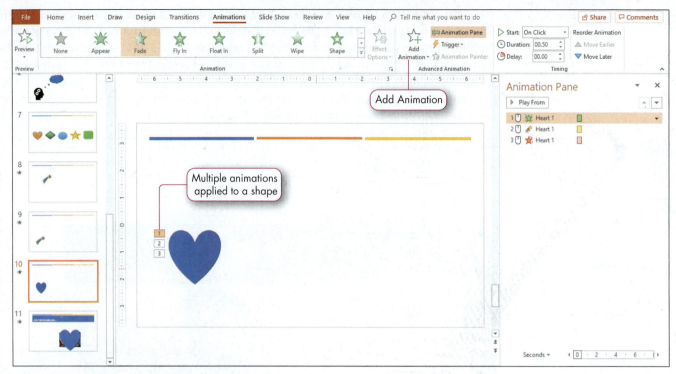

FIGURE 2.29 Multiple Animations Applied to a Shape

Apply a Motion Path

Because the eye is naturally drawn to motion, using a ***motion path*** (a predetermined path that an object follows as part of an animation) to animate an object can capture and focus a viewer's attention on key objects or text. For example, during an awards show, a motion path could be used to drag a shape off a text box to reveal the award recipient's name. PowerPoint includes a variety of interesting motion paths such as arcs, turns, shapes, and loops. You can also draw a custom path for the object to follow.

To apply a motion path animation, select the object. On the Animation tab, click More in the Animation group. Locate the Motion Paths category by scrolling down and selecting the motion path animation to apply it to the object. You can see how each motion path works by using Preview.

Once you have applied the motion path animation to an object, the motion path displays as a dotted line on the slide. A small arrow indicates the starting point for the animation, and a red arrow with a line indicates the ending point. If it is a closed path, like a circle, only the starting point displays. Figure 2.30 shows an example of a motion path animation applied.

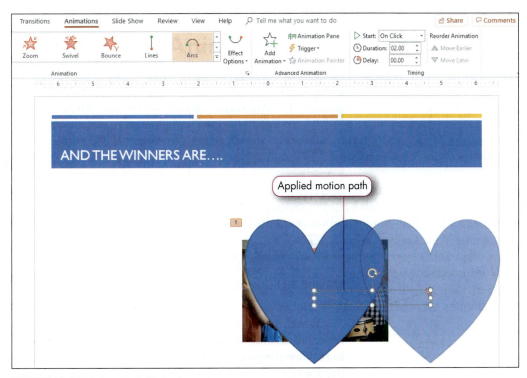

FIGURE 2.30 Motion Path Example

A *custom path* is an animation path that can be created freehand instead of following a preset path. For example, in a presentation explaining the importance of honey bees, you include a slide showing flowers and a bee graphic. A custom path could be used to move the bee from flower to flower. Because the path is drawn onto the slide, it would more accurately depict how the bee uses a unique flight path as it gathers pollen.

To create a custom path, complete the following steps:

1. Select the object and click the Animations tab. Click More in the Animation group.
2. Select the Custom Path animation from the Motion Paths section.
3. Position the cross-hair pointer in the approximate center of the object you want to animate.
4. Drag in the direction you want the object to follow. Drag the cross-hair pointer until you have completed the path.
5. Double-click to end the path.
6. Click Preview to see that the path works as you intended.

STEP 3 ▸ Animate Text

Although animating non-bulleted text in placeholders and text boxes uses the same method as other objects, bullet text has additional animation options. You can bring text onto the slide by animating the text as one object, all paragraphs to come in at once, or sequencing the text to come in by paragraph. A paragraph in PowerPoint, similar to Word, can be a line of text, several lines of text, or even a blank line. Whenever you press Enter to move the insertion point to a new line, you create a new paragraph. For further control of text animation, you can control text so it displays one word or one letter at a time by clicking the arrow next to the animation in the Animation pane, and then selecting Effect Options. In the dialog box, on the Effect tab under Enhancements, click the arrow next to Animate text and select By word or By letter.

If the text has three or more levels of bullet points, the default effect is to group the bullets by the paragraph that brings each main bullet point and all sub bullet points in as a group. If you want to animate individual bullets or group them by different levels other than by the first level (by the main bullet point), you can group the level of bullet points by using the Group Text option on the Text Animation tab in the Animation dialog box.

STEP 4 ▸ Specify Animation Settings and Timings

Attaching timing settings to animations frees you from constantly advancing to the next object and enables you to concentrate on delivering your message. These timings include Start, Duration, and Delay. Start is used to specify when an animation should begin, such as On Click, With Previous, or After Previous. Duration determines how long the animation takes to play out. Delay specifies how many seconds pass before the animation begins. After selecting an object, you can set these timing options in the Timing group on the Animations tab.

STEP 5 ▸ Use the Animation Pane

As you work with complex animations, the Animation Pane displays helpful information. The Animation Pane summarizes the animation effects used. To open the Animation Pane, click the Animations tab and click Animation Pane in the Advanced Animation group.

The display begins with a number indicating the animation order followed by an icon indicating how the animation starts. If there is a mouse icon next to the number, that indicates that animation begins with a click. If there is no mouse icon, then it begins with the previous animation. If there is a clock, then it starts after the previous animation. On the right, a star icon displays that represents the type of animation effect applied. Animation effects are color-coded by type of animation: green indicates an entrance animation; red indicates an exit animation; yellow indicates an emphasis animation; and blue indicates motion paths.

Next, a portion of the name of the animated object displays. This is followed by a color-coded timeline that displays the duration of an animation as a bar that can be used to adjust timing. Although the timing is often better controlled by using the Timing feature on the Animation tab, you can adjust the timing of any animation by dragging the edge of the timeline bar. This is useful when you have multiple animations for a shape on a slide or applied to several objects on a slide to ensure that the animations have the desired timing applied to each animation on the slide. Figure 2.34 shows these features in an open Animation Pane.

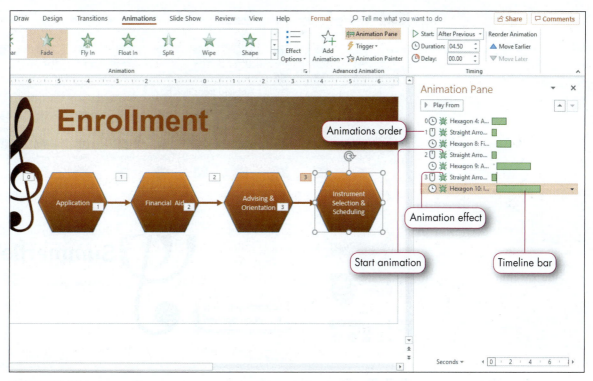

FIGURE 2.34 Animation Pane

TIP: SIZING THE ANIMATION PANE

The size of the Animation Pane can be adjusted by positioning the pointer along the left edge of the pane. When it changes to a double-headed arrow, drag it to the left. A wider pane may make it easier to adjust the timing.

STEP 6 ▶ Apply a Transition

Transitions can help focus or re-focus attention on a presentation. A transition provides visual interest as a slide is replaced by another slide. Like animations, well-planned transitions can help you keep the audience's attention.

Transitions are found on the Transitions tab. To display all the transitions, click More to open the gallery. Like animations, transitions have effect options and timings. A transition, by default, is applied to one slide, but it can be applied to all slides. When a transition is applied, a star displays next to the slide thumbnail. Click Preview to see the transition applied to the slide. Figure 2.35 displays the Transitions gallery.

In special circumstances, you may want to add sound to introduce special content on a slide. For example, as you transition to a slide that reveals the winner of award, you can add a drumroll or applause. Click the slide or object on the slide and click the Transitions tab. Then click the Sound arrow in the Timing group. You can select from several prerecorded sounds. But be careful with this option. The addition of sound during a transition could startle the audience or be off-putting.

You may decide that you no longer want to include transitions in your presentation. To delete a transition, select the slide with the transition that you want to delete. Click the Transitions tab, and then click None in the Transition to This Slide group. Click Apply to All in the Timing group if you want to remove all transitions.

FIGURE 2.35 Transitions Gallery

Quick Concepts

9. Describe three reasons why animations and transitions are useful to include in a presentation. *p. 870*

10. Explain how applying a motion path to an object or text can enhance your presentation. *p. 872*

11. Describe the animation effects that are edited and controlled in the Animation Pane. *p. 876*

Hands-On Exercises

Skills covered: Apply Animation to an Object • Apply Multiple Animations to an Object • Apply a Motion Path • Animate Text • Specify Animation Settings and Timings • Use the Animation Pane • Apply a Transition

3 Animations and Transitions

The director of the Summerfield Music School tells you that the presentation has a great design and uses shapes well. He also thinks that it delivers the message about the school's services. However, he thinks the presentation needs something to capture the audience's attention. You show him how animation and transition features can be applied to some of the slide content to enhance the message of the presentation.

STEP 1 **APPLY ANIMATION TO AN OBJECT**

You begin to add animation to the slide show by controlling how individual shapes enter a slide. Refer to Figure 2.36 as you complete Step 1.

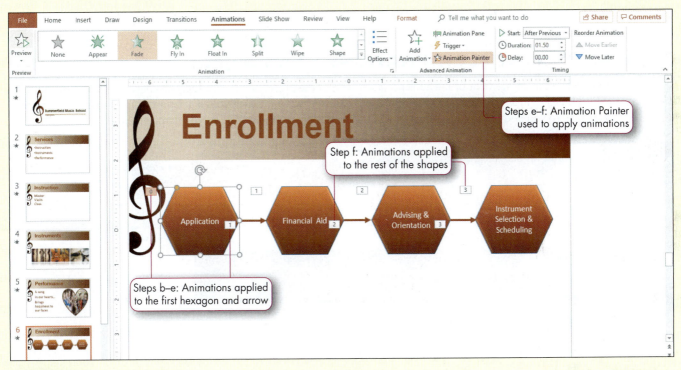

FIGURE 2.36 Shapes with Animation

---

a. Open *p02h2Music_LastFirst* if you closed it at the end of Hands-On Exercise 2, and save it as **p02h3Music_LastFirst**, changing h2 to h3.

b. Click **Slide 6** and select the hexagon shape, **Application.**

c. Click the **Animations tab** and click **Fade** in the Animation group.

The Fade animation is applied to the shape.

d. Click **Preview** in the Preview group.

You notice the shape displays shortly after the slide displays and that there is a reasonable length of time in which to read the text on the shape. You decide to apply the same animation to the rest of the shapes.

e. Ensure the Application shape is still selected. Double-click the **Animation Painter** in the Advanced Animation group. Click the **arrow** between Application shape and Financial Aid shape.

The animation automatically previews for you. You see that the arrow connecting to the second shape of the enrollment process now displays automatically after the audience has had a chance to read the first shape.

f. Click the **Financial Aid shape** and the next **arrow** to apply the animation using the Animation Painter. Click the **Advising & Orientation shape** and the next **arrow**. Click the **Instrument Selection & Scheduling shape** after the preview of the third arrow ends. Click **Animation Painter** in the Advanced Animation group to toggle it off.

Animation tags display next to each hexagon and each arrow indicating the order in which the shape will display on the slide when the slide show is run.

g. Click the **Slide Show tab** and click **From Current Slide**. Click the **first hexagon** to display it. Click the **first arrow** and click the second hexagon. Continue clicking each arrow to get the Press **Esc** after viewing the animation.

All four shapes and three arrows display the animation one after another as you click each shape and arrow in sequence.

h. Save the presentation.

STEP 2 ## APPLY MULTIPLE ANIMATIONS TO AN OBJECT

To maintain the engagement of the audience at the end of the presentation, you apply an entrance, emphasis, and exit animation to an image. After testing the animations, you see that using such bold animations could be distracting to the audience, so you decide to modify the animation choices. Refer to Figure 2.37 as you complete Step 2.

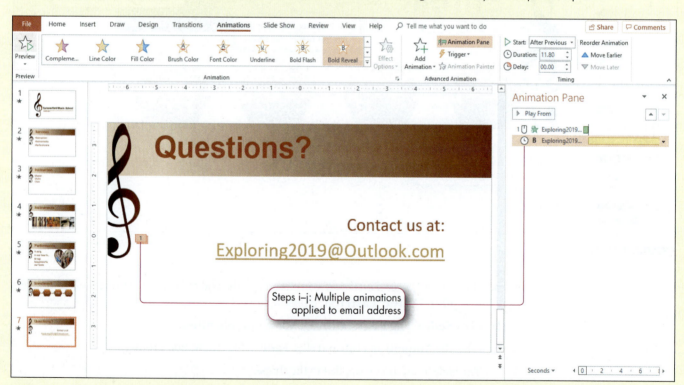

FIGURE 2.37 Multiple Animations Applied to an Object

a. Click **Slide 7**, select the **email address**, and ensure the Animations tab is selected.

b. Click **More** in the Animation group and select **Bounce** in the Entrance category.

The Bounce animation previews, and an animation tag numbered 1 is assigned to the placeholder.

c. Click **Add Animation** in the Advanced Animation group.

> **MAC TROUBLESHOOTING:** To add a second animation, click the object again, and then click the Teeter animation in Step d.

d. Select **Teeter** in the Emphasis category.

The Teeter animation previews, and an animation tag numbered 2 is assigned to the placeholder.

e. Ensure email is selected and click **Add Animation** in the Advanced Animation group.

f. Scroll down the Animation gallery and select **Float Out** in the Exit category.

The Float Out animation previews, and more animation tag numbers are assigned to the image.

g. Click the **Slide Show tab** and click **From Current Slide**. Click after each animation displays. Press **Esc** after viewing the animation.

The animation sequence displays without regard to how each animation is set to start. You notice how the animations distract rather than emphasize the message. The audience will likely have a hard time focusing on the email address to use for asking questions.

h. Click the **content placeholder**, click the **Animations tab,** and then select **None** in the Animation group.

You have removed all of the animations and will start over. This time you will apply only an Entrance and Emphasis animation.

i. Select the email address and click **More** in the Animation group. Click **Random Bars** in the Entrance category.

j. Select the email address again and click **Add Animation** in the Advanced Animation group. Select **Bold Reveal** in the Emphasis category.

k. Click the **Slide Show tab** and click **From Current Slide** in the Start Slide Show group. Click to play each animation in the animation sequence. Press **Esc** after viewing.

Because the animations were created using the default *Start: On Click* timing option, you must click to start each animation in the sequence. You decide to modify this at a later time.

l. Save the presentation.

If you want to use a video other than from YouTube, you can embed a video from any online video website that offers an embed code. Generally, embed codes are found in a sharing option for the video. When you embed video from the online site, you copy and paste the embed code from the site into the *From a Video Embed Code* box (refer to Figure 2.42). If you embed video from an online site, you must be connected to the Internet when you display the presentation. Not all online videos will have an embed code. In that case, you need to find a different video, or save the file to your computer and insert it from your computer into the presentation.

Whether you have inserted your own video or a video from a website, the video will include a Media Controls bar with a Play/Pause button, a Move Back button, a Move Forward button, a time notation, and a Mute/Unmute control slider. The Move Back and Move Forward buttons aid you when editing your own video. However, these controls may auto-hide and become visible only when the pointer is moved. Additionally, videos inserted from websites may use their own control bars instead of the PowerPoint Media Controls bar shown in Figure 2.43. The video should be checked after inserting it to make sure that it will play the way you intended. You can click Play in the Preview group on either the Format or Playback tabs to see the video in Normal view. You can also check it in Slide Show view.

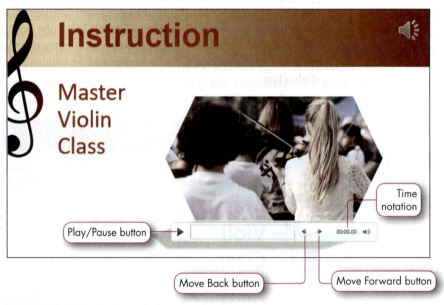

FIGURE 2.43 Media Controls Bar

Format a Video

PowerPoint includes tools for working with video. You can format the video's brightness and contrast, color, and style. You can apply most artistic image effects, add or remove bookmarks, trim the video, and set fade in or fade out effects. When you select an inserted video, the Video Tools contextual tab displays with two subtabs: the Format tab and the Playback tab.

The Format tab includes options for playing the video for preview purposes, adjusting the video, applying a style to the video, arranging a video on the slide, and cropping and sizing the video.

Using the Adjust group, you can adjust video contrast and brightness, and you can recolor a video as you did when you worked with images. The Adjust group also includes the **Poster Frame** option, which enables you to choose a still frame (or image) from within the video or any image file from your storage device. This image is displayed on the PowerPoint slide when the video is not playing. Figure 2.44 shows a video with a Poster Frame option set to the current frame.

FIGURE 2.44 Poster Frame Options

To create a Poster Frame from a video, complete the following steps:

1. Select the video and click Play in the Preview group to display the video.
2. Pause the video when the frame you want to use as the poster frame displays.
3. Click Poster Frame in the Adjust group.
4. Select Current Frame.

If you want to use an image stored on your computer, such as a company logo, as a poster frame, select the video. Click Poster Frame and select Image from File. Select the image you want to use and click Insert.

Adding Audio and Using Audio Tools

Audio can draw on common elements of any language or culture—music, laughter, cheers—to add excitement, provide a pleasurable background, set the mood, or serve as a wake-up call for the audience. Harnessing the emotional impact of sound in your presentation can transform your presentation from good to extraordinary. On the other hand, use sound incorrectly, and you can destroy your presentation, leaving your audience confused or distracted. Keep in mind the guideline emphasized throughout this text—any object you add to the presentation should enhance, not detract from, your message.

STEP 4 ▶ Insert Audio from a File

Your computer needs speakers to play audio. In a classroom or computer laboratory, you will need a headset, headphones, or earbuds for playback so that you do not disturb other students. You can locate and play sounds and music from the Insert Audio dialog box or from any storage device. You can also record your own sounds, music, or narration to play from PowerPoint.

Various formats can be used for sound in presentations. Table 2.4 lists the commonly used types of audio file formats supported by PowerPoint.

TABLE 2.4	Commonly Used Audio File Formats Supported by PowerPoint	
File Format	**Extension**	**Description**
MIDI File	.mid or .midi	**Musical Instrument Digital Interface:** Standard format for interchange of musical information between musical instruments, synthesizers, and computers
MP3 Audio File	.mp3	**MPEG Audio Layer 3:** Sound file that has been compressed by using the MPEG Audio Layer 3 codec (developed by the Fraunhofer Institute)
Windows Audio File	.wav	**Wave Form:** Stores sounds as waveforms. Depending on various factors, one minute of sound can occupy as little as 644 kilobytes or as much as 27 megabytes of storage
Windows Media Audio File	.wma	**Windows Media Audio:** Sound format used to distribute recorded music, usually over the Internet. Compressed using the Microsoft Windows Media Audio codec

You can insert audio from a file on the Insert tab using the Audio command in the Media group. The Audio on My PC option enables you to browse and locate the file you want. Select the file and click Insert. A speaker icon, representing the audio file, displays in the center of the slide with a Media Controls bar beneath it. The same controls are available when you select audio as when you select video.

> **TIP: HIDING THE SOUND ICON DURING A PRESENTATION**
> When audio is added to a presentation, the sound icon shows on the slide. However, you may not want the icon to display during the presentation. To hide the icon during a presentation, click the icon, click the Audio Tools Playback tab, and select Hide During Show in the Audio Options group.

Record and Insert Audio

Sometimes you may find it helpful to add recorded audio to a slide show. Although you could record music, *narration* (spoken commentary) is more common. You might want to include audio in your presentations to create an association between words and an image on the screen. This could be helpful for a group learning a new language or for helping young children build their vocabulary.

Another example of a use for recorded narration is when you want to create a self-running presentation, such as a presentation displaying in a kiosk at the mall or online. Rather than adding narration prior to a presentation, you could create the narration during the presentation. For example, recording the discussion and decisions made during a meeting would create an archive of the meeting.

Before creating the narration, keep in mind the following:

- Your computer will need a microphone.
- Voice narration takes precedence over any other sounds during playback, making it possible for a voice to play over other audio files.
- PowerPoint records the amount of time it takes you to narrate each slide, and if you save the slide timings, you can use them to create an automatic slide show.
- You can pause and resume recording during the process.

To begin recording narration, click the Slide Show tab. Then in the Set Up group choose either Record from Current Slide or Record from Beginning. The Set Up group provides the other options of Play Narrations (to play back narrations during the slide show), Use Timings (to use set rehearsal timings during the slide show), and Show Media Controls (to show controls for playing audio and video clips during the presentation).

To record an audio clip, complete the following steps:

1. Click the Insert tab and click Audio in the Media group. Select Record Audio.
2. Type a name for the recording and click Record (see Figure 2.47).
3. Record your message. When you have finished, click Stop.
4. Click Play to check the recording. Then click OK.

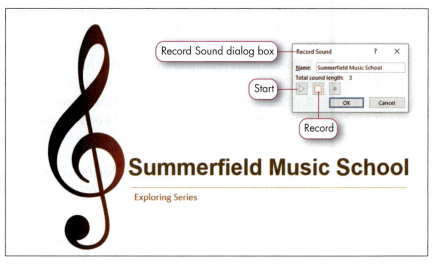

FIGURE 2.47 Record Sound Dialog Box

TIP: CREATE NOTES OF YOUR NARRATION
A transcript of your narration should be available for those in your audience who are hearing impaired. Doing so ensures the presentation meets accessibility guidelines and lets everyone in the audience benefit from your presentation. A convenient way to provide a transcript is to put it in the Notes pane so it can be printed out whenever it is needed.

STEP 5 **Change Audio Settings**

When the icon for an inserted audio clip is selected, the Audio Tools Format and Playback tabs display. The Format tab provides options relating to the inserted sound icon. The Playback tab provides options for playing and pausing the audio clip, adding a bookmark, trimming, fading in and out, adjusting volume, determining starting method, hiding the audio icon while playing, looping, and rewinding after playing. All of these features work similarly to the video features, except that the Trim audio feature displays an audio timeline rather than a video preview window.

Hands-On Exercises

MyLab IT HOE4 Sim Training

▶ Watch the Video for this Hands-On Exercise!

Skills covered: Insert Video Files • Format a Video • Set Video Playback Options • Insert Audio from a File • Record and Insert Audio • Change Audio Settings • Animate an Audio Sequence • Play Sound Over Multiple Slides • Record a Screen Recording

4 Video and Audio

The director of Summerfield Music School wants to strongly engage the audience as they watch the presentation that you are developing. You suggest including multimedia in the presentation because video and audio add interest for many people. You insert a video, add a poster frame, and set the video playback options. Then you add audio from a file and change audio settings.

STEP 1 INSERT VIDEO FILES

You want to show how well the students play their instruments. You decide to add a video showing some children participating in one of the school's recent events, a master violin class. Refer to Figure 2.50 as you complete Step 1.

FIGURE 2.50 Inserted Video File

a. Open *p02h3Music_LastFirst* if you closed it at the end of Hands-On Exercise 3, and save it as **p02h4Music_LastFirst**, changing h3 to h4.

b. Click **Slide 3**. Click the **right content placeholder**. Click the **Insert Video icon**.

c. Click **Browse** in the From a file section of the Insert Video dialog box.

d. Navigate to the *p02h4Music_Media* folder, select *p02h4Video.mp4*, and then click **Insert**.

e. Click **Play/Pause** on the Media Controls bar.

f. Save the presentation.

You decide to use a Poster Frame showing as many students as possible as an attractive image on display before the video begins. You also decide that a shape softening the edges of the video would be an improvement. Finally, you add a shadow video effect. Refer to Figure 2.51 as you complete Step 2.

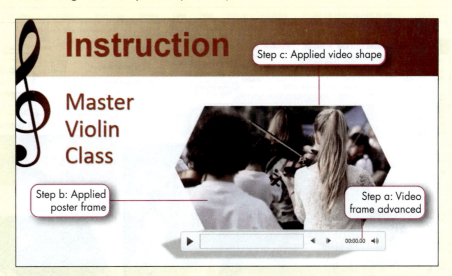

FIGURE 2.51 Formatted Video File

a. Ensure the video object is selected and click **Move Forward 0.25 Seconds** on the Media Controls bar located beneath the video to advance the video to the frame at **00:00.75 seconds**.

b. Click the **Poster Frame** in the Adjust group on the Format tab and select **Current Frame**.

   The frame you selected becomes the poster frame and displays on the slide.

c. Click **Video Shape** in the Video Styles group and select **Hexagon** in the Basic Shapes category.

   The video shape changes to a hexagon.

> **MAC TROUBLESHOOTING:** Click the Crop arrow in the Size group on the Video Format tab, point to Change Shape, and then click Hexagon.

d. Click **Video Effects** in the Video Styles group, point to **Shadow**, and then select **Perspective: Lower Left** in the Perspective category.

   The shadow displays in a hexagon shape with a perspective view.

e. Click the **Slide Show tab** and click **From Current Slide** in the Start Slide Show group.

   Slide 3 opens with the video displayed on the slide. The poster frame shows several students with the video shadow below the image.

f. Move the pointer to the bottom of the video to display the Media Controls bar and click **Play**. Press **Esc** when you have completed your review of the video.

g. Save the presentation.

Because it is not necessary to hear the entire audio clip to convey the message of the slide, you use the Trim Audio setting to shorten the clip. You also set the clip to fade in and out so the audience will not be startled by the music as it begins and ends. Refer to Figure 2.54 as you complete Step 5.

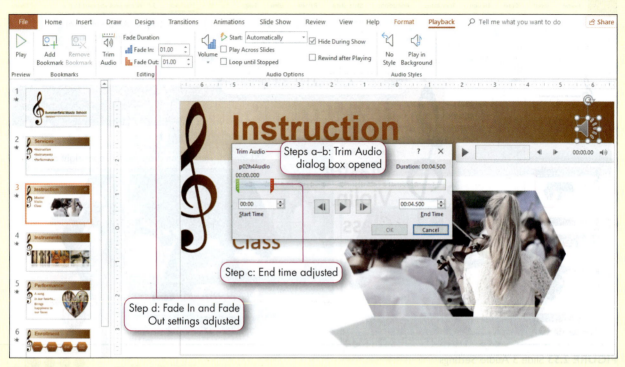

FIGURE 2.54 Audio Playback Options

a. Select the **sound icon** on the top-right of Slide 3.

b. Click the **Playback tab**. Click **Trim Audio** in the Editing group.

c. Drag the red **End Time marker** on the slider until **00:04.500** appears in the End Time box. Click **OK**.

   Alternatively, you can type 00:04.500 in the End Time box.

d. Click the **Fade In spin bar** to the setting **01.00**. Click the **Fade Out spin bar** to the setting **01.00**.

e. Play the slide show and note the music plays on the third slide. Press **Esc**.

f. Click **File**, and under **Info**, click **Compress Media**. Select **Standard (480p)**. Click **Close**.

> **MAC TROUBLESHOOTING:** Click the File menu and click Compress Pictures. Click the Picture Quality arrow and click On-screen (150 ppi). Click OK.

g. Save and close the presentation. Exit PowerPoint. Based on your instructor's directions, submit p02h4Music_LastFirst.

Chapter Objectives Review

After reading this chapter, you have accomplished the following objectives:

1. Examine slide show design principles.

- Understand media-specific design principles: Know the media to be used and the venue for the presentation to make the best design choices for your presentation.
- Plan design elements: Background, colors, images, and text contribute to the overall appeal and professionalism of your presentation.
- Apply design principles: Use basic slide show principles (contrast, alignment, repetition, and proximity) to make presentations more polished and professional.
- Use Designer: Designer is an intelligent tool that provides suggestions for layouts that match your presentation content. Designer works if you have Office 365, are connected to the Internet, are using a PowerPoint theme instead of a custom theme, and if only one person is editing a slide at the time.

2. Create shapes.

- Create a shape: Shapes can be used to create an illustration or to provide information visually.
- Create a text box: Text boxes can be used to provide text in slide layouts that do not include a content placeholder.
- Draw lines and connectors: Lines are used to point to information, connect shapes, or divide a slide into sections.

3. Format shapes.

- Apply Quick Styles and customize shapes: Quick Styles provides a combination of formats that can be selected from a gallery to quickly add a professional look to shapes.
- Change shape fills: Customize shapes by adding a solid color fill, picture fill, gradient fill, texture fill, or no fill.
- Change shape outlines: Outlines form a border around a shape that can be changed for color, style, or line weight.
- Change shape effects: There are many shape effects available, including preset three-dimensional, shadows, reflections, glows, soft edge bevels, and 3-D rotation effects.

4. Apply animation to slide content.

- Apply animation to an object: Four animation types that can be applied to an object include Entrance, Emphasis, Exit, and Motion Paths.
- Apply multiple animations to an object: Multiple animations can be applied to any object present on a slide, but care must be taken to ensure the animations are not distracting.
- Apply a motion path: A motion path can capture and focus a viewer's attention to key objects or text. You can create your own motion path and then resize, move, or rotate the path until it fits its intended purpose.

5. Control animation and interactivity.

- Animate text: Text animation keeps the audience focused and prevents them from reading ahead in a presentation.

- Specify animation settings and timings: Each animation has associated settings that free you from constantly advancing to the next object, so you can focus on delivering your message. These settings vary according to the animation.
- Use the Animation Pane: The Animation Pane provides a summary of all animations in use, showing when each starts, how each is started, the order of the animations, the type of animation, and the timing of the animation.
- Apply a transition: Transitions are applied to a slide or slides as one is replaced by another to maintain or re-focus audience attention.

6. Add video and use video tools.

- Insert video files: You can link or embed videos found on the Internet or your computer into your presentations. Be sure to check for copyright clearance.
- Format a video: The Video Tools contextual tab includes the Format tab, which enables you to format a video's brightness, contrast, color, or style; set a Poster Frame; arrange the video on the slide; crop the video; and size the video.
- Set video playback options: The Playback tab gives options when displaying the video such as bookmarking, editing, trimming, and setting fade in and fade out options.

7. Add audio and use audio tools.

- Insert audio from a file: Recorded sound can be added to your presentation and controlled during the presentation by using the Media Controls bar.
- Record and insert audio: Music or spoken word can be recorded and added to a presentation if your computer has speakers and a microphone.
- Change audio settings: The Audio Tools contextual tab includes the Format tab, with options relating to the inserted sound icon, and the Playback tab, with options for playing and pausing the audio clip, adding a bookmark, trimming the audio clip, fading in and out, adjusting volume, determining the starting method, hiding the audio icon during playback, looping, and rewinding the audio clip after playing.
- Animate an audio sequence: The Playback tab contains options for starting an audio sequence with a click or automatically. The Timings group on the Animations tab enables you to choose whether the audio clip plays with or after a previous event.
- Play sound over multiple slides: You can change the default setting from playing an audio clip until it ends or until the next slide is shown. Instead, the audio clip can be set to play or loop until the clip is stopped or the presentation ends.
- Record a screen recording: Screen recordings show what is happening on a screen. Pairing it with audio is useful for providing instructions, navigating settings on a computer, or using in training.

1 Social Media Marketing Plan

You have a bright, creative, and energetic personality, and you are using these talents in college. You plan to work in social media marketing after graduating. The Marketing 331 course you are taking this semester requires every student to create a social media marketing plan for a fictional company and to present an overview of the company. This presentation will be shown through a projection device to the class. It will include the company information as well as information about developing a social media marketing plan. Refer to Figure 2.55 as you complete this exercise.

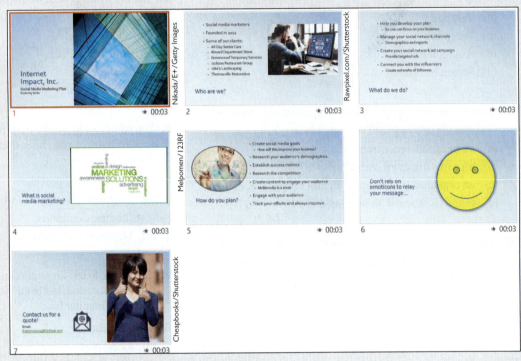

FIGURE 2.55 Social Media Marketing Plan

a. Open *p02p1Social*, and save it as **p02p1Social_LastFirst**.

b. Replace *Student Name* on Slide 1 with your name.

c. Change the title font color to **Blue-Gray, Accent 1** (fifth column, first row). Click **Slide 6** and change the title font color to **Blue-Gray, Accent 1**. Repeat on **Slide 7**.

d. Click **Slide 2** and type a question mark after the phrase *Who are we* in the Title placeholder. Select the first bullet in the content placeholder. Click **Change Case** in the Font group on the Home tab and select **Sentence case**.

e. Click **Slide 3** and type another question mark after the phrase *What do we do*.

f. Click **Slide 6**. Click the right content placeholder. Click **Bullets** in the Paragraph group on the Home tab to toggle off the bullets. Click **Shapes** in the Illustrations group on the Insert tab. Select the **Smiley Face** in the Basic Shapes category. Click in the right content placeholder. Set the height of the shape to **5"** and the width to **5"**. Click the Dialog Box Launcher in the Size group. Click Position in the Format Shape task pane to expand it. Set the Horizontal position to **6.5"** from Top Left Corner and Vertical position to **1.5"** from Top Left Corner. Close the Format Shape task pane.

g. Click Shape Fill arrow in the Shape Styles group and select **Yellow** in the Standard colors. Click Shape Outline arrow in the Shape Styles group and select **Dark Blue** in the Standard colors. Add the shape effect **Glow: 18 point; Blue-Gray, Accent color 1**.

h. Click **Slide 2** and click the content placeholder. Click the **Animations tab.** Click **Float In** in the Animation group. Click the **Start arrow** and select **After Previous.** Ensure the Duration is set to **01.00.** Use the **Delay arrow** to change to **01.50.**

i. Click **Slide 3** and click the **content placeholder.** Click **Fade** in the Animation group.

j. Click the **Animations Pane** in the Advanced Animation group. Click the animation numbered **1** in the Animation Pane and click the **arrow.** Select **Effect Options** and click **After animation arrow** on the Effect tab. Select **White** (first color).

k. Click the **Timing tab.** Click the **Duration arrow** and select **3 seconds (Slow).** Click **OK.**

l. Click **Slide Show tab.** Click **From Current Slide** in the Start Slide Show group. Test the animation sequence in Slide Show view to ensure that the animations play correctly. Press **Esc** after viewing Slide 3, and close the Animation Pane.

m. Click **Slide 5** and click the **right content placeholder** to select it. Click **Float In** in the Animation group on the Animations tab. Click the **Animation Dialog Box Launcher** to display the Float Up dialog box. Click the **After animation arrow** on the Effects tab and select **White** (first color).

n. Click the **Text Animation tab** in the Float Up dialog box, click the **Group text arrow**, and then select **By 2nd Level Paragraphs.** Click the **Automatically after check box** to select it and click the **spin arrow** to **3.** Click **OK.** Close the Animation Pane.

MAC TROUBLESHOOTING: MAC users may not be able to animate text..

---

o. Click the **Transitions tab** and click **Push** in the Transition to This Slide group. Click **Apply to All** in the Timing group.

p. Select the **Slide 1,** click the **Effect Options arrow** in the Transitions to This Slide group, and then select **From Left.** Click **Apply to All** in the Timing group.

q. Click **On Mouse Click** check box in Timing group to deselect it. Click the **After check box** and click the **spin arrow** to set it for **00:03.00.** Click **Apply to All** in the Timing group.

r. Click the **Slide Show tab.** Click **From Beginning** in the Start Slide Show group. Press **Esc** after reviewing the presentation.

s. Click **Slide 4.** Click the **Insert tab.** Click **Video** in the Media group. Select **Online Video**, type **social media marketing** in the Search YouTube box, and then click **Search.** Select the first result and click **Insert.**

MAC TROUBLESHOOTING: To insert the video, click the Insert tab, click Video, and then click Movie from File. Navigate to your student data files, locate the *p02p1SocialVideo.mp4* video and click Insert.

---

t. Click the **Size Dialog Box Launcher.** Set Height at **4.5"** and Width to **8.22"** in the Size section. Set Horizontal position at **5"** from the Top Left Corner. Set Vertical position at **1.25"** from the Top Left Corner in the Position section. Close the Format Video pane.

u. Click **Video Shape arrow** in the Video Styles group and select **Rectangle** in the Rectangles category. Click the **Video Border arrow** and select **Green** in the Standard Colors. Click **Play/Pause** to check the recording.

MAC TROUBLESHOOTING: On the Video Format tab, in the Size group, click the Crop arrow and click Change Shape.

Mid-Level Exercises

1 Learning from an Expert

CREATIVE CASE

Video-sharing sites such as YouTube.com make it possible to learn from PowerPoint industry experts as well as everyday PowerPoint users. You can learn through step-by-step instructions or by inspiration after seeing others use PowerPoint. The video source may also refer you to a professional website that will provide you with a wealth of tips and ideas for creating slide shows that move your work from ordinary to extraordinary. In this exercise, you will view a YouTube video featuring the work of Nancy Duarte, a well-known PowerPoint industry expert. After viewing the video and using good design principles, you will use shapes, text boxes, animation, transition, and video to illustrate each one of the rules in Duarte's presentation. You will end up with a six-slide presentation that illustrates your understanding of the rules plus a title slide. Apply the design skills you learned about in this chapter as you create each slide.

a. Access the Internet and go to www.youtube.com. Search for the video *Duarte Design's Five Rules for Presentations by Nancy Duarte.* View the video and take notes on how to apply the five rules to your presentations.

b. Open *p02m1Duarte* and rename it **p02m1Duarte_LastFirst**.

c. Click the **subtitle text box** on Slide 1. Replace *Student Name* with your name.

d. Click **Slide 2** and type **Treat Your Audience Well** as the title. Select the **bulleted text** and apply the **Fade Entrance effect**. Set the animation to start **After Previous** with a Duration of **03.00** and a Delay of **03.00**.

e. Click the **Animation Dialog Box Launcher** to access the Fade dialog box. Set the After animation to **Orange** on the Effect tab.

f. Click **Slide 3** and type **Use Movement to Express Your Ideas** as the title. Search for a video on YouTube with the words **Design principles** (Mac users: insert *p02m1DuarteVideo.mp4* from the starting files). Insert the first video and apply a **video shape**. Apply a **video border**. Set both the Fade In and Fade Out durations.

g. Click **Slide 4** and type **Show Meaningful Visuals** as the title.

h. Click **Slide 5** and type **Design for impact** as the title. Type **Don't decorate** in the subtitle placeholder and change the font size to **44**. Apply the **Fade Entrance effect**. Set the animation to start **After Previous** with a duration and a delay.

i. Click **Slide 6** and type **Talk to the Audience** as the title. Insert a text box in the subtitle content placeholder and type **Relationships matter.** Size the text box to a height of **0.7"** and a width of **5.75"**. Position it horizontally at **6.25"** from the Top Left Corner and vertically at **2.5"** from the Top Left Corner. Apply the **Heart motion path**. Set the animation to start **After Previous** with a Duration of **03.00** and a Delay of **02.00**.

j. Click **Slide 1** and apply a **transition**. Set an Effect Option and apply to all slides.

k. View the presentation. Click **File** and **Compress Media**. Select **Standard (480p)**.

> **MAC TROUBLESHOOTING:** Click the File menu, click Compress Pictures, click the Picture Quality arrow, and then click On-screen (150 ppi).

l. Save and close the file. Exit PowerPoint. Based on your instructor's directions, submit p02m1Duarte_LastFirst.

CREATIVE
CASE
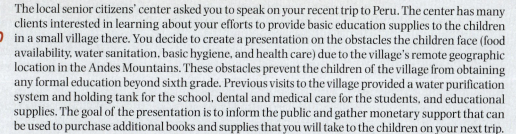
FROM
SCRATCH

The local senior citizens' center asked you to speak on your recent trip to Peru. The center has many clients interested in learning about your efforts to provide basic education supplies to the children in a small village there. You decide to create a presentation on the obstacles the children face (food availability, water sanitation, basic hygiene, and health care) due to the village's remote geographic location in the Andes Mountains. These obstacles prevent the children of the village from obtaining any formal education beyond sixth grade. Previous visits to the village provided a water purification system and holding tank for the school, dental and medical care for the students, and educational supplies. The goal of the presentation is to inform the public and gather monetary support that can be used to purchase additional books and supplies that you will take to the children on your next trip.

a. Open PowerPoint and search for the **Chalkboard education presentation** template in the Education category. Create the template and save it as **p02m2Education_LastFirst**.

b. Click the **Title Layout slide** and type **Children of Peru** as the title. Replace the subtitle with your name.

c. Click **Slide 2**. Develop slide content that details the major obstacles listed above (food availability, water sanitation, basic hygiene, and health care).

d. Insert a **Title and Content layout slide** after Slide 2. Type **Obstacles Prevent Education** on the new Slide 3 as the title. Add shapes, lines, and arrows that can convey the relationship between the obstacles and the children's education.

e. Insert another **Title and Content layout slide** after Slide 3. Type **Daily Activity** on the new Slide 4 as the title. Search for a video on YouTube of Peruvian children going about their daily tasks with their families and insert it (Mac users: insert *p02m2EducationVideo.mp4* from the starting files). Add a shape to the video and a border. Set the video option to start automatically.

f. Delete **Slides 5–12**. Click the last slide and type **Please help** as the title. Type **Your contribution would mean so much to the children** and increase the font size to **24**. Search the Internet and insert a picture in the left content placeholder, of a Peruvian scene (Mac users: insert *p02m2EducationImage.jpg* from the starting files).

g. Create a brief recording of you saying "**Your contribution would mean so much to the children.**" Insert that on the last slide. Drag the speaker icon to the top right of the slide. Set the audio option to start automatically and to hide during the show.

h. Review the presentation to ensure that is adheres to slide show design principles. Compress the video and audio.

i. Save and close the file. Exit PowerPoint. Based on your instructor's directions, submit p02m2Education_LastFirst.

Running Case

New Castle County Technical Services

New Castle County Technical Services (NCCTS) provides technical support for several companies in the greater New Castle County, Delaware, area. As a trainer in the Human Resources department, you were asked to provide a training seminar for managers. In Chapter 1 you began building your presentation. You continue to improve the presentation by adding additional content about adding shapes, animations, transitions, and video using the good design principles. You will apply a Designer idea to the last slide.

a. Open *p02r1Guidelines* and save the presentation as **p02r1Guidelines_LastFirst**.

b. Add a new slide with the **Title Only layout** after Slide 23. In the Title Placeholder type **Simple Shape Design**.

c. Type the following in the speaker notes in the Notes pane of the new slide: **There are many interesting designs you can create with the shape options in PowerPoint. Here is an example using simple shapes to introduce main points to the audience.**

d. Ensure you are still on the new slide. Click the **Insert tab** and click **Shapes** in the Illustrations group. Select **Rectangle: Top Corners Rounded** in the Rectangles group and draw the shape on the slide. Make the following changes to the shape:

- Apply the **Intense Effect – Plum, Accent 2** shape style.
- Set the shape height to **3.7"** and the shape width to **3.3"**.
- Set the Horizontal position to **0.96"** from the Top Left Corner and the Vertical position to **3.8"** from the Top Left Corner.
- Click in the shape and type **Main Point**. Increase the font size to **28 pt**.

e. Copy the shape and paste it on the slide. Set the Horizontal position to **5.1"** from the Top Left Corner and the Vertical position to **3.8"** from the Top Left Corner.

f. Copy the shape again to create a third Rectangle: Top Corners Rounded shape and paste on the slide. Set the Horizontal position to **9.25"** from the Top Left Corner and the Vertical position to **3.8"** from the Top Left Corner.

g. Click the **Insert tab** and click **Shapes** in the Illustrations group. Select **Oval** in the Basic Shapes group and draw the shape on the slide. Make the following changes to the shape:

- Change the shape style to **Intense Effect – Black, Dark 1**.
- Change the shape outline to **Blue, Accent 1** and the weight to **4½ pt**.
- Set the shape height to **1.25"** and the shape width to **1.25"**.
- Set the Horizontal position to **0.7"** from the Top Left Corner and the Vertical position to **3.3"** from the Top Left Corner.
- Type the number **1** in the shape and change the font size to **36 pt**.

h. Copy the shape and paste it on the slide. Set the Horizontal position to **4.8"** from the Top Left Corner and the Vertical position to **3.3"** from the Top Left Corner. Change the number 1 to number **2** in the shape.

i. Copy the shape again to create a third oval shape and paste on the slide. Set the Horizontal position to **9.0"** from the Top Left Corner and the Vertical position to **3.3"** from the Top Left Corner. Change the number to **3**.

j. Click **Slide 12**. Animate the bullet points with the **Fly In animation**. Make the following changes to the animation:

- Set each bullet point to appear **After Previous**.
- Set the Effect Options **From Top**.

k. Click **Slide 22**. Apply the following animation to the text on the slide:

- Select the first bullet point and apply the **Bounce Entrance animation** under More Entrance Effects. Set the animation to start **After previous** with a delay of .25.
- Select the image of the basketball and apply the **Bounce Entrance animation**. Set the animation to start **With Previous**.
- Select the second bullet point and apply the **Spinner animation** (located under More Entrance Effects) with a duration of **0.50**. Set the animation to begin **After Previous**.

- Select the image of the top. Set the animation to **Spinner** and to begin **With Previous**.
- Select the last bullet point and apply the **Float In animation** with a delay of **0.25**. Set the animation to begin **After Previous.**

l. Insert a new slide with the **Title and Content layout** after Slide 10. Type **Death by PowerPoint** in the Title placeholder. Type the following speaker note in the Notes pane: **This humorous video by Don McMillan gives you an idea of the concept.** Search for a video on YouTube with the words **Don McMillan Life After Death by PowerPoint** and use the embed code to insert the video. Make the following changes:

- Change the width of the video to **6.9"**.
- Set the Horizontal position to **2.6"** from the Top Left Corner and the Vertical position to **2.8"** from the Top Left Corner.
- Apply the **Center Shadow Rectangle** video style.
- Apply a **Plum, Accent 2 video border** and set the Weight of the border to **6 pt**.

m. Click **Slide 26**. On the Design, in the Designer group, click **Design Ideas**. Choose an option that enhances the content of the slide.

n. Click the Transitions tab and click **Push** in the Transition to This Slide group. Click **Apply to All** in the Timing group.

o. Save and close the file. Exit PowerPoint. Based on your instructor's directions, submit p02r1Guidelines_LastFirst.

Disaster Recovery

Predators

Your friend who teaches in a middle school asked you to fix the presentation she created about sharks to make it more interesting for her students. Open *p02d1Predators* and save the new presentation as **p02d1Predators_LastFirst**. View the presentation and note the visually jarring font that was applied throughout as well as shapes that are positioned poorly. If you have an Office 365 subscription, use Designer to help you fix the presentation.

Convert the title text on Slide 1 so that the font type used is appropriate for being projected in a classroom. Add your first and last names as the subtitle text. Convert the bulleted text on Slide 2 so that the font type used is appropriate. Then apply animations to the bullets to focus the students' attention. Convert the bulleted text on Slide 3 into a series of shapes demonstrating the food chain. Use the following as labels for the shapes: Predators, Secondary Consumers, Primary Consumers, and Primary Producers. Work with the shapes on Slide 4 to show a relationship between the shapes and image. Search for a video on YouTube of a shark swimming and insert it on Slide 5 (Mac users: insert *p02d1PredatorsVideo.mp4* from the starting files). Trim the video and format the style. Apply a transition to all slides and set the timing to advance each slide after 00:01.00. View the slide show and review the slides. Edit layouts, fonts, and other style elements as needed to make the slides readable and effectively convey the message of the presentation. Compress the video. Save and close the file. Exit PowerPoint. Based on your instructor's directions, submit p02d1Predators_LastFirst.

Capstone Exercise

The Science Club

The Science Club at your school wants to raise awareness of the fragility of the world's oceans. You volunteer to create a slide show that can be used at promotional events put on by the club. In this activity, you will create a presentation that meets slide show design principles, create and modify shapes and text boxes, apply and control animation, and add video and audio.

Examine Slide Show Design Principles

A few months ago, another member of the Science Club started a presentation about our oceans but did not complete it. You decide this is good way to get started on the presentation. You notice most of the presentation follows good design principles, but there is a problem with the font used on some of the slides. And although you feel the background is appropriate for the topic of the presentation, there is a problem with the contrast between the background and the text.

1. Open the file named *p02c1Oceans* and save it as **p02c1Oceans_LastFirst**. Replace *Student Name* on Slide 1 with your first and last names.
2. Change the title font type to **Tw Cen MT (Headings)** and ensure the font size is **48**. Change the font color to **Black, Text 1**. Change the subtitle font type to **Tw Cen MT (Body)** and ensure the font size is **22**. Change the font color to **White, Background 1, Darker 50%**.
3. Click **Slide 4** and change the title font color to **Black, Text 1**. Change the bulleted text font color to **Black, Text 1**.
4. Click **Slide 5**. Change the title font type to **Tw Cen MT (Headings)** and ensure the font size is **32**. Change the font color to **Black, Text 1**.
5. Click **Slide 6** and change the title font color to **Black, Text 1**. Change the bulleted text font color to **Black, Text 1**. Leave the email address alone.

Create and Modify Shapes and Text Boxes

You want to add visual interest to the presentation by inserting shapes and text boxes. You start by adding text to the image of the whale's tail. Then you use repetitive shapes and arrows to show the food chain as well as add a title to that slide.

6. Click **Slide 2**, create a text box, and then size it to a height of **0.5"** and a width of **4"**. Type **Whales are amazing creatures**. Apply **Tight Reflection: Touching** as a text effect. Drag the text box to the lower-right corner.
7. Click **Slide 3** and use Lock Drawing Mode to add four **Ovals**. Size them to a height of **2"** and a width of **3.44"**. Arrange them from the lower left corner to

the upper right corner of the slide. Change the fill to **Blue**. Add a **Line Arrow** connecting each oval to the next higher oval. Change the weight to **4½ pt** and the outline color to **Blue**.
8. Type **Primary Producer** in the lowest oval. Type **Primary Consumer** in the next oval. Type **Secondary Consumer** in the third oval. Type **Top Predator** in the highest oval.
9. Create a text box and type **THE FOOD CHAIN**. Change the font type to **Tw Cen MT (Headings)** and the size to **32**. Drag the text box to the upper-left corner.
10. View and save the presentation.

Apply and Control Animation

After viewing the presentation, you decide to make some modifications. The shapes on Slide 3 would be more interesting with some animation added.

11. Click **Slide 3**. Select the *Primary Producer* oval and add the **Wheel Entrance animation**. Next, select the *Primary Consumer* oval and add the **Wheel Entrance animation**. Then, select the *Secondary Consumer* oval and add the **Wheel Entrance animation**. Finally, select the *Top Predator* oval and add the **Wheel Entrance animation**. Select **After Previous** in the Start box. Adjust the Delay to **00.50**.
12. View the slide. Press **Esc**. Open the Animation Pane. Click each of the three lower ovals and select **After Previous**. Close the Animation Pane.
13. Click **Slide 4** and select the **bulleted text** and apply the **Fade Entrance effect**. Set the animation to start **After Previous** with a Duration of **02.00** and a Delay of **01.75**.
14. Click the **Animation Pane** to access the Fade dialog box. Set the After animation to **Green** on the Effect tab.
15. Click **Slide 1** and add the **Fade transition**. Set it to apply to all. Set the slides to advance automatically after **00:02.00**.
16. Save the presentation.

Add Video and Audio

You insert a video clip of the ocean and modify the settings. Then you add a narration.

17. Click **Slide 5**. Search for a video on YouTube of jellyfish swimming underwater and insert it (Mac users: insert *p02c1OceansVideo.mp4* from the starting files).
18. Set the video to start **Automatically**.

19. Change the Video Options to **Hide While Not Playing** and to **Rewind after Playing**.

20. Format the video into an **Oval**. Apply a **Simple Frame, White Subtle** video style.

21. Click **Slide 2**. Create a recording of you saying "**Whales are amazing creatures.**" Drag the speaker icon to the lower left of the slide. Set the audio option to start automatically and to hide during the show.

22. View the presentation and then compress the video.

23. Save and close the file. Exit PowerPoint. Based on your instructor's directions, submit p02c1Oceans_LastFirst.

Work with SmartArt

In addition to creating SmartArt from a bulleted list as you learned in Chapter 1, you can create SmartArt from scratch, adding both text and pictures. SmartArt graphics enable you to create a visual representation of information, making it easier to understand. Why use a boring bulleted or numbered list when you can create a vibrant graphic to better communicate your information? Once created, you can customize the SmartArt graphic to improve its appearance to better fit your presentation.

In this section you will learn to create and modify SmartArt graphics. You will change layouts, colors and effects, and apply a SmartArt style. In addition, you will learn to add, promote, demote, reorder, and change SmartArt shapes.

STEP 1 Creating SmartArt

Several different types of SmartArt are available to assist with illustrating a concept. Within each type are several layouts you can choose from depending on what information you want to convey. Some layouts simply add visual appeal to a bulleted list, whereas others are designed to portray specific kinds of information. For example, the Process layout shows the steps to complete a task, whereas the Hierarchy layout illustrates the structure of an organization with an organizational chart. Figure 3.2 compares a text-based slide in the common bullet format to a slide showing the information in a SmartArt graphic. The arrows and colors make it easier for the audience to remember the message and understand the concept as a process required to build teams.

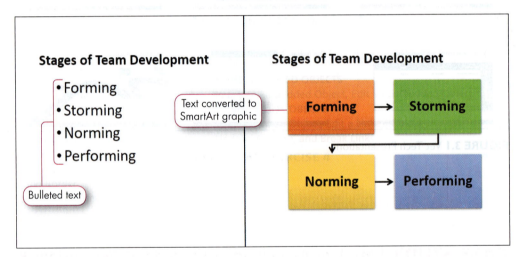

FIGURE 3.2 Bulleted Text and SmartArt Comparison

Choose Layouts

To create a SmartArt graphic, first choose a type that fits your message. The SmartArt gallery has nine types: List, Process, Cycle, Hierarchy, Relationship, Matrix, Pyramid, Picture, and Office.com. At the top of the list is All, which you can click to display all SmartArt graphics. Each type includes a description of the information appropriate for the layouts within the type. Table 3.1 shows the SmartArt types and their purposes.

TABLE 3.1	SmartArt Types and Purposes
Type	**Purpose**
List	Shows nonsequential information.
Process	Displays steps in a process or a timeline.
Cycle	Shows a continual process.
Hierarchy	Displays a decision tree, organization chart, or pedigree.
Relationship	Illustrates connections.
Matrix	Displays how parts relate to a whole.
Pyramid	Shows proportional relationships with the largest component on the top or bottom.
Picture	Displays nonsequential or grouped blocks of information. Maximizes both horizontal and vertical display space for shapes.
Office.com	Shows SmartArt graphics available from layouts on Office.com.

After you have narrowed down a potential SmartArt type, there are layouts from which to further choose. Figure 3.3 shows the Choose a SmartArt Graphic dialog box. The pane on the left shows the types of SmartArt graphics available. Each type includes layouts that are displayed in the center pane. Clicking one of the layouts enlarges the selected graphic and displays it in the preview pane on the right side. The preview pane describes purposes for which the SmartArt layout can be used effectively. Some of the descriptions include tips for the type of text to enter.

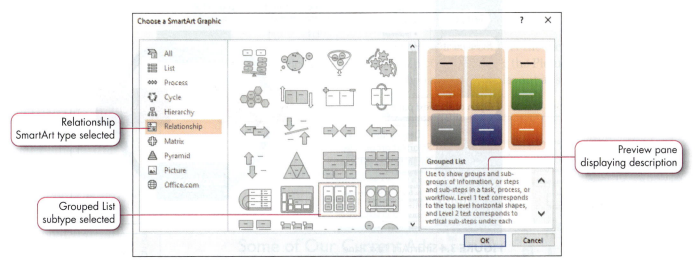

FIGURE 3.3 Choose a SmartArt Graphic Gallery

> **To insert a SmartArt graphic, complete the following steps:**
>
> 1. Click the Insert tab, and click SmartArt in the Illustrations group or click the SmartArt icon on the icon palette of a layout.
> 2. Select the type of SmartArt graphic you want in the left pane.
> 3. Select the SmartArt layout you want in the center pane.
> 4. Preview the selected SmartArt and layout in the right pane.
> 5. Click OK.

STEP 3 Modifying SmartArt

Once you have selected the appropriate SmartArt and added the necessary text, it can be designed to match the look and feel of your presentation. PowerPoint displays two contextual tabs that enable you to modify the design and format of your SmartArt graphics: the SmartArt Tools Design tab and the SmartArt Tools Format tab. You can change the color, add a SmartArt style, or even change the layout without having to start over.

Change SmartArt Colors

By default, when you insert a SmartArt graphic, it displays using the first accent color of the color scheme in the applied theme. To change the color of a SmartArt graphic, select the SmartArt graphic, and then click Change Colors to display the Colors gallery (see Figure 3.7). The gallery contains Primary Theme Colors, Colorful, and Accent color schemes. Select a color variation to apply it to the SmartArt graphic.

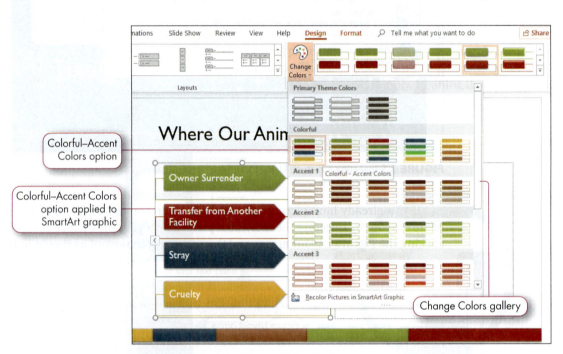

FIGURE 3.7 SmartArt Theme Color Options

Individual shapes and borders can also be modified using the Shape Styles group on the SmartArt Format tab as shown in Figure 3.8. To change the color of a shape, click the individual shape, and then click the Shape Fill arrow. Select a color from the Theme Colors or Standard Colors or click More Fill Colors for more options. Changing the shape border is similar to changing the shape fill; click the shape, click the Shape Outline arrow, and then click a color choice. In addition, you can change the weight and style of the border by clicking the Shape Outline arrow.

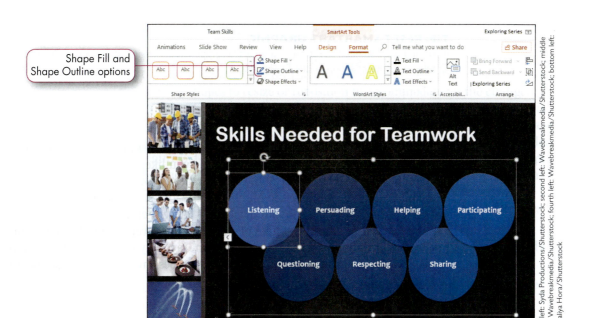

FIGURE 3.8 Shape Fill and Outline Options

Apply a SmartArt Style

You can quickly change the overall look and effects of SmartArt graphics by using the built-in SmartArt on the Design tab. Using a style can enhance the appearance of a SmartArt and often can make the text easier to read and interpret. A SmartArt Style combines several effects, such as line styles, different shape fills, shadows, or a 3-D style. Like many of the other galleries across Office, this gallery has an automatic Live Preview to show what the graphic could look like with the styles applied.

To apply a SmartArt style, select the SmartArt graphic. In the SmartArt Styles group, click More to display the SmartArt Styles gallery as shown in Figure 3.9, and then select a style.

FIGURE 3.9 SmartArt Styles Gallery

Promote, Demote, and Reorder Shapes

The Create Graphic group on the SmartArt Tools Design tab also includes several commands that enable you to organize the content in the SmartArt graphic as shown in Figure 3.12. For example, you can promote, demote, or reorder objects to customize the graphic exactly the way you want. Be aware that like other options in the Create Graphic group, the availability of these buttons is dependent on the SmartArt type and what object is selected.

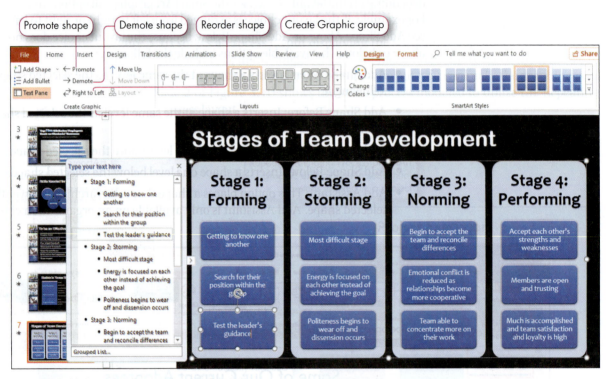

FIGURE 3.12 SmartArt Create Graphic Options

To move a shape to a higher level, click Promote in the Create Graphic group on the Design tab. To move a shape to a lower level, click Demote. This process is similar to changing the indent level of items in a bulleted list or Word outline. You can also demote and promote shapes from within the Text pane. With the insertion point in the Text pane, press Tab to demote a shape. Press Backspace or Shift+Tab to promote a shape.

You can reorder the shapes on the same level by using the Move Up, Move Down, and Right to Left options in the Create Graphic group. Move Up will move the selected shape up in a sequence, Move Down will move the selected object down in the sequence, and the Right to Left option will change the layout from the right to the left.

Modify Shapes

You can make modifications to the default shapes in a SmartArt graphic by using the commands in the Shapes group on the SmartArt Tools Format tab. If you want to change the default shapes, click Change Shape on the Format tab. For example, if you added a Basic Block List SmartArt the default shape is a basic rectangle, but you could change this to an oval shape as shown in Figure 3.13.

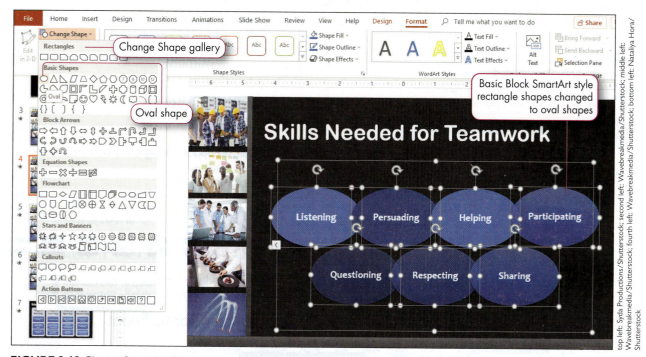

FIGURE 3.13 Change SmartArt Shapes

To change a SmartArt default shape, complete the following steps:

1. Select the shape or shapes you want to change. To select multiple shapes, press Ctrl while clicking each of the shapes you want to change.
2. Click the SmartArt Tools Format tab.
3. Click Change Shape in the Shapes group. The Shape gallery will display.
4. Select the shape.

Shapes can also be resized by selecting the Larger or Smaller commands in the Shapes group on the Format tab. You can continue clicking the command until you reach the size you want. To change the size of all of the shapes at the same time, press and hold Ctrl, and then select each of the shapes to be changed.

Quick Concepts

1. Describe how typing text in a SmartArt Text pane works like an outline. *p. 918*
2. Explain when the option to add a shape to a SmartArt graphic may not be available, and give an example. *p. 923*
3. Give two suggestions for SmartArt text to ensure consistency in a SmartArt graphic. *p. 918*

The pictures are automatically inserted into the picture style SmartArt graphic on the slide and in the Text pane.

> **MAC TROUBLESHOOTING:** Delete the images on Slide 4. Click the Insert tab and click the SmartArt arrow. Point to Picture and select Bending Picture Caption. Double-click the picture icon in the Text pane, navigate to the p03h1MacImages folder, and then click *p03h1Bailey.jpg*. Click Insert. Repeat until all eight images have been inserted in the SmartArt graphic. Note: You will need to click Add after inserting the third image and before inserting all remaining images.

c. Ensure the Text pane is open. Click in the first bullet point in the Text pane, and type **Max**. Continue adding names to the bullet points in this order: **Shadow**, **Lily**, **Buster**, **Millie**, **Bailey**, **Ollie**, and **Bella**. Close the Text pane.

d. Save the presentation.

> **TROUBLESHOOTING:** The order of your images and names may not match Figure 3.15. The layout of the SmartArt is dependent on the order in which the images are selected. To ensure they are selected correctly, click the first picture in the upper left-corner, press and hold Ctrl and then select each of the remaining pictures in the first row, moving to the bottom right-corner and selecting the remaining images in the bottom row in order. Make the necessary name changes to match the images in Figure 3.15.

STEP 3 MODIFY SMARTART

You decide that a few modifications to the inserted SmartArt would be a better way to showcase the information. Refer to Figure 3.16 as you complete Step 3.

FIGURE 3.16 SmartArt with Modifications

a. Ensure the SmartArt graphic on Slide 4 is selected.

b. Click the **SmartArt Tools Design tab**. In the Layouts group, click **More**, and then select **Titled Picture Blocks**.

The SmartArt is changed to the new layout.

c. Click **Intense Effect** in the SmartArt Styles group, click **Change Colors**, and then select **Colorful – Accent Colors**.

d. Click **Slide 7** and select the **SmartArt graphic**.

e. Click **Intense Effect** in the SmartArt Styles group on the Design tab, click **Change Colors**, and then select **Colorful – Accent Colors**.

Both of the SmartArt graphics now have the same colors and SmartArt styles applied.

f. Save the presentation.

STEP 4 # WORK WITH SMARTART SHAPES

You realize that you need to add an additional shape to the SmartArt graphic on Slide 7 in the presentation, and you want to reorder one of the shapes. Refer to Figure 3.17 as you complete Step 4.

FIGURE 3.17 Shapes Modified

a. Click **Slide 7** and click the **SmartArt graphic**. Click **Text Pane** in the Create Graphic group on the Design tab to open the Text pane of the SmartArt.

b. Place the insertion point at the end of the text *Cruelty* in the Text pane and press **Enter**.

A new bullet point will be added to the Text pane, and an additional shape will display on the slide.

c. Type **Transfer from Another Facility** and close the Text pane.

d. Select the **Transfer from Another Facility shape**, click the **Design tab**, and then click **Move Up** in the Create Graphic group twice.

The shape is now the second text shape.

e. Select the first shape with text, press and hold **Ctrl**, and then select the three additional shapes with the text inserted.

f. Click the **Format tab**. Click **Change Shape** in the Shapes group and click **Arrow: Pentagon** in the Block Arrows group.

g. Save the presentation. Keep the presentation open if you plan to continue with the next Hands-On Exercise. If not, close the presentation and exit PowerPoint.

To draw a table, complete the following steps:

1. Click the Insert tab.
2. Click Table in the Tables group.
3. Click Draw Table. As you move the pointer over the document, it resembles a pen.
4. Drag a rectangle, and then draw horizontal and vertical lines to create rows and columns within the rectangular table space.
5. Press Esc when the table is complete.

Add Text to a Table

Table data on a slide should be as simple as possible to convey your message. When working with text-based tables, limit the number of rows and columns to keep the font size large enough to read. For example, rather than listing 20 items in a table, list the top 5. If the audience needs the complete list, consider using a handout that the audience can refer to later.

To navigate the table, you move the insertion point from cell to cell in the table using the pointer or by pressing Tab. Additionally, you can use the keyboard arrows to move from cell to cell. Pressing Tab in the last cell of a table creates a new blank row at the end of the table.

As you type text in a cell, the text will wrap to the next line when it reaches the right edge of the cell, adjusting row height as necessary to accommodate cell contents. To force text to a new line in a cell (before reaching the right cell border), press Enter.

Insert a Picture into a Table Cell

You can add pictures or other background fills to an individual cell or to the table. This can add an interesting element to the background of the table or to individual cells. For example, as shown in Figure 3.21, an image of a heart has been set in the background of the cells in the middle of the table, adding a divider between the two columns of warning signs to give the table more visual appeal.

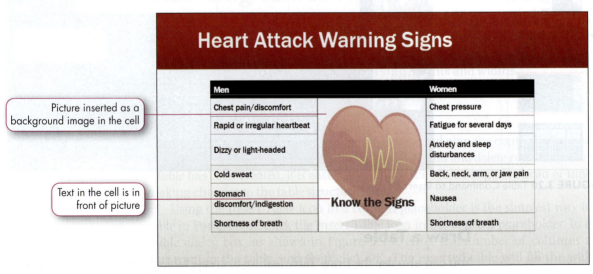

Picture inserted as a background image in the cell

Text in the cell is in front of picture

FIGURE 3.21 Inserted Picture in Table

When an image is placed in a table cell in PowerPoint, the image is not the cell content. Rather, it is treated as a background image, enabling you to type text over the top of the image (refer to Figure 3.21). Copying and pasting an image might seem like a likely method to insert an image, but it does not work. If you try and do this in a table created in PowerPoint, the image free-floats on the slide but does not become part of the cell content.

When you insert a picture into a cell as a background, the picture is resized to fit into the cell, often resulting in distorted images. You may need to resize the image in a photo image software application or resize the height or width of the cell to fix the issue. Resizing a cell is covered later in this chapter.

To insert a picture into a table cell, complete the following steps:

1. Right-click in the cell you want to add the image.
2. Click Format Shape on the shortcut menu.
3. Click Fill in the Format Shape task pane and click Picture or texture fill.
4. Click File. In the Insert Picture dialog box, navigate to the location of the picture you want to insert, and click Insert. The picture is inserted into the cell and automatically sized to fit the size of the cell.

STEP 2 — Modifying a Table Layout

It is often necessary to modify the layout of a table. You may find the need to add or delete rows or columns, merge or split cells, or resize the table to better accommodate the information.

Add and Delete Rows and Columns

Suppose you have inserted a table and you realize as you enter data into the last row that an additional row is needed. You can press Tab to begin a new row. You can continue entering data and pressing Tab to create new rows until the table is complete. However, you will occasionally need to insert a row above or below an existing row when the row is not the last row in the table. You might even want to insert a column to the left or right of an existing column. To add a column or row to a table, place the insertion point in a cell adjacent to the location where you want to add a new row or column. In the Rows & Columns group on the Table Tools Layout tab, to add a row, select either Insert Above or Insert Below. To add a column, select Insert Left or Right in the Rows & Columns group shown in Figure 3.22.

FIGURE 3.22 Rows & Columns Group

When you delete rows and columns, the table automatically resizes to account for the removal of the data. You may need to resize the table after removing a column or row. You will learn about resizing a table in a later section. To delete a row or column in a table, place the insertion point in the cell where you want to delete a column or row. In the Rows & Columns group on the Table Tools Layout tab, click Delete, and then select Delete Columns or Delete Rows.

> **TIP: DELETE OR ADD MULTIPLE ROWS OR COLUMNS AT THE SAME TIME**
> To add or delete multiple rows/columns at once, select the number of rows/columns that you want to add or delete, and then click the appropriate choice from the Rows & Columns group.

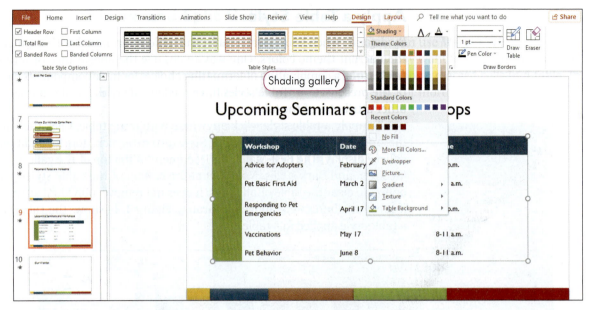

FIGURE 3.26 Shading Gallery

Certain styles include borders, but you can add them manually, as well. Change border style, weight, and color by using the pen options located in the Draw Borders group on the Table Tools Design tab as shown in Figure 3.27. The Pen Style option changes the style of the line used to draw borders and includes options for dotted and dashed lines. The Pen Weight option changes the width of the border and the Pen Color option changes the color of the border. After selecting the style, weight, and color of a border, click the border you want to change with the pencil. You can also drag to include additional borders.

If you have multiple borders to change, however, it is faster to use Borders in the Table Styles group on the Table Tools Design tab. Select the cell or cells you want to change or select the entire table. You can choose to have no border; all cells bordered; only outside borders; only inside borders; just a top, bottom, left, or right border; inside horizontal or vertical borders; or diagonal down or up borders. Figure 3.27 shows the line thickness of the outside border changed to 6 pt.

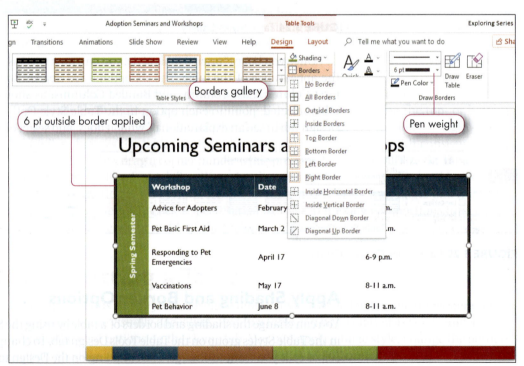

FIGURE 3.27 Border Weight Changed for Outside Borders

Align Text Within Cells, Rows, and Columns

You may find for better readability that you need to change the alignment of text within the table or adjust the margins inside the cell. To add variety, you may want to rotate the direction of text within a cell. The Alignment group on the Table Tools Layout tab includes features to accomplish these tasks.

To change the alignment of text within the table, select the text you want to change the alignment for, and then click the Table Tools Layout tab. Select Align Left, Center, or Align Right in the Alignment group to align text horizontally. Select Align Top, Center Vertically, or Align Bottom in the Alignment group to align text vertically.

If space is needed between the border of a cell and the text, you can change the internal margin spacing of a cell from the default 0.05″ for top and bottom margins and 0.1″ for left and right margins to no margins, narrow margins, wide margins, or custom margins. To change the margins, click Cell Margins in the Alignment group on the Table Tools Layout tab and select an option from the gallery.

To change the direction of text within a cell, click Text Direction in the Alignment group on the Table Tools Layout tab and select Horizontal, Rotate All Text 90°, Rotate All Text 270°, or Stacked in the Alignment group. Rotate All Text 90° positions text vertically facing to the right, and Rotate All Text 270° positions text vertically facing to the left. Stacked changes the text orientation from horizontal to vertical for each individual character. Figure 3.28 shows a table with text rotated 270° within a column.

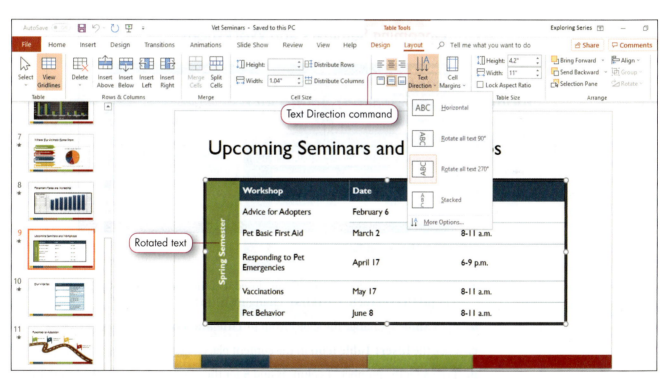

FIGURE 3.28 Rotated Text

Quick Concepts

4. Explain when it is better to draw a table instead of using the Insert Table feature. ***p. 931***

5. Describe some of the options available to format a table and when they might be used. ***p. 934***

6. Explain the different ways you can resize a column or row in a table. ***p. 934***

TABLE 3.3 Chart Elements

Element	Description
Axes	Charts typically have two axes that are used to measure and categorize the data. • A vertical axis (also known as value axis or y-axis) • A horizontal axis (also known as category axis or x-axis)
Axis title	Label that describes the category or value axes.
Chart area	The background area of the entire chart and its elements.
Chart title	A heading that describes the chart information.
Data label	Descriptive label used to identify the exact value or name of a data point.
Data table	A grid that contains the data source values and labels.
Error bars	Graphically express the potential error amounts relative to each data marker in a data series.
Gridlines	Horizontal or vertical lines that extend from the tick marks across the plot area, which can help make it easier to estimate the value of specific data points.
Legend	The key that identifies each data series by color.
Plot area	Region containing the graphical representation of the values in the data series; surrounded by two axes.
Trendline	Used to graphically display the trends in data and to analyze the problems of prediction.

Modify Chart Titles

A chart includes the placeholder text *Chart Title*. You should give the chart a meaningful and descriptive title to ensure that the audience is able to interpret the information correctly. Click inside the Chart Title placeholder and type the title. Format the text by using the Font commands on the Home tab.

By default, the chart title displays centered above the chart. Although this is a typical location for a chart title, you can position the chart title in other locations. You can drag the title text placeholder to a new location on the plot area or you can access other chart title options in Chart Elements, as shown in Figure 3.36.

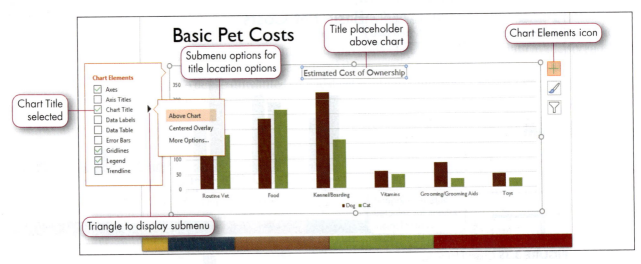

FIGURE 3.36 Chart Title Options

Add Data Labels

Data labels make a chart easier to understand because they show details about a data series or its individual data points. A data label shows the exact value or name of a data point, as shown in Figure 3.37. Use either Add Chart Element or the Design tab to display data labels. You can determine the position of the data labels by selecting a data label option in Add Chart Element. For example, you can specify Center or Outside End.

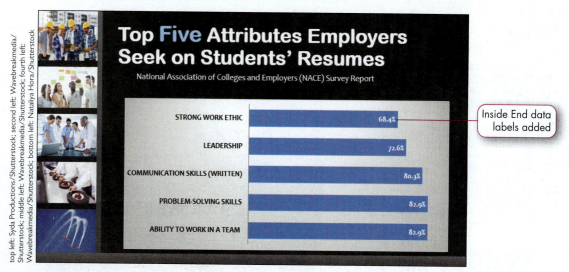

FIGURE 3.37 Chart with Data Labels

Modify a Chart Axis

The numeric scale to be used for the axes in a chart is determined automatically, with the minimum usually set at zero and the maximum slightly larger than the highest value. You can adjust the scale and make formatting changes to the axes. For example, you may want to set the vertical axis to start at a value other than zero, change the number format of the axis values to currency, or increase the font size for readability.

To make changes to an axis, double-click the axis you want to change to open the Format Axis task pane (see Figure 3.38). Use Axis Options to specify the bounds, units, display units, labels, and number formatting for an axis. In addition, you can use the font options on the Home tab to format the axis values.

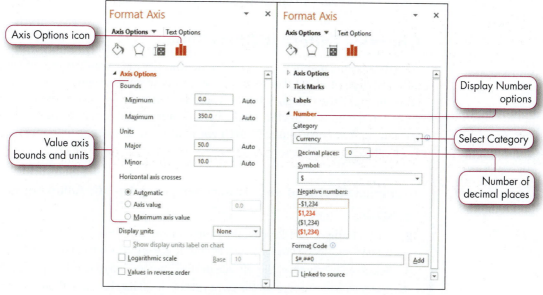

FIGURE 3.38 Format Axis Task Pane

Apply a Quick Layout

Instead of manually adding or changing chart elements, you can apply a predefined layout to the chart with a single click. Each layout contains predefined chart elements, as shown in Figure 3.39. To apply a Quick Layout, select the chart, and then click Quick Layout on the Chart Tools Design tab. Select the layout in the Quick Layout gallery.

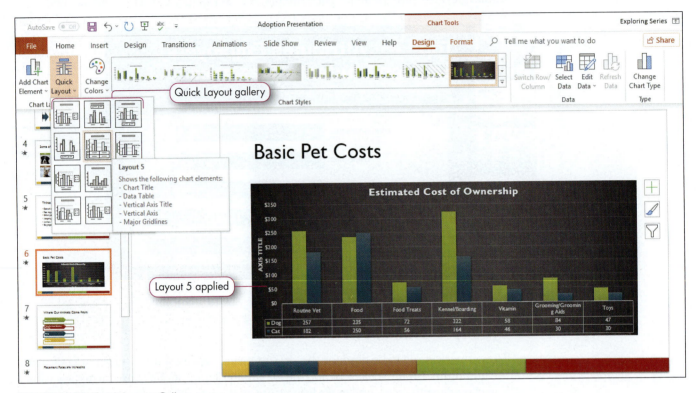

FIGURE 3.39 Quick Layout Gallery

Modifying a Chart

There are several ways to modify a chart using the Chart Tools Design tab. PowerPoint enables you to change the chart type, rearrange a chart's data, and even change the color and style of a chart. In addition, you may want to resize or move the chart on the slide.

Choose a Different Chart Type

After you create a chart, you may decide that the data would be better represented by a different type of chart. For example, you may want to change a column chart to a bar chart because the category labels would fit better in that arrangement. Or, the data in a clustered column chart might be better represented in a line chart if it contains data with dates. Use the Change Chart Type command to change a chart to a different type of chart.

> **To change the type of an existing chart, complete the following steps:**
>
> 1. Select the chart.
> 2. Click Change Chart Type on the Design tab in the Type group to open the Change Chart Type dialog box (which is similar to the Insert Chart dialog box).
> 3. Select a chart type on the left side of the Change Chart Type dialog box.
> 4. Select a chart subtype on the right side of the dialog box, and then click OK.

STEP 3 Apply a Chart Style and Change Chart Colors

To apply formatting to an entire chart, you can use a chart style. A **chart style** is a collection of formatting that controls the colors of the chart area, plot area, and data series, as well as the font and font size of the titles. To apply a chart style, select the chart, and then click More in the Chart Styles group on the Chart Tools Design tab to display the Chart Styles gallery. Select a style from the Chart Styles gallery.

Use Change Colors in the Chart Styles group on the Design tab to select a different set of predefined colorful or monochromatic combinations of the colors defined by the presentation theme. The colorful set includes different color options, whereas the monochromatic colors displays different shades of the same color, as shown in Figure 3.40.

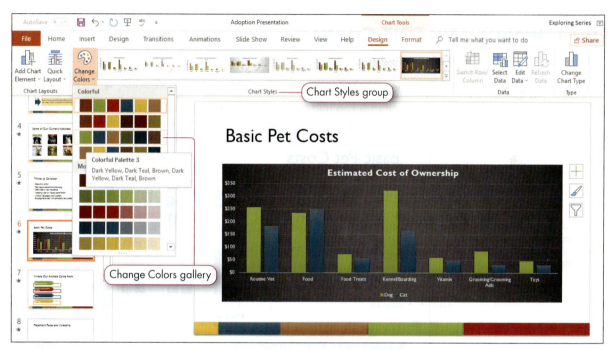

FIGURE 3.40 Change Color Gallery

Move or Resize a Chart

A chart can be resized manually by dragging a corner or middle sizing handle. To keep the ratio of height to width consistent when resizing the chart, drag a corner handle while pressing Shift; this will size the chart in both the vertical and horizontal directions simultaneously. If you want to size the chart to a specific size, use the Height and Width options in the Size group of the Chart Tools Format tab.

To move a chart, click on the border of the chart. When you see the four-headed pointer, drag and drop the chart in a new location on the slide.

Quick Concepts ✓

7. Describe the most common chart types and their purposes. *p. 942*

8. Explain the difference between a single series chart and a multi-series chart. *p. 942*

9. Explain what a chart element is, and give three examples. *p. 946*

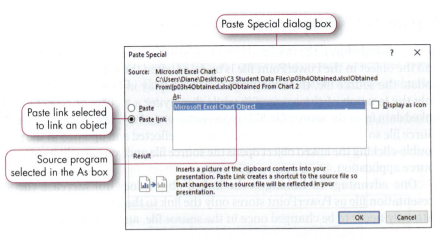

FIGURE 3.47 Link an Object Using Paste Special

Edit a Linked Object

When you double-click a linked object on a PowerPoint slide, the source application opens, and you edit the source file directly. This is different, as you recall, from embedding. When you double-click the embedded object, the source application ribbon opens within PowerPoint without opening the source application itself. Changes made in the source file will be reflected and updated in the PowerPoint file. Additionally, you can right-click the linked object and select Linked Worksheet Object (Excel) or Linked Document Object (Word), and then select Edit, as shown in Figure 3.48.

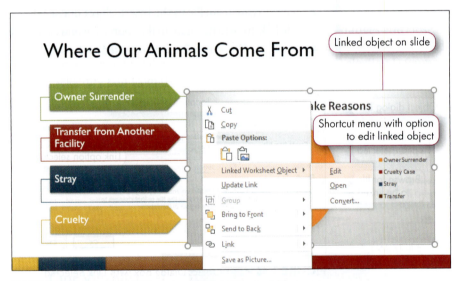

FIGURE 3.48 Edit Linked Worksheet Object Shortcut Menu

STEP 4 › Update, Change, and Break Links

When you open a presentation with a linked file, a security warning indicating that Microsoft has identified a security concern is displayed. If you are familiar with the source of the file, click Update Links, as shown in Figure 3.49, and any changes made to the source file while the PowerPoint presentation was closed will be updated in the PowerPoint file. You can manually update a linked object by right-clicking the linked object and clicking Update Link.

There may be situations when you do not want the PowerPoint object to reflect any changes in the linked source file. In that case, you can choose to Cancel and not update the links, and the data in the presentation will remain unchanged.

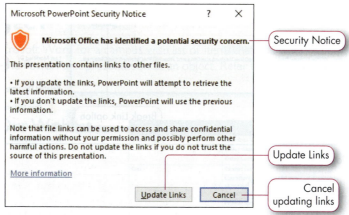

FIGURE 3.49 Update Links

If the location of the destination or source file of a linked object has changed, when you open the presentation containing an object that is linked, an error message displays when you try to edit the data. To fix this, you can either change the source of the broken link or remove it.

To change the source or break a link, complete the following steps:

1. Click the File tab in PowerPoint.
2. Click Info on the left side.
3. Click Edit Links to Files.
4. Click Change Source in the Links dialog box (see Figure 3.50) if you want to change the location of the link or click Break Link to remove the link.

g. Double-click the embedded table.

The Word ribbon displays within the PowerPoint window.

> **MAC TROUBLESHOOTING:** Double-click the table, click Document Object, and then select Open.

h. Click the **Table Tools Design tab**. Select **Grid Table 4–Accent 4** in the Table Styles group.

i. Click the **Table Tools Layout tab**. Click **Align Center Left** in the Alignment group.

j. Click anywhere on the slide to close the Word ribbon and return to PowerPoint.

The changes are reflected in the embedded table on the slide.

> **MAC TROUBLESHOOTING:** Click Update (the Save Icon on the Quick Access Toolbar) in the Word document and return to PowerPoint.

k. Save the presentation.

STEP 2 INSERT A LINKED OBJECT

Placement statistics and where the animals have been obtained from are in an Excel worksheet. You want to add these items as links to the presentation. Refer to Figure 3.52 as you complete Step 2.

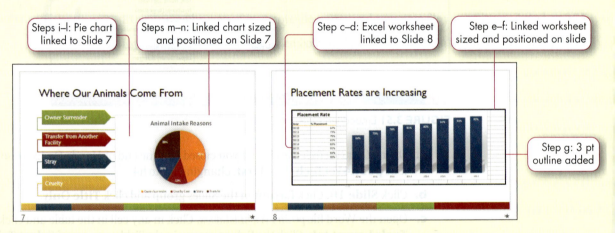

FIGURE 3.52 Linked Objects

a. Open the Excel file *p03h4Placement.xlsx* and save the file as **p03h4Placement_LastFirst.xlsx** Close the Excel file.

b. Click **Slide 8**. Click **Layout** in the Slides group and click **Title Only**.

c. Click the **Insert tab** and click **Object** in the Text group.

The Object dialog box opens.

d. Click **Create from file** in the Insert Object dialog box, click **Browse**, navigate to the folder containing your student files, select **p03h4Placement_LastFirst.xlsx**, and then click **OK**. Click to select the **Link check box** in the Insert Object dialog box and click OK.

The Excel worksheet is added to the slide as a linked object. The copy is a link to the original data file so that changes to the source data file are reflected in the presentation.

> **MAC TROUBLESHOOTING:** Linking is not an option in Mac for Excel. Paste the file as an object on the slide. Changes to the source file will not be automatically reflected in the file.

e. Click the **Format tab**. Change the Shape Height to **4"** in the Size group and press **Enter**.

f. Click the **Dialog Box Launcher** in the Size group to open the Format Object task pane. Click **Position**. Set the Horizontal position to **1.1"** from the Top Left Corner and the Vertical position to **1.9"** from the Top Left corner. Close the Format Object task pane.

g. Click the **Shape Outline arrow** in the Shape Styles group, click **Weight**, and then select **3 pt**.

h. Click **Slide 7**. Delete the empty content placeholder on the right.

i. Open the Excel file *p03h4Obtained.xlsx* and save the file as **p03h4Obtained_LastFirst.xlsx**.

j. Select the **pie chart** and click **Copy** in the Clipboard group on the Home tab. Minimize Excel. Click **PowerPoint** on the taskbar to make it active again.

k. Click the **Paste arrow** in the Clipboard group on the Home tab and click **Paste Special**.

l. Click the **Paste link option** in the Paste Special dialog box. Click **Microsoft Excel Chart Object** in the *As* box and click **OK**.

> **TROUBLESHOOTING:** If you closed the *p03h4Obtained_LastFirst.xlsx* Excel file instead of minimizing the file, the Paste link option may be grayed out. Reopen the file and repeat Steps k–l.

> **MAC TROUBLESHOOTING:** The Paste Link option is not available. Click Microsoft Graphic Object.

m. Click the **Format tab**, type **4.5"** in the Shape Height box in the Size group, and then press **Enter**.

n. Click the **Dialog Box Launcher** in the Size group. Set the Horizontal position to **5.35"** from the Top Left Corner and the Vertical position to **2.3"** from the Top Left corner. Close the Format Object task pane.

> **MAC TROUBLESHOOTING:** Click the Format pane on the Format tab to set positions.

o. Close Excel. Save the presentation.

Chapter Objectives Review

After reading this chapter, you have accomplished the following objectives:

1. Create SmartArt.

- SmartArt graphics are diagrams that present information visually to effectively communicate a message.
- Choose layouts: Select a diagram type from one of the nine categories of diagrams in the SmartArt gallery. Refer to the description of the layout to ensure that it is appropriate to the information type.
- Add text to SmartArt: SmartArt graphics include a Text pane, which enables you to type text in the pane like you would type an outline.
- Insert pictures into SmartArt: Many of the SmartArt layouts include placeholders to insert pictures.

2. Modify SmartArt.

- Change SmartArt colors: SmartArt graphics can be modified to fit nearly any color scheme.
- Apply a SmartArt style: There are several built-in SmartArt styles to change the overall look of the graphic.
- Change the SmartArt layout: Once a SmartArt graphic type has been selected, it can easily be converted to another layout.

3. Work with SmartArt shapes.

- Add and delete shapes: SmartArt can be modified to include additional shapes or to delete shapes. Some SmartArt types are limited in the number of shapes possible, due to the design of the SmartArt type, such as Opposing Arrows, which only enables two shapes.
- Promote, demote, and reorder shapes: Once a SmartArt graphic is created, you can promote, demote, and reorder objects to customize it exactly as you want.
- Modify shapes: Shapes can be modified from the default shape. Shapes can also be resized, and borders and shading can be applied to individual shapes.

4. Insert tables.

- Create a table: Tables can be inserted with or without a content placeholder. When a table is created, you specify the number of columns and rows.
- Draw a table: If your table has various sized columns and rows, using the Draw Table feature may be a better choice rather than modifying the dimensions later.
- Add text to a table: Simplify the information you add to a table. Limiting the number of rows and columns keeps the font size readable.
- Insert a picture into a table cell: Pictures are inserted as backgrounds in a table cell in PowerPoint. Text can be typed over the image.

5. Modify a table layout.

- Add and delete rows and columns: You can insert rows below or above an existing row, or insert columns to the left and right of an existing column to accommodate additional information. Delete columns and rows when the layout of the table needs to change.
- Merge and split cells: Merging cells enables you to combine two or more cells. This is common for the title row of a table. Splitting cells divides a cell into two or more cells.
- Change row height, column width, and table size: Change the size of a cell or table to better accommodate the information or call attention to it.

6. Format a table.

- Apply a table style: A table style is applied by default when you create a table, using a Quick Style from the theme. You can change the appearance of a table using one of the built-in table styles.
- Apply shading and border options: You can change the shading of any of the cells in a table. Border styles, weight, and color can be changed using the pen options.
- Align text within cells, rows, and columns: You can change the alignment within a table to align the text both vertically and horizontally. Text can also be rotated in a cell.

7. Insert and edit charts.

- Understand basic chart types: A chart is a visual representation of data. Choose the type of chart that best portrays the data.
- Insert a chart: A chart can be inserted with or without a content placeholder.
- Enter and edit data: When you enter data into a chart, a spreadsheet opens with sample data to be replaced. The chart and spreadsheet are linked. As you input data in the spreadsheet, the chart updates on the slide.

8. Identify and modify chart elements.

- Modify chart titles: The chart area is made up of the chart and all its elements. When a chart is created, a placeholder is included for a chart title. Chart titles give meaning to the data for the audience to interpret the information correctly.
- Add data labels: Data labels add meaning to a chart because they show details about a data series or individual data point.
- Modify a chart axis: To help clarify information, a chart axis may need to be modified. A numeric scale is created automatically with the minimum and maximum set.
- Apply a Quick Layout: A predefined layout can be applied to a chart that includes style elements.

9. Modify a chart.

- Choose a different chart type: Each chart type organizes and emphasizes data differently. Select the chart type that conveys the intended message of the chart.

- Apply a chart style and change chart colors: Several built-in chart styles are available. Chart styles control the formatting of the chart elements. Available chart colors are determined by the theme colors of the presentation.
- Move or resize a chart: Charts can be sized manually by dragging the sizing handles or you can set a specific height and width for the chart on the slide on the ribbon.

10. Embed objects.
- Insert an embedded object: When you embed an object, a connection is established in PowerPoint to the source file and the object is inserted into PowerPoint, with the source file formatting. The embedded object becomes part of the destination file.
- Edit an embedded object: Double-clicking an embedded object opens the source application ribbon within PowerPoint. Changes you make will be reflected in the destination file but will not be made in the source file.

11. Link objects.
- Insert a linked object: When you link an object, the information is stored in the source file. The destination file stores only the location of the source file.
- Edit a linked object: Double-clicking a linked object opens the source file for editing. Any changes made to the source file will be updated in both the source and destination files.
- Update, change, and break links: When a link is established, each time you open the PowerPoint presentation a security warning is displayed asking if you want to update the link. If either the source file or destination file location is changed, the link will be broken and will need to be re-established. If you no longer need the link to the source file, you can break the link.

Practice Exercises

Request for Venture Capital

Security Specialists is a successful company looking to expand its operation by requesting venture capital. You have been asked to assist the company with creating a presentation it will use for this purpose. Some of the data needed for the presentation has been created in Excel, which you can incorporate into your presentation without having to recreate the tables and charts. Refer to Figure 3.55 as you complete this exercise.

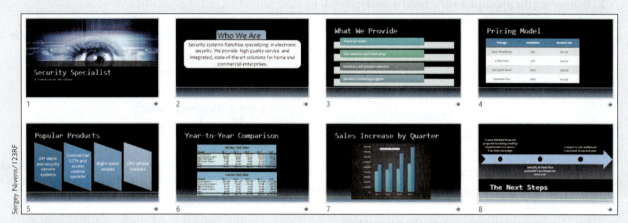

FIGURE 3.55 Security Specialists

a. Open *p03p1SecuritySpecialist* and save it as **p03p1SecuritySpecialist_LastFirst**.

b. Click **Slide 3**. Click the **Insert a SmartArt Graphic icon** in the content placeholder.

c. Select **List**, select the subtype **Vertical Box List**, and then click **OK**.

d. Type the following into the Text pane:

   Financial model

   Site selection and initial setup

   Inventory and product selection

   Detailed marketing program

e. Click the **SmartArt Tools Design tab**. Select **Intense Effect** in the SmartArt Styles group. Click the **Change Colors arrow** and select **Colorful – Accent Colors** in the Colorful group.

f. Click **Slide 5**. Select all of the shapes in the SmartArt graphic. Click the **Format tab**. Click the **Change Shape arrow** in the Shapes group and select **Flowchart: Data** in the Flowchart group.

g. Click the **Design tab**. Select **Intense Effect** in the SmartArt Styles group. Click the **Change Colors arrow** and select **Gradient Range – Accent 1** in the Accent 1 group.

h. Click **Slide 4**. Click **Insert Table** in the content placeholder. Insert a 3x5 table. Type the following information into the table:

Package	Installation	Monthly Fee
Basic Monitoring	$99	$37.99
2-Way Voice	$99	$42.99
Cell Guard Alarm	$199	$49.99
Essentials Plus	$199	$53.99

i. Click **More** in the Table Styles group and select **Medium Style 3 – Accent 1**.

j. Select the table and click the **Layout tab**. Select **Center** in the Alignment group and select **Center Vertically**. Change the Height in the Table Size group to **4.3"** and the Width to **9.3"**.

k. Open the *p03p1Sales.xlsx* Excel workbook.

l. Click on the **Previous Year worksheet**. Select the range **A1:F8** in Excel. Click **Copy** in the Clipboard group on the Home tab. Switch to PowerPoint and click **Slide 6**. Click the **Paste arrow** in the Clipboard group on the Home tab and select **Paste Special**.

m. Ensure that Paste is selected in the Paste Special dialog box, click **Microsoft Excel Worksheet Object** in the *As* box if it is not selected by default, and then click **OK**.

n. Select the embedded table and click the **Format tab**. Change the Shape Height in the Size group to **2.3"**. Click the **Dialog Box Launcher** in the Size group, and change the Horizontal position to **2.1"** from the Top Left Corner and the Vertical position to **2"** from the Top Left Corner. Click anywhere on the slide to deselect the inserted object.

o. Switch to Excel and click on the **Current Year worksheet**. Select the range **A1:F8** in Excel. Click **Copy** in the Clipboard group on the Home tab. Switch to PowerPoint and click **Slide 6**. Click the **Paste arrow** in the Clipboard group on the Home tab and select **Paste Special**.

p. Ensure that Paste in the Paste Special dialog box is selected, click **Microsoft Excel Worksheet Object** in the *As* box if it is not selected by default, and then click **OK**.

q. Select the pasted table and click the **Format tab**. Change the Shape Height in the Size group to **2.3"**. Click the **Dialog Box Launcher** in the Size group, and change the Horizontal position to **2.1"** from the Top Left Corner and the Vertical position to **4.6"** from the Top Left Corner.

r. Switch to Excel. Click on the **Sales Increase by Quarter worksheet**. Select the chart. Click **Copy** in the Clipboard group on the Home tab.

s. Switch to PowerPoint and click **Slide 7**. Click the **Paste arrow** in the Clipboard group on the Home tab and select **Paste Special**.

t. Click **Paste link** in the Paste Special dialog box, click **Microsoft Excel Chart Object** in the *As* box if it is not selected by default, and then click **OK**. Close Excel.

u. Select the linked chart and click the **Format tab**. Change the Shape Height in the Size group to **5.5"**. Click the **Dialog Box Launcher** in the Size group, change the Horizontal position to **2.4"** from the Top Left Corner and the Vertical position to **1.8"** from the Top Left Corner. Click anywhere on the slide to deselect the inserted chart.

v. Save and close the file. Based on your instructor's directions, submit p03p1SecuritySpecialist_LastFirst.

Mid-Level Exercises

1 Teamwork

You are a recruiter for Sperry Consults and have been asked to put together a workshop on teamwork. Your presentation will be used at various events sponsored by the company. You decide to add a chart to show the results of a survey on the benefits of working on a team. You will add a SmartArt graphic to illustrate teamwork skills. Finally, you will create a table that describes the roles of team members.

a. Open *p03m1Teamwork* and save it as **p03m1Teamwork_LastFirst**.

b. Click **Slide 3**. Insert a **Clustered Column chart**.

c. Replace the spreadsheet data with the following:

Attribute	% of Respondents
Ability to work in a team	82.9%
Problem-solving skills	82.9%
Communication skills (written)	80.3%
Leadership	72.6%
Strong work ethic	68.4%

d. Change the chart type to a **Clustered Bar chart**.

e. Make the following modification to the chart:
   - Apply the **Style 3 chart style**.
   - Remove the legend, chart title, horizontal axis, and gridlines.
   - Change the font size to **16 pt**, font color to **Black, Text 2**, and apply **Bold** on the vertical axis.
   - Change the data labels font size to **16 pt**.

f. Click **Slide 4**. Insert an **Interconnected Rings SmartArt graphic** from the Relationship category.

g. Type the following list items into the Text pane:

   Listening

   Questioning

   Persuading

   Respecting

   Helping

   Sharing

   Participating

h. Make the following changes to the SmartArt graphic.
   - Apply the SmartArt **Intense Effect** style.
   - Change the font color text for all shapes to **White, Background 1** and apply **Bold**.

i. Click **Slide 6**. Insert a **3×9 table**.

j. Merge the cells in column 1, rows 1, 2, and 3. Select rows 4, 5 and 6, and merge the cells. Select rows 7, 8, and 9, and merge the cells.

k. Type the following information into the table starting in the first cell of the first row:

Action Oriented Roles	**Shaper**	**Challenges the team to improve**
	Implementer	**Puts ideas into action**
	Completer/Finisher	**Ensures thorough, timely completion**
People Oriented Roles	**Coordinator**	**Acts as a chairperson**
	Team Worker	**Encourages cooperation**
	Resources Investigator	**Explores outside opportunities**
Thought Oriented Roles	**Plant**	**Presents new ideas and approaches**
	Monitor/Evaluator	**Analyzes the options**
	Specialist	**Provides specialized skills**

l. Make the following changes to the table:
- Apply the **No Style, Table Grid** table style.
- Change the font color for the text in the table to **White, Background 1**.
- **Center Vertically** the text in the table.
- Apply **Dark Blue, Accent 1 shading** to the cells in Column 1.

m. Click **Slide 7**. Convert the list to a **Grouped List SmartArt graphic**.

n. Apply the **Intense Effect** SmartArt style.

o. Select the text **Stage 1: Forming, Stage 2: Storming, Stage 3: Norming**, and **Stage 4: Performing** and change the font color to **Black, Text 2** and apply **Bold**.

p. Save and close the presentation. Based on your instructor's directions, submit p03m1Teamwork_LastFirst.

---

2 | Heart Healthy—Know the Warning Signs MyLab IT Grader

As a nursing student you often need to put together presentations on various health related topics for your courses. You have been asked to prepare a presentation on understanding the warning signs of a heart attack and risk factors for heart disease.

a. Open *p03m2Heart* and save it as **p03m2Heart_LastFirst**.

b. Click **Slide 3**. Insert a **Basic Block List SmartArt graphic** (first row, first column in the List category).

c. Type the following list items into the Text pane:

Family history of heart disease

High blood pressure

Overweight or obese

Lack of exercise

Use of tobacco products

Diabetes or other diseases

For women, use of birth control pills

d. Select all of the individual shapes in the SmartArt graphic. Change the shapes to **Frame** in the Basic Shapes group. Click **Larger** in the Shapes group three times to increase the size of the shape borders. Change the font color to **Black, Text 1** for all shapes.

e. Ensure the shapes are still selected and change the Shape Width to **3.8"**.

f. Open *p03m2HeartData.xlsx* and select the **clustered column chart**. Click **Copy** in the Clipboard group on the Home tab. Minimize Excel.

g. Return to PowerPoint and click **Slide 4**. Click the **Paste arrow** in the Clipboard group on the Home tab and click **Paste Special**.

Bryce Adventure Camp is a successful outdoor retreat dedicated to the appreciation of the splendor and inspiration of nature for good health. The operation has been so successful in its two years of operation that the owners opened retreats in two additional locations. They now want to open another retreat so even more people can enjoy the exhilaration of nature in magnificent settings. They are meeting with officers of a venture capital corporation that offers funding for unique opportunities. The representatives have asked for an overview of Bryce Adventure Camp's philosophy, services and activities, sales for this year and last year, a year-to-year comparison, and charts showing the increase. The owners of Bryce Adventure Camp asked you for help in preparing the presentation for the meeting.

Create and Modify SmartArt Graphics

To add interest and appeal to the presentation, you want to add and modify SmartArt graphics in the presentation.

1. Open *p03c1BryceAdventureCamp* and save it as **p03c1BryceAdventureCamp_LastFirst**.
2. Click **Slide 1**. Insert a Title and Content layout slide.
3. Type **Agenda** in the Title Placeholder.
4. Click the **Insert SmartArt icon** in the content placeholder.
5. Select **Vertical Box List** in the List category. Type the following in the Text pane:

    Highlights and Activities

    Lodging

    Income

    Revenue

    Balance Sheet

    Assets

    Stock Performance
6. Change the SmartArt graphic to a **Lined List**.
7. Click **Slide 4**. Convert the bulleted list to a **Horizontal Bullet List SmartArt graphic**. Change the width to **10.5″**. Apply the **Intense Effect** and change the color to **Colored Fill – Accent 6**.

Create an Activity Costs Table

To showcase the Adventure packages you have to offer, you decide to place the information into a table to help organize the information into an easy to read and understand format.

8. Create a new slide following Slide 4 using the Title and Content layout.
9. Type the title **Adventure Prices: $10 per voucher**.
10. Create a **4×7 table**. Do not worry about width or height of rows or columns.

11. Type the following table:

Adventure	Duration	Vouchers Required Private	Vouchers Required Group (min 3 people)
Guided hike	1 hour	3	1
Rappelling	2 hours	8	4
ATV tours	2 hours	10	4
Fitness classes	1 hour	3	1
Horseback riding	2 hours	6	2
Zip line	1 ride	1	

Modify Table Structure and Format Table

The table structure needs to be modified by adding an additional row. You also format the table to obtain a professional appearance. Size the table and apply a table style.

12. Change the table structure by adding an additional row at the bottom of the table. Merge the cells in the new row. Type **Camp Package: 10 Adventure Vouchers/$90 (All vouchers are non-refundable)** in the new row.
13. Set the table size to a height of **4.7″** and a width of **11.7″**.
14. Apply the **Medium Style 3 - Accent 6** table style to the table.
15. Select the table and **Center Vertically** the text. Select the column headings and change the font size to **20 pt**.
16. Select the text in rows 2–6 of the third and fourth columns, and align **Center**. Select the text in the last row and apply **Italic**.

Embed and Edit an Excel Chart

Bryce Adventure Camp's owners have tables and charts showing sales figures for this year and the previous year. These figures show that all three branches of their Adventure Camp have increased revenue and profit each year, and the charts emphasize the data. You will embed the chart that shows the increase by camp data.

17. Insert a Title Only slide after Slide 5 and type **Increase by Camp** as the slide title.
18. Open the *p03c1Campprofits.xlsx* workbook in Excel and click the **Increase by Camp worksheet**. Copy the chart. Click **Paste Special** and embed the chart on the slide.

19. Double-click the chart. Change the chart colors to **Colorful Palette 1**.

20. Apply the **Layout 10** Quick Layout to the chart.

21. Size the chart to a height of **4.2"**. Position the chart horizontally at **1.37"** from the Top Left Corner and vertically at **2.1"** from the Top Left Corner.

22. Select the chart, click **Shape Outline**, and then select **Black, Text 1**. Change the weight to **3 pt**.

23. Close Excel.

Create a Bar Chart

To identify their guests' reasons for visiting the adventure camps, the owners included this question in a guest satisfaction survey. They provide the answers as a bar chart to make the venture capitalists aware that demand for the camp is unlikely to go down.

24. Create a **Title and Content** slide after Slide 6, and type **Top Five Reasons for Visiting Camp** as the title of the new Slide 7.

25. Create a bar chart using the default Clustered Bar type with the following data:

Location/Sight-seeing	52%
Adventure Opportunities	22%
Relaxation	13%
Children's Activities	8%
Spa and Fitness Facilities	5%

26. Apply **Chart Style 13** to the chart.

27. Change the colors of the chart to **Monochromatic Palette 2**.

28. Remove the title, legend, and x-axis.

29. Increase the font size of the Y-axis to **16 pt** and apply **Bold**.

30. Add **Outside End Data Labels**. Change the font size of data labels to **16 pt** and apply **Bold**.

31. Save and close the file. Based on your instructor's directions, submit p03c1BryceAdventureCamp_LastFirst.

PowerPoint

Presentation Refinement

LEARNING OUTCOME You will refine a presentation by manipulating objects, transforming pictures, and enhancing animations and transitions.

OBJECTIVES & SKILLS: After you read this chapter, you will be able to:

CASE STUDY | United Animal Services

United Animal Services (UAS) is a non-profit organization that operates throughout the country to match rescued animals with new families. The newly formed chapter in your city is trying to develop its funding and support network by holding many promotional activities over the next few weeks. One of the first activities is a speaking engagement at the monthly Chamber of Commerce luncheon. You create the presentation to explain the services the organization offers.

As you prepare the presentation, you work with shapes and objects to convey the organization's purpose. You edit images to show some of the successful pet placements that UAS has facilitated. You also animate some objects in the presentation to engage the audience. You use transition enhancements to add interest to the presentation and to create a presentation that can be shown to many audience types.

CHAPTER 4

Manipulating Objects and Presentation Effects

FIGURE 4.1 United Animal Services

CASE STUDY | United Animal Services

Starting Files	File to be Submitted
p04h1Animal **p04h2Animal_Media folder** **p04h3Animal_Media folder**	**p04h3Animal_LastFirst**

MyLab IT Grader An alternate version of this project is available as a MyLab IT Grader Assessment

Object Manipulation

As you add objects to your slides, you may want to arrange them differently on the slide or recolor them. Perhaps you have created several shapes, and you want to align them at their left edges or arrange them by their center points, and then determine the order of the shapes. You may have inserted an image and find that the colors used in the image do not match the presentation theme colors. You may have added an image and decide that it would work well as a background for the slide.

In this section, you will learn to modify objects. You will group and ungroup objects, convert SmartArt into shapes, use gridlines and guides to place objects, align and distribute shapes, as well as order and stack them. You also will learn several methods to edit pictures.

Grouping and Ungrouping Objects

Some images are graphic drawings that are usually created in pieces, layered, and then grouped to create the final image. *Grouping* enables multiple objects to act or move as though they were a single object. For example, a group of shapes like a circle, triangle, and text box can be used to form a logo. You would group those items so they stay in exactly the same place every time you manipulate them. Grouping makes it easier to move, resize, or format the grouped objects as one. On the other hand, grouped objects can be *ungrouped*, or broken apart, so you can modify or delete the individual pieces.

STEP 1 ▸ Group and Ungroup Objects

Graphic drawings that are composed of grouped objects are often created and saved as vector graphics. *Vector graphics* are math-based graphics. Drawing programs such as Adobe Illustrator are used to create vector graphic images. Common vector graphics file formats include .svg, .cdr, and .dwf, and .u3d for 3D vector files. The advantage of vector files is that they retain perfect clarity when edited or resized because the computer simply recalculates the math used to create the image. Vector files also use a smaller amount of storage space compared to their pixel-based counterparts such as photographs.

In some instances, vector graphics need to be ungrouped to manipulate some of the individual components. For example, you may need to recolor a component of the graphic or delete part of it. However, vector graphics must be converted into a drawing object before they can be ungrouped. The feature to ungroup the image enables you to separate the parts of the image and edit or adjust each component to tailor it to your needs.

To convert a vector graphic into a drawing object of grouped shapes, right-click the graphic on the slide and select the Edit Picture option. Click Yes to respond to the message asking you if you want to convert the picture into a drawing object. Note that if the Edit Picture option is not available after right-clicking the graphic, it cannot be converted into a drawing object.

To ungroup a drawing object, right-click and point to Group or click Group in the Arrange group on the Format tab. Then select Ungroup to see each individual shape surrounded by adjustment handles. Click outside of the image borders to deselect the shapes.

> **TIP: AN IMAGE THAT WILL NOT UNGROUP**
> If your selected image will not ungroup for editing, it is not in a vector format. Often pictures from the Web are in .bmp, .jpg, .gif, and .png formats, which are not vector-based images and cannot be ungrouped.

Some images may have more than one grouping. The artist may create an image from individual shapes, group it, layer it on other shapes, and then group it again. If this occurs, the Ungroup option will be available to repeat again. You can ungroup as many times as necessary to break the image down to all shapes. Figure 4.2 shows a graphic that has been ungrouped to its lowest level. All individual parts are selected, and Ungroup is no longer available as an option.

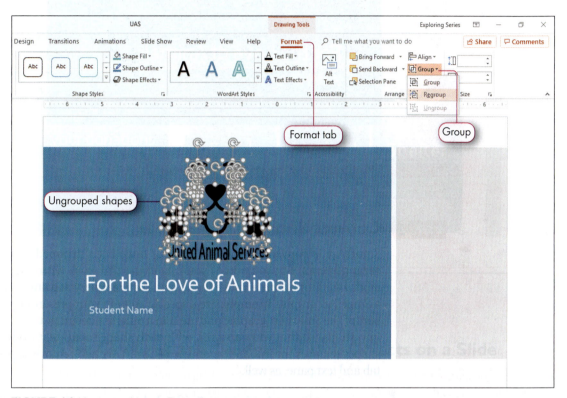

FIGURE 4.2 Ungrouped Image Example

When working with the individual shapes of an image, it is helpful to zoom in on, or magnify, the image. Zooming in enables you to make sure you have the correct shape before you make modifications. Figure 4.3 shows selected shapes that have their fill changed to a theme color. Once you have made all changes, press and hold Ctrl as you click all the shapes of the image, and then group or regroup the image. Alternatively, you can drag over the shapes by using Select Objects. Click Select in the Editing group on the Home tab. Then with Select Objects activated, drag to create a box over all the objects. If you do not group the image, you risk moving the individual pieces inadvertently.

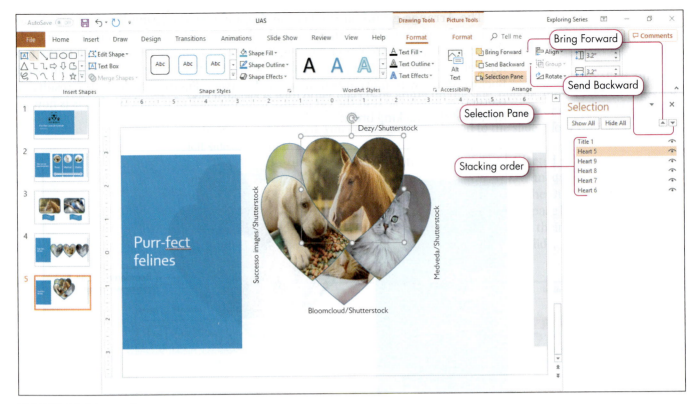

FIGURE 4.9 Selection Pane

1. Explain why you would you ungroup a shape. **p. 980**

2. Describe how rulers, a grid, and drawing guides are used when aligning objects. **pp. 983–985**

3. Explain why the Selection Pane is useful. **p. 987**

Hands-On Exercises

Skills covered: Group and Ungroup Objects • Convert SmartArt to Shapes • Use Gridlines and Guides to Place Objects on a Slide • Align and Distribute Shapes • Order and Stack Objects

1 Object Manipulation

As you prepare the UAS presentation, you realize that the ability to manipulate shapes by grouping and ungrouping and using other techniques with slide objects offers unlimited possibilities for creativity. You look forward to making a presentation that will engage your audience and compel them to help the organization.

STEP 1 GROUP AND UNGROUP OBJECTS

The UAS has recently revised its logo, and this presentation is the first time the logo will be used publicly. You tweak it just a bit more on the Title slide of the presentation, so the concept of animal love stands out. To do so, you must ungroup the image to modify just one component of the logo, and then regroup everything so the logo can be resized. Refer to Figure 4.10 as you complete Step 1.

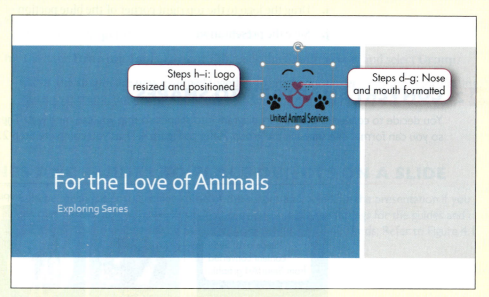

FIGURE 4.10 Image Ungrouped

a. Open *p04h1Animal* and save it as **p04h1Animal_LastFirst**.

> **TROUBLESHOOTING:** If you make any major mistakes in this exercise, you can close the file, open *p04h1Animal* again, and then start this exercise over.

b. Click the **subtitle placeholder** on **Slide 1.** Replace *Student Name* with your name.

c. Click the **top of the image**. Click the **Format tab**, click **Group** in the Arrange group, and then select **Ungroup**.

The image is ungrouped, and each individual component of the image is selected.

Picture Transformation

Vector graphics can be sized easily and still retain their clarity but are not photorealistic. Bitmap images represent a much more complex range of colors and shades. Many pictures that you take yourself, or find online, are bitmap images.

Computers can read and interpret bitmap images to create a photorealistic image. Unlike vector graphics, which are created by mathematical statements, **bitmap images** are created by bits or pixels placed on a grid or map. In a bitmap image, each pixel contains information about the color to be displayed. A bitmap image is required to have the realism necessary for a photograph. Think of vector graphics as connect-the-dots and bitmap images as paint-by-number, and you begin to see the difference in the methods of representation.

In this section, you will learn to manipulate a picture by removing its background. You will learn to correct a picture, recolor a picture, and use artistic effects to refine a picture. You will use a picture as a slide background and learn about compression.

Transforming a Picture

Once you insert a picture onto a slide, PowerPoint provides tools on the Picture Tools Format tab that you can use to adjust the image (see Figure 4.15). These tools are designed to enable you to modify an image background, correct image problems, manipulate image color, or add artistic or stylized effects. You can also arrange, crop, or resize an image using the Picture Tools Format tab. Alternatively, when you right-click on the picture and select Format Picture, the Format Picture task pane displays where you can access these same tools.

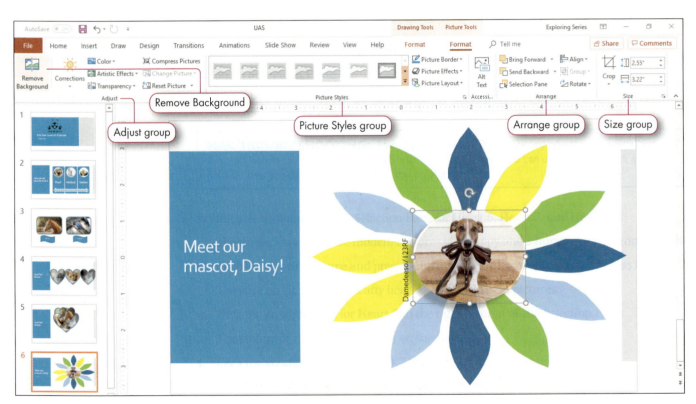

FIGURE 4.15 Picture Tools Format Tab

STEP 1 Remove a Picture Background

Pictures can be used in many ways that will take your presentations to the next level. For example, a picture can be modified so it coordinates better with the overall design concept of the presentation. Or a picture can become the slide background.

Many pictures contain a subject against a complex background such as a person in front of a garden or an animal with its trainer. In some instances, you may just want to focus on the subject and remove the distracting background. Removing that unwanted background of a picture creates a stronger message for the presentation.

The Remove Background tool in the Adjust group on the Format tab enables you to remove portions of a picture you do not want to keep. When you select a picture and click Remove Background, PowerPoint creates an automatic marquee selection area in the picture that determines the **background**, or area to be removed, and the **foreground**, or area to be kept. PowerPoint identifies the background selection with magenta coloring. You then adjust PowerPoint's automatic selection by marking areas you want to keep, marking areas you want to remove, and deleting any markings you do not want. You can discard all changes you have made if you change your mind or keep your changes. Figure 4.16 shows a picture in which the Remove Background tool has created a marquee identifying the foreground and background.

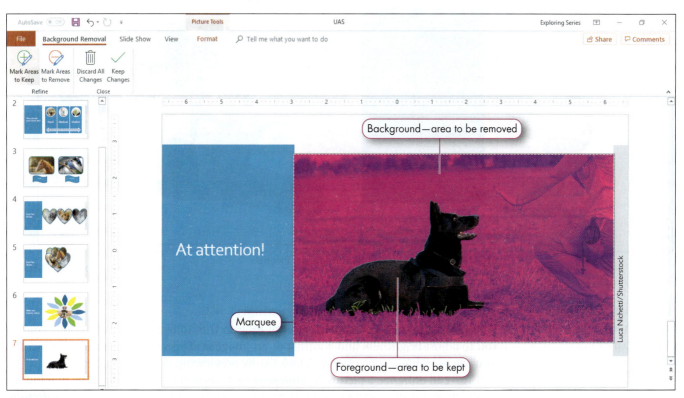

FIGURE 4.16 Remove Background Marquee, Foreground, and Background

Once the background has been identified by the marquee, you can refine the marquee size and shape so that it contains everything you want to keep without extra areas.

To resize the marquee, complete the following steps:

1. Select the picture and click the Remove Background button on the Picture Format tab.
2. Refine the picture further by using the tools available on the Background Removal tab (see Figure 4.17):
   - Use the *Mark Areas to Keep* tool to add to the foreground, which keeps the area.
   - Use the *Mark Areas to Remove* tool to add to the background, which eliminates the area.
3. Press Esc or click away from the selection to see what the picture looks like. Note that the thumbnail also shows what the image will look like with the changes applied.

You can use the Picture Corrections Options at the bottom of the Corrections gallery to make fine adjustments to the amount of brightness or contrast in the image. On the Format Picture pane, drag the Brightness and Contrast sliders or enter percentages in the boxes next to the sliders until you get the result you want. Figure 4.20 shows the Format Picture pane and the same picture adjusted for brightness.

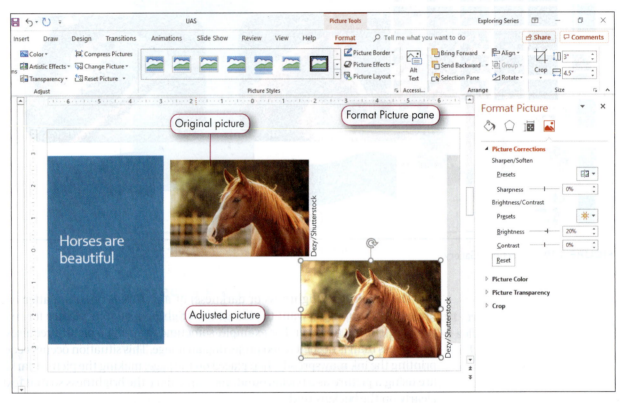

FIGURE 4.20 Format Picture Pane and Adjusted Picture

STEP 2   Change Picture Color

You can change the saturation and tone of a picture's colors with PowerPoint's Color tools. The pictures can be recolored to create a different feel to the picture or to coordinate the picture with the color scheme being used in the presentation. For example, a presentation on a historical event might use sepia or only black-and-white pictures to express that "old time" genre.

You can change a picture's saturation. The ***saturation*** of a picture is the intensity of the colors in an image. A high saturation level makes the colors more vivid, whereas 0% saturation converts the picture to grayscale. Figure 4.21 shows a picture at its original (100%) saturation and at 0% saturation.

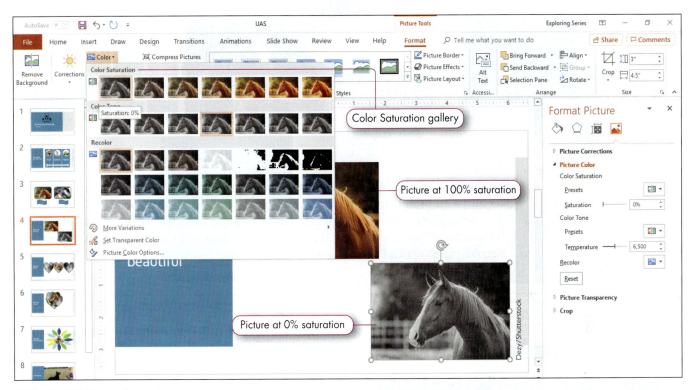

FIGURE 4.21 Picture Saturation

The ***tone***, or temperature, of a color is a characteristic of lighting in pictures. It is measured in ***kelvin*** (K) units of absolute temperature. Lower color temperatures are cool colors and appear blueish white, whereas higher color temperatures are warm colors and appear yellowish to red. PowerPoint enables you to increase or decrease a picture's temperature to enhance its details. Point to a thumbnail in the Color gallery to see the amount of temperature in kelvin units that would be applied. Figure 4.22 shows a picture with its original tone and a copy of the picture at a lower temperature with a cooler tone.

To use a picture as a background, use the Format Background command on the Design tab rather than the Insert Picture feature. Figure 4.25 shows a picture inserted as a background. It is automatically placed behind the placeholders and resized to fit the slide. The Transparency can be adjusted to improve the readability of any text on the slide.

To create a background from a picture, complete the following steps:

1. Click the Design tab.
2. Click Format Background in the Customize group.
3. Click Picture or Texture fill.
4. Click File and navigate to the location where the picture is stored.
5. Click the picture file and click Insert.
6. Adjust the transparency for the picture by dragging the Transparency slider.
7. Click Close to apply the picture background to the current slide or click Apply to All to apply it to all slides in the presentation.

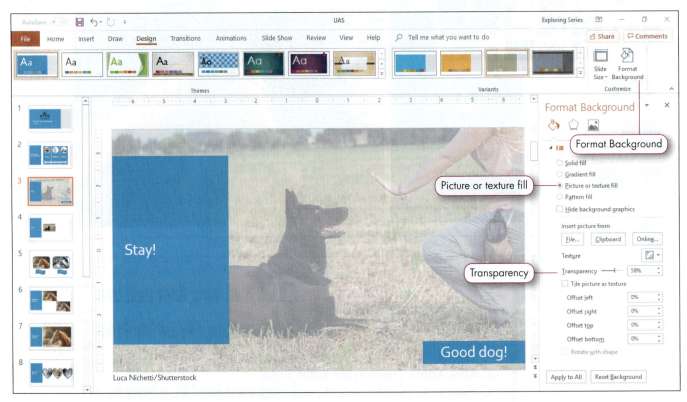

FIGURE 4.25 Background from Format Background Option

Insert Picture can be used to create a background on the slide, but it requires resizing the image to fit the slide. You may need to change the order of the objects on the slide so that the placeholders are visible. The transparency must be adjusted as well. Figure 4.26 shows an image inserted using Insert Picture. Notice that adjustments need to be made.

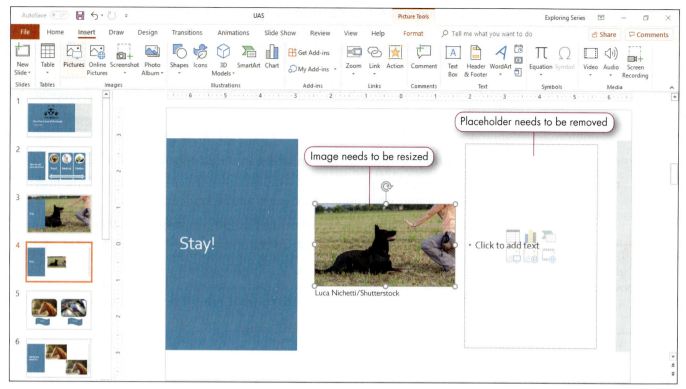

FIGURE 4.26 Background from Insert Picture Option

When the background of the picture is too busy or not transparent enough, it can make the presentation difficult to read or distract the audience. Test several images and settings to confirm there is enough contrast between the picture and the text to ensure easy reading of the text. Some other picture characteristics to watch out for that support text readability include:

- Pictures with a good amount of white space
- Blurred areas of the picture
- Gradient areas of the picture
- Non-distracting textures

Understand Compression

A bitmap image can be a large file, so *compression*, a method applied to data to reduce the amount of space required for file storage, may be applied to reduce the size. Certain formats can be either lossy or lossless.

The JPEG image file is a common lossy format. Lossy compression reduces a file by permanently eliminating certain data, especially redundant data. This makes the file size smaller. However, when the file is uncompressed, only a part of the original data is still there. The picture can become pixelated (individual pixels are visible and display square edges for a jagged effect) especially when the picture is enlarged.

Alternatively, with lossless compression, data that were originally in the file remain after the file is uncompressed. All compressed data are completely restored. The Graphics Interchange File (GIF) image format provides lossless compression.

e. Locate the *p04h2Animal1.jpg* picture in the p04h2Animal_Media folder and select the picture. Click Insert. Close the Design Ideas pane.

The picture is inserted on the slide.

f. Click the **Dialog Box Launcher** in the Size group on the Format tab to open the Format Picture task pane. Ensure the Lock aspect ratio check box is selected. Delete the existing text in the Height box and type **6"**. Press **Enter**.

Typing 6" in the Height box automatically sets the Width to 9.39" because the Lock aspect ratio check box is selected.

> **MAC TROUBLESHOOTING:** Ensure the picture is selected and click Format pane on Picture Format tab. Click the Size & Position icon, and make the size and position settings as indicated in Steps f and g.

g. Click **Position** in the Format Picture pane, and set the Horizontal position to **4.5"** from the Top Left Corner and the Vertical position to **1"** from the Top Left Corner.

h. Click **Remove Background** in the Adjust group on the Format tab. Click **Keep Changes**.

The background is removed, but the dog appears to be floating on the slide.

i. Click **Remove Background** again. Click **Discard All Changes** to restore the picture to its original state.

j. Click Remove Background again. Click **Mark Areas to Keep** and use the pencil to carefully draw around the border of the white street marker on the right beneath the dog's feet over to the left edge of the white street marker on the left side of the dog.

Some of the road is now visible, giving the dog and his handler something to stand on.

k. Click **Keep Changes** in the Close group on the Background Removal tab. Close the Format Picture pane.

The background is removed from the picture.

l. Save the presentation.

You want to include two pictures of dogs that have been successfully placed in new homes in the presentation, but the pictures were taken in different lighting conditions. You will use PowerPoint's correction tools to balance the differences between the pictures. You will experiment with the options available with these tools to see the impact they have on the pictures. You will also apply an artistic effect to a picture. Refer to Figure 4.28 as you complete Step 2.

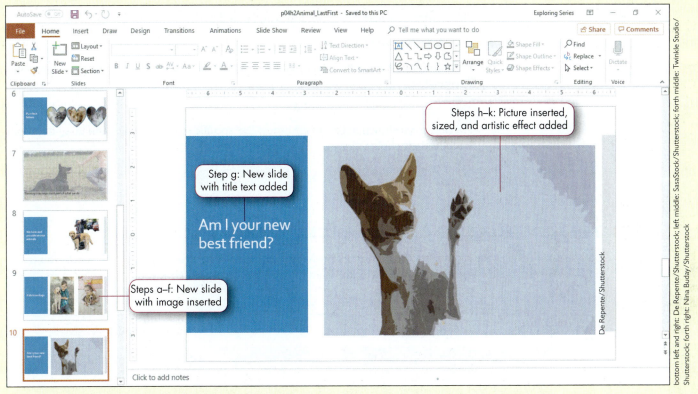

FIGURE 4.28 Picture Correction and Color Tone Adjustment

a. Insert a new **Slide 9** with the **Two Content** layout. Type **Kids love dogs** in the title placeholder.

b. Insert *p04h2Animal2.jpg* in the left placeholder and *p04h2Animal3.jpg* in the right placeholder. Close the Design Ideas pane.

c. Click to deselect Lock Aspect Ratio check box in the Format Picture pane. Size each picture to a height of **5.95"** and a width of **3.97"**. Reposition pictures back into placeholders using the Smart Guides as a guide.

d. Select the image on the right, and click **Corrections** in the Adjust group on the Format tab. select **Brightness: 0% (Normal) Contrast: -20%** (second row, third column of the Brightness/Contrast section).

The image becomes slightly darker.

e. Select the image on the left and click **Corrections** in the Adjust group. Click **Brightness: 0% (Normal) Contrast: +20%** (fourth row, third column of the Brightness/Contrast section).

The brightness is reduced in the image.

f. Select **both images** and click **More** in the Picture Styles group. Click **Center Shadow Rectangle** (second row, sixth column).

g. Insert a new **Slide 10** with the **Title and Content** layout. Type **Am I your new best friend?** in the title placeholder.

h. Insert *p04h2Animal4.jpg* in the right placeholder. Click to deselect Lock Aspect Ratio check box in the Format Picture pane. Size the picture to a height of **6"** and width of **8.44"**. Position the picture Horizontally at **4.3"** from the Top Left Corner and Vertically at **0.84"** from the Top Left Corner. Close the **Format Picture pane**.

i. Click **Color** in the Adjust group on the Format tab and select **Temperature: 4700 K** in the Color Tone section. Click **Corrections** in the Adjust group and select **Brightness: 0% (Normal) Contrast: −20%** (second row, third column).

The picture now features cooler tones and matches the theme better.

j. Click **Artistic Effects** in the Adjust group on the Format tab.

The Artistic Effects gallery opens. Point to the effects, and watch how each effect impacts the image.

k. Select **Cutout** (first column, last row).

The dog breed shown in the image is now less specific so the audience can imagine a dog breed of their choice.

l. Save the presentation.

STEP 3 USE A PICTURE AS A SLIDE BACKGROUND

You notice that one of the slides has a very important message but no graphics to help engage the audience. You will add an image as a background for that slide. Refer to Figure 4.29 as you complete Step 3.

FIGURE 4.29 Background Created from a Picture

a. Click **Slide 7** and click the **Design tab**.

b. Click **Format Background** in the Customize group.

The Format Background task pane displays.

c. Click **Picture or texture fill** and click **File** to open the Insert Picture dialog box.

d. Select *p04h2Animal5.jpg* in the p04h2Animal_Media folder, and click **Insert.**

e. Adjust the transparency for the picture by dragging the Transparency slider to **50%.**

The transparency is applied only to this image in the presentation.

f. Click the **text box** and click the **Format pane**. Set the width to **13.33"** in the Size group. Click **Align** in the Arrange group. Select **Align Center**. Click **Align** and Select **Align Bottom**.

g. Click the Shape Styles Dialog Box Launcher. Click **Solid Fill** in the Format Shape pane. Click the **Color arrow** and select **White, Background 1, Darker 25%**. Set the Transparency to **50%.**

h. Change the font color to **Black, Text 1**. Close the **Format Shape pane.**

i. Click **Slide 8** and click the **picture**. Click the **Format tab** and click **Compress Pictures** in the Adjust group. Deselect **Apply only to this picture**. Click **Use Default Resolution**. Click **OK.**

j. Save the presentation. Keep the presentation open if you plan to continue with the next Hands-On Exercise. If not, close the presentation and exit PowerPoint.

Animation and Transition Enhancement

Animation and transitions provide movement on a slide that engages the audience or emphasizes key points of the message. Typically, you set the movement to start with a mouse click or to start automatically after the previous event such as a new slide displaying. But you can also control movement and turn it into interactivity by using a trigger.

Text is commonly animated, but you can also animate other objects on a slide such as SmartArt or charts. The process of animating text or other objects is similar and produces equally engaging results. Transitions occur as slides are changed during a presentation. PowerPoint provides a wide range of transition styles to introduce motion into your presentation.

In this section, you will learn how to animate objects such as SmartArt, charts, tables, and 3D models. You will learn about triggers. You will also learn about Morph transitions and experiment with the Zoom tools.

Animating Objects

You have already learned how to animate text and how useful adding animations can be to keep the audience engaged while delivering your message effectively. Because you might have slides that contain just a SmartArt graphic, a chart, or a table, it is important to know how to apply similar animations to these types of objects. After you animate the object, you can apply effect options and timings to further control the animation. Other settings include ways of specifying the number of times the animation is repeated, setting the animation to rewind when it is done playing, and determining how the animation is initiated.

STEP 1 Animate a SmartArt Graphic

As you have learned, SmartArt is used to provide information in a visual form. Ideas are conveyed through a combination of shapes and text. After inserting a SmartArt diagram into a presentation, you can animate the entire graphic by clicking the Animations tab while the graphic is selected. Click More in the Animation group to see all animation choices and select the animation that you want to use. You can use Preview in the Preview group to see the animation in Normal view. Alternatively, to view the animation as it will be seen when you deliver your presentation, you can use From Current Slide in the Start Slide Show group on the Slide Show tab.

Although controlling how the object enters or exits the slide during a presentation is useful, there may be situations where you want to animate individual shapes. Similar to animating bullet points, you can control how different parts of the SmartArt enter or exit the screen, or how individual SmartArt shapes are animated. For example, you can create an organization chart and use animation to highlight specific positions in the company as you discuss each during your presentation. Or animate individual shapes in the Basic Process SmartArt diagram to show each step in a workflow or process. Figure 4.30 shows a SmartArt graphic that uses animation to help explain an organization chart.

Using Effect Options in the Animation group, you can control the animation by layers or objects in a SmartArt graphic. The number 1 that was placed on the slide when the entire SmartArt graphic was animated will be replaced by numbers representing the individual components. If you stop and play the animation, you may notice that there are components of the SmartArt graphic that you do not want to animate at all. Or you may notice that you want to group objects, similar to how text and pictures can be grouped, to enter all at the same time. The Animation Pane is very useful to manage

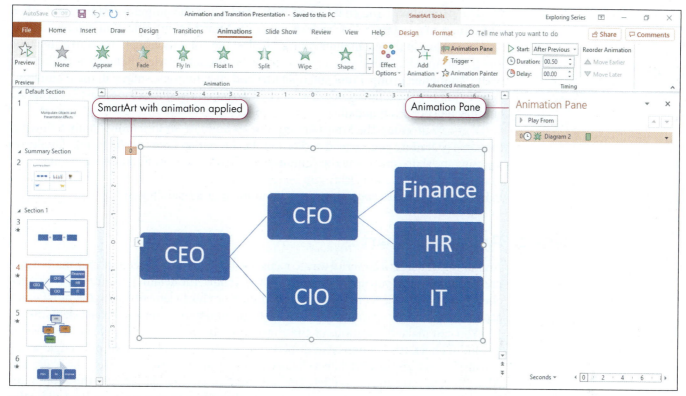

FIGURE 4.30 Animated Organization Chart

the tasks associated with the multiple animations. To further manage the animation of individual shapes within the SmartArt graphic, display the Animation Pane and click the double arrows to expand the listing of the individually animated shapes in the SmartArt. Figure 4.31 shows the open Animation Pane indicating multiple animated shapes.

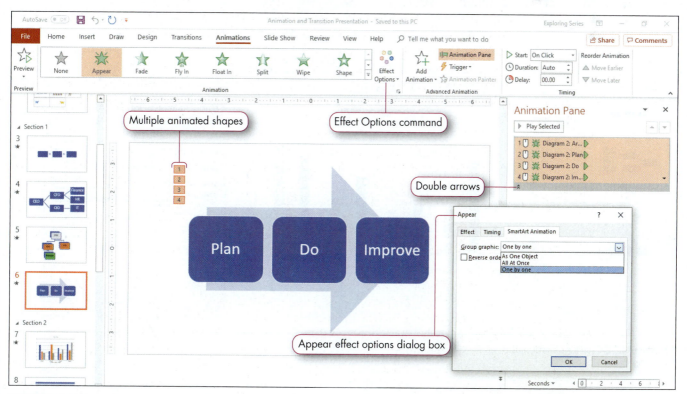

FIGURE 4.31 Animation Pane Showing Animated Shapes

The Animation Pane enables you to control when the animation starts, and other effect and timing options, for each shape in the SmartArt graphic. You can also right-click any shape in the Animation Pane and select the animations options from a shortcut menu. For any shape that you do not want to be animated, select Remove or click None in the Animation group. Press and hold Ctrl and click multiple shapes in the Animation Pane to remove the animations all at once. The shapes remain in the SmartArt graphic, but they will not be animated.

You can ungroup the SmartArt graphic to animate shapes individually following the same procedure you learned earlier. Set the animation for each shape individually by selecting the shape and using the Animations tab to apply the animation you want to use. The Start, Duration, and Delay can be set for each individual shape. Or the Animation Painter can be used to apply the same animation to multiple shapes.

STEP 2 ## Animate a Chart

Animating a chart is a powerful way to focus the audience on key pieces of information in a presentation. When you apply an animation to a chart, the default is to animate the entire chart with no specific focus on any piece of data or chart element. To highlight different aspects of the chart separately, you can apply animations to individual chart elements.

You can make the sections of the chart enter in various sequences. For example, in a column chart, the columns can display one at a time, or all columns of a single series can display as a group. Click Effect Options in the Animation group to select the sequence. Alternatively, you can access Effect Options from the Animation Pane. In the Animation Pane, click the arrow for the animation and select Effect Options. The dialog box for the selected animation displays. Click the Chart Animation tab and select from among the Group chart options. Figure 4.32 shows the Chart Animation tab and the animation options available.

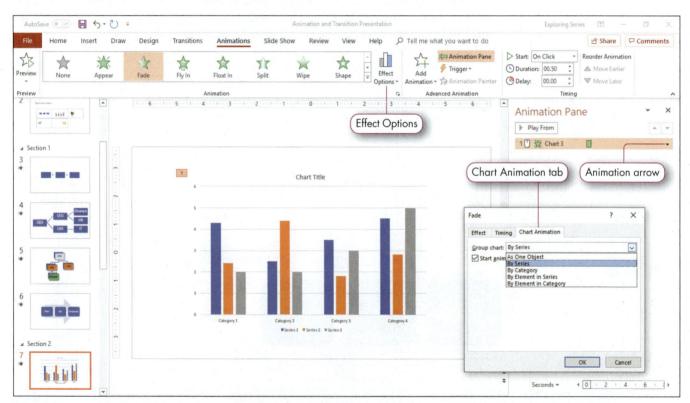

FIGURE 4.32 Chart Animation Tab

The default option, As One Object, animates the entire chart. The option By Series animates the chart by the data represented in the legend. For a pie chart, this would be each slice, whereas for a column chart, this would be each column of the same color. Using the By Category option displays the x-axis information with each category animating individually. The option By Element in Series, when used for a column chart, displays each column individually, completing all columns of one series before displaying the columns of the next series, and so on. Finally, the option By Element in Category displays each column individually within a category before moving on to the next category to animate each individual column there.

> **TIP: START ANIMATION BY DRAWING THE CHART BACKGROUND**
> Drawing the chart background provides a clear frame of reference for the audience. The option to do so is available on the Chart Animation tab. When selected, the y-axis and x-axis are displayed before any chart data are added. If it is not selected, then the focus for the audience is on the columns (or data points) that display on top of the already existing y-axis and x-axis.

You can use the Timing tab to set the Start, Delay, Duration, and Repeat for the animation. The Effects tab controls the Settings and Enhancements, such as dimming after the animation. For example, after you display a specific budget item during a presentation being used at a fund-raising dinner, each part of the chart could dim after you discuss it.

STEP 3 ▸ **Animate a Table**

When you include a table in a presentation, it can be met with a couple of different reactions. For some, the numbers are intimidating. The audience just wants you to quickly give the conclusion. For others, they will try to make sense out of the numbers and find a relationship among them. That type of audience is no longer listening to you and your objectives for presenting the table data. To regain control over both audience reactions, animate your table so that the data are presented incrementally.

The method of applying an animation to a table is different from that with SmartArt or a chart. Instead, the table needs to be converted into a set of drawing objects similar to converting a SmartArt object into individual objects. By changing the table into a set of drawing objects, you can ungroup them so that you can animate them separately. Use this method if the individual components of the table are to be animated.

Keep in mind that after you make the conversion from table to drawing objects, you will no longer be able to edit or update the table with new information. Because of this, begin by adding a blank slide so you can copy the table and use Paste Special to put the table on the new slide so you have a duplicate of the slide with the table in case you make a mistake during the process.

To convert a table to objects, you must first change the table into a picture, and ungroup the picture to reveal the individual components. On a Mac, you cannot convert a table to objects.

To convert a table to objects, complete the following steps:

1. Click the slide in Slide thumbnail pane.
2. Click the Home tab.
3. Click Copy in the Clipboard group.
4. Click Paste and select Paste Special.
5. Click Picture (Enhanced Metafile).
6. Select the table, and click the Format tab.
7. Click Group in the Arrange group and select Ungroup.
8. Click Yes if you are prompted to change the picture into a Microsoft drawing object.

Every component of the table picture is now an object. For example, each cell is an object that contains a text box and data as objects. Press and hold Ctrl as you select the parts of the table picture that you want to animate, such as grouping data by columns or by rows. Alternatively, you could use Select Objects to draw a box around the larger group or use the Selection Pane to select individual components. Click the Animate tab and click Add Animation in the Advanced Animation group. At this point, you can add an entrance, emphasis, or exit animation. You can also set the Start, Duration, or Delay for the animation as you do for any animation.

Copying and pasting the table, ungrouping, and then manipulating each component can be a complex and time-consuming process. You can use another method for animating a table. Create separate tables for the parts you want to animate and align them to appear as if the parts are all one table. For example, you can create one table that is comprised of one row to create the header row of the table. Then create another table with data and align the bottom of the header table with the top of the data table and the left sides of both tables. From there, you can animate each individual table to provide emphasis for your message. Figure 4.33 shows the preparation for creating an animated table using the second method.

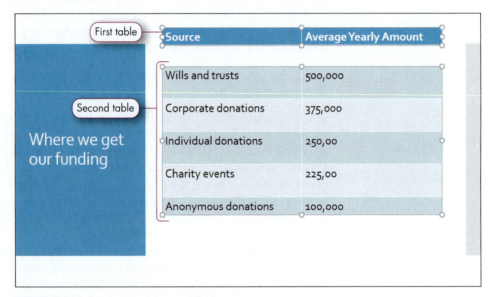

FIGURE 4.33 Creating an Animated Table

STEP 4 > Animate a 3D Model

PowerPoint supports the animation of 3D objects in a presentation. For example, you can use 3D animation to show specific features of a product or to illustrate a point about your topic. Two-dimensional objects can be manipulated for height and width. But with a 3D object, you can turn it 360° to view from any angle—either while you are in the presentation or as you are creating the presentation.

You add a 3D model to your presentation just like adding pictures or shapes. You can use a 3D model previously created or you can select one from online sources. To search, click From Online Sources in the Illustrations group on the Insert tab and search Remix 3D. Remix 3D is an online catalog created by a community of users who share 3D models with each other. You are responsible for respecting others' rights, including copyright, as a condition of using the catalog. Several categories of models are available, so you can either type a keyword or scroll through the categories.

When a 3D model is selected, the 3D Model Tools tab displays with its contextual Format tab. You can size and arrange 3D objects just as you do with any other shape. For more control over a view or to resize the object, you can use the **Pan & Zoom** tool. Pan & Zoom controls how the image fits within the frame (zoom) and turns it any direction (pan), taking full advantage of the 3D nature of the object. Click and drag the object within the frame to move it. Use the Size Dialog Box Launcher to open the Format 3D Model pane, which offers tools that are very similar to the tools you have already used in the Format Shapes pane. Figure 4.34 shows a 3D model with some of the tools available.

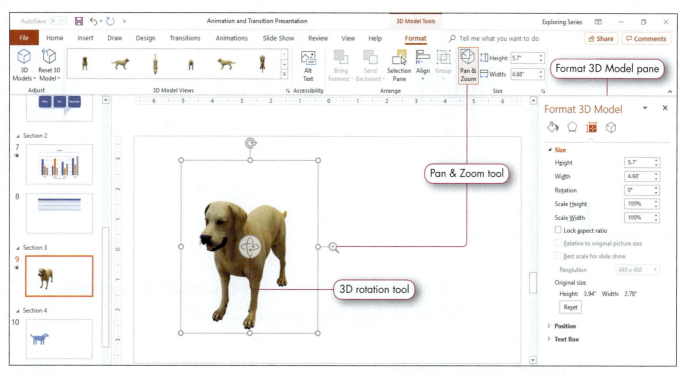

FIGURE 4.34 3D Model Tools Format Tab

As with other shapes, you can animate a 3D model using the Animations tab. A unique set of animations is available for 3D models. The 3D animations include Arrive, Turntable, Swing, Jump & Turn, and Leave. These are color-coded, similar to other animations you are already familiar with: Entrance (green), Emphasis (yellow), and Exit (red). You can also apply most of the animations that you use on other objects to 3D models. Effect options for 3D models include Direction, Intensity, and Rotation Axis. The Direction option dictates the directional focus for the 3D model. For example, if an Entrance animation has been applied to a 3D model, it can be set to start from the Right, Left, Up, Down, Clockwise, or Counterclockwise. Options for Intensity include Subtle, Moderate, or Strong. Rotation Axis options are View Center or Object Center.

Many other features that you are already familiar with are available for 3D models. This includes the Animation Pane, control of timing, and the ability to add multiple animations to the model. Figure 4.35 shows many options available for 3D models.

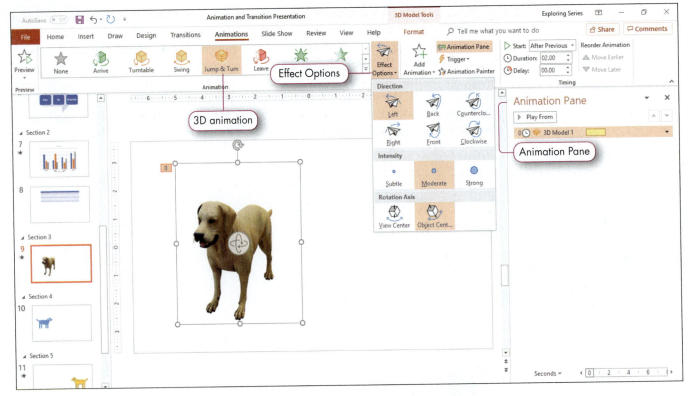

FIGURE 4.35 Available Options for 3D Animations

> **TIP: ADD ALT TEXT TO INCREASE THE ACCESSIBLITY OF 3D MODELS**
> You add Alt Text (used by screen readers) for 3D models after selecting the model and clicking the Alt Text option in the Accessibility group on the 3D Models Format tab.

STEP 5 ## Use a Trigger

So far you have learned how to control animated objects with a mouse click. This type of control is used primarily by the presenter. When you want the viewer to be able to control the animation, or to use a specific object to initiate an animation, then a trigger can be used. A ***trigger*** launches an animation that displays when you click an associated object or a bookmarked location in a media object. The presentation is designed so that when a certain area of a slide or an object is clicked, the presentation responds with the animation. Triggers are a way to add interactivity to presentations. Remember this key point about triggers: a trigger must use animation.

Figure 4.36 displays a slide where you click the text box, which is the trigger, and an image displays on the slide. The Animation Pane is open on the right side of the slide and shows the object and the animation or action associated with the trigger. The slide is interactive because the viewer initiates the process by clicking the trigger.

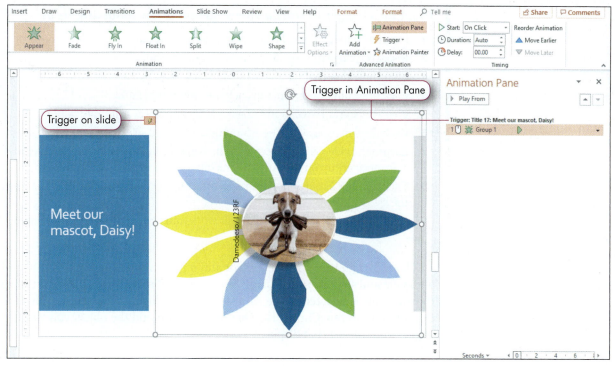

FIGURE 4.36 Create a Trigger

> **To set up a trigger, complete the following steps:**
>
> 1. Select the object that you want to animate.
> 2. Click the Animations tab and click Add Animation in the Advanced Animation group.
> 3. Add the animation effect of your choice from the Animation group.
> 4. Open the Animation Pane.
> 5. Click Trigger in the Advanced Animation group.
> 6. Select the *On Click of* option.
> 7. Select the object that will launch the animation from the displayed list.
> 8. Click Preview to see how the trigger works after being applied to the slide.

A trigger can be used to start a video without first displaying the video on a slide. It can also be used to start audio even if the sound icon has been set to hide during the slide show or it has been set to play automatically. This is helpful to keep an audience engaged with your presentation's message while providing a level of interactivity to the presentation. You can make your point about the slide content, and then a video or audio clip seemingly begins automatically to further explain or illustrate the point. For example, you may be presenting a slide show on how to bathe a dog. You show a slide that details the supplies needed such as tub, water, soap, and towels listed in a SmartArt graphic. After talking about these supplies, you can set up a trigger so that when you click a SmartArt graphic, a video showing a dog being bathed with these supplies plays.

To set up a trigger to start a video, complete the following steps:

1. Insert a shape that will be used as the trigger on slide.
2. Insert the video file and drag the file off of the slide.
3. Click the Video Tool Playback tab and click Play Full Screen.
4. Click the Animations tab and click the Animation Pane.
5. Click the Start arrow on the Playback tab and select Automatically.
6. Click the video arrow in the Animation Pane and select Remove.
7. Ensure the video is still selected in the Animation Pane and click Trigger in the Advanced group on the Animations tab.
8. Click the *On Click of* option and select the object you want to use as the trigger from the list.
9. Click Preview to see how the trigger works after being applied to the slide.

Triggers can be set up to control audio files in a similar way. You would insert the audio file and set it to Hide During Show on the Playback tab. Just as with video, ensure the audio file is selected in the Animation Pane. Click Trigger in the Advanced group of the Animations tab. Choose the *On Click of* option and the object you want to use as the trigger from the list that displays.

Enhancing Transitions

Another determination you make when planning a presentation is what type of transitions to use for moving between slides. The goal is to provide some movement without being jarring or distracting. In addition to the types of transitions you have already learned about, there are the Morph transitions and the Zoom tools that have specific transitional roles. **Morph** is a transition that creates a cinematic motion by seamlessly animating between two slides. It can create motion, formatting, zoom in or out, or change one shape into another. As the next slide displays, you will not notice the change to the new slide. The movement is so gradual that the objects slowly morph into new positions or formatting such as a color change.

Zoom enables you to be able to jump to and from specific slides and portions of your presentation in an order that you decide while you are presenting. A Summary Zoom slide acts as both an agenda slide and a section slide. This gives the benefit of customized presentations based on the needs of the audience.

STEP 6 › Use Morph

Morph offers a convenient way to represent motion across slides. You do not control how the changes occur; PowerPoint takes care of that for you. Using Morph saves time and many steps when developing a presentation with this type of motion. Morph can be used to create entrance, emphasis, exit, and motion path animations. It can also be used to animate words; create 3D rotations; zoom in, scroll, flip, and crop images; or morph a shape into another shape. The Morph transition takes the beginning slide and gradually morphs the changes into the ending slide. You create a beginning slide and then another slide that is the endpoint. Modify the objects on the ending slide for color, size, rotation, or location on the slide. Table 4.1 explains how Morph can be used to create the main animation types.

TABLE 4.1 Morph Transition Used for Main Animation Types

Type	Method
Entrance	Add a new object to the ending slide after duplicating the beginning slide but before applying the transition.
Emphasis (Rotation)	Select the object and use the Rotate handle to turn the object on the ending slide to where you would like to see it rotate to during the Morph transition.
Exit	Delete the object on the ending slide after duplicating the beginning slide but before applying the transition.
Motion path	Move the object on the ending slide to the destination position where it will end after the Morph transition.

To create a Morph transition, complete the following steps:

1. Create a slide with the objects in their starting position and formats.
2. Click the Slide thumbnail pane and click the Home tab.
3. Click Copy and select Duplicate to insert the second slide after the original slide.
4. Make the changes to the second slide.
5. Ensure the second slide is selected in the Slide thumbnail pane and click the Transitions tab.
6. Click Morph (see Figure 4.37).
7. Click Preview to see how the transition works after it is applied to the slide.

Once the transition has been applied, you can use Effect Options to control how the transition takes place. The Objects option moves entire objects like shapes or pictures. The Words option moves objects (such as text boxes) and individual words. For example, if you had a quote but wanted to change the quote, you could use Morph. The Characters option moves objects and individual letters. Note that it is important that you keep the capitalization the same when using either Words or Characters. Figure 4.37 shows an example of using Morph with the Objects effect option.

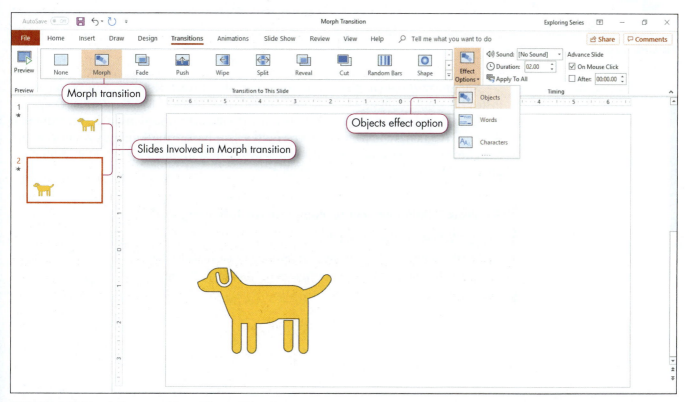

FIGURE 4.37 Morph Transition Using Objects Effect Option

STEP 7 ▶ **Use Zoom**

While you carefully plan for your presentation based on the audience, the venue, and the message you want to convey, it is helpful to have the option to modify your planned presentation order. At times you may find that you need to customize your presentation quickly and easily based on the needs of the audience or the direction you need to take your intended message. Zoom is a tool that can help you do that. Zoom has different options available; among them are Summary Zoom, Slide Zoom, and Section Zoom. Figure 4.38 shows an example of a Summary Zoom Slide.

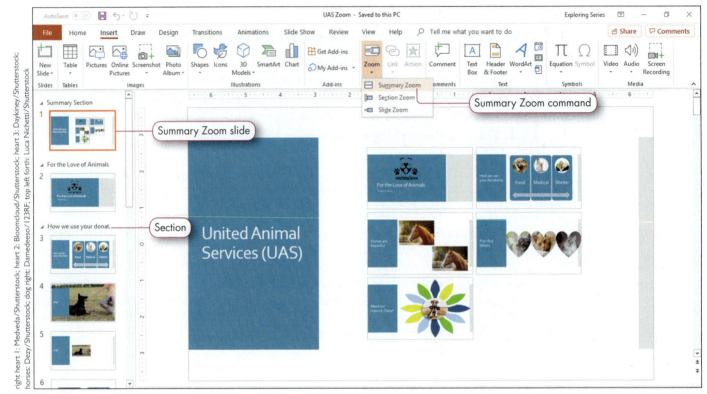

FIGURE 4.38 Summary Zoom Slide

Summary Zoom enables you to move quickly between slides in your presentation instead of sequentially as a typical presentation runs. Think of it as an interactive agenda slide that includes thumbnails of selected slides that mark off sections in the presentation. After each section is completed, the presentation goes back to the Summary Zoom slide and then transitions to the section represented by the next thumbnail. On a Mac, Summary, Slide, and Section Zoom are not available.

To create a Summary Zoom, complete the following steps:

1. Click Zoom on the Insert tab.
2. Select Summary Zoom to open the Summary Zoom dialog box.
3. Click the slides you want to include in the Summary Zoom.
4. Click Insert.

After the Summary Zoom slide is created, it is displayed as a new slide inserted just ahead of the first slide you selected in the Summary Zoom choices. You can edit the Summary Zoom whenever there are changes to your presentation. Edits you make in the Summary Zoom do not impact the actual presentation. For example, if you delete slides from the Summary Zoom, the slides will still be part of the presentation. However, any changes that are made to the slides that are part of the Summary Zoom will be automatically updated in the Summary Zoom slide.

Slide Zoom also uses selected slides from your presentation. It can be used to easily present only specific parts of a presentation. Slide Zoom can help you work through multiple pieces of information while feeling like you are staying on the same canvas. With Slide Zoom, you navigate directly to another part of the presentation, and then continue to the end from that slide. Figure 4.39 shows how a Slide Zoom can be inserted into a presentation by selecting certain slides.

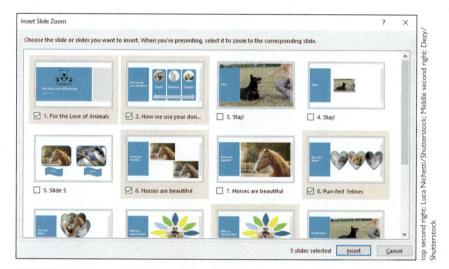

FIGURE 4.39 Insert Slide Zoom Dialog Box

Creating a Slide Zoom is similar to creating a Summary Zoom. On the Insert tab, click Zoom and select Slide Zoom. A dialog box opens enabling you to select the slides you want to include. Click Insert to create the Slide Zoom. As an alternative, you can quickly create a Slide Zoom by selecting a slide in the Slide thumbnail pane and dragging it to the slide you are using as the Slide Zoom slide. This is an efficient way to change slides or rearrange them just by clicking and dragging.

When you want to highlight certain sections of your presentation, you can use a Section Zoom. This tool is useful for long presentations where you have already created sections within the presentation. It enables you to emphasize those sections geared to specific audiences. After viewing the section, you return to the Section Zoom slide.

By default, the Summary Zoom and Slide Zoom slides will display a preview image as a thumbnail of each slide, but you can select another image to represent the slide instead. For example, if you have a series of slides showing details of a particular topic, you may want to have an image representing that topic instead of the actual slides and slide content. To change the preview image, click the Slide Zoom slide and click the Format tab. Click Change Image in the Zoom Options group. Click Zoom Options to open the Insert Pictures dialog box. You can choose to insert a picture from a file, get an online picture, or make a selection from the icon collection.

The Zoom Tools Format tab offers many options to modify the Zoom. These options are available when creating either a Summary Zoom, Slide Zoom, or Section Zoom. For example, when working with a Summary Zoom or Section Zoom, you return to the Zoom slide by default. A Slide Zoom moves on to the next slide by default. You can control this default for any Zoom type by working with the Return to Zoom option on the Format tab. Other options you can use include selecting a Zoom style and adding a border, effect, or background. You can arrange a Zoom, size a Zoom, position it, or add Alt text for the Zoom. Figure 4.40 shows the Zoom Tools Format tab.

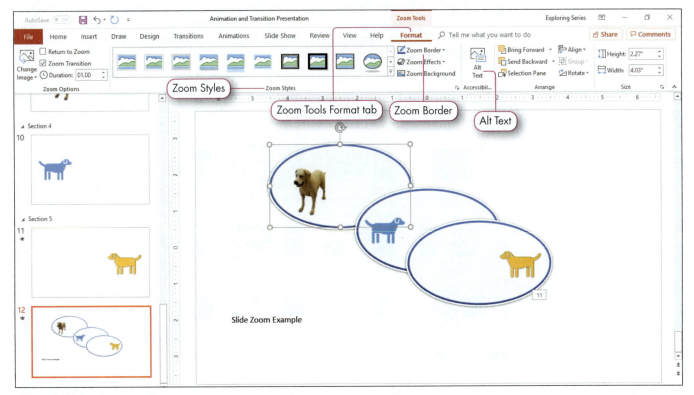

FIGURE 4.40 Zoom Tools Format Tab

7. Explain why you would animate a table. **p. 1015**

8. Describe two benefits of using Morph. **p. 1020**

9. Explain how Zoom is useful when delivering a presentation. **p. 1022**

Hands-On Exercises

MyLab IT HOE3 Sim Training

 Watch the Video for this Hands-On Exercise!

Skills covered: Animate a SmartArt Graphic • Animate a Chart • Animate a Table • Animate a 3D Model • Use a Trigger • Use Morph • Use Zoom

3 Animation and Transition Enhancement

The presentation for UAS does a good job in delivering the emotional message of placing rescue pets in new homes. You want to strengthen the financial message and refine the options for presenting the slide show to various audiences. You animate a SmartArt graphic, a chart, a table, and a 3D model. Then you will add a trigger to an object to engage the audience in a major point of a slide. Finally, you apply a Morph transition to illustrate an important point and create a Zoom to modify the presentation for a different audience.

STEP 1 **ANIMATE A SMARTART GRAPHIC**

The adoption process for a rescue animal is multifaceted and can be confusing for prospective pet families. You decide to animate a SmartArt graphic that depicts the adoption process to make each step clearer. Refer to Figure 4.41 as you complete Step 1.

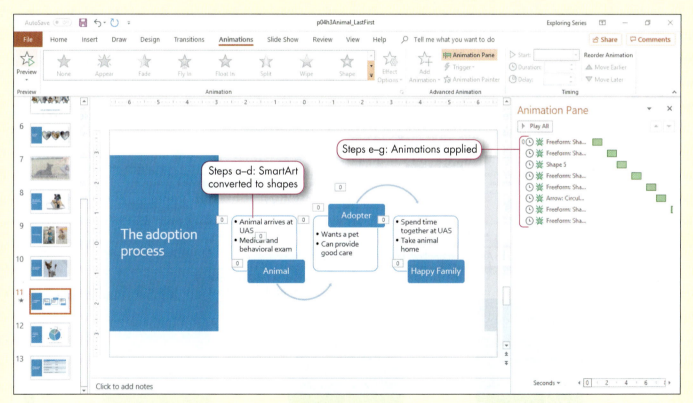

FIGURE 4.41 Animated SmartArt

    a. Open *p04h2Animal_LastFirst* if you closed it at the end of Hands-On Exercise 2, and save it as **p04h3Animal_LastFirst**, changing h2 to h3.

    b. Click **Slide 11** and select the **SmartArt graphic**.

    c. Click the SmartArt Tools Design tab and click **Convert** in the Reset group. Select **Convert to Shapes**.

    Given all the components of the SmartArt graphic, and the need to animate only the bulleted text box, you convert the graphic to shapes.

a. Click **Slide 13** and select the **header row** of the table.

The table on the slide is comprised of two separate tables that are aligned to display as one table. The first table is a single row with two columns that functions as a header row for the second table. The second table is five rows and two columns.

b. Click **More** in the Animation group. Click **Zoom** in the Entrance Effects section. Set Start to **After Previous** in the Timing group. Set the Duration to **01.00** and the Delay to **00.50**.

The first table is now animated.

c. Click the **second table**. Click **Fade**. Set Start to **After Previous**. Set the Duration to **01.50** and the Delay to **01.00**. Close the Animation Pane.

The second table is now animated. It displays after a short delay to help the audience focus before seeing the data.

d. Run the presentation from the current slide to test the animation.

e. Save the presentation.

STEP 4 ▶ ANIMATE A 3D MODEL

You want to make sure the audience knows how much pets appreciate their new family. You animate a 3D pet to show the joyful side of pet adoption. Refer to Figure 4.44 as you complete Step 4.

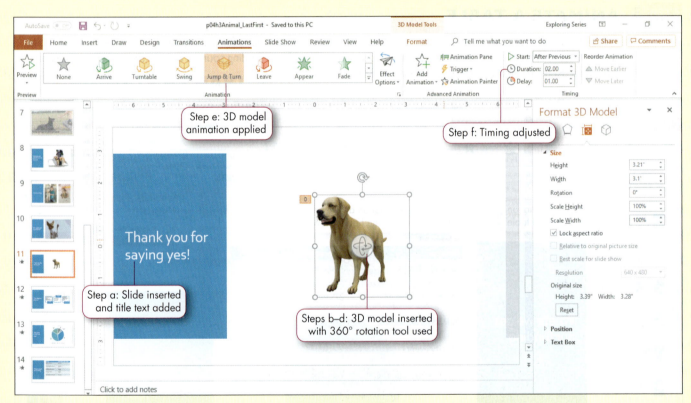

FIGURE 4.44 Animated 3D Model

a. Click **Slide 10**. Insert a new **Slide 11** using the **Title and Content** layout. Type **Thank you for saying yes!** in the title placeholder.

b. Click the **Insert tab** and then click **3D Models arrow** in the Illustrations group. Select **From Online Sources**.

c. Type **Golden Retriever** in the search box and press Enter. Select the 3D model that matches the 3D model shown in Figure 4.44 and click **Insert(1)**.

> **TROUBLESHOOTING:** If a golden retriever is not available, any dog or cat 3D model would work.

d. Click the **360° rotation tool** and drag it to rotate the dog so it faces the left side of the slide.

e. Click the **Animations tab** and click **Jump & Turn**, in the Animation group.

f. Set Start to **After Previous**. Leave the Duration at **02.00** and set the Delay to **01.00**.

g. Run the presentation from the current slide to test the animation.

If the animation does not work as expected, go back through the steps to resolve any issues.

h. Save the presentation.

USE A TRIGGER

You use a trigger to make an image of a friendly dog display on one of the slides in the presentation. Refer to Figure 4.45 as you complete Step 5.

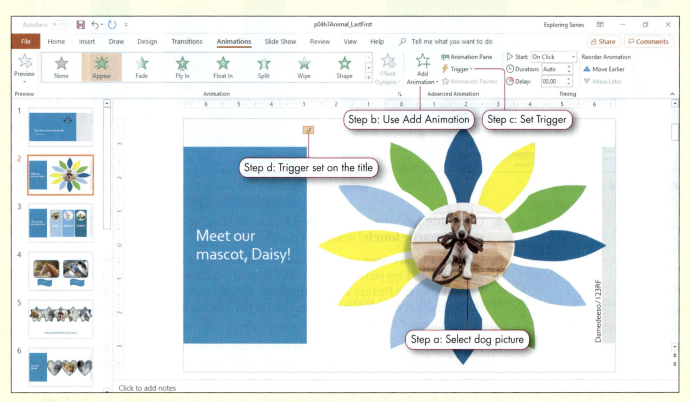

FIGURE 4.45 Applied Trigger

a. Click **Slide 2** and double-click the **dog picture**.

b. Click **Add Animation** in the Advanced Animation group on the Animations tab. Click **Appear**.

The animation has been added to the picture of the dog.

c. Click **Trigger** in the Advanced Animation group. Select **On Click of** and select **Title 17**.

When the words in the title placeholder are clicked, the picture of the dog will display.

d. Run the presentation from the current slide to test the animation.

e. Save the presentation.

After reading this chapter, you have accomplished the following objectives:

1. Group and ungroup objects.

- Group and ungroup objects: Vector graphics can be ungrouped so that each part of the graphic can be edited. When you have finished adjusting the graphic, the parts can be regrouped.
- Convert SmartArt to shapes: Separating the shapes enables you to modify, format, or animate each shape that makes up the SmartArt.
- Use gridlines and guides to place objects on a slide: Using Smart Guides and grids enables you to position objects quickly and precisely on a slide.
- Align and distribute shapes: You can align objects by lining up the side, middle, top, or bottom edges with each other or with the slide edges. The distribute options enable you to assign an equal amount of space between the shapes.
- Order and stack objects: The Selection Pane lists all objects on a slide and enables you to select, multi-select, show, hide, or change the order of the objects on the slide.

2. Transform a picture.

- Remove a picture background: The Remove Background tool enables you to remove portions of a picture you do not want to keep.
- Correct a picture: You can enhance a picture by sharpening or softening it, or you can increase or decrease a picture's brightness and contrast.
- Change picture color: Use the color tools to adjust the saturation and tone of pictures.
- Apply an artistic effect: With artistic effects, you can change the appearance of a picture so that it looks like it was created with a marker, as a pencil sketch, or with other artist tools.
- Use a picture as a slide background: Pictures can make appealing backgrounds. Adjusting the transparency makes it easier to read any text that might be on the slide.
- Understand compression: Compression reduces the amount of space required for file storage. The term can be used when discussing specific file formats as in lossy (JPEG) or lossless (GIF) compression. The term is also used when discussing a method to reduce overall presentation size by compressing one or all pictures used in a presentation.

3. Animate objects.

- Animate a SmartArt graphic: You can animate an entire SmartArt graphic or animate individual shapes to provide emphasis as you discuss the SmartArt graphic during the presentation.
- Animate a chart: Chart animation is a powerful way to help the audience focus on key pieces of data during a presentation.
- Animate a table: Animating a table enables you to present the table data incrementally and helps ensure your audience is paying attention to the data as it is presented.
- Animate a 3D model: 3D animation can be used to highlight specific features of a product or illustrate a point. You can search online for 3D models if you do not have your own models.
- Use a trigger: Triggers are a way to add interactivity to a presentation. The process is initiated by clicking the trigger to reveal an object or action associated with the trigger.

4. Enhance transitions.

- Use Morph: Morph creates a seamless cinematic transition between two slides. Start with objects on a beginning slide and create a second slide that shows the objects as they should display in the end. PowerPoint takes care of the transition movements between the two slides.
- Use Zoom: Summary Zoom serves as a landing page where you can go from one slide to another. Slide Zoom enables you work through multiple slides of information while feeling like you are staying on the same canvas. Section Zoom is used when a section has already been created in a presentation.

Key Terms Matching

Match the key terms with their definitions. Write the key term letter by the appropriate numbered definition.

a. Background
b. Bitmap image
c. Brightness
d. Contrast
e. Foreground
f. Grid
g. Group
h. Morph
i. Recolor
j. Saturation
k. Selection Pane
l. Sharpening
m. Smart Guide
n. Softening
o. Stacking order
p. Tone
q. Trigger
r. Ungroup
s. Vector graphic
t. Zoom

1. _____ A technique to break apart a grouped object into individual objects. **p. 980**

2. _____ Multiple objects connected so they move as though they are a single object. **p. 980**

3. _____ An image created by a mathematical statement. **p. 980**

4. _____ A guide that displays when an object is moved that helps align objects in relation to other objects. **p. 985**

5. _____ Intersecting guides on a slide that are hidden by default but can be used to align objects and keep them evenly spaced. **p. 983**

6. _____ A pane designed to help select objects. **p. 987**

7. _____ The order of objects placed on top of one another. **p. 986**

8. _____ An image created by bits or pixels placed on a grid to form a picture. **p. 996**

9. _____ The portion of a picture that can be deleted when removing part of a picture. **p. 997**

10. _____ The portion of the picture that is kept when removing the background of a picture. **p. 997**

11. _____ A technique that enhances the edges of the content in a picture to make the boundaries more prominent. **p. 998**

12. _____ A technique that blurs the edges of the content in a picture to make boundaries less prominent. **p. 998**

13. _____ A picture correction that controls the lightness or darkness of a picture. **p. 999**

14. _____ The difference between the darkest and lightest areas of a picture. **p. 999**

15. _____ A characteristic of color that controls its intensity. **p. 1001**

16. _____ A characteristic of lighting that controls the temperature of a color. **p. 1001**

17. _____ The process of changing a picture by adjusting the image's colors. **p. 1002**

18. _____ An object that launches an animation that takes place when you click an associated object or a bookmarked location in a media object. **p. 1018**

19. _____ A transition that creates a cinematic motion by seamlessly animating between two slides. **p. 1020**

20. _____ A tool that enables you to move from a landing slide to another slide in the presentation without that slide being sequential to the landing slide. **p. 1020**

g. Click the **Design tab** and click **Format Background** in the Customize group. Click **Picture or texture fill** in the Format Background pane, click **File**, locate, and select *p04p1Travel1.jpg* in the p04p1Travel_Media folder, and then click **Insert**. Drag the Transparency slider to **55%**. Close the Format Background pane.

h. Click **Slide 4**. Click the **Insert tab** and click **Pictures** in the Images group. Select *p04p1Travel2.jpg* and click **Insert**. Click **Height** in the Size group, type **5"**. Click **Align** and select **Align Right**. Click Align and select **Align Bottom**.

i. Click **Remove Background** in the Adjust group and click **Keep Changes** in the Close group.

j. Click **Slide 5** and click the **Pictures icon** in the right placeholder. Insert *p04p1Travel3.jpg* and size height to **5"**. Click **Align** and **Align Right**. Click **Align** again and select **Align Middle**.

k. Ensure the picture is selected and the Format tab is displayed. Click **Corrections** in the Adjust group. Select **Sharpen: 25%**. Click **Corrections** and select **Brightness: 0% (Normal) Contrast +20%**. Click **Artistic Effects** and select **Pencil Grayscale**. Click **Compress Pictures** in the Adjust group. Click the **Apply only to this picture check box** to deselect it. Click **OK**.

l. Click **Slide 6** and click the **SmartArt graphic**. Click the **Animations tab**. Click **Fade** in the Animation group. Click **Effect Options** and select **One by One**. Click the **Start arrow** in the Timing group and select **After Previous**. Set Duration to **01.50** and Delay to **00.50**.

> **MAC TROUBLESHOOTING:** Open the Animation Pane to set Delay timing in PowerPoint for Mac.

m. Click **Slide 7** and click the **chart**. Click **Fade** in the Animation group. Click **Effect Options** and select **By Category**. Set start in the Timing group, to **After Previous**. Set Duration to **01.00** and Delay to **00.25**.

n. Click **Slide 8**. Click the **bottom table** and use **Smart Guides** to align it to the bottom of the top table. Click the **top table** and click **Appear** in the Animation group. Set Start to **After Previous**. Set Duration to **01.00** and Delay to **00.25**. Click the **bottom table** and click **Appear**. Set Start to **After Previous**. Set Duration to **01.50** and Delay to **00.50**.

o. Click **Slide 9** and click the **world** (3D model). Select **Turntable** in the Animation group. Set Start to **After Previous**. Set Duration to **15.00**.

p. Click **Slide 10** and click the **Home tab**. Click the **Copy arrow** in the Clipboard group and select **Duplicate**.

q. Click the new **Slide 11** and delete the frowning face icon. Click the **Insert tab** and click **Icons** in the Illustrations group. Click the **Faces** category on the left, and select the **smiling face**. Click **Insert**. Click **Graphics Fill** in the Graphics Styles group and select **Gold, Accent 4**.

r. Click the left placeholder and replace the text *Go From This* with the text **To This**. Click the **Transitions tab** and click **Morph**.

s. Click **Slide 2** and click the **Insert tab**. Click **Zoom** in the Links group. Select **Summary Zoom**. Click **Slides 2**, **10**, and **11**. Click **Insert**. Type **Grayson Travel Agency** in the title placeholder of the new Slide 1.

> **MAC TROUBLESHOOTING:** Summary Zoom is not available in PowerPoint for Mac.

t. Click **Slide 5** and click the picture. Click the **Format tab** and click **Compress Pictures** in the Adjust group. Ensure **Apply only to this picture** is deselected. Click **OK**.

u. Run the presentation from the beginning to test the animations, Morph transition, and Summary Zoom.

v. Save and close the file. Exit PowerPoint. Based on your instructor's directions, submit p04p1Travel_LastFirst.

A lot of research mentions camping as a wonderful activity to support good health. You will develop a presentation on its benefits that can be shown at the sporting goods store where you work. Refer to Figure 4.49 as you complete this exercise.

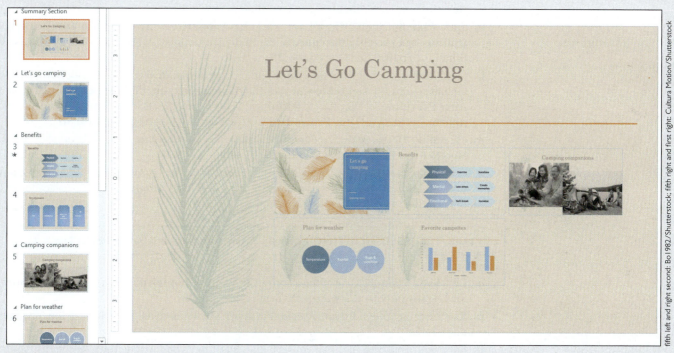

FIGURE 4.49 Let's Go Camping Presentation

a. Open the *p04p2Camp* and save it as **p04p2Camp_LastFirst**.

b. Click the subtitle placeholder on **Slide 1**. Replace *Student Name* with your name.

c. Click **Slide 2** and click the **SmartArt graphic**. Click the **Animations tab** and click **Fly In** in the Animation group. Click **Effect Options** and select **From Left** in the Direction section. Click **Effect Options** and select **One by One** in the Sequence section. Set Start in the Timing group to **After Previous**. Set Duration to **01.00** and Delay to **00.25**.

d. Click **Slide 3**. Click the **View tab** and click the **Guides check box** in the Show group to select it. Drag each shape to position the bottom edge on the lower guide.

e. Press and hold **Ctrl** and select each shape. Click **Format** and click **Align** in the Arrange group. Select **Align to Slide**. Click **Align** again and select **Distribute Horizontally**. Click the **View tab** and click the **Gridlines check box** in the Show group to deselect it.

f. Click **Slide 4**. Click the **Insert tab** and click **Pictures** in the Images group. Click the picture file *p04p2Camp1.jpg* in the p04p2Camp_Media folder and click **Insert**. Click the **Size Dialog Box Launcher**. Click **Lock Aspect Ratio** to deselect it. Click the height box in the Sizing group and type **5"**. Click Position in the Format Picture pane to expand it. Position it Horizontally at 0" from Top Left Corner and Vertically at **1.48"** from Top Left Corner. Click the **Insert tab**. Click **Pictures** and click *p04p2Camp2.jpg*. Click **Insert**. Size the picture to **5"** tall. Click **Align** and select **Align Right**. Click **Align** and select **Align Bottom**.

g. Press and hold **Ctrl** and click the second picture so both pictures are selected. Click **Color** in the Adjust group and select **Sepia**. Click **Compress Pictures**. Click the **Apply only to this picture check box** to deselect it. Click **OK**.

h. Click **Slide 6** and click the **Home tab**. Click the **Copy arrow** and click **Duplicate**.

i. Click the new **Slide 7** and delete the rain cloud icon. Click the **Insert** tab and click **Icons** in the Illustrations group. Click the **Weather and seasons** category and click the **cloud and sun icon**. Click **Insert**. Click the **Format tab**. Click **Graphics Fill** in the Graphic Styles group and select **Ice Blue, Accent 1, Darker 25%**.

j. Click the right placeholder and replace the text *Rain or . . .* with the text **Shine**. Click the **Transitions tab** and click **Morph** in the Transition to This Slide group.

k. Click **Slide 8** and click the **Chart**. Click the **Animations tab**. Select **Fly In**. Click **Effect Options** and select **By Category** in the Sequence section. Set Start to **After Previous**. Set Duration to **01.00** and Delay to **00.25**.

l. Click **Slide 9**. Click the **bottom table** and use **Smart Guides** to align it to the bottom of the top table. Click the **top table** and click the **Animations tab**. Click **Appear** and set Start to **After Previous**. Set Duration to **01.00** and Delay to **00.25**. Click the **bottom table** and click **Appear**. Set Start to **After Previous**. Set Duration to **01.50** and Delay to **00.50**.

m. Click **Slide 10** and select the **campfire** (3D model). Click **Swing** in the Animation group. Set Start to **After Previous**. Set Duration to **15.00**.

n. Click **Slide 2** and click the **Insert tab**. Click **Zoom** in the Links group. Select **Summary Zoom**. Click **Slides 1**, **2**, **4**, **5**, and **8**. Click **Insert**. Type **Let's Go Camping** in the title placeholder of the new Slide 1.

> **MAC TROUBLESHOOTING:** Summary Zoom is not available in PowerPoint for Mac.

o. Click **Slide 5** and click one of the pictures. Click the **Format tab** and click **Compress Pictures**. Click **Apply only to this picture** to deselect it. Click **OK.**

p. Run the presentation from the beginning to test the animations, Morph transition, and Summary Zoom.

q. Save and close the file. Exit PowerPoint. Based on your instructor's directions, submit p04p2Camp_LastFirst.

Mid-Level Exercises

1 Impressionist Paintings

You are preparing a presentation on Impressionism as your final project in your art history class. You will mention some of the major artists, show a couple of the paintings from this movement, and provide information about where the original artworks may be seen.

a. Open the *p04m1Painting* presentation, and save it as **p04m1Painting_LastFirst**.

b. Click **Slide 1** and change the subtitle *Student Name* to your name.

c. Click the **Design tab** and click **Format Background**. Click the *p04m1Painting1.jpg* picture in the p04m1Painting_Media folder and click **Insert** as the background. Set the Transparency at **75%**.

d. Click **Slide 2** and click the **SmartArt graphic**. Click the **Animations tab** and click **Wipe**. Set the Effect Options to **From Right** in the Directions section and **One by One** in the Sequence section. Set Start to **After Previous**. Set Duration to **02.50** and Delay to **00.25**.

e. Click **Slide 3** and select the **picture**. Click the **Format tab** and click **Remove Background**. Click **Keep Changes**.

f. Click **Slide 4** and click the **top table**. Click the **Animations tab** and click **Split**. Set the Effect Option to **Vertical Out**. Set Start to **After Previous**. Set Duration to **01.50** and set Delay to **00.25**. Click the **bottom table** and click **Split**. Set the Effect Option to **Vertical Out**. Set Start to **After Previous**. Set Duration to **01.25** and set Delay to **00.50**.

g. Click **Slide 5** and click the **chart**. Click the **Animations tab** and click **Shape**. Set the Effect Option to **Out**. Set Start to **After Previous**. Set Duration to **02.50** and set Delay to **00.25**.

h. Click **Slide 6** and then click the **Home tab**. Click the **Copy arrow** and select **Duplicate**. Delete the **picture** on the new Slide 7. Insert *p04m1Painting2.jpg*. Click the **Transitions tab** and click **Morph**.

i. Click the **picture of the dancers** and click **Format**. Click **Compress Pictures** and deselect **Apply only to this picture**. Click **OK**.

j. Click **Slide 2**. Click the **Insert tab** and click **Zoom**. Select **Summary Zoom**. Click **Slides 1**, **2**, **4**, and **5**. Click **Insert**. Type **Impressionism** in the new slide title placeholder.

> **MAC TROUBLESHOOTING:** Summary Zoom is not available in PowerPoint for Mac.

k. Run the presentation from the beginning to test the animations, Morph transition, and Summary Zoom.

l. Save and close the file. Exit PowerPoint. Based on your instructor's directions, submit p04m1Painting_LastFirst.

2 Red Butte Garden

You visited Red Butte Garden, a part of the University of Utah, and enjoyed the natural gardens and the botanical garden. You want to create a presentation that features some of the best things you saw and learned that day.

a. Open the *p04m2Garden* presentation and save it as **p04m2Garden_LastFirst**.

b. Click **Slide 1** and change the subtitle *Student Name* to your name.

c. Click **Slide 2** and select all three shapes. Click **Drawing Tools Format tab** and click the Size Dialog Box Launcher. Click the **Lock Aspect Ratio check box** to select it. Change the height to **2.5"**.

d. Click **Align** in the Arrange group and select **Align to Slide**. Click **Distribute Horizontally** and click **Align Middle**. Click **Group** in the Arrange group and select **Group**.

e. Click **Slide 3** and select the **picture**. Click the **Format tab** and click **Corrections**. Select **Sharpen: 25%**. Select **Brightness: +20% Contrast: +20%**. Apply the **Plastic Wrap** artistic effect. Click **Compress Pictures** and deselect **Apply only to this picture**. Click **OK**. Close the Format pane.

f. Click **Slide 4** and select the **picture** (3D model). Click the **Animations tab** and click **Turntable**. Set the Effect Option to **Object Center**. Set Start to **After Previous**. Set Delay to **00.25**.

g. Click **Slide 2**. Click the **Insert tab** and click **Zoom**. Select **Summary Zoom**. Click **Slides 2** and **4**. Click **Insert**. Type **Cactus Shapes** in the new slide title placeholder.

> **MAC TROUBLESHOOTING:** Summary Zoom is not available in PowerPoint for Mac.

h. Run the presentation from the beginning to test the animations and Summary Zoom.

i. Save and close the file. Exit PowerPoint. Based on your instructor's directions, submit p04m2Garden_LastFirst.

Running Case

New Castle County Technical Services

New Castle County Technical Services (NCCTS) provides technical support for a number of companies in the greater New Castle County, Delaware, area. As a trainer in the Human Resources department, you were asked to provide a training seminar for managers. In Chapters 1, 2, and 3 you worked on building your presentation. You will continue to add additional content by working with images, adding animation to a SmartArt graphic, converting a SmartArt graphic to shapes, and inserting a Summary Zoom slide.

a. Open *p04r1Guidelines* and save the presentation as **p04r1Guidelines_LastFirst**.

b. Click the **subtitle placeholder** on Slide 1. Replace *Student Name* with your name.

c. Click **Slide 24**. Insert *p04r1Background.jpg* as a background image on the slide. Set the transparency to **15%**.

d. Click the **title placeholder** and change the Shape Fill to **Light Gray, Background 2**. Set the transparency to **50%**.

e. Click **Slide 21**. Select the **heart image** in the right content placeholder. Use Remove Background to remove the white background of the heart image.

f. Click **Slide 22** and complete the following:
   - Click after the **first bullet point** in the SmartArt Text pane and type **Original**.
   - Click after the second bullet point and type **Chalk Sketch**. Click the **picture icon** associated with the second bullet point and change the Artistic Effect to **Chalk Sketch** in the Artistic Effect gallery.
   - Click after the third bullet point and type **Paint Brush**. Click the **picture icon** associated with the bullet point and change the Artistic Effect to **Paint Brush** in the Artistic Effect gallery.
   - Click after the last bullet point and type **Glass**. Click the **picture icon** associated with the bullet point and change the Artistic Effect to **Glass** in the Artistic Effect gallery.

g. Click **Slide 28**. Select the **SmartArt graphic**. Convert the SmartArt graphic to shapes on the slide.

h. Make the following changes to the converted SmartArt:
   - Delete the two-way arrow.
   - Select the first circle shape, press **Ctrl**, and then select the other two circle shapes. Change the Shape Fill to **Black, Text 1** for the three selected shapes.
   - Select the **first circle shape** on the left and set the horizontal position to **0.67"** and the vertical position to **2.26"**. Type **1** in the circle shape.
   - Select the **middle circle shape** and set the horizontal position to **4.79"** and the vertical position to **2.26"**. Type **2** in the circle shape.
   - Select the circle shape on the right and set the horizontal position to **8.66"** and the vertical position to **2.26"**. Type **3** in the circle shape.
   - Select the first circle shape, press **Ctrl**, and then select the other two circle shapes. On the Home tab, in the Paragraph group, set the text alignment to **Center** and the Align Text to **Middle**. Increase the font size to **28 pt** for each of the numbers.
   - Type **Main Point** in each of the rounded rectangle shapes.

   i. Click **Slide 34**. Select the SmartArt graphic. Apply the **Fly In** animation (Entrance category). Change the Effect Options to **One by One**. Set the animation to start **After Previous**.

   j. Click **Slide 1** and click the **Insert tab**. Click **Zoom** in the Links group. Select **Summary Zoom**. Click **Slides 1**, **3**, **7**, **12**, **15**, **19**, **25**, **29**, and **32**. Click **Insert**. Type **New Castle County Technical Services** in the title placeholder of the new Slide 1.

   > **MAC TROUBLESHOOTING:** Summary Zoom is not available in PowerPoint for Mac.

   k. Save and close the presentation. Based on your instructor's directions, submit p04r1Guidelines_LastFirst.

Disaster Recovery

Our Earth's Ecosystems

You are working with another student to a create slide show about Earth's ecosystems as the project for your science class. The other student has already created a presentation that you can use for the project. After looking at the presentation, you see some revisions that would help the presentation provide a more impactful message. Open *p04d1Ecosystem* and save it as p04d1Ecosystem_LastFirst. Add your first and last names to the first slide. Align the shapes on Slide 2 in the middle of the slide. Distribute them horizontally and group them together. Animate the entire chart on Slide 3. Set the Start, Duration, and Delay. Align Bottom the pictures on Slide 4 and apply a different artistic effect to each picture. Animate the SmartArt graphic on Slide 5 so each shape moves individually. Set the Start, Duration, and Delay. Format the background for Slide 6 with *p04d1Ecosystem1.jpg*. Compress all pictures in the presentation. Create a Summary Zoom slide using Slides 1, 3, 5, and 6. Type **Our Earth's Ecosystems** as the title.

Run the presentation to review the animations and the Summary Zoom. Save and close the file. Exit PowerPoint. Based on your instructor's directions, submit p04d1Ecosystem_LastFirst.

Word Application Capstone Exercise

You are enrolled in an independent study graduate class in which you are reading and analyzing a book, *Cognitive Creativity*. As the final project for the class, you prepare a paper providing an overview of the book and its application to decision-making strategy. You will use MLA style as a basis for the paper, but you are allowed to deviate from the style with respect to the inclusion of a cover page and various other elements. A table included in the paper summarizes data and includes a formula to provide numerical analysis.

Edit and Format the Document

The rough draft includes text that you will begin with, but you must format the text and you will reword a bit as well. Because headings are formatted in preset styles, you will modify those styles to suit your purposes. By adjusting paragraph and line spacing, you will produce an attractive document that is well designed.

1. Open *wApp_Cap1_Thinking* and save it as **wApp_Cap1_Thinking_LastFirst**.
2. Display nonprinting characters. Note that the document includes a blank first page, as evidenced by the page break designation on the first page. Change the document theme to **Retrospect** and select Colors of **Blue Warm**. Select all text in the document and change the font to **Times New Roman**. View the Ruler.
3. Remove the word *why* from the second sentence in the first body paragraph on page 2. Change the word *believes* in the *Prospect Theory* section on page 3 to **proposes**.
4. Remove the space following the word *Cognitive* in the last sentence of the first body paragraph on page 2 and insert a **Nonbreaking Space symbol** between *Cognitive* and *Creativity*.
5. Insert **black check mark bullets** on the three single-line paragraphs following the first body paragraph, beginning with *the irrationality of humans* and ending with *the nature of well-being*. Decrease indent to position bullets at the left margin and ensure that each bulleted text begins with a capital letter.
6. Change margins to **1"** top, bottom, left, and right. Change to **Outline View**. Change the Show Level setting to **Level 2**. Drag *Stages of Prospect Theory* directly below the heading *Prospect Theory* so that it becomes the first sublevel in the *Prospect Theory* section. Close Outline View.
7. **Bold** the bulleted items on page 2. Select all text in the document and adjust paragraph spacing Before and After to **0 pt**. **Double-space** the document. Add a First line indent of **0.5"** to the first body paragraph on page 2 (beginning with *The study of behavioral economics*).
8. Center the title and subtitle (*Cognitive Creativity* and *An Analysis*). Change the line spacing of the *Cognitive Creativity* title to **1.0**.
9. Modify document properties to include **Parker Adams** as the author, removing any existing author.
10. Modify Heading 1 style to include a font of **Times New Roman**, **14 pt**, **Black, Text 1**. Modify Heading 2 style to include a font of **Times New Roman** with a font color of **Black, Text 1**. Changes in style should apply to the current document only.

Insert and Format a Table

To support the report summary, you will develop a table to describe various decision-making strategies. You will ensure that the table is well organized and attractive, inserting rows where appropriate and merging and splitting others. A table style adds to the design, while borders improve the table's readability. You will also include a formula to summarize a column numerically.

11. Select the lines of tabbed text near the top of page 3 (beginning with *System 1* and ending with *0.39*). Whether you select the final paragraph mark on the last line is irrelevant. Convert the selection to a table, accepting all default settings.
12. Insert a row above the first row of the new table, merge all cells, and then type **Systems of Decision Making**. Apply **Align Center** alignment to text in the first row.

13. Insert a row below the first row. Split cells in the new row, adjusting the number of columns shown in the dialog box to **4** and ensuring that *Merge cells before split* is selected. Select the table and choose **Distribute Columns** on the Table Tools Layout tab to align all columns.

14. Type the following text in row 2:

System Theory	Characterized by	Percentage Employed	Probability Factor

15. Insert a row at the end of the table and merge the first three cells in the row. Type **Average Probability** in the merged cell on the last row and apply **Align Center** alignment to the text. In the last cell on the last row, include a formula to average numbers in the column above. You do not need to select a number format.

16. Apply a table style of **List Table 3 – Accent 1**. Deselect **First Column** in the Table Style Options group to remove bold formatting from the first column. **Bold** text on the second row. Select the table and change the font size to **10 pt**. Apply **Align Center** alignment to all text in rows 2, 3, and 4. Apply **Align Center** alignment to the numeric value in the last cell on the last row.

17. Add a caption below the table of **Table 1: Decision-Making Strategies**.

18. Change the probability factor for *System 1* (in row 3) to **0.62**. Update the field in the last cell on the last row to reflect the change in probability.

19. Select **rows 2**, **3**, and **4**, click the **Table Tools Design tab**, and then choose a Pen Color of **Black, Text 1**. Ensure that the line style is a single line and the line weight is **½ pt**. Apply the border selection to **All Borders**.

Edit and Format a Report

The report is near completion but must be formatted to adhere to guidelines supplied by your instructor and loosely based on the MLA writing style. You will include a header to identify yourself as the author and you will provide a footnote with additional information on a report topic. Including a table of contents assists readers with moving quickly to topics, while a cover page provides an introduction to the report. You will include a picture as a design element on the cover page and insert a watermark to identify the report as a draft copy. You will include citations to properly acknowledge sources and include those sources in a Works Cited page.

20. Click after the period that ends the last sentence in the first body paragraph under *System Biases* (ending in *economical solutions to problems*). Insert a footnote with the text, **For more information on theory-induced blindness, visit http://cognitivecreativity.com/ theory.** (Include the period.) Right-click the footnote and modify the style to include **Times New Roman, 12 pt font.**

21. Shade the first two lines on page 2, *Cognitive Creativity* and *An Analysis* in **Blue, Accent 2, Lighter 60%**. Add a **½ pt Box border** to the shaded text, ensuring that the color is **Black, Text 1**.

22. Insert a **DRAFT 1 watermark**, colored **Red** (second column in Standard Colors).

23. Click before the *Cognitive Creativity* heading at the top of page 2 (in the shaded area) and insert a page break. Click before the new page break indicator on the newly inserted page 2 and insert a Table of Contents, selecting **Automatic Table 1**. (On a Mac, select Classic.)

24. Click before the word *Contents* at the top of the table of contents and insert a **Continuous section break**. Click before the page break indicator on the first page and insert text from the file *wApp_Cap1_Cover*. Choose from options in the Page Setup dialog box to center the cover page vertically. Ensure that the settings apply to the current section only. (On a Mac, click before the word Table at the top of the table of contents.)

25. Click before the fourth blank paragraph below the words *An Analysis* on the Cover page. Insert the picture file *wApp_Cap1_QuestionMark.png*. Change the picture height to **1.5"** and choose **Top and Bottom text wrapping**. Apply an artistic effect of **Paint Strokes** to the picture (row 2, column 2).

11. Click **cell C9** and insert a VLOOKUP function that looks up the code in cell B9, compares it to the codes and types of art in the range B2:C6, and then returns the type of art. Copy the function in cell C9 to the **range C9:C54**. Hide column B that contains the codes.

12. Click **cell K9** and insert an IF function that determines if the Issue Price is equal to the Current Value. If the values are the same, display **Same as Issue** (using the cell reference K2); otherwise, display **Increased in Value** (using the cell reference K3). Copy the function from cell K9 to the **range K10:K54**.

13. Display the Purchase worksheet and insert a row above Monthly Payment. Type **Payments in 1 Year** in **cell A5** and type **12** in **cell B5**.

14. Click **cell B6** and insert the PMT function to calculate the monthly payment using cell references, not numbers, in the function, and make sure the function displays a positive result. Apply **Accounting Number Format** and the **Output cell style** to **cell B6**.

Create a Column Chart

The Types of Art input section on the Christensen worksheet displays the total of the issue prices and the total current values of each type of art that Raymond owns. You will create a chart so that Raymond can compare the purchase price to the current value of each type of art.

15. Display the Christensen worksheet, select the **range C1:E6**, and create a clustered column chart.

16. Cut the chart and paste it in **cell C57**, change the height to **4"**, and change the width to **7"**.

17. Customize the chart by doing the following:
    - Type **Raymond's Art Collection** for the chart title, apply **bold**, and then apply **Black, Text 1 font color**.
    - Place the legend at the top of the chart.
    - Add **Primary Minor Horizontal gridlines**.
    - Add Alt Text **The column chart compares total issue prices to total current values by type of art. Most of the art value comes from the Limited Edition Canvas category.** (including the period).

Create a Pie Chart

To further analyze the data for Raymond, you will create a pie chart that shows the proportion each type of art contributes to the total current value.

18. Create a pie chart using the **ranges C2:C6** and **E2:E6** and move the chart to a new chart sheet named **Current Values**. Move the Current Values sheet to the right of the Purchase sheet.

19. Customize the chart by doing the following:
    - Type **Percentage of Total Current Value** as the chart title and change the font size to **18 pt**.
    - Remove the legend.
    - Add data labels for categories and percentages; remove value data labels. Change the font size to **16 pt**, **bold**, and **Black, Text 1 font color** for the data labels.
    - Choose **Colorful Palette 3** for the chart colors.
    - Explode the Masterwork Anniversary Edition slice by **15%** and change the fill color to **Light Blue**.
    - Add the Alt Text **Masterwork Anniversary Editions account for 17% of the total value. Other canvas editions account for 58% of the total value.** (including the period).

Insert a Table, Sort and Filter Data, and Apply Conditional Formatting

You will format the main dataset as a table and apply a table style. Then you will apply conditional formatting to highlight art that has increased in value, sort the data so that it is more easily reviewed, and set a filter to focus on a specific art category. Finally, you will add a total row to display summary totals.

20. Display the Christensen worksheet, click in any cell within the dataset, convert the data to a table, assign a table name **Collection**, and then apply **Green, Table Style Light 14.**

21. Apply a conditional format to the **range J9:J54** that highlights cells where the value is greater than 200% with **Green Fill with Dark Green Text.**

22. Sort the dataset by Type of Art and then within Type of Art, sort by Current Value from largest to smallest.

23. Set a filter to display art that has a **Sold Out** status.

24. Add a total row to display the sum of the Issue Price, Paid, and Current Values columns. Remove the total for the Note column.

Select Page Setup Options

You are ready to finalize the workbook so that you can show it to Raymond.

25. Select the Purchase sheet, set **2"** top margin, and then center horizontally on page.

26. Select the Christensen sheet, select **Landscape orientation**, **Legal paper size**, set **0.2"** left and right margins, **0.5"** top and bottom margins, and then set row 8 to repeat at the top of pages.

27. Change the width of **column A** to **27**, the width of **column D** to **11**, and the width of **column J** to **12**. Wrap text in **cell A1** and **cell J8.**

28. Create a footer with your name on the left side, the sheet tab code in the center, and file name code on the right side on all sheets.

29. Display the workbook in Normal View.

30. Save and close the file. Based on your instructor's directions, submit eApp_Cap1_Collection_LastFirst.

Create a Form

Hideo Sasaki, the department's administrative assistant, will handle data entry. He asked you to simplify the way he inputs information into the new table. You will create a form based on the new Transfer Schools table.

27. Create a Split Form using the Transfer Schools table as the source.

28. Change the height of the AdmittingSchool field to be approximately half the current height. Remove the layout from all the labels and fields. Shrink each field so it is approximately as large as it needs to be.

29. Click record **123455** in the bottom half of the split form. Make sure all fields are still visible in the top half of the form. If not, adjust the controls so all values are visible.

30. Move the CreditsTransferred field so it is to the right of the CreditsEarned field on the same row. Move the RegistrationFee field so it is just below the CreditsEarned field. Move the TuitionDue field so it is just below the CreditsTransferred field.

31. Change the title of the form to **Transfer Schools Overview** and save the form as **Transfer Schools Form**. Close the form.

Create a Report

Cala is hoping you can create a more print-friendly version of the query you created earlier for her to distribute to the Board of Trustees. You will create a report based on the Transfer Calculations query.

32. Create a report using the Report Wizard. Add the **Major**, **FirstName**, **LastName**, **Class**, **GPA**, and **LostCredits** fields from the Transfer Calculations query. Do not add any grouping or sorting. Ensure that the report is in Landscape orientation.

33. Save the report as **Transfer Students Report** and view the report in Layout view.

Format a Report

Now that you have included the fields Cala asked for, you will work to format the report to make the information more obvious.

34. Apply the **Wisp theme**.

35. Group the report by the Major field. Sort the records within each group by LastName then by FirstName, both in ascending order.

36. Adjust the text boxes so the values for the Major field are completely visible.

37. Switch to Print Preview mode and verify that the report is only one page wide (Note: it may be a number of pages long).

38. Export the results as a PDF document saving the file as **aApp_Cap1_Transfer_LastFirst.pdf**.

39. Save and close the report.

Close and Submit the Database

40. Create a backup of the database. Accept the default name for the backup.

41. Close all database objects and exit Access.

42. Based on your instructor's directions, submit the following:

aApp_Cap1_Advising_LastFirst

aApp_Cap1_Advising_LastFirst_*CurrentDate*

aApp_Cap1_Transfer_LastFirst.pdf

PowerPoint Application Capstone Exercise

As a member of the local school district's STEM (Science, Technology, Engineering, and Math) committee, you have been asked to create a presentation on STEM education to be used to build interest in expanding the STEM curriculum with the local school district and to seek funding from local business owners and taxpayers. You began a presentation and now need to add the content to the presentation.

Create the Presentation

You open the original presentation, rename it, and then save the presentation. You want to change the presentation colors and fonts.

1. Open *pApp_Cap1_Stem* and save it as **pApp_Cap1_Stem_LastFirst**.
2. Change the theme colors to **Aspect**.
3. Change the theme fonts to **Gill Sans MT**.
4. Replace *Student Name* with your name on **Slide 1**.

Insert Pictures and Video

You want to include several pictures and a video in your presentation to showcase students in STEM courses. You insert a video, apply a video and border style, and then set the video to start automatically. You add several pictures to the presentation, applying picture and border styles, cropping, sizing, and repositioning the images on the slides. Additionally, you will add a picture to the background of one of the slides and change the transparency.

5. Click **Slide 8**. Insert *pApp_Cap1_Microscope.jpg* in the left placeholder. Apply the **Metal Oval picture style**. Change the Picture Border fill to **Dark Gray, Background 2, Lighter 10%**.
6. Click **Slide 10**. In the left content placeholder, insert the *pApp_Cap1_ElementarySchool.jpg* image. In the right content placeholder, insert the *pApp_Cap1_ElementarySchool2.jpg* image. Apply the **Simple Frame, White picture style** to both images. Change the Picture Border fill for both images to **Dark Gray, Background 2, Lighter 10%**.
7. Click **Slide 11**. Insert the *pApp_Cap1_MiddleSchool.jpg* image. Make the following changes to the inserted image:
   - Crop the left side of the image so that most of the white area is removed.
   - Change the Shape Height of the image to **5.2"**.
   - Apply the **Simple Frame, White picture style**.
   - Change the Picture Border to **Dark Gray, Background 2, Lighter 10%**.
   - Set the Horizontal position of the image to **3.6"** and the Vertical position to **1.9"**.
8. Click **Slide 12**. Insert the *pApp_Cap1_HS.mp4* video file. Make the following changes to the video:
   - Apply the **Simple Frame, White video style**.
   - Change the Video Border to **Dark Gray, Background 2, Lighter 10%**.
   - Set the video to start **Automatically**.
9. Click **Slide 4**. Insert the image *pApp_Cap1_WorldMap.jpg* as a background image on the slide. Change the transparency to **40%**.

Add SmartArt, WordArt, and Shapes

You create a SmartArt graphic with a picture layout to explain the meaning of the acronym STEM, and convert a bulleted list to a SmartArt graphic. Next, you change text to a WordArt style and apply formatting changes to the WordArt. Finally, you insert shapes to emphasize data on a slide.

10. Click **Slide 2**. Insert a **Picture Caption List SmartArt graphic**. Complete the following:
    - Ensure the insertion point is in the first bullet point in the Text pane. Type **Science** and insert *pApp_Cap1_Science.jpg* as the image for the first bullet point.

- Click the second bullet point, type **Technology**, and then add the *pApp_Cap1_Technology.jpg* image.
- Click the third bullet point, type **Engineering**, and then add the image *pApp_Cap1_Engineering.jpg*.
- Click the last bullet point, type **Math**, and then add the image *pApp_Cap1_Math.jpg*.
- Apply the **Intense Effect** SmartArt Style to the SmartArt graphic.

11. Click **Slide 6**. Convert the bulleted list to a **Lined List SmartArt graphic** and change the colors to **Colorful–Accent Colors**.

12. Click **Slide 3**. Apply the **Gradient Fill: Dark Purple, Accent color 5, Reflection WordArt style** to the text *Why Stem?* Make the following changes to the WordArt:
    - Increase the font size to **96 pt**.
    - Change the Text Fill to **Orange, Accent 1**.
    - Apply the **Wave Up text effect** in the Transform gallery (Mac users: Apply the Wave 2 text effect in the Transform gallery).
    - Change the Shape Height to **2.8"**.

13. Click **Slide 4**. Insert an **Oval shape** on the slide. Make the following changes to the Oval shape:
    - Change the Shape Height to **3.9"** and the Shape Width to **3.9"**.
    - Type **40th in Mathematics** in the shape, change the font color to **Black, Background 1**, and then increase the font size to **36 pt**.
    - Change the Shape Fill to **White, Text 1** and the Shape Outline to **No Outline**.
    - Change the Transparency to **36%**.
    - Set the Horizontal position of the shape to **2"** and the Vertical position to **2.5"**.

14. Make a copy of the formatted oval shape and paste on the slide. Set the Horizontal position of the new shape to **7"** and the Vertical position to **2.5"**. Highlight the text in the shape and type **25th in Science**.

Add a Table

To showcase the STEM curriculum at each level, you create and format a table.

15. Click **Slide 9**. Insert a **2x6 table**. Make the following changes to the table structure:
    - Apply the **No Style, Table Grid table style**.
    - Merge rows 1 and 2 in column 1. In column 1, select rows 3 and 4 and merge the cells, and select rows 5 and 6 and merge the cells.
    - Click in the first cell in the first column, and change the Table Column Width in the Cell Size group to **2.8"**.
    - Click in the first cell in the second column and change the Table Column Width in the Cell Size group to **8.2"**.

16. Type the following information into the table starting in the first cell of the first row:

Elementary School	Focuses on introductory STEM courses and awareness of STEM occupations
	Provides structured inquiry-based and real-world problem-based learning, connecting all four of the STEM subjects
Middle School	Courses become more rigorous and challenging
	Student exploration of STEM-related careers begins at this level
High School	Focuses on the application of the subjects in a challenging and rigorous manner
	Courses and pathways are now available in STEM fields and occupations

17. Set the Table Height to **4.8"**. Select the first column, click **Center**, and then **Center Vertically**. Select the second column of the table and click **Center Vertically**.

18. Click in the cell with the text *Elementary School* and change the Shading to **Red, Accent 2**. Click in the cell with the text *Middle School* and change the Shading to **Orange, Accent 1**. Click in the cell with the text *High School* and change the Shading to **Dark Blue, Accent 3**.

Create a Column Chart

You have information on the growth of STEM occupations that you want to put into a chart to reinforce why STEM curriculum is so important.

19. Click **Slide 5**. Insert a **Clustered Column chart**. Replace the spreadsheet information with the following information:

	Percentage
All Occupations	14%
Mathematics	16%
Computer Systems Analysts	22%
Systems Software Developers	32%
Medical Scientists	36%
Biomedical Engineers	62%

20. Make the following changes to the chart:
- Remove any unneeded sample data in the spreadsheet.
- Remove the chart title, gridlines, legend, and vertical axis.
- Increase the font size of the x-axis (horizontal) to **16 pt**.
- Add **Outside End data labels** and change the font size to **18 pt**.
- Change the color of the All Occupations data point to **Red, Accent 2**.

Add Content

Another STEM committee member has put together some slides on careers in the STEM field that you will add to your presentation. Additionally, she has an Excel chart you want to embed on one of the slides.

21. Click **Slide 13** and use the Reuse Slides option to insert **Slides 2–5** from *pApp_Cap1_Careers*. Click **Keep source formatting** to retain the formatting from the original presentation.

> **MAC TROUBLESHOOTING:** Open pApp_Cap1_Careers. Select Slides 2–5. Click Copy. Navigate back to the pApp_Cap1_Stem_LastName file. Click Slide 13. Click Paste Special and select Keep Source Formatting.

22. Open the *pApps_Cap1_Data.xlsx* Excel workbook, and copy the **Bar Chart**. Minimize Excel.

23. Click **Slide 13**. Click **Paste Special** and embed the chart on the slide. (On a Mac, click the Paste arrow and select Paste as Picture.)

24. Change the Shape Height to **4.8"**. Set the Horizontal position to **1.4"** and the Vertical position to **1.9"**.

25. Select Excel on the taskbar, and close **Excel** without saving.

Add Animation

You add animation to the opening slide and to a column chart to add emphasis. On the first slide, you will group the icons and circle shape for each animation.

26. Click **Slide 1**. Select the **blue circle shape**, press **Shift**, and then select the **inserted icon**. Group the shapes.

27. Repeat Step 26 for the three remaining shapes on the first slide to group each of the circle shapes with their associated icons.

28. Select the grouped **blue circle shape** and apply the **Zoom animation** (Entrance category). Set the animation to start **After Previous** with a Duration of **00.50** and a Delay of **00.50**.

29. Use the **Animation Painter** to set the same animation and animation settings to the other circle shapes, moving from left to right (orange, red, green).

30. Click **Slide 5**. Apply the **Fly In animation** (Entrance category) to the chart. Set the animation to start **After Previous**. Set the Effect Options Sequence to **By Element in Category**.

Finalize the Presentation

You want to put the final touches on the presentation. You have one slide that needs to be deleted. You add slide numbers and apply a transition. Next, you add a speaker note to the first slide and check the presentation for possible spelling errors. Finally you compress the size of the video and view the presentation in Presenter view to ensure it looks professional.

31. Delete **Slide 7**.

32. Add **page numbers** to all slides with the exception of the first slide.

33. Add the **Split transition** to all slides.

34. Click **Slide 1**. Type **Welcome to our presentation on STEM education.** (including the period) as a speaker note.

35. Check the presentation for spelling errors and correct any errors.

36. Save the presentation. Click the **File tab** and ensure Info is selected. In the Info pane, click **Compress Media** and select **Standard (480p)**. In the Compress Video dialog box, click **Close** when the video is finished compressing.

37. Change to Presenter view and navigate through the presentation. Return to Normal view.

38. Save and close the presentation. Based on your instructor's directions, submit pApp_Cap1_Stem_LastFirst.

MOS Obj #	MOS Objective	Exploring Chapter	Exploring Section Heading
4. Create and Manage References			
4.1 Create and manage reference elements			
4.1.1	Insert footnotes and endnotes	**Chapter 4**: Research and Collaboration	Create Footnotes and Endnotes
4.1.2	Modify footnote and endnote properties	**Chapter 4**: Research and Collaboration	Create Footnotes and Endnotes
4.1.3	Create and modify bibliography citations sources	**Chapter 4**: Research and Collaboration	Create a Source and Include a Citation
4.1.4	Insert citations for bibliographies	**Chapter 4**: Research and Collaboration	Create a Source and Include a Citation
4.2 Create and manage reference tables			
4.2.1	Insert tables of contents	**Chapter 4**: Research and Collaboration	Create a Table of Contents
4.2.2	Customize tables of contents	**Chapter 4**: Research and Collaboration	Create a Table of Contents
4.2.3	Insert bibliographies	**Chapter 4**: Research and Collaboration	Create a Bibliography
5. Insert and Format Graphic Elements			
5.1 Insert illustrations and text boxes			
5.1.1	Insert shapes	Online Appendix	Online Appendix
5.1.2	Insert pictures	Online Appendix	Online Appendix
5.1.3	Insert 3D models	Online Appendix	Online Appendix
5.1.4	Insert SmartArt graphics	Online Appendix	Online Appendix
5.1.5	Insert screenshots and screen clippings	**Chapter 2**: Document Presentation	Inserting and Formatting Objects
5.1.6	Insert text boxes	**Chapter 2**: Document Presentation	Inserting and Formatting Objects
5.2 Format illustrations and text boxes			
5.2.1	Apply artistic effects	**Chapter 2**: Document Presentation	Modify a Picture
5.2.2	Apply picture effects and picture styles	**Chapter 2**: Document Presentation	Modify a Picture
5.2.3	Remove picture backgrounds	**Chapter 2**: Document Presentation	Modify a Picture
5.2.4	Format graphic elements	Online Appendix	Online Appendix
5.2.5	Format SmartArt graphics	Online Appendix	Online Appendix
5.2.6	Format 3D models	Online Appendix	Online Appendix
5.3 Add text to graphic elements			
5.3.1	Add and modify text in text boxes	**Chapter 2**: Document Presentation	Inserting and Formatting Objects
5.3.2	Add and modify text in shapes	Online Appendix	Online Appendix
5.3.3	Add and modify SmartArt graphic content	Online Appendix	Online Appendix

MOS Obj #	MOS Objective	Exploring Chapter	Exploring Section Heading
5.4	**Modify graphic elements**		
5.4.1	Position objects	**Chapter 2**: Document Presentation	Inserting and Formatting Objects
5.4.2	Wrap text around objects	**Chapter 2**: Document Presentation	Inserting and Formatting Objects
5.4.3	Add alternative text to objects for accessibility	Online Appendix	Online Appendix

6. Manage Document Collaboration

MOS Obj #	MOS Objective	Exploring Chapter	Exploring Section Heading
6.1	**Add and manage comments**		
6.1.1	Add comments	**Chapter 4**: Research and Collaboration	Add a Comment
6.1.2	Review and reply to comments	**Chapter 4**: Research and Collaboration	View Comments Reply to Comments
6.1.3	Resolve comments	**Chapter 4**: Research and Collaboration	View Comments Reply to Comments
6.1.4	Delete comments	**Chapter 4**: Research and Collaboration	Add a Comment
6.2	**Manage change tracking**		
6.2.1	Track changes	**Chapter 4**: Research and Collaboration	Use Track Changes
6.2.2	Review tracked changes	**Chapter 4**: Research and Collaboration	Use Track Changes
6.2.3	Accept and reject tracked changes	**Chapter 4**: Research and Collaboration	Accept and Reject Changes
6.2.4	Lock and unlock change tracking	**Chapter 4**: Research and Collaboration	Tracking Changes

MOS Obj #	MOS Objective	Exploring Chapter	Exploring Section Heading
3.3	**Filter and sort table data**		
3.3.1	Filter records	**Chapter 4**: Datasets and Tables	Filtering Data
3.3.2	Sort data by multiple columns	**Chapter 4**: Datasets and Tables	Sorting Data

4. Perform Operations by using Formulas and Functions

MOS Obj #	MOS Objective	Exploring Chapter	Exploring Section Heading
4.1	**Insert references**		
4.1.1	Insert relative, absolute, and mixed references	**Chapter 2**: Formulas and Functions	Using Relative, Absolute, and Mixed References in Formulas
4.1.2	Reference named ranges and named tables in formulas	Online Appendix	Online Appendix
4.2	**Calculate and transform data**		
4.2.1	Perform calculations by using the AVERAGE(), MAX(), MIN(), and SUM() functions	**Chapter 2**: Formulas and Functions	Inserting Basic Math and Statistics Functions
4.2.2	Count cells by using the COUNT(), COUNTA(), and COUNTBLANK() functions	**Chapter 2**: Formulas and Functions	Inserting Basic Math and Statistics Functions
4.2.3	Perform conditional operations by using the IF() function	**Chapter 2**: Formulas and Functions	Using the IF Function
4.3	**Format and modify text**		
4.3.1	Format text by using RIGHT(), LEFT(), and MID() functions	Online Appendix	Online Appendix
4.3.2	Format text by using UPPER(), LOWER(), and LEN() functions	Online Appendix	Online Appendix
4.3.3	Format text by using the CONCAT() and TEXTJOIN() functions	Online Appendix	Online Appendix

5. Manage Charts

MOS Obj #	MOS Objective	Exploring Chapter	Exploring Section Heading
5.1	**Create charts**		
5.1.1	Create charts	**Chapter 3**: Charts	Creating a Basic Chart Using Other Methods to Create a Chart Creating Other Charts
5.1.2	Create chart sheets	**Chapter 3**: Charts	Move a Chart
5.2	**Modify charts**		
5.2.1	Add data series to charts	**Chapter 3**: Charts	Change the Data Source
5.2.2	Switch between rows and columns in source data	**Chapter 3**: Charts	Switch Row and Column Data
5.2.3	Add and modify chart elements	**Chapter 3**: Charts	Chart Elements
5.3	**Format charts**		
5.3.1	Apply chart layouts	**Chapter 3**: Charts	Apply a Quick Layout
5.3.2	Apply chart styles	**Chapter 3**: Charts	Applying a Chart Style and Colors
5.3.3	Add alternative text to charts to accessibility	**Chapter 3**: Charts	Include Alt Text

Microsoft Office 2019 Specialist Access

Online Appendix materials can be found in the Student Resources located at **www.pearsonhighered.com/exploring**.

MOS Obj #	MOS Objective	Exploring Chapter	Exploring Section Heading
1.	**Manage Databases**		
1.1	**Modify database structure**		
1.1.1	Import objects or data from other sources	**Access Chapter 2**: Tables and Queries in Relational Databases	Multitable Queries
1.1.2	Delete database objects	Online Appendix	Online Appendix
1.1.3	Hide and display objects in the Navigation Pane	**Access Chapter 1**: Introduction to Access	Databases Are Everywhere!
1.2	**Manage table relationships and keys**		
1.2.1	Understand relationships	**Access Chapter 2**: Tables and Queries in Relational Databases	Multitable Queries
1.2.2	Display relationships	**Access Chapter 2**: Tables and Queries in Relational Databases	Multitable Queries
1.2.3	Set primary keys	**Access Chapter 2**: Tables and Queries in Relational Databases	Table Design, Creation, and Modification
1.2.4	Enforce referential integrity	**Access Chapter 2**: Tables and Queries in Relational Databases	Multitable Queries
1.2.5	Set foreign keys	**Access Chapter 2**: Tables and Queries in Relational Databases	Table Design, Creation, and Modification
1.3	**Print and export data**		
1.3.1	Configure print options for records, forms, and reports	**Access Chapter 4**: Basic Forms and Reports	Create Basic Reports to Present Information
1.3.2	Export objects to alternative formats	**Access Chapter 4**: Basic Forms and Reports	Create Basic Reports to Present Information
2.	**Create and Modify Tables**		
2.1	**Create tables**		
2.1.1	Import data into tables	**Access Chapter 2**: Tables and Queries in Relational Databases	Multitable Queries
2.1.2	Create linked tables from external sources	**Access Chapter 2**: Tables and Queries in Relational Databases	Multitable Queries
2.1.3	Import tables from other databases	**Access Chapter 2**: Tables and Queries in Relational Databases	Multitable Queries
2.2	**Manage tables**		
2.2.1	Hide fields in tables	**Access Chapter 2**: Tables and Queries in Relational Databases	Table Design, Creation, and Modification
2.2.2	Add total rows	**Access Chapter 3**: Query Calculations and Expressions	Aggregate Functions
2.2.3	Add tables descriptions	**Access Chapter 1**: Introduction to Access	Databases Are Everywhere!

MOS Obj #	MOS Objective	Exploring Chapter	Exploring Section Heading
2.3	**Manage table records**		
2.3.1	Find and replace data	**Access Chapter 1**: Introduction to Access	Filters and Sorts
2.3.2	Sort records	**Access Chapter 1**: Introduction to Access	Filters and Sorts
2.3.3	Filter records	**Access Chapter 1**: Introduction to Access	Filters and Sorts
2.4	**Create and modify fields**		
2.4.1	Add and remove fields	**Access Chapter 2**: Tables and Queries in Relational Databases	Table Design, Creation, and Modification
2.4.2	Add validation rules to fields	**Access Chapter 2**: Tables and Queries in Relational Databases	Table Design, Creation, and Modification
2.4.3	Change field captions	**Access Chapter 2**: Tables and Queries in Relational Databases	Table Design, Creation, and Modification
2.4.4	Change field sizes	**Access Chapter 2**: Tables and Queries in Relational Databases	Table Design, Creation, and Modification
2.4.5	Change field data types	**Access Chapter 2**: Tables and Queries in Relational Databases	Table Design, Creation, and Modification
2.4.6	Configure fields to auto-increment	**Access Chapter 2**: Tables and Queries in Relational Databases	Table Design, Creation, and Modification
2.4.7	Set default values	**Access Chapter 2**: Tables and Queries in Relational Databases	Table Design, Creation, and Modification
2.4.8	Apply built-in input masks	**Access Chapter 2**: Tables and Queries in Relational Databases	Table Design, Creation, and Modification

3. Create and Modify Queries

MOS Obj #	MOS Objective	Exploring Chapter	Exploring Section Heading
3.1	**Create and run queries**		
3.1.1	Create simple queries	**Access Chapter 2**: Tables and Queries in Relational Databases	Single-Table Queries
3.1.2	Create basic crosstab queries	Online Appendix	Online Appendix
3.1.3	Create basic parameter queries	Online Appendix	Online Appendix
3.1.4	Create basic action queries	Online Appendix	Online Appendix
3.1.5	Create basic multi-tab queries	**Access Chapter 2**: Tables and Queries in Relational Databases	Multitable Queries
3.1.6	Save queries	**Access Chapter 2**: Tables and Queries in Relational Databases	Single-Table Queries
3.1.7	Run queries	**Access Chapter 2**: Tables and Queries in Relational Databases	Single-Table Queries
3.2	**Modify queries**		
3.2.1	Add, hide, and remove fields in queries	**Access Chapter 2**: Tables and Queries in Relational Databases	Multitable Queries
3.2.2	Sort data within queries	**Access Chapter 2**: Tables and Queries in Relational Databases	Single-Table Queries
3.2.3	Filter data within queries	**Access Chapter 2**: Tables and Queries in Relational Databases	Single-Table Queries

MOS Obj #	MOS Objective	Exploring Chapter	Exploring Section Heading
4. Modify Forms in Layout View			
4.1 Configure form controls			
4.1.1	Add, move, and remove form controls	**Access Chapter 4**: Basic Forms and Reports	Create Basic Forms to Simplify Data Management
4.1.2	Set form control properties	**Access Chapter 4**: Basic Forms and Reports	Create Basic Forms to Simplify Data Management
4.1.3	Add and modify form labels	**Access Chapter 4**: Basic Forms and Reports	Create Basic Forms to Simplify Data Management
4.2 Format forms			
4.2.1	Modify tab order on forms	Online Appendix	Online Appendix
4.2.2	Sort records by form field	**Access Chapter 4**: Basic Forms and Reports	Create Basic Forms to Simplify Data Management
4.2.3	Modify form positioning	**Access Chapter 4**: Basic Forms and Reports	Create Basic Forms to Simplify Data Management
4.2.4	Insert information in form headers and footers	Online Appendix	Online Appendix
4.2.5	Insert images on forms	**Access Chapter 4**: Basic Forms and Reports	Create Basic Forms to Simplify Data Management
5. Modify Reports in Layout View			
5.1 Configure report controls			
5.1.1	Group and sort fields on reports	**Access Chapter 4**: Basic Forms and Reports	Create Basic Reports to Present Information
5.1.2	Add report controls	**Access Chapter 4**: Basic Forms and Reports	Create Basic Reports to Present Information
5.1.3	Add and modify labels on reports	**Access Chapter 4**: Basic Forms and Reports	Create Basic Reports to Present Information
5.2 Format reports			
5.2.1	Format a report into multiple columns	**Access Chapter 4**: Basic Forms and Reports	Create Basic Reports to Present Information
5.2.2	Modify report positioning	**Access Chapter 4**: Basic Forms and Reports	Create Basic Reports to Present Information
5.2.3	Format report elements	**Access Chapter 4**: Basic Forms and Reports	Create Basic Reports to Present Information
5.2.4	Change report orientation	**Access Chapter 4**: Basic Forms and Reports	Create Basic Reports to Present Information
5.2.5	Insert information in report headers and footers	**Access Chapter 4**: Basic Forms and Reports	Create Basic Reports to Present Information
5.3.6	Insert images on reports	**Access Chapter 4**: Basic Forms and Reports	Create Basic Reports to Present Information

Microsoft Office 2019 Specialist PowerPoint

Online Appendix materials can be found in the Student Resources located at **www.pearsonhighered.com/exploring**.

MOS Obj #	MOS Objective	Exploring Chapter	Exploring Section Heading
I.	**Manage Presentations**		
1.1	**Modify slide masters, handout masters, and note masters**		
1.1.1	Change the slide master theme or background	Online Appendix	Online Appendix
1.1.2	Modify slide master content	Online Appendix	Online Appendix
1.1.3	Create slide layouts	Online Appendix	Online Appendix
1.1.4	Modify slide layouts	Online Appendix	Online Appendix
1.1.5	Modify the handout master	Online Appendix	Online Appendix
1.1.6	Modify the notes master	Online Appendix	Online Appendix
1.2	**Change presentation options and views**		
1.2.1	Change slide size	Online Appendix	Online Appendix
1.2.2	Display presentations in different views	**Chapter 1**: Introduction to PowerPoint	Use Views
1.2.3	Set basic file properties	Online Appendix	Online Appendix
1.3	**Configure print settings of presentations**		
1.3.1	Print all or part of a presentation	**Chapter 1**: Introduction to PowerPoint	Print Full Page Slides
1.3.2	Print notes pages	**Chapter 1**: Introduction to PowerPoint	Print Notes Pages
1.3.3	Print handouts	**Chapter 1**: Introduction to PowerPoint	Print Handouts
1.3.4	Print in color, grayscale, or black and white	**Chapter 1**: Introduction to PowerPoint	Print Full Page Slides
1.4	**Configure and present slide shows**		
1.4.1	Create custom slide shows	Online Appendix	Online Appendix
1.4.2	Configure slide show options	Online Appendix	Online Appendix
1.4.3	Rehearse slide show timing	Online Appendix	Online Appendix
1.4.4	Set up slide show recording options	Online Appendix	Online Appendix
1.4.5	Present slide shows by using Presenter View	**Chapter 1**: Introduction to PowerPoint	Use Presenter View
1.5	**Prepare presentations for collaboration**		
1.5.1	Restrict editing	Online Appendix	Online Appendix
1.5.2	Protect presentations by using passwords	Online Appendix	Online Appendix
1.5.3	Inspect presentations for issues	Online Appendix	Online Appendix
1.5.4	Add and manage comments	Online Appendix	Online Appendix
1.5.5	Preserve presentation content	**Chapter 2**: Effective Presentation Development	Video and Audio
1.5.6	Export presentations to other formats	Online Appendix	Online Appendix

MOS Obj #	MOS Objective	Exploring Chapter	Exploring Section Heading
2. Manage Slides			
2.1 Insert slides			
2.1.1	Import Word document outlines	Online Appendix	Online Appendix
2.1.2	Insert slides from another presentation	**Chapter 1**: Introduction to PowerPoint	Reuse Slides from Another Presentation
2.1.3	Insert slides and select slide layouts	**Chapter 1**: Introduction to PowerPoint	Add New Slides
2.1.4	Insert Summary Zoom slides	**Chapter 4**: Presentation Refinement	Enhancing Transitions
2.1.5	Duplicate slides	**Chapter 4**: Presentation Refinement	Enhancing Transitions
2.2 Modify slides			
2.2.1	Hide and unhide slides	Online Appendix	Online Appendix
2.2.2	Modify individual slide backgrounds	Online Appendix	Online Appendix
2.2.3	Insert slide headers, footers, and page numbers	**Chapter 1**: Introduction to PowerPoint	Insert a Header and Footer
2.3 Order and group slides			
2.3.1	Create sections	Online Appendix	Online Appendix
2.3.2	Modify slide order	**Chapter 1**: Introduction to PowerPoint	Rearrange Slides
2.3.3	Rename sections	Online Appendix	Online Appendix
3. Insert and Format Text, Shapes, and Images			
3.1 Format text			
3.1.1	Apply built-in styles to text	**Chapter 1**: Introduction to PowerPoint	Change Theme Fonts Using the Design Tab
3.1.2	Format text in multiple columns	Online Appendix	Online Appendix
3.1.3	Create bulleted and numbered lists	**Chapter 1**: Introduction to PowerPoint	Create Bulleted and Numbered Lists
3.2 Insert links			
3.2.1	Insert hyperlinks	Online Appendix	Online Appendix
3.2.2	Insert Sections Zoom links and Slide Zoom links	**Chapter 4**: Presentation Refinement	Enhancing Transitions
3.3 Insert and format images			
3.3.1	Resize and crop images	**Chapter 1**: Introduction to PowerPoint	Resize and Position a Picture Crop a Picture
3.3.2	Apply built-in styles and effects to images	**Chapter 1**: Introduction to PowerPoint	Apply Picture Styles
3.3.3	Insert screenshots and screen clippings	Online Appendix	Online Appendix

MOS Obj #	MOS Objective	Exploring Chapter	Exploring Section Heading
3.4	**Insert and format graphic elements**		
3.4.1	Insert and change shapes	**Chapter 2**: Effective Presentation Development	Creating Shapes
3.4.2	Draw by using digital ink	Online Appendix	Online Appendix
3.4.3	Add text to shapes and text boxes	**Chapter 2**: Effective Presentation Development	Creating Shapes
3.4.4	Resize shapes and text boxes	**Chapter 2**: Effective Presentation Development	Creating Shapes
3.4.5	Format shapes and text boxes	**Chapter 2**: Effective Presentation Development	Formatting Shapes
3.4.6	Apply built-in styles to shapes and text boxes	**Chapter 2**: Effective Presentation Development	Formatting Shapes
3.4.7	Add alt text to graphic elements for accessibility	Online Appendix	Online Appendix
3.5	**Order and group objects on slides**		
3.5.1	Order shapes, images, and text boxes	**Chapter 4**: Presentation Refinement	Group and Ungroup Objects
3.5.2	Align shapes, images, and text boxes	**Chapter 4**: Presentation Refinement	Group and Ungroup Objects
3.5.3	Group shapes and images	**Chapter 4**: Presentation Refinement	Group and Ungroup Objects
3.5.4	Display alignment tools	**Chapter 4**: Presentation Refinement	Group and Ungroup Objects

4. Insert Tables, Charts, SmartArt, 3D Models, and Media

MOS Obj #	MOS Objective	Exploring Chapter	Exploring Section Heading
4.1	**Insert and format tables**		
4.1.1	Create and insert tables	**Chapter 3**: Presentation Enhancement	Insert a Linked Object Insert an Embedded Object
4.1.2	Insert and delete table rows and columns	**Chapter 3**: Presentation Enhancement	Add and Delete Rows and Columns
4.1.3	Apply built-in table styles	**Chapter 3**: Presentation Enhancement	Apply a Table Style
4.2	**Insert and modify charts**		
4.2.1	Create and insert charts	**Chapter 3**: Presentation Enhancement	Insert a Chart
4.2.2	Modify charts	**Chapter 3**: Presentation Enhancement	Modifying a Chart
4.3	**Insert and format SmartArt graphics**		
4.3.1	Insert SmartArt graphics	**Chapter 3**: Presentation Enhancement	Creating SmartArt
4.3.2	Convert lists to SmartArt graphics	**Chapter 1**: Introduction to PowerPoint	Convert Text to SmartArt
4.3.3	Add and modify SmartArt graphic content	**Chapter 3**: Presentation Enhancement	Working with SmartArt Shapes
4.4	**Insert and modify 3D models**		
4.4.1	Insert 3D models	**Chapter 4**: Presentation Refinement	Animating Objects
4.4.2	Modify 3D models	**Chapter 4**: Presentation Refinement	Animating Objects

MOS Obj #	MOS Objective	Exploring Chapter	Exploring Section Heading
4.5 **Insert and manage media**			
4.5.1	Insert audio and video clips	**Chapter 2**: Effective Presentation Refinement	Video and Audio
4.5.2	Create and insert screen recordings	**Chapter 2**: Effective Presentation Refinement	Video and Audio
4.5.3	Configure media playback options	**Chapter 2**: Effective Presentation Refinement	Video and Audio
5. Apply Transitions and Animations			
5.1 **Apply and configure slide transitions**			
5.1.1	Apply basic and 3D slide transitions	**Chapter 2**: Effective Presentation Refinement	Controlling Animation and Interactivity
5.1.2	Configure transition effects	**Chapter 2**: Effective Presentation Refinement	Controlling Animation and Interactivity
5.2 **Animate slide contents**			
5.2.1	Animate text and graphic elements	**Chapter 2**: Effective Presentation Refinement	Controlling Animation and Interactivity
5.2.2	Animate 3D models	**Chapter 4**: Presentation Refinement	Animate a 3D Model
5.2.3	Configure animation effects	**Chapter 2**: Effective Presentation Refinement	Controlling Animation and Interactivity
5.2.4	Configure animation paths	**Chapter 2**: Effective Presentation Refinement	Controlling Animation and Interactivity
5.2.5	Reorder animations on a slide	**Chapter 2**: Effective Presentation Refinement	Controlling Animation and Interactivity
5.3 **Set timing for transitions and animations**			
5.3.1	Set transition effect duration	**Chapter 2**: Effective Presentation Refinement	Controlling Animation and Interactivity
5.3.2	Configure transition start and finish options	**Chapter 2**: Effective Presentation Refinement	Controlling Animation and Interactivity

Glossary

100% stacked bar chart A chart type that places (stacks) data in one bar per category, with each bar the same width of 100%.

100% stacked column chart A chart type that places (stacks) data in one column per category, with each column the same height of 100%.

Absolute cell reference A designation that indicates a constant reference to a specific cell location; the cell reference does not change when you copy the formula.

Accessibility Checker A feature that locates elements in a document that might cause difficulty for people with disabilities to read.

Accounting Number Format A number format that displays $ on the left side of a cell, formats a value with a comma for every three digits on the left side of the decimal point, and displays two digits to the right of the decimal point.

Active cell The current cell in a worksheet. It is indicated by a dark green border, and the Name Box shows the location of the active cell.

Active sheet The currently displayed worksheet.

Add-in A custom program or additional command that extends the functionality of a Microsoft Office program.

Adjustment handle A yellow circle on a shape that is used to change the shape.

Aggregate function A calculation performed on an entire column of data that returns a single value. Includes functions such as Sum, Avg, and Count.

Align A feature that enables you to line up shapes and objects. You can align objects by lining up the sides, middles, or top/bottom edges of objects.

Alignment (Excel) The placement of data within the boundaries of a cell.

Alignment (Word) The positioning of text relative to the margins.

Alignment guide A horizontal or vertical green bar that displays as you move an object, assisting with aligning the object with text or with another object.

All Markup A markup view that shows the document with all the revisions, markups, and comments using the formats predefined in Track Changes options.

Alt text (Alternative text) Also known as *alternative text*, an accessibility compliance feature where you enter text and a description for an objective, such as a table or a chart. A special reader can read the alt text to a user.

AND logical operator A condition in a query, returns only records that meet all criteria.

Animation A motion applied to text and objects.

APA (American Psychological Association) A writing style established by the American Psychological Association with rules and conventions for documenting sources and organizing a research paper (used primarily in business and the social sciences).

Application part A feature that enables you to add a set of common Access components to an existing database, such as a table, a form, and a report for a related task.

Area chart A chart type that emphasizes magnitude of changes over time by filling in the space between lines with a color.

Argument A positional reference contained within parentheses in a function such as a cell reference or value, required to complete a function and produce output.

Auto Fill A feature that helps you complete a sequence of months, abbreviated months, quarters, weekdays, weekday abbreviations, or values. Auto Fill also can be used to fill or copy a formula down a column or across a row.

AutoComplete A feature that searches for and automatically displays any other text in that column that matches the letters you type.

AutoCorrect A feature that automatically corrects various spelling and word usage errors as they are typed.

AutoNumber A number that automatically increments each time a record is added.

AutoRecover A feature that enables Word to recover a previous version of a document.

AutoSave A feature that saves files every few seconds if those files are housed on OneDrive, OneDrive for Business, or SharePoint Online.

AVERAGE function A statistical function that calculates the arithmetic mean, or average, of values in a range of cells.

Axis title A label that describes either the category axis or the value axis. Provides clarity, particularly in describing the value axis.

Back Up Database A utility that creates a duplicate copy of the entire database to protect from loss or damage.

Background The portion of a picture that can be deleted when removing the background of a picture.

Backstage view A component of Office that provides a concise collection of commands related to an open file.

Bar chart A chart type that compares values across categories using horizontal bars where the length represents the value; the longer the bar, the larger the value. In a bar chart, the horizontal axis displays values and the vertical axis displays categories.

Bibliography A list of sources consulted by an author during research for a paper.

Bitmap image An image created by bits or pixels placed on a grid to form a picture.

Bookmark A method used to mark a specific location in a video.

Border Lines that display at the top, bottom, left, or right of a paragraph, a page, a table, or an image.

Border (Excel) A line that surrounds a cell or a range of cells to offset particular data from the rest of the data in a worksheet.

Border Painter A feature that enables you to choose border formatting and click on any table border to apply the formatting.

Breakpoint The lowest value for a category or in a series.

Brightness A picture correction that controls the lightness or darkness of a picture.

Bulleted list A list of points that is not sequential; each point is typically identified by a graphic element that itemizes and separates bulleted items.

Calculated field A field that displays the result of an expression rather than data stored in a field.

Callout A shape that can be used to add notes, often used in cartooning.

Cancel A command to the left of the Formula Bar that is used to cancel data being entered or edited into the active cell. The Cancel command changes from gray to red when you position the pointer over it.

Caption A descriptive title for a table.

Caption property A property that is used to create a more understandable label than a field name that displays in the top row in Datasheet view and in forms and reports.

Cascade Delete Related Records When the primary key value is deleted in a primary table, Access will automatically delete all records in related tables that contain values that match the primary key.

Cascade Update Related Fields An option that directs Access to automatically change all foreign key values in a related table when the primary key value is modified in a primary table.

Category axis The chart axis that displays descriptive labels for the data points plotted in a chart. The category axis labels are typically text contained in the first column of worksheet data (such as job titles) used to create the chart.

Cell The intersection of a column and row in a Word table, PowerPoint table, or Excel worksheet.

Cell address The unique identifier of a cell, starting with the column letter and then the row number, such as C6.

Cell style A collection of format characteristics (font, font color, font size, borders, fill colors, and number formatting) to provide a consistent appearance within a worksheet and among similar workbooks.

Center alignment Positions text horizontally in the center of a line, with an equal distance from both the left and right margins.

Chart A visual representation of numeric data.

Chart area A container for the entire chart and all of its elements, including the plot area, titles, legends, and labels.

Chart element A component of a chart that helps complete or clarify the chart.

Chart filter A setting that controls what data series and categories are displayed or hidden in a chart.

Chart sheet A sheet within a workbook that contains a single chart and no spreadsheet data.

Chart style A collection of formatting that controls the color of the chart area, plot area, and data series, as well as the font and font size of the titles.

Chart title The label that describes the entire chart. The title is usually placed at the top of the chart area.

Chicago Manual of Style A writing style established by the University of Chicago with rules and conventions for preparing an academic paper for publication.

Citation A brief, parenthetical reference placed at the end of a sentence or paragraph that directs a reader to a source of information you used.

Cloud storage A technology used to store files and to work with programs that are stored in a central location on the Internet.

Clustered bar chart A type of chart that groups, or clusters, bars displayed horizontally to compare several data points among categories.

Clustered column chart A type of chart that groups, or clusters, columns set side by side to compare several data points among categories.

Codec (coder/decoder) A digital video compression scheme used to compress a video and decompress for playback.

Color scale A conditional format that displays a particular color based on the relative value of the cell contents to the other selected cells.

Column A format that separates document text into side-by-side vertical blocks, often used in newsletters.

Column chart A type of chart that compares values vertically in columns where the height represents the value; the taller the column, the larger the value. In a column chart, the vertical axis displays values and the horizontal axis displays categories.

Column heading The alphabetical letter above a column in a worksheet. For example, B is the column heading for the second column.

Column index number The column number in the lookup table that contains the return values.

Column width The horizontal measurement of a column in a table or a worksheet.

Combo chart A chart that combines two chart types, such as column and line, to plot different types of data, such as quantities and percentages.

Comma Style A number format that formats a value with a comma for every three digits on the left side of the decimal point and displays two digits to the right of the decimal point.

Command A button or area within a group that you click to perform tasks.

Comment A note, annotation, or additional information to the author or another reader about the content of a document.

Comment balloon A feature that displays as a boxed note in the margin and, when selected, highlights the text to which the comment is applied.

Compact and Repair Database A utility that reduces the size of a database and fixes any errors that may exist in the file.

Comparison operator An operator such as greater than (>), less than (<), greater than or equal to (>=), and less than or equal to (<=) used to limit query results that meet the criteria.

Compression A method applied to data to reduce the amount of space required for file storage.

Conditional formatting A set of rules that applies specific formatting to highlight or emphasize cells that meet specific conditions.

Connector A line with connection points at each end.

Constant A value that does not change.

Contextual tab A tab that contains a group of commands related to the selected object.

Contrast The difference between the darkest and lightest areas of a picture.

Control A text box, button, label, or other tool you use to add, edit, and display the data in a form or report.

Copy A command used to duplicate a selection from the original location and place a copy in the Office Clipboard.

Copyright The legal protection afforded to a written or artistic work.

COUNT function A statistical function that tallies the number of cells in a range that contain values you can use in calculations, such as numeric and date data, but excludes blank cells or text entries from the tally.

COUNTA function A statistical function that tallies the number of cells in a range that are not blank—that is, cells that contain data, whether a value, text, or a formula.

COUNTBLANK function A statistical function that tallies the number of cells in a range that are blank.

Cover page The first page of a report, including the report title, author, and other identifying information.

Criteria row A row in the query design grid that determines which records will be selected.

Crop The process of trimming edges that you do not want to display.

Cropping The process of eliminating unwanted portions of an image.

Cropping handles Dark, thick lines around the four corners and on the left, right, top, and bottom sides of the selected image.

Currency format A number format that displays $ to the immediate left of the value, formats a value with a comma for every three digits on the left side of the decimal point, and displays two digits to the right of the decimal point.

Current List A list that includes all citation sources you use in the current document.

Custom path An animation path that can be created freehand instead of following a preset path.

Cut A command used to remove a selection from the original location and place it in the Office Clipboard.

Data bar Data bar formatting applies a gradient or solid fill bar in which the width of the bar represents the current cell's value compared relatively to other cells' values.

Data label An identifier that shows the exact value of a data point in a chart. Appears above or on a data point in a chart. May indicate percentage of a value to the whole on a pie chart.

Data point An individual value in a cell that is plotted in a chart.

Data redundancy The unnecessary storing of duplicate data in two or more tables.

Data series A group of related data points that displays in rows or columns in a worksheet.

Data source A list of information that is merged with a main document during a mail merge procedure.

Data structure The organization method used to manage multiple data points within a dataset.

Data table A grid that contains the data source values and labels to plot data in a chart. A data table may be placed below a chart or hidden from view.

Data type Determines the type of data that can be entered and the operations that can be performed on that data.

Database A collection of data organized as meaningful information that can be accessed, managed, stored, queried, sorted, and reported.

Database Management System (DBMS) A software system that provides the tools needed to create, maintain, and use a database.

Datasheet view A grid containing fields (columns) and records (rows) used to view, add, edit, and delete records.

Deck A collection of slides.

Design view (form/report) A view that gives users advanced design settings not available in Layout view, (such as changing the tab order of a form) providing more control over the form and report design. Also used to create a new report or form from scratch by adding fields and controls manually to a blank object.

Design view (query) A detailed view of a query's structure and is used to create and/or modify a query's design by specifying the tables, fields, and criteria required for output.

Design view (table) A view that gives users a detailed view of the table's structure and is used to create and modify a table's design by specifying the fields it will contain, the fields' data types, and their associated properties.

Designer An intelligent tool that aids you in designing a PowerPoint presentation.

Destination file The file that contains the inserted or embedded object.

Dialog box A box that provides access to more precise, but less frequently used, commands.

Dialog Box Launcher A button that when clicked opens a corresponding dialog box.

Document Inspector A feature that checks for and removes certain hidden and personal information from a document.

Document properties Data elements that are saved with a document but do not appear in the document as it is shown onscreen or is printed.

Document theme A unified set of design elements, including font style, color, and special effects, that is applied to an entire document.

Draft view A view that shows a great deal of document space, but no margins, headers, footers, or other special features.

Embed The process of placing a copy of a video on a slide.

Embedded object An object that becomes part of the destination file in which the source file program is used for editing within PowerPoint.

Endnote A citation that appears at the end of a document.

Enhanced ScreenTip A small message box that displays when you place the pointer over a command button. The purpose of the command, short descriptive text, or a keyboard shortcut, if applicable, will display in the box.

Enter A command to the left of the Formula Bar that is used to accept data typed in the active cell and keep the current cell active. The Enter command changes from gray to blue when you position the pointer over it.

Error bars Visual that indicates the standard error amount, a percentage, or a standard deviation for a data point or marker in a chart.

Exploded pie chart A chart type in which one or more pie slices are separated from the rest of the pie chart for emphasis.

Expression A combination of elements that produces a value.

Expression Builder An Access tool that helps you create more complicated expressions.

Eyedropper A tool used to recreate an exact color.

Field The smallest data element contained in a table, such as first name, last name, address, and phone number.

Field property A characteristic of a field that determines how it will look and behave.

Fill color The background color that displays behind the data in a cell so that the data stand out.

Fill handle A small green square at the bottom-right corner of the active cell. You can position the pointer on the fill handle and drag it to repeat the contents of the cell to other cells or to copy a formula in the active cell to adjacent cells down the column or across the row.

Filter A feature that enables users to specify conditions to display only those records that meet those conditions.

Filter By Form A more versatile method of selecting data, enabling users to display records based on multiple criteria.

Filtering The process of specifying conditions to display only those records that meet those conditions.

First line indent Marks the location to indent only the first line in a paragraph.

Flash Fill A feature that fills in data or values automatically based on one or two examples you enter using another part of data entered in a previous column in the dataset.

Font A combination of typeface and type style.

Footer Information that displays at the bottom of a document page.

Footnote A citation that appears at the bottom of a page.

Foreground The portion of the picture that is kept when removing the background of a picture.

Foreign key A field in a related table that is the primary key of another table.

Form A database object that is used to view data, add data to, or edit data in a table.

Form letter A letter with standard information that you personalize with recipient information, which you might print or email to many people.

Form tool A tool used to create data entry forms for customers, employees, products, and other tables.

Form view A view that provides a simplified user interface primarily used for data entry; does not enable you to make changes to the layout.

Format Painter A feature that enables you to quickly and easily copy all formatting from one area to another in Word, PowerPoint, and Excel.

Formatting The process of modifying text by changing font and paragraph characteristics.

Formula A combination of cell references, operators, values, and/or functions used to perform a calculation.

Formula AutoComplete A feature that displays a list of functions and defined names that match letters as you type a formula.

Formula Bar A bar below the ribbon and to the right of the Insert Function command that shows the contents (text, value, date, formula, or function) stored in the active cell. You enter or edit cell content here.

Freezing The process of keeping rows and/or columns visible onscreen at all times even when you scroll through a large dataset.

Fully qualified structured reference A structured formula that contains the table name.

Function A predefined computation that simplifies creating a complex calculation and produces a result based on inputs known as arguments.

Function ScreenTip A small pop-up description that displays the function's arguments.

Gallery An Office feature that displays additional formatting and design choices.

Go To Navigation feature to go to a specific page in Word or a specific cell in Excel.

Gradient fill A fill that contains a blend of two or more colors or shades.

Grid Intersecting lines on a slide that enable you to align objects.

Gridline A horizontal or vertical line that extends from the tick marks on the value axis across the plot area to guide the reader's eyes across the chart to identify values.

Group A subset of a tab that organizes similar tasks together.

Group (PowerPoint) Multiple objects connected so they are able to move as though they are a single object.

Grouping A method of summarizing data by the values of a field.

Guide A nonprinting, temporary vertical or horizontal line placed on a slide to enable you to align objects or determine regions of the slide.

Hanging indent The first line of a paragraph begins at the left margin, but all other lines in the source are indented.

Header An area with one or more lines of information at the top of each page.

Header row The first row in a data source, that contains labels describing the data in rows beneath.

Histogram A chart that is similar to a column chart. The category axis shows bin ranges (intervals) where data are aggregated into bins, and the vertical axis shows frequencies.

HLOOKUP function A lookup and reference function that accepts a value, looks the value up in a horizontal lookup table with data organized in rows, and returns a result.

Horizontal alignment The placement of cell data between the left and right cell margins. By default, text is left-aligned, and values are right-aligned.

Icon set A set of symbols or signs that classifies data into three, four, or five categories, based on values in a range.

Ideas feature A task pane that provides intelligent analysis of a dataset to recommend potentially useful charts.

IF function A logical function that evaluates a condition and returns one value if the condition is true and a different value if the condition is false.

Immersive Reader A document view that is an add-in learning tool designed to help readers pronounce words correctly, read quickly and accurately, and to understand what is read.

Indent (Excel) A format that offsets data from its default alignment. For example, if text is left-aligned, the text may be indented or offset from the left side to stand out. If a value is right-aligned, it can be indented or offset from the right side of the cell.

Indent (Word) A setting associated with how part of a paragraph is distanced from the margin.

Index Used to locate a topic of interest in a book.

Infringement of copyright A situation that occurs when a right of the copyright owner is violated.

Input area A range of cells in a worksheet used to store and change the variables used in calculations.

Input mask Simplifies data entry by providing literal characters that are typed for every entry.

Insert control An indicator that displays between rows or columns in a table; click the indicator to insert one or more rows or columns.

Insert Function A command that displays the Insert Function dialog box to search for and select a function to insert into the active cell. The Insert Function command changes from gray to green when you position the pointer over it.

Insertion point Blinking bar that indicates where text that you next type will appear.

Join line A line used to create a relationship between two tables using a common field.

Justified alignment Spreads text evenly between the left and right margins, so that text begins at the left margin and ends uniformly at the right margin.

Kelvin The unit of measurement for absolute temperature used to measure the tone of an image.

Keyboard shortcut A combination of two or more keys pressed together to initiate a software command.

Kiosk An interactive computer terminal available for public use.

Label Wizard A feature that enables you to easily create mailing labels, name tags, and other specialized tags.

Landscape orientation A document layout when a page is wider than it is tall.

Layout control A tool that provides guides to help keep controls aligned horizontally and vertically and give your form a uniform appearance.

Layout view A view that enables users to make changes to a layout while viewing the data in the form or report.

Leaders The series of dots or hyphens that leads the reader's eye across the page to connect two columns of information.

Left alignment Begins text evenly at the left margin, with a ragged right edge.

Left indent A setting that positions all text in a paragraph an equal distance from the left margin.

Legend A key that identifies the color or pattern assigned to each data series in a chart.

Line chart A chart type that displays lines connecting data points to show trends over equal time periods, such as months, quarters, years, or decades.

Line spacing The vertical spacing between lines in a paragraph.

Line weight The width or thickness of a shape's outline.

Link A connection from the presentation to another location such as a storage device or website.

Linked object The information is stored in the source file (such as Excel or Word), and the object in the PowerPoint file is updated when the source file changes.

Live Layout Feature that enables you to watch text flow around an object as you move it, so you can position the object exactly as you want it.

Live Preview An Office feature that provides a preview of the results of a selection when you point to an option in a list or gallery. Using Live Preview, you can experiment with settings before making a final choice.

Live Preview (Word) An Office feature that enables you to select text and see the effects without finalizing the selection.

Lock Drawing Mode Enables the creation of multiple shapes of the same type.

Logical test An expression that evaluates to true or false.

Lookup table A range that contains data for the basis of the lookup and data to be retrieved.

Lookup value The cell reference of the cell that contains the value to look up.

Macro A stored series of commands that carry out an action; often used to automate simple tasks.

Mail Merge A process that combines content from a main document and a data source.

Main document A document that contains the information that stays the same for all recipients in a mail merge.

Margin The area of blank space that displays to the left, right, top, and bottom of a document or worksheet.

Markup A feature to help customize how tracked changes are displayed in a document.

Master List A database of all citation sources created in Word on a particular computer.

MAX function A statistical function that identifies the highest value in a range.

MEDIAN function A predefined formula that identifies the midpoint value in a set of values.

Merge field An item that serves as a placeholder for the variable data that will be inserted into the main document during a mail merge procedure.

Merged cells Combining two or more cells together in a table.

Microsoft Access A relational database management system in which you can record and link data, query databases, and create forms and reports.

Microsoft Excel An application that makes it easy to organize records, financial transactions, and business information in the form of worksheets.

Microsoft Office A productivity software suite including a set of software applications, each one specializing in a particular type of output.

Microsoft PowerPoint An application that enables you to create dynamic presentations to inform groups and persuade audiences.

Microsoft Word A word processing software application used to produce all sorts of documents, including memos, newsletters, forms, tables, and brochures.

MIN function A predefined formula that displays the lowest value in a range.

Mini Toolbar A toolbar that provides access to the most common formatting selections, such as adding bold or italic, or changing font type or color. Unlike the Quick Access Toolbar, the Mini Toolbar is not customizable.

Mixed cell reference A designation that combines an absolute cell reference with a relative cell reference. The absolute part does not change but the relative part does when you copy the formula.

MLA (Modern Language Association) A writing style established by the Modern Language Association, with rules and conventions for preparing research papers (used primarily in the area of humanities).

Module An advanced object written using the VBA (Visual Basic for Applications) programming language.

Morph A transition that creates a cinematic motion by seamlessly animating between two slides.

Motion path A predetermined path that an object follows as part of an animation.

Multimedia Various forms of media used to entertain or inform an audience.

Multiple Items form A form that displays multiple records in a tabular layout like a table's Datasheet view, with more customization options than a datasheet.

Multi-series chart A chart that represents two or more sets of data.

Name Box A rectangular area located below the ribbon that displays the address (or name) of the active cell, selected chart, or selected table. Use the Name Box to go to a cell or table; select a range; or assign a name to one or more cells.

Narration Spoken commentary that is added to a presentation.

Navigation Form User interface that enables users to switch between various forms and reports in a database.

Navigation Pane An Access interface element that organizes and lists the objects in an Access database.

New sheet Button used to insert a new worksheet to the right of the current worksheet.

No Markup A markup view that provides a completely clean view of a document, temporarily hiding all comments and revisions, and displays the document as it would if all changes were applied and does not show any of the markups or comments.

Nonadjacent range A collection of multiple ranges (such as D5:D10 and F5:F10) that are not positioned in a contiguous cluster in an Excel worksheet.

Normal view (Excel) The default view of a worksheet that shows worksheet data but not margins, headers, footers, or page breaks.

Normal view (PowerPoint) The default PowerPoint workspace.

Notes Page view Used for entering and editing large amounts of text to which the speaker can refer when presenting.

NOW function A date and time function that calculates the current date and military time that you last opened the workbook using the computer's clock.

Nper Total number of payment periods.

Number format A setting that controls how a value appears in a cell.

Numbered list A list that sequences items by displaying a successive number beside each item.

Object An item, such as a picture or text box, that can be individually selected and manipulated in a document.

Object (Access) A component created and used to make the database function (such as a table, query, form, or report).

Object Linking and Embedding (OLE) A feature in Microsoft Office that enables you to insert an object into a presentation either as an embedded or linked object.

Office Clipboard An area of memory reserved to temporarily hold selections that have been cut or copied and enables you to paste the selections.

OneDrive Microsoft's cloud storage system. Saving files to OneDrive enables them to sync across all Windows devices and to be accessible from any Internet-connected device.

One-to-many relationship When the primary key value in the primary table can match many of the foreign key values in the related table.

Opaque A solid fill, one with no transparency.

OR condition A query condition that returns records meeting any of the specified criteria.

Order of operations A set of rules that controls the sequence in which arithmetic operations are performed. Also called the *order of precedence*.

Original Markup A markup view that displays the document in its original form, as it was before any changes were applied.

Outline view A structural view of a document that can be collapsed or expanded as necessary.

Outline view (PowerPoint) A view showing the presentation in an outline format displayed in levels according to the points and any subpoints on each slide.

Output area The range of cells in an Excel worksheet that contains formulas dependent on the values in the input area.

Page break An indication of where data will start on another printed page.

Page Break Preview A view setting that displays page breaks within the worksheet.

Page Layout view A view setting that displays the worksheet data, margins, headers, and footers.

Pan & Zoom A tool that controls how the image fits within the frame.

Paragraph spacing The amount of space before or after a paragraph.

Paste A command used to place a cut or copied selection into another location.

Paste Options button A button that displays near the bottom-right corner of the pasted data immediately after using the Paste command. It enables the user to apply different paste options.

PDF (Portable Document Format) A file type that was created for exchanging documents independent of software applications and operating system environments.

PDF Reflow A Word feature that converts a PDF document into an editable Word document.

Percent Style A number format that displays a value as if it was multiplied by 100 and with the % symbol. The default number of decimal places is zero if you click Percent Style in the Number group or two decimal places if you use the Format Cells dialog box.

Picture A graphic file that is retrieved from storage media or the Internet and placed in an Office project.

Picture fill Inserts an image from a file into a shape.

Pie chart A chart type that shows each data point in proportion to the whole data series as a slice in a circle. A pie chart depicts only one data series.

Placeholder A container that holds text, images, graphs, or other objects to be used in a presentation.

Plagiarizing The act of using and documenting the works of another as one's own.

Plot area The region of a chart containing the graphical representation of the values in one or more data series. Two axes form a border around the plot area.

PMT function A financial function that calculates the periodic loan payment given a fixed rate, number of periods (also known as *term*), and the present value of the loan (the principal).

Point (pt) The smallest unit of measurement used in typography, $1/72$ of an inch.

Pointing The process of using the pointer to select cells while building a formula. Also known as *semi-selection*.

Portable Document Format (PDF) A file type that was created for exchanging documents independent of software applications and operating system environment.

Portrait orientation A document layout when a page is taller than it is wide.

Poster Frame The image that displays on a slide when a video is not playing.

PowerPoint presentation An electronic slide show that can be edited or delivered in a variety of ways.

Presenter view Specialty view that delivers a presentation on two monitors simultaneously.

Primary key The field (or combination of fields) that uniquely identifies each record in a table.

Print area The range of cells within a worksheet that will print.

Print Layout view View that closely resembles the way a document will look when printed.

Print order The sequence in which the pages are printed.

Print Preview A view that enables you to see exactly what the report will look like when it is printed.

Property Sheet The location where you change settings such as number format and number of decimal places.

Public domain The rights to a literary work or property owned by the public at large.

Pv An argument in the PMT function representing the present value of the loan.

Query A question about the data stored in a database; answers provided in a datasheet.

Quick Access Toolbar A toolbar located at the top-left corner of any Office application window; provides fast access to commonly executed tasks such as saving a file and undoing recent actions.

Quick Analysis A set of analytical tools you can use to apply formatting, create charts or tables, and insert basic functions.

Quick Style A combination of formatting options that can be applied to a shape or graphic.

QuickStarter A feature that creates a collection of slides to provide research and design suggestions based on a presentation topic.

Radar chart A chart type that compares aggregate values of three or more variables represented on axes starting from the same point.

Range A group of adjacent or contiguous cells in a worksheet. A range can be adjacent cells in a column (such as C5:C10), in a row (such as A6:H6), or a rectangular group of cells (such as G5:H10).

Range_lookup An argument that determines how the VLOOKUP and HLOOKUP functions handle lookup values that are not an exact match for the data in the lookup table.

Rate The periodic interest rate; the percentage of interest paid for each payment period; the first argument in the PMT function.

Read Mode View in which text reflows automatically between columns to make it easier to read.

Reading View Displays the slide show full screen, one slide at a time, complete with animations and transitions.

Real-time co-authoring A Word feature that shows several authors simultaneously editing the document in Word or Word Online.

Real Time Typing A Word feature that shows where co-authors are working, and what their contributions are as they type.

Recolor The process of changing a picture by adjusting the image's colors.

Record A group of related fields representing one entity, such as data for one person, place, event, or concept.

Record source The table or query that supplies the records for a form or report.

Referential integrity Rules in a database that are used to preserve relationships between tables when records are added, deleted, or changed.

Relationship A connection between two tables using a common field.

Relative cell reference A designation that indicates a cell's relative location from the original cell containing the formula; the cell reference changes when the formula is copied.

Report A database document that outputs meaningful, professional-looking, formatted information from underlying tables or queries.

Report tool A tool used to instantly create a tabular report based on the table or query currently selected.

Report view A view that enables you to determine what a printed report will look like in a continuous onscreen page layout.

Report Wizard A feature that prompts you for input and then uses your answers to generate a customized report.

Revision mark Markings that indicate where text is added, deleted, or formatted while the Track Changes feature is active.

Ribbon The command center of Office applications. It is the long bar located just beneath the title bar, containing tabs, groups, and commands.

Right alignment Begins text evenly at the right margin, with a ragged left edge.

Right indent A setting that positions all text in a paragraph an equal distance from the right margin.

Rotation handle A circular arrow at the top of the placeholder that allows rotation of the placeholder.

ROUND function A statistical function that rounds a number to a specified number of digits.

Row heading A number to the left side of a row in a worksheet. For example, 3 is the row heading for the third row.

Row height The vertical measurement of the row in a worksheet.

Sans serif font A font that does not contain a thin line or extension at the top and bottom of the primary strokes on characters.

Saturation A characteristic of color that controls its intensity.

Screen recording A recording of the computer screen and the related audio that can be inserted onto a slide.

Section A part of a document that contains its own page format settings, such as those for margins, columns, and orientation.

Section break An indicator that divides a document into parts, enabling different formatting for each section.

Select All The triangle at the intersection of the row and column headings in the top-left corner of the worksheet used to select everything contained in the active worksheet.

Selection filter A method of selecting that displays only the records that match a criterion you select.

Selection pane A pane designed to help select objects.

Semi-selection The process of using the pointer to select cells while building a formula. Also known as *pointing*.

Serif font A font that contains a thin line or extension at the top and bottom of the primary strokes on characters.

Shading A background color that appears behind text in a paragraph, page, or table element.

Shape A geometric or non-geometric object, such as a rectangle or an arrow, used to create an illustration or highlight information.

Sharpening A technique that enhances the edges of the content in a picture to make the boundaries more prominent.

Sheet tab A label that looks like a file folder tab, located between the bottom of the worksheet and the status bar, that shows the name of a worksheet contained in the workbook.

Sheet tab scroll button A button to the left of the sheet tabs, used to scroll through sheet tabs; not all the sheet tabs are displayed at the same time.

Shortcut menu A menu that provides choices related to the selection or area at which you right-click.

Simple Markup A Word feature that simplifies the display of comments and revision marks, resulting in a clean, uncluttered look.

Simple Query Wizard Provides a step-by-step guide to help you through the query design process.

Single-series chart A chart that represents one set of data.

Sizing handle A series of dots on the outside border of a selected object; enables the user to adjust the height and width of the object.

Sizing handle (Excel) One of eight circles that display on the outside border of a chart—one on each corner and one on each middle side—when the chart is selected; enables the user to adjust the height and width of the chart.

Slide The most basic element of a presentation that can include text, bulleted lists, images, tables, charts, SmartArt, video, and audio.

Slide layout The position of placeholders on a slide; each slide layout is defined by the type and placement of placeholders.

Slide show A series of slides displayed onscreen for an audience.

Slide Show view Displays the completed presentation full screen to an audience as an electronic presentation.

Slide Sorter view Displays thumbnails of presentation slides, enabling a view of multiple slides.

Smart Guide A guide that displays when an object is moved that helps align objects in relation to other objects.

Smart Lookup A feature that provides information about tasks or commands in Office and can also be used to search for general information on a topic, such as *President George Washington*.

SmartArt A visual representation of information that can be created to effectively communicate a list, process, or relationship.

Softening A technique that blurs the edges of the content in a picture to make the boundaries less prominent.

Sort A feature that lists records in a specific sequence.

Sorting The process of arranging records by the value of one or more fields within a table or data range.

Source A publication, person, or media item that is consulted in the preparation of a paper and given credit.

Source file The file that contains the original table or data used or copied to create a linked or embedded object, such as an Excel worksheet.

Sparkline A small line, column, or win/loss chart contained in a single cell to provide a simple visual illustrating one data series.

Speaker notes Notes added to slides to assist the speaker with preparing or delivering a presentation.

Split cells Dividing a cell into two or more cells in a table.

Split form A form that combines two views of the same record source—one section is displayed in a stacked layout and the other section is displayed in a tabular layout.

Spreadsheet An electronic file that contains a grid of columns and rows used to organize related data and to display results of calculations, enabling interpretation of quantitative data for decision making.

Stacked bar chart A chart type that places stacks of data in segments in one bar, with each category in the data series represented by a different color.

Stacked column chart A chart type that shows the relationship of individual data points to the whole category by stacking data in segments in one column, with each segment represented by a different color.

Stacked layout Arrangement that displays fields in a vertical column.

Stacking order The order of objects placed on top of one another.

Status bar A bar located at the bottom of the program window that contains information relative to the open file. It also includes tools for changing the view of the file and for changing the zoom size of onscreen file contents.

Stock chart A chart type that shows fluctuation in stock prices.

Storyboard A visual plan of a presentation that displays the content of each slide in the slide show.

Structured reference A tag or use of a table element, such as a field label, as a reference in a formula. Field labels are enclosed in square brackets, such as [Amount] within the formula.

Style A named collection of formatting characteristics that can be applied to text or paragraphs.

Style manual A guide to a particular writing style outlining required rules and conventions related to the preparation of papers.

Style set Predefined combinations of font, style, color, and font size that can be applied to selected text.

SUBTOTAL function A predefined formula that calculates an aggregate value, such as totals, for displayed values in a range, a table, or a database.

SUM function A statistical function that calculates the total of values contained in one or more cells.

Surface chart A chart type that displays trends using two dimensions on a continuous curve.

Symbol A character or graphic not normally included on a keyboard.

Syntax A set of rules that governs the structure and components for properly entering a function.

Tab Located on the ribbon, each tab is designed to appear much like a tab on a file folder, with the active tab highlighted.

Tab selector The small box at the leftmost edge of the horizontal ruler.

Tab stop A marker on the horizontal ruler specifying the location where the insertion point stops after Tab is pressed to align text in a document.

Table (Access) The location where all data are stored in a database; organizes data into columns and rows.

Table (Excel) A structured range that contains related data organized in a method that increases the capability to manage and analyze information.

Table (PowerPoint; Word) A grid of columns and rows that organizes data.

Table alignment The horizontal position of a table between the left and right margins.

Table array The range that contains the lookup table.

Table of contents A page that lists headings in the order in which they appear in a document and the page numbers on which the entries begin.

Table style (Excel; Word) A named collection of color, font, and border designs that can be applied to a table.

Table style (PowerPoint) A combination of formatting choices for table components available to you based on the theme.

Tabular layout Arrangement that displays fields horizontally across the screen or page.

Tag A data element or metadata that is added as a document property. Tags help in indexing and searching.

Task pane A window of options specific to a feature in an Office application. The task pane name and options change based on the selected range, object, or feature.

Tell me box A box located to the right of the last tab that enables you to search for help and information about a command or task you want to perform and also displays a shortcut directly to that command.

Template A predesigned file that contains suggested content, formatting, and other elements that can be modified to conform to the user's specific needs.

Template (Access) A predefined database that includes professionally designed tables, forms, reports, and other objects that you can use to jumpstart the creation of your database.

Text Any combination of letters, numbers, symbols, and spaces not used in Excel calculations.

Text box (PowerPoint) An object that provides space for text anywhere on a slide; it can be formatted with a border, shading, and other characteristics.

Text box (Word) A bordered area you can use to draw attention to specific text.

Text pane A pane that displays beside a SmartArt diagram, enabling you to enter text.

Texture fill Inserts a texture such as canvas, denim, marble, or cork into a shape.

Theme A collection of design choices that includes colors, fonts, and special effects used to give a consistent look to a document, workbook, presentation, or database form or report.

Thesaurus A tool used to quickly find a synonym (a word with the same meaning as another).

Three-part indent marker An icon located at the left side of the ruler that enables you to set a left indent, a hanging indent, or a first line indent.

Thumbnail A miniature view of a slide that appears in the Slides pane and Slide Sorter view.

Title bar The long bar at the top of each window that displays the name of the folder, file, or program displayed in the open window and the application in which you are working.

TODAY function A date and time function that displays the current date.

Toggle command A button that acts somewhat like a light switch that you can turn on and off. You select the command to turn it on, then select it again to turn it off.

Tone A characteristic of lighting that controls the temperature of a color; see also *Kelvin*.

Total row A method to display aggregate function results as the last row in Datasheet view of a table or query.

Totals query A way to display aggregate data when a query is run.

Track Changes A Word feature that monitors all additions, deletions, and formatting changes you make in a document.

Transition A specific animation that is applied as the previous slide is replaced by a new slide while displayed in Slide Show view or Reading view.

Transparency The visibility of fill.

Trendline A line that depicts trends or helps forecast future data in a chart. For example, if the plotted data includes 2015, 2020, 2025, and 2030, a trendline can help forecast values for 2030 and beyond.

Trigger An object that launches an animation that takes place when you click an associated object or a bookmarked location in a media object.

Ungroup A process that divides a combined single object into individual objects that comprise it.

Unqualified reference The use of field headings without row references in a structured formula.

Validation rule Checks the data for allowable value when the user exits the field.

Value A number that represents a quantity or a measurable amount.

Value axis The chart axis that displays incremental numbers to identify approximate values, such as dollars or units, of data points in a chart.

Value_if_false The value that is returned if Logical_test is FALSE, if omitted, the word FALSE is returned.

Value_if_true The value that is returned if Logical_test is TRUE, if omitted, the word TRUE is returned.

Variant A variation on a chosen design theme.

Vector graphic An image created by a mathematical statement.

Vertical alignment The placement of cell data between the top and bottom cell margins.

View The various ways a file can display on the screen.

View controls Buttons on the right side of the status bar that enable you to change to Normal, Page Layout, or Page Break view to display the worksheet.

VLOOKUP function A lookup and reference function that accepts a value, looks the value up in a vertical lookup table with data organized in columns, and returns a result.

Watermark Text or graphics that display behind text.

Web Layout view A view that displays the way a document will look when posted on the Internet.

Wildcard A special character that can represent one or more characters in the criterion of a query.

Word Online An online component of Office Online consisting of a Web-based version of Word with sufficient capabilities to enable you to edit and format a document online.

Word processing software A computer application, such as Microsoft Word, used primarily with text to create, edit, and format documents.

Word wrap The feature that automatically moves words to the next line if they do not fit on the current line.

WordArt A feature that modifies text to include special effects, such as color, shadow, gradient, and 3-D appearance.

Workbook A collection of one or more related worksheets contained within a single file.

Works Cited A list of sources cited by an author in his or her work.

Worksheet A single spreadsheet that typically contains descriptive labels, numeric values, formulas, functions, and graphical representations of data.

Wrap text An alignment option that word-wraps data on multiple lines within a cell.

Writing style Provides a set of rules that results in standardized documents that present citations in the same manner and that include the same general page characteristics.

X Y (scatter) chart A chart type that shows a relationship between two variables using their X and Y coordinates. Excel plots one coordinate on the horizontal X-axis and the other variable on the vertical Y-axis. Scatter charts are often used to represent data in education, scientific, and medical experiments.

X-axis Also known as the *horizontal axis*; the horizontal border that provides a frame of reference for measuring data left to right on a chart.

Y-axis Also known as the *vertical axis*; the vertical border that provides a frame of reference for measuring data up and down on a chart.

Zoom A tool that enables you to move from a landing slide to another slide in the presentation without that slide being sequential to the landing slide.

Zoom slider A feature that displays at the far right side of the status bar. It is used to increase or decrease the magnification of the file.

Index

T